ROAD ATLAS EU[ROPE]

GW00402877

Contents

2 – 3	Distance map and chart
4	International road signs
5	Key to map pages
6 – 17	Route planning maps 1:4 500 000
18 – 197	Road maps 1:1 000 000
198 – 203	Road maps 1:750 000
204 – 207	Index to place names 1:750 000

208 – 219	City [maps]
208	Amst[erdam],
209	Berlin, Birmingham, Bonn, Bruxelles
210	Bucureşti, Budapest, Dublin, Edinburgh
211	Frankfurt, Glasgow, Göteborg, Den Haag
212	Hamburg, Helsinki, İstanbul, København
213	Köln, Leipzig, Lisboa, London
214	Lyon, Madrid, Manchester, Marseille
215	Milano, München, Napoli, Oslo
216	Palermo, Paris, Praha, Roma
217	Rotterdam, Sevilla, Sofiya, Stockholm
218	Strasbourg, Torino, Toulouse, Valencia
219	Venezia, Warszawa, Wien, Zürich
220 – 280	Index to place names 1:1 000 000

Country identifiers

A	Austria	Autriche	Österreich	
AL	Albania	Albanie	Albanien	
AND	Andorra	Andorre	Andorra	
B	Belgium	Belgique	Belgien	
BG	Bulgaria	Bulgarie	Bulgarien	
BIH	Bosnia - Herzegovina	Bosnie Herzégovine	Bosnien-Herzegowina	
BY	Belarus	Bélarus	Belarus	
CH	Switzerland	Suisse	Schweiz	
CY	Cyprus	Chypre	Zypern	
CZ	Czech Republic	République tchèque	Tschechische Republik	
D	Germany	Allemagne	Deutschland	
DK	Denmark	Danemark	Dänemark	
DZ	Algeria	Algérie	Algerien	
E	Spain	Espagne	Spanien	
EST	Estonia	Estonie	Estland	
F	France	France	Frankreich	
FIN	Finland	Finlande	Finnland	
FL	Liechtenstein	Liechtenstein	Liechtenstein	
FO	Faroe Islands	Iles Féroé	Färöer-Inseln	
GB	United Kingdom GB & NI	Grande-Bretagne	Grossbritannien	
GBA	Alderney	Alderney	Alderney	
GBG	Guernsey	Guernsey	Guernsey	
GBJ	Jersey	Jersey	Jersey	
GBM	Isle of Man	île de Man	Insel Man	
GBZ	Gibraltar	Gibraltar	Gibraltar	
GR	Greece	Grèce	Griechenland	
H	Hungary	Hongrie	Ungarn	
HR	Croatia	Croatie	Kroatien	
I	Italy	Italie	Italien	
IRL	Ireland	Irlande	Irland	
IS	Iceland	Islande	Island	
L	Luxembourg	Luxembourg	Luxemburg	
LT	Lithuania	Lituanie	Litauen	
LV	Latvia	Lettonie	Lettland	
M	Malta	Malte	Malta	
MA	Morocco	Maroc	Marokko	
MC	Monaco	Monaco	Monaco	
MD	Moldova	Moldavie	Moldawien	
MK	Macedonia (F.Y.R.O.M.)	Ancienne République yougoslave de Macédoine	Ehemalige jugoslawische Republik Mazedonien	
MNE	Montenegro	Monténégro	Montenegro	
N	Norway	Norvège	Norwegen	
NL	Netherlands	Pays-Bas	Niederlande	
P	Portugal	Portugal	Portugal	
PL	Poland	Pologne	Polen	
RO	Romania	Roumanie	Rumänien	
RSM	San Marino	Saint-Marin	San Marino	
RUS	Russian Federation	Russie	Russische Föderation	
S	Sweden	Suède	Schweden	
SK	Slovakia	République slovaque	Slowakei	
SLO	Slovenia	Slovénie	Slowenien	
SRB	Serbia	Sérbie	Serbien	
TN	Tunisia	Tunisie	Tunisien	
TR	Turkey	Turquie	Türkei	
UA	Ukraine	Ukraine	Ukraine	

Road Atlas Europe

Collins
An imprint of HarperCollins Publishers
77-85 Fulham Palace Road
London W6 8JB

Revised edition

Printed and bound in Thailand

ISBN 978 0 00 726784 2

All mapping in this title is generated from Collins Bartholomew™ digital databases.
Collins Bartholomew™, the UK's leading independent geographical information supplier, can provide a digital, custom, and premium mapping service to a variety of markets.
For further information:
tel: +44 (0) 141 306 3752
e-mail: collinsbartholomew@harpercollins.co.uk
or visit our website: www.collinsbartholomew.com

We also offer a choice of books, atlases and maps that can be customized to suit a customer's own requirements.
For further information:
tel: +44 (0) 306 3209
e-mail: business.gifts@harpercollins.co.uk

www.collins.co.uk

Distance map

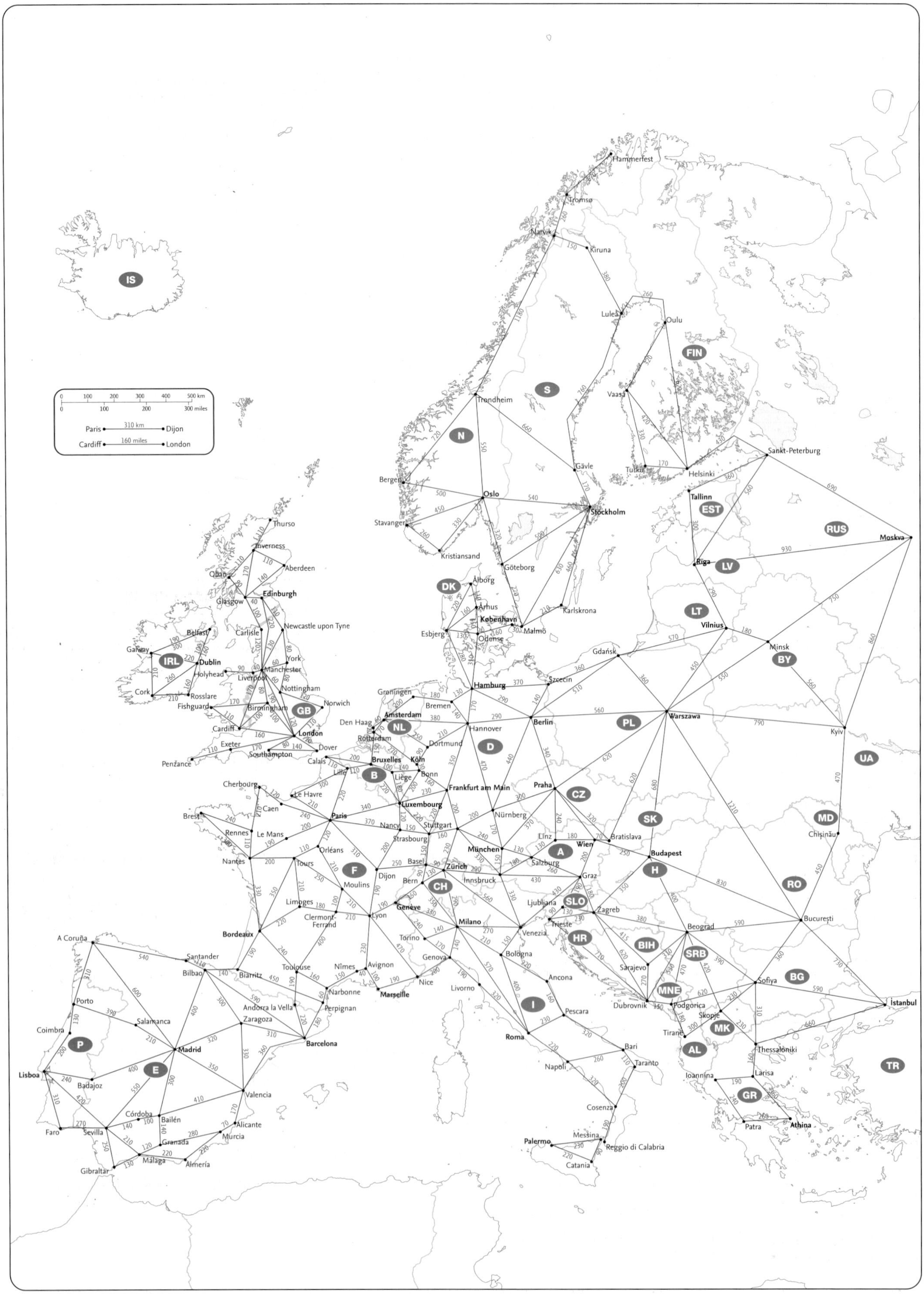

km

Distances in kilometres.
The distances given in this chart are obtained by following main routes and are not necessarily the shortest routes.

880 1160 1220 1680 2270 1390 1730 1970 910 510 2690 1370 840 2520 1140 1280 1760 390 550 2300 260 760 2780 440 880 460 1190 1100 1410 210 1070 660 1620 2970 3230 | **Amsterdam**

2600 2050 2360 2810 3400 3780 2430 3100 2310 3380 3570 3700 2400 2930 2490 3030 4180 2950 3550 4830 2930 3100 420 2990 2750 2740 4200 4100 1740 3190 3500 2700 3560 1690 | **Ankara**

2530 1810 2250 2850 3440 3470 2450 3140 2130 2940 3340 3460 2210 2970 2210 2750 3880 2600 3200 4530 2740 2880 1130 2770 2530 2530 3840 3750 1570 2810 3400 2470 3250 | **Athina**

1090 1760 2450 2930 3520 2740 1410 3220 1690 1110 2370 2720 1430 3770 1040 500 630 750 1560 1280 1350 2110 3060 1790 770 1340 2200 2110 2020 1410 660 1840 | **Barcelona**

850 660 560 1010 1020 1490 1300 340 1090 2450 1000 590 1850 1010 1520 2350 1160 1170 3000 570 390 2290 290 1080 530 1810 1720 910 780 1660 | **Berlin**

970 1720 2300 2880 3420 2430 1540 3160 1540 560 2500 2410 1300 3670 1000 630 690 880 980 1230 1020 1800 3020 1480 710 1030 1620 1530 1990 860 | **Bordeaux**

660 1120 1340 1870 2490 1550 1520 2160 910 300 2480 1530 790 2710 930 1070 1550 220 390 2090 220 920 2650 600 680 410 1030 940 1370 | **Bruxelles**

1010 250 680 1130 1720 1920 1250 1720 570 1460 2210 1900 690 1970 1010 1530 2620 1200 1760 3240 1160 1290 1320 1200 1280 970 2400 2310 | **Budapest**

1500 2060 2280 2810 3320 2490 2360 3100 1860 1000 3320 2470 1690 3092 1770 1760 2220 1150 550 2870 1130 1860 3560 1540 1480 1350 500 | **Dublin**

1620 2150 2370 2820 3410 2580 2450 3110 1950 1090 3410 2560 1800 3660 1860 1850 2310 1240 640 2960 1250 1950 3650 1630 1570 1440 | **Edinburgh**

430 720 1100 1650 2240 1440 1280 1940 500 570 2240 1420 380 2490 720 1000 1820 230 800 2470 200 810 2320 490 570 | **Frankfurt am Main**

280 1010 1550 2080 2670 2010 910 2370 930 510 1870 1990 570 2920 330 430 1400 490 930 2050 710 1380 2330 1060 | **Genève**

820 950 850 1300 1890 950 1680 1690 630 920 2640 930 780 2140 1200 1450 2170 630 990 2710 430 320 2560 | **Hamburg**

2230 1570 1940 2390 2980 3300 2260 2680 1890 2750 3150 3280 1980 2510 2020 2560 3690 2420 3010 4340 2510 2680 | **İstanbul**

1240 1040 970 2350 2360 630 2000 2060 740 1240 2960 610 1090 2610 1520 1770 2490 950 1310 3050 750 | **København**

500 910 1130 1600 2190 1380 1470 1890 700 490 2430 1360 570 2440 880 1000 1740 200 610 2360 | **Köln**

2230 3000 3530 4250 4840 3660 2690 4540 2910 1790 3650 3640 2700 5040 2300 1780 650 2130 2320 | **Lisboa**

1030 1510 1730 2180 2770 1940 1810 2470 1310 450 2770 1920 1160 3020 1220 1210 1670 600 | **London**

420 930 1350 1980 2470 1580 1300 2170 730 340 2260 1560 530 2720 710 820 1590 | **Luxembourg**

1690 2380 2930 3700 4200 3120 2040 3990 2310 1250 3000 3100 2050 4320 1670 1130 | **Madrid**

710 1370 1980 2600 3190 2400 910 2890 1360 770 1870 2380 1010 3440 540 | **Marseille**

300 820 1510 2090 2680 2150 590 2380 870 820 1550 2130 530 2930 | **Milano**

2640 1978 1290 930 1040 1560 3780 930 1910 3060 4740 2090 2280 | **Moskva**

300 440 990 1440 2030 1720 950 1730 370 860 1870 1700 | **München**

1830 1660 1490 3330 3130 540 2610 3440 1350 1850 3570 | **Oslo**

1840 2030 2720 3620 4210 3590 960 3910 2250 2360 | **Palermo**

580 1200 1620 2220 2810 1870 1400 2510 1000 | **Paris**

670 320 620 1070 1660 1370 1290 1360 | **Praha**

2090 1420 740 290 310 2900 2950 | **Rīga**

890 1140 1830 2320 3060 2630 | **Roma**

1860 1680 1470 3190 2590 | **Stockholm**

2390 1730 1040 590 | **Tallinn**

1800 1140 450 | **Vilnius**

1350 690 | **Warszawa**

750 | **Wien**

Zürich

Distance chart

Be aware!

On the spot fines for motoring offences are common in many European countries, including France, Spain, and Italy. For each fine an official receipt should be issued.

Speed camera detectors are illegal in many European countries whether in use or not. You should ensure that they are removed from your vehicle. In France you are liable to a prison sentence, a fine, and confiscation of the device and your vehicle. GPS/satellite navigation systems which show speed camera locations are legal.

In Austria and Switzerland all vehicles using motorways and expressways must display a motorway vignette. Failure to do so will result in a heavy, on the spot fine. Vignettes are available at major border crossing points and major petrol stations in both Austria and Switzerland. A vignette for Switzerland can be purchased in advance in the UK from the Switzerland Travel Centre.

Dipped headlights are compulsory when using road tunnels in Austria, Switzerland and Germany.

Penalties for speeding or drink-driving in many European countries are often more severe than in the UK. In Belgium the fine for exceeding the speed limit by 40km/h can be as much as €2750, and for drink-driving can range from €1100 to €11 000.

In Nordic countries you must drive with dipped headlights at all times.

In Denmark you must indicate when changing lanes on a motorway.

In Spain you must carry two red warning triangles to be placed in front and behind the vehicle in the event of accident or breakdown.

In many European countries, as in the UK and Ireland, the use of mobile phones while driving is not permitted unless 'hands-free'.

Fluorescent waistcoats and warning triangles should be carried inside the car and not in the boot.

In Sweden, by law, all Swedish registered cars must have winter tyres fitted between 1 December and 31 March. Foreign cars are exempt but winter tyres are advisable in this period.

International road signs

Informative signs

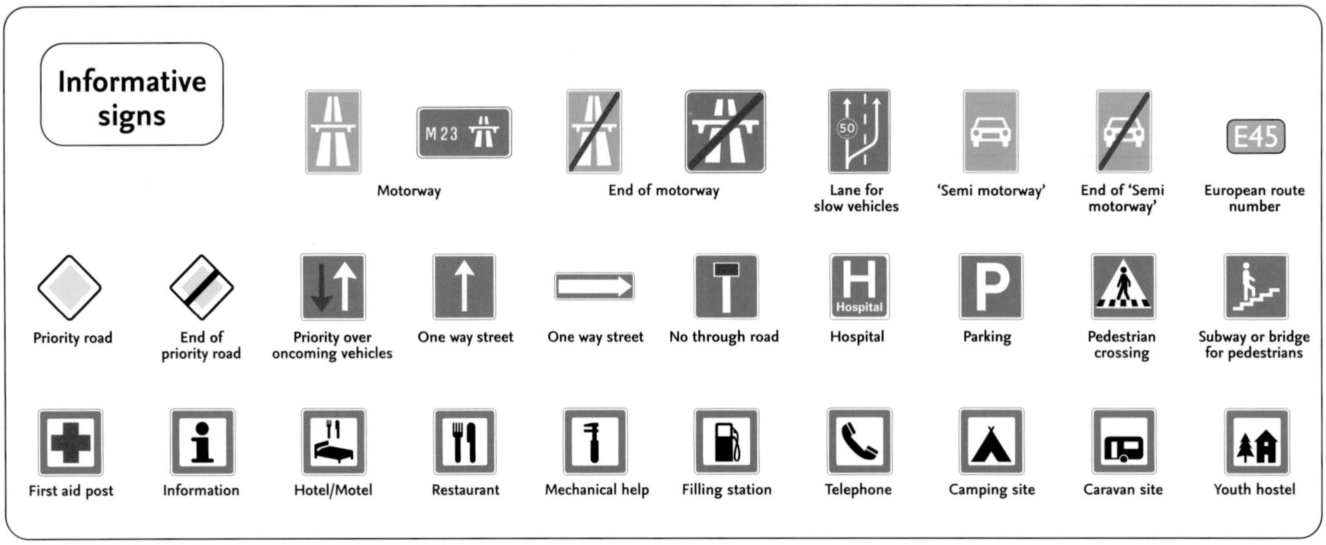
Motorway
End of motorway
Lane for slow vehicles
'Semi motorway'
End of 'Semi motorway'
European route number
Priority road
End of priority road
Priority over oncoming vehicles
One way street
One way street
No through road
Hospital
Parking
Pedestrian crossing
Subway or bridge for pedestrians
First aid post
Information
Hotel/Motel
Restaurant
Mechanical help
Filling station
Telephone
Camping site
Caravan site
Youth hostel

Warning signs

Right bend
Left bend
Double bend
Roundabout
Intersection with non-priority road
Traffic merges from left
Traffic merges from right
Road narrows
Road narrows at left
Road narrows at right
Give way
Slippery road
Uneven road
Steep hill – descent
Tunnel
Opening bridge
Road works
Loose chippings
Level crossing with barrier
Level crossing without barrier
Tram
'Count down' posts
'Danger' level crossing
Low flying aircraft
Falling rocks
Cross wind
Quayside or river bank
Two-way traffic
Traffic signals ahead
Pedestrians
Children
Animals
Wild animals
Other dangers
Width of carriageway
Beginning of regulation
Repetition sign
End of regulation

Regulative signs

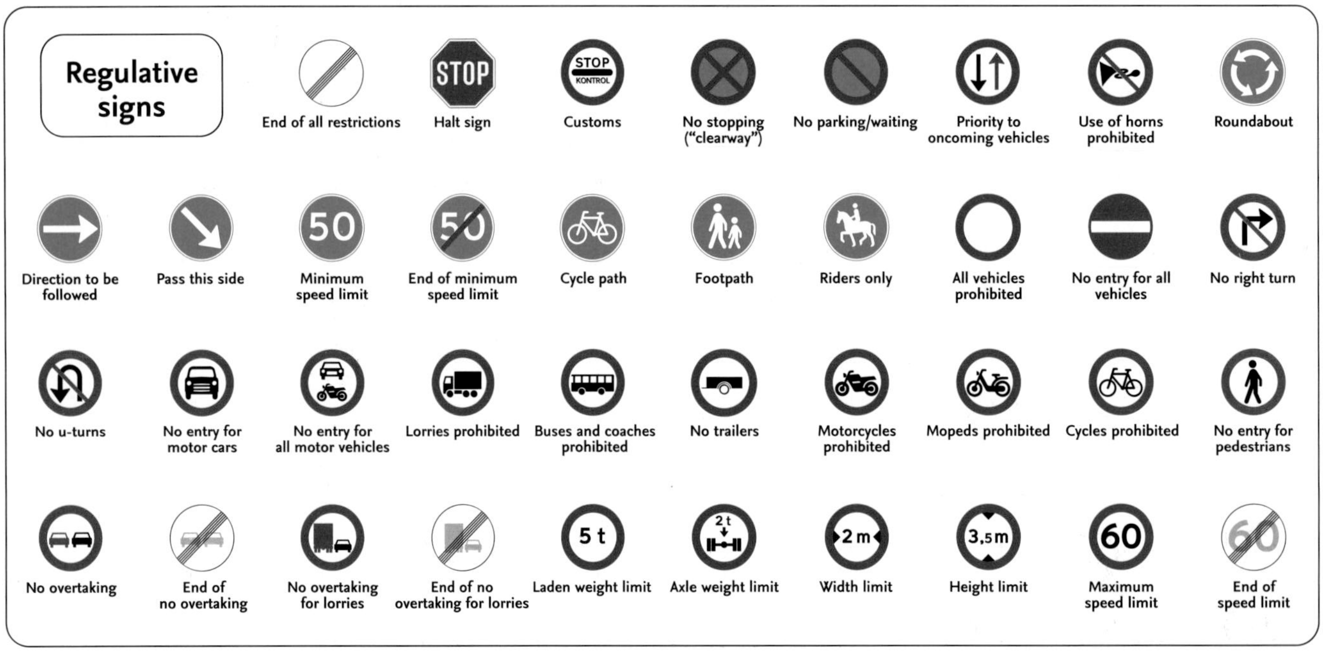
End of all restrictions
Halt sign
Customs
No stopping ("clearway")
No parking/waiting
Priority to oncoming vehicles
Use of horns prohibited
Roundabout
Direction to be followed
Pass this side
Minimum speed limit
End of minimum speed limit
Cycle path
Footpath
Riders only
All vehicles prohibited
No entry for all vehicles
No right turn
No u-turns
No entry for motor cars
No entry for all motor vehicles
Lorries prohibited
Buses and coaches prohibited
No trailers
Motorcycles prohibited
Mopeds prohibited
Cycles prohibited
No entry for pedestrians
No overtaking
End of no overtaking
No overtaking for lorries
End of no overtaking for lorries
Laden weight limit
Axle weight limit
Width limit
Height limit
Maximum speed limit
End of speed limit

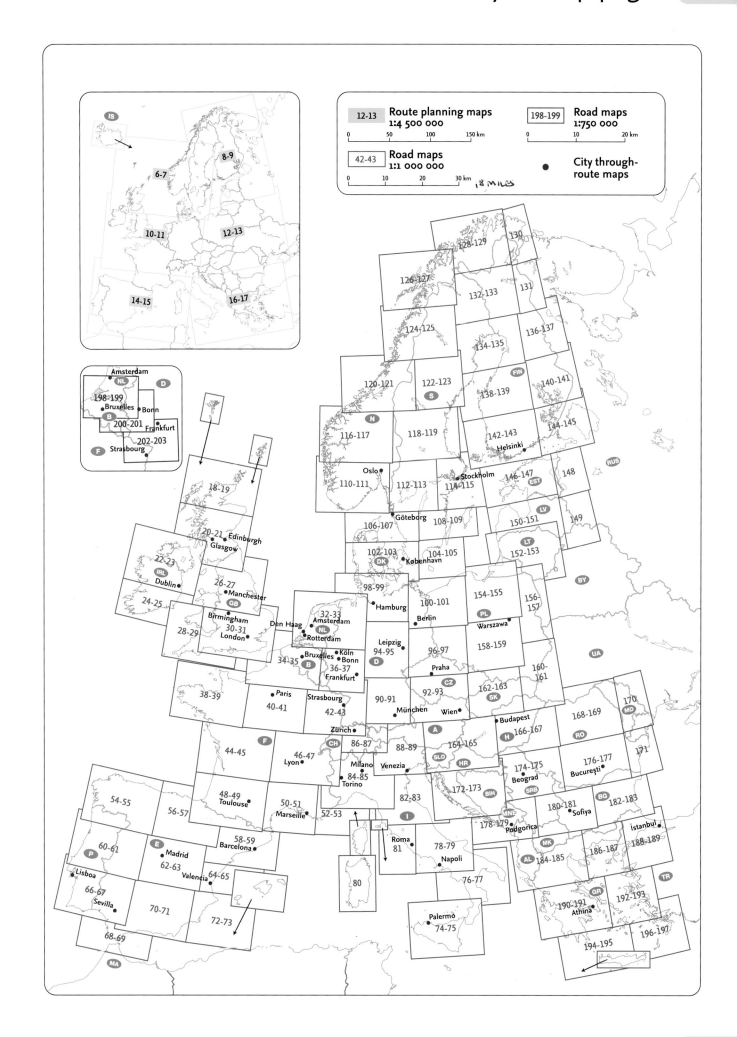

Route planning maps 12-13
1:4 500 000
0   50   100   150 km

Road maps 42-43
1:1 000 000
0   10   20   30 km
18 MILES

Road maps 198-199
1:750 000
0   10   20 km

● City through-route maps

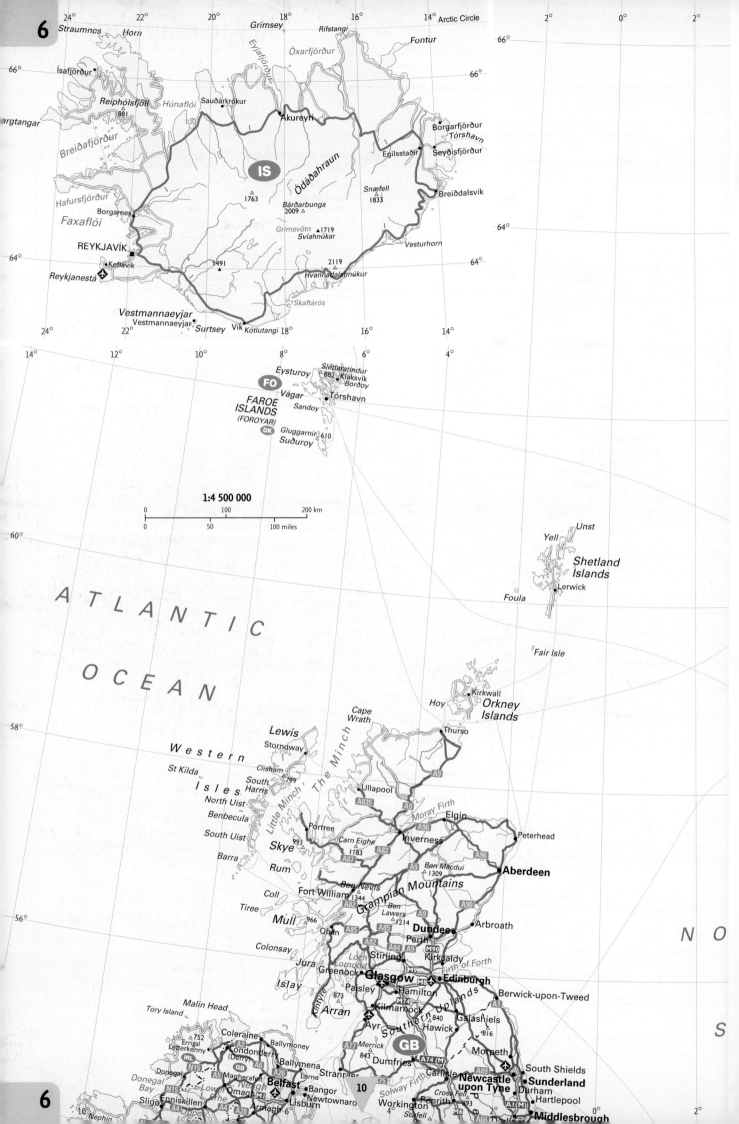

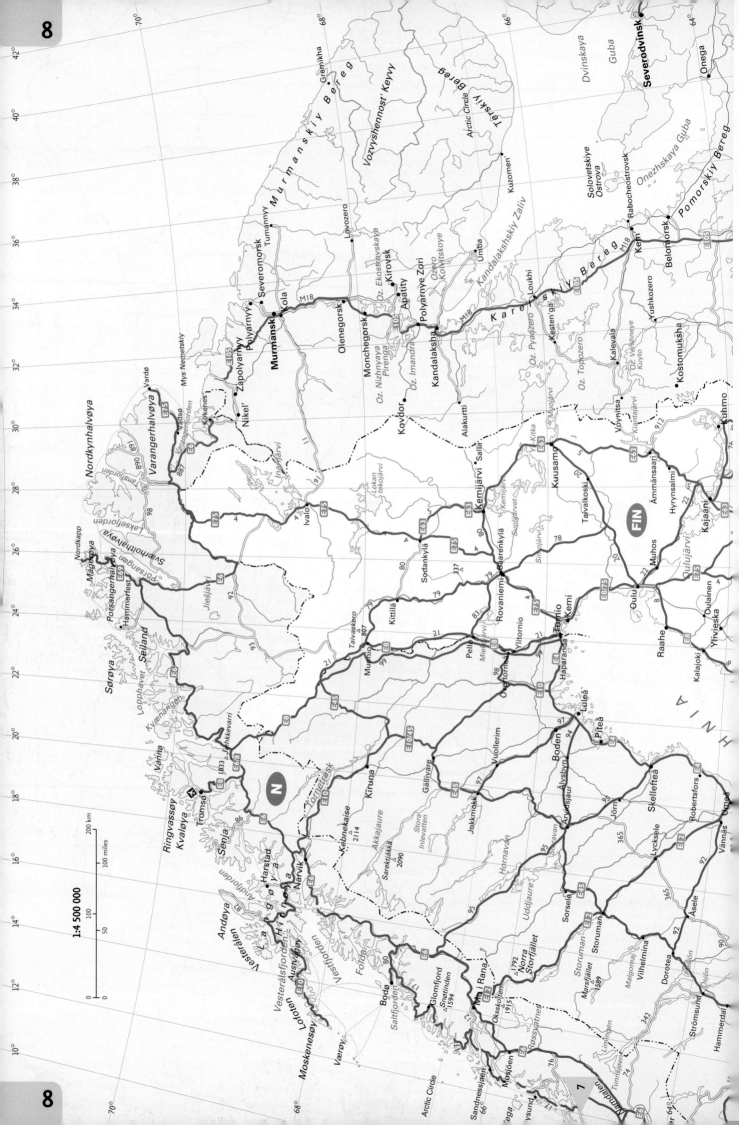

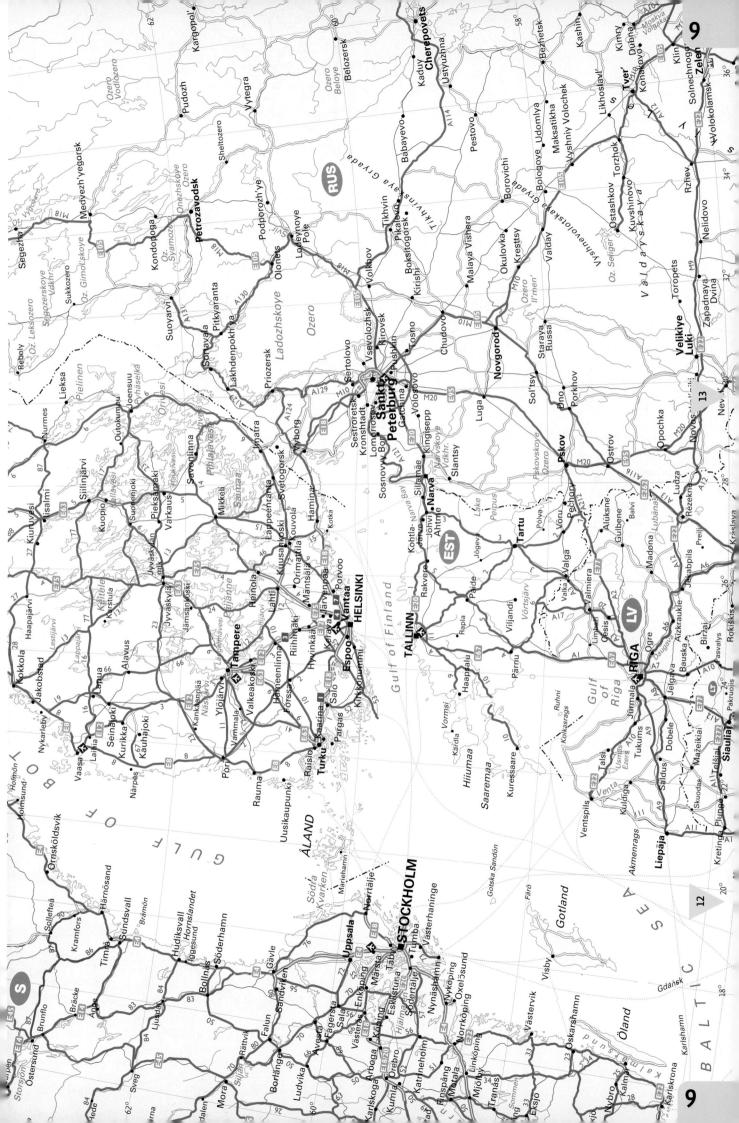

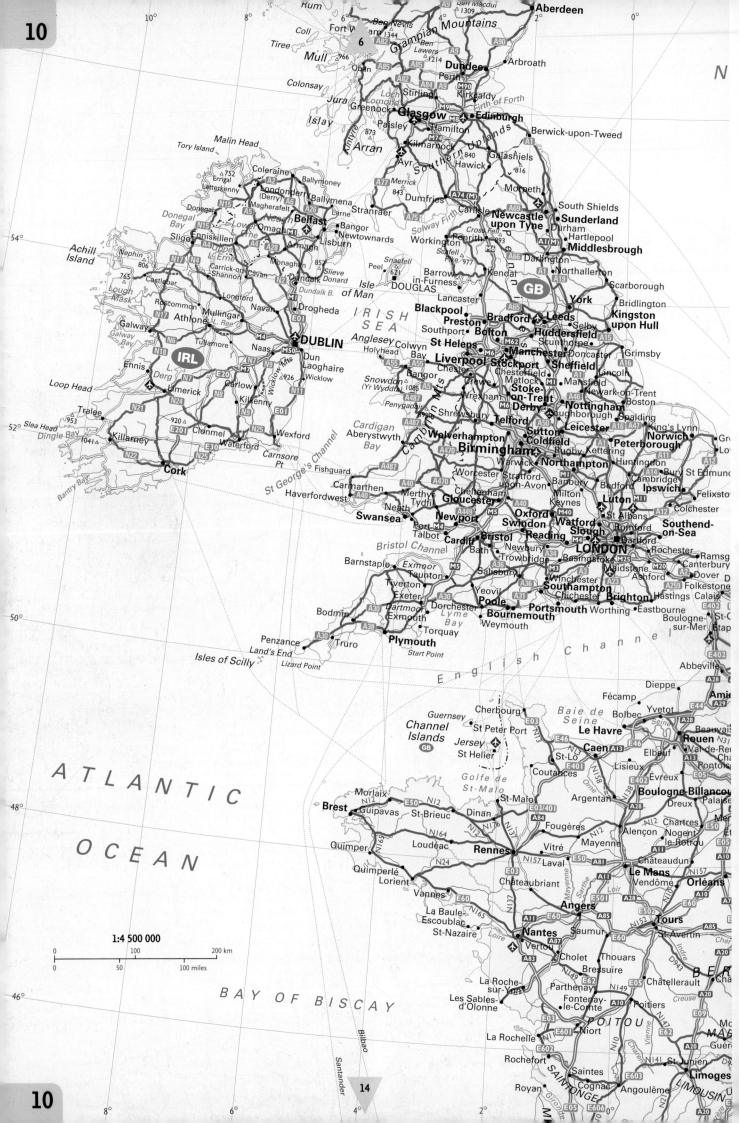

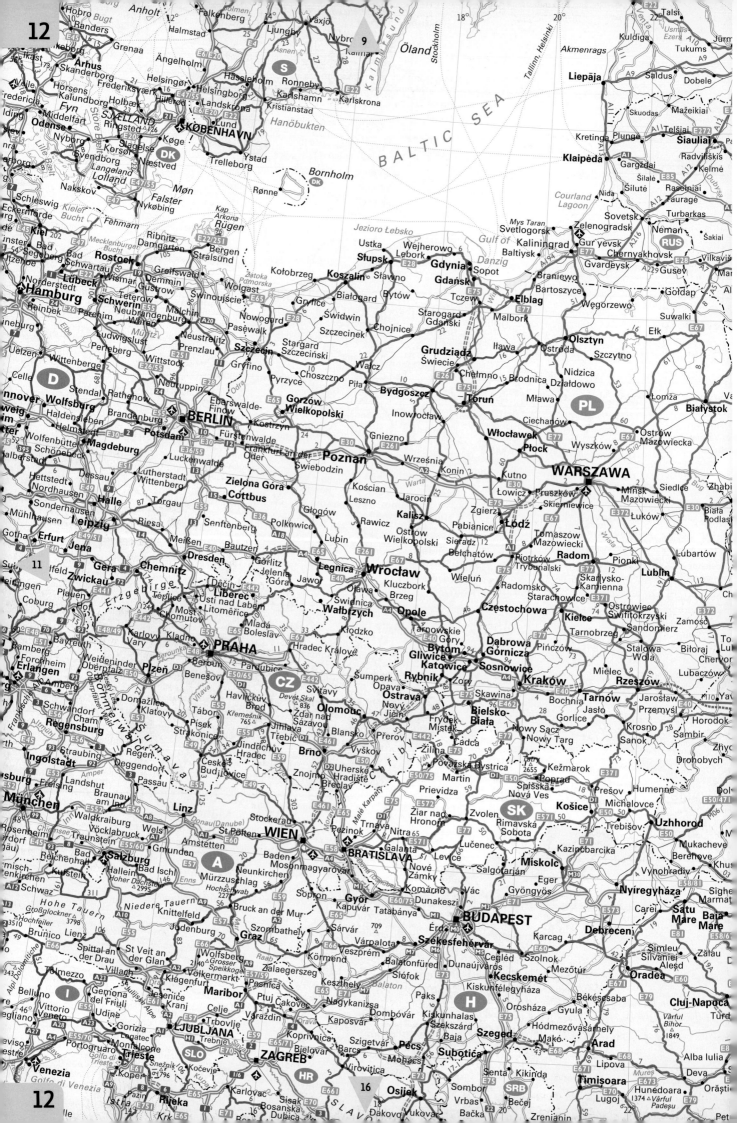

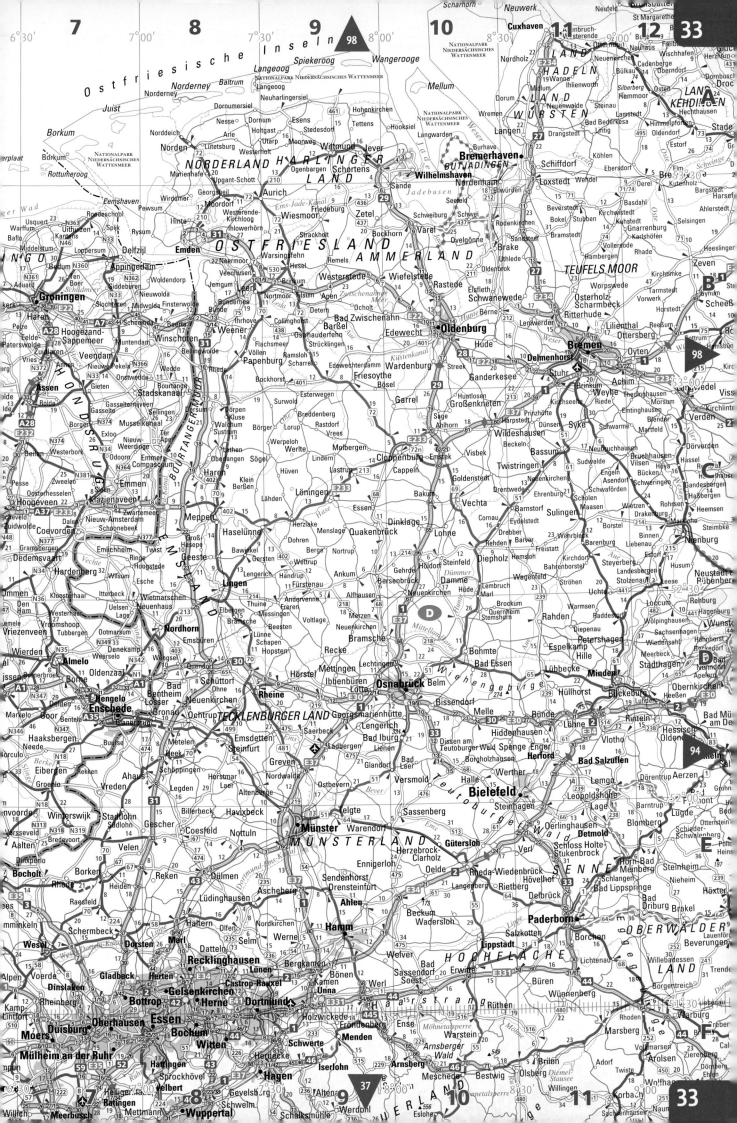

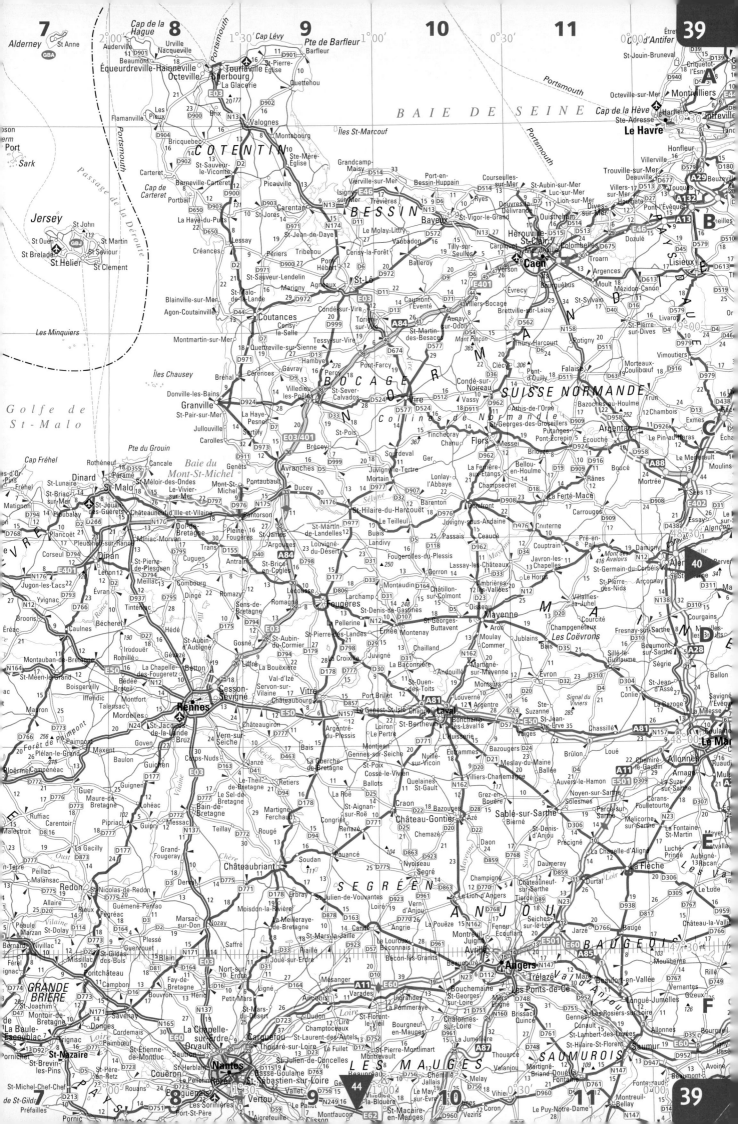

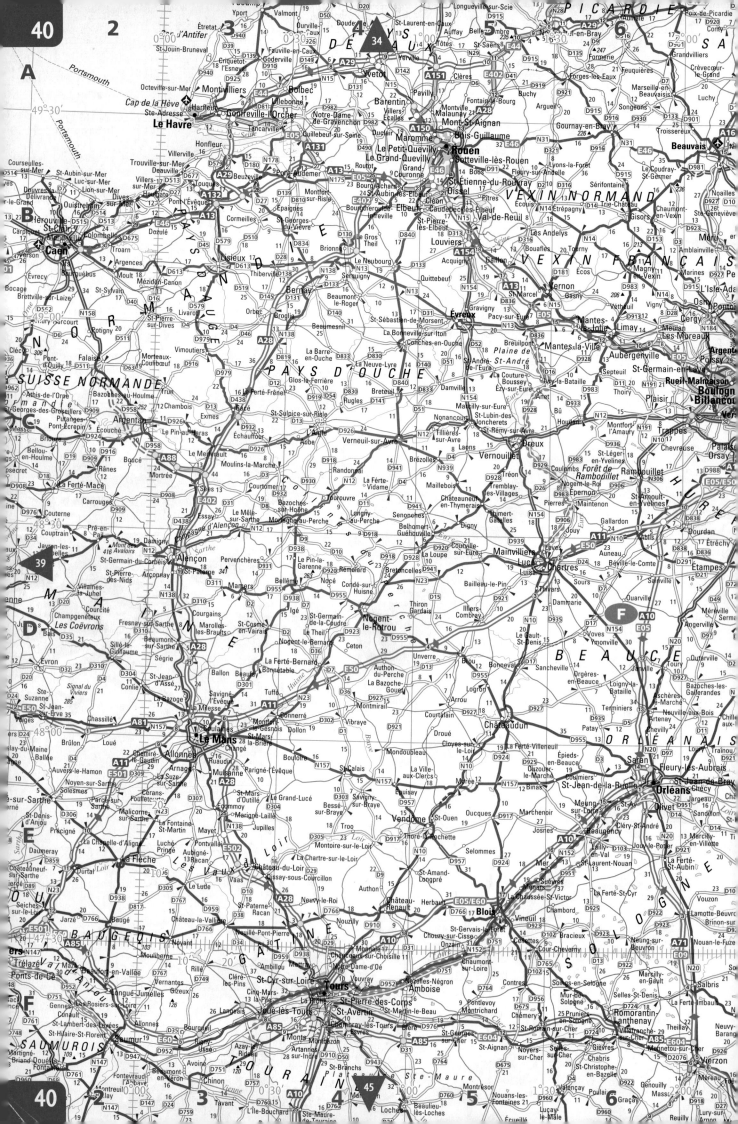

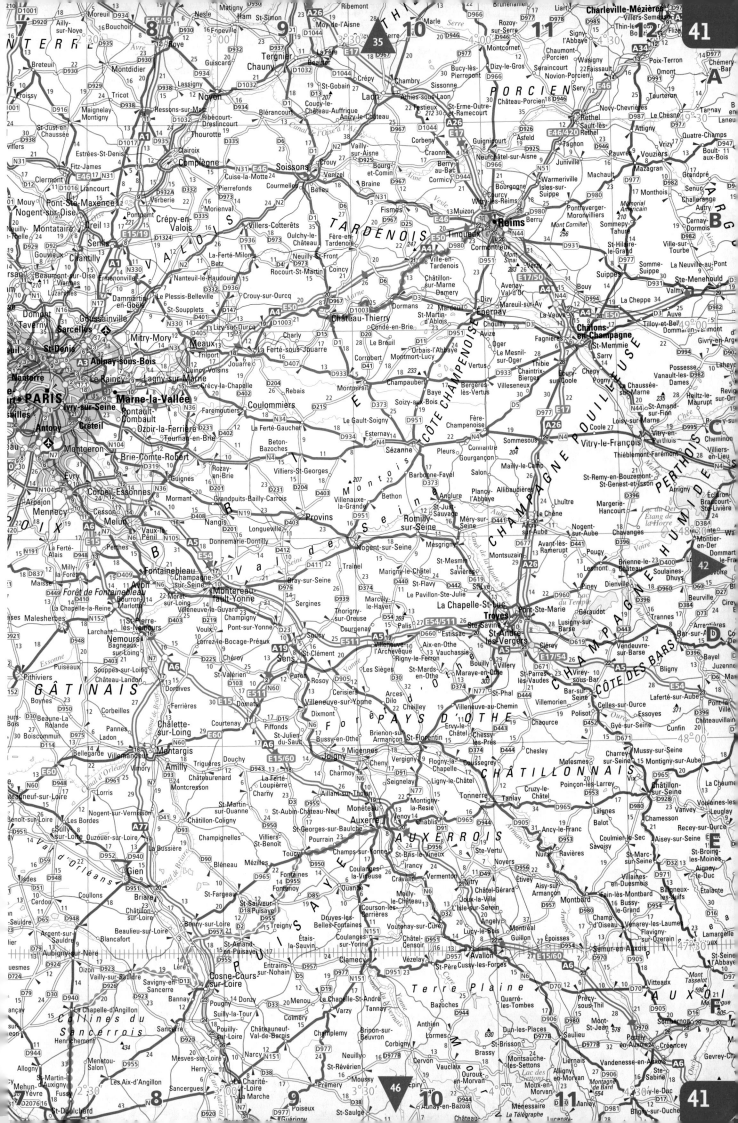

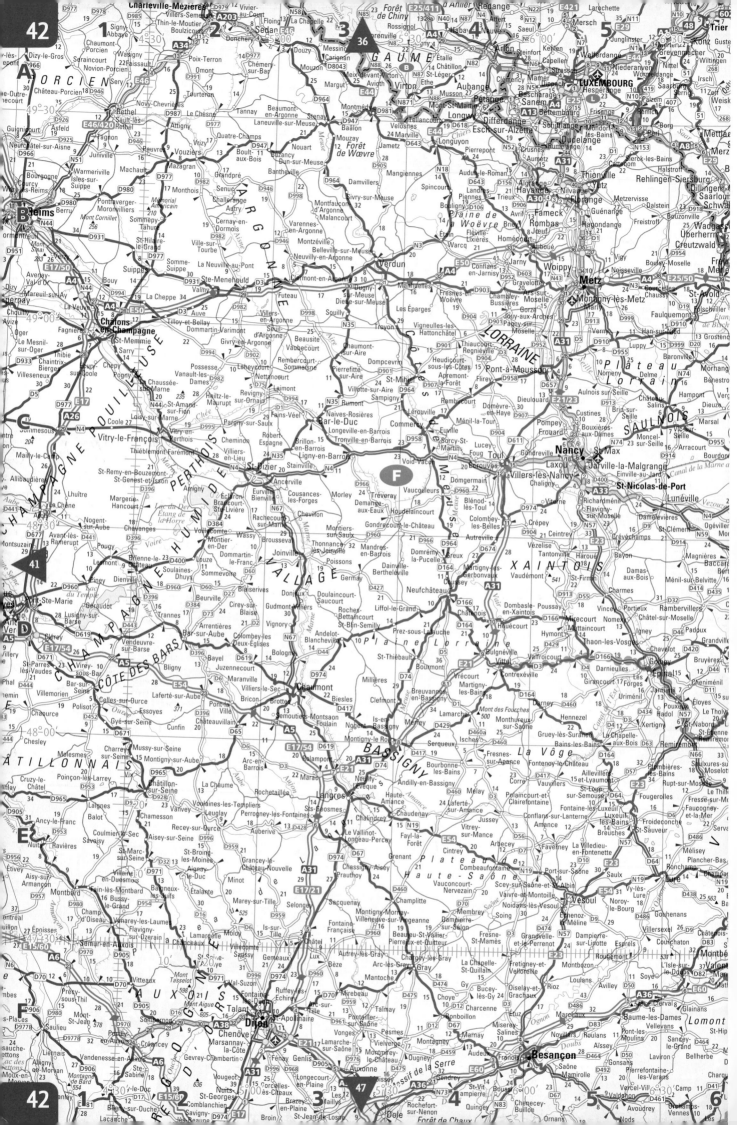

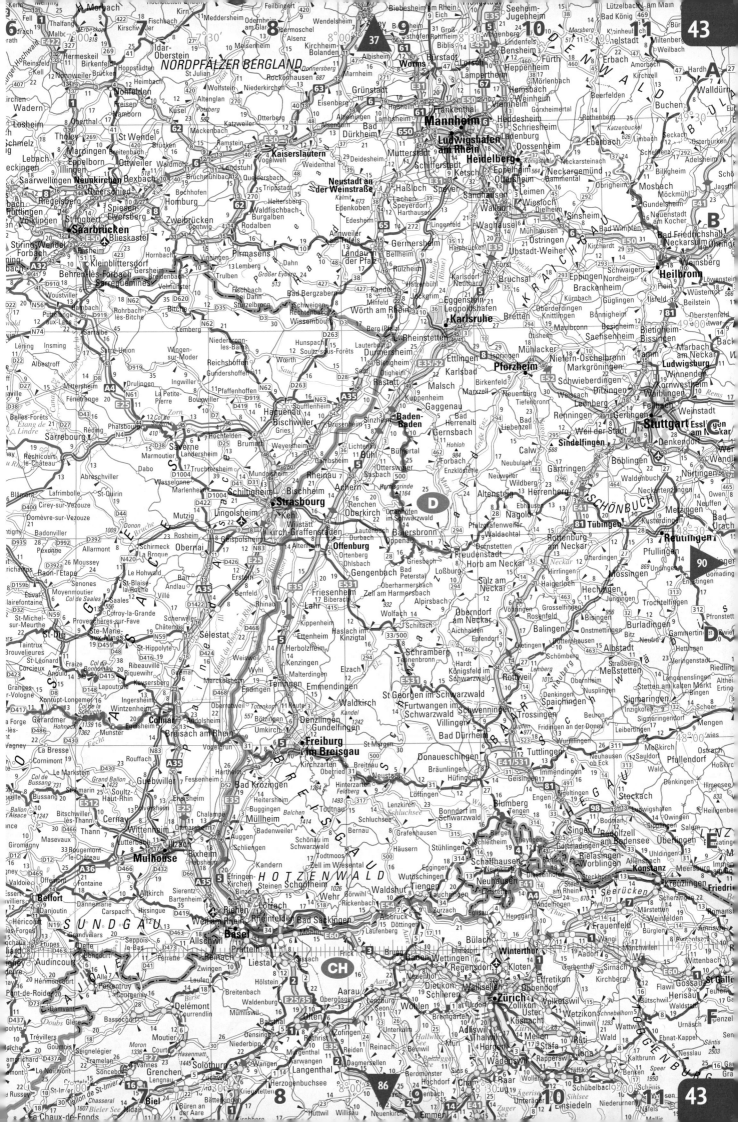

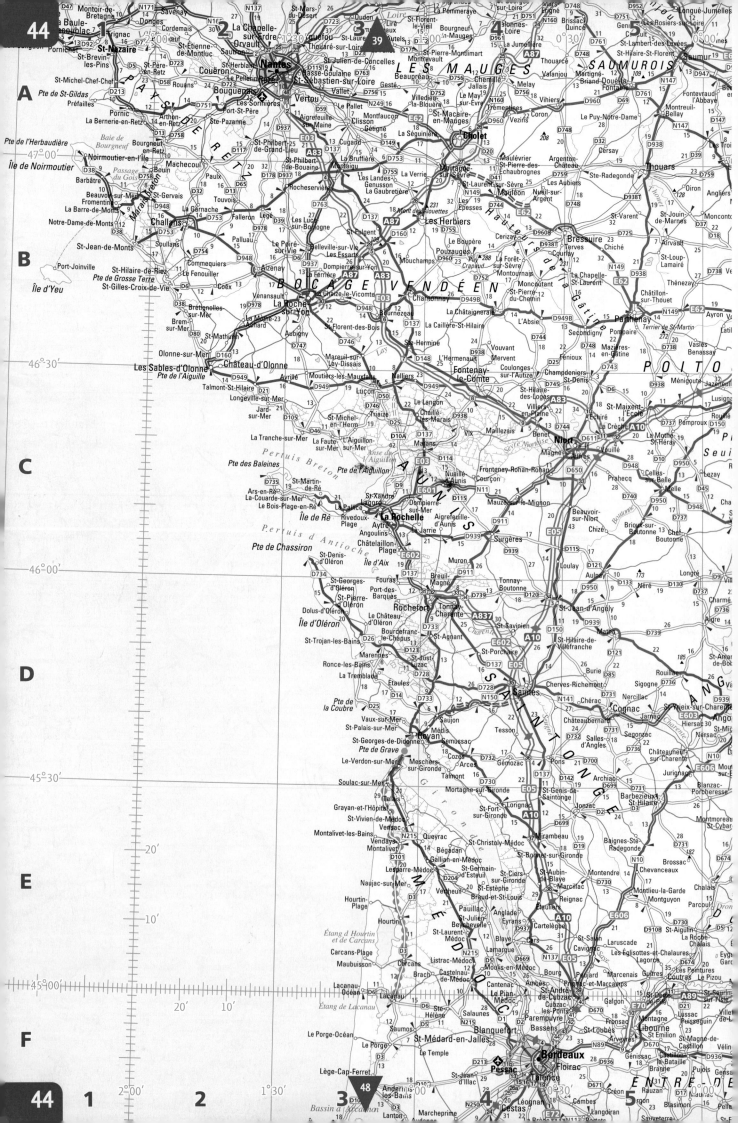

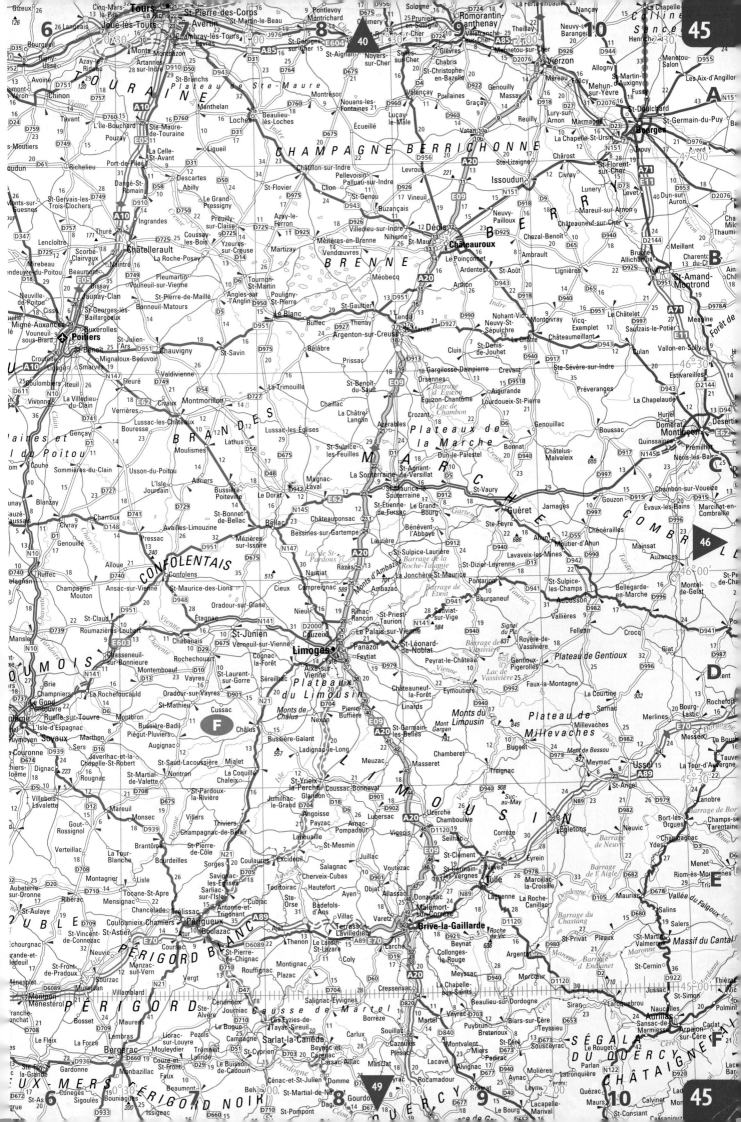

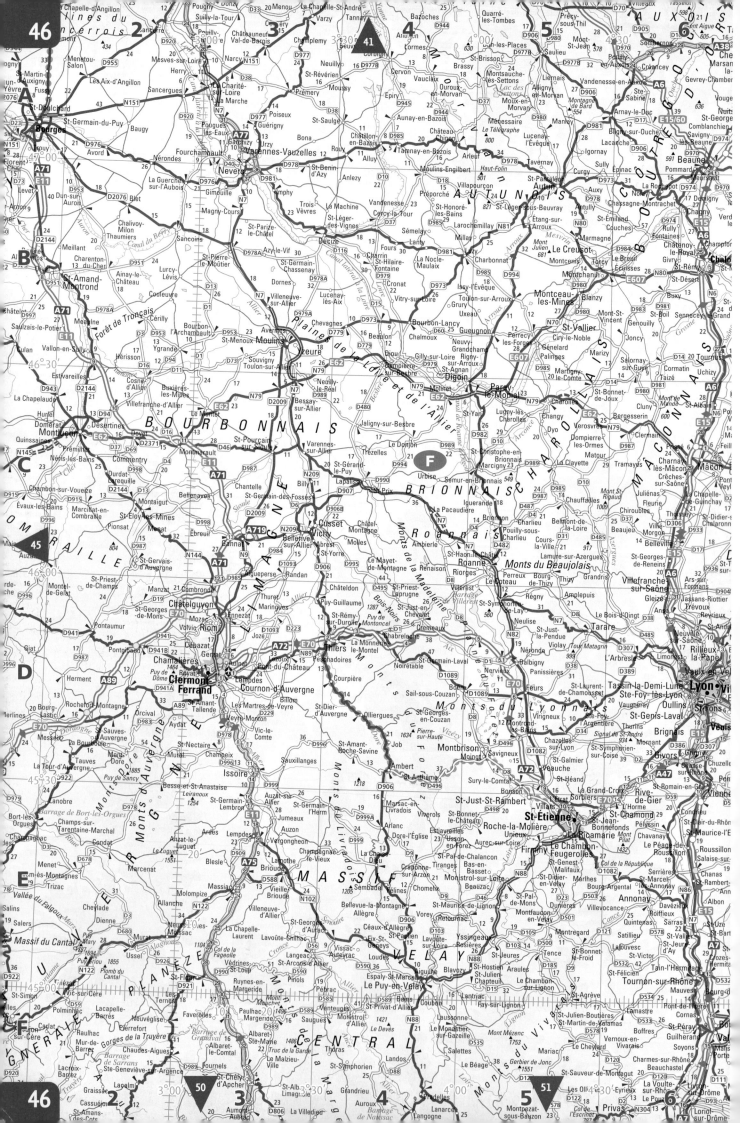

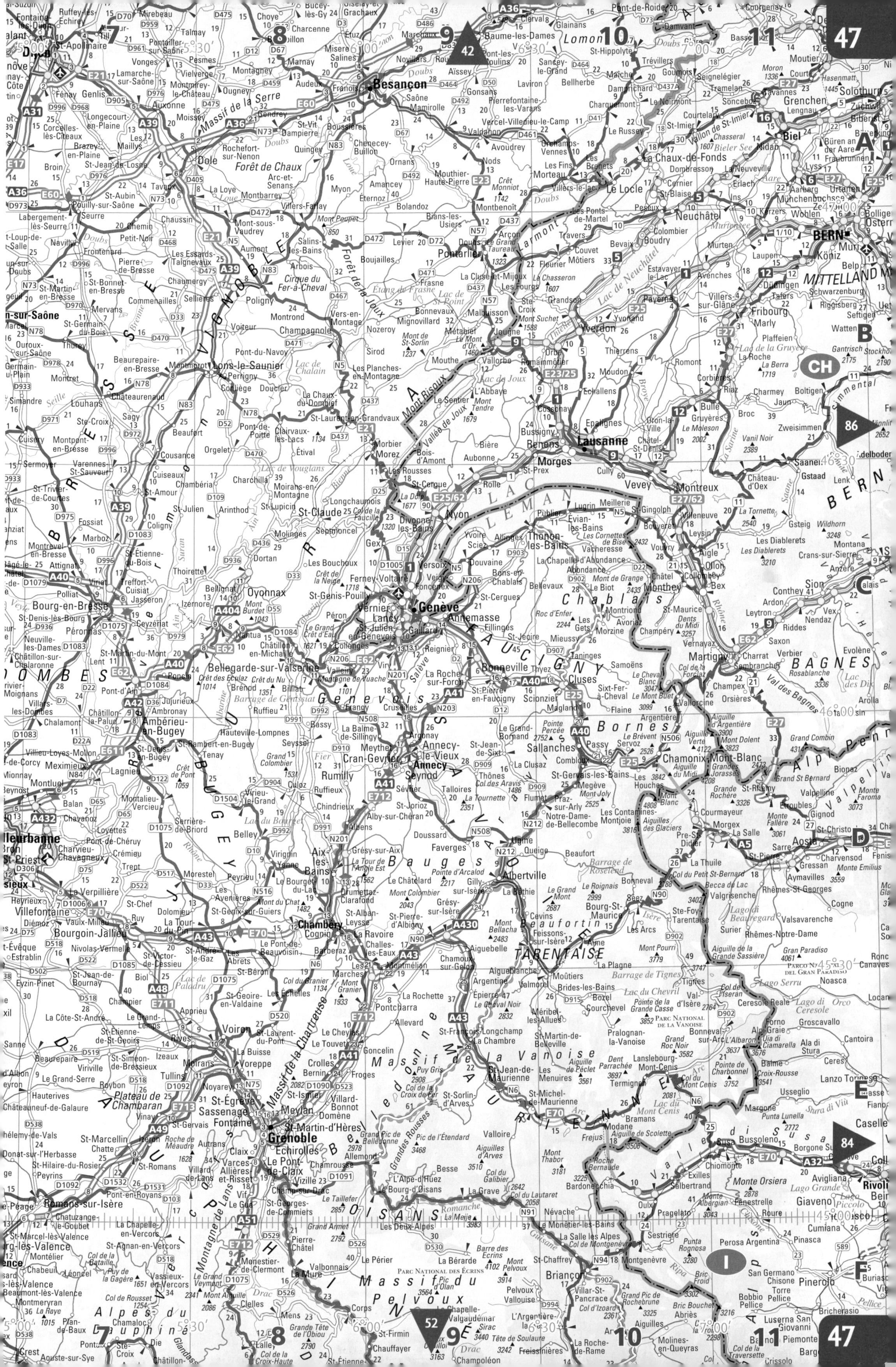
Dijon
Besançon
Dole
Forêt de Chaux
Massif de la Serre
Auxonne
Seurre
Lons-le-Saunier
Poligny
Arbois
Salins-les-Bains
Champagnole
Pontarlier
Morteau
Le Locle
La Chaux-de-Fonds
Neuchâtel
Lac de Neuchâtel
Biel
Solothurn
Grenchen
BERN
MITTELLAND
Fribourg
Yverdon
Lausanne
Morges
Vevey
Montreux
Nyon
Genève
Annemasse
Thonon-les-Bains
Évian-les-Bains
LAC LÉMAN
Chablais
Sion
Martigny
BAGNES
Bourg-en-Bresse
Oyonnax
St-Claude
Bellegarde-sur-Valserine
Annecy
Cran-Gevrier
Seynod
Rumilly
Aix-les-Bains
Chambéry
Bauges
Albertville
Beaufortin
TARENTAISE
Chamonix-Mont-Blanc
Sallanches
Bornes
Cluses
Bonneville
FAUCIGNY
Genevois
BUGEY
Villeurbanne
Bron
St-Priest
Villefontaine
Bourgoin-Jallieu
Voiron
Grenoble
Échirolles
Massif de la Chartreuse
Plateau de Chambaran
Romans-sur-Isère
Valence
VERCORS
OISANS
Massif du Pelvoux
La Vanoise
MAURIENNE
St-Jean-de-Maurienne
Modane
Briançon
Courmayeur
Aosta
Pinerolo
Rivoli
Val di Susa
Gran Paradiso
Parc National des Écrins
Alpes du Dauphiné
CH
I
42
52
84
86
A
B
C
D
E
F
7
8
9
10
11

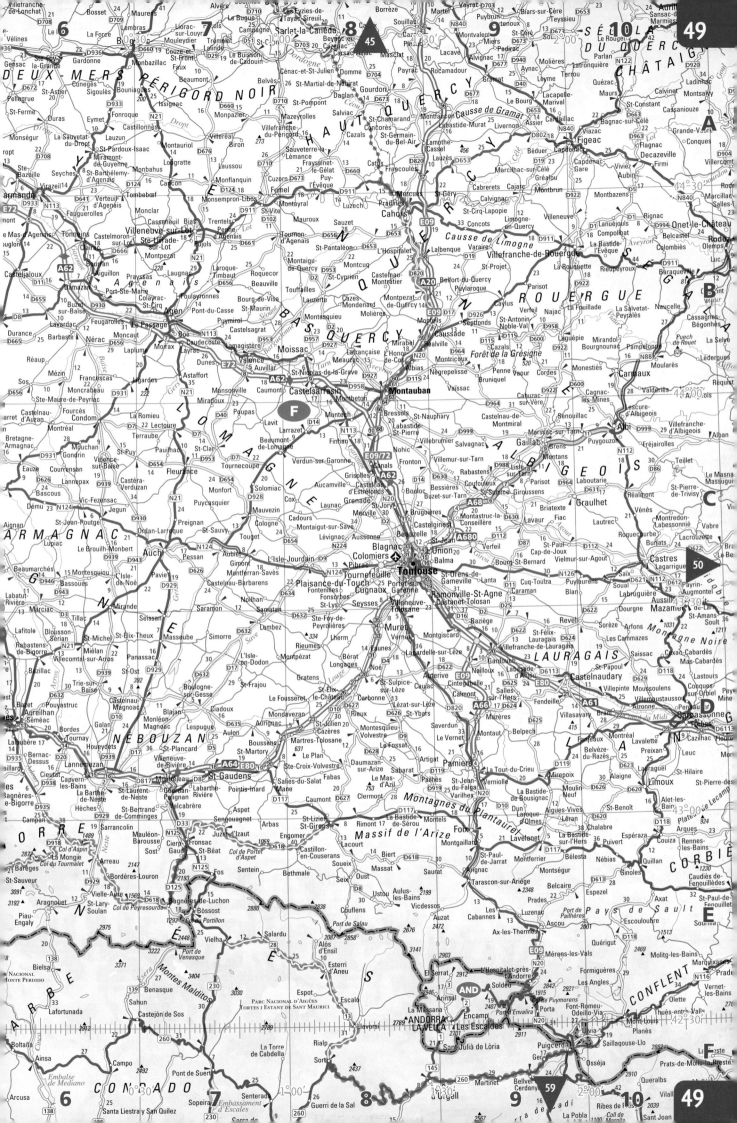

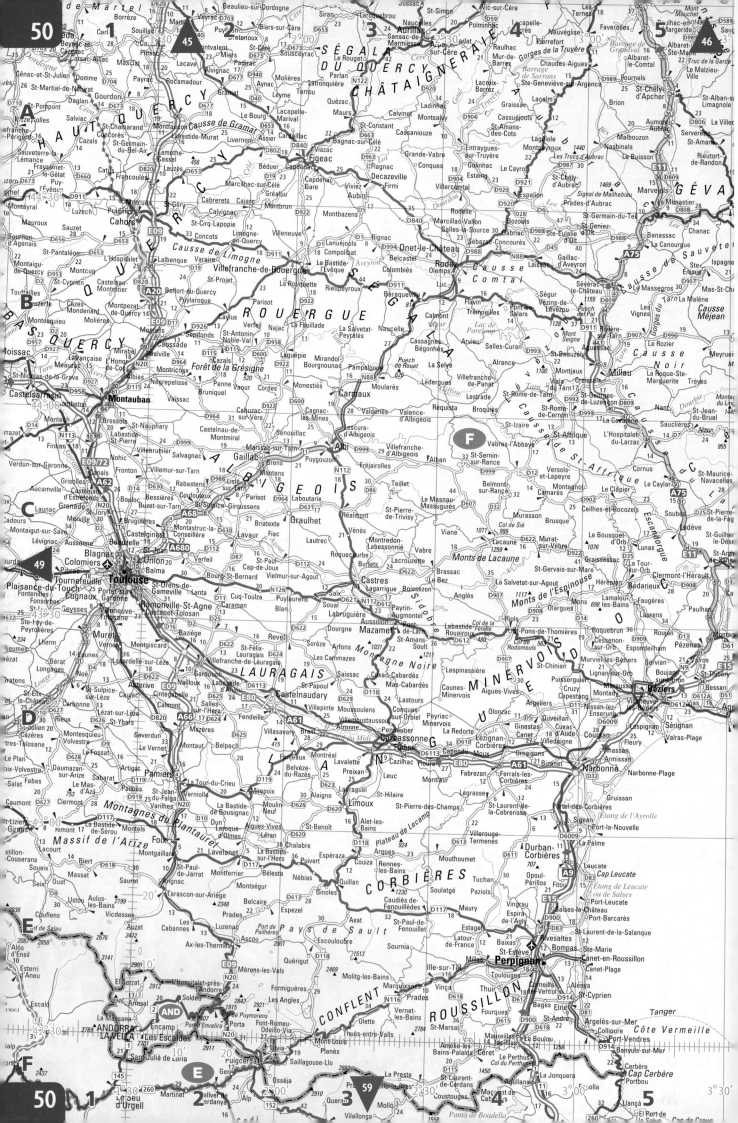

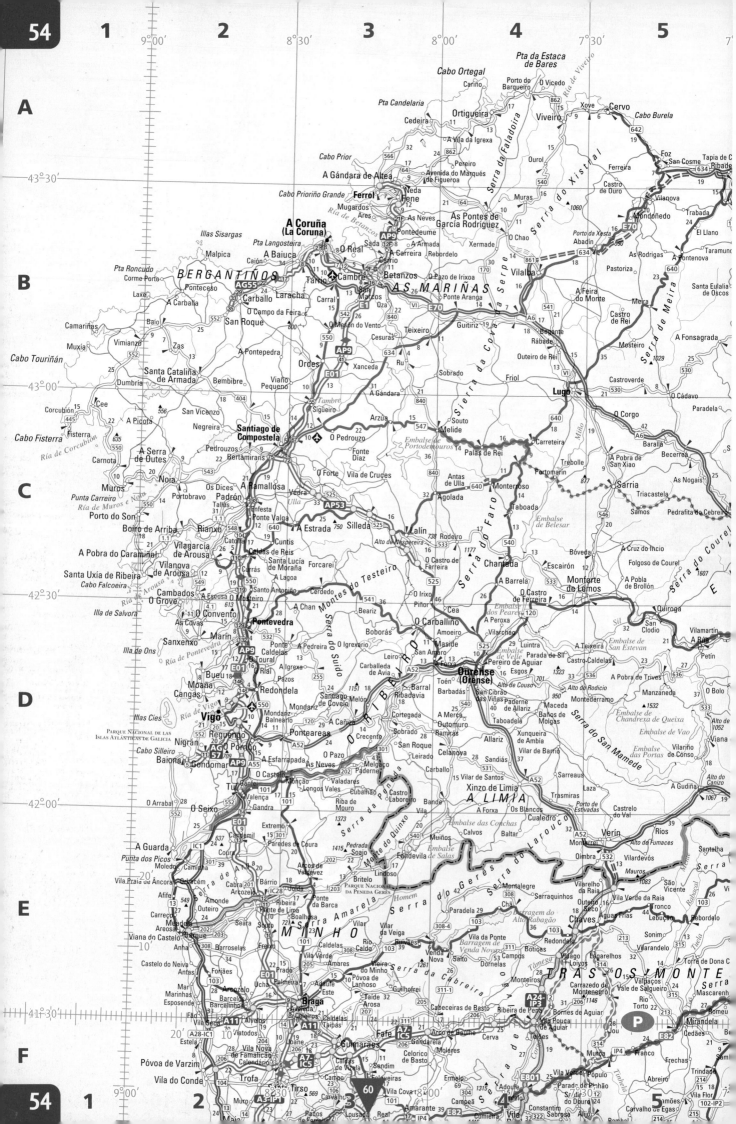

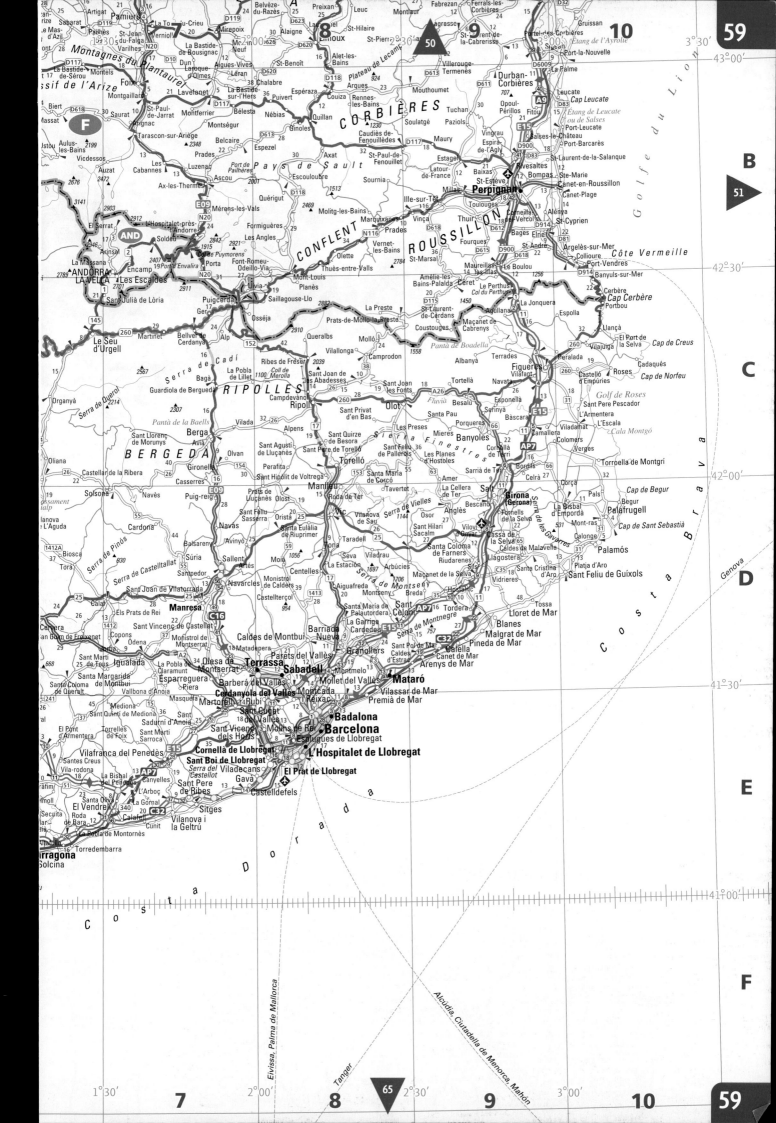

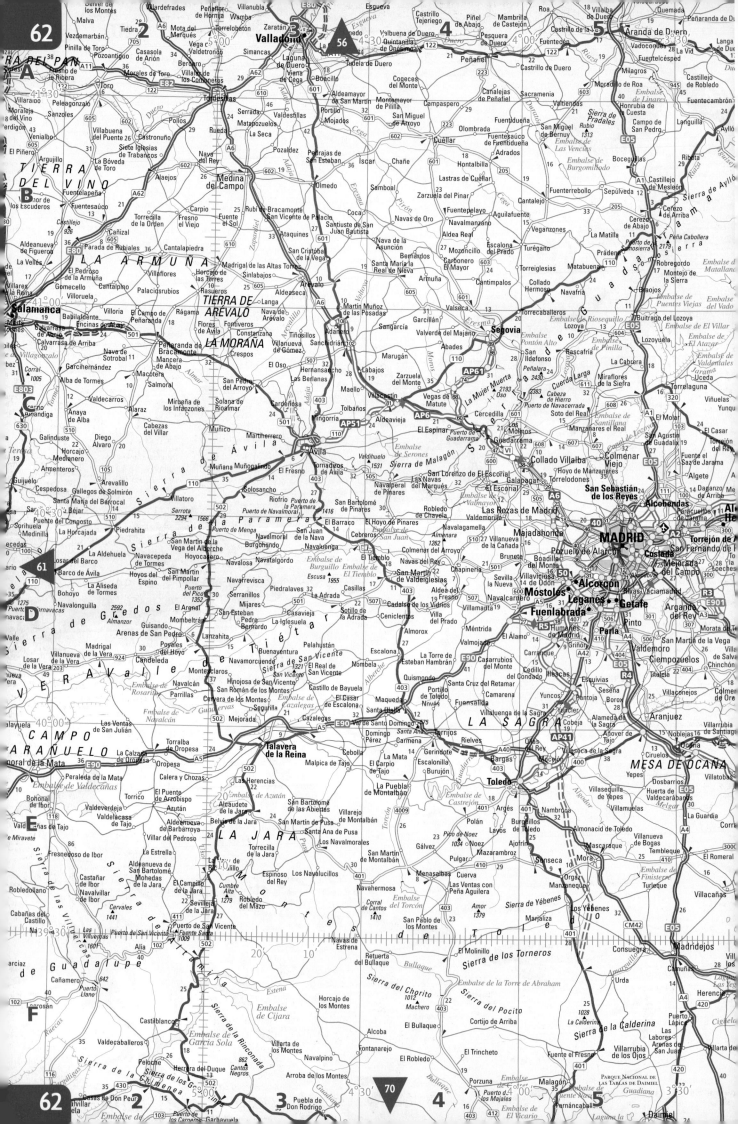

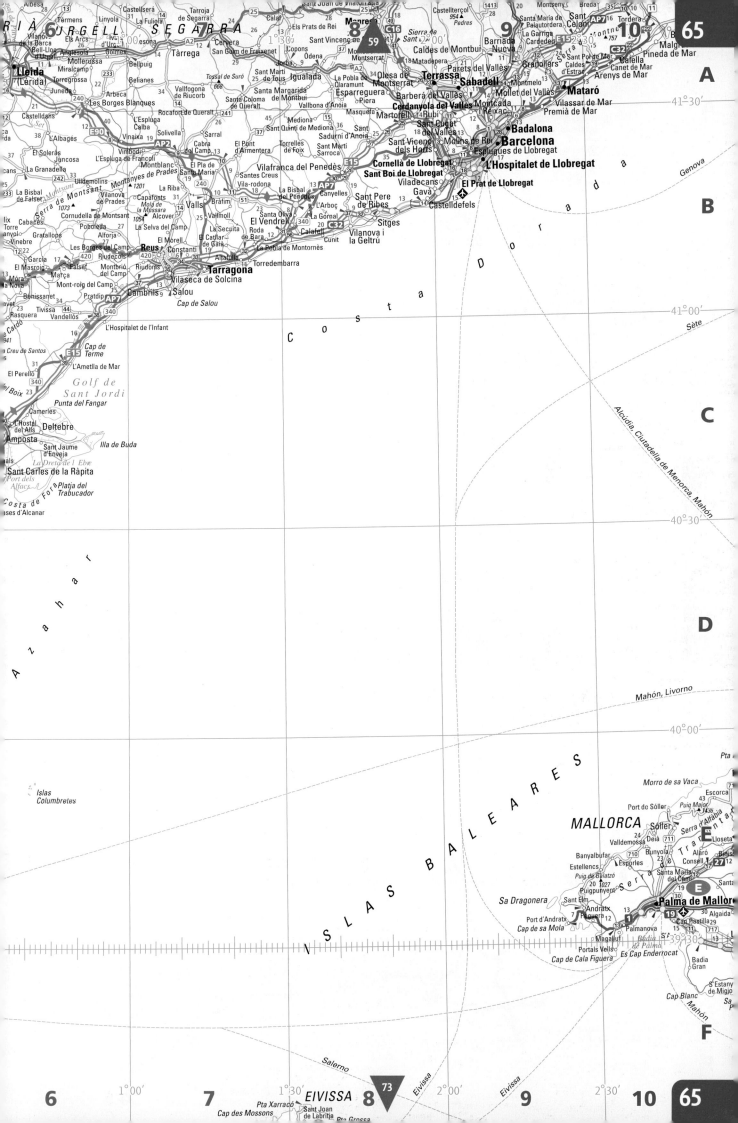

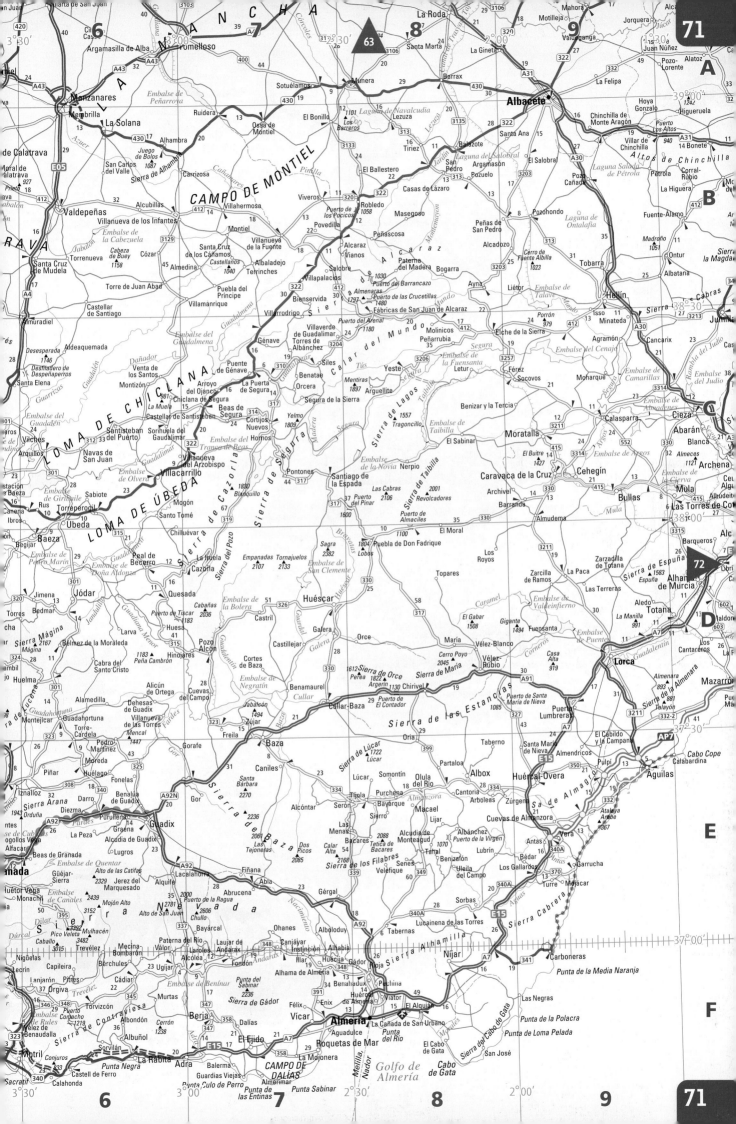

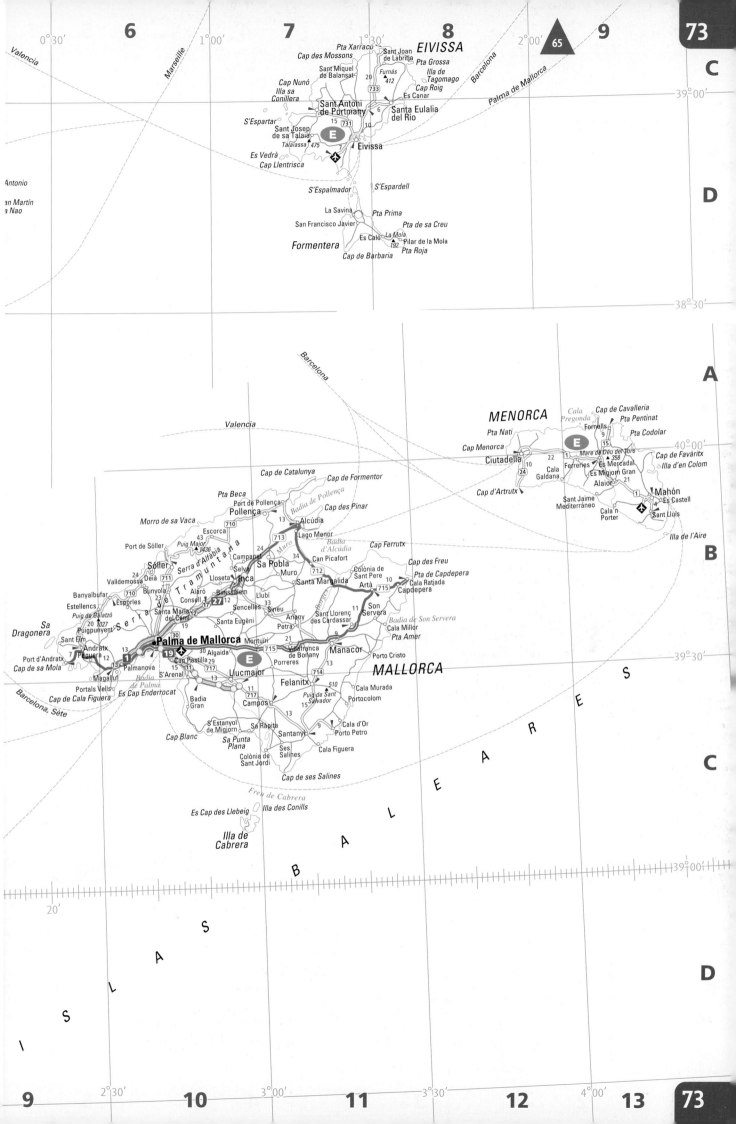

6   **7**   **8**   EIVISSA   65   **9**   73

C

0°30'   1°00'   2°00'

Pta Xarraco
Cap des Mossons
Sant Joan
de Labritja   Pta Grossa
Sant Miquel   Illa de
de Balansat   20   Furnás   Tagomago
412   Cap Roig
Cap Nunó   733   Es Canar
Illa sa
Conillera   731   Sant Antoni
de Portmany   6   Santa Eulalia
del Río
S'Espartar   15
Sant Josep   10
de sa Talaia
Talaiassa 475   E
7   Eivissa
Es Vedrà
Cap Llentrisca

Valencia

Marseille

Barcelona

Palma de Mallorca

39°00'

D

Antonio
an Martín
a Nao

S'Espalmador   S'Espardell

La Savina   Pta Prima
San Francisco Javier   Pta de sa Creu
Es Caló   La Mola   Pilar de la Mola
192   Pta Roja
Formentera
Cap de Barbaria

38°30'

Barcelona

A

Valencia

MENORCA   Cala
Pregonda   Cap de Cavalleria
Pta Nati   Fornells   Pta Pentinat
Cap Menorca   E   Pta Codolar
9   15
Cap de Catalunya   Cap de Formentor   Ciutadella   22   1   Mare de Déu del Toro   Cap de Favàritx
Pta Beca   Ferreries   358   Illa d'en Colom
Port de Pollença   Cap des Pinar   24   Cala   Es Mercadal
Pollença   13   Alcúdia   Galdana   Es Migjorn Gran   40°00'
Morro de sa Vaca   710   Lago Menor   Alaior   21
Escorca   713   Muro   Badia   Sant Jaime   Cala n   1   Mahón
Port de Sóller   43   d'Alcúdia   Mediterráneo   Porter   Es Castell
Puig Major   24   Campanet   34   Can Picafort   Cap d'Artrutx   Sant Lluís
1436   Selva   Sa Pobla   Cap Ferrutx
Sóller   711   Lloseta   Muro   712   Colònia de   Cap des Freu   B
Serra d'Alfàbia   Inca   Santa Margalida   Sant Pere   Pta de Capdepera   Illa de l'Aire
Valldemossa   24   Alaró   Binissalem   Artà   10   Cala Ratjada
Deià   710   Bunyola   Consell   27   12   715   Capdepera
Banyalbufar   Santa Maria   Llubí   11   Son
Estellencs   710   del Camí   Sineu   Sant Llorenç   Servera
Puig de Galatzó   23   Sencelles   19   Anany   des Cardassar   Cala Millor   Badia de Son Servera
Sa   20   1027   Santa Eugèni   Petra   Pta Amer
Dragonera   Puigpunyent   Villafranca
Sant Elm   Montuïri   21   de Bonany   Manacor
Andratx   13   30   Algaida   715   13   Porto Cristo   39°30'
Port d'Andratx   Figuera   12   Palma de Mallorca   Can Pastilla   Porreres   MALLORCA   C
Cap de sa Mola   7   1   S'Arenal   717   714   Cala Murada
Palmanova   15   11   13   Felanitx   510   Portocolom
Magaluf   Badia   Llucmajor   Puig de Sant   15   Portocolom
Portals Vells   de Palma   717   Salvador   Cala d'Or
Cap de Cala Figuera   Es Cap Enderrocat   Campos   9   Porto Petro
Barcelona, Sète   Badia   13   Cala Figuera
Gran   S'Estanyol   Santanyí
de Migjorn
Cap Blanc   Sa Ràpita   Ses
Sa Punta   Salines
Plana   Colònia de
Sant Jordi   Cap de ses Salines

B   A   L   E   A   R   E   S

Freu de Cabrera

Es Cap des Llebeig   Illa des Conills

Illa de
Cabrera   C

39°00'

20'

D

I
S
L
A
S

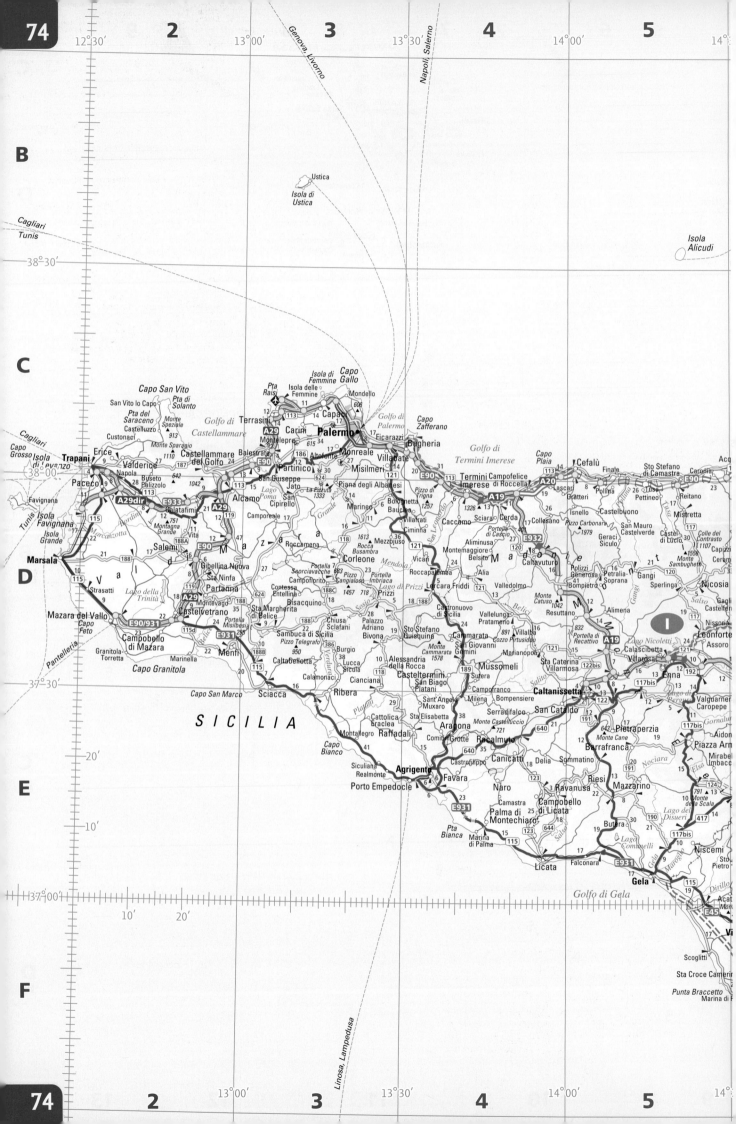

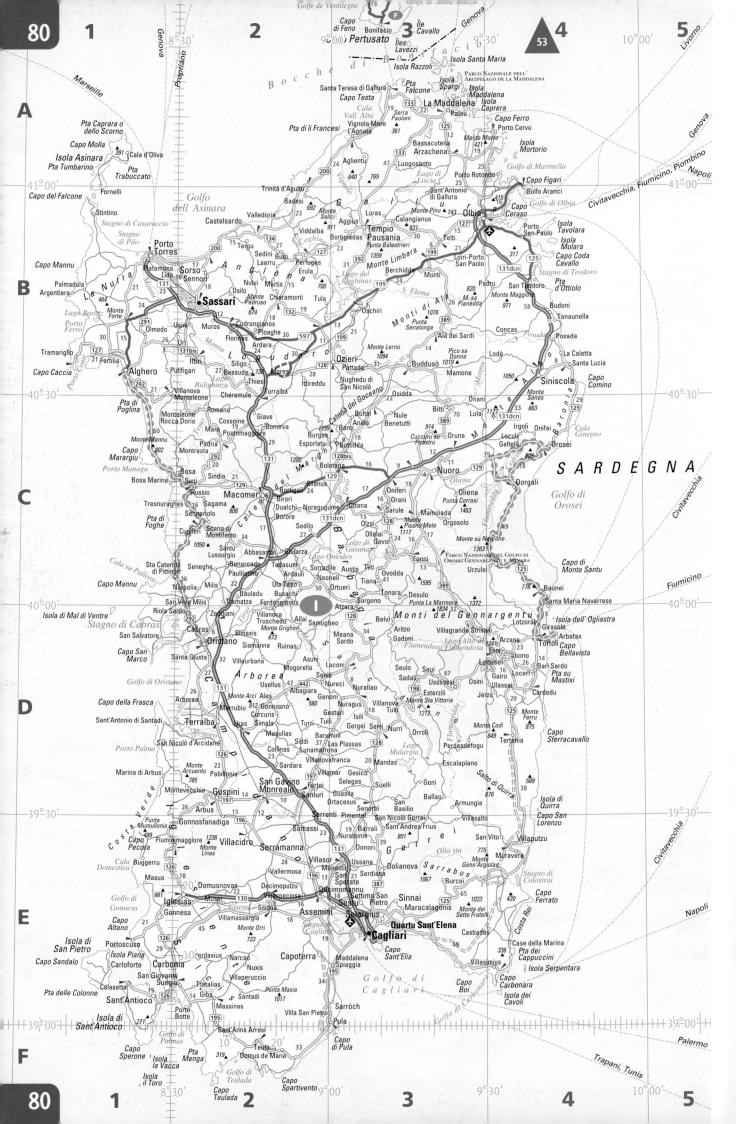

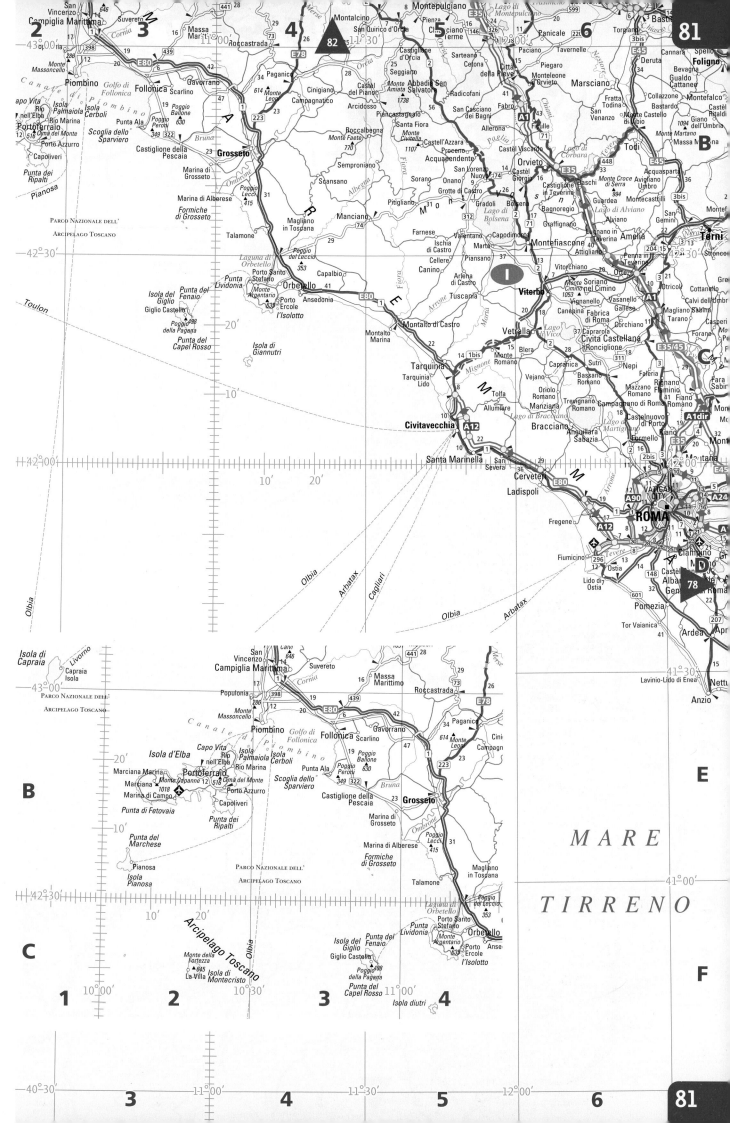

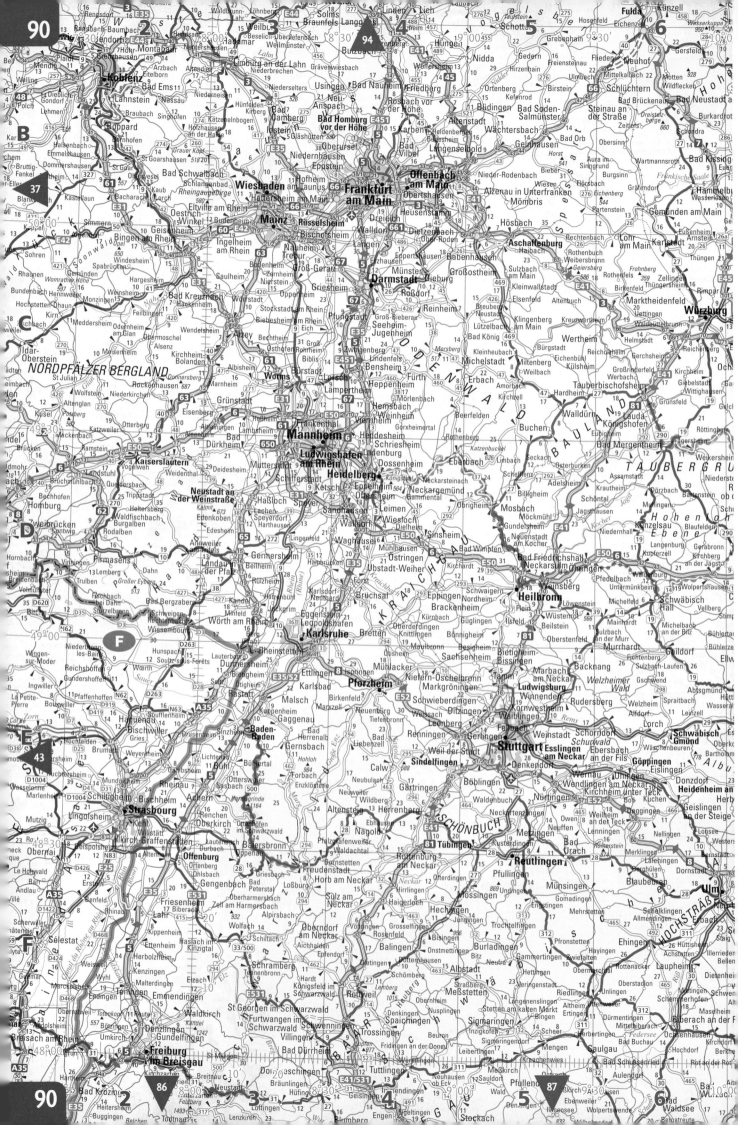

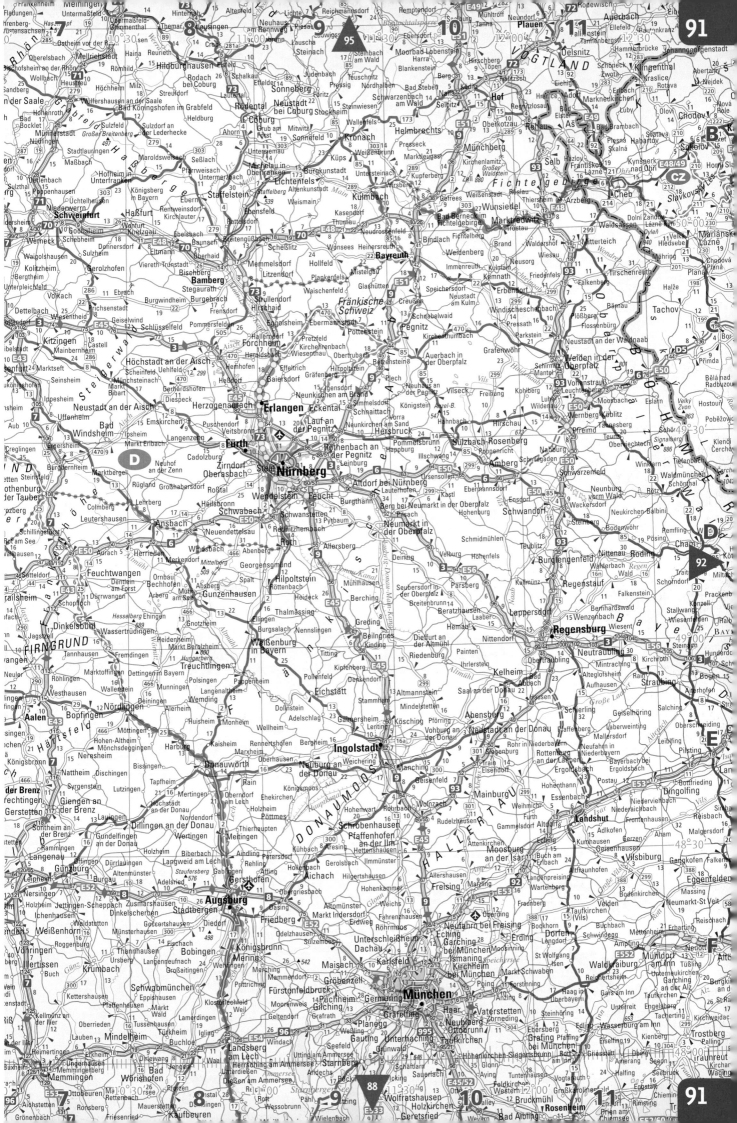

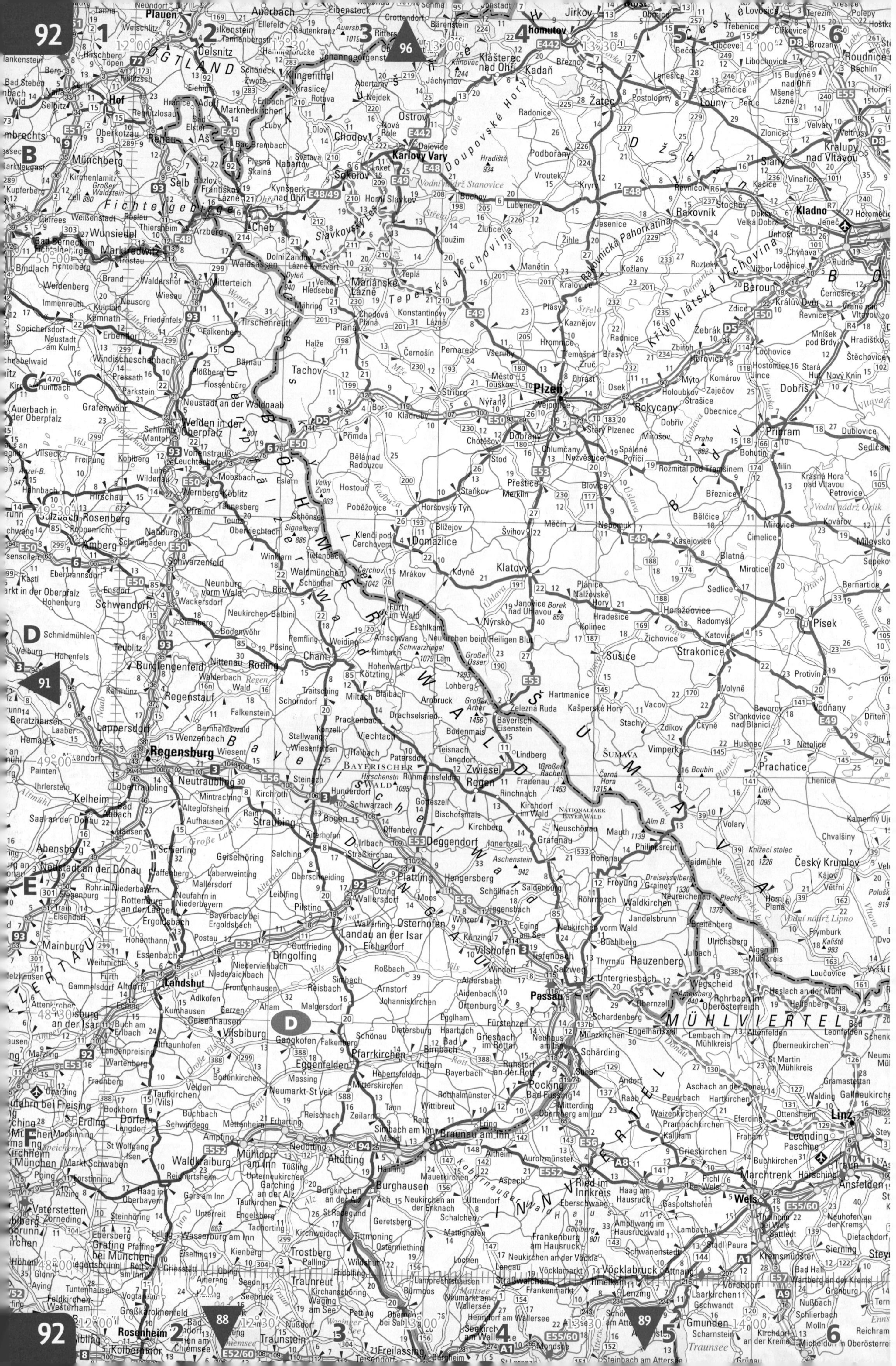

96

91

B

C

D

E

F

Plauen
Auerbach
Eibenstock
Jirkov
Chomutov
Kadaň
Žatec
Louny

Hof
Münchberg
Selb
Cheb
Karlovy Vary
Sokolov
Rakovník
Kladno
Slaný

Marktredwitz
Mariánské Lázně
Plasy
Beroun

Tachov
Stříbro
Plzeň
Rokycany
Příbram

Weiden in der Oberpfalz
Domažlice
Klatovy
Horažďovice
Písek

Amberg
Schwandorf
Cham
Furth im Wald
Sušice
Strakonice

Regensburg
Bayerischer Wald
Zwiesel
Regen
Šumava
Prachatice
Český Krumlov

Straubing
Deggendorf
Grafenau
Freyung

Landshut
Vilshofen
Passau
MÜHLVIERTEL
Linz
Wels

Mühldorf am Inn
Burghausen
Braunau am Inn
Ried im Innkreis

Rosenheim
Traunstein
Freilassing
Gmunden

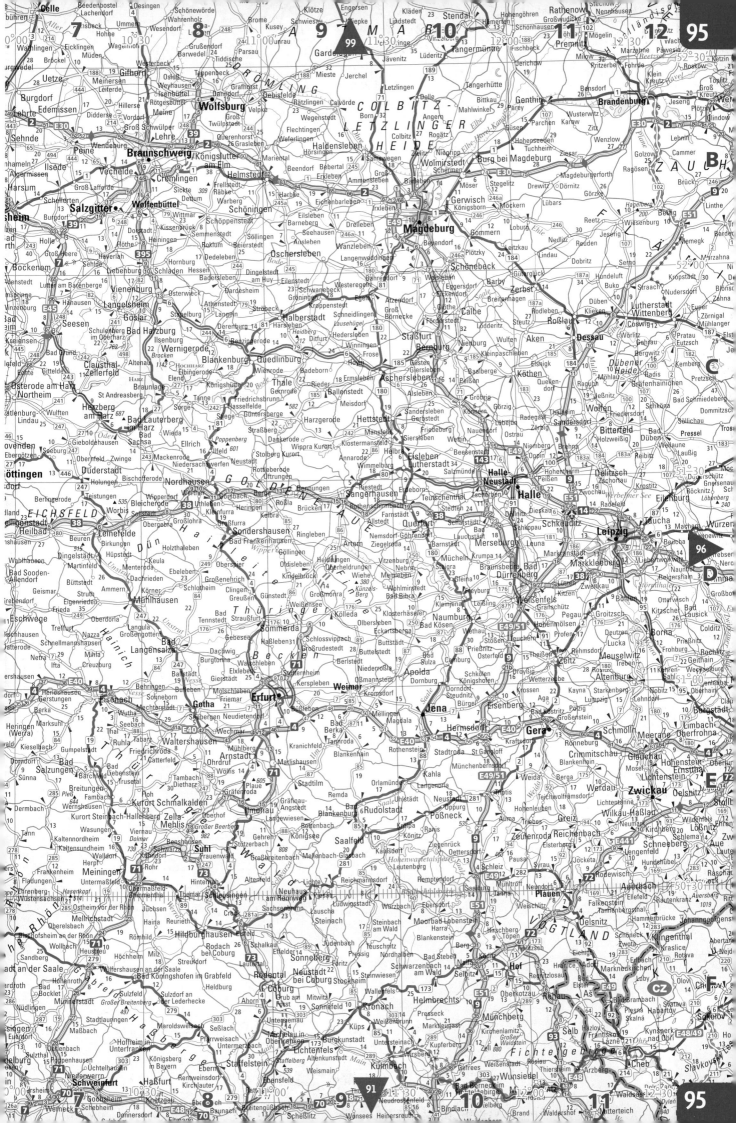

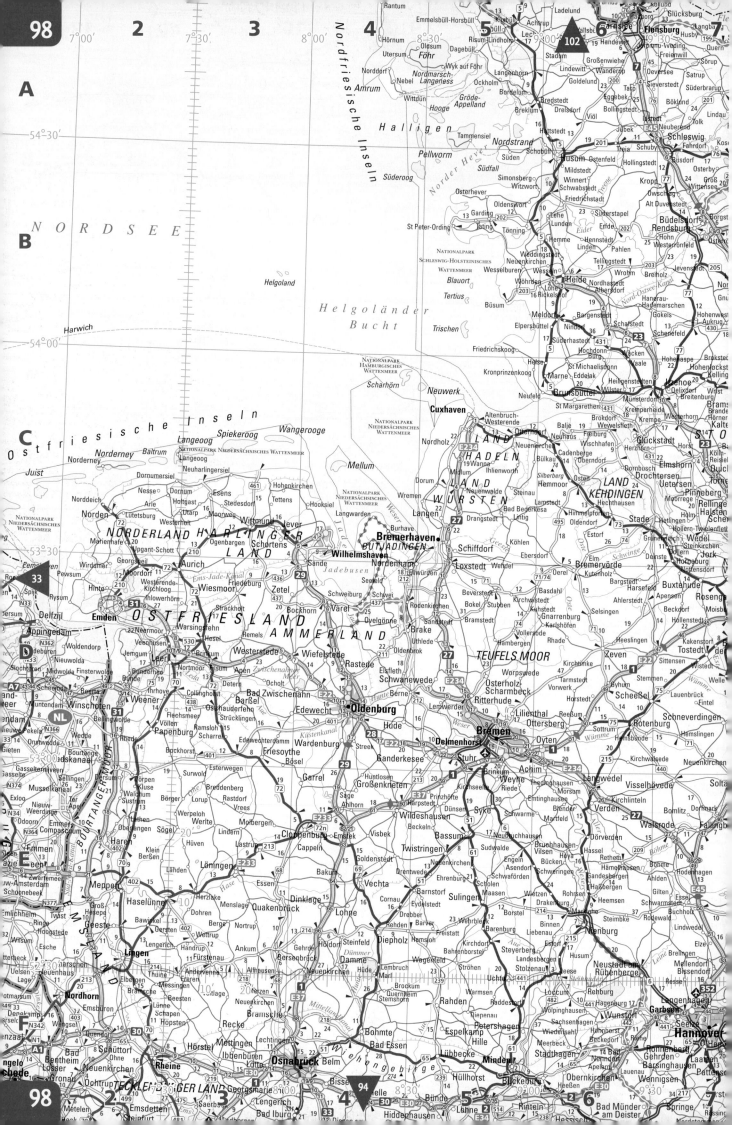

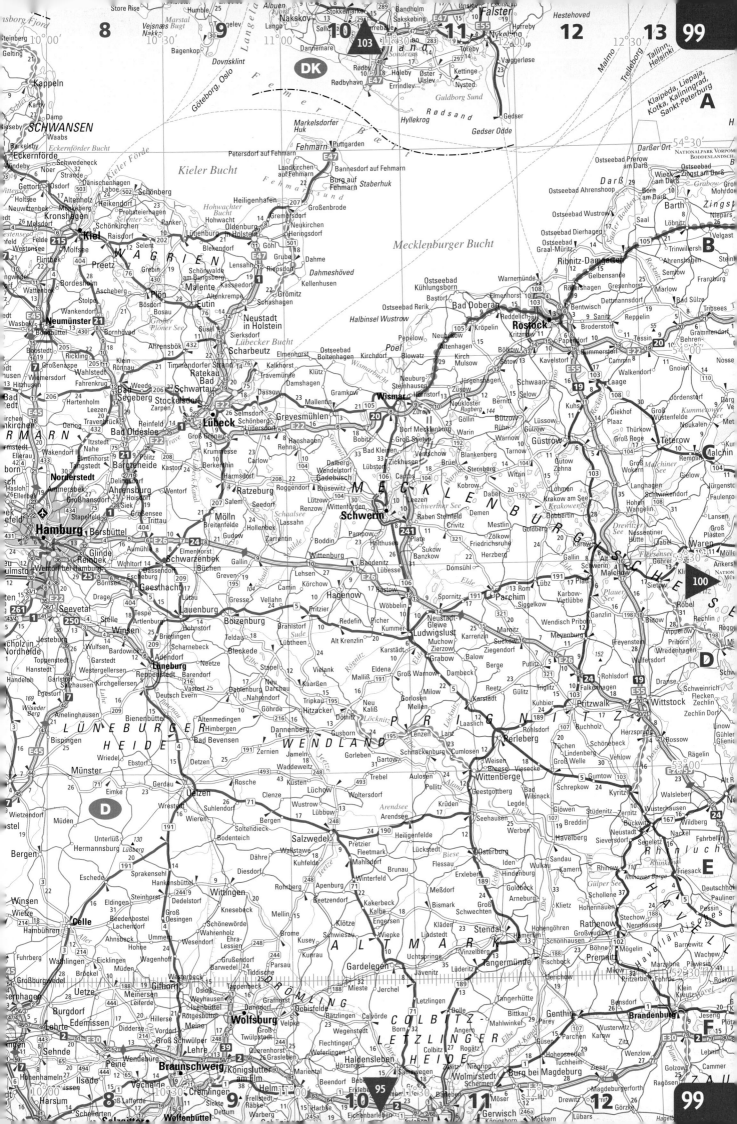

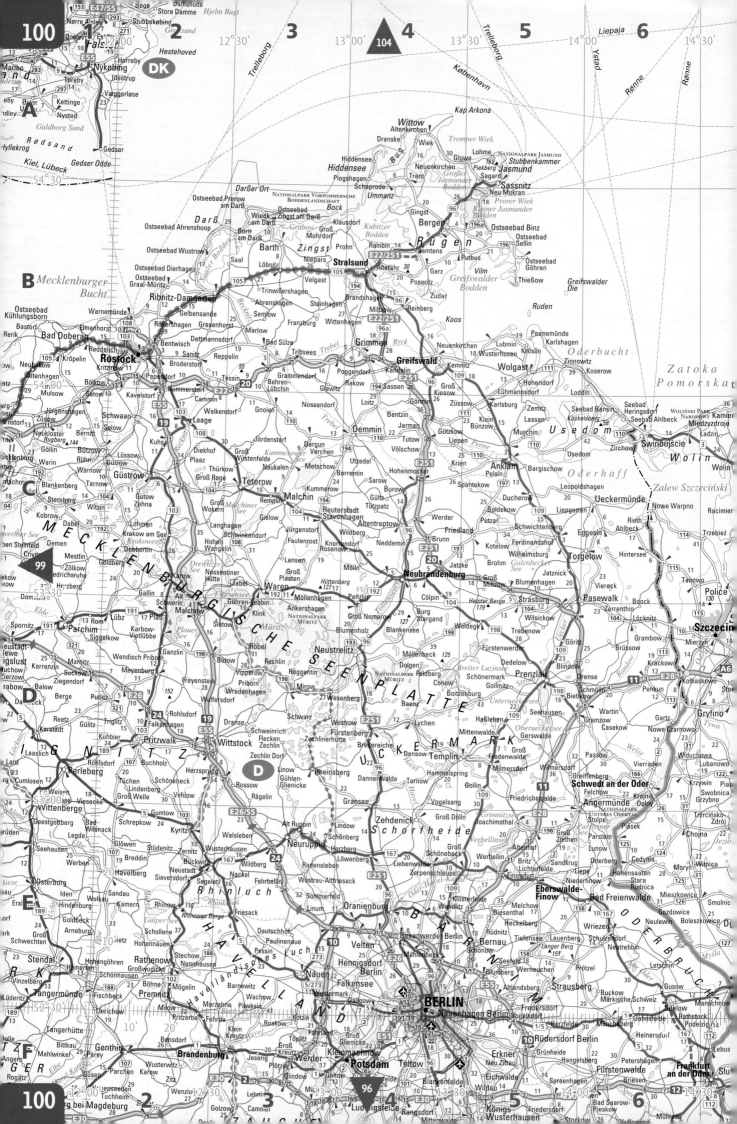

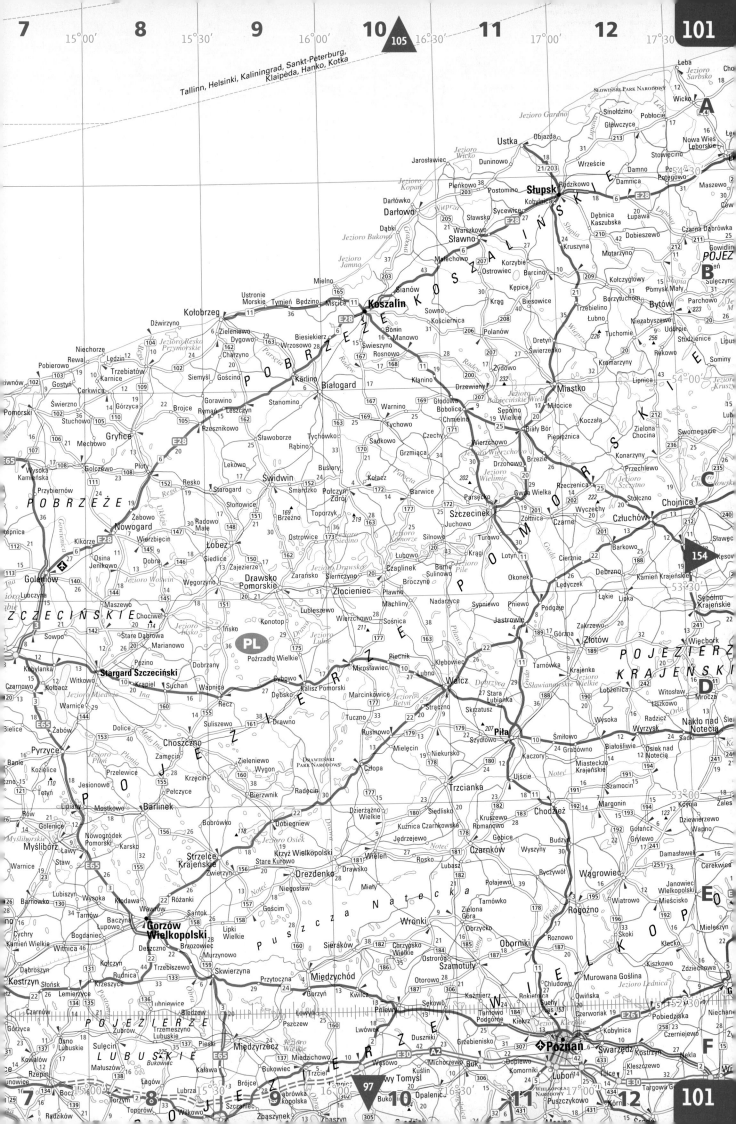

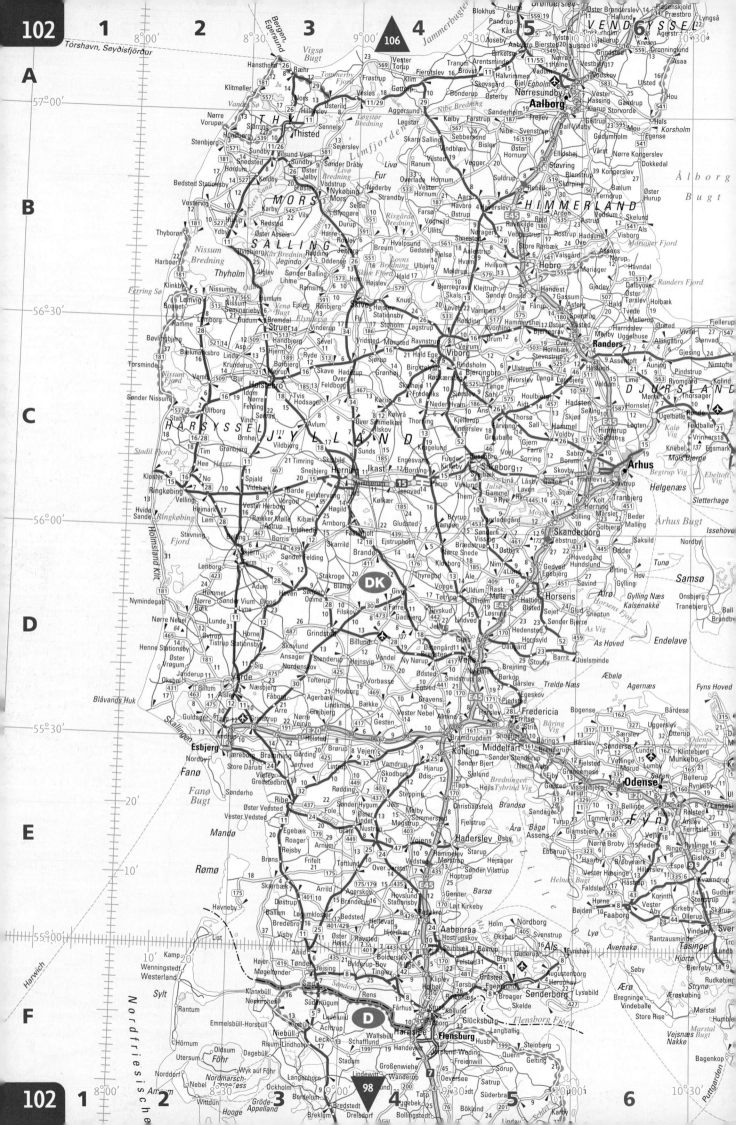

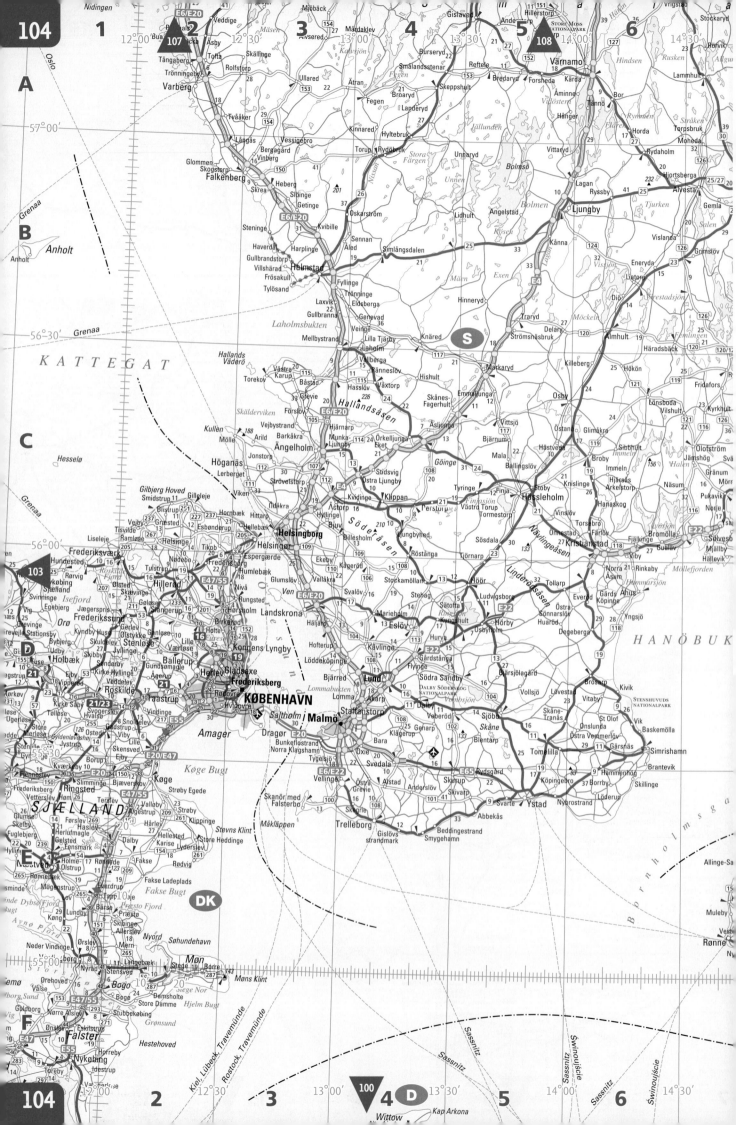

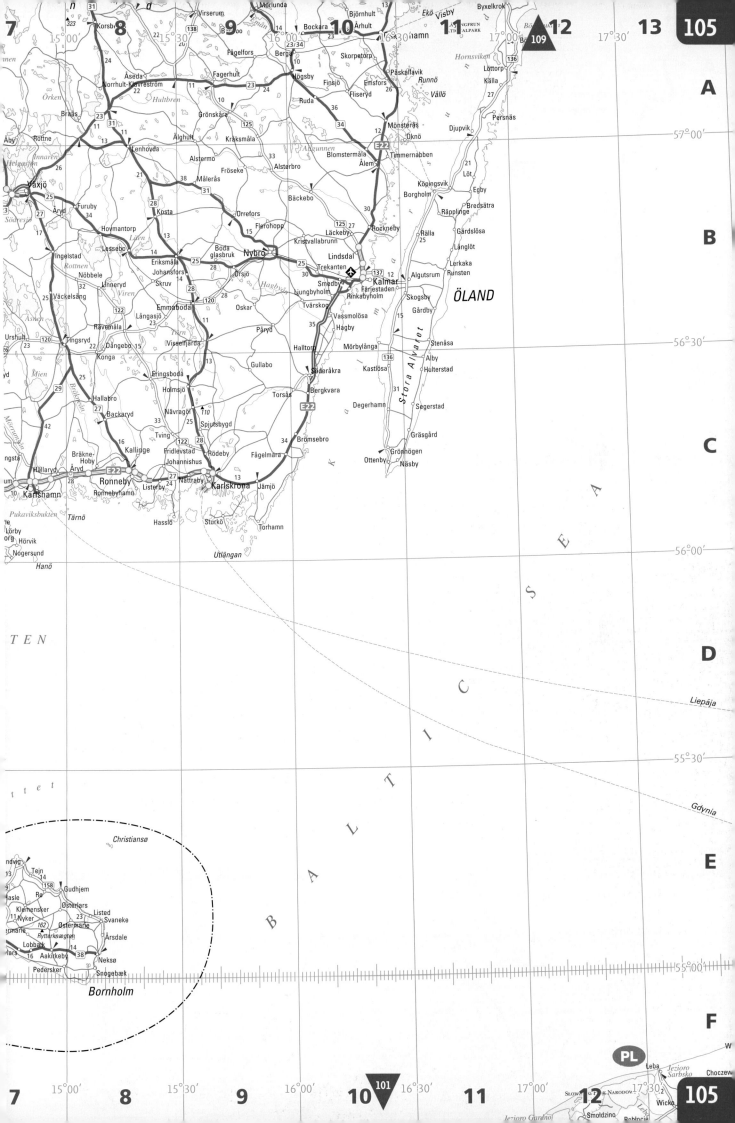

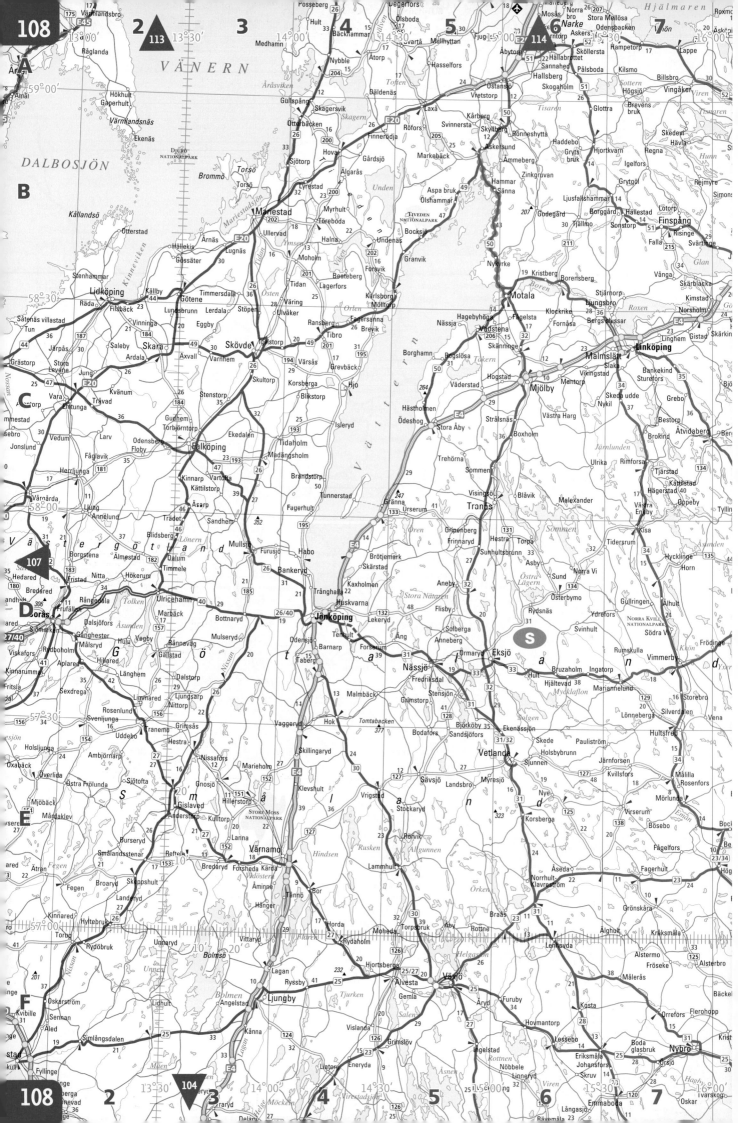

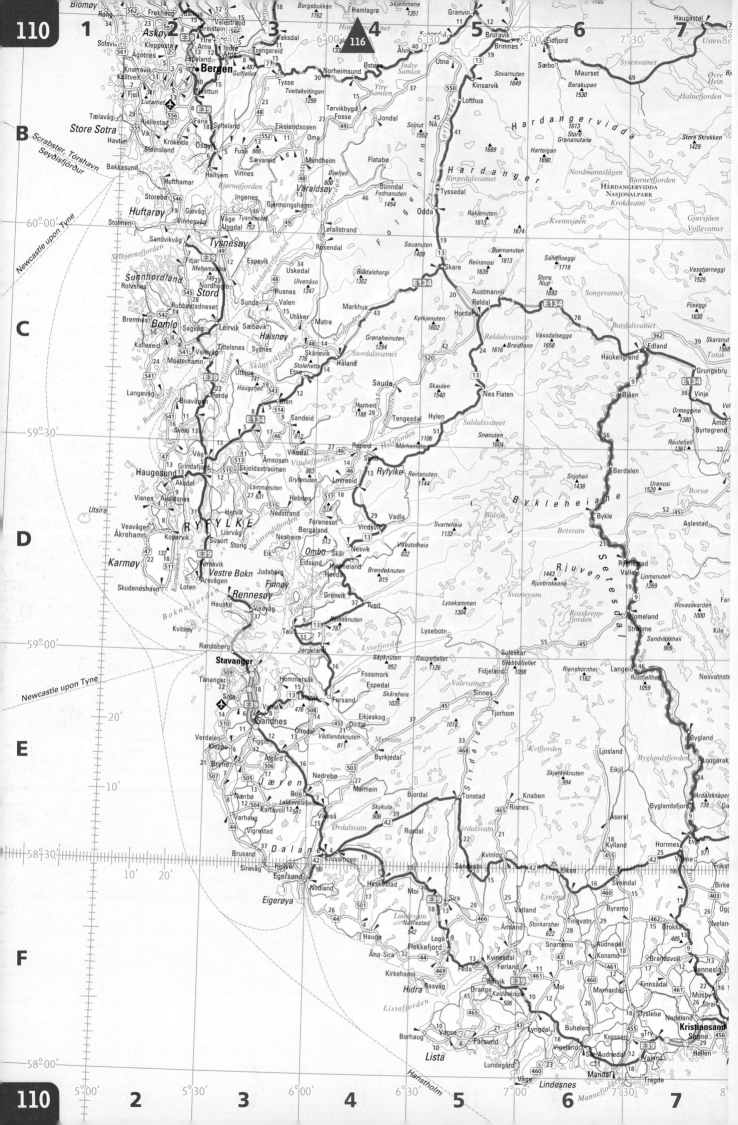

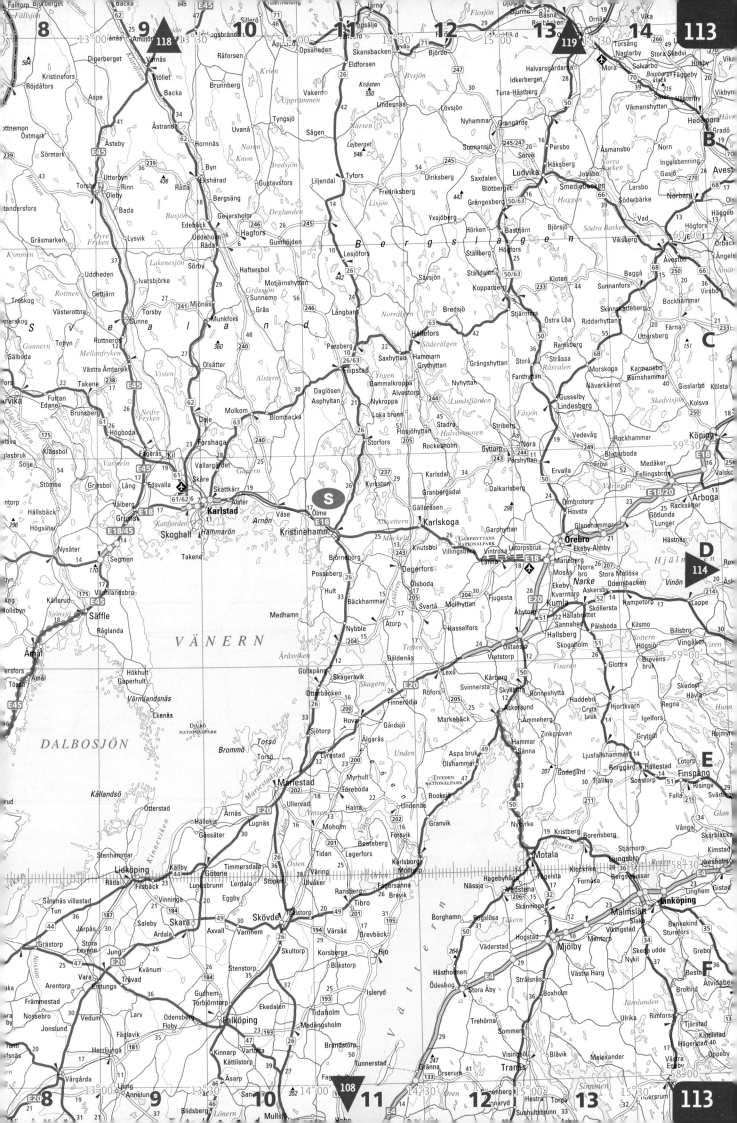

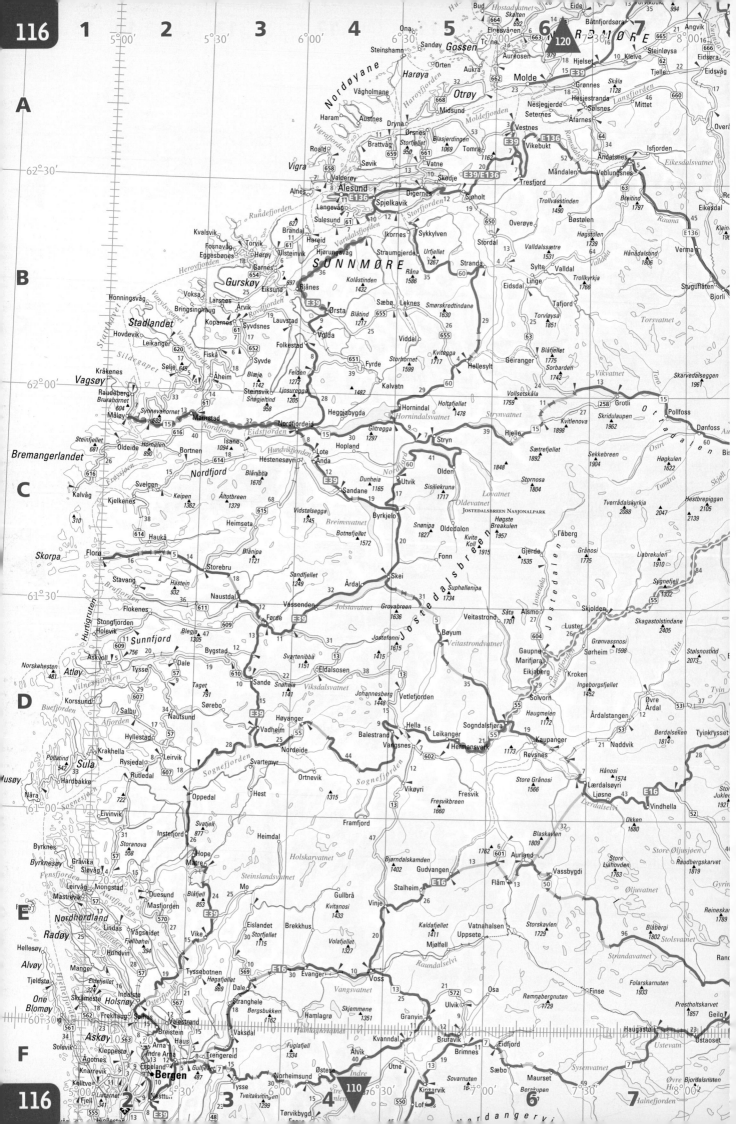

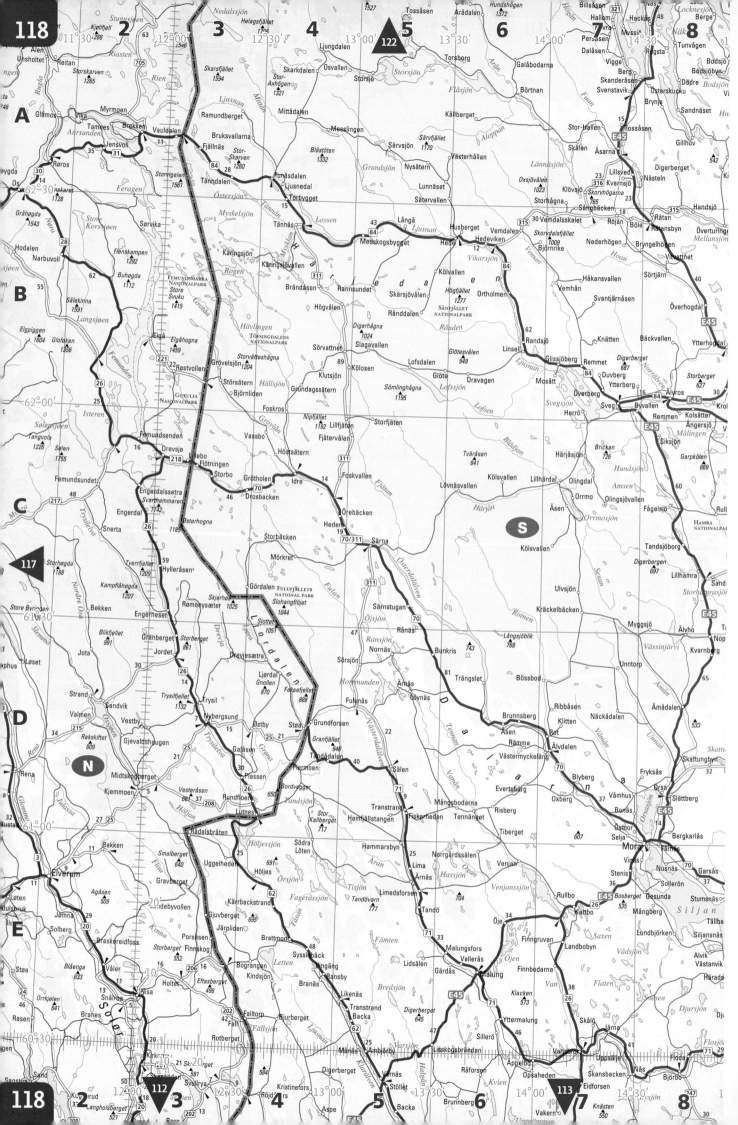

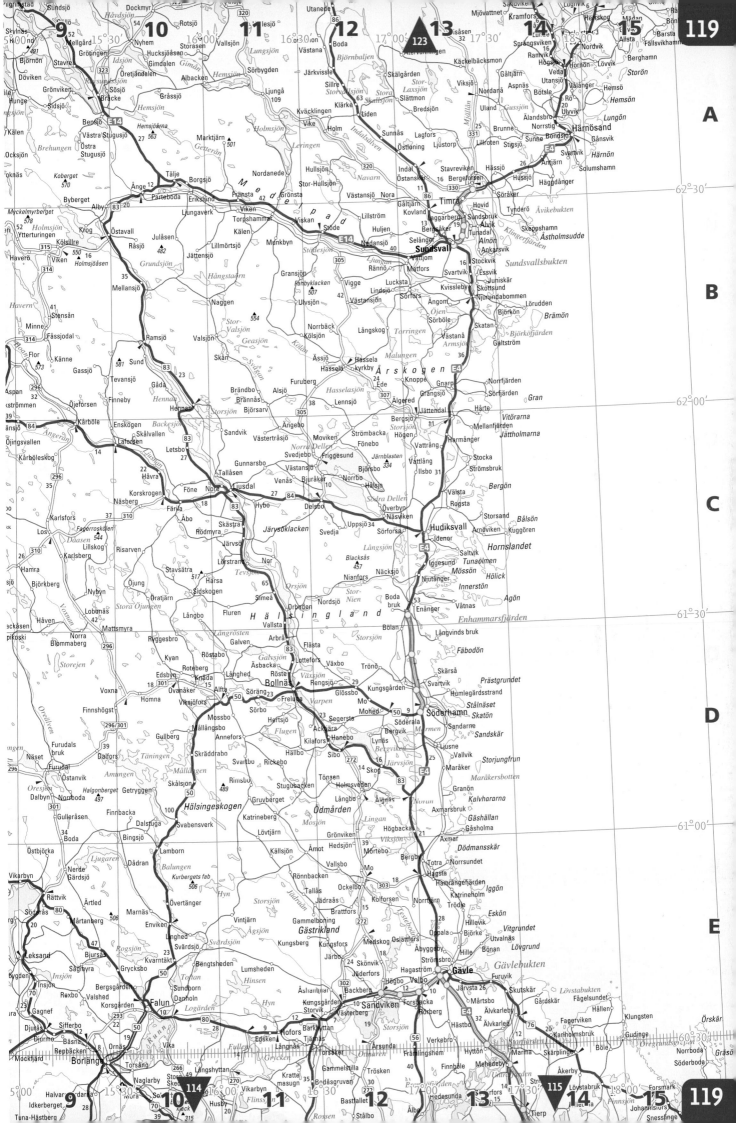

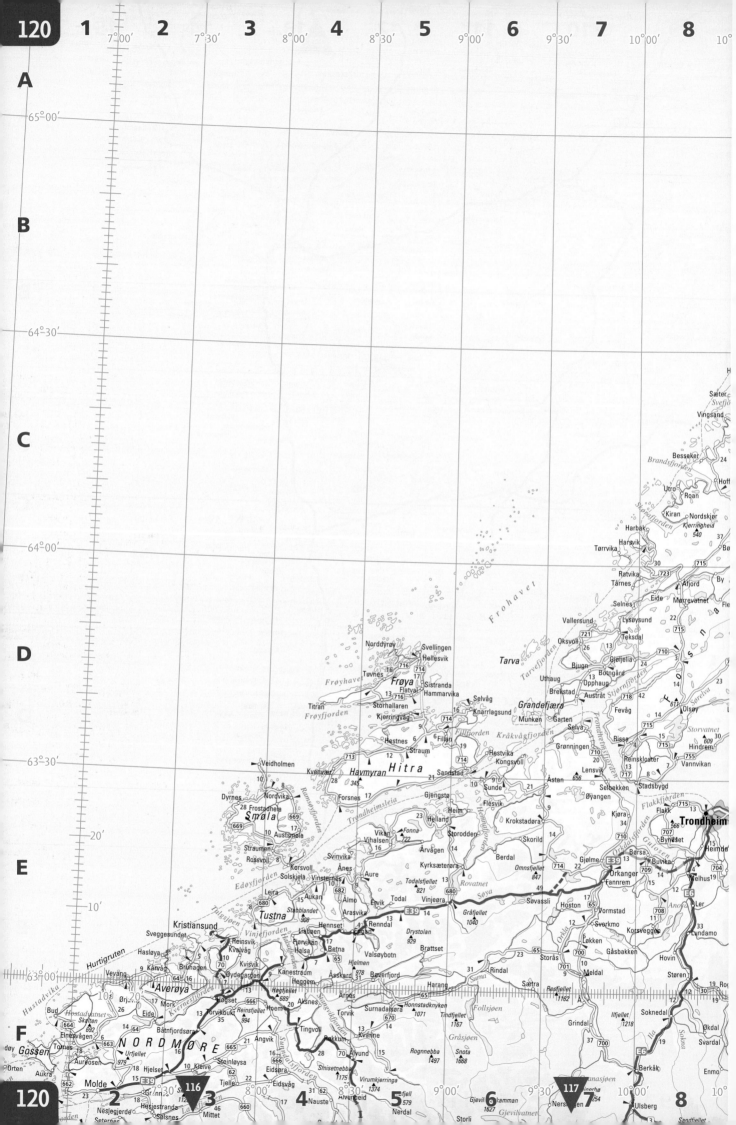

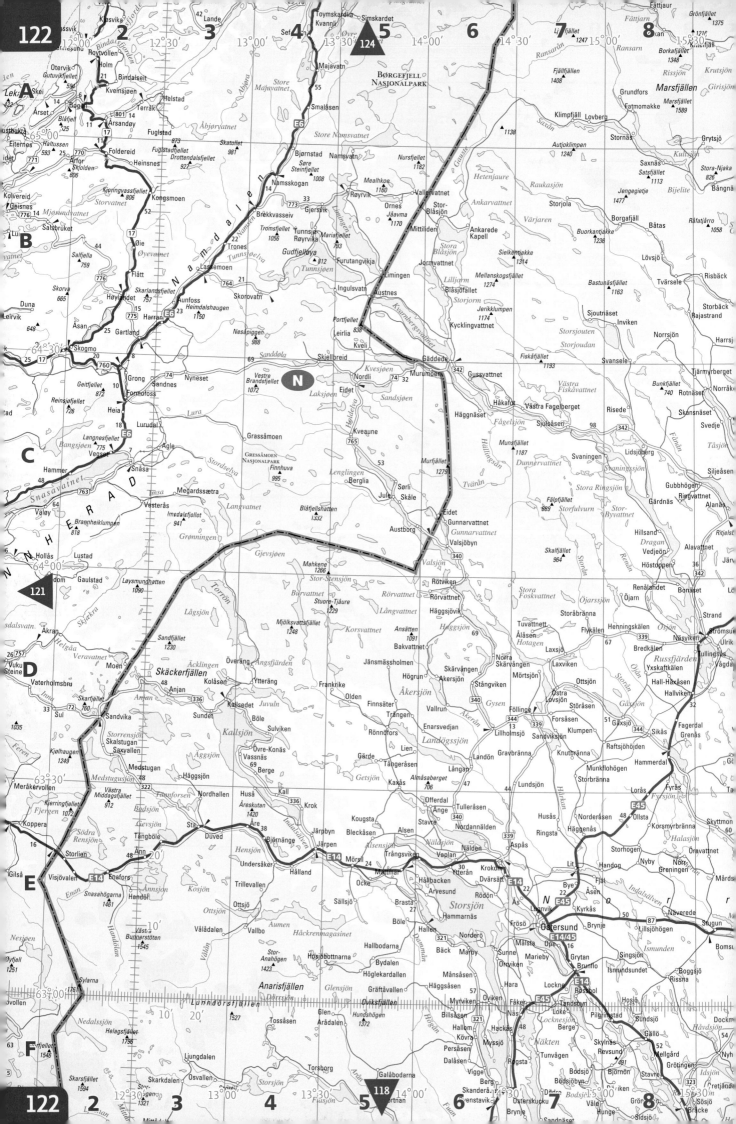

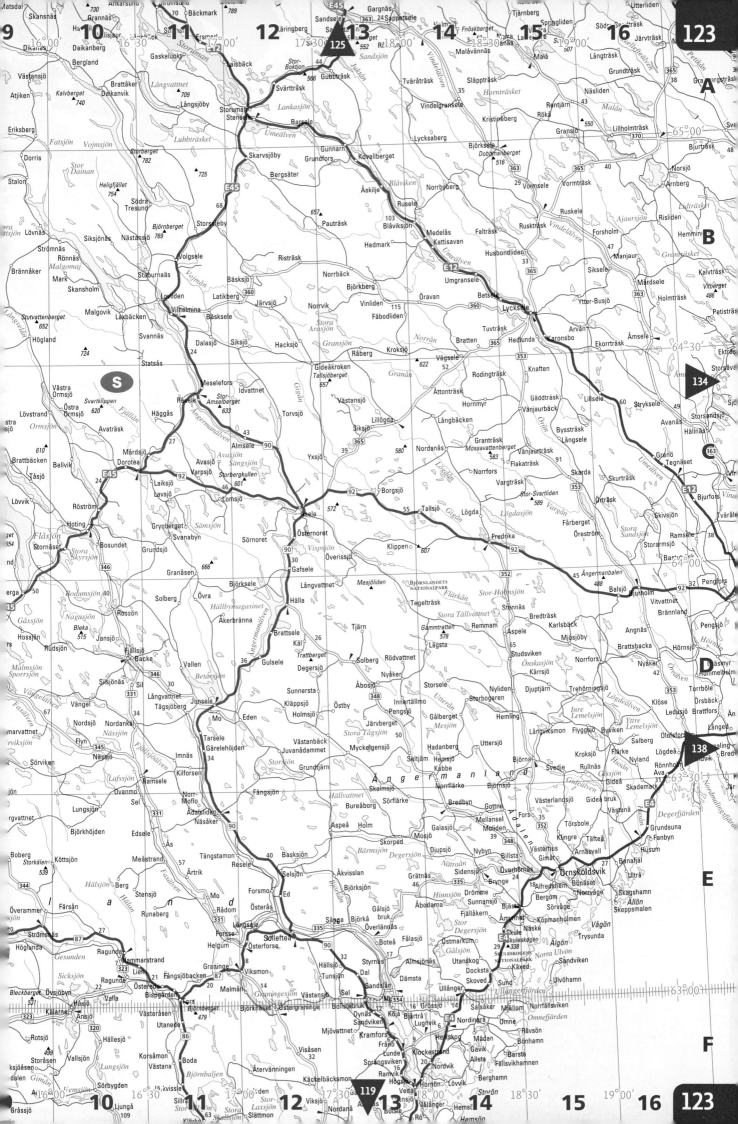

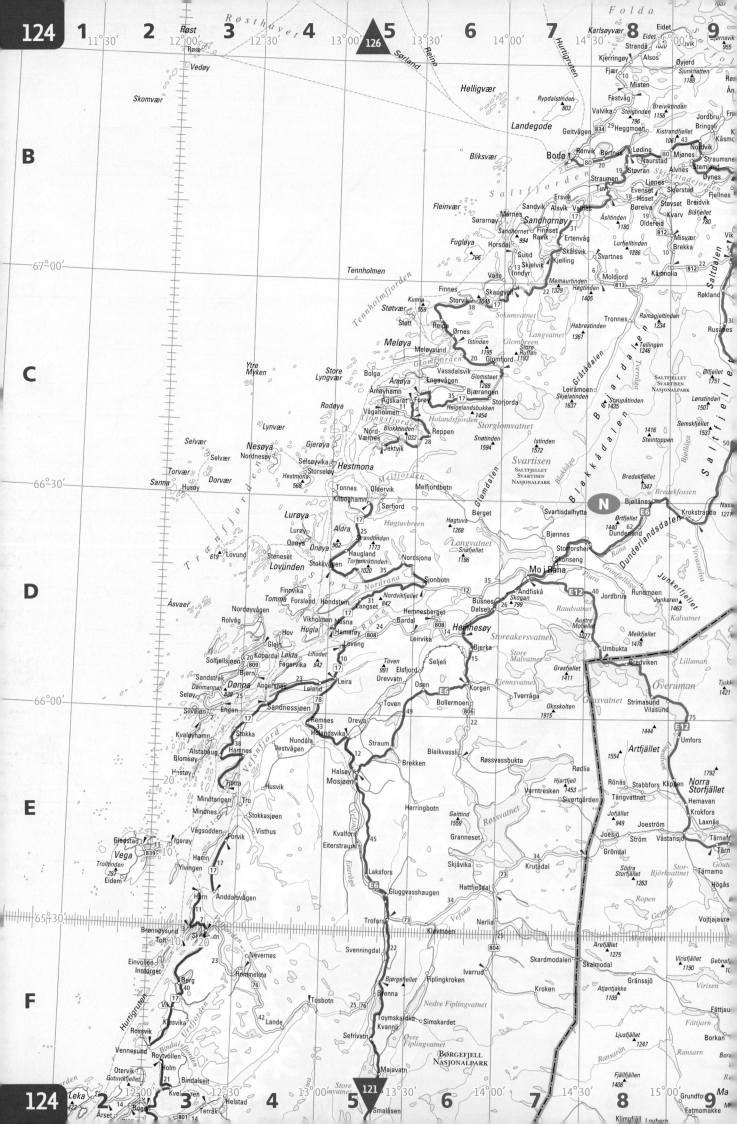

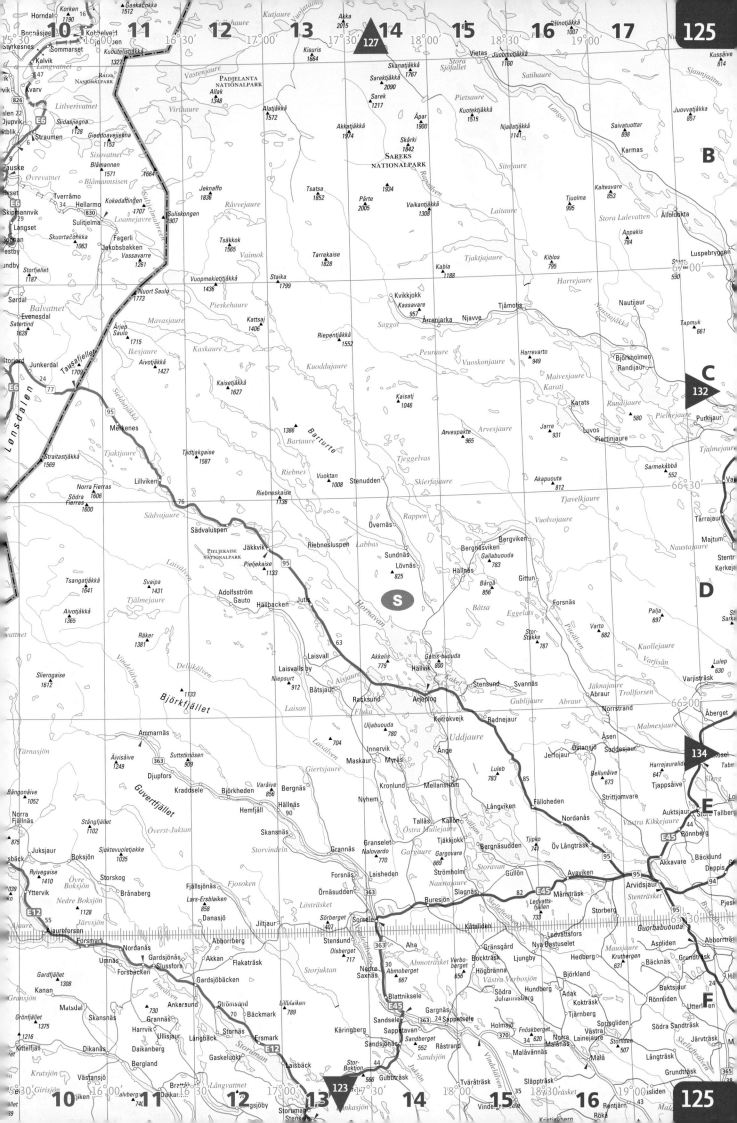

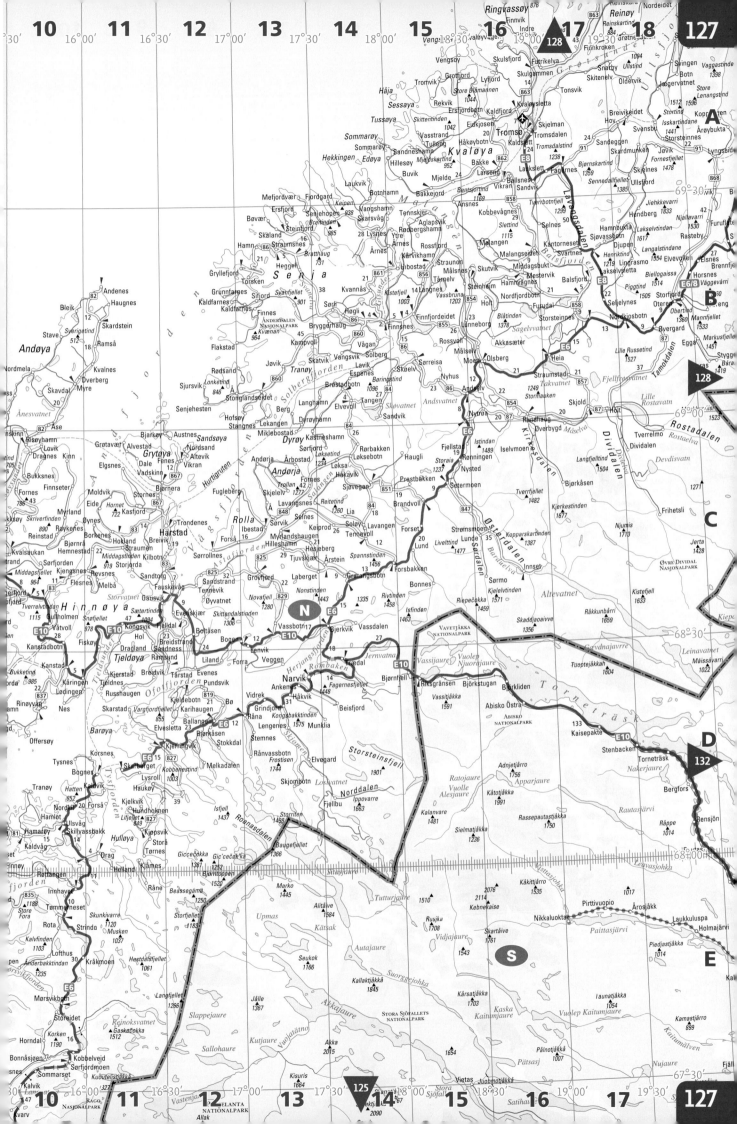

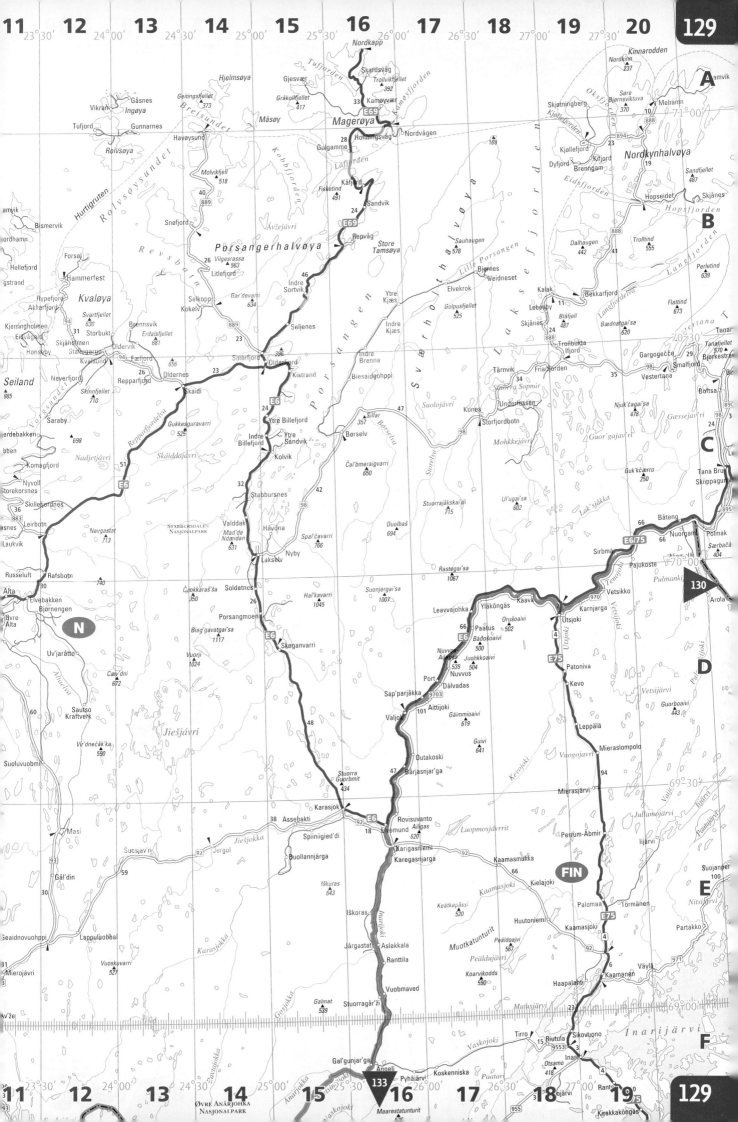

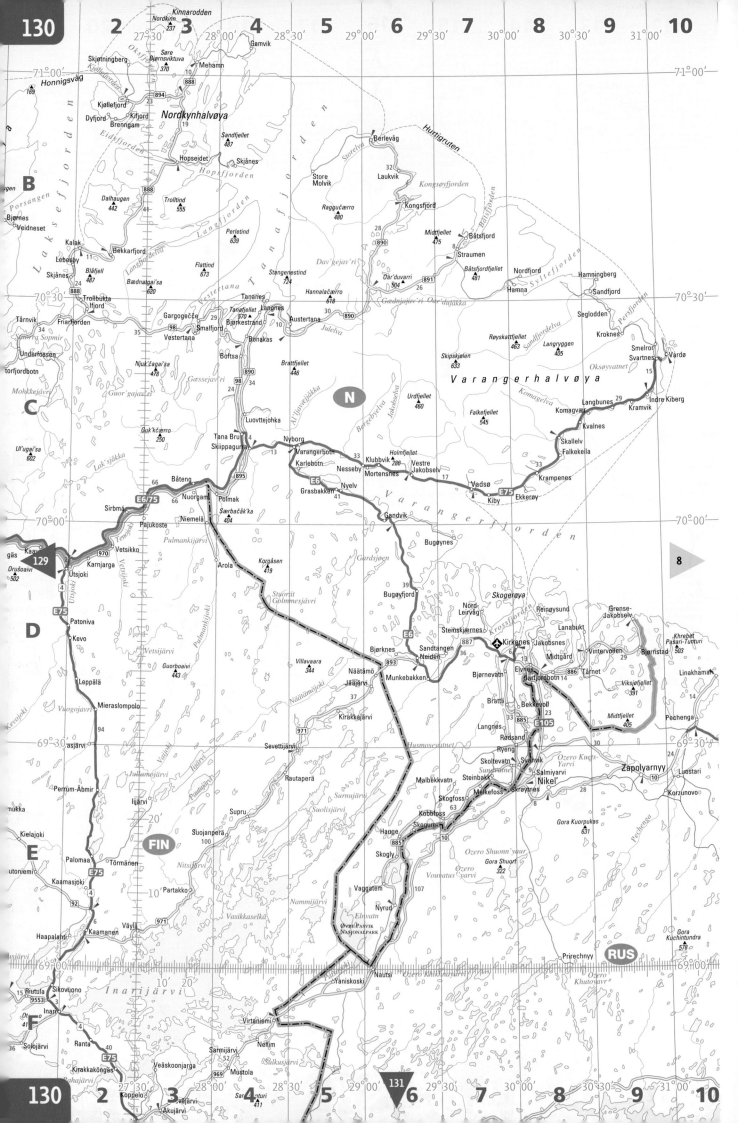

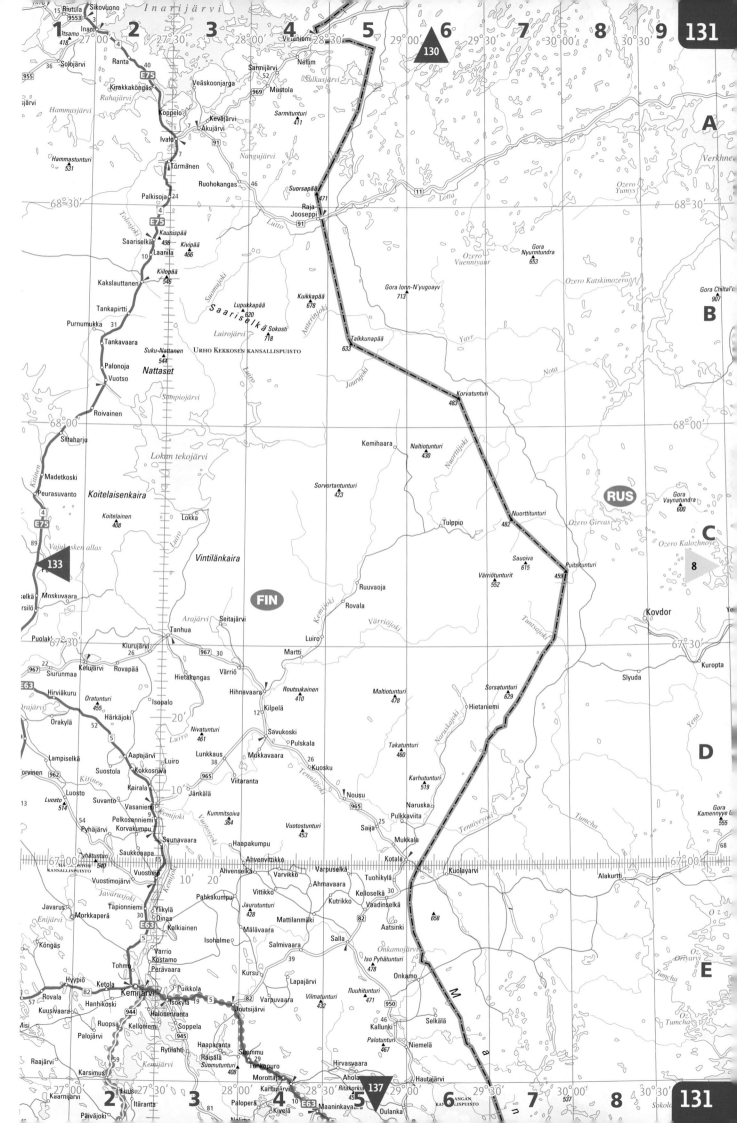

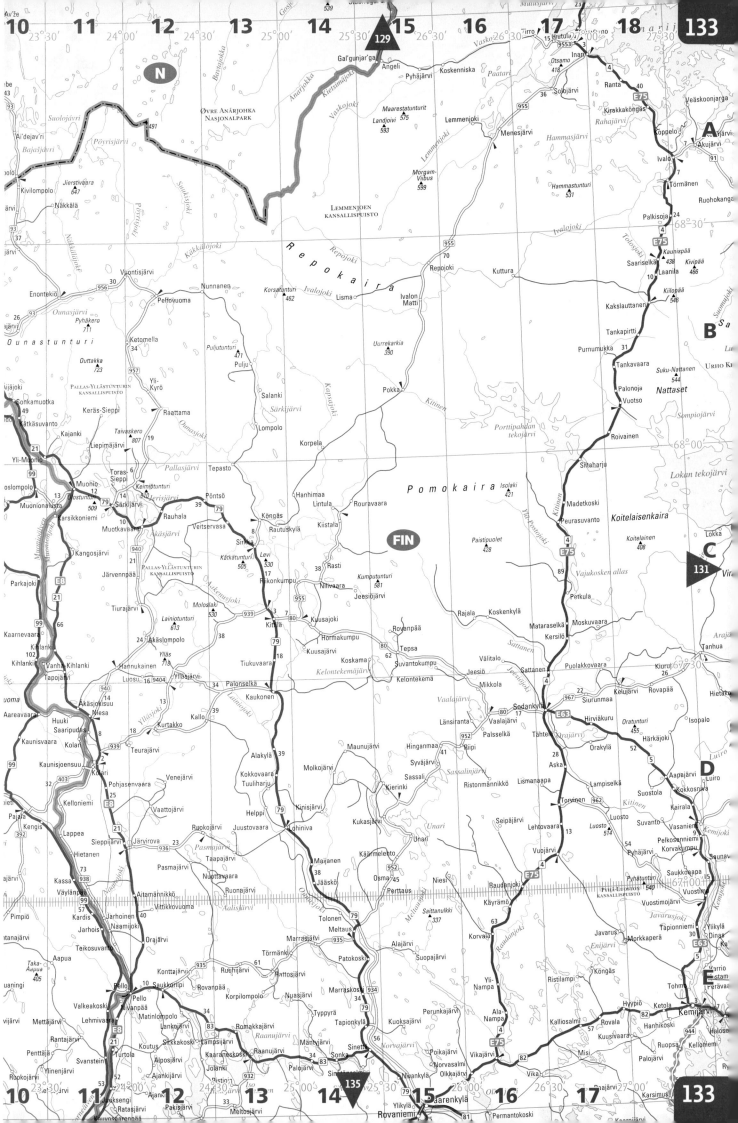

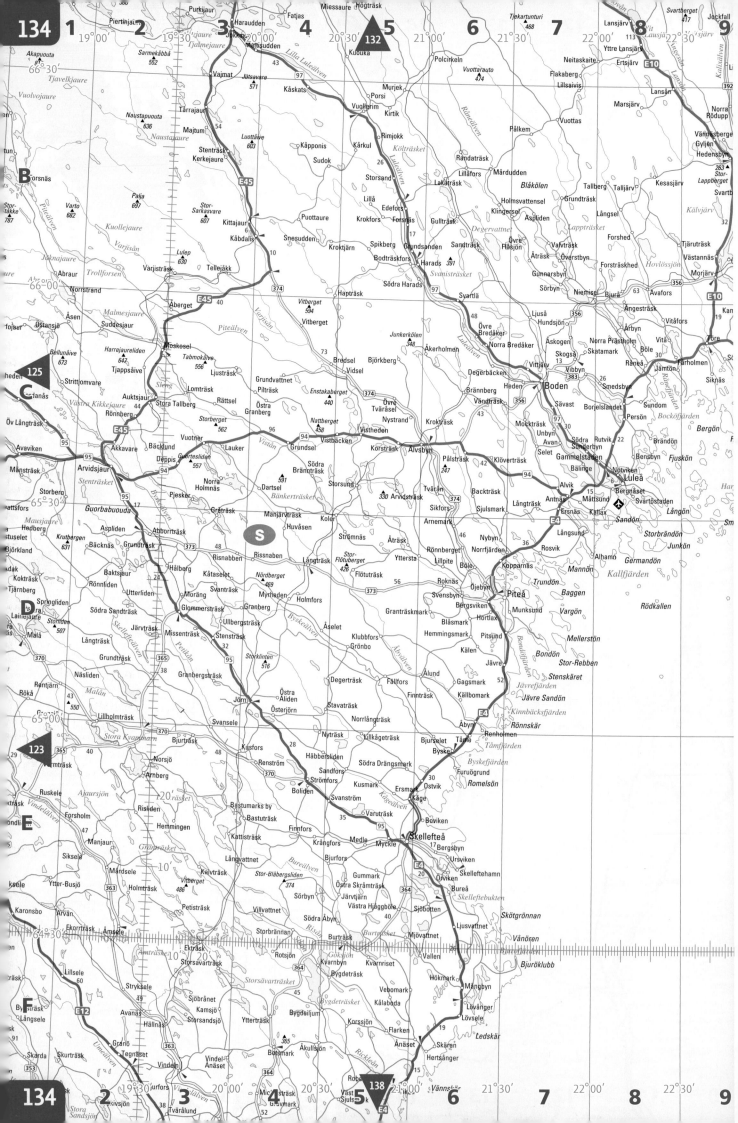

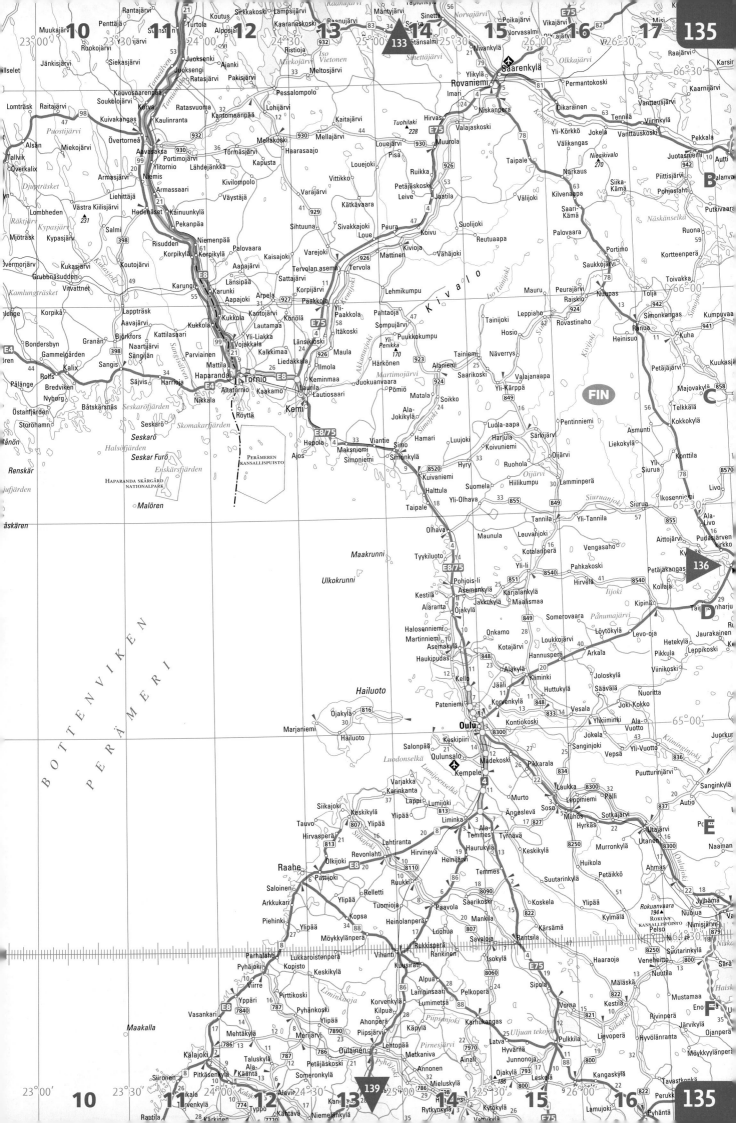

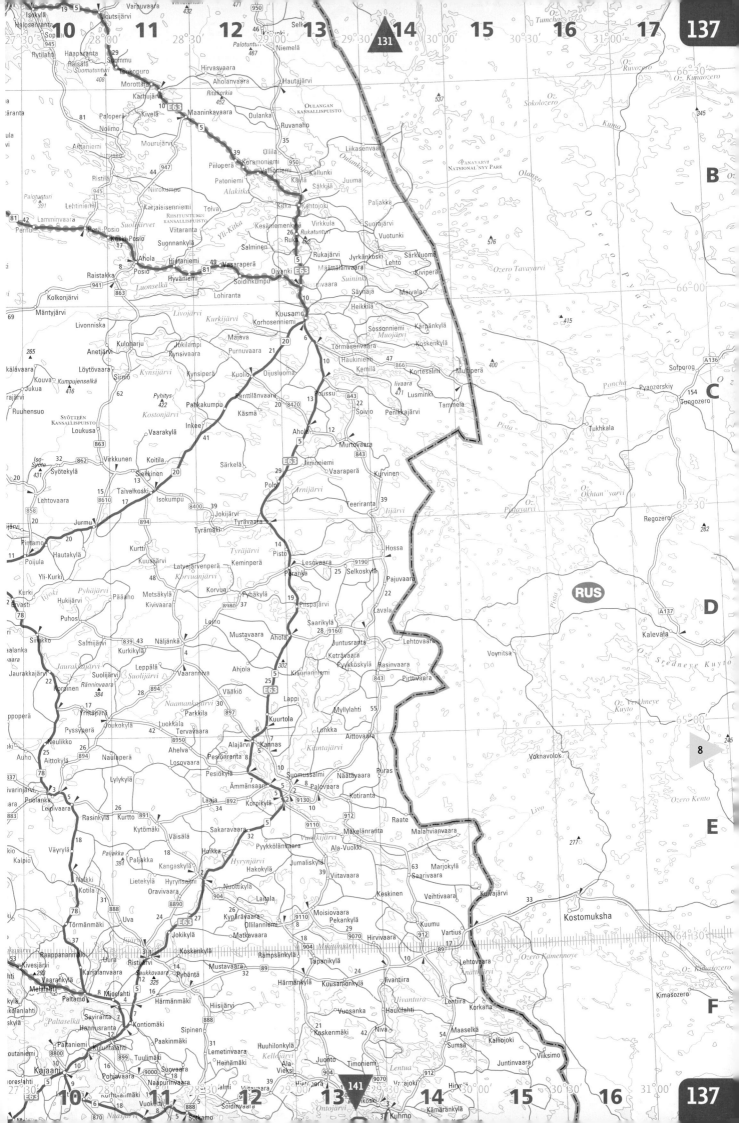

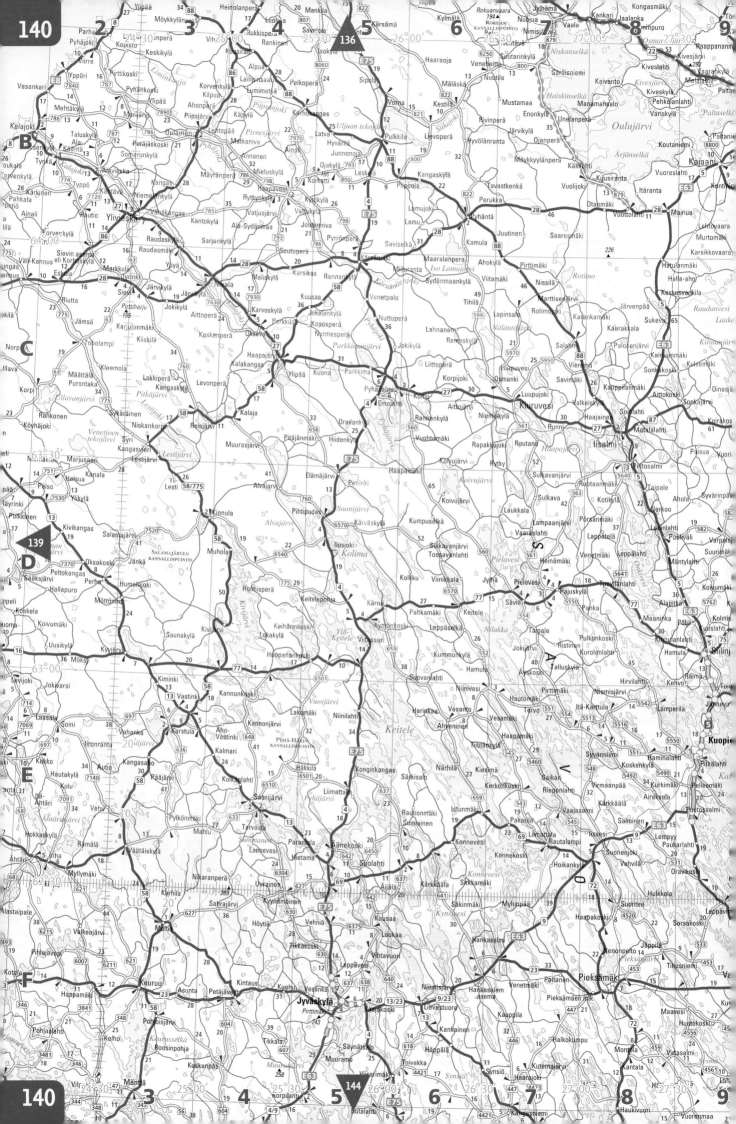

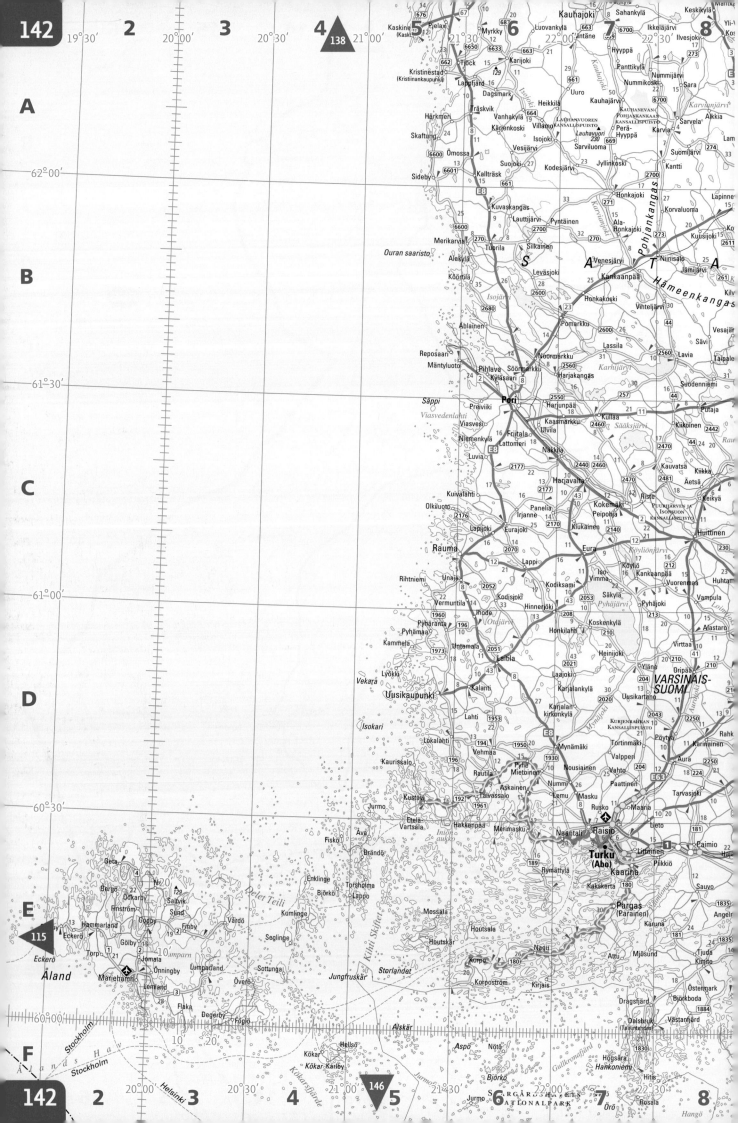

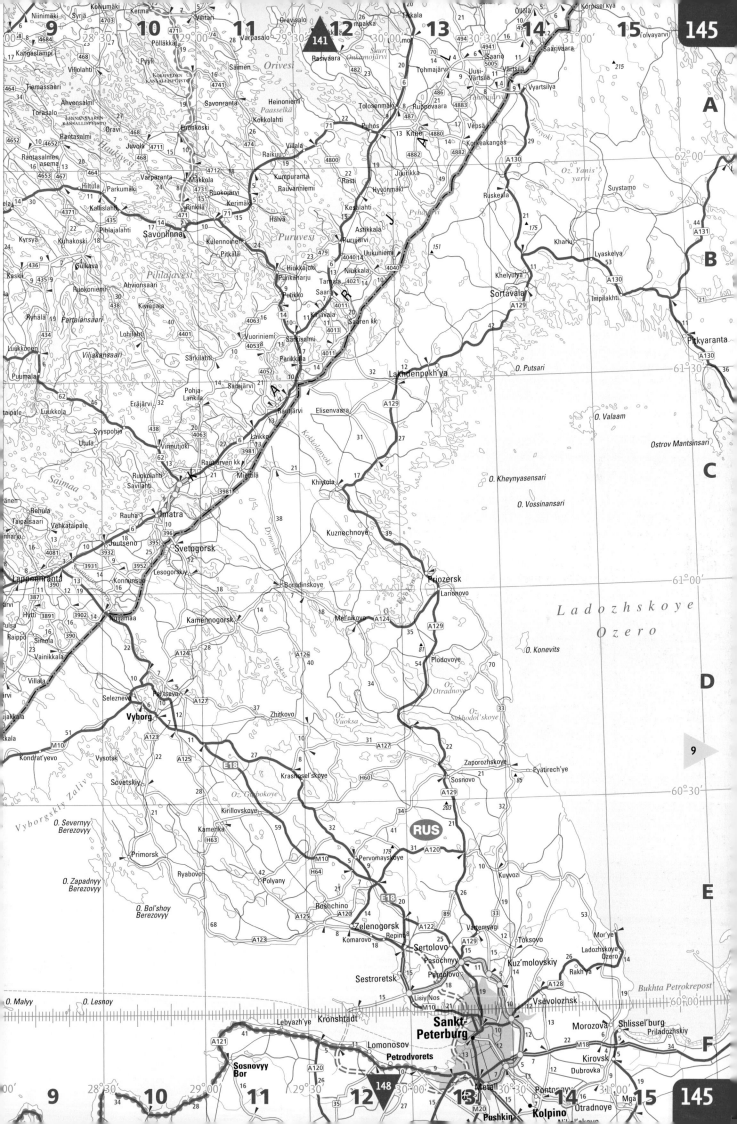

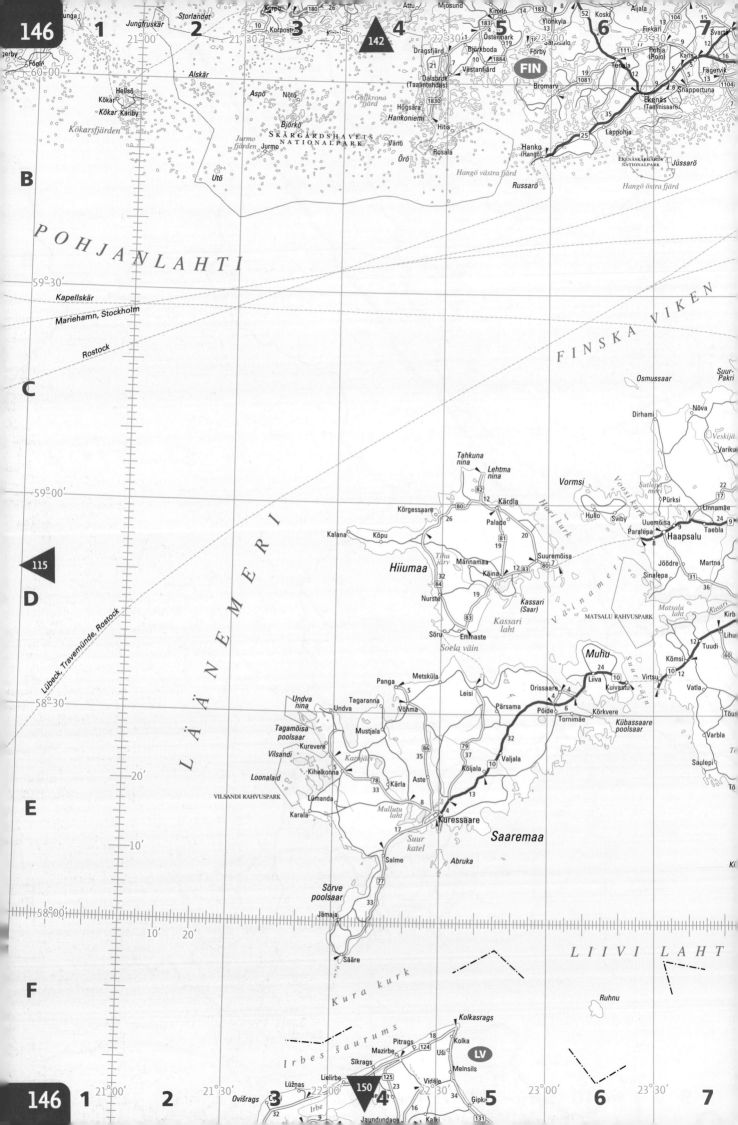

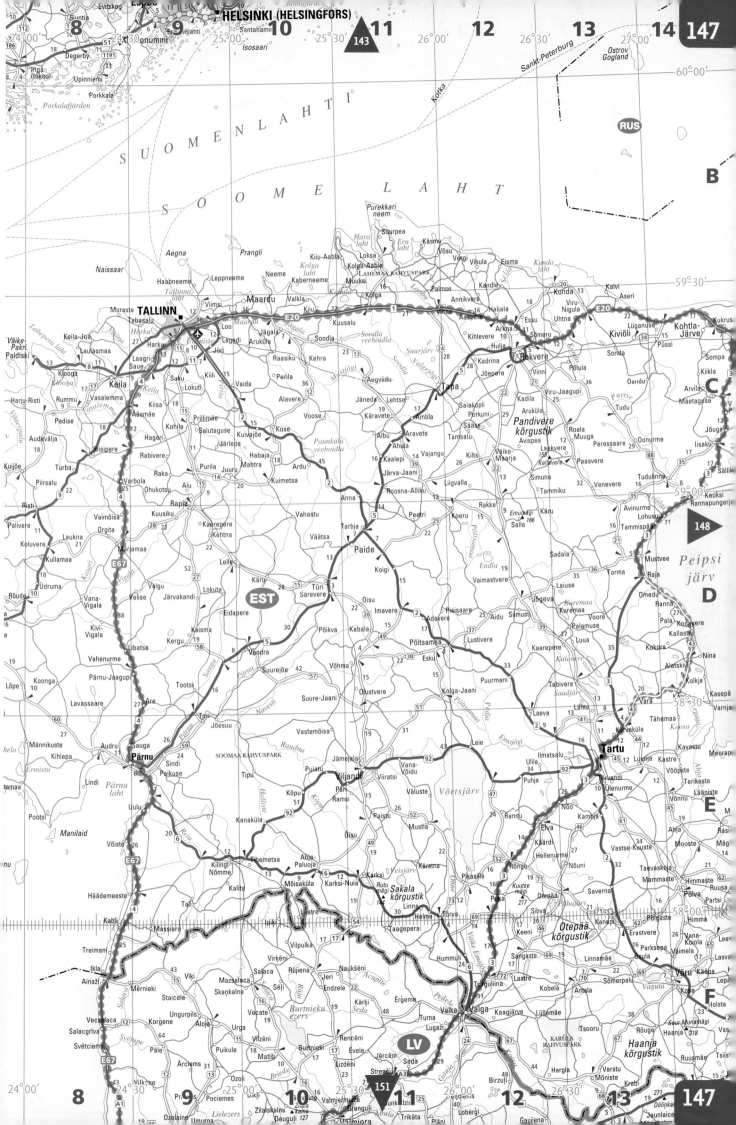

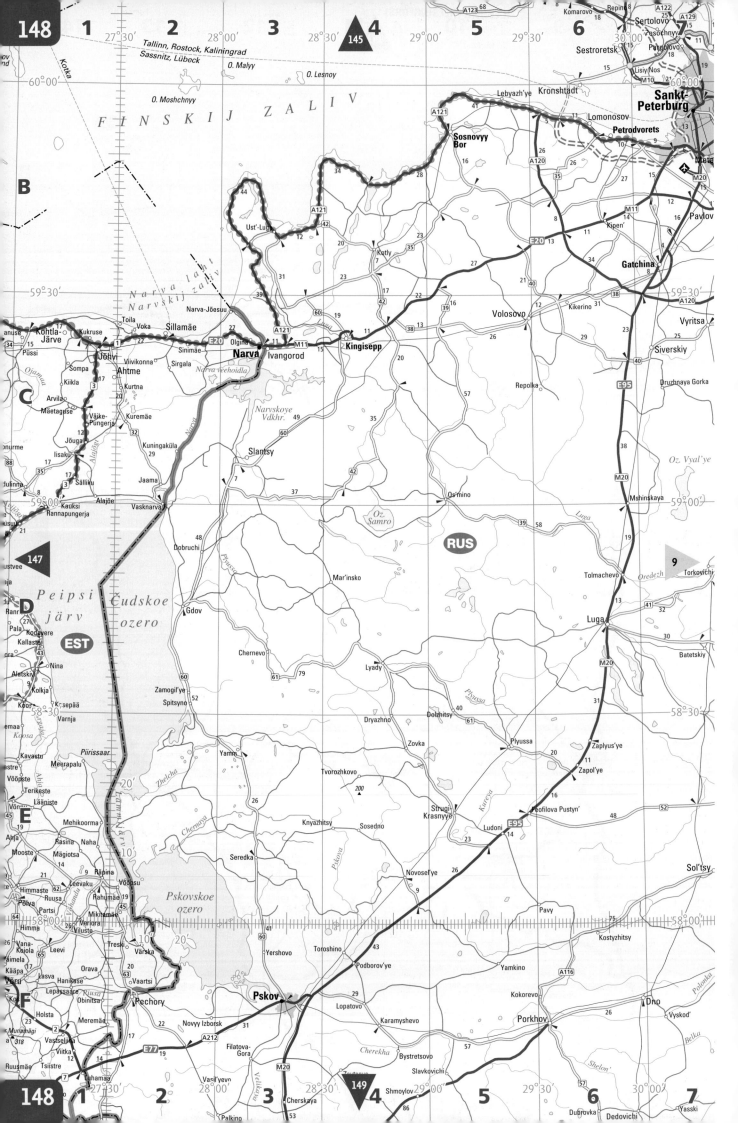

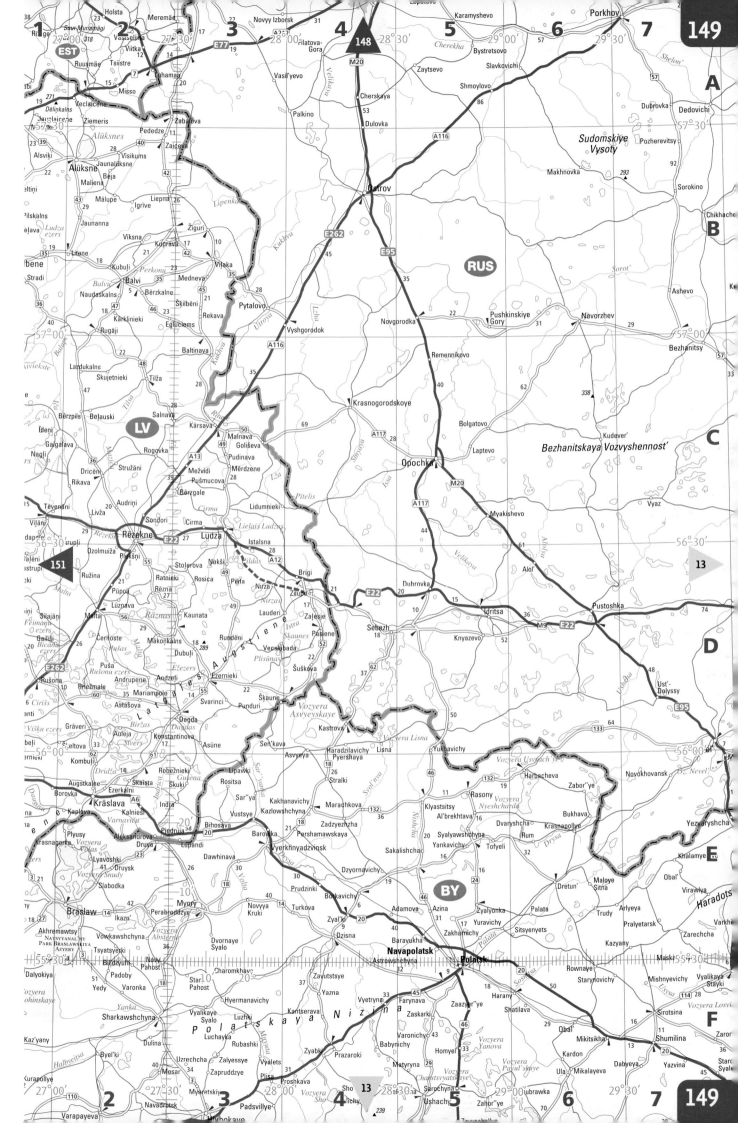

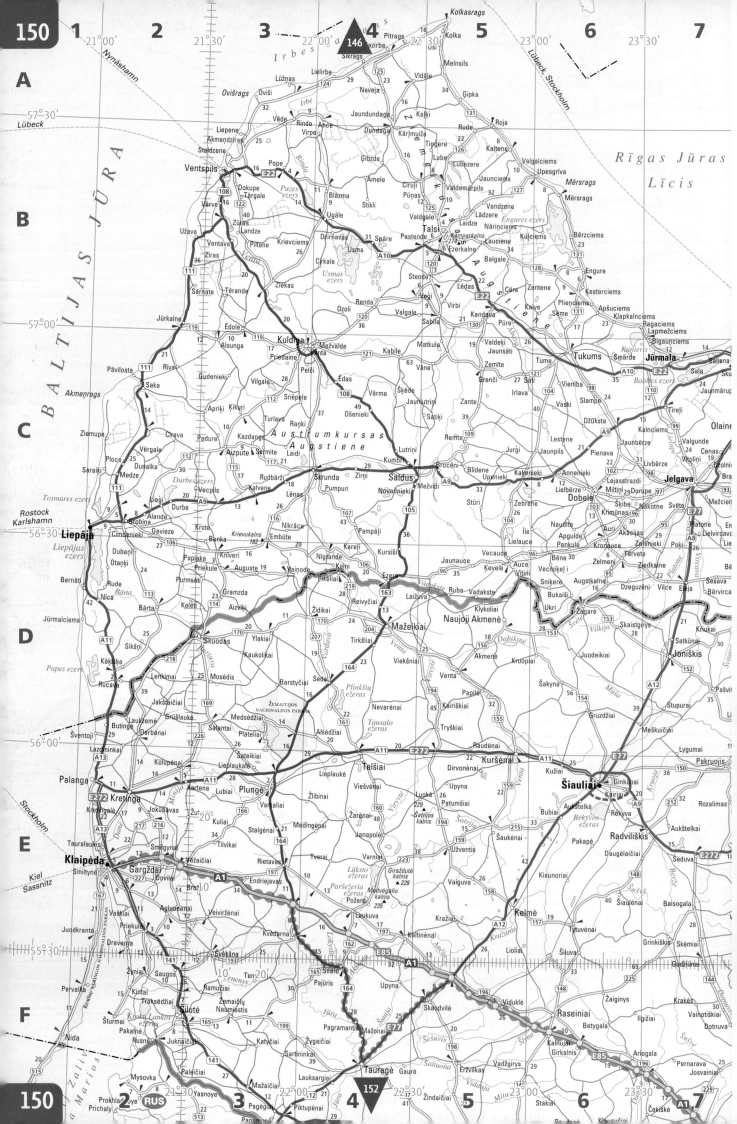

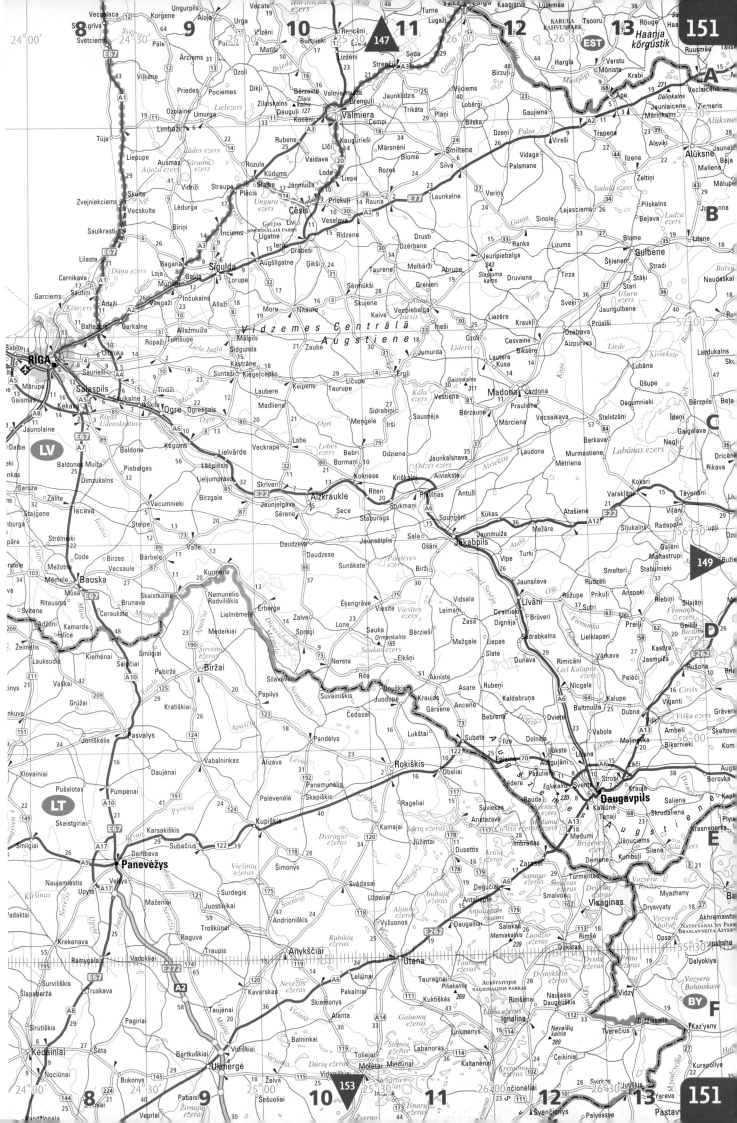

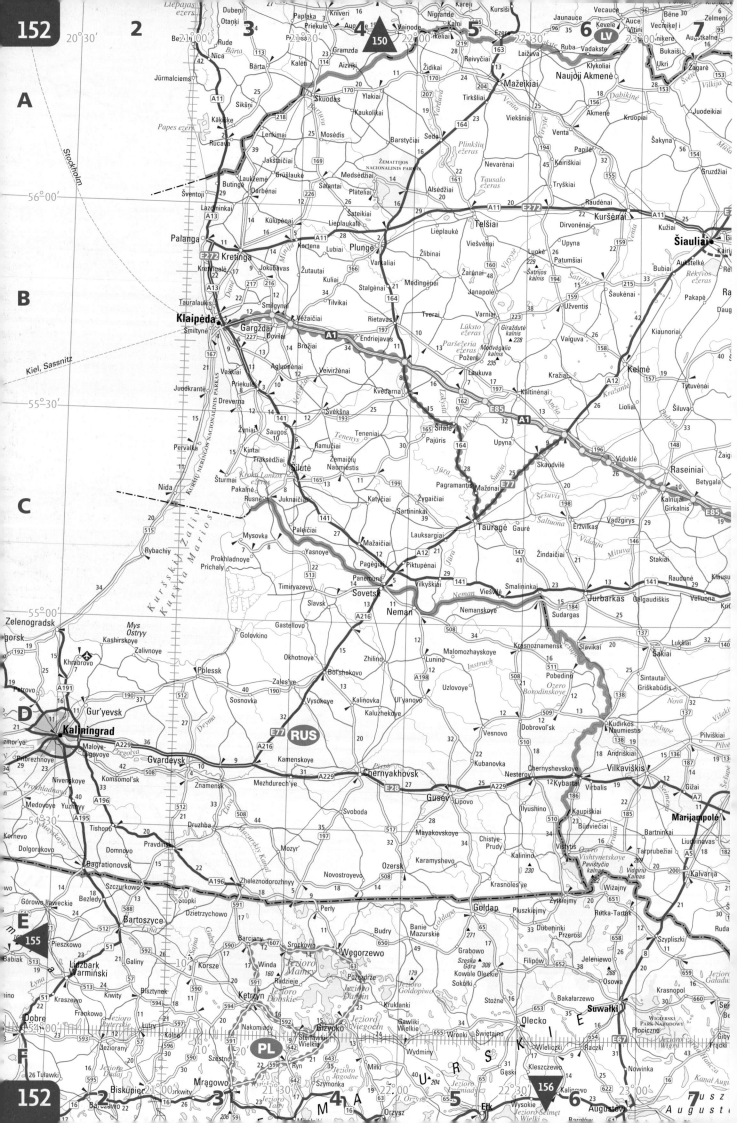

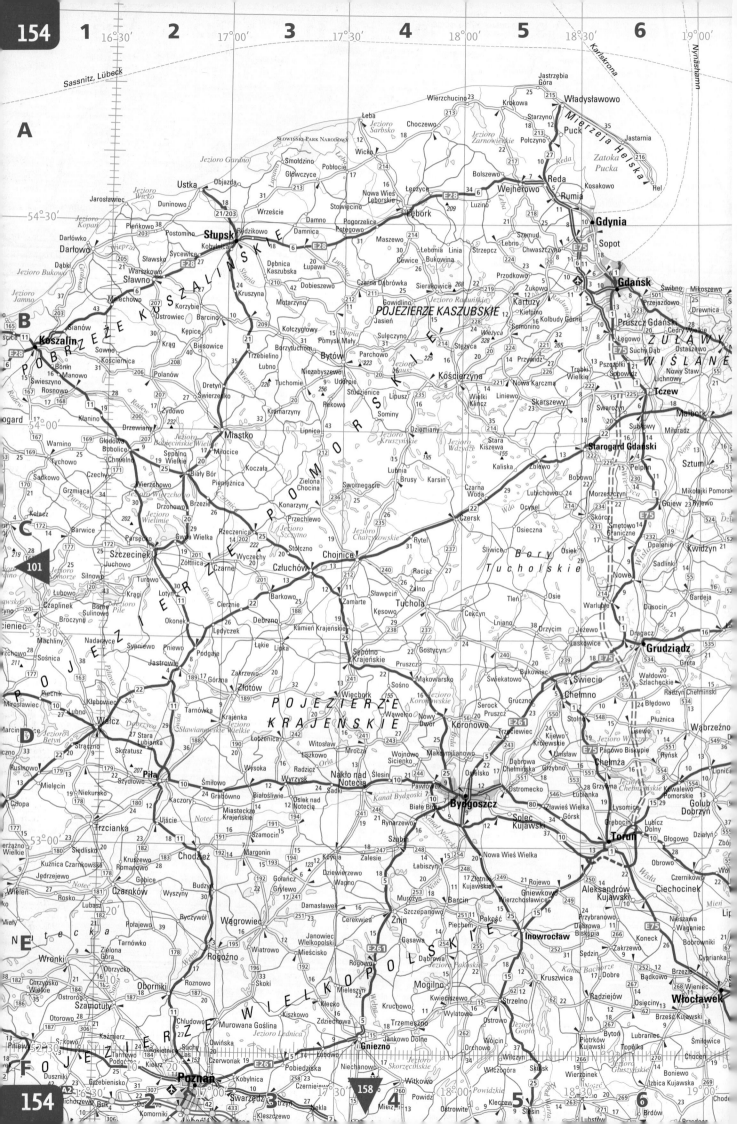

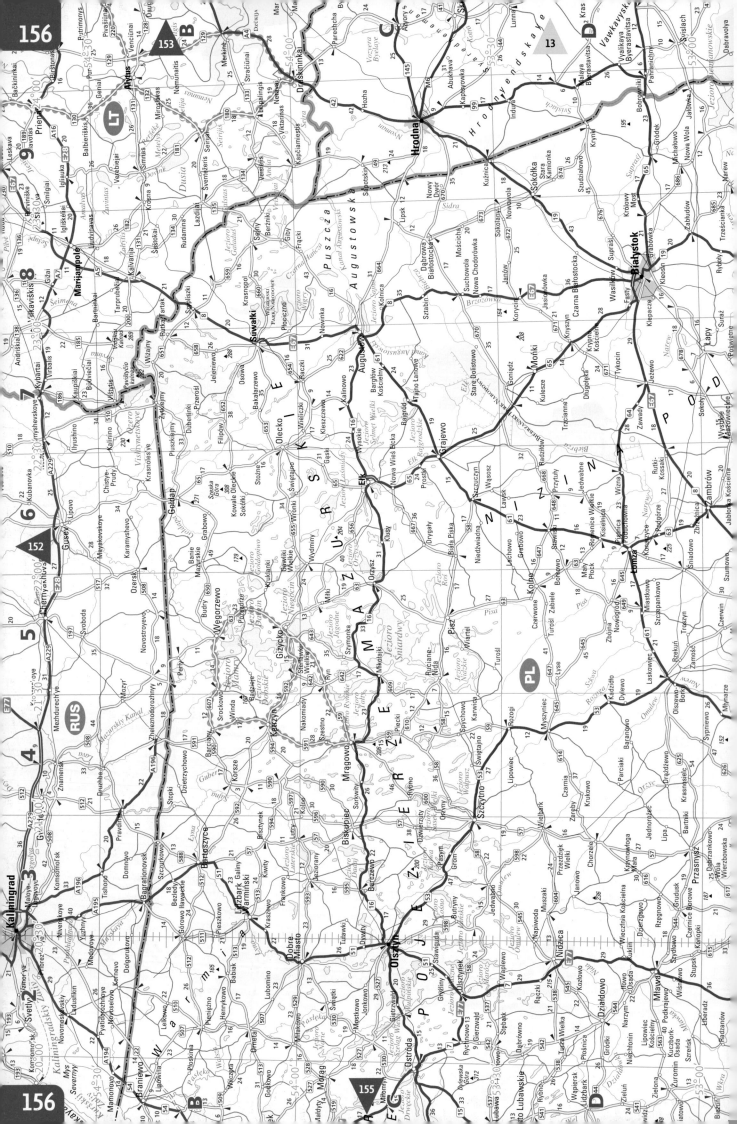

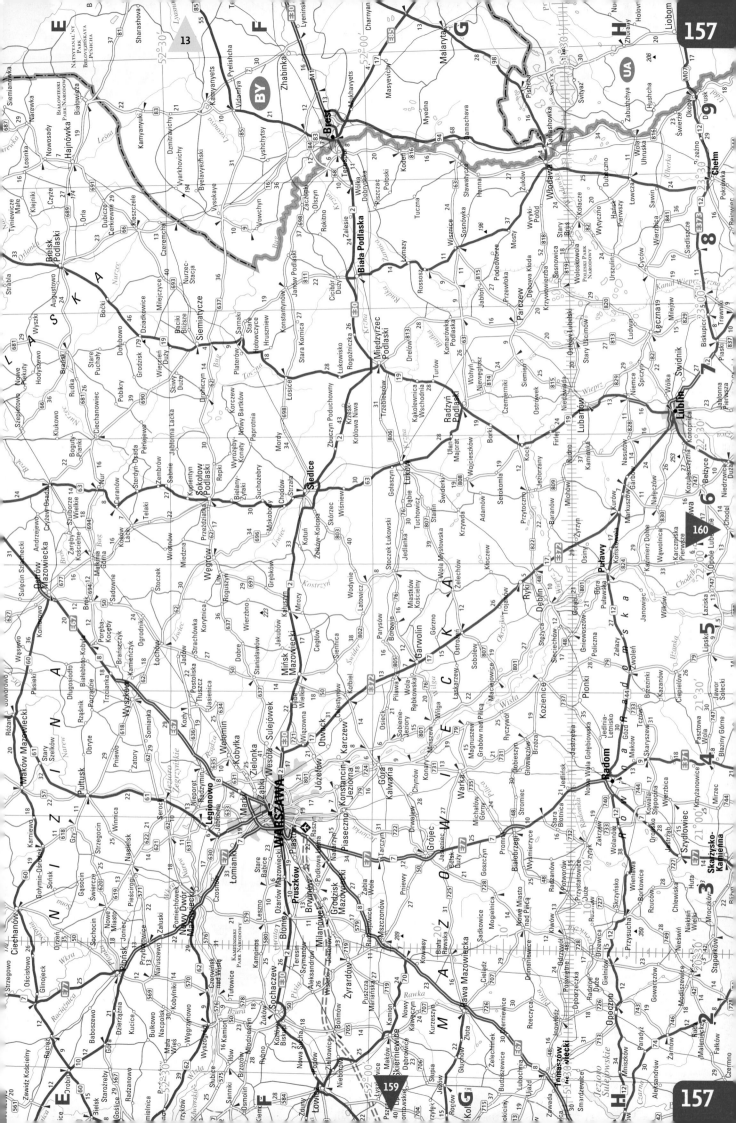

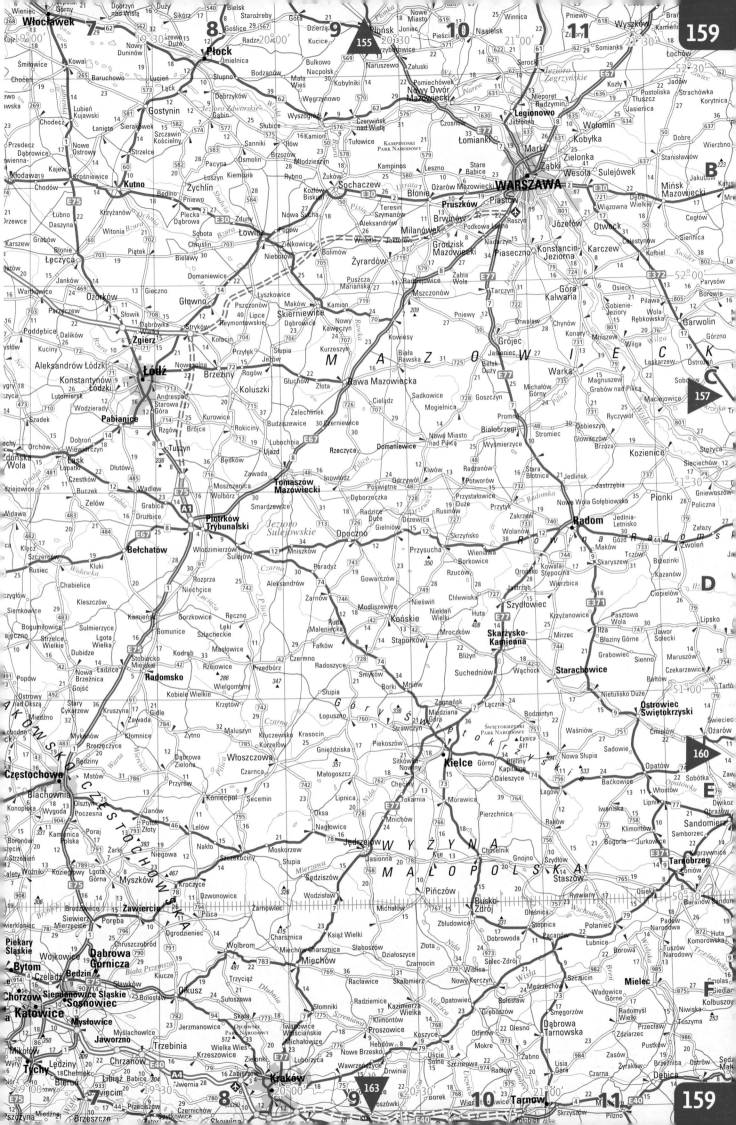

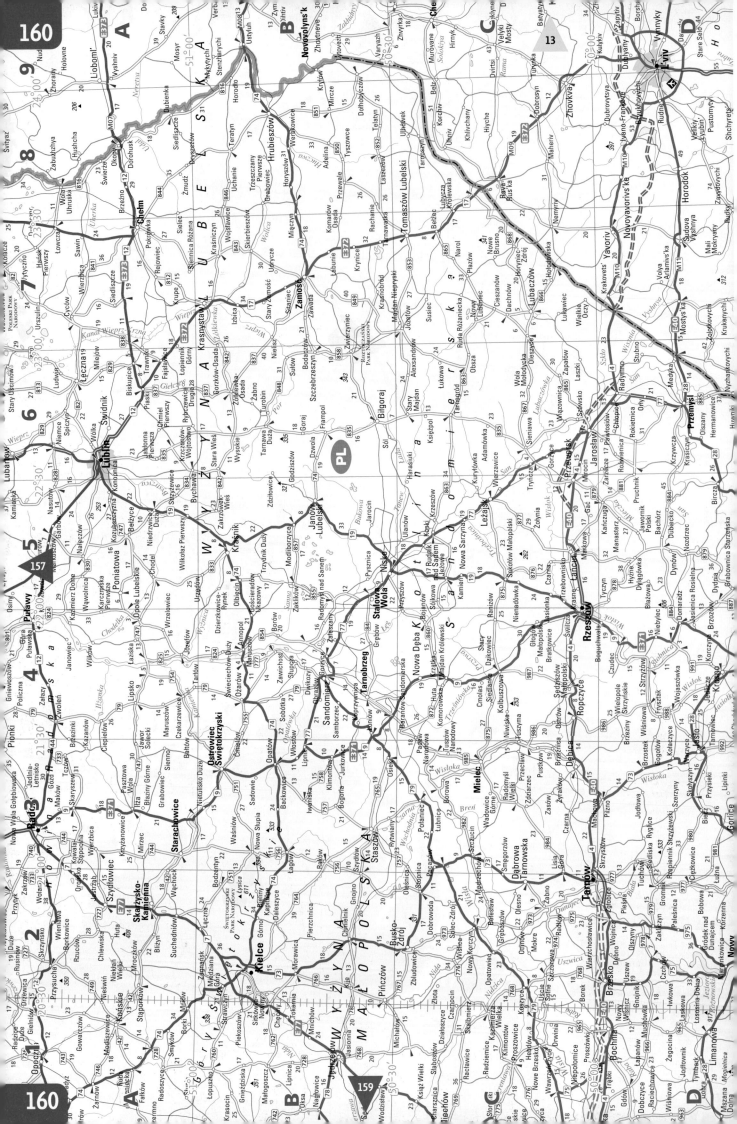

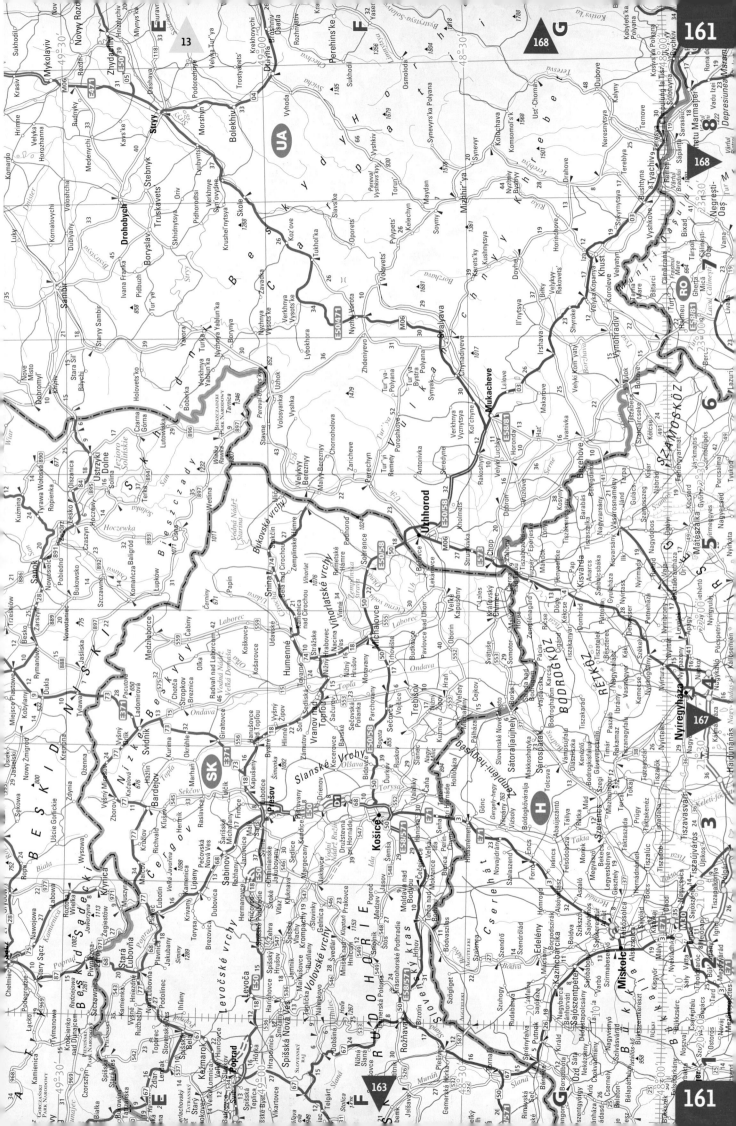

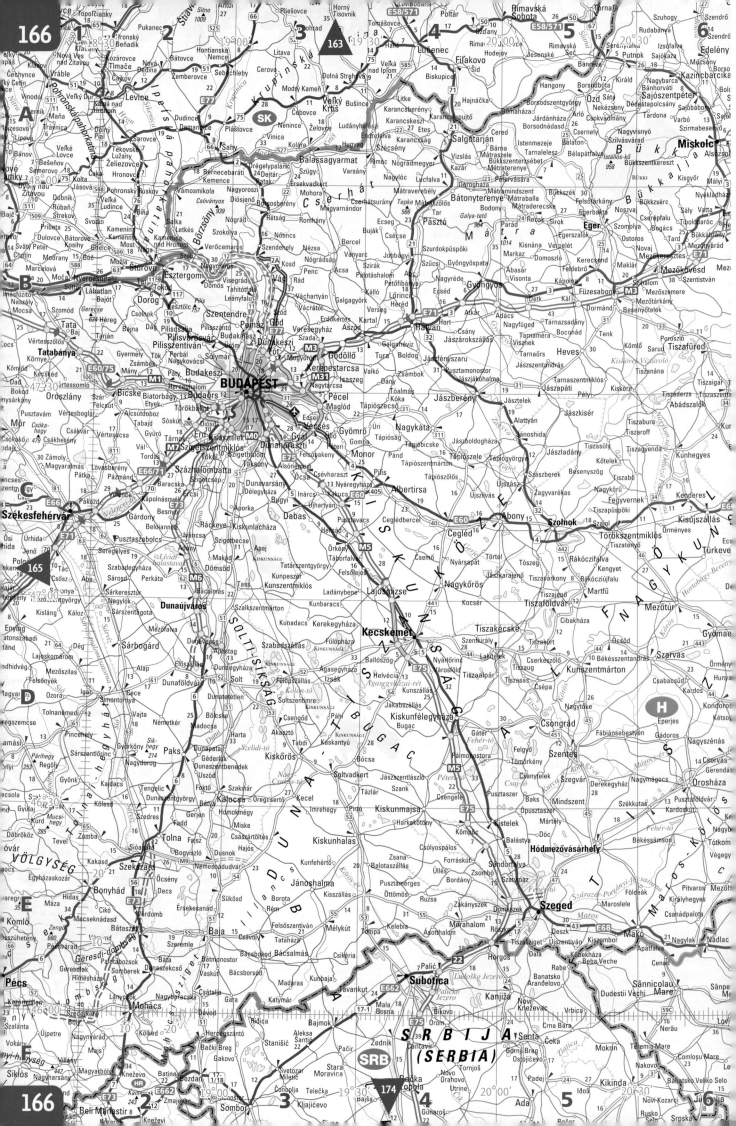

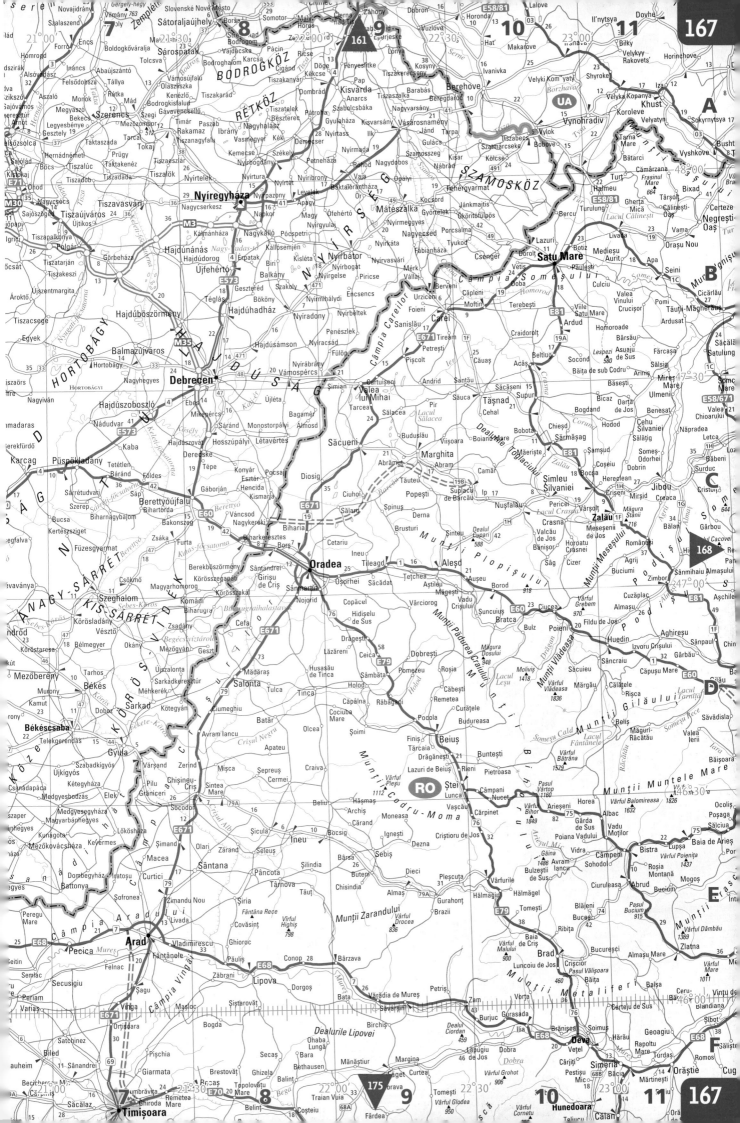

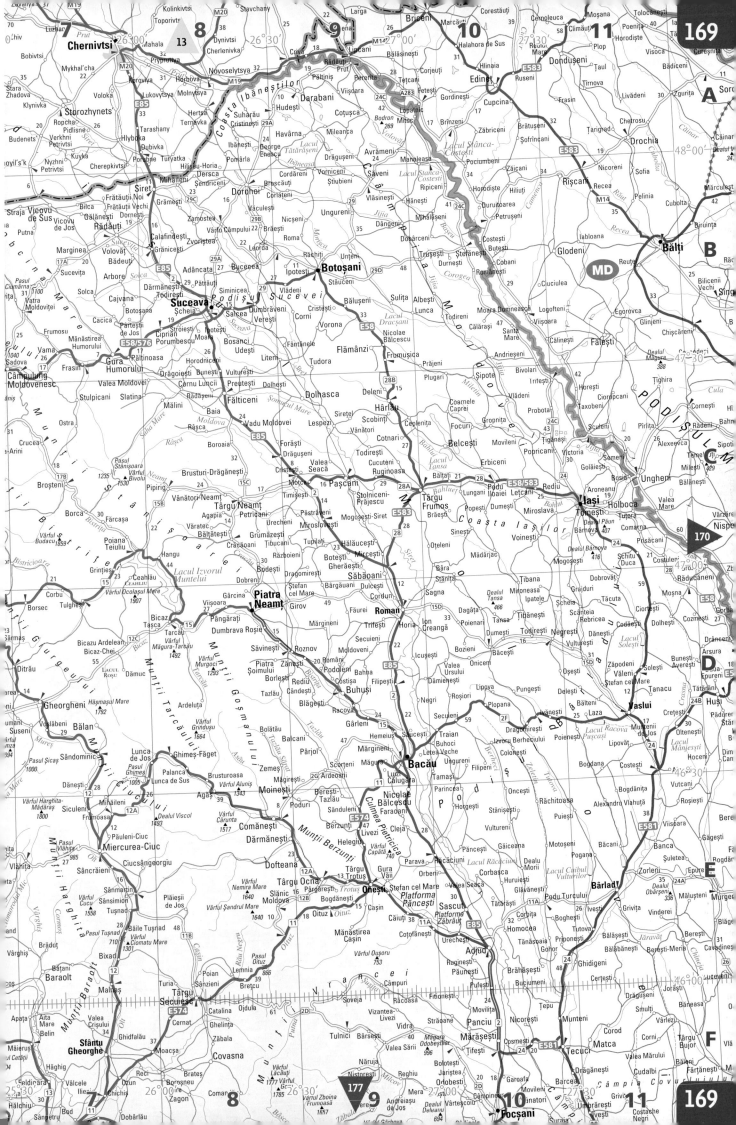

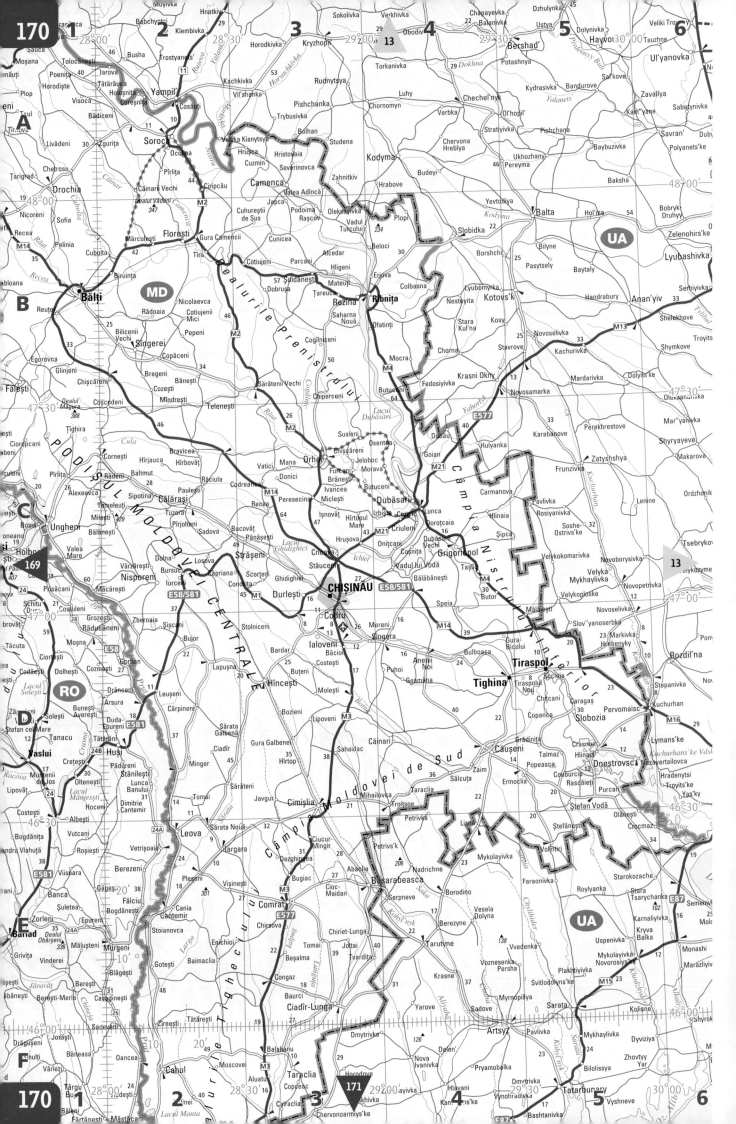

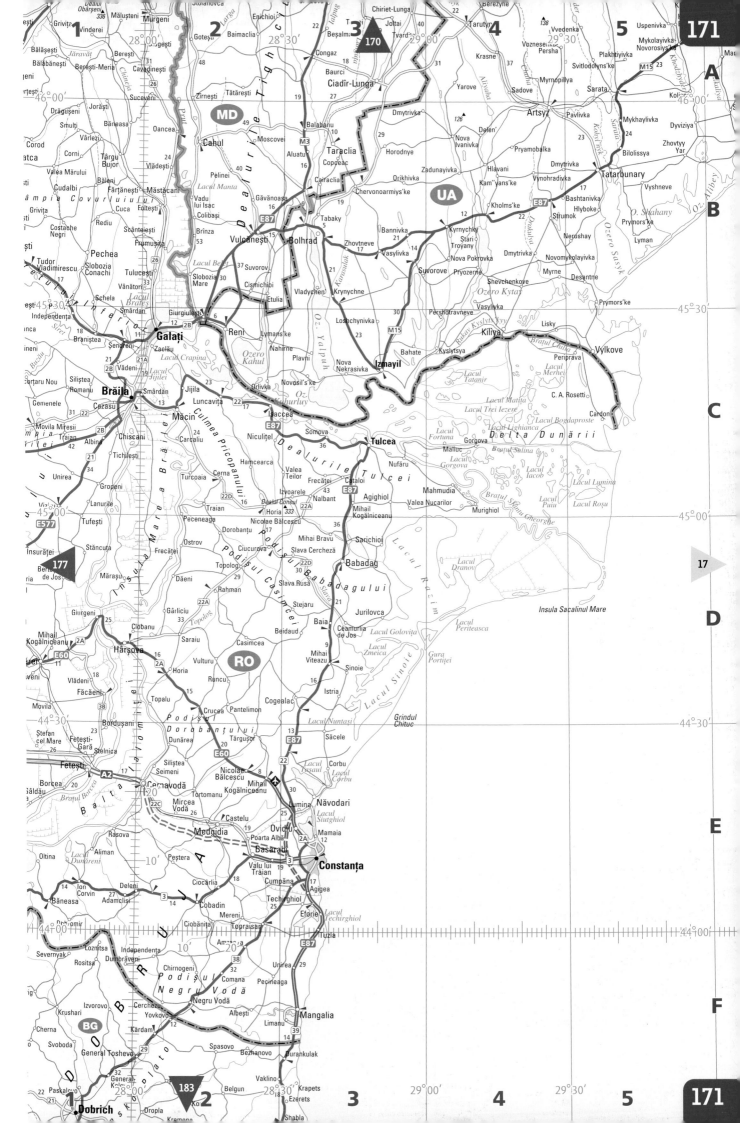

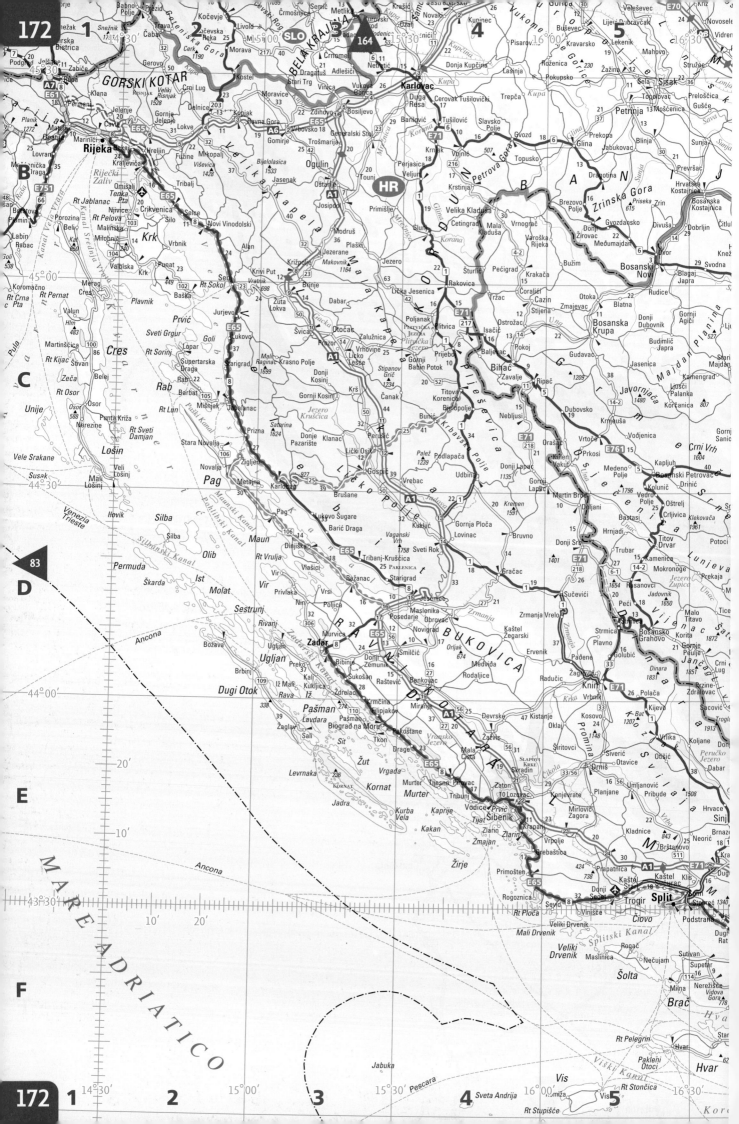

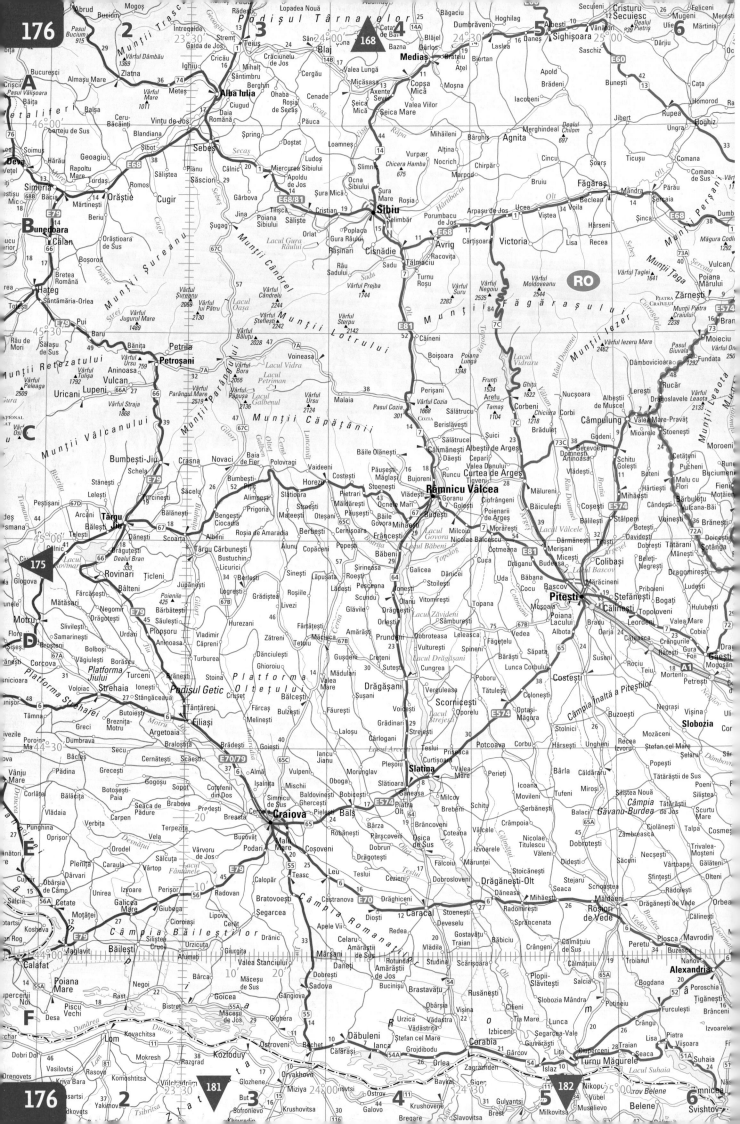

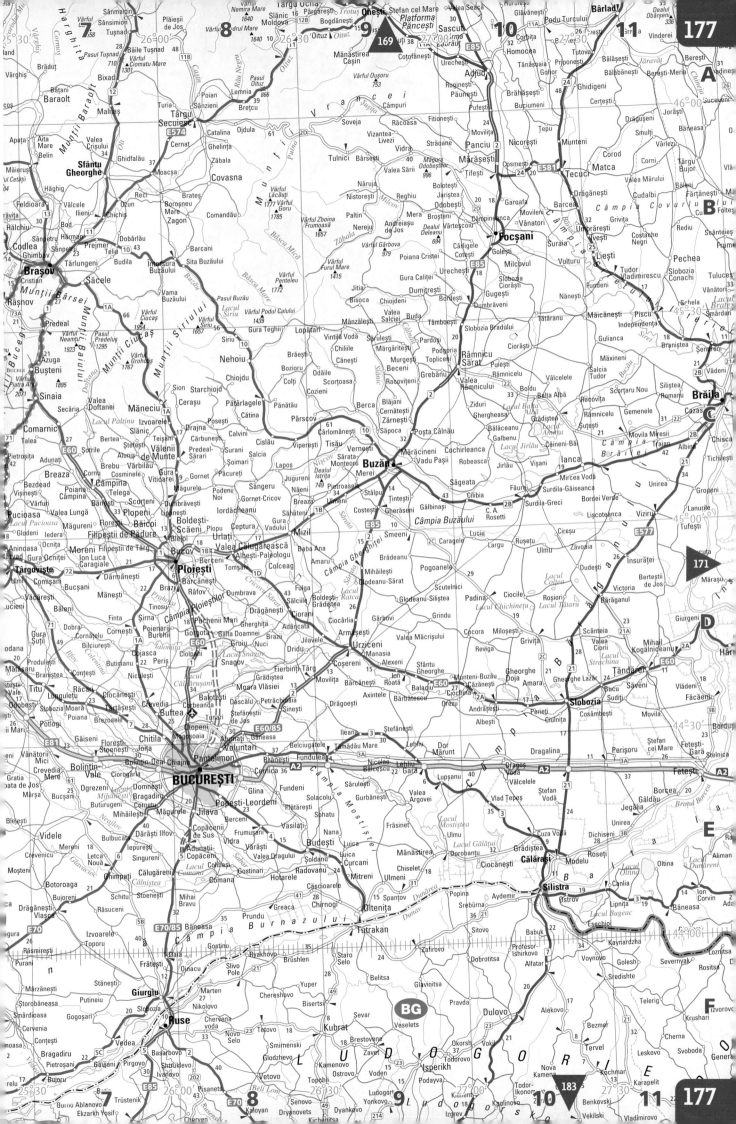

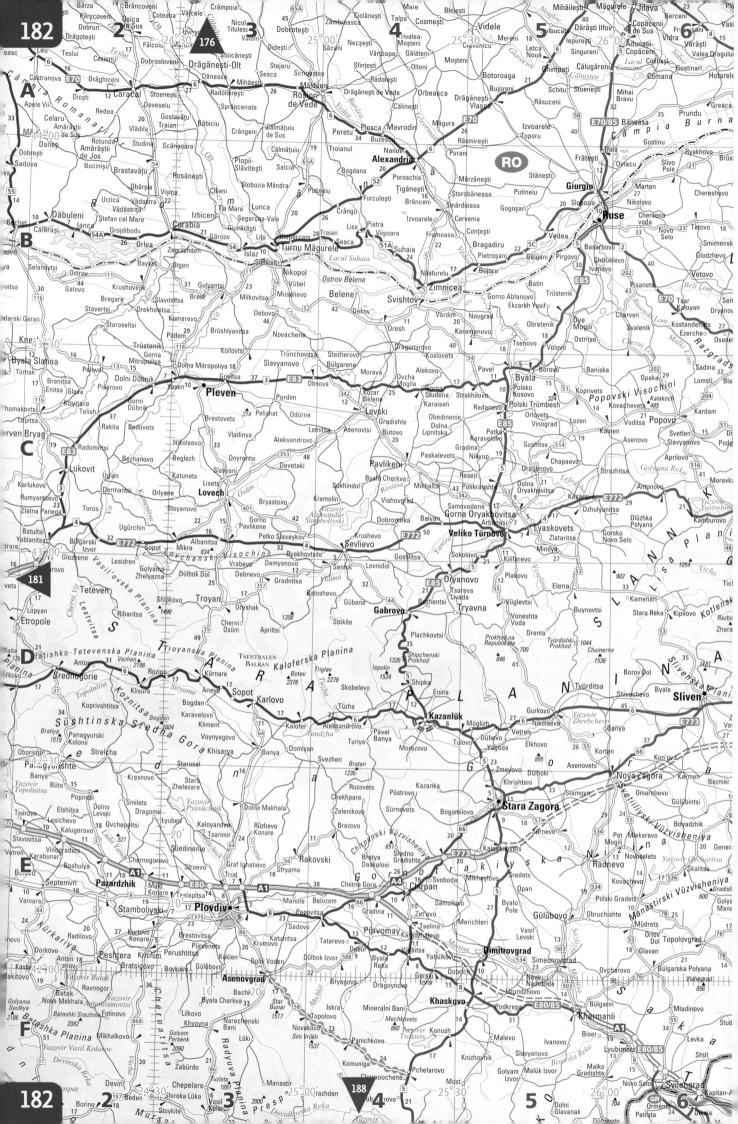

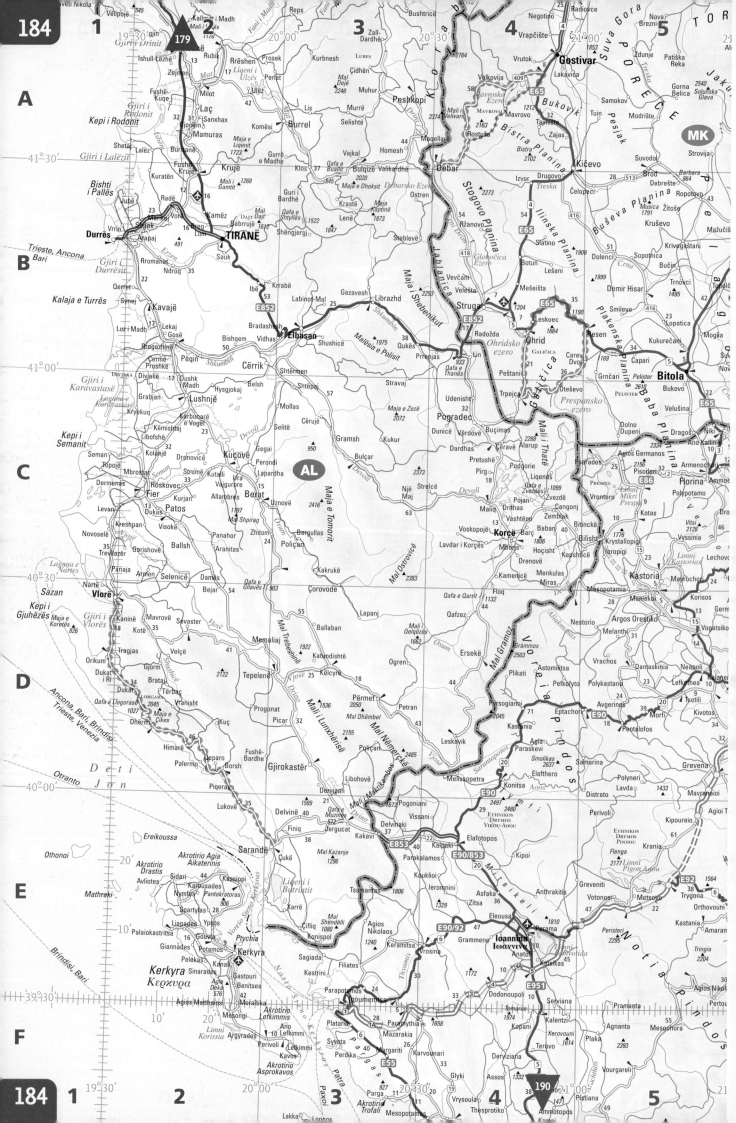

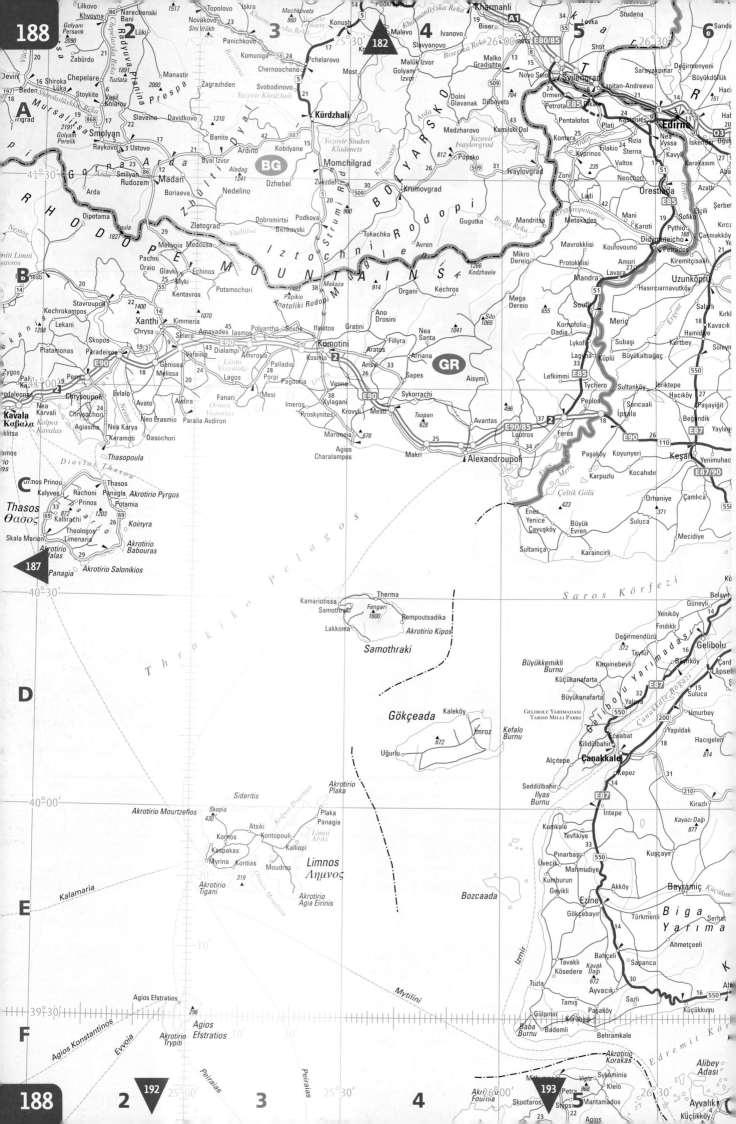

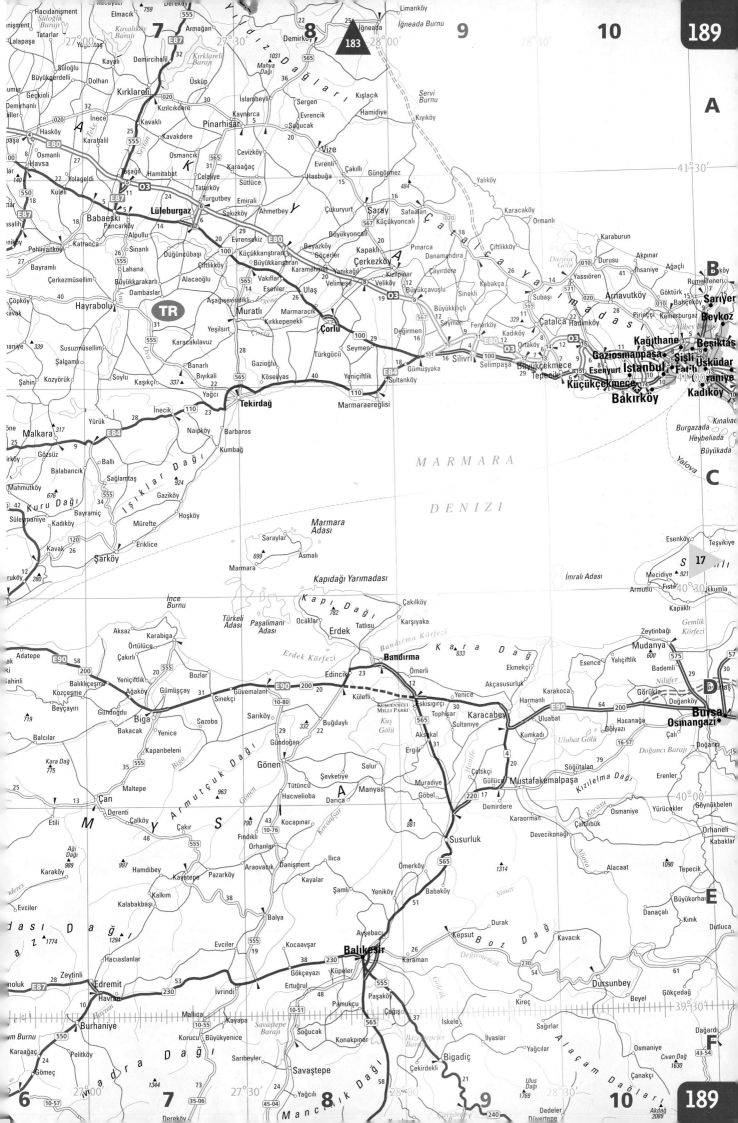

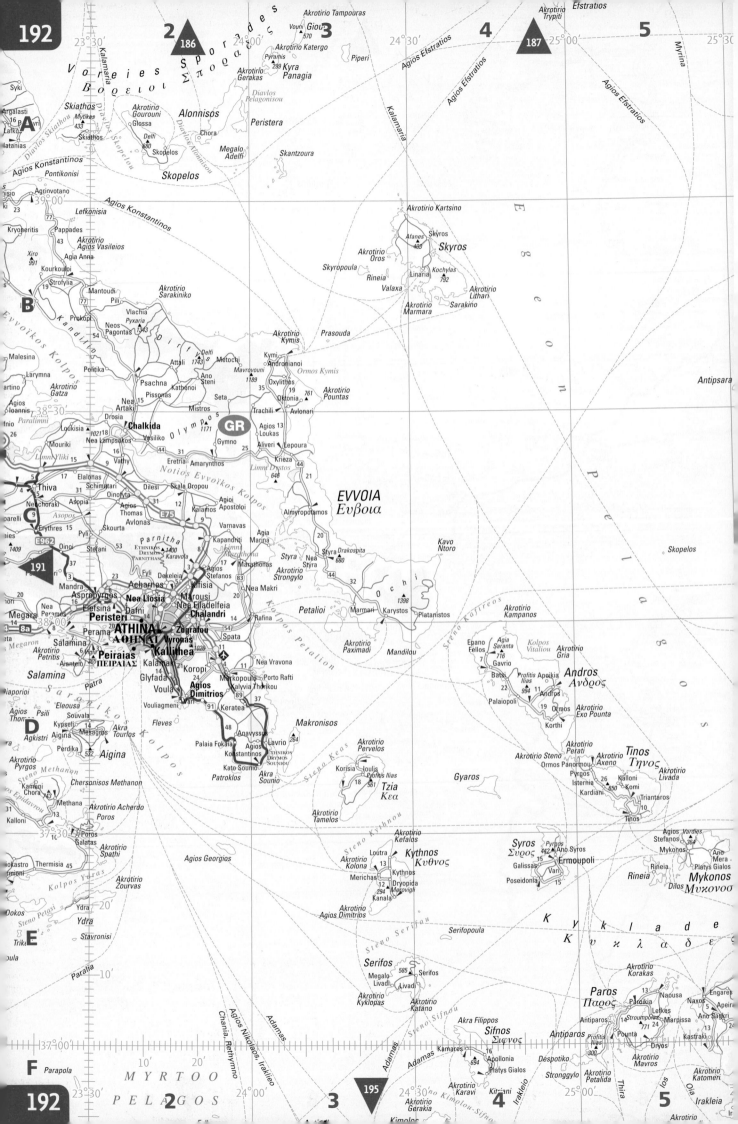

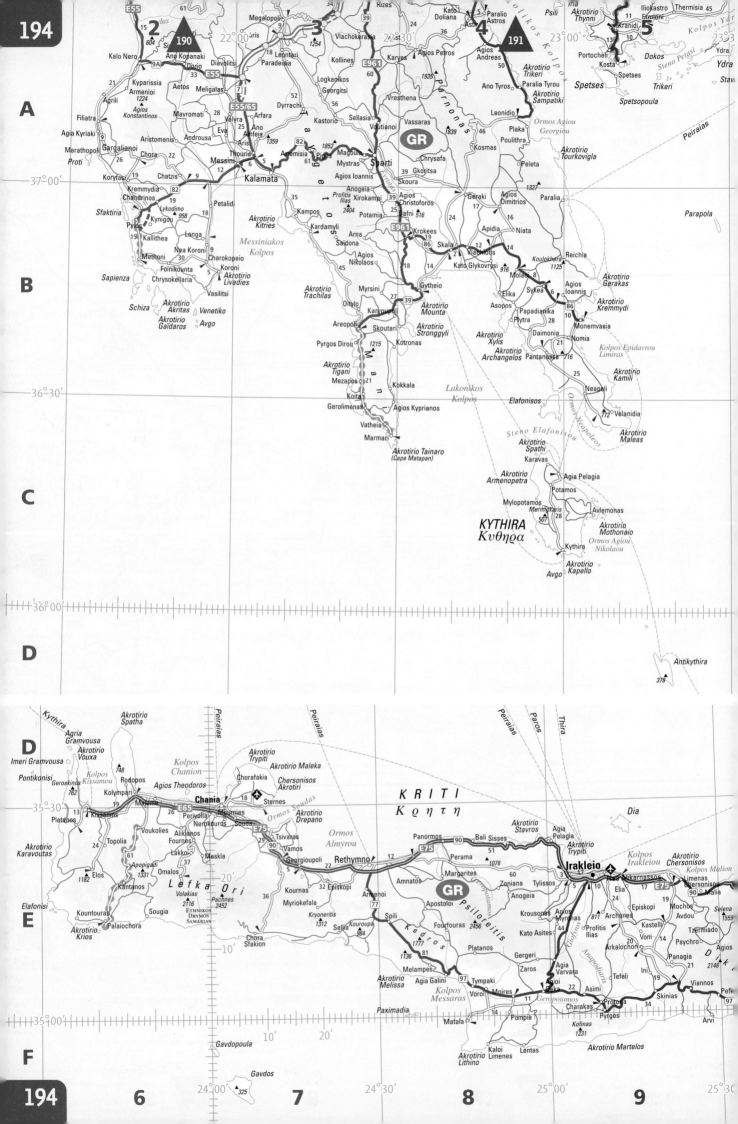

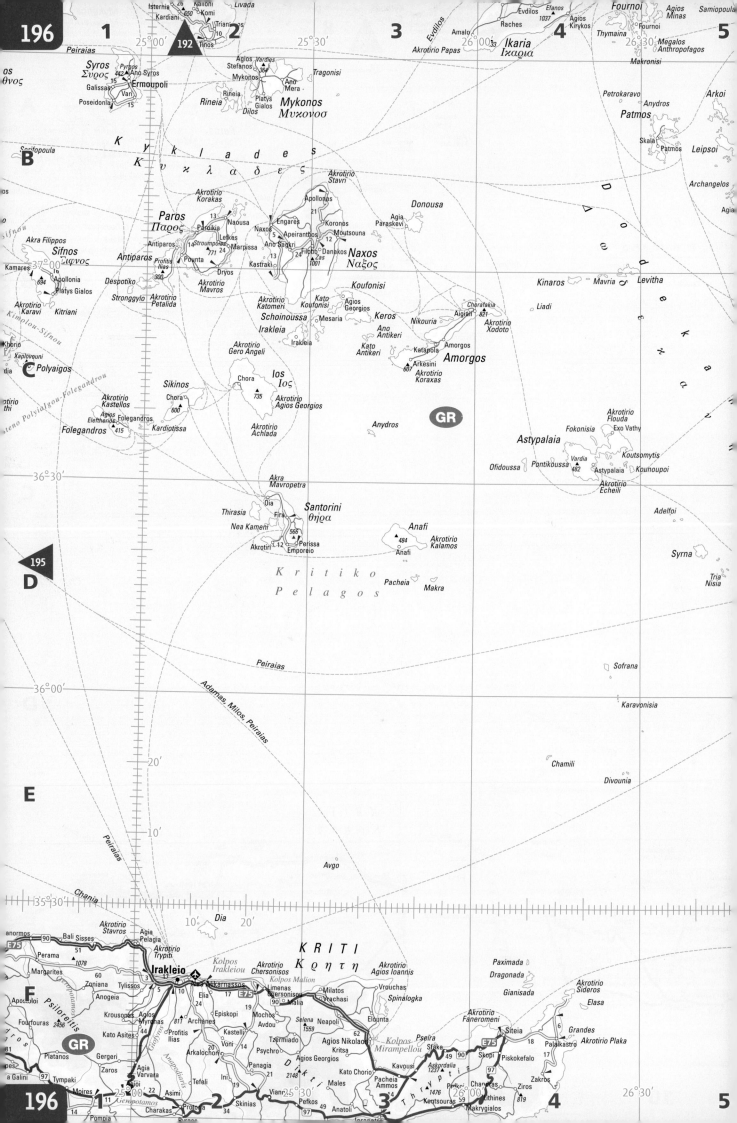

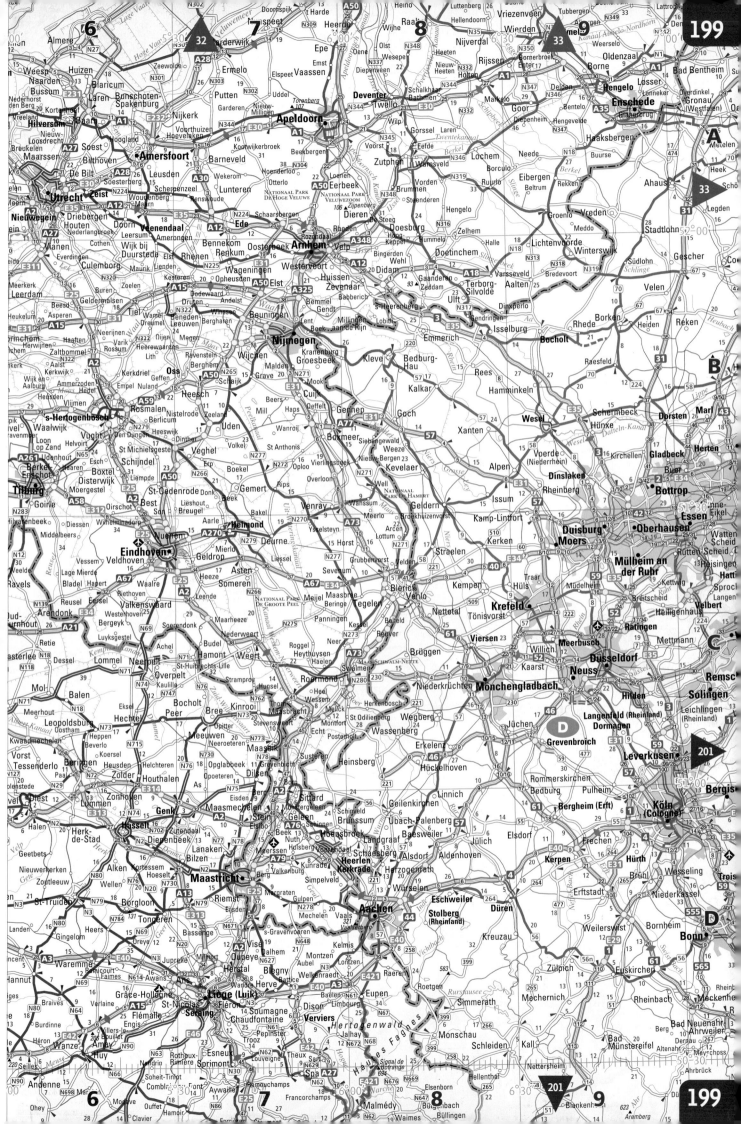

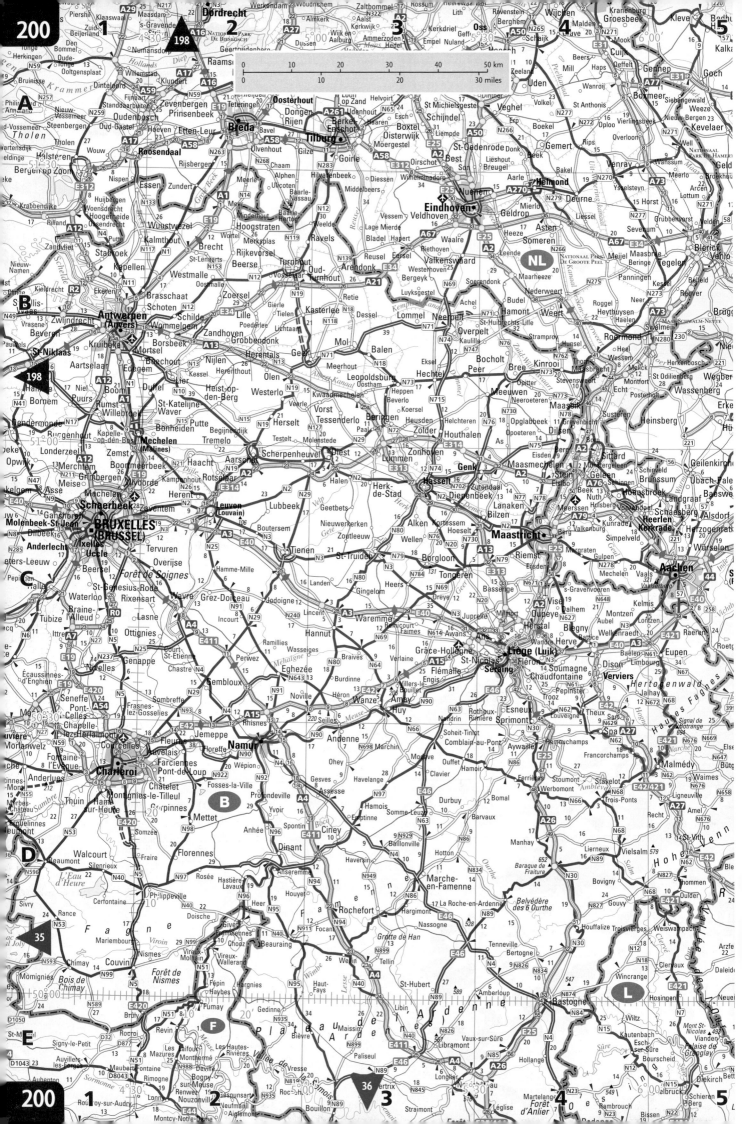

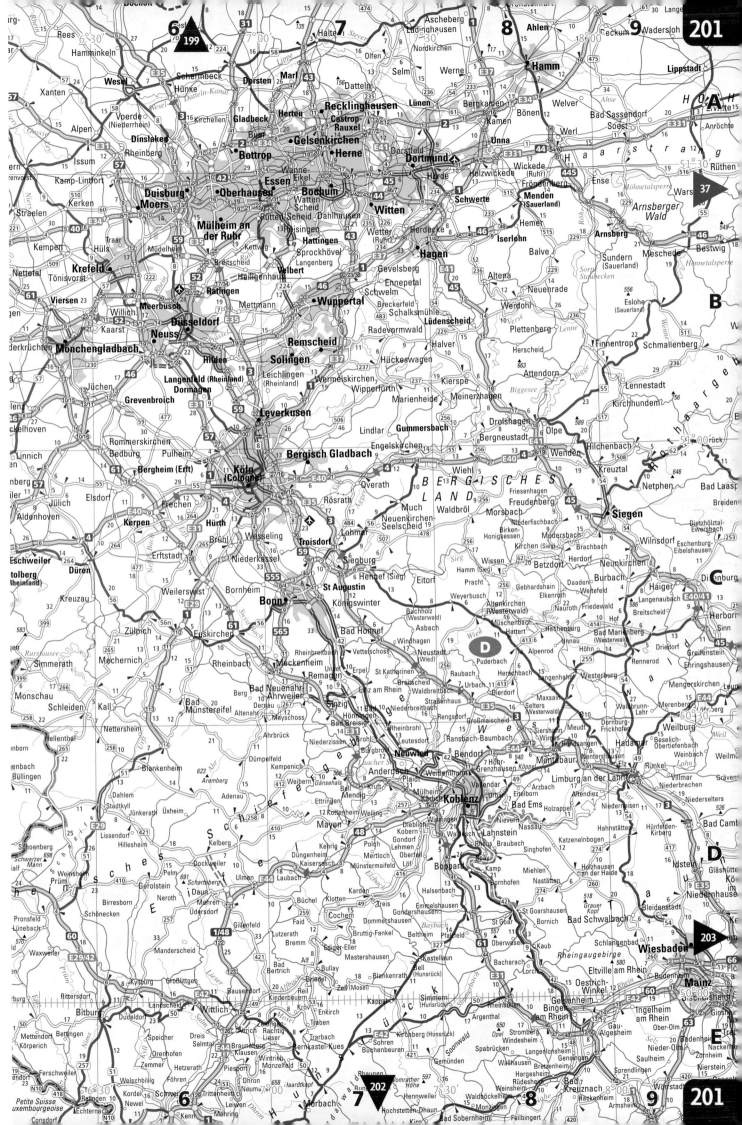

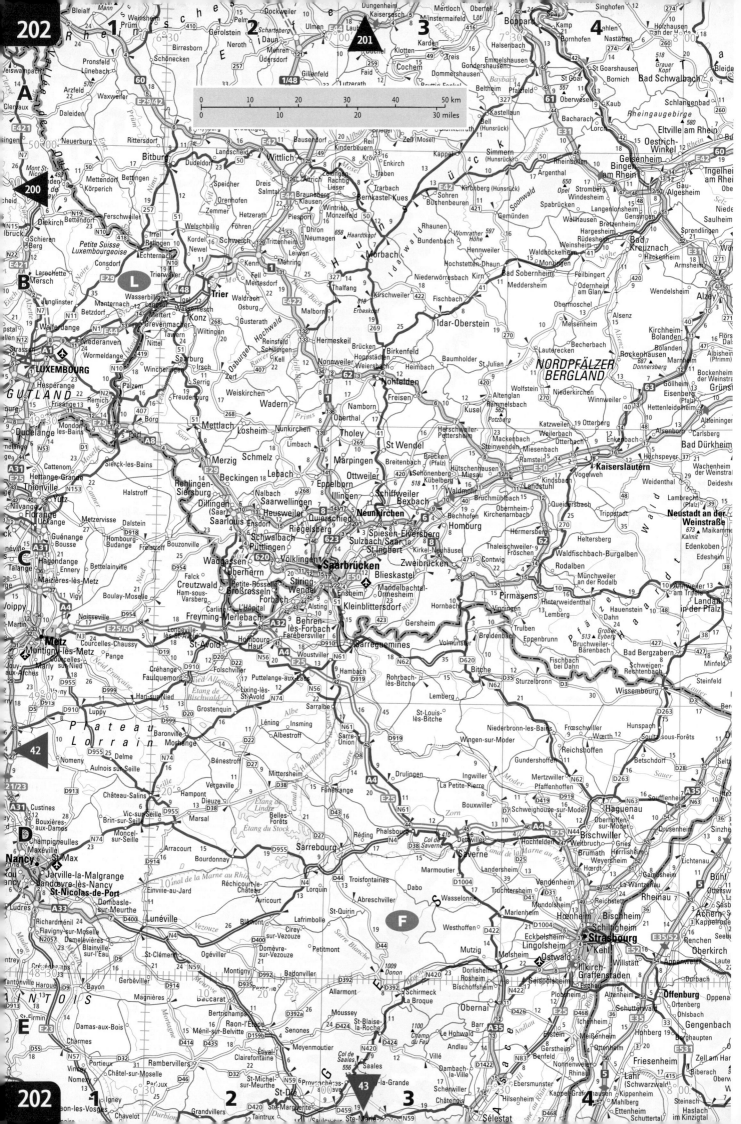

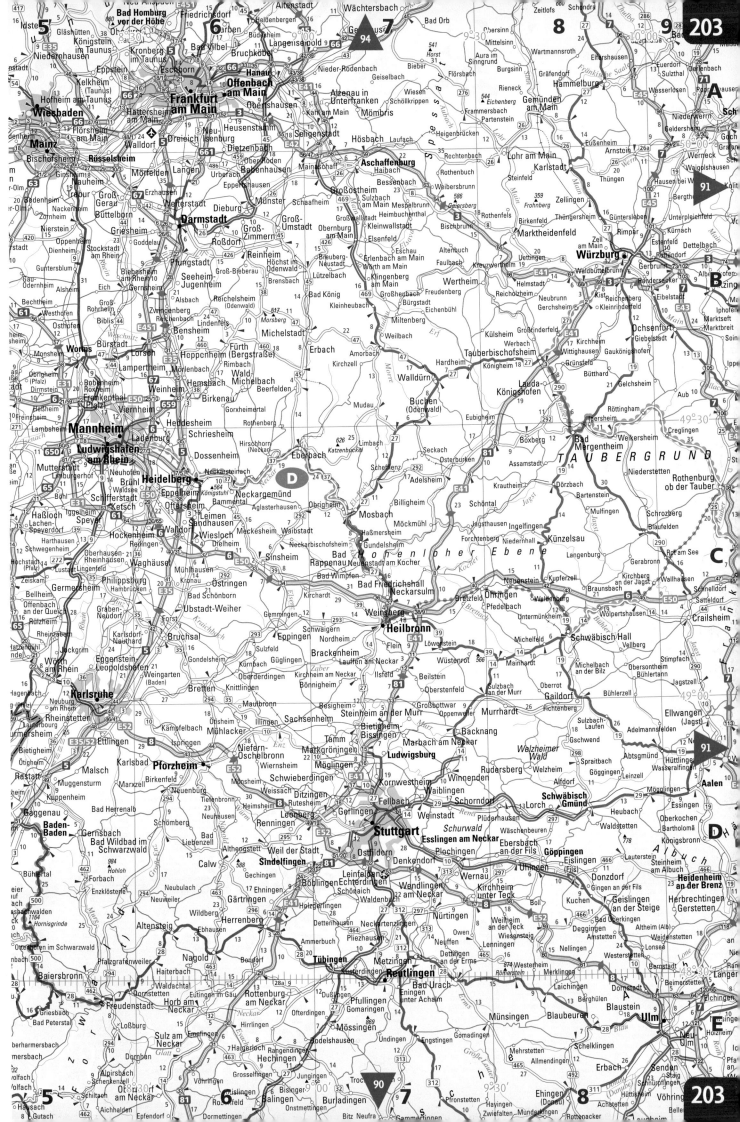

A

Aachen D 199 D8
Aalen D 203 D9
Aalsmeer NL 198 A5
Aalst B 198 D4
Aalst NL 199 B6
Aalten NL 199 B9
Aalter B 198 C2
Aardenburg NL 198 C2
Aarle NL 199 C7
Aarschot B 198 D5
Aartrijke B 198 C2
Aartselaar B 198 C4
Abcoude NL 198 A5
Abreschviller F 202 D3
Abtsgmünd D 203 D8
Achel B 199 C6
Achern D 202 D5
Achstetten D 203 E8
Adegem B 198 C2
Adelmannsfelden D 203 D8
Adelsheim D 203 C7
Adenau D 201 D6
Aglasterhausen D 203 C6
Ahaus D 199 A10
Ahlen D 201 A8
Ahrbrück D 199 E9
Aichhalden D 203 E5
Aiglemont F 200 E2
Albergen NL 199 A9
Albertshofen D 203 B9
Albestroff F 202 D2
Albisheim (Pfrimm) D 202 B5
Alblasserdam NL 198 B5
Aldenhoven D 199 D8
Alf D 201 D7
Alfdorf D 203 D8
Alken B 199 D6
Allarmont F 202 E3
Allmendingen D 203 E8
Almelo NL 199 A9
Almere NL 199 A6
Almkerk NL 198 B5
Alost B 198 D4
Alpen D 199 B9
Alpenrod D 201 C8
Alphen NL 198 C5
Alphen aan den Rijn NL 198 A5
Alpirsbach D 203 E5
Alsbach D 203 B6
Alsdorf D 199 D8
Alsenborn D 202 C4
Alsenz D 202 B4
Alsheim D 201 E9
Alsting F 202 C2
Altena D 201 B8
Altenahr D 199 D9
Altenbuch D 203 B7
Altendiez D 201 D8
Altenglan D 202 B3
Altenheim D 202 E4
Altenkirchen (Westerwald) D 201 C8
Altenstadt D 203 A6
Altensteig D 203 D6
Altheim (Alb) D 203 D9
Althengstett D 203 D6
Altleiningen D 202 B5
Altrich D 201 E6
Alzenau in Unterfranken D 203 A7
Alzey D 202 B5
Amay B 199 D6
Amberloup B 200 D4
Ameide NL 198 B5
Amel B 200 D5
Amerongen NL 199 B6
Amersfoort NL 199 A6
Ammerbuch D 203 D6
Ammerzoden NL 199 B6
Amnéville F 202 C1
Amorbach D 203 B7
Amstelveen NL 198 A5
Amsterdam NL 198 A5
Amstetten D 203 D8
Andelst NL 199 B7
Andenne B 199 E6
Anderlecht B 198 D4
Anderlues B 198 E4
Andernach D 201 D7
Andlau F 202 E3
Anhée B 200 D2
Annœullin F 198 D1
Annweiler am Trifels D 202 C4
Anröchte D 201 A9
Ans B 199 D7
Anseremme B 200 D2
Antoing B 198 D2
Antwerpen B 198 C4
Anvers B 198 C4
Anzegem B 198 D2
Apeldoorn NL 199 A7
Appenweier D 202 D4
Arcen NL 199 C8
Ardooie B 198 D2
Arendonk B 199 C6
Argenthal D 201 E8
Armentières F 198 D1
Armsheim D 201 E9
Arnemuiden NL 198 C3
Arnhem NL 199 B7
Arnsberg D 201 B9
Arnstein D 203 B8
Arracourt F 202 D2
Arry F 202 C1
Arzbach D 201 D8
Arzfeld D 201 D5
As B 199 C7
Asbach D 201 C7
Aschaffenburg D 203 B7
Ascheberg D 201 A8
Asperen NL 199 B6
Assamstadt D 203 C8
Asse B 198 D4
Assenede B 198 C3
Assesse B 200 D3
Asten NL 199 C7
Ath B 198 D3
Attendorn D 201 B8
Aub D 203 B9
Aubel B 199 D7
Aubenton F 200 E1
Auby F 198 E2
Aulnois sur-Seille F 202 D1
Aura im Sinngrund D 203 A8
Auvelais B 198 E5
Auvillers-les-Forges F 200 E1
Avelgem B 198 D2
Avricourt F 202 D2
Awans B 199 D6
Axel NL 198 C3
Aywaille B 199 E7

B

Baarle-Hertog B 198 C5
Baarle-Nassau NL 198 C5
Baarn NL 199 A6
Babberich NL 199 B8
Babenhausen D 203 B6
Baccarat F 202 E2
Bacharach D 201 D8
Backnang D 203 D7
Bad Bentheim D 199 A10
Bad Bergzabern D 202 C4
Bad Berleburg D 201 B9
Bad Bertrich D 201 D7
Bad Breisig D 201 D7
Bad Camberg D 201 D9
Bad Dürkheim D 203 C5
Bad Ems D 201 D8
Baden-Baden D 203 D5
Bad Friedrichshall D 203 C7
Bad Herrenalb D 203 D5
Badhoevedorp NL 198 A5
Bad Homburg vor der Höhe D 203 A6
Bad Honnef D 201 C7
Bad Hönningen D 201 C7
Bad Kissingen D 203 A9
Bad König D 203 B7
Bad Kreuznach D 201 E8
Bad Laasphe D 201 C9
Bad Liebenzell D 203 D6
Bad Marienberg (Westerwald) D 201 C8
Bad Mergentheim D 203 C8
Bad Münstereifel D 199 D9
Bad Neuenahr-Ahrweiler D 199 D10
Badonviller F 202 D2
Bad Orb D 203 A7
Bad Peterstal D 203 E5
Bad Rappenau D 203 C7
Bad Sassendorf D 201 A9
Bad Schönborn D 203 C6
Bad Schwalbach D 201 D9
Bad Sobernheim D 201 E8
Bad Überkingen D 203 D8
Bad Urach D 203 E7
Bad Vilbel D 203 A6
Bad Wildbad im Schwarzwald D 203 D6
Bad Wimpfen D 203 C7
Baelen B 199 D7
Baesweiler D 199 D8
Baiersbronn D 203 D5
Baillonville B 200 D3
Bakel NL 199 C7
Balen B 199 C6
Balingen D 203 E6
Balve D 201 B8
Bammental D 203 C6
Barneveld NL 199 A7
Baronville F 202 D2
Barr F 202 E3
Bartenstein D 203 C8
Bartholomä D 203 D8
Barvaux B 200 D3
Basècles B 198 D3
Bassenge B 199 D7
Bastogne B 200 D4
Bathmen NL 199 A8
Battice B 199 D7
Baumholder D 202 B3
Bausendorf D 201 D6
Bavel NL 198 B5
Bayon F 202 E1
Beaumont B 200 D1
Beauraing B 200 D2
Becherbach D 202 B4
Bechhofen D 202 C3
Bechtheim D 203 B5
Beckingen D 202 C2
Beckum D 201 A9
Bedburg D 199 D9
Bedburg-Hau D 199 B8
Beek NL 199 B7
Beek NL 199 B7
Beek NL 199 D7
Beekbergen NL 199 A7
Beerfelden D 203 B6
Beernem B 198 C2
Beers NL 199 B7
Beerse B 198 C5
Beersel B 198 D4
Beerst B 198 C1
Beesd NL 199 B6
Begijnendijk B 198 C5
Behren-lès-Forbach F 202 C2
Beilstein D 203 C7
Beimerstetten D 203 E8
Belfeld NL 199 C8
Bell D 201 D7
Bell (Hunsrück) D 201 D7
Bellenberg D 203 E9
Belles-Forêts F 202 D2
Bellheim D 203 C5
Belœil B 198 D3
Beltheim D 201 D7
Beltrum NL 199 A9
Bemmel NL 199 B7
Bendorf D 201 D8
Beneden-Leeuwen NL 199 B6
Bénestroff F 202 D2
Benfeld F 202 E4
Bennebroek NL 198 A5
Bennekom NL 199 A7
Bensheim D 203 B6
Bentelo NL 199 A9
Berchem B 198 D3
Berg D 199 D9
Berg L 200 E5
Berg NL 199 D7
Berg NL 199 D7
Berg (Pfalz) D 203 D5
Bergen op Zoom NL 198 C4
Bergeyk NL 199 C6
Bergharen NL 199 B7
Berghaupten D 202 E4
Bergheim (Erft) D 199 D9
Berghem NL 199 B7
Berghülen D 203 E8
Bergisch Gladbach D 199 D10
Bergkamen D 201 A8
Bergneustadt D 201 B8
Bergschenhoek NL 198 B5
Bergtheim D 203 B9
Beringe NL 199 C7
Beringen B 199 C6
Berkel NL 198 B4
Berkel-Enschot NL 199 B6
Berlicum NL 199 B6
Bernissart B 198 E3
Bernkastel-Kues D 201 E7
Bernstadt D 203 D9
Bertogne B 200 D4
Bertrange L 202 B1
Bertrichamps F 202 E2
Bertrix B 200 E3
Beselich-Obertiefenbach D 201 D9
Besigheim D 203 D7
Bessenbach D 203 B7
Best NL 199 B6
Bestwig D 201 B9
Betschdorf F 202 D4
Bettelainville F 202 C1
Bettembourg L 202 B1
Bettendorf L 200 E5
Bettingen D 201 E5
Betzdorf D 201 C8
Betzdorf L 202 B1
Beuningen NL 199 B7
Beuvrages F 198 E2
Beveren B 198 C4
Beverlo B 199 C6
Bexbach D 202 C3
Biberach D 202 E5
Biblis D 203 B5
Bieber D 203 A7
Biebesheim am Rhein D 203 B5
Bietigheim D 203 D5
Bietigheim-Bissingen D 203 D7
Bièvre B 200 E3
Billigheim D 203 C7
Bilthoven NL 199 A6
Bilzen B 199 D7
Binche B 198 E4
Bingen am Rhein D 201 E8
Bingerden NL 199 B8
Birkenau D 203 B6
Birkenfeld D 202 B3
Birkenfeld D 203 B8
Birkenfeld D 203 D6
Birken-Honigsessen D 201 C8
Birresborn D 201 D6
Bischbrunn D 203 B7
Bischheim F 202 D4
Bischoffsheim F 202 E3
Bischofsheim D 201 E9
Bischwiller F 202 D4
Bisingen D 203 E6
Bissen L 200 E5
Bitburg D 201 E6
Bitche F 202 C3
Bladel NL 199 C6
Blainville-sur-l'Eau F 202 D1
Blâmont F 202 D2
Blankenberge B 198 C2
Blankenheim D 199 E9
Blankenrath D 201 D7
Blaricum NL 199 A6
Blaton B 198 D3
Blaubeuren D 203 E8
Blaufelden D 203 C8
Blaustein D 203 E8
Blegny B 199 D7
Bléharies B 198 D2
Bleialf D 201 D5
Bleidenstadt D 201 D9
Bleiswijk NL 198 A5
Blerick NL 199 C8
Bleskensgraaf NL 198 B5
Blieskastel D 202 C3
Bobenheim-Roxheim D 203 B5
Böblingen D 203 D7
Bocholt B 199 C7
Bocholt D 199 B9
Bochum D 201 B7
Bockenheim an der Weinstraße D 203 B5
Bodegraven NL 198 A5
Bodelshausen D 203 E6
Bodenheim D 201 E9
Boechout B 198 C4
Boekel NL 199 B7
Boekhoute B 198 C3
Bogny-sur-Meuse F 200 E2
Böhl D 203 C5
Bolanden D 202 B5
Boll D 203 D8
Bolnes NL 198 B5
Bomal B 200 D4
Bondorf D 203 D6
Bondues F 198 D2
Bönen D 201 A8
Bonheiden B 198 C5
Bonn D 199 D10
Bönnigheim D 203 C7
Boom B 198 C4
Boortmeerbeek B 198 D5
Boppard D 201 D8
Borculo NL 199 A9
Borg D 202 B1
Borgloon B 199 D6
Borken D 199 B9
Born NL 199 C7
Borne NL 199 A9
Bornem B 198 C4
Bornerbroek NL 199 A9
Bornheim D 199 D9
Bornhofen D 201 D8
Bornich D 201 D8
Borssele NL 198 C3
Boskoop NL 198 A5
Bottrop D 199 B9
Bouillon B 200 E3
Boulay-Moselle F 202 C1
Bourdonnay F 202 D2
Bourscheid L 200 E5
Bousse F 202 C1
Boussu B 198 E3
Boutersem B 198 D5
Bouxières-aux-Dames F 202 D1
Bouxwiller F 202 D3
Bouzonville F 202 C2
Bovigny B 200 D4
Boxberg D 203 C8
Boxmeer NL 199 B7
Boxtel NL 199 B6
Brachbach D 201 C8
Brackenheim D 203 C7
Braine-l'Alleud B 198 D4
Braine-le-Comte B 198 D4
Braives B 199 D6
Brakel B 198 D3
Brasschaat B 198 C4
Braubach D 201 D8
Brauneberg D 201 E6
Braunfels D 201 C9
Braunsbach D 203 C8
Brecht B 198 C5
Breckerfeld D 201 B7
Breda NL 198 B5
Bredene B 198 C1
Bredevoort NL 199 B9
Bree B 199 C7
Breidenbach F 202 C3
Breitenbach D 202 C3
Breitscheid D 199 C9
Breitscheid D 201 C7
Breitscheid D 201 C9
Bremm D 201 D7
Brensbach D 203 B6
Breskens NL 198 C3
Bretten D 203 C6
Bretzenheim D 201 E8
Bretzfeld D 203 C7
Breuberg-Neustadt D 203 B7
Breugel NL 199 B7
Breukelen NL 199 A6
Briedel D 201 D7
Brielle NL 198 B4
Brin-sur-Seille F 202 D1
Broekhuizenvorst NL 199 C8
Brohl D 201 D7
Brouvelieures F 202 E2
Brouwershaven NL 198 B3
Bruchköbel D 203 A6
Bruchmühlbach D 202 C3
Bruchsal D 203 C6
Bruchweiler-Bärenbach D 202 C4
Brücken D 202 B3
Brücken (Pfalz) D 202 C3
Brugelette B 198 D3
Bruges B 198 C2
Brugge B 198 C2
Brüggen D 199 C8
Brühl D 199 D9
Brühl D 203 C6
Bruinisse NL 198 B4
Brûly B 200 E2
Brumath F 202 D4
Brummen NL 199 A8
Brunehamel F 200 E1
Brunssum NL 199 D7
Brussel B 198 D4
Bruttig-Fankel D 201 D7
Bruxelles B 198 D4
Büchel D 201 D7
Buchen (Odenwald) D 203 B7
Büchenbeuren D 201 E7
Buchholz (Westerwald) D 201 C7
Budel NL 199 C7
Budenheim D 201 D9
Büdesheim D 203 A6
Buer D 199 B10
Buggenhout B 198 C4
Bühl D 202 D5
Bühlertal D 203 D5
Bühlertann D 203 C8
Bühlerzell D 203 C8
Bullay D 201 D7
Büllingen B 199 E8
Bundenbach D 201 E7
Bunschoten-Spakenburg NL 199 A6
Burbach D 201 C9
Burdinne B 199 D6
Buren NL 199 B6
Burgbrohl D 201 D7
Burgh-Haamstede NL 198 B3
Burgsinn D 203 A8
Bürgstadt D 203 B7
Burladingen D 203 E7
Bürstadt D 203 B5
Bussum NL 199 A6
Bütgenbach B 199 E8
Büttelborn D 203 B6
Bütthard D 203 B8
Buurse NL 199 A9

C

Calw D 203 D6
Capelle aan de IJssel NL 198 B5
Carling F 202 C2
Carlsberg D 202 C5
Carvin F 198 E1
Castrop-Rauxel D 201 A7
Cattenom F 202 C1
Ceintrey F 202 D1
Celles B 198 D2
Cerfontaine B 200 D1
Chaam NL 198 C5
Chaligny F 202 D1
Champigneulles F 202 D1
Chapelle-lez-Herlaimont B 198 E4
Charleroi B 198 E4
Charmes F 202 E1
Chastre B 198 D5
Château-Salins F 202 D2
Châtelet B 200 D2
Châtel-sur-Moselle F 202 E1
Châtenois F 202 E3
Chaudfontaine B 199 D7
Chavelot F 202 E1
Chièvres B 198 D3
Chimay B 200 D1
Chooz F 200 D2
Ciney B 200 D3
Cirey-sur-Vezouze F 202 D2
Clavier B 199 E6
Clervaux L 200 D5
Clinge NL 198 C4
Cochem D 201 D7
Coesfeld D 199 B10
Colijnsplaat NL 198 B3
Colroy-la-Grande F 202 E3
Comblain-au-Pont B 199 E7
Comines B 198 D1
Condé-sur-l'Escaut F 198 E3
Consdorf L 202 B1
Contwig D 202 C3
Cothen NL 199 A6
Courcelles B 198 E4
Courcelles-Chaussy F 202 C1
Courcelles-sur-Nied F 202 C1
Courrières F 198 E1
Courtrai B 198 D2
Court-St-Etienne B 198 D5
Couvin B 200 D2
Crailsheim D 203 C9
Creglingen D 203 C9
Créhange F 202 C2
Creutzwald F 202 C2
Crévéchamps F 202 D1
Cuijk NL 199 B7
Culemborg NL 199 B6
Custines F 202 D1
Cysoing F 198 D2

D

Daaden D 201 C8
Dabo F 202 D3
Dahlem D 201 D6
Dahlhausen D 199 C10
Dahn D 202 C4
Daknam B 198 C3
Daleiden D 200 D5
Dalhem B 199 D7
Dalstein F 202 C1
Damas-aux-Bois F 202 E1
Dambach-la-Ville F 202 E3
Damelevières F 202 D1
Damme B 198 C2
Darmstadt D 203 B6
Datteln D 201 A7
Daun D 201 D6
De Bilt NL 199 A6
Deerlijk B 198 D2
Deggingen D 203 D8
De Haan B 198 C2
Deidesheim D 203 C5
Deinze B 198 D3
Delden NL 199 A9
Delft NL 198 A4
Delme F 202 D1
De Meern NL 199 A6
Den Bommel NL 198 B4
Denderleeuw B 198 D4
Dendermonde B 198 C4
Den Dungen NL 199 B6
Denekamp NL 199 A10
Den Haag NL 198 A4
Denkendorf D 203 D7
Dentergem B 198 D2
Dernau D 199 D10
Dessel B 199 C6
De Steeg NL 199 A8
Destelbergen B 198 C3
Dettelbach D 203 B9
Dettenhausen D 203 D7
Dettingen an der Erms D 203 D7
Dettwiller F 202 D3
Deurne NL 199 C7
Deventer NL 199 A8
Deville F 200 E2
Dhron D 201 E6
Didam NL 199 B8
Dieblich D 201 D7
Dieburg D 203 B6
Diekirch L 200 E5
Dielheim D 203 C6
Diemen NL 198 A5
Dienheim D 201 E9
Diepenbeek B 199 D6
Diepenheim NL 199 A9
Diepenveen NL 199 A8
Dierdorf D 201 C8
Dieren NL 199 A8
Diessen NL 199 C6
Diest B 199 D6
Dietzenbach D 203 A6
Dietzhölztal-Ewersbach D 201 C9
Dieuze F 202 D2
Dikkebus B 198 D1
Diksmuide B 198 C1
Dilbeek B 198 D4
Dillenburg D 201 C9
Dillingen (Saar) D 202 C2
Dilsen B 199 C7
Dinant B 200 D2
Dinslaken D 199 B9
Dinteloord NL 198 B4
Dinther NL 199 B6
Dinxperlo NL 199 B8
Dirksland NL 198 B4
Dirmstein D 203 B5
Dison B 199 D7
Ditzingen D 203 D7
Dockweiler D 201 D6
Dodewaard NL 199 B7
Doesburg NL 199 A8
Doetinchem NL 199 B8
Doische B 200 D2
Dombasle-sur-Meurthe F 202 D1
Domburg NL 198 B3
Domèvre-sur-Vezouze F 202 D2
Dommershausen D 201 D7
Dongen NL 198 B5
Donk NL 199 B7
Donzdorf D 203 D8
Doorn NL 199 A6
Doornspijk NL 199 A7
Dordrecht NL 198 B5
Dorlisheim F 202 D3
Dormagen D 199 C9
Dornburg-Frickhofen D 201 C9
Dornhan D 203 E6
Dornstadt D 203 E8
Dornstetten D 203 E5
Dorsten D 199 B9
Dorstfeld D 201 A7
Dortmund D 201 A7
Dörzbach D 203 C8
Dossenheim D 203 C6
Dreieich D 203 A6
Dreis D 201 E6
Drensteinfurt D 201 A8
Dreumel NL 199 B6
Driebergen NL 199 A6
Driedorf D 201 C9
Drolshagen D 201 B8
Drongen B 198 C3
Drulingen F 202 D3
Drusenheim F 202 D4
Druten NL 199 B7
Dudelange L 202 C1
Dudeldorf D 201 E6
Duffel B 198 C5
Duisburg D 199 C9
Dümpelfeld D 199 E9
Düngenheim D 201 D7
Durbach D 202 D5
Durbuy B 200 D3
Düren D 199 D8
Durmersheim D 203 D5
Düsseldorf D 199 C9
Dussen NL 198 B5
Dußlingen D 203 E7

E

Eberbach D 203 C6
Ebersbach an der Fils D 203 D8
Ebersmunster F 202 E4
Ebhausen D 203 D6
Écaussinnes-d'Enghien B 198 D4
Echt NL 199 C7
Echternach L 201 E5
Eckbolsheim F 202 D4
Ede NL 199 A7
Edegem B 198 C4
Edenkoben D 202 C5
Edesheim D 202 C5
Ediger-Eller D 201 D7
Eefde NL 199 A8
Eeklo B 198 C3
Eerbeek NL 199 A8
Eernegem B 198 C2
Eersel NL 199 C6
Eggenstein-Leopoldshafen D 203 C5
Eghezée B 198 D5
Ehingen (Donau) D 203 E8
Ehningen D 203 D6
Ehringshausen D 201 C9
Eibelstadt D 203 B9
Eibergen NL 199 A9
Eich D 203 B5
Eichenbühl D 203 B7
Eijsden NL 199 D7
Eindhoven NL 199 C6
Einville-au-Jard F 202 D1
Eisden B 199 D7
Eisenberg (Pfalz) D 202 B5
Eislingen (Fils) D 203 D8
Eitelborn D 201 D8
Eitorf D 201 C7
Ekeren B 198 C4
Eksaarde B 198 C3
Eksel B 199 C6
Elchingen D 203 E9
Elfershausen D 203 A8
Elkenroth D 201 C8
Ellenberg D 203 C9
Ellezelles B 198 D3
Ellwangen (Jagst) D 203 D9
Elsdorf D 199 D9
Elsenborn B 199 E8
Elsenfeld D 203 B7
Elsloo NL 199 D7
Elspeet NL 199 A7
Elst NL 199 B6
Elst NL 199 B7
Eltville am Rhein D 201 D9
Elz D 201 D9
Emmelshausen D 201 D8
Emmerich D 199 B8
Empel NL 199 B6
Empfingen D 203 E6
Emptinne B 200 D3
Emst NL 199 A7
Engden D 199 A10
Engelskirchen D 201 C7
Enghien B 198 D4
Engis B 199 D6
Engstingen D 203 E7
Eningen unter Achalm D 203 E7
Enkenbach D 202 C4
Enkirch D 201 E7
Ennepetal D 201 B7
Ennery F 202 C1
Enschede NL 199 A9
Ensdorf D 202 C2
Ense D 201 B9
Ensheim D 202 C3
Enter NL 199 A9
Enzklösterle D 203 D5
Epe NL 199 A7
Epfendorf D 203 E6
Eppelborn D 202 C2
Eppelheim D 203 C6
Eppenbrunn D 202 C4
Eppertshausen D 203 B6
Eppingen D 203 C6
Eppstein D 203 A5
Erbach D 203 B7
Erbach D 203 E8
Erftstadt D 199 D9
Erkelenz D 199 C8
Erlenbach am Main D 203 B7
Ermelo NL 199 A7
Erndtebrück D 201 C9
Erp NL 199 B7
Erpel D 201 C7
Erquelinnes B 200 D1
Erstein F 202 E4
Ertvelde B 198 C3
Erwitte D 201 A9
Erzhausen D 203 B6
Esch NL 199 B6
Eschau D 203 B7
Eschau F 202 E4
Eschborn D 203 A6
Eschenburg-Eibelshausen D 201 C9
Esch-sur-Sûre L 200 E4
Eschweiler D 199 D8
Eslohe (Sauerland) D 201 B9
Esneux B 199 D7
Essen B 198 C4
Essen D 199 C10
Essingen D 203 D9
Esslingen am Neckar D 203 D7
Estaimpuis B 198 D2
Estenfeld D 203 B9
Étival-Clairefontaine F 202 E2
Ettelbruck L 200 E5
Ettenheim D 202 E4
Etten-Leur NL 198 B5
Ettlingen D 203 D5
Ettringen D 201 D7
Eubigheim D 203 B8
Euerdorf D 203 A9
Eupen B 199 D8
Euskirchen D 199 D9
Eußenheim D 203 A8
Eutingen im Gäu D 203 E6
Everdingen NL 199 B6
Evergem B 198 C3

F

Faches-Thumesnil F 198 D2
Faid D 201 D7
Faimes B 199 D6
Falck F 202 C2
Fameck F 202 C1
Farciennes B 198 E5
Farébersviller F 202 C2
Faulbach D 203 B7
Faulquemont F 202 C2
Feilbingert D 201 E8
Fell D 202 B2
Fellbach D 203 D7
Fénétrange F 202 D3
Fépin F 200 D2
Ferrières B 199 E7
Ferschweiler D 201 E5
Fichtenberg D 203 D8
Fijnaart NL 198 B4
Finnentrop D 201 B8
Fischbach D 202 B3
Fischbach bei Dahn D 202 C4
Flavigny-sur-Moselle F 202 D1
Flein D 203 C7
Flémalle B 199 D6
Fléron B 199 D7
Flers-en-Escrebieux F 198 E2
Fleurus B 198 E5
Flines-lez-Raches F 198 E2
Florange F 202 C1
Floreffe B 198 E5
Florennes B 200 D2
Flörsbach D 203 A7
Flörsheim am Main D 203 A5
Flörsheim-Dalsheim D 203 B5
Focant B 200 D3
Föhren D 201 E6
Folschviller F 202 C2
Fontaine-l'Évêque B 198 E4
Forbach D 203 D5
Forbach F 202 C2
Forchtenberg D 203 C8
Forst D 203 C6
Fosses-la-Ville B 200 D2
Fraire B 200 D2
Frameries B 198 E3
Frammersbach D 203 A7
Francorchamps B 199 E7
Frankenthal (Pfalz) D 203 B5
Frankfurt am Main D 203 A6
Frasnes-lez-Buissenal B 198 D3
Frasnes-lez-Gosselies B 198 D4
Frechen D 199 D9
Freinsheim D 203 B5
Freisen D 202 B3
Freistroff F 202 C1
Fresnes-sur-Escaut F 198 E3
Freudenberg D 201 C8
Freudenberg D 203 B7
Freudenburg D 202 B2
Freudenstadt D 203 E5
Freyming-Merlebach F 202 C2
Friedewald D 201 C8
Friedrichsdorf D 203 A6
Friesenhagen D 201 C8
Friesenheim D 202 E4
Frisange L 202 B1
Frœschwiller F 202 D4
Fromelennes F 200 D2
Fröndenberg D 201 B8
Frouard F 202 D1
Fumay F 200 E2
Fürth D 203 B6

G

Gaanderen NL 199 B8
Gaggenau D 203 D5
Gaildorf D 203 D8
Gambsheim F 202 D4
Gammertingen D 203 E7
Gand B 198 C3
Ganshoren B 198 D4
Garderen NL 199 A7
Gärtringen D 203 D6
Gau-Algesheim D 201 E9
Gaukönigshofen D 203 B8
Gau-Odernheim D 201 E9
Gavere B 198 D3
Gebhardshain D 201 C8
Gechingen D 203 D6
Gedinne B 200 E2
Geel B 199 C6
Geertruidenberg NL 198 B5
Geesteren NL 199 A9
Geetbets B 199 D6
Geffen NL 199 B6
Geilenkirchen D 199 D8
Geiselbach D 203 A7
Geisenheim D 201 E8
Geislingen D 203 E6
Geislingen an der Steige D 203 D8
Geispolsheim F 202 D4
Gelchsheim D 203 B9
Geldermalsen NL 199 B6
Geldern D 199 B8
Geldersheim D 203 A9
Geldrop NL 199 C7
Geleen NL 199 D7
Gelnhausen D 203 A7
Gelsenkirchen D 199 B10
Gembloux B 198 D5
Gemert NL 199 B7
Gemmingen D 203 C6
Gemünden D 201 E7
Gemünden am Main D 203 A8
Genappe B 198 D4
Gendringen NL 199 B8
Gendt NL 199 B7
Gengenbach D 202 E5
Genk B 199 D7
Gennep NL 199 B7
Gensingen D 201 E8
Gent B 198 C3
Geraardsbergen B 198 D3
Gerabronn D 203 C8
Gerbéviller F 202 E2
Gerbrunn D 203 B8
Gerchsheim D 203 B8
Gerlingen D 203 D7
Germersheim D 203 C5
Gernsbach D 203 D5
Gernsheim D 203 B5
Gerolstein D 201 D6
Gerpinnes B 200 D2
Gersheim D 202 C3
Gerstetten D 203 D9
Gerstheim F 202 E4
Gescher D 199 B10
Gespunsart F 200 E2
Gesves B 200 D3
Gevelsberg D 201 B7
Ghislenghien B 198 D3
Giebelstadt D 203 B8
Gierle B 198 C5
Gillenfeld D 201 D6
Gilze NL 198 B5
Gingelom B 199 D6
Gingen an der Fils D 203 D8
Ginsheim D 201 E9
Gistel B 198 C1
Givet F 200 D2
Gladbeck D 199 B9
Glanerbrug NL 199 A9
Glashütten D 203 A5
Goch D 199 B8
Goddelau D 203 B6
Goedereede NL 198 B3
Goes NL 198 B3
Göggingen D 203 D8
Goirle NL 199 B6
Göllheim D 202 B5
Gomadingen D 203 E7

Gomaringen D 203 E7
Gondelsheim D 203 C6
Gondershausen D 201 D7
Gondorf D 201 D7
Goor NL 199 A9
Göppingen D 203 D8
Gorinchem NL 198 B5
Gorssel NL 199 A8
Gorxheimertal D 203 B6
Gouda NL 198 A5
Goudswaard NL 198 B4
Gouvy B 200 D4
Graben-Neudorf D 203 C5
Grâce-Hollogne B 199 D6
Gräfendorf D 203 A8
Grafenrheinfeld D 203 B9
Grandvillers F 202 E2
Grave NL 199 B7
Greifenstein D 201 C9
Grevenbicht NL 199 C7
Grevenbroich D 199 C9
Grevenmacher L 202 B1
Grez-Doiceau B 198 D5
Gries F 202 D4
Griesbach D 203 E5
Griesheim D 203 B6
Grimbergen B 198 D4
Grobbendonk B 198 C5
Groenlo NL 199 A9
Groesbeek NL 199 B7
Gronau (Westfalen) D 199 A10
Groß-Bieberau D 203 B6
Großbottwar D 203 D7
Grosselfingen D 203 E6
Groß-Gerau D 203 B5
Großheubach D 203 B7
Großlangheim D 203 B9
Großlittgen D 201 D6
Großmaischeid D 201 C8
Großostheim D 203 B7
Großrinderfeld D 203 B8
Groß-Rohrheim D 203 B5
Großrosseln D 202 C2
Groß-Umstadt D 203 B6
Großwallstadt D 203 B7
Groß-Zimmern D 203 B6
Grostenquin F 202 D2
Grubbenvorst NL 199 C8
Grünsfeld D 203 B8
Grünstadt D 203 B5
Gschwend D 203 D8
Guénange F 202 C1
Güglingen D 203 C6
Gulpen NL 199 D7
Gummersbach D 201 B8
Gundelsheim D 203 C7
Gundershoffen F 202 D4
Guntersblum D 201 E9
Güntersleben D 203 B8
Gusterath D 202 B2
Gutach (Schwarzwaldbahn) D 203 E5

H

Haacht B 198 D5
Haaften NL 199 B6
Haaksbergen NL 199 A9
Haaltert B 198 D4
Haaren NL 199 B6
Haarlem NL 198 A5
Haastrecht NL 198 B5
Hachenburg D 201 C8
Hackenheim D 201 E8
Hadamar D 201 D9
Haelen NL 199 C7
Hagen D 201 B7
Hagenbach D 203 C5
Hagondange F 202 C1
Haguenau F 202 D4
Hahnstätten D 201 D9
Haibach D 203 B7
Haiger D 201 C9
Haigerloch D 203 E6
Haiterbach D 203 D6
Halen B 199 D6
Halfweg NL 198 A5
Halle B 198 D4
Halle NL 199 B8
Halluin B 198 D2
Halsenbach D 201 D8
Halsteren NL 198 B4
Halstroff F 202 C1
Haltern D 199 B10
Halver D 201 B7
Hambach F 202 C3
Hambrücken D 203 C6
Hamm D 201 A8
Hamm (Sieg) D 201 C8
Hamme B 198 C4
Hammelburg D 203 A8
Hamme-Mille B 198 D5
Hamminkeln D 199 B9
Hamoir B 199 E7
Hamois B 200 D3
Hamont B 199 C7
Hampont F 202 D2
Ham-sous-Varsberg F 202 C2
Ham-sur-Heure B 200 D1
Hanau D 203 A6
Handzame B 198 C2
Hannut B 199 D6
Han-sur-Nied F 202 D1
Hapert NL 199 C6
Haps NL 199 B7
Harderwijk NL 199 A7
Hardheim D 203 B7
Hardinxveld-Giessendam NL 198 B5
Harelbeke B 198 D2
Hargesheim D 201 E8
Hargimont B 200 D3
Hargnies F 200 D2
Harmelen NL 198 A5
Harnes F 198 E1
Haroué F 202 E1
Harthausen D 203 C5
Haslach im Kinzigtal D 202 E5
Hasselt B 199 D6
Haßloch D 203 C5
Haßmersheim D 203 C7
Hastière-Lavaux B 200 D2
Hattersheim am Main D 203 A5
Hattert D 201 C8
Hattingen D 199 C10
Hatzenbühl D 203 C5
Haubourdin F 198 D1
Hauenstein D 202 C4
Hausach D 203 E5
Hausen bei Würzburg D 203 B9
Haut-Fays B 200 D3
Havelange B 200 D3
Haversin B 200 D3
Hayange F 202 C1
Haybes F 200 D2
Hayingen D 203 E7
Hazerswoude-Rijndijk NL 198 A5
Hechingen D 203 E6
Hechtel B 199 C6
Heddesheim D 203 C6
Hedel NL 199 B6
Heek D 199 A10
Heel NL 199 C7
Heemstede NL 198 A5
Heenvliet NL 198 B4
Heer B 200 D2
Heerde NL 199 A8
Heerewaarden NL 199 B6
Heerlen NL 199 D7
Heers B 199 D6
Heesch NL 199 B7
Heeswijk NL 199 B6
Heeten NL 199 A8
Heeze NL 199 C7
Heidelberg D 203 C6
Heiden D 199 B9
Heidenheim an der Brenz D 203 D9
Heigenbrücken D 203 A7
Heilbronn D 203 C7
Heiligenhaus D 199 C9
Heimbach D 202 B3
Heimbuchenthal D 203 B7
Heimsheim D 203 D6
Heinkenszand NL 198 C3
Heino NL 199 A8
Heinsberg D 199 C8
Heisingen D 199 C10
Heist-op-den-Berg B 198 C5
Hekelgem B 198 D4
Helchteren B 199 C6
Heldenbergen D 203 A6
Hellendoorn NL 199 A8
Hellenthal D 199 E8
Hellevoetsluis NL 198 B4
Helmond NL 199 C7
Helmstadt D 203 B8
Heltersberg D 202 C4
Helvoirt NL 199 B6
Hem F 198 D2
Hemer D 201 B8
Hemsbach D 203 B6
Hengelo NL 199 A8
Hengelo NL 199 A9
Hengevelde NL 199 A9
Hénin-Beaumont F 198 E1
Hennef (Sieg) D 201 C7
Hennweiler D 201 E7
Heppen B 199 C6
Heppenheim (Bergstraße) D 203 B6
Herbeumont B 200 E3
Herborn D 201 C9
Herbrechtingen D 203 D9
Herdecke D 201 B7
Herdorf D 201 C8
Herent B 198 D5
Herentals B 198 C5
Herenthout B 198 C5
Herk-de-Stad B 199 D6
Herkenbosch NL 199 C8
Herkingen NL 198 B4
Hermersberg D 202 C4
Hermeskeil D 202 B2
Herne B 198 D4
Herne D 201 A7
Héron B 199 D6
Herrenberg D 203 D6
Herrlisheim F 202 D4
Herschbach D 201 C8
Herscheid D 201 B8
Herschweiler-Pettersheim D 202 C3
Herselt B 198 C5
Herstal B 199 D7
Herten D 199 B10
Herve B 199 D7
Herwijnen NL 199 B6
Herzele B 198 D3
Herzogenrath D 199 D8
Hespérange L 202 B1
Heßheim D 203 B5
Hettange-Grande F 202 C1
Hettenleidelheim D 202 B5
Hetzerath D 201 E6
Heubach D 203 D8
Heukelum NL 199 B6
Heusden B 199 C6
Heusden NL 199 B6
Heusenstamm D 203 A6
Heusweiler D 202 C2
Heythuysen NL 199 C7
Hilchenbach D 201 C9
Hilden D 199 C9
Hillegom NL 198 A5
Hillesheim D 201 D6
Hilsenheim F 202 E4
Hilvarenbeek NL 199 C6
Hilversum NL 199 A6
Hinterweidenthal D 202 C4
Hirrlingen D 203 E6
Hirschhorn (Neckar) D 203 C6
Hochfelden F 202 D4
Hochspeyer D 202 C4
Hochstadt (Pfalz) D 203 C5
Hochstetten-Dhaun D 201 E7
Höchst im Odenwald D 203 B6
Hockenheim D 203 C6
Hoek NL 198 C3
Hoek van Holland NL 198 B4
Hoenderloo NL 199 A7
Hœnheim F 202 D4
Hoensbroek NL 199 D7
Hœrdt F 202 D4
Hoeselt B 199 D6
Hoevelaken NL 199 A6
Hoeven NL 198 B5
Hof D 201 C9
Hofheim am Taunus D 203 A5
Hohberg D 202 E4
Höhn D 201 C8
Höhr-Grenzhausen D 201 D8
Hollange B 200 E4
Holten NL 199 A8
Holzappel D 201 D8
Holzgerlingen D 203 D7
Holzhausen an der Haide D 201 D8
Holzheim D 203 E9
Holzwickede D 201 A8
Hombourg-Budange F 202 C1
Hombourg-Haut F 202 C2
Homburg D 202 C3
Hoofddorp NL 198 A5
Hoogerheide NL 198 C4
Hoog-Keppel NL 199 B8
Hoogland NL 199 A6
Hoogstraten B 198 C5
Hoogvliet NL 198 B4
Hoornaar NL 198 B5
Hoppstädten D 202 B3
Horb am Neckar D 203 E6
Hörde D 201 B7
Hornbach D 202 C3
Horst NL 199 C8
Hösbach D 203 A7
Hosingen L 200 D5
Hotton B 200 D3
Houffalize B 200 D4
Houten NL 199 A6
Houthalen B 199 C6
Houthulst B 198 D1
Houyet B 200 D3
Hückelhoven D 199 C8
Hückeswagen D 201 B7
Huijbergen NL 198 C4
Huissen NL 199 B7
Huizen NL 199 A6
Hüls D 199 C8
Hulsberg NL 199 D7
Hulst NL 198 C4
Hummelo NL 199 A8
Hundsangen D 201 D8
Hünfelden-Kirberg D 201 D9
Hunsel NL 199 C7
Hunspach F 202 D4
Hünxe D 199 B9
Hürth D 199 D9
Hütschenhausen D 202 C3
Hüttisheim D 203 E8
Hüttlingen D 203 D9
Huy B 199 D6
Hymont F 202 E1

I

Ichenheim D 202 E4
Ichtegem B 198 C2
Idar-Oberstein D 202 B3
Idstein D 201 D9
Ieper B 198 D1
Iffezheim D 203 D5
Igel D 202 B2
Igersheim D 203 C8
Iggelheim D 203 C5
Igney F 202 E1
IJsselstein NL 199 A6
IJzendijke NL 198 C3
Illingen D 202 C3
Illingen D 203 D6
Illkirch-Graffenstaden F 202 D4
Ilsfeld D 203 C7
Incourt B 198 D5
Ingelfingen D 203 C8
Ingelheim am Rhein D 201 E9
Ingelmunster B 198 D2
Ingwiller F 202 D3
Insming F 202 D2
Iphofen D 203 B9
Ippesheim D 203 B9
Irrel D 201 E5
Irsch D 202 B2
Iserlohn D 201 B8
Ispringen D 203 D6
Isselburg D 199 B8
Issum D 199 B8
Ittre B 198 D4
Ixelles B 198 D4
Izegem B 198 D2

J

Jabbeke B 198 C2
Jagsthausen D 203 C7
Jagstzell D 203 C9
Jalhay B 199 D7
Jarville-la-Malgrange F 202 D1
Jemeppe B 198 E5
Jockgrim D 203 C5
Jodoigne B 198 D5
Jouy-aux-Arches F 202 C1
Jüchen D 199 C8
Jülich D 199 D8
Jungingen D 203 E7
Junglinster L 202 B1
Jünkerath D 201 D6
Juprelle B 199 D7
Jurbise B 198 D3

K

Kaarst D 199 C9
Kaatsheuvel NL 199 B6
Kahl am Main D 203 A7
Kaisersesch D 201 D7
Kaiserslautern D 202 C4
Kalkar D 199 B8
Kall D 199 D9
Kalmthout B 198 C4
Kamen D 201 A8
Kamerik NL 198 A5
Kamp D 201 D8
Kampenhout B 198 D5
Kämpfelbach D 203 D6
Kamp-Lintfort D 199 C9
Kandel D 203 C5
Kapelle NL 198 C3
Kapellen B 198 C4
Kapelle-op-den-Bos B 198 C4
Kappel D 201 E7
Kappel-Grafenhausen D 202 E4
Kappelrodeck D 202 D5
Kaprijke B 198 C3
Karben D 203 A6
Karden D 201 D7
Karlsbad D 203 D6
Karlsdorf-Neuthard D 203 C6
Karlsruhe D 203 C5
Karlstadt D 203 B8
Kastellaun D 201 D7
Kasterlee B 198 C5
Katwijk aan Zee NL 198 A4
Katzenelnbogen D 201 D8
Katzweiler D 202 B4
Kaub D 201 D8
Kaulille B 199 C7
Kautenbach L 200 E5
Kehl D 202 D4
Kehlen L 202 B1
Kehrig D 201 D7
Kelberg D 201 D6
Kelkheim (Taunus) D 203 A5
Kell D 202 B2
Kelmis B 199 D8
Kempen D 199 C8
Kempenich D 199 E10
Kenn D 201 E6
Kerkdriel NL 199 B6
Kerken D 199 C8
Kerkrade NL 199 D8
Kerkwijk NL 199 B6
Kerpen D 199 D9
Kessel B 198 C5
Kessel NL 199 C8
Kesteren NL 199 B7
Ketsch D 203 C6
Kettwig D 199 C9
Kevelaer D 199 B8
Kieldrecht B 198 C4
Kierspe D 201 B8
Kinderbeuern D 201 D7
Kindsbach D 202 C4
Kinrooi B 199 C7
Kippenheim D 202 E4
Kirchardt D 203 C6
Kirchberg (Hunsrück) D 201 E7
Kirchberg an der Jagst D 203 C8
Kirchellen D 199 B9
Kirchen (Sieg) D 201 C8
Kirchheim D 203 B8
Kirchheim am Neckar D 203 C7
Kirchheim-Bolanden D 202 B5
Kirchheim unter Teck D 203 D7
Kirchhundem D 201 B9
Kirchzell D 203 B7
Kirkel-Neuhäusel D 202 C3
Kirn D 201 E7
Kirschweiler D 202 B3
Kist D 203 B8
Kitzingen D 203 B9
Klaaswaal NL 198 B4
Klausen D 201 E6
Kleinblittersdorf D 202 C3
Kleinheubach D 203 B7
Kleinrinderfeld D 203 B8
Kleinwallstadt D 203 B7
Kleve D 199 B8
Klingenberg am Main D 203 B7
Kloetinge NL 198 C3
Kloosterzande NL 198 C4
Klotten D 201 D7
Klundert NL 198 B5
Knesselare B 198 C2
Knittlingen D 203 C6
Knokke-Heist B 198 C2
Kobern D 201 D7
Koblenz D 201 D8
Koekelare B 198 C1
Koersel B 199 C6
Koewacht NL 198 C3
Kolitzheim D 203 B9
Köln D 199 D9
Königheim D 203 B8
Königsbronn D 203 D9
Königstein im Taunus D 203 A5
Königswinter D 201 C7
Konz D 202 B2
Kootwijkerbroek NL 199 A7
Kopstal L 202 B1
Kordel D 201 E6
Kornwestheim D 203 D7
Körperich D 201 E5
Kortemark B 198 C2
Kortenhoef NL 199 A6
Kortessem B 199 D6
Kortgene NL 198 B3
Kortrijk B 198 D2
Kottenheim D 201 D7
Koudekerke NL 198 C3
Krabbendijke NL 198 C4
Kranenburg D 199 B8
Krautheim D 203 C8
Krefeld D 199 C9
Kreuzau D 199 D8
Kreuztal D 201 C8
Kreuzwertheim D 203 B8
Krimpen aan de IJssel NL 198 B5
Kronau D 203 C6
Kronberg im Taunus D 203 A5
Kröv D 201 E7
Kruft D 201 D7
Kruibeke B 198 C4
Kruiningen NL 198 C4
Kruishoutem B 198 D3
Kuchen D 203 D8
Külsheim D 203 B8
Kunrade NL 199 D7
Künzelsau D 203 C8
Kupferzell D 203 C8
Kuppenheim D 203 D5
Kürnach D 203 B9
Kürnbach D 203 C6
Kusel D 202 B3
Kusterdingen D 203 D7
Kuurne B 198 D2
Kwaadmechelen B 199 C6
Kyllburg D 201 D6

L

Laarne B 198 C3
La Broque F 202 E3
Lachen-Speyerdorf D 203 C5
Ladenburg D 203 C6
Lafrimbolle F 202 D3
Lage Mierde NL 199 C6
Lahnstein D 201 D8
Lahr (Schwarzwald) D 202 E4
Laichingen D 203 E8
Laifour F 200 E2
Lallaing F 198 E2
La Louvière B 198 E4
Lambersart F 198 D2
Lambrecht (Pfalz) D 202 C5
Lambsheim D 203 B5
Lampertheim D 203 B5
Lanaken B 199 D7
Landau in der Pfalz D 202 C5
Landen B 199 D6
Landersheim F 202 D3
Landgraaf NL 199 D8
Landscheid D 201 E6
Landsmeer NL 198 A5
Landstuhl D 202 C4
Langemark B 198 D1
Langen D 203 B6
Langenau D 203 E9
Langenaubach D 201 C9
Langenberg D 199 C10
Langenberg D 201 A9
Langenburg D 203 C8
Langenfeld (Rheinland) D 199 C9
Langenhahn D 201 C8
Langenlonsheim D 201 E8
Langenselbold D 203 A7
Langsur D 202 B2
Lannoy F 198 D2
La Petite-Pierre F 202 D3
Laren NL 199 A6
Laren NL 199 A8
La Roche-en-Ardenne B 200 D4
Larochette L 202 B1
Lasne B 198 D4
Lattrop NL 199 A9
Laubach D 201 D7
Lauda-Königshofen D 203 B8
Lauf D 202 D5
Laufach D 203 A7
Lauffen am Neckar D 203 C7
Lautenbach D 202 D5
Lauterbourg F 203 D5
Lauterecken D 202 B4
Lauterstein D 203 D8
La Wantzenau F 202 D4
Laxou F 202 D1
Lebach D 202 C2
Le Ban-St-Martin F 202 C1
Lebbeke B 198 C4
Lede B 198 D3
Ledegem B 198 D2
Leende NL 199 C7
Leerdam NL 199 B6
Leersum NL 199 A6
Leffinge B 198 C1
Leforest F 198 E2
Legden D 199 A10
Léglise B 200 E4
Lehmen D 201 D7
Le Hohwald F 202 E3
Leichlingen (Rheinland) D 199 C10
Leiden NL 198 A5
Leiderdorp NL 198 A5
Leidschendam NL 198 A4
Leimen D 203 C6
Leimuiden NL 198 A5
Leinfelden-Echterdingen D 203 D7
Leinzell D 203 D8
Leiwen D 201 E6
Lembeke B 198 C3
Lemberg D 202 C4
Lemberg F 202 C3
Lendelede B 198 D2
Léning F 202 D2
Lennestadt D 201 B9
Lenningen D 203 D7
Lens B 198 D3
Lent NL 199 B7
Leonberg D 203 D7
Leopoldsburg B 199 C6
Les Hautes-Rivières F 200 E2
Les Mazures F 200 E2
Lessines B 198 D3
Leun D 201 C9
Leusden NL 199 A6
Leutesdorf D 201 D7
Leuven B 198 D5
Leuze-en-Hainaut B 198 D3
Leverkusen D 199 C9
L'Hôpital F 202 C2
Libin B 200 E3
Libramont B 200 E3
Lichtaart B 198 C5
Lichtenau D 202 D5
Lichtenvoorde NL 199 B9
Lichtervelde B 198 C2
Liège B 199 D7
Liempde NL 199 B6
Lienden NL 199 B7
Lier B 198 C5
Lierneux B 200 D4
Lieser D 201 E7
Lieshout NL 199 B7
Liessel NL 199 C7
Ligneuville B 200 D5
Lille B 198 C5
Lille F 198 D2
Limbach D 202 C2
Limbach D 203 C7
Limbourg B 199 D7
Limburg an der Lahn D 201 D9
Limburgerhof D 203 C5
Lincent B 199 D6
Lindenfels D 203 B6
Lindlar D 201 B7
Lingenfeld D 203 C5
Lingolsheim F 202 D4
Linnich D 199 D8
Linz am Rhein D 201 C7
Lippstadt D 201 A9
Lisse NL 198 A5
Lissendorf D 201 D6
Lith NL 199 B6
Lixing-lès-St-Avold F 202 C2
Lobith NL 199 B8
Lochem NL 199 A8
Lochristi B 198 C3
Loenen NL 199 A8
Löf D 201 D7
Lohmar D 201 C7
Löhnberg D 201 C9
Lohr am Main D 203 B8
Lokeren B 198 C4
Lomme F 198 D1
Lommel B 199 C6
Londerzeel B 198 D4
Longeville-lès-St-Avold F 202 C2
Longlier B 200 E3
Lonneker NL 199 A9
Lonny F 200 E2
Lonsee D 203 D8
Lontzen B 199 D8
Loon op Zand NL 199 B6
Loos F 198 D2
Lopik NL 198 B5
Lorch D 201 D8
Lorch D 203 D8
Lorquin F 202 D2
Lorsch D 203 B6
Losheim D 202 B2
Loßburg D 203 E5
Losser NL 199 A9
Lotenhulle B 198 C2
Lottum NL 199 C8
Louvain B 198 D5
Louveigné B 199 D7
Lovendegem B 198 C3
Löwenstein D 203 C7
Lubbeek B 198 D5
Lüdenscheid D 201 B8
Lüdinghausen D 201 A7
Ludres F 202 D1
Ludwigsburg D 203 D7
Ludwigshafen am Rhein D 203 C5
Luik B 199 D7
Lummen B 199 D6
Lünebach D 201 D5
Lünen D 201 A8
Lunéville F 202 D1
Lunteren NL 199 A7
Luppy F 202 D1
Lustadt D 203 C5
Luttenberg NL 199 A8
Lützelbach D 203 B7
Lutzerath D 201 D7
Luxembourg L 202 B1
Luyksgestel NL 199 C6

M

Maarheeze NL 199 C7
Maarn NL 199 A6
Maarssen NL 199 A6
Maarssenbroek NL 199 A6
Maasbracht NL 199 C7
Maasbree NL 199 C8
Maasdam NL 198 B5
Maaseik B 199 C7
Maasland NL 198 B4
Maasmechelen B 199 D7
Maassluis NL 198 B4
Maastricht NL 199 D7
Machelen B 198 D4
Mackenbach D 202 C4
Made NL 198 B5
Magnières F 202 E2
Mahlberg D 202 E4
Maikammer D 202 C5
Mainaschaff D 203 B7
Mainbernheim D 203 B9
Mainhardt D 203 C8
Mainz D 201 D9
Maissin B 200 E3
Maizières-lès-Metz F 202 C1
Malborn D 202 B2
Maldegem B 198 C2
Malden NL 199 B7
Malines B 198 C4
Malmédy B 199 E8
Malsch D 203 D5
Manage B 198 E4
Mandelbachtal-Ormesheim D 202 C3
Manderscheid D 201 D6
Manhay B 200 D4
Mannheim D 203 C5
Manternach L 202 B1
Marange-Silvange F 202 C1
Marbach am Neckar D 203 D7
Marche-en-Famenne B 200 D3
Marchiennes F 198 E2
Marchin B 199 E6
Marcq-en-Barœul F 198 D2
Margraten NL 199 D7
Mariembourg B 200 D2
Marienheide D 201 B8
Markelo NL 199 A9
Markgröningen D 203 D7
Marktbreit D 203 B9
Marktheidenfeld D 203 B8
Marktseft D 203 B9
Marl D 199 B10
Marlenheim F 202 D4
Marly F 202 C1
Marmoutier F 202 D3
Marnheim D 202 B5
Marpingen D 202 C3
Marsal F 202 D2
Martelange B 200 E4
Marxzell D 203 D5
Maßbach D 203 A9
Mastershausen D 201 D7
Mattaincourt F 202 E1
Maubert-Fontaine F 200 E1
Maulbronn D 203 D6
Maurik NL 199 B6
Maxéville F 202 D1
Maxsain D 201 C8
Mayen D 201 D7
Mayschoss D 199 D10
Mechelen B 198 C4
Mechelen NL 199 D7
Mechernich D 199 D9
Meckenheim D 199 D10
Meckesheim D 203 C6
Meddersheim D 202 B4
Meddo NL 199 A9
Meer B 198 C5
Meerbusch D 199 C9
Meerhout B 199 C6
Meerkerk NL 198 B5
Meerle B 198 C5
Meerlo NL 199 B8
Meerssen NL 199 D7
Meetkerke B 198 C2
Meeuwen B 199 C7
Megen NL 199 B7
Mehren D 201 D6
Mehring D 201 E6
Mehrstetten D 203 E8
Meijel NL 199 C7
Meinerzhagen D 201 B8
Meise B 198 D4
Meisenheim D 202 B4
Meißenheim D 202 E4
Melick NL 199 C8
Meliskerke NL 198 B3
Melle B 198 C3
Menden (Sauerland) D 201 B8
Mendig D 201 D7
Menen B 198 D2
Mengerskirchen D 201 C9
Ménil-sur-Belvitte F 202 E2
Menin B 198 D2
Merbes-le-Château B 200 D1
Merchtem B 198 D4
Mere B 198 D3
Merelbeke B 198 D3
Merenberg D 201 C9
Merklingen D 203 D8
Merksplas B 198 C5
Mersch L 202 B1
Mertert L 202 B1
Mertesdorf D 202 B2
Mertloch D 201 D7
Mertzwiller F 202 D4
Merzig D 202 C2
Meschede D 201 B9
Mespelbrunn D 203 B7
Metelen D 199 A10
Mettendorf D 201 E5
Mettet B 200 D2
Mettlach D 202 C2
Mettmann D 199 C9
Metz F 202 C1
Metzervisse F 202 C1
Metzingen D 203 D7
Meudt D 201 D8
Meulebeke B 198 D2
Michelbach an der Bilz D 203 C8
Michelfeld D 203 C8
Michelstadt D 203 B7
Middelbeers NL 199 C6
Middelburg NL 198 B3
Middelharnis NL 198 B4
Middelkerke B 198 C1
Miehlen D 201 D8
Mierlo NL 199 C7
Miesau D 202 C3
Miesenbach D 202 C4
Mijdrecht NL 198 A5
Mill NL 199 B7
Millingen aan de Rijn NL 199 B8
Milmort B 199 D7
Miltenberg D 203 B7
Minderhout B 198 C5
Minfeld D 202 C5
Mirecourt F 202 E1
Mittelsinn D 203 A8
Mittersheim F 202 D2
Möckmühl D 203 C7
Modave B 199 E6
Moerbeke B 198 C3
Moergestel NL 199 B6
Moerkerke B 198 C2
Moers D 199 C9
Mögglingen D 203 D8
Möglingen D 203 D7
Mol B 199 C6
Molenbeek-St-Jean B 198 D4
Molenstede B 199 C6
Molsheim F 202 D3
Mömbris D 203 A7
Momignies B 200 D1
Moncel-sur-Seille F 202 D1
Mönchengladbach D 199 C8
Mondorf-les-Bains L 202 B1
Mons B 198 E3
Monschau D 199 D8
Monsheim D 203 B5
Mönsheim D 203 D6
Monster NL 198 A4
Montabaur D 201 D8
Montcy-Notre-Dame F 200 E2
Montfoort NL 198 A5
Montfort NL 199 C7
Monthermé F 200 E2
Montignies-le-Tilleul B 200 D1
Montigny F 202 D2
Montigny-lès-Metz F 202 C1
Montzen B 199 D7
Monzelfeld D 201 E7
Monzingen D 201 E8
Mook NL 199 B7
Moorslede B 198 D2
Morbach D 201 E7
Mörfelden D 203 B6
Morhange F 202 D2
Morlanwelz B 198 E4
Mörlenbach D 203 B6
Morsbach D 201 C8
Mortsel B 198 C4
Mosbach D 203 C7
Mössingen D 203 E7
Mouscron B 198 D2
Moussey F 202 E3
Moyenmoutier F 202 E2
Much D 201 C7
Mudau D 203 B7
Müdelheim D 199 C9
Mudersbach D 201 C8
Muggensturm D 203 D5
Mühlacker D 203 D6
Mühlhausen D 203 C6
Mulfingen D 203 C8
Mülheim an der Ruhr D 199 C9
Mülheim-Kärlich D 201 D7
Münchweiler an der Rodalb D 202 C4
Munderkingen D 203 E8
Mundolsheim F 202 D4
Munkzwalm B 198 D3
Münnerstadt D 203 A9
Münsingen D 203 E7
Münster D 203 B6
Munstergeleen NL 199 D7
Münstermaifeld D 201 D7
Murrhardt D 203 D8
Müschenbach D 201 C8
Mutterstadt D 203 C5
Mutzig F 202 D3

N

Naaldwijk NL 198 B4
Naarden NL 199 A6
Nackenheim D 201 E9
Nagold D 203 D6
Nalbach D 202 C2
Namborn D 202 B3
Namur B 198 E5
Nancy F 202 D1
Nandrin B 199 D6
Nassau D 201 D8
Nassogne B 200 D3
Nastätten D 201 D8
Nauheim D 203 B5
Nauroth D 201 C8
Neckarbischofsheim D 203 C6
Neckargemünd D 203 C6
Neckarsteinach D 203 C6
Neckarsulm D 203 C7
Neckartenzlingen D 203 D7
Nederhorst den Berg NL 199 A6
Nederlangbroek NL 199 A6
Nederweert NL 199 C7
Neede NL 199 A9
Neer NL 199 C8
Neerijnen NL 199 B6
Neeroeteren B 199 C7
Neerpelt B 199 C6
Nellingen D 203 D8
Nentershausen D 201 D8
Neroth D 201 D6
Nersingen D 203 E9
Netphen D 201 C9
Nettersheim D 199 E9
Nettetal D 199 C8
Neubrunn D 203 B8
Neubulach D 203 D6
Neuburg am Rhein D 203 D5
Neuenbürg D 203 D6
Neuenkirchen-Seelscheid D 201 C7
Neuenrade D 201 B8
Neuenstadt am Kocher D 203 C7
Neuenstein D 203 C8
Neuerburg D 201 D5
Neufchâteau B 200 E3

Neuffen D 203 D7
Neufmanil F 200 E2
Neufra D 203 E7
Neuhausen D 203 D6
Neuhofen D 203 C5
Neu-Isenburg D 203 A6
Neuler D 203 D9
Neumagen D 201 E6
Neunkirchen D 201 C9
Neunkirchen D 202 C3
Neuss D 199 C9
Neustadt (Wied) D 201 C7
Neustadt an der Weinstraße D 202 C5
Neu-Ulm D 203 E9
Neuves-Maisons F 202 D1
Neuweiler D 203 D6
Neuwied D 201 D7
Nevele B 198 C3
Newel D 201 E6
Niederanven L 202 B1
Niederbrechen D 201 D9
Niederbreitbach D 201 C7
Niederbronn-les-Bains F 202 D4
Niederfischbach D 201 C8
Niederkassel D 199 D10
Niederkirchen D 202 B4
Niederkrüchten D 199 C8
Niederneisen D 201 D9
Niedernhall D 203 C8
Niedernhausen D 201 D9
Nieder-Olm D 201 E9
Nieder-Rodenbach D 203 A7
Niederselters D 201 D9
Niederstetten D 203 C8
Niederwerrn D 203 A9
Niederwörresbach D 202 B3
Niederzissen D 201 D6
Niefern-Öschelbronn D 203 D6
Niel D 198 C4
Nierstein D 201 E9
Nieuw-Bergen NL 199 B8
Nieuwegein NL 199 A6
Nieuwerkerk NL 198 B4
Nieuwerkerk aan de IJssel NL 198 B5
Nieuwerkerken B 199 D6
Nieuwe-Tonge NL 198 B4
Nieuw-Heeten NL 199 A8
Nieuwkoop NL 198 A5
Nieuw-Loosdrecht NL 199 A6
Nieuw-Milligen NL 199 A7
Nieuwveen NL 198 A5
Nieuw-Vennep NL 198 A5
Nieuw-Vossemeer NL 198 B4
Nievern D 201 D8
Nijkerk NL 199 A6
Nijlen B 198 C5
Nijmegen NL 199 B7
Nijverdal NL 199 A8
Nilvange F 202 C1
Ninove B 198 D4
Nismes B 200 D2
Nispen NL 198 C4
Nistelrode NL 199 B7
Nittel D 202 B1
Nivelles B 198 D4
Nohfelden D 202 B3
Noisseville F 202 C1
Nomeny F 202 D1
Nomexy F 202 E2
Nonnenweier D 202 E4
Nonnweiler D 202 B2
Noordwijk aan Zee NL 198 A4
Noordwijk-Binnen NL 198 A4
Noordwijkerhout NL 198 A5
Nootdorp NL 198 A4
Nordheim D 202 C2
Nordkirchen D 201 A8
Nouzonville F 200 E2
Noville B 198 D5
Nüdlingen D 203 A9
Nuenen NL 199 C7
Nuland NL 199 B6
Numansdorp NL 198 B4
Nunkirchen D 202 C2
Nunspeet NL 199 A7
Nürtingen D 203 D7
Nuth NL 199 D7

O

Oberderdingen D 203 C6
Oberfell D 201 D7
Oberharmersbach D 202 E5
Oberhausen D 199 C9
Oberhausen-Rheinhausen D 203 C5
Oberhoffen-sur-Moder F 202 D4
Oberkirch D 202 D5
Oberkochen D 203 C9
Obermoschel D 202 B4
Obernai F 202 E3
Obernburg am Main D 203 B7
Oberndorf am Neckar D 203 E6
Obernheim-Kirchenarnbach D 202 C4
Ober-Olm D 201 E9
Ober-Roden D 203 B6
Oberrot D 203 C8
Obersinn D 203 A8
Obersontheim D 203 C8
Oberstenfeld D 203 C7
Oberthal D 202 B3
Oberthulba D 203 A8
Obertshausen D 203 A6
Oberursel (Taunus) D 203 A6
Oberwesel D 201 D8
Oberwolfach D 203 E5
Obrigheim D 203 C7
Obrigheim (Pfalz) D 203 B5
Ochsenfurt D 203 B9
Ochtrup D 199 A10
Odernheim am Glan D 202 B4
Oedelem B 198 C2
Oeffelt NL 199 B8
Oegstgeest NL 198 A5
Oene NL 199 A8
Oerlenbach D 203 A9
Oestrich-Winkel D 201 D8
Offenbach am Main D 203 A6
Offenbach an der Queich D 203 C5
Offenburg D 202 E4
Ofterdingen D 203 E7
Oftersheim D 203 C6
Ogéviller F 202 D2
Ohey B 199 E6
Ohlsbach D 202 E4
Öhringen D 203 C7
Oignies F 198 E1

Oijen NL 199 B6
Oirschot NL 199 B6
Oisterwijk NL 199 B6
Oldenzaal NL 199 A9
Olen B 198 C5
Olfen D 201 A7
Olpe D 201 B8
Olst NL 199 A8
Onstmettingen D 203 E6
Ooltgensplaat NL 198 B4
Oostakker B 198 C3
Oostburg NL 198 C2
Oostende B 198 C1
Oosterbeek NL 199 B7
Oosterhout NL 198 B5
Oosterland NL 198 B4
Oosterzele B 198 D3
Oostham B 199 C6
Oostkamp B 198 C2
Oostkapelle NL 198 B3
Oostmalle B 198 C5
Oost-Souburg NL 198 C3
Oostvoorne NL 198 B4
Ootmarsum NL 199 A9
Opglabbeek B 199 C7
Opheusden NL 199 B7
Opitter B 199 C7
Oploo NL 199 B7
Opoeteren B 199 C7
Oppenau D 203 E5
Oppenheim D 201 E9
Oppenweiler D 203 D7
Opwijk B 198 D4
Orchies F 198 E2
Orenhofen D 201 E6
Oreye B 199 D6
Ortenberg D 202 E4
Osburg D 202 B2
Oss NL 199 B7
Ossenfeld NL 198 C4
Ostend B 198 C1
Osterburken D 203 C7
Ostfildern D 203 D7
Osthofen D 203 B5
Ostricourt F 198 E2
Östringen D 203 C6
Ostwald F 202 D4
Ötigheim D 203 D5
Ötisheim D 203 D6
Ottenheim D 202 E4
Ottenhöfen im Schwarzwald D 203 D5
Otterbach D 202 C4
Otterberg D 202 B4
Otterlo NL 199 A7
Ottersweier D 202 D5
Ottignies B 198 D5
Ottweiler D 202 C3
Oud-Beijerland NL 198 B4
Ouddorp NL 198 B3
Oudenaarde B 198 D3
Oudenbosch NL 198 B5
Oudenburg B 198 C2
Oude-Tonge NL 198 B4
Oudewater NL 198 A5
Oud-Gastel NL 198 B4
Oud-Turnhout B 198 C5
Oud-Vossemeer NL 198 B4
Oudzele B 198 C2
Ouffet B 199 E6
Oulder B 200 D5
Oupeye B 199 D7
Overath D 201 C7
Overdinkel NL 199 A10
Overijse B 198 D5
Overloon NL 199 B7
Overpelt B 199 C6
Ovezande NL 198 C3
Owen D 203 D7

P

Paal B 199 C6
Padoux F 202 E2
Paliseul B 200 E3
Palzem D 202 B1
Pange F 202 C1
Panningen NL 199 C7
Papendrecht NL 198 B5
Partenstein D 203 A8
Pâturages B 198 E3
Pecq B 198 D2
Peer B 199 C6
Pelm D 201 D6
Pepingen B 198 D4
Pepinster B 199 D7
Perl D 202 C1
Péruwelz B 198 D3
Perwez B 198 D5
Petite-Rosselle F 202 C2
Petitmont F 202 D2
Pexonne F 202 E2
Pfaffenhofen an der Roth D 203 E9
Pfaffenhoffen F 202 D4
Pfalzfeld D 201 D8
Pfalzgrafenweiler D 203 D6
Pfedelbach D 203 C7
Pforzheim D 203 D6
Pfronstetten D 203 E7
Pfullingen D 203 E7
Pfungstadt D 203 B6
Phalsbourg F 202 D3
Philippeville B 200 D2
Philippine NL 198 C3
Philippsburg D 203 C5
Piershil NL 198 B4
Piesport D 201 E6
Pijnacker NL 198 A4
Pirmasens D 202 C4
Pittem B 198 C2
Plaidt D 201 D7
Plettenberg D 201 B8
Pliezhausen D 203 D7
Plobsheim F 202 E4
Plochingen D 203 D7
Ploegsteert B 198 D1
Plüderhausen D 203 D8
Poederlee B 198 C5
Polch D 201 D7
Polsbroek NL 198 B5
Pompey F 202 D1
Pont-à-Celles B 198 D4
Pont-à-Marcq F 198 E2
Pont-de-Loup B 198 E5
Poppenhausen D 203 A9
Portieux F 202 E2
Posterholt NL 199 C8
Poussay F 202 E1
Pracht D 201 C8
Prinsenbeek NL 198 B5
Profondeville B 200 D2

Pronsfeld D 201 D5
Provenchères-sur-Fave F 202 E3
Prüm D 201 D5
Puderbach D 201 C8
Pulheim D 199 C9
Putte B 198 C5
Putte NL 198 C4
Puttelange-aux-Lacs F 202 C2
Putten NL 199 A7
Püttlingen D 202 C2
Puurs B 198 C4

Q

Quaregnon B 198 E3
Queidersbach D 202 C4
Quendorf D 199 A10
Quesnoy-sur-Deûle F 198 D2
Quierschied D 202 C3
Quiévrain B 198 E3
Quiévrechain F 198 E3

R

Raalte NL 199 A8
Raamsdonksveer NL 198 B5
Radevormwald D 201 B7
Raeren B 199 D8
Raesfeld D 199 B9
Ralingen D 201 E6
Rambervillers F 202 E2
Rambrouch L 200 E4
Ramillies B 198 D5
Rammelsbach D 202 B3
Rammingen D 203 D9
Ramstein D 202 C4
Rance B 200 D1
Randersacker D 203 B8
Rangendingen D 203 E6
Ransbach-Baumbach D 201 D8
Ranst B 198 C5
Raon-l'Étape F 202 E2
Rastatt D 203 D5
Ratingen D 199 C9
Raubach D 201 C8
Ravels B 198 C5
Ravenstein NL 199 B7
Rebecq B 198 D4
Réchicourt-le-Château F 202 D2
Recht B 200 D5
Rechtenbach D 203 B8
Recklinghausen D 199 B10
Réding F 202 D3
Rees D 199 B8
Rehlingen-Siersburg D 202 C2
Reichelsheim (Odenwald) D 203 B6
Reichenbach D 203 B6
Reichenberg D 203 B8
Reicholzheim D 203 B8
Reichshoffen D 202 D4
Reichstett F 202 D4
Reil D 201 D7
Reilingen D 203 C6
Reinheim D 203 B6
Reinsfeld D 202 B2
Reken D 199 B10
Rekken NL 199 A9
Remagen D 201 D6
Remich L 202 B1
Remicourt B 199 D6
Remouchamps B 199 E7
Remscheid D 199 C10
Renchen D 202 D5
Renesse NL 198 B3
Rengsdorf D 201 C7
Renkum NL 199 B7
Rennerod D 201 C9
Renningen D 203 D6
Renswoude NL 199 A7
Renwez F 200 E2
Retie B 199 C6
Reusel NL 199 C6
Reutlingen D 203 E7
Reuver NL 199 C8
Revin F 200 E2
Rhaunen D 201 E7
Rhede D 199 B9
Rheden NL 199 A8
Rheinau D 202 D4
Rheinbach D 199 D9
Rheinberg D 199 B9
Rheinböllen D 201 E8
Rheinbreitbach D 201 C7
Rheinbrohl D 201 D7
Rheinstetten D 203 D5
Rheinzabern D 203 C5
Rhenen NL 199 B7
Rhens D 201 D8
Rhinau F 202 E4
Rhisnes B 198 D5
Rhoon NL 198 B4
Richardménil F 202 D1
Ridderkerk NL 198 B5
Riegelsberg D 202 C2
Riemst B 199 D7
Rieneck D 203 A8
Riethoven NL 199 C6
Rijen NL 198 B5
Rijnsburg NL 198 A4
Rijsbergen NL 198 B5
Rijssen NL 199 A9
Rijswijk NL 198 A4
Rilland NL 198 C4
Rimbach D 203 B6
Rimogne F 200 E2
Rimpar D 203 B8
Rips NL 199 B7
Rittersdorf D 201 D5
Rixensart B 198 D5
Rochefort B 200 D3
Rochehaut B 200 E3
Rochin F 198 E2
Rockanje NL 198 B4
Rockenhausen D 202 B4
Rocroi F 200 E2
Rodalben D 202 C4
Roermond NL 199 C7
Roeselare B 198 D2
Roetgen D 199 D8
Roggel NL 199 C7
Röhlingen D 203 D9
Rohrbach-lès-Bitche F 202 C3
Rombas F 202 C1
Rommerskirchen D 199 C9
Ronse B 198 D3
Roosendaal NL 198 B4
Rosée F 200 D2
Rosenfeld D 203 E6
Rosheim F 202 D3

Rosmalen NL 199 B6
Rösrath D 201 C7
Roßdorf D 203 B6
Rossum NL 199 B6
Rot am See D 203 C9
Rothenberg D 203 B6
Rothenbuch D 203 B7
Rothenburg ob der Tauber D 203 C9
Rothenfels D 203 B8
Rotheux-Rimière B 199 D6
Rotselaar B 198 D5
Rottenacker D 203 E8
Rottenburg am Neckar D 203 E6
Rottendorf D 203 B9
Rotterdam NL 198 B5
Röttingham D 203 B8
Roubaix F 198 D2
Roulers B 198 D2
Rouvroy F 198 E1
Rouvroy-sur-Audry F 200 E2
Rozenburg NL 198 B4
Rozendaal NL 199 A7
Ruddervoorde B 198 C2
Rudersberg D 203 D8
Rüdesheim D 201 E8
Ruiselede B 198 C2
Rülzheim D 203 C5
Rumes B 198 D2
Rumigny F 200 E1
Rumst B 198 C4
Runkel D 201 D9
Rüsselsheim D 203 A5
Ruteshoim D 203 D6
Rüthen D 201 B9
Rütten-Scheid D 199 C9
Ruurlo NL 199 A8

S

Saales F 202 E3
Saarbrücken D 202 C2
Saarburg D 202 B2
Saarlouis D 202 C2
Saarwellingen D 202 C2
Sachsenheim D 203 D7
St-Amand-les-Eaux F 198 E2
St-Avold F 202 C2
St-Blaise-la-Roche F 202 E3
St-Clément F 202 E2
St-Dié F 202 E2
Ste-Marguerite F 202 E2
Ste-Marie-aux-Mines F 202 E3
St-Firmin F 202 E1
St-Ghislain B 198 E3
St-Hubert B 200 D3
St-Louis-lès-Bitche F 202 D3
St-Max F 202 D1
St-Michel F 200 E1
St-Michel-sur-Meurthe F 202 E2
St-Nicolas B 199 D7
St-Nicolas-de-Port F 202 D1
St-Oedenrode NL 199 B6
St-Quirin F 202 D3
St-Vith B 200 D5
Salmtal D 201 E6
Sandhausen D 203 C6
Sankt Augustin D 201 C7
Sankt Goar D 201 D8
Sankt Goarshausen D 201 D8
Sankt Ingbert D 202 C3
Sankt Julian D 202 B3
Sankt Katharinen D 201 C7
Sankt Wendel D 202 C3
Santpoort NL 198 A5
Sarralbe F 202 C3
Sarrebourg F 202 D3
Sarreguemines F 202 C3
Sarre-Union F 202 D3
Sart B 199 D7
Sasbach D 202 E4
Sasbachwalden D 202 D5
Sassenheim NL 198 A5
Sas Van Gent NL 198 C3
Satteldorf D 203 C9
Saulheim D 201 E9
Saverne F 202 D3
Schaafheim D 203 B7
Schaarsbergen NL 199 A7
Schaerbeek B 198 D4
Schaesberg NL 199 D8
Schaijk NL 199 B7
Schalkhaar NL 199 A8
Schalksmühle D 201 B8
Scharendijke NL 198 B3
Schebheim D 203 B9
Schefflenz D 203 C7
Schelklingen D 203 E8
Schenkenzell D 203 E5
Schermbeck D 199 B9
Scherpenheuvel B 198 D5
Scherpenzeel NL 199 A6
Scherwiller F 202 E3
Schiedam NL 198 B5
Schieren L 200 E5
Schifferstadt D 203 C5
Schiffweiler D 202 C3
Schijndel NL 199 B6
Schilde B 198 C5
Schillingen D 202 B2
Schiltach D 203 E5
Schiltigheim F 202 D4
Schinnen D 199 D7
Schinveld NL 199 D7
Schipluiden NL 198 B4
Schirmeck F 202 E3
Schlangenbad D 201 D9
Schleiden D 199 D8
Schmallenberg D 201 B9
Schmelz D 202 C2
Schnelldorf D 203 C9
Schnürpflingen D 203 E8
Schoenberg B 201 D5
Schöllkrippen D 203 A7
Schömberg D 203 D6
Schömberg D 203 E6
Schondra D 203 A8
Schönecken D 201 D5
Schönenberg-Kübelberg D 202 C3
Schöntal D 203 C8
Schoondijke NL 198 C3
Schoonhoven NL 198 B5
Schorndorf D 203 D7
Schoten B 198 C4
Schriesheim D 203 C6
Schrozberg D 203 C8
Schuttertal D 202 E4
Schutterwald D 202 E4
Schüttorf D 199 A10
Schwäbisch Gmünd D 203 D8
Schwäbisch Hall D 203 C8

Schwaigern D 203 C7
Schwalbach D 202 C2
Schwegenheim D 203 C5
Schweich D 201 E6
Schweigen-Rechtenbach D 202 C4
Schweighouse-sur-Moder F 202 D4
Schweinfurt D 203 A9
Schwelm D 201 B7
Schwerte D 201 A8
Schwieberdingen D 203 D7
Seckach D 203 C7
Seebach D 203 D5
Seeheim-Jugenheim D 203 B6
Seilles B 199 E6
Seinsheim D 203 B9
Sélestat F 202 E3
Selm D 201 A7
Selters (Westerwald) D 201 C8
Seltz F 202 D5
Senden D 203 E9
Seneffe B 198 D4
Senones F 202 E2
Seraing B 199 D7
Serooskerke NL 198 B3
Serrig D 202 B2
Sevenum NL 199 C8
's-Gravendeel NL 198 B5
's-Gravenhage NL 198 A4
's-Gravenmoer NL 198 B5
's-Gravenpolder NL 198 C3
's-Gravenvoeren B 199 D7
's-Gravenzande NL 198 B4
's-Heerenberg NL 199 B8
's-Heerenhoek NL 198 C3
's-Hertogenbosch NL 199 B6
Siebengewald NL 199 B8
Siegburg D 201 C7
Siegen D 201 C9
Sierck-les-Bains F 202 C1
Siershahn D 201 D8
Signy-le-Petit F 200 E1
Sijsele B 198 C2
Silenrieux B 200 D1
Simmerath D 199 D8
Simmern (Hunsrück) D 201 E8
Simpelveld NL 199 D7
Sindelfingen D 203 D6
Singhofen D 201 D8
Sinn D 201 C9
Sinsheim D 203 C6
Sint Annaland NL 198 B4
Sint Anthonis NL 199 B7
Sint-Genesius-Rode B 198 D4
Sint-Gillis-Waas B 198 C4
Sint-Huibrechts-Lille B 199 C6
Sint Jansteen NL 198 C4
Sint-Kateljine-Waver B 198 C5
Sint-Lenaarts B 198 C5
Sint Maartensdijk NL 198 B4
Sint-Margriete B 198 C3
Sint-Maria-Lierde B 198 D3
Sint Michielsgestel NL 199 B6
Sint-Niklaas B 198 C4
Sint Odilienberg NL 199 C8
Sint-Pauwels B 198 C4
Sint Philipsland NL 198 B4
Sint-Pieters-Leeuw B 198 D4
Sint-Truiden B 199 D6
Sinzheim D 203 D5
Sinzig D 201 C7
Sittard NL 199 D7
Sivry B 200 D1
Sleidinge B 198 C3
Sliedrecht NL 198 B5
Sluis NL 198 C2
Sluiskil NL 198 C3
Soerendonk NL 199 C7
Soest D 201 A9
Soest NL 199 A6
Soesterberg NL 199 A6
Soheit-Tinlot B 199 E6
Sohren D 201 E7
Soignies B 198 D4
Solingen D 199 C10
Sombreffe B 198 D5
Someren D 199 C7
Somme-Leuze B 200 D3
Somzée B 200 D2
Son NL 199 B6
Soufflenheim F 202 D4
Soultz-sous-Forêts F 202 D4
Soumagne B 199 D7
Spa B 199 E7
Spabrücken D 201 E8
Spay D 201 D8
Speicher D 201 E6
Speyer D 203 C5
Spiere B 198 D2
Spiesen-Elversberg D 202 C3
Spijkenisse NL 198 B4
Spontin B 200 D3
Spraitbach D 203 D8
Sprendlingen D 201 E8
Sprimont B 199 D7
Sprockhövel D 201 B7
Stabroek B 198 C4
Staden B 198 D2
Stadtkyll D 201 D6
Stadtlohn D 199 B9
Staig D 203 E9
Standdaarbuiten NL 198 B5
Stavelot B 199 D8
Stavenisse NL 198 B4
Steenbergen NL 198 B4
Steenderen NL 199 A8
Stein NL 199 D7
Steinach D 202 E5
Steinfeld D 203 B8
Steinheim am Albuch D 203 D9
Steinheim an der Murr D 203 D7
Steinsfeld D 203 C9
Steinwenden D 202 C4
Stekene B 198 C4
Stellendam NL 198 B4
Stevensweert NL 199 C7
Stimpfach D 203 C9
Stiring-Wendel F 202 C2
Stockstadt am Rhein D 203 B5
Stolberg (Rheinland) D 199 D8
Stoumont B 199 E7
Straelen D 199 C8
Straimont B 200 E3
Stramproy NL 199 C7
Strasbourg F 202 D4
Strassen L 202 B1

Straßenhaus D 201 C8
Strijen D 198 B5
Stromberg D 201 E8
Sturzelbronn F 202 C4
Stuttgart D 203 D7
Suddendorf D 199 A10
Südlohn D 199 B9
Sulz am Neckar D 203 E6
Sulzbach am Main D 203 B7
Sulzbach an der Murr D 203 C7
Sulzbach-Laufen D 203 D8
Sulzbach/Saar D 202 C3
Sulzfeld D 203 C6
Sulzthal D 203 A9
Sundern (Sauerland) D 201 B9
Susteren NL 199 C7
Swalmen NL 199 C8

T

Taintrux F 202 E2
Talange F 202 C1
Tamm D 203 D7
Tantonville F 202 E1
Tauberbischofsheim D 203 B8
Tawern D 202 B2
Tegelen NL 199 C8
Tellin B 200 D3
Templeuve F 198 D2
Temse B 198 C4
Tenneville B 200 D4
Ter Aar NL 198 A5
Terborg-Silvolde NL 199 B8
Terheijden NL 198 B5
Terneuzen NL 198 C3
Tervuren B 198 D5
Tessenderlo B 199 C6
Testelt B 198 D5
Teteringen NL 198 B5
Thaleischweiler-Fröschen D 202 C4
Thalfang D 202 B2
Thaon-les-Vosges F 202 E1
Theux B 199 D7
Thionville F 202 C1
Tholen NL 198 B4
Tholey D 202 C3
Thommen B 200 D5
Thorn NL 199 C7
Thuin B 200 D1
Thüngen D 203 B8
Thüngersheim D 203 B8
Tiefenbronn D 203 D6
Tiel NL 199 B6
Tielen B 198 C5
Tielt B 198 C2
Tienen B 198 D5
Tilburg NL 199 B6
Tongeren B 199 D6
Tönisvorst D 199 C8
Torhout B 198 C2
Tourcoing F 198 D2
Tournai B 198 D2
Traar D 199 C9
Traben D 201 E7
Trarbach D 201 E7
Trebur D 203 B5
Treis D 201 D7
Tremelo B 198 D5
Trier D 202 B2
Trierweiler D 202 B2
Trippstadt D 202 C4
Trittenheim D 201 E6
Trochtelfingen D 203 E7
Troisdorf D 199 D10
Troisfontaines F 202 D3
Trois-Ponts B 200 D4
Troisvierges L 200 D5
Trooz B 199 D7
Truchtersheim F 202 D4
Trulben D 202 C4
Tubbergen NL 199 A9
Tübingen D 203 D7
Tubize B 198 D4
Turnhout B 198 C5
Twello NL 199 A8

U

Übach-Palenberg D 199 D8
Überherrn D 202 C2
Ubstadt-Weiher D 203 C6
Üchtelhausen D 203 A9
Uckange F 202 C1
Uddel NL 199 A7
Udenhout NL 199 B6
Üdersdorf D 201 D6
Uettingen D 203 B8
Uffenheim D 203 B9
Uhingen D 203 D8
Uithoorn NL 198 A5
Ulft NL 199 B8
Ulicoten NL 198 C5
Ulm D 203 E8
Ulmen D 201 D6
Unkel D 201 C7
Unna D 201 A8
Unnau D 201 C8
Untermünkheim D 203 C8
Unterpleichfeld D 203 B9
Urbach D 203 D8
Urbar D 201 D8
Urberach D 203 B6
Utrecht NL 199 A6
Üxheim D 201 D6

V

Vaals NL 199 D8
Vaassen NL 199 A8
Valkenburg NL 199 D7
Valkenswaard NL 199 C6
Vallendar D 201 D8
Vandœvre-lès-Nancy F 202 D1
Varik NL 199 B6
Varsseveld NL 199 B8
Veendendaal NL 199 A7
Veere NL 198 B3
Veerle B 198 C5
Veghel NL 199 B6
Velbert D 199 C10
Veldegem B 198 C2
Velden D 199 C8
Veldhoven NL 199 C6

Velen D 199 B9
Vellberg D 203 C8
Velp NL 199 B7
Vendenheim F 202 D4
Venlo NL 199 C8
Venray NL 199 B7
Vergaville F 202 D2
Verlaine B 199 D6
Verny F 202 C1
Verviers B 199 D7
Vessem NL 199 C6
Vettelschoss D 201 C7
Vianden L 200 E5
Vianen NL 199 B6
Vic-sur-Seille F 202 D2
Vielsalm B 200 D4
Vierlingsbeek NL 199 B7
Viernheim D 203 B6
Viersen D 199 C8
Vieux-Condé F 198 E3
Vigy F 202 C1
Villé F 202 E3
Villeneuve-d'Ascq F 198 D2
Villers-le-Bouillet B 199 D6
Villers-lès-Nancy F 202 D1
Villmar D 201 D9
Vilvoorde B 198 D4
Vincey F 202 E1
Vinkt B 198 C2
Vinningen D 202 C4
Vireux-Molhain F 200 D2
Vireux-Wallerand F 200 D2
Visé B 199 D7
Vlaardingen NL 198 B4
Vleuten NL 199 A6
Vlijmen NL 199 B6
Vlissingen NL 198 C3
Voerde (Niederrhein) D 199 B9
Voerendaal NL 199 D7
Vogelenzang NL 198 A5
Vogelweh D 202 C4
Vöhringen D 203 E6
Vöhringen D 203 E9
Volkach D 203 B9
Volkel NL 199 B7
Völklingen D 202 C2
Volmunster F 202 C3
Voorburg NL 198 A4
Voorhout NL 198 A4
Voorschoten NL 198 A4
Voorst NL 199 A8
Voorthuizen NL 199 A7
Vorden NL 199 A8
Vorst B 199 C6
Vosselaar B 198 C5
Vrasene B 198 C4
Vreden D 199 A9
Vreeland NL 199 A6
Vresse B 200 E2
Vriezenveen NL 199 A9
Vrouwenpolder NL 198 B3
Vught NL 199 B6

W

Waalre NL 199 C6
Waalwijk NL 199 B6
Waarschoot B 198 C3
Wachenheim an der Weinstraße D 203 C5
Wachtebeke B 198 C3
Wächtersbach D 203 A7
Waddinxveen NL 198 A5
Wadern D 202 B2
Wadersloh D 201 A9
Wadgassen D 202 C2
Wageningen NL 199 B7
Waghäusel D 203 C6
Waiblingen D 203 D7
Waibstadt D 203 C6
Waigolshausen D 203 B9
Waimes B 199 D8
Walcourt B 200 D1
Waldachtal D 203 E6
Waldböckelheim D 201 E8
Waldbreitbach D 201 C7
Waldbröl D 201 C8
Waldbrunn-Lahr D 201 C9
Waldbüttelbrunn D 203 B8
Waldenbuch D 203 D7
Waldenburg D 203 C8
Waldesch D 201 D8
Waldfischbach-Burgalben D 202 C4
Wald-Michelbach D 203 B6
Waldmohr D 202 C3
Waldrach D 202 B2
Waldsee D 203 C5
Waldstetten D 203 D8
Walferdange L 202 B1
Walldorf D 203 A6
Walldorf D 203 C6
Walldürn D 203 B7
Wallhausen D 201 E8
Wallhausen D 203 C9
Wamel NL 199 B6
Wandre B 199 D7
Wanne-Eikel D 199 B10
Wanroij NL 199 B7
Wanssum NL 199 B8
Wanze B 199 D6
Wapenveld NL 199 A8
Waregem B 198 D2
Waremme B 199 D6
Warmond NL 198 A5
Warnsveld NL 199 A8
Warstein D 201 B9
Wartmannsroth D 203 A8
Wäschenbeuren D 203 D8
Waspik NL 198 B5
Wasseiges B 199 D6
Wasselonne F 202 D3
Wassenaar NL 198 A4
Wassenberg D 199 C8
Wasseralfingen D 203 D9
Wasserbillig D 202 B1
Wasserliesch D 202 B2
Wasserlosen D 203 A9
Wateringen NL 198 A4
Waterland-Oudeman B 198 C3
Waterloo B 198 D4
Watten-Scheid D 199 C10
Wavre B 198 D5
Wavrin F 198 D1
Waxweiler D 201 D5
Waziers F 198 E2
Weelde B 198 C5
Weerselo NL 199 A9
Weert NL 199 C7
Weesp NL 199 A6
Weeze D 199 B8
Wegberg D 199 C8

Wehl *NL* 199 B8
Weibern *D* 199 E10
Weibersbrunn *D* 203 B7
Weidenstetten *D* 203 D8
Weidenthal *D* 202 C4
Weiersbach *D* 202 B3
Weikersheim *D* 203 C8
Weilbach *D* 203 B7
Weilburg *D* 201 D9
Weil der Stadt *D* 203 D6
Weilerbach *D* 202 C4
Weilerswist *D* 199 D9
Weilheim an der Teck *D* 203 D8
Weilmünster *D* 201 D9
Weinbach *D* 201 D9
Weingarten (Baden) *D* 203 C6
Weinheim *D* 203 B6
Weinsberg *D* 203 C7
Weinsheim *D* 201 D5
Weinsheim *D* 201 E8
Weinstadt *D* 203 D7
Weiskirchen *D* 202 B2
Weissach *D* 203 D6
Weißenhorn *D* 203 E9
Weißenthurm *D* 201 D7
Weiswampach *L* 200 D5
Weitbruch *F* 202 D4
Weitefeld *D* 201 C8
Weiterstadt *D* 203 B6
Wekerom *NL* 199 A7
Welkenraedt *B* 199 D7
Well *NL* 199 B8

Wellen *B* 199 D6
Wellin *B* 200 D3
Welling *D* 201 D7
Welschbillig *D* 201 E6
Welver *D* 201 A8
Welzheim *D* 203 D8
Wemeldinge *NL* 198 B4
Wendelsheim *D* 202 B5
Wenden *D* 201 C8
Wendlingen am Neckar *D* 203 D7
Wenduine *B* 198 C2
Wengsel (Isterberg) *D* 199 A10
Wépion *B* 198 E5
Werbach *D* 203 B8
Werbomont *B* 200 D4
Werdohl *D* 201 B8
Werkendam *NL* 198 B5
Werl *D* 201 A8
Wermelskirchen *D* 201 B7
Wernau *D* 203 D7
Werne *D* 201 A8
Werneck *D* 203 B9
Wertheim *D* 203 B8
Wervik *B* 198 D2
Wesel *D* 199 B9
Wesepe *NL* 199 A8
Wesseling *D* 199 D9
Wessem *NL* 199 C7
Westerburg *D* 201 C8
Westerhem *D* 203 D8
Westerhoven *NL* 199 C6

Westerlo *B* 198 C5
Westerstetten *D* 203 D8
Westervoort *NL* 199 B7
Westhausen *D* 203 D9
Westhofen *D* 203 B5
Westhoffen *F* 202 D3
Westkapelle *NL* 198 B2
Westmalle *B* 198 C5
Wetter (Ruhr) *D* 201 B7
Wetteren *B* 198 C3
Wevelgem *B* 198 D2
Weyerbusch *D* 201 C8
Weyersheim *F* 202 D4
Wichelen *B* 198 C3
Wickede (Ruhr) *D* 201 B8
Wiehl *D* 201 C8
Wielsbeke *B* 198 D2
Wierden *NL* 199 A9
Wiernsheim *D* 203 D6
Wiesbaden *D* 201 D9
Wiesen *D* 203 A7
Wiesensteig *D* 203 D8
Wiesloch *D* 203 C6
Wijchen *NL* 199 B7
Wijhe *NL* 199 A8
Wijk bij Duurstede *NL* 199 B6
Wijk en Aalburg *NL* 199 B6
Wildberg *D* 203 D6
Wilhelminadorp *NL* 199 C6
Willebroek *B* 198 C4
Willemstad *NL* 198 B4
Willich *D* 199 C9

Willstätt *D* 202 D4
Wilnis *NL* 198 A5
Wilnsdorf *D* 201 C9
Wilp *NL* 199 A8
Wiltingen *D* 202 B2
Wiltz *L* 200 E4
Wincheringen *D* 202 B1
Wincrange *L* 200 D4
Windesheim *D* 201 E8
Windhagen *D* 201 C7
Wingene *B* 198 C2
Wingen-sur-Moder *F* 202 D3
Winnenden *D* 203 D7
Winningen *D* 201 D8
Winnweiler *D* 202 B4
Winssen *NL* 199 B7
Winterswijk *NL* 199 B9
Wintrich *D* 201 E6
Wipperfürth *D* 201 B7
Wirges *D* 201 D8
Wissembourg *F* 202 C4
Wissen *D* 201 C8
Wissenkerke *NL* 198 B3
Witten *D* 201 B7
Wittighausen *D* 203 B8
Wittlich *D* 201 E6
Woensdrecht *NL* 198 C4
Woerden *NL* 198 A5
Wœrth *F* 202 D4
Woippy *F* 202 C1
Wolfach *D* 203 E5
Wolfstein *D* 202 B4

Wolpertshausen *D* 203 C8
Wolphaartsdijk *NL* 198 B3
Wommelgem *B* 198 C5
Wormeldange *L* 202 B1
Worms *D* 203 B5
Wortel *B* 198 C5
Wörth am Main *D* 203 B7
Wörth am Rhein *D* 203 C5
Woudenberg *NL* 199 A6
Woudrichem *NL* 198 B5
Woustviller *F* 202 C3
Wouw *NL* 198 B4
Wuppertal *D* 199 C10
Würselen *D* 199 D8
Würzburg *D* 203 B8
Wüstenrot *D* 203 C7
Wuustwezel *B* 198 C5

X

Xanten *D* 199 B8

Y

Yerseke *NL* 198 C4
Ysselsteyn *NL* 199 C7
Yutz *F* 202 C1
Yvoir *B* 200 D2

Z

Zaamslag *NL* 198 C3
Zaandam *NL* 198 A5
Zaltbommel *NL* 199 B6
Zandhoven *B* 198 C5
Zandvliet *B* 198 C4
Zandvoort *NL* 198 A5
Zarren *B* 198 C1
Zaventem *B* 198 D4
Zeddam *NL* 199 B8
Zedelgem *B* 198 C2
Zeebrugge *B* 198 C2
Zeeland *NL* 199 B7
Zeewolde *NL* 199 A7
Zeiskam *D* 203 C5
Zeist *NL* 199 A6
Zeitlofs *D* 203 A8
Zele *B* 198 C4
Zelhem *NL* 199 A8
Zell (Mosel) *D* 201 D7
Zell am Harmersbach *D* 202 E5
Zell am Main *D* 203 B8
Zellingen *D* 203 B8
Zeltingen-Rachtig *D* 201 E7
Zelzate *B* 198 C3
Zemmer *D* 201 E6
Zemst *B* 198 D4
Zerf *D* 202 B2
Zevenaar *NL* 199 B8
Zevenbergen *NL* 198 B5
Zierikzee *NL* 198 B3

Zoelen *NL* 199 B6
Zoersel *B* 198 C5
Zoetermeer *NL* 198 A4
Zolder *B* 199 C6
Zomergem *B* 198 C3
Zonhoven *B* 199 D6
Zonnebeke *B* 198 D1
Zornheim *D* 201 E9
Zottegem *B* 198 D3
Zoutleeuw *B* 199 D6
Zuid-Beijerland *NL* 198 B4
Zuidland *NL* 198 B4
Zuienkerke *B* 198 C2
Zülpich *D* 199 D9
Zulte *B* 198 D2
Zundert *NL* 198 C5
Zutendaal *B* 199 D7
Zutphen *NL* 199 A8
Zweibrücken *D* 202 C3
Zwevegem *B* 198 D2
Zwevezele *B* 198 C2
Zwijndrecht *B* 198 C4
Zwijndrecht *NL* 198 B5
Zwiefalten *D* 203 E7
Zwingenberg *D* 203 B6

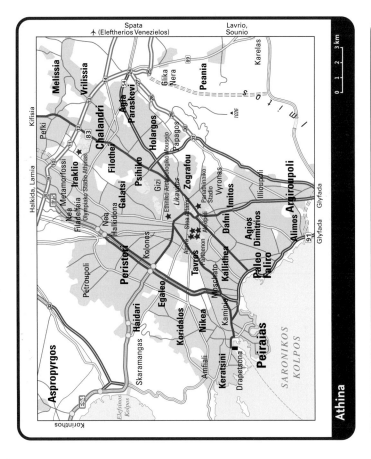

Athina

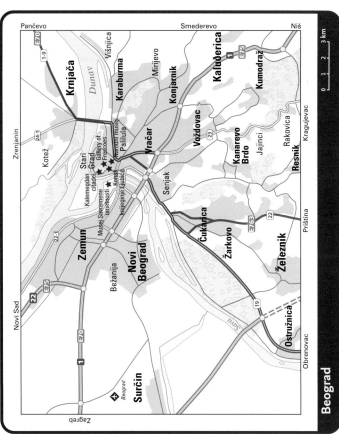

Beograd

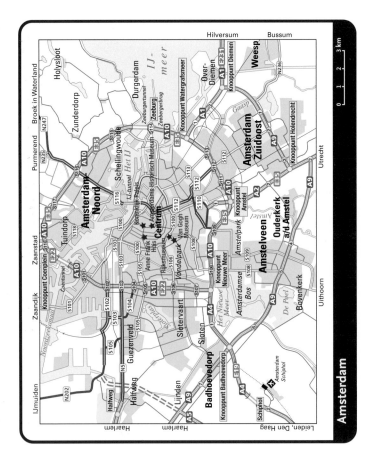

Amsterdam

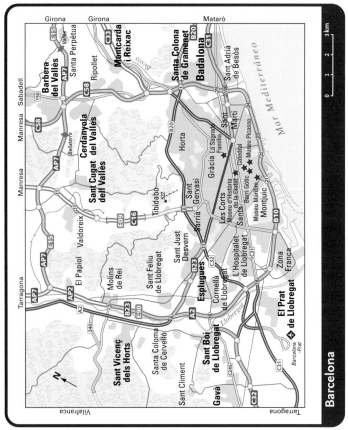

Barcelona

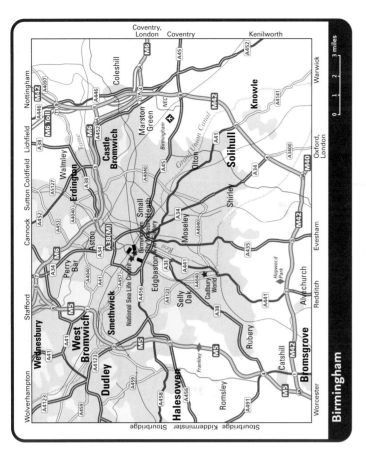

Birmingham

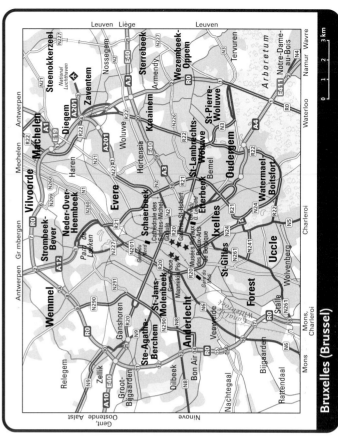

Bruxelles (Brussel)

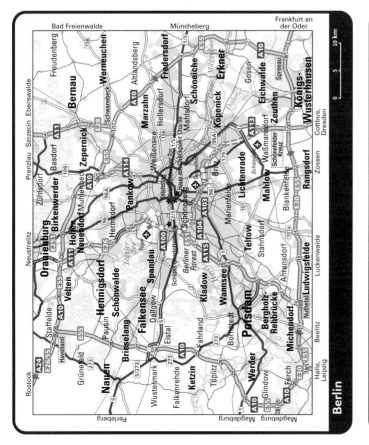

Berlin

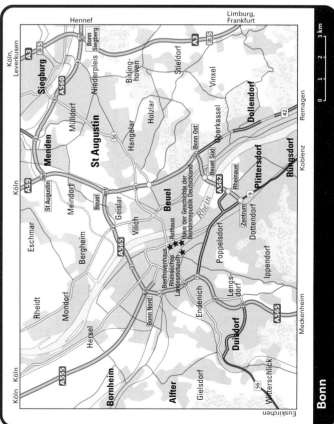

Bonn

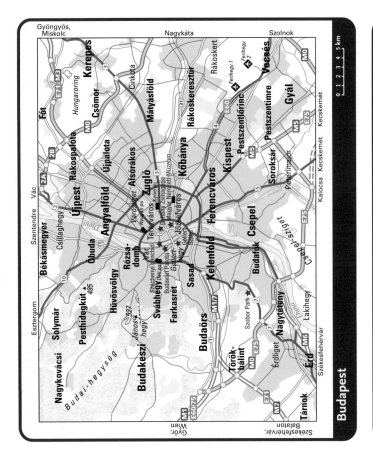

Budapest

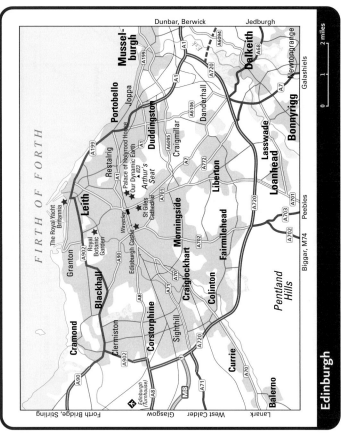

Edinburgh

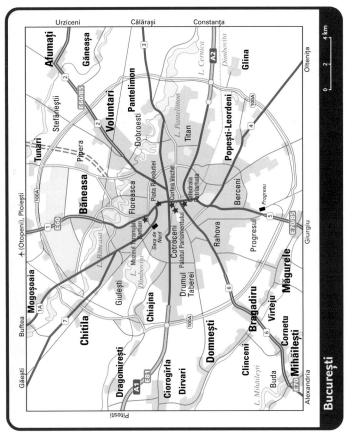

Bucureşti

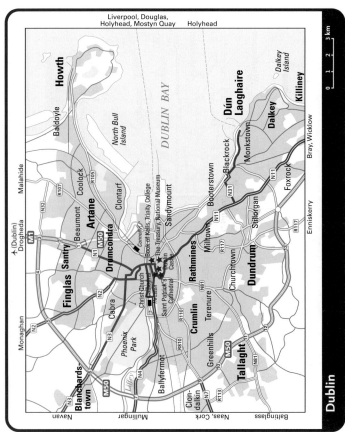

Dublin

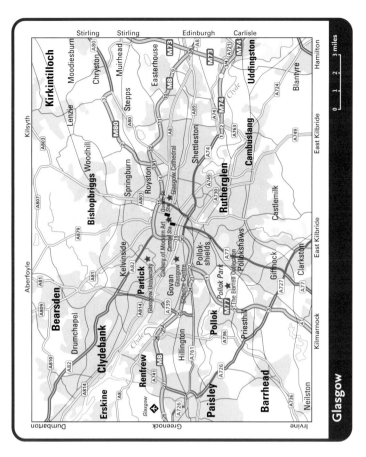

Glasgow

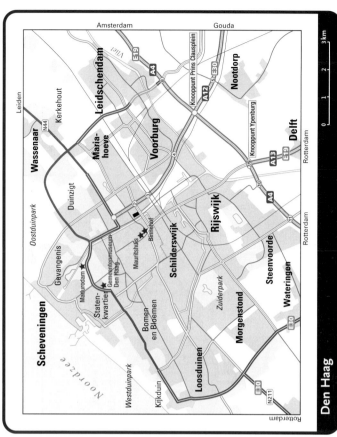

Den Haag

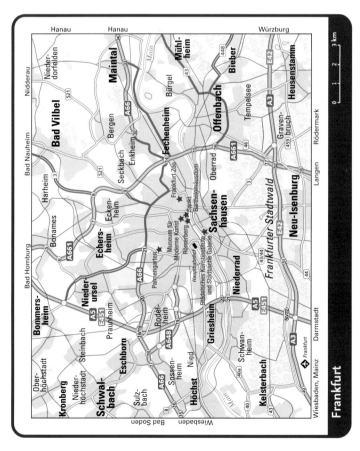

Frankfurt

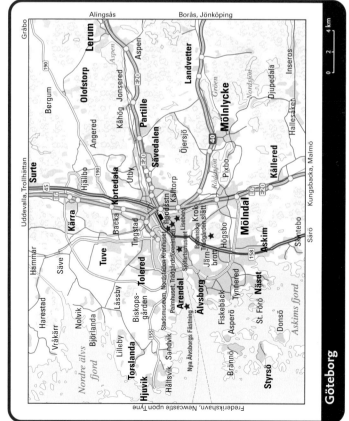

Göteborg

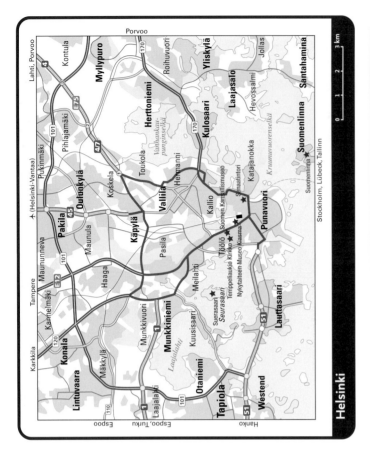

Helsinki

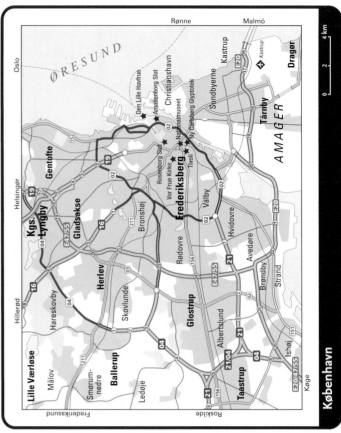

København

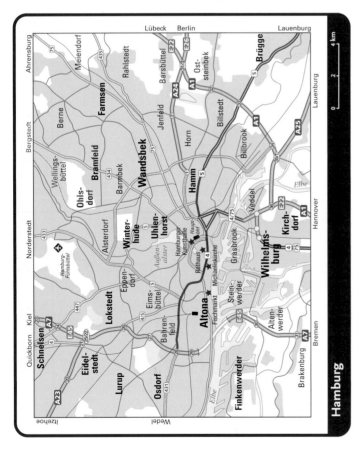

Hamburg

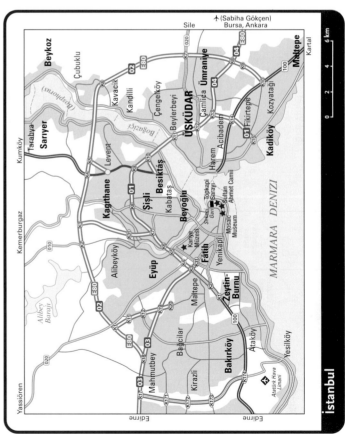

İstanbul

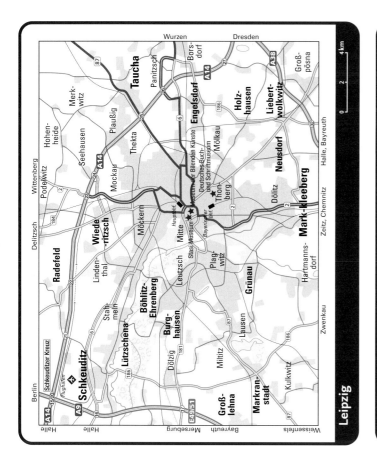

Leipzig

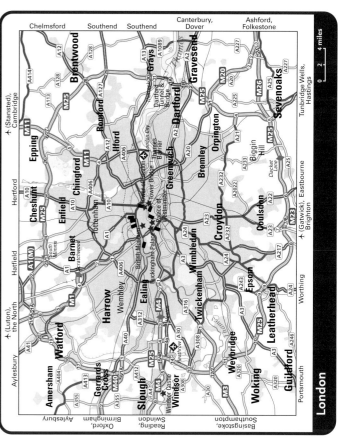

London

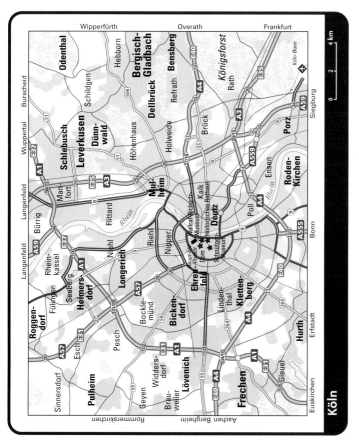

Köln

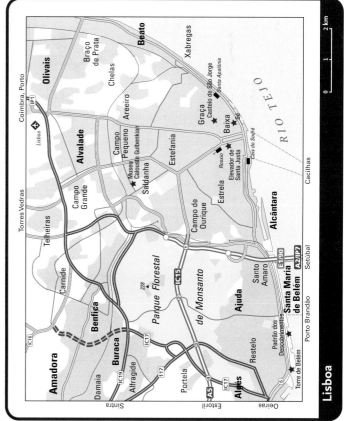

Lisboa

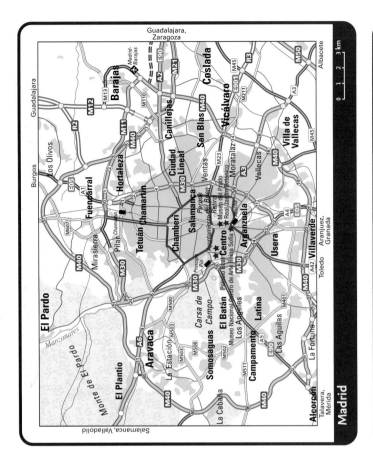

Madrid

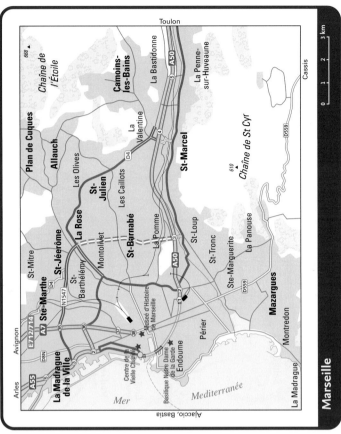

Marseille

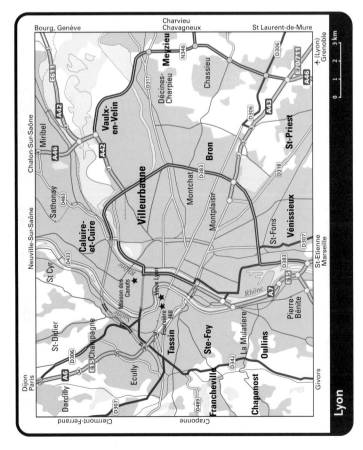

Lyon

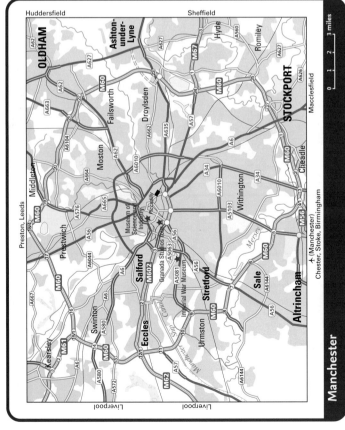

Manchester

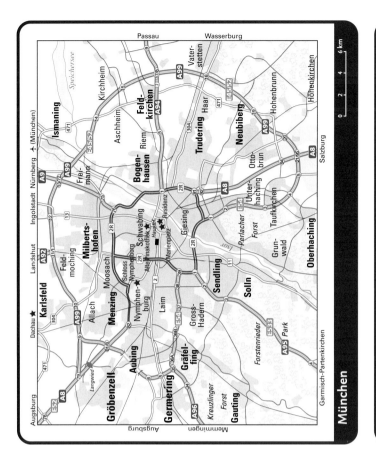

München

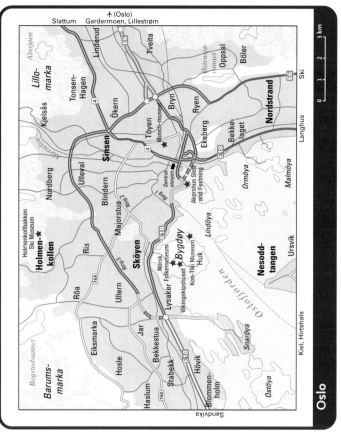

Oslo

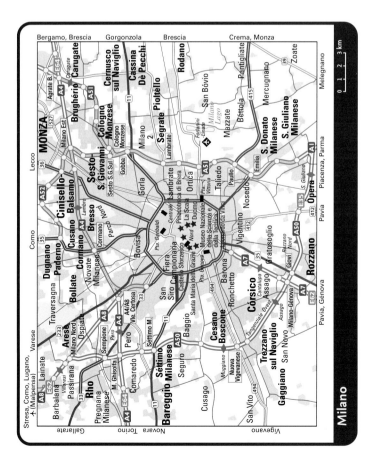

Milano

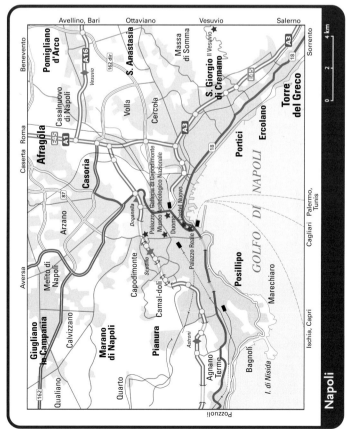

Napoli

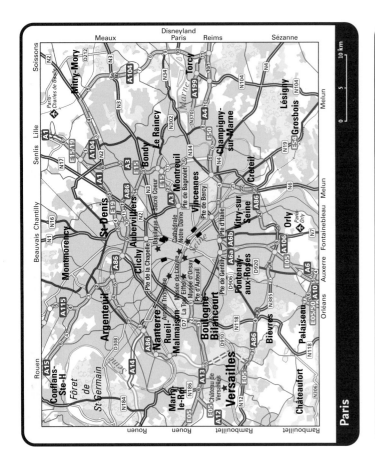

Paris

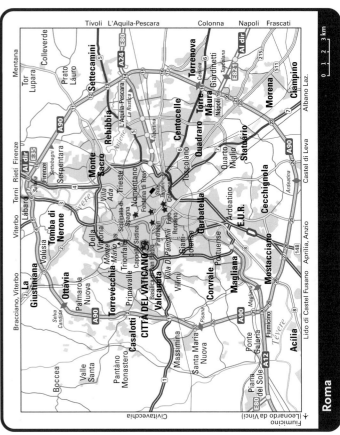

Roma

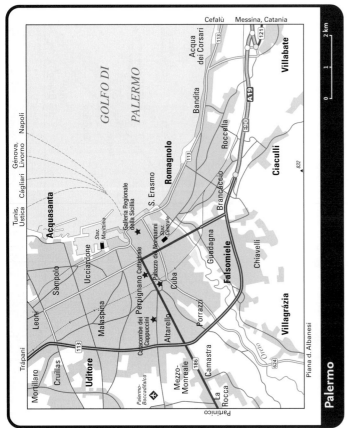

Palermo

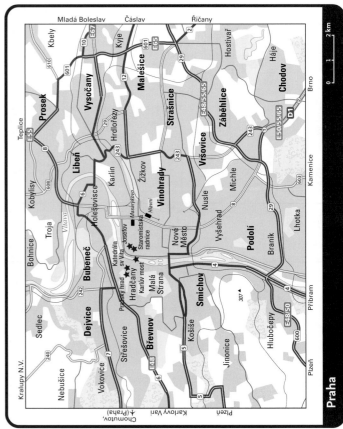

Praha

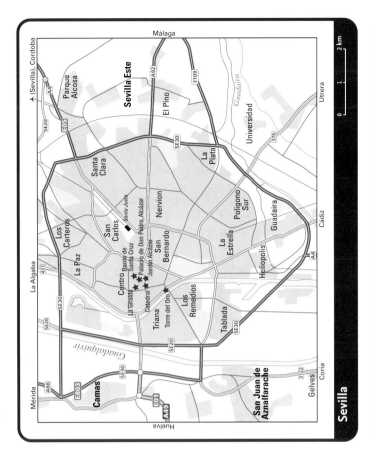

Sevilla

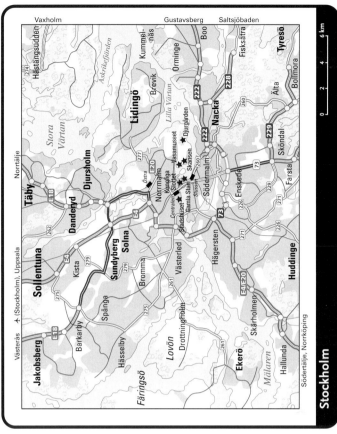

Stockholm

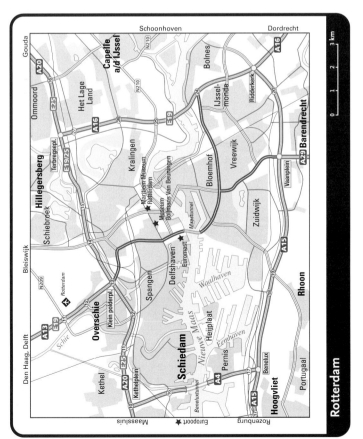

Rotterdam

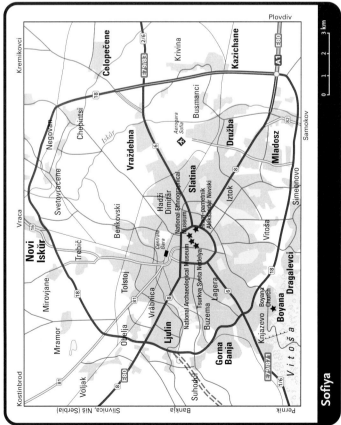

Sofiya

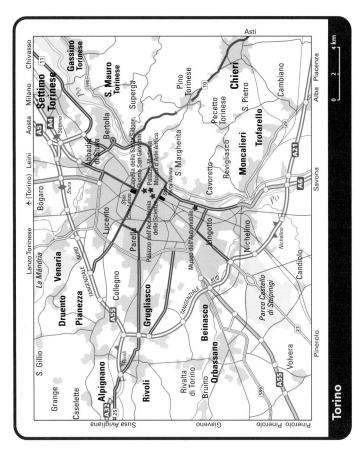

Torino

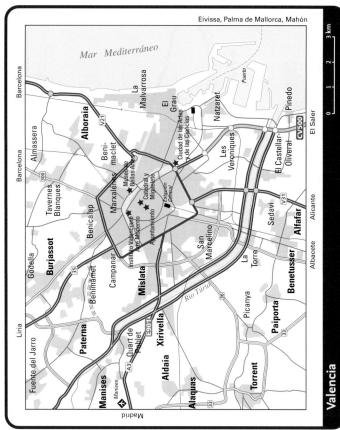

Valencia

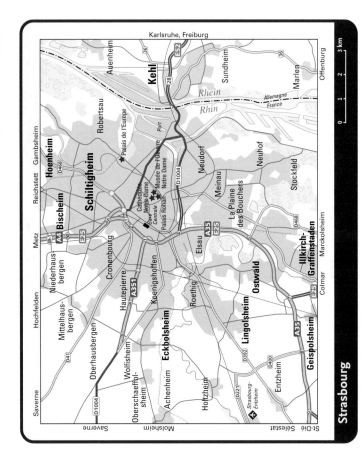

Strasbourg

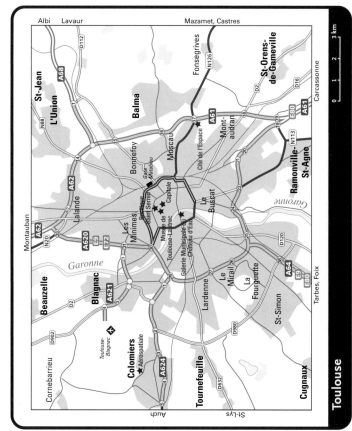

Toulouse

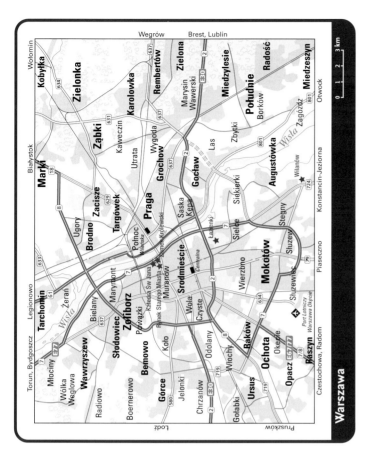

Warszawa

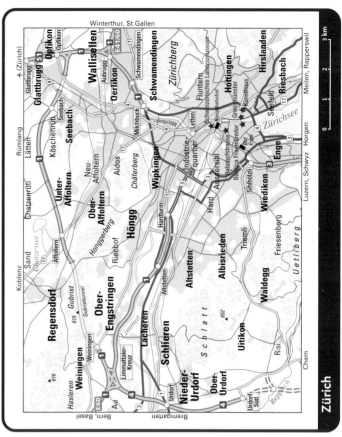

Zürich

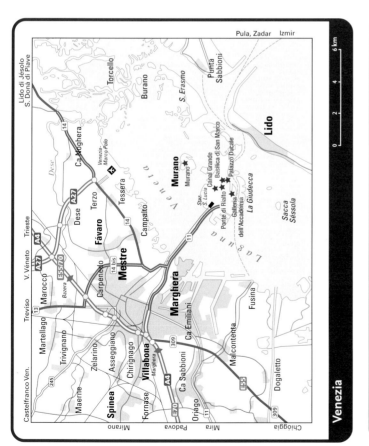

Venezia

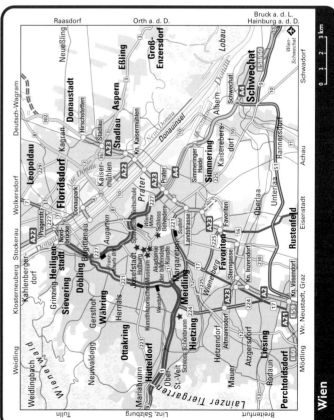

Wien

A

Å N 120 F7
Å N 126 E4
Å N 127 B12
Å N 127 C13
Aabenraa DK 102 E4
Aabla EST 147 B11
Aabybro DK 102 A5
Aachen D 36 C6
Aadorf CH 43 F10
Aakirkeby DK 105 E7
Aalborg DK 102 A5
Aalen D 91 E7
Aalestrup DK 102 B4
Aalsmeer NL 32 D3
Aalst B 35 C9
Aalst NL 199 B6
Aalten NL 33 E7
Aalter B 35 B7
Äänekoski FIN 139 E15
Aapajärvi FIN 131 D2
Aapajärvi FIN 135 B12
Aapajoki FIN 135 B12
Aapua S 133 E11
Aarau CH 43 F9
Aarberg CH 47 A11
Aardenburg NL 35 B7
Aareavaara S 133 D10
Aarle NL 32 F5
A Armada E 54 B3
Aars DK 102 B5
Aarschot B 35 C10
Aartrijke B 198 C2
Aartselaar B 35 B9
Aarup DK 102 E6
Aarwangen CH 43 F8
Aasleagh IRL 22 E3
Ääsmäe EST 147 C9
Aaspere EST 147 C12
Aatsinki FIN 131 E5
Aavajärvi S 135 C11
Aavasaksa FIN 135 B11
Aba H 165 B11
Abaclia MD 170 E3
Abades E 62 C4
Abadín E 54 B5
Abadiño-Zelaieta E 57 B6
Abádszalók H 166 C6
A Baiuca E 54 B3
Abak TR 197 A7
Abalar TR 188 A6
Abánades E 63 C8
Abanilla E 72 E2
Abano Terme I 82 B4
Abarán E 71 C10
A Barrela E 54 C4
Abasár H 166 B5
Abaújszántó H 161 G3
Abbadia San Salvatore I 78 B1
Abbasanta I 80 C2
Abbekås S 103 E13
Abbeville F 34 D4
Abbey IRL 22 F6
Abbeydorney IRL 24 D3
Abbeyfeale IRL 24 D4
Abbeyleix IRL 25 C8
Abbey Town GB 21 F10
Abbiategrasso I 85 C6
Abborrberg S 125 F12
Abborreberget S 114 D8
Abborrträsk S 125 F17
Abbotsbury GB 29 D9
Abbots Langley GB 31 D8
Abcoude NL 32 D3
Abejar E 56 E6
Abejuela E 64 E3
Abela P 66 C2
Abelvær N 121 B10
Abenberg D 91 D8
Abenójar E 70 B4
Abensberg D 91 E10
Aberaeron GB 28 A6
Aberaman GB 29 B8
Aberchirder GB 19 K11
Aberdare GB 29 B8
Aberdaron GB 26 F2
Aberdeen GB 19 L12
Aberdovey GB 26 F3
Aberfeldy GB 21 B9
Aberffraw GB 26 E3
Aberford GB 27 D9
Aberfoyle GB 21 C8
Abergavenny GB 29 B8
Abergele GB 26 E4
Åberget S 125 E18
Abergwaun GB 28 B5
Abergynolwyn GB 26 F4
Aberlady GB 21 C11
Aberlour GB 19 L10
Abernethy GB 21 C10
Aberporth GB 28 A5
Abersoch GB 26 F2
Abertamy CZ 91 B12
Abertawe GB 29 B7
Abertillery GB 29 B8
Abertura E 61 F9
Aberuthven GB 21 C9
Aberystwyth GB 28 A6
Abetone I 82 D2
Abfaltersbach A 88 C6
Abhainnsuidhe GB 18 K2
Abia de la Obispalía E 63 D8
Abiego E 58 C3
Abild DK 102 F3
Abilly F 45 B7
Abingdon GB 29 B12
Abington GB 21 E9
Abisko Östra S 127 D16
Abja-Paluoja EST 147 E10
Abla E 71 E7
Ablis F 40 C6
Ablitas E 57 E8
Abmelaseter N 128 E6
Abo FIN 142 E7
Åbo S 119 C10
Åbodarna S 123 E14
Åbogen N 112 B7
Abondance F 47 C10
Abony H 166 C5
Åbosjö S 123 D13
Aboyne GB 21 A11
Abragão P 60 B4
Abram RO 167 C9
Abrămuț RO 167 C9
Abrantes P 60 F4
Abraur S 125 D16
Abreiro P 54 F5
Abreschviller F 43 C7
Abrest F 46 C3
Abriès F 47 F10
Abrigada P 60 F2
Abriola I 76 B5
Abrucena E 71 E7
Abrud RO 167 E11
Abrupe LV 151 B11
Absam A 88 B4
Absberg D 91 D8
Absdorf A 93 F9
Abtenau A 89 A7
Abtsgmünd D 90 E6
Abukhava BY 156 C10
Åby S 105 A7
Åby S 109 B8
Åbyen DK 106 D7
Åbyggeby S 119 E13
Åbyn S 134 D6
Åbytorp S 108 A6
Acaill IRL 22 E3
A Cañiza E 54 D3
A Carballa E 54 B2
Acarlar TR 193 D10
A Carreira E 54 B3
Acâș RO 167 B10
Acate I 74 E5
Accadia I 76 A4
Acceglio I 52 C5
Accettura I 76 C6
Acciano I 78 C5
Acciaroli I 76 C4
Accous F 48 E4
Accrington GB 27 D7
Accumoli I 78 B4
Acebo E 61 D7
Acedera E 61 F9
Acedo E 48 E1
Acehuche E 61 E7
Aceituna E 61 D8
Acered E 63 B9
Acerenza I 76 B5
Acerno I 76 B4
Acerra I 76 B2
Aceuchal E 67 B7
Ach A 92 F3
Achadh Mòr GB 18 J3
A Chan E 54 D3
Acharacle GB 20 B5
Acharnes GR 191 C8
Achavanich GB 19 J10
Achel B 199 C6
Achenkirch A 88 A4
Achern D 43 C9
Acheux-en-Amiénois F 34 D6
Achicourt F 34 D6
Achill IRL 22 E3
Achilleio GR 191 A6
Achim D 33 B12
Achintee GB 18 L6
Achladochori GR 185 B10
Achladokampos GR 191 D6
Achnacroish GB 20 B6
Achnasheen GB 18 K6
Achosnich GB 20 B4
Achstetten D 87 A9
Achtrup D 98 A6
Aci Castello I 75 D7
Aci Catena I 75 D7
Acireale I 75 D7
Aci Sant'Antonio I 75 D7
Aci Trezza I 75 D7
Acktjära S 119 D11
Acle GB 31 B12
A Coruña E 54 B3
Acquacalda I 75 B6
Acqualagna I 83 E6
Acquanegra sul Chiese I 82 B1
Acquapendente I 78 B1
Acquappesa I 76 E5
Acquaro I 75 B9
Acquarossa CH 87 E7
Acquasanta Terme I 78 B4
Acquasparta I 78 B3
Acquaviva Picena I 78 B5
Acquedolci I 75 C6
Acquigny F 40 B5
Acqui Terme I 53 B8
Acri I 77 E6
A Cruz do Incio E 54 C5
Ács H 165 A10
Acsa H 166 B3
Acuto I 78 D4
Ada SRB 166 F5
Adács H 166 B4
Adahuesca E 58 C3
Adak S 125 F16
Ådalsliden S 123 E11
Adamas GR 195 B7
Adamclisi RO 171 E1
Adamov CZ 93 D11
Adamova BY 149 E4
Adamów PL 157 G6
Adamówka PL 160 C6
Adamstown IRL 25 D9
Adămuș RO 168 E4
Adamuz E 69 A7
Adâncata RO 169 B8
Adâncata RO 177 D8
Ádánd H 165 C10
Adanero E 62 C3
Adão P 61 D6
Adare IRL 24 C5
Adatepe TR 189 D6
Adaúfe P 54 E3
Adavere EST 147 D11
Ādaži LV 151 B8
Adderbury GB 29 A12
Addlestone GB 31 E8
Adegem B 198 C2
Adelboden CH 47 C12
Adelebsen D 94 C6
Adelfia I 77 A7
Adelina PL 160 B8
Adelmannsfelden D 203 D8
Adelschlag D 91 E9
Adelsheim D 43 B11
Adelsried D 91 F8
Ademuz E 63 D10
Adenau D 37 D7
Adendorf D 99 D8
Adendro GR 185 C8
Adenstedt D 94 B6
Adjud RO 169 E10
Adlešiči SLO 164 E4
Adliswil CH 43 F10
Adlkofen D 91 E11
Admont A 89 A9
Adolfsström S 125 D12
Adony H 165 B11
Adorf D 91 B11
Adorf (Diemelsee) D 33 F11
Adoufe P 54 F4
Adra E 71 F6
Adradas E 57 F7
Adrados E 57 F8
Adrano I 75 D6
Adria I 82 B5
Adriani GR 187 B6
Adriers F 45 C7
Aduard NL 33 B6
Adulsbruk N 117 E14
Ådum DK 102 D3
Adunați RO 177 C7
Adunații-Copăceni RO 177 E8
Adutiškis LT 151 F13
Adzaneta de Albaida E 72 D4
Adžūni LV 151 D8
Aegviidu EST 147 C11
Aerino GR 185 F8
Ærøskøbing DK 102 F6
Aerzen D 33 D12
A Escusa E 54 C2
A Esfarrapada E 54 D2
A Estrada E 54 C3
Aetos GR 185 C6
Aetos GR 190 B3
Aetos GR 190 E4
Äetsä FIN 142 C8
Afantou GR 197 D8
Åfarnes N 116 A7
A Feira do Monte E 54 B4
Affing D 91 F8
Afife P 54 E2
Afissos GR 185 F9
Åfjord N 120 D8
Aflenz Kurort A 89 A11
A Fonsagrada E 54 B5
A Forxa E 54 D4
A Forxa E 54 D4
Åfoss N 106 A6
Afragola I 76 B2
Afritz A 89 C8
Afumați RO 176 E2
Afumați RO 177 D8
Afytos GR 185 D9
Aga D 95 E11
Ağaçlı TR 189 B10
Ağaköy TR 189 D7
Agalas GR 190 D2
Agallas E 61 D8
A Gándara E 54 B3
A Gándara de Altea E 54 A3
Agapia RO 169 C8
Agăș RO 169 D8
Ágasegyháza H 166 D3
Agde F 50 D5
Agen F 49 B7
Åger E 58 C5
Agerbæk DK 102 D3
Agerskov DK 102 E4
Agersted DK 102 A6
Ågerup DK 103 D10
Ägfalva H 165 A7
Aggersund DK 102 A4
Aggius I 80 B3
Aggsbach Markt A 93 F8
Aghaboe IRL 25 C7
Aghagallon GB 23 C10
Aghalee GB 23 C10
Aghanloo GB 20 E3
Aghaville IRL 24 E4
Aghern IRL 24 D6
Aghione F 53 G10
Aghireșu RO 167 D11
Aghleam IRL 22 D2
Aghnagar Bridge IRL 24 E2
Agia GR 185 E8
Agia Anna GR 191 B7
Agia Anna GR 191 C6
Agia Effimia GR 190 C2
Agia Efthymia GR 190 C5
Agia Galini GR 194 E8
Agia Kyriaki GR 190 E4
Agia Marina GR 191 B6
Agia Marina GR 191 C9
Agia Marina GR 193 E8
Agia Paraskevi GR 184 D4
Agia Paraskevi GR 190 A3
Agia Paraskevi GR 193 E6
Agia Pelagia GR 194 C4
Agia Pelagia GR 194 E9
Agiasma GR 187 C7
Agiasos GR 193 A7
Agia Triada GR 190 D4
Agia Triada GR 191 D6
Agia Varvara GR 185 D7
Agia Varvara GR 194 E9
Agigea RO 171 E3
Agighiol RO 171 C3
Agino Selo BIH 173 C7
Agiofyllo GR 185 E6
Agioi Anargyroi GR 185 E7
Agioi Apostoloi GR 191 C8
Agioi Deka GR 194 E8
Agioi Theodoroi GR 185 E5
Agioi Theodoroi GR 191 A6
Agioi Theodoroi GR 191 D7
Agiokampos GR 185 E8
Agiokampos GR 191 B7
Agionori GR 191 D6
Agios Andreas GR 191 E6
Agios Athanasios GR 185 C8
Agios Athanasios GR 187 B6
Agios Charalampos GR 187 C9
Agios Christoforos GR 191 F5
Agios Dimitrios GR 185 D7
Agios Dimitrios GR 191 D8
Agios Dimitrios GR 191 F6
Agios Efstratios GR 187 E7
Agios Georgios GR 185 C7
Agios Georgios GR 190 B4
Agios Georgios GR 191 C6
Agios Georgios GR 193 F6
Agios Georgios GR 194 E9
Agios Germanos GR 184 C5
Agios Ioannis GR 190 E5
Agios Ioannis GR 191 C7
Agios Ioannis GR 194 B4
Agios Kirykos GR 193 D7
Agios Konstantinos GR 190 B3
Agios Konstantinos GR 190 D5
Agios Konstantinos GR 191 B6
Agios Konstantinos GR 191 D9
Agios Kyprianos GR 194 C3
Agios Leon GR 190 D2
Agios Loukas GR 185 C7
Agios Loukas GR 191 C9
Agios Mamas GR 185 D9
Agios Matthaios GR 184 F2
Agios Myronas GR 194 E9
Agios Nikolaos GR 184 E3
Agios Nikolaos GR 184 E5
Agios Nikolaos GR 185 D10
Agios Nikolaos GR 190 B2
Agios Nikolaos GR 190 B4
Agios Nikolaos GR 190 B4
Agios Nikolaos GR 194 B3
Agios Nikolaos GR 195 E10
Agios Panteleïmonas GR 185 C6
Agios Paraskevi GR 187 F10
Agios Petros GR 185 C8
Agios Petros GR 190 B2
Agios Petros GR 191 E6
Agios Spyridonas GR 185 D7
Agios Spyridonas GR 190 A2
Agios Stefanos GR 191 C8
Agios Stefanos GR 192 E5
Agios Thomas GR 191 C8
Agios Vasileios GR 185 C9
Agios Vasileios GR 191 D6
Agira I 75 D6
Agivey GB 20 E3
Agkathia GR 185 C7
Agkistro GR 185 B9
Aglapsvik N 127 B15
Aglasterhausen D 203 C6
Agle N 121 C13
Aglen N 121 B10
Agliana I 82 E3
Aglientu I 80 A3
Aglish IRL 25 D7
Agluonėnai LT 150 E2
Agnadello I 85 C8
Agnagar Bridge IRL 24 E2
Agnanta GR 184 F5
Agnantero GR 185 F6
Agneaux F 39 B9
Agnita RO 168 F5
Agno CH 85 A6
Agnone I 79 D6
Agolada E 54 C3
Agoncillo E 48 F1
Agon-Coutainville F 39 B8
Agordo I 88 D5
Agost E 72 E3
Agos-Vidalos F 48 D5
Ågotnes N 110 B2
Agra GR 193 A7
Agramón E 71 C9
Agramunt E 58 D6
Agrate Brianza I 85 B7
Agreda E 57 E8
Agrés E 72 D4
Agria GR 185 F9
Agridi GR 190 D4
Agrigento I 74 E4
Agrij RO 167 C11
Agrili GR 190 E4
Agrinio GR 190 B3
Agriovotano GR 191 A7
Agrochão P 55 E5
Agropoli I 76 C3
Ågskaret N 124 C5
Aguadulce E 69 B7
Aguadulce E 71 F7
A Guarda E 54 E2
Aguarón E 57 F9
Aguas E 58 C3
Águas Belas P 60 E4
Aguas de Busot E 72 D4
Águas de Moura P 66 B2
Águas Frias P 54 E5
Aguaviva E 58 F3
A Gudiña E 54 D5
Agudo E 70 B3
Águeda P 60 C4
Aguessac F 50 B5
Agugliano I 83 E7
Aguiar P 66 C4
Aguiar da Beira P 60 C5
Aguilafuente E 62 B4
Aguilar de Alfambra E 58 F2
Aguilar de Campóo E 56 C3
Aguilar de la Frontera E 69 A7
Aguilar del Río Alhama E 57 E8
Águilas E 71 E9
Agullana E 50 F4
Agullent E 72 D3
Aha S 125 F14
Ahafona IRL 24 C3
Aham D 91 E11
Ahascragh IRL 22 F6
Ahaus D 33 D8
Åheim N 116 B3
Ahelva FIN 137 E11
Ahigal E 61 D8
Ahigal de Villarino E 61 B8
Ahillones E 67 C8
Ahja EST 147 E14
Ahjola FIN 137 D12
Ahlainen FIN 142 B6
Ahlatlı TR 183 E8
Ahlbeck D 100 C6
Ahlbeck, Seebad D 100 C6
Ahlden (Aller) D 98 E7
Ahlen D 33 E9
Ahlerstedt D 33 B12
Ahlhorn D 33 C10
Ahmas FIN 135 E17
Ahmavaara FIN 131 E4
Ahmetbey TR 189 B8
Ahmetbeyli TR 193 C9
Ahmetçeeli TR 188 E6
Ahmetli TR 193 C9
Ahmovaara FIN 141 D13
Ahnsbeck D 95 A7
Ahoghill GB 20 F4
Ahoinen FIN 143 D11
Ahokylä FIN 139 C17
Ahola FIN 137 B11
Ahola FIN 137 C13
Ahola FIN 137 D13
Ahola FIN 140 D9
Aholanvaara FIN 131 E5
Ahonperä FIN 135 F13
Ahorn D 91 B8
Aho-Vastinki FIN 139 E14
Ahrbrück D 37 D7
Ahrensbök D 99 B9
Ahrensburg D 99 C8
Ahrenshagen D 99 B13
Ahrenshoop, Ostseebad D 99 B12
Ähtäri FIN 139 E12
Ähtärinranta FIN 139 E12
Ahtme EST 148 C1
Ahula EST 147 C11
Ahun F 45 C10
Åhus S 104 D6
Ahveninen FIN 139 E16
Ahvenisto FIN 143 C16
Ahvensalmi FIN 141 F10
Ahvenselkä FIN 131 E4
Ahvenvittikko FIN 131 D4
Ahvionsaari FIN 145 B10
Aiani GR 185 D6
Aianteio GR 191 D7
Aibar E 48 E3
Aibl A 89 C11
Aichach D 91 F9
Aichhalden D 43 D9
Aichstetten D 87 B10
Ai'dejav'ri N 133 A10
Aidenbach D 92 E4
Aidipsos GR 191 B7
Aidone I 74 E5
Aidonochori GR 185 C10
Aidt DK 102 C5
Aidu EST 147 D12
Aiello Calabro I 75 A9
Aielo de Malferit E 72 D3
Aieta I 76 D5
Aiffres F 44 C5
Aigeira GR 190 C5
Aigen im Ennstal A 89 A9
Aigen im Mühlkreis A 92 E5
Aigiali GR 193 F6
Aigina GR 191 D7
Aiginio GR 185 D8
Aigio GR 190 C5
Aigle CH 47 C10
Aiglemont F 200 E2
Aignan F 49 C6
Aignay-le-Duc F 41 E12
Aigre F 44 D6
Aigrefeuille-d'Aunis F 44 C4
Aigrefeuille-sur-Maine F 44 A3
A Igrexa E 54 D3
Aiguafreda E 59 D8
Aiguebelle F 47 D9
Aigueblanche F 47 D10
Aigueperse F 46 C3
Aigues-Mortes F 51 C7
Aigues-Vives F 49 E9
Aigues-Vives F 50 D4
Aigues-Vives F 51 C7
Aiguilhe F 46 E4
Aiguilles F 47 F10
Aiguillon F 49 B6
Aigurande F 45 C9
Äijäjoki FIN 132 B10
Äijälä FIN 139 E16
Aijala FIN 143 E9
Aijänneva FIN 139 F11
Aillant-sur-Tholon F 41 E9
Aillas F 48 B5
Aillevillers-et-Lyaumont F 42 E5
Ailly-le-Haut-Clocher F 34 D4
Ailly-sur-Noye F 34 E5
Ailly-sur-Somme F 34 E5
Ailt an Chorráin IRL 22 C6
Aimargues F 51 C7
Aime F 47 D10
Ainali FIN 135 F14
Ainali FIN 139 B11
Ainay-le-Château F 45 B11
Ainaži LV 147 F8
Aindling D 91 E8
Ainet A 89 C6
Ainsa E 49 F6
Ainzón E 57 E9
Airaines F 34 E4
Airaksela FIN 140 E8
Airasca I 47 F11
Aird Asaig GB 18 K3
Airdrie GB 21 D9
Aire-sur-l'Adour F 48 C5
Aire-sur-la-Lys F 34 C5
Airidh a'Bhruaich GB 18 J3
Airola I 76 A3
Airole I 53 D7
Airolo CH 87 D7
Airvault F 44 B5
Aisey-sur-Seine F 41 E12
Aissey F 42 F5
Aisymi GR 187 B9
Aisy-sur-Armançon F 41 E11
Aitamännikkö FIN 133 D12
Aita Mare RO 169 F7
Aiterhofen D 91 E12
Aith GB 19 E14
Aith GB 19 G11
Aitolahti FIN 143 B10
Aitoliko GR 190 C3
Aiton RO 168 D3
Aitona E 58 E4
Aitoo FIN 143 C11
Aitrach D 87 B10
Aitrang D 87 B11
Aittaniemi FIN 137 B10
Aittijoki FIN 129 D17
Aittojärvi FIN 135 D17
Aittojärvi FIN 139 C16
Aittokoski FIN 140 C8
Aittokylä FIN 137 E10
Aittoperä FIN 139 C13
Aittovaara FIN 137 D13
Aiud RO 168 E3
Aiviekste LV 151 C11
Aix-en-Othe F 41 D10
Aix-en-Provence F 51 C9
Aixe-sur-Vienne F 45 D8
Aix-les-Bains F 47 D8
Aizenay F 44 B2
Aizkraukle LV 151 C10
Aizpún E 48 E2
Aizpurves LV 151 C12
Aizpute LV 150 C3
Aizviķi LV 150 D3
Ajaccio F 53 H9
Ajanki FIN 133 E12
Ajankijärvi FIN 133 E12
Ajat F 45 E8
Ajaureforsen S 125 E10
Ajdovščina SLO 89 E8
Ajka H 165 B9
Ajnovce SRB 180 D4
Ajo E 56 B4
Ajofrín E 62 E5
Ajos FIN 135 C13
Akācijas LV 150 C6
Åkarp S 103 D12
Äkäsjokisuu FIN 133 D11
Äkäslompolo FIN 133 C12
Akasztó H 166 D3
Akçaova TR 197 B7
Akçasusurluk TR 189 D9
Akeld GB 21 D12
Aken D 95 C11
Åkerbränna S 123 D11
Åkerby S 115 B9
Åkerholmen S 134 C6
Åkersberga S 115 D10
Akersjön S 121 D16
Åkers styckebruk S 114 D8
Åkerstrømmen N 117 C14
Akheloy BG 183 D9
Akhremawtsy BY 149 E2
Akhtopol BG 183 E9
Akkan S 125 F12
Akkarfjord N 129 B12
Akkarvik N 128 C5
Akkasæter N 127 B16
Akkavare S 125 E17
Akkerhaugen N 111 D10
Akköy TR 187 E10
Akköy TR 193 E9
Akkrum NL 32 B5
Akmeņdziras LV 150 B3
Akmenė LT 150 D5
Åknes N 126 C9
Aknīste LV 151 D11
Akonkoski FIN 137 F13
Akonpohja FIN 141 D10
Akpınar TR 189 B10
Akraifnio GR 191 C7
Åkran N 121 D12
Akrata GR 190 C5
Åkrehamn N 110 D2
Akrini GR 185 D6
Akrolimni GR 185 C7
Akropotamos GR 186 C6
Akrotiri GR 195 C9
Aksakal TR 189 D9
Aksaz TR 189 D7
Aksdal N 110 D2
Aksnes N 120 F4
Akujärvi FIN 130 F3
Åkullsjön S 134 F5
Åkvisslan S 123 E13
Ål N 117 E9
Ala I 85 B11
Ala S 109 E13
Alacaat TR 189 E10
Alacaoğlu TR 189 B7
Alaçatı TR 193 C7
Alà dei Sardi I 80 B3
Ala di Stura I 47 E11
Alaejos E 55 F9
Alagna Valsesia I 84 B4
A Lagoa E 54 C2
Alagoa P 60 F5
Alagón E 57 E9
Alahärmä FIN 138 D9
Ala-Honkajoki FIN 142 B7
Alaigne F 49 D10
Alaior E 73 B13
Alájar E 67 D6
Alajärvi FIN 133 E15
Alajärvi FIN 137 E12
Alajärvi FIN 139 D11
Alajõe EST 148 C1
Ala-Jokikylä FIN 135 C14
Ala-Kääntä FIN 135 F12
Ala-Keyritty FIN 141 D10
Alakurtti RUS 131 E8
Alakylä FIN 133 D13
Alakylä FIN 135 D15
Alakylä FIN 142 B6
Ala-Livo FIN 135 D17
Alameda E 69 B7
Alameda de Cervera E 63 F6
Alameda de la Sagra E 62 D5
Alamedilla E 71 D6
Alamillo E 70 B3
Alan HR 83 B10
Ala-Nampa FIN 133 E16
Alanäs S 122 C9
Ålande LV 150 C2
Alandroal P 66 B5
Ålandsbro S 119 A14
Alange E 67 B7
Alaniemi FIN 135 C14
Alanís E 67 C8
Alanta LT 151 F10
Alap H 165 C11
Alapitkä FIN 140 D9
Alaquàs E 64 F4
Alaranta FIN 135 D14
Alaraz E 61 C10
Alarcón E 63 E8
Alar del Rey E 56 C3
Alaró E 65 E10
Alarup AL 184 C4
Alåsen S 122 D7
Alaskylä FIN 143 B8
Alassio I 53 C8
Alastaipale FIN 139 F11
Alastaro FIN 142 D8
Ala-Sydänmaa FIN 139 B14
Alata F 53 H9
Ala-Temmes FIN 135 E15
Alatoz E 63 F10
Alatri I 78 D4
Alatskivi EST 147 D14
Alattyán H 166 C5
Ala-Valli FIN 139 F9
Alavattnet S 122 C9
Alavere EST 147 C10
Ala-Vieksi FIN 137 F12
Alavieska FIN 135 F12
Ala-Viirre FIN 139 B11
Ala-Vuokki FIN 137 E13
Ala-Vuotto FIN 135 D16
Alavus FIN 139 E11
Alba I 53 B8
Alba Adriatica I 78 B5
Albac RO 167 E10
Albacete E 71 A9
Albacken S 119 A11
Alba de Tormes E 61 C9
Ålbæk DK 106 D7
Albagiara I 80 D2
Albaida E 72 D4
Alba Iulia RO 168 E3
Albaladejo E 71 B7
Alba-la-Romaine F 51 A8
Albalate de Arzobispo E 58 E3
Albalate de Cinca E 58 D4
Albalate de las Nogueras E 63 D8
Albalate de Zorita E 63 D7
Albalatillo E 58 D3
Alban F 49 C10
Albánchez E 71 E8
Albanella I 76 C4
Albanitsa BG 181 C10
Albano di Lucania I 76 B6
Albano Laziale I 78 D3
Albano Vercellese I 84 C5
Albanyà E 59 C9
Albaredo per San Marco I 85 A8
Albaret-le-Comtal F 46 F3
Albareto I 85 E8
Albaret-Ste-Marie F 46 F3
Albaron F 51 C7
Albarracín E 63 D10
Albatana E 71 B9
Albatàrrec E 58 D5
Albatera E 72 E3
Albbruck D 43 E9
Albelda E 58 D4
Albelda de Iregua E 57 D7
Albella E 48 F5
Albendea E 63 C8
Albendín E 69 A8
Albenga I 53 C8
Albeni RO 176 C3
Albens F 47 D8
Albentosa E 64 D3
Ålberga S 109 B9
Ålberga S 114 D6
Albergaria-a-Velha P 60 C4
Albergaria dos Doze P 60 E3
Albergen NL 199 A9
Alberic E 64 F4
Alberndorf in der Riedmark A 93 F6
Albernoa P 66 D4
Albero Alto E 57 D11
Alberobello I 77 B8
Alberona I 76 A4
Alberoni I 82 B5
Alberschwende A 87 C9
Albersdorf D 98 B6
Albert F 34 E6
Albertacce F 53 G9
Alberta Ligure I 53 B10
Albertirsa H 166 C4
Albertshofen D 203 B9
Albertville F 47 D9
Alberuela de Tubo E 58 D3
Albesa E 58 D5
Albești RO 168 E5
Albești RO 169 B10
Albești RO 169 D11
Albești RO 171 F2
Albești RO 177 D10
Albeștii de Argeș RO 176 C5
Albeștii de Muscel RO 176 C6
Albești-Paleologu RO 177 D8
Albestroff F 43 C6
Albi F 49 C10
Albias F 49 B8
Albidona I 77 D6
Albignasego I 82 B4
Albina RO 171 C1
Albino I 85 B8
Albires E 55 D9
Albisheim (Pfrimm) D 37 E10
Albisola Marina I 53 C9
Albisola Superiore I 53 C9
Alblasserdam NL 32 E3
Ålbo S 114 B7
Albocàsser E 64 D5
Alboloduy E 71 E7
Albolote E 69 B9
Albon F 46 E6
Albondón E 71 F6
Alboraya E 64 E4
Alborea E 63 F10
Albota RO 176 D5
Albox E 71 E8
Albrechtice nad Orlicí CZ 93 B10
Al'brekhtava BY 149 E5
Albstadt D 43 D11
Albu EST 147 C11
Albudeite E 71 C10
Albufeira P 66 E3
Albujón E 72 F2
Albuñol E 71 F6
Albuñuelas E 69 C9
Alburquerque E 61 F7
Alby S 105 C11
Alby S 119 A9
Alby-sur-Chéran F 47 D9
Alcácer E 64 F4
Alcácer do Sal P 66 C2
Alcáçovas P 66 C3
Alcadozo E 71 B9
Alcafozes P 61 E6
Alcaine E 58 F2
Alcains P 60 E6
Alcalá de Guadaira E 67 E8
Alcalá de Gurrea E 57 D10
Alcalá de Henares E 62 D6
Alcalá del Júcar E 63 F10
Alcalá de los Gazules E 68 D5
Alcalá del Río E 67 D8
Alcalá del Valle E 67 F9
Alcalà de Xivert E 64 D5
Alcalá la Real E 69 B9
Alcalalí E 72 D4
Alcamo I 74 D2
Alcampell E 58 D4
Alcanadre E 48 F1
Alcanede P 60 F3
Alcanena P 60 F3
Alcanhões P 60 F3
Alcañices E 55 E7
Alcañiz E 58 E3
Alcántara E 61 E7
Alcantarilla E 72 F2
Alcantud E 63 C8
Alcaracejos E 70 C3
Alcara li Fusi I 75 C6
Alcaraz E 71 B8
Alcaria Ruiva P 66 D4
Alcarràs E 58 D5
Alcaucín E 69 C8
Alcaudete E 69 A8
Alcaudete de la Jara E 62 E3
Alçay-Alçabéhéty-Sunharette F 48 D4
Alcázar del Rey E 63 D7
Alcázar de San Juan E 63 F6
Alcedar MD 170 B3
Alcester GB 29 A11
Alçıtepe TR 187 D10
Alcoba E 62 F4
Alcobaça P 60 E3
Alcobendas E 62 C5
Alcocer E 63 D7
Alcocero de Mola E 56 D5
Alcochete P 66 B2
Alcoentre P 60 F3
Alcolea E 69 A7
Alcolea E 71 F7
Alcolea de Calatrava E 70 B4
Alcolea de Cinca E 58 D4
Alcolea del Pinar E 63 B8
Alcolea del Río E 67 D8
Alcollarín E 61 F9
Alconchel E 67 B5
Alconétar E 61 E7
Alcorcón E 62 D5
Alcorisa E 58 F3
Alcoroches E 63 C9
Alcossebre E 64 D5
Alcoutim P 66 E5
Alcover E 58 E6
Alcoy-Alcoi E 72 D4
Alcsútdoboz H 165 B11
Alcubierre E 57 E11
Alcubilla de Avellaneda E 56 E5
Alcubillas E 71 B6
Alcublas E 64 E3
Alcúdia E 73 B11
Alcudia de Guadix E 71 E6
Alcudia de Monteagud E 71 E8
Alcuéscar E 61 F8
Aldbrough GB 27 D11

Aldeacentenera E 61 E9
Aldeadávila de la Ribera E 61 B7
Aldea del Cano E 61 F8
Aldea del Obispo E 61 C7
Aldea del Fresno E 62 D4
Aldea del Rey E 70 B5
Aldea de Trujillo E 61 E9
Aldealafuente E 57 E7
Aldealpozo E 57 E7
Aldeamayor de San Martín E 55 E10
Aldeanueva de Barbarroya E 61 E10
Aldeanueva de Ebro E 57 D8
Aldeanueva de Figueroa E 61 B9
Aldeanueva de la Vera E 61 D9
Aldeanueva del Camino E 61 D9
Aldeanueva de San Bartolomé E 61 E10
Aldeaquemada E 71 C6
Aldea Real E 62 B4
Aldearrodrigo E 61 B9
Aldeaseca E 62 B3
Aldeatejada E 61 C9
Aldeavieja E 62 C4
Aldeburgh GB 31 C12
Aldehuela de la Bóveda E 61 C8
Aldehuela de Yeltes E 61 C8
Aldeia da Mata P 60 F5
Aldeia da Ponte P 61 D7
Aldeia de João Pires P 61 D6
Aldeia do Bispo P 61 D6
Aldeia dos Elvas P 66 D3
Aldeia dos Fernandes P 66 D3
Aldeia dos Palheiros P 66 D3
Aldeia Velha P 60 F3
Aldenhoven D 36 C6
Aldeno I 85 B11
Alderbury GB 29 C11
Alderholt GB 29 D11
Alderley Edge GB 27 E7
Aldersbach D 92 F4
Aldershot GB 31 E7
Aldinac SRB 180 B5
Aldingham GB 26 C5
Aldinci MK 180 F3
Aldomirovtsi BG 181 D6
Aldover E 58 F5
Aldridge GB 27 F8
Aldudes F 48 D3
Åle DK 102 D5
Åled S 103 B11
Aledo E 71 D9
Alekovo BG 177 F10
Alekovo BG 182 C4
Aleksandriškės LT 153 D10
Aleksandrovac SRB 175 E7
Aleksandrovac SRB 179 C11
Aleksandrovo BG 181 C10
Aleksandrovo BG 182 D4
Aleksandrovo BG 183 E7
Aleksandrów PL 157 F2
Aleksandrów PL 157 H1
Aleksandrów Kujawski PL 154 E6
Aleksandrów Łódzki PL 159 C7
Aleksa Šantić SRB 166 F3
Aleksinac SRB 180 B4
Ålem S 105 B10
Ålen N 117 A14
Alençon F 39 D12
Alenya F 50 E4
Alerheim D 91 E8
Aléria F 53 G11
Alerre E 57 D11
Alès F 51 B7
Ales I 80 D2
Aleşd RO 167 C9
Alesón E 57 D7
Alessandria I 53 B9
Alessandria del Carretto I 77 D6
Alessandria della Rocca I 74 D3
Alessano I 77 D10
Ålesund N 116 B4
Alet-les-Bains F 49 D10
Alexandreia GR 185 C7
Alexandria GB 20 C7
Alexandria RO 176 F6
Alexandroupoli GR 187 C9
Alexandru Vlahuță RO 169 E11
Alexeevca MD 169 C11
Alexeni RO 177 D9
Alexandrów PL 160 C6
Alezio I 77 C10
Alf D 37 D8
Alfacar E 69 B9
Alfafar E 64 F4
Alfaiates P 61 D7
Alfajarín E 57 E10
Alfambra E 58 F1
Alfambras P 66 E2
Alfamén E 57 F9
Alfândega da Fé P 55 F6
Alfântega E 58 D4
Alfarim P 66 C1
Alfaro E 57 D8
Alfarràs E 58 D5
Alfatar BG 177 F10
Alfdorf D 90 E6
Alfedena I 78 D6
Alfeizerão P 60 E2
Alfeld (Leine) D 94 C6
Alfena P 60 B3
Alferce P 66 E3
Alfhausen D 33 C9
Alfonsine I 82 C5
Alford GB 19 L11
Alford GB 27 E12
Alforja E 58 E5
Alfredshem S 123 E15
Alfreton GB 27 E9
Alfta S 119 D11
Alfundão P 66 C3
Algaida E 73 B10
Algajola I 53 F9
Algámitas E 69 B6
Algar E 68 C5
Ålgård N 110 E3
Algarinejo E 69 B8
Algarrobo E 69 C8
Algeciras E 69 D6
Algemesí E 64 F4
Algered S 119 B12
Algerri E 58 D5
Algestrup DK 103 E10
Algete E 62 C5
Alghero I 80 B1
Ålghult S 105 A9
Alginet E 64 F3

Ålgnäs S 119 D12
Algodonales E 67 F9
Algodor P 66 D4
Algora E 63 C7
Algorta E 56 B5
Algoso P 55 F6
Algoz P 66 E3
Alguaire E 58 D5
Alguazas E 72 E2
Algueirão-Mem Martins P 66 B1
Algueña E 72 E3
Algutsrum S 105 B11
Alhabia E 71 F7
Alhama de Almería E 71 F7
Alhama de Aragón E 57 F8
Alhama de Granada E 69 B9
Alhama de Murcia E 71 D10
Alhambra E 71 B6
Alhamn S 134 D7
Alhaurín de la Torre E 69 C7
Alhaurín el Grande E 69 C7
Alhendín E 69 B9
Alhojärvi FIN 143 B13
Alhóndiga E 63 D7
Alhult S 108 D7
Alía E 61 F10
Aliaga E 58 F2
Aliağa TR 193 B8
Aliaguilla E 63 E10
Aliano I 76 C6
Aliartos GR 191 C7
Alibunar SRB 175 C6
Alicante E 72 E4
Alicún de Ortega E 71 D6
Alife I 76 A2
Alija del Infantado E 55 D8
Alijó P 54 F5
Alikianos GR 194 E6
Alikylä FIN 139 C11
Aliman RO 171 E1
Alimena I 74 D5
Aliminusa I 74 D4
Alimpeşti RO 176 C3
Alingsås S 107 D10
Alino BG 181 E7
Alionys 1 LT 153 C11
Aliseda E 61 F7
Alistrati GR 186 B5
Alì Terme I 75 C7
Aliveri GR 191 C7
Alixan F 47 F7
Alizava LT 151 E10
Aljaraque E 67 E5
Aljezur P 66 E2
Aljinovići SRB 179 C8
Aljucén E 67 A7
Aljustrel P 66 D3
Alken B 35 C11
Alkkia FIN 138 F9
Alkmaar NL 32 C3
Allai I 80 D2
Allaire F 39 E7
Allambre AL 184 C2
Allan F 51 A8
Allanche F 46 E2
Allariz E 54 D4
Allarmont F 43 D7
Allassac F 45 E8
Allažì LV 151 B9
Allažmuiža LV 151 B9
Alle CH 43 F7
Alleghe I 88 D5
Allègre F 46 E4
Alleins F 51 C9
Allemond F 47 E9
Allen IRL 23 F9
Allendale Town GB 21 F12
Allendorf (Eder) D 37 B11
Allenheads GB 21 F12
Allensbach D 43 E11
Allensteig A 93 E8
Allenwood IRL 23 F9
Allepuz E 58 F2
Allerona I 78 B1
Allersberg D 91 D10
Allershausen D 91 F10
Allerslev DK 103 E10
Allevard F 47 E9
Allex F 46 F6
Allibaudières F 41 C11
Alligny-en-Morvan F 41 F11
Allihies IRL 24 E2
Allingâbro DK 102 C6
Allinges F 47 C9
Allinge-Sandvig DK 105 E7
Alliste I 77 D10
Allmendingen D 90 F6
Allo E 48 E1
Alloa GB 21 C9
Allogny F 41 F7
Ålloluokta S 125 B17
Allonnes F 39 E12
Allonnes F 39 F12
Allons F 48 B5
Allos F 52 C5
Alloue F 45 C7
Alloza E 58 F2
Allschwil CH 43 E8
Allsta S 119 A15
Allstad N 126 D6
Allstedt D 95 D9
Allumiere I 78 C1
Alluy F 46 A4
Almacelles E 58 D4
Almáchar E 69 C8
Almada P 66 B1
Almadén E 70 B3
Almadén de la Plata E 67 D7
Almadenejos E 70 B3
Almagro E 70 B5
Almăj RO 176 D3
Almajano E 57 E7
Almalaguês P 60 D4
Almaluez E 57 F7
Almansa E 71 B11
Almansil P 66 E3
Almanza E 55 D9
Almaraz E 61 E9
Almargen E 69 B6
Almarza E 57 E7
Almaş RO 167 E9
Almaşu RO 168 C3
Almaşu Mare RO 167 E11
Almázan E 57 F6
Almazora E 64 E4
Almazul E 57 F7
Almedina E 71 B7
Almedinilla E 69 B7
Almeida de Sayago E 55 F7

Almeirim P 60 F3
Almelo NL 33 D7
Almenar E 58 D5
Almenara E 64 E4
Almenar de Soria E 57 E7
Almendra E 61 B8
Almendra P 61 B6
Almendral E 67 B6
Almendralejo E 67 B7
Almendricos E 71 E9
Almendros E 63 E7
Almere NL 32 D4
Almería E 71 F8
Almerimar E 71 F7
Almeston E 58 D5
Åmhult S 104 B6
Almind DK 102 D4
Almkerk NL 32 E3
Almo N 120 E4
Almodôvar P 66 D3
Almodóvar del Campo E 70 B4
Almodóvar del Pinar E 63 E9
Almodóvar del Río E 69 A6
Almofala P 60 D6
Almogía E 69 C7
Almograve P 66 D2
Almoguera E 63 D7
Almoharín E 61 F8
Almonacid de la Sierra E 57 F9
Almonacid del Marquesado E 63 E7
Almonacid del Zorita E 63 D7
Almonacid de Toledo E 62 E5
Almonaster la Real E 67 D6
Almondsbury GB 29 B9
Almonte E 67 E6
Almoradí E 72 E3
Almorchón E 67 B9
Almorox E 62 D4
Almoster P 60 E4
Almscle S 123 C12
Almsjönäs S 123 E14
Ålmsta S 115 C11
Almstedt D 95 B6
Almudema I 71 C9
Almudévar E 57 D10
Almuñécar E 69 C9
Almunge S 115 C10
Almuniente E 57 D10
Almünster A 89 A8
Álmuradiel E 71 B6
Almussafes E 64 F4
Almvik S 109 D9
Almyropotamos GR 191 C7
Almyros GR 191 A6
Alnes N 116 B3
Alness GB 19 K8
Alnwick GB 21 E13
Alobras E 63 D10
Alocén E 63 C7
Aloja LV 147 F9
Alonia GR 185 D8
Álora E 69 C7
Alonsotegi E 56 B6
Alos d'Ensil E 49 E8
Alosno E 67 D5
Alost B 35 C9
Alovera E 63 C6
Alozaina E 69 C7
Alp E 49 F9
Alpalhão P 60 F5
Alpanseque E 57 F6
Alpbach A 88 A4
Alpedrinha P 60 D6
Alpedriz P 60 E3
Alpen D 33 E7
Alpenrod D 37 C9
Alpens E 59 C8
Alpera E 72 D2
Alphen NL 32 F3
Alphen aan den Rijn NL 32 D3
Alpiarça P 60 F3
Alpirsbach D 43 D9
Alpnach CH 86 D6
Aposjärvi FIN 133 E12
Alpua FIN 135 F13
Alpuente E 63 E11
Alpullu TR 189 B7
Alquería de la Condesa E 72 D4
Alquerías E 72 E2
Alqueva P 66 C4
Alquife E 71 E6
Alrance F 50 B4
Alrewas GB 27 F8
Als DK 102 B6
Alsager GB 27 E7
Alsàn S 135 B9
Alsbach D 203 B6
Alsdorf D 36 C6
Alsédžiai LT 150 D4
Alsen S 121 E15
Alsenborn D 37 F9
Alseno I 85 B8
Alsenz D 37 C12
Alsfeld D 37 C11
Alsheim D 201 C6
Alsike S 115 C9
Alsjö S 119 B11
Alsleben (Saale) D 95 C10
Alslev DK 102 D2
Alsmo N 116 D6
Alsónémedi H 166 C3
Alsópáhok H 165 C8
Alsos N 124 A8
Alsóvadász H 145 G3
Alsószölca H 161 G2
Alsta N 117 A9
Ålta N 129 D11
Älta S 115 D10
Altafulla E 59 E6
Altaharju E 135 D11
Altaseica RO 176 D3
Altare I 53 C8
Altavilla Irpina I 76 B3
Altavilla Silentina I 76 B4
Altdöbern D 96 C6
Altdorf CH D7

Altdorf D 91 E11
Altdorf bei Nürnberg D 91 D9
Alt Duvenstedt D 98 B7
Alte P 66 E3
Altea E 72 D4
Altefähr D 100 B4
Altegolfsheim D 91 E11
Alteidet N 128 C9
Altena D 33 F9
Altenahr D 37 C7
Altenau D 95 C7
Altenberg D 96 E5
Altenberge D 33 D8
Altenbruch-Westerende D 33 A11
Altenburg D 95 E11
Altendiez D 37 D9
Altenfeld D 91 A8
Altenfelden A 92 F5
Altenglan D 37 E8
Altenhagen D 99 D8
Altenheim D 43 D8
Altenhof D 100 C5
Altenholz D 99 B8
Altenkirchen D 100 A4
Altenkirchen (Westerwald) D 37 C9
Altenkrempe D 99 B9
Altenkunstadt D 91 B9
Altenmarkt an der Triesting A 93 F9
Altenmarkt bei Sankt Gallen A 89 A10
Altenmarkt im Pongau A 89 B7
Altenmedingen D 99 D9
Altenmünster D 91 E8
Altenstadt D 87 A10
Altenstadt D 87 B9
Altensteig D 43 C10
Altentreptow D 99 D12
Alter do Chão P 60 F5
Altes Lager D 96 B4
Altfraunhofen D 91 F11
Altheim A 92 F4
Altheim D 43 D11
Altheim (Alb) D 203 D9
Althengstett D 203 C6
Altier F 51 B6
Altimir BG 181 B8
Altina RO 168 F4
Altinoluk TR 188 E6
Altinova TR 193 A8
Altintaş TR 197 A8
Altkirch F 43 F7
Alt Krenzlin D 99 D10
Altlandsberg D 96 A5
Altleiningen D 37 E10
Altmannstein D 91 E10
Altnaharra GB 18 J8
Altofonte I 74 C3
Altomonte I 76 D6
Altomünster D 91 F9
Alton GB 27 F8
Alton GB 30 E7
Altopascio I 82 E2
Altorricón E 58 D4
Altötting D 91 F12
Altrich D 201 E6
Altrincham GB 27 E7
Alt Ruppin D 100 E3
Altsasu E 48 E1
Alt Schwerin D 99 C12
Altshausen D 87 B9
Altstätten CH 87 C9
Alttärnby S 132 C5
Altura E 64 E4
Altusried D 87 B10
Aluatu MD 170 F1
Alūksne LV 149 B2
Ålund S 134 D6
Alunda S 115 B10
Aluniş RO 168 D5
Aluniş RO 177 C2
Alupu RO 176 C3
Alva EST 147 C9
Alvaiázere P 60 E4
Alvajarvi FIN 139 D14
Alvalade P 66 D3
Alvaneu CH 87 D9
Ālvängen S 107 D11
Alvarenga P 60 D4
Álvares P 60 D4
Álvaro P 60 E5
Alvdal N 117 B13
Älvdalen S 118 D7
Alvega P 60 F4
Aveley GB 29 A10
Avelos P 54 E2
Alverca P 66 B1
Alverca da Beira P 61 C8
Alvesta S 104 B7
Alvestorp S 113 C12
Alvettula FIN 143 C11
Alvhem S 107 C11
Älvho S 118 D8
Alvignac F 45 F9
Ålvik N 110 B4
Alvik S 118 B8
Alvik S 119 B13
Alvik S 134 C7
Alvito I 78 D5
Alvito P 66 C4
Älvkarleby S 119 E13
Älvkarleö S 115 A8
Alvnes N 124 B9
Alvnes N 126 B9
Alvoco da Serra P 60 D5
Ålvros S 118 B8
Älvsbyn S 134 C6
Älvsered S 103 A11
Ålvund N 117 A9
Alwernia PL 159 F6
Alyki GR 190 A3
Alyth GB 21 B10
Alytus LT 153 E9
Alzano I 53 C7
Alzenau in Unterfranken D 37 D12
Alzey D 37 E10
Alzira E 64 F4
Alzon F 50 C5
Alzonne F 49 D10

Åmådalen S 118 D8
Amadora P 66 B1
Amaiur-Maia E 48 D3
Åmål S 107 A12
Åmål S 107 B12
Amalfi I 76 B3
Amaliada GR 190 D3
Amaliapoli GR 191 A6
Amalo GR 193 D6
Amance F 42 E5
Amancey F 47 A9
Amandola I 78 B5
Amantea I 76 E6
Amara RO 177 D10
Amarante P 54 F3
Amarantos GR 184 E5
Amărăşti RO 176 D4
Amărăştii de Jos RO 176 F4
Amărăştii de Sus RO 176 F4
Amareleja P 67 C5
Amares P 54 E3
Amaroni I 75 B9
Amaru RO 177 D9
Amarynthos GR 191 C8
Amaseno I 78 E4
Amatrice I 78 B4
Amaxades GR 187 B8
Amay B 35 C11
Ambasaguas E 55 C9
Ambazac F 45 D8
Ambel E 57 E8
Amberg D 91 D10
Ambergate GB 27 E9
Ambérieu-en-Bugey F 47 D7
Amberloup B 35 D12
Ambert F 46 D4
Ambès F 44 E4
Ambierle F 46 C4
Ambilou F 40 F3
Ambjörby S 113 B9
Ambjörnarp S 107 E13
Ambla EST 147 D11
Amblainville F 40 B7
Amble GB 21 E13
Ambleside GB 26 C6
Ambleteuse F 31 F12
Amboise F 40 F4
Ambon F 38 E6
Åmbra EST 147 D11
Ambrault F 45 B9
Ambrières-les-Vallées F 39 D10
Ambrosden GB 29 B12
Åmdals Verk N 111 D10
Ameglia I 85 B8
Ameide NL 198 B5
Ameixial P 66 D4
Amel B 36 D6
Amele LV 150 B4
Amelia I 78 B2
Amélie-les-Bains-Palalda F 50 F4
Amelinghausen D 99 D8
Amêndoa P 60 E4
Amendoeira P 66 D4
Amendolara I 77 D7
Amer E 59 C9
Amerang D 91 G11
Amerongen NL 199 B6
Amersfoort NL 32 D4
Amersham GB 31 D7
Amesbury GB 29 C11
Amezketa E 48 D1
Amfikleia GR 191 B6
Amfilochia GR 190 B3
Amfipoli GR 185 C10
Amfissa GR 190 B5
Amieira P 66 C4
Amiens F 34 E5
Amilly F 41 E8
Åminne FIN 138 E7
Åminne S 103 A14
Åmland N 110 E5
Åmli N 106 A3
Åmli N 106 B3
Amlwch GB 26 E3
Ämmälänkylä FIN 139 E9
Ammanford GB 28 B7
Ämmänsaari FIN 137 E12
Ammarnäs S 125 E11
Ämmeberg S 108 B6
Ammenäs S 107 C10
Ammerbuch D 203 D6
Ammern D 95 D7
Ammersbek D 99 C8
Ammerzoden NL 199 B6
Ammochori GR 185 C6
Ammotopos GR 184 F4
Ammoudia GR 185 D6
Amnatos GR 194 E8
Åmot N 110 C6
Åmot N 111 B11
Åmot N 111 C8
Åmot N 111 C11
Åmot N 119 E11
Åmotfors S 112 C7
Åmøyhamn N 124 C5
Ampelakia GR 191 B9
Ampelakia GR 192 D4
Ampeleia GR 185 F7
Ampelokipoi GR 185 E7
Ampelonas GR 185 E7
Ampezzo I 89 D6
Ampfing D 91 F11
Ampflwang im Hausruckwald A 92 F5
Amplepuis F 46 D5
Amposta E 58 F5
Ampthill GB 31 C8
Ampudia E 55 E10
Ampuero E 56 B5
Amriswil CH 43 E11
Åmsele S 123 B16
Åmsosen N 110 C3
Amstelveen NL 32 D3
Amsterdam NL 32 D3
Amstetten A 93 F7
Amstetten D 203 D8
Amulree GB 21 B9
Amurrio E 56 B6
Amusco E 56 D3
Amvrosia GR 187 B8
Amygdaleonas GR 187 C6

Amygdalia GR 190 C5
Åmynnet S 123 E15
Amyntaio GR 185 C6
Amzacea RO 171 F2
Anacapri I 76 B2
Anadia P 60 D4
Anafi GR 196 D3
Anafonitria GR 190 D2
Anagairo IRL 22 B6
Anagni I 78 D4
Anarcs H 161 G5
Anargyroi GR 185 C6
Anarrachi GR 185 D6
Ånäset S 134 F6
Ana-Sira N 110 F4
Anatazavë LT 151 E11
Anatoli GR 185 E8
Anatoli GR 185 E8
Anatoli GR 195 E10
Anatoliki Fragkista GR 190 B4
Anatoliko GR 185 C6
Anatoliko GR 185 C8
Anavatos GR 193 C7
Anavra GR 190 A5
Anavra GR 191 A6
Anavyssos GR 191 C8
Anaya de Alba E 61 C10
An Baile Breac IRL 24 E2
An Baile Nua IRL 24 D5
An Bhlarna IRL 24 E5
An Bun Beag IRL 22 B6
An Cabhán IRL 23 E8
An Caiseal IRL 22 F3
An Caisleán Riabhach IRL 22 E6
An Caisleán Nua IRL 23 F10
An Caisleán Nua IRL 24 D4
An Cathair IRL 25 D7
Ance LV 150 A4
Ancelle F 52 B4
Ancene LV 151 D11
Ancenis F 39 F9
Ancerville F 42 C3
An Charraig IRL 22 C5
An Cheathru Rua IRL 22 F3
An Chill IRL 23 E9
Ancín E 48 E2
An Cionn Garbh IRL 22 C6
An Clochán IRL 22 E3
An Clochán Liath IRL 22 C6
An Cóbh IRL 24 E6
An Coimín IRL 23 C7
An Coireán IRL 24 E2
Ancona I 83 E8
Ancroft GB 21 D11
Ancrum GB 21 D11
Ancy-le-Franc F 41 E11
An Daingean IRL 24 D2
Andalo I 85 A11
Åndalsnes N 116 A7
Andau A 165 A8
Andavías E 55 E8
Anddalsvägen N 124 E3
Andebu N 111 D12
Andechs D 91 G9
Andeer CH 87 D8
Andelfingen CH 43 E10
Andelot-Blancheville F 42 D3
Andelst NL 32 E5
Andenes N 127 B11
Andenne B 35 D9
Anderlecht B 35 C9
Anderlues B 35 D9
Andermatt CH 87 D7
Andernach D 201 D7
Andernos-les-Bains F 44 F3
Andersbo S 115 B9
Anderslöv S 103 E12
Anderstorp S 104 A5
Andervenne D 33 D7
Andfiska N 124 D7
Andijk NL 32 C5
Andilly-en-Bassigny F 42 E4
Andlau F 43 D7
Andoain E 48 D1
Andocs H 165 C9
Andolsheim F 43 D7
Andorf A 92 F5
Andorno Micca I 84 B5
Andorra E 58 F2
Andorra la Vella AND 49 E9
Andosilla E 58 F1
Andouillé F 39 D10
Andover GB 29 C11
Andrano I 77 D10
Andratx E 65 E10
Andreas GBM 26 C3
Andreiaşu de Jos RO 169 F9
Andrespol PL 159 C7
Andrest F 49 D6
Andretta I 76 B4
Andria I 76 A6
Andrid RO 167 B9
Andrieşeni RO 169 B10
Andrijaševci HR 173 B10
Andrijevica MNE 179 D8
Andrioniškis LT 151 E10
Andriškiai LT 152 D6
Andritsaina GR 190 E4
Andronianoi GR 191 B9
Andros GR 192 D4
Androusa GR 190 E4
Andrup DK 102 D3
Andrupene LV 149 D2
Andrychów PL 163 B8
Andrzejewo PL 157 E6
Andselv N 127 C13
Andsnes N 128 C7
Andújar E 69 A8
Anduze F 51 B6
Andzeļi LV 149 D3
An Eachléim IRL 22 D2
Ænes N 110 C4
Aneby N 111 B13
Aneby S 108 D5
Anela I 80 C3
Anet F 40 C4
Anetjärvi FIN 137 C10
Anevo BG 181 D9
Aneza GR 190 A2
An Fál Carrach IRL 22 B6
An Féar Bán IRL 23 F7
An Fhairche IRL 22 E4

Ång S 108 D5
Anga S 109 E13
Änge S 121 E16
Ånge S 119 A10
Änge S 125 E14
An Geata Mór IRL 22 D2
Ängebo S 119 C11
Angeja P 60 C3
Ängelholm S 103 C11
Angeli FIN 129 F16
Angelniemi FIN 143 E8
Angelochori GR 185 C8
Angelokastro GR 190 B3
Angelokastro GR 191 D6
Ängelsberg S 113 C15
Angelstad S 103 B13
Angely F 41 E11
Anger D 89 A6
Angera I 84 B6
Angermünde D 100 D6
Angern an der March A 93 F11
Angers F 39 F10
Ångersjö S 118 C8
Ångersjö S 123 D16
Angersnes N 124 D4
Angerville F 40 D7
Angerville F 40 D7
Ångesån S 132 C8
Ängeslevä FIN 135 C15
Anghiari I 82 E5
Anglade F 44 E4
Angle GB 28 C2
Anglès E 59 D9
Anglès F 50 C2
Anglesola E 58 D6
Anglesona S 58 D5
Angles-sur-l'Anglin F 45 B7
Anglet F 48 D2
Angliers F 45 B6
Anglure F 41 C10
Agnäs S 123 D16
Angoisse F 45 D8
Ångom S 119 B13
An Gort IRL 22 F5
Angoulême F 45 D6
Angoulins F 44 C3
Angri I 76 B3
Angrie F 39 F9
Angüés E 58 C3
Anguiano E 56 D6
Anguillara Sabazia I 78 C2
Anguillara Veneta I 82 B4
Anguita E 63 B8
Angvik N 116 A8
Anha P 54 E2
Anhée B 35 D10
Anholt DK 103 B9
Aniane F 51 C6
Aniche F 35 D7
Anif A 89 A7
Anina RO 175 C8
Aninoasa RO 176 C2
Aninoasa RO 176 C3
Aninoasa RO 176 D2
Aninoasa RO 177 C6
Anizy-le-Château F 35 E7
Anjalankoski FIN 144 D6
Anjan S 121 D13
Anjum NL 32 B6
Ankaran SLO 89 E8
Ankarede Kapell S 121 B16
Ankarsrum S 109 D8
Ankarsund S 125 F12
Ankarsvik S 119 B13
Ankenes N 127 D13
Ankerlia N 128 E6
Ankershagen D 100 D3
Anklam D 100 C5
Ankum D 33 C9
Anlaby GB 27 D11
An Leadhb Gharbh IRL 22 C5
Anlezy F 46 B4
An Longfort IRL 23 E7
An Mám IRL 22 E3
An Mhala Raithní IRL 22 E3
An Móta IRL 23 F7
An Muileann gCearr IRL 23 E8
Ånn S 121 E13
Anna E 72 C2
Anna EST 147 C11
Annaberg A 93 G8
Annaberg-Buchholtz D 96 E4
Annaburg D 96 C4
Annagassan IRL 23 E10
Annagry IRL 22 B6
Annahilt GB 23 D10
Annahütte D 96 C5
Annalong GB 23 D11
Annamoe IRL 23 F10
Annan GB 21 F10
Anna Paulowna NL 32 C3
An Nás IRL 23 F9
Annayalla IRL 23 D9
Annbank GB 20 E7
Anneberg S 107 D11
Anneberg S 108 D5
Annecy F 47 D9
Annecy-le-Vieux F 47 D9
Annefors S 119 D11
Annelund S 107 D13
Annemasse F 47 C9
Annen NL 33 B7
Annenieki LV 150 C6
Annestown IRL 25 D8
Anneyron F 46 E6
Annikvere EST 147 C12
Annæullin F 198 D2
Annonay F 46 E6
Annonen FIN 135 F14
Annopol PL 160 B4
Annot F 52 C5
Annweiler am Trifels D 37 F9
Ano Agios Vlasios GR 190 B4
Ano Chora GR 190 B4
Ano Diakofto GR 190 C5
Ano Drosini GR 187 B9
Anoeta E 48 D1
Anogeia GR 190 D5
Anogeia GR 194 E8
Ano Kallinikis GR 184 C5
Ano Kardamyla GR 193 C7
Ano Kavallari GR 185 C9
Ano Komi GR 185 D6
Ano Kopanaki GR 190 E4
Ano Lechonia GR 185 F9
Ano Lefkimmi GR 184 F3
Ano Mera GR 192 D5
Añón E 57 E8
Ano Poroia GR 185 B9

Anor F 35 E9
Añora E 70 C3
Ano Sagkri GR 192 E5
Ano Steni GR 191 B8
Ano Syros GR 192 E4
Ano Trikala GR 190 D5
Ano Tyros GR 191 E6
Anould F 43 D6
Añover de Tajo E 62 E5
Ano Vrontou GR 185 B10
Anquela del Ducado E 63 C8
Anras A 88 C6
An Rinn IRL 25 D7
Anröchte D 201 A9
An Ros IRL 23 E10
Ans B 35 C12
Ans DK 102 C5
Ansac-sur-Vienne F 45 D7
Ansager DK 102 D3
Ansbach D 91 D8
An Sciobairin IRL 24 E4
Anse F 46 D6
Ansedonia I 81 C4
Anseremme B 35 D10
Ansfelden A 92 F6
Ansião P 60 E4
Ansızca TR 193 C9
Ansjö S 119 A11
Ansnes N 127 B15
Ansó E 48 E4
An Spidéal IRL 22 F4
Anspoki LV 151 D13
Ansprung D 96 E4
Ånstad N 126 C8
Anstruther GB 21 C11
Ånsvik N 125 B9
Antalieptė LT 151 E11
Antanhol P 60 D4
An tAonach IRL 24 C6
Antas E 71 E9
Antas P 54 E2
Antas P 60 C6
Antas de Ulla E 54 C4
An Teampall Mór IRL 25 C7
An Tearmann IRL 23 B7
Antequera E 69 B7
Anterselva di Sopra I 88 C5
Anthéor F 52 E5
Anthien F 41 F10
Anthili GR 191 B5
Anthotopos GR 191 A6
Anthrakitis GR 184 E4
Antibes F 52 D6
Antigonos GR 185 C6
Antikyra GR 191 C6
Antillo I 75 D7
Antimacheia GR 193 F9
An tInbhear Mór IRL 25 C10
Antiparos GR 192 E5
Antirrio GR 190 C4
Antisanti F 53 G10
Antissa GR 187 F9
Antjärn S 119 A14
Antnäs S 134 C7
Antoing B 35 C7
Antol SK 163 E7
Anton BG 181 D9
Anton Ivanov BG 181 E9
Antonivka UA 161 F6
Antonne-et-Trigonant F 45 E7
Antonovo BG 182 C6
Antony F 41 C7
Antraigues-sur-Volane F 46 F5
Antrain F 39 D9
Antrim GB 20 F4
Antrodoco I 78 C4
An tSeanga Mheáin IRL 22 C6
Antsla EST 147 F13
Anttis S 132 D9
Anttola FIN 144 B8
An Tulch IRL 25 C9
Antully F 46 B5
Antunovac Tenjski HR
165 F11
Antuži LV 151 C11
Antwerpen B 35 B9
Antzuola E 48 D1
An Uaimh IRL 23 E9
Anvers B 35 B9
Anvers B 198 C4
Anvin F 34 D5
Anykščiai LT 151 E10
Anzano di Puglia I 76 A4
Anzat-le-Luguet F 46 E3
Anzegem B 35 C7
Anzère CH 47 C11
Anzi I 76 B5
Anzin F 35 D7
Anzing D 91 F10
Anzio I 78 E3
Aoiz E 48 E3
Aoradh GB 20 D4
Aós E 48 E3
Aosta I 47 D11
Aouste-sur-Sye F 47 F7
Apa RO 167 B11
Apagy H 161 H4
Apahida RO 168 D3
Apaj H 166 C3
Apața RO 169 F7
Apateu RO 167 D8
Apátfalva H 166 E6
Apatin SRB 174 B2
Apatovac HR 165 D7
Apc H 166 B4
Ape LV 147 F13
Apecchio I 82 E5
A Pedreira E 54 D3
Apeiranthos GR 193 E6
Apeldoorn NL 32 D5
Apelern D 33 D12
Apele Vii RO 176 E4
Apen D 33 B9
Apenburg D 99 E10
Apensen D 98 D7
Aperi GR 197 E6
A Peroxa E 54 D4
Apgulde LV 150 C6
Apice I 76 A3
A Picota E 54 C2
Apidia GR 191 F6
Apiro I 83 F7
Aplared S 107 D13
A Pobla de Brollón E 54 C5
A Pobra de San Xiao E 54 C5
A Pobra de Trives E 54 D5
A Pobra do Caramiñal E 54 C2
Apoikia GR 192 D4
Apolakkia GR 197 D7
Apold RO 168 E5
Apolda D 95 D10
Apoldu de Jos RO 168 F3
Apollona GR 197 D7
Apollonas GR 193 E6
Apollonia GR 192 F4
A Pontenova E 54 B5
A Pontepedra E 54 B2
Áporka H 166 C3
Apostag H 165 C11
Apostoloi GR 194 E8
Äppelbo S 113 B11
Appenweier D 202 D4
Appenzell CH 43 F11
Appiano sulla Strada del Vino I
88 D3
Appietto F 53 G9
Appignano I 83 F7
Appingedam NL 33 B7
Appleby-in-Westmorland GB
26 B7
Appleby Magna GB 27 F8
Appledore GB 28 C6
Appledore GB 31 E10
Apprieu F 47 E7
Apremont-la-Forêt F 42 C4
Aprica I 85 A9
Apricena I 79 D8
Aprigliano I 77 E6
Apriki LV 150 C3
Aprilia I 78 D3
Aprilovo BG 182 C6
Apriltsi BG 181 D10
A Proba E 55 C6
Apsalos GR 185 C7
Apšuciems LV 150 B6
Apt F 51 C9
Aquaviva delle Fonti I 77 B7
Aquilonia I 76 B4
Aquilué E 48 F5
Aquino I 78 E5
Aracena E 67 D6
Arachnaio GR 191 D6
Arachova GR 191 C6
Aračinovo MK 180 E4
Arad RO 167 E7
Aradac SRB 174 C5
Arådalen S 118 A6
Aradeo I 77 C10
Aragnouet F 49 E6
Aragona I 74 E4
Aragoncillo E 63 C8
Araia E 48 E1
A Ramallosa E 54 C2
Aramits F 48 D4
Aramon F 51 C8
Aranda de Duero E 56 E4
Aranda de Moncayo E 57 E8
Aranđelovac SRB 174 E6
Aranhas P 61 D6
Aranitas AL 184 C2
Aranjuez E 62 D5
Arano E 48 D2
Aranzueque E 63 D6
Araovacık TR 189 E7
Arapaj AL 184 B2
Arapiles E 61 C9
Aras E 48 E1
Aras de Alpuente E 63 E10
Arasvika N 120 E4
Aratos GR 187 B9
Araules F 46 E5
Aravete EST 147 C11
Aravissos GR 185 C7
Arazede P 60 D3
Arbanasi BG 182 C5
Arbas F 49 E7
Arbatax I 80 D4
Arbeca E 58 D5
Arbecey F 42 E4
Arbedo CH 85 A7
Arbéost F 48 E5
Arberg D 91 D8
Arbesbach A 93 E7
Arbeteta E 63 C8
Arboga S 113 D14
Arbois F 47 B8
Arboleas E 71 E8
Arbon CH 43 E11
Arbore RO 169 B7
Arborea I 80 D2
Arborio I 84 C5
Årbostad N 127 C13
Arbrå S 119 D11
Arbroath GB 21 B11
Arbúcies E 59 D9
Arbus I 80 D2
Årby DK 103 D8
Årbyn S 134 C8
Arcachon F 48 A3
Arcangues F 48 D2
Arcani RO 175 C11
Arce I 78 D5
Arcen NL 32 F6
Arc-en-Barrois F 42 E3
Arces F 44 D4
Arces-Dilo F 41 D10
Arc-et-Senans F 47 A8
Arcevia I 83 E6
Archaia Epidavros GR 191 D7
Archaia Korinthos GR 191 D6
Archaia Olympia GR 190 D4
Archanes GR 194 E9
Archangelos GR 197 D8
Archar BG 175 F10
Archena E 71 C10
Archiac F 44 D5
Archidona E 69 B8
Archipoli GR 197 D8
Archiș RO 167 E9
Archivel E 71 C9
Arcidosso I 81 B5
Ārciems LV 147 F9
Arcis-sur-Aube F 41 C11
Arc-lès-Gray F 42 F4
Arco I 85 B10
Arco de Baúlhe P 54 F4
Arcola I 85 E8
Arçon F 47 B9
Arçonnay F 39 D12
Arcos E 56 D4
Arcos P 66 B4
Arcos de Jalón E 63 B8
Arcos de la Frontera E 68 C5
Arcos de las Salinas E 63 E10
Arcos de Valdevez P 54 E3
Arcozelo P 54 E2
Arcozelo P 54 E2
Arc-sur-Tille F 42 F3
Arcusa E 49 F6
Arda BG 187 B7
Ardagger Markt A 93 F7
Ardagh IRL 24 D4
Årdal N 116 C4
Ardala S 107 C13
Ardales E 69 C7
Årdalstangen N 116 D7
Ardanairy IRL 25 C10
Ardanaz E 48 E3
Ard an Rátha IRL 22 C6
Ardara I 80 B2
Ardara IRL 22 C6
Ardauli I 80 C2
Ardea I 78 D3
Ardee IRL 23 E9
Ardeluța RO 169 D8
Arden DK 102 B5
Arden GB 20 C7
Ardentes F 45 B9
Ardeoani RO 169 D9
Ardersier GB 19 K8
Ardes F 46 E3
Ardez CH 87 D10
Ardfern GB 20 C5
Ardfert IRL 24 D3
Ardfinnan IRL 25 D7
Ardgay GB 19 K8
Ardglass GB 23 D11
Ardgroom IRL 24 E3
Ardino BG 187 A8
Ardkeen GB 23 D11
Ardlui GB 20 C7
Ardlussa GB 20 C5
Ardmair GB 18 K6
Ardminish GB 20 D5
Ardmore IRL 22 F3
Ardmore IRL 25 E7
Ardon CH 47 C11
Ardooie B 35 C7
Ardore I 75 C9
Ardpatrick IRL 24 D5
Ardrahan IRL 22 F5
Ardre S 109 E13
Ardres F 34 C4
Ardrishaig GB 20 C6
Ardrossan GB 20 D7
Ardscull IRL 23 F9
Ardtoe GB 20 B5
Ardu EST 147 C10
Ardud RO 167 B10
Ardusat RO 167 B11
Ardvasar GB 20 A5
Are EST 147 D9
Åre S 121 E14
Areatza E 56 B6
Arefu RO 176 C5
Areias P 60 E4
Aremark N 112 D6
Arén E 58 C5
Arenas de Iguña E 56 B3
Arenas del Rey E 69 C9
Arenas de San Juan E 62 F6
Arenas de San Pedro E 61 D10
Arendal N 106 C4
Arendonk B 32 F4
Arendsee (Altmark) D 99 E10
Arengosse F 48 B4
Arenillas E 56 F6
Arenshausen D 95 D6
Arentorp S 107 C12
Arentsminde DK 102 A5
Arenys de Mar E 59 D9
Arenzano I 53 C9
Areopoli GR 194 B3
Areosa P 54 E2
Ares E 54 B3
Arès F 44 F3
Ares del Maestre E 64 D4
Aresing D 91 E9
Arespalditza E 56 B5
Arethousa GR 185 C10
Arette F 48 D4
Arette-Pierre-St-Martin F 48 E4
Aretxabaleta E 57 B7
Arevalillo E 61 C10
Arévalo E 62 B3
Arezzo I 82 F4
Arfara GR 190 E5
Arfons F 49 D10
Årfor N 121 B11
Argalasti GR 185 F9
Argallón E 67 C9
Argamasilla de Alba E 63 F6
Argamasilla de Calatrava E
70 B4
Argamasón E 71 B8
Arganda del Rey E 62 D6
Arganil P 60 D4
Arganza E 55 C6
Årgård N 121 C10
Argegno I 85 B7
Argelès-Gazost F 48 E5
Argelès-sur-Mer F 50 E5
Argeliers F 50 D4
Argelita E 64 D4
Argenbühl D 87 B9
Argences F 39 B11
Argenta I 82 C4
Argentan F 39 C11
Argentat F 45 E9
Argente E 63 C10
Argentera I 52 C5
Argenteuil F 41 C7
Argenthal D 37 E9
Argentiera I 80 B1
Argentière F 47 D10
Argentine F 47 E9
Argenton-Château F 44 B5
Argenton-sur-Creuse F 45 B9
Argentre F 39 D10
Argentré-du-Plessis F 39 D9
Argent-sur-Sauldre F 41 E7
Argés E 62 E4
Argetoaia RO 175 D11
Arginonta GR 193 E8
Argonay F 47 D9
Argos GR 191 D6
Argos Orestiko GR 184 D5
Argostoli GR 190 C1
Argouges F 39 D9
Arguedas E 57 D8
Argueil F 34 E4
Arguellite E 71 C8
Arguís E 48 F5
Arguisuelas E 63 E9
Argujillo E 55 F8
Argyrades GR 184 F2
Argyropouli GR 185 E7
Århult S 105 A10
Århus DK 102 C6
Ariano Irpino I 76 A4
Ariano nel Polesine I 82 C5
Ariany E 73 B11
Aribe E 48 E3
Ariccia I 78 D3
Aridaia GR 185 C7
Arieșeni RO 167 E10
Arignac F 49 E9
Arija E 56 C4
Arild S 103 C11
Arileod GB 20 B3
Arilje SRB 174 F5
Arinagour GB 20 B3
Ariniș RO 167 C11
Ariño E 58 E2
Arinsal AND 49 E8
Arinthod F 47 C8
Ariogala LT 150 F6
Aris GR 190 E5
Arisaig GB 20 B5
Aristomenis GR 190 E4
Arisvi GR 187 B9
Aritzo I 80 D3
Ariz P 60 C5
Ariza E 57 F7
Arizgoiti E 56 B6
Arizola E 48 E2
Årjäng S 112 D7
Arjeplog S 125 D14
Arjona E 69 A8
Arjonilla E 69 A8
Arkala FIN 135 D16
Arkalochori GR 194 E9
Arkasa GR 197 F6
Arkelstorp S 104 C6
Arkesini GR 196 C3
Arkitsa GR 191 B7
Arkkukari FIN 135 E12
Arklow IRL 25 C10
Arkna EST 147 C12
Arkösund S 109 C9
Ärla S 114 D7
Arlanc F 46 E4
Arlanzón E 56 D5
Arle (Großheide) D 33 A8
Arlena di Castro I 78 C1
Arles F 51 C8
Arleuf F 46 A5
Arleux F 35 D7
Arligbo S 114 B8
Arló H 161 G1
Arlon B 35 E12
Arluno I 85 B6
Arlyeya BY 149 E6
Armação de Pêra P 66 E3
Armadale GB 21 D9
Armağan TR 183 F8
Armagh GB 23 D9
Armallones E 63 C8
Armamar P 60 B5
Armășești RO 177 D9
Armasjärvi S 135 B11
Armassaari FIN 135 B11
Armen AL 184 C2
Armenioi GR 190 E4
Armeniș RO 175 C9
Armenistis GR 193 D7
Armeno I 84 B5
Armenochori GR 184 C5
Armenoi GR 194 E7
Armenteros E 61 C10
Armentières F 34 C6
Armento I 76 C6
Armilla E 69 B9
Armissan F 50 D5
Armolia GR 193 C7
Armoy GB 20 E4
Armsheim D 201 E9
Armuña E 62 B4
Armungia I 80 D3
Armunia E 55 C8
Armutalanı TR 197 C8
Armutlu TR 189 C10
Armutlu TR 193 C10
Arna GR 190 F5
Arnac-Pompadour F 45 E8
Arnad I 84 B4
Arnage F 39 E12
Arnaia GR 185 D10
Årnäs S 107 B14
Årnäs S 118 D5
Årnäs S 118 E5
Arnäsvall S 123 E15
Arnavutköy TR 189 B10
Arnay-le-Duc F 41 F11
Arnberg S 123 B16
Arnborg DK 102 C3
Arnbruck D 92 D3
Arneburg D 99 E12
Arnedillo E 57 D7
Arnedo E 57 D7
Arnéguy F 48 D3
Arnemark S 134 D6
Arnemuiden NL 32 F1
Arnes E 58 F4
Årnes N 111 B14
Årnes N 120 F5
Årnes N 127 B15
Arnfels A 164 C4
Arnhem NL 32 E5
Arnionys 1 LT 153 C12
Arnissa GR 185 C6
Arnö S 109 B10
Arnol GB 18 J3
Arnold GB 27 E9
Arnoldstein A 89 C8
Arnót H 161 G2
Arnöviken S 119 C13
Arnøyhamn N 128 C6
Arnprior GB 21 C8
Arnsberg D 33 F10
Arnschwang D 92 D3
Arnstadt D 95 E8
Arnstein D 90 C6
Arnstorf D 92 E3
Arnum DK 102 E3
Aroania GR 190 D5
Ároktő H 167 B6
Arola FIN 129 D20
Arolla CH 47 C11
Arolsen D 33 F12
Aron F 39 D10
Arona I 84 B6
Aroneanu RO 169 C11
Aronkylä FIN 138 F8
Åros N 111 C12
Arosa CH 87 D9
Arosa P 54 E3
Årosjäkk S 127 E17
Arouca P 60 C4
Årøybukta N 127 A19
Årøysund N 106 A7
Arpajon F 41 C7
Arpajon-sur-Cère F 45 F10
Arpașu de Jos RO 168 F5
Arpela FIN 135 B12
Arpino I 78 D5
Arquata del Tronto I 78 B4
Arquata Scrivia I 53 B9
Arques F 34 C5
Arques F 49 E10
Arques-la-Bataille F 34 E3
Arquillos E 71 C6
Arrabalde E 55 D8
Arracourt F 42 C6
Arradon F 38 E6
Arraiolos P 66 B4
Arrakoski FIN 143 C13
Arranhó P 66 B1
Arras F 34 D6
Arrasate E 57 B7
Årre DK 102 D3
Arreau F 49 E6
Arredondo E 56 B4
Arrën AL 179 F9
Årrenjarka S 125 C15
Arrentières F 41 D12
Arriach A 89 C8
Arriana GR 187 B9
Arriate E 69 C6
Arrifana P 61 C6
Arrigny F 41 C12
Arrigorriaga E 56 B6
Arrild DK 102 E3
Arriondas E 55 B9
Arroba de los Montes E 62 F3
Arrochar GB 20 C7
Arronches P 61 F6
Arrone I 78 B3
Arroniz E 48 E1
Arrou F 40 D5
Arroyal E 56 C3
Arroyo de la Luz E 61 E7
Arroyo del Ojanco E 71 C7
Arroyo de San Serván E 67 B7
Arroyomolinos de León E 67 C7
Arruda dos Vinhos P 66 B1
Arry F 202 C1
Årsandøy N 121 A12
Årsdale DK 105 E8
Arseni GR 185 C7
Ars-en-Ré F 44 C2
Årset N 121 A11
Arsiè I 88 E4
Arsiero I 85 B11
Årslev DK 102 E6
Arsoli I 78 C4
Ars-sur-Formans F 46 D6
Ars-sur-Moselle F 42 B5
Årstein N 127 C14
Årsunda S 114 A7
Arsura RO 169 D12
Arsvågen N 110 D2
Artà E 73 B11
Arta GR 190 A2
Artajona E 48 E2
Artana E 64 E4
Artannes-sur-Indre F 40 F4
Artemisia GR 190 E5
Artemisio GR 190 D5
Artemisio GR 191 A7
Artèn I 88 D4
Artena I 78 D3
Artenay F 40 D6
Artern (Unstrut) D 95 D9
Artés E 59 D7
Artesa de Segre E 58 D6
Artesiano GR 185 F6
Arth CH 87 C7
Arthez-d'Asson F 48 D5
Arthez-de-Béarn F 48 D4
Arthon F 45 B9
Arthon-en-Retz F 39 F8
Artieda E 48 E4
Artigarvan GB 20 F2
Artigat F 49 D8
Artix F 48 D4
Artjärvi FIN 143 D15
Ärtled S 119 E9
Artlenburg D 99 D8
Artogne I 85 B9
Ärtrik S 123 E11
Artsyz UA 170 F4
Artziniega E 56 B5
A Rúa E 54 D5
Arudy F 48 D5
Aruküla EST 147 C10
Aruküla EST 147 C12
Arundel GB 31 F7
Årvågen N 120 E5
Arvagh IRL 23 E7
Arvån S 123 B16
Arvesund S 121 E16
Arveyres F 44 F5
Arvi GR 194 F9
Arvidsjaur S 125 E17
Arvidsträsk S 134 C5
Arvieu F 50 B4
Arvieux F 47 F10
Årvik N 116 B3
Arvika S 113 C8
Årviksand N 128 C6
Arvila EST 147 C14
Aryd S 105 B7
Åryd S 105 C8
Arzachena I 80 A3
Arzacq-Arraziguet F 48 C5
Arzana I 80 D4
Aržano HR 173 E7
Arzbach D 37 D9
Arzberg D 91 B11
Arzberg D 96 C4
Arzfeld D 36 D6
Arzignano I 82 A3
Arzl im Pitztal A 87 C11
Arzúa E 54 C3
As B 35 B12
Aš CZ 91 B11
Ås N 111 C13
Ås N 121 E11
Ås S 112 C7
Ås S 113 C12
Ås S 122 E7
Ås S 123 E11
Åsa N 111 B12
Åsa S 107 E11
Asaa DK 102 A6
Aşağıçobanisa TR 193 B10
Aşağısevindikli TR 189 B8
Åsan N 121 B12
Ašanja SRB 174 D5
Asare LV 151 D11
Åsarna S 118 A7
Åsarp S 107 C14
Asasp-Arros F 48 D4
Asbach D 37 C8
Åsbacka S 119 D11
Åsby S 103 A10
Åsby S 108 D6
Ascain F 48 D2
Ascea I 76 C4
Aschach an der Donau A 92 F6
Aschaffenburg D 37 E12
Aschbach Markt A 93 F7
Ascheberg D 33 E9
Ascheberg (Holstein) D 99 B8
Aschères-le-Marché F 40 D7
Aschersleben D 95 C9
Așchileu RO 167 D11
Asciano I 82 F4
Ascó E 58 E5
Asco F 53 G10
Ascoli Piceno I 78 B5
Ascoli Satriano I 76 A5
Ascona CH 84 A6
Ascou F 49 E9
As Covas E 54 D2
Åse N 127 B10
Åsebyn S 112 D7
Åseda S 105 A8
Åsegg N 121 C9
Åsele S 123 C12
Åselet S 134 D4
Asemakylä FIN 135 D14
Asemankylä FIN 135 D14
Asemanseutu FIN 139 E11
Åsen N 121 D10
Åsen S 118 C7
Åsen S 118 D6
Åsen S 122 E7
Åsen S 125 E16
Åsenbruk S 107 B11
Asendorf D 33 C12
Asenovets BG 182 D5
Asenovgrad BG 181 E10
Asenovo BG 182 C6
Asenovtsi BG 181 C11
Åseral N 106 B1
Aseri EST 147 C13
A Serra de Outes E 54 C2
Asfaka GR 184 E4
Asfeld F 35 F9
Asfendiou GR 193 F9
Asferg DK 102 B5
Asgårstrand N 111 D12
Ash GB 31 E7
Åshammar S 119 E12
Ashbourne GB 27 E8
Ashbourne IRL 23 E10
Ashburton GB 29 D7
Ashbury GB 29 B11
Ashby de la Zouch GB 27 F9
Ashcott GB 29 C9
Ashevo RUS 149 B7
Ashford GB 29 D11
Ashford GB 31 E10
Ashford IRL 23 F10
Ashford IRL 24 D4
Ashill GB 31 B10
Ashington GB 21 E13
Ashkirk GB 21 E11
Ashley GB 31 C9
Ashmyany BY 153 D13
Ashmyany BY 153 E12
Ashton-under-Lyne GB 27 E7
Ashurst GB 29 D11
Ashwick GB 29 C9
Asiago I 88 E4
Asikkala FIN 143 C14
Asilah MA 68 F4
Asimi GR 194 E9
Asín E 48 F3
Asiros GR 185 C9
Ask N 111 B14
Aska FIN 133 D17
Askainen FIN 142 D6
Askeaton IRL 24 C5
Asker N 111 C12
Askern GB 27 D9
Askersby S 108 A6
Askersund S 108 B5
Åskilje S 123 B13
Askim N 111 C14
Asklipieio GR 191 D7
Asklipieio GR 197 D7
Åskogen S 134 C7
Askola FIN 143 D14
Asköping S 108 A8
Askos GR 185 C9
Askvoll N 116 D2
Aslakkala FIN 129 E16
Aslestad N 110 D7
Åsli N 117 E11
Åsljunga S 103 C12
Asmalı TR 189 C8
Åsmansbo S 113 B13
Åsmarka N 117 D13
Asmunti FIN 135 C17
Asnæs DK 103 D8
As Neves E 54 B3
As Neves E 54 D3
As Nogais E 54 C5
Asola I 82 B1
Asolo I 88 E4
Asopia GR 191 C8
Asopos GR 194 B4
Asos GR 190 C2
Ásotthalom H 166 E4
Asp DK 102 C3
Aspa S 109 B10
Aspa bruk S 108 B5
Aspach A 92 F4
Aspan S 118 B8
Aspang-Markt A 164 A6
Asparn an der Zaya A 93 E10
Asparukhovo BG 183 D8
Aspås S 122 E6
Aspatria GB 21 F10
Aspe E 72 E3
Aspe S 113 B8
Aspeå S 123 E12
Aspele S 123 D14
Asperen NL 199 B6
Aspet F 49 D7
Asphyltan S 113 C11
Aspliden S 125 F17
Aspliden S 134 B7
Aspnäs S 115 B8
Aspnäs S 119 A14
As Pontes de García Rodríguez
E 54 B4
Aspremont F 51 A10
Aspres-sur-Buëch F 51 A10
Aspropyrgos GR 191 C8
Asprovalta GR 185 C10
Aspudden S 132 E3
As Rodrigas E 54 B5
Assamstadt D 90 D6
Asse B 35 C9
Assebakti N 129 E15
Asseiceira P 60 E4
Assemini I 80 E3
Assen NL 33 B7
Assendelft NL 32 D3
Assenede B 32 F2
Assens DK 102 B6
Assens DK 102 E5
Assentoft DK 102 C6
Assérac F 39 F7
Assergi I 78 C5
Assesse B 35 D11
Assier F 49 A9
Assisi I 78 A3
Åssjö S 119 B12
Åsskard N 120 E5
Aßlar D 37 C10
Assling A 89 C6
Asso I 85 B7
Asson F 48 D5
Assoro I 74 D5
Assos GR 184 F4
Assumar P 60 F6
Åsta N 117 D14
Astaffort F 49 B7
Astakos GR 190 B3
Åstan N 120 E7
Astašova LV 149 D2
Aste EST 146 E4
Åsteby S 113 B9
Astee IRL 24 C3
Asten A 92 F6
Asten NL 32 F5
Asti I 53 B8
Astikkala FIN 145 B12
Aștileu RO 167 C9
Astomilitsa GR 184 D4
Aston Clinton GB 31 D7
Astorga E 55 D7
Åstorp S 103 C11
Åstrand S 113 B9
Astravyets BY 153 D12
Astros GR 191 E6
Astrowna BY 149 F7
Astrowshchyna BY 149 F4
Astrup DK 102 B5
Astrup DK 102 C3
Astrup DK 106 E7
Astudillo E 56 D3
Astypalaia GR 196 C4
Asuaju de Sus RO 167 B11
Asūne LV 149 D3
Asuni I 80 D2
Asunta FIN 139 F13
Ásványráró H 162 F5
Asvestopetra GR 185 D6
Asvyeya BY 149 D4
Aszaló H 161 G2
Aszód H 166 B3
Atalaia P 60 F4
Atalaia P 60 F5
Atalanti GR 191 B7
Atalaya del Cañavate E 63 E8
Ataquines E 62 B3
Atarfe E 69 B9
Atašiene LV 151 C12
Atea E 63 B9
Ateca E 57 F8
A Teixeira E 54 D5
Ațel RO 168 E4
Ateleta I 79 D6
Atella I 76 B5
Atena Lucana I 76 C5
Ätervänningen S 119 A13
Atessa I 79 C6
Ath B 35 C8
Athani GR 190 B2
Áth an Sceire IRL 23 F10
Athboy IRL 23 E9
Athea IRL 24 D4
Athenry IRL 22 F5
Athenstedt D 95 C8
Atheras GR 190 C1
Atherington GB 28 D6
Atherstone GB 27 F8
Athies F 34 E6
Athies-sous-Laon F 35 E8
Athikia GR 191 D6
Athina GR 191 D8
Athis-de-l'Orne F 39 C11
Athleague IRL 22 E6
Athlone IRL 23 F7
Áth Trasna IRL 24 D4
Athy IRL 23 G9
Athyra GR 185 C8
Atid RO 168 E6
Atienza E 63 B7
Atina I 78 D5
Ațintiș RO 168 E4
Atjiken S 123 A9
Atkár H 166 B4
Atna N 117 C13
Åtorp S 108 A4
Atouguia da Baleia P 60 F2
Åtran S 103 A11
Åträsk S 134 B7
Åträsk S 134 D5
Atri I 78 B5
Atripalda I 76 B3
Atsiki GR 187 E8
Attadale GB 18 L6
Attala H 165 D10
Attali GR 191 B8
Attanagh IRL 25 C8
Attavalley IRL 22 D3
Attendorn D 37 B9
Attenkirchen D 91 E10
Attersee A 89 A8
Attert B 35 E12
Attica GB 23 D10
Attigliano I 78 B2
Attignat F 47 C7
Attigny F 35 F10
Attleborough GB 31 B11
Attnang A 92 F5
Åttonträsk S 123 C14
Attu FIN 142 E7
Atur F 45 E7
Åtvidaberg S 108 C7
Atzara I 80 D3
Atzenbrugg A 93 F9
Atzendorf D 95 C10
Atzeneta del Maestrat E 64 D4
Au A 87 C9
Au CH 87 C9
Aub D 91 C7
Aubagne F 51 D10
Aubange B 35 E12
Aube F 40 C4
Aubel B 199 D7
Aubenas F 51 A7
Aubenton F 35 E9
Aubergenville F 40 C6
Auberive F 42 E3
Aubeterre-sur-Dronne F 45 E6
Aubiet F 49 C7
Aubignan F 51 B9
Aubigné-Racan F 39 E12
Aubignosc F 51 B10
Aubigny F 44 B3
Aubigny-en-Artois F 34 D6
Aubigny-sur-Nère F 41 F7
Aubin F 49 A10

Aubonne CH 47 B9
Aubord F 51 C7
Aboué F 36 F5
Aubusson F 45 D10
Auby F 35 D7
Aucamville F 49 C8
Auce LV 150 D5
Auch F 49 C7
Auchallater GB 21 B10
Auchenbreck GB 20 D6
Auchencairn GB 21 F9
Auchencrow GB 21 D12
Auchnagatt GB 19 L12
Auchterarder GB 21 C9
Auchtermuchty GB 21 C10
Auchy-au-Bois F 34 C5
Aucun F 48 E5
Audenge F 48 A3
Auderville F 39 A8
Audeux F 42 F4
Audevälja EST 147 C8
Audierne F 38 D2
Audlem GB 26 F6
Audley GB 27 E7
Audnedal N 106 C1
Audon F 48 C4
Audresselles F 31 F12
Audriņi LV 149 C2
Audru EST 147 E8
Audruicq F 34 C5
Audun-le-Roman F 36 F5
Aue D 95 E12
Auerbach D 91 A11
Auerbach in der Oberpfalz D 91 C10
Auersthal A 93 F11
Auffay F 34 E3
Aufhausen D 91 E11
Augbrim IRL 22 F5
Auggen D 43 E8
Augher GB 23 D8
Aughnacloy GB 23 D9
Aughrim IRL 22 F5
Aughrim IRL 25 C10
Aughton GB 27 E9
Augsburg D 91 F8
Augšlīgatne LV 151 B10
Augstkalne LV 149 E2
Augstkalne LV 150 D6
Augusta I 75 E7
Auguste LV 150 D3
Augustenborg DK 102 F5
Augustów PL 152 F6
Augustowo PL 157 E8
Augustusburg D 96 E4
Auho FIN 137 E10
Aukan N 120 E4
Aukra N 116 A5
Aukrug D 98 B7
Aukštadvaris LT 153 D10
Aukštelkai LT 150 E7
Aukštelkė LT 150 E6
Auktsjaur S 125 E17
Auleja LV 149 D2
Auletta I 76 B4
Aulla I 85 E8
Aullène F 53 H10
Aulnat F 46 D3
Aulnay F 44 C5
Aulnay-sous-Bois F 41 C8
Aulnois-sur-Seille F 42 C5
Aulnoye-Aymeries F 35 D8
Aulon F 49 D7
Aulosen D 99 E11
Ault F 34 D3
Aultbea GB 18 K5
Aultguish Inn GB 18 K7
Aulus-les-Bains F 49 E8
Auma D 95 E10
Aumale F 34 E4
Aumetz F 36 F5
Aumont F 47 B8
Aumont-Aubrac F 46 F3
Aumühle D 99 C8
Aunay-en-Bazois F 41 F10
Aunay-sur-Odon F 39 B10
Auneau F 40 D6
Aunegrenda N 121 F10
Aunfoss N 121 B13
Auning DK 102 C6
Auñón E 63 C7
Aups F 52 D4
Aurach D 91 D8
Aurach bei Kitzbühel A 88 B5
Aura im Sinngrund D 90 B6
Auran N 121 E9
Auray F 38 E6
Aurdal N 117 E10
Aure N 120 E5
Aurec-sur-Loire F 46 E5
Aureilhan F 49 D6
Aureille F 51 C8
Aurel F 51 A9
Aurel F 51 B9
Aurensan F 48 C5
Aureosen N 116 A6
Auri LV 150 C6
Aurich D 33 B8
Aurignac F 49 D7
Aurillac F 45 F10
Auriol F 51 D10
Aurisina I 89 E8
Auritz E 48 E3
Aurland N 116 E6
Aurolzmünster A 92 F4
Auron F 52 C5
Auronzo di Cadore I 88 C5
Auros F 48 A5
Auroux F 46 F4
Aurskog N 111 C14
Ausa-Corno I 89 E7
Ausejo E 48 F1
Auseu RO 167 C10
Ausleben D 95 B9
Ausmas LV 151 B9
Ausonia I 78 E5
Außervillgraten A 88 C5
Aussillon F 49 C10
Aussonne F 49 C8
Austad N 106 C2
Austbø N 111 C8
Austertana N 130 C5
Austfjord N 121 B9
Austis I 80 C3
Austmannli N 110 C5
Austnes N 116 A4
Austnes N 121 B15
Austnes N 127 C12

Austråt N 120 D7
Austsmøla N 120 E4
Auterive F 49 D8
Authon F 40 E4
Authon F 52 C4
Authon-du-Perche F 40 D4
Autio FIN 135 E17
Autio FIN 139 E13
Autol E 57 D7
Autrans F 47 E8
Autreville F 42 D4
Autrey-lès-Gray F 42 F3
Autry F 35 F10
Autti FIN 135 B18
Auttoinen FIN 143 C13
Autun F 46 B5
Auve F 41 C11
Auvelais B 35 D10
Auvers-le-Hamon F 39 E11
Auvillar F 49 B7
Auvillers-les-Forges F 200 E1
Auxerre F 41 E10
Auxi-le-Château F 34 D5
Auxonne F 42 F3
Auxy F 46 B5
Auzances F 45 C10
Auzat F 49 E8
Auzat-sur-Allier F 46 E3
Auzon F 46 E3
Åva FIN 142 E5
Ava S 123 D16
Availles-Limouzine F 45 C7
Avaldsnes N 110 D2
Avallon F 41 E10
Avan S 134 C7
Avanäs S 123 C17
Avança P 60 C3
Avançon F 52 B4
Avantas GR 187 C9
Avant lès Ramerupt F 41 D11
Avasjö S 123 C11
Avato GR 187 C7
Avaträsk S 123 C10
Avaviken S 125 E16
Avdira GR 187 C7
Avdou GR 194 E9
A Veiga E 55 D6
Aveiras de Cima P 60 F3
Aveiro P 60 C3
Avelar P 60 D4
Avelås de Caminho P 60 D4
Aveleda P 55 D4
Aveleda S 55 E6
Avelgem B 35 C7
Avella I 76 B3
Avellino I 76 B3
Avenay-Val-d'Or F 41 B11
Avenches CH 47 B11
Avenhorn NL 32 C3
Avenida do Marquês de Figueroa E 54 A3
Avermes F 46 B3
Aversa I 76 B1
Avesnes-le-Comte F 34 D6
Avesnes-sur-Helpe F 35 D8
Avesta S 114 B6
Åvestbo S 113 C14
Avetrano I 77 C9
Avezzano I 78 C4
Avgerinos GR 184 D5
Avià E 59 C7
Aviano I 89 D6
Aviemore GB 19 L9
Avigliana I 47 E11
Avigliano I 76 B5
Avigliano Umbro I 78 B2
Avignon F 51 C8
Ávila E 62 C3
Avilley F 42 F5
Avintes P 60 B3
Avinurme EST 147 D13
Aviñyó E 59 D7
Avio I 85 B10
Avion F 34 C6
Avioth F 35 E11
Avis P 60 F5
Avispea EST 147 C12
Åvist FIN 138 D8
Avize F 41 C11
Avižieniai LT 153 D11
Avlakia GR 193 D8
Avlemonas GR 194 C5
Avliotes GR 184 E2
Avlonari GR 191 B9
Avlonas GR 191 C8
Avlum DK 102 C3
Avoca IRL 25 C10
Avoine F 39 F12
Avola I 75 F7
Avon F 41 D8
Avonmouth GB 29 B9
Avord F 45 A11
Avoriaz F 47 C10
Avoudrey F 42 F5
Avrämeni RO 169 A9
Avrämeşti RO 168 E6
Avram Iancu RO 167 D10
Avram Iancu RO 167 E10
Avranches F 39 C9
Avren BG 187 B9
Avricourt F 202 D2
Avrig RO 168 F4
Avril F 36 F5
Avrillé F 39 E10
Avrillé F 44 C3
Avtovac BIH 173 F10
Av'ze N 128 E12
Awans B 199 D6
Axams A 88 B3
Axat F 49 E10
Axel NL 32 F1
Axente Sever RO 168 E4
Axintele RO 177 D9
Axioupoli GR 185 C8
Ax-les-Thermes F 49 E9
Axmar S 119 D13
Axmarsbruk S 119 D13
Axminster GB 29 D9
Axos GR 185 C2
Axvall S 107 C14
Ayamonte E 66 E5
Aycliffe GB 21 F13
Aydat F 46 D3
Aydemir BG 177 E10
Ayen F 45 E8
Ayerbe E 48 F4
Aying D 88 A4
Aylesbury GB 31 D7

Ayllón E 56 F5
Aylsham GB 31 B11
Âĵcles RO 175 E11
Bacoli I 76 B2
Bacúmanu F 37 C6
Bacquevile-en-Caux F 34 E2
Ayora E 63 F10
Ayr GB 20 E7
Ayrancılar TR 193 C9
Ayron F 44 B6
Aysebacı TR 189 E10
Aysgarth GB 27 C8
Åyskoski FIN 139 D17
Aytos E 59 E8
Aytré F 44 C3
Ayvacık TR 187 E10
Ayvalık GB 35 D12
Azagra E 48 F2
Azaila E 57 F11
Azambuja P 60 F3
Azanja SRB 175 E6
Azanúy E 58 D4
Azaña P 66 B4
Azatlı TR 188 B6
Azay-le-Ferron F 45 B8
Azay-le-Rideau F 40 F3
Azé F 39 E10
Azerables F 45 C8
Azina BY 149 E5
Azinhaga P 60 F3
Azinhal P 66 E5
Azinheira dos Barros P 66 C3
Azinhoso P 55 F6
Azkoitia E 48 D1
Aznalcázar E 67 E7
Aznalcóllar E 67 D7
Azóia P 66 C1
Azpeitia E 48 D1
Azuaga E 67 C8
Azuara E 57 F10
Azuelo E 48 E1
Azuel E 70 C4
Azután E 61 E10
Azy-le-Vif F 46 B3
Azyory BY 156 C10
Azzano Decimo I 89 E6
Azzone I 85 B9

B

Baalberge D 95 C10
Baällon F 35 F11
Baar CH 87 B9
Baarle-Hertog B 32 F3
Baarle-Nassau NL 32 F3
Baarn NL 32 D4
Baba Ana RO 177 D8
Babadag RO 171 D3
Babaeski TR 189 B7
Babaköy TR 189 C9
Baban AL 184 C4
Bābana RO 176 D5
Babberich NL 199 B8
Babchyntsi UA 170 A2
Babenhausen D 37 E11
Băbeni RO 167 C11
Băbeni RO 176 C3
Babiak PL 152 E1
Babiak PL 154 F6
Babice CZ 162 C4
Babice PL 159 F7
Babice nad Svitavou CZ 93 D11
Babići BIH 173 D7
Băbiciu RO 176 E5
Babigoszcz PL 100 D6
Babilafuente E 61 C10
Babimost PL 97 B9
Babin SK 163 C8
Babina Greda HR 173 B3
Babino Polje HR 178 D4
Babīte LV 150 C5
Babócsa H 165 D6
Bábolna H 165 A9
Baborów PL 158 F4
Babòt H 165 A8
Babrruje AL 184 B2
Babtai LT 153 C8
Babuk BG 177 E10
Babušnica SRB 180 C5
Babyak BG 181 F8
Babynichy BY 149 F4
Baċ MNE 179 D7
Bač SRB 174 C3
Băcani RO 169 E11
Bacares E 71 E8
Baccarat F 43 D6
Baceno I 84 A5
Băcești RO 169 D10
Bach A 87 C10
Bacharach D 37 D9
Bachkovo BG 181 F10
Bachórz PL 160 D5
Băcia RO 167 F11
Baciki Bliższe PL 157 F7
Baciu RO 168 D3
Băck S 121 E16
Backa S 107 B10
Backa S 113 A9
Backa S 113 D9
Backaland GB 19 G11
Bačka Palanka SRB 174 C3
Backaryd S 105 C9
Bačka Topola SRB 166 F4
Backberg S 119 E12
Backe S 123 D10
Backe S 125 B10
Bäckefors S 107 B13
Bäckhammar S 107 A15
Bäcki Breg SRB 166 F2
Bački Brestovac SRB 174 B3
Bački Jarak SRB 174 C4
Bački Monoštor SRB 166 F2
Bačkininkai LT 153 D8
Bački Petrovac SRB 174 C4
Bäcklund S 125 E17
Bäckmark S 123 A11
Backnang D 43 C11
Bäcknäs S 125 F17
Bačko Dobro Polje SRB 174 C4
Bačko Gradište SRB 174 C5
Bačko Novo Selo SRB 173 B11
Bačko Petrovo Selo SRB 174 B5
Baćkowice PL 159 E11

Backträsk S 134 C6
Bäckvalen S 118 B8
Bacău RO 169 D9
Bad Abbach D 91 E11
Bad Aibling D 88 A5
Badalona E 59 E8
Badalucco I 53 D7
Bădames E 56 B5
Badarán E 56 D6
Bad Bederkesa D 33 A11
Bad Bentheim D 33 D8
Bad Bergzabern D 43 D9
Bad Berka D 95 E9
Bad Berleburg D 37 B10
Bad Berneck im Fichtelgebirge D 91 B10
Bad Bertrich D 37 D8
Bad Bevensen D 99 D9
Bad Bibra D 95 D10
Bad Birnbach D 92 F4
Bad Blankenburg D 95 E9
Bad Bocklet D 91 B7
Bad Brambach D 91 B11
Bad Bramstedt D 99 C7
Bad Breisig D 201 D7
Bad Brückenau D 90 B6
Bad Buchau D 87 E11
Bad Camberg D 37 D10
Badcaul GB 18 K6
Badderen N 128 D9
Bad Doberan D 99 B11
Bad Driburg D 33 E12
Bad Düben D 95 C12
Bad Dürkheim D 37 E10
Bad Dürrenberg D 95 D11
Bad Dürrheim D 43 D10
Badeborn D 95 C9
Badefols-d'Ans F 45 E8
Bad Elster D 91 B11
Bademler TR 193 C8
Bademli TR 189 D10
Bademli TR 193 B8
Bad Ems D 37 D9
Baden A 93 F10
Baden CH 43 F9
Baden F 38 E6
Bådenas E 63 B10
Baden-Baden D 43 C9
Bad Endorf D 88 A5
Badenweiler D 43 E8
Baderna HR 83 B8
Badersleben D 95 C8
Badesi I 80 B2
Bad Essen D 33 C10
Bădeuţi RO 169 B8
Bad Feilnbach D 88 A5
Bad Frankenhausen (Kyffhäuser) D 95 D9
Bad Freienwalde D 100 E6
Bad Friedrichshall D 37 F12
Bad Füssing D 92 F4
Bad Gams A 89 C11
Bad Gandersheim D 95 C7
Badgastein A 89 B7
Bad Gleichenberg A 164 C5
Bad Goisern A 89 A8
Bad Grönenbach D 87 F10
Bad Grund (Harz) D 95 C7
Bad Hall A 92 F6
Bad Harzburg D 95 C8
Bad Hersfeld D 94 E6
Badhoevedorp NL 198 A5
Bad Hofgastein A 89 B7
Bad Homburg vor der Höhe D 37 D11
Bad Honnef D 37 C8
Bad Hönningen D 201 C7
Badia I 75 B10
Badia Calavena I 85 B11
Badia Gran E 65 F10
Badia Polesine I 82 B3
Badia Tedalda I 82 E5
Bad Iburg D 33 D10
Bădiceni MD 169 A12
Bad Ischl A 89 B8
Bad Karlshafen D 94 C5
Bad Kissingen D 91 B7
Bad Kleinen D 99 C10
Bad Kleinkirchheim A 89 C8
Bad König D 37 E12
Bad Königshofen im Grabfeld D 91 B7
Bad Kösen D 95 D10
Bad Köstritz D 95 E11
Bądkowo PL 154 E6
Bad Kreuzen A 93 F7
Bad Kreuznach D 37 E8
Bad Krozingen D 43 E8
Bad Laasphe D 37 C10
Bad Laer D 33 D10
Bad Langensalza D 95 D8
Bad Lauchstädt D 95 D10
Bad Lausick D 95 D12
Bad Lauterberg im Harz D 95 C7
Bad Leonfelden A 92 E6
Bad Liebenstein D 95 E7
Bad Liebenwerda D 96 C4
Bad Liebenzell D 43 C10
Bad Lippspringe D 33 E11
Badljevina HR 165 B6
Bad Marienberg (Westerwald) D 37 C9
Bad Mergentheim D 90 D6
Bad Mitterndorf A 89 A8
Bad Münder am Deister D 94 B5
Bad Münstereifel D 201 D6
Bad Muskau D 97 C7
Bad Nauheim D 37 D11
Bad Nenndorf D 33 D12
Bad Neuenahr-Ahrweiler D 37 C8
Bad Neustadt an der Saale D 91 B7
Badolato I 75 B10
Badolatosa E 69 B7
Bad Oldesloe D 99 C8
Badonviller F 43 C6

Bad Orb D 37 D12
Badovinci SRB 174 D3
Bad Peterstal D 43 D9
Bad Pirawarth A 93 F11
Bad Pyrmont D 33 E12
Bad Radkersburg A 164 C5
Bad Ragaz CH 87 C9
Bad Rappenau D 203 C7
Bad Reichenhall D 89 A6
Bad Saarow-Pieskow D 96 B6
Bad Sachsa D 95 C8
Bad Säckingen D 43 E8
Bad Salzdetfurth D 95 B7
Bad Salzuflen D 33 D11
Bad Salzungen D 95 E7
Bad Sankt Leonhard im Lavanttal A 89 C10
Bad Sassendorf D 33 E10
Bad Schandau D 96 E6
Bad Schmiedeberg D 95 C12
Bad Schönborn D 203 C6
Bad Schussenried D 87 E10
Bad Schwalbach D 37 D10
Bad Schwartau D 99 C9
Bad Segeberg D 99 C8
Bad Sobernheim D 201 E8
Bad Soden-Salmünster D 90 B5
Bad Sooden-Allendorf D 95 D6
Bad Steben D 91 B10
Bad Sulza D 95 D10
Bad Sülze D 99 B13
Bad Tennstedt D 95 D8
Bad Tölz D 88 A4
Bad Überkingen D 203 D8
Bailo E 48 E4
Baimaclia MD 170 E2
Bainbridge GB 27 C7
Bain-de-Bretagne F 39 E8
Baindt D 87 B9
Bains F 46 E4
Bains-les-Bains F 42 D5
Bainton GB 27 D10
Baio E 54 B2
Baiona E 54 E2
Bais F 39 D11
Baiso I 82 D2
Băişoara RO 167 D11
Baisogala LT 150 E7
Băiţa RO 167 E10
Băiţa de sub Codru RO 167 B11
Baix F 51 A8
Baixa da Banheira P 66 B1
Baixas F 50 E4
Baj H 165 A10
Baja H 166 E2
Bajč SK 162 F5
Bajgora SRB 179 D11
Bajina Bašta SRB 174 E4
Bajmok SRB 166 F4
Bajna H 165 A11
Bajót H 165 A11
Bajovo Polje MNE 173 F10
Bajram Curri AL 179 E9
Bajša SRB 166 F4
Bak H 165 C7
Baka SK 162 F4
Bakacak TR 189 D7
Bakafarzewo PL 152 E6
Bakar HR 83 B10
Bakel NL 32 F5
Bakır TR 193 A10
Bakırköy TR 189 C10
Bakkasund N 110 B2
Bakke N 127 A16
Bakkeby N 128 C6
Bakkejord N 127 A15
Bakken N 111 C9
Bakonszeg H 167 C7
Bakonybél H 165 B9
Bakonycsernye H 165 B10
Bakonysárkány H 165 B10
Bakonyszentkirály H 165 B9
Bakonyszentlászló H 165 B9
Bakonyszombathely H 165 B9
Bakov nad Jizerou CZ 93 D7
Baks H 166 D5
Baksa H 165 E9
Baktalórántháza H 161 H5
Baktsjaur S 125 F17
Bäl S 109 D13
Bala RO 175 D10
Bala RO 175 D10
Bălăbăneşti MD 170 C4
Bălăbăneşti RO 169 E11
Balabanu MD 170 E4
Bălăceanu RO 177 C10
Balaci RO 176 E5
Bălăciţa RO 175 E11
Balaciu RO 177 D9
Bălan RO 167 C11
Bălan RO 169 D7
Bălan F 47 D7
Bălăneşti MD 170 D4
Bălăneşti RO 176 C2
Balanivka UA 170 A6
Balaruc-les-Bains F 51 D6
Bălăşeşti RO 169 E11
Bălăsineşti MD 169 A9
Balassagyarmat H 163 E8
Balástya H 166 E5
Balat TR 193 D9
Balaton H 161 G1
Balatonalmádi H 165 B10
Balatonberény H 165 C8
Balatonboglár H 165 C9
Balatonederics H 165 C8
Balatonfenyves H 165 C8
Balatonföldvár H 165 C9
Balatonfőzfő H 165 B10
Balatonkenese H 165 B10
Balatonlelle H 165 C9
Balatonszabadi H 165 C10
Balatonszárszó H 165 C9
Balatonvilágos H 165 C10
Bălăuşeri RO 168 E5
Balázsfalva RO 168 E4
Balbeggie GB 21 C10
Balbigny F 46 D5
Balbriggan IRL 23 E10
Balcani RO 169 D9
Bălceşti RO 176 D2
Balchik BG 183 C10
Balciler TR 189 D6
Balçova TR 193 C9

Baile an Mhóta IRL 22 D5
Baile an Mhuilinn IRL 24 D2
Baile an Róba IRL 22 E4
Baile an Sceilg IRL 24 E2
Baile Átha Bui IRL 23 E9
Baile Átha Cliath IRL 23 F10
Baile Átha Fhirdhia IRL 23 E9
Baile Átha Luain IRL 23 F7
Baile Átha Troim IRL 23 E9
Baile Brigín IRL 23 E10
Baile Comín IRL 23 F9
Băile Govora RO 176 C3
Băile Herculane RO 175 D9
Baile Loch Riach IRL 22 F5
Băile Mhistéale IRL 24 D4
Bileştí RO 176 E2
Băile Olănesti RO 176 C4
Bileştí RO 176 E2
Băile Tuşnad RO 169 E7
Baile Uílcín IRL 23 E10
Bailieborough IRL 23 E9
Baillargues F 51 C7
Bailleau-le-Pin F 40 D5
Bailleul F 34 C6
Bailonville B 35 D11
Bailo E 48 E4
Baimaclia MD 170 E2
Bainbridge GB 27 C7
Bain-de-Bretagne F 39 E8
Baindt D 87 B9
Bains F 46 E4
Bains-les-Bains F 42 D5
Bainton GB 27 D10
Baio E 54 B2
Baiona E 54 E2
Bais F 39 D11
Baiso I 82 D2
Băişoara RO 167 D11
Baisogala LT 150 E7
Băiţa RO 167 E10
Băiţa de sub Codru RO 167 B11
Baix F 51 A8
Baixa da Banheira P 66 B1
Baixas F 50 E4
Baj H 165 A10
Baja H 166 E2
Bajč SK 162 F5
Bajgora SRB 179 D11
Bajina Bašta SRB 174 E4
Bajmok SRB 166 F4
Bajna H 165 A11
Bajót H 165 A11
Bajovo Polje MNE 173 F10
Bajram Curri AL 179 E9
Bajša SRB 166 F4
Bak H 165 C7
Baka SK 162 F4
Bakacak TR 189 D7
Bakafarzewo PL 152 E6
Bakar HR 83 B10
Bakel NL 32 F5
Bakır TR 193 A10
Bakırköy TR 189 C10
Bakkasund N 110 B2
Bakke N 127 A16
Bakkeby N 128 C6
Bakkejord N 127 A15
Bakken N 111 C9
Bakonszeg H 167 C7
Bakonybél H 165 B9
Bakonycsernye H 165 B10
Bakonysárkány H 165 B10
Bakonyszentkirály H 165 B9
Bakonyszentlászló H 165 B9
Bakonyszombathely H 165 B9
Bakov nad Jizerou CZ 93 D7
Baks H 166 D5
Baksa H 165 E9
Baktalórántháza H 161 H5
Baktsjaur S 125 F17
Bäl S 109 D13
Bala RO 175 D10
Bala RO 175 D10
Bălăbăneşti MD 170 C4
Bălăbăneşti RO 169 E11
Balabanu MD 170 E4
Bălăceanu RO 177 C10
Balaci RO 176 E5
Bălăciţa RO 175 E11
Balaciu RO 177 D9
Bălan RO 167 C11
Bălan RO 169 D7
Balan F 47 D7
Bălăneşti MD 170 D4
Bălăneşti RO 176 C2
Balanivka UA 170 A6
Balaruc-les-Bains F 51 D6
Bălăşeşti RO 169 E11
Bălăsineşti MD 169 A9
Balassagyarmat H 163 E8
Balástya H 166 E5
Balat TR 193 D9
Balaton H 161 G1
Balatonalmádi H 165 B10
Balatonberény H 165 C8
Balatonboglár H 165 C9
Balatonederics H 165 C8
Balatonfenyves H 165 C8
Balatonföldvár H 165 C9
Balatonfőzfő H 165 B10
Balatonkenese H 165 B10
Balatonlelle H 165 C9
Balatonszabadi H 165 C10
Balatonszárszó H 165 C9
Balatonvilágos H 165 C10
Bălăuşeri RO 168 E5
Balázsfalva RO 168 E4
Balbeggie GB 21 C10
Balbigny F 46 D5
Balbriggan IRL 23 E10
Balcani RO 169 D9
Bălceşti RO 176 D2
Balchik BG 183 C10
Balciler TR 189 D6
Balçova TR 193 C9

Balderton GB 27 E10
Baldone LV 151 C8
Baldones Muiža LV 151 C8
Baldovineşti RO 176 E4
Bale HR 83 B8
Baleizão P 66 C4
Balemartine GB 20 C3
Balen B 35 B11
Băleni RO 169 F11
Băleni RO 177 D7
Balephuil GB 20 C3
Balerma E 71 F7
Băleşti RO 175 C11
Balestrand N 116 D5
Balestrate I 74 C3
Balfour GB 19 G11
Balfron GB 21 C9
Balgale LV 150 B5
Balgown GB 18 K4
Bali GR 194 C5
Baligród PL 161 E5
Balikesir TR 189 E8
Balıkliçeşme TR 189 D7
Balıkliova TR 193 C8
Bălileşti RO 176 C5
Bälinge S 115 C9
Bälinge S 134 C7
Balingen D 43 D10
Balinka H 165 B10
Balint RO 167 F8
Balintore GB 19 K9
Balje D 33 A12
Baljevac BIH 172 C4
Baljevac SRB 179 C10
Baljvine BIH 173 D7
Balk NL 32 C5
Balkány H 167 B8
Balkbrug NL 32 C6
Balla IRL 22 E4
Ballaban AL 184 D3
Ballabio I 85 B7
Ballachulish GB 20 B6
Ballaghaderreen IRL 22 E5
Ballaghkeen IRL 25 D10
Ballangen N 127 D12
Ballantrae GB 20 E6
Ballao I 80 D3
Ballasalla GBM 26 C2
Ballater GB 21 A10
Ballaugh GBM 26 C2
Balle DK 103 C7
Ballée F 39 E11
Ballee GB 23 D11
Ballen DK 102 E7
Ballenstedt D 95 C9
Balleroy F 39 B10
Ballerup DK 103 D10
Ballesteros de Calatrava E 70 B5
Ballı TR 189 C7
Ballina IRL 22 D4
Ballina IRL 24 C6
Ballinaboy IRL 22 F2
Ballinafad IRL 22 D6
Ballinagar IRL 23 F8
Ballinagh IRL 23 E8
Ballinakill IRL 25 C8
Ballinalack IRL 23 E8
Ballinalee IRL 23 E7
Ballinamallard GB 23 D7
Ballinamore IRL 23 D7
Ballinamult IRL 25 C7
Ballinasloe IRL 22 F6
Ballincollig IRL 24 E5
Ballindine IRL 22 E5
Ballindooly IRL 22 F4
Ballineen IRL 24 E5
Ballingarry IRL 24 D5
Ballingarry IRL 25 C7
Ballingeary IRL 24 E4
Ballingry GB 21 C10
Ballinglöw S 103 C13
Ballinlurteen IRL 22 F5
Ballinhassig IRL 24 E5
Ballinlough IRL 22 E5
Ballinluig GB 21 B9
Ballinrobe IRL 22 E4
Ballinskelligs IRL 24 E2
Ballinspittle IRL 24 E5
Ballintober IRL 22 E5
Ballintoy GB 20 E4
Ballintra IRL 22 C6
Ballintubber IRL 22 E4
Ballinure IRL 25 C7
Ballivor IRL 23 E9
Ballobar E 58 D3
Ballon F 39 D12
Ballon IRL 25 C9
Ballószög H 166 D4
Ballots F 39 F11
Ballsh AL 184 C2
Ballsnes N 127 A16
Ballstad N 126 D6
Ballstädt D 95 D8
Ballum DK 102 E3
Ballum NL 32 B5
Ballure GB 22 C6
Ballybay IRL 23 D9
Ballybofey IRL 23 C7
Ballybrack IRL 23 F10
Ballybrack IRL 24 E2
Ballybrittas IRL 23 F8
Ballybunion IRL 24 C3
Ballybunnion IRL 24 C3
Ballycahill IRL 25 C7
Ballycanew IRL 25 C10
Ballycarry GB 20 F5
Ballyclare GB 20 F5
Ballycolla IRL 25 C8
Ballyconneely IRL 22 F2
Ballyconnell IRL 23 D7
Ballycotton IRL 24 E6
Ballycroy IRL 22 D3
Ballydavid IRL 22 F5
Ballydehob IRL 24 F4
Ballydesmond IRL 24 D4
Ballydonegan IRL 24 F2
Ballyduff IRL 24 C3
Ballyduff IRL 24 C6
Ballyfarnan IRL 22 D6
Ballyfarnon RO 22 D6
Ballyfeard IRL 24 E6
Ballyferriter IRL 24 D2
Ballyforan IRL 22 F6
Ballygar IRL 22 E6
Ballygarrett IRL 25 C10
Ballygawley GB 23 D8
Ballyglass IRL 22 E5
Ballygorman IRL 20 E2

Ballygowan GB 23 C11
Ballyhaise IRL 23 D8
Ballyhalbert GB 23 D12
Ballyhale IRL 25 D8
Ballyhaunis IRL 22 E5
Ballyhean IRL 22 E4
Ballyheigue IRL 24 D3
Ballyjamesduff IRL 23 E8
Ballykeeran IRL 23 F7
Ballykelly GB 20 E2
Ballykilleen IRL 23 F8
Ballylanders IRL 24 D6
Ballylaneen IRL 25 D8
Ballylickey IRL 24 E4
Ballyliffen IRL 20 E2
Ballyliffin IRL 20 E2
Ballylynan IRL 25 C8
Ballymacarberry IRL 25 D7
Ballymacmague IRL 25 D7
Ballymadog IRL 25 E7
Ballymagorry GB 20 F2
Ballymahon IRL 23 E7
Ballymakeery IRL 24 E4
Ballymartin GB 23 D11
Ballymena GB 20 F4
Ballymoney GB 20 E3
Ballymore IRL 23 F7
Ballymote IRL 22 D5
Ballymurphy IRL 25 C9
Ballymurry IRL 22 E6
Ballynacally IRL 24 C4
Ballynafid IRL 23 E8
Ballynahinch GB 23 D11
Ballynahowen IRL 23 F7
Ballynakill IRL 23 F7
Ballynamona IRL 24 D5
Ballyneaner GB 20 F2
Ballynunty IRL 25 C7
Ballynure GB 20 F5
Ballyporeen IRL 24 D6
Ballyragget IRL 25 C8
Ballyroan IRL 25 C8
Ballyronan GB 20 F3
Ballyshannon IRL 22 C6
Ballyvaldon IRL 25 D10
Ballyvaughan IRL 22 F4
Ballyvoy GB 20 E4
Ballyvoyle IRL 25 D7
Ballywalter GB 23 C12
Ballyward GB 23 D10
Balma F 49 C9
Balmaha GB 20 C7
Balmaseda E 56 B5
Balmazújváros H 167 B7
Balme I 47 E11
Balmedie GB 19 L12
Balmuccia I 84 B5
Balnacra GB 18 L6
Balnapaling GB 19 K8
Balneario de Panticosa Huesca E 48 E5
Balninkai LT 151 F10
Balocco I 84 C5
Balogunyom H 165 B7
Balot F 41 E11
Balotaszállás H 166 E4
Balotești RO 177 D8
Balow D 99 D11
Balrath IRL 23 E10
Balș RO 176 E4
Balșa RO 167 E11
Balsa de Ves E 63 F10
Balsa Pintada E 72 F2
Balsareny E 59 D7
Balsfjord N 127 B17
Balsicas E 72 F3
Balsjö S 123 D16
Balsorano I 78 D5
Bålsta S 115 C9
Balsthal CH 43 F8
Balta RO 175 D10
Balta UA 170 B5
Balta Albă RO 177 C10
Balta Berilovac SRB 180 C5
Balta Doamnei RO 177 D8
Baltanás E 56 E3
Baltar E 54 E4
Baltasound GB 19 D15
Bălțătești RO 169 C8
Bălțați RO 169 C10
Bălțeni RO 169 D11
Bâlteni RO 175 D11
Baltezers LV 151 B8
Bălți MD 169 B11
Baltimore IRL 24 F4
Baltinava LV 149 C3
Baltinglass IRL 25 C9
Baltiysk RUS 155 A8
Baltmuiža LV 151 D13
Baltoji Vokė LT 153 E11
Baltora S 115 C11
Bałtów PL 159 D12
Baltray IRL 23 E10
Bălușeni RO 169 B9
Balvan BG 182 C4
Bălvănești RO 175 D10
Balvano I 76 B5
Balve D 33 F9
Balvi LV 149 B2
Balvicar GB 20 C5
Balya TR 189 E8
Balzers FL 87 C9
Bamberg D 91 C8
Bamburgh GB 21 D13
Bammental D 37 F11
Bampini GR 190 B3
Bampton GB 29 B11
Bampton GB 29 D8
Bana H 165 A9
Banafjäl S 123 E16
Banagher IRL 23 F7
Banarlı TR 189 B7
Banassac F 50 B5
Banatski Brestovac SRB 175 D6
Banatski Dvor SRB 174 B6
Banatski Karlovac SRB 175 C7
Banatsko Aranđelovo SRB 166 E5
Banatsko Karađorđevo SRB 174 B6
Banatsko Novo Selo SRB 175 D6
Banatsko Veliko Selo SRB 166 F6
Banbridge GB 23 D10
Banbury GB 29 A12
Banca RO 169 E11
Banchory GB 21 A12
Band RO 168 D4
Bande E 54 D4
Bandenitz D 99 D10
Bandholm DK 99 A10
Bandırma TR 189 D8
Bandol F 51 D10
Bandon IRL 24 E5
Bandurove UA 170 A5
Băneasa RO 169 F11
Băneasa RO 171 E1
Băneasa RO 177 E8
Bănești MD 170 B2
Bănești RO 177 C7
Banevo BG 183 D8
Banff GB 19 K11
Bångnäs S 122 B9
Bangor GB 20 F5
Bangor GB 26 E3
Bangor IRL 22 D3
Bangor Erris IRL 22 D3
Bangsund N 121 C10
Banham GB 31 C11
Bánhorváti H 161 G2
Bănia RO 175 D9
Banie PL 101 D7
Banie Mazurskie PL 152 E5
Baniska BG 182 C5
Bănișor RO 167 C10
Bănița RO 175 C11
Banite BG 187 A8
Banitsa BG 181 C8
Banja BIH 174 F3
Banja SRB 179 B8
Banja Lučica BIH 173 D10
Banja Luka BIH 173 C7
Banjani SRB 174 D4
Banja Vrućia BIH 173 C8
Bankekind S 108 C7
Bankeryd S 108 D4
Bankfoot GB 21 B9
Bankya BG 181 D6
Bankya BG 181 D7
Banloc RO 175 C7
Bannalec F 38 E4
Bannay F 41 F8
Bannesdorf auf Fehmarn D 99 B10
Bannewitz D 96 E5
Bannivka UA 171 B3
Bannockburn GB 21 C9
Bañobárez E 61 C7
Bañón E 63 C10
Banon F 51 B10
Baños de la Encina E 70 C5
Baños de Molgas E 54 D4
Baños de Montemayor E 61 D9
Baños de Río Tobía E 56 D6
Baños de Valdearados E 56 E4
Bánov CZ 162 D5
Bánov SK 162 E6
Banova Jaruga HR 165 F7
Bánovce nad Bebravou SK 162 D6
Banovići BIH 173 D10
Bánréve H 161 G1
Bansin, Seebad D 100 C6
Banská Belá SK 163 E7
Banská Bystrica SK 163 D8
Banská Štiavnica SK 163 E7
Banské SK 161 F4
Bansko BG 181 F7
Bant NL 32 C5
Banteer IRL 24 D5
Banteln D 94 B6
Bantheville F 35 F11
Bantry IRL 24 E4
Banya BG 181 D10
Banya BG 181 E9
Banya BG 181 F8
Banya BG 182 D5
Banya BG 183 D9
Banyalbufar E 65 E10
Banyeres de Mariola E 72 D3
Banyliv UA 168 A6
Banyliv-Pidhirnyy UA 168 A7
Banyoles E 59 C9
Banyuls-sur-Mer F 50 F5
Banzi I 76 B6
Banzkow D 99 C11
Bapaume F 34 D6
Bar MNE 179 E7
Bara RO 167 F8
Bâra RO 169 C10
Bara S 103 D12
Barabás H 161 G5
Baracska H 165 B11
Bărăganul RO 177 D11
Baragiano I 76 B5
Barahona E 57 F6
Barajas de Melo E 63 D7
Barajevo SRB 174 D5
Barakaldo E 56 B6
Barakovo BG 181 E7
Baralla E 54 C5
Barañain E 48 E2
Baranbio E 56 B6
Baránd H 167 C7
Baranello I 79 D7
Baranjsko Petrovo Selo HR 165 E10
Barano d'Ischia I 78 F5
Baranów PL 157 G6
Baranów PL 158 D5
Baranowo PL 155 D11
Baranów Sandomierska PL 159 F12
Barão de São João P 66 E2
Baraolt RO 169 E7
Baraqueville F 49 B10
Barásoain E 48 E2
Barassie GB 20 D7
Bărăști RO 176 D5
Baravukha BY 149 E5
Barbacena P 67 B5
Barbadás E 54 D4
Barbadillo de Herreros E 56 D5
Barbadillo del Mercado E 56 D5
Barbadillo del Pez E 56 D5
Barban HR 83 B9
Barbarano Vicentino I 82 B4
Barbaraville GB 19 K8
Barbaros TR 189 C7
Barbaste F 49 B6
Barbastro E 58 C4
Barbat HR 83 C10
Barbate de Franco E 68 D5
Bărbătescu RO 177 D9
Bărbătești RO 176 D3
Barbatovac SRB 180 C3
Barbâtre F 44 B1
Barbele LV 151 D9
Barbentane F 51 C8
Barberá del Vallès E 59 D8
Barberaz F 47 D8
Barberino di Mugello I 82 D3
Barbezieux-St-Hilaire F 44 E5
Barbonne-Fayel F 41 C10
Bărbulețu RO 176 C6
Barbullush AL 179 F8
Barby (Elbe) D 95 C10
Barç AL 184 C4
Barca E 57 F6
Bârca RO 176 F3
Barcabo E 58 C4
Barcada BIH 173 B8
Barca de Alva P 61 B7
Bărcănești RO 177 D8
Bărcănești RO 177 D9
Barcani RO 177 B8
Barcarrota E 67 B6
Barcea RO 169 F10
Barcelinhos P 54 E2
Barcellona Pozzo di Gotto I 75 C7
Barcelona E 59 E8
Barcelonne-du-Gers F 48 C5
Barcelonnette F 52 C5
Barcelos P 54 E2
Bárcena del Monasterio E 55 B6
Bárcena de Pie de Concha E 56 B3
Barcenillas de Cerezos E 56 B4
Barchfeld D 95 E7
Barciany PL 152 E3
Barcillonnette F 51 B10
Barcin PL 154 E4
Barcino PL 101 B11
Barcis I 88 D6
Barcones E 56 F6
Barcos P 60 B5
Barcs H 165 E8
Barcus F 48 D4
Barczewo PL 152 F2
Bardal N 124 D5
Bardar MD 170 D3
Barde DK 102 C3
Bardejov SK 161 E3
Bárdena E 57 D9
Bardenitz D 96 B3
Bårdesø DK 102 D6
Bardi I 85 D8
Bardineto I 53 C8
Bardney GB 27 E11
Bardo PL 93 B11
Bardolino I 82 A2
Bardonecchia I 47 E10
Bardos F 48 D3
Bardowick D 99 D8
Bardsea GB 26 C5
Bárdudvarnok H 165 D9
Bare BIH 173 E10
Bare SRB 174 E6
Bare SRB 179 C8
Barefield IRL 24 C5
Barèges F 49 E6
Barenburg D 33 C11
Barendorf D 99 D9
Bärenklau D 97 C7
Bärenstein D 92 B4
Bärenstein D 96 E5
Barentin F 34 E2
Barenton F 39 C10
Barevo BIH 173 D7
Barfleur F 39 A9
Barga I 82 D1
Bargagli I 53 C10
Bargas E 62 E4
Bârgăuani RO 169 D9
Barge I 47 F11
Bargemon F 52 D5
Bargen CH 43 E10
Bargenstedt D 98 B6
Barghe I 85 B9
Bârghiș RO 168 F5
Bargischow D 100 C5
Bargłów Kościelny PL 156 C7
Bargoed GB 29 B8
Bargrennan GB 20 E7
Bargstedt D 33 B12
Bargteheide D 99 C8
Bargullas AL 184 C3
Barham GB 31 E11
Bar Hill GB 31 C9
Bari I 77 A7
Barić Draga HR 172 D3
Barile I 76 B5
Barilović HR 164 F5
Barinas E 72 E2
Båring DK 102 E5
Barì Sardo I 80 D4
Barisciano I 78 C5
Barjac F 51 B7
Bårjasnjar'ga N 129 D15
Barjols F 51 C11
Barkåkar N 111 D12
Barkåkra S 103 C11
Barkald N 117 C13
Barkarö S 114 C7
Barkava LV 151 C13
Barkelsby D 99 A7
Barkhyttan S 119 E11
Barkowo PL 101 C12
Barkston GB 27 F10
Bârla RO 176 E5
Bârlad RO 169 E11
Barleben D 95 B10
Bar-le-Duc F 42 C3
Barles F 52 C4
Barletta I 76 A6
Barley GB 31 C9
Barlinek PL 101 E8
Barlingbo S 109 D12
Barmouth GB 26 F3
Barmstedt D 98 C7
Bârna H 163 E9
Barna IRL 22 F4
Bârna RO 175 B9
Barnaderg IRL 22 F5
Barnard Castle GB 27 B8
Barnarp S 108 D4
Barnatra IRL 22 D3
Bârnau D 91 C11
Barnbach A 89 B11
Barneberg D 95 B9
Barneveld NL 32 D5
Barneville-Carteret F 39 B8
Barnewitz D 95 A12
Barneycarroll IRL 22 E5
Barnoldswick GB 27 D7
Bârnova RO 169 C11
Barnowko PL 101 E7
Barnsley GB 27 D9
Barnstädt D 95 D10
Barnstaple GB 28 C6
Barnstorf D 33 C11
Barntrup D 33 E12
Baronissi I 76 B3
Baronville F 42 C6
Baroševac SRB 174 E5
Barovo MK 185 B7
Barowka BY 149 E3
Barqueros E 71 D10
Barquinha P 60 F4
Barr F 43 D7
Barr GB 20 E7
Barracas E 64 D3
Barrachina E 63 C10
Barraduff IRL 24 D4
Barrafranca I 74 E5
Barral E 54 D3
Barrali I 80 E3
Barranco do Velho P 66 E4
Barrancos P 67 C6
Barranda E 71 C9
Barrapoll GB 20 C3
Barrax E 71 A8
Barre-des-Cévennes F 51 B6
Barreiro P 66 B1
Bärrek S 114 B7
Barrême F 52 D4
Barrhead GB 21 D8
Barrhill GB 20 E7
Barriada Nueva E 59 D8
Bárrio P 54 E2
Barrio del Peral E 72 F3
Barrio Mar E 64 E4
Barrit DK 102 D5
Barr na Trá IRL 22 D3
Barroca P 60 D5
Barroselas P 54 E2
Barrowby GB 27 F10
Barrow-in-Furness GB 26 C5
Barruecopardo E 61 B7
Barruelo de Santullan E 56 C3
Barry GB 29 C8
Barry IRL 23 E7
Bârsa RO 167 E9
Barsac F 48 A5
Bârsana RO 161 H9
Bârsău RO 167 B11
Barsbüttel D 99 C8
Bårse DK 103 E9
Barsele S 123 A12
Bârsești RO 169 F9
Barsinghausen D 94 B5
Barßel D 33 B9
Barsta S 119 A15
Barstyčiai LT 150 D3
Bar-sur-Aube F 41 D12
Bar-sur-Seine F 41 D11
Bārta LV 150 D2
Bartenheim F 43 E7
Bartenstein D 90 D6
Barth D 99 B13
Bartholomä D 90 E6
Bartholomäberg A 87 C9
Bartkušškiai LT 151 F9
Bartkuškis LT 153 D10
Bartnes N 121 C10
Bartniki PL 155 D10
Bartninkai LT 152 E7
Barton GB 26 D6
Barton-upon-Humber GB 27 D11
Bartoszyce PL 152 E2
Baru RO 175 C11
Baruchowo PL 155 F7
Barulho P 61 F6
Barumini I 80 D3
Baruth D 96 B5
Barvas GB 18 J3
Barvaux B 35 D11
Barver D 33 C11
Barwedel D 95 A8
Barwice PL 101 C10
Barxeta E 72 C4
Bârza RO 176 E4
Bárzana E 55 B8
Bârzava RO 167 E9
Barzio I 85 B7
Bašaid SRB 174 B5
Basarabeasca MD 170 E3
Basarabi RO 171 E2
Basarbovo BG 177 F7
Bascara E 59 C9
Bascharage L 36 E5
Baschi I 78 B2
Baschurch GB 26 F6
Basciano I 78 B5
Basconcillos del Tozo E 56 C4
Bascons F 48 C5
Bascous F 49 C6
Bascov RO 176 D5
Basdahl D 33 B12
Basècles B 35 C8
Basel CH 43 E8
Baselga di Pinè I 85 A11
Baselice I 76 A3
Bas-en-Basset F 46 E5
Băsești RO 167 C11
Båsheim N 111 B10
Bashtanivka UA 170 F4
Basigo E 56 B6
Basildon GB 31 D9
Basiliano I 89 D7
Basingstoke GB 29 C12
Baška CZ 162 B6
Baška HR 83 C10
Baška Voda HR 173 F6
Baskemölla S 104 D6
Bäsksele S 123 B11
Bäsksjö S 123 B12
Basksjön S 123 E12
Baslow GB 27 E8
Bäsna S 113 A13
Bassacutena I 80 A3
Bassano del Grappa I 88 E4
Bassano Romano I 78 C2
Bassecourt CH 43 F7
Basse-Goulaine F 39 F9
Bassenge B 35 C12
Bassens F 44 F4
Bassiano I 78 D4
Bassoues F 49 C6
Bassum D 33 C11
Bassy F 47 D8
Bast FIN 139 C10
Båstad S 103 C11
Bastardo I 78 B3
Bastasi BIH 172 D5
Bastasi BIH 173 F10
Bastelica F 53 G10
Bastelicaccia F 53 H9
Bastennes F 48 C4
Bastfallet S 114 B7
Bastia F 53 F10
Bastia I 78 A3
Bastogne B 35 D12
Bastorf D 99 B11
Basttjärn S 113 B12
Bastumarks by S 134 E3
Bastuträsk S 123 C16
Bastuträsk S 134 E4
Báta H 165 D11
Bata RO 167 E9
Batajnica SRB 174 D5
Batak BG 181 F9
Batalha P 60 E3
Bățani RO 169 E7
Batăr RO 167 D8
Bătarci RO 161 G7
Båtas S 122 B8
Bátaszék H 165 D11
Batea E 58 E4
Batelov CZ 93 D8
Båteng N 129 C20
Baterno E 70 B3
Batetskiy RUS 148 D7
Bath GB 29 C10
Bathford GB 29 C10
Bathgate GB 21 D9
Bathmen NL 32 D6
Batin BG 177 F7
Batina HR 165 E11
Batizovce SK 161 E1
Batković BIH 174 D3
Batlava SRB 180 D3
Batley GB 27 D8
Bátmonostor H 166 E2
Båtnfjordsøra N 116 A7
Batočina SRB 175 E7
Bátonyterenye H 163 F9
Bátorove Kosihy SK 162 F6
Batoș RO 168 D5
Batoshevo BG 182 D4
Bátovce SK 163 E7
Batovo BG 183 C9
Batrina HR 173 B8
Båtsfjord N 130 B7
Batsi GR 192 D4
Båtsjaur S 125 D13
Båtskärsnäs S 135 C10
Battenberg (Eder) D 37 B11
Bätterkinden CH 43 F8
Battice B 199 D7
Battipaglia I 76 B3
Battle GB 31 F9
Battonya H 167 E7
Batultsi BG 181 C9
Bátya H 166 E2
Batyatychi UA 160 C9
Batz-sur-Mer F 38 F7
Baucina I 74 D4
Baud F 38 E5
Bauduen F 52 D4
Bauen CH 87 D7
Baugé F 39 E11
Baugy F 41 F8
Bauladu I 80 C2
Baulon F 39 E8
Baume-les-Dames F 42 F5
Baumholder D 202 B3
Baunach D 91 C8
Baunei I 80 C4
Baurci MD 170 E3
Bausendorf D 37 D7
Bauska LV 151 D8
Băuțar RO 175 B10
Bautzen D 96 D6
Bavanište SRB 175 D6
Bavay F 35 D8
Bavel NL 198 B5
Baveno I 84 B6
Bavilliers F 43 E6
Bavorov CZ 92 D6
Bawdeswell GB 31 B11
Bawdsey GB 31 C11
Bawinkel D 33 C8
Bawn Cross Roads IRL 24 D5
Bayárcal E 71 E7
Bayarque E 71 E8
Baybuzivka UA 170 A5
Baye F 41 C10
Bayel F 41 D12
Bayerbach D 92 F4
Bayerbach bei Ergoldsbach D 91 E11
Bayerisch Eisenstein D 92 D4
Bayersoien D 87 B12
Bayeux F 39 B10
Bayındır TR 193 C10
Bayır TR 197 B8
Bayırköy TR 188 D6
Baykal BG 176 F4
Bayon F 42 D5
Bayonne F 48 D3
Bayramiç TR 188 E6
Bayramiç TR 189 C6
Bayramlı TR 189 B6
Bayreuth D 91 C10
Bayrischzell D 88 A5
Bayston Hill GB 26 F6
Baytaly UA 170 B5
Bayubas de Abajo E 56 E6
Baza E 71 D7
Bázakerettye H 165 C7
Bazar"yanka UA 170 F6
Bazas F 48 B5
Bazet F 49 D6
Baziège F 49 D9
Bazillac F 49 D6
Bazna RO 168 E4
Bazoches F 41 F10
Bazoches-au-Houlme F 39 C11
Bazoches-les-Gallerandes F 40 D7
Bazoches-sur-Hoëne F 40 C3
Bazougers F 39 D10
Bazouges F 39 E10
Bazzano I 82 D3
Beaconsfield GB 31 D7
Beadnell GB 21 D13
Beagh IRL 22 E5
Bealach A Doirín IRL 22 E5
Bealach Conglais IRL 25 C9
Bealach Feich IRL 23 C7
Bealaclugga IRL 22 F4
Béal an Átha IRL 22 D4
Béal an Mhuirthead IRL 22 D3
Béal Átha an Ghaorthaidh IRL 24 E4
Béal Átha Beithe IRL 23 D9
Béal Átha hAmhnais IRL 22 E5
Béal Átha Liag IRL 23 E7
Béal Átha na Muice IRL 22 E5
Béal Átha na Sluaighe IRL 22 F6
Béal Átha Seanaidh IRL 22 C6
Béal Deirg IRL 22 D3
Béal Easa IRL 22 E4
Bealnablath IRL 24 E5
Beaminster GB 29 D9
Beamud E 63 D9
Beannchar IRL 23 F7
Beantraí IRL 24 E4
Beariz E 54 D3
Bearna IRL 22 F4
Bearsden GB 21 D8
Beas E 67 E6
Beasain E 48 D1
Beas de Granada E 69 B10
Beas de Segura E 71 C7
Beateberg S 108 B4
Beattock GB 21 E10
Beaucaire F 51 C8
Beaucamps-le-Vieux F 34 E4
Beauchastel F 46 F6
Beaucouzé F 39 F10
Beaufay F 40 D3
Beaufort F 47 B7
Beaufort F 47 D10
Beaufort IRL 24 D3
Beaufort-en-Vallée F 39 F11
Beaugency F 40 E6
Beaujeu F 46 C6
Beaujeu F 52 C4
Beaujeu-St-Vallier-Pierrejux-et-Quitteur F 42 E4
Beaulieu F 51 C7
Beaulieu-lès-Loches F 40 F5
Beaulieu-sur-Dordogne F 45 F9
Beaulieu-sur-Loire F 41 E8
Beaulon F 46 B4
Beauly GB 18 L8
Beaumarchés F 49 C6
Beaumaris GB 26 E3
Beaumesnil F 40 B4
Beaumetz-lès-Loges F 34 D6
Beaumont B 35 D9
Beaumont F 39 A8
Beaumont F 45 B6
Beaumont F 45 F7
Beaumont-de-Lomagne F 49 C7
Beaumont-de-Pertuis F 51 C10
Beaumont-en-Argonne F 35 E11
Beaumont-en-Véron F 39 F12
Beaumont-le-Roger F 40 B4
Beaumont-lès-Valence F 46 F6
Beaumont-sur-Oise F 41 B7
Beaumont-sur-Sarthe F 39 D12
Beaune F 46 A6
Beaune-La Rolande F 41 D7
Beaupréau F 39 F10
Beauquesne F 34 D5
Beauraing B 35 D10
Beaurepaire F 47 E7
Beaurepaire-en-Bresse F 47 B7
Beaurières F 51 A10
Beausite F 42 C3
Beausoleil F 53 D6
Beautor F 35 E7
Beauvais F 34 F5
Beauval F 34 D5
Beauvezer F 52 C5
Beauville F 49 B7
Beauvoir-sur-Mer F 44 B1
Beauvoir-sur-Niort F 44 C5
Beauzac F 46 E5
Beauzelle F 49 C8
Beba Veche RO 166 E5
Bebertal D 95 B9
Bebington GB 26 E5
Bebra D 94 E6
Bebrene LV 151 D12
Bebri LV 151 C10
Bebrina HR 173 B8
Beccles GB 31 C12
Becedas E 61 D9
Beceite E 58 F4
Bečej SRB 174 B5
Beceni RO 177 C9
Becerreá E 54 C5
Becerril de Campos E 55 D10
Becherbach D 202 B4
Bécherel F 39 D8
Bechet RO 176 F3
Bechhofen D 37 F8
Bechhofen D 91 D8
Bechlín CZ 92 B6
Bechtheim D 37 E10
Bechyně CZ 93 D6
Becicherecu Mic RO 167 F7
Bečići MNE 179 E6
Becilla de Valderaduey E 55 D9
Beçin TR 197 B7
Beckdorf D 98 D7
Beckedorf D 33 D12
Beckeln D 33 C11
Beckingen D 37 F7
Beckingham GB 27 E10
Beckov SK 162 D5
Beckum D 33 E10
Beclean RO 168 C4
Beclean RO 168 F5
Bécon-les-Granits F 39 F10
Bečov CZ 92 B5
Becsehely H 165 D7
Becsvölgye H 165 C7
Bečváry CZ 93 C8
Bedale GB 27 C8
Bédar E 71 E9
Bédarieux F 50 C5
Bédarrides F 51 B8
Bedburg D 37 C7
Bedburg-Hau D 199 B8
Beddgelert GB 26 E3
Beddingestrand S 103 E12
Bédée F 39 D8
Bedekovčina HR 164 D5
Beden BG 181 F9
Beder DK 102 C6
Bedford GB 31 C8
Bedihošť CZ 93 D12
Będków PL 159 C8
Bedlington GB 21 E13
Bedlno PL 159 B8
Bedmar E 69 A10
Bednja HR 164 D5
Bédoin F 51 B9
Bedollo I 85 A11
Bedonia I 53 B11
Bedous F 48 D4
Bedsted DK 102 E4
Bedsted Stationsby DK 102 B2
Béduer F 49 A9
Bedum NL 33 B7
Bedwas GB 29 B8
Bedworth GB 29 A12
Będzin PL 159 F7
Będzino PL 101 B9
Beedenbostel D 95 A7
Beeford GB 27 D11
Beek NL 32 E5
Beek NL 32 E5
Beek NL 199 D7
Beekbergen NL 199 A7
Beelitz D 96 B3
Beendorf D 95 B9
Beenz D 100 D4
Beerfelden D 37 E11
Beernem B 35 B7
Beers NL 32 E5
Beerse B 32 F3
Beersel B 35 C9
Beerst B 198 C1
Beerta NL 33 B8
Beesd NL 199 B6
Beesenstedt D 95 C10
Beeskow D 96 B6
Beesten D 33 D9
Beeston GB 27 F9
Beetsterzwaag NL 32 B6
Beetzendorf D 99 E10
Bégaar F 48 C4
Bégadan F 44 E4
Begaljica SRB 174 D6
Bégard F 38 C5
Begejci SRB 174 B6
Beğendik TR 188 C6
Begíjar E 69 A9
Begijnendijk B 35 B10
Beglezh BG 181 C10
Begnište MK 185 B6
Begonte E 54 B4
Begur E 59 D10
Behramkale TR 187 F10
Behren-lès-Forbach F 43 B6
Behren-Lübchin D 99 B13
Behringen D 95 D8
Beica de Jos RO 168 D5
Beidaud RO 171 D3
Beierfeld D 95 E12
Beierstedt D 95 B8
Beilen NL 33 C7
Beilngries D 91 D9
Beilstein D 43 B11
Beimerstetten D 203 E8
Beinasco I 53 A7
Beinette I 53 C7
Beinwil CH 43 F9
Beirã P 60 F6
Beisfjord N 127 D14
Beisland N 106 C3
Beith GB 20 D7
Beitostølen N 117 D9
Beitstad N 121 C10
Beiuș RO 167 D9
Beja LV 149 B2
Beja P 66 C4
Bejar AL 184 D2
Béjar E 61 D9
Bejís E 64 E3
Bekecs H 161 G3
Békés H 167 D7
Békéscsaba H 167 D7
Békéssámson H 166 E6
Békésszentandrás H 166 D5
Bekkarfjord N 129 B19
Bekken N 117 C15
Bekkevoll N 130 D8
Belá SK 163 C7
Bélâbre F 45 B8
Bela Crkva SRB 175 D7
Beladice SK 162 E6
Belá-Dulice SK 163 C7
Belalcázar E 67 B9
Belá nad Cirochou SK 161 F5
Bělá nad Radbuzou CZ 91 C12
Belanica SRB 179 E10
Belanovce MK 180 E4
Belanovica SRB 174 E5
Bela Palanka SRB 180 C5
Bélapátfalva H 161 G1
Bělá pod Bezdězem CZ 93 A7
Bělá pod Pradědem CZ 93 B12
Belascoáin E 48 E2
Belauski LV 149 C2
Belava LV 151 B13
Belazaima do Chão P 60 C4
Belcaire F 49 E9
Belcastel F 49 B10
Belcești RO 169 C10
Bełchatów PL 159 D7
Belchin BG 181 E7
Belchite E 57 F10
Bělčice CZ 92 C5
Belciugatele RO 177 E8
Belclare IRL 22 F5
Belcoo GB 23 D7
Belderg IRL 22 D3
Beldibi TR 197 C8
Beled H 165 B8
Belegiš SRB 174 C5
Belej HR 83 C9
Belene BG 176 F6
Bélesta F 49 E9
Beleți-Negrești RO 176 D6
Belevi TR 193 C9
Belezna H 165 D7
Belfast GB 23 C11
Belfeld NL 32 F6
Belford GB 21 D13
Belfort F 43 E6
Belfort-du-Quercy F 49 B9
Belforte del Chienti I 83 F7
Belgern D 96 D4
Belgershain D 95 D12
Belgioioso I 85 C7
Belgodère F 53 F10
Belgooly IRL 24 E6
Belgun BG 171 F2
Belhomert-Guéhouville F 40 C5
Beli HR 83 B9
Belianes E 58 D6
Belica HR 165 D7
Beli Iskŭr BG 181 E8
Beli Izvor BG 181 C7
Beli Manastir HR 165 E11
Belin RO 169 F7
Belin-Béliet F 48 B4
Belinchón E 63 D6
Belint RO 167 F8
Beli Potok SRB 180 B5
Beliș RO 167 D11
Belišće HR 165 E10
Belitsa BG 177 F9
Belitsa BG 181 D8
Belitsa BG 181 F8
Beliu RO 167 E9
Bělkovice-Lašťany CZ 162 B4
Bell D 37 D8
Bell (Hunsrück) D 201 D7
Bella I 76 B5
Bellac F 45 C8
Bellacorick IRL 22 D3
Bellaghy GB 20 F3
Bellaghy IRL 22 E5
Bellagio I 85 B7
Bellahy IRL 22 E5
Bellano I 85 A7
Bellante I 78 B5
Bellaria I 82 D5
Bellavary IRL 22 E4
Bellavista E 67 E8
Bellclaire d'Urgell E 58 D5
Belleek GB 23 D10

Bellegarde F 41 E7
Bellegarde F 51 C8
Bellegarde-en-Marche F 45 D10
Bellegarde-sur-Valserine F 47 C8
Belle-Isle-en-Terre F 38 C5
Bellême F 40 D4
Bellenaves F 46 C3
Bellenberg D 87 A10
Bellencombre F 34 E3
Bellerive-sur-Allier F 46 C3
Belles-Forêts F 43 C6
Belleu F 35 F7
Bellevaux F 47 C10
Belleville F 46 C6
Belleville-sur-Meuse F 42 B3
Belleville-sur-Vie F 44 B3
Bellevue-la-Montagne F 46 E4
Belley F 47 D8
Bellheim D 37 F10
Bellherbe F 42 F6
Bellignat F 47 C8
Bellinge DK 102 E6
Bellingham GB 21 E12
Bellingwolde NL 33 B8
Bellinzago Novarese I 84 B6
Bellinzona CH 85 A7
Bellizzi I 76 B3
Bell-Lloc d'Urgell E 58 D5
Bello E 63 C10
Bellou-en-Houlme F 39 C11
Bellpuig E 58 D6
Bellreguard E 72 D4
Bellshill GB 21 D8
Belluno I 88 D5
Bellver de Cerdanya E 49 F9
Bellvik S 123 C10
Belm D 33 D10
Bélmegyer H 167 D7
Bélmez E 67 C9
Bélmez de la Moraleda E 69 A10
Belmont GB 19 D15
Belmont-de-la-Loire F 46 C5
Belmonte E 55 B7
Belmonte E 63 E7
Belmonte P 61 D6
Belmonte Calabro I 76 E6
Belmonte del Sannio I 79 D6
Belmonte in Sabina I 78 C3
Belmontejo E 63 E8
Belmont-sur-Rance F 50 C4
Belmullet IRL 22 D3
Belo Brdo SRB 179 C10
Beloci MD 170 B4
Belœil B 35 C8
Belogradchik BG 175 F10
Beloiannisz H 165 B11
Belojin SRB 180 C3
Belo Polje SRB 179 D10
Belorado E 56 D5
Beloslav BG 183 C9
Bělotín CZ 162 B5
Belotintsi BG 181 B6
Belovo BG 181 E9
Belozem BG 182 E4
Belp CH 47 B11
Belpasso I 75 D6
Belpech F 49 D9
Belper GB 27 E9
Belsay GB 21 E13
Belsh AL 184 C2
Belsk Duży PL 157 G3
Beltheim D 37 D8
Beltinci SLO 164 C6
Beltiug RO 167 B10
Beltra IRL 22 D5
Beltra IRL 22 E4
Beltrum NL 199 A9
Belturbet IRL 23 D8
Beluša SK 162 C6
Belušić SRB 175 F7
Belvédère-Campomoro F 53 H9
Belvedere Marittimo I 76 D5
Belvedere Ostrense I 83 E7
Belver de Cinca E 58 D4
Belver de los Montes E 55 E9
Belvès F 45 F8
Belvèze-du-Razès F 49 D10
Belvì I 80 D3
Belville IRL 22 D4
Belvís de la Jara E 62 E3
Belz F 38 E5
Belz UA 160 C9
Bełżec PL 160 C7
Belzig D 95 B12
Bełżyce PL 157 H6
Bembibre E 54 B2
Bembibre E 55 C7
Bemmel NL 32 E5
Bemposta P 55 F7
Bemposta P 60 F4
Bempton GB 27 C11
Benabarre E 58 C4
Benacazón E 67 E7
Benahadux E 71 F8
Benahavís E 69 C6
Benalmádena E 69 C7
Benalúa de Guadix E 71 E6
Benalúa de las Villas E 69 B9
Benalup de Sidonia E 68 D5
Benamargosa E 69 C8
Benamaurel E 71 D7
Benamejí E 69 B7
Benamocarra E 69 C8
Benaocaz E 69 C6
Benaoján E 69 C6
Benasal E 64 D4
Benasau E 72 D4
Benasque E 49 E7
Benassay F 44 B6
Benatae E 71 C7
Benátky nad Jizerou CZ 93 B7
Benavente E 55 D8
Benavente P 66 B2
Benavides de Orbigo E 55 D8
Benavila P 60 F5
Benburb GB 23 D9
Bencatel P 66 B5
Bendorf D 37 D9
Bēne LV 150 D6
Benecko CZ 97 E9
Beneden-Leeuwen NL 32 E4
Benediktbeuren D 88 A3
Benedita P 60 F3
Benegiles E 55 E8
Bénéjacq F 48 D5
Benejama E 72 D3
Benejúzar E 72 E3
Benesat RO 167 C11
Benešov CZ 93 C7
Benešov nad Černou CZ 93 E7
Benešov nad Ploučnicí CZ 96 E6
Bénesse-Maremne F 48 C3
Benestare I 75 C9
Bénestroff F 43 C6
Benet F 44 C4
Benetutti I 80 C3
Bene Vagienna I 53 B7
Bénévent-l'Abbaye F 45 C9
Benevento I 76 A3
Benfeld F 43 D8
Benfica do Ribatejo P 60 F3
Bengești-Ciocadia RO 176 C3
Bengtsfors S 107 A11
Bengtsheden S 119 E10
Benia de Onís E 55 B10
Beniarbeig E 72 D5
Beniarrés E 72 D4
Beničanci HR 165 E10
Benicarló E 64 D5
Benicasim E 64 D5
Benidorm E 72 D4
Beniel E 72 E3
Benifaió E 64 F4
Benifallet E 58 F5
Benifallim E 72 D4
Benigánim E 72 D4
Benilloba E 72 D4
Benissa E 72 D5
Benissanet E 58 E5
Benitachell E 72 D5
Benitses GR 184 E2
Benizalón E 71 E8
Benizar y la Tercia E 71 C9
Benken CH 43 F11
Benkovac HR 172 D4
Benkovski BG 177 F10
Benkovski BG 187 B8
Benllech GB 26 E3
Benlloch E 64 D5
Bennebroek NL 198 A5
Bennekom NL 199 A7
Bennewitz D 95 D12
Bennungen D 95 D9
Bénodet F 38 E3
Benquerença P 61 D6
Benquerenças P 60 E5
Benquerencia de la Serena E 67 B9
Benquet F 48 C4
Bensafrim P 66 E2
Bensbyn S 134 C8
Bensdorf D 95 B11
Benshausen D 95 E8
Bensheim D 37 E11
Bensjö S 119 A9
Benson GB 29 B12
Bentelo NL 33 D7
Bentivoglio I 82 C3
Bentley GB 27 D9
Bentwisch D 99 B12
Bentzin D 100 C4
Beňuš SK 163 D9
Benzingerode D 95 C8
Beočin SRB 174 C4
Beograd SRB 174 D5
Bera de Bidasoa E 48 D2
Beragh GB 23 C8
Berane MNE 179 D8
Beranga E 56 B4
Berango E 56 B6
Berantevilla E 56 C6
Berat AL 184 C2
Bérat F 49 D8
Beratzhausen D 91 D10
Berbegal E 58 D3
Berbești RO 176 C3
Berca RO 177 C9
Bercedo E 56 B5
Bercel H 163 F8
Berceni RO 177 D8
Berceni RO 177 E8
Bercero E 55 E9
Berceto I 85 D8
Berchem B 35 C8
Berchidda I 80 B3
Berching D 91 D9
Berchtesgaden D 89 A7
Bérchules E 71 F6
Bercianos del Páramo E 55 D8
Berck F 31 G12
Bercu RO 161 H6
Berdal N 120 E6
Berdalen N 110 D6
Berducedo E 55 B6
Berdún E 48 E4
Bere Alston GB 28 E6
Beregdaróc H 161 G6
Bereguardo I 85 C7
Berehomet UA 168 A6
Berehove UA 161 G6
Berek HR 165 E7
Berekböszörmény H 167 C8
Berekfürdő H 166 C6
Beremend H 165 E10
Berești RO 169 E11
Berești-Meria RO 169 E11
Berești-Tazlău RO 169 E9
Berettyóújfalu H 167 C8
Berevoești RO 176 C5
Berezeni RO 170 E2
Berezyne UA 170 E4
Berg D 87 B9
Berg D 91 B10
Berg D 199 D9
Berg L 36 E6
Berg N 112 B7
Berg N 124 F3
Berg N 127 B13
Berg NL 35 C12
Berg NL 199 D7
Berg S 108 C8
Berg S 118 A7
Berg S 123 E10
Berg (Pfalz) D 43 C9
Berga D 95 D9
Berga D 95 E11
Berga E 59 C7
Berga S 105 A10
Bergagård S 103 B11
Bergaland N 110 D4
Bergama TR 193 A9
Bergamo I 85 B8
Bergantino I 82 B3
Bergara E 48 D1
Bergasa E 48 F1
Bergatreute D 87 B9
Berg bei Neumarkt in der Oberpfalz D 91 D9
Bergby S 119 E13
Berge D 33 C9
Berge D 99 D11
Berge E 58 F3
Berge S 118 A8
Berge S 121 D14
Bergeforsen S 119 A13
Bergeggi I 53 C8
Bergen D 89 A6
Bergen D 99 E7
Bergen D 100 B4
Bergen N 110 B2
Bergen NL 32 C3
Bergen (Dumme) D 99 E9
Bergen op Zoom NL 32 F2
Berger N 111 C12
Bergerac F 45 F6
Bergères-lès-Vertus F 41 C11
Bergesserin F 46 C6
Berget N 124 D6
Bergeyk NL 32 F4
Bergfors S 127 D18
Berghamn S 119 A15
Bergharen NL 199 B7
Berghaupten D 202 E4
Bergheim A 89 A7
Bergheim D 91 E9
Bergheim (Edertal) D 37 B12
Bergheim (Erft) D 37 C7
Berghem NL 32 E5
Berghem S 107 E12
Berghin RO 168 E3
Berghülen D 90 F6
Berg im Drautal A 89 C7
Bergisch Gladbach D 37 C8
Bergkamen D 33 E9
Bergkarlås S 118 D8
Bergkvara S 105 C10
Bergland S 123 A10
Berglia N 121 C15
Bergmo N 128 D7
Bergnäs S 125 E13
Bergnäset S 134 C8
Bergnäsudden S 125 E15
Bergnäsviken S 125 D15
Bergneustadt D 201 B8
Bergö FIN 115 B13
Bergö FIN 138 E6
Bergom S 123 F15
Bergsåker S 119 B13
Bergsäng S 113 B10
Bergsäter S 123 B12
Bergsbyn S 134 E6
Bergschenhoek NL 198 B5
Bergsgården S 119 E10
Bergshamra S 115 C11
Bergsjö S 119 C13
Bergsnov N 121 B9
Bergs slussar S 108 C7
Bergstod N 111 D9
Bergstrøm N 112 D6
Bergsviken S 134 D6
Bergtheim D 91 C7
Bergues F 34 C5
Bergün CH 87 D9
Bergvik S 119 D12
Bergviken S 125 D16
Bergwitz D 95 C12
Berhida H 165 B10
Beringe NL 199 C7
Beringel P 66 C4
Beringen B 35 B11
Berislăvești RO 176 C4
Beriu RO 167 F11
Berja E 71 F7
Berka D 95 E7
Berkåk N 117 A12
Berkel NL 32 E2
Berkel-Enschot NL 32 E4
Berkeley GB 29 B10
Berkenthin D 99 C9
Berkheim D 87 A10
Berkhout NL 32 C4
Berkovići BIH 173 F9
Berkovitsa BG 181 C7
Berlanga E 67 C8
Berlanga de Duero E 56 F6
Berlești RO 176 D3
Berlevåg N 130 B6
Berlicum NL 199 B6
Berlin D 96 A4
Berlingerode D 95 D7
Berliște RO 175 D7
Berlstedt D 95 D9
Bermatingen D 43 E11
Bermeo E 56 B6
Bermillo de Sayago E 55 F7
Bern CH 47 B11
Bernac-Dessus F 49 D6
Bernalda I 77 C7
Bernardos E 62 B4
Bernartice CZ 92 D6
Bernartice CZ 97 E9
Bernāti LV 150 D1
Bernau D 43 E9
Bernau D 100 E5
Bernau am Chiemsee D 88 A5
Bernaville F 34 D5
Bernay F 40 B4
Bernbeuren D 87 B11
Bernburg (Saale) D 95 C10
Berndorf A 93 G10
Berne D 33 B10
Bernecebaráti H 163 E7
Bernedo E 57 C7
Bernhardsthal A 93 E11
Bernhardswald D 91 D11
Bernin F 47 E8
Bernis F 51 C7
Bernisdale GB 18 L4
Bernissart B 35 D8
Bernitt D 99 C11
Bernkastel-Kues D 37 E8
Bernolákovo SK 162 E4
Bernsdorf D 96 D6
Bernshammar S 113 C14
Bernstadt D 90 E7
Bernstadt D 97 D7
Bernstein A 164 B6
Beromünster CH 43 F9
Beronovo BG 183 D7
Beroun CZ 92 C6
Berovo MK 181 F6
Berra I 82 C4
Berre-l'Étang F 51 D9
Berriedale GB 19 J9
Berrien F 38 D4
Berriozar E 48 E2
Berru F 35 F9
Berry-au-Bac F 35 F8
Bersenbrück D 33 C9
Bershad' UA 170 A5
Beršići SRB 174 E5
Bersone I 85 B10
Bērstele LV 151 D7
Bertamirans E 54 C2
Bertea RO 177 C7
Berteștii de Jos RO 171 D1
Bertinoro I 82 D5
Bertnes N 124 B8
Bertogne B 35 D12
Bertrange L 202 B1
Bertrichamps F 43 D6
Bertrix B 35 E11
Běrunice CZ 93 B8
Berveni RO 167 B9
Bērvircava LV 150 D7
Berwick-upon-Tweed GB 21 D12
Bērzaine LV 147 F10
Berzasca RO 175 D8
Bērzaune LV 151 C12
Bērzciems LV 150 B6
Berzence H 165 D8
Bērzgale LV 149 C3
Bērzieši LV 151 D11
Bērzkalne LV 149 B2
Berźniki PL 153 E7
Berzovia RO 175 C8
Bērzpils LV 149 C2
Berzunți RO 169 E9
Beșalma MD 170 E3
Besalú E 59 C9
Besançon F 42 F5
Besande E 55 C10
Bescanó E 59 D9
Beselich-Obertiefenbach D 37 D10
Bešeňov SK 162 E6
Besenyőtelek H 166 B5
Besenyszög H 166 C5
Besigheim D 43 C11
Beşiktaş TR 189 B11
Beška SRB 174 C5
Besko PL 161 D4
Besni Fok SRB 174 D5
Besnyő H 165 B11
Besozzo I 84 B6
Bessacarr GB 27 D9
Bessaker N 120 C8
Bessan F 50 D5
Bessay-sur-Allier F 46 C3
Bessbrook GB 23 D10
Besse F 47 E9
Besse-et-St-Anastaise F 46 D2
Bessèges F 51 B7
Bessenbach D 203 B7
Bessé-sur-Braye F 40 E4
Besse-sur-Issole F 52 E4
Bessières F 49 C9
Bessines-sur-Gartempe F 45 C8
Bessude I 80 B2
Best NL 32 E4
Bestensee D 96 B5
Bestorp S 108 C7
Bestwig D 33 F10
Bestwina PL 163 B8
Beszterec H 161 G4
Betanzos E 54 B3
Betelu E 48 D2
Bétera E 64 E4
Beteta E 63 C8
Bethausen RO 167 F8
Betheln D 94 B6
Bethesda GB 26 E3
Bethmale F 49 E8
Bethon F 41 C10
Béthune F 34 C6
Betna N 120 E4
Beton-Bazoches F 41 C9
Betschdorf F 202 D4
Betsele S 123 B15
Bettelainville F 202 C1
Bettembourg L 36 E6
Bettendorf L 36 E6
Bettingen D 36 E6
Bettna S 109 B9
Bettola I 53 B11
Betton F 39 D8
Bettyhill GB 19 H8
Bettystown IRL 23 E10
Betws-y-coed GB 26 E4
Betxi E 64 E4
Betygala LT 150 F6
Betz F 41 B8
Betzdorf D 37 C9
Betzdorf L 202 B1
Betzenstein D 91 C9
Betzigau D 87 B10
Beucha D 95 D12
Beuil F 52 C5
Beuningen NL 32 E5
Beuren D 95 D7
Beuron D 43 D10
Beurville F 41 D12
Beuvrages F 198 E2
Beuvry F 34 C6
Beuzeville F 34 F1
Bevagna I 78 B3
Bevaix CH 47 B10
Beveren B 35 B9
Beverley GB 27 D11
Beverlo B 199 C6
Bevern D 94 C5
Beverstedt D 33 B11
Beverungen D 37 A12
Beverwijk NL 32 D3
Béville-le-Comte F 40 D6
Bewdley GB 29 A10
Bex CH 47 C11
Bexbach D 37 F8
Bexhill GB 31 F9
Beyağaç TR 197 B9
Beyazköy TR 189 B8
Beyçayırı TR 189 D6
Beyel TR 189 E10
Beyendorf D 95 B10
Beykoz TR 189 B11
Beynac-et-Cazenac F 45 F8
Beynat F 45 E9
Beynost F 47 D7
Beyoba TR 193 B10
Beyobası TR 197 C9
Bezas E 63 D10
Bezau A 87 C9
Bezdan SRB 166 F2
Bezdead RO 177 C6
Bezdonys LT 153 D12
Bèze F 42 E3
Bezenye H 162 F4
Bezhanitsy RUS 149 C7
Bezhanovo BG 171 F2
Bezhanovo BG 181 C9
Béziers F 50 D5
Bezledy PL 152 E2
Bezmer BG 177 F10
Bezmer BG 182 E6
Bezouce F 51 C8
Bežovce SK 161 F5
Biadki PL 158 C4
Biała PL 158 F4
Biała-Parcela Pierwsza PL 158 D5
Biała Piska PL 155 C13
Biała Podlaska PL 157 F8
Biała Rawska PL 157 G2
Białe Błota PL 154 D4
Białebłoto-Kobyla PL 155 E12
Białka PL 161 E1
Białobrzegi PL 157 G3
Białogard PL 101 C9
Białośliwie PL 101 D12
Białowieża PL 157 E9
Biały Bór PL 101 C11
Biały Dunajec PL 163 C10
Białystok PL 156 D8
Biancavilla I 75 D6
Bianco I 75 C9
Biandrate I 84 C5
Bians-les-Usiers F 47 B9
Bianzè I 84 C5
Biar E 72 D3
Biarritz F 48 D2
Biarrotte F 48 C3
Biars-sur-Cère F 45 F9
Bias F 48 B3
Bias F 49 B7
Biasca CH 87 E7
Biatorbágy H 165 B11
Bibbiena I 82 E4
Bibbona I 82 F2
Biberach D 43 D9
Biberach an der Riß D 87 A9
Biberbach D 91 E8
Biberist CH 43 F8
Bibinje HR 172 D3
Bibione I 89 E7
Biblis D 37 E10
Bibury GB 29 B11
Bicaz RO 167 C11
Bicaz RO 169 D8
Bicaz-Chei RO 169 D7
Bicazu Ardelean RO 169 D7
Biccari I 76 A4
Bicester GB 29 B12
Bichiș RO 168 F4
Bichl D 88 A3
Bichlbach A 87 C11
Bickleigh GB 29 D7
Bicorp E 64 F3
Bicos P 66 D3
Bicske H 165 A11
Bicton GB 26 F6
Bidache F 48 D3
Bidart F 48 D2
Biddenden GB 31 E10
Biddinghuizen NL 32 D5
Biddulph GB 27 E7
Bideford GB 28 C6
Bidjovagge N 128 E10
Bidos F 48 D4
Bidovce SK 161 F3
Bie S 109 A8
Bieber D 37 D12
Biebesheim am Rhein D 37 E10
Biecz PL 160 D3
Biedenkopf D 37 C11
Biel CH 43 F7
Biel E 48 F4
Bielany-Żytaki PL 157 F6
Bielawa PL 97 E11
Bielawy PL 159 B8
Bielefeld D 33 D11
Bielice PL 101 D7
Bieliny Kapitulne PL 159 E10
Biella I 84 B5
Bielle F 48 D5
Bielsa E 49 E6
Bielsk PL 155 E8
Bielsko-Biała PL 163 B8
Bielsk Podlaski PL 157 E8
Bienenbüttel D 99 D8
Bieniów PL 97 C8
Bienno I 85 B9
Bienservida E 71 B7
Bienvenida E 67 C7
Bierawa PL 158 F5
Bierdzany PL 158 E5
Bière CH 47 B9
Bierge E 58 C3
Bierné F 39 E10
Biersted DK 102 A5
Biert F 49 E8
Biertan RO 168 E5
Bieruń PL 159 F7
Bierutów PL 158 D4
Bierzwienna-Długa PL 158 B6
Bierzwnik PL 101 D9
Biesaidgohppi N 129 C16
Biescas E 48 E5
Biesenthal D 100 E5
Biesiekierz PL 101 B10
Biesles F 42 D3
Biesowice PL 101 B11
Biessenhofen D 87 B11
Bietigheim D 43 C9
Bietigheim-Bissingen D 43 C11
Bietikow D 100 D5
Bièvre B 35 E11
Bieżuń PL 155 E8
Biga TR 189 D7
Bigadiç TR 189 F9
Biganos F 48 A4
Bigastro E 72 E3
Bigauņciems LV 150 C7
Bigbury-on-Sea GB 29 E7
Biggar GB 21 D9
Biggleswade GB 31 C8
Bignan F 38 E6
Bignasco CH 87 E7
Bigor MNE 179 E7
Bigüézal E 48 E3
Biguglia F 53 F10
Bihać BIH 172 C4
Biharia RO 167 C8
Biharkeresztes H 167 C8
Biharnagybajom H 167 C7
Bihartorda H 167 D8
Biharugra H 167 D8
Bihosava BY 149 E3
Bijela MNE 179 E6
Bijele Poljane MNE 179 D6
Bijeljani BIH 173 F9
Bijeljina BIH 174 D3
Bijelo Brdo HR 165 E11
Bijelo Bučje BIH 173 D8
Bijelo Polje MNE 179 C8
Biķernieki LV 151 E13
Bikovo SRB 166 F4
Biksēre LV 151 C12
Bílá Lhota CZ 93 C11
Bilalovac BIH 173 D9
Bilbao E 56 B6
Bilbo E 56 B6
Bilbor RO 169 C7
Bilca RO 169 B7
Bilciurești RO 177 D7
Bil'dzyuhi BY 149 F2
Bileća BIH 178 D5
Biled RO 167 F6
Biłgoraj PL 160 B6
Bilicenii Vechi MD 169 B12
Bílina CZ 96 E5
Bilisht AL 184 C4
Biljača SRB 180 E4
Bilje HR 165 E11
Bilky UA 161 G7
Billdal S 107 D10
Billerbeck D 33 E8
Billère F 48 D5
Billericay GB 31 D9
Billesholm S 103 C11
Billiat F 47 C8
Billigheim D 37 F12
Billingham GB 27 B9
Billinghay GB 27 E11
Billingsfors S 107 B11
Billingshurst GB 31 E8
Billom F 46 D3
Billsåsen S 121 F16
Billsbro S 108 A7
Billsta S 123 E15
Billum DK 102 D2
Billund DK 102 D4
Billy F 46 C3
Bilolissya UA 170 F5
Bílovec CZ 162 B6
Bílovice CZ 162 C5
Bilska LV 151 B11
Bilston GB 21 D10
Bilthoven NL 32 D4
Bilto N 128 E7
Bilton GB 27 D11
Bilyayivka UA 170 E6
Bilychi UA 161 E6
Bilyn UA 168 A4
Bilyne UA 170 B5
Bilzen B 35 C12
Bimbister GB 19 G10
Bíňa SK 163 F7
Binaced E 58 D4
Binas F 40 E5
Binasco I 85 C7
Binbrook GB 27 E11
Binche B 35 D9
Bindalseit N 121 A12
Bindlach D 91 C10
Bindslev DK 106 D7
Binefar E 58 D4
Bingen D 43 D11
Bingen am Rhein D 37 E9
Bingerden NL 199 B8
Bingham GB 27 F10
Binghamstown IRL 22 D2
Bingley GB 27 D8
Bingsjö S 119 D10
Binic F 38 C6
Biniés E 48 E4
Binissalem E 65 E10
Binnen D 33 C12
Binz, Ostseebad D 100 B5
Binzen D 43 E8
Biograd na Moru HR 172 E3
Biokovina BIH 173 D7
Biol F 47 E7
Bionaz I 47 D11
Biorra IRL 23 F7
Biosca E 59 D6
Biot F 52 D6
Biota E 57 D9
Birchington GB 31 E11
Birchiș RO 167 F9
Bircza PL 160 D5
Birdhill IRL 24 C6
Birgittelyst DK 102 C4
Biri H 167 B8
Biri N 117 E13
Bīriņi LV 151 B9
Biristrand N 117 D12
Birkeland N 106 C3
Birkelse DK 102 A5
Birkenau D 203 B6
Birkenfeld D 37 E8
Birkenfeld D 43 C10
Birkenfeld D 90 C6
Birkenhead GB 26 E5
Birken-Honigsessen D 201 C8
Birkenwerder Berlin D 100 E4
Birkerød DK 103 D10
Birket DK 103 F8
Birketveit N 106 C2
Birkfeld A 164 B5
Birkungen D 95 D7
Birmingham GB 29 A11
Birnbaum A 89 C6
Biron F 49 A7
Birori I 80 C2
Birr IRL 23 F7
Birresborn D 37 D7
Birsay GB 19 G10
Birstall GB 27 F9
Birstein D 37 D12
Birštonas LT 153 D9
Birtavarre N 128 E6
Birtley GB 21 F13
Biruința MD 169 B12
Biržai LT 151 D9
Birzes LV 151 D8
Birzgale LV 151 C9
Birži LV 151 D11
Birzuļi LV 147 F12
Biš SLO 164 C5
Bisaccia I 76 A4
Bisacquino I 74 D3
Biscarrosse F 48 B3
Biscarrosse-Plage F 48 B3
Bisceglie I 77 A7
Bischberg D 91 C8
Bischbrunn D 203 B7
Bischhausen (Waldkappel) D 94 D6
Bischheim F 43 C8
Bischoffen D 37 C10
Bischofferode D 95 D7
Bischoffsheim F 202 E3
Bischofsheim D 37 E10
Bischofsheim an der Rhön D 90 B7
Bischofshofen A 89 B7
Bischofsmais D 92 E4
Bischofswerda D 96 D6
Bischofswiesen D 89 A6
Bischofszell CH 43 E11
Bischwiller F 43 C8
Bisenti I 78 B5
Biser BG 182 F5
Bisertsi BG 177 F9
Bishop Auckland GB 21 F13
Bishop's Castle GB 26 G6
Bishop's Cleeve GB 29 B10
Bishop's Lydeard GB 29 C8
Bishop's Stortford GB 31 D9
Bishop's Waltham GB 29 D12
Bishqem AL 184 B2
Bisignano I 76 D6
Bisingen D 43 D10
Biskupice PL 157 H7
Biskupice PL 158 D5
Biskupice SK 163 E9
Biskupiec PL 152 F2
Biskupiec PL 155 C7
Bislev DK 102 B5
Bismark (Altmark) D 99 E11
Bismervik N 129 B11
Bismo N 117 C8
Bisoca RO 177 B9
Bispgården S 123 E11
Bispingen D 99 D8
Bissen L 36 E6
Bissendorf D 33 D10
Bissendorf (Wedemark) D 94 A6
Bissingen D 91 E8
Bistagno I 53 B8
Bistarac BIH 173 C10
Bistra RO 167 E11
Bistra RO 168 B4
Bistražin SRB 179 E10
Bistreț RO 176 F3
Bistrets BG 183 E8
Bistrica BIH 173 B7
Bistrica BIH 173 C7
Bistrica BIH 173 E8
Bistrica BIH 173 E10
Bistrica SLO 89 D9
Bistrica SLO 164 D5
Bistričak BIH 173 D8
Bistrița RO 168 C5
Bistrița Bârgăului RO 168 C5
Bistritsa BG 181 D7
Bistritsa BG 181 E7
Bisztynek PL 152 E2
Bitburg D 37 E7
Bitche F 43 B7
Bitetto I 77 A7
Bitinckë AL 184 C4
Bitola MK 184 B5
Bitonto I 77 A7
Bitritto I 77 A7
Bitschwiller-lès-Thann F 43 E7
Bitterfeld D 95 C11
Bitterstad N 126 C9
Bitti I 80 C3
Bittkau D 95 B10
Bitton GB 29 C10
Bitz D 43 D11
Biurrun E 48 E2
Bivio CH 87 E9
Bivolari RO 169 B10
Bivona I 74 D3
Bixad RO 161 H7
Bixad RO 169 E7
Bixter GB 19 E14
Bıyıkalı TR 189 B7
Bıyıklı TR 193 D10
Bizanet F 50 D4
Bizanos F 48 D5
Bizovac HR 165 E10
Bjåen N 110 C6
Bjærangen N 124 C6
Bjæverskov DK 103 E10
Bjännberg S 138 C3
Bjarkøy N 127 C12
Bjärnum S 103 C13
Bjärred S 103 D12
Bjärsjölagård S 103 D13
Bjärtrå S 123 F13
Bjästa S 123 E15
Bjela BIH 173 F10
Bjelajci BIH 173 B6
Bjelopolje HR 172 C4
Bjelovar HR 165 E7
Bjergby DK 106 D7
Bjerge DK 103 D8
Bjerka N 124 D6
Bjerkvik N 127 C14
Bjerreby DK 102 F7
Bjerregrav DK 102 B5
Bjerringbro DK 102 C5
Bjøllånes N 124 C8
Bjoneroa N 111 A12
Bjønnes N 124 D7
Björbo S 113 B12
Björboholm S 107 D11
Bjordal N 110 E4
Bjørgen N 121 F9
Bjørgo N 117 E10
Björkå S 123 E13
Bjørkåsen N 127 C17
Bjørkåsen N 127 D12
Björkberg S 119 C9
Björkberg S 123 B13
Björkberg S 134 C5
Björkboda FIN 142 E8
Björke S 109 D12
Björke S 119 E13
Bjørkeflåta N 111 B9
Bjørkelangen N 111 C15
Bjørkeset N 111 C10
Bjørkestrand N 130 C4
Björketorp S 107 E12
Björkfors S 135 C10
Björkheden S 125 E12
Björkhöjden S 123 E10
Björkholmen S 125 C17
Björkland S 125 F16
Bjørklia N 121 E9
Björkliden S 127 D16
Björklinge S 115 B9
Björknäset S 123 F12
Bjørknes N 112 B6
Bjørknes N 130 D6
Björkö FIN 142 E4
Björköby FIN 138 D6
Björköby S 108 D5
Björkön S 119 B14
Björksele S 123 B15
Björksele S 123 D12
Björksjön S 123 E13
Björkstugan S 127 D15
Björkvik S 109 B9
Bjorli N 116 B8
Bjørn N 124 D4
Björna S 123 D15
Björnänge S 121 E14
Björndalen S 107 C11
Björneborg S 113 D11
Bjørnengen N 129 D11
Bjørnera N 127 C12
Bjørnes N 129 B18
Bjørnevatn N 130 D7
Bjørnfjell N 127 D15
Björnhult S 105 A10
Björnliden S 118 B3

Björnlunda S 109 A10
Björnön S 119 A9
Bjørnrå N 127 C10
Björnrike S 118 B6
Björnsjö S 123 D14
Björnskinn N 127 B10
Bjørnstad N 121 B14
Bjørnstad N 130 D9
Björsarv S 119 B11
Björsäter S 108 C8
Björsbo S 119 C12
Björsjö S 113 B13
Bjugn N 120 D7
Bjurå S 119 B8
Bjuråker S 119 C12
Bjurberget S 113 A8
Bjurfors S 123 C17
Bjurfors S 134 E5
Bjurholm S 123 D16
Bjursås S 119 E9
Bjurselet S 134 E6
Bjurträsk S 123 B17
Bjuv S 103 C11
Blace MK 180 E3
Blace SRB 179 E10
Blace SRB 180 C3
Blachownia PL 159 E6
Black Bourton GB 29 B11
Black Bull IRL 23 F10
Blackburn GB 19 L12
Blackburn GB 21 D9
Blackburn GB 26 D7
Blackmoor Gate GB 29 C7
Blackpool GB 26 D5
Blackrock IRL 23 E10
Blackstad S 109 D8
Blacktown GB 23 C7
Blackwater IRL 25 D10
Blackwaterfoot GB 20 D6
Blackwood GB 29 B8
Bladel NL 32 F4
Blaenau Ffestiniog GB 26 F4
Blaenavon GB 29 B8
Blagaj BIH 173 F8
Blagaj Japra BIH 172 B5
Blagdon GB 29 C9
Blăgeşti RO 169 D9
Blăgeşti RO 169 E12
Blagnac F 49 C8
Blagoevgrad BG 181 E7
Blagoevo BG 182 C6
Blåhøj DK 102 D4
Blaibach D 91 D12
Blain F 39 E8
Blainville-sur-l'Eau F 202 D1
Blainville-sur-Mer F 39 B8
Blair Atholl GB 21 B9
Blairgowrie GB 21 B10
Blaiserives F 41 D12
Blaj RO 168 E3
Blajan F 49 D7
Blăjani RO 177 C9
Blăjel RO 168 E4
Blăjeni RO 167 E10
Blakeney GB 29 B10
Blakeney GB 31 B11
Blakstad N 106 C4
Blåmont F 43 C6
Blan F 49 C10
Blanca E 71 C10
Blancafort F 41 E8
Blancas E 63 C10
Blandford Forum GB 29 D10
Blandiana RO 167 F11
Blanes E 59 D9
Blaney GB 23 D7
Blangy-sur-Bresle F 34 E4
Blankaholm S 109 D9
Blankenberg D 99 C11
Blankenberge B 35 B7
Blankenburg (Harz) D 95 C8
Blankenhain D 95 E9
Blankenhain D 95 E11
Blankenheim D 37 D7
Blankenrath D 37 D8
Blankensee D 100 D4
Blankenstein D 91 B10
Blanquefort F 44 F4
Blans DK 102 F5
Blansko CZ 93 D11
Blanzac-Porcheresse F 44 E6
Blanzay F 45 C6
Blanzy F 46 B5
Blaricum NL 199 A6
Blarney IRL 24 E5
Blasimon F 44 F5
Blåsjöfallet S 121 B16
Blåsmark S 134 D6
Błaszki PL 158 C5
Blatec MK 180 E3
Blatets BG 183 D7
Blatna CZ 93 D10
Blatná CZ 92 D5
Blatné SK 162 E4
Blatnica BIH 173 D8
Blato HR 178 D2
Blaton B 198 D3
Blattniksele S 125 F14
Blaubeuren D 90 F6
Blaufelden D 90 D6
Blausasc F 53 D6
Blaustein D 203 E8
Blåvik S 108 C6
Blåviksjön S 123 B14
Blavozy F 46 E4
Blaye F 44 E4
Blaževo SRB 179 C10
Blažiny Górne PL 157 H4
Błażma LV 150 B4
Blažovice CZ 93 D11
Błażowa PL 160 D5
Blázquez E 67 C9
Blažuj BIH 173 E9
Blecksåsen S 121 E15
Bleckede D 99 D9
Blecua E 58 C3
Bled SLO 89 D9
Błędowo PL 154 D6
Bledzew PL 97 A8
Blegny B 35 C12
Bléharies B 35 C7
Bleialf D 36 D6
Bleiburg A 89 C10
Bleicherode D 95 D8
Bleidenstadt D 201 D9
Bleik N 127 B10
Bleikvassli N 124 E6
Bleiswijk NL 198 A5
Blejești RO 177 E7
Blejoi RO 177 D8
Blekendorf D 99 B9
Bleket S 107 D10

Blender D 33 C12
Bléneau F 41 E8
Blénod-lès-Toul F 42 C4
Blenstrup DK 102 B6
Blentarp S 103 D13
Blera I 78 C2
Blérancourt F 35 E7
Bléré F 40 F4
Blerick NL 32 F6
Blesa E 58 E2
Bleskensgraaf NL 198 B5
Blessington IRL 23 F9
Blet F 45 B11
Bletchley GB 31 D7
Blidene LV 150 C5
Blidsberg S 107 D14
Blieskastel D 37 F8
Bligny F 41 D12
Bligny-sur-Ouche F 41 F12
Blikstorp S 107 C15
Bliksund N 106 C3
Blimea E 55 B8
Blindow D 100 D5
Blinja HR 165 F6
Blistrup DK 103 C10
Blixterboda S 113 D13
Blizanów PL 158 C5
Blíževoz CZ 92 D3
Blížkovice CZ 93 E9
Bliznatsi BG 183 C9
Bliżyn PL 157 H3
Blois F 40 E5
Blokhus DK 102 A5
Blokzijl NL 32 C5
Blombacka S 113 C10
Blomberg D 33 E12
Blome LV 151 B8
Blome LV 151 B13
Blomsøy N 124 E5
Boé F 49 B7
Boechout B 35 B9
Boecillo E 55 E10
Boekhoute B 198 C3
Boën F 46 D5
Boeslunde DK 103 E8
Boeza E 55 C7
Boffres F 46 F6
Boffzen D 37 A12
Boftsa N 129 C21
Bogács H 161 H2
Bogajo E 61 C7
Bogarra E 71 B8
Bogati RO 176 D6
Bogatić SRB 174 B5
Bogatići BIH 173 C7
Bogatynia PL 97 E7
Bogazici TR 193 C10
Bogda RO 167 F8
Bogdan BG 181 D10
Bogdana RO 169 D11
Bogdana RO 176 F6
Bogdanci MK 185 B7
Bogdand RO 167 C10
Bogdănești RO 169 E9
Bogdănești RO 170 E2
Bogdaniec PL 101 E8
Bogdănița RO 169 E11
Bogdanoci RO 174 B6
Boge S 109 D13
Bogen D 91 E12
Bogen N 121 A11
Bogen N 127 C12
Bogense DK 102 D6
Boggsjö S 122 E8
Boghești RO 169 E10
Bogílice BIH 173 F3
Bogliasco I 53 C10
Bognanco I 84 A5
Bognes N 127 C10
Bognor Regis GB 31 F7
Bogny-sur-Meuse F 200 E2
Bogø DK 103 F10
Bogodol BIH 173 F8
Bogojevo SRB 173 A11
Bogomilovo BG 182 E5
Bogoria PL 159 E11
Bogorojca MK 185 B8
Bogovina SRB 175 F8
Bogovinje MK 179 F10
Bogoy N 124 B6
Bograngen S 118 E4
Boguchwała PL 160 D4
Bogumiłowice PL 159 D7
Boguszów-Gorce PL 97 E10
Boguty-Pianki PL 157 E6
Bogyiszló PL 97 B9
Bohain-en-Vermandois F 35 E7
Bohars F 38 D3
Bohdalov CZ 93 D9
Bohdan UA 168 A4
Bohdíkov CZ 93 C9
Boherboy IRL 24 D4
Boherbue IRL 24 D4
Bohinjska Bistrica SLO 89 D8
Böhl D 203 C5
Böhlen D 95 D11
Böhme D 98 E6
Bohmte D 33 D10
Böhne D 95 A11
Bohola IRL 22 E4
Bohonal de Ibor E 61 E10
Böhönye H 165 B8
Bohoyo E 61 D10
Bohumín CZ 162 B5
Bohuňovice CZ 162 B4
Bohuslavice CZ 162 B6
Bohutín CZ 92 C5
Boianu Mare RO 167 C10
Boiro de Arriba E 54 C2
Boiscommun F 41 D7
Bois-d'Amont F 47 B9
Boisgervilly F 39 D7
Bois-Guillaume F 34 F3
Boişoara RO 176 C4
Boisseron F 49 C10
Boisset-et-Gaujac F 51 B7
Boisezon F 49 C10
Boitzenburg D 100 D5
Boiu Mare RO 168 C3
Boizenburg D 99 D9
Bojadła PL 97 C9
Bojano I 79 E6
Bojanów PL 160 C4
Bojanowo PL 97 C12
Bojkovice CZ 162 C5
Bojná SK 162 D6
Bojnice SK 163 D7
Bojničky SK 162 E5
Bojszowy PL 159 F7
Bojszów PL 158 F5

Boda glasbruk S 105 B9
Bodajk H 165 B10
Bodåsgruvan S 114 B6
Bodbacka FIN 138 E6
Bodbyn S 138 B4
Boddam GB 19 F14
Boddam GB 19 L13
Boddin D 99 C10
Bodegraven NL 198 A5
Bodelshausen D 203 E6
Boden S 134 C7
Bodenfelde D 94 C6
Bodenham GB 29 A9
Bodenheim D 37 E10
Bodenmais D 92 D4
Bodenteich D 99 E9
Bodenwerder D 94 C6
Bodenwöhr D 91 D11
Bodești RO 169 C8
Bodman D 43 E11
Bodmin GB 28 E5
Bodnegg D 87 B9
Bodø N 124 B7
Bodom N 121 D11
Bodonal de la Sierra E 67 C6
Bodoney GB 23 C8
Bodony H 163 F10
Bodroghalom H 161 G4
Bodrogkisfalud H 161 G3
Bodrum TR 193 E4
Bodsjö S 118 A8
Bodsjöbyn S 118 A8
Bodträskfors S 119 B8
Bódvaszilas H 161 F2
Bodyke IRL 24 C5
Bodzanów PL 155 E9
Bodzanów PL 158 F3
Bodzentyn PL 159 E10
Boechout B 35 B9
Boën F 46 D5
Boeslunde DK 103 E8

Bojszowy PL 159 F7
Boka SRB 175 C6
Bokel D 33 B11
Böklund D 98 A7
Bokod H 165 A10
Bököny H 167 B8
Bokšić HR 165 E9
Boksjön S 125 E10
Bol HR 172 F6
Bölan S 119 D12
Bolanden D 202 B5
Bolandoz F 47 A9
Bolaños de Calatrava E 70 B5
Bolăşău RO 169 D8
Bolayır TR 189 C6
Bolbaite E 72 C3
Bolbec F 34 E1
Bolboși RO 175 D10
Boldekow D 100 C5
Bolderslev DK 102 F4
Boldești-Grădiştea RO 177 D9
Boldești-Scăeni RO 177 C8
Boldog H 166 B4
Boldogkőváralja H 161 G3
Bolderslev DK 102 F4
Boldre GB 29 D11
Boldu RO 177 C10
Boldur RO 167 F8
Boldva H 161 G2
Bôle S 115 D10
Bôle S 118 B7
Bôle S 121 E15
Böle S 134 C5
Böle S 134 D6
Bolea E 57 D10
Bolekhiv UA 161 E10
Boleráz SK 162 E5
Bolesław PL 159 D8
Bolesław PL 157 F2
Bolesławiec PL 97 D9
Bolesławiec PL 158 D5
Boleszkowice PL 100 E7
Bolga N 124 C5
Bolgatovo RUS 149 C5
Bolhás H 165 B8
Bolhrad UA 171 B3
Boliden S 134 E4
Bolimów PL 157 F2
Bolintin-Deal RO 177 E7
Bolintin-Vale RO 177 E7
Boliqueime P 66 E3
Boljanić BIH 173 C9
Boljanići MNE 179 C7
Boljevac SRB 175 F8
Boljevci SRB 174 B5
Bôlkow D 99 B11
Bolków PL 97 E10
Boll D 90 E6
Bollebygd S 107 D12
Bollène F 51 B8
Bollengo I 84 C4
Bollermoen N 124 D6
Bolligen CH 47 B11
Bolling DK 102 D3
Bollingstedt D 98 A6
Bollnäs S 119 D11
Bollsbyn S 107 A12
Bollstabruk S 123 E13
Bollullos Par del Condado E 67 E6
Bolmen NL 198 B5
Bolnhurst GB 31 C8
Bologna I 82 D3
Bologne F 42 D3
Bolognetta I 74 D3
Bolognola I 78 C4
Bolotana I 80 D2
Boltești RO 169 F10
Bolsena I 78 A1
Bol'shakovo RUS 152 D4
Bolsover GB 27 E9
Bolsward NL 32 B5
Bolszewo PL 154 A5
Boltaña E 49 F6
Boltenhagen, Ostseebad D 99 C10
Bøltien CH 47 B10
Bolton GB 21 D11
Bolton GB 27 D7
Bölüntü TR 197 A7
Bolvaşnița RO 175 C9
Bolventor GB 28 D5
Bóly H 165 E11
Bolyarovo BG 183 E7
Bolzano I 88 D3
Bomal B 35 D12
Bomba I 79 C6
Bombarral P 60 F2
Bömlitz D 98 E6
Bompas F 50 E4
Bompensiere I 74 D4
Bompietro I 74 D5
Bomporto F 82 C3
Bomsund S 123 E9
Bona F 46 A3
Bonaduz CH 87 D8
Bonakas N 129 C21
Bônan S 119 E13
Bonanza E 68 C4
Boñar E 55 C9
Bonar Bridge GB 19 K8
Bonarcado I 80 C2
Bonares E 67 E6
Bonås S 118 D7
Bônäset S 122 E8
Bônäset S 123 E15
Bonassola I 53 C11
Bonawe GB 20 C6
Bonbillon F 42 E4
Bonchamp-lès-Laval F 39 D10
Bonchester Bridge GB 21 E11
Boncourt CH 43 F7
Bondeno I 82 C3
Bondersbyn S 135 C2
Bonderup DK 102 A4
Bondorf D 203 D6
Bondsjö S 119 A14
Bondues F 198 D2
Bônebüttel D 99 B8
Bonefro I 79 D7
Bönen D 33 E9
Bönhamn S 119 A15
Bonheiden B 35 B10
Boniches E 63 E9
Boniewo PL 154 F6
Bonifacio I 52 J10
Bonifati I 76 D5
Bönigen CH 86 D5
Bonin PL 101 B10

Bonn D 37 C8
Bonnåsjøen N 125 A10
Bonnat F 45 C9
Bonndorf im Schwarzwald D 43 E9
Bonnes N 127 C15
Bonnet DK 102 B2
Bonnétable F 40 D3
Bonneuil-Matours F 45 B7
Bonneval F 40 D5
Bonneval F 47 D10
Bonneval-sur-Arc F 47 E11
Bonnevaux F 47 B8
Bonneville F 47 C9
Bonnières F 51 C9
Bonnieux F 51 C9
Bönnigheim D 43 B11
Bonnyrigg GB 21 D10
Bonny-sur-Loire F 41 E8
Bono I 80 C3
Bono I 80 C3
Bonorva I 80 C2
Bons-en-Chablais F 47 C9
Bonțida RO 168 D3
Bôný H 165 A9
Bonyhád H 165 D11
Booa S 115 D10
Boock D 100 D6
Boom B 35 B9
Boortmeerbeek B 35 C10
Boostedt D 99 B8
Bootle GB 26 D6
Bopfingen D 91 E7
Boppard D 37 D9
Bor CZ 91 C12
Bor S 104 A6
Bor SRB 175 E9
Borač SRB 174 F6
Borås S 107 D12
Borăscu RO 176 D2
Borba P 66 B5
Borbjerg DK 102 C3
Borca RO 169 C7
Borchen D 33 E11
Borci BIH 173 C7
Borci BIH 173 E9
Börcs H 165 A9
Borculo NL 33 D7
Bordalba E 57 F7
Bordány H 166 E5
Bordeaux F 44 F4
Bordeira P 66 E2
Bordei Verde RO 177 C11
Bordères-Louron F 49 E6
Bordères-sur-l'Échez F 49 D6
Bordes E 48 D5
Bordes F 49 D6
Bordesholm D 99 B8
Bordeşti RO 177 B10
Bordighera I 53 D7
Bordils E 59 C9
Bording DK 102 C4
Bordón E 58 F3
Borduşani RO 171 E1
Bore I 85 D8
Boreham GB 31 D10
Borehamwood GB 31 D8
Borek PL 159 F10
Borek Strzeliński PL 97 E12
Borek Wielkopolski PL 97 C12
Boreland GB 21 E10
Børeiva N 124 D6
Børselv N 129 C16
Borensberg S 108 B6
Borg D 36 F6
Borgå FIN 143 E14
Borgafjäll S 122 B8
Borgentreich D 33 E12
Börger D 33 C8
Borgentreich D 33 E12
Borger NL 33 C7
Borggård S 108 B6
Borghamn S 108 C5
Borgheim N 106 A7
Borghetto d'Arroscia I 53 C7
Borghetto di Borbera I 53 B9
Borghetto di Vara I 85 E8
Borghetto Santo Spirito I 53 C8
Borgholm S 105 B11
Borgholzhausen D 33 D10
Borgia I 75 D7
Borgloon B 35 C11
Børglum DK 106 C3
Borgo F 53 F10
Borgo a Mozzano I 82 E2
Borgo d'Ale I 84 C5
Borgoforte I 82 B2
Borgofranco d'Ivrea I 84 B4
Borgo Grappa I 77 C10
Borgo-lavezzaro I 84 C6
Borgomanero I 84 B5
Borgomaro I 53 D7
Borgone Susa I 47 E11
Borgonovo Val Tidone I 85 C7
Borgo Pace I 82 E5
Borgorose I 78 C4
Borgo San Dalmazzo I 53 C6
Borgo San Lorenzo I 82 E3
Borgo San Martino I 84 C5
Borgosesia I 84 B5
Borgo Tossignano I 82 D4
Borgo Val di Taro I 85 E8
Borgo Valsugana I 88 D3
Borgo Velino I 78 C4
Borgo Vercelli I 84 C5
Borgsjö S 119 A13
Borgsjö S 123 E12
Borgstedt D 98 B7
Bort-les-Orgues F 45 E10
Bortan BG 181 C8
Bortnen N 116 C2
Borum DE 102 C6
Borup DK 103 E9
Borve GB 18 L3
Borynya UA 161 E6
Borysław UA 161 E6
Borzęciczki PL 97 C12
Borzonasca I 53 C10
Borzytuchom PL 101 B12
Bosa I 80 C2
Bošáca SK 162 D5
Bosanci RO 169 B8
Bosanska Rača BIH 174 C3
Bosanska Dubica BIH 173 B6
Bosanska Gradiška BIH 173 B7
Bosanska Kostajnica BIH 172 B5
Bosanska Krupa BIH 172 C5
Bosanski Brod BIH 173 B8
Bosanski Kobas BIH 173 B8
Bosanski Novi BIH 173 B6
Bosanski Petrovac BIH 172 C6
Bosanski Šamac BIH 173 B9
Bosansko Grahovo BIH 172 D6
Bošany SK 162 D6
Bôsárkány H 165 A8
Bosau D 99 B9
Boscastle GB 28 D5
Boscesem D 82 E5
Borgvattnet S 123 D8
Bosco Chiesanuova I 85 B11
Bosco Marengo I 84 C6
Boscotrecase I 76 B2
Bösdorf D 99 B9
Bôsebo S 105 A9
Bôsel D 33 B9
Bosham GB 31 F7
Boshulya BG 181 E9
Bosia RO 169 C11
Bosilegrad SRB 180 E5
Bosiljevo HR 164 F3
Boskoop NL 32 D3
Boskovice CZ 93 D11
Bošnjace SRB 180 D4
Bošnjaci HR 173 B10
Bošnjane SRB 175 F7
Bosórod RO 175 B11
Bossbod S 118 D7
Bosset F 45 F6

Bossolasco I 53 B8
Bôssost E 49 E7
Bostad N 126 D6
Bostan BIH 173 E7
Bøstølen N 116 B6
Boston GB 27 F11
Boston Spa GB 27 D9
Bostrak N 106 A4
Bosundet S 123 C10
Botão P 60 D3
Boteå S 123 E13
Boteni RO 176 C6
Botesdale GB 31 C11
Botești RO 169 D8
Botești RO 176 C6
Botevgrad BG 181 D8
Botevo BG 183 C9
Bothel GB 21 F10
Boticas P 54 E4
Botiz RO 167 B10
Botiza RO 168 B4
Botn N 126 E9
Botn N 127 A18
Botn N 128 D6
Botngård N 120 D7
Botnhamn N 127 A14
Botoroaga RO 177 E7
Botorrita E 57 E9
Botoş SRB 174 C6
Botoşana RO 169 B7
Botoşani RO 169 B9
Botoşeşti-Paia RO 175 C11
Botricello I 77 F7
Bötsle S 119 A12
Botsmark S 134 F4
Bottendorf (Burgwald) D 37 B11
Bottesford GB 27 D10
Bottidda I 80 C2
Bottnaryd S 107 D14
Bottrop D 33 E7
Botun MK 184 B4
Bötzingen D 43 D8
Bouaflès F 40 B5
Boucau F 48 C3
Bouc-Bel-Air F 51 D9
Boucé F 39 C11
Bouchain F 35 D7
Bouchemaine F 39 F10
Bouchoir F 34 E6
Boudry CH 47 B10
Boué F 35 D8
Bouglon F 49 B6
Bouguenais F 39 F8
Bouillargues F 51 C7
Bouillon B 35 E11
Bouilly F 41 D10
Bouin F 44 B1
Boujailles F 47 B9
Boujan-sur-Libron F 50 D5
Boulay-Moselle F 42 B5
Boulazac F 45 E7
Boulbon F 51 C8
Bouligny F 35 F12
Bouloc F 49 C8
Boulogne-Billancourt F 41 C7
Boulogne-sur-Gesse F 49 D7
Boulogne-sur-Mer F 31 F12
Bouloire F 40 E4
Boulouris F 52 D1
Boult-aux-Bois F 35 F10
Boulzicourt F 35 E10
Bouniagues F 45 F7
Bøur FO 18 A2
Bourbon-Lancy F 46 B4
Bourbon-l'Archambault F 46 B3
Bourbonne-les-Bains F 42 E4
Bourbourg F 34 C6
Bourbriac F 38 D5
Bourcefranc-le-Chapus F 44 D3
Bourdeaux F 51 A9
Bourdeilles F 45 E7
Bourdonnay F 43 C6
Bouresse F 45 C7
Bourg F 44 E4
Bourg-Achard F 34 F2
Bourganeuf F 45 D9
Bourg-Argental F 46 E6
Bourg-de-Péage F 47 D7
Bourg-de-Thizy F 46 C5
Bourg-de-Visa F 49 B7
Bourg-Dun F 34 E2
Bourg-en-Bresse F 47 C7
Bourges F 45 A10
Bourg-et-Comin F 35 F8
Bourg-Lastic F 45 D11
Bourg-lès-Valence F 46 F6
Bourgneuf-en-Mauges F 39 F10
Bourgneuf-en-Retz F 44 A2
Bourgogne F 35 F9
Bourgoin-Jallieu F 47 D7
Bourg-St-Andéol F 51 B8
Bourg-St-Bernard F 49 C8
Bourg-St-Maurice F 47 D10
Bourgtheroulde-Infreville F 34 F2
Bourguébus F 39 B11
Bourgueil F 39 F12
Bourmont F 42 D4
Bourne GB 27 E10
Bourneneu F 48 B5
Bourran F 49 B6
Bourriot-Bergonce F 48 B5
Bourron-Marlotte F 41 D8
Bourscheid D 200 E5
Bourtange NL 33 B8
Bourton GB 29 C10
Boussac F 45 C10
Bousse F 202 C1
Boussens F 49 D7
Boussières F 42 F4
Boussois F 35 D9
Boussu B 35 D8
Boutersem B 35 C10
Bouveret CH 47 C10
Bouvières F 51 A9
Bouvron F 39 F8
Bouxières-aux-Dames F 42 C5
Bouxwiller F 43 C7
Bouy F 41 B11
Bouzonville F 37 F7
Bouzov CZ 93 C11
Bova I 75 C8
Bøvær N 127 A13
Bovalino I 75 C9
Bovallstrand S 107 C9
Bova Marina I 75 D8
Bovan SRB 175 F8
Bovec SLO 89 D8
Bóveda E 54 C4
Boveda E 56 C5
Bovegno I 85 B9
Bovenden D 94 C6

Bøverfjord N 120 E5
Boves F 34 E5
Boves I 53 C7
Bovigny B 36 D5
Boviken S 134 E6
Boville Ernica I 78 D4
Bovino I 76 A4
Bøvlingbjerg DK 102 C2
Bovolone I 82 B3
Bovrup DK 102 F5
Bow GB 19 H10
Bowes GB 27 B7
Bowmore GB 20 D4
Box FIN 143 E13
Boxberg D 97 D7
Boxberg D 203 C8
Boxdorf D 96 D5
Boxholm S 108 C6
Boxmeer NL 32 E5
Boxtel NL 32 E4
Boyadzhik BG 182 E6
Boyanovo BG 183 E7
Boychinovtsi BG 181 C7
Boykovo BG 181 E10
Boyle IRL 22 E6
Bøylefoss N 106 B4
Boynes F 41 D7
Boynitsa BG 175 F10
Bøyum N 116 D5
Božava HR 83 D10
Bozburun TR 197 C8
Bozeat GB 31 C7
Bozel F 47 E10
Boževac SRB 175 D7
Bożewo PL 155 E8
Bozhentsi BG 182 D4
Božica SRB 180 D5
Božice CZ 93 E10
Bozieni MD 170 D3
Bozieni RO 169 D10
Bozioru RO 177 C8
Božjakovina HR 164 E6
Bozlar TR 189 D7
Bozouls F 50 B4
Bozovici RO 175 D9
Bozveliysko BG 183 C8
Bra I 53 B7
Braås S 105 A8
Bråbo S 105 A10
Brabova RO 176 E2
Bracadale GB 18 L4
Bracciano I 78 C2
Brach F 44 E4
Brachbach D 201 C8
Bracieux F 40 E6
Bräcke S 119 A9
Brackenheim D 43 B11
Brackley GB 29 A12
Bracknagh IRL 23 F8
Bracknell GB 31 E7
Braco GB 21 C9
Brad RO 167 E10
Bradashesh AL 184 B3
Brădeanu RO 177 D9
Brădeni RO 168 E5
Brădești RO 168 E6
Brădești RO 176 E3
Bradford GB 27 D8
Bradford-on-Avon GB 29 C10
Bradpole GB 29 D9
Bradu RO 176 D5
Brăduleţ RO 176 C5
Brădut RO 169 E7
Bradwell GB 31 D11
Bradwell Waterside GB 31 D10
Brae GB 19 E14
Brædstrup DK 102 D5
Braehead of Lunan GB 21 B11
Braemar GB 21 A10
Brăești RO 169 B8
Brăești RO 169 C10
Brăești RO 177 C9
Bråfim E 59 E6
Braga P 54 E3
Bragadiru RO 177 E7
Bragadiru RO 177 F7
Bragança P 55 E6
Bragar GB 18 J3
Brăhăşeşti RO 169 E10
Brahlstorf D 99 D9
Brăila RO 171 C1
Brailsford GB 27 F8
Braine F 35 F8
Braine-l'Alleud B 35 C9
Braine-le-Comte B 35 C9
Braintree GB 31 D10
Braives B 35 C11
Brajković BIH 173 D8
Brake (Unterweser) D 33 B10
Brakel B 35 C8
Brakel D 33 E12
Bråkne-Hoby S 105 C8
Bråland S 107 B11
Bralin PL 158 D4
Brallo di Pregola I 53 B10
Bralos GR 190 B5
Bralostiţa RO 176 D3
Bram F 49 D10
Bramans F 47 E10
Bramberg am Wildkogel A 88 B5
Bramdrupdam DK 102 D4
Bramming DK 102 E3
Brampton GB 21 F11
Brampton GB 31 C12
Bramsche D 33 D8
Bramsche D 33 D10
Bramstedt D 33 B11
Bran RO 176 B6
Brånaberg S 125 E11
Branäs S 118 E4
Brancaleone I 75 D9
Brancaster GB 31 B10
Brânceni RO 176 F6
Brâncoveneşti RO 168 D5
Brâncoveni RO 176 E4
Brand A 87 C9
Brand D 91 C10
Brandal N 116 B4
Brändåsen S 118 B4
Brändbu S 119 B11
Brandbu N 111 B13
Brande DK 102 D4
Brande-Hörnerkirchen D 98 C7
Brandenberg A 88 B4
Brandenburg D 95 B12
Brand-Erbisdorf D 96 E4
Branderup DK 102 E4
Brandis D 95 D11
Brand-Nagelberg A 93 E8

Brando F 53 F10
Brändö FIN 142 E5
Brandon GB 31 C10
Brändön S 134 C8
Brändövik FIN 138 D6
Brandshagen D 100 B4
Brandstorp S 108 C4
Brandsvoll N 106 C2
Brandval N 114 B7
Brandvoll N 127 C15
Brandýs nad Labem-Stará
Boleslav CZ 93 B7
Brandýs nad Orlicí CZ 93 B10
Branes N 112 A6
Brănești RO 176 C6
Brănești RO 177 E7
Brănești RO 177 E8
Branice PL 158 F4
Braniewo PL 155 B8
Brănişca RO 167 F10
Branişte RO 171 C1
Branişte RO 177 D7
Brankas LV 150 C7
Bränna S 107 B11
Brännåker S 123 B9
Brännås S 119 B11
Brännberg S 134 C6
Branne F 44 F5
Brännland S 123 D16
Brännland S 138 C4
Brañosera E 56 C4
Braňsk PL 157 E7
Branston GB 27 E11
Brantevik S 104 D6
Brantice CZ 158 F4
Brantôme F 45 E7
Branzi I 85 A8
Braojos E 62 B5
Braone I 85 B9
Brasaljce SRB 180 E3
Braslaw BY 149 E2
Brașov RO 177 B7
Brassac F 49 C9
Brasschaat B 32 F2
Brassy F 41 F10
Brasta S 121 E16
Brastad S 107 C10
Brastăvăţu RO 176 F4
Břasy CZ 92 C5
Brataj AL 184 D2
Bratca RO 167 D10
Bråte N 111 C14
Brateiu RO 168 E4
Brateljevici BIH 173 D10
Brateş RO 169 F8
Bratislava SK 93 F12
Bratkowice PL 160 C4
Bratovoești RO 176 E3
Bratsigovo BG 181 E9
Brattåker S 123 A11
Bratten S 123 B14
Brattfors S 119 E12
Brattfors S 123 D17
Brattli N 130 D7
Brattmon S 118 E4
Bratton GB 29 D10
Brattsbacka S 123 D16
Brattsele S 123 D12
Brattset N 120 E5
Brattvåg N 116 A4
Bratunac BIH 174 E3
Brătuşeni MD 169 A10
Bratya Daskalovi BG 182 E4
Braubach D 37 D9
Braud-et-St-Louis F 44 E4
Braunau am Inn A 92 F4
Brauneberg D 201 E6
Braunfels D 37 C10
Braunlage D 95 D10
Bräunlingen D 43 E9
Braunsbach D 203 C8
Braunsbedra D 95 D10
Braunschweig D 95 B8
Braunton GB 28 C6
Bravicea MD 170 C2
Bravnica BIH 173 D7
Bray IRL 23 F10
Bray-sur-Seine F 41 D9
Bray-sur-Somme F 34 E6
Brazey-en-Plaine F 42 F3
Brazi RO 177 D7
Brazii RO 167 D9
Brazii RO 177 D8
Brbinj HR 83 D11
Brčko BIH 173 C10
Brdów PL 154 F6
Bré IRL 23 F10
Brea E 57 E8
Brea de Tajo E 63 D10
Breaghva IRL 24 C3
Breascleit GB 18 J3
Breasta RO 176 E3
Breaza RO 168 B6
Breaza RO 168 C5
Breaza RO 177 C7
Breaza RO 177 C9
Brebeni RO 176 E4
Brebu RO 175 C9
Brebu RO 177 C7
Brebu Nou RO 175 C9
Brécey F 39 D8
Brech F 38 E6
Brechfa GB 28 B6
Brechin GB 21 B11
Brecht B 32 F1
Breckerfeld D 201 B7
Břeclav CZ 93 E11
Brecon GB 29 B8
Breda I 59 E14
Breda NL 32 E3
Bredared S 107 D12
Bredaryd S 103 A13
Bredbyn S 119 C11
Breddenberg D 33 C9
Breddin D 99 E12
Bredebro DK 102 E3
Bredene B 34 B6
Bredereiche D 100 D4
Bredevoort NL 33 E7
Bredkälen S 122 D8
Bredsätra S 105 B11
Bredsel S 134 C4
Bredsjö S 113 C13
Bredsjön S 119 A13
Bredstedt D 98 A5

Bredsten DK 102 D4
Bredträsk S 123 D15
Bredvik S 123 D17
Bredviken S 124 C8
Bredviken S 135 C10
Bree B 35 B12
Breese D 99 D11
Bregana HR 164 E4
Breganze I 88 E4
Bregare BG 181 B9
Bregeni MD 169 B12
Bregenz A 87 B9
Breg-Lum AL 179 E9
Breg-Lum AL 184 B2
Bregninge DK 102 F6
Bregovo BG 175 D9
Bréhal F 39 C8
Bréhan F 38 C8
Brehna D 95 D11
Breidenbach D 37 C10
Breidenbach F 43 B7
Breidstrand N 127 C12
Breiknik BG 181 D6
Breidvik N 124 B9
Breidvik N 126 C8
Breidvik N 126 E9
Breidvik N 127 D11
Breiholz D 98 B7
Breil CH 87 D8
Breil-sur-Roya F 53 D7
Breisach am Rhein D 43 D8
Breistein N 110 B2
Breitenbach CH 43 F8
Breitenbach D 37 C7
Breitenbach (Schauenburg) D
33 F12
Breitenbach am Herzberg D
94 E6
Breitenbach am Inn A 88 B4
Breitenberg D 92 E5
Breitenbrunn D 91 D10
Breitenburg D 98 C7
Breitenfelde D 99 C9
Breitengüßbach D 91 C8
Breitenhagen D 95 C10
Breitnau D 43 E9
Breitscheid D 199 C9
Breitscheid D 201 C7
Breitscheid D 201 E9
Breitungen D 95 E7
Breivik N 127 C12
Breivik N 128 B9
Breivikbotn N 128 B9
Breivikeidet N 127 A18
Brejning DK 102 D5
Brekka N 124 B6
Brekken N 124 E5
Brekkestø N 106 C3
Brekkhus N 116 B4
Brekkvasselv N 121 C11
Breklum D 98 A5
Brekovo SRB 174 E5
Breksillan N 121 B10
Brekstad N 120 D7
Brélès F 38 D2
Brelingen (Wedemark) D 94 A6
Bremdal DK 102 B3
Bremen D 33 B11
Bremerhaven D 33 B11
Bremervörde D 33 B12
Bremgarten CH 43 F9
Bremm D 37 D8
Bremnes N 110 C2
Bremnes N 126 C9
Brem-sur-Mer F 44 B2
Brenderup DK 102 E5
Brenes E 51 D8
Brengulï LV 147 F11
Brenitsa BG 181 C9
Brenna N 124 F5
Brenna N 126 B9
Brenna PL 163 B7
Brennero I 88 C4
Brennes N 128 D5
Brennfjell N 128 E5
Brenngam N 129 B19
Brennmo N 121 E11
Brennsvik N 129 B13
Breno I 85 B9
Brénod F 47 C8
Brens F 49 C8
Brensbach D 203 B6
Brent Knoll GB 29 C9
Brentwood GB 31 D9
Brenzone I 85 B10
Brescello I 82 C2
Brescia I 82 C1
Breskens NL 32 F1
Bresnica HR 83 D11
Bressana Bottarone I 85 C7
Bressanone I 88 C4
Bressols F 49 C8
Bressuire F 44 B5
Brest BG 176 F5
Brest BY 157 F7
Brest F 38 D3
Brestak BG 183 C9
Brestanica SLO 164 E4
Bresternica SLO 164 C5
Brestova HR 83 B9
Brestovac RO 169 E8
Brestovac SRB 180 C4
Brestovac Požeški HR 165 F9
Brestovăţ RO 167 F8
Brestovene BG 161 E10
Brestovets BG 181 C10
Brestovitsa BG 181 E10
Bretagne-d'Armagnac F 49 C6
Breţcu RO 169 E8
Bretea Română RO 175 B11
Breteil F 39 D8
Bretenoux F 45 F9
Breteuil F 34 E5
Breteuil F 40 C4
Brétignolles-sur-Mer F 44 B2
Bretnig D 96 D6
Bretocino E 55 E8
Bretoncelles F 40 D4
Bretten D 43 B10
Bretten GB 26 E6
Brettheim D 203 B9
Bretten GB 26 E6
Bretzenheim D 201 E8
Breuberg-Neustadt D 37 E12
Breuches F 42 E5
Breugel NL 199 B7
Breuil-Cervinia I 84 B4
Breuil-Magné F 44 D3
Breuilpont F 40 C5
Breukelen NL 32 D4
Breum DK 102 B4

Breuna D 33 F12
Breuvannes-en-Bassigny F
42 D1
Brevens bruk S 108 A7
Brevik N 106 A6
Brevik S 108 C4
Brevik S 109 A12
Brevik S 115 D10
Breviken S 112 B7
Brevörde D 94 C5
Breza BIH 173 D9
Brežana BG 181 B7
Breže-Lum AL 179 E9
Brežđe SRB 174 E5
Breze SLO 164 D4
Brezhani BG 181 F7
Brezi CZ 93 E11
Brezičani BIH 173 B6
Brežice SLO 164 E5
Brezna SRB 179 B10
Breznica HR 164 D6
Breznica SK 161 E4
Březnice CZ 92 C5
Breznik BG 181 F8
Brezniţa-Motru RO 175 D11
Brezniţa-Ocol RO 175 D10
Breznitsa BG 181 F8
Brezno CZ 92 B4
Brezno SK 163 D9
Brezoaele RO 177 D7
Brézolles F 40 C5
Březolupy CZ 162 C5
Březová CZ 162 D5
Březová nad Svitavou CZ 93 C11
Brezová pod Bradlom SK 162 D5
Brezovica SK 161 E2
Brezovica SLO 89 D9
Brezovo BG 182 E4
Brezovo Polje BIH 173 C10
Brezovo Polje HR 172 B5
Briançon F 47 F10
Briare F 41 E8
Briatexte F 49 C9
Briceni MD 169 A10
Bricherasio I 47 F11
Bricon F 42 E3
Bricquebec F 39 B8
Brides-les-Bains F 47 E10
Brideswell IRL 23 F6
Bridgeland IRL 26 L5
Bridgend GB 20 C6
Bridgend GB 20 D6
Bridgend GB 29 B8
Bridge of Cally GB 21 B10
Bridge of Don GB 19 L12
Bridge of Dye GB 21 A11
Bridge of Earn GB 21 C10
Bridge of Orchy GB 20 B7
Bridge of Weir GB 20 D7
Bridgetown IRL 25 D9
Bridgnorth GB 27 F7
Bridgwater GB 29 C8
Brídičná CZ 162 B4
Bridlington GB 27 C11
Bridport GB 29 D9
Brie F 45 D6
Briec F 38 D4
Brie-Comte-Robert F 41 C8
Briedel D 201 D7
Brielle NL 32 E2
Brienne-le-Château F 41 D12
Briennon F 46 C5
Brienon-sur-Armançon F 41 E10
Brienz CH 86 D6
Brienza I 76 C5
Briesen D 96 D5
Brieske D 96 D5
Brieskow-Finkenheerd D 97 B7
Briesnig D 97 C7
Brietlingen D 99 D8
Briey F 36 F5
Brig CH 84 A4
Brigg GB 27 D11
Brighouse GB 27 D8
Brighstone GB 29 D12
Brightlingsea GB 31 D11
Brighton GB 31 F8
Brigi LV 149 D4
Brignais F 46 D6
Brignogan-Plage F 38 C3
Brignoles F 52 E4
Brigstock GB 31 C7
Brihuega E 63 C7
Brijesta HR 178 D4
Brillon-en-Barrois F 42 C3
Brilon D 33 F11
Brimington GB 27 E9
Brimnes N 110 B5
Brinches P 66 C4
Brincones E 61 E10
Brindisi I 77 B9
Brindisi Montagna I 76 B5
Bringsli N 124 B9
Brinian GB 19 G11
Brinje HR 83 B11
Brinkum D 33 B8
Brinkum D 33 B11
Brinlack IRL 22 B6
Brinon-sur-Beuvron F 41 F9
Brinon-sur-Sauldre F 41 E7
Brin-sur-Seille F 42 C5
Brînza MD 171 A10
Brînzeni MD 169 A10
Brion F 46 F3
Briones E 56 C6
Brionne F 40 B4
Brioude F 46 E4
Brioux-sur-Boutonne F 44 C5
Briouze F 39 C11
Briscous F 48 D3
Brisighella I 82 D4
Brissac-Quincé F 39 F11
Bristol GB 29 C9
Briston GB 31 B11
Britelo P 54 E3
Briton Ferry GB 29 B7
Brittas IRL 23 F10
Brittas Bay IRL 25 C10
Britvica BIH 173 E8
Britz D 100 E5
Brive-la-Gaillarde F 45 E9
Briviesca E 56 C5
Brix F 39 A8
Brixen im Thale A 88 B5
Brixham GB 29 E8
Brixworth GB 31 A7
Brka BIH 173 C10
Brløžnik BIH 173 D11
Brna HR 178 E5
Brnaze HR 173 E6
Brniště CZ 97 E7

Breuna D 33 F12
Brnjica SRB 175 D8
Brnjica SRB 179 C9
Brno CZ 93 D11
Bro S 109 D12
Bro S 115 C9
Broadford GB 18 L5
Broadford IRL 24 C5
Broadford IRL 24 D5
Broad Haven GB 25 E12
Broadheath GB 29 A10
Broadstairs GB 31 E11
Broadway GB 29 A11
Broadwey GB 29 D10
Broadwindsor GB 29 D9
Broager DK 102 F5
Broaryd S 103 A12
Broby S 104 C3
Broby S 115 C11
Brobyværk DK 102 E6
Broc CH 47 B11
Broćanac BIH 173 F7
Brocas F 48 B4
Broceni LV 150 C5
Bröckel D 95 A7
Brockum D 33 C10
Brockworth GB 29 B10
Broczyno PL 101 C10
Brod BIH 173 F10
Brod MK 184 A5
Brod MK 185 C6
Brod SRB 179 D7
Brod SRB 180 E3
Brodalen S 107 C10
Brodarevo SRB 179 C8
Broddbo S 114 C6
Broddetorp S 107 C13
Brodek u Prostějova CZ 93 D12
Broderstorf D 99 B12
Brodica SRB 175 D8
Brodick GB 20 D6
Brodilovo BG 183 E9
Brodina RO 168 B6
Brodnica PL 97 B11
Brodnica PL 155 D7
Brodosavce SRB 179 E10
Brodské SK 93 E12
Brodski Stubnik HR 173 B8
Brody PL 97 B8
Brody PL 97 C7
Broekhuizenvorst NL 199 C8
Broglie F 40 B4
Brohl D 201 D7
Brohm D 100 C5
Broin F 42 F3
Brójce PL 97 B9
Brójce PL 101 C8
Brójce PL 159 C8
Brok PL 155 E12
Brokdorf D 33 A12
Brokind S 108 C7
Brokka N 106 C2
Brokstedt D 99 C7
Brolo I 75 C6
Bromarv FIN 143 F9
Brome D 95 A8
Bromnes N 128 C2
Bromölla S 104 C5
Brömsebro S 105 C10
Bromsgrove GB 29 A10
Bromyard GB 29 A9
Bron F 46 D6
Bronchales E 63 C9
Brønderslev DK 102 A5
Broni I 85 C7
Bronice PL 97 C7
Brønnøysund N 124 F3
Bronnytsya UA 170 A1
Brønsholm DK 102 B3
Bronte I 75 D6
Bronzani Majdan BIH 173 C6
Brooke GB 31 B11
Brookeborough GB 23 D8
Broons F 39 D7
Broquiès F 50 B4
Brørup DK 102 E4
Brösarp S 104 D6
Broscăuţi RO 169 B8
Broseley GB 26 F6
Broshniv Osada UA 161 F9
Brossac F 44 E5
Brøstadbotn N 127 B14
Broşteni RO 169 C7
Broşteni RO 169 F10
Broşteni RO 175 D10
Brotas P 66 B3
Brötjemark S 108 D4
Broto E 48 E5
Brottby S 115 C10
Brottes F 42 D3
Brotton GB 27 B10
Brøttum N 117 D13
Brou F 40 D5
Brough GB 19 H10
Brough GB 27 B7
Broughshane GB 20 F4
Broughton GB 26 E5
Broughton GB 31 C11
Broughton in Furness GB 26 C5
Broughton Astley GB 27 F9
Broughty Ferry GB 21 C11
Broumov CZ 97 E10
Brousseval F 42 D2
Broutzaiika GR 191 D6
Brouvelieures F 42 D6
Brouwershaven NL 32 E1
Brovst DK 102 A5
Brownhills GB 27 F8
Broxburn GB 21 D10
Brozany CZ 92 B6
Brozas E 61 E7
Brožiai LT 150 E3
Brozzo I 85 B9
Brštanovo HR 172 E5
Brtnice CZ 93 D9
Bruay-la-Bussière F 34 D6
Bruchhausen-Vilsen D 33 C12
Bruchköbel D 37 D8
Bruchmühlbach D 37 B8
Bruchsal D 43 B10
Bruchweiler-Bärenbach D
202 C4
Brück D 95 B12
Brücken D 37 B8
Brücken (Helme) D 95 D9
Brücken (Pfalz) D 37 E8
Brückl A 89 C10
Brückner I 75 E6
Bruchianico I 79 C6
Buccinasco I 85 C7
Buccino I 76 B4
Bucelas P 66 B1
Buceş RO 167 E10
Bucey-lès-Gy F 42 F4
Buch D 87 A10
Buch am Erlbach D 91 F11
Buchbach D 91 F11
Buchei Jenbach A 88 B4
Buchboden A 87 C9
Büchel D 37 D8
Büchen D 99 D9
Buchen (Odenwald) D 43 A11
Büchenbeuren D 201 E8
Buchholz D 99 D12
Buchholz (Aller) D 98 E7
Buchholz D 99 D11
Buchholz (Westerwald) D 37 C8
Buchin Prohod BG 181 D7
Buchkirchen A 92 F6
Büchlberg D 92 E5
Buchloe D 87 A11
Buchlovice CZ 162 C4
Bucholz in der Nordheide D
99 D7
Buchs CH 87 C9
Buchy F 34 E3
Bučim MK 180 F5
Buçimas AL 184 C4
Bučin MK 185 B6
Bucine I 82 F4
Bucinişu RO 176 F4
Bučiште MK 180 F5
Bucium RO 167 E11
Buciumeni RO 169 F10
Buciumeni RO 177 C6
Buciumi RO 167 C11
Bučje SRB 175 F9
Bučje SRB 179 C7
Buckden GB 27 C7
Bückeburg D 33 D12
Bücken D 33 C12
Buckfastleigh GB 29 E7
Buckhaven GB 21 C10
Buckie GB 19 K11
Buckingham GB 30 D7
Buckley GB 26 E5
Buckode IRL 22 D6
Buckow Märkische Schweiz D
96 A6
Bückwitz D 99 E12
Bucoşniţa RO 175 C9
Bucov RO 177 D8
Bucovăţ MD 170 C2
Bucovăţ RO 176 E3
Bucovica BIH 173 E7
Bučovice CZ 93 D12
Bucsa H 167 C7
Bucşani RO 177 D7
Bucşani RO 177 D11
Bucu RO 177 D11
Bucureşci RO 167 E10
Bucureşti RO 177 E8
Bucy-lès-Pierrepont F 35 E8
Bucz PL 97 B10
Buczek PL 159 D7
Bud N 116 A5
Buda RO 177 E9
Budacu de Jos RO 168 C5
Budakalász H 166 B3
Budakeszi H 165 A11
Budakovo MK 184 B5
Budaörs H 166 B3
Budapest H 166 C3
Budča SK 163 D8
Buddusò I 80 B3
Bude GB 28 D5
Budeasa RO 176 D5
Budel NL 32 F5
Büdelsdorf D 98 B7
Budenheim D 37 D10
Budens P 66 E2
Büdesheim D 37 D11
Budeşti RO 168 D3
Budeşti RO 168 D4
Budeşti RO 176 D4
Budeşti RO 177 E8
Budeyi UA 170 A4
Budia E 63 D7
Budila RO 177 B7
Budimci HR 165 F10
Budimlić Japra BIH 172 C5
Budinå SK 163 E8
Büdingen D 37 D12
Budinščina HR 164 D6
Budišov CZ 93 D9
Budišov nad Budišovkou CZ
162 B5
Budkovce SK 161 F4
Budleigh Salterton GB 29 D8
Budmerice SK 162 E4
Budoia I 88 D5
Budoni I 80 B4
Budrio I 82 C4
Budry PL 152 E4
Budureasa RO 167 D10
Budusláu RO 167 C9
Budva MNE 179 E6
Būdviečiai LT 152 D6
Budynė nad Ohří CZ 92 B6
Budziszewice PL 157 G1
Budzów PL 163 B9
Budzyń PL 101 E11
Bue N 110 E3
Bueña E 63 C10
Buenache de Alarcón E 63 E8
Buenache de la Sierra E 63 D8
Buenaventura E 62 D3
Buenavista de Valdavia E 55 C10
Buendía E 63 D7
Buer D 199 B10
Buer N 112 D6
Bueu E 54 D2
Bufleben D 95 D8
Buftea RO 177 D7
Bugac H 166 D4
Bugarra E 64 E3
Buğdaylı TR 189 D8
Bugeat F 45 D9
Buggenhout B 198 C4
Buggerru I 80 E1
Buggingen D 43 E8
Bugnara I 78 D5
Bugnein F 48 D4
Bugojno BIH 173 D8
Bugøyfjord N 130 D6
Bugøynes N 130 D7
Bugyi H 166 C3
Bühl D 43 C9
Bühlertal D 43 C9
Bühlertann D 90 D6
Bühlertann D 90 D6
Buhoci RO 169 D10

Buhølen N 106 C1
Buhuşi RO 169 D9
Buia I 89 D7
Builth Wells GB 29 A8
Buis-les-Baronnies F 51 B9
Buitenpost NL 32 B6
Buitrago del Lozoya E 62 C5
Buivydiškės LT 153 D11
Būivydžiai LT 153 D12
Buják H 163 F9
Bujalance E 69 A8
Bujan AL 179 E9
Bujanovac SRB 180 E4
Bujaraloz E 58 E3
Buje HR 83 B8
Bujor MD 170 D2
Bujoreni BG 181 D8
Bujoreni RO 177 E7
Bujoru RO 177 F7
Bük H 165 B7
Buk PL 97 B11
Bukhava BG 149 E6
Bukhovo BG 181 D8
Bukhovtsi BG 183 C7
Bükkábrány H 161 H2
Bükkösd H 165 D9
Bükksnes N 127 C10
Bükkszék H 161 H1
Bükkszentkereszt H 161 G2
Bükkszérc H 161 H2
Buko D 95 C11
Bukonys LT 151 F8
Bukova Gora BIH 173 E7
Bukovče SRB 175 E10
Bukovec CZ 163 B7
Bukovets BG 181 D8
Bukovje SLO 89 E9
Buków PL 97 B9
Bukowe PL 158 B4
Bukowice PL 97 D12
Bukowiec PL 97 B10
Bukowiec PL 154 D5
Bukowina PL 154 B4
Bukowina Tatrzańska PL 161 E1
Bukownica PL 158 C5
Bukowsko PL 161 E5
Bülach CH 43 E10
Bulboaca MD 170 D4
Bulbucata RO 177 E7
Bulçar AL 184 C3
Buldoo GB 19 H9
Bulford GB 29 C11
Bŭlgarene BG 181 C11
Bŭlgarevo BG 183 C10
Bŭlgari BG 183 E9
Bŭlgarovo BG 183 D8
Bŭlgarska Polyana BG 182 E6
Bŭlgarski Izvor BG 181 C9
Bulgnéville F 42 D4
Bŭlkau D 33 A11
Bulkington GB 29 A12
Bulkowo PL 155 E9
Bullas E 71 C9
Bullaun IRL 22 F5
Bullay D 37 D8
Bulle CH 47 B11
Bullerup DK 102 E6
Büllingen D 36 D6
Bullmark S 138 B4
Bully-les-Mines F 34 D6
Bulqizë AL 184 A3
Bultei I 80 C3
Bulz RO 167 D10
Bulzeşti RO 176 C4
Bulzeştii de Sus RO 167 E10
Bulzi I 80 B2
Bumbeşti-Jiu RO 176 C2
Bumbeşti-Piţic RO 176 C3
Buna BIH 173 F8
Bunacurry IRL 22 E3
Bunalty IRL 22 F5
Bun an Churraigh IRL 22 E3
Bun an Phobail IRL 22 C5
Bun an Tábhairne IRL 24 E6
Bunbeg IRL 22 B6
Bunclody IRL 25 C9
Bun Clóidí IRL 25 C9
Buncrana IRL 20 E2
Bun Cranncha IRL 20 E2
Bunde D 33 B8
Bünde D 33 D11
Bundenbach D 37 E8
Bunderhee D 33 B8
Bun Dobhrain IRL 22 C6
Bundoran IRL 22 C6
Bunessan GB 20 C4
Buneşti RO 168 E6
Buneşti RO 169 B8
Buneşti-Avereşti RO 169 D11
Bungay GB 31 C11
Bunge S 109 D14
Bunić HR 172 C4
Buniel E 56 D4
Bunila RO 175 B10
Bunka LV 150 D3
Bunkeflostrand S 103 D11
Bunkris S 118 D5
Bunmahon IRL 25 D8
Bunnaglass IRL 22 F5
Bun na hAbhna IRL 22 D3
Bunnahowen IRL 22 D3
Bun na Leaca IRL 22 B6
Bunnanaddan IRL 22 D5
Bunnanadden IRL 22 D5
Buñol E 64 F3
Bunschoten-Spakenburg NL 32 D4
Bunteşti RO 167 D10
Buntingford GB 31 D8
Bunyola E 65 E10
Buoač BIH 173 C7
Buochs CH 87 D6
Buollannjárga N 129 E15
Buonabitacolo I 76 C5
Buonalbergo I 76 A3
Buonconvento I 82 F3
Buonvicino I 76 D5
Bur DK 102 C2
Buran N 121 D11
Burbach D 37 C10
Burbage GB 29 C11
Burbáguena E 63 B10
Burcei I 80 E3
Bŭrdarski Geran BG 181 B8
Burdinne B 35 C11
Bureå S 134 E6
Bureåborg S 123 E13
Büren D 33 E11
Buren NL 199 B6

Büren an der Aare CH 43 F7
Bures GB 31 D10
Buresjön S 125 E14
Burfjord N 128 D9
Burford GB 29 B11
Burg D 96 C6
Burg (Dithmarschen) D 98 C6
Burganes de Valverde E 55 E8
Burgas BG 183 E8
Burgau A 164 B6
Burgau D 91 F7
Burgau P 66 E2
Burg auf Fehmarn D 99 B10
Burg bei Magdeburg D 95 B10
Burgberg im Allgäu D 87 B10
Burgbernheim D 91 D7
Burgbrohl D 91 D7
Burgdorf CH 86 C5
Burgdorf D 95 B7
Burgdorf D 95 B7
Burgebrach D 91 C8
Bürgel D 95 E10
Burgess Hill GB 31 F8
Burghausen D 92 F3
Burghclere GB 29 C12
Burghead GB 19 K10
Burgh-Haamstede NL 32 E1
Burgh le Marsh GB 27 E12
Burgio I 74 D3
Burgkirchen an der Alz D 91 F12
Burgkunstadt D 91 B9
Bürglen CH 43 E11
Bürglen CH 87 D7
Burglengenfeld D 91 D11
Burgohondo E 62 D3
Burgos E 56 D4
Burgos I 80 C2
Burgsalach D 91 D9
Burgsinn D 90 B6
Bürgstadt D 37 E12
Burgstädt D 95 E12
Burg Stargard D 100 D4
Burgsvik S 109 E12
Burgthann D 91 D9
Burgtonna D 95 D8
Burgui E 48 E3
Burguillos E 67 D8
Burguillos del Cerro E 67 C6
Burguillos de Toledo E 62 E5
Burgum NL 32 B6
Burgwindheim D 91 C8
Burhaniye TR 189 F6
Burhave (Butjadingen) D 33 A10
Buriasco I 47 F11
Burie F 44 D5
Burila Mare RO 175 E10
Burizanë AL 184 A2
Burjassot E 64 F4
Burjuc RO 167 F10
Burkardroth D 91 B7
Burkhardtsdorf D 96 E3
Burlada E 48 E2
Burladingen D 43 D11
Burlats F 49 C9
Bürmoos A 92 G3
Burnchurch IRL 25 C8
Burness GB 19 G11
Burnfoot GB 20 E3
Burnfoot GB 20 E2
Burnham GB 31 D7
Burnham Market GB 31 B10
Burnham-on-Crouch GB 31 D10
Burnham-on-Sea GB 29 C9
Burniston GB 27 C11
Burnley GB 27 D7
Burntisland GB 21 D10
Burntwood Green GB 27 F8
Burón E 55 B9
Buronzo I 84 C5
Buros F 48 D5
Burovac SRB 175 E7
Burow D 100 C4
Burøysund N 128 C4
Burravoe GB 19 E14
Burrel AL 184 A3
Burren GB 23 D10
Burren IRL 22 F4
Burriana E 64 E4
Burry Port GB 28 B6
Bürs A 87 C9
Burs S 109 D13
Bursa TR 189 D11
Burscough Bridge GB 26 D6
Burseryd S 103 A12
Bursfelde D 94 C6
Bürstadt D 37 E10
Burstow GB 31 E8
Bursuc MD 170 C2
Burtnieki LV 147 F10
Burton-in-Kendal GB 26 C6
Burton Latimer GB 31 C7
Burtonport IRL 22 C6
Burton upon Trent GB 27 F8
Burträsk S 134 E5
Buru RO 168 D3
Burujón E 62 E4
Burwarton GB 29 A9
Burwash GB 31 F9
Burwell GB 31 C9
Burwick GB 19 H11
Bury GB 27 D7
Bury St Edmunds GB 31 C10
Burzenin PL 158 D6
Busachi I 80 C2
Busalla I 53 B9
Busana I 82 D1
Busano I 84 C4
Bušanski Dubočac BIH 173 B8
Busca I 53 B6
Buscemi I 75 E6
Busdorf D 98 B7
Buseto Palizzolo I 74 C2
Buševec HR 164 E6
Busha UA 169 A12
Bushmills GB 20 E3
Bushtricë AL 179 F9
Bushtyna UA 161 G7
Busigny F 35 D7
Busilovac SRB 175 F7
Bušince SK 163 E8
Byske S 134 E6

Büßleben D 95 E9
Bussolengo I 82 B2
Bussoleno I 47 C4
Bussum NL 32 D4
Bussy-en-Othe F 41 D10
Bussy-le-Grand F 41 E12
Busto Arsizio I 85 B6
Busturi-Axpe E 57 B6
Büsum D 98 B5
Büta BG 181 E9
Butan BG 176 F3
Buteni RO 170 D3
Buteni RO 167 E9
Butera I 74 E5
Buteşti MD 169 B10
Bütgenbach B 36 D6
Butimanu RO 177 D7
Butoieşti RO 176 D2
Butor MD 170 C4
Butovo BG 182 C5
Bütow D 99 D12
Butrimonys LT 153 D9
Butrimonys LT 153 E11
Butryny PL 155 C10
Butschwil CH 43 F11
Büttelborn D 203 B6
Buttelstedt D 95 D10
Buttermere GB 26 B5
Buttevant IRL 24 E5
Butthard D 203 B8
Buttigliera d'Asti I 53 A7
Buttle GB 109 E13
Büttstädt D 95 D9
Büttstedt D 95 D7
Butuceni MD 169 B8
Butuceni MD 170 C3
Butzbach D 37 D11
Bützow D 99 C11
Buurse NL 33 D7
Buvåg N 126 D9
Buvik N 120 E8
Buxerolles F 45 B6
Buxheim D 87 B10
Buxières-les-Mines F 46 C2
Buxted GB 31 F9
Buxtehude D 98 D7
Buxton GB 27 E8
Buxy F 46 B6
Buynovtsi BG 182 D5
Büyükada TR 189 C11
Büyükaltuağaç TR 187 B10
Büyükanafarta TR 187 D10
Büyükbelen TR 193 B10
Büyükçavuşlu TR 189 B10
Büyükçekmece TR 189 B10
Büyükçiğli TR 193 C10
Büyükdöllük TR 183 F7
Büyük Evren TR 187 C10
Büyükgerdelli TR 183 F7
Büyükkarakarlı TR 189 B7
Büyükkarıştıran TR 189 B8
Büyükkılıçlı TR 189 B9
Büyükkorhan TR 189 E10
Büyükyenice TR 189 F7
Büyükyoncalı TR 189 B8
Buza RO 168 D4
Buzançais F 45 B8
Buzancy F 35 F10
Buzescu RO 176 E6
Buzet HR 83 B8
Buzet-sur-Baïse F 49 B6
Buzet-sur-Tarn F 49 C9
Buziaş RO 175 B8
Buzica SK 161 F3
Buziim BIH 172 B5
Buzoeşti RO 176 D5
Buzsák H 165 C9
By N 120 D8
Byala BG 182 D5
Byala BG 182 D6
Byala BG 183 D9
Byala Cherkva BG 182 C5
Byala Cherkva BG 182 C4
Byala Reka BG 182 D7
Byala Reka BG 183 D7
Byal Izvor BG 187 A8
Byalo Pole BG 182 E5
Byberget S 119 A9
Bybjerg DK 103 D9
Bychawa PL 160 A6
Bycina PL 158 F6
Byczyna PL 158 D5
Bydgoszcz PL 154 D5
Bye S 122 E7
Byelavyezhski BY 157 F8
Byel'ki BY 149 F2
Byenyakoni BY 153 E11
Byershty BY 153 F9
Byfield GB 31 C6
Bygdeå S 138 B5
Bygdeträsk S 134 E5
Bygdsiljum S 134 F5
Bygland N 106 B2
Byglandsfjord N 106 B2
Bykle N 110 D6
Bylchau GB 26 E4
Bylderup-Bov DK 102 F4
Byn S 113 B10
Byneset N 120 E8
Byremo N 106 C1
Byrkjedal N 110 E4
Byrkjelo N 116 C5
Byrknes N 116 C1
Byrtegrend N 110 C7
Byrum DK 103 A7
Byšice CZ 93 B7
Byske S 134 E6

Bystrzyca PL 158 E3
Bystrzyca Kłodzka PL 93 B11
Bytča SK 163 C7
Bytnica PL 97 B8
Bytom PL 159 F6
Bytom Odrzański PL 97 C9
Bytoń PL 154 E6
Bytów PL 101 B12
Byvallen S 118 B7
Byviken S 123 D16
Byxelkrok S 105 A12
Bzenec CZ 162 D4
Bzince pod Javorinou SK 162 D5

C

Cabacés E 58 E5
Cabaj-Čápor SK 162 E6
Cabanac-et-Villagrains F 48 A4
Cabañaquinta E 55 B8
Cabañas del Castillo E 61 E9
Cabanas de Viriato P 60 D5
Cabañas Raras E 55 C6
Cabanes E 64 D5
Cabanillas E 57 C8
Cabannes F 51 C8
Čabar HR 89 E10
Cabasse F 52 E4
Cabeça Gorda P 66 D4
Cabeção P 66 B3
Cabeceiras de Basto P 54 E4
Cabeço de Vide P 60 F5
Cabella Ligure I 53 B9
Căbeşti RO 167 D9
Cabeza del Villar E 61 C10
Cabezas Rubias E 67 D5
Cabezón de Cameros E 57 D6
Cabezón de la Sal E 56 B3
Cabezón de Liébana E 55 B10
Cabezuela del Valle E 61 D9
Cabo de Palos E 72 F3
Cabolafuente E 63 B8
Cabra E 69 B8
Cabração P 54 E2
Cabra del Camp E 58 E6
Cabra del Santo Cristo E 71 D6
Cabra de Mora E 64 D3
Cabras I 80 D2
Cabrejas del Pinar E 56 E5
Cabrela P 49 A9
Cabrerets F 49 A9
Cabrières-d'Aigues F 51 C10
Cabril P 60 D5
Cabrillanes E 55 C7
Cabrillas E 61 C8
Cabuna HR 165 B7
Cacabelos E 55 C6
Čačak SRB 174 F4
Caçarelhos P 55 E7
Caccamo I 74 D4
Caccuri I 77 E7
Cacém P 66 B1
Cáceres E 61 F8
Cachopo P 66 E4
Cachtice SK 162 D5
Cacica RO 169 B7
Cacín E 69 B9
Čačinci HR 165 B7
Cadalso de los Vidrios E 62 D4
Cadamstown IRL 23 F7
Cadaqués E 59 C10
Cadaval P 60 F2
Čadavica BIH 173 D6
Čadavica HR 165 B9
Čadavica Gornja BIH 173 C11
Čadca SK 163 C7
Cadelbosco di Sopra I 82 C1
Cadenazzo CH 85 A6
Cadenberge D 33 A12
Cadenet F 51 C9
Cadeo I 85 D8
Cádiar E 71 E6
Cadillac F 48 A5
Cádiz E 68 C4
Cadolzburg D 91 D8
Cadoneghe I 82 B4
Cadours F 49 C8
Cadrete E 57 D8
Cadrete E 57 D8
Caen F 39 B11
Caerau GB 29 C8
Caerdydd GB 29 C8
Caerfyrddin GB 28 B6
Caergybi GB 26 D2
Caerhun GB 26 D4
Caerleon GB 29 B9
Caernarfon GB 26 D4
Caerphilly GB 29 B8
Cafasse I 47 E12
Caggiano I 76 B5
Cagli I 82 E6
Cagliari I 80 E3
Čaglin HR 165 F9
Cagnac-les-Mines F 49 C10
Cagnano Varano I 79 D9
Cagnes-sur-Mer F 52 D6
Caherconlish IRL 24 C6
Cahermore IRL 24 E2
Cahir IRL 25 D7
Cahirciveen IRL 24 E2
Cahors F 49 B8
Cahul MD 170 F3
Cahuzac-sur-Vère F 49 C9
Căianu RO 168 D3
Căianu Mic RO 168 C4

Caissargues F 51 C7
Caister-on-Sea GB 31 B12
Caistor GB 27 E11
Căiuţi RO 169 E9
Caivano I 76 B2
Cajarc F 49 B9
Čajetina SRB 174 F4
Čajkov SK 163 E7
Čajniče BIH 173 E11
Čajvana RO 169 B7
Čaka SK 162 E6
Cakajovce SK 162 E6
Çakılköy TR 189 A8
Çakıllı TR 189 A8
Çakır TR 189 E7
Çakırlı TR 189 D9
Çakmakköy TR 188 B6
Çal TR 189 E7
Çalabardina E 71 E9
Calabritto I 76 B4
Calaceite E 58 E4
Cala d'Oliva I 80 A1
Cala d'Or E 73 C11
Cala Figuera E 73 C11
Calafat RO 175 F10
Calafell E 59 E7
Calafindeşti RO 169 B8
Cala Galdana E 73 B12
Calahonda E 69 C10
Calahorra E 48 F2
Calais F 31 F12
Calalzo di Cadore I 88 D5
Calamandrana I 53 B8
Cala Millor E 73 B11
Calamocha E 63 C10
Calamonaci I 74 D3
Calamonte E 67 B7
Cala Murada E 73 C11
Călan RO 167 F11
Calañas E 67 D6
Calanda E 58 F3
Calangianus I 80 B3
Calanna I 75 C8
Cala'n Porter E 73 B13
Calaşaţuca MD 170 A1
Călăraşi MD 169 C11
Călăraşi RO 168 E3
Călăraşi RO 169 B10
Călăraşi RO 176 F4
Cala Ratjada E 73 B11
Calascibetta I 74 D5
Calasetta I 80 E1
Calasparra E 71 C9
Calatayud E 57 F8
Călăţele RO 167 D11
Calatorao E 57 E9
Calau D 96 C5
Calbe (Saale) D 95 C10
Calcatoggio I 53 G9
Calcinato I 82 B1
Calcio I 85 B8
Căldăraru RO 176 D5
Caldarola I 83 F7
Caldaro sulla Strada del Vino I 88 D3
Caldas da Rainha P 60 F2
Caldas de Reis E 54 C2
Caldas de Vizela P 54 F3
Caldbeck GB 21 F10
Caldearenas E 48 E4
Caldecott GB 27 F10
Caldelas P 54 E3
Caldelas Taipas P 54 F3
Calden D 37 B12
Caldercruix GB 21 D9
Caldes de Malavella E 59 D9
Caldes de Montbui E 59 D8
Caldes d'Estrac E 59 D9
Caldicot GB 29 B9
Caldogno I 88 B4
Caldonazzo I 85 A11
Calella E 59 D9
Calendário P 54 F2
Calenzana F 53 F9
Calenzano I 82 E3
Calera de León E 67 C7
Calera y Chozas E 61 E10
Calerueca E 56 F5
Calfsound GB 19 G11
Calgary GB 20 C4
Çalı TR 189 D10
Calig E 58 G4
Călimăneşti RO 176 C4
Calimera I 77 C10
Călineşti MD 169 B10
Călineşti RO 168 B3
Călineşti RO 176 E6
Călineşti-Oaş RO 161 H7
Calitri I 76 B4
Calizzano I 53 C8
Çalköy TR 189 E9
Callac F 38 D4
Callain IRL 25 C8
Callan IRL 25 C8
Callander GB 21 C8
Callanish GB 18 J3
Callas F 52 D5
Callen F 48 B5
Callian F 52 D5
Calliano I 53 A8
Callington GB 28 F5
Callosa d'En Sarrià E 72 C2
Callosa de Segura E 72 E3
Čalma SRB 174 C4
Călmăţuii RO 176 E5
Călmăţuiu de Sus RO 176 E5
Calmont F 49 B11
Calmont F 49 D9
Calne GB 29 C10
Câlnic RO 168 F3
Câlnic RO 175 D11
Calolziocorte I 85 B7
Calomarde E 63 D9
Calonge E 59 D10
Calopăr RO 176 E3
Čalovec SK 162 F5
Calpe E 72 D2
Caltabellotta I 74 D3
Caltagirone I 75 E6
Caltanissetta I 74 E5
Caltavuturo I 74 D4
Caltignaga I 84 B6
Çaltılıbük TR 189 E10
Caltojar E 57 F6
Caltra IRL 22 F6

Călugăreni RO 177 E7
Caluso I 84 C4
Calvão P 66 D2
Calvarrasa de Abajo E 61 C9
Calvarrasa de Arriba E 61 C9
Calvello I 76 C5
Calverstown IRL 23 F9
Calvi F 53 F9
Calvi dell'Umbria I 78 C3
Calvignac F 49 B9
Calvinet F 45 F10
Calvini RO 177 D8
Calvi Risorta I 76 A2
Calvisson F 51 C7
Calvörde D 95 B9
Calvos E 54 E4
Calw D 43 C10
Calzada de Calatrava E 70 B5
Calzada de Valdunciel E 61 B9
Calzadilla E 61 D7
Calzadilla de los Barros E 67 C7
Camaldoli I 82 E4
Camaleño E 55 B10
Camallera E 59 C10
Camañas E 63 C10
Camar RO 167 C10
Camarasa E 58 D5
Câmăraşu RO 168 D4
Camarena E 62 D4
Camarena de la Sierra E 63 D10
Camarès F 50 C4
Camaret-sur-Aigues F 51 B8
Camaret-sur-Mer F 38 D2
Camarillas E 58 F2
Camariñas E 54 B1
Câmărzana RO 161 H7
Camarzana de Tera E 55 D7
Camas E 67 D7
Camastra I 74 E4
Cambados E 54 C2
Camberley GB 31 E7
Cambes F 44 A5
Cambil E 69 A9
Cambo-les-Bains F 48 D3
Camborne GB 28 E4
Cambra de Baixo P 60 C4
Cambrai F 35 C7
Cambre E 54 B3
Cambridge GB 31 C9
Cambrils E 58 E6
Cambron F 34 D4
Cambs D 99 C11
Camburg D 95 D10
Camelford GB 28 D5
Camenca MD 170 A3
Camerano I 83 E8
Camerino I 83 F7
Cameri I 84 B6
Camerles E 58 F5
Camerota I 76 C4
Camici TR 193 E10
Camigliatello Silano I 77 E6
Camin D 99 D9
Caminha P 54 E2
Caminomorisco E 61 D8
Camineal E 63 C10
Çamlıca TR 188 C6
Çamlık TR 193 D9
Cammarata I 74 D4
Cammin D 99 C12
Camogli I 53 C10
Camolin IRL 25 C10
Camon F 38 E6
Camors F 38 E6
Campagna I 76 B4
Campagnano di Roma I 78 C2
Campagnatico I 81 B4
Campagne F 45 F7
Campagne-lès-Hesdin F 31 G12
Campan F 48 D6
Campana I 77 E7
Campanario I 67 B9
Campanet E 73 B10
Câmpani RO 167 D10
Campano E 68 D4
Campaspero E 56 F3
Campbeltown GB 20 E5
Campbon F 39 F7
Campdevànol E 59 C8
Campea P 54 F4
Campello I 78 E2
Campello sul Clitunne I 78 B3
Campelo P 60 F2
Campelos P 60 F2
Campénéac F 39 E7
Câmpeni RO 167 E11
Campertogno I 84 B5
Câmpia Turzii RO 168 D3
Campi Bisenzio I 82 E3
Campiglia Marittima I 81 A3
Campiglia Soana I 47 D12
Campillo de Alto Buey E 63 E9
Campillo de Arenas E 69 A9
Campillo de Dueñas E 63 C9
Campillo de Llerena E 67 B8
Campillos E 69 B7
Campillos-Paravientos E 63 E9
Câmpina RO 177 C7
Câmpineanca RO 169 F10
Campinho P 66 C5
Campişábalos E 56 F5
Campi Salentina I 77 C10
Campli I 78 B5
Campo E 49 F6
Campo P 54 F3
Campobasso I 79 D7
Campobello di Licata I 74 E4
Campobello di Mazara I 74 D2
Campodarsego I 82 A4
Campo de Caso E 55 B9
Campo de Criptana E 63 F7
Campo de San Pedro E 56 F4
Campodimele I 78 D5
Campo di Trens I 88 C3
Campodolcino I 85 D8
Campofelice di Roccella I 74 D4
Campofiorito I 74 D3
Campoformido I 89 D7
Campofranco I 74 D4
Campofrío E 67 D6
Campo Ligure I 53 B9
Campo Lugar E 61 F10
Campo Maior P 67 A5
Campomanes E 55 B8
Campomarino I 79 D8
Campomoro F 53 H9
Camponaraya E 55 C6
Camponogara I 82 B5
Campora San Giovanni I 75 A9

Camporeale I 74 D3
Campo Redondo P 66 D2
Camporgiano I 82 D1
Camporosso I 53 D7
Camporrells E 58 D5
Camporrobles E 63 E10
Campos E 73 C11
Campos P 54 E4
Camposampiero I 82 A3
Camposanto I 82 C3
Campotéjar E 69 A9
Campotosto I 78 B4
Campo Tures I 88 C4
Camptown GB 21 E11
Câmpulung RO 176 C6
Câmpulung la Tisa RO 161 H8
Câmpulung Moldovenesc RO 169 B7
Câmpuri RO 169 E9
Camrose GB 28 B3
Camuñas E 62 F6
Çamyaylı TR 197 B8
Çan TR 189 D7
Caña SK 161 F3
Cañada E 72 D2
Cañada de Benatanduz E 58 F2
Cañada del Hoyo E 63 E8
Cañada Vellida E 58 F2
Canak AR 177 C10
Çanakçı TR 189 F10
Çanakkale TR 187 C10
Canale I 53 B7
Canale-di-Verde F 53 G10
Canalejas del Arroyo E 63 D8
Canalejas de Peñafiel E 56 E3
Canals E 72 D3
Canals F 49 C8
Canàl San Bovo I 88 D4
Cañamares E 63 D8
Cañamero E 61 F10
Canaples F 34 D5
Canari F 53 F10
Canaro I 82 C4
Cañaveral E 61 E8
Cañaveral de León E 67 C6
Cañaveras E 63 D8
Cañavereulas E 63 D7
Canazei I 88 D4
Cancale F 39 C8
Cancarix E 71 C9
Cancellara I 76 B5
Cancello ed Arnone I 76 A2
Cancon F 49 A7
Candanchú E 48 E4
Çandarlı TR 193 B8
Candás E 55 B8
Candasnos E 58 D4
Candé F 39 E9
Candela I 76 A5
Candelario E 61 D9
Candeleda E 61 D10
Candelo I 84 B5
Candemil P 54 E2
Cândeşti RO 169 D9
Cândeşti RO 176 C6
Candia Lomellina I 84 C6
Candilichera E 57 E7
Candin E 55 C6
Canedo P 60 B4
Canelli I 53 B8
Canena I 69 A6
Canepina I 78 C2
Canero I 55 A7
Canet E 72 D4
Canet F 50 D5
Canet de Mar E 59 D9
Cañete E 63 D9
Cañete de las Torres E 69 A8
Cañete la Real E 69 C6
Canet-en-Roussillon F 50 E5
Canet lo Roig E 58 F4
Canet-Plage F 50 E5
Cangas E 54 D2
Cangas del Narcea E 55 B6
Cangas de Onís E 55 B9
Cangonj AL 184 C4
Canha P 66 B2
Canhestros P 66 C3
Cania MD 170 E3
Canicattì I 74 E4
Canicattini Bagni I 75 E7
Canicosa de la Sierra E 56 E5
Caniles E 71 E7
Canillas de Aceituno E 69 C8
Canino I 78 C1
Cañizal E 61 B10
Cañizares E 63 C8
Cañizo E 55 E9
Canjáyar E 71 E7
Canlia RO 177 E11
Canna I 77 C7
Cannara I 78 B3
Cannero Riviera I 84 A6
Cannes F 52 D6
Canneto I 75 C6
Canneto I 82 E2
Canneto sull'Oglio I 82 B1
Cannich GB 18 L7
Canningstown IRL 23 E8
Cannington GB 29 C8
Cannobio I 84 A6
Cannock GB 27 F7
Cano P 66 B4
Canolo I 75 C9
Canonbie GB 21 E11
Canosa di Puglia I 76 A6
Cánovas P 72 F2
Can Pastilla E 65 E10
Can Picafort E 73 B11
Canredondo E 63 C8
Cansano I 78 D6
Cantagallo I 82 D3
Cantalapiedra E 61 B10
Cantalejo E 56 F4
Cantalice I 78 C3
Cantalpino E 61 B10
Cantanhede P 60 D3
Cantavieja E 58 F3
Čantavir SRB 166 F4
Cantemir MD 170 E2
Cantenac F 44 E4
Canteras F 72 F2
Canterbury GB 31 E11
Cantiano I 82 F6
Cantillana E 67 D8
Cantimpalos E 62 B4
Cantoira I 47 D11
Cantoria E 71 E8
Cantù I 85 B7
Canvey Island GB 31 D10
Cany-Barville F 34 E2

Canyelles E 59 E7
Caolas GB 20 B3
Caorle I 89 E6
Capaccio I 76 C4
Capaci I 74 C3
Capafonts E 58 E6
Capalbio I 81 C4
Căpâlna RO 167 D9
Căpâlnița RO 169 E6
Capannoli I 82 E2
Capannori I 82 E2
Caparde BIH 173 D10
Capari MK 184 B5
Caparica P 66 B1
Caparrosa P 60 C4
Caparroso E 48 F2
Cap-Blanc E 64 F4
Capbreton F 48 C3
Cap d'Agde F 50 D6
Capdenac F 49 A10
Capdenac-Gare F 49 A10
Capdepera E 73 B11
Capel Curig GB 26 E4
Capelins P 67 B5
Capelle aan de IJssel NL 32 E3
Capellen L 36 E6
Capel St Mary GB 31 C11
Capendu F 50 D4
Capestang F 50 D5
Capestrano I 78 C5
Cap Ferret F 48 A3
Capileira E 71 F6
Capilla E 70 B2
Capinha P 60 D6
Capistrello I 78 D4
Capizzi I 74 D5
Căpleni RO 167 B10
Čaplje BIH 173 C6
Čapljina BIH 173 F8
Capodimonte I 78 B1
Capo di Ponte I 85 A9
Capo d'Orlando I 75 C6
Capoliveri I 81 B2
Capolona I 82 E4
Caposele I 76 B4
Capoterra I 80 E2
Cappadocia I 78 C4
Cappagh White IRL 24 C6
Cappamore IRL 24 C6
Cappawhite IRL 24 C6
Cappeen IRL 24 E5
Cappelle sul Tavo I 78 C6
Cappeln (Oldenburg) D 33 C10
Cappercleuch GB 21 E10
Cappoquin IRL 25 D7
Capracotta I 79 D6
Capraia Isola I 81 A1
Capranica I 78 C2
Caprarola I 78 C2
Căpreni RO 176 D3
Capri I 76 B2
Căpriana MD 170 C2
Capriati a Volturno I 79 E6
Capri Leone I 75 C6
Caprino Bergamasco I 85 B7
Caprino Veronese I 85 B10
Captieux F 48 B5
Capua I 76 A2
Capurso I 77 A7
Căpușu Mare RO 167 D11
Capvern-les-Bains F 49 D6
Carabaña E 63 D6
Caracal RO 176 E4
Caracuel de Calatrava E 70 B4
Caragaș MD 170 D5
Caragele RO 177 D10
Caraglio I 53 C6
Caraman F 49 C9
Caramanico Terme I 78 C6
Caramulo P 60 C4
Cărand RO 167 E9
Caranga E 55 B7
Caranguejeira P 60 E3
Caransebeș RO 175 C9
Carantec F 38 C4
Carapelle I 76 A5
Carapinheira P 60 D3
Carasco I 53 C10
Carașova RO 175 C8
Caraula RO 175 E11
Caravaca de la Cruz E 71 C9
Caravaggio I 85 C8
Carbajales de Alba E 55 E8
Carballeda de Avia E 54 D3
Carballo E 54 B2
Carballo E 54 D4
Carbellino E 61 B8
Carbonera de Frentes E 57 E6
Carboneras E 71 F9
Carboneras de Guadazaón E 63 E9
Carbonero El Mayor E 62 B4
Carboneros E 70 C5
Carbonia I 80 E2
Carbonìn I 88 C5
Carbonne F 49 D8
Carbost GB 18 L4
Carbost GB 18 L4
Cărbunari RO 175 D8
Cărbunești RO 177 C8
Carbury IRL 23 F9
Carcaboso E 61 D8
Carcabuey E 69 B8
Carcaixent E 64 F4
Carcaliu RO 171 C2
Carcans F 44 E3
Carcans-Plage F 44 E3
Carção P 55 E6
Cárcar E 48 F2
Carcare I 53 C8
Carcassonne F 49 D10
Carcastillo E 48 F3
Carcelén E 63 F10
Carcès F 52 E4
Carchelejo E 69 A9
Carcoforo I 84 B5
Cardaillac F 45 F9
Çardak TR 188 D6
Cardedeu E 59 D8
Cardedu I 80 D4
Cardeña E 70 C4
Cardeñadijo E 56 D4
Cardenden GB 21 C10
Cardenete E 63 E9
Cardeñosa E 62 C3
Cardeto I 75 C8
Cardiff GB 29 C8
Cardigan GB 28 A5
Cardigos P 60 E4
Cardinale I 75 B9
Cardito I 78 D5
Cardon RO 171 C5
Cardona E 59 D7
Cardosas P 66 E2
Carei RO 167 B9
Carenas E 57 F8
Carentan F 39 B9
Carentoir F 39 E7
Carevdar HR 165 D7
Carev Dvor MK 184 B5
Cargenbridge GB 21 E9
Cargèse F 53 G9
Carhaix-Plouguer F 38 D4
Caria P 60 D6
Cariati I 77 E7
Caridade P 66 C4
Carife I 76 A4
Carignan F 35 E11
Carignano I 53 B7
Cariñena E 57 F9
Carini I 74 C3
Carinish GB 18 K2
Cariño E 54 A4
Carinola I 76 A1
Carisio I 84 C5
Carisolo I 85 A10
Cârjiți RO 167 F10
Carland GB 23 C9
Carlanstown IRL 23 E9
Carlantino I 79 D7
Carlat F 45 F11
Carlentini I 75 E7
Carlet E 64 F3
Cârlibaba RO 168 B6
Cârligele RO 169 F10
Carling F 202 C2
Carlingford IRL 23 D10
Carlisle GB 21 F11
Carloforte I 80 E1
Cârlogani RO 176 D4
Cârlomănești RO 177 C9
Carlopoli I 75 A9
Carlops GB 21 D10
Carlow D 99 C9
Carlow IRL 25 C9
Carloway GB 18 J3
Carlsberg D 202 C5
Carlton GB 27 F9
Carlton Colville GB 31 C12
Carluke GB 21 D9
Carlux F 45 F8
Carmagnola I 53 B7
Carmanova MD 170 C5
Carmarthen GB 28 B6
Carmaux F 49 B10
Carmena E 62 E4
Cármenes E 55 C8
Carmiano I 77 C10
Carmona E 67 E8
Carmonita E 61 F8
Carmyllie GB 21 B11
Carnac F 38 E5
Carnagh GB 23 D9
Carndonagh IRL 20 E2
Carnew IRL 25 C10
Carnforth GB 26 C6
Carnières F 35 D7
Carnikava LV 151 B8
Carnlough GB 20 F5
Carno GB 26 F4
Carnota E 54 C1
Carnoules F 52 E4
Carnoustie GB 21 B11
Carnoux-en-Provence F 51 D10
Carnteel GB 23 D9
Carnwath GB 21 D9
Carolei I 76 E6
Carolles F 39 C8
Carona I 85 A8
Caronia I 74 C5
C. A. Rosetti RO 171 C5
C. A. Rosetti RO 177 C10
Carosino I 77 C8
Carovigno I 77 B9
Carovilli I 79 D6
Carpaneto Piacentino I 85 D8
Carpegna I 82 E5
Carpen RO 175 E11
Carpenedolo I 82 B1
Carpentras F 51 B9
Carpi I 82 C2
Carpignano Salentino I 77 C10
Carpignano Sesia I 84 B5
Cărpineni MD 170 D2
Cărpinet RO 167 E10
Carpineti I 82 D1
Carpineto Romano I 78 D4
Cărpiniș RO 167 F6
Carpino I 79 D9
Carpinone I 79 D6
Carpio E 56 F1
Carpiquet F 39 B11
Carquefou F 39 F9
Carqueiranne F 52 E4
Carracastle IRL 22 E5
Carracedelo E 55 C6
Carradale East GB 20 D6
Carragh IRL 23 F9
Carraig Airt IRL 23 B7
Carraig na Siuire IRL 25 D8
Carraig Thuathail IRL 24 E6
Carral E 54 B3
Carranque E 62 D5
Carrapateira P 66 E2
Carrapichana P 60 C6
Carrara I 85 E9
Carraroe IRL 22 F3
Carrascal del Obispo E 61 C9
Carrascosa E 63 C8
Carrascosa del Campo E 63 D7
Carratraca E 69 C7
Carrazeda de Ansiães P 61 B6
Carrazedo de Montenegro P 54 E5
Carrbridge GB 19 L9
Carreço P 54 E2
Carregado P 66 A2
Carregal do Sal P 60 D5
Carregueiros P 60 E4
Carreira P 60 E3
Carreña E 55 B10
Carreteira E 54 C4
Carriazo E 56 B4
Carrick IRL 22 C5
Carrick IRL 25 D9
Carrickart IRL 23 B7
Carrickfergus GB 20 F5
Carrickmacross IRL 23 E9
Carrickmore GB 20 F2
Carrick-on-Shannon IRL 22 E6
Carrick-on-Suir IRL 25 D8
Carriço P 60 E3
Carrigaholt IRL 24 C3
Carrigallen IRL 23 E7
Carriganima IRL 24 E4
Carriganimmy IRL 24 E4
Carrigart IRL 23 B7
Carrigkerry IRL 24 D4
Carrig Mhachaire IRL 23 E9
Carrigtohill IRL 24 E6
Carrigtwohill IRL 24 E6
Carrio E 54 B3
Carrión de Calatrava E 70 A5
Carrión de los Céspedes E 67 E7
Carrión de los Condes E 55 D10
Carrizo de la Ribera E 55 C8
Carrizosa E 71 B7
Carronbridge GB 21 E9
Carros F 53 D6
Carrouges F 39 C11
Carrowkeel IRL 20 E2
Carrowkeel IRL 23 B7
Carrowkennedy IRL 22 E3
Carrù I 53 C7
Carryduff GB 23 C11
Carry-le-Rouet F 51 D9
Cars F 44 E4
Carsac-Aillac F 45 F8
Carsluith GB 21 F8
Carsoli I 78 C4
Carspach F 43 E7
Carsphairn GB 21 E8
Carstairs GB 21 D9
Cartagena E 72 F3
Cártama E 69 C7
Cartaxo P 60 F3
Cartaya E 67 E5
Cartelègue F 44 E4
Carteret F 39 B8
Carterton GB 29 B11
Cartes E 56 B3
Cârțișoara RO 168 F5
Cartoceto I 83 E6
Carucedo E 55 D6
Carunchio I 79 D7
Carvalhal P 60 E4
Carvalhal P 66 C2
Carvalho de Egas P 54 F5
Carvalhosa P 54 F3
Carviçais P 61 B7
Carvin F 34 D6
Carvoeira P 60 F2
Carvoeiro P 66 E3
Čáry SK 93 E12
Casabermeja E 69 C8
Casabona I 77 E7
Casa Branca P 66 B3
Casa Branca P 66 B4
Casacalenda I 79 D7
Casagiove I 76 A2
Casaglione F 53 G9
Casa l'Abate I 77 C10
Casalanguida I 79 C6
Casalarreina E 56 C6
Casalbordino I 79 C7
Casalbore I 76 A4
Casalborgone I 84 C4
Casalbuono I 76 C5
Casalbuttano ed Uniti I 85 C8
Casàl Cermelli I 53 B9
Casàl di Principe I 76 A2
Casalecchio di Reno I 82 D3
Casale Monferrato I 84 C5
Casaletto Spartano I 76 C5
Casalfiumanese I 82 D4
Casalgrande I 82 C2
Casalgrasso I 53 B7
Casalmaggiore I 82 C1
Casalnuovo Monterotaro I 79 D8
Casalpusterlengo I 85 C8
Casalvecchio di Puglia I 79 D8
Casàl Velino I 76 C4
Casamassima I 77 B7
Casamozza F 53 F10
Casarabonela E 69 C7
Casarano I 77 C10
Casar de Cáceres E 61 E8
Casar de Palomero E 61 D8
Casarejos E 56 E5
Casares E 55 B7
Casares E 69 D6
Casares de las Hurdes E 61 D8
Casariche E 69 B7
Casarrubios del Monte E 62 D4
Casarsa della Delizia I 89 E6
Casarza Ligure I 53 C10
Casas Altas E 63 D10
Casas Bajas E 63 D10
Casas de Benitez E 63 F8
Casas de Don Pedro E 61 F10
Casas de Fernando Alonso E 63 F8
Casas de Haro E 63 F8
Casas de Juan Gil E 63 F10
Casas de Juan Núñez E 63 F9
Casas de Lázaro E 71 B8
Casas del Monte E 61 D9
Casas de los Pinos E 63 F8
Casas del Puerto E 72 E2
Casas de Millán E 61 E8
Casas de Reina E 67 C8
Casas de Ves E 63 F10
Casas-Ibáñez E 63 F10
Casasimarro E 63 F8
Casas Novas de Mares P 66 B5
Casasola de Arión E 55 E9
Casatejada E 61 E9
Casatenovo I 85 B7
Casavieja E 62 D3
Cascais P 66 B1
Cascante E 57 D8
Cascante del Río E 63 D10
Cascia I 78 B4
Casciana Terme I 82 E2
Cascina I 82 E2
Căscioarele RO 177 E8
Casebres P 66 B2
Cáseda E 48 E3
Case della Marina I 80 E4
Casei Gerola I 53 A9
Cășeiu RO 168 C3
Casekow D 100 D6
Casella I 53 B9
Caselle in Pittari I 76 C5
Caselle Torinese I 84 C4
Case Perrone I 77 B7
Caseras E 58 E4
Caserta I 76 A2
Casével P 66 D3
Cashel IRL 22 E5
Cashel IRL 22 F3
Cashel IRL 23 B7
Cashel IRL 23 G8
Cashel IRL 25 C7
Cashla IRL 22 F5
Casillas E 62 D3
Casillas de Flores E 61 D7
Casimcea RO 171 D2
Cașin RO 169 E9
Casina I 82 C1
Casinos E 64 E3
Casla IRL 22 F3
Čáslav CZ 93 C8
Casnewydd GB 29 B9
Casola in Lunigiana I 82 D1
Casola Valsenio I 82 D4
Casole d'Elsa I 82 F3
Casoli I 79 C6
Casoria I 76 B2
Caspe E 58 E3
Casperia I 78 C3
Cassà de la Selva E 59 D9
Cassagnes-Bégonhès F 49 B11
Cassaniouze F 45 F10
Cassano allo Ionio I 77 D6
Cassano delle Murge I 77 B7
Cassano Magnano I 85 B6
Cassano Spinola I 53 B9
Cassaro I 75 E6
Cassel F 34 C5
Casseneuil F 49 B7
Casserres E 59 C7
Cassibile I 75 F7
Cassine I 53 B9
Cassino I 78 E5
Cassis F 51 D10
Cassola I 88 E4
Cassuéjouls F 46 F2
Častá SK 162 E4
Castagliona Olona I 85 B6
Castagnaro I 82 B3
Castagneto Carducci I 82 F2
Castagnole delle Lanze I 53 B8
Castagnole Monferrato I 53 B8
Castalla E 72 D3
Castañar de Ibor E 61 E10
Castañares de Rioja E 56 C6
Castanet-Tolosan F 49 C9
Castanheira P 60 C6
Castanheira de Pêra P 60 D4
Castano Primo I 84 B6
Castasegna CH 85 A8
Casteggio I 53 A10
Castejón E 57 D8
Castejón del Puente E 58 D4
Castejón de Monegros E 58 D3
Castejón de Sos E 49 E6
Castejón de Valdejasa E 57 E10
Castelbellino I 83 F7
Castèl Bolognese I 82 D4
Castelbuono I 74 D5
Castelcivita I 76 C4
Castèl d'Ario I 82 B2
Castel de Cabra E 58 F2
Casteldelfino I 52 B6
Castèl del Monte I 78 C5
Castèl del Piano I 81 B5
Castèl del Rio I 82 D4
Castèl di Iudica I 75 E6
Castèl di Lama I 78 B5
Castèl di Lucio I 74 D5
Castèl di Sangro I 78 D6
Casteleiro P 61 D6
Castelfidardo I 83 F8
Castelfiorentino I 82 E2
Castelflorite E 58 D3
Castèl Focognano I 82 E4
Castelforte I 78 E5
Castelfranci I 76 B4
Castelfranco di Sopra I 82 E4
Castelfranco di Sotto I 82 E2
Castelfranco Emilia I 82 C3
Castelfranco in Miscano I 76 A4
Castelfranco Veneto I 88 E4
Castèl Frentano I 79 C6
Castèl Gandolfo I 78 D3
Castelginest F 49 C8
Castèl Giorgio I 78 B1
Castèl Goffredo I 82 B1
Castelgrande I 76 B4
Casteljaloux F 49 B6
Castell D 91 C7
Castellabate I 76 C3
Castell'Alfero I 53 B8
Castellalto I 78 B5
Castellammare del Golfo I 74 C2
Castellammare di Stabia I 76 B2
Castellamonte I 84 C4
Castellana Grotte I 77 B8
Castellane F 52 D5
Castellaneta I 77 B7
Castellanos de Castro E 56 D3
Castellarano I 82 C2
Castellar de la Frontera E 69 D6
Castellar de la Muela E 63 C9
Castellar de la Ribera E 59 C6
Castellar de Santiago E 71 B6
Castellar de Santisteban E 71 C6
Castell'Arquato I 85 D8
Castell'Azzara I 78 B1
Castellazzo Bormida I 53 B9
Castelldans E 58 E5
Castell de Cabres E 58 F4
Castell de Castells E 72 D4
Castelldefels E 59 E7
Castell de Ferro E 71 F6
Castelleone I 85 C8
Castelletto sopra Ticino I 84 B6
Castellfort E 58 F3
Castellina in Chianti I 82 F3
Castellina Marittima I 82 F2
Castelliri I 78 D5
Castellnou de Bassella E 59 C6
Castellnovo E 64 E4
Castello d'Argile I 82 C3
Castelló de Farfanya E 58 D5
Castelló d'Empúries E 59 C10
Castelló de Rugat E 72 D4
Castello di Annone I 53 B8
Castellón de la Plana E 64 E4
Castellote E 58 F3
Castello Tesino I 88 D4
Castellserá E 58 D5
Castellterçol E 59 D8
Castellucchio I 82 B2
Castelluccio dei Sauri I 76 A4
Castelluccio Inferiore I 76 C5
Castellucio Valmaggiore I 76 A4
Castell'Umberto I 75 C6
Castelluzzo I 74 C2
Castell-y-Nedd GB 29 B7
Castèl Madama I 78 D3
Càstel Maggiore I 82 C3
Castelmagno I 53 C6
Castelmassa I 82 B3
Castelmauro I 79 D7
Castelmoron-sur-Lot F 49 B6
Castelnau-Barbarens F 49 C7
Castelnaudary F 49 D9
Castelnau-d'Auzan F 49 C6
Castelnau-de-Médoc F 44 E4
Castelnau-de-Montmiral F 49 C9
Castelnau d'Estréfonds F 49 C8
Castelnau-le-Lez F 51 C6
Castelnau-Magnoac F 49 D7
Castelnau-Montratier F 49 B8
Castelnau-Rivière-Basse F 48 C5
Castelnovo di Sotto I 82 C2
Castelnovo ne'Monti I 82 D1
Castelnuovo Berardenga I 82 F4
Castelnuovo della Daunia I 79 D8
Castelnuovo di Garfagnana I 82 D1
Castelnuovo di Porto I 78 C3
Castelnuovo di Val di Cecina I 82 F2
Castelnuovo Don Bosco I 84 C4
Castelnuovo Rangone I 82 C2
Castelnuovo Scrivia I 53 B9
Castelo Bom P 61 C7
Castelo Branco P 55 F6
Castelo Branco P 60 E6
Castelo de Paiva P 60 B4
Castelo de Vide P 60 F6
Castelo do Neiva P 54 E2
Castelões P 60 B4
Castelplanio I 83 F7
Castelraimondo I 83 F7
Castèl Ritaldi I 78 B3
Castelrotto I 88 C4
Castelsagrat F 49 B7
Castèl San Giovanni I 85 C7
Castèl San Lorenzo I 76 C4
Castèl San Niccolò I 82 E4
Castèl San Pietro Terme I 82 D4
Castèl Sant'Angelo I 78 C4
Castelsantangelo sul Nera I 78 B4
Castelsaraceno I 76 C5
Castelsardo I 80 B2
Castelsarrasin F 49 B8
Castelseras E 58 F3
Casteltermini I 74 D4
Castelu RO 171 E2
Castelverde I 85 C8
Castelvetere in Val Fortore I 76 A3
Castelvetrano I 74 D2
Castelvetro Placentino I 85 C8
Castèl Viscardo I 78 B2
Castèl Volturno I 76 A1
Castenaso I 82 C3
Castéra-Verduzan F 49 C6
Castetnau-Camblong F 48 D4
Castets F 48 C3
Castiadas I 80 E4
Castielfabib E 63 D10
Castiello de Jaca E 48 E4
Castiglioncello I 82 F1
Castiglione dei Pepoli I 82 D3
Castiglione del Lago I 82 F5
Castiglione della Pescaia I 81 B3
Castiglione della Stiviere I 82 B1
Castiglione di Sicilia I 75 D7
Castiglione d'Orcia I 81 A5
Castiglione in Teverina I 78 B2
Castiglione Messer Marino I 79 D6
Castiglion Fiorentino I 82 F4
Castignano I 78 B5
Castilblanco E 61 F10
Castilblanco de los Arroyos E 67 D8
Castiliscar E 48 F3
Castilleja de la Cuesta E 67 E7
Castillejar E 71 D7
Castillejo de Martin Viejo E 61 C7
Castillejo de Mesleón E 56 F4
Castillejo de Robledo E 56 E5
Castillo de Bayuela E 62 D3
Castillo de Garcimuñoz E 63 E8
Castillo de Locubín E 69 A9
Castillon-en-Couserans F 49 E8
Castillon-la-Bataille F 44 F5
Castillonnès F 49 A7
Castillo-Nuevo E 48 E3
Castilruiz E 57 E7
Castione della Presolana I 85 B9
Castiòns di Strada I 89 E7
Castlebar IRL 22 E4
Castlebay GB 20 B2
Castlebellingham IRL 23 E10
Castleblakeney IRL 22 F6
Castleblayney IRL 23 D9
Castlebridge IRL 25 D10
Castle Carrock GB 21 F11
Castle Cary GB 29 C9
Castlecomer IRL 25 C8
Castleconnell IRL 24 C5
Castlecor IRL 24 D5
Castledawson GB 20 F3
Castlederg GB 20 F1
Castledermot IRL 25 C9
Castle Douglas GB 21 F9
Castleellis IRL 25 D10
Castlefinn IRL 20 F1
Castleford GB 27 D9
Castlegal IRL 22 D6
Castlegregory IRL 24 D2
Castlehill IRL 22 D4
Castleisland IRL 24 D4
Castle Kennedy GB 20 F7
Castlellis IRL 25 D10
Castlemaine IRL 24 D3
Castlemartin GB 28 B4
Castlemartyr IRL 24 E6
Castleplunket IRL 22 E6
Castlepollard IRL 23 E8
Castlerea IRL 22 E6
Castlereagh GB 23 C11
Castlerock GB 20 E3
Castletown GB 19 H10
Castletown GB 27 F7
Castletown GBM 26 C2
Castletown IRL 23 G8
Castletown Bere IRL 24 E3
Castletownshend IRL 24 E4
Castlewellan GB 23 D11
Castranova RO 176 E4
Castrejón de la Peña E 55 C10
Castrelo do Val E 54 E5
Castres F 49 C10
Castricum NL 32 C3
Castries F 51 C6
Castrignano del Capo I 77 D10
Castril E 71 D7
Castrillo de Don Juan E 56 E3
Castrillo de Duero E 56 E3
Castrillo de la Reina E 56 E5
Castrillo de la Vega E 56 E4
Castrillo Tejeriego E 56 E3
Castro I 77 C10
Castrobarto E 56 B5
Castrocalbón E 55 D8
Castro Caldelas E 54 D5
Castrocaro Terme I 82 D4
Castrocontrigo E 55 D7
Castro Daire P 60 C5
Castro dei Volsci I 78 D5
Castro del Río E 69 A8
Castro de Ouro E 54 A5
Castro de Rei E 54 B5
Castrofilippo I 74 E4
Castrogonzalo E 55 E8
Castrojeriz E 56 D3
Castro Laboreiro P 54 D3
Castro Marim P 66 E5
Castromocho E 55 D10
Castromonte E 55 E9
Castronuevo E 55 E8
Castronuño E 55 F9
Castronuovo di Sant'Andrea I 76 C6
Castronuovo di Sicilia I 74 D4
Castropignano I 79 D7
Castropodame E 55 C7
Castropol E 55 A5
Castrop-Rauxel D 33 E8
Castroreale I 75 C7
Castro-Urdiales E 56 B5
Castroverde E 54 B5
Castro Verde P 66 D3
Castroverde de Campos E 55 E9
Castrovillari I 76 D6
Castuera E 67 B8
Cața RO 168 E6
Catadau E 64 F3
Çatalca TR 189 B9
Catalina RO 169 F8
Cataloi RO 171 C3
Catania I 75 E7
Catanzaro I 75 B10
Catanzaro Marina I 75 B10
Catarroja E 64 F4
Câtcău RO 168 C3
Căteasca RO 176 D6
Catenanuova I 75 D6
Caterham GB 31 E8
Cateri F 53 F9
Cathair Dónall IRL 24 E2
Cathair na Mart IRL 22 E3
Cathair Saidhbhín IRL 24 E2
Catherdaniel IRL 24 E2
Catí E 58 G4
Čatići BIH 173 D9
Catignano I 78 C5
Cătina RO 168 D4
Cătina RO 177 C8
Cativelos P 60 C5
Catoira E 54 C2
Caton GB 26 C6
Catral E 72 E3
Cattenom F 36 F6
Catterfeld D 95 E8
Catterick GB 27 C8
Catterline GB 21 B12
Cattolica I 83 E6
Cattolica Eraclea I 74 E3
Cătunele RO 175 D10
Catus F 49 A8
Căuaș RO 167 B10
Caudan F 38 E5
Caudebec-lès-Elbeuf F 34 F3
Caudecoste F 49 B7
Caudete E 72 D3
Caudete de las Fuentes E 63 E10
Caudiel E 64 E3
Caudiès de-Fenouillèdes F 49 E10
Caudry F 35 D7
Caujac F 49 D8
Caulnes F 39 D7
Caulonia I 75 C9
Caumont F 49 B8
Caumont F 49 D8
Caumont-l'Éventé F 39 B10
Caumont-sur-Durance F 51 C8
Caunes-Minervois F 50 D4
Cauro F 53 H9
Căușeni MD 170 D4
Causeway IRL 24 D3
Causeway Head GB 20 E3
Caussade F 49 B9
Cautano I 76 A3
Cauterets F 48 E5
Cava de'Tirreni I 76 B3
Cavadinești RO 169 E12
Cavaglià I 84 C5
Cavaillon F 51 C9
Cavalaire-sur-Mer F 52 E5
Cavaleiro P 66 D2
Cavalese I 88 D3
Cavallermaggiore I 53 B7
Cavallino I 82 B6
Cava Manara I 85 C7
Cavan IRL 23 E8
Cavanagarven IRL 23 D9
Cavargna I 85 A7
Cavarzere I 82 B5
Cavazzo Carnico I 89 D7
Cave I 78 D3
Cave del Predìl I 89 D8
Caveirac F 51 C7
Cavezzo I 82 C3
Cavignac F 44 E5
Čavle HR 83 B9
Cavnic RO 168 B3
Cavour I 84 D3
Cavriago I 82 C2
Cavriglia I 82 E3
Cavtat HR 178 D5
Çavuşköy TR 187 C10
Cawdor GB 19 K9
Cawood GB 27 D9
Cawston GB 31 B11
Caxarias P 60 E3
Çaybaşı TR 193 C9
Çayboyu TR 197 B8
Cayeux-sur-Mer F 34 D4
Çayırdere TR 189 B9
Caylus F 49 B9
Cazalegas E 62 D3
Cazalilla E 69 A9
Cazalla de la Sierra E 67 D8
Cazals F 49 A8
Cazals F 49 B9
Căzănești RO 175 D10
Căzănești RO 177 D10
Cazasu RO 171 C1
Cazaubon F 48 C5
Cazères F 49 D8
Cazes-Mondenard F 49 B8
Cazilhac F 49 D10
Cazin BIH 172 C4
Cazis CH 87 D8
Cažma HR 165 E7
Cazorla E 71 D7
Cazoulès F 45 F8
Cea E 54 D4
Cea E 55 D10
Ceahlău RO 169 C7
Ceamurlia de Jos RO 171 D3
Ceanannus Mór IRL 23 E9
Ceann Toirc IRL 24 D5
Ceann Trá IRL 24 D2
Ceanu Mare RO 168 D3
Cearsiadar GB 18 J3
Ceatharlach IRL 25 C9
Ceaucé F 39 D10
Ceaușu de Câmpie RO 168 D5
Céaux-d'Allègre F 46 E4
Cébazat F 46 D3
Čebín CZ 93 D10
Cebolla E 62 E3
Čebovce SK 163 E8
Cebreros E 62 D4
Ceccano I 78 D4
Cece H 165 C11
Čečejovce SK 161 F3
Čechtice CZ 93 C8
Čechynce SK 162 E6
Cecina I 82 F2
Ceclavín E 61 E7
Cecuni MNE 179 D8
Cedães P 54 F5
Čedasai LT 151 D10
Cedegolo I 85 A9
Cedeira E 54 A3
Cedillo E 60 E6
Cedillo del Condado E 62 D5
Cedrillas E 64 D3
Cedry Wielkie PL 154 B6
Cedynia PL 100 E6
Cee E 54 C1
Cefa RO 167 D8
Cefalù I 74 C5
Cefn-mawr GB 26 F5
Ceggia I 89 E6
Cegléd H 166 C4
Ceglédbercel H 166 C4
Ceglie Messapica I 77 B9
Cegłów PL 157 F5
Čegrane MK 179 F10
Cehal RO 167 C10
Cehegín E 71 C9
Cehu Silvaniei RO 167 C11
Ceica RO 167 D9
Ceikiniai LT 151 F12
Ceilhes-et-Rocozels F 50 C5
Ceinos de Campos E 55 D9
Ceintrey F 42 C5
Ceira P 60 D4
Čejč CZ 93 E11
Cejkov SK 161 G4
Cekcyn PL 154 C5
Çekirdekli TR 189 F9
Čekiškė LT 150 F7
Ceków-Kolonia PL 158 C5
Celadas E 63 D10
Čeladná CZ 162 B6
Čelákovice CZ 93 B7
Celaliye TR 189 A7
Celano I 78 C5
Celanova E 54 D4
Čelarevo SRB 174 C4
Celaru RO 176 E4
Celbridge IRL 23 F9
Čelebić BIH 173 E6
Čelebići BIH 173 F10
Celeiros P 54 E3
Celenza Valfortore I 79 D7
Celestynów PL 157 F4
Čelič BIH 173 C10
Celico I 77 E6
Čelinac Donji BIH 173 C7
Celje SLO 164 D4
Cella E 63 D10
Celldömölk H 165 B8
Celle D 95 A7
Celle Ligure I 53 C9
Cellere I 78 C1
Celles B 35 C7
Celles-sur-Belle F 44 C5
Celles-sur-Ource F 41 D11
Cellettes F 40 E5
Cellino Attanasio I 78 B5
Cellole I 78 E5
Čelopeci MK 184 B5
Čelopek MK 180 F3
Celorico da Beira P 60 C6
Celorico de Basto P 54 F4
Celrà E 59 C9
Çeltikçi TR 189 D9
Cembra I 85 A11
Čemerno BIH 173 F10
Cempi LV 151 A11
Cénac-et-St-Julien F 45 F8
Cenad RO 166 E6
Cenade RO 168 E4
Cenas LV 150 C7
Cencenighe Agordino I 88 D4
Cendras F 51 B7
Cendrieux F 45 F7
Cenei RO 175 B6
Ceneselli I 82 B3
Cengio I 53 C8
Cenicero E 57 D6
Ceniclentos E 62 D4
Čenta SRB 174 C5
Centallo I 53 B7
Centelles E 59 D8
Cento I 82 C3
Centola I 76 C4
Centuri F 53 F10
Centuripe I 75 D6
Cepagatti I 78 C6
Cepari RO 176 C5
Čepin HR 165 E11
Ceplenița RO 169 C9
Čepovan SLO 89 D8
Ceppaloni I 76 A3
Ceppo Morelli I 84 B5
Ceprano I 78 D5
Ceptura RO 177 C8
Čeralije HR 165 E9
Cerami I 75 D6
Cerani BIH 173 C8
Cerano I 84 C6
Ceranów PL 157 E6
Cérans-Foulletourte F 39 E12
Cerasi I 75 C8
Ceraso I 76 C4
Cerașu RO 177 C8
Cerăt RO 176 E3
Ceraukste LV 151 D8
Çëravë AL 184 C4

Cerbăl RO 167 F10
Cerbère F 50 F5
Cercal P 60 F3
Cercal P 66 D2
Čerčany CZ 93 C7
Cercedilla E 62 C4
Cerchezu RO 171 F2
Cerchiara di Calabria I 77 D6
Cerchio I 78 C5
Cercy-la-Tour F 46 B4
Cerda I 74 D4
Cerdanyola del Vallès E 59 E8
Cerdedo E 54 C3
Cerdeira P 60 D5
Cerdon F 41 E7
Cēre LV 150 B5
Cerea I 82 B3
Cered H 163 E9
Ceregnano I 82 B4
Cerekwica PL 101 E13
Cérences F 39 C9
Ceres GB 21 C11
Ceres I 47 E11
Ceresole Reale I 47 E11
Céreste F 51 C10
Céret F 50 F4
Čerević SRB 174 C4
Cerezo de Abajo E 62 B5
Cerezo de Arriba E 56 F4
Cerezo de Ríotirón E 56 C5
Cerfontaine B 200 D1
Cergău RO 168 E3
Cergy F 40 B7
Cerhenice CZ 93 B8
Ceriale I 53 C8
Ceriana I 53 D7
Cerignola I 76 A5
Cérilly F 46 B2
Čerín BIH 173 F8
Cerisano I 76 E6
Cerisiers F 41 D9
Cerisy-la-Forêt F 39 B10
Cerisy-la-Salle F 39 B9
Cerizay F 44 B4
Çerkezköy TR 189 B9
Çerkezmüsellim TR 189 B7
Cerklje SLO 89 D9
Cerklje SLO 164 E5
Cerknica SLO 89 E9
Cerkno SLO 89 D8
Cerkwica PL 101 B8
Cermei RO 167 D8
Çermë-Proshkë AL 184 B2
Cermignano I 78 B5
Cerna HR 173 B10
Cerna RO 171 C2
Cernache do Bonjardim P 60 E4
Černá Hora CZ 93 D11
Cernat RO 169 F8
Cernătești RO 176 E2
Cernătești RO 177 C9
Cernavodă RO 171 E2
Cernay F 43 E7
Cernay-en-Dormois F 35 F10
Černčice CZ 92 B5
Cernégula E 56 C4
Cernele RO 176 E3
Cernești RO 168 C3
Cernica RO 177 E8
Černík SK 162 E6
Černilov CZ 93 B9
Cernișoara RO 176 C4
Cernobbio I 85 B7
Cernoleuca MD 169 A11
Černošice CZ 92 C6
Černošín CZ 92 C3
Černoste LV 149 D2
Černovice CZ 93 D7
Černožice CZ 93 B9
Cerová SK 162 D4
Cerovac SRB 175 E6
Cerovak Tušilovički HR 164 F5
Ceroviljani BIH 173 B7
Cerovlje HR 83 B9
Cerovo SK 163 E8
Cerralbo E 61 C7
Cerreto d'Esi I 83 F6
Cerreto di Spoleto I 78 B3
Cerreto Sannita I 76 A3
Cerrigydrudion GB 26 E4
Cērrik AL 184 B2
Cerro al Volturno I 78 D6
Cersay F 44 A5
Cersosimo I 77 C6
Certaldo I 82 E3
Certeju de Sus RO 167 F10
Certeşti RO 169 E11
Certeze RO 161 H7
Certosa di Pavia I 85 C7
Certosa di Pesio I 53 C7
Ceru-Băcăinţi RO 167 F11
Cërujë AL 184 C3
Cerva P 54 F4
Cervaro I 78 E5
Cervatos de la Cueza E 55 D10
Červená Voda CZ 93 B11
Cervenia RO 177 F6
Červenka CZ 93 C12
Červený Kostelec CZ 93 B10
Cervera E 58 D6
Cervera de la Cañada E 57 F8
Cervera del Llano E 63 E8
Cervera del Maestre E 64 D5
Cervera de los Montes E 62 D3
Cervera del Río Alhama E 57 D8
Cervera de Pisuerga E 56 C3
Cerveteri I 78 D5
Cervia I 82 D5
Cervignano del Friuli I 89 E7
Cervinara I 76 A3
Červivá Řečice CZ 93 C8
Cervione F 53 G10
Cervo E 54 A5
Cervo I 53 D8
Cervon F 41 E11
Cerzeto I 76 E6

Český Brod CZ 93 B7
Český Dub CZ 97 E7
Český Krumlov CZ 92 E6
Český Těšín CZ 163 C7
Çeşme TR 193 C7
Cespedosa E 61 C9
Cessalto I 89 E6
Cessenon-sur-Orb F 50 D5
Cessnaria P 61 A9
Cessole I 53 B8
Cesson F 41 C8
Cesson-Sévigné F 39 D8
Cestas F 44 F4
Čestobrodica SRB 174 F5
Cesuras E 54 B3
Cesvaine LV 151 C12
Cetariu RO 167 C9
Cetate RO 175 E11
Cetatea de Baltă RO 168 E4
Cetăţeni RO 176 C6
Cetina E 57 F8
Cetinje MNE 179 E6
Ceto I 85 A9
Ceton F 40 D4
Cetona I 78 B1
Cetraro I 76 E5
Ceuta WHAT 69 E6
Ceutí E 72 E2
Ceva I 53 C8
Cevico de la Torre E 56 E3
Cevico Navero E 56 E3
Cevins F 47 F10
Cevio CH 84 A6
Cevizköy TR 189 A8
Čevo MNE 179 D6
Cewice PL 101 B13
Ceyrat F 46 F3
Ceyreste F 51 D10
Ceyzériat F 47 C7
Cezieni RO 176 E4
Chã P 54 E4
Chaam NL 32 F3
Chabanais F 45 D7
Chabeuil F 47 F7
Chabielice PL 159 D2
Chablis F 41 E10
Chabówka PL 163 B9
Chabreloche F 46 D4
Chabris F 40 F6
Chacim P 55 E6
Chagford GB 29 D7
Chagny F 46 B6
Chaïkali GR 190 C4
Chaillac F 45 C8
Chailland F 39 D10
Chaillé-les-Marais F 44 C3
Chailley F 41 D9
Chalabre F 49 E10
Chalais CH 47 C12
Chalais F 44 E6
Chalamera E 58 D4
Chalamont F 47 C7
Chalampé F 43 E8
Chalandri GR 191 C8
Chalandritsa GR 190 C4
Chalastra GR 185 C8
Chale GB 29 D12
Chaleix F 45 D9
Châlette-sur-Loing F 41 D8
Chalford GB 29 B10
Chalgrove GB 29 B12
Chaligny F 42 C5
Chalin PL 155 E7
Chalindrey F 42 E4
Chalivoy-Milon F 45 B11
Chalki GR 185 E8
Chalki GR 197 D7
Chalkiades GR 185 F7
Chalkiades GR 190 A2
Chalkida GR 191 C8
Chalkio GR 191 D6
Challans F 44 B2
Challerange F 35 E10
Challes-les-Eaux F 47 D8
Chalmoux F 46 B4
Chalonnes-sur-Loire F 39 F10
Châlons-en-Champagne F 41 C11
Chalon-sur-Saône F 46 B6
Châlus F 45 D8
Cham CH 43 F9
Cham D 91 D12
Chamalières F 46 D3
Chamaloc F 47 F7
Chambéret F 45 D9
Chambéria F 47 C8
Chambéry F 47 D8
Chambley-Bussières F 42 B4
Chambois F 39 C12
Chambon-sur-Voueize F 45 C10
Chambord F 40 E6
Chamboulive F 45 D9
Chambray-lès-Tours F 40 F4
Chambry F 35 E8
Chamesson F 41 E12
Chamonix-Mont-Blanc F 47 D10
Chamoux-sur-Gelon F 47 D9
Champagnac F 45 E10
Champagnac-de-Belair F 45 E7
Champagnac-le-Vieux F 46 D4
Champagne-Mouton F 45 C6
Champagne-sur-Seine F 41 D8
Champagney F 42 E6
Champagnole F 47 C8
Champaubert F 41 C10
Champdeniers-St-Denis F 44 C5
Champeix F 46 D3
Champéry CH 47 C10
Champex CH 47 C11
Champforgeuil F 46 B6
Champgénéteux F 39 D11
Champier F 47 E7
Champigné F 39 E10
Champignelles F 41 E9
Champigneulles F 202 D1
Champigny F 45 B11
Champigny F 40 F6
Champlemy F 41 F10
Champlitte F 42 E4
Champniers F 45 D6
Champoléon F 47 F9
Champoluc I 84 B4
Champsecret F 39 C10
Champs-sur-Tarentaine-Marchal F 45 E11
Champs-sur-Yonne F 41 E10
Champ-sur-Drac F 47 E8
Champtoceaux F 39 F9
Chamrousse F 47 E8

Chamusca P 60 F4
Chanac F 50 B5
Chanas F 46 E6
Chança P 60 F5
Chanceaux F 41 E12
Chanceaux-sur-Choisille F 40 F4
Chancelade F 45 E7
Chancelaria P 60 E3
Chandras GR 195 E11
Chandrinos GR 190 F4
Chañe E 56 F3
Changé F 39 D10
Changé F 39 E12
Changy F 46 C5
Chania GR 194 D7
Chaniotis GR 185 D10
Chantada E 54 C4
Chantelle F 46 C3
Chantilly F 41 B7
Chantonnay F 44 B3
Chanu F 39 C10
Chaource F 41 D11
Chapaevo BG 182 D5
Chapayevka UA 170 A5
Chapel-en-le-Frith GB 27 E8
Chapelle-lez-Herlaimont B 198 E4
Chapeltown GB 27 E9
Chapinería E 62 D4
Charakas GR 194 E7
Charavgi GR 185 D6
Charbonnat F 46 B5
Charcenne F 42 F4
Charchilla F 47 C8
Chard GB 29 D9
Chardstock GB 29 D9
Charenton-du-Cher F 45 B11
Charfield GB 29 B10
Chargey-lès-Gray F 42 F4
Charlbury GB 29 B12
Charlemont GB 23 D9
Charleroi B 35 D9
Charlestown IRL 22 D4
Charleville IRL 24 D5
Charleville-Mézières F 35 E10
Charlieu F 46 C5
Charlottenberg S 112 C7
Charlton GB 29 C12
Charlton Kings GB 29 B10
Charly F 41 C9
Charmé F 45 D6
Charmes F 42 D5
Charmes-sur-Rhône F 46 F6
Charmey CH 47 B11
Charmouth GB 29 D9
Charmoy F 41 E9
Charnay-lès-Mâcon F 46 C6
Charny F 41 E9
Charokopeio GR 194 B2
Charolles F 46 C5
Charomkhava BY 149 F3
Charopo GR 185 B9
Chârost F 45 B10
Charquemont F 43 F6
Charrat CH 47 C11
Charrey-sur-Seine F 41 E12
Charrin F 46 B4
Charroux F 45 C6
Charsznica PL 159 F8
Chartres F 40 D5
Charvieu-Chavagneux F 47 D7
Charzyno PL 101 B9
Chassagne-Montrachet F 46 B6
Chasseneuil-sur-Bonnieure F 45 D6
Chasseradès F 51 A6
Chasse-sur-Rhône F 46 D6
Chassigny-Aisey F 42 E3
Chassillé F 39 D11
Chastre B 35 C10
Château-Arnoux F 51 B10
Châteaubernard F 44 D5
Châteaubourg F 39 D9
Châteaubriant F 39 E9
Château-Chinon F 46 A4
Château-d'Oex CH 47 C11
Château-d'Olonne F 44 B2
Château-du-Loir F 40 E3
Châteaudun F 40 D5
Châteaugiron F 39 D8
Château-Gontier F 39 E10
Château-Landon F 41 D8
Château-la-Vallière F 40 E3
Châteaulin F 38 D3
Châteaumeillant F 45 B10
Châteauneuf-de-Galaure F 47 E6
Châteauneuf-de-Randon F 51 A6
Châteauneuf-d'Ille-et-Vilaine F 39 C8
Châteauneuf-du-Faou F 38 D4
Châteauneuf-en-Thymerais F 40 C5
Châteauneuf-la-Forêt F 45 D9
Châteauneuf-les-Martigues F 51 D9
Châteauneuf-sur-Charente F 44 D5
Châteauneuf-sur-Cher F 45 B10
Châteauneuf-sur-Loire F 41 E7
Châteauneuf-sur-Sarthe F 39 E11
Châteauneuf-Val-de-Bargis F 41 F9
Châteauponsac F 45 C8
Château-Porcien F 35 E9
Châteauredon F 52 C4
Châteaurenard F 45 E8
Châteaurenard F 51 C8
Châteaurenaud F 47 B7
Château-Renault F 40 E4
Châteauroux F 45 B9
Châteauroux F 52 B5
Château-Salins F 42 C5
Château-Thierry F 41 B9
Châteauvillain F 41 D12
Châtel F 47 C10
Châtelaillon-Plage F 44 C3
Châtelaudren F 38 C6
Châtel-Censoir F 41 E10
Châteldon F 46 D4
Châtelet B 35 D10
Châtel-Gérard F 41 E11
Châtelguyon F 46 D3
Châtellerault F 45 B7
Châtel-Montagne F 46 C4
Châtel-St-Denis CH 47 B10
Châtel-sur-Moselle F 42 D5
Châtelus-Malvaleix F 45 C10
Châtenois F 42 D4
Châtenois F 43 D7

Chianni I 82 E2
Châtenoy-le-Royal F 46 B6
Chatham GB 31 E10
Châtillon I 84 B4
Châtillon I 83 E7
Châtillon-Coligny F 41 E8
Châtillon-en-Bazois F 46 A4
Châtillon-en-Diois F 51 A9
Châtillon-en-Michaille F 47 C8
Châtillon-la-Palud F 37 D7
Châtillon-sur-Chalaronne F 47 C6
Châtillon-sur-Colmont F 39 D10
Châtillon-sur-Indre F 45 B8
Châtillon-sur-Loire F 41 E8
Châtillon-sur-Marne F 41 B10
Châtillon-sur-Seine F 41 E12
Châtillon-sur-Thouet F 44 B5
Chatte F 47 E7
Chatteris GB 31 C9
Chatton GB 21 D13
Chatuzange-le-Goubet F 47 F7
Chatzis GR 190 E4
Chaudenay F 42 E4
Chaudes-Aigues F 46 F3
Chaudeyrac F 51 A6
Chaudfontaine B 35 C12
Chauffailles F 46 C5
Chauffayer F 47 F8
Chaulnes F 34 E6
Chaumergy F 47 B7
Chaumont F 42 D3
Chaumont-en-Vexin F 34 F4
Chaumont-Porcien F 35 E9
Chaumont-sur-Aire F 42 C3
Chaumont-sur-Loire F 40 F5
Chaunay F 45 C6
Chauny F 35 E7
Chaussin F 47 B7
Chauvigny F 45 B7
Chavanay F 46 E6
Chavanges F 41 C12
Chavanoz F 47 D7
Chavari GR 190 C3
Chavelot F 42 D5
Chaves P 54 E5
Chazelles-sur-Lyon F 46 D5
Cheadle GB 27 F8
Cheadle GB 27 C12
Cheb CZ 91 B11
Checa E 63 C9
Chechel'nyk UA 170 A4
Cheçiny PL 159 E9
Chécy F 40 E7
Cheddar GB 29 C9
Chef-Boutonne F 44 C5
Chekhpare BG 182 E4
Cheles E 67 A5
Chella E 72 C3
Chełm PL 157 H8
Chełmek PL 159 F6
Chełmiec PL 161 D2
Chełmno PL 154 E5
Chełmno PL 158 B6
Chelmsford GB 31 D9
Chełmża PL 154 E5
Cheltenham GB 29 B10
Chelva E 63 E11
Chemazé F 39 E10
Chemillé F 39 F10
Chemin F 47 B7
Cheminon F 41 C12
Chemiré-le-Gaudin F 39 E11
Chemnitz D 96 E3
Chenecey-Buillon F 42 F4
Chénérailles F 45 C10
Cheniménil F 42 D6
Chenôve F 41 E10
Cheny F 41 E10
Chepelare BG 181 F10
Chepintsi BG 181 D7
Chepstow GB 29 B9
Chepy F 41 C11
Chera E 64 E3
Chérac F 44 D5
Cheraute F 48 D4
Cherbourg F 39 A8
Cheremule I 80 B2
Cherepkivtsi UA 169 A7
Chereshovo BG 177 F8
Cherlenivka UA 169 A8
Cherna BG 171 F1
Cherna Gora BG 182 E4
Chernevo RUS 148 D3
Cherni Osŭm BG 181 D10
Cherni Vrŭkh BG 183 E8
Cherno More BG 183 D8
Chernoochene BG 182 F4
Chernyakhovsk RUS 152 D2
Chernyshevskoye RUS 152 D6
Chéroy F 41 D8
Cherskaya RUS 148 F3
Cherso GR 185 B8
Chervena Voda BG 177 F8
Chervena voda BG 177 F8
Cherven BG 177 F8
Cherven Bryag BG 181 C9
Chervenisi BG 183 B8
Cherves-Richemont F 44 D5
Chervona Hreblya UA 170 A6
Chervonoarmiys'ka UA 170 C3
Chervonohrad UA 160 C9
Chesham GB 31 D7
Cheshunt GB 31 D8
Chesley F 41 E11
Chessy-les-Prés F 41 D10
Cheste E 64 F3
Chester GB 26 E6
Chesterfield GB 27 E9
Chester-le-Street GB 21 F13
Chețani RO 168 E4
Chetrosu MD 169 A11
Chevagnes F 46 B4
Chevanceaux F 44 E5
Chevereşu Mare RO 175 B7
Chevillon F 42 C3
Chevilly F 40 D6
Chevreuse F 40 C7
Cheylade F 46 E3
Cheylard-Benoît F 45 B10
Chèze F 48 E5
Chiajna RO 177 E8
Chiampo I 82 A3
Chianciano Terme I 78 A1

Chianni I 82 E2
Chiaramonte Gulfi I 75 E6
Chiaramonti I 80 B2
Chiaravalle I 83 E7
Chiaravalle Centrale I 75 B9
Chiari I 85 B8
Chiaromonte I 76 C5
Chiasso I 85 B7
Chiavari I 53 C10
Chiavenno I 85 A7
Chiché F 44 B5
Chichester GB 31 F7
Chichiş RO 169 F7
Chiclana de la Frontera E 68 D4
Chiclana de Segura E 71 C5
Chieming D 88 A6
Chienes I 88 C4
Chieri I 53 A7
Chiesa in Valmalenco I 85 A8
Chieşd RO 167 C10
Chiesina Uzzanese I 82 E2
Chieti I 79 D8
Chieuti I 79 D8
Chieveley GB 29 C12
Chièvres B 35 C8
Chigwell GB 31 D9
Chiheru de Jos RO 168 D5
Chikhachevo RUS 149 B7
Chilches E 64 E4
Chilcompton GB 29 C9
Chilham GB 31 E10
Chiliile RO 177 C9
Chiliomodi GR 191 D6
Chilleurs-aux-Bois F 40 D7
Chillón E 70 B3
Chilluévar E 71 C6
Chiloeches E 63 C6
Chimay B 35 D9
Chimeneas E 69 B9
Chinanale I 52 B6
Chinchilla de Monte Aragón E 71 B9
Chinchón E 62 D6
Chindrieux F 47 D8
Chinon F 39 F12
Chinteni RO 168 D3
Chiochiş RO 168 D4
Chioggia I 82 B5
Chiojdeni RO 177 B9
Chiojdu RO 177 C8
Chiomonte I 47 E10
Chiona GR 190 C4
Chionata GR 190 C2
Chios GR 193 C7
Chiperceni MD 170 B3
Chipiona E 68 C5
Chippenham GB 29 C10
Chipping Campden GB 29 A11
Chipping Norton GB 29 B12
Chipping Ongar GB 31 D9
Chipping Sodbury GB 29 B10
Chippis CH 47 C12
Chiprana E 58 E4
Chiprovtsi BG 181 C6
Chirbury GB 26 F5
Chirivel E 71 D8
Chirk GB 26 F5
Chirnogeni RO 171 F2
Chirnogi RO 177 E9
Chirnside GB 21 D12
Chiroubles F 46 C6
Chirpan BG 182 E4
Chirpăr RO 168 F5
Chirsova MD 170 E3
Chişcani RO 171 C6
Chişcăreni MD 169 B12
Chişcăreni MD 170 C3
Chiselet RO 177 E9
Chişinău MD 170 C3
Chisindia RO 167 E9
Chişinau-Criş RO 167 D8
Chistye-Prudy RUS 152 D5
Chiţcani MD 170 D5
Chitignano I 82 E4
Chitila RO 177 E8
Chiuiești RO 168 C3
Chiuro I 85 A8
Chiusa I 88 C4
Chiusa di Pesio I 53 C7
Chiusaforte I 89 D7
Chiusanecchia I 53 D7
Chiusdino I 82 F3
Chiusi I 78 A1
Chiusi della Verna I 82 E4
Chiuza RO 168 C4
Chiva E 64 F3
Chivasso I 84 C4
Chizé F 44 C5
ChlebiČov CZ 162 B5
Chlebnice SK 163 C9
Chlebowo PL 97 B7
Chlewiska PL 157 H3
Chłopice PL 160 D6
Chludowo PL 97 A11
Chlumčany CZ 96 C5
Chlumec CZ 96 E5
Chlumec nad Cidlinou CZ 93 B8
Chlum u Třeboně CZ 93 E7
Chmielnik PL 159 E9
Chmielno PL 101 C10
Chmielno PL 101 C10
Chobienia PL 97 C10
Chobienice PL 97 B9
Choceň CZ 93 B10
Choceň PL 154 F7
Chochołów PL 163 B9
Chocianów PL 97 C8
Chocicza PL 97 B12
Chociwel PL 101 D8
Chocz PL 158 C4
Choczewo PL 154 A5
Chodecz PL 154 F7
Chodel PL 157 H6
Chodov CZ 91 B12
Chodová Planá CZ 91 C12
Chodów PL 157 F6
Chodów PL 159 B7
Chodzież PL 101 E11
Chojna PL 100 D6
Chojnice PL 154 C4
Chojno PL 101 C13
Chojno PL 97 C12
Chojnów PL 97 D9
Chomakovtsi BG 181 D9
Chomelix F 46 E4
Chomérac F 51 A8
Chomutov CZ 92 B4
Chonikas GR 191 D6

Cill Chomhghaill IRL 23 F10
Cill Chormaic IRL 23 F7
Cill Chuillin IRL 23 F9
Cill Dalua IRL 24 C7
Cill Dara IRL 23 F9
Cill Dhéagláin IRL 23 E10
Cill Droichid IRL 23 F9
Cille Bhrighde GB 18 L2
Cilleros E 61 D7
Cill Mhantáin IRL 23 G10
Cill Mocheallóg IRL 24 D5
Cill na Mallach IRL 24 D5
Cill Orglan IRL 24 D3
Cill Rois IRL 24 C4
Cill Rónáin IRL 22 F3
Cilybebyll GB 29 B7
Cimanes del Tejar E 55 C8
Cimballa E 63 B9
Cimdenieki LV 150 C2
Čimelice CZ 92 D5
Ciminna I 74 D4
Cimişlia MD 170 D3
Cimolais I 88 D5
Çinarcık TR 189 C11
Cinco Casas E 63 F6
Cinderford GB 29 B10
Cincu RO 168 F5
Ciñera E 55 C8
Ciney B 35 D11
Cinfães P 60 B4
Cinge TR 193 A9
Cingoli I 83 F7
Cinigiano I 81 B4
Cinisello Balsamo I 85 B7
Cinn Mhara IRL 22 F3
Cinobaňa SK 163 E9
Cinq-Mars-la-Pile F 40 F3
Cinquefrondi I 75 C9
Cintegabelle F 49 D9
Cintrey F 42 E4
Cintruénigo E 57 D8
Ciobăniţa RO 171 E2
Ciobanu RO 171 D1
Čiobiškis LT 153 D10
Ciocănești RO 177 D9
Ciocănești RO 177 C8
Ciocârlia RO 171 E2
Ciocârlia RO 177 D9
Ciochina RO 177 D10
Ciocile RO 177 D10
Cioc-Maidan MD 170 E3
Ciofrângeni RO 176 C5
Ciolineanca IRL 23 F7
Ciolănești RO 176 E5
Ciolpani RO 177 D8
Cionn tSáile IRL 24 E5
Ciorani RO 177 D9
Ciorăşti RO 177 C10
Ciorogârla RO 176 E7
Cioroiaşi RO 176 E2
Cioropcani MD 169 C11
Ciorteşti RO 169 D11
Ciprian Porumbescu RO 169 B8
Cirat E 64 D4
Cirauqui E 48 E3
Cīrava LV 150 C2
Circello I 76 A3
Cireşu RO 175 D10
Cireşu RO 175 D10
Cirey-sur-Blaise F 42 D2
Cirey-sur-Vezouze F 43 C6
Ciria E 57 E8
Ciriè I 84 C4
Cirigliano I 76 C6
Ciripcău MD 170 A3
Cirkale LV 150 B4
Cirma LV 149 C3
Cirò I 77 E8
Cirò Marina I 77 E8
Çırpı TR 193 C10
Cirsinieki LV 151 D12
Ciruelos E 62 E5
Ciruelos del Pinar E 63 B8
Círulji LV 150 B4
Ciry-le-Noble F 46 B5
Cisano sul Neva I 53 C8
Cisek I 158 F5
Cislău RO 177 C8
Cişmichioi MD 171 B2
Cisna PL 161 E5
Cisnădie RO 176 B4
Cisneros E 55 D10
Cisón de Valmarino I 88 E5
Cissé F 45 B6
Cista Provo HR 173 E6
Cisterna di Latina I 78 D3
Cisternino I 77 B8
Cistierna E 55 C9
Citerna I 82 F5
Čitluk BIH 173 B6
Čitluk BIH 173 F7
Cittadella I 88 E4
Città della Pieve I 78 B2
Città di Castello I 82 F5
Cittanova I 75 C9
Cittareale I 78 B4
Città Sant'Angelo I 78 B6
Cittiglio I 84 B6
Ciucea RO 167 D10
Ciuchici RO 175 D8
Ciuciuleaa MD 169 B11
Ciucsângeorgiu RO 169 E7
Ciucur-Mingir MD 170 E3
Ciucurova RO 171 D2
Ciudad Real E 70 B5
Ciudad Rodrigo E 61 C7
Ciudanoviţa RO 175 C8
Ciugud RO 168 E3
Ciuhoi RO 167 C9
Ciulniţa RO 177 D10
Ciumani RO 169 D7
Ciumeghiu RO 167 D8
Ciuperceni RO 175 D10
Ciuperceni RO 176 F5
Ciuperceni Noi RO 175 D10
Ciurila RO 168 D3
Ciuruleasa RO 167 E11
Ciutadella E 73 A12
Cĺvaux F 45 C7
Cividale del Friuli I 89 D7
Civita I 77 D6
Civita Castellana I 78 C2
Civita d'Antino I 78 D4
Civitanova del Sannio I 79 D6
Civitanova Marche I 83 F8
Civitaquana I 78 C5
Civitavecchia I 78 C1
Civitella Casanova I 78 C5
Civitella del Tronto I 78 B5
Civitella di Romagna I 82 D4

Civitella in Val di Chiana I 82 F4
Civitella Roveto I 78 D4
Civray F 45 B10
Civray F 45 C6
Çizer RO 167 C10
Čížkovice CZ 92 B6
Čkyně CZ 92 D5
Clabhach GB 20 B3
Clachan GB 18 L4
Clachan GB 20 C7
Clachan of Glendaruel GB 20 C6
Clachtoll GB 18 J6
Clackmannan GB 21 C9
Clacton-on-Sea GB 31 D11
Cladich GB 20 C6
Clady GB 20 F1
Clady GB 20 F3
Claggan GB 20 B5
Clairac F 49 B6
Clairoix F 34 F6
Clairvaux-les-Lacs F 47 B8
Claix F 47 E8
Clamecy F 41 F10
Clane IRL 23 F9
Clans F 52 C6
Claonadh IRL 23 F9
Claonaig GB 20 D6
Clapham GB 27 C7
Clapham GB 31 C8
Clara IRL 23 F7
Clár Chlainne Mhuiris IRL 22 E5
Clarecastle IRL 24 C5
Claremorris IRL 22 E5
Claret F 51 B10
Claro CH 85 A7
Clary F 35 D7
Clashmore IRL 25 D7
Clashnessie GB 18 J6
Claudy GB 20 F2
Clausnitz D 96 E4
Claußnitz D 96 E3
Clausthal-Zellerfeld D 95 C7
Claut I 88 D6
Clauzetto I 89 D6
Clavering GB 31 D9
Clavier B 35 D11
Clay Cross GB 27 E9
Claydon GB 31 C11
Clayton GB 31 F8
Cleady IRL 24 E3
Cleat GB 19 H11
Cleator Moor GB 26 B4
Clécy F 39 C11
Cléder F 38 C3
Cleethorpes GB 27 D11
Clefmont F 42 D4
Cléguérec F 38 D5
Cleja RO 169 E9
Clelles F 47 F8
Clémency L 36 E5
Clenze D 99 E9
Cleobury Mortimer GB 29 A10
Cléon F 34 F3
Cléon-d'Andran F 51 A8
Cléré-les-Pins F 40 F3
Clères F 34 E3
Clérey F 41 D11
Clermain F 46 C6
Clermont F 34 F5
Clermont F 49 D8
Clermont-en-Argonne F 42 B3
Clermont-Ferrand F 46 D3
Clermont-l'Hérault F 50 C5
Clerval F 42 F6
Clervaux L 36 D6
Cléry-St-André F 40 E6
Cles I 88 D3
Clevedon GB 29 C9
Cleveleys GB 26 D5
Clifden IRL 22 F2
Cliffe GB 31 E9
Cliffoney IRL 22 D6
Climăuți MD 169 A11
Clinge NL 32 F2
Clingen D 95 D8
Clion F 45 B8
Clisson F 44 A3
Clitheroe GB 27 D7
Cloch na Rón IRL 22 F3
Clogh GB 20 F4
Clogh IRL 25 C7
Clogh IRL 25 C8
Clogh IRL 25 C10
Cloghan IRL 23 C7
Cloghan IRL 23 F7
Clogheen IRL 24 D7
Clogher GB 23 D8
Clogherhead IRL 23 E10
Cloghy GB 23 D12
Clohars-Carnoët F 38 E4
Clohernagh IRL 25 D8
Cloich na Coillte IRL 24 E5
Clonakilty IRL 24 E5
Clonaslee IRL 23 F7
Clonbern IRL 22 E5
Clonbulloge IRL 23 F8
Clonbur IRL 22 E4
Clondrohid IRL 24 E4
Clondulane IRL 24 D6
Clonea IRL 25 D8
Clonee IRL 23 F10
Cloneen IRL 25 D7
Clones IRL 23 D8
Clonmel IRL 25 D7
Clonmellon IRL 23 E8
Clonoulty IRL 25 C7
Clonroche IRL 25 D9
Clontibret IRL 23 D9
Clonygowan IRL 23 F8
Cloonbannin IRL 24 D4
Cloonboo IRL 22 F4
Cloonfad IRL 22 E5
Cloonfad IRL 22 F6
Cloonkeen IRL 22 E4
Cloppenburg D 33 C10
Closeburn GB 21 E9
Clough GB 23 D11
Cloughjordan IRL 24 C6
Cloughmills GB 20 E4
Cloughton GB 27 C11
Clova GB 21 B10
Clovelly GB 28 D6
Clovullin GB 20 B6
Cloyes-sur-le-Loir F 40 E5
Cloyne IRL 24 E6
Cluain Bú IRL 22 F4
Cluain Eois IRL 23 D8
Cluainín IRL 22 D6
Cluain Meala IRL 25 D7
Cluis F 45 B9
Cluj-Napoca RO 168 D3
Clumanc F 52 C4
Clun GB 29 A8
Cluny F 46 C6
Cluses F 47 C10
Clusone I 85 B8
Clydach GB 29 B7
Clydebank GB 21 D8
Clynderwen GB 28 B5
Clyro GB 29 A8
Ćmielów PL 159 E12
Cmolas PL 159 F12
Coachford IRL 24 E5
Coagh GB 20 F3
Coalburn GB 21 D9
Coalisland GB 23 C9
Coalville GB 27 F9
Coaña E 55 A6
Coarnele Caprei RO 169 C10
Coarraze F 48 D5
Coast GB 18 K5
Coatbridge GB 21 D8
Cobadin RO 171 E2
Cobani MD 169 B10
Cobeja E 62 D5
Cobeta E 63 C8
Cobh IRL 24 E6
Cobia RO 176 D6
Coburg D 91 B8
Coca E 62 B3
Cocentaina E 72 D4
Cochem D 37 D8
Cochirleanca RO 177 C10
Cociuba Mare RO 167 D9
Cockburnspath GB 21 D12
Cockenzie and Port Seton GB 21 D11
Cockerham GB 26 D6
Cockermouth GB 21 F10
Cockett GB 28 B7
Cocora RO 177 D10
Cocu RO 176 D5
Cocumont F 48 B6
Codăești RO 169 D11
Coddington GB 27 E10
Code LV 151 D8
Codevigo I 82 B5
Codigoro I 82 C5
Codlea RO 177 B6
Codogno I 85 C8
Codos E 57 F9
Codreanca MD 170 C3
Codroipo I 89 E6
Codrongianos I 80 B2
Codru MD 170 D3
Coesfeld D 33 E8
Coevorden NL 33 C7
Coëx F 44 B2
Cofrentes E 63 F10
Cogealac RO 171 D3
Cogeces del Monte E 56 E3
Coggeshall GB 31 D10
Coggia F 53 G9
Coggiola I 84 B5
Cogîlniceni MD 170 B3
Çöğmen TR 197 C10
Cognac F 44 D5
Cognac-la-Forêt F 45 D8
Cogne I 47 D11
Cognin F 47 D8
Cogoleto I 53 C9
Cogolin F 52 E5
Cogollos E 56 D4
Cogollos Vega E 69 B9
Cogolludo E 63 C6
Cogula P 61 C6
Coillan Chollaigh IRL 23 E9
Coimbra P 60 D4
Coimbrão P 60 E3
Coín E 69 C7
Coincy F 41 B9
Coja P 60 D5
Cojasca RO 177 D7
Cojocna RO 168 D3
Čoka SRB 166 F5
Colares P 66 B1
Colayrac-St-Cirq F 49 B7
Colbasna MD 170 B4
Cölbe D 37 C11
Colbitz D 95 B10
Colbordola I 83 E6
Colceag RO 177 D8
Colchester GB 31 D10
Coldingham GB 21 D12
Colditz D 95 D12
Coldstream GB 21 D12
Coleford GB 29 B9
Coleraine GB 20 E3
Colibași MD 171 B2
Colibași RO 176 D5
Colibași RO 177 E8
Colibița RO 168 C5
Colico I 85 A7
Coligny F 47 C7
Colijnsplaat NL 198 B3
Colindres E 56 B5
Colintraive GB 20 D6
Collado Hermoso E 62 B5
Collado Villalba E 62 C5
Collagna I 82 D1
Collanzo E 55 B8
Collarmele I 78 C5
Collazzone I 78 B2
Collecchio I 82 C1
Collecorvino I 78 C5
Colledara I 78 B5
Colle di Val d'Elsa I 82 F3
Colleferro I 78 D4
Collegno I 84 C4
Colle Isarco I 88 C3
Collelongo I 78 D5
Collepardo I 78 D4
Collepasso I 77 C10
Collesalvetti I 82 E1
Colle Sannita I 76 A3
Collesano I 74 D4
Colletorto I 79 D7
Colliano I 76 B4
Colli a Volturno I 78 D6
Collieston GB 19 L13
Collinas I 80 D2
Collinée F 38 D6
Collinghorst (Rhauderfehn) D 33 B9
Collio I 85 B9
Collioure F 50 E5
Collobrières F 52 E4
Collombey CH 47 C10
Collon IRL 23 E10
Collonges F 47 C8
Collonges-la-Rouge F 45 E9
Collooney IRL 22 D6
Colmar F 43 D7
Colmars F 52 C5
Colmberg D 91 D7
Colmeal P 60 D5
Colmenar E 69 C8
Colmenar del Arroyo E 62 D4
Colmenar de Montemayor E 61 D9
Colmenar de Oreja E 62 D6
Colmenar Viejo E 62 C5
Colméry F 41 F9
Colmonell GB 20 E7
Colne GB 27 D7
Colobraro I 77 C6
Cologna Veneta I 82 B3
Cologne F 49 C7
Cologno al Serio I 85 B8
Colombelles F 39 B11
Colombey-les-Belles F 42 C4
Colombey-les Deux-Églises F 41 D12
Colombier CH 47 B10
Colombiès F 49 B10
Colombres E 55 B10
Colomers E 59 C9
Colomiers F 49 C8
Colonești RO 169 D10
Colonești RO 176 D5
Colònia de Sant Jordi E 73 C11
Colònia de Sant Pere E 73 B11
Colonnella I 78 B5
Colorno I 82 C1
Colos P 66 D3
Cölpin D 100 C4
Colquhar GB 21 D10
Colroy-la-Grande F 43 D7
Colsterworth GB 27 F10
Colți RO 177 C8
Coltishall GB 31 B11
Colunga E 55 B9
Colwyn Bay GB 26 E4
Coly F 45 E8
Colyford GB 29 D8
Comacchio I 82 C5
Comana RO 168 F6
Comana RO 171 F2
Comana RO 177 E8
Comana de Sus RO 168 F6
Comandău RO 169 F8
Comănești RO 169 E8
Comares E 69 C8
Comarna RO 169 C11
Comarnic RO 177 C7
Combeaufontaine F 42 E4
Combe Martin GB 28 C6
Comber GB 23 C11
Comberton GB 31 C9
Comblain-au-Pont B 35 D12
Comblanchien F 42 F2
Combles F 34 D6
Combloux F 47 D10
Combourg F 39 D8
Combronde F 46 D3
Comeglians I 89 C6
Comèlico Superiore I 88 C6
Comillas E 56 B3
Comines B 34 C6
Comișani RO 177 D7
Comiso I 75 F6
Comitini I 74 E4
Comloșu Mare RO 166 F6
Commeen IRL 23 C7
Commenailles F 47 B7
Commensacq F 48 B4
Commentry F 46 C2
Commequiers F 44 B2
Commer F 39 D10
Commercy F 42 C4
Como I 85 B7
Cómpeta E 69 C9
Compiano I 53 B11
Compiègne F 34 F6
Compolibat F 49 B10
Comporta P 66 C2
Compreignac F 45 D8
Comps-sur-Artuby F 52 D5
Comrat MD 170 E3
Comrie GB 21 C9
Comunanza I 78 B4
Cona I 82 B5
Conca F 53 H10
Concarneau F 38 E4
Concas I 80 B4
Conceição P 66 E4
Concesio I 85 B9
Concha E 56 B5
Conches-en-Ouche F 40 C4
Concordia Sagittaria I 89 E6
Concorès F 49 A8
Concots F 49 B9
Condat F 46 E2
Condé-en-Brie F 41 B10
Condeixa-a-Nova P 60 D4
Condé-sur-Huisne F 40 D4
Condé-sur-l'Escaut F 198 E3
Condé-sur-Noireau F 39 C10
Condé-sur-Vire F 39 B9
Condino I 85 B10
Condofuri I 75 C8
Condom F 49 C6
Condove I 47 E11
Condrieu F 46 E6
Condrița MD 170 C3
Conegliano I 88 E5
Conflans-en-Jarnisy F 42 B4
Conflans-sur-Lanterne F 42 E5
Conflenti I 75 A9
Confolens F 45 C7
Cong IRL 22 E4
Congaz MD 170 E3
Congdon's Shop GB 28 D6
Congleton GB 27 E7
Congosto E 55 C7
Congosto de Valdavia E 55 C10
Congrier F 39 E9
Conil de la Frontera E 68 D4
Coningsby GB 27 E11
Coniston GB 26 C5
Conlie F 39 D11
Conliège F 47 B8
Conlig GB 20 F5
Connah's Quay GB 26 E5
Connantre F 41 C10
Connaux F 51 B8
Connel GB 20 C6
Connerré F 40 D3
Connolly IRL 24 C4
Connor GB 20 F4
Conon Bridge GB 18 K8
Conop RO 167 E8
Čonoplja SRB 166 F3
Conow D 100 D4
Conques F 49 A10
Conques-sur-Orbiel F 49 D10
Conquista E 70 C3
Consandolo I 82 C4
Consdorf L 202 B1
Conselice I 82 C4
Consell E 65 E10
Conselve I 82 B4
Consett GB 21 F13
Constância P 60 F4
Constanța RO 171 E3
Constantí E 58 E6
Constantim P 54 F4
Constantim P 55 E7
Constantina E 67 D8
Constantin Daicoviciu RO 175 B9
Constanzana E 62 C3
Consuegra E 62 F5
Contarina I 82 B5
Contes F 53 D6
Contessa Entellina I 74 D3
Conțești RO 177 D7
Conțești RO 177 F6
Conthey CH 47 C11
Contigliano I 78 C3
Contis-Plage F 48 B3
Contres F 40 F5
Contrexéville F 42 D4
Controne I 76 B4
Contursi Terme I 76 B4
Contwig D 37 F8
Conty F 34 E5
Conversano I 77 B8
Convoy IRL 23 C7
Conwy GB 26 E4
Conza della Campania I 76 B4
Cookstown GB 20 F3
Coola IRL 22 D6
Coolbaun IRL 22 G6
Coole F 41 C11
Coole IRL 23 E8
Coolmore IRL 22 C6
Coombe Bissett GB 29 C11
Cootehill IRL 23 D8
Copăcel RO 167 D9
Copăcele RO 175 C9
Copăceni MD 170 B2
Copăceni RO 176 D3
Copăcenii de Sus RO 177 E8
Copalnic-Mănăștur RO 168 B3
Copanca MD 170 D5
Copanello I 75 B10
Copceac MD 170 F3
Copertino I 77 C10
Çöpköy TR 189 B6
Copley GB 21 F13
Copons E 59 D7
Copparo I 82 C4
Coppeen IRL 24 E5
Copplestone GB 29 D7
Coppull GB 26 D6
Copșa Mică RO 168 E4
Copythorne GB 29 D11
Corabia RO 176 F4
Cora Chaitlín IRL 24 C5
Cora Droma Rúisc IRL 22 E6
Čoralići BIH 172 C4
Corato I 77 A6
Coray F 38 D4
Corbalán E 63 D11
Corbally IRL 22 D4
Corbasca RO 169 E10
Corbeanca RO 177 D8
Corbeil-Essonnes F 41 C7
Corbeilles F 41 D8
Corbeni RO 176 C5
Corbeny F 35 F8
Corbera E 64 F4
Corbera d'Ebre E 58 E4
Corbi RO 176 C5
Corbie F 34 E6
Corbières CH 47 B11
Corbières F 51 C10
Corbigny F 41 F10
Corbii Mari RO 177 D6
Corbița RO 169 E10
Corbridge GB 21 F12
Corbu RO 169 D7
Corbu RO 171 E3
Corbu RO 176 D5
Corby GB 27 G10
Corçà E 59 D10
Corcaigh IRL 24 E6
Corcelles-lès-Cîteaux F 42 F3
Corchiano I 78 C2
Corciano I 82 F5
Corcieux F 43 D6
Corcova RO 175 D11
Corcubión E 54 C1
Cordăreni RO 169 B9
Cordemais F 39 F8
Cordenòns I 89 E6
Cordes F 49 B9
Córdoba E 69 A7
Cordobilla de Lácara E 61 F8
Corduente E 63 C9
Cordun RO 169 D9
Coreglia Antelminelli I 82 D2
Corella E 57 D8
Coreses E 55 E8
Corestăuți MD 169 A10
Corfe Castle GB 29 D10
Corfinio I 78 C5
Cori I 78 D3
Coria E 61 E7
Coria del Río E 67 E7
Coriano I 82 E6
Corigliano Calabro I 77 D7
Corinaldo I 83 E7
Coripe E 67 F9
Corjeuți MD 169 A10
Cork IRL 24 E6
Corlătel RO 175 E10
Corlăteni RO 169 B9
Corlay F 38 D5
Corlea IRL 23 E7
Corleone I 74 D3
Corleto Perticara I 76 C6
Çorlu TR 189 B8
Cormatin F 46 B6
Cormeilles F 34 F1
Corme Porto E 54 B2
Cormicy F 35 F8
Cormons I 89 E7
Cormontreuil F 36 F2
Cornafulla IRL 22 F7
Cornago E 57 D7
Cornamona IRL 22 E4
Cornaredo I 85 B7
Cornas F 46 F6
Cornățelu RO 177 D7
Cornau D 33 C10
Cornea RO 175 C9
Cornedo all'Isarco I 88 D3
Cornedo Vicentino I 85 B11
Corneilla-del-Vercol F 50 E4
Cornellà de Llobregat E 59 E8
Cornellà de Terri E 59 C9
Cornellana E 55 B7
Cornereva RO 175 C9
Cornești MD 169 C12
Cornești RO 168 C3
Cornești RO 177 D7
Cornetu RO 177 E7
Corni RO 169 B9
Corni RO 169 F11
Corniglio I 85 E9
Cornimont F 43 E6
Cornu RO 177 C7
Cornuda I 88 E5
Cornudella de Montsant E 58 E5
Cornudilla E 56 C5
Cornu Luncii RO 169 C8
Cornus F 50 C5
Corod RO 169 F11
Corofin IRL 24 C4
Coroieni RO 168 C3
Coroisânmărtin RO 168 E5
Coron F 39 F10
Çorovodë AL 184 C3
Corps F 47 F8
Corps-Nuds F 39 E8
Corral de Almaguer E 63 E6
Corral de Calatrava E 70 B4
Corrales E 55 F8
Corral-Rubio E 71 B10
Corre F 42 E5
Correggio I 82 C2
Corrèze F 45 E9
Corridonia I 83 F8
Corrie GB 20 D6
Corris GB 26 F4
Corr na Móna IRL 22 E4
Corrobert F 41 C10
Corry IRL 22 D6
Corsano I 77 D10
Corseul F 39 D7
Corsham GB 29 C10
Corsico I 85 C7
Corsock GB 21 E9
Cortale I 75 B9
Corte F 53 G10
Corteconcepción E 67 D7
Corte de Peleas E 67 B6
Cortegada E 54 D3
Cortegana E 67 D6
Cortemilia I 53 B8
Corteno Golgi I 85 A9
Corteolona I 85 C7
Cortes E 57 E9
Cortes de Aragón E 58 F2
Cortes de Arenoso E 64 D3
Cortes de Baza E 71 D7
Cortes de la Frontera E 69 C6
Cortes de Pallás E 64 F3
Cortiçadas do Lavre P 66 B3
Cortijo de Arriba E 62 F4
Cortijos Nuevos E 71 C7
Cortina d'Ampezzo I 88 C5
Corton GB 31 B12
Cortona I 82 F4
Coruche P 66 B2
Corullón E 55 C6
Corund RO 168 E6
Corvara in Badia I 88 C4
Corvera E 72 F2
Corwen GB 26 F5
Coryton GB 31 D10
Cosa E 63 C10
Cosâmbești RO 177 D10
Cosăuți MD 170 A2
Coșbuc RO 168 C4
Cosby GB 27 F9
Coșcodeni MD 169 B12
Coscurita E 57 F7
Coșeiu RO 167 C11
Cosenza I 76 E6
Coșereni RO 177 D9
Coșești RO 176 C5
Coshieville GB 21 B9
Ćosići BIH 173 D8
Cosio di Arroscia I 53 C7
Coslada E 62 D5
Cosmești RO 169 F10
Cosmești RO 176 E6
Cosminele RO 177 C7
Cosne-Cours-sur-Loire F 41 F8
Cosne-d'Allier F 46 C2
Coșnița MD 170 C4
Cosoleto I 75 C8
Coșoveni RO 176 E3
Cossato I 84 B5
Cossé-le-Vivien F 39 E10
Cossoine I 80 C2
Cossonay CH 47 B10
Costacciaro I 83 F6
Costache Negri RO 169 F11
Costa da Caparica P 66 B1
Costa di Rovigo I 82 B4
Costa Volpino I 85 B9
Coșteiu RO 167 F8
Costelloe IRL 22 F3
Costești MD 169 B10
Costești MD 170 D3
Costești RO 169 D11
Costești RO 176 C4
Costești RO 176 D5
Costești RO 177 C9
Costeștii din Vale RO 177 D6
Costigliole Saluzzo I 53 B6
Costișa RO 169 D9
Costuleni RO 169 C11
Cosuenda E 57 F9
Coswig D 95 C11
Coswig D 96 D5
Coteana RO 176 E4
Cotești RO 177 B10
Cothen NL 32 D4
Coti-Chiavari F 53 H9
Cotignac F 52 D4
Cotignola I 82 D4
Cotiujeni MD 170 B3
Cotiujenii Mici MD 170 B2
Cotmeana RO 176 D5
Cotnari RO 169 C9
Cotofănești RO 169 E9
Coțofenii din Dos RO 176 E3
Cotronei I 77 E7
Cottanello I 78 C3
Cottbus D 96 C6
Cottenham GB 31 C9
Cottesmore GB 27 F10
Cottingham GB 27 F10
Cotușca RO 169 A9
Coubon F 46 E4
Couburciu MD 170 D5
Couches F 46 B6
Couço P 66 B3
Coucy-le-Château-Auffrique F 35 E7
Coudekerque-Branche F 34 B5
Couëron F 39 F8
Couflens F 49 E8
Coufouleux F 49 C9
Couhé F 45 C6
Couiza F 49 E10
Coulaines F 39 D12
Coulanges-la-Vineuse F 41 E10
Coulanges-sur-Yonne F 41 E10
Coulaures F 45 E7
Couleuvre F 46 B2
Coullons F 41 E7
Coulmier-le-Sec F 41 E11
Coulmiers F 40 E6
Coulogne F 31 F12
Coulombiers F 45 C6
Coulombs F 40 C6
Coulommiers F 41 C9
Coulonges-sur-l'Autize F 44 C4
Coulounieix-Chamiers F 45 E7
Coulport GB 20 C7
Coupar Angus GB 21 B10
Couptrain F 39 D11
Coura P 54 E2
Courcelles B 198 E4
Courcelles-Chaussy F 42 B5
Courcelles-sur-Nied F 202 C1
Courchaton F 42 E6
Courchevel F 47 E10
Cour-Cheverny F 40 E5
Courcité F 39 D11
Courçon F 44 C4
Courcy F 35 F9
Courgains F 39 D12
Courgenay CH 43 F7
Courgenay F 41 D10
Courlay F 44 B4
Courmayeur I 47 D10
Courmelles F 35 F7
Cournon-d'Auvergne F 46 D3
Courpière F 46 D4
Courrendlin CH 43 F7
Courrensan F 49 C6
Courrières F 198 E1
Coursac F 45 E7
Coursan F 50 D5
Coursegoules F 52 D6
Courseulles-sur-Mer F 39 B11
Cours-la-Ville F 46 C5
Courson-les-Carrières F 41 E9
Court CH 43 F7
Courtalain F 40 D5
Courtelary CH 43 F7
Courtenay F 41 D9
Courthézon F 51 B8
Courtmacsherry IRL 24 E5
Courtomer F 40 C3
Courtown IRL 25 C10
Courtrai B 35 C7
Courtrai B 198 D2
Court-St-Etienne B 35 C10
Courville-sur-Eure F 40 D5
Cousance F 47 B7
Cousances-les-Forges F 42 C3
Coussac-Bonneval F 45 D8
Coussay-les-Bois F 45 B7
Coussegrey F 41 E11
Coussey F 42 D4
Coustouges F 50 F4
Coutances F 39 B9
Couterne F 39 C11
Couto de Cima P 60 C5
Coutras F 44 E5
Couvet CH 47 B10
Couvin B 35 D10
Couze-et-St-Front F 45 F7
Couzeix F 45 D8
Covaleda E 56 E6
Covarrubias E 56 D5
Covăsinț RO 167 E8
Covasna RO 169 F8
Cove GB 18 K5
Cove Bay GB 19 L12
Coventry GB 29 A11
Covilhã P 60 D6
Cowbit GB 27 F11
Cowbridge GB 29 C8
Cowdenbeath GB 21 C10
Cowes GB 29 D12
Cox E 72 E3
Cox F 49 C8
Coxheath GB 31 E9
Coxhoe GB 21 F13
Coylumbridge GB 19 L9
Cózar E 71 B6
Cozes F 44 D4
Cozești MD 170 B2
Cozieni RO 177 C9
Cozmești RO 169 D11
Cozzano F 53 H10
Craanford IRL 25 C10
Crăcăoani RO 169 C8
Crach F 38 E5
Crăciunelu de Jos RO 168 E3
Crăciunești RO 168 E5
Craco I 77 C6
Craidorolț RO 167 B10
Craig GB 18 L6
Craigavad GB 20 F5
Craigavon GB 23 D10
Craigellachie GB 19 L10
Craignure GB 20 C5
Crail GB 21 C11
Crailsheim D 91 D7
Craiova RO 176 E3
Craiva RO 167 D8
Cramlington GB 21 E13
Crâmpoia RO 176 E5
Cranage GB 27 E7
Cranagh GB 20 F2
Cranford IRL 23 B7
Crângeni RO 176 E5
Cran-Gevrier F 47 D9
Crângu RO 176 F6
Crângurile RO 176 D6
Cranleigh GB 31 E8
Crans-sur-Sierre CH 47 C11
Craon F 39 E10
Craonne F 35 F8
Craponne-sur-Arzon F 46 E4
Crask Inn GB 18 J7
Crasna RO 167 C10
Crasna RO 176 C3
Crasnoe MD 170 D5
Crathie GB 21 A10
Crato P 60 F5
Cravagliana I 84 B5
Cravant F 41 E10
Craven Arms GB 29 A9
Crawfordjohn GB 21 E9
Crawfordsburn GB 20 F5
Crawley GB 31 E8
Creaca RO 167 C11
Creagh IRL 24 E4
Creagorry GB 18 L2
Creamhghort IRL 23 B7
Créances F 39 B8
Créancey F 41 F12
Crecente E 54 D3
Crêches-sur-Saône F 46 C6
Crécy-en-Ponthieu F 34 D4
Crécy-la-Chapelle F 41 C8
Crécy-sur-Serre F 35 E8
Credenhill GB 29 A9
Crediton GB 29 D7
Creeslough IRL 23 B7
Creevagh IRL 22 D4
Creggan GB 20 F2
Creggan GB 23 D9
Cregganbaun IRL 22 E3
Creggs IRL 22 E6
Creglingen D 91 C7
Cregneash GBM 26 C2
Créhange F 202 C2
Creil F 34 F5
Creil NL 32 C5
Creissels F 50 B5
Crema I 85 C8
Cremeaux F 46 D4
Crémenes E 55 C9
Crémieu F 47 D7
Cremlingen D 95 B8
Cremona I 85 C9
Črenšovci SLO 164 C6
Créon F 44 F5
Crepaja SRB 174 C6
Crépey F 42 C4
Crépy F 35 E8
Crépy-en-Valois F 34 F6
Cres HR 83 C9
Crescentino I 84 C5
Crespina I 82 E2
Crespino I 82 C4
Crespos E 62 C3
Cressensac F 45 E9
Crest F 47 F7
Creswell GB 27 E9
Cretas E 58 F4
Créteil F 41 C7
Crețeni RO 176 D4
Crețești RO 169 D11
Creußen D 91 C10
Creutzwald F 37 F7
Creuzburg D 95 D7
Crevalcore I 82 C3
Crevant F 45 C9
Crévéchamps F 42 C5
Crèvecœur-le-Grand F 34 E5
Crevedia RO 177 D7
Crevedia Mare RO 177 E7
Crevenicu RO 177 E7
Crevillente E 72 E3
Crevoladossola I 84 A5
Crewe GB 26 E7
Crewkerne GB 29 D9
Crianlarich GB 20 C7
Cricău RO 168 E3
Criccieth GB 26 F3
Criciova RO 175 B9
Crickhowell GB 29 B8
Cricklade GB 29 B11
Cricova MD 170 C3
Crieff GB 21 C9
Criel-sur-Mer F 34 D3
Crikvenica HR 83 B10
Crimmitschau D 95 E11
Crimond GB 19 K13
Crinan GB 20 C5
Cringleford GB 31 B11
Crinitz D 96 C5
Cripán E 57 C7
Cripp's Corner GB 31 F10
Criquetot-l'Esneval F 34 E1
Crișcior RO 167 E10
Crișeni RO 167 C11
Crispiano I 77 B8
Crissolo I 47 F11
Cristești RO 168 D4
Cristești RO 169 B9
Cristești RO 169 C9
Cristian RO 168 F4
Cristian RO 177 B6
Cristinești RO 169 A8
Criștioru de Jos RO 167 E10
Cristóbal E 61 D9
Cristolț RO 167 C11
Cristuru Secuiesc RO 168 E6
Criuleni MD 170 C4
Criva MD 169 A9
Crivitz D 99 C11
Crkvice BIH 173 D8
Crkvice HR 178 D3
Crkvice MNE 179 D6
Crkvina BIH 173 B9
Crkvine SRB 179 C9
Crljivica BIH 172 D5
Crmjan SRB 179 E9
Črmošnjice SLO 89 E11
Črna SLO 89 D10
Crna Bara SRB 166 F5
Crna Bara SRB 174 D3
Crnac HR 165 E9
Crnajka SRB 175 E9
Crna Trava SRB 180 D5
Crnča SRB 174 E3
Crni Lug BIH 172 D6
Crni Lug HR 83 B10
Crnjelovo BIH 173 C11
Črnkovci HR 165 E10
Crnokliště SRB 180 C5
Crnoljevo SRB 179 E10
Črnomelj SLO 164 E4
Crock D 91 B8
Crocketford GB 21 E9
Crockets Town IRL 22 D4
Crockmore IRL 23 C7
Crocmaz MD 170 E5
Crocq F 45 D10
Crodo I 84 A5
Crofty GB 28 B6
Croghan IRL 22 E6
Crognaleto I 78 B4
Croisilles F 34 D6
Croithlí IRL 22 B6
Crolles F 47 E8
Crolly IRL 22 B6
Cromadh IRL 24 C5
Cromarty GB 19 K8
Cromer GB 31 B11
Cromhall GB 29 B10
Cronat F 46 B4
Crook GB 21 F13
Crookham GB 21 D12
Crookhaven IRL 24 F3
Crookstown IRL 24 E5
Croom IRL 24 C5

Cropalati I 77 D7
Cropani I 75 B10
Crosbost GB 18 J4
Crosby GB 26 E5
Crosia I 77 D7
Cross IRL 22 E4
Crossaig GB 20 D6
Crossakeel IRL 23 E8
Cross Barry IRL 24 E5
Crossdoney IRL 23 E8
Crossgar GB 23 D11
Crossgare GB 20 D4
Crossgates GB 29 A8
Crosshands GB 21 D8
Crosshaven IRL 24 E6
Crosshill GB 20 E7
Cross Inn GB 28 A6
Cross Keys IRL 23 E9
Crossmaglen GB 23 D9
Crotone I 77 E8
Crots F 52 B4
Crottendorf D 92 B3
Croughton GB 29 B12
Croutelle F 45 B6
Crouy F 35 F7
Crouy-sur-Ourcq F 41 B9
Crowborough GB 31 E9
Crowland GB 27 F11
Crowle GB 27 D10
Crowthorne GB 31 E7
Croy GB 19 K8
Croyde GB 28 C6
Crozant F 45 C9
Crozes-Hermitage F 46 E6
Crozon F 38 D3
Cruas F 51 A8
Crucea RO 169 C7
Crucea RO 171 D2
Crucișor RO 167 C10
Crucoli I 77 E7
Cruden Bay GB 19 L13
Cruglic MD 170 C4
Crumlin GB 20 D7
Cruseilles F 47 C9
Cruşeţ RO 176 D3
Crusheen IRL 24 C5
Crusnes F 36 F5
Cruzy F 50 D4
Cruzy-le-Châtel F 41 E11
Crvenka SRB 174 B3
Crymych GB 28 B3
Csabacsüd H 166 D6
Csabrendek H 165 B8
Csákánydoroszló H 165 C7
Csákbárény H 165 B10
Csákvár H 165 B10
Csanádapáca H 167 D6
Csanádpalota H 166 E6
Csány H 166 B4
Csanytelek H 166 D5
Császár H 165 A10
Császártöltés H 166 E3
Csátalja H 166 E3
Csávoly H 166 E3
Csécse H 163 F9
Csemő H 166 C4
Csengele H 166 D4
Csenger H 167 B10
Csengőd H 166 D3
Csépa H 166 D5
Csepreg H 165 B7
Cserépfalu H 161 H2
Cserhátsurány H 163 F8
Cserkeszőlő H 166 D5
Csernely H 161 G1
Csesztreg H 165 C7
Csetény H 165 B9
Csévharaszt H 166 C3
Csikéria H 166 E3
Csókakő H 165 B10
Csökmő H 167 C7
Csököly H 165 D9
Csokonyavisonta H 165 D8
Csokvaomány H 161 G1
Csolnok H 165 A11
Csólyospálos H 166 E4
Csongrád H 166 D5
Csopak H 165 C9
Csór H 165 B10
Csorna H 165 A8
Csörnyeföld H 165 D7
Csorvás H 166 D6
Csősz H 165 B10
Csót H 165 B9
Csurgó H 165 D8
Cuacos de Yuste E 61 D9
Cuadros E 55 C8
Cualedro E 54 E4
Cuarte de Huerva E 57 E10
Cuba P 66 C4
Cubalhão P 54 D3
Cubells E 58 D5
Cubjac F 45 E7
Cubla E 63 D10
Cubo de Bureba E 56 C5
Cubo de la Solana E 57 E7
Cubzac-les-Ponts F 44 F5
Cuca RO 169 F11
Cuca RO 176 D5
Cucalón E 63 B10
Cucerdea RO 168 E4
Cuci RO 168 E4
Cuckfield GB 31 E8
Cucuron F 51 C9
Cucuteni RO 169 C9
Cudalbi RO 169 F11
Cudillero E 55 A7
Čudniči BIH 173 D8
Cudos F 48 B5
Cuéllar E 56 F3
Cuenca E 63 D8
Cuenca de Campos E 55 D9
Cuers F 52 E4
Cuerva E 62 E4
Cueva de Agreda E 57 E8
Cuevas Bajas E 69 B8
Cuevas de Almanzora E 71 E9
Cuevas del Becerro E 69 C7
Cuevas del Campo E 71 D7
Cuevas de San Clemente E 56 D4
Cuevas de San Marcos E 69 B8
Cuevas Labradas E 58 G1
Cuffley GB 31 D8
Cugand F 44 A3
Cuges-les-Pins F 51 D10
Cugir RO 167 F11
Cuglieri I 80 C2
Cuguen F 39 D8
Cuhureşti de Sus MD 170 B3

Cuijk NL 32 E5
Cúil an tSúdaire IRL 23 F8
Cuiseaux F 47 C7
Cuise-la-Motte F 34 F7
Cuisery F 47 B6
Cujmir RO 175 E10
Culan F 45 B10
Culciu RO 167 B11
Culdaff IRL 20 E2
Culdrain GB 19 L11
Culemborg NL 32 E4
Culjković SRB 174 D4
Culla E 64 D4
Cullahill IRL 25 C8
Cúllar-Baza E 71 D7
Cullen GB 19 K11
Cullera E 64 F4
Cullivoe GB 19 D14
Cullompton GB 29 D8
Cullybackey GB 20 D4
Cullyhanna GB 23 D9
Culmstock GB 29 D8
Culnaknock GB 18 K4
Culoz F 47 D8
Culswick GB 19 E13
Cumbernauld GB 21 D9
Cumbres de San Bartolomé E 67 C6
Cumbres Mayores E 67 C6
Cumeada P 66 E3
Cumiana I 47 F11
Cumieira P 54 F4
Cumiestown GB 19 K12
Cumlosen D 99 D11
Cumnock GB 21 E8
Cumpăna RO 171 E3
Cunault F 39 F11
Cunegès F 45 F6
Cuneo I 53 F7
Cunewalde D 97 D7
Cunfin F 41 D12
Cungrea RO 176 D3
Cunha P 45 D2
Cunicea MD 170 B3
Ćuništa BIH 173 D10
Cunit E 59 E7
Cunningsburgh GB 19 E14
Cuntis E 54 C2
Cuorgnè I 47 E11
Cupar GB 21 C10
Cupcina MD 169 A10
Cupello I 79 C7
Cupra Marittima I 78 A5
Cupramontana I 83 F7
Ćuprija SRB 175 E7
Cupşeni RO 168 B3
Cuq-Toulza F 49 C9
Curățele RO 167 D9
Curcani RO 177 E9
Curcuris I 80 D2
Cureggio I 84 B5
Cureşniţa MD 169 A12
Curgy F 46 B5
Curinga I 75 B9
Curon Venosta I 87 D11
Curracloe IRL 25 D10
Curraghroe IRL 22 E6
Curragh West IRL 22 E5
Currás F 54 C2
Curry IRL 22 E5
Curry Rivel GB 29 C9
Cursi I 77 C10
Curtea RO 167 F9
Curtea de Argeş RO 176 C5
Curtici RO 167 E7
Curtişoara RO 176 E4
Curtuişeni RO 167 B9
Ćurug SRB 174 C5
Cusano Mutri I 76 A3
Cushendall GB 20 D4
Cushendun GB 20 D4
Cushina IRL 23 F8
Cussac F 45 D7
Cusset F 46 C3
Cussy-les-Forges F 41 F11
Custines F 42 C5
Custonaci I 74 C2
Cutigliano I 82 D2
Cutro I 77 E7
Cutrofiano I 77 C10
Cuxac-Cabardès F 49 D10
Cuxac-d'Aude F 50 D4
Cuxhaven D 33 A11
Cuza Vodă RO 177 E10
Cuzmin MD 170 A3
Cuzorn F 49 A7
Cvikov CZ 97 E7
Cwmafan GB 29 B7
Cwmbrân GB 29 B9
Cybinka PL 97 B7
Cybowo PL 101 D9
Cychry PL 101 E7
Cyców PL 157 H8
Cydweli GB 28 B6
Cynghordy GB 29 A7
Cynwyl Elfed GB 28 B6
Cyprianka PL 154 E7
Cysoing F 198 D2
Czacz PL 97 B11
Czajków PL 158 D5
Czajlink PL 101 C10
Czarna PL 159 F11
Czarna PL 160 C5
Czarna Białostocka PL 156 D8
Czarna Dąbrówka PL 101 B13
Czarna Górna PL 161 E6
Czarna Woda PL 154 C5
Czarncza PL 159 E8
Czarne PL 101 C11
Czarnia PL 155 D11
Czarnków PL 101 E11
Czarnocin PL 159 F10
Czarnów PL 97 A5
Czarnowąsy PL 158 E4
Czarnożyły PL 158 D6
Czarny Bór PL 97 E10
Czarny Dunajec PL 163 C9
Czastary PL 158 D5
Czaszyn PL 161 E5
Czchów PL 160 D2
Czechowice-Dziedzice PL 163 B8
Czechy PL 101 C11
Czechy PL 159 C6
Czekarzewice PL 159 D12
Czeladź PL 159 F7
Czemierniki PL 157 G7
Czempiń PL 97 B11
Czeremcha PL 157 E8
Czermin PL 158 C4

Czermno PL 157 H2
Czernica PL 97 D13
Czernice Borowe PL 155 D10
Czernichów PL 159 G8
Czernichów PL 163 B8
Czerniejewo PL 101 F12
Czernikowo PL 154 E6
Czernina PL 97 C11
Czersk PL 154 B5
Czerwieńsk PL 97 B8
Czerwin PL 155 E12
Czerwińsk nad Wisłą PL 155 F9
Czerwionka-Leszczyny PL 158 F6
Czerwonak PL 97 B11
Czerwone PL 155 D12
Czerwone PL 155 F10
Czestków PL 159 C7
Czeszów PL 97 D12
Częstochowa PL 159 E7
Człopa PL 101 D10
Człuchów PL 101 C12
Czmoń PL 97 B12
Czorsztyn PL 161 E1
Czosnów PL 155 F10
Czudec PL 160 D4
Czyże PL 157 E8
Czyżew-Osada PL 157 E6

D

Daaden D 201 C8
Dăbâca RO 168 D3
Dabar HR 172 C3
Dabar HR 172 E6
Dabas H 166 C3
Dabel D 99 C11
Dąbie PL 97 B8
Dąbie PL 157 G6
Dąbie PL 158 B6
Dabo F 43 C7
Dąbki PL 101 B10
Daborgrad BIH 173 C9
Dabrac BIH 173 D7
Dabrica BIH 173 F9
Dąbroszyn PL 97 A7
Dąbroszyn PL 158 B6
Dąbrowa PL 154 E4
Dąbrowa PL 158 E4
Dąbrowa Białostocka PL 156 C8
Dąbrowa Biskupia PL 154 E6
Dąbrowa Chełmińska PL 154 D5
Dąbrowa Górnicza PL 159 F7
Dąbrowa Tarnowska PL 159 F10
Dąbrowa Zielona PL 159 E8
Dąbrowice PL 157 G2
Dąbrowice PL 158 B5
Dąbrówka Wielka PL 159 C7
Dąbrówka Wielkopolska PL 97 B9
Dąbrówno PL 155 D9
Dąbuleni RO 176 F4
Dabyeya BY 149 F7
Dachau D 91 F9
Dachnów PL 160 C7
Dachrieden D 95 D8
Dachwig D 95 D8
Dačice CZ 93 D8
Dacre GB 21 F11
Dad H 165 A10
Dadia GR 187 B10
Dâdran S 119 E10
Dăeni RO 171 D2
Dăeşti RO 176 C4
Dáfjord N 128 D3
Dafnes GR 197 E8
Dafni GR 175 D7
Dafni GR 190 D5
Dafni GR 191 B6
Dafni GR 191 F6
Dág H 165 A10
Daganzo de Arriba E 62 C6
Dağardı TR 189 E11
Dağâţa RO 169 D10
Dagda LV 149 D3
Dagebüll D 98 A5
Dağkızılca TR 193 C9
Daglan F 45 F8
Daglösen S 113 C11
Dağpınar TR 197 B8
Dagsmark FIN 138 T
Dahlem D 37 D7
Dahlen D 96 D4
Dahlenburg D 99 D9
Dahlhausen D 99 C9
Dahme D 96 C4
Dahme S 123 E13
Dahn D 43 B8
Dähre D 99 E9
Daia RO 177 E7
Daia Română RO 168 E3
Daikanberg S 123 A10
Daikanvik S 123 A10
Dailly GB 20 E7
Daimiel E 62 F5
Daimonia GR 194 B4
Daingean IRL 23 F8
Dainville F 34 D6
Dainville-Berthéléville F 42 D4
Dairsie GB 21 C11
Daknam B 198 C3
Đakovica SRB 179 E9
Đakovo HR 165 F10
Dal N 111 B14
Dal S 123 E13
Dala SRB 166 E5
Dalabrog GB 18 L2
Dalaman TR 197 C9
Dalarö S 109 A12
Dalasjö S 123 B11
Dalbe LV 151 C7
Dalbeattie GB 21 F9
Dardes AL 184 C4
Dardha AL 184 C4
Darė I 85 A10
Darfo Boario Terme I 85 B7
Dargun D 99 C13
Darıca TR 189 B10
Darıcı TR 189 F10
Dârjiu RO 168 E6
Darkley GB 23 D9
Darlington GB 27 B8
Dârlos RO 168 E5
Darłówko PL 101 B10
Darłowo PL 101 B10
Dărmăneşti RO 169 C8
Dârmăneşti RO 169 D9
Dărmăneşti RO 169 E9
Dârmăneşti RO 176 C5

Dalen N 106 A5
Dalen N 110 D7
Dalen N 110 D7
Dalesyce PL 159 E10
Dalfors S 119 D9
Dalfsen NL 32 C6
Dalgety Bay GB 21 C10
Dalham GB 31 C10
Dalhem B 35 C12
Dalhem S 109 D13
Dalholen N 117 A14
Dalías E 71 F7
Dalików GB 159 C7
Dalj HR 173 B10
Dalkarlsberg S 113 D12
Dalkeith GB 21 D10
Dalkey IRL 23 F11
Dallas GB 19 K10
Dallgow D 96 A4
Dall Villaby DK 103 E8
Dalmally GB 20 C7
Dalmand H 165 D10
Dalmellington GB 21 E8
Dalmine I 85 B8
Dalmose DK 103 E8
Dalovice CZ 92 B3
Dalry GB 20 D7
Dalrymple GB 20 E7
Dalsbruk FIN 142 E8
Dalsjöfors S 107 D13
Dals Långed S 107 C11
Dalstein F 36 F6
Dalston GB 21 F11
Dalstorp S 107 D14
Dalstuga S 119 D10
Dalton-in-Furness GB 26 C5
Daluis F 52 C5
Dalum S 107 D13
Dalur FO 18 B3
Dàlvadas FIN 129 C17
Dalwhinnie GB 21 B8
Dalyan TR 197 C9
Dalyokiya BY 151 F13
Dalystown IRL 22 F6
Damachava BY 157 G9
Damasi GR 185 E7
Damaskinia GR 184 D5
Damasławek PL 101 E13
Damazan F 49 B6
Dambach-la-Ville F 202 E3
Dambaslar TR 189 B7
Dâmbovicioara RO 176 C6
Damelevières F 42 C5
Damerstown IRL 25 C8
Damery F 41 B10
Dameš AL 184 C2
Damgan F 38 E6
Damhead GB 20 D3
Damhliag IRL 23 E10
Dămieneşti RO 169 D9
Damigny F 39 D12
Dammarie F 40 D6
Dammartin-en-Goële F 41 B8
Damme B 35 B7
Damme D 33 C10
Damnica PL 101 B12
Damnjane SRB 179 E9
Damno PL 101 A12
Damp D 99 A7
Dampierre F 42 F4
Dampierre-sur-Linotte F 42 E5
Dampierre-sur-Salon F 42 E4
Damprichard F 43 F6
Damshagen D 99 C10
Damshölte DK 103 F10
Dämsta S 123 E13
Damvant CH 43 F6
Damville F 40 C5
Damvillers F 35 F11
Damwoude NL 32 B6
Damyanovo BG 181 D10
Danaçalı TR 189 E9
Danakos GR 195 E6
Danamandıra TR 189 B9
Danasjö S 125 F12
Dăncigeşti RO 176 D3
Dăneasa RO 176 E4
Daneş RO 168 E5
Danesfort IRL 25 C8
Dănești RO 169 D7
Dăneşti RO 169 D11
Dănești RO 176 D4
Daneți RO 176 E4
Dângebo S 105 B8
Dângeni RO 169 B9
Dangé-St-Romain F 45 B7
Danholn S 119 E10
Dănicei RO 176 D4
Daniec PL 158 E5
Danilovgrad MNE 179 D7
Dänischenhagen D 99 B8
Danişment TR 189 E8
Danjoutin F 43 E6
Dankerode D 95 D8
Danndorf D 95 A8
Dannemare DK 99 A10
Dannemarie F 43 E7
Dannemora S 115 B9
Dannenberg (Elbe) D 99 D10
Dannenwalde D 100 D4
Dány H 166 B4
Daon F 39 E10
Daoulas F 38 D3
Darabani RO 169 A9
Dărăşti Ilfov RO 177 E8
Darbénai LT 150 D2
Dar Ben Karricha el Behri MA 69 E6
Darby's Bridge IRL 24 D2
Dar Chaoui MA 68 E5
Darda HR 165 E11

Dărmăneşti RO 177 D7
Darmstadt D 37 E11
Darney F 42 D5
Darnieulles F 42 D5
Darnózseli H 162 F4
Daroca E 63 B10
Darova RO 175 B8
Darque P 54 E2
Darra GB 19 L12
Darragh IRL 24 C4
Darro E 71 E6
Dartford GB 31 E9
Dartmeet GB 29 D7
Dartmouth GB 29 E7
Darton GB 27 D8
Dartsel S 134 C4
Daruvar HR 165 E8
Dârvari RO 175 E11
Darwen GB 26 D7
Daščău RO 177 D8
Dashava UA 161 E9
Dašice CZ 93 B9
Dasing D 91 F9
Dasochori GR 185 B9
Dasochori GR 187 C7
Dassel D 94 C6
Dassendorf D 99 D8
Dassow D 99 C9
Daszyna PL 159 B7
Datça TR 197 C7
Datteln D 33 E8
Datterode (Ringgau) D 95 D7
Daudzese LV 151 C10
Daudzeva LV 151 C10
Daugai LT 153 E9
Daugailiai LT 151 E13
Daugavpils LV 151 E13
Daugârd DK 102 D5
Daugelaičiai LT 150 E7
Daugulji LV 151 A10
Daujėnai LT 151 E9
Daumazan-sur-Arize F 49 D8
Daumeray F 39 E11
Daun D 37 D7
Dauphin F 51 C10
Daventry GB 29 A12
Davézieux F 46 E6
Davidesti RO 176 C6
Davidkovo BG 181 F10
Daviot GB 19 L8
Davle CZ 92 C6
Davleia GR 191 B6
Dávod H 166 E2
Davoli I 75 B9
Davor HR 173 B8
Davos CH 87 D9
Davutlar TR 193 D9
Davydiv UA 160 D9
Dawlish GB 29 D8
Dax F 48 C3
Deal GB 31 E11
Dealu RO 168 E6
Dealu Morii RO 169 E10
Dearham GB 21 F9
Deauville F 39 B12
Deba E 48 D1
Debar MK 184 A4
Debeli Lug SRB 175 E8
Debeljača SRB 174 C6
Debenham GB 31 C11
Dębe Wielkie PL 157 F4
Dębica PL 159 F11
Dęblin PL 157 G5
Debnevo BG 181 D10
Dębnica Kaszubska PL 101 B12
Dębno PL 101 E7
Dębno PL 159 G10
Dęborzęczka PL 157 H2
Debovo BG 181 B10
Dębowa Kłoda PL 157 G8
Dębowa Łąka PL 154 D7
Dębowiec PL 163 D7
Debrc SRB 174 D4
Debrecen H 167 B8
Debreşte MK 184 B5
Debrzno PL 101 C12
Dębsko PL 101 D9
Dečani SRB 179 D9
Decazeville F 49 A10
Dechtice SK 162 D5
Decimomannu I 80 E2
Decimoputzu I 80 E2
Děčín CZ 96 E6
Decize F 46 B3
De Cocksdorp NL 32 B3
Decollatura I 75 A9
Deda RO 168 D5
Deddington GB 29 B12
Dedeler TR 189 F9
Dedelow D 100 D5
Dedelstorf D 99 E9
Dedemsvaart NL 33 C6
Dédestapolcsány H 161 G2
Dedham GB 31 D11
Dedovichi RUS 148 F5
Deensen D 94 C6
Deerlijk B 35 C7
Dég H 165 C10
Degaña E 55 D7
Degeberga S 104 D6
Degerbäcken S 134 C6
Degerby FIN 115 B14
Degerby FIN 143 E11
Degerfors S 108 A4
Degerhamn S 105 C10
Degersjö S 123 D12
Degerträsk S 134 C4
Deggendorf D 92 E6
Değirmen TR 189 B9
Değirmendere TR 193 C9
Değirmendüzü TR 187 D10
Değirmenyeni TR 183 F7
Dego I 37 C8
Degučiai LT 151 E12
Degumnieki LV 151 C13
De Haan B 198 B1
Dehesa de Campoamor E 72 F3
Dehesas de Guadix E 71 D6
Deià E 65 F10
Deidenberg B 201 E8
Deidesheim D 37 F10
Deifontes E 69 B9
Deilão P 55 E6
Deining D 91 D8
Deiningen D 91 E8
Deinste D 33 A12
Deinze B 35 C8

Dărmăneşti RO 177 D7
Deiva Marina I 53 C11
Dej RO 168 C3
Deje S 113 C9
Dejtár H 163 E8
Dekani SLO 83 E8
De Koog NL 32 B3
De Kooy NL 32 C3
Dekov BG 181 B11
Delabole GB 28 D5
Delary S 103 B13
Delbrück D 33 E11
Delčevo MK 181 F6
Delden NL 33 D7
Delegyháza H 166 C3
Deleitosa E 61 E9
Đelekovec HR 165 D7
Delémont CH 43 F7
Delen' UA 161 C6
Deleni RO 169 C9
Deleni RO 171 E2
Deleria GR 185 E7
Deleşti RO 169 D11
Delfoi GR 191 C6
Delft NL 32 D2
Delfzijl NL 33 B7
Delia I 74 E4
Delianuova I 75 C8
Deliblato SRB 175 D7
Deliceto I 76 A4
Deligrad SRB 175 F8
Deliktaş TR 193 B8
Delingsdorf D 99 C8
Delitzsch D 95 C11
Delle F 43 E7
Delligsen D 94 C6
Dello I 82 B1
Delme F 42 C5
Delmenhorst D 33 B11
Delnice HR 83 B10
Delsbo S 119 C12
Deltebre E 58 F5
Delvin IRL 23 E9
Delvinaki GR 184 E3
Delvinë AL 184 E3
Demandice SK 163 E7
Demange-aux-Eaux F 42 C3
Demba LT 151 E8
Demecser H 161 G4
Demen D 99 C11
Demene LT 151 E13
Demigny F 46 B6
Demiraj AL 179 F9
Demircihalil TR 183 F8
Demirdere TR 189 D9
Demirhanlı TR 189 D7
Demir Hisar MK 184 B5
Demirköy TR 183 F9
Demirli TR 197 C9
Demirtaş TR 189 D11
Demmin D 100 C4
Demonte I 53 C6
Dému F 49 C6
Denain F 35 D7
Denbigh GB 26 E5
Den Bommel NL 198 B4
Den Burg NL 32 B3
Denderleeuw B 198 D4
Dendermonde B 35 B9
Den Dungen NL 32 E4
Denekamp NL 33 D8
Deneral Janković SRB 180 E3
Denguin F 48 D5
Den Haag NL 32 D2
Den Ham NL 33 D7
Den Helder NL 32 C3
Denholm GB 21 E11
Denia E 72 D5
Denkendorf D 43 C11
Denkendorf D 91 E9
Denkingen D 43 D11
Denkingen D 43 E11
Denklingen D 87 B11
Dennewitz D 96 C3
Dennhausen (Fuldabrück) D 94 D5
Denny GB 21 C9
Den Oever NL 32 C4
Densow D 100 D4
Densuş RO 175 B10
Denta RO 175 C7
Dentergem B 35 C7
Dentlein am Forst D 91 D7
Denver GB 27 F12
Denzlingen D 43 E8
Déols F 45 B9
De Panne B 34 B6
Deppis S 125 E18
Derăsbrenna N 121 C10
Derby GB 27 F9
Derecske H 167 C8
Dereham GB 31 B10
Derekegyház H 166 D5
Dereköy TR 183 F8
Dereköy TR 189 F7
Derenti TR 189 F8
De Rijp NL 32 C3
Dermantsi BG 181 C9
Dermbach D 95 E7
Dermenas AL 184 C2
Derna RO 167 C9
Derrään HU 22 D4
Derreendaragh IRL 24 D3
Derreeny Bridge IRL 24 E4
Derry GB 20 F7
Derrygonnelly GB 23 D7
Derrylin GB 23 D8
Derrymore IRL 24 D3
Derrynawilt GB 23 D8
Derryrush IRL 22 F3
Derrywode IRL 22 E5
Dersca RO 169 B8
Dersingham GB 27 F13
Dersum D 33 C8
Derutti I 78 B2
Dervaig GB 20 B4
Derval F 39 E8
Dervenakia GR 191 D6
Derveni GR 190 C5
Derventa BIH 173 C8
Derviçan AL 184 D3
Derviziana GR 184 F4
Dervock GB 20 D4
Desa RO 175 F11
Desana I 84 C5
Desantne UA 171 B5

Descargamaría E 61 D8
Descartes F 45 B7
Desenzano del Garda I 82 B2
Désertines F 45 C11
Deseşti RO 168 B3
Desfina GR 191 C6
Deskati GR 185 E6
Deskle SLO 89 D8
Despotovac SRB 175 E7
Despotovo SRB 174 C4
Dessau D 95 C11
Dessel B 32 F4
Destelbergen B 35 B8
Deštná CZ 93 D7
Destriana E 55 C7
Desulo I 80 C3
Desvres F 31 F12
Deszczno PL 101 E8
Deszk H 166 E5
Deta RO 175 C7
Detern D 33 B8
Detk H 166 B5
Detkovac HR 165 E9
Dětmarovice CZ 162 B6
Detmold D 33 E11
Dettelbach D 91 C7
Dettenhausen D 203 D7
Dettingen an der Erms D 203 D7
Dettmannsdorf D 99 B13
Dettum D 95 B8
Dettwiller F 202 D3
Detva SK 163 D8
Deurne NL 32 F5
Deutsch Evern D 99 D8
Deutschfeistritz A 164 B4
Deutschhof D 100 E3
Deutschkreutz A 165 A7
Deutschlandsberg A 89 C11
Deutschneudorf D 96 E4
Deutsch-Wagram A 93 F11
Deutzen D 95 D11
Deva RO 167 F11
Dévaványa H 167 C6
Devecikonağı TR 189 E10
Devecser H 165 B8
Devene BG 181 C8
Deventer NL 32 D6
Devesel RO 175 E10
Deveselu RO 176 E4
Devetaki BG 181 D10
Deville F 200 E2
Devil's Bridge GB 29 A7
Devin BG 181 F9
Devizes GB 29 C11
Devletliağaç TR 183 F8
Devnya BG 183 C9
Đevrske HR 172 E4
De Wijk NL 32 C6
Dewsbury GB 27 D8
Deza E 57 F7
Dežanovac HR 165 E8
Dezghingea MD 170 E3
Dezna RO 167 D9
Dhërmi AL 184 D2
Dhron D 201 E7
Diafani GR 197 E6
Diakofto GR 190 C5
Dialampi GR 187 B8
Diamante I 76 D5
Dianalund DK 103 D8
Diano d'Alba I 53 B8
Diano Marina I 53 C8
Diavata GR 185 C8
Diavolitsi GR 194 B5
Dichiseni RO 177 E11
Dicomano I 82 E4
Didam NL 32 E6
Didcot GB 29 B12
Didderse D 95 B7
Dideşti RO 176 E5
Didyma GR 191 E7
Didymoteicho GR 187 B10
Didžiasalis LT 151 F13
Die F 47 F7
Dieblich D 37 D8
Dieburg D 37 E11
Dieci RO 167 E9
Diedorf D 91 F8
Diego Álvaro E 61 C10
Diekhof D 99 C12
Diekholzen D 94 B6
Diekirch L 36 E6
Dielheim D 37 F11
Dielmissen D 94 C6
Dielsdorf CH 43 F9
Diemen NL 32 D3
Diémoz F 47 D7
Dienheim D 201 E9
Dienne F 46 E2
Dienville F 41 D12
Diepenau D 33 D10
Diepenbeek B 35 C11
Diepenheim NL 198 A8
Diepenveen NL 199 A8
Diepholz D 33 C10
Dieppe F 34 E3
Dierdorf D 37 C9
Dieren NL 32 D6
Dierhagen, Ostseebad D 99 B12
Diesdorf D 99 E9
Dieskau D 95 D11
Diespeck D 91 C8
Diessen NL 199 C6
Dießen am Ammersee D 88 A3
Diessenhofen CH 43 E10
Diest B 35 C11
Dietachdorf A 93 F6
Dietenheim D 87 A10
Dietersburg D 92 E5
Dietfurt an der Altmühl D 91 D10
Dietikon CH 43 F9
Dietingen D 43 D10
Dietmanns A 93 E8
Dietmanns A 93 E8
Dietmannsried D 87 B10
Dietzenbach D 37 D11
Dietzhölztal-Ewersbach D 201 C9
Dieue-sur-Meuse F 42 B3
Dieulefit F 51 A9
Dieulouard F 42 C5
Dieuze F 42 C6
Dieveniškės LT 153 E12
Diever NL 32 C5
Diex A 89 C10
Dizma E 71 E6
Differdange L 36 F5
Digerberget S 113 B9
Digerberget S 118 A8
Digermulen N 126 D8

Digernes N 116 B5
Dignac F 45 D6
Dignāja LV 151 D12
Dignano I 89 D6
Digne-les-Bains F 52 C4
Digny F 40 C5
Digoin F 46 C4
Dihtiv UA 160 B9
Dijon F 42 F3
Dikaia GR 182 F6
Dikanäs S 123 A10
Dikance SRB 179 E10
Dikili TR 193 A8
Dikkebus B 34 C6
Dikļi LV 147 F10
Diksmuide B 34 B6
Dilar E 69 B9
Dilbeek B 198 D4
Dilesi GR 191 C8
Dilinata GR 190 C2
Dillenburg D 37 C10
Dilling N 111 D13
Dillingen (Saar) D 37 F7
Dillingen an der Donau D 91 E7
Dilove UA 161 H9
Dilsen B 35 B12
Dimaro I 87 E11
Diminio GR 185 F8
Dimitrie Cantemir RO 169 D12
Dimitritsi GR 185 C9
Dimitrovgrad BG 182 E5
Dimitrovgrad SRB 181 C6
Dimitsana GR 190 D5
Dimovo BG 175 F10
Dimzukalns LV 151 C8
Dinami I 75 B9
Dinan F 39 D7
Dinant B 35 D10
Dinard F 39 C7
Dingé F 39 D8
Dingelstädt D 95 D7
Dingelstedt am Huy D 95 C8
Dingle IRL 24 D2
Dingle S 107 B10
Dingolfing D 91 E12
Dingtuna S 114 C6
Dingwall GB 18 K8
Dinjiška HR 83 D11
Dinkelsbühl D 91 D7
Dinkelscherben D 91 F8
Dinklage D 33 C10
Dinnet GB 21 A11
Dinslaken D 33 E7
Dinteloord NL 32 E2
Dinther NL 199 B6
Dinxperlo NL 33 E6
Diö S 104 B6
Dion GR 185 D7
Diósd H 165 B11
Diosig RO 167 C9
Diósjenő H 163 F8
Dioști RO 176 E4
Diou F 46 B4
Dipignano I 76 E6
Dipotama GR 187 B7
Dippach L 36 E6
Dippoldiswalde D 96 E5
Dirdal N 110 E4
Dirhami EST 146 C7
Dirivaara S 132 E8
Dirkshorn NL 32 C3
Dirksland NL 32 E2
Dirlewang D 87 A11
Dirmstein D 203 B5
Dirvonėnai LT 150 E5
Dischingen D 91 E7
Disentis Muster CH 87 D7
Diseröd S 107 D11
Dison B 35 C12
Diss GB 31 C11
Dissay F 45 B6
Dissay-sous-Courcillon F 40 E3
Dissen am Teutoburger Wald D 33 D10
Distington GB 26 B4
Distomo GR 191 C6
Distrato GR 184 D5
Ditfurt D 95 C9
Ditrău RO 169 D7
Ditton GB 31 E9
Ditzingen D 43 C11
Divača SLO 89 E8
Divarata GR 190 C2
Diva Slatina BG 181 C6
Divci SRB 174 E5
Divčibare SRB 174 E5
Dives-sur-Mer F 39 B11
Dividalen N 127 C18
Divieto I 75 C7
Divín SK 163 E9
Divina SK 163 C7
Divion F 34 D6
Divišov CZ 93 C7
Divjakë AL 184 C2
Divonne-les-Bains F 47 C9
Divuša HR 172 B5
Dixmont F 41 D9
Dizy F 41 B10
Dizy-le-Gros F 35 E9
Djäkneboda S 138 B5
Djäkneböle S 138 C4
Djupen N 127 B18
Djupfjord N 126 C9
Djupfors S 125 E11
Djupsjö S 123 E14
Djuptjärn S 123 D15
Djupvik N 125 B10
Djupvik N 128 D5
Djupvik S 105 A11
Djura S 119 E8
Djurås S 113 A13
Djurmo S 113 A13
Djurö S 115 D11
Dlhá nad Oravou SK 163 C8
Dlouhá Loučka CZ 93 C12
Dlouhá Třebová CZ 93 C10
Długołęka PL 97 D12
Długołęka PL 156 D7
Długosiodło PL 155 E12
Dłutów PL 159 C7
Dlŭzhka Polyana BG 182 C6
Dmytrivka UA 170 F3
Dmytrivka UA 170 F4
Dmytrivka UA 171 B4
Dnestrovsc MD 170 D5
Dno RUS 148 F6
Doagh GB 20 F4
Doba RO 167 B10
Dobanovci SRB 174 D5
Dobârceni RO 169 B10
Dobârlău RO 169 F7
Dobbertin D 99 C12
Dobbiaco I 88 C5
Dobczyce PL 160 D1
Dobele LV 150 C6
Döbeln D 96 D4
Doberlug-Kirchhain D 96 C5
Döbern D 97 C7
Dobersberg A 93 E8
Doberschütz D 95 D12
Dobiegniew PL 101 E9
Dobieszewo PL 101 B12
Dobieszyn PL 157 G4
Doboj BIH 173 C9
Dobova SLO 164 E5
Doboz H 167 D7
Dobrá CZ 162 B6
Dobra PL 101 C8
Dobra PL 158 C6
Dobra PL 160 D1
Dobra RO 167 F10
Dobra RO 177 D7
Dobra SRB 175 D8
Dobrá Niva SK 163 E8
Dobřany CZ 92 C4
Dobrčane SRB 180 E4
Dobre PL 154 E6
Dobre PL 155 F12
Dobre Miasto PL 152 F1
Dobreni RO 169 D8
Dobrešinci MK 185 A8
Dobrești RO 167 D9
Dobrești RO 176 D6
Dobrești RO 176 F3
Dobrevo MK 180 E5
Dobrica SRB 175 C6
Dobričevo SRB 175 D7
Dobrich BG 171 F1
Dobrich BG 182 E5
Dobri Do SRB 180 D3
Dobri Dol BG 175 F11
Dobrin RO 167 C11
Dobrinishte BG 181 F8
Dobříš CZ 92 C6
Dobritz D 95 B11
Dobřív CZ 92 C5
Dobrljin BIH 172 B5
Dobrna SLO 89 D11
Dobrnič SLO 89 E10
Dobrnja BIH 173 C7
Dobrnja BIH 173 C10
Dobrnje SRB 175 E7
Dobro E 56 C4
Dobrodzień PL 158 E5
Döbrököz H 165 D10
Dobromierz PL 97 E10
Dobromir RO 171 E1
Dobromirka BG 182 C4
Dobromirtsi BG 187 B8
Dobromyl' UA 161 D6
Dobroń PL 159 C7
Dobron' UA 161 G5
Dobronín CZ 93 D9
Dobro Polje BIH 173 E10
Dobro Polje SRB 175 F9
Dobrošane MK 180 E4
Dobrosloveni RO 176 E4
Dobrosyn UA 160 C8
Dobroszyce PL 97 D12
Dobroteasa RO 176 D4
Dobrotești RO 176 E5
Dobrotić SRB 180 C4
Dobrotich BG 183 C8
Dobrotino MK 185 B6
Dobrotitsa BG 177 F9
Dobrovăț RO 169 D11
Dobrovci BIH 173 C9
Dobrovice CZ 93 B7
Dobrovnik SLO 165 C6
Dobrovol'sk RUS 152 D5
Dobrowoda PL 159 F10
Dobruchi RUS 148 D2
Dobrun BIH 174 F3
Dobrun RO 176 E4
Dobrușa MD 170 B3
Dobruševo MK 185 B5
Dobruška CZ 93 B10
Dobrzankowo PL 155 E10
Dobrzany PL 101 D8
Dobrzeń Wielki PL 158 E4
Dobrzyca PL 158 C4
Dobrzyków PL 155 F8
Dobrzyń nad Wisłą PL 155 E7
Dobšiná SK 161 F1
Dóc H 166 E5
Docking GB 31 B10
Dockmyr S 119 A10
Docksta S 123 E14
Dockweiler D 37 D7
Doclin RO 175 C8
Doddington GB 21 D12
Dodewaard NL 199 B7
Dodonoupoli GR 184 E4
Dödre S 118 A8
Doesburg NL 32 D6
Doetinchem NL 32 E6
Dofteana RO 169 E9
Doğanbey TR 193 C8
Doğanbey TR 193 D9
Doğancı TR 189 D10
Doğanköy TR 189 D10
Döge H 161 G5
Dogliani I 53 B7
Dognecea RO 175 C8
Döğüşbelen TR 197 C9
Dohna D 96 E5
Dohňany SK 162 C6
Dohren D 33 C9
Doicești RO 176 D6
Doïrani GR 185 B8
Doire Iorrais IRL 22 F3
Doische B 35 D10
Dojč SK 162 D4
Dojkinci SRB 181 C6
Dokka N 117 E12
Dokkas S 132 D6
Dokkedal DK 102 B6
Dokkum NL 32 B5
Doksy CZ 92 B6
Doksy CZ 97 E7
Doktor Yosifovo BG 181 C7
Dokupe LV 150 B3
Dolanog GB 26 F5
Dolbenmaen GB 26 F3
Dolceacqua I 53 D7
Dol-de-Bretagne F 39 C8
Dole BIH 173 D10
Dole F 42 F3
Dølemo N 106 B3
Dolenci MK 184 B5
Dolenja Vas SLO 89 E10
Dolenjske Toplice SLO 89 E11
Dolgarrog GB 26 E4
Dolgellau GB 26 F4
Dolgen D 100 D4
Dolgorukovo RUS 152 E2
Dolhan TR 183 F8
Dolhasca RO 169 C9
Dolhești RO 169 C9
Dolhești RO 169 D11
Dołhobyczów PL 160 B9
Dolianova I 80 E3
Dolice PL 101 D8
Dolichi GR 185 D7
Doljani BIH 173 E8
Doljani HR 172 D5
Doljevac SRB 180 C4
Dolla IRL 24 C6
Dolle D 95 B10
Dollern D 98 C7
Döllnitz D 95 D11
Dollnstein D 91 E9
Dollon F 40 D4
Dolna MD 170 C2
Dolna Banya BG 181 E8
Dolna Dikanya BG 181 E7
Dolna Gradeshnitsa BG 181 F7
Dolnāja LV 151 D12
Dolná Krupá SK 162 E5
Dolna Lipnitska BG 182 C4
Dolna Makhala BG 181 E10
Dolna Melna BG 180 D6
Dolna Mitropoliya BG 181 C10
Dolna Oryakhovitsa BG 182 C5
Dolná Strehová SK 163 E8
Dolná Súča SK 162 D6
Dolná Tižina SK 163 C7
Dolna Vasilitsa BG 181 E8
Dolné Orešany SK 162 E4
Dolné Vestenice SK 162 D6
Dolní Bousov CZ 93 B8
Dolní Bukovsko CZ 93 D7
Dolní Čermná CZ 93 C11
Dolni Chiflik BG 183 D9
Dolní Dobrouč CZ 93 C11
Dolni Dŭbnik BG 181 C9
Dolní Dvořiště CZ 93 E6
Dolni Glavanak BG 182 F5
Dolní Kounice CZ 93 D10
Dolni Lom BG 181 C6
Dolní Loučky CZ 93 D10
Dolní Němčí CZ 162 D5
Dolní Podluží CZ 97 E7
Dolní Újezd CZ 93 C10
Dolní Újezd CZ 162 B5
Dolni Voden BG 181 E10
Dolní Žandov CZ 91 B12
Dolno Dupeni MK 184 C5
Dolno Ezerovo BG 183 D8
Dolno Kamartsi BG 181 D8
Dolno Konjare MK 180 F4
Dolno Levski BG 181 E9
Dolno Osenovo BG 181 F7
Dolno Selo BG 180 E5
Dolno Tserovene BG 175 F11
Dolno Uyno BG 180 E6
Dolný Hričov SK 163 C7
Dolný Kubín SK 163 C8
Dolný Pial SK 162 E6
Dolný Štál SK 162 F5
Dolo I 82 B5
Dolomieu F 47 D8
Dolores E 72 E3
Dolovo SRB 175 D6
Dölsach A 89 C6
Dolsk PL 97 C12
Dołubowo PL 157 E7
Dolus-d'Oléron F 44 D3
Dolyna UA 161 F8
Dolynivka UA 170 A5
Dolyns'ke UA 170 B5
Dolzhitsy RUS 148 D5
Domaháza H 163 E10
Domaniewice PL 157 G2
Domaniewice PL 159 B8
Domanín CZ 162 C4
Domaradz PL 160 D4
Domart-en-Ponthieu F 34 D5
Domaševo BIH 178 D5
Domašinec HR 165 D7
Domașnea RO 175 C9
Domaszek H 166 E5
Domaszków PL 93 B11
Domaszowice PL 158 D4
Domat Ems CH 87 D8
Domats F 41 D9
Domažlice CZ 92 D3
Dombås N 117 B10
Dombasle-en-Xaintois F 42 D4
Dombasle-sur-Meurthe F 202 D1
Dombegyház H 167 E7
Dombóvár H 165 D10
Dombrád H 161 G4
Dombresson CH 47 A10
Domburg NL 32 E1
Domegge di Cadore I 88 D5
Domeikava LT 153 D8
Domène F 47 E8
Domeniko GR 185 E7
Domérat F 45 C11
Domèvre-en-Haye F 42 C4
Domèvre-sur-Vezouze F 43 C6
Domfront F 39 C10
Domgermain F 42 C4
Domince HR 178 D3
Domingo Pérez E 62 E4
Dömitz D 99 D10
Domlyan BG 181 D10
Dommartin-le-Franc F 42 D2
Dommartin-Varimont F 41 C12
Domme F 45 F8
Dommershausen D 37 D8
Dommitzsch D 96 C3
Domnești RO 176 C5
Domnești RO 177 E7
Domnitsa GR 190 B4
Domnovo RUS 152 E2
Domodossola I 84 A5
Domokos GR 190 A5
Domont F 41 B7
Domorovce SRB 180 D4
Dömös H 165 A11
Domoszló H 163 F10
Dompcevrin F 42 C3
Dompierre-les-Ormes F 46 C5
Dompierre-sur-Besbre F 46 B4
Dompierre-sur-Mer F 44 C3
Dompierre-sur-Yon F 44 B3
Domrémy-la-Pucelle F 42 D4
Dömsöd H 166 C3
Domsühl D 99 D11
Domus de Maria I 80 F2
Domusnovas I 80 E2
Domvaina GR 191 C6
Domžale SLO 89 D10
Donada I 82 B5
Donagh GB 23 D8
Donaghadee GB 20 F5
Donaghmore GB 23 C9
Donaghmore IRL 23 F10
Đonaj SRB 179 E10
Don Álvaro E 67 B7
Doña Mencía E 69 A8
Donard IRL 23 F9
Donaueschingen D 43 E9
Donauwörth D 91 E8
Don Benito E 67 B8
Doncaster GB 27 D9
Donchery F 35 E10
Donduşeni MD 169 A11
Donegal IRL 22 C6
Doneraile IRL 24 D5
Doneztebe E 48 D2
Dønfoss N 116 C8
Dongen NL 32 E3
Donges F 39 F7
Dongo I 85 A7
Donici MD 170 C3
Doñinos de Salamanca E 61 C9
Donja Bela Reka SRB 175 E9
Donja Brela HR 173 F6
Donja Bukovica MNE 179 C7
Donja Dubnica SRB 180 D3
Donja Dubrava HR 165 D7
Donja Kupčina HR 164 E5
Donja Mahala BIH 173 B10
Donja Motičina HR 165 F10
Donja Šatornja SRB 174 E6
Donja Stubica HR 164 E5
Donja Višnjica HR 164 D6
Donja Vrijeska HR 165 E8
Donja Zelina HR 164 E6
Donje Pazarište HR 83 C11
Donjeux F 42 D3
Donji Andrijevci HR 173 B9
Donji Čaglić HR 165 F8
Donji Dubovnik BIH 172 C5
Donji Dušnik SRB 180 C5
Donji Kosinj HR 172 C3
Donji Krčin SRB 175 F7
Donji Krivodol SRB 181 C6
Donji Lapac HR 172 C4
Donji Miholjac HR 165 E10
Donji Milanovac SRB 175 E9
Donji Proložac HR 173 F7
Donji Rujani BIH 173 E5
Donji Seget HR 172 E5
Donji Srb HR 172 D5
Donji Striževac SRB 180 C5
Donji Svilaj BIH 173 B9
Donji Vakuf BIH 173 D7
Donji Vijačani BIH 173 C8
Donji Zemunik HR 172 D3
Donji Žirovac HR 172 B5
Donk NL 199 B7
Donkerbroek NL 32 B6
Donnalucata I 75 F6
Donnas I 84 B4
Donnemarie-Dontilly F 41 D9
Donnersbach A 89 B9
Donnersdorf D 91 C7
Donohill IRL 24 C6
Donori I 80 E3
Donostia-San Sebastián E 48 D2
Donskoye RUS 155 A8
Donville-les-Bains F 39 C8
Donzdorf D 90 E6
Donzenac F 45 E9
Donzère F 51 B8
Donzy F 41 F9
Dooagh IRL 22 E2
Doochary IRL 22 C6
Dooish GB 20 F2
Doolin IRL 22 F4
Doon IRL 24 C6
Doonbeg IRL 24 C3
Doorn NL 32 D4
Doornspijk NL 199 A7
Dopiewo PL 97 B11
Đorče Petrov MK 180 E3
Dorchester GB 29 D10
Dørdal N 106 B5
Dordives F 41 D8
Dordrecht NL 32 E3
Dore-l'Église F 46 E4
Dörentrup D 33 D12
Dores GB 19 L8
Dorfen D 91 F11
Dorfgastein A 89 B7
Dorfmark D 98 E7
Dorf Mecklenburg D 99 C10
Dorgali I 80 C4
Dorgoș RO 167 E8
Dorio GR 190 E4
Dorking GB 31 E8
Dorkovo BG 181 E9
Dorlisheim F 202 D3
Dormagen D 37 B7
Dormánd H 166 B5
Dormans F 41 B10
Dor Mărunt RO 177 E9
Dorna-Arini RO 168 C6
Dorna Candrenilor RO 168 C6
Dornava SLO 164 D5
Dörnberg (Habichtswald) D 33 F12
Dornbirn A 87 C9
Dornburg (Saale) D 95 D10
Dornburg-Frickhofen D 201 C9
Dornbusch D 33 A12
Dorndorf D 95 E7
Dorndorf-Steudnitz D 95 D10
Dornelas P 54 E4
Dornes F 46 B3
Dornești RO 169 B8
Dornhan D 203 E6
Dornie GB 18 L5
Dornișoara RO 168 C6
Dörnitz D 95 B11
Dorno I 85 C6
Dornoch GB 19 K8
Dornstadt D 90 F6
Dornstetten D 43 D9
Dornum D 33 A8
Dornumersiel D 33 A8
Dorobanțu RO 171 D2
Dorobanțu RO 177 E9
Dorog H 165 A11
Dorogháza H 163 F9
Dorohoi RO 169 B8
Dorohusk PL 157 H9
Dorolț RO 167 B10
Dorotcaia MD 170 C4
Dorotea S 123 C10
Dörpen D 33 C8
Dorras N 128 D8
Dorris S 123 B9
Dorstadt D 95 B8
Dorsten D 33 E7
Dorstfeld D 201 A7
Dortan F 47 C8
Dortmund D 33 E8
Dörttepe TR 193 E10
Doruchów PL 158 D5
Dorum D 33 A11
Dorupe LV 150 C7
Dörverden D 33 C12
Dörzbach D 90 D6
Dos Aguas E 64 F3
Dosbarrios E 62 E6
Dos Hermanas E 67 E8
Dospat BG 181 F9
Dossenheim D 37 F11
Doștat RO 168 F3
Dos Torres E 70 C3
Døstrup DK 102 E3
Dotnuva LT 150 F7
Dotternhausen D 43 D10
Döttingen CH 43 E9
Douai F 35 D7
Douarnenez F 38 D3
Doubrava CZ 163 B7
Doubravice nad Svitavou CZ 93 D11
Doubs F 47 B9
Douchy F 41 E9
Douchy-les-Mines F 35 D7
Doucier F 47 B8
Doudeville F 34 E2
Doudleby nad Orlicí CZ 93 B10
Doué-la-Fontaine F 39 F11
Douglas GB 21 D9
Douglas GBM 26 C3
Douglas IRL 24 E6
Douglas Bridge GB 20 F2
Doulaincourt-Saucourt F 42 D3
Doullens F 34 D5
Dounaiika GR 190 D3
Doune GB 21 C8
Dounreay GB 19 H9
Dour B 35 D8
Dourdan F 40 C7
Dourgne F 49 D10
Douriez F 34 D4
Doussard F 47 D9
Douvaine F 47 C9
Douvres-la-Délivrande F 39 B11
Douzy F 35 E11
Dovadola I 82 D4
Dover GB 31 E11
Dovhe UA 161 G7
Döviken S 119 A9
Dovilai LT 150 E2
Dovre N 117 C10
Dowally GB 21 B9
Downham Market GB 27 F12
Downpatrick GB 23 D11
Downton GB 29 D11
Dowra IRL 22 D6
Dowsby GB 27 F11
Doxato GR 187 B6
Doyet F 46 C2
Doyrentsi BG 181 C10
Dozulé F 39 B11
Drabeši LV 151 B10
Dråby DK 102 C7
Dračevo BIH 178 D5
Dračevo MK 180 F4
Drachhausen D 96 C6
Drachselsried D 92 D4
Drachten NL 32 B6
Drag N 121 B10
Drag N 127 D11
Dragacz PL 154 C6
Dragalijevac BIH 173 C11
Dragalina RO 177 E10
Dragalovci BIH 173 C8
Drăgănești RO 167 D9
Drăgănești RO 169 F10
Drăgănești RO 177 D8
Drăgănești de Vede RO 176 E6
Drăgănești-Olt RO 176 E5
Drăgănești-Vlașca RO 177 E7
Draganići HR 164 E5
Draganovo BG 182 C5
Drăganu RO 176 D5
Dragaš SRB 179 E10
Drăgășani RO 176 D4
Dragatuš SLO 83 A11
Drage D 99 D8
Drage HR 172 E4
Drăgești RO 167 D9
Drăghiceni RO 176 E4
Draginac SRB 174 D3
Draginje SRB 174 D4
Draginovo BG 181 E8
Dragland N 127 C11
Dragnes N 127 C10
Dragnić BIH 173 D7
Dragobi AL 179 E8
Dragočaj BIH 173 C7
Dragocvet SRB 175 F7
Dragodana RO 176 D6
Drăgoești RO 176 D4
Drăgoești RO 177 D9
Dragoevo BG 183 C7
Dragoevo MK 180 F5
Drăgoiești RO 169 B8
Dragoman BG 181 D6
Dragomance MK 180 E4
Dragomir BG 181 E9
Dragomirești RO 168 B4
Dragomirești RO 169 C9
Dragomirești RO 169 D10
Dragomirești RO 176 D6
Dragomirovo BG 182 B4
Dragoni I 76 A2
Dragør DK 103 D11
Dragoš MK 184 C5
Dragoslavele RO 176 C6
Dragoș Vodă RO 177 E10
Drăgotești RO 175 D11
Drăgotești RO 176 E4
Dragotina HR 172 B5
Dragović HR 165 F8
Dragovishtitsa BG 181 E6
Dragoychintsi BG 180 D5
Dragoynovo BG 182 F4
Dragsfjärd FIN 142 E7
Draguignan F 52 D4
Drăgușeni RO 169 A9
Drăgușeni RO 169 C8
Drăgușeni RO 169 F11
Drăgutești RO 175 D11
Drahnsdorf D 96 C5
Drahovce SK 162 D5
Drahove UA 161 G8
Drahovica Donja BIH 173 C9
Drajna RO 177 C8
Draka BG 183 E8
Drakenburg D 33 C12
Draksenić BIH 173 B6
Dralfa BG 183 C6
Drama GR 186 B6
Drammen N 111 C12
Drânceni RO 169 D12
Drange N 110 F5
Drangedal N 106 A5
Drangstedt D 33 A11
Drănic RO 176 E3
Dranse D 99 D13
Dransfeld D 94 D6
Dranske D 100 A4
Draperstown GB 20 F3
Drasenhofen A 93 E11
Draßmarkt A 165 A6
Drávafok H 165 E9
Dravagen S 118 B6
Draviskos GR 186 C5
Dravograd SLO 89 C11
Drawno PL 101 D9
Drawsko PL 101 E10
Drawsko Pomorskie PL 101 C9
Drayton GB 31 B11
Drążdżewo PL 155 D11
Dražen Vrh SLO 164 C5
Draževac SRB 174 D5
Dražgoše SLO 89 D9
Drebber D 33 C10
Drebkau D 96 C6
Drégelypalánk H 163 E8
Dreieich D 37 D11
Dreileben D 95 B9
Dreis D 37 E7
Drelów PL 157 G7
Drelsdorf D 98 A6
Drem GB 21 C11
Drenchia I 89 D8
Drenovac SRB 175 F7
Drenovci HR 173 C10
Drenovë AL 184 C4
Drenovets BG 175 F10
Drenovicë AL 184 C2
Drenovo MK 180 F4
Drenovo MK 185 B6
Drense D 100 D5
Drensteinfurt D 33 E9
Drenta BG 182 D5
Drentwede D 33 C11
Drepano GR 185 D6
Drepano GR 191 D6
Dresden D 96 D5
Dretun' BY 149 E6
Dretyń PL 101 B11
Dreumel NL 199 B6
Dreux F 40 C5
Dreverna LT 150 E2
Drevja N 124 E5
Drevjesætra N 118 D4
Dřevohostice CZ 162 C5
Drevsjø N 118 C3
Drevvatn N 124 D5
Drewitz D 95 B11
Drewnica PL 154 B6
Drezdenko PL 101 E9
Drežnica BIH 173 E8
Drežnik SRB 174 F4
Dricēni LV 149 C2
Dridu RO 177 D8
Driebergen NL 32 D4
Driebes E 63 D6
Driedorf D 201 C9
Drienov SK 161 F3
Drietoma SK 162 D5
Driffield GB 27 C11
Drimmo IRL 23 F7
Drimnin GB 20 B5
Drimoleague IRL 24 E4
Drinić BIH 172 C5
Drinjača BIH 173 D11
Drinovci BIH 173 F7
Dripsey IRL 24 E5
Drisht AL 179 E8
Dříteň CZ 92 D6
Drithas AL 184 C4
Driva N 117 A11
Drivstua N 117 B11
Drmno SRB 175 D7
Drnholec CZ 93 E11
Drniš HR 172 E5
Drnje HR 165 D7
Drnovice CZ 93 D11
Drnovice CZ 93 D11
Dro I 85 B10
Drøbak N 111 C13
Drobeta-Turnu Severin RO 175 D10
Drobin PL 155 E8
Drochia MD 169 A11
Drochtersen D 33 A12
Drogheda IRL 23 E10
Drohiczyn PL 157 F7
Drohobych UA 161 E8
Droichead Abhann IRL 24 C5
Droichead Átha IRL 23 E10
Droichead na Bandan IRL 24 E5
Droichead Nua IRL 23 F9
Droitwich Spa GB 29 A10
Drolshagen D 201 B8
Drolsum N 111 B12
Dromara GB 23 D10
Dromina IRL 24 D5
Drommahane IRL 24 D5
Drömme S 123 E14
Dromod IRL 23 E7
Dromore GB 23 C8
Dromore GB 23 D10
Dromore West IRL 22 D5
Dronero I 53 C6
Dronfield GB 27 E9
Drongan GB 21 E8
Drongen B 198 C3
Dronninglund DK 102 A6
Dronrijp NL 32 B5
Dronten NL 32 C5
Dropla BG 171 F2
Drosato GR 185 B8
Drosbacken S 118 C3
Drosendorf A 93 E9
Drosia GR 191 C8
Drösing A 93 E11
Drosopigi GR 184 C5
Droué F 40 D5
Droyßig D 95 D11
Drugan BG 181 E7
Drugovo MK 184 B4
Druid GB 26 F5
Druimdrishaig GB 20 D5
Drulingen F 43 C7
Drumandoora IRL 22 G5
Drumanespick IRL 23 E8
Drumatober IRL 22 F6
Drumbeg GB 18 J6
Drumbilla IRL 23 D10
Drumcard GB 23 D7
Drumcollogher IRL 24 D5
Drumcondra IRL 23 E9
Drumconrath IRL 23 E9
Drumcree IRL 23 E8
Drumettaz-Clarafond F 47 D8
Drumevo BG 183 C8
Drumfree IRL 20 E2
Drumkeeran IRL 22 D6
Drumlea IRL 23 D7
Drumlish IRL 23 E7
Drumlithie GB 21 B12
Drummin IRL 25 D9
Drummore GB 20 F7
Drumnadrochit GB 18 L8
Drumquin GB 20 F2
Drumshanbo IRL 22 D6
Drung IRL 23 D8
Drusenheim F 43 C8
Druskininkai LT 153 F9
Drusti LV 151 B11
Druten NL 199 B7
Druviena LV 151 B12
Druya BY 149 E2
Druyes-les-Belles-Fontaines F 41 E9
Druysk BY 149 E2
Drużbice PL 159 D7
Druzhba RUS 152 E3
Druzhnaya Gorka RUS 148 C7
Družstevná pri Hornáde SK 161 F3
Drvenik HR 173 F7
Drwalew PL 157 G4
Drwinia PL 159 F9
Dryanovets BG 177 F8
Dryanovo BG 182 D4
Dryazhno RUS 148 E4
Drygały PL 155 C13
Drymaia GR 191 B6
Drymen GB 21 C8
Drymos GR 185 C8
Dryna N 116 A5
Dryopida GR 191 E9
Dryos GR 192 E5
Drysvyaty BY 151 E13
Dryszczów PL 160 A8
Drzewce PL 158 B6
Drzewiany PL 101 C11
Drzewica PL 157 H2
Drzonowo PL 101 C11
Drzycim PL 154 C5
Duagh IRL 24 D4
Dualchi I 80 C2
Dually IRL 25 C7
Duas Igrejas P 55 F7
Dub SRB 174 F4
Dubá CZ 93 A7
Dubăsari MD 170 C4
Dubăsarii Vechi MD 170 C4
Duba Stonska HR 178 D4
Dubău MD 170 C4
Dubeczno PL 157 H8
Düben D 95 C11
Duben D 96 C5
Dübendorf CH 43 F10
Dubeņi LV 150 D2
Dubeninki PL 152 E6
Dubí CZ 96 E5
Dubičiai LT 153 E10
Dubicko CZ 93 C11
Dubicze Cerkiewne PL 157 E8
Dubidze PL 159 D7
Dubiecko PL 160 D5
Dubienka PL 160 A8
Dubingiai LT 153 C11
Dubino I 85 A7
Dubivka UA 169 A8
Dublin IRL 23 F10
Dublje SRB 174 D4
Dublovice CZ 92 C6
Dublyany UA 160 D9
Dublyany UA 161 E7
Dubna LV 151 D13
Dub nad Moravou CZ 162 C4
Dubňany CZ 93 E12
Dubnica nad Váhom SK 162 D6
Dubník SK 162 F6
Duboštica BIH 173 D9
Dubova RO 175 D9
Dubovac SRB 175 D7
Dubove UA 161 G8
Dŭbovets BG 182 F5
Dubovica SK 161 E2
Dŭbovo BG 182 D5
Dubovo SRB 180 C4
Dubovsko BIH 172 C5
Dubrava BIH 173 C8
Dubrava HR 165 E7
Dubrave BIH 173 C10
Dubrave BIH 173 D6
Dubrave BIH 173 D10
Dubravica BIH 173 D8
Dubravica HR 164 E5
Dubravica SRB 175 D7
Dúbravy SK 163 D8
Dubrawka BY 149 F6
Dubrovka RUS 145 F14
Dubrovka RUS 148 F6
Dubrovka RUS 149 D5
Dubrovnik HR 178 D5
Dubrovytsya UA 160 D8
Dubulti LV 149 D3
Dubynove UA 170 A6
Ducey F 39 C9
Ducherow D 100 C5
Duchov CZ 96 E5
Duck End GB 31 D9
Duclair F 34 F2
Duda-Epureni RO 169 D12
Dudar H 165 B9
Duddo GB 21 D12
Dudelange L 36 F6
Dudeldorf D 37 E7
Duderstadt D 95 C7
Dudești RO 177 D10
Dudeștii Vechi RO 166 E5
Dudince SK 163 E7
Düdingen CH 47 B11
Dudley GB 27 F7
Dudovica SRB 174 E5
Dueñas E 56 E2
Duesund N 116 E2
Dueville I 88 E4
Duffel B 35 B10
Dufftown GB 19 L10
Duga Poljana SRB 179 C9
Duga Resa HR 164 F5
Dugi Rat HR 172 F6
Dugny-sur-Meuse F 42 B3
Dugopolje HR 172 E6
Dugo Selo HR 164 E6
Düğüncübaşı TR 189 B7
Duhort-Bachen F 48 C5
Duino I 89 E8

Duirinish GB 18 L5
Duisburg D 33 F7
Dukas AL 184 C2
Dukat AL 184 D2
Dukat i Ri AL 184 D1
Dukla PL 161 D4
Dükštas LT 151 E12
Dŭlboki BG 182 E5
Dŭlbok Dol BG 181 D10
Dŭlbok Izvor BG 182 E4
Dulcești RO 169 D9
Duleek IRL 23 E10
Dŭlgodeltsi BG 176 F2
Dŭlgopol BG 183 C8
Dulina BY 149 F2
Duljci BIH 173 D7
Dullingham GB 31 C9
Dülmen D 33 E8
Dulnain Bridge GB 19 L9
Dulovce SK 162 F6
Dulovka RUS 149 A4
Dulovo BG 177 F10
Dulverton GB 29 C7
Dumbarton GB 20 D7
Dumbrava RO 167 F9
Dumbrava RO 175 D11
Dumbrava RO 177 D8
Dumbrava Rosie RO 169 D8
Dumbrăveni RO 168 E5
Dumbrăveni RO 169 B8
Dumbrăveni RO 171 F1
Dumbrăveni RO 177 B10
Dumbrăvești RO 177 C7
Dumbrăvița RO 167 F7
Dumbrăvița RO 168 B3
Dumbrăvița RO 169 F6
Dumbría E 54 B1
Dumești RO 169 C10
Dumești RO 169 D10
Dumfries GB 21 E9
Dumitra RO 168 C4
Dumitrești RO 177 B9
Dummerstorf D 99 C12
Dümpelfeld D 37 D7
Dun N 121 B11
Duna N 121 B11
Dunaegyháza H 165 C11
Dunaföldvár H 165 C11
Dunaharaszti H 166 C3
Dunajská Lužná SK 162 E4
Dunajská Streda SK 162 F5
Dunakeszi H 166 B3
Dunalka LV 150 C2
Dún an Rí IRL 23 E9
Dunapataj H 166 D3
Dunărea RO 171 E2
Dunaszeg H 165 A9
Dunaszekcső H 165 E11
Dunaszentbenedek H 165 C11
Dunaszentgyörgy H 165 C11
Dunasziget H 162 F4
Dunatetétlen H 166 D3
Dunaújváros H 165 C11
Dunava LV 151 D12
Dunavarsány H 166 C3
Dunavecse H 166 D2
Dunavtsi BG 175 F10
Dunbar GB 21 C11
Dunbeath GB 19 J10
Dunblane GB 21 C9
Dunboyne IRL 23 A12
Dún Búinne IRL 23 F10
Duncannon IRL 25 D9
Dún Chaoin IRL 24 D2
Dunchurch GB 29 A12
Dundaga LV 150 A4
Dundalk IRL 23 D10
Dún Dealgan IRL 23 D10
Dun Dealgan IRL 23 D10
Dundee GB 21 C11
Dunderland N 124 D8
Dundonald GB 23 C11
Dundreggan GB 18 L7
Dundrennan GB 21 F9
Dundrum GB 23 D11
Dundrum IRL 24 C6
Dunecht GB 19 L12
Dunes F 49 B7
Dunfanaghy IRL 23 B7
Dunfermline GB 21 C10
Dungannon GB 23 C9
Dún Garbhán IRL 25 D7
Dungarvan IRL 25 C8
Dungarvan IRL 25 D7
Düngenheim D 201 D7
Dungiven GB 20 F3
Dungloe IRL 22 C6
Dungourney IRL 24 E6
Dunholme GB 27 E11
Duniče AL 184 B5
Dunières F 46 E5
Duninowo PL 101 A11
Dunje MK 185 B6
Dunkeld GB 21 B9
Dunkerque F 34 B5
Dunkerrin IRL 25 C7
Dunkitt IRL 25 D8
Dún Laoghaire IRL 23 F10
Dunlavin IRL 23 F9
Dunleer IRL 23 E10
Dún Léire IRL 23 E10
Dun-le-Palestel F 45 C9
Dun-les-Places F 41 F11
Dunlop GB 20 D7
Dunloy GB 20 E4
Dún Mámhaí IRL 24 E4
Dunmanway IRL 24 E4
Dún Mór IRL 25 D9
Dunmore IRL 22 E5
Dunmore East IRL 25 D9
Dunmurry GB 23 C11
Dunnamanagh GB 20 F2
Dún na nGall IRL 22 C6
Dunning GB 21 C9
Dunoon GB 20 D7
Dunquin IRL 24 D2
Duns GB 21 D12
Dunscore GB 21 E9
Dünsen D 33 C11
Dunshaughlin IRL 23 E9
Dunstable GB 31 D7
Dunster GB 29 C8
Dun-sur-Auron F 45 B11
Dun-sur-Meuse F 35 F11
Dunure GB 20 E7
Dunvant GB 28 B6
Dunvegan GB 18 L3
Duplica SLO 89 D10
Dupnitsa BG 181 E7
Durach D 87 B10
Durak TR 189 E9
Đurakovac SRB 179 D9

Durana E 57 C6
Durance F 49 B6
Durango E 57 B6
Durankulak BG 171 F3
Duras F 49 C7
Durbach D 43 C9
Durban-Corbières F 50 E4
Durbe LV 150 C2
Durbuy B 200 D3
Dúrcal E 69 C9
Durdat-Larequille F 45 C11
Đurđenovac HR 165 E10
Đurđevac HR 165 E10
Đurđevića Tara MNE 179 C7
Đurđevik BIH 173 D7
Đurđevo SRB 174 C5
Đurđevo SRB 175 E6
Düren D 36 C6
Durfort F 51 C6
Durham GB 21 F13
Durlas IRL 25 C7
Durlești MD 170 C3
Durmanec HR 164 D5
Dürmentingen D 87 A9
Durmersheim D 43 C9
Durness GB 18 H7
Durnești RO 169 B10
Dürnkrut A 93 F11
Durrës AL 184 B1
Durrington GB 29 C11
Dürrlauingen D 91 F7
Durrow IRL 25 C8
Durrus IRL 24 E3
Dürrwangen D 91 D7
Dursley GB 29 B10
Dursunbey TR 189 E10
Durtal F 39 E11
Duruelo de la Sierra E 56 E6
Duruitoarea MD 169 B10
Durup DK 102 B3
Durusu TR 189 B10
Dusetos LT 151 E11
Dushk i Madh AL 184 C2
Dusina BIH 173 E8
Dúskotna BG 183 D8
Duškovci SRB 174 F5
Dusmenys LT 153 E9
Dusnok H 166 E2
Dusocin PL 154 D6
Düsseldorf D 37 B7
Dussen NL 32 E3
Dußlingen D 203 E7
Düßnitz D 95 C12
Duszniki PL 97 B10
Dutluca TR 189 E11
Dutovlje SLO 89 E7
Duved S 118 E7
Düvertepe TR 189 E10
Duži BIH 178 D5
Dvärsätt S 122 E6
Dvaryshcha BY 149 E6
Dve Mogili BG 177 F7
Dverberg N 127 B10
Dviete LV 151 D12
Dvirtsi UA 160 C9
Dvor HR 172 B5
Dvorce CZ 162 B5
Dvornaye Syalo BY 149 E3
Dvorníky SK 162 E5
Dvory nad Žitavou SK 162 F6
Dvůr Králové CZ 93 B9
Dwikozy PL 160 B4
Dwingeloo NL 32 C6
Dyan GB 23 D9
Dyankovo BG 177 F9
Dybvad DK 106 C7
Dyce GB 19 L12
Dychów PL 160 D5
Dydnia PL 161 D5
Dyffryn GB 28 A5
Dyfjord N 129 B19
Dygowo PL 101 B9
Dyke GB 19 K9
Dykehead GB 21 B11
Dykhtyets' UA 168 A6
Dylągówka PL 160 D5
Dylaki PL 158 E5
Dylewo PL 155 D11
Dymchurch GB 31 E10
Dymock GB 29 B10
Dynäs S 123 F13
Dynivtsi UA 169 A8
Dynów PL 160 D5
Dyo F 46 C5
Dyping N 126 E9
Dyrnes N 120 D3
Dyrøyhamn N 127 B13
Dyrrachi GR 190 E5
Dyulevo BG 183 D8
Dyulino BG 183 D9
Dyviziya UA 170 F5
Dywity PL 152 F7
Dzęgzęni LV 150 D6
Dzelzava LV 151 C12
Dzeni LV 151 B12
Dzērbene LV 151 B11
Dzherman BG 181 E7
Dzhulynka UA 170 A5
Dzhulyunitsa BG 182 C5
Dzhuriv UA 168 A6
Dzhurovo BG 181 D9
Dziadkowice PL 157 E7
Działdowo PL 155 D9
Działoszyce PL 159 F10
Działoszyn PL 158 D6
Dziafyń PL 154 B4
Dziemiany PL 154 B4
Dziergowice PL 158 F5
Dzierzążnia PL 155 E9
Dzierżążno Wielkie PL 101 E10
Dzierzgoń PL 155 C7
Dzierzgowo PL 155 D10
Dzierzkowice-Rynek PL 160 B5
Dzierżoniów PL 97 E11
Dzietrzniki PL 158 D6
Dziewierzewo PL 101 E13
Dżigolj SRB 180 C3
Dzirnavas LV 150 B4
Dzisna BY 149 E4
Dziwnów PL 101 B8
Dziwnówek PL 101 B8
Dzukste LV 150 C5
Dżwierzuty PL 155 D10
Dźwirzyno PL 101 B8
Dzwola PL 160 B6
Dzwonowice PL 159 E8
Dzyornavichy BY 149 E4

E

Éadan Doire IRL 23 F8
Eaglesfield GB 21 E10
Eardisley GB 29 A8
Earith GB 31 C9
Earl Shilton GB 27 D12
Earls Barton GB 31 C11
Earl Stonham GB 31 C11
Earsairidh GB 20 B2
Easdale GB 20 C5
Easington GB 21 F14
Easington GB 27 E12
Easingwold GB 27 C9
Easky IRL 22 D5
Eastbourne GB 31 F9
Eastburn GB 27 D12
Eastfield GB 27 C11
Eastgate GB 21 F12
East Grinstead GB 31 E8
East Harling GB 31 C10
East Kilbride GB 21 D8
Eastleigh GB 29 D12
East Linton GB 21 D11
East Looe GB 28 E6
Eastoft GB 27 D10
Easton GB 29 D10
East Retford GB 27 E10
Eastriggs GB 21 F10
Eastry GB 31 E11
East Wemyss GB 21 C10
East Wittering GB 31 F7
Eastwood GB 27 E9
Eaton Socon GB 31 C8
Eaunes F 49 D8
Eauze F 49 C6
Ebberup DK 102 E5
Ebbw Vale GB 29 B8
Ebebecik TR 197 A9
Ebeleben D 95 D8
Ebelsbach D 91 B8
Ebeltoft DK 102 C7
Ebene Reichenau A 89 C8
Eben im Pongau A 89 B7
Ebensee A 89 A8
Ebensfeld D 91 B8
Ebenthal A 89 C9
Ebenweiler D 87 B9
Eberbach D 37 F11
Ebergötzen D 95 C7
Ebermannsdorf D 91 C10
Ebermannstadt D 91 C9
Ebern D 91 C9
Eberndorf A 89 C10
Ebersbach D 96 D5
Ebersbach D 96 E5
Ebersbach an der Fils D 90 E6
Ebersberg D 91 C9
Eberschwang A 92 F5
Ebersdorf A 164 B5
Ebersdorf D 33 A12
Ebersdorf D 91 B10
Ebersmunster F 202 E4
Eberstein A 89 C10
Eberswalde-Finow D 100 E5
Ebes H 167 C8
Ebhausen D 43 C10
Ebikon CH 43 F9
Ebnat-Kappel CH 43 F11
Eboli I 76 B4
Ebrach D 91 C7
Ebreichsdorf A 93 G10
Ébreuil F 46 C3
Ebsdorfergrund-Dreihausen D 37 C11
Ebstorf D 99 D8
Écaussinnes-d'Enghien B 198 D4
Ecclefechan GB 21 E10
Eccles GB 21 D12
Eccleshall GB 27 F7
Eceabat TR 187 D10
Echallens CH 47 B10
Echarri E 48 E2
Échauffour F 40 C3
Échenoz-la-Méline F 42 E5
Eching D 91 E11
Eching D 91 F10
Echinos GR 187 B7
Échiré F 44 C4
Échirolles F 47 E8
Échourgnac F 45 E6
Echsenbach A 93 E8
Echt GB 19 L12
Echt NL 35 B12
Echte D 95 C7
Echternach L 36 E6
Écija E 69 A6
Ečka SRB 174 C5
Eckartsberga D 95 D10
Eckbolsheim F 202 D4
Eckental D 91 C9
Eckernförde D 99 B7
Eckerö FIN 115 B13
Eckington GB 27 E9
Eckington GB 29 A10
Éclaron-Braucourt-Ste-Livière F 41 C12
Écommoy F 39 E12
Écos F 40 B6
Écouché F 39 C11
Écouflant F 39 E10
Écouis F 34 F3
Écroures F 42 A5
Écs H 165 A9
Ecséd H 166 B4
Ecseg H 163 F9
Ecsegfalva H 167 C6
Écueillé F 45 A8
Écuisses F 46 B6
Écueillé F 45 A8
Écury-sur-Coole F 41 C11
Ed S 123 E12
Eda glasbruk S 112 C7
Edam NL 32 C4
Edane S 113 C9
Ēdas LV 150 C4
Eddelak D 98 C6
Edderton GB 19 K8
Eddleston GB 21 D10
Ede NL 32 D5
Ede S 119 F12
Edebäck S 113 B10
Edefors S 134 B5
Edegem B 35 B9
Edelény H 161 G2
Edelschrott A 89 B11
Edemissen D 95 B7
Eden GB 20 F5

Eden S 123 D12
Edenderry IRL 23 F8
Edenkoben D 37 F9
Edermünde D 94 D5
Ederny GB 23 C7
Edesheim D 37 F10
Edessa GR 185 C7
Edewecht D 33 B9
Edewechterdamm D 33 B9
Edgeworthstown IRL 23 E7
Edgmond GB 27 F7
Ediger-Eller D 37 D8
Edinburgh GB 21 D10
Edincik TR 189 D8
Edineț MD 169 A11
Edirne TR 187 A11
Edland N 110 C7
Edling D 91 F11
Edlingham GB 21 E13
Edlitz A 164 A6
Edmondstown IRL 22 E5
Edmundbyers GB 21 F13
Édole LV 150 B3
Edolo I 85 A9
Edremit TR 189 E7
Edrosa P 55 E6
Edroso P 55 E6
Edsbro S 115 C10
Edsbruk S 109 C8
Edsbyn S 119 D10
Edsele S 123 E11
Edsken S 114 A6
Edsvalla S 113 D9
Edzell GB 21 B11
Eefde NL 199 A8
Eeklo B 35 B8
Eelde-Paterswolde NL 33 B7
Eerbeek NL 32 D6
Eernegem B 198 C2
Eersel NL 32 F4
Eferding A 92 F6
Effelder D 91 B9
Effeltrich D 91 C9
Effretikon CH 43 F10
Efkarpia GR 185 B8
Efkarpia GR 185 C10
Eforie RO 171 E3
Efpalio GR 190 C4
Efringen-Kirchen D 43 E8
Eftimie Murgu RO 175 D9
Efxeinoupoli GR 191 A6
Egby S 105 B10
Egebæk DK 102 E3
Egebjerg DK 102 E5
Egebjerg DK 103 D9
Egeln D 95 C9
Egense DK 102 B6
Eger H 161 H1
Egerbakta H 161 H1
Egernsund D 102 F5
Egersund N 110 F4
Egerszalók H 161 H1
Egervár H 165 C7
Egeskov DK 102 E5
Egestorf D 99 D8
Egg A 87 C9
Eggby S 107 C14
Eggebek D 98 A6
Eggenburg A 93 E9
Eggenfelden D 91 F12
Eggesin D 100 C6
Eggingen D 43 E9
Eggiwil CH 86 D5
Egglham D 92 E4
Eggolsheim D 91 C9
Eggstätt D 88 A5
Eggum N 126 D6
Eghezée B 35 C10
Eging am See D 92 E4
Eglaine LV 151 E11
Égletons F 45 E10
Egling D 88 A4
Eglingham GB 21 E13
Eglinton GB 20 E3
Eglisau CH 43 E10
Eglish GB 23 D9
Egliciems LV 149 B2
Eglwys Fach GB 28 A5
Eglwyswrw GB 28 A5
Egmond aan Zee NL 32 C3
Egna I 85 A11
Egorovca MD 169 B11
Egremont GB 26 C4
Egsmark DK 102 D7
Egtved DK 102 D4
Éguilles F 51 C9
Éguzon-Chantôme F 45 C9
Egyek H 167 B6
Egyházaskozár H 165 D10
Ehekirchen D 91 E9
Ehingen D 91 E8
Ehingen (Donau) D 87 A9
Ehningen D 203 D6
Ehra-Lessien D 95 A8
Ehrenberg-Wüstensachsen D 90 B7
Ehrenburg D 33 C11
Ehrenfriedersdorf D 96 E3
Ehrenhausen A 164 C5
Ehringshausen D 37 C10
Eibar E 57 B7
Eibelstadt D 91 C7
Eibenstock D 91 B12
Eibergen NL 33 D7
Eibiswald A 164 C4
Eich D 37 E10
Eichenbarleben D 95 B9
Eichenbühl D 43 A11
Eichendorf D 92 E3
Eichenzell D 90 B6
Eichgraben A 93 F9
Eichigt D 91 B11
Eichstätt D 91 E9
Eichwalde D 96 B5
Eickendorf D 95 D7
Eicklingen D 95 A7
Eidapere EST 147 D9
Eide N 116 A6
Eide N 120 D8
Eide N 127 C11
Eidem N 121 D15
Eidet N 121 C16
Eidet N 124 A9
Eidet N 127 A14
Eidfjord N 110 B6

Eiði FO 18 A2
Eidkjosen N 127 A16
Eidsbugarden N 117 D8
Eidsdal N 116 B6
Eidsfjord N 126 C3
Eidshaug N 121 B10
Eidsnes N 128 C10
Eidsøra N 116 A8
Eidstranda N 127 A19
Eidsund N 110 D3
Eidsvåg N 116 A8
Eidsvoll N 111 B14
Eidsvoll Verk N 111 B14
Eidvågeid N 129 B12
Eigeltingen D 43 E10
Eigenrieden D 95 D7
Eijsden NL 199 D7
Eik N 110 D3
Eikelandsosen N 110 B3
Eiken N 110 F6
Eikesdal N 116 B8
Eikjaberg N 116 D6
Eikjeskog N 110 E4
Eikjiil N 106 B3
Eiksund N 116 B3
Eilenburg D 95 D12
Eilenstedt D 95 B9
Eilsleben D 95 B9
Eime D 94 B6
Eimen D 94 C6
Eimke D 99 E8
Eina N 117 E13
Einacleit GB 18 J3
Einbeck D 94 C6
Eindhoven NL 32 F4
Einsiedeln CH 43 F10
Einville-au-Jard F 42 C5
Einvollen N 124 F3
Eisden D 199 D7
Eiselfing D 91 F11
Eisenach D 95 E7
Eisenberg D 95 E10
Eisenberg (Pfalz) D 37 E9
Eisenerz A 89 A10
Eisenhüttenstadt D 97 B7
Eisenstadt A 93 G11
Eisfeld D 91 B8
Eišiškės LT 153 E9
Eislandet N 116 E3
Eisleben Lutherstadt D 95 C10
Eislingen (Fils) D 90 E6
Eisma EST 147 B12
Eitelborn D 37 D9
Eiterfeld D 94 B6
Eiternes N 121 B11
Eiterstraum N 124 E5
Eitorf D 37 C8
Eivinvik N 116 E2
Eivissa E 73 D7
Eja P 60 B4
Ejby DK 102 E5
Ejby DK 103 C10
Ejby DK 103 E10
Ejea de los Caballeros E 57 D9
Ejsing DK 102 B3
Ejstrupholm DK 102 D4
Ejulve E 58 F2
Ekeby DK 102 E5
Ekeby S 103 C11
Ekeby S 108 A6
Ekeby S 115 D9
Ekeby-Almby S 113 D13
Ekedalen S 107 C14
Ekenäs FIN 143 H9
Ekenäs S 107 B13
Ekenäs S 109 B9
Ekenässjön S 108 E6
Ekengräve LV 151 D11
Ekeren B 198 C4
Ekerö S 115 B11
Eket S 103 C12
Ekkerøy N 130 C14
Ekmekçi TR 189 D9
Ekola FIN 138 D9
Ekorrträsk S 123 B16
Eksaarde B 198 C3
Eksel B 199 C6
Ekshärad S 113 B9
Eksjö S 108 D5
Eksta S 109 E12
Ekträsk S 134 F3
Ekzarkh-Antimovo BG 183 D7
Ekzarkh Yosif BG 177 F7
Elafos GR 185 B10
Elafotopos GR 184 E4
Elaiochori GR 187 C6
Elaionas GR 185 B10
Elaionas GR 190 B4
Elaionas GR 191 C7
El Álamo E 62 D5
El Algar E 72 F3
El Almendro E 67 D6
El Alquián E 71 E9
Elämäjärvi FIN 139 D15
El Arahal E 67 E8
El Arenal E 61 D10
Elassona GR 185 E7
El Astillero E 56 B4
Elateia GR 191 B6
Elati GR 185 D6
Elati GR 185 E6
Elatochori GR 185 C7
Elatou GR 190 B4
Elnesvågen N 116 A6
Elorrio E 57 B7
Elorz E 48 E2
Elos GR 194 E6
El Oso E 62 C3
El Palmar E 72 F2
El Palo E 69 C8
El Payo E 61 D7
El Pedernoso E 63 F7
El Pedroso E 67 D8
El Pedroso de la Armuña E 61 B10
El Peral E 63 E9
El Perdigón E 55 F8
El Perelló E 58 F5
El Perelló E 64 F4
El Picazo E 63 E8
El Pinell de Bray E 58 E5
El Piñero E 55 E6
El Pla de Santa María E 59 E6
El Pobo E 58 F2
El Pobo de Dueñas E 63 C9

El Casar de Escalona E 62 D3
El Castellar E 64 D3
El Castillo de las Guardas E 67 D7
El Catllar de Gaià E 59 E6
El Centenillo E 70 C5
El Cerro de Andévalo E 67 D6
Elche de la Sierra E 71 C8
Elche-Elx E 72 E3
Elchingen D 203 E9
Elciego E 57 E7
Elçili TR 188 B6
El Coronil E 67 E8
El Cubo de Don Sancho E 61 C8
El Cubo de Tierra del Vino E 55 F8
El Cuervo E 66 F3
El Cuervo E 67 F7
Elda E 72 E2
Eldalsosen N 116 D4
Eldena D 99 D10
Eldforsen S 113 B11
Eldingen D 99 E8
Eldsberga S 103 B12
Elduvik FO 18 A3
Elefsina GR 191 C8
Elefthero GR 184 D4
Eleftheres GR 187 C6
Eleftheroupoli GR 187 C6
Eleja LV 150 D7
El Ejido E 71 F7
Elek H 167 D7
Elektrėnai LT 153 D10
Elemir SRB 174 C5
Elena BG 182 D5
Elend D 95 C8
Eleousa GR 184 E4
El Escorial E 62 C4
Eleshnitsa BG 181 F8
El Espinar E 62 C4
El Estrecho E 72 F3
Elexalde E 56 B6
El Fendek MA 69 E5
Elfershausen D 203 A8
El Fresno E 62 C3
Elgå N 117 B15
El Garrobo E 67 D7
Elgersundet D
(Schauenburg) D 37 B12
Elgeta E 57 B7
Elgin GB 19 K10
Elgoibar E 57 B7
Elgol GB 18 L4
El Grado E 58 C4
El Granado E 66 D5
El Grau de Borriana E 64 E4
Elgsnes N 127 C11
El Herrumblar E 63 F9
El Hito E 63 D7
El Hoyo de Pinares E 62 C4
Elia GR 194 E9
Elice I 78 B5
Elie GB 21 C11
Elika GR 194 F6
Elimäki FIN 143 D15
Eling GB 29 D12
Elini I 80 D7
Elin Pelin BG 181 D8
Elisenvaara RUS 145 C12
Eliseyna BG 181 C8
Elizondo E 48 D2
Eljas E 61 D7
Efk PL 152 E5
Elkenroth D 201 C8
Elkhovo BG 182 D5
Elkhovo BG 183 E7
Elkšni LV 151 D11
Ellan S 115 B11
Elland GB 27 D7
Ellenberg D 203 C9
Ellerau D 99 C7
Ellerbek D 99 C7
Ellesmere GB 26 F6
Ellesmere Port GB 26 E6
Ellezelles B 35 C8
Ellídshøj DK 102 B5
Elling DK 106 C7
Ellingen D 91 D8
Ellington GB 21 E13
El Llano E 54 B5
Ellmau A 88 A5
Ellon GB 19 L12
Ellös S 107 C9
Ellrich D 95 C8
Ellwangen (Jagst) D 91 E7
Ellwürden D 33 B10
Elm CH 87 D8
Elm D 33 A12
Elm (Wedemark) D 94 A6
Elmbrun F 32 B4
Elmebakken N 129 D11
Elvegard N 127 D13
Elvekrok N 129 B17
Elvelund N 128 C6
Elvemund N 129 E16
Elven F 38 E6
El Vendrell E 59 E7
El Verger E 72 D5
Elverum N 117 E15
Elvesletta N 127 D12
Elvevoll N 127 B14
Elvevollen N 127 B18
El Villar de Arnedo E 48 F1
Elvington GB 27 D10
El Viso E 70 C3
El Viso del Alcor E 67 E8
Elvnes N 130 D8
Elxleben D 95 D8
Ely GB 29 C8
Ely GB 31 C9
Elz D 201 D9
Elzach D 43 D9
Elze D 94 B6
Elze (Wedemark) D 94 A6
Embid E 63 C9
Embid de Ariza E 57 F8
Embleton GB 21 E13
Embrun F 52 B4
Emburga LV 151 C7
Embûte LV 150 C3
Emden D 33 B8
Emecik TR 197 C7
Emiralem TR 193 C8
Emirali TR 189 B7
Emlichheim D 33 C7
Emly IRL 24 D6
Emmaboda S 105 B9
Emmaljunga S 103 C13
Emmamäste EST 146 D5
Emmeloord NL 32 C5
Emmelsbüll-Horsbüll D 98 A5
Emmelshausen D 37 D8
Emmen CH 43 F8
Emmen NL 33 C7
Emmendingen D 43 D8
Emmer-Compascuum NL 33 C8
Emmerich D 32 E6
Emmoo IRL 23 F7
Emőd H 161 H2
Emolahti FIN 139 C15
Empel NL 32 E4
Empesos GR 190 A3
Empfingen D 203 E6
Empoli I 82 E2
Emponas GR 197 D7
Emporeio GR 195 C9
Emporeios GR 193 C7
Emptinne B 35 D11
Emsbüren D 33 D8
Emsdetten D 33 D9
Emsfors S 105 A10
Emskirchen D 91 C8
Emst NL 32 D5
Emstek D 33 C10
Emsworth GB 31 F7
Emtinghausen D 33 C11
Emtunga S 107 C12
Emyvale IRL 23 D8
Enäjärvi FIN 144 D2
Enånger S 119 C14
Enarsvedjan S 121 D16
Encamp AND 49 E9
Encinas de Abajo E 61 C10
Encinasola E 67 C6
Encinas Reales E 69 B8
Encinedo E 55 D6
Enciso E 57 E7
Encs H 161 G3
Encsencs H 167 B9
Endingen D 43 D8

Endre S 109 D12
Endrefalva H 163 E9
Endriejavas LT 150 E3
Endrinal E 61 C9
Endzele LV 147 F10
Enebakk N 111 C14
Enego I 88 E4
Eneryda S 104 B6
Enese H 165 A8
Enez TR 187 C10
Enfesta E 54 C2
Enfield IRL 23 F9
Engan N 117 B11
Engan N 120 E4
Engan N 124 D3
Engares GR 192 E5
Engden D 199 A10
Engelberg CH 87 D6
Engelhartstetten A 93 F11
Engelhartszell A 92 E5
Engeln D 33 C11
Engelsberg S 91 F12
Engelskirchen D 37 C8
Engen D 43 E10
Enger D 33 D11
Engerdal N 117 C15
Engerdalssetra N 117 C15
Engerneset N 118 C3
Engersen D 95 A9
Engesland N 106 B3
Engesvang DK 102 C4
Enghien B 35 C9
Engis B 35 C11
Englefontaine F 35 D8
Engomer F 49 E8
Engstingen D 43 D11
Enguera E 72 D3
Enguidanos E 63 E9
Engure LV 150 B6
Engvik N 128 C2
Enhagen-Ekbacken S 114 C7
Enichioi MD 170 F2
Enina BG 182 D4
Eningen unter Achalm D 203 E7
Enitsa BG 181 C9
Enix E 71 F7
Enkenbach D 202 C4
Enkhuizen NL 32 C4
Enkirch D 37 E8
Enklinge FIN 115 B15
Enköping S 114 C7
Enmo N 117 A12
Enna I 74 D5
Ennepetal D 201 B7
Ennery F 202 C1
Ennezat F 46 D3
Ennigerloh D 33 E10
Ennis IRL 24 C5
Enniscorthy IRL 25 C9
Enniscrone IRL 22 D4
Enniskean IRL 24 E5
Enniskerry IRL 23 F10
Enniskillen GB 23 D7
Ennistymon IRL 24 C4
Enns A 93 F6
Eno FIN 141 E14
Enonkoski FIN 141 F11
Enonkylä FIN 135 F12
Enontekiö FIN 133 B11
Ens NL 32 C5
Enschede NL 33 D7
Ensdorf D 91 D10
Ensdorf D 202 C2
Ense D 33 F10
Ensheim D 37 F8
Ensisheim F 43 E7
Enskogen S 119 C9
Ensuès-la-Redonne F 51 D9
Enter NL 199 A9
Enterknfoot GB 21 E9
Entlebuch CH 86 D6
Entracque I 53 C6
Entradas P 66 D3
Entraigues-sur-la-Sorgue F 51 B8
Entrains-sur-Nohain F 41 F9
Entrammes F 39 E10
Entraunes F 52 C5
Entraygues-sur-Truyère F 49 A10
Entrena E 57 D6
Entrevaux F 52 D5
Entroncamento P 60 F4
Envendos P 60 E5
Envermeu F 34 E3
Enviken S 119 E10
Enying H 165 C10
Enzklösterle D 43 C9
Eochaill IRL 25 E7
Eoropaidh GB 18 H4
Épaignes F 34 F1
Epalinges CH 47 B10
Epano Fellos GR 192 D4
Epe NL 32 D5
Eperjes H 166 D6
Eperjeske H 161 G5
Épernay F 41 B10
Épernon F 40 C6
Epfendorf D 43 D10
Épieds-en-Beauce F 40 E6
Épierre F 47 E9
Épila E 57 E9
Épinac F 46 B6
Épinal F 42 D5
Épiry F 41 F10
Episcopia I 76 C6
Episkopi GR 185 C7
Episkopi GR 194 E7
Episkopi GR 194 E9
Epitalio GR 190 D3
Époisses F 41 E11
Epoo FIN 143 E14
Eppelborn D 37 F7
Eppelheim D 37 F11
Eppenbrunn D 202 C4
Eppertshausen D 37 E11
Eppeville F 35 E7
Epping GB 31 D9
Eppingen D 43 B10
Eppishausen D 87 A11
Eppstein D 37 D10
Epsom GB 31 E8
Eptachori GR 184 D5
Épuisay F 40 E4
Epureni RO 169 D11
Epworth GB 27 D10
Équeurdreville-Hainneville F 39 A8
Eraclea I 89 C6
Eraclea Mare I 83 A6
Er ähijärvi FIN 143 B12
Erähijärvi FIN 145 C10

Erastvere EST 147 F13
Erateini GR 190 C5
Eratyra GR 185 D6
Erba I 85 B7
Erbach D 37 E12
Erbach D 90 F6
Erbendorf D 91 C11
Erberge LV 151 D10
Erbiceni RO 169 C10
Erbray F 39 D7
Erchie I 77 C9
Ercsi H 165 B11
Érd H 165 B11
Erdeborn D 95 D10
Erdek TR 189 D8
Erdelli TR 193 B10
Erdeven F 38 E5
Erdevik SRB 174 C3
Erding D 91 F10
Erdőkertes H 166 B3
Erdut HR 173 A11
Erdweg D 91 F9
Erdželija MK 180 F5
Éréac F 39 D7
Eremitu RO 168 D5
Eremiya BG 181 E6
Erenler TR 189 D8
Eresos GR 193 A6
Eretria GR 185 F8
Eretria GR 191 C8
Erfde D 98 B6
Erftstadt D 37 C7
Erfurt D 95 E7
Érgeme LV 147 E9
Ergersheim D 91 C7
Ergili TR 189 D8
Ergli LV 151 C11
Ergoldsbach D 91 E11
Ergué-Gabéric F 38 D3
Erharting D 91 F12
Eribill GB 18 J7
Erice E 48 E2
Erice I 74 C2
Ericeira P 66 B1
Eriklice TR 189 C7
Eriksberg S 123 A9
Erikslund S 119 A10
Eriksmåla S 105 B8
Erikssund S 115 C9
Ering D 92 F4
Eringsboda S 105 C8
Eriswil CH 86 C5
Erjova MD 170 B4
Erkelenz D 36 B6
Erkheim D 87 A10
Erkner D 96 B5
Erla E 57 D10
Erlach CH 47 A11
Erlangen D 91 C7
Erlauf A 93 F8
Erlbach D 91 B11
Erlenbach am Main D 203 B7
Erli I 53 C8
Ermelo NL 32 D5
Ermelo P 54 F4
Ermenonville F 41 B8
Ermesinde P 60 B3
Ermidas do Sado P 66 C3
Ermioni GR 191 E7
Ermoclia MD 170 D5
Ermoupoli GR 192 E4
Ermsleben D 95 C9
Ermua E 57 B6
Erndtebrück D 37 C10
Ernée F 39 D10
Ernei RO 168 D5
Ernestinovo HR 165 F11
Ernstbrunn A 93 E10
Erp NL 32 E5
Érpatak H 167 B8
Erpel D 37 C8
Erquelinnes B 200 D1
Erquy F 38 C6
Erra P 66 A3
Errenteria E 48 D2
Errezil E 48 D1
Erribera E 57 B7
Errill IRL 25 C7
Errindlev DK 99 A11
Erritsø DK 102 D5
Errogie GB 19 L8
Érsekcsanád H 166 E2
Érsekë AL 184 D4
Érsekvadkert H 163 E8
Ersfjord N 127 B13
Ersfjordbotn N 127 A16
Ersmark S 123 A11
Ersmark S 134 C5
Ersmark S 138 C4
Ersnäs S 134 C7
Erstein F 43 D8
Erstfeld CH 87 D7
Ersvik N 124 B7
Ertenvåg N 124 B7
Ertingen D 87 A8
Erto I 88 D5
Ertsjärv S 132 E8
Ertuğrul TR 189 E9
Ertvelde B 198 C3
Erula I 80 B2
Ervalla S 113 D13
Ervasti FIN 137 D9
Ervedosa do Douro P 60 B6
Ervenik HR 172 D4
Ervidel P 66 D3
Ervik N 116 B1
Ervillers F 34 D6
Ervy-le-Châtel F 41 D10
Erwitte D 33 E10
Erxleben D 95 B9
Erxleben D 99 E11
Erythres GR 191 C7
Erzhausen D 37 E11
Eržvilkas LT 150 E5
Esanatoglia I 83 F6
Esbjerg DK 102 E2
Esbo FIN 143 E13
Esbønderup DK 103 C10
Escairón E 54 C4
Escalante E 56 B5
Escalaplano I 80 D3
Escalhão P 61 C7
Escaló E 49 E8
Es Caló E 73 D7
Escalona E 62 D4
Escalona del Prado E 62 B4
Escalonilla E 62 E4
Escalos de Baixo P 60 E6
Escalos de Cima P 60 E6
Escamilla E 63 D7
Es Canar E 73 C8
Escañuela E 69 A8
Escariche E 63 D6

Escarigo P 61 D6
Escároz E 48 E3
Es Castell E 73 B13
Escatrón E 58 E3
Esch NL 199 B6
Eschau D 203 B7
Eschau F 202 E4
Eschborn D 203 A6
Esche D 33 C7
Escheburg D 99 D8
Eschede D 99 E8
Eschenbach CH 43 F9
Eschenbach D 91 C10
Eschenburg-Eibelshausen D 37 C10
Eschenstruth (Helsa) D 94 D6
Eschershausen D 94 C6
Eschlkam D 92 D3
Escholzmatt CH 86 D5
Esch-sur-Alzette L 36 F5
Esch-sur-Sûre L 36 E5
Eschwege D 95 D7
Eschweiler D 36 C6
Escombreras E 72 F3
Escorca E 65 E10
Escorihuela E 58 F2
Escos F 48 D3
Escouloubre F 49 E10
Escource F 48 B3
Escout F 48 D4
Escragnolles F 52 D5
Escucha E 58 F2
Escurial E 61 F9
Escúzar E 69 B9
Esechioi RO 171 E2
Esence TR 189 D10
Esenköy TR 189 C10
Esenler TR 189 B8
Esens D 33 A9
Esenyurt TR 189 B10
Esgos E 54 D4
Esgueira P 60 C3
Eskdalemuir GB 21 E10
Eskelhem S 109 E12
Eskişehir TR 193 C12
Eskilstrup DK 100 A1
Eskilstuna S 114 D7
Eskioba TR 193 C10
Eskisigirçi TR 189 D9
Eskogen S 115 D10
Eskola FIN 139 C12
Eskoriatza E 57 B6
Eslarn D 91 C12
Eslava E 48 E3
Eslohe (Sauerland) D 33 F10
Eslöv S 103 D12
Es Mercadal E 73 B13
Es Migjorn Gran E 73 B13
Esnes F 35 D7
Esneux B 35 C12
Espa N 117 E14
Espadañedo E 55 D7
Espalion F 50 A4
Espaly-St-Marcel F 46 E4
Esparragalejo E 67 B7
Esparragosa E 67 B7
Esparragosa de la Serena E 67 B8
Esparreguera E 59 D7
Esparron F 51 C10
Esparza de Salazar E 48 E3
Espe FIN 142 C6
Espedal N 110 B2
Espeja E 61 C7
Espeja de San Marcelino E 56 E5
Espejo E 69 A7
Espejón E 56 E5
Espel NL 32 C5
Espeland N 110 B2
Espelette F 48 D3
Espelkamp D 33 D11
Espenau D 94 D5
Espenes N 127 B14
Espera E 67 F8
Esperança P 61 F6
Espéraza F 49 E10
Espergærde DK 103 D11
Esperia I 78 E5
Espevik N 110 C3
Espezel F 49 E10
Espiel E 70 C3
Espinama E 55 B10
Espinasses F 52 B4
Espinhal P 60 D4
Espinho P 60 B3
Espinilla E 56 B3
Espinosa de Cerrato E 56 E4
Espinosa de Henares E 63 C6
Espinosa de los Monteros E 56 B4
Espinoso del Rey E 62 E3
Espira-de-l'Agly E 50 E4
Espírito Santo P 66 D4
Espite P 60 E3
Espluegares E 63 D8
Esplugues de Llobregat E 59 E8
Esplús E 58 D4
Espolla E 50 F5
Espondeilham F 50 D5
Esponellà E 59 C9
Espoonlahti FIN 143 E12
Esporles E 65 E10
Esposende P 54 E2
Espot E 49 E8
Esprels F 42 E5
Esquivias E 62 D5
Esrange S 132 C6
Essay F 39 C12
Esse FIN 139 C10
Essel D 98 D7
Essen B 32 F2
Essen D 37 B7
Essen (Oldenburg) D 33 C9
Essenbach D 91 F11
Essert F 43 E6
Essingen D 90 E7
Esslingen am Neckar D 43 C11
Essoyes F 41 D10
Essu EST 147 C12
Essvik S 119 B13

Este I 82 B4
Este P 54 E3
Estela P 54 F2
Estella E 48 E1
Estellencs E 65 E10
Estenfeld D 203 B9
Estepa E 69 B7
Estepar E 56 D4
Estepona E 69 D6
Esteras de Medinaceli E 63 B8
Estercuel E 58 F2
Esternay F 41 C10
Esterwegen D 33 C9
Esterzili I 80 D3
Estiavreilles F 46 E5
Estissac F 41 D10
Estivareilles F 45 C11
Estói P 66 E4
Estômbar P 66 E3
Estorf D 33 A11
Estorf D 33 D9
Estoril P 66 B1
Estoublon F 52 B4
Estrablin F 47 D6
Estreito P 60 D5
Estrela P 67 C5
Estremera E 63 D6
Estremoz P 66 B4
Estriégala E 63 B7
Esvres F 40 F4
Esztár H 167 C8
Esztergom H 165 A11
Étables-sur-Mer F 38 C6
Étagnac F 45 D8
Étain F 35 F12
Étais-la-Sauvin F 41 E9
Étalante F 41 E12
Étalle B 35 F12
Étampes F 40 D7
Étang-sur-Arroux F 46 D3
Étaples F 31 F12
Étaules F 44 D3
Étauliers F 44 E4
Eteläinen FIN 143 C12
Etelä-Vartsala FIN 142 D5
Etelhem S 109 E13
Éternoz F 47 A9
Étes H 163 E9
Ethe B 35 F12
Etholmen N 107 A9
Etili TR 189 E6
Étival F 47 B8
Étival-Clairefontaine F 43 D6
Etna N 117 E11
Etne N 110 C3
Étoile F 46 F6
Etropole BG 181 D9
Etroubles I 47 D11
Ettelbruck L 36 E6
Ettenheim D 43 D8
Etten-Leur NL 32 E3
Ettington GB 29 A11
Ettlingen D 43 C9
Ettringen D 37 D8
Etulia MD 171 B2
Étupes F 43 E6
Etwall GB 27 F8
Etxalar E 48 D2
Etxarri-Aranatz E 48 E1
Etyek H 165 B10
Eu F 34 D3
Eubigheim D 90 C6
Euerdorf D 90 B7
Eugénie-les-Bains F 48 C5
Eugmo FIN 138 C9
Eulate E 48 E1
Eupen B 36 C6
Euper D 95 C12
Eura FIN 142 C6
Eurajoki FIN 142 C6
Eurasburg D 88 A3
Eurville-Bienville F 42 C3
Euskirchen D 37 C7
Eußenheim D 90 B6
Eutin D 99 B9
Eutingen im Gäu D 203 E6
Eutzsch D 95 C12
Euville F 42 C4
Eva GR 190 D5
Evanger N 110 B4
Evanton GB 19 K8
Évaux-les-Bains F 45 C10
Evciler TR 189 B9
Evciler TR 189 E7
Evdilos GR 193 D7
Évele LV 147 F11
Evenes N 127 D12
Evenesdal N 125 C10
Evenset N 124 B8
Evenskjær N 127 C12
Evenstad N 117 D14
Everdingen N 199 B6
Everdrup DK 103 E9
Evergem B 35 B8
Everöd S 104 D6
Evertsberg S 118 D6
Evesham GB 29 A11
Évian-les-Bains F 47 C10
Evijärvi FIN 139 D10
Evisa F 53 G9
Evitskog FIN 143 E11
Evje N 106 B2
Evlalo GR 187 C8
Evolène CH 47 C12
Évora P 66 B4
Évora-Monte P 66 B4
Evosmos GR 185 C8
Évran F 39 D8
Évrecy F 39 B10
Evrencik TR 189 A8
Evrenli TR 189 B10
Evrensekiz TR 189 B7
Évreux F 40 B5
Évron F 39 D11
Évry F 41 C8
Evzonoi GR 185 B8
Ewhurst GB 31 E8
Examilia GR 191 D6
Exaplatanos GR 185 C7
Exarchos GR 191 B6
Excideuil F 45 E8
Exebridge GB 29 C7

Exeter GB 29 D7
Exilles I 47 E10
Exloo NL 33 C7
Exmes F 39 C12
Exminster GB 29 D8
Exmouth GB 29 D8
Exochi GR 185 B10
Exochi GR 185 D7
Exo Chora GR 190 D2
Exo Vathy GR 196 C4
Extremo P 54 E3
Eydehavn N 106 B4
Eydelstedt D 33 C11
Eye GB 27 F11
Eye GB 31 C11
Eyemouth GB 21 D12
Eyeries IRL 24 E3
Eyguians F 51 B10
Eyguières F 51 C9
Eygurande-et-Gardedeuil F 45 E6
Eymet F 49 A6
Eymoutiers F 45 D9
Eynsham GB 29 B12
Eyragues F 51 C8
Eyrans F 44 E4
Eyrecourt IRL 22 F6
Eyrein F 45 E9
Eyzin-Pinet F 47 E6
Ezcaray E 56 D6
Ezerche BG 171 F3
Ezere LV 150 D4
Ežerėlis LT 153 D8
Ezerets BG 183 B15
Ezerets BG 181 F7
Ezeriş RO 175 C10
Ezerkalne LV 149 C12
Ezerkalni LV 149 C7
Ezernieki LV 149 D3
Ezine TR 187 E10
Ezkurra E 48 D2
Ézy-sur-Eure F 40 C5

F

Faaborg DK 102 E6
Fabara E 58 E4
Fabas F 49 D8
Fåberg N 124 C6
Fåberg N 117 D12
Fabero E 55 C6
Fábiánháza H 161 H5
Fabiánki PL 154 E7
Fábiánsebestyén H 166 D5
Fåbodliden S 123 B13
Fåborg DK 102 D3
Fabrègues F 51 C6
Fabrezan F 50 D4
Fabriano I 83 F6
Fabrica di Roma I 78 C2
Fábricas de San Juan de Alcaraz E 71 B8
Fabrizia I 75 C9
Fabro I 78 B2
Făcăeni RO 171 D1
Faches-Thumesnil F 198 D2
Facinas E 68 D5
Fadd H 165 D11
Faedis I 89 D7
Fæfjord N 129 C13
Fafe P 54 F3
Fagagna I 89 D7
Făgăraş RO 168 F5
Fågelfors S 105 B9
Fågelmara S 105 C9
Fågeljö S 118 D6
Fågelsjö S 118 C6
Fågelsundet S 119 E14
Fagerås S 113 C9
Fagerdal S 122 D8
Fagerhaug N 117 A11
Fagerhult S 105 A9
Fagerhult S 107 C11
Fagerhult S 108 C4
Fageri N 125 B11
Fagernes N 117 E10
Fagernes N 127 A17
Fagersanna S 108 C4
Fagerstad S 113 C14
Fagervik FIN 143 E10
Fagervik N 124 C9
Fagervika N 115 A9
Fåget RO 167 F9
Fägetelu RO 176 D5
Fåggeby S 113 B14
Fågåvik S 107 B11
Fahan IRL 20 E2
Fahrdorf D 99 C8
Fahrenkrug D 99 C8
Fahrenzhausen D 91 F10
Fahrland D 96 B4
Faiccchio I 76 A2
Faid D 37 D8
Faido CH 87 E7
Failde P 55 E6
Faimes B 35 C11
Fain-lès-Montbard F 41 E11
Fains-Véel F 42 C3
Fairlie GB 20 D7
Fair Oak GB 29 D12
Faissault F 35 F10
Fajão P 60 D5
Fajarda P 66 A2
Fajsławice PL 160 A6
Fajsz H 165 D11
Fakenham GB 31 B10
Fakija BG 183 E8
Fakovići BIH 174 E4
Faksdal N 121 B10
Fakse DK 103 E10
Fakse Ladeplads DK 103 E10
Falaise F 39 C11
Falani GR 185 E7
Fålåsjö S 123 E13
Falcade I 88 D4
Falces E 48 F2
Fălciu RO 170 E2
Falck D 202 E2
Fălciu RO 170 E2
Falconara I 74 E5
Falconara Marittima I 83 E7
Falcone I 75 C7
Faldsled DK 102 E6
Fale N 117 A9
Faleria I 78 C2

Falerna I 75 A9
Falerone I 78 A4
Falerum S 109 C8
Fălesti MD 169 B11
Falkeberg S 91 C11
Falkeberg D 91 F12
Falkenberg D 96 C4
Falkenberg S 103 B11
Falkenhagen D 99 D12
Falkenhain D 95 D12
Falkensee D 96 A4
Falkenstein D 91 B11
Falkenstein D 91 D11
Falkirk GB 21 D9
Falkland GB 21 C10
Falkopeng S 107 C14
Fałków PL 157 H2
Fall N 113 A8
Falla S 108 B7
Falleron F 44 B2
Fällfors S 134 C5
Fallingbostel D 98 E7
Fålloheden S 125 E15
Fällsvikhamnen S 119 A15
Falltorp S 113 A8
Falmenta I 84 A6
Falmouth GB 28 E4
Falset E 58 E5
Falstad N 121 D10
Fălticeni RO 169 C8
Faltrask S 123 B15
Falun S 119 E10
Famalicão P 60 B6
Fambach D 95 E7
Fámjin FO 18 B3
Fana N 110 B2
Fanano I 82 D2
Fanari GR 187 C8
Fanbyn S 123 E16
Fångsjöbacken S 123 C11
Fångsjön S 123 E12
Fanjeaux F 49 D10
Fanlo E 48 E5
Fannrem N 120 E7
Fano I 83 E7
Fanore IRL 22 F4
Fanos GR 185 B7
Fântânele RO 168 E5
Fântânele RO 168 E5
Fanthyttan S 113 C13
Fão P 54 E2
Fara Filiorum Petri I 79 C6
Fărăgău RO 168 D5
Fara in Sabina I 78 C3
Faraoani RO 169 E9
Fara San Martino I 79 C6
Faraonivka UA 170 E5
Farasdues E 57 D9
Fărău RO 168 E4
Fårberget S 123 C15
Fårbo S 109 E8
Fărcaş RO 176 E3
Fărcaşa RO 168 E3
Fărcaşa RO 169 C7
Fărcăşeşti RO 175 D11
Farchant D 88 A3
Fardal N 106 A3
Fårdala I 76 C6
Fardhem S 109 E12
Fardrum IRL 23 F7
Faréberchtsville F 202 C2
Fareham GB 29 D12
Faremoutiers F 41 C9
Fårevejle DK 103 D8
Fårevejle Stationsby DK 103 D8
Färgelanda S 107 B11
Fargues-St-Hilaire F 48 A5
Färholmen S 134 C8
Fårhus DK 102 F5
Färila S 119 C10
Faringdon GB 29 B11
Farini I 85 D8
Fariza de Sayago E 55 F7
Färjestaden S 105 B10
Farkadona GR 185 E7
Farlete E 57 E10
Fårliug RO 175 B8
Färlöv S 104 C6
Färna S 113 C14
Färnäs S 118 D8
Farnborough GB 31 E7
Farndon GB 26 E6
Farnese I 78 B1
Farnham GB 31 E7
Farnstädt D 95 D10
Faro P 66 E4
Fårö S 109 D14
Faro do Alentejo P 66 C4
Fårösund S 109 D14
Farr GB 19 L8
Farra d'Alpago I 88 D5
Farranfore IRL 24 D3
Farre DK 102 C4
Farre DK 102 D4
Farsala GR 185 F7
Fårsån S 123 E14
Farsø DK 102 B4
Farstrup DK 102 B4
Farsund N 110 F4
Fårt DK 102 B4
Fårvang DK 102 B5
Farynava BY 149 F5
Fasano I 77 B8
Fåset N 117 B13
Fåssjodal S 119 B9
Fasterholt DK 102 C4
Fasty PL 156 D8
Fatela P 60 D6
Fatih TR 189 B10
Fátima P 60 E3
Fatjas S 123 B18
Fatmomakke S 122 A8
Fatnica BIH 173 F9
Fättjaur S 122 A8
Faucogney-et-la-Mer F 42 E6
Faugères F 50 C5
Fauguerolles F 49 B6
Faulbach D 203 B7
Fauldhouse GB 21 D9
Faulenrost D 99 C13
Faulquemont F 42 B6
Fauquembergues F 34 C5
Faura E 64 E4
Fauske N 125 B11
Fauskevåg N 127 C12
Fauville-en-Caux F 34 E2
Faux F 45 F7
Faux-la-Montagne F 45 D9
Favaios P 54 F5
Favale di Malvaro I 53 C10
Fåvang N 117 D12
Favara E 64 F4
Favara I 74 E4
Faverges F 47 D9
Faverney F 42 E5
Faverolles F 46 F4
Faversham GB 31 E10
Favignana I 74 D1
Fawley GB 29 D12
Fay-de-Bretagne F 39 F8
Fayence F 52 D5
Fayl-la-Forêt F 42 E4
Fayón E 58 E4
Fay-sur-Lignon F 46 F5
Fažana HR 83 C8
Fazeley GB 27 F8
Feakle IRL 24 C5
Fécamp F 34 E1
Feda N 110 F5
Fedamore IRL 24 C5
Feeny N 116 E1
Fedosiyivka UA 170 B4
Feeard IRL 24 C5
Feeny GB 20 E2
Fégréac F 39 E7
Fegyvernek H 166 C6
Fehérgyarmat H 161 H6
Fehrbellin D 99 E13
Fehring A 164 C6
Feijó P 66 B1
Feilbingert D 37 E9
Feilitzsch D 91 B10
Fcillens F 46 C6
Feissons-sur-Isère F 47 D9
Feistritz im Rosental A 89 C9
Feistritz ob Bleiburg A 89 C10
Feiteira P 66 E4
Feketić SRB 174 B4
Felanitx E 73 C11
Felchow D 100 D6
Felcsút H 165 B11
Feld am See A 89 C8
Feldbach A 164 C5
Feldballe DK 102 C7
Feldberg D 100 D4
Felde D 99 B7
Feldebrő H 163 F10
Feldioara RO 169 F7
Feldkirch A 87 C9
Feldkirchen in Kärnten A 89 C9
Feldkirchen-Westerham D 88 A4
Feldru RO 168 C5
Feleacu RO 168 D3
Felgar P 61 B7
Felgueiras P 54 F3
Felgyő H 166 D5
Feliceni RO 168 E6
Felindre GB 29 A8
Félines F 46 E4
Felino I 82 C1
Felitto I 76 C4
Félix E 71 F7
Felixdorf A 93 G10
Felixstowe GB 31 D11
Felizzano I 53 B8
Fell D 37 E7
Fellbach D 43 C11
Felletin F 45 D10
Fellingsbro S 113 D14
Felnac RO 167 F2
Felsberg D 37 B12
Felsődobsza H 161 G3
Felsőlajos H 166 C4
Felsőnyék H 165 C10
Felsőpakeny H 166 C4
Felsőszentiván H 166 E4
Felsőtárkány H 161 H1
Felsőzsolca H 161 G2
Felsted DK 102 F4
Felton GB 21 E13
Feltre I 88 D4
Feltwell GB 27 G13
Femundsenden N 117 C15
Femundsundet N 117 C15
Fénay F 42 F3
Fendeille F 49 D9
Fene S 84 B3
Fenerköy TR 189 B9
Fenes N 127 C12
Fenestrelle I 47 E11
Fénétrange F 43 C7
Feneu F 39 F10
Fengersfors S 107 B11
Fenioux F 45 C5
Fenis I 47 D11
Fenit IRL 24 D3
Feniton GB 29 D8
Fensmark DK 103 E9
Fenstanton GB 31 C8
Fenwick GB 21 D13
Fényeslitke H 161 G5
Feofilova Pustyn' RUS 148 E5
Feolin Ferry GB 20 D4
Feonanagh IRL 24 D5
Fépin F 35 D10
Ferbane IRL 23 F7
Ferdinanda I 75 B9
Ferdinandovac HR 165 D8
Ferdinandshof D 100 C5
Fère-Champenoise F 41 C10
Fère-en-Tardenois F 41 B10
Férel F 39 F7
Ferentillo I 78 B3
Ferentino I 78 D4
Feres GR 187 C10
Férez E 71 C8
Feria E 67 B6
Feričanci HR 165 E9
Ferlach A 89 C9
Fermignano I 82 F6
Fermo I 83 F7
Fermoselle E 55 F7
Fermoy IRL 24 D6
Fernáncaballero E 62 F5
Fernán Núñez E 69 A7
Ferndown GB 29 D11
Ferness GB 19 L9
Ferney-Voltaire F 47 C9
Fernitz A 164 C5
Ferns IRL 25 C9
Feroleto Antico I 75 B9
Ferrals-les-Corbières F 50 D4
Ferrandina I 77 C6

Ferrara I 82 C4
Ferrazzano I 79 D7
Ferreira E 54 A5
Ferreira do Alentejo P 66 C3
Ferreira do Zêzere P 60 E4
Ferrel P 60 F2
Ferreras de Abajo E 55 E7
Ferreras de Arriba E 55 E7
Ferrere I 53 B7
Ferreries E 73 B13
Ferreruela de Huerva E 63 B10
Ferreruela de Tábara E 55 E7
Ferrette F 43 E7
Ferriere I 53 B11
Ferrières B 35 D12
Ferrières F 41 D8
Ferritslet DK 102 E7
Ferrol E 54 B3
Ferrybank IRL 25 C10
Ferryhill GB 21 F13
Ferschweiler D 201 E5
Fertilia I 80 B1
Fertőd H 165 A7
Fertőrákos H 165 A7
Fertőszentmiklós H 165 A7
Ferwert NL 32 B5
Feshiebridge GB 19 L9
Fessenheim F 43 E8
Festieux F 35 E8
Festvåg N 124 B8
Fetești RO 171 E1
Fetești-Gară RO 171 E1
Fethard IRL 25 D7
Fethard IRL 25 D9
Fetsund N 111 C14
Fettercairn GB 21 B11
Feucht D 91 D9
Feuchtwangen D 91 D7
Feugarolles F 49 B6
Feuquières F 34 E4
Feuquières-en-Vimeu F 34 C4
Feurs F 46 D5
Fevåg N 120 D7
Fevik N 106 C4
Feytiat F 45 D8
Ffestiniog GB 26 F4
Ffostrasol GB 28 A6
Fiac F 49 C9
Fiamignano I 78 C4
Fiano I 47 E12
Fiano Romano I 78 C3
Fiavè I 85 B10
Ficarazzi I 74 C3
Ficarolo I 82 C3
Fichtelberg D 91 D10
Fichtenberg D 90 E6
Fichti GR 191 D6
Ficulle I 78 B2
Fiddown IRL 25 D8
Fide S 109 E12
Fidenza I 85 D9
Fidjeland N 110 E5
Fiè allo Sciliar I 88 C4
Fieberbrunn A 88 B6
Fieni RO 176 C6
Fier AL 184 C2
Fiera di Primiero I 88 D4
Fierbinți-Târg RO 177 D8
Fierzë AL 179 E9
Fiesch CH 86 E6
Fiesole I 82 E3
Fiesso Umbertiano I 82 C4
Figanières F 52 D4
Figari F 53 J10
Figeac F 49 A10
Figeholm S 109 E9
Figgio N 110 E3
Figline Valdarno I 82 E3
Figueira da Foz P 60 D3
Figueira de Castelo Rodrigo P 61 C7
Figueira e Barros P 60 F5
Figueiredo de Alva P 60 C5
Figueiró da Granja P 60 C6
Figueiró dos Vinhos P 60 E4
Figueres E 59 C9
Figueroles E 64 D4
Figueruela de Arriba E 55 E7
Fijnaart NL 198 B4
Filadelfia I 75 B9
Filakio GR 187 A10
Fiľakovo SK 163 E9
Filatova-Gora RUS 148 F3
Filattiera I 85 E8
Fildu de Jos RO 167 D11
Filettino I 78 D4
Filey GB 27 C11
Filiano I 76 B5
Filiași RO 176 D3
Filiates GR 184 E3
Filiatra GR 190 E4
Filicudi Porto I 75 B6
Filipeni RO 169 D10
Filipești RO 169 D9
Filipeşti de Pădure RO 177 D7
Filipeştii de Târg RO 177 D7
Filipjakov HR 172 E3
Filipovtsi BG 181 D6
Filipów PL 152 E6
Filippiada GR 190 A2
Filipstad S 113 C11
Filisur CH 87 D9
Fillan N 120 D5
Fillinges F 47 C9
Fillyra GR 187 B9
Filotas GR 185 C6
Filottin I 83 F7
Filsbäck S 107 C13
Filskov DK 102 D4
Filsum D 33 B9
Filton GB 29 B9
Filzmoos A 89 B8
Fimber GB 27 C10
Finale I 74 C5
Finale Emilia I 82 C3
Finale Ligure I 53 C8
Fiñana E 71 E7
Finavon GB 21 B11
Finby FIN 115 B14
Finby FIN 143 E8
Findern GB 27 F8
Findhorn GB 19 K9
Fındıklı TR 188 D6
Fındıklı TR 189 E8
Findochty GB 19 K11
Findon GB 31 F8
Finestrat E 72 D4
Finhan F 49 C8
Finiq AL 184 E3
Finiș RO 167 D9
Finja S 103 C13

Finkenstein A 89 C8
Finnbacka S 119 D10
Finnbodarna S 118 E7
Finnböle S 114 B8
Finnbyen N 126 D5
Finneby S 119 B9
Finnea IRL 23 E8
Finneidfjord N 124 C6
Finnentrop D 37 B9
Finnerödja S 108 B4
Finnes N 124 C6
Finnfjordeidet N 127 B15
Finnfors S 134 E4
Finngruvan S 118 E7
Finnholt N 112 B6
Finningham GB 31 C11
Finnkroken N 127 A17
Finnøy N 127 D9
Finnsådal N 106 C2
Finnsäter S 121 D15
Finnset N 117 B8
Finnset N 126 A7
Finnset N 126 D9
Finnseter N 117 D12
Finnshögst S 119 D9
Finnskog N 118 E3
Finnsnes N 127 B14
Finntorp S 112 D7
Finnträsk S 134 D6
Finnvik N 127 A16
Finnvika N 124 D4
Finnygaud GB 19 K11
Fino Mornasco I 85 B7
Finowfurt D 100 E5
Finse N 116 E7
Finsjö S 105 A10
Finspång S 108 B7
Finsterwalde D 96 C5
Finsterwolde NL 33 B8
Finström FIN 115 B13
Finta RO 177 D7
Fintel D 98 D7
Fintice SK 161 E3
Fintona GB 23 D8
Fintown IRL 22 C6
Finuge IRL 24 D3
Finvoy GB 20 E4
Fiodh Ard IRL 25 D7
Fionnphort GB 20 C4
Fiorano Modense I 82 C2
Fiorenzuola d'Arda I 85 D8
Fiplingkroken N 124 F6
Fira GR 195 C9
Firenze I 82 E3
Firenzuola I 82 D3
Firlej PL 157 G7
Firmi F 49 A10
Firminy F 46 E5
Firmo I 76 D6
Fiscal E 48 E5
Fischach D 91 F8
Fischbach A 164 B5
Fischbach D 37 E8
Fischbachau D 88 A4
Fischbach bei Dahn D 43 B8
Fischbeck D 95 A11
Fischen im Allgäu D 87 C10
Fishguard GB 28 B5
Fiskå N 116 B3
Fiskardo GR 190 C2
Fiskarheden S 118 D5
Fiskari FIN 143 E10
Fiskebäckskil S 107 C9
Fiskebøl N 126 C9
Fiskefjord N 126 C9
Fiskö FIN 142 E4
Fisksbøy N 127 C11
Fisksätra S 115 D10
Fismes F 35 F8
Fisterra E 54 C1
Fistikli TR 189 D10
Fitero E 57 D8
Fitionești RO 169 F10
Fitjar N 110 C2
Fitou F 50 E4
Fitz-James F 34 F5
Fiuggi I 78 D4
Fiumalbo I 82 D2
Fiumefreddo Bruzio I 76 E6
Fiumefreddo di Sicilia I 75 D7
Fiumicino I 78 D3
Fiunary GB 20 B5
Fivemiletown GB 23 D8
Fivizzano I 82 D1
Fix-St-Geneys F 46 E4
Fizeşu Gherlii RO 168 C3
Fjær N 124 B8
Fjäl S 122 E7
Fjälkinge S 104 C6
Fjäll S 112 C7
Fjällåkern S 123 E14
Fjällåsen S 132 C4
Fjällbacka S 107 D9
Fjällnäs S 118 A3
Fjällsjö S 123 D10
Fjällsjönäs S 125 D12
Fjärås Kyrkby S 107 E11
Fjärdhundra S 114 C7
Fjätervålen S 118 C5
Fjell N 110 B2
Fjellbu N 127 C12
Fjelldal N 127 C12
Fjelle N 121 C10
Fjellerup DK 102 B7
Fjellnes N 127 C15
Fjellstad N 127 C15
Fjelsø DK 102 B4
Fjelsted DK 102 E6
Fjelstervang DK 102 C3
Fjelstrup DK 102 E5
Fjennneslev DK 103 E9
Fjerritslev DK 102 A4
Fjone N 106 A3
Fjordgard N 127 A14
Fjørvikan N 120 E4
Fjugesta S 108 A5
Flå N 111 B10
Flachau A 89 B7
Flachsmere D 33 B8
Fladungen D 91 A7
Flagnac F 49 A10
Flaine F 47 C10
Flaka FIN 115 B14
Flakaberg S 132 E7
Flakaträsk S 123 C15
Flakaträsk S 125 E12
Flakk N 120 E8
Flakkebjerg DK 103 E8
Flakstad N 127 B13
Flåm N 116 E6
Flamanville F 39 A8
Flåmânzi RO 169 B9
Flamborough GB 27 C11

Flamouria GR 185 C7
Flampouro GR 185 C10
Flärke S 123 D16
Flarken S 134 F5
Flästa S 119 D11
Flåten N 128 D6
Flatåbø N 110 B4
Flåten N 121 B12
Flatтраск S 134 D6
Flatval N 120 D5
Flauenskjold DK 102 A6
Flavigny-sur-Moselle F 42 C5
Flavigny-sur-Ozerain F 41 E12
Flavin F 50 B4
Flawil CH 43 F11
Flayosc F 52 D4
Flechtingen D 95 B9
Flecken Zechlin D 99 D13
Fleet GB 31 E7
Fleetmark D 99 E10
Fleetwood GB 26 D5
Flein D 43 B11
Flekkefjord N 110 F5
Flémalle B 35 C11
Flen S 109 A9
Flensburg D 98 A6
Flenstad N 120 D8
Fleringe S 109 D13
Flermoen N 118 D4
Flerohopp S 105 B9
Fléron B 35 C12
Flers F 39 C10
Flers-en-Escrebieux F 198 D2
Flesberg N 111 C10
Flesnes N 127 C10
Flessau D 99 E11
Flesvik N 120 E6
Fleurance F 49 C7
Fleuré F 45 C7
Fleurie F 46 B6
Fleurier CH 47 B10
Fleurus B 35 D10
Fleury F 50 D5
Fleury-les-Aubrais F 40 E6
Fleury-sur-Andelle F 34 F3
Fléville-Lixières F 35 F12
Flieden D 90 B6
Fließ A 87 C11
Flimby GB 21 F9
Flims CH 87 D8
Flines-lez-Raches F 198 D2
Flint GB 26 E5
Flintbek D 99 B8
Flirey F 42 C4
Flisa N 118 E3
Flisby S 108 D5
Fliseryd S 105 A10
Flix E 58 E5
Flixecourt F 34 D5
Flize F 35 E10
Floby S 107 C13
Floda S 107 D11
Floda S 113 A12
Flodden GB 21 E10
Flogned S 112 C7
Floh D 95 E7
Floing F 35 E10
Floirac F 44 F4
Flokenes N 116 D2
Floq AL 184 C4
Flor S 119 B9
Florac F 51 B6
Florange F 36 F6
Floreffe B 35 D10
Florennes B 35 D10
Florenville B 35 E11
Flores de Ávila E 61 C10
Floresta I 75 D6
Florești MD 169 B12
Florești RO 168 D3
Florești RO 175 D10
Florești RO 177 C7
Florești-Stoenești RO 177 E7
Floriada GR 190 A3
Florida de Liébana E 61 B9
Floridia I 75 E7
Florina GR 184 C5
Florinas I 80 B2
Florø N 116 C2
Flörsbach D 90 B5
Flörsheim am Main D 203 A5
Flörsheim-Dalsheim D 203 B5
Flosjöhyttan S 113 C12
Flossenbürg D 91 C11
Flöthe D 95 B7
Flötningen S 118 C3
Flötuträsk S 134 D5
Floure F 49 D9
Flovika N 126 D8
Fluberg N 117 E12
Flüelen CH 87 D7
Flühli CH 86 D6
Flumeri I 76 A4
Fluminimaggiore I 80 E2
Flums CH 43 F11
Fluren S 119 C11
Flurkmark S 138 C4
Flussio I 80 C2
Fly DK 102 C4
Flyggsjö S 123 D15
Flyinge S 103 D12
Flykälen S 122 D8
Flyn S 123 D10
Fobello I 68 B5
Foča BIH 173 F10
Foça TR 193 B8
Focant B 35 D11
Fochabers GB 19 K10
Focşani RO 169 F10
Focuri RO 169 C10
Foëcy F 40 F7
Foeni RO 175 B6
Foggia I 79 E9
Foglianise I 76 A3
Föglö FIN 115 B14
Fohnsdorf A 89 B10
Fohrde D 95 B11
Föhren D 37 E7
Foiano della Chiana I 82 F4
Foieni RO 167 B9
Foinikounta GR 194 B2
Foix F 49 E9
Fojnica BIH 173 E8
Foktő H 165 C11
Földeák H 166 E6
Földes H 167 C7
Fole DK 102 E4

Fole S 109 D13
Folegandros GR 195 B8
Folgarìa I 85 B11
Folgoso de Courel E 54 C5
Folgoso de la Ribera E 55 C7
Folia GR 186 C6
Folignano I 78 B5
Foligno I 78 B3
Folkestad N 116 B4
Folkestone GB 31 E11
Folkingham GB 27 F11
Follafoss N 121 D10
Folldal N 117 B12
Follebu N 117 D12
Føllenslev DK 103 D8
Follina I 88 E5
Follingbo S 109 D12
Föllinge S 122 D7
Follonica I 81 B3
Folly Gate GB 28 D6
Fölsbyn S 112 D7
Folschviller F 42 B6
Foltești RO 171 B2
Fonàltika GR 190 D3
Fondevila E 54 E3
Fondi I 78 E4
Fondón E 71 F7
Föne S 119 C10
Föneşo S 119 C12
Fonelas E 71 E6
Fonfría E 55 E7
Fonfría E 58 E1
Fønhus N 117 E11
Fonni I 80 C3
Fonroque F 45 F6
Fonsorbes F 49 C8
Fontaine F 43 E6
Fontaine F 47 E8
Fontainebleau F 41 D8
Fontaine-Française F 42 E3
Fontaine-le-Bourg F 34 E2
Fontaine-le-Dun F 34 E2
Fontaine-lès-Dijon F 42 E3
Fontaine-lès-Luxeuil F 42 E5
Fontaine-l'Évêque B 35 D9
Fontainemore I 84 B4
Fontaines F 41 E9
Fontaines F 46 B6
Fontan F 53 C7
Fontanar E 63 C6
Fontanarejo E 62 F3
Fontane I 53 C7
Fontanelice I 82 D3
Fontanellato I 82 C1
Fontanès F 51 C7
Fontanigorda I 53 B10
Fontanosas I 76 B3
Fontecchio I 78 C5
Fonte Díaz E 54 B3
Fontellas E 57 D8
Fontenay-le-Comte F 44 C4
Fontenilles F 49 C8
Fontenoy F 41 E9
Fontenoy-le-Château F 42 E5
Fontes P 60 D5
Fontevraud-l'Abbaye F 39 F12
Fontiveros E 62 C3
Font-Romeu-Odeillo-Via F 49 E10
Fontstown IRL 23 F9
Fontvieille F 51 C8
Fonyód H 165 C9
Fonz E 58 C4
Fonzaso I 88 D4
Foppolo I 85 A8
Forano I 78 C3
Forăşti RO 169 C8
Forbach D 43 C9
Forbach F 43 B6
Förby FIN 142 E8
Forcall E 58 F3
Forcalquier F 51 C10
Forcarei E 54 C3
Force I 78 B4
Forchheim D 91 C9
Forchtenberg D 203 A6
Forchtenstein A 165 A6
Ford GB 20 C6
Ford GB 21 D12
Ford IRL 25 C10
Førde N 110 C2
Førde N 116 D2
Förderstedt D 95 C10
Fordham GB 31 C9
Fordingbridge GB 29 D11
Fordongianus I 80 D2
Fordoun GB 21 B12
Fore N 124 B8
Foreneset N 110 D4
Forenza I 76 B5
Føresvik N 110 D2
Forfar GB 21 B11
Forges-les-Eaux F 34 E4
Forgie GB 19 K10
Forino I 76 B3
Forio I 78 F5
Föritz D 91 B9
Forjães P 54 E2
Forkhill GB 23 D10
Førland N 110 F5
Forlev DK 103 E8
Forlì I 82 D5
Forlimpopoli I 82 D5
Formazza I 84 B5
Formby GB 26 D5
Formello I 78 C3
Formerie F 34 E4
Formia I 78 E5
Formiche Alto I 64 D3
Formicola I 76 A2
Formigine I 82 C2
Formigliana I 84 C5
Formignana I 82 C4
Formiguères F 49 E10
Formofoss N 121 C12
Fornåsa S 108 C6
Fornelli I 80 A1
Fornells E 73 A13
Fornells de la Selva E 59 D9
Fornes N 127 C10
Fornes N 127 D11
Forni Avoltri I 89 C6
Forni di Sopra I 88 D6
Forni di Sotto I 89 D6
Forno Alpi Graie I 47 E11
Forno di Zoldo I 88 D5
Fornos P 61 B7
Fornos de Algodres P 60 C5
Fornovo du Taro I 82 C1
Foros de Vale Figueira P 66 B3
Foros do Arrão P 60 F4
Forotic RO 175 D9

Forøy N 124 C6
Forra N 127 D13
Forráskút H 166 E4
Forres GB 19 K9
Forró H 161 G3
Fors S 114 B6
Fors S 123 E11
Fors S 123 E15
Forså N 127 C12
Forså N 127 D11
Forsand N 110 E4
Forsåsen S 122 D7
Forsbäck S 125 E9
Forsbacka S 119 E14
Forsbacken N 127 C14
Forsby FIN 138 C9
Forsby FIN 143 E14
Forserum S 108 D4
Forset S 127 C15
Forshaga S 113 C9
Forshed S 134 B8
Forsheda S 103 A13
Forsholm S 123 B16
Forsinard GB 19 J9
Forsland N 124 C6
Førslev DK 103 C11
Forsmark S 115 B10
Forsmark S 125 F11
Formo S 123 E12
Forsnäs S 125 E12
Forsnäs S 125 E13
Forsnäs S 135 E9
Forsnes N 120 E4
Forsøl N 129 B8
Forsse S 123 E11
Forssjö S 109 B8
Forst D 37 C7
Forstinning D 91 F10
Forsträskhed S 134 B8
Forsvik S 108 B5
Fortanete E 58 F2
Fort Augustus GB 18 L7
Forter GB 21 B10
Fortezza I 88 C4
Forth GB 21 D9
Fortios P 60 F6
Fort-Mahon-Plage F 34 C4
Fortrose GB 19 K8
Fortuna E 72 E2
Fortuneswell GB 29 D10
Fort William GB 20 B6
Forvik N 124 C5
Fos F 49 E7
Fosdinovo I 85 E9
Foskros S 118 B4
Foskvallen S 118 C4
Fosnavåg N 116 B3
Fosnesvågen N 121 B10
Fossacesia I 79 B7
Fossato di Vico I 83 F6
Fossby S 107 A13
Fosse N 110 E4
Fosser N 111 C14
Fosses-la-Ville B 35 D10
Fossheim N 128 D5
Fossiat F 47 C7
Fossing N 106 B5
Fossmork N 110 E4
Fossombrone I 83 E6
Fos-sur-Mer F 51 D8
Fót H 166 B3
Fotherby GB 27 E11
Fotinovo BG 181 F9
Fotolivos GR 186 B6
Foucarmont F 34 E4
Fouesnant F 38 E3
Foug F 42 C4
Fougères F 39 D9
Fougerolles F 42 E5
Fougerolles-du-Plessis F 39 D10
Fouilloy F 34 E4
Foulain F 42 D3
Foulayronnes F 49 B7
Fountain Cross IRL 24 C4
Fouras F 44 D3
Fourcès F 49 C6
Fourchambault F 46 A3
Four Mile Bridge GB 26 E2
Fourfouras GR 194 E8
Fourmies F 35 D10
Fourna GR 190 A4
Fournels F 46 F3
Fournes GR 194 E6
Fournoi GR 193 D7
Fourques F 50 D4
Fourques F 51 C8
Fours F 46 B3
Foustani GR 185 B7
Fownhope GB 29 B9
Foxdale GBM 26 F2
Foxford IRL 22 E4
Foxhall IRL 22 E4
Foygh IRL 23 F7
Foynes IRL 24 C4
Foz E 54 A5
Foz P 60 F3
Foz do Arelho P 60 F2
Foz Giraldo P 60 E5
Frabosa Soprana I 53 C7
Fracki PL 160 F6
Frades de la Sierra E 61 C9
Fraga E 58 D4
Fragagnano I 77 C8
Fraham A 92 F6
Frailes E 69 B9
Fraire B 35 D7
Fraize F 43 D7
Frameries B 35 D8
Framlev DK 102 C6
Framlingham GB 31 C11
Frammersbach D 203 A7
Främmestad S 107 C12
Frampol PL 160 B6
Frampton GB 27 F11
Francavilla al Mare I 79 C6
Francavilla Fontana I 77 C8
Francavilla in Sinni I 76 C6
Francescas F 49 B6
Frâncești RO 176 C4
Franco P 54 F5
Francofonte I 75 E6
Francorchamps B 36 D5
Francoulès F 49 A8

Francova Lhota CZ 162 C6
Frändefors S 107 C11
Franeker NL 32 B5
Frangy F 47 C9
Frankenau D 37 B11
Frankenberg D 96 E4
Frankenberg (Eder) D 37 B11
Frankenburg am Hausruck A 92 F4
Frankenfels A 93 G8
Frankenheim D 91 A7
Frankenmarkt A 92 G4
Frankenthal (Pfalz) D 37 E10
Frankfurt am Main D 37 D11
Frankfurt an der Oder D 97 B7
Frankowo PL 152 C2
Frankrike S 121 D15
Fränö S 119 A14
Franois F 42 F4
Fränsta S 119 A11
Františkovy Lázně CZ 91 B11
Franzburg D 99 B13
Frascati I 78 D3
Frascineto I 76 D6
Fraserburgh GB 19 K12
Frasin MD 169 A11
Frasin RO 169 B7
Fräsinet RO 177 E8
Frasne F 47 B9
Frasnes-lez-Buissenal B 35 C8
Frasnes-lez-Gosselies B 35 C9
Frassinoro I 82 D2
Frasso Telesino I 76 A3
Frastanz A 87 C9
Frata RO 168 D4
Frătăuții Noi RO 169 B7
Frătăuții Vechi RO 169 B7
Fratel P 60 E5
Frătești RO 177 F7
Fratta Polesine I 82 B4
Fratta Todina I 78 B2
Fraubrunnen CH 47 A12
Frauenau D 92 E14
Frauenfeld CH 43 E10
Frauenkirchen A 93 G11
Frauental an der Laßnitz A 164 C4
Frauenwald D 95 E8
Frauenberg D 91 F10
Frayssinet-le-Gélat F 49 A8
Frečăței RO 171 C3
Frečăței RO 171 D2
Frechas P 54 F5
Frechen D 37 C7
Frechilla E 55 D10
Freckleton GB 26 D6
Fredensborg DK 103 D10
Fredericia DK 102 E5
Frederiks DK 102 C4
Frederiksberg DK 103 D11
Frederiksberg DK 103 E9
Frederikshavn DK 106 E8
Frederikssund DK 103 D10
Frederiksværk DK 103 D10
Fredrika S 123 C14
Fredriksberg S 113 B11
Fredriksdal S 108 D5
Fredrikstad N 107 A8
Freemount IRL 24 D5
Fregenal de la Sierra E 67 C6
Fregene I 78 D2
Freginals E 58 F5
Fréhel F 39 C7
Freiberg D 96 E4
Freiberg (Elbe) D 33 A12
Freiburg im Breisgau D 43 D8
Freiensteinau D 90 B5
Freienwill D 98 A6
Freihung D 91 C10
Freila E 71 D7
Freilassing D 89 A6
Freinsheim D 203 B5
Freisen D 37 E8
Freising D 91 F10
Freissinières F 47 F10
Freistadt A 93 C11
Freistatt D 33 C11
Freistroff F 36 F6
Freital D 96 E5
Freixedas P 61 C6
Freixianda P 60 E4
Freixiosa P 60 C5
Freixo P 54 F4
Fréjairolles F 49 C10
Frejlev DK 102 A5
Frejlev DK 102 E7
Frösö S 122 E7
Frekhaug N 110 A2
Fremdingen D 91 E7
Fremington GB 28 C6
Frenchpark IRL 22 E6
Frencq F 31 F12
Frensdorf D 91 C8
Frenštát pod Radhoštěm CZ 162 B6
Freren D 33 D9
Fresach A 89 C8
Fresagrandinaria I 79 D7
Freshford IRL 25 C8
Freshwater GB 29 D11
Fresne-Saint-Mamès F 42 E4
Fresneda de la Sierra E 63 D8
Fresnedoso de Ibor E 61 E9
Fresnes-en-Woëvre F 42 B4
Fresnes-sur-Apance F 42 E4
Fresnes-sur-Escaut F 198 E3
Fresno Alhándiga E 61 C9
Fresno de la Ribera E 55 E8
Fresno de Sayago E 55 E8
Fresno el Viejo E 61 B10
Fresnoy-Folny F 34 E3
Fresnoy-le-Grand F 35 E7
Fresse-sur-Moselle F 42 E5
Fressingfield GB 31 C11
Fresvik N 116 D6
Freswick GB 19 H10
Fretigney-et-Velloreille F 42 F4
Freudenberg D 203 B7
Freudenberg D 43 D7
Freudenstadt D 43 D9
Frévent F 34 D5
Freyburg (Unstrut) D 95 D10
Freyenstein D 99 D12
Freyming-Merlebach F 43 B6
Freyung D 92 E14
Friarfjorden N 129 C18
Friárias P 54 E4
Frías E 56 C5

Fribourg CH 47 B11
Frick CH 43 E9
Fríčovce SK 161 E2
Fridafors S 104 C7
Fridalen N 125 B9
Fridaythorpe GB 27 C10
Fridingen an der Donau D 43 D10
Fridlevstad S 105 C9
Fridolfing D 92 G3
Frieda (Meinhard) D 95 D7
Friedberg A 164 B6
Friedberg D 91 F8
Friedberg (Hessen) D 37 D11
Friedburg (Saale) D 95 C10
Friedenfels D 91 C11
Friedersdorf D 95 C11
Friedersdorf D 96 B5
Friedewald D 94 E6
Friedewald D 201 C8
Friedland D 94 D6
Friedland D 96 B6
Friedland D 100 C5
Friedrichroda D 95 E8
Friedrichsbrunn D 95 C8
Friedrichsdorf D 203 A6
Friedrichshafen D 87 B9
Friedrichskoog D 98 B5
Friedrichstadt D 98 B5
Friedrichswalde D 100 D5
Frielendorf D 37 C12
Friemar D 95 E8
Friesach A 89 C9
Friesack D 99 E12
Friesenhagen D 201 C8
Friesenheim D 43 D8
Friesenried D 87 B11
Friesoythe D 33 B9
Frifelt DK 102 E4
Frigento I 76 A4
Friggesund S 119 C12
Frigiliana E 69 C9
Frihetsli N 127 C15
Friitala FIN 142 C6
Frikes GR 190 C2
Frikstad N 106 B2
Frillesås S 107 E11
Frinnaryd S 108 D5
Frinton-on-Sea GB 31 D11
Friockheim GB 21 B11
Friol E 54 B4
Frisange L 36 E6
Fristad S 107 D13
Fritsla S 107 D12
Fritzens A 88 B4
Fritzlar D 37 B12
Friville-Escarbotin F 34 D4
Frizington GB 26 B5
Frŏdba FO 18 B3
Frödinge S 108 D8
Frodsham GB 26 E6
Frœschwiller F 202 D4
Froges F 47 E8
Frogmore GB 31 E7
Frohburg D 95 D12
Frohnleiten A 164 B4
Froidconche F 42 E4
Froissy F 34 E5
Frójel S 109 E12
Froland N 106 B4
Frolosh BG 181 E6
Frombork PL 155 B8
Frome GB 29 D10
Fromelennes F 200 D2
Fromentine F 44 B1
Frómista E 56 D3
Fröndenberg D 33 F9
Fronhausen D 37 C11
Fronsac F 44 F5
Fronsac F 49 E7
Fronteira P 60 F5
Frontenard F 47 B7
Frontenay-Rohan-Rohan F 44 C4
Frontenhausen D 91 E12
Frontignan F 51 D6
Fronton F 49 C8
Frösakull S 103 B11
Frose D 95 C9
Fröseke S 105 B9
Frosinone I 78 D4
Frosta N 121 D9
Frostadheia N 128 D4
Frøstrup DK 102 A3
Frouard F 42 C5
Frövi S 113 D13
Frufällan S 107 D12
Fruges F 34 C5
Frumoara RO 169 E7
Frumoasa RO 177 F6
Frumosu RO 169 B7
Frumuşani RO 177 E8
Frumușica RO 169 B9
Frumuşiţa RO 171 B2
Frunzivka UA 170 D5
Frutigen CH 86 D5
Fry GR 197 F5
Frýdek-Místek CZ 162 B6
Frýdlant CZ 97 E8
Frýdlant nad Ostravicí CZ 162 B6
Frygnowo PL 155 C9
Fryksås S 118 D8
Frymburk CZ 92 E6
Fryšták CZ 162 C5
Frysztak PL 160 D5
Fubine I 53 B8
Fucecchio I 82 E2
Fuchstal D 87 B11
Fuencaliente E 70 C4
Fuendejalón E 57 E9
Fuengirola E 69 C7
Fuenmayor E 57 D6
Fuensalida E 62 D4
Fuensanta E 63 E7
Fuensanta E 71 D9
Fuensanta de Martos E 69 A9
Fuente-Álamo E 71 F8
Fuente Álamo E 72 F2
Fuentealbilla E 63 E9
Fuentecambrón E 56 E5
Fuentecén E 56 E4
Fuente de Cantos E 67 C7
Fuente del Arco E 67 C8
Fuente del Maestre E 67 B7

Fuente de Pedro Naharro E 63 E6
Fuente de Piedra E 69 B7
Fuente el Fresno E 62 F5
Fuente el Saz de Jarama E 62 C6
Fuente el Sol E 62 B3
Fuenteguinaldo E 61 D7
Fuentelapeña E 55 F9
Fuentelcésped E 56 E4
Fuentelespino de Haro E 63 E7
Fuentelespino de Moya E 63 E10
Fuentelmonge E 57 F7
Fuentenovilla E 63 D6
Fuente Obejuna E 67 C9
Fuentepalmera E 69 A6
Fuentepelayo E 62 B4
Fuentepinilla E 56 E6
Fuenterodos E 57 F10
Fuenterrebollo E 56 F4
Fuenterroble de Salvatierra E 61 C9
Fuentesaúco E 61 B10
Fuentesaúco de Fuentidueña E 56 F3
Fuentes-Claras E 63 C10
Fuentes de Andalucía E 67 E9
Fuentes de Ebro E 57 E10
Fuentes de Jiloca E 57 F8
Fuentes de León E 67 C6
Fuentes de Nava E 55 D10
Fuentes de Oñoro E 61 C7
Fuentes de Ropel E 55 E8
Fuentespalda E 58 F4
Fuente-Tójar E 69 A8
Fuente Vaqueros E 69 B9
Fuentidueña E 56 F4
Fuerte del Rey E 69 A9
Fuertescusa E 63 D8
Fügen A 88 B4
Fuglafjørður FO 18 A3
Fugleberg N 127 C12
Fuglebjerg DK 103 E8
Fuglstad N 121 A13
Fuhrberg (Burgwedel) D 94 A6
Fulda D 90 A6
Fulford GB 27 D9
Fulga RO 177 D10
Fulham GB 31 E8
Fullbro S 109 A11
Fulnek CZ 162 B5
Fülöp H 167 B9
Fülöpháza H 166 D3
Fülöpszállás H 166 D3
Fulunäs S 118 A4
Fundada P 60 E4
Fundão P 60 D6
Fundata RO 176 C6
Fundeni RO 177 B11
Fundeni RO 177 E8
Funder Kirkeby DK 102 C4
Fundulea RO 177 E9
Fundu Moldovei RO 168 B6
Funes E 48 F2
Funes I 88 C4
Funzie GB 19 D15
Furadouro P 60 C3
Furceni MD 170 C3
Furci I 79 C7
Furci Siculo I 75 D7
Furiani I 75 C7
Furnace GB 20 C6
Furnari I 75 C7
Furraleigh IRL 25 D8
Fürstenau D 33 C9
Fürstenberg D 37 A12
Fürstenberg D 100 D4
Fürstenberg (Lichtenfels) D 37 B11
Fürstenfeld A 164 B6
Fürstenfeldbruck D 91 F9
Fürstenwalde D 96 B6
Fürstenwerder D 100 D5
Fürstenzell D 92 E4
Furta H 167 C7
Furtan S 113 C8
Furtei I 80 D2
Fürth D 37 E11
Fürth D 91 B8
Fürth D 91 E11
Furth bei Göttweig A 93 F9
Furth im Wald D 92 D3
Furtwangen im Schwarzwald D 43 D9
Furuberg S 119 B12
Furuby S 105 B8
Furudal N 127 B16
Furudal S 119 D9
Furudals bruk S 119 D9
Furuflaten N 127 B19
Furugrund S 134 E6
Furusjö S 107 E10
Furusund S 115 C11
Furutangvika N 121 B14
Furuvik S 119 E13
Fusa N 110 B3
Fuscaldo I 76 E6
Fushë-Arrëz AL 179 E9
Fushë-Bardhe AL 184 D3
Fushë-Krujë AL 184 B2
Fushë-Kuqe AL 184 A2
Fusignano I 82 D4
Fußach A 87 C9
Füssen D 87 B11
Fussy F 41 F7
Fustiñana E 57 D9
Futeau F 42 B3
Futog SRB 174 C4
Futrikelva N 127 A17
Füzesabony H 166 B5
Füzesgyarmat H 167 C7
Fužine HR 83 B10
Fyfield GB 31 D9
Fylaki GR 185 F8
Fyli GR 191 C8
Fyllinge S 103 B11
Fyllo GR 185 F7
Fynshav DK 102 F5
Fyrås S 122 D8
Fyrde N 116 B4
Fyresdal N 106 A3
Fyteies GR 190 B3
Fyvie GB 19 L12

G

Gaal A 89 B10
Gaanderen NL 199 B8

Gabaldón E 63 E9
Gabare BG 181 C8
Gabarret F 48 C6
Gabčíkovo SK 162 F5
Gabela BIH 173 F8
Gabér BG 181 D6
Gabia la Grande E 69 B9
Gabicce Mare I 83 E6
Gabin PL 155 F8
Gablenz D 91 F8
Gablingen D 91 F8
Gablitz A 93 F10
Gáborján H 167 C8
Gabriac F 50 B4
Gabrnik SLO 164 D5
Gabrovnitsa BG 181 B7
Gabrovo BG 182 D4
Gaby I 84 B4
Gać PL 160 C5
Gacé F 39 C12
Gacko BIH 173 F10
Gåda S 119 B10
Gadbjerg DK 102 D4
Gäddede S 121 B16
Gäddträsk S 123 C15
Gadebusch D 99 C10
Gadmen CH 86 D5
Gadoni I 80 D3
Gádor E 71 F8
Gádoros H 166 D6
Gadstrup DK 103 D10
Gadžin Han SRB 180 C5
Gaeiras P 60 E2
Gærum DK 106 D7
Găeşti RO 177 D7
Gaeta I 78 E5
Gafanha da Boa Hora P 60 C3
Gafanha da Nazaré P 60 C3
Gafanha do Carmo P 60 C3
Gafanhoeira P 66 B3
Gáfete P 60 F5
Gafsele S 123 C12
Gaganitsa BG 181 C7
Găgeşti RO 169 E11
Gaggenau D 43 C9
Gaggi I 75 D7
Gaggio Montano I 82 D2
Gaglianico I 84 B5
Gagliano Castelferrato I 75 D6
Gagliano del Capo I 77 D10
Gagnef S 119 E9
Gagnières F 51 B7
Gagsmark S 134 C6
Găiceana RO 169 E10
Gaigalava LV 149 C2
Gaildorf D 90 E6
Gailīši LV 149 D7
Gaillac F 49 C9
Gaillac-d'Aveyron F 50 B4
Gaillard F 47 C9
Gaillimh IRL 22 F4
Gaillon F 40 B5
Gaimersheim D 91 E9
Gaiole in Chianti I 82 F3
Gaios GR 190 A1
Gairloch GB 18 K5
Gairo I 80 D4
Gais CH 87 C8
Gais I 88 C4
Găiseni RO 177 D7
Gaishorn A 89 A10
Gaismas LV 151 C8
Gaj SRB 175 D7
Gajanejos E 63 C7
Gajary SK 93 F11
Gakovo SRB 166 F3
Galåbodarna S 118 A6
Galambok H 165 C8
Galan F 49 D6
Gălăneşti RO 169 B7
Gălăniitu N 128 F10
Galanta SK 162 E5
Galapagar E 62 C5
Galaroza E 67 D6
Galashiels GB 21 D11
Galашiels GB 21 D11
Galasjö S 123 C14
Galata BG 183 C9
Galatades GR 185 C7
Galatas GR 191 E7
Galatas GR 191 E7
Gălăteni RO 176 E6
Galați RO 171 C2
Galați Bistriţei RO 168 D4
Galati Mamertino I 75 C6
Galatin BG 181 C8
Galatina I 77 C10
Galatini GR 185 C5
Galatista S 185 D9
Galatone I 77 C10
Gălăuţaş RO 168 D5
Galaxidi GR 190 C5
Galbally IRL 24 D6
Galbarra E 48 E1
Galbenu RO 177 C10
Gălberget S 123 D18
Galbún RO 177 C10
Galda de Jos RO 168 E3
Gâldău RO 177 E11
Gál'din N 129 E12
Galeata I 82 E4
Galende E 55 D6
Galēni LV 151 D13
Galera E 71 D7
Galéria F 53 G9
Găleşti RO 168 E5
Galewice PL 158 D5
Galgagyörk H 166 B4
Galgahévíz H 166 B4
Gâlgău RO 168 C3
Galgon F 44 F5

Gallin D 99 C12
Gallio I 88 E4
Gallipoli I 77 D10
Gällivare S 132 D5
Gallizien A 89 C10
Gallneukirchen A 92 F6
Gällö S 119 A9
Gällstad S 107 D13
Galluccio I 76 A1
Gallur E 57 E9
Galovo BG 176 F4
Galros IRL 23 F7
Galston GB 21 D8
Galten DK 102 C5
Galterud N 112 B6
Gâltjärn S 119 A13
Gâltjärn S 119 A14
Galtström S 119 B13
Galtür A 87 D10
Galve E 63 C10
Galve de Sorbe E 63 B6
Galveias P 60 F5
Galven S 119 D11
Gálvez E 62 E4
Gama E 56 B5
Gamaches F 34 E4
Gamarde-les-Bains F 48 C4
Gamás H 165 C9
Gambara I 82 B1
Gambarie I 75 C8
Gambassi Terme I 82 E2
Gambatesa I 79 D7
Gambettola I 82 D5
Gambolò I 85 C6
Gambsheim F 43 C8
Gaming A 93 G8
Gamleby S 109 D8
Gamlingay GB 31 C8
Gamlitz I 165 C9
Gammalkroppa S 113 C11
Gammelboning S 119 E11
Gammelgården S 135 C10
Gammelgarn S 109 E13
Gammel Rye DK 102 C5
Gammelsdorf D 91 E10
Gammelstaden S 134 C8
Gammelstilla S 114 B7
Gammertingen D 43 D11
Gams CH 87 C8
Gamvik N 128 C7
Gamvik N 129 A21
Gamvik N 129 B11
Gan F 48 D5
Ganagobie F 51 B10
Gand B 35 B8
Gand B 198 C3
Gandarela P 54 F3
Gandellino I 85 B8
Ganderkesee D 33 B11
Gandesa E 58 E4
Gandesbergen D 33 C12
Gandia GR 72 D4
Gandino I 85 B8
Gandra P 54 F2
Gandrup DK 102 A6
Gandvik N 130 C6
Găneasa RO 176 E4
Găneasa RO 177 D8
Gănești RO 168 E4
Ganfei P 54 E2
Ganges F 51 C6
Gânghester S 107 D13
Gangi I 74 D5
Găngiova RO 176 F3
Gangkofen D 91 F12
Ganløse DK 103 D10
Gannat F 46 C3
Gänserndorf A 93 F11
Ganshoren B 35 C9
Gânsvik S 119 A15
Ganzlin D 99 D12
Gaoth Dobhair IRL 22 B6
Gap F 52 B4
Gaperhult S 107 B13
Gara H 166 E3
Garaballa E 63 E10
Garagarza E 48 D1
Garaguso I 76 B6
Gara Khitrino BG 183 C7
Gara Oreshets BG 175 F10
Gârbău RO 167 D11
Gârbova RO 168 F3
Gârbovi RO 177 D10
Garbów PL 157 H6
Garbsen D 94 B6
Garching an der Alz D 91 F12
Garching bei München D 91 F10
Garchizy F 46 A3
Garcia E 58 E5
Garciaz E 61 F9
Garciems LV 151 B8
Garcihernández E 61 C10
Garcillán E 62 C4
Garčin HR 157 B9
Gârcina RO 169 D8
Garcinarro E 63 D7
Gârcov RO 176 F5
Garda I 85 B10
Gârda de Sus RO 167 E10
Gardanne F 51 D9
Gârdås S 118 E6
Gårdby S 105 B11
Garde S 109 E13
Gärde S 121 D15
Gardeja PL 150 F4
Gardelegen D 95 A9
Gardenstown GB 19 K12
Garderen NL 199 A7
Gardermoen N 111 B14
Gardiki GR 190 B4
Garding D 98 B5
Gardone Riviera I 85 B10
Gardone Val Trompia I 85 B9
Gardonne F 45 F6
Gárdony H 165 B11
Gardouch F 49 D9
Gârdsjø S 108 B4
Gardsjöbäcken S 125 F12
Gardsjönäs S 125 F11
Gårdskär S 119 E9
Gårds Köpinge S 104 D6
Gardstånga S 103 D12
Gåre N 118 A1

Garein F 48 B4
Gårelehöjden S 123 D11
Garelochhead GB 20 C7
Garéoult F 52 E4
Garforth GB 27 D9
Gargaliánoi GR 190 E4
Gargáligas E 61 F9
Gargallo E 58 F2
Garganta la Olla E 61 D9
Gargazzone I 88 C3
Gargnano I 85 B10
Gargnäs S 123 A13
Gargogečče N 129 C20
Gargždai LT 150 E2
Garijp NL 32 B5
Garkalne LV 151 B8
Gârla Mare RO 175 E10
Gârleni RO 169 D9
Garlenz A 89 A10
Garliava LT 153 D8
Gârliciu RO 171 D2
Garlieston GB 21 F8
Garlin F 48 C5
Garlitos E 70 B2
Garlstorf D 99 D8
Garmisch-Partenkirchen D 88 B3
Garnes N 116 B3
Gârnic RO 175 D8
Garoafa RO 169 F11
Garons F 51 C7
Garpenberg S 114 B6
Garphyttan S 113 D12
Garrafe de Torio E 55 C8
Garralda E 48 D3
Garrane IRL 24 E4
Garray E 57 E7
Garrel D 33 C10
Garrison GB 22 D6
Garristown IRL 23 E10
Garrovillas E 61 E7
Garrucha E 71 E9
Garrynahine GB 18 J3
Garryvoe IRL 24 E6
Gars am Inn D 91 F11
Gars am Kamp A 93 E9
Garsås S 118 E8
Gârsene LV 151 D11
Gârslev DK 102 D5
Gârsnäs S 104 D7
Garstang GB 26 D6
Garstedt D 99 D8
Garsten N 120 D7
Garth GB 29 A7
Garthmyl GB 26 F5
Gartow D 99 D10
Gartringen D 43 C10
Gartz D 100 D6
Garvagh GB 20 F3
Garvagh IRL 23 E7
Garvaghy GB 23 D8
Garvald GB 21 D11
Garvamore GB 21 A8
Garvão P 66 D3
Garvard GB 20 C4
Garvary GB 23 D7
Garve GB 18 K7
Garwolin PL 157 G5
Garz D 100 B5
Gąsawa PL 154 E4
Gąşanep RO 177 E11
Gåsbakken N 120 E7
Gaschurn A 87 D10
Gascueña E 63 D7
Gåsholma S 119 D13
Gasjö S 113 B14
Gaskeluokt S 123 A11
Gåsnes N 129 A13
Gåsnes N 129 B11
Gasny F 40 B6
Gąsocin PL 155 E10
Gasperina I 75 B10
Gaspoltshofen A 92 F5
Gasselte NL 33 C7
Gasselternijveen NL 33 C7
Gassino Torinese I 84 C4
Gassjö S 119 B9
Gassum DK 102 B6
Gastellovo RUS 152 C4
Gastes F 48 B3
Gastouni GR 190 D3
Gastouri GR 184 E2
Gata E 61 D7
Gata de Gorgos E 72 D5
Gâtaia RO 175 C7
Gatchina RUS 148 B7
Gatehouse of Fleet GB 21 F8
Gátér H 166 D4
Gateshead GB 21 F13
Gátova E 64 E3
Gattendorf A 93 F11
Gatteo a Mare I 82 D5
Gattières F 53 D6
Gattinara I 84 B5
Gaubodo DK 102 D4
Gaucín E 69 C6
Gaucín E 69 C6
Gauja LV 151 B9
Găujani RO 177 F7
Gaujiena LV 147 C13
Gaukönigshofen D 90 C6
Gaulstad N 121 D12
Gau-Odernheim D 201 E9
Gauré E 61 D9
Gausvik N 127 C11
Gautestad N 106 B2
Gauting D 91 F9
Gauto S 125 D12
Gavà E 59 E8
Gavalou GR 190 B4
Gavardo I 85 B9
Gavarnie F 48 E5
Găvănoasa MD 171 B2
Gavardo P 66 D3
Gavi I 53 B9
Gavieze LV 150 C2
Gavik S 119 A15
Gavirate I 84 B6
Gävle S 119 E13
Gavoi I 80 C3
Gavorrano I 81 B3
Gavray F 39 C7

Gavrio GR 192 D4
Gavrolimni GR 190 C4
Gåvsta S 115 C9
Gaweinstal A 93 F11
Gawliki Wielkie PL 152 F5
Gaworzyce PL 97 D9
Gāxsjö S 122 D8
Gaytanovo BG 185 B10
Gayton GB 27 F13
Gazimir TR 193 C9
Gaziköy TR 189 C7
Gazioğlu TR 189 B8
Gaziosmanpaşa TR 189 B10
Gazolaz E 48 E2
Gazoldo degli Ippoliti I 82 B2
Gazoros GR 185 B10
Gazzo Veronese I 82 B3
Gazzuolo I 82 B2
Gbelce SK 163 F7
Gbely SK 93 E12
Gdańsk PL 154 B6
Gdinj HR 173 F6
Gdów PL 160 D1
Gdynia PL 154 A6
Geaca RO 168 D4
Gea de Albarracín E 63 D10
Geaidnovuohppi N 129 E12
Geamăna MD 170 D4
Geashill IRL 23 F8
Geaune F 48 C5
Gebesee D 95 D7
Gebhardshain D 37 C9
Gębice PL 101 E11
Gechingen D 203 D8
Geddington GB 31 C7
Gedern D 37 D12
Gedinne B 35 F10
Gedney Drove End GB 27 F12
Gèdre F 48 E6
Gedser DK 99 A11
Gedsted DK 102 B4
Gedved DK 102 D5
Geel B 35 B11
Geertruidenberg NL 32 E3
Geeste D 33 C8
Geesteren NL 199 A9
Geestgottberg D 99 E11
Geesthacht D 99 D8
Geetbets B 35 C11
Geffen NL 199 B6
Gefrees D 91 B10
Gefyra GR 185 C8
Gefyria GR 185 F7
Gegai AL 184 C2
Geguzinė LT 153 D9
Gehrde D 33 C10
Gehrden D 94 B6
Gehren D 95 E9
Geijersholm S 113 B10
Geilenkirchen D 36 C6
Geilo N 111 A8
Geiranger N 116 B6
Geisa D 94 E6
Geiselbach D 203 A7
Geiselhöring D 91 E11
Geiselwind D 91 C8
Geisenfeld D 91 E10
Geisenhausen D 91 F11
Geisenheim D 37 E9
Geising D 96 E5
Geisingen D 43 E10
Geislingen D 203 B6
Geislingen an der Steige D 90 E4
Geismar D 95 D7
Geisnes N 121 B11
Geispolsheim F 43 C8
Geisthal A 89 B11
Geithain D 95 D11
Geithus N 111 C11
Geitvågen N 124 B8
Gela I 74 F5
Gelbensande D 99 B12
Gelchsheim D 90 C7
Geldern D 32 E6
Geldermalsen NL 32 E4
Geldersheim D 91 B7
Geldrop NL 32 F5
Geleen NL 35 C12
Gelgaudiškis LT 152 C6
Gelibolu TR 188 D2
Gellénháza H 165 C7
Gelligaer GB 29 B8
Gelnhausen D 37 D12
Gelnica SK 161 F2
Gelos F 48 D5
Gelsa E 57 F11
Gelse I 165 C7
Gelsenkirchen D 33 C6
Gelsted DK 102 E5
Gelsted DK 103 E9
Gelsenkirchen D 33 C6
Geltendorf D 87 A12
Gelting D 99 A7
Geltow D 96 B3
Gelvonai LT 153 C10
Gembloux B 35 C10
Gemeaux F 42 F3
Gemenele RO 171 C1
Gémenos F 51 D10
Gemerská Hôrka SK 161 F1
Gemerská Poloma SK 161 F1
Gemert NL 32 E5
Gemla S 105 B8
Gemmingen D 203 C6
Gemona del Friuli I 89 D7
Gémozac F 44 D4
Gemünden D 37 E8
Gemünden am Main D 90 B6
Genappe B 35 C9
Genarp S 103 D12
Génave E 71 C7
Genazzano I 78 D3
Gençay F 45 C6
Gencsapáti H 165 B7
Gendrey F 42 F4
Gendringen NL 32 E6
Gendt NL 32 E5
Génelard F 46 B5
Genemuiden NL 32 D6
General-Inzovo BG 183 C6
General-Kolevo BG 171 F1
General Toshevo BG 171 F2
Genesin F 42 E5
Genestoso E 55 B7
Genêts F 39 C7
Genevad S 103 B12
Genève CH 47 C9
Genevilla E 48 E1
Genga I 83 F6
Gengenbach D 43 D9

Ghergheasa RO 177 C10
Gherghiţa RO 177 D8
Gherla RO 168 C3
Gherta Mică RO 161 H7
Ghidfalău RO 169 F7
Ghidigeni RO 169 E10
Ghidighiei MD 170 C3
Ghiffa I 84 B6
Ghilarza I 80 C2
Ghimbav RO 177 B7
Ghimes-Făget RO 169 D8
Ghimpaţi RO 177 E7
Ghindari RO 168 E5
Ghioroc RO 167 E8
Ghioroiu RO 176 D3
Ghiroda RO 167 F6
Ghislenghien B 35 C8
Ghisonaccia F 53 G10
Ghisoni F 53 G10
Ghizela RO 167 F8
Ghyvelde F 34 B6
Gialtra GR 191 B6
Giannades GR 184 E2
Giannitsa GR 185 C7
Giannouli GR 185 E7
Giano dell'Umbria I 78 B3
Giardinello RO 167 F7
Giardini-Naxos I 75 D7
Giarmata RO 167 F7
Giarratana I 75 E6
Giarre I 75 D7
Giave I 80 C2
Giaveno I 47 E11
Giba I 80 F2
Gibellina Nuova I 74 D2
Gibostad N 127 B15
Gibraléon E 67 E5
Gibraltar GBZ 69 D6
Giby PL 152 E7
Gibzde LV 150 B4
Gideå S 123 E15
Gideå bruk S 123 L14
Gideåkroken S 123 C12
Gidle PL 159 E7
Giebelstadt D 90 C6
Gieboldehausen D 95 C7
Gieczno PL 159 C7
Giedraičiai LT 153 C11
Gielniów PL 157 H12
Gielow D 99 C13
Gien F 41 E8
Giengen an der Brenz D 91 E7
Giera RO 175 C6
Gierle B 198 C5
Giersleben D 95 C10
Gierstädt D 95 D8
Gierzwałd PL 155 C9
Gießen D 37 C11
Gieten NL 33 B7
Gietrzwałd PL 155 C9
Gièvres F 40 F6
Giffnock GB 21 D8
Gifford GB 21 C11
Gifhorn D 95 B8
Gigean F 51 C6
Gigen BG 176 F4
Gighera RO 176 F3
Giglio Castello I 81 C3
Gignac F 51 C6
Gignac F 51 C10
Gignod F 47 C10
Gijón-Xixón E 55 A8
Gikši LV 151 B10
Gîlău RO 167 D11
Gilching D 91 F9
Gilena E 69 B7
Gilette F 53 D6
Gilford GB 23 D10
Gillberga S 113 C10
Gilleleje DK 103 C10
Gillenfeld D 37 D7
Gillhov S 118 A8
Gillingham GB 29 C10
Gillingham GB 31 C6
Gilling West GB 27 C8
Gilly-sur-Isère F 47 D9
Gilly-sur-Loire F 46 B4
Gilmerton GB 21 C9
Gilså N 121 E11
Gilserberg D 37 C12
Gilsland GB 21 F11
Gilten D 98 E7
Gilwern GB 29 B8
Gilze NL 32 E3
Gimât S 123 E15
Gimdalen S 119 A10
Gimigliano I 75 B10
Gimo S 115 B10
Gimont F 49 C7
Gimouille F 46 B3
Gimsøy N 126 F3
Ginasservis F 51 C10
Ginestas F 50 D4
Gingelom B 35 C11
Gingen an der Fils D 203 D8
Gingst D 100 B4
Ginkūnai LT 150 E6
Ginoles F 49 E10
Ginosa I 77 B7
Ginostra I 75 B7
Ginsheim D 201 E9
Gintsi BG 181 C7
Giões P 66 D4
Gioi I 76 C4
Gioia dei Marsi I 78 D5
Gioia del Colle I 77 B7
Gioia Sannitica I 76 A2
Gioia Tauro I 75 C8
Gioiosa Ionica I 75 C9
Gioiosa Marea I 75 C6
Giornico I 87 A7
Giovinazzo I 77 A7
Gipka S/rva I 146 F5
Giraltovce SK 161 E4
Girancourt F 42 D5
Girasole I 80 D4
Girifalco I 75 B9
Girişu de Criş RO 167 C8
Girkalnis LT 150 E6
Giroc RO 175 B7
Giromagny F 43 E6
Girona E 59 C9
Gironde-sur-Dropt F 48 A5
Gironella E 59 C7
Giroussens F 49 C9
Girov RO 169 D8
Girvan GB 20 E7
Gislaved S 104 A5
Gislev DK 102 E7
Gislinge DK 103 D9
Gislövs strandmark S 103 E13
Gisloy N 126 C9
Gisors F 34 F4
Gissi I 79 C7

Gisslarbo S 113 C14
Gistad S 108 C7
Gistel B 34 B6
Gistrup DK 102 B5
Giswil CH 86 D6
Gittelde D 95 C7
Gittun S 125 D16
Giubega RO 176 E2
Giubiasco CH 85 A7
Giugliano in Campania I 76 B2
Giuleşti RO 168 B3
Giulianova I 78 B5
Giulvăz RO 175 B6
Giuncugnano I 82 D1
Giurgeni RO 177 D1
Giurgiţa RO 176 E3
Giurgiu RO 177 F7
Giurgiuleşti MD 171 C2
Giuvărăşti RO 176 F5
Give DK 102 D4
Givet F 35 D10
Givors F 46 D6
Givry B 35 D9
Givry F 46 B6
Givry-en-Argonne F 41 C12
Givskud DK 102 D4
Gizai LT 152 D7
Gizafki PL 158 B4
Gizeux F 39 F12
Giżycko PL 152 E4
Gizzeria I 75 B9
Gjærnes N 106 B5
Gjegjan AL 179 E9
Gjegjan AL 179 F9
Gjengstø N 120 E6
Gjerde N 116 C6
Gjerdebakken N 129 C11
Gjerdrum N 111 B14
Gjerlev DK 102 B6
Gjermungshamn N 110 B3
Gjern DK 102 C5
Gjerrild DK 103 C7
Gjerstad N 106 B5
Gjersvik N 121 B14
Gjesing DK 102 C6
Gjesvær N 129 A15
Gjevaldshaugen N 117 D15
Gjirokastër AL 184 D3
Gjógv FO 18 A3
Gjøl DK 102 A5
Gjøljelia N 120 D7
Gjølme N 120 E7
Gjonëm AL 184 A2
Gjøra N 117 A10
Gjorm AL 184 D2
Gjøvåg N 110 B2
Gjøvik N 117 E13
Gjuvberget N 118 E3
Gkoritsa GR 191 E6
Gladbeck D 33 D7
Gladenbach D 37 C11
Gladsaxe DK 103 D10
Gladstad N 124 E2
Glainans F 42 F6
Glamis GB 21 B11
Glamoč BIH 173 D6
Glåmos N 117 A14
Glamsbjerg DK 102 E6
Glandage F 51 A10
Glandon F 45 E8
Glandore IRL 24 E4
Glandorf D 33 D10
Glanegg A 89 C9
Glanerbrug NL 33 D7
Glanshammar S 113 D13
Glanworth IRL 24 D6
Glarryford GB 20 F4
Glarus CH 87 C8
Glasbury GB 29 A8
Glasgow GB 21 D8
Gläshütten D 37 D10
Glashütten D 91 C9
Glaslough IRL 23 D9
Glassan IRL 23 F7
Glastonbury GB 29 C9
Glaubitz D 96 D4
Glauchau D 95 E12
Glava BG 181 C9
Glava S 113 C8
Glava glasbruk S 112 C7
Glavan BG 182 E6
Glăvăneşti RO 169 E10
Glavanovtsi BG 180 D6
Glavatičevo BIH 173 F9
Glavice HR 173 E6
Glavičice BIH 173 C11
Glăvile RO 176 D3
Glavinitsa BG 177 F9
Glavki GR 187 B7
Glavnik SRB 180 E3
Gleann Cholm Cille GB 22 C5
Gleann Doimhin IRL 23 C7
Gleann na Muaidhe IRL 22 D3
Gledica SRB 179 C9
Glein N 124 D4
Gleina D 95 D10
Gleisdorf A 164 B5
Gleizé F 46 D6
Glejbjerg DK 102 D3
Glemsford GB 31 C10
Glen S 118 A6
Glenade IRL 22 D6
Glenamaddy IRL 22 E5
Glenamoy IRL 22 D3
Glenariff GB 20 E4
Glenarm GB 20 E5
Glenavy GB 23 C10
Glenbarr GB 20 B5
Glenbeg GB 20 B5
Glenbeigh IRL 24 D3
Glencaple GB 21 E9
Glencar IRL 22 D6
Glencoe GB 20 B6
Glencolumbkille IRL 22 C5
Glendowan IRL 23 C7
Gleneagles GB 21 C9
Glenealy IRL 23 G9
Gleneely IRL 20 D7
Glenegedale GB 20 D4
Glenela GB 18 L5
Glenfield GB 27 E11
Glenfinnan GB 20 B6
Glengarriff IRL 24 E3
Glengavlen IRL 23 D7
Glenhead GB 20 E2
Glenluce GB 20 F7
Glenmore IRL 25 D8
Glenoe GB 20 F5
Glenrothes GB 21 C10
Glenties IRL 22 C6
Glère F 43 F6
Glesborg DK 103 C7

Gletsch CH 87 D6
Glewitz D 100 B3
Glibaći MNE 179 C7
Glimäkra S 104 C6
Glimboca RO 175 C9
Glin IRL 24 C4
Glina HR 164 F5
Glina RO 177 E8
Glindow D 95 B12
Glinjeni MD 169 B11
Glinojeck PL 155 E9
Glinsce IRL 22 F3
Glinsk IRL 22 F3
Glinton GB 27 F11
Glissjöberg S 118 B7
Gliwice PL 158 F6
Globočica SRB 180 E3
Glodeanu-Sărat RO 177 D9
Glodeanu-Siliştea RO 177 D9
Glodeni MD 169 B11
Glodeni RO 168 D5
Glodeni RO 177 C6
Glödnitz A 89 C9
Głodowa PL 101 C11
Glodzhevo BG 177 F8
Gloggnitz A 164 A5
Glogova RO 175 D10
Glogovac SRB 175 E7
Glogovac SRB 179 D10
Głogów PL 97 C10
Głogówek PL 158 F4
Głogów Małopolski PL 160 C4
Głogowo PL 154 D6
Glomfjord N 124 C6
Glommen S 103 B10
Glommersträsk S 123 A17
Glonn D 91 G10
Glória P 66 B4
Glória do Ribatejo P 60 F3
Glos-la-Ferrière F 40 C4
Glossa GR 191 A8
Glössbo S 119 D12
Glossop GB 27 E8
Glöte S 118 B5
Glöthe D 95 C10
Glottra S 108 B6
Gloucester GB 29 B10
Glounthaune IRL 24 E6
Głowaczów PL 157 G4
Głowaczyce PL 101 A12
Glowe D 100 A4
Głowno PL 159 C8
Głożan SRB 174 C4
Glozhene BG 186 F5
Glozhene BG 181 C9
Głubczyce PL 158 F4
Głuchołazy PL 158 F3
Głuchów PL 157 G2
Glücksburg (Ostsee) D 98 A7
Glückstadt D 33 A12
Glud DK 102 D5
Gludsted DK 102 D4
Gluggvasshaugen N 124 E5
Glumslöv S 103 D11
Glumsø DK 103 E9
Glusburn GB 27 D8
Glušci SRB 174 D4
Głuszyca PL 97 E10
Głuszyn PL 154 D6
Glyfa GR 191 B6
Glyfada GR 191 D8
Glyki GR 184 F4
Glyn Ceiriog GB 26 F5
Glyngøre DK 102 B3
Glynn GB 20 E5
Glynn IRL 25 D9
Glynneath GB 29 B7
Gmünd A 89 B7
Gmünd A 93 E7
Gmund am Tegernsee D 88 A4
Gmunden A 89 A8
Gnarp S 119 B13
Gnarrenburg D 33 B12
Gneisenaustadt Schildau D
96 D3
Gnesta S 109 A10
Gniebing A 164 C5
Gniew PL 154 C6
Gniewkowo PL 154 E5
Gniewoszów PL 157 H5
Gnieżdziska PL 159 E9
Gniezno PL 101 E13
Gnisvärd S 109 D12
Gnjilane SRB 180 E3
Gnocchetta I 82 C5
Gnoien D 99 C13
Gnojna PL 157 G6
Gnojnice BIH 173 F8
Gnojnik PL 160 D2
Gnojno PL 159 D14
Gnosall GB 27 F7
Gnosjö S 107 E14
Gnotzheim D 91 D8
Gnutz D 98 B7
Göbel TR 189 D9
Gobowen GB 26 F5
Göçbeyli TR 193 A9
Göcek TR 197 C9
Göçerler TR 189 B8
Goch D 32 E6
Gochsheim D 91 B7
Goczałkowice-Zdrój PL 163 B7
Godal N 111 D11
Godalming GB 31 E7
Godby FIN 115 B13
Goddelau D 203 B6
Goddelsheim (Lichtenfels) D
37 B11
Godeanu RO 175 D10
Godech BG 181 C7
Godega di Sant'Urbano I 88 E5
Godegård S 108 B6
Godelleta E 64 F3
Godeni RO 176 C5
Goderville F 34 E1
Godiasco I 53 B10
Godimilje BIH 173 D8
Godineşti RO 175 C10
Godinje MNE 179 E7
Godkowo PL 155 B8
Godmanchester GB 31 C8
Gödöllő H 166 B3
Godovič SLO 89 E9
Gödre H 165 D9
Godstone GB 31 E8
Goduš BIH 173 C10
Góra PL 97 C11
Góra PL 155 E9
Górafe E 71 E6
Goraj PL 160 B4
Góra Kalwaria PL 157 G4
Goranu RO 176 C4

Góra Puławska PL 157 H5
Gorawino PL 101 C8
Goražde BIH 173 E10
Gorban RO 169 D12
Görbeháza H 167 B8
Görcsöny H 165 E10
Gördalen S 118 C3
Gordaliza del Pino E 55 D9
Gordes F 51 C9
Gordeşti RO 169 C11
Gordoşu RO 175 E10
Goghi D 99 B9
Gohor RO 169 E10
Gohrau D 95 C11
Göhrde D 99 E8
Göhren, Ostseebad D 100 B5
Göhren-Lebbin D 99 D13
Goian MD 170 C4
Goicea RO 176 F3
Goieşti RO 176 E3
Goirle NL 32 E4
Góis P 60 D4
Goizueta E 48 D2
Gojść N 159 D2
Gökçealan TR 193 D9
Gökçebayır TR 187 E10
Gökçedağ TR 189 E10
Gökçeören TR 197 B9
Gökçeyazı TR 189 E8
Gokels D 98 B6
Gökova TR 197 B8
Göktepe TR 197 B9
Göktürk TR 189 B10
Gol N 117 E9
Gola HR 165 D8
Gołąb PL 157 H5
Golac SLO 83 A9
Golăieşti RO 169 C11
Golaj AL 179 E9
Gołańcz PL 101 E12
Gołaszyn PL 157 G6
Golbey F 42 D5
Gölby FIN 115 B13
Gölcük TR 189 F8
Golčův Jeníkov CZ 93 C8
Golczewo PL 101 C7
Goldach CH 87 C9
Goldberg D 99 E11
Goldberg D 99 C12
Goldegg A 89 B7
Goldelund D 98 A4
Golden IRL 25 D7
Golden Pot GB 30 E7
Goldenstedt D 33 C10
Goleen IRL 24 F3
Golegã P 44 F4
Golemanovo BG 175 F9
Golema Rakovitsa BG 181 D8
Golema Rečica MK 179 F10
Golenice PL 101 E7
Golenovi PL 101 C7
Golesh BG 177 F11
Goleşti RO 169 F10
Goleşti RO 176 C4
Golfo Aranci I 80 B4
Golina PL 158 B5
Golinhac F 49 A11
Goliševa LV 149 C3
Gölköy TR 193 D9
Gölle I 165 D10
Göllersdorf A 93 F10
Göllheim D 202 B5
Gollin D 99 C11
Gollin D 100 D5
Golling an der Salzach A 89 A7
Göllingen D 95 D9
Gollmitz D 100 D5
Golmes E 58 D5
Golnik SLO 89 D9
Gøløse DK 103 D10
Golovkino RUS 152 D3
Golpejas E 61 B9
Gols S 43 G11
Golspie GB 19 K9
Golßen D 96 C5
Golubac SRB 175 D8
Golub-Dobrzyń PL 154 D7
Golubić HR 172 D5
Golubinje SRB 175 D9
Golyama Zhelyazna BG 181 D9
Golyam Izvor BG 182 F5
Golyam Manastir BG 182 E6
Golyamo Belovo BG 181 E8
Gölyazı TR 189 D10
Gomadingen D 43 D11
Gómara E 57 E7
Gomaringen D 203 D7
Gomati GR 185 D10
Gomba H 166 C4
Gomecello E 61 B9
Gomes Aires P 66 D3
Gomirje HR 83 B11
Gommern D 95 B10
Gomotartsi BG 175 E10
Gomunice PL 159 D7
Gönc H 161 G3
Gonçalo P 60 D6
Goncelin F 47 E8
Gondelsheim D 203 C6
Gondershausen D 201 D7
Gondomar E 54 D2
Gondomar P 60 B3
Gondrecourt-le-Château F
42 C4
Gondreville F 42 C4
Gondrin F 49 C6
Gönen TR 189 D8
Gonfaron F 52 E4
Goni I 80 D3
Goniądz PL 156 D7
Goniana S 80 E1
Gonnoi GR 185 E7
Gonnosfanadiga I 80 E2
Gonnosnò I 80 D2
Gonsans F 42 F5
Gönyú H 165 A9
Gonzaga I 82 C2
Goodwick GB 28 A5
Goole GB 27 D10
Goonhavern GB 28 E4
Goor NL 33 D7
Göppingen D 90 E6
Gor E 71 E6
Góra PL 97 C11
Góra PL 155 E9
Gorafe E 71 E6
Goraj PL 160 B4
Góra Kalwaria PL 157 G4
Goranu RO 176 C4

Gorzów Wielkopolski PL 101 E8
Górzyca PL 97 B7
Górzyca PL 101 C8
Gorzyce PL 160 B4
Gorzyce PL 160 C5
Gorzyce PL 162 B6
Gorzyń PL 97 A9
Górzyn PL 97 C7
Gosaldo I 88 D4
Gosau A 89 A8
Gosberton GB 27 F11
Gościeradów Ukazowy PL
160 B4
Gościm PL 101 E9
Gościno PL 101 B9
Gościszów PL 97 D8
Gosdorf A 164 C5
Gosè AL 184 B2
Gosfield GB 31 D10
Gosforth GB 21 E13
Gosforth GB 26 C5
Goslar D 95 C7
Goślice PL 155 E8
Gosné F 39 E8
Gospić HR 172 C3
Gospodinci SRB 174 C4
Gosport GB 29 D12
Gössäter S 107 B13
Gossau CH 43 F11
Gössendorf A 164 C5
Gößl A 89 A8
Gostavățu RO 176 E5
Gostil AL 179 E9
Gostilitsa BG 182 C4
Gostinari RO 177 E8
Gostinu RO 177 E8
Gostivar MK 179 F10
Göstling an der Ybbs A 89 A10
Gostovići BIH 173 D9
Gostycyn PL 154 D4
Gostyń PL 97 C12
Gostyń PL 101 B7
Gostynin PL 155 F7
Goszcz PL 158 D3
Goszczyn PL 157 G3
Goszczanów PL 158 C5
Göta S 107 C11
Göteborg S 107 D10
Götene S 107 B13
Goteşti MD 170 E2
Gotha D 95 E8
Gothem S 109 D13
Götlunda S 113 D14
Gotse Delchev BG 185 A10
Gottböle FIN 138 F6
Gotteszell D 91 E12
Gottfrieding D 91 E12
Göttingen D 94 D6
Gottmadingen D 43 E10
Gottröra A 93 F9
Gottsdorf D 95 B8
Götzis A 87 C9
Gouarec F 38 D5
Gouda NL 32 D3
Goudoswaard NL 198 B5
Gouesnou F 38 D3
Gouhenans F 42 E5
Gould GB 41 C9
Goult F 51 C9
Goumenissa GR 185 C9
Goumois F 43 F6
Gourdan-Polignan F 49 D7
Gourdon F 45 F8
Gourdon GB 21 B12
Gourette F 48 E5
Gourgançon F 41 C11
Gouria GR 190 C3
Gourin F 38 D4
Gournay-en-Bray F 34 F4
Goussainville F 41 B7
Gout-Rossignol F 45 E6
Gouveia P 60 D5
Gouvia GR 184 E2
Gouvieux F 41 B7
Gouvy B 36 D5
Gouzon F 45 C10
Gove P 60 B5
Govedari BIH 178 D3
Govedartsi BG 181 D7
Goven F 38 D4
Gowarczów PL 157 H2
Gowidlino FIN 154 B5
Goworowo PL 155 E12
Gowran IRL 25 C8
Goxhill GB 27 D11
Göynükbelen TR 189 E11
Gózd PL 157 H4
Gozdnica PL 97 D8
Gozdowice PL 100 E6
Gozzano I 84 B5
Górno PL 159 D10
Gorno Ablanovo BG 177 F7
Gorno Aleksandrovo BG 183 D7
Gorno Orizari MK 180 F4
Gorno Ozirovo BG 181 C7
Gorno Pavlikene BG 181 C10
Goro I 82 C5
Gorobinci MK 180 F4
Gorodok RO 175 C8
Gorodok RO 176 C4

Gradefie E 55 C9
Gradets BG 175 E10
Gradets BG 183 D7
Gradevo BG 181 F7
Gradina BG 182 C5
Gradina BG 183 D7
Gradina BG 182 E4
Gradina BIH 173 F9
Gradina BIH 173 D9
Gradina BIH 178 D5
Gradina MNE 179 E7
Gradinari RO 176 D4
Gradinari SRB 174 D4
Grădinarita MD 170 D5
Gradishte BG 182 C4
Gradište HR 173 B10
Gradište SRB 180 C5
Gradište SRB 180 C5
Grădiştea RO 176 D3
Grădiştea RO 177 D8
Grădiştea RO 177 D8
Grădiştea RO 177 E10
Gradište Bekteško HR 165 F9
Gradnitsa BG 181 D10
Grado E 55 B7
Grado I 89 E7
Grado S 113 B15
Gradojević SRB 174 D4
Gradoli I 78 B2
Gradsko MK 185 A6
Gradskovo SRB 175 E9
Graena E 71 E6
Græsted DK 103 C10
Gräfelfing D 91 F9
Grafenau D 92 E4
Gräfenberg D 91 C9
Gräfendorf D 90 B6
Grafendorf bei Hartberg A
164 B5
Gräfenhainichen D 95 C11
Grafenhausen D 43 E9
Grafenrheinfeld D 203 B9
Gräfenroda D 95 E8
Grafenstein A 89 C9
Grafenwöhr D 91 C10
Grafenworth A 93 F9
Graffignano I 78 B2
Grafhorst D 95 B8
Graf Ignatievo BG 181 E10
Gräfinau-Angstedt D 95 E9
Grafing bei München D 91 F10
Grafrath D 91 F9
Gragnano I 76 B3
Grahovac MNE 179 D6
Grahovo SLO 89 D8
Gráig na Manach IRL 25 C9
Graigue IRL 25 C9
Graiguenamanagh IRL 25 C9
Grain GB 31 E9
Grainau D 87 C12
Grainet D 92 E4
Graissac F 46 F2
Graissessac F 50 C5
Graja de Iniesta E 63 E9
Grajal de Campos E 55 D9
Grajduri RO 169 D11
Grajewo PL 156 C6
Grållsta S 114 C7
Grålum N 111 D14
Gram DK 102 E4
Gramada BG 175 F10
Gramastetten A 92 F6
Gramat F 45 F9
Gramatikovo BG 183 E8
Grambow D 100 D6
Grămeşti RO 169 B8
Grambow D 99 C10
Grammatiko GR 185 F7
Grammendorf D 99 B13
Grammenitsa GR 190 A2
Grammeno GR 184 E4
Grammichele I 75 E6
Gramsbergen NL 33 C7
Gramsh AL 184 C3
Gramzda LV 150 D3
Gramzow D 100 D6
Gran N 111 B13
Granabeg IRL 23 F10
Granada E 69 B9
Granån S 135 C10
Granard IRL 23 E8
Granarolo dell'Emilia I 82 C3
Granberg S 134 C7
Granberget N 118 D3
Granbergsdal S 113 D12
Granbergsträsk S 123 A17
Grancey-le-Château-Neuvelle F
42 E3
Grandas E 55 B6
Grandcamp-Maisy F 39 B7
Grand-Champ F 38 E6
Grand-Couronne F 34 F3
Grande-Synthe F 34 B5
Grande-Vabre F 49 A10
Grand-Fort-Philippe F 34 B5
Grand-Fougeray F 39 E8
Grândola P 66 C2
Grandpré F 35 F10
Grandpuits-Bailly-Carrois F
41 C8
Grandrieu F 46 F4
Grandris F 46 C5
Grandson CH 47 B9
Grandtully GB 21 B9
Grandvelle-et-le-Perrenot F
42 E5
Grandvillars F 43 E6
Grandvilliers F 34 E4
Grañén E 57 E11
Grängärde S 113 B12
Grange IRL 25 E7
Grange IRL 22 D6
Grangemouth GB 21 C9
Grange-over-Sands GB 26 C6
Grängesberg S 113 B13
Granges-sur-Vologne F 43 D6
Grängshyttan S 113 C12
Grängsjö S 119 B13
Granhult S 132 D7
Grăniceri RO 167 D7
Grănicești RO 169 B8
Graninge S 123 B13
Granitola-Torretta I 74 D2
Granitsa GR 190 A4
Granja P 60 B3
Granja de Moreruela E 55 E8
Granja de Torrehermosa E 67 C8
Granja do Ulmeiro P 60 D3

Gränna S 108 C4
Grannäs S 123 A10
Grannäs S 125 E13
Granö S 123 C16
Granön S 123 C17
Granollers E 59 D8
Granowiec PL 158 D4
Granowo PL 97 B11
Granschütz D 95 D11
Gransee D 100 D4
Granselet S 125 E14
Gränsgård S 125 F15
Gransjö S 123 A15
Gransjön S 119 B11
Gränsjö S 124 F8
Grantham GB 27 F10
Grantown-on-Spey GB 19 L9
Granträsk S 123 C14
Gränträsk S 123 C16
Granträskmark S 134 D6
Grantshouse GB 21 D12
Gränum S 104 C7
Granvik S 108 B5
Granville F 39 C8
Granvin N 110 A5
Grapska BIH 173 C9
Gräs S 113 C10
Grasbakken N 130 C5
Gräsgård S 105 C11
Grasleben D 95 B9
Gräsmarken S 113 B8
Grasmere GB 26 C5
Gräsmyr S 123 D17
Grassau I 76 B6
Grassau D 88 A5
Grasse F 52 D5
Grassington GB 27 C8
Gråssjö S 119 A10
Gråsten DK 102 F5
Grästorp S 107 C12
Gratallops E 58 E5
Gratangsbotn N 127 C14
Gratens F 49 D8
Gratia RO 177 E6
Gratini GR 187 B7
Gratkorn A 164 B4
Grätnäs S 123 E14
Gråträsk S 134 D3
Gratteri I 74 D4
Gratwein A 164 B4
Graubälle DK 102 C5
Graulhet F 49 C9
Graupa D 96 D6
Graus E 58 C4
Grávalos E 57 D8
Gravberget N 118 E3
Gravbränna S 122 D7
Gravdal N 126 D6
Grave NL 32 E5
Gravedona I 85 A7
Gravelines F 34 B5
Gravellona Toce I 84 B5
Gravelotte F 42 B6
Gravens DK 102 D4
Grävenwiesbach D 37 D10
Gräveri LV 149 D3
Gravesend GB 31 E9
Gravia GR 190 B5
Gravigny F 40 B5
Gråvika N 116 E1
Gravina di Catania I 75 D7
Gravina in Puglia I 77 B6
Gravmark S 134 F4
Gray F 42 F4
Grayan-et-l'Hôpital F 44 E3
Grays GB 31 E9
Graz A 164 B4
Grazalema E 69 C6
Grążawy PL 155 D8
Grazzanise I 76 A2
Grčak SRB 179 C10
Grdelica SRB 180 D5
Greaca RO 177 E8
Greåker N 111 D14
Gréalou F 49 A9
Great Baddow GB 31 D9
Great Bircham GB 31 B10
Great Clifton GB 21 F7
Great Cornard GB 31 C10
Great Dunmow GB 31 D9
Great Glen GB 27 F9
Great Gonerby GB 27 F10
Greatham GB 27 B9
Great Harwood GB 27 D7
Great Haywood GB 27 F8
Great Linford GB 31 C7
Great Malvern GB 29 A10
Great Ponton GB 27 F10
Great Salkeld GB 21 F11
Great Shelford GB 31 C9
Great Torrington GB 28 D6
Great Wakering GB 31 E10
Great Yarmouth GB 31 B12
Grebănu RO 177 C9
Grebaštica HR 172 E4
Grebbestad S 107 B9
Grebci BIH 178 D4
Grebenac SRB 175 D7
Grebendorf (Meinhard) D 95 D7
Grebenhain D 37 D12
Grebenişu de Câmpie RO
168 D4
Grebenstein D 37 B12
Grebin D 99 B8
Grębków PL 157 F5
Grebo S 108 C7
Grębocin PL 154 D6
Greboszów PL 159 F10
Grębów PL 160 B4
Greccio I 78 C3
Grecești RO 176 E2
Greci I 76 A4
Gredelj BIH 173 F10
Greding D 91 D9
Gredstedbro DK 102 E3
Greencastle GB 21 D8
Greencastle GB 20 D3
Greencastle IRL 20 D3
Greene D 94 C6
Greengairs GB 21 D9
Greenhead GB 21 F11
Greenigo GB 19 H10
Greenisland GB 20 F5
Greenlaw GB 21 D11
Greenloaning GB 21 C9
Greenock GB 20 D7
Greenodd GB 26 C5
Greenway GB 28 B5
Greggio I 84 C5
Greifenburg A 89 C7

Greifendorf D 96 D4
Greifenstein D 37 C10
Greiffenberg D 100 D5
Greifswald D 100 B4
Grein A 93 F7
Greiz D 95 E11
Gremersdorf D 99 B9
Grenade F 49 C8
Grenade-sur-l'Adour F 48 C5
Grenant F 42 E4
Grenås S 122 D8
Grenchen CH 43 F7
Grenči LV 150 C5
Grenoble F 47 E8
Grense-Jakobselv N 130 D9
Gréoux-les-Bains F 51 C10
Gresenhorst D 99 B12
Gress GB 18 J4
Gressan F 47 D11
Gresse D 99 D9
Gressoney-la-Trinite I 84 B4
Gressvik N 107 A8
Gresten A 93 G8
Grésy-sur-Aix F 47 D8
Grésy-sur-Isère F 47 D9
Gretna GB 21 F10
Greußen D 95 D8
Greux F 42 D4
Grevbäck S 108 C4
Greve in Chianti I 82 E3
Greven D 33 D9
Greven D 99 D9
Grevena GR 184 D5
Grevenbicht NL 199 C7
Grevenbroich D 37 B7
Greveniti GR 184 E5
Grevenmacher L 36 E6
Grevesmühlen D 99 C10
Grevie S 103 C11
Grevinge DK 103 D9
Greyabbey GB 23 C11
Greystoke GB 21 F11
Greystones IRL 23 F10
Grez-Doiceau B 35 C10
Grez-en-Bouère F 39 E10
Grgar SLO 89 D8
Grgurevci SRB 174 C4
Griegos E 63 D9
Gries F 43 C8
Gries am Brenner A 88 B3
Griesbach D 43 D9
Griesbach im Rottal D 92 F4
Griesheim D 37 E11
Grieskirchen A 92 F5
Grießen D 97 C7
Griesstätt D 91 G11
Griffen A 89 C10
Grignan F 51 B8
Grigno I 88 D4
Grignols F 48 B5
Grigny F 46 D6
Grigoriopol MD 170 C4
Grijota E 56 D2
Grijpskerk NL 32 B6
Grillby S 114 C8
Grillon F 51 B8
Grimaldi I 76 A4
Grimaud F 52 E5
Grimbergen B 35 C9
Grimma D 95 D12
Grimmen D 100 B4
Grimoldby DK 27 E12
Grimsås S 107 E14
Grimsby GB 27 D11
Grimslöv S 104 B7
Grimstad N 106 A6
Grimston GB 27 F13
Grimstorp S 108 D5
Grimstrup DK 102 D3
Grindafjord N 110 D2
Grindaheim N 117 D9
Grindal N 117 A11
Grindelwald CH 86 D6
Grinder N 112 B7
Grindjord N 127 D13
Grindsted DK 102 A6
Grindsted DK 102 D3
Grindu RO 177 D10
Grinkiškis LT 150 E7
Griñón E 62 D5
Grins A 87 C11
Grinsbol S 113 D8
Grințies RO 169 C7
Gripenberg S 108 D5
Grisén E 57 E9
Grisolles F 49 C8
Grisslehamn S 115 B11
Gritley GB 19 H11
Grivița RO 169 E11
Grivița RO 169 F11
Grivița RO 177 D10
Grivitsa BG 181 C10
Grkinja SRB 180 C4
Grljan SRB 175 F9
Grnčari MK 184 B5
Grobbendonk B 35 B10
Gröbenzell D 91 F9
Grobina LV 150 C2
Gröbming A 89 B8
Gröbzig D 95 C10
Grocka SRB 174 D6
Gródby S 109 A11
Gródek PL 156 D9
Gródek nad Dunajcem PL 160 D2
Gröden D 96 D5
Grödig A 89 A7
Gröditz D 96 D4
Gródki PL 155 D9
Grodków PL 158 E3
Grodziczno PL 155 D8
Grodziec PL 158 B5
Grodzisk PL 157 E7
Grodzisk Mazowiecki PL 157 F3
Grodzisk Wielkopolski PL 97 B10
Groenlo NL 33 D7
Groesbeek NL 199 B8
Grohnde (Emmerthal) D 94 B5
Groitzsch D 95 D11
Groix F 38 E5
Grojdibodu RO 176 F4
Grójec PL 157 G3
Grom PL 155 C10
Gromadka PL 97 D9
Grömitz D 99 B9
Gromnik PL 160 D2

Gromo I 85 B8
Gronau (Westfalen) D 33 D8
Grønbjerg DK 102 C3
Grönbo S 134 C6
Gröndal S 124 E8
Grönenbach D 87 B10
Grong N 121 C12
Grönhögen S 105 C10
Grønhøj DK 102 C4
Gröningen D 95 C9
Groningen NL 32 B6
Grønnemose DK 102 E6
Grønnes N 116 A6
Grønning N 126 E9
Grønningen N 120 D7
Gronowo PL 155 B7
Grönsinka S 114 B7
Grönskåra S 105 A9
Grönsta S 119 A11
Grønvik N 110 D4
Grönviken S 119 A9
Grönviken S 119 E12
Groomsport GB 20 F5
Grootegast NL 32 B6
Gropello Cairoli I 85 C6
Gropeni RO 171 C1
Gropnița RO 169 C10
Grorud N 111 D11
Groscavallo I 47 E11
Grosi RO 168 B3
Grosio I 85 A9
Grošnica SRB 175 F6
Grosotto I 85 A9
Großaitingen D 87 A11
Groß Ammensleben D 95 B10
Großarl A 89 B7
Groß-Bieberau D 37 E11
Groß Börnecke D 95 C9
Großbothen D 95 D12
Großbottwar D 43 C11
Großbreitenbach D 95 E9
Großburgwedel (Burgwedel) D 94 B6
Groß Dölln D 100 E5
Grosselfingen D 43 D10
Großenaspe D 99 C7
Großenbrode D 99 B10
Großenehrich D 95 D9
Groß Engersdorf D 93 F11
Großengottern D 95 D8
Großenhain D 96 D5
Großenkneten D 33 C10
Großenlüder D 94 E6
Großensee D 99 C8
Großenstein D 95 E11
Großenwiehe D 98 A6
Groß-Enzersdorf D 93 F11
Grosseto I 81 B4
Grosseto-Prugna F 53 H9
Groß Fredenwalde D 100 D5
Großfurra D 95 D9
Groß-Gerau D 37 E10
Groß-Gerungs A 93 E8
Groß Glienicke D 99 E12
Großgmain D 89 A6
Groß Grönau D 99 C9
Großhabersdorf D 91 D8
Großhansdorf D 99 C8
Großharras A 93 E11
Großhartmannsdorf D 96 E4
Groß Heere (Heere) D 95 B7
Großhennersdorf D 97 E7
Groß-Hesepe D 33 C8
Großheubach D 203 B7
Grössjö S 123 F14
Großkarolinenfeld D 88 A5
Groß Kiesow D 100 C5
Großklein A 164 C4
Groß Köris D 96 B5
Groß Kreutz D 95 B12
Großkrut A 93 E11
Groß Lafferde (Lahstedt) D 95 B7
Großlangheim D 203 B9
Groß Leine D 96 B6
Groß Leuthen D 96 B6
Großlittgen D 37 D7
Großlohra D 95 D8
Großmaischeid D 201 C8
Großmehlen D 96 D5
Groß Miltzow D 100 C5
Groß Mohrdorf D 100 B3
Großmonra D 95 D9
Groß Naundorf D 96 D5
Großnaundorf D 96 D5
Groß Nemerow D 100 D4
Groß Oesingen D 95 A7
Großolbersdorf D 96 E4
Groß Oßnig D 96 C6
Großostheim D 37 E12
Großpetersdorf A 165 B6
Groß Plasten D 99 C13
Großraming A 89 A10
Großräschen D 96 C6
Großrinderfeld D 90 C6
Groß Roge D 99 C13
Groß-Rohrheim D 37 E10
Großröhrsdorf D 96 D6
Grosrosseln D 202 C2
Großrudestedt D 95 D9
Großrußbach A 93 F10
Groß Sankt Florian A 164 C4
Groß Särchen D 96 D6
Großschirma D 96 E4
Großschönau A 93 E7
Groß Schönebeck D 100 E5
Groß Schwechten D 95 A9
Groß Schwülper (Schwülper) D 95 B7
Groß-Siegharts A 93 E8
Groß Stieten D 99 C10
Großthiemig D 96 C3
Groß Twülpstedt D 95 B8
Groß-Umstadt D 203 B6
Großwallstadt D 37 E12
Groß Warnow D 99 D11
Großweikersdorf A 93 F9
Groß Welle D 99 D12
Groß Wittensee D 98 B7
Groß Wokern D 99 C13
Großwudicke D 95 A11
Groß-Zimmern D 203 B6
Groß Ziethen D 100 E5
Grostenquin F 43 D6
Grosuplje SLO 89 E10
Grøtavær N 127 C11
Grotfjord N 127 A16
Gröthlein S 118 C4
Grötingen S 119 A9
Grotli N 116 B7
Grötlingbo S 109 E12

Grøtnesdalen N 127 A18
Grottaferrata I 78 D3
Grottaglie I 82 F6
Grottaminarda I 76 A4
Grottammare I 78 B5
Grottazzolina I 78 A5
Grotte I 74 E4
Grotte di Castro I 78 B1
Grotteria I 75 C9
Grottole I 77 B6
Grou NL 32 B5
Grova N 106 A4
Grove GB 29 B12
Gröveslsjön S 118 B3
Grovfjord N 127 C13
Grozd'ovo BG 183 C9
Grozești RO 169 D12
Grub am Forst D 91 B9
Grubbenvorst NL 199 C8
Grubbnäsudden S 135 B10
Grube D 99 B10
Grubišno Polje HR 165 E8
Gruczno PL 154 D5
Gruda HR 178 D5
Grude BIH 173 F7
Grudusk PL 155 D10
Grudziądz PL 154 D6
Gruey-lès-Surance F 42 D5
Grugliasco I 84 C4
Gruia RO 175 E10
Gruissan F 50 D5
Gruiu RO 177 D8
Grullos E 55 B7
Grumăzești RO 169 C8
Grumbach D 96 D5
Grumo Appula I 77 A7
Grums S 113 D9
Grünau A 89 A8
Grünau A 93 F9
Grünberg D 37 C10
Grünburg A 92 G6
Grundagssätern I 118 B4
Grundfors S 122 A8
Grundfors S 123 B13
Grundforsen S 118 A4
Grundsanden S 134 B5
Grundsel S 134 C4
Grundsund S 107 C9
Grundtjärn S 123 C11
Grundträsk S 123 A16
Grundträsk S 125 F17
Grundträsk S 134 B7
Grundvattnet S 134 C4
Grünendeich D 98 C7
Grünewald D 96 D5
Grünewalde D 96 C5
Grüngebru N 110 C7
Grünheide D 96 B5
Grünkraut D 87 B9
Grunnfarnes N 127 B12
Grunnfjord N 128 C4
Grunnførfjord N 126 D8
Grunow D 96 B6
Grünsfeld D 90 C6
Grünstadt D 37 E10
Grünwald D 91 F10
Grupčin MK 180 E3
Grury F 46 B4
Grüšlaukė LT 150 D2
Grußendorf (Sassenburg) D 95 A8
Gruta PL 154 D6
Gruvberget S 119 D11
Gruyères CH 47 B11
Gruža SRB 175 F6
Grüžai LT 151 D8
Gružďiai LT 150 D6
Grybów PL 161 D2
Grycksbo S 119 E13
Gryfice PL 101 C8
Gryfino PL 100 D6
Gryfów Śląski PL 97 D8
Grygov CZ 162 B4
Grylewo PL 101 E12
Gryllefjord N 127 B13
Grynberget S 123 C11
Gryt S 109 C9
Grytan S 122 E7
Grytgöl S 108 B7
Grythyttan S 113 C12
Gryts bruk S 108 B7
Grytsjö S 122 A9
Gryttjom S 115 B8
Gryżlyny PL 155 C9
Grzebienisko PL 97 B11
Grzmiąca PL 101 C10
Grzybno PL 100 D7
Grzybno PL 154 D5
Grzymiszew PL 158 B5
Grzywna PL 154 D6
Gschnitz A 88 B3
Gschwandt A 89 A8
Gschwend D 90 D6
Gstaad CH 47 C11
Gsteig CH 47 C11
Guadahortuna E 69 A10
Guadajoz E 67 D8
Guadalajara E 63 C9
Guadalaviar E 63 D9
Guadalcanal E 67 C8
Guadalcázar E 69 A7
Guadalen E 72 D4
Guadalmez E 70 B3
Guadalupe E 64 F4
Guadarrama E 62 C4
Guadassuar E 64 F4
Guadix E 71 E6
Guagno F 53 G9
Guájar-Faraguit E 69 C9
Gualalv S 104 C6
Gualdo Cattaneo I 78 B3
Gualdo Tadino I 83 F6
Gualtieri I 78 D4
Guarcino I 78 D4
Guarda P 61 C6
Guardamar del Segura E 72 E3
Guardavalle I 75 C9
Guardea I 78 B2
Guardiagrele I 79 C6
Guardia Lombardi I 76 B4
Guardia Perticara I 76 C5
Guardia Piemontese I 76 E6
Guardia Sanframondi I 76 A3
Guardias Viejas E 71 F7
Guardiola de Berguedà E 59 C7
Guardo E 55 C10
Guardrama E 61 B8
Guareña E 67 B7
Guaro E 69 C7
Guarromán E 70 C5
Guasila I 80 D3
Guastalla I 82 C2

Gubaveeny IRL 23 D7
Gubbhögen S 122 C9
Gubbio I 82 F6
Gubbträsk S 123 A13
Guben D 97 C7
Gubin PL 97 C7
Gübene BG 182 D4
Gučin RO 177 B9
Guča SRB 174 F5
Guča Gora BIH 173 D8
Gudar E 64 D3
Gudavac BIH 172 C5
Gudbjerg DK 102 E7
Gudenieki LV 150 C3
Guderup DK 102 F5
Gudhem S 107 C14
Gudhjem DK 105 E7
Gudiena LT 153 D9
Gudinge S 115 A9
Gudme DK 103 E7
Gudmont-Villiers F 42 D3
Gudow D 99 D9
Gudum DK 102 C3
Gudumholm DK 102 B6
Gudvangen N 116 E5
Gudžiūnai LT 150 E7
Guebwiller F 43 E7
Guégon F 38 E6
Güéjar-Sierra E 69 B10
Guémar F 43 D7
Guémené-Penfao F 39 E8
Guémené-sur-Scorff F 38 D5
Guénange F 36 F6
Güeñes E 56 B5
Guenrouet F 39 E8
Guer F 39 E7
Guérande F 38 F3
Guéret F 45 C9
Guérigny F 41 F9
Guerri de la Sal E 49 F8
Güesa E 48 E3
Gueugnon F 46 B5
Gueures F 34 E5
Gueux F 35 F8
Guéthary E 48 D3
Gueugnon F 46 B5
Gugești RO 177 B10
Güglingen D 43 B10
Guglionesi I 79 D7
Gugutka BG 187 B9
Gühlen-Glienicke D 99 D13
Guia P 60 E3
Guia P 66 E3
Guichen F 39 E8
Guidel F 38 E5
Guide Post GB 21 E13
Guidizzolo I 82 B2
Guidonia-Montecelio I 78 D3
Guiglia I 82 D2
Guignen F 39 E8
Guignes F 41 C8
Guignicourt F 35 F8
Guijo de Coria E 61 D8
Guijo de Galisteo E 61 D8
Guijo de Granadilla E 61 D8
Guijuelo E 61 C9
Guildford GB 31 E7
Guilers F 38 D2
Guilford GB 31 E7
Guilheim F 38 E6
Guilherand F 46 F6
Guilhofrei P 54 E3
Guillalumes F 52 C5
Guillena E 67 D7
Guillestre F 52 B5
Guilliers F 38 D7
Guillon F 41 E10
Guillos F 48 A4
Guilvinec F 38 E3
Guimarães P 54 F3
Guînes F 31 F12
Guingamp F 38 C5
Guipavas F 38 D3
Guipry F 39 E8
Guisando E 61 D10
Guiscard F 35 E7
Guise F 35 E8
Guissény F 38 C3
Guissona E 58 D6
Guist GB 31 B10
Guîtres F 44 E5
Guitiriz E 54 B4
Gujan-Mestras F 48 A3
Gulács I 161 G5
Gülbahçe TR 193 C8
Gulbene LV 151 B12
Guldager DK 102 D2
Guldborg DK 100 A1
Gulen N 116 E2
Gulgame F 48 A3
Gulianca RO 177 C11
Gullabo S 105 C9
Gullane GB 21 C11
Gullberg S 119 D11
Gullbrå S 116 E4
Gullbrandstorp S 103 B11
Gullbranna S 103 B11
Gulleråsen S 119 D9
Gullholmen S 107 C10
Gullön S 125 E15
Gullringen S 108 D7
Gullspång S 107 B15
Gullträsk S 134 B6
Güllübahçe TR 193 D9
Güllüce TR 189 D9
Güllük TR 193 E10
Gullverket N 111 B14
Gülpinar TR 187 E10
Gulsele S 123 D12
Gulsvik N 111 B11
Gültz D 100 C4
Gülübintsi BG 182 E6
Gülübovo BG 181 E10
Gülübovo BG 182 E5
Gulyantsi BG 176 F5
Gumhöjden S 113 B10
Gumiel de Hizán E 56 E6
Gumiel de Mercado E 56 E4
Gummark S 134 C5
Gummersbach D 37 B9
Gumpelstadt D 95 E7
Gumtow D 99 E12
Gümüşçay TR 189 D7
Gümüşsuyu TR 193 C9
Gümüşyaka TR 189 B9
Gümzovo BG 175 D10
Gunaroš SRB 166 E5
Gunja HR 173 C10

Güneyli TR 188 D6
Gunja HR 173 C10
Gunnarn S 123 A13
Gunnarnes N 124 A9
Gunnarsbo S 119 C11
Gunnarsbyn S 134 B7
Gunnarskog S 113 C8
Gunnarvattnet S 121 C16
Gunnebo S 109 D9
Günstedt D 95 D9
Güntersberge D 95 C8
Guntersblum D 201 E9
Guntersdorf A 93 E10
Guntramsdorf A 93 F10
Günzburg D 91 F7
Gunzenhausen D 91 D8
Gura-Biculului MD 170 D4
Gura Calitei RO 177 B9
Gura Camencii MD 170 B2
Gura Foii RO 176 D6
Gura Galbenei MD 170 D3
Gurahont RO 167 E9
Gura Ocniței RO 176 D6
Gura Râului RO 168 F3
Gurasada RO 167 F10
Gura Șuții RO 176 D6
Gura Teghii RO 177 C8
Gura Vadului RO 177 D8
Gura Văii RO 169 C9
Gura Vitioarei RO 177 C8
Gurbănești RO 177 E8
Gurghiu RO 168 D5
Guri i Bardhë AL 184 B3
Guri i Zi AL 179 E8
Gurk A 89 C9
Gurkovo BG 182 D5
Gurkovo BG 183 C10
Gûrlyano BG 180 D5
Gurrea de Gállego E 57 D10
Gurrë e Madhe AL 184 A3
Gurteen IRL 22 E6
Gur'yevsk RUS 152 D2
Gusborn D 99 D9
Gušče HR 165 F7
Güsen D 95 B10
Gusev RUS 152 D5
Gusinje MNE 179 D8
Gușoeni RO 176 D4
Gusow D 99 A6
Guspini I 80 D2
Gusselby S 113 C13
Güssing A 165 B6
Gussola I 82 B1
Gußswattnet S 121 C16
Gußwerk A 164 A4
Gustavsberg S 115 D10
Gustavsfors S 113 B10
Güsten D 95 C10
Gusterath D 37 E7
Güstrow D 99 C12
Gutach (Schwarzwaldbahn) D 203 E5
Gutau A 93 F7
Gutcher GB 19 D14
Güterfelde D 96 B4
Güterglück D 95 C10
Gütersloh D 33 C10
Guthrie GB 21 B11
Gutorfölde H 165 C7
Gutow D 99 C12
Guttannen CH 86 D6
Guttaring A 89 C10
Gützkow D 100 C4
Guvåg N 126 C8
Güvemalani TR 189 D7
Güvercinlik TR 193 E10
Guxhagen D 94 D5
Güzelbahçe TR 193 D8
Güzelçamlı TR 193 D9
Gvardeysk RUS 152 D3
Gvarv N 111 D10
Gvozd HR 164 F5
Gvozd MNE 179 D7
Gvozdansko HR 172 B5
Gwda Wielka PL 101 C11
Gweedore IRL 22 B6
Gwithian GB 28 E4
Gy F 42 F4
Gyál H 166 C3
Gyarmat H 165 B8
Gyékényes H 165 D8
Gyenesdiás H 165 C8
Gyermely H 165 A11
Gyé-sur-Seine F 41 D11
Gyhum D 33 B12
Gyljen S 134 B8
Gymno GR 191 C8
Gyomaendrőd H 166 D6
Gyömöre H 165 A9
Gyömrő H 166 C3
Gyöngyös H 166 B4
Gyöngyöspata H 166 B4
Gyönk H 165 C10
Győr H 165 A9
Győrköny H 165 C9
Győrság H 165 A9
Győrszemere H 165 A9
Győrtelek H 161 H5
Győrújbarát H 165 A9
Győrújfalu H 165 A9
Győrzámoly H 165 A9
Gyrstinge DK 103 E9
Gysinge S 114 B7
Gytheio GR 194 F5
Gyttorp S 113 C12
Gyueshevo BG 180 E5
Gyula H 167 D7
Gyulaháza H 161 G5
Gyulaj H 165 D10
Gyúró H 165 A11
Gzy PL 155 E10

H

Haabneeme EST 147 B9
Haacht B 35 C10
Häädemeeste EST 147 E8
Haaften NL 199 B6
Haag N 93 F7
Haag am Hausruck A 92 F5
Haag in Oberbayern D 91 F11
Haajainen FIN 140 C7
Haaksbergen NL 33 D7
Haaltert B 35 C9
Haanja EST 147 F14
Haapa-Kimola FIN 143 D15
Haapajärvi FIN 139 C14

Haapakoski FIN 139 E10
Haapakoski FIN 140 F8
Haapakumpu FIN 131 D3
Haapalahti FIN 129 C19
Haapaluoma FIN 139 E10
Haapamäki FIN 131 C16
Haapamäki FIN 139 E10
Haapamäki FIN 139 F12
Haapamäki FIN 141 E10
Haaparanta FIN 131 E3
Haapavesi FIN 135 F11
Haapsalu EST 146 D7
Haar D 91 F10
Haarajoki FIN 139 F17
Haarajoki FIN 143 E13
Haaraoja FIN 135 F16
Haarasaajo FIN 135 B12
Haarbach D 92 E4
Haarby DK 102 E6
Haaren NL 32 E3
Haarlem NL 32 C3
Haastrecht NL 32 C3
Haavisto FIN 143 D11
Habaja EST 147 C10
Habartov CZ 91 B12
Habas F 48 C4
Habay-la-Neuve B 35 E12
Häbbersliden S 134 E4
Habiller TR 183 F7
Hablingbo S 109 E12
Habo S 107 D15
Håbol S 107 B11
Hábovka SK 163 C9
Habry CZ 93 C8
Hachenburg D 37 C7
Hacıaslanlar TR 189 F7
Hacıdanişment TR 183 F7
Hacıeylen TR 188 D6
Hacıköy TR 188 C6
Hacinas E 56 E5
Hacırahmanlı TR 193 B10
Hacıumur TR 183 F7
Hacıvelioba TR 189 D8
Hackås S 118 A8
Hackenheim D 37 E8
Hacketstown IRL 25 C9
Hackleton GB 31 B7
Hacksjö S 123 B12
Hadamar D 37 D10
Hadanberg S 123 D14
Haddeo S 108 B6
Haddington GB 21 D11
Haddiscoe GB 31 B12
Haderslev DK 102 E4
Haderup DK 102 C3
Hadımköy TR 189 B10
Hadleigh GB 31 C10
Hadleigh GB 31 D9
Hadley GB 26 F7
Hadol F 42 D5
Hadres A 93 E10
Hadsel N 126 C8
Hadsten DK 102 C6
Hadsund DK 102 B6
Hadžići BIH 173 E9
Haelen NL 199 C7
Hafnerbach A 93 F8
Haftersbol S 113 C10
Haga S 114 B8
Haganj HR 165 E7
Hagastrom S 119 E13
Hagby S 105 B10
Hagebyhöga S 108 C5
Hagen D 37 B8
Hagenbach D 203 C5
Hagenburg D 33 D12
Hagenow D 99 D10
Hagenwerder D 97 D7
Hageri EST 147 C9
Hägerstad S 108 C7
Hagetaubin F 48 C4
Hagetmau F 48 C4
Hagfors S 113 B10
Häggås S 123 C17
Hägge S 119 E11
Häggdånger S 119 A14
Häggebäcken S 114 B6
Häggenås S 122 E7
Häggsåsen S 121 E16
Häggsjön S 121 D13
Häggsjövik S 121 D16
Häghig RO 169 F7
Hagley GB 29 A9
Hagondange F 36 F6
Hagsta S 119 E13
Haguenau F 43 C8
Hahausen D 95 C7
Hahnbach D 91 C10
Hahnstätten D 201 D9
Hahót F 165 C7
Haibach D 37 E12
Haidmühle D 92 E5
Haiger D 37 C10
Haigerloch D 43 D10
Häijää FIN 143 B9
Hailsham GB 31 F9
Hailuoto FIN 135 D13
Haiming D 92 F3
Haimoo FIN 143 E11
Hainlé AL 179 F8
Haina D 91 B9
Haina (Kloster) D 37 B11
Hainburg an der Donau A 93 F11
Hainfeld A 93 F9
Hainichen D 96 E4
Haiterbach D 203 D6
Haitzendorf A 93 F9
Hajala FIN 143 F8
Hajdúböszörmény H 167 B8
Hajdúdorog H 167 B8
Hajdúhadház H 167 B8
Hajdúnánás H 167 B8
Hajdúsámson H 167 B8
Hajdúszoboszló H 167 C7
Hajdúszovát H 167 C7
Hajmáskér H 165 B9
Hajmel AL 179 F8
Hajnówka PL 157 E9
Hajós H 166 E3
Hakadal N 111 B13
Håkafot S 121 C16
Hakkas S 132 C5
Hakenberg D 99 D12
Håkkila FIN 139 E14
Hakokylä FIN 137 E12
Håkøybotn N 127 A16
Håksberg S 113 B13
Hakstabben N 128 C11

Håkvik N 127 D13
Halahora de Sus MD 169 A10
Håland N 110 C4
Halapić BIH 173 D6
Halászi F 162 F4
Halásztelek H 166 C3
Hălăucești RO 169 C9
Halbe D 96 B5
Halbenrain A 164 C5
Hålberg S 125 F18
Halberstadt D 95 C9
Halbjerg DK 106 E7
Halblech D 87 B11
Halbturn A 93 G11
Hălchiu RO 169 F7
Hald DK 102 B4
Hald DK 102 C4
Haldarsvík FO 18 A2
Hald Ege DK 102 C4
Halden N 107 A7
Haldensleben D 95 B9
Hale GB 27 E7
Halen B 199 C6
Halenkov CZ 162 C6
Halenkovice CZ 162 C4
Halesowen GB 29 A10
Halesworth GB 31 C12
Halfing D 88 A5
Halfway IRL 24 E5
Halfweg NL 32 D3
Halhjem N 110 B2
Halič SK 163 E9
Halifax GB 27 D8
Halikko FIN 143 E9
Halimba H 165 B9
Halitpaşa TR 193 B10
Halkia FIN 143 D13
Halkirk GB 19 H10
Halkivaha FIN 143 C9
Halkokumpu FIN 140 F7
Hall S 109 D13
Hälla S 123 D12
Halla-aho FIN 140 C9
Hallabro S 105 C8
Hällabrottet S 108 A6
Halla Heberg S 107 E10
Halland GB 31 F9
Hålland S 121 E14
Hallapuro FIN 139 D14
Hällaryd S 105 C7
Hällbacken S 121 E16
Hällbacken S 125 D12
Hällberga S 114 D7
Hällbo S 119 D11
Hallbodarna S 121 E15
Hällbybrunn S 114 D6
Halle S 35 C9
Halle D 94 D6
Halle NL 199 B8
Halle (Saale) D 95 D11
Halle (Westfalen) D 33 D10
Hällefors S 113 C12
Hälleforsnäs S 109 A9
Hallein A 89 A7
Hällekis S 107 B13
Hällen S 114 B8
Hallen S 121 E16
Hallenberg D 37 B11
Hallencourt F 34 E4
Hallerndorf D 91 C8
Hällestad S 108 B7
Hälleviksstrand S 107 C9
Hall-Häksåns S 122 D10
Hallingby N 111 B12
Hallingeberg S 109 D8
Hällinmäki FIN 140 F9
Hall in Tirol A 88 B4
Hällnäs S 123 C17
Hällnäs S 125 D15
Hällnäs S 125 E13
Hallom S 118 A7
Hallow GB 29 A10
Hällsbäck S 113 D8
Hallsberg S 108 A6
Hällsjö S 123 E13
Hällsta S 114 C6
Hallstahammar S 114 C6
Hallstatt A 89 A8
Hallstavik S 115 B11
Halltorp S 105 C9
Halluin B 35 C7
Hallund DK 102 A6
Hällvik S 125 D14
Hallviken S 122 D8
Hallworthy GB 28 F5
Hălmăgel RO 167 E10
Hălmagiu RO 167 E10
Halmeu RO 161 H7
Halmstad S 103 B11
Halna S 108 A4
Halosenniemi FIN 135 D14
Halosenranta FIN 131 E2
Halovo SRB 175 F9
Hals DK 102 B6
Halsa N 120 E4
Halsenbach D 37 D9
Hal'shany BY 153 E13
Hälsingby FIN 138 D7
Hälsjö S 119 C12
Halsøy N 124 E3
Halskov DK 103 E8
Halstead GB 31 D10
Halstenbek D 99 C7
Halsteren NL 32 E2
Halstroff F 36 F6
Halsua FIN 139 C12
Haltdalen D 33 D8
Halttula FIN 135 C14
Haltwhistle GB 21 F12
Halvarsgårdarna S 113 B13
Halver D 37 B9
Halvrimmen DK 102 A5
Halwell GB 29 E7
Halže CZ 91 C12
Ham F 35 E7
Ham GB 19 E12
Hamar N 117 E14
Hamari FIN 135 C14
Hamarøy N 124 D5
Hamarøy N 127 D10
Hambach F 43 B7
Hambergen D 33 B11
Hamble-le-Rice GB 29 D12
Hambrücken D 37 F10
Hambühren D 95 A6

Hamburg D 99 C7
Hamburgsund S 107 B9
Hambye F 39 C9
Hamcearca RO 171 C2
Hamdibey TR 189 E7
Hämeenkoski FIN 143 C13
Hämeenkyrö FIN 143 B9
Hämeenlinna FIN 143 D11
Hämelhausen D 33 C12
Hameln D 33 D12
Hämerten D 95 A10
Hamica HR 164 E5
Hamidiye TR 183 F9
Hamidiye TR 188 B6
Hamilton GB 21 D8
Hamilton's Bawn GB 23 D9
Hamina FIN 144 D7
Haminalahti FIN 140 E9
Hamit TR 197 C9
Hamitabat TR 189 A7
Hamlagrø N 110 A4
Hamlot N 127 D10
Hamm D 33 E9
Hamm (Sieg) D 201 C8
Hammar S 108 B5
Hammarland FIN 115 B13
Hammarn S 113 C12
Hammarnäs S 121 E16
Hammarsbyn S 118 E5
Hammarstrand S 123 E10
Hammarvika N 120 D5
Hamme B 35 B9
Hammel DK 102 C5
Hammelburg D 90 B6
Hammelev DK 102 E4
Hammelspring D 100 D4
Hamme-Mille B 35 C10
Hammenhög S 104 D6
Hammer N 121 C12
Hammerbrücke D 91 B11
Hammerdal S 122 D8
Hammerfest N 129 B12
Hammershøj DK 102 C5
Hammerum DK 102 C4
Hamminkeln D 33 E7
Hamn N 124 E3
Hamn N 127 B13
Hamna N 130 B8
Hamnavoe GB 19 D14
Hamnavoe GB 19 E14
Hamnbukt N 128 C8
Hamnbukta N 127 B18
Hamneidet N 128 D6
Hamnes N 121 B10
Hamnes N 124 E4
Hamnes N 128 D6
Hamningberg N 130 B9
Hamnøy N 126 E5
Hamnvågnes N 127 B16
Hamoir B 35 D12
Hamois B 35 D11
Hamont B 32 F5
Hampen DK 102 C4
Hampetorp S 108 A7
Håmpjåkk S 132 D4
Hampont F 42 C6
Hampreston GB 29 D11
Hamra S 109 F12
Hamra S 119 C9
Hamrångefjärden S 119 E13
Hamre N 128 C4
Hamry nad Sázavou CZ 93 C9
Ham-sous-Varsberg F 202 C2
Hamstreet GB 31 E10
Hamsund N 127 D10
Ham-sur-Heure B 35 D9
Hamula FIN 139 D16
Hamula FIN 140 D9
Hamzabeyli TR 183 F7
Hanaskog S 104 C6
Hanau D 203 A6
Handbjerg DK 102 C3
Handeloh D 99 D7
Handen S 109 A12
Handest DK 102 B5
Handewitt D 98 A6
Handlová SK 163 D7
Handog S 122 E7
Handöl S 121 E12
Handrabury UA 170 B5
Handrup D 33 C9
Handsjö S 118 B8
Handstein N 124 D4
Handzame B 198 C2
Hanebo S 119 D12
Hanerau-Hademarschen D 98 B6
Hanestad N 117 C13
Hăneşti RO 169 B9
Hangastenmaa FIN 144 B7
Hangelsberg D 96 B5
Hånger S 103 A13
Hangö FIN 143 F8
Hangony H 161 G1
Hangu RO 169 C8
Hangvar S 109 D13
Hanhikoski FIN 131 E2
Hanhimaa FIN 133 C14
Hanikase EST 148 F1
Haniska SK 161 F3
Hankamäki FIN 141 D10
Hankasalem asema FIN 139 F16
Hankasalmi FIN 139 F16
Hankensbüttel D 99 E9
Han Knežica BIH 173 B6
Hanko FIN 143 F8
Hanna PL 157 G9
Hannäs S 109 C8
Hannover D 94 B6
Hannoversch Münden D 94 D6
Hannukainen FIN 133 C11
Hannusperä FIN 135 D15
Hannusranta FIN 137 F10
Hannut B 35 C11
Hanøy N 126 D9
Han-Pijesak BIH 173 D10
Hanshagen D 99 C10
Hańsk Pierwszy PL 157 H8
Hansnes N 128 D4
Hanstedt D 99 D8
Hanstholm DK 102 A3
Han-sur-Nied F 42 C5
Hanušovce nad Topľou SK 161 E4
Hanušovice CZ 93 B11
Hanvec F 38 D3
Haparanda S 135 C12
Hapert NL 199 C6
Häppälä FIN 139 F16
Happburg D 91 D9
Happisburgh GB 31 B12
Haps NL 199 B7
Hapträsk S 134 B4
Hara S 122 E6
Härad S 114 D7
Haradok BY 149 F7
Harads S 134 B5
Häradsbäck S 104 B6
Häradsbygden S 119 E9
Haradshammar S 109 B9
Haradzilavichy Pyershaya BY 149 D4
Haraldseng N 128 B9
Haram N 116 A4
Harang N 120 E6
Harany BY 149 F6
Harasiuki PL 160 C5
Hărău RO 167 F10
Haraudden S 132 E3
Harbacheva BY 149 E6
Harbak N 120 C8
Harbke D 95 B9
Harbo S 114 B8
Harboør DK 102 B2
Harbost GB 18 J4
Harburg (Schwaben) D 91 E8
Harbury GB 29 A12
Hard A 87 C9
Hardbakke N 116 D1
Hardegg A 93 E9
Hardegsen D 94 C6
Hardelot-Plage F 31 F12
Hardenberg NL 33 C7
Harderwijk NL 32 D5
Hardheim D 43 A11
Hardinxveld-Giessendam NL 198 B5
Hardt D 43 D9
Hareid N 116 B4
Harelbeke B 35 C7
Haren NL 33 B7
Haren (Ems) D 33 C8
Hare Street GB 31 D9
Harestua N 111 B13
Harfleur F 39 A12
Harg S 115 B10
Hargesheim D 37 E9
Hargimont B 35 D11
Hargla EST 147 F12
Hargnies F 35 D10
Hargshamn S 115 B10
Harichovce SK 161 F2
Harinkaa FIN 139 E16
Harjakangas FIN 142 B6
Härjäro S 115 D8
Härjåsjön S 118 C7
Harjavalta FIN 142 C7
Harjula FIN 135 C15
Harjumaa FIN 144 B7
Harjunkylä FIN 138 E7
Harjunpää FIN 142 C6
Harju-Risti EST 147 C7
Harka H 165 A7
Härkäjoki FIN 131 D2
Harkakötöny H 166 E4
Harkány H 165 E10
Härkmeri FIN 138 F6
Härkönen FIN 135 C13
Harku EST 147 C9
Hârlău RO 169 C9
Harlech GB 26 F3
Harleston GB 31 C11
Hårlev DK 103 E10
Harlingen NL 32 B4
Harlow GB 31 D9
Harly F 35 E7
Hărman RO 169 F7
Harmånger S 119 C13
Härmänkylä FIN 137 F13
Harmanlı TR 189 D9
Härmänmäki FIN 137 F11
Harmannsdorf A 93 F10
Harmelen NL 198 A5
Harmoinen FIN 143 C13
Harmsdorf D 99 C9
Harmston GB 27 E10
Harnes F 34 D6
Härnösand S 119 A14
Haro E 56 C6
Harodz'ki BY 153 E13
Haroldswick GB 19 D15
Haroué F 42 D5
Härpe FIN 143 E14
Harpefoss N 117 C11
Harpenden GB 31 D8
Harplinge S 103 B11
Harpstedt D 33 C11
Harra D 91 B10
Harrachov CZ 97 E8
Harran N 121 B13
Harre DK 102 B3
Harridslev DK 102 C6
Harrietfield GB 21 C9
Harrioja S 135 C11
Harrislee D 98 A6
Harrogate GB 27 D8
Harrsjö S 122 B9
Harrström FIN 138 E6
Harrvik S 123 A10
Harsa S 119 C10
Hårsbäck S 114 C7
Harsefeld D 98 D7
Hârseni RO 168 F6
Harseşti RO 176 D5
Harsleben D 95 C9
Hårslev DK 102 D6
Hârşova RO 171 D1
Harsprånget S 132 E3
Harstad N 127 C12
Harsum D 94 B6
Harsvik N 120 C8
Harta H 166 D3
Hartberg A 164 B5
Hårte S 119 C13
Hartenholm D 99 C8
Hartha D 96 D3
Harthausen D 37 F10
Hartheim D 43 E8
Hârtieşti RO 176 C6
Hart im Zillertal A 88 B4
Hartkirchen A 92 F5
Hartland GB 28 D6
Hartlepool GB 27 B9
Hartmanice CZ 92 D4
Hartola FIN 143 B15
Harwich GB 31 D11
Harzgerode D 95 C9
Hasanağa TR 189 D10
Hasbuğa TR 189 A8
Haselünne D 33 C8
Hasırcıarnavutköy TR 187 B10
Håsjö S 123 F10
Hasköy TR 189 A6
Hasköy TR 193 C9
Haslach an der Mühl A 92 E6
Haslach im Kinzigtal D 43 D9
Hasle CH 86 C5
Hasle DK 104 E7
Haslemere GB 31 E7
Haslev DK 103 E9
Hasloh D 99 C7
Hasløya N 120 E2
Haslund DK 102 C6
Hăşmaş RO 167 D9
Hasparren F 48 D3
Haßbergen D 33 C12
Hassel (Weser) D 33 C12
Hassela S 119 B12
Hassela kyrkby S 119 B12
Hasselfelde D 95 C8
Hasselfors S 108 A5
Hasselt B 35 C11
Hasselt NL 32 C6
Haßfurt D 91 B8
Hassi FIN 143 B13
Hässjö S 119 A14
Haßleben D 95 D9
Haßleben D 100 D5
Hässleholm S 103 C13
Hasslö S 105 C8
Haßloch D 37 F10
Hasslöv S 103 C12
Haßmersheim D 203 C7
Hästbo S 119 E13
Hästholmen S 108 C5
Hastière-Lavaux B 35 D10
Hastings GB 31 F10
Hästnäs S 113 D14
Håstrup DK 102 E6
Hästveda S 103 C13
Hasvåg N 121 C9
Hasvik N 128 C9
Hať CZ 162 B6
Hat' UA 161 G6
Haţeg RO 175 B10
Hatfield GB 27 D10
Hatherleigh GB 28 D6
Hätilä FIN 143 C11
Hatipkışlası TR 197 B7
Hatsola FIN 144 B8
Hattarvík FO 18 A4
Hattem NL 32 D6
Hattersheim am Main D 37 D10
Hattert D 37 C9
Hattfjelldal N 124 E6
Hatting DK 102 D5
Hattingen D 33 F8
Hatton GB 19 L13
Hattstedt D 98 A6
Hattula FIN 143 C11
Hattuvaara FIN 141 E16
Hatulanmäki FIN 140 C8
Hatunkylä FIN 141 D15
Hatvan H 166 B4
Hatzenbühl D 43 B9
Hatzendorf A 164 C6
Hatzfeld (Eder) D 37 C11
Haubourdin F 34 C6
Hauenstein D 202 C4
Haugan N 121 D9
Haugastøl N 110 A7
Hauge N 110 F4
Hauge N 130 E6
Haugen N 126 D7
Haugesund N 110 D2
Haugh of Urr GB 21 F9
Haugland N 124 D5
Haugli N 127 C15
Haugnes N 127 B11
Haugnes N 128 C6
Haugset N 128 D7
Hauho FIN 143 C12
Haukå N 116 C2
Haukela FIN 141 B14
Haukeligrend N 110 C7
Haukijärvi FIN 143 B9
Haukilahti FIN 137 F13
Haukiniemi FIN 137 C13
Haukipudas FIN 135 D14
Haukivaara FIN 141 E15
Haukivuori FIN 140 F8
Haukøy N 127 D11
Haulerwijk NL 32 B6
Haurukylä FIN 135 E15
Haus A 89 B8
Haus N 110 B2
Hausach D 203 E5
Hausen D 91 E11
Hausen bei Würzburg D 203 B9
Häusern D 43 E9
Hausham D 88 A4
Hausjärvi FIN 143 D12
Hauske N 110 D3
Hausleiten A 93 F10
Hausmannstätten A 164 C5
Hautajärvi FIN 131 E6
Hautakylä FIN 137 D10
Hautakylä FIN 139 E12
Haute-Amance F 42 E4
Hautefort F 45 E8
Hauterives F 47 E7
Hauteville-Lompnes F 47 D8
Haut-Fays B 200 D3
Hautmont F 35 D8
Hautomäki FIN 139 E17
Haux F 48 D4
Hauzenberg D 92 E5
Havant GB 30 F7
Havårna RO 169 A9
Havbro DK 102 B4
Havdhem S 109 E12
Håvdna N 129 C15
Havelange B 35 D11
Havelberg D 99 E12
Havelte NL 32 C6
Håven S 119 C9
Haverdal S 103 B11
Haverfordwest GB 28 B5
Haverhill GB 31 C9
Haverlah D 95 B7
Haverö S 119 B9
Haversin B 35 D11
Haverslev DK 102 B5
Håverud S 107 B11
Havířov CZ 162 B6
Havixbeck D 33 E8
Hävla S 108 B7
Havlíčkův Brod CZ 93 C9
Havndal DK 102 B6
Havneby DK 102 E3
Havnebyen DK 103 D8
Havnsø DK 103 D8
Havøysund N 129 A14
Håvra S 119 C10
Havran TR 189 E7
Havrebjerg DK 103 E8
Havsa TR 189 A6
Havsskogen S 115 B11
Havtun N 110 B2
Hawarden GB 26 E5
Hawes GB 27 C7
Hawick GB 21 E11
Hawkhurst GB 31 E10
Hawkinge GB 31 E11
Haxby GB 27 C9
Hayange F 36 F6
Haybes F 200 D2
Haydarlı TR 193 D10
Haydere TR 197 A8
Haydon Bridge GB 21 F12
Haydon Wick GB 29 B11
Hayingen D 87 A8
Hayle GB 28 E4
Hay-on-Wye GB 29 A8
Hayrabolu TR 189 B7
Hayton GB 27 D10
Hayvoron UA 170 A5
Haywards Heath GB 31 F8
Hazebrouck F 34 C6
Hazerswoude-Rijndijk NL 198 A5
Haźlach PL 163 B7
Hažlín SK 161 E3
Hazlov CZ 91 B11
Heacham GB 27 F12
Headcorn GB 31 E10
Headford IRL 22 F4
Healeyfield GB 21 F13
Heanor GB 27 E9
Heathfield GB 31 F9
Hebdów PL 159 F9
Hebenhausen (Neu-Eichenberg) D 94 D6
Heberg S 103 B11
Hebertsfelden D 92 F3
Hebnes N 110 D3
Heby S 114 C7
Hèches F 49 D6
Hechingen D 43 D10
Hecho E 48 E4
Hechtel B 35 B11
Hechthausen D 33 A12
Heckelberg D 100 E5
Heckington GB 27 F11
Hedared S 107 D12
Hedberg S 125 F16
Heddesheim D 37 F11
Hédé F 39 D8
Hede S 114 B6
Hede S 118 B6
Hedekas S 107 B10
Hedel NL 32 E4
Hedemora S 113 B14
Heden DK 102 E6
Heden S 118 C4
Heden S 134 C7
Hedenäset S 135 B11
Hedensbyn S 134 B9
Hedensted DK 102 D5
Hedersleben D 95 C9
Hédervár H 162 F4
Hedesunda S 114 B8
Hedeviken S 118 B6
Hedge End GB 29 D12
Hedlunda S 123 B15
Hedmark S 123 B13
Hedsjön S 119 E12
Hee DK 102 C2
Heeg NL 32 C5
Heek D 33 D8
Heel NL 199 C7
Heemsen D 33 C12
Heemskerk NL 32 C3
Heemstede NL 32 D3
Heenvliet NL 198 B4
Heer B 35 D10
Heerde NL 32 D6
Heerenveen NL 32 C5
Heerewaarden NL 199 B6
Heerhugowaard NL 32 C3
Heerlen NL 36 C5
Heers B 35 C11
Heesch NL 32 E5
Heeslingen D 33 B12
Heeßen D 33 D12
Heeswijk NL 32 E4
Heeten NL 199 A8
Heeze NL 32 F5
Heggeli N 127 B13
Heggem N 120 E4
Heggenes N 117 D10
Heggjabygda N 116 C4
Heggland N 106 A5
Heggmoen N 124 B8
Hegra N 121 E10
Hegyeshalom H 162 F4
Hehlen D 94 C5
Heia N 121 C12
Heia N 127 B17
Heide D 98 B6
Heideck D 91 D9
Heidelberg D 37 F11
Heiden D 33 E7
Heidenau D 96 E5
Heidenheim D 91 D8
Heidenheim an der Brenz D 91 E7
Heidenreichstein A 93 E8
Heigenbrücken D 203 A7
Heikendorf D 99 B8
Heikkilä FIN 137 C14
Heikkilä FIN 138 F7
Heiland N 106 B4
Heilbronn D 43 B11
Heilbrunn A 164 B5
Heiligenberg D 43 E11
Heiligenfelde D 99 E10
Heiligenhafen D 99 B9
Heiligenhaus D 33 F7
Heiligenkreuz am Waasen A 164 C5
Heiligenkreuz im Lafnitztal A 164 C6
Heiligenstadt Heilbad D 95 D7
Heiligenstedten D 98 C6
Heiloo NL 32 C3
Heilsbronn D 91 D8
Heiltz-le-Maurupt F 41 C12
Heim N 120 E6
Heimbach D 37 E8
Heimbuchenthal D 203 B7
Heimdal N 116 E3
Heimdal N 120 E8
Heimertingen D 87 A10
Heimseta N 116 C3
Heimsheim D 203 D6
Heinade D 94 C6
Heinämaa FIN 143 D14
Heinämäki FIN 137 F12
Heinämäki FIN 139 D17
Heinävaara FIN 141 E14
Heinävesi FIN 141 F11
Heinebach (Alheim) D 94 D6
Heinersbrück D 97 C7
Heinersdorf D 96 B6
Heinersreuth D 91 C10
Heinijärvi FIN 135 E14
Heinijoki FIN 142 D7
Heiningen D 95 B8
Heinisuo FIN 135 C16
Heinkenszand NL 32 F1
Heinlahti FIN 144 E6
Heino NL 199 A8
Heinola FIN 143 C15
Heinolan kirkonkylä FIN 143 C15
Heinolanperä FIN 135 E14
Heinoniemi FIN 141 F13
Heinsberg D 36 B6
Heinsen D 94 C5
Heinsnes N 121 B12
Heisingen D 199 C10
Heistadmoen N 111 C11
Heist-op-den-Berg B 35 B10
Heitersheim D 43 E8
Heituinlahti FIN 144 C8
Hejls DK 102 E5
Hejnice CZ 97 E8
Hejnsvig DK 102 D4
Hejőpapi H 161 H2
Hejsager DK 102 E5
Hekelgem B 35 C9
Hel PL 154 A6
Helbra D 95 C9
Helchteren B 199 C6
Heldburg D 91 B8
Heldenbergen D 37 D11
Heldrungen D 95 D9
Helechal E 67 B9
Helegiu RO 169 E9
Helensburgh GB 20 C7
Helfenberg A 92 E6
Helgenes N 126 C9
Helgeroa N 106 B6
Helgum S 123 E11
Hell N 121 E9
Hella N 116 D5
Helland N 120 E5
Helland N 127 D11
Hellanmaa FIN 138 D9
Hellarmo N 125 B10
Helle N 106 B5
Hellebæk DK 103 C11
Hellefjord N 129 B11
Hellendoorn NL 199 A8
Hellenthal D 36 D6
Hellenurme EST 147 E12
Hellesøy N 116 E1
Hellested DK 103 E10
Hellesvik N 120 D5
Hellesylt N 116 B5
Hellevad DK 102 E4
Hellevoetsluis NL 32 E2
Helligskogen N 128 E6
Hellín E 71 B9
Hellingly GB 31 F9
Hellnes N 128 C6
Hellsö FIN 142 F4
Hellvi S 109 D13
Hellvik N 110 F3
Helmbrechts D 91 B10
Helme EST 147 E11
Helmond NL 32 F5
Helmsdale GB 19 J9
Helmsley GB 27 C9
Helmstadt D 90 C6
Helmstedt D 95 B9
Helpa SK 163 D9
Helppi FIN 133 D13
Helpringham GB 27 F11
Helse D 98 C6
Helsingborg S 103 C11
Helsinge DK 103 C10
Helsingfors FIN 143 E12
Helsingør DK 103 C11
Helsinki FIN 143 E12
Helstad N 121 A12
Helston GB 28 E4
Heltersberg D 37 F9
Helvacı TR 193 B9
Helvécia H 166 D4
Helvoirt NL 199 B6
Hem DK 102 B3
Hem F 198 D2
Hemau D 91 D10
Hemavan S 124 E9
Hemeiuş RO 169 D9
Hemel Hempstead GB 31 D8
Hemer D 201 B8
Hemfjäll S 125 E12
Hemfjällstangen S 118 D5
Hemhofen D 91 C8
Hemling S 123 D15
Hemme D 98 B6
Hemmet DK 102 D2
Hemmingen D 94 B6
Hemmingen S 123 B17
Hemmingsmark S 134 D6
Hemmoor D 33 A12
Hemnesberget N 124 D6
Hemnestad N 127 C11
Hempnall GB 31 C11
Hempstead GB 31 C9
Hemsbach D 37 E11
Hemsbünde D 98 D6
Hemsby GB 31 B12
Hemse S 109 E12
Hemsedal N 117 E9
Hemsjö S 123 D14
Hemslingen D 98 D7
Hemsloh D 33 C11
Hemsö S 119 A15
Hemyock GB 29 D8
Henån S 107 C10
Hénanbihen F 39 C7
Henarejos E 63 E10
Hencida H 167 C8
Hendaye F 48 D2
Hendon GB 31 D8
Hengelo NL 32 D6
Hengelo NL 33 D7
Hengersberg D 92 E4
Hengevelde NL 199 A9
Henggart CH 43 E10
Hengoed GB 29 B8
Hénin-Beaumont F 34 D6
Henley-on-Thames GB 31 D7
Hennan S 119 B10
Henndorf am Wallersee A 89 A7
Hennebont F 38 E5
Hennef (Sieg) D 37 C8
Hennes N 126 C9
Henne Stationsby DK 102 D2
Hennezel F 42 D5
Hennickendorf D 96 B4
Hennigsdorf Berlin D 96 A4
Henningskälen S 122 D8
Henningsvær N 126 D7
Hennseid N 106 A5
Hennset N 120 E4
Hennstedt D 98 B6
Hennweiler D 37 E8
Henrichemont F 41 F8
Henryków PL 97 E12
Henrykowo PL 155 B9
Henstridge GB 29 D10
Hepola FIN 135 C13
Heppen B 199 C6
Heppenheim (Bergstraße) D 37 E11
Herálec CZ 93 C8
Herálec CZ 93 C9
Herbault F 40 E5
Herbertingen D 43 D11
Herbertstown IRL 24 C6
Herbés E 58 F3
Herbeumont B 200 E3
Herbignac F 39 F7
Herbolzheim D 43 D8
Herborn D 37 C10
Herbrechtingen D 91 E7
Herbstein D 37 C12
Herby PL 158 E6
Herceghalom H 165 A11
Herceg-Novi MNE 178 E6
Hercegovac HR 165 E8
Hercegszántó H 166 F2
Herdecke D 33 F8
Herdorf D 37 C9
Hereclean RO 167 C11
Heréd H 166 B4
Hereford GB 29 A9
Héreg H 165 A11
Herencia E 62 F6
Herend H 165 B9
Herent B 35 C10
Herentals B 35 B10
Herenthout B 198 C5
Hérépian F 50 C5
Herford D 33 D11
Hergatz D 87 B9
Hergiswil CH 86 D6
Herguijuela E 61 F9
Héric F 39 F8
Héricourt F 43 E6
Hérimoncourt F 43 F6
Heringen (Helme) D 95 D8
Heringen (Werra) D 95 E7
Heringsdorf D 99 B10
Heringsdorf, Seebad D 100 C6
Heriot GB 21 D11
Herisau CH 43 F11
Hérisson F 45 B11
Herk-de-Stad B 35 C11
Herkenbosch NL 199 C8
Herkingen NL 198 B4
Herleshausen D 95 D7
Herlev DK 103 D10
Herlufmagle DK 103 E9
Herm F 48 C3
Hermagor A 89 C7
Hermannsburg D 99 E8
Hermanovce SK 161 E3
Hermanowice PL 160 D6
Hermansverk N 116 D5
Heřmanův Městec CZ 93 C9
Herment F 45 D11
Hermersberg D 202 C4
Hermeskeil D 37 E7
Hermisende E 55 E6
Hermsdorf D 95 E10
Hernád H 166 C3
Hernádnémeti H 161 G2
Hernani E 48 D2
Hernansancho E 62 C3
Herne B 35 C9
Herne D 33 E8
Herne Bay GB 31 E11
Herning DK 102 C3
Heroldsbach D 91 C8
Héron B 35 C11
Hérouville-St-Clair F 39 B11
Herøy N 116 B3
Herpf D 95 E7
Herrala FIN 143 D13
Herramélluri E 56 C5
Herräng S 115 B11
Herré F 48 C5
Herre N 106 A6
Herrenberg D 43 C10
Herrera E 69 B7
Herrera del Duque E 61 F10
Herrera de los Navarros E 58 E1
Herrera de Pisuerga E 56 C3
Herrería E 63 C9
Herreruela E 61 F7
Herrestad S 107 C10
Herrieden D 91 D8
Herringbotn N 124 E6
Herrlisheim F 202 D4
Herrljunga S 107 C13
Herrnhut D 97 D7
Herrö S 118 B7
Herrsching am Ammersee D 91 G9
Herrskog S 119 A15
Herrvik S 109 E13
Herry F 41 F8
Hersbruck D 91 C9
Herschbach D 37 C9
Herscheid D 37 B9
Herschweiler-Pettersheim D 202 C3
Herselt B 35 B10
Herslev DK 102 D5
Herstal B 35 C12
Herstmonceux GB 31 F9
Herston GB 19 H11
Herten D 33 E8
Hertford GB 31 D8
Hertník SK 161 E3
Hertsa UA 169 A8
Hertsånger S 134 F6
Hertsjö S 119 D11
Herve B 35 C12
Hervik N 110 D3
Herwijnen NL 199 B6
Herzberg D 96 C4
Herzberg D 99 C11
Herzberg D 100 E3
Herzberg am Harz D 95 C7
Herzebrock-Clarholz D 33 E10
Herzele B 35 C8
Herzfelde D 96 B5
Herzhorn D 33 A12
Herzlake D 33 C9
Herzogenaurach D 91 C8
Herzogenbuchsee CH 43 F8
Herzogenburg A 93 F9
Herzogenrath D 199 D8
Herzsprung D 99 D12
Hesdin F 34 D5
Hesel D 33 B9
Hesjeberg N 127 C13
Hesjestranda N 116 A6
Heskestad N 110 F4
Hespérange L 36 E6
Heßdorf D 91 C8
Hesselager DK 103 E7
Hessen D 95 B8
Hessfjorden N 128 D3
Heßheim D 37 E10
Hessisch Lichtenau D 94 D6
Hessisch Oldendorf D 33 D12
Hest N 116 D3
Hestenesøyri N 116 C4
Hestnes N 120 D5
Hestøy N 124 E3
Hestra S 107 E14
Hestra S 108 D6
Hestvik N 121 B10
Hestvika N 120 D6
Heswall GB 26 E5
Hetekylä FIN 135 D17
Hetés H 165 D9
Hethersett GB 31 B11
Hetlingen D 98 C7
Hettange-Grande F 202 C1
Hettenleidelheim D 202 B5
Hettenshausen D 91 E10
Hettingen D 43 D11
Hetton GB 27 C7
Hettstedt D 95 C10
Hetzerath D 37 E7
Heubach D 203 D8
Heuchelheim D 37 C11
Heuchin F 34 D5
Heudicourt-sous-les-Côtes F 42 C4
Heukelum NL 32 E4
Heusden B 35 B11
Heusden NL 199 B6
Heusenstamm D 37 D11
Heustreu D 91 B7
Heusweiler D 202 C2
Heves H 166 B5
Hévíz H 165 C8
Hevlín CZ 93 E10
Hexham GB 21 F12
Heyrieux F 47 D7
Heysham GB 26 C6
Heythuysen NL 35 B12
Heywood GB 27 D7
Hida RO 167 C11
Hidas H 165 D10
Hidasnémeti H 161 G3
Hiddenhausen D 33 D11
Hiddensee D 100 A4
Hıdırköylü TR 193 D10
Hidişelu de Sus RO 167 D9
Hieflau A 89 A10
Hiendelaencina E 63 B7
Hiersac F 44 D5
Hietakangas FIN 131 D3
Hietama FIN 139 E15
Hietanen FIN 133 D11
Hietanen FIN 144 B7
Hietaniemi FIN 131 D6
Hietaniemi FIN 137 B11
Hietaperä FIN 137 F13
Higham Ferrers GB 31 C7
Highampton GB 28 D6
High Bentham GB 26 C6
Highbridge GB 29 C9
Highclere GB 29 C12
High Halden GB 31 E10
High Hawsker GB 27 C10
High Hesket GB 21 F11
High Lorton GB 21 F10
Highnam GB 29 B10
Highworth GB 29 B11
High Wycombe GB 31 D7
Higuera de Arjona E 69 A9
Higuera de la Serena E 67 B8
Higuera de la Sierra E 67 D7
Higuera de Llerena E 67 C8
Higuera de Vargas E 67 C6
Higuera la Real E 67 C6
Higueruela E 71 B10
Higueruelas E 64 E3
Hiihnavaara FIN 131 D4
Hiidenkylä FIN 139 C15
Hiidenlahti FIN 141 E10
Hiilikumpu FIN 135 C15
Hiirikylä FIN 141 C10
Hiirola FIN 144 B7
Hiisijärvi FIN 137 F12
Híjar E 58 E3
Hikiä FIN 143 D12
Hilbersdorf D 96 E4
Hilchenbach D 37 C10
Hildburghausen D 91 B8
Hilden D 37 B7
Hilders D 95 E7
Hilderthorpe GB 27 C11
Hildesheim D 94 B6
Hilgertshausen D 91 F9
Hilişeu-Horia RO 169 A8
Hiliuţi MD 169 B10
Hillared S 107 D13
Hille D 33 D11
Hille S 119 E13
Hillebola S 115 B9
Hillegom NL 32 D3
Hillerød DK 103 D10
Hillerse D 95 B7
Hillerslev DK 102 A3
Hillerslev DK 102 E6
Hillerstorp S 104 A5
Hilleshamn N 127 C13
Hillesheim D 37 D7
Hillesøy N 127 A15
Hillevik S 119 E13
Hilli FIN 139 C11
Hilliä FIN 139 B11
Hill of Fearn GB 19 K9
Hillosensalmi FIN 144 C6
Hillsand S 122 C8
Hillsborough GB 23 D10
Hillside GB 21 B12
Hillswick GB 19 E14
Hilltown GB 23 D10
Hilpoltstein D 91 D9
Hilsenheim F 202 E4
Hilton GB 27 F8
Hiltpoltstein D 91 C9
Hiltula FIN 145 B9
Hilvarenbeek NL 199 C6
Hilversum NL 32 D4
Himalansaari FIN 144 C8
Himanka FIN 139 B11

Himarë AL 184 D2
Himberg A 93 F10
Himbergen D 99 D9
Himesháza H 165 D11
Himmaste EST 147 E14
Himmelberg A 89 C9
Himmelpforten D 33 A12
Hîncești MD 170 D3
Hinckley GB 27 F9
Hindås S 107 D11
Hindelang D 87 B10
Hindenburg D 99 E11
Hinderwell GB 27 B10
Hindhead GB 31 E7
Hindley GB 26 D6
Hindon GB 29 C10
Hindrem N 120 D8
Hinganmaa FIN 133 D15
Hingham GB 31 B10
Hinnerjöki FIN 142 C6
Hinnerup DK 102 C6
Hinneryd S 103 B13
Hinojal E 61 E8
Hinojales E 67 C6
Hinojares E 71 D7
Hinojasas de Calatrava E 70 B4
Hinojos E 67 E7
Hinojosa E 63 B9
Hinojosa de Duero E 61 C7
Hinojosa de Jarque E 58 F2
Hinojosa del Duque E 67 B9
Hinojosa del Valle E 67 C7
Hinojosa de San Vicente E 62 D3
Hinova RO 175 D10
Hinte D 33 B8
Hinterhermsdorf D 96 E6
Hinternah D 91 A8
Hinterrhein CH 87 D8
Hintersee A 89 A7
Hintersee D 100 C6
Hinterweidenthal D 202 C4
Hinterzarten D 43 E9
Hinthaara FIN 143 E13
Hinwil CH 43 F10
Hinx F 48 C4
Hippolytushoef NL 32 C3
Hîrbovăț MD 170 C2
Hîrjauca MD 170 C2
Hırka TR 197 B9
Hirnyk UA 160 C9
Hirrlingen D 43 D10
Hirschaid D 91 C9
Hirschau D 91 C10
Hirschberg D 91 B10
Hirschfeld D 96 D5
Hirschhorn (Neckar) D 203 C6
Hirsilä FIN 143 B11
Hirsingue F 43 E7
Hirson F 35 E9
Hîrtop MD 170 D3
Hîrtopul Mare MD 170 C3
Hirtshals DK 106 D6
Hirvas FIN 135 B14
Hirvaskoski FIN 136 D9
Hirvasperä FIN 135 E13
Hirvasvaara FIN 131 E5
Hirvelä FIN 135 D16
Hirvelä FIN 137 F14
Hirvensalmi FIN 144 B6
Hirviäkuru FIN 131 D1
Hirvihaara FIN 143 D13
Hirvijoki FIN 139 E10
Hirvikylä FIN 139 F9
Hirvilahti FIN 140 D8
Hirvineva FIN 135 E14
Hirvivaara FIN 137 E13
Hirvlax FIN 138 D8
Hirwaun GB 29 B7
Hirzenhain D 37 D12
Hisarönü TR 197 C8
Hishult S 103 C12
Hissjön S 138 C4
Histon GB 31 C9
Hita E 63 C6
Hitchin GB 31 D8
Hitis FIN 142 F8
Hittarp S 103 C11
Hittisau A 87 C9
Hitzacker D 99 D10
Hitzendorf A 164 B4
Hitzhusen D 99 C7
Hiukkajoki FIN 145 B12
Hiyche UA 160 C8
Hjåggsjö S 138 C3
Hjallerup DK 102 A6
Hjältevad S 108 D6
Hjärnarp S 103 C11
Hjärsås S 104 C6
Hjärtum S 107 C11
Hjarup DK 102 E4
Hjelle N 116 C6
Hjellestad N 110 B2
Hjellsand N 126 C8
Hjelmeland N 110 D4
Hjelset N 116 A7
Hjerkinn N 117 B11
Hjerm DK 102 C3
Hjo S 108 C4
Hjordkær DK 102 E4
Hjørring DK 106 E7
Hjorted S 109 D8
Hjortkvarn S 108 B6
Hjortsberga S 104 B6
Hjørungavåg N 116 B4
Hjuvik S 107 D10
Hlavani UA 170 F4
Hlebine HR 165 D7
Hligeni MD 170 B3
Hlinaia MD 169 A10
Hlinaia MD 170 C4
Hlinaia MD 170 D5
Hliník nad Hronom SK 163 D7
Hlinné SK 161 F4
Hlinsko CZ 93 C9
Hlohovec SK 162 E5
Hlubočky CZ 162 B4
Hluboká nad Vltavou CZ 93 D6
Hlučín CZ 162 B6
Hlyboka UA 169 A7
Hlybokaye BY 149 F3
Hlyboke UA 171 B5
Hnatkiv UA 170 A2
Hněvotín CZ 93 C12
Hniezdné SK 161 E2
Hnizdychiv UA 161 E9
Hnojník CZ 163 B7
Hnúšťa SK 163 D9
Hobol H 165 D9
Hobøl N 111 C13
Hobro DK 102 B5
Hoburg S 109 F12
Hoča Zagradska SRB 179 E10
Hoceni RO 169 D12
Hochdonn D 98 B6
Hochdorf CH 43 F9
Hochdorf D 87 A9
Hochfelden F 43 C8
Höchheim D 91 B7
Hochspeyer D 202 C4
Hochstadt (Pfalz) D 203 C5
Höchstadt an der Aisch D 91 C8
Höchstädt an der Donau D 91 E8
Hochstetten-Dhaun D 37 E8
Höchst im Odenwald D 203 B6
Hoçisht AL 184 C4
Hockenheim D 203 C6
Hoczew PL 161 E5
Hodac RO 168 D5
Hodalen N 117 B14
Hoddesdon GB 31 D8
Hodejov SK 163 E10
Hodenhagen D 98 E7
Hodkovice nad Mohelkou CZ 97 E8
Hódmezővásárhely H 166 E5
Hodnet GB 26 F6
Hodod RO 167 C11
Hodonice CZ 93 E10
Hodonín CZ 93 E12
Hodoșa RO 168 D5
Hodruša-Hámre SK 163 E7
Hodsager DK 102 C3
Hodyszewo PL 157 E7
Hoek NL 32 F1
Hoek van Holland NL 32 E2
Hoem N 120 F4
Hoenderloo NL 199 A7
Hœnheim F 202 D4
Hoensbroek NL 35 C12
Hœrdt F 202 D4
Hoeselt B 35 C11
Hoevelaken NL 32 D4
Hoeven NL 32 E3
Hof D 37 C10
Hof D 91 B10
Hof N 111 C12
Hofbieber D 94 E6
Hoffstad N 120 C8
Hofgeismar D 37 B12
Hofheim am Taunus D 37 D10
Hofheim in Unterfranken D 91 B8
Hofles N 121 B11
Hofors S 114 A6
Hofsøy N 127 B13
Hofterup S 103 D11
Höganäs S 103 C11
Högås S 124 E9
Högbacka S 119 D12
Högbo S 119 E12
Högboda S 113 C9
Högbränna S 125 F15
Högen S 119 C13
Högfors S 113 B15
Högfors S 113 C13
Hoghilag RO 168 E5
Hoghiz RO 168 F6
Høgild DK 102 C3
Högland S 123 B9
Höglekardallen S 121 E15
Høgli N 127 B14
Höglunda S 123 E9
Högrun S 121 D16
Högsåra FIN 142 F7
Högsäter S 107 B11
Högsäter S 112 C6
Högsäter S 113 D8
Högsby S 105 A10
Høgset N 120 F3
Högsjö S 108 A7
Högsjö S 119 A14
Hogstad S 108 C6
Hogstorp S 107 C10
Högträsk S 132 E5
Högvålen S 118 B4
Hőgyész H 165 C10
Hohberg D 202 E4
Hohen-Altheim D 91 E8
Hohenaspe D 98 C7
Hohenau D 92 E5
Hohenau an der March A 93 E11
Hohenberg A 93 G9
Hohenbocka D 96 D6
Hohenbucko D 96 C4
Hohenburg D 91 D10
Hohendorf D 100 B5
Hoheneich A 93 E8
Hohenems A 87 C9
Hohenfels D 91 D10
Hohenfurch D 87 B11
Hohengöhren D 95 A11
Hohenhameln D 95 B7
Hohenkammer D 91 F10
Hohenkirchen D 33 A9
Höhenkirchen-Siegertsbrunn D 91 F10
Hohenleuben D 95 E11
Hohenlockstedt D 98 C7
Hohenmocker D 100 C4
Hohenmölsen D 95 D11
Hohennauen D 99 E12
Hohenpeißenberg D 87 B12
Hohenroth D 91 B7
Hohensaaten D 100 E6
Hohenseeden D 95 B11
Hohenstein-Ernstthal D 95 E12
Hohenthann D 91 E11
Hohenthurm D 95 C11
Hohen Wangelin D 99 C12
Hohenwart D 91 E9
Hohenwarth D 92 D3
Hohenwestedt D 98 B7
Höhn D 37 C9
Hohn D 98 B7
Hohne D 95 A7
Hohnhorst D 33 D12
Hohnstorf (Elbe) D 99 D9
Höhr-Grenzhausen D 37 D9
Hohwacht (Ostsee) D 99 B9
Hoikankylä FIN 140 E7
Hoikka FIN 137 E12
Hoisdorf D 99 C8
Hoisko FIN 139 D11
Højby DK 102 E6
Højby DK 103 D9
Højer DK 102 F3
Højmark DK 102 C2
Højslev DK 102 B4
Højslev Stationsby DK 102 B4
Hok S 108 D4
Hökåsen S 114 C7
Hökerum S 107 D13
Hökhult S 107 A13
Hökhuvud S 115 B10
Hokka FIN 144 B6
Hokkaskylä FIN 139 E12
Hokksund N 111 C11
Hokland N 127 C11
Hökmark S 134 F6
Hökön S 104 C6
Hol N 117 E8
Hol N 127 C11
Holand N 126 D9
Holandsvika N 124 E5
Holasovice CZ 158 G4
Holbæk DK 102 B6
Holbæk DK 103 D9
Holbeach GB 27 F12
Holboca RO 169 C11
Holbøl DK 102 F4
Holbrook GB 31 D11
Holdorf D 33 C10
Holeby DK 99 A10
Hølen N 111 C13
Holešov CZ 162 C5
Holevik N 116 D1
Holguera E 61 E8
Holíč SK 93 E12
Holice CZ 93 B9
Höljes S 118 E4
Holkestad N 126 E8
Holkonkylä FIN 139 E11
Hollabrunn A 93 E10
Hollandscheveld NL 33 C7
Hollange B 35 E12
Hollås N 121 C11
Holle D 95 B7
Høllen N 106 C2
Hollenbach D 91 F9
Hollenbek D 99 C9
Hollenegg A 89 C11
Hollenstedt D 98 D7
Hollenstein an der Ybbs A 89 A10
Hollern-Twielenfleth D 98 C7
Hollfeld D 91 C9
Hollingstedt D 98 B6
Hollington GB 31 F10
Hollingworth GB 27 E8
Hollóháza H 161 F3
Hollola FIN 143 D14
Hollum NL 32 B5
Hollybush GB 20 E7
Hollyford IRL 24 C6
Hollywood IRL 23 F9
Holm D 98 C7
Holm DK 102 E5
Holm N 121 A12
Holm N 126 C9
Holm S 119 A12
Holm S 123 E13
Hol'ma UA 170 B5
Holmajärvi S 127 E18
Holme-Olstrup DK 103 E9
Holme-on-Spalding-Moor GB 27 D10
Holmestrand N 111 D12
Holmfirth GB 27 D8
Holmfors S 134 D4
Holmisperä FIN 139 D14
Holmsjö S 105 C9
Holmsjö S 123 A14
Holmsjö S 123 D12
Holmsund S 138 C4
Holmsvattensel S 134 B6
Holmsveden S 119 D12
Holmträsk S 123 B16
Hölö S 109 A11
Holod RO 167 D9
Hołodowska PL 160 C7
Holoșnița MD 169 A12
Holoubkov CZ 92 C5
Holovets'ko UA 161 E6
Holovne UA 157 H10
Holsbybrunn S 108 E6
Holsljunga S 107 E12
Holsta EST 147 F14
Holstebro DK 102 C3
Holsted DK 102 D3
Hölstein CH 43 F8
Holsworthy GB 28 D6
Holt GB 26 E6
Holt GB 31 B11
Holt N 127 B16
Holt N 127 B17
Holte DK 103 D10
Holten NL 33 D6
Holtet N 118 E3
Holtgast D 33 A9
Holthusen D 99 C10
Holtsee D 99 B7
Holungen D 95 D7
Holwerd NL 32 B5
Holycross IRL 25 C7
Holyhead GB 26 E2
Holywell GB 23 D7
Holywell GB 26 E5
Holywood GB 20 F5
Holzappel D 201 D8
Holzen D 94 C6
Holzgerlingen D 203 D7
Holzhausen an der Haide D 37 D9
Holzheim D 37 D11
Holzheim D 91 E8
Holzheim D 91 E8
Holzheim D 91 F7
Holzkirchen D 88 A4
Holzminden D 37 A12
Holzthaleben D 95 D8
Holzweißig D 95 C11
Holzwickede D 33 E9
Høm DK 103 E9
Homberg (Efze) D 37 B12
Homberg (Ohm) D 37 C11
Hombourg-Budange F 202 C1
Hombourg-Haut F 202 C2
Homburg D 37 F8
Homécourt F 36 F5
Homersfield GB 31 C11
Homesh AL 184 A3
Hommelstø N 124 F4
Hommelvik N 121 E9
Hommersåk N 110 E3
Homna S 119 D10
Homocea RO 169 E10
Homokmégy H 166 E3
Homokszentgyörgy H 165 D9
Homoroade RO 167 B11
Homorod RO 168 E6
Homrogd H 161 G2
Homyel' BY 149 F5
Hondarribia E 48 D2
Hondón de las Nieves E 72 E3
Hondón de los Frailes E 72 E3
Hondschoote F 34 C6
Hône I 84 B4
Hønefoss N 111 B12
Honfleur F 39 B12
Høng DK 103 D8
Honiton GB 29 D8
Honkajoki FIN 138 G8
Honkakoski FIN 142 B7
Honkakylä FIN 138 E9
Honkilahti FIN 142 D7
Honley GB 27 D8
Honningsvåg N 116 B2
Honningsvåg N 129 B16
Hönö S 107 D10
Honoratka PL 158 B5
Honrubia E 63 E8
Honrubia de la Cuesta E 56 F4
Hønseby N 129 B11
Hontacillas E 63 E8
Hontalbilla E 56 F3
Hontanaya E 63 E7
Hontianske Nemce SK 163 E7
Hontoria de la Cantera E 56 D4
Hontoria del Pinar E 56 E5
Hontoria de Valdearados E 56 E4
Hoofddorp NL 32 D3
Hoogerheide NL 32 F2
Hoogersmilde NL 32 C6
Hoogeveen NL 33 C6
Hoogezand-Sappemeer NL 33 B7
Hoogkarspel NL 32 C4
Hoog-Keppel NL 199 B8
Hoogkerk NL 33 B6
Hoogland NL 199 A6
Hoogstede D 33 C7
Hoogstraten B 32 F3
Hoogvliet NL 32 E2
Hook GB 27 D10
Hook GB 30 E7
Hooksiel D 33 A10
Höör S 103 D13
Hoorn NL 32 C4
Hoornaar NL 198 B5
Hopârta RO 168 E3
Hope GB 26 E5
Hope N 116 E3
Hopeman GB 19 K10
Hopen N 127 E10
Hopfgarten im Brixental A 88 B5
Hopfgarten in Defereggen A 88 C6
Hopland N 116 C4
Hoppstädten D 37 E8
Hoppula FIN 131 F2
Hopseidet N 129 B20
Hopsten D 33 D9
Hopton GB 31 B12
Hoptonheath GB 29 A9
Hoptrup DK 102 E4
Horam GB 31 F9
Horažďovice CZ 92 D5
Horb am Neckar D 43 D10
Horbova UA 169 A8
Hörbranz A 87 B9
Hørby DK 106 E7
Hörby S 103 D13
Horcajo de las Torres E 61 B10
Horcajo de los Montes E 62 F3
Horcajo de Santiago E 63 E7
Horcajo Medianero E 61 C10
Horda N 110 C5
Horda S 104 A6
Hörde D 201 B7
Horden GB 27 B9
Hordum DK 102 B3
Horea RO 167 E10
Horeb GB 28 A6
Horești MD 169 C11
Horezu RO 176 C3
Horgen CH 43 F10
Horgenzell D 87 B9
Horgești RO 169 E10
Horgoš SRB 166 E4
Horia RO 169 D9
Horia RO 171 C2
Horia RO 171 D2
Hořice CZ 93 B9
Horinchove UA 161 G7
Horitschon A 165 A7
Horjul SLO 89 D9
Horka D 97 D7
Hôrka SK 161 E1
Hörken S 113 B12
Horley GB 31 E8
Hörlitz D 96 C5
Hormakumpu FIN 133 C14
Hormilla E 56 D6
Horn A 93 E9
Horn N 111 A12
Horn N 124 E3
Horn S 108 D7
Hornachos E 67 B7
Hornachuelos E 67 D9
Horná Kraľová SK 162 E5
Horná Potôň SK 162 E4
Horná Streda SK 162 D5
Horná Štubňa SK 163 D7
Horná Súča SK 162 D5
Horná Ves SK 162 D6
Hornbach D 37 F8
Horn-Bad Meinberg D 33 E11
Hornbæk DK 103 C10
Hornburg D 95 B8
Hornby GB 26 C6
Horncastle GB 27 E11
Horndal N 125 A10
Horndal S 114 B6
Horndean GB 30 F6
Horne DK 102 D3
Horne DK 102 E6
Horne DK 106 D6
Horneburg D 98 C7
Hörnefors S 138 C3
Horné Obdokovce SK 162 E6
Horné Orešany SK 162 E4
Horné Saliby SK 162 E5
Horné Srnie SK 162 C6
Horní Bečva CZ 162 C6
Horní Benešov CZ 162 B5
Horní Beřkovice CZ 92 B6
Horní Cerekev CZ 93 D8
Horní Jelení CZ 93 B10
Horní Jiřetín CZ 96 E5
Horní Lideč CZ 162 C6
Horní Maršov CZ 97 E9
Horní Moštěnice CZ 162 C4
Hornindal N 116 C5
Hørning DK 102 C6
Horní Planá CZ 92 E6
Horní Slavkov CZ 91 B12
Horní Štěpánov CZ 93 C11
Horní Stropnice CZ 93 E7
Horní Suchá CZ 162 B6
Hornmyr S 123 C14
Hornnäs S 113 B9
Hornnes N 106 B2
Hornön S 119 A14
Hornos E 71 C7
Hornow D 97 C7
Hornoy-le-Bourg F 34 E4
Hornsea GB 27 D11
Hörnsjö S 123 D17
Hornslet DK 102 C6
Hornstorf D 99 C11
Hornsyld DK 102 D5
Hörnum D 98 A4
Hornum DK 102 B4
Horný Bar SK 162 F4
Horný Tisovník SK 163 E8
Horný Vadičov SK 163 C7
Horoatu Crasnei RO 167 C10
Horodiște MD 169 A11
Horodiște MD 169 B10
Horodkivka UA 170 A3
Horodło PL 160 B9
Horodniceni RO 169 B8
Horodnye UA 170 F3
Horodok UA 160 D8
Horoměřice CZ 92 B6
Horonda UA 161 G6
Horonkylä FIN 138 E7
Hořovice CZ 92 C5
Horrabridge GB 28 D6
Horreby DK 99 A11
Horred S 107 E11
Hörsching A 92 F6
Horsdal N 124 B7
Horseleap IRL 22 F5
Horsens DK 102 D5
Horsforth GB 27 D8
Horsham GB 31 E8
Hørsholm DK 103 D10
Hörsingen D 95 B9
Horslunde DK 103 F8
Horsmanaho FIN 141 E12
Horsnes N 127 B18
Horšovský Týn CZ 92 C3
Horsskog S 114 B8
Horst NL 32 F6
Horst (Holstein) D 98 C7
Horstedt D 33 B12
Hörstel D 33 D9
Horstmar D 33 D8
Hort H 166 B4
Horten N 111 D12
Hortezuela E 56 F6
Hortigüela E 56 D5
Hortlax S 134 D6
Hortobágy H 167 B7
Horton in Ribblesdale GB 27 C7
Høruphav DK 102 F5
Hørve DK 103 D8
Hörvik S 105 C7
Horw CH 86 C6
Horwich GB 26 D6
Horyniec-Zdrój PL 160 C7
Horyszów PL 160 B8
Hösbach D 37 D12
Hosena D 96 D6
Hosenfeld D 90 A5
Hoset N 124 B8
Hosingen L 36 D6
Hosio FIN 135 C15
Hosjö S 122 E8
Hosjöbottnarna S 121 E15
Hoşköy TR 189 C7
Hospital IRL 24 D6
Hossa FIN 137 D14
Hössjö S 138 C3
Hossjön S 123 D9
Hoßkirch D 43 E11
Hosszúhetény H 165 D10
Hosszúpályi H 167 C8
Hosszúpereszteg H 165 B8
Hošťálková CZ 162 C5
Hostalríc E 59 D9
Hostens F 48 B4
Hostěradice CZ 93 E10
Hostie SK 162 E6
Hostinné CZ 97 E9
Hošťka CZ 92 B6
Hostomice CZ 92 C6
Hostomice CZ 96 E5
Hoston N 120 E7
Höstoppen S 122 C8
Hostouň CZ 91 C12
Hostrupskov DK 102 E4
Höstsätern S 118 C4
Hot AL 179 E7
Hotarele RO 177 E8
Hoting S 123 C10
Hotinja vas SLO 164 D5
Hotonj BIH 178 D4
Hotton B 35 D11
Hou DK 102 A6
Houbie GB 19 D15
Houdain F 34 D6
Houdan F 40 C6
Houdelaincourt F 42 C3
Houécourt F 42 D4
Houeillès F 48 B6
Houeydets F 49 D6
Houffalize B 35 D12
Houghton le Spring GB 21 F14
Houghton Regis GB 31 D7
Houlbjerg DK 102 C5
Houlgate F 39 B11
Hourtin F 44 E3
Hourtin-Plage F 44 E3
Houten NL 32 D4
Houthalen B 35 B11
Houthulst B 34 C6
Houton GB 19 H10
Houtsala FIN 142 E6
Houtskär FIN 142 E5
Houyet B 200 D3
Hov DK 102 D6
Hov N 117 E12
Hov N 124 D4
Hov N 127 A18
Hova S 108 B4
Hovborg DK 102 D3
Hovda N 110 D4
Hovde N 106 B4
Hovden N 126 C8
Hovdevik N 116 B2
Hove GB 31 F8
Hovedgård DK 102 D5
Hövelhof D 33 E11
Hoven DK 102 D3
Hoveton GB 31 B11
Hověží CZ 162 C6
Hovid S 119 B13
Hovin N 120 E8
Hovingham GB 27 C10
Hovmantorp S 105 B8
Høvringen N 117 C10
Hovslund Stationsby DK 102 E4
Hovsta S 113 D13
Howden GB 27 D10
Howth IRL 23 F10
Höxter D 33 E12
Hoya D 33 C12
Hoya Gonzalo E 71 B9
Høyanger N 116 D4
Høydal N 106 A5
Hoyerswerda D 96 D6
Hoylake GB 26 E5
Høylandet N 121 B12
Hoym D 95 C9
Hoyocasero E 62 D3
Hoyo de Manzanares E 62 C5
Hoyos E 61 D7
Hoyos del Espino E 61 D10
Höytiä FIN 139 F14
Hoyvik FO 18 A3
Hozha BY 153 F8
Hrabove UA 170 A4
Hrabyně CZ 162 B6
Hradec Králové CZ 93 B9
Hradec nad Moravicí CZ 162 B5
Hradec nad Svitavou CZ 93 C10
Hrádek CZ 163 B7
Hrádek nad Nisou CZ 97 E7
Hradenytsi UA 170 D6
Hradešice CZ 92 D5
Hradište SK 162 D6
Hradište pod Vrátnom SK 162 D5
Hradištko CZ 92 C6
Hraň SK 161 F4
Hranice CZ 91 B11
Hranice CZ 162 B5
Hranovnica SK 161 F1
Hrasnica BIH 173 E9
Hrastnik SLO 89 D11
Hrawzhyshki BY 153 E12
Hrebenyky UA 170 D5
Hreljin HR 83 B10
Hrhov SK 161 F2
Hrimne UA 161 D8
Hriňová SK 163 D9
Hristovaia MD 170 A3
Hrnjadi BIH 172 D5
Hrob CZ 96 E5
Hrochot SK 163 D8
Hrochův Týnec CZ 93 C9
Hrodna BY 156 C9
Hromnice CZ 92 C4
Hronec SK 163 D9
Hronov CZ 93 B10
Hronovce SK 163 E7
Hronský Beňadik SK 163 E7
Hrotovice CZ 93 D10
Hroznová Lhota CZ 162 D4
Hrtkovci SRB 174 D4
Hrubieszów PL 160 B8
Hrușca MD 170 A3
Hrušky CZ 93 E11
Hrușova MD 170 C3
Hrušovany SK 162 E6
Hrušovany nad Jevišovkou CZ 93 E10
Hruštín SK 163 C8
Hruszniew PL 157 F7
Hrvaćani BIH 173 C7
Hrvace HR 172 E6
Hrvatska Dubica HR 173 B6
Hrvatska Kostajnica HR 172 B6
Hrynyava UA 168 B5
Huaröd S 104 D5
Huarte E 48 E2
Hubová SK 163 C8
Hückelhoven D 36 B6
Hückeswagen D 37 B8
Hucknall GB 27 E9
Hucksjöåsen S 119 A10
Hucqueliers F 31 F12
Huddersfield GB 27 D8
Hüde D 33 C10
Hude (Oldenburg) D 33 B10
Hudești RO 169 A9
Hudiksvall S 119 C13
Huécija E 71 F7
Huedin RO 167 D11
Huélago E 71 E6
Huelgoat F 38 D4
Huelma E 69 A10
Huelva E 67 E6
Huelves E 63 D7
Huércal de Almería E 71 F8
Huércal-Overa E 71 E9
Huérguina E 63 D9
Huérmeces E 56 C4
Huerta del Marquesada E 63 D9
Huerta del Rey E 56 E5
Huerta de Valdecarábanos E 62 E5
Huertahernando E 63 C8
Huerto E 58 D3
Huesa E 71 D6
Huesa del Común E 58 E2
Huesca E 57 D11
Huéscar E 71 D7
Huete E 63 D7
Huétor-Tájar E 69 B8
Huétor-Vega E 69 B9
Huévar E 67 E7
Hüfingen D 43 E9
Hufthamar N 110 B2
Hugh Town GB 28 F2
Hugulia N 117 D11
Hugyag H 163 E8
Huhdasjärvi FIN 143 C16
Huhmarkoski FIN 139 D10
Huhtamo FIN 143 C8
Huhti FIN 143 C10
Huhtilampi FIN 141 F14
Huhus FIN 141 E15
Huijbergen NL 198 C4
Huikola FIN 135 E16
Huisheim D 91 E8
Huisinis GB 18 K2
Huissen NL 32 E5
Huissinkylä FIN 138 E8
Huittinen FIN 142 C8
Huizen NL 32 D4
Hujakkala FIN 144 D8
Hukijärvi FIN 137 D10
Hukkajärvi FIN 141 B14
Hulín CZ 162 C4
Hulja EST 147 C12
Huljen S 119 B12
Hulkkola FIN 140 E8
Hüllhorst D 33 D11
Hullo EST 146 D6
Hullsjön S 119 A12
Hüls D 199 C8
Hulsberg NL 199 D7
Hulst NL 32 F2
Hult S 107 A15
Hult S 108 D6
Hulterstad S 105 C11
Hultsfred S 108 D7
Hulu S 107 D13
Hulubești RO 176 D6
Hulyanka UA 170 C4
Hum BIH 173 F10
Hum BIH 178 D5
Humalajoki FIN 139 D13
Humanes de Madrid E 62 D5
Humanes de Mohernando E 63 C6
Humberston GB 27 D11
Humbie GB 21 D11
Humble DK 99 A9
Humenné SK 161 F4
Humilladero E 69 B7
Humlebæk DK 103 D11
Humlegärdsstrand S 119 D13
Humlum DK 102 B3
Hummelholm S 123 D17
Hummelo NL 199 A8
Hummelsta S 114 C7
Hummuli EST 147 F12
Hum na Sutli HR 164 D5
Humpolec CZ 93 C8
Humppila FIN 143 D9
Humshaugh GB 21 E12
Huncovce SK 161 E1
Hundåla N 124 E4
Hundberg N 127 B18
Hundberg S 125 F16
Hundborg DK 102 B3
Hundeluft D 95 C11
Hunderdorf D 91 E12
Hundested DK 103 D9
Hundholmen N 127 D11
Hundorp N 117 C11
Hundsangen D 37 D9
Hundshübel D 95 E12
Hundsjön S 134 C7
Hundslund DK 102 D6
Hundvin N 116 E2
Hune DK 102 A5
Hunedoara RO 167 F10
Hünfeld D 94 E6
Hünfelden-Kirberg D 37 D10
Hunge S 119 A9
Hungen D 37 D11
Hungerford GB 29 C11
Hunnebostrand S 107 C9
Hunsel NL 35 B12
Hunspach F 43 C8
Hunstanton GB 27 F12
Huntingdon GB 31 C8
Huntlosen D 33 C10
Huntly GB 19 L11
Hünxe D 199 B9
Hunya H 167 D6
Huopanankoski FIN 139 D15
Hüpstedt D 95 D7
Hurbanovo SK 162 F6
Hurdal N 111 B14
Hurdalsverk N 111 B14
Hurezani RO 176 D3
Huriel F 45 C10
Hurissalo FIN 144 C8
Hurler's Cross IRL 24 C5
Hursley GB 29 C12
Hurst Green GB 31 E9
Hurstpierpoint GB 31 F8
Hurteles E 57 D7
Hürth D 37 C7
Huruiești RO 169 E10
Huruksela FIN 144 D6
Hurup DK 102 B2
Hurva S 103 D12
Huså S 121 E14
Husås S 122 E7
Husasău de Tinca RO 167 D8
Husbands Bosworth GB 29 A12
Husberget S 118 B6
Husbondliden S 123 B15
Husby D 98 A7
Husby S 113 B15
Husby S 115 B9
Hushcha UA 157 H9
Huși RO 169 D12
Husinec CZ 92 D5
Husjorda N 127 D9
Huskvarna S 108 D4
Husnes N 110 C3
Husnicioara RO 175 D10
Husøy N 124 D3
Hussjö S 119 A14
Hustopeče CZ 93 E11
Hustopeče nad Bečvou CZ 162 B5
Husum D 33 C12
Husum D 98 B6
Husum S 123 E16
Husvik N 124 E4
Huta PL 157 H3
Huta Komorowska PL 159 F12
Hutisko-Solanec CZ 162 C6
Hutovo BIH 178 D4
Hütschenhausen D 202 C3
Hüttau A 89 B7
Hüttenberg A 89 C10
Hüttisheim D 90 F6
Hüttlingen D 91 E7
Huttoft GB 27 E12
Hüttschlag A 89 B7
Huttukylä FIN 135 D15
Huttwil CH 43 F8
Huuhilonkylä FIN 137 F13
Huuki S 133 D11
Huutijärvi FIN 143 C11
Huutokoski FIN 140 F9
Huutokoski FIN 141 E12
Huutoniemi FIN 129 E18
Huvåsen S 134 D4
Hüven D 33 C9
Huwniki PL 161 D6
Huy B 35 C11
Hvalpsund DK 102 B4
Hvalsø DK 103 D9
Hvalvik FO 18 A2
Hvam DK 102 B5
Hvannasund FO 18 A3
Hvar HR 172 F5
Hvidbjerg DK 102 B3
Hvide Sande DK 102 C2
Hvidovre DK 103 D10
Hvilsom DK 102 B5
Hvittingfoss N 111 D11
Hvorslev DK 102 C5
Hwlffordd GB 28 B5
Hybe SK 163 C9
Hybo S 119 C11

Hycklinge S 108 D7
Hyères F 52 E4
Hyermanavichy BY 149 F3
Hyervyaty BY 153 D13
Hylen N 110 C5
Hylleråsen N 118 C3
Hyllestad N 116 D2
Hyllinge DK 103 E9
Hyllinge S 103 C11
Hyltebruk S 103 A12
Hymont F 42 D5
Hyönölä FIN 143 E10
Hyrkäs FIN 135 E16
Hyry FIN 135 C14
Hyrynsalmi FIN 137 E11
Hysgjokaj AL 184 C2
Hyssna S 107 D12
Hythe GB 29 D12
Hythe GB 31 E11
Hytti FIN 145 D9
Hyttön S 115 B8
Hyväneula FIN 143 D13
Hyväniemi FIN 137 B11
Hyvärilä FIN 135 F15
Hyvikkälä FIN 143 D12
Hyvinkää FIN 143 D12
Hyvölänranta FIN 135 F16
Hyvönmäki FIN 145 B12
Hyypiö FIN 131 E1
Hyyppä FIN 138 F8
Hyżne PL 160 D5

I

Iablanița RO 175 D9
Iabloana MD 169 B11
Iacobeni RO 168 C6
Iacobeni RO 168 E5
Ialoveni MD 170 D3
Iam RO 175 C7
Ianca RO 176 F4
Ianca RO 177 C10
Iancu Jianu RO 176 E4
Iara RO 168 D3
Iargara MD 170 E2
Iarova MD 169 A12
Iași RO 169 C11
Iasmos GR 187 B8
Ibahernando E 61 F9
Iballë AL 179 E9
Ibănești RO 168 D5
Ibănești RO 169 A8
Ibarra E 48 D1
Ibbenbüren D 33 D9
Ibdes E 63 B9
Ibë AL 184 B2
Ibeas de Juarros E 56 D4
Ibestad N 127 C13
Ibi E 72 D3
Ibos F 48 D5
Ibrány H 161 G4
İbriktepe TR 187 B10
Ibros E 69 A10
Ibstock GB 27 F9
Ichenhausen D 91 F7
Ichenheim D 202 E4
Ichtegem B 34 B7
Icking D 88 A3
Icklesham GB 31 F10
Icklingham GB 31 C10
Iclănzel RO 168 D4
Iclod RO 168 D3
Icoana RO 176 E5
Icușești RO 169 D9
Idanha-a-Nova P 61 E6
Idanha-a-Velha P 61 E6
Idar-Oberstein D 37 E8
Ideciu de Jos RO 168 D5
Iden D 99 E11
Ideņi LV 149 C1
Idenor S 119 C13
Idestrup DK 99 A11
Idiazabal E 48 D1
Idivuoma S 132 B8
Idkerberget S 113 B13
Idmiston GB 29 C11
Idocin E 48 E3
Idom DK 102 C2
Iđoš SRB 166 F5
Idre S 118 C4
Idrigil GB 18 K4
Idrija SLO 89 D9
Idritsa RUS 149 D5
Idro I 85 B9
Idron-Ousse-Sendets F 48 D5
Idstedt D 98 A7
Idstein D 37 D10
Idvattnet S 123 C12
Iecava LV 151 C8
Iedera RO 177 C7
Ieper B 34 C6
Iepurești RO 177 E7
Ierapetra GR 195 E10
Ieriķi LV 151 B10
Ierissos GR 186 D5
Iernut RO 168 E4
Ieromnini GR 184 E4
Ieropigi GR 184 C5
Ieșelnița RO 175 D9
Ifaistos GR 187 B8
Iffendic F 39 D7
Iffezheim D 203 D5
Ifjord N 129 C19
Ifs F 39 B11
Ifta D 95 D7
Ig SLO 89 E10
Igal H 165 C9
Igalo MNE 178 E6
Igar H 165 C11
Igé F 40 D4
Igea E 57 D7
Igel D 202 B2
Igelfors S 108 B7
Igelstorp S 107 C14
Igensdorf D 91 C9
Igerøy N 124 E3
Igersheim D 90 D6
Iggelheim D 203 C5
Iggensbach D 92 E4
Iggesund S 119 C13
Ighiu RO 168 E3
Igis CH 87 D9
Iglesias I 80 E2
Igliauka LT 153 D8
Igling D 87 A11
Igliškėliai LT 153 D8
Ignalina LT 151 F12
Ignatievo BG 183 C9
İğneada TR 183 F9
Ignești RO 167 E9
Igney F 42 D5
Igornay F 46 A5
Igoumenitsa GR 184 E3
Igralishte BG 185 A9
Igrejinha P 66 B4
Igrici H 161 H2
Igrīve LV 149 B2
Igualada E 59 D7
Igualeja E 69 C6
Igueña E 55 C7
Iguerande F 46 C5
Iharosberény H 165 D8
Ihľany SK 161 E2
Ihlienworth D 33 A11
Ihlowerhörn (Ihlow) D 33 B9
Ihode FIN 142 D6
Iholdy F 48 D3
Ihrhove D 33 B8
Ihrlerstein D 91 E10
İhsaniye TR 189 B10
Ii FIN 135 D14
Iijärvi FIN 129 E20
Iinattijärvi FIN 137 D9
Iironranta FIN 139 E12
Iisalmi FIN 140 C8
Iisvesi FIN 140 E8
Iitti FIN 143 D15
Iitto FIN 132 A6
Iivantiira FIN 137 F13
IJlst NL 32 B5
IJmuiden NL 32 D3
IJsselmuiden NL 32 C5
IJsselstein NL 32 D4
IJzendijke NL 32 F1
Ikaalinen FIN 143 B9
Ikast DK 102 C4
Ikazn' BY 149 E2
Ikervár H 165 B7
Ikhtiman BG 181 E8
İkizdere TR 193 D10
Ikkala FIN 139 F11
Ikkala FIN 143 E11
Ikkeläjärvi FIN 138 F9
Ikla EST 147 F8
Ikornes N 116 B5
Ikosenniemi FIN 135 C17
Ikrény H 165 A9
Ikšķile LV 151 C8
Ilandža SRB 175 C6
Ilanz CH 87 D8
Ilava SK 162 D6
Iława PL 155 C8
Ilbono I 80 D4
Ilchester GB 29 C9
Ildır TR 193 C7
Île LV 150 C6
Ileana RO 177 D9
Ileanda RO 168 C3
Ilfeld D 95 C8
Ilford GB 31 D9
Ilfracombe GB 28 C6
Ilgižiai LT 150 F6
Ílhavo P 60 C3
Ilia RO 167 F10
Ilıca TR 189 E8
Ilidža BIH 173 E9
Ilieni RO 169 F7
Ilijaš BIH 173 E9
Ilindentsi BG 181 F7
Iliokastro GR 191 E7
Ilirska Bistrica SLO 89 E9
Ilk H 161 G5
Ilkeston GB 27 F9
Ilkley GB 27 D8
Illana E 63 D7
Illar E 71 F7
Illats F 48 A5
Illerrieden D 87 A10
Illertissen D 87 A10
Illescas E 62 D5
Ille-sur-Têt F 50 E4
Illiers-Combray F 40 D5
Illingen D 37 F8
Illingen D 203 D6
Illkirch-Graffenstaden F 43 C8
Illmensee D 43 E11
Illmitz A 165 A7
Íllora E 69 B9
Illschwang D 91 D10
Illueca E 57 E8
Illzach F 43 E7
Ilmajoki FIN 138 E9
Ilmatsalu EST 147 E13
Ilmenau D 95 E8
Ilminster GB 29 D9
Ilmmünster D 91 F10
Ilmola FIN 135 C13
Il'nytsya UA 161 G7
Ilok HR 174 C3
Ilola FIN 143 E14
Ilomantsi FIN 141 E15
Ilosjoki FIN 139 D15
Ilovăț RO 175 D10
Ilovica MK 185 B8
Ilovice BIH 173 E9
Ilovița RO 175 D9
Iłów PL 155 F9
Iłowa PL 97 C8
Iłowo Osada PL 155 D9
Ilsbo S 119 C13
Ilsede D 95 B7
Ilsenburg (Harz) D 95 C8
Ilseng N 117 E14
Ilsfeld D 43 B11
Ilskov DK 102 C4
Ilūkste LV 151 E12
Ilva Mare RO 168 C5
Ilva Mică RO 168 C5
Ilvesjoki FIN 138 F9
İlyaslar TR 189 F9
Ilyushino RUS 152 D6
Ilz A 164 B5
Iłża PL 157 H4
Ilze LV 151 D12
Ilzene LV 151 B13
Imari FIN 135 B15
Imatra FIN 145 C10
Imavere EST 147 D11
Imbradas LT 151 E12
Imeľ SK 162 F6
Imèr I 88 D4
Imeros GR 187 C8
Imielnica PL 155 E8
Immeln S 104 C6
Immendingen D 43 E10
Immenhausen D 94 D5
Immenreuth D 91 C10
Immenstaad am Bodensee D 43 E11
Immenstadt im Allgäu D 87 B10
Immingham GB 27 D11
Imnäs S 123 D11
Imola I 82 D4
Imotski HR 173 F7
Imperia I 53 D8
Imphy F 46 B3
Impilakhti RUS 145 B15
Impiö FIN 136 C9
Impruneta I 82 E3
Imrehegy H 166 E3
İmroz TR 187 D9
Imst A 87 C11
Ina FIN 139 D11
Inagh IRL 24 C4
Ináncs H 161 G3
Inárcs H 166 C3
Inari FIN 129 F19
Inari FIN 141 D15
Inca E 73 B10
Inch IRL 24 D3
Inch IRL 25 C10
Inchbare GB 21 B11
Incheville F 34 D3
Inchigeelagh IRL 24 E4
Inchnadamph GB 18 J7
Inciems LV 151 B9
Incinillas E 56 C4
İncirliova TR 193 D10
Incisa in Val d'Arno I 82 E3
Incourt B 35 C10
Inčukalns LV 151 B9
Indal S 119 A13
Indalstø N 116 E2
Independența RO 171 C1
Independența RO 171 F2
Inđija SRB 174 C5
Indra LV 149 E3
Indreabhán IRL 22 F4
Indre Arna N 110 B2
Indre Billefjord N 129 C15
Indre Brenna N 129 B16
Indre Kårvik N 127 A16
Indre Kiberg N 130 C9
Indre Kjæs N 129 B16
Indre Sortvik N 129 B15
Indura BY 156 D9
Indzhe Voyvoda BG 183 E8
İnece TR 183 F8
İnecik TR 189 C7
Ineši LV 151 B11
Ineu RO 167 C9
Ineu RO 167 E8
Infiesto E 55 B9
Ingå FIN 143 E11
Ingared S 107 D11
Ingatestone GB 31 D9
Ingatorp S 108 D6
Ingelfingen D 203 C8
Ingelheim am Rhein D 37 E10
Ingelmunster B 35 C7
Ingelstad S 105 B7
Ingenes N 110 B3
Ingersheim F 43 D7
Ingleton GB 21 F13
Ingleton GB 26 C7
Ingoldmells GB 27 E12
Ingolsbenning S 113 B14
Ingolstadt D 91 E9
Ingrandes F 39 F10
Ingrandes F 45 B7
Ingstrup DK 106 E6
Inguiniel F 38 E5
Ingulsvatn N 121 B14
Ingwiller F 43 C7
Inha FIN 139 E12
Ini GR 194 E9
Iniesta E 63 F9
Inis IRL 24 C5
Inis Córthaidh IRL 25 C9
Inis Diomáin IRL 24 C4
Inistioge IRL 25 D8
Injevo MK 185 A7
Inkberrow GB 29 A11
Inke H 165 D8
Inkee FIN 137 C12
Inkere FIN 143 E9
Inkoo FIN 143 E11
Inndyr N 124 B7
Innerbraz A 87 C9
Innerleithen GB 21 D10
Innernzell D 92 E4
Innertällmo S 123 D13
Innertavle S 138 C4
Innertkirchen CH 86 D6
Innervik S 125 E14
Innervillgraten A 88 C5
Innhavet N 127 E10
Inniscrone IRL 22 D4
Innishannon IRL 24 E5
Innsbruck A 88 B3
Innset N 127 C16
Inntorget N 124 F3
Inowłódz PL 157 G2
Inowrocław PL 154 E5
Ins CH 47 A11
Insch GB 19 L11
Insjön S 119 E9
Ińsko PL 101 D9
Insming F 43 C6
Instefjord N 116 E2
Instinción E 71 F7
Însurăței RO 177 D11
İntepe TR 187 D10
Interlaken CH 86 D5
Întorsura Buzăului RO 177 B8
Întregalde RO 167 E11
Introbio I 85 B7
Inturkė LT 151 F11
Inver IRL 22 C6
Inverallochy GB 19 K13
Inveran IRL 22 F4
Inveraray GB 20 C6
Inverarity GB 21 B11
Inverarnan GB 20 C7
Inverbervie GB 21 B12
Invercassley GB 18 K7
Invercharnan GB 20 B6
Invergarry GB 20 A7
Invergordon GB 19 K8
Inverkeilor GB 21 B11
Inverkeithing GB 21 C10
Invermoriston GB 18 L7
Inverness GB 19 L8
Inverurie GB 19 L12
Inviken S 122 B8
Inzell D 89 A6
Inzigkofen D 43 D11
Inzing A 88 B3
Inzinzac-Lochrist F 38 E5
Ioannina GR 184 E4
Ion Corvin RO 171 E1
Ion Creangă RO 169 D9
Ionești RO 176 D2
Ionești RO 176 D4
Ion Luca Caragiale RO 177 D7
Ion Roată RO 177 D9
Iordăcheanu RO 177 C8
Ioulis GR 191 D9
Ip RO 167 C10
Ipatele RO 169 D10
Iphofen D 203 B9
Ipiķi LV 147 E10
Ipotești RO 169 B8
Ipotești RO 169 B9
Ippesheim D 91 C7
Ipplepen GB 29 E7
İpsala TR 187 C10
Ipsheim D 91 C7
Ipstones GB 27 E8
Ipswich GB 31 C11
Irakleia GR 185 B9
Irakleia GR 190 B5
Irakleia GR 192 F5
Irakleio GR 194 E9
Irancy F 41 E10
Iratoșu RO 167 E7
Irdning A 89 A9
Irechekovo BG 183 E7
Iregszemcse H 165 C10
Irgoli I 80 C4
Iria GR 191 E7
Irig SRB 174 C4
Irishtown IRL 22 E5
Irissarry F 48 D3
Irjanne FIN 142 C6
Irlava LV 150 C5
Irlbach D 91 E12
Irninniemi FIN 137 C13
Irodouër F 39 D8
Ironbridge GB 26 F7
Irrel D 36 E6
Irsch D 37 E7
Irsee D 87 B11
Irshava UA 161 G7
Irši LV 151 C11
Irsina I 76 B6
Irsta S 114 C7
Irueste E 63 C7
Irun E 48 D2
Irunea E 48 E2
Irurita E 48 D2
Irurozqui E 48 E3
Irurtzun E 48 E2
Irvine GB 20 D7
Irvinestown GB 23 D7
Irxleben D 95 B9
Isaba E 48 E4
Isaccea RO 171 C2
Isačić BIH 172 C4
Isalnița RO 176 E3
Isane N 116 C3
Isaris GR 190 E5
Isaszeg H 166 B3
Isätra S 114 C7
Isbergues F 34 C5
Isbister GB 19 D14
Íscar E 56 F2
Isches F 42 D4
Ischgl A 87 C10
Ischia I 76 B1
Ischia di Castro I 78 B1
Ischitella I 79 D9
Isdes F 41 E8
Iselvmoen N 127 C16
Isen D 91 F11
Is-en-Bassigny F 42 D3
Isenbüttel D 95 B8
Isenvad DK 102 C4
Iseo I 85 B9
Iserlohn D 33 F9
Isernhagen D 94 B6
Isernia I 79 D6
Isfjorden N 116 A7
İshakçelebi TR 193 B10
Ishull-Lezhë AL 179 F8
Isigny-sur-Mer F 39 B9
Isili I 80 D3
İskele TR 189 F9
İskender TR 188 A6
Iškoras N 129 E16
Iskra BG 182 F4
Iskrets BG 181 D7
Isla Cristina E 67 E5
İslambeyli TR 183 F9
Isla Plana E 72 F2
Išlaužas LT 153 D8
Islaz RO 176 F5
Isle F 45 D8
Isle of Whithorn GB 21 F8
Isleryd S 108 C4
Isles-sur-Suippe F 35 F9
Īslīce LV 151 D8
İsmailli TR 193 B9
Ismaning D 91 F10
Ismundsundet S 122 E8
Isna P 60 E5
Isnäs FIN 143 E15
Isnello I 74 D5
Ișnovăț MD 170 C3
Isny im Allgäu D 87 B10
Iso-Äiniö FIN 143 C13
Iso-Evo FIN 143 C13
Isohalme FIN 131 E3
Isojoki FIN 138 F7
Isokumpu FIN 137 C11
Isokylä FIN 131 E3
Isokylä FIN 135 F14
Isokyrö FIN 138 E8
Isola F 52 C6
Isola 2000 F 53 C6
Isola d'Asti I 53 B8
Isola del Gran Sasso d'Italia I 78 B5
Isola della Scala I 82 B3
Isola delle Femmine I 74 C3
Isola del Liri I 78 D5
Isola di Capo Rizzuto I 77 F8
Isole del Cantone I 53 B9
Isona E 58 C6
Isopalo FIN 131 D2
Isorella I 82 B1
Iso-Vimma FIN 142 C7
Ispagnac F 51 B6
Isperikh BG 177 F9
Ispica I 75 F6
Ispoure F 48 D3
Ispra I 84 B6
Ispringen D 43 C10
Issakka FIN 141 C10
Isselburg D 33 E6
Issigeac F 45 F7
Issime I 84 B4
Isso E 71 C9
Issogne I 84 B4
Issoire F 46 D3
Issoudun F 45 B9
Issum D 33 E6
Is-sur-Tille F 42 E3
Issy-l'Évêque F 46 B4
Istalsna LV 149 D3
Istán E 69 C7
İstanbul TR 189 B10
Istead Rise GB 31 E9
Istebna PL 163 B7
Istebné SK 163 C8
Istenmezeje H 163 E10
Isternia GR 192 D5
Isthmia GR 191 D7
Istiaia GR 191 B7
Istibanja MK 180 F5
Istok SRB 179 D9
Istres F 51 C8
Istria RO 171 D3
Istrio GR 197 D7
Istunmäki FIN 139 E16
Isuerre E 48 F3
Iszkaszentgyörgy H 165 B10
Itä-Ähtäri FIN 139 E12
Itä-Aure FIN 139 F10
Itä-Karttula FIN 140 E8
Itäkoski FIN 135 C13
Itäkoski FIN 141 C9
Itäkylä FIN 139 D11
Itäranta FIN 131 F2
Itäranta FIN 136 F9
Itea GR 185 C6
Itea GR 185 D6
Itea GR 185 F7
Itea GR 190 C5
Itero de la Vega E 56 D3
Iteuil F 45 C6
Ithaki GR 190 C2
Itrabo E 69 C9
Itri I 78 E5
Itterbeck D 33 C7
Ittireddu I 80 B2
Ittiri I 80 B2
Ittre B 35 C9
Ituero de Azaba E 61 D7
Itzehoe D 98 C7
Itzstedt D 99 C8
Iurceni MD 170 C2
Ivalo FIN 131 A3
Ivalon Matti FIN 133 B15
Iván H 165 B7
Ivana Franka UA 161 E7
Ivancea MD 170 C3
Ivančice CZ 93 D10
Ivančići BIH 173 D9
Iváncsa H 165 B11
Ivanec HR 164 D6
Ivănești RO 169 D10
Ivangorod RUS 148 C3
Ivanić-Grad HR 165 E6
Ivanivka UA 161 G6
Ivanjica SRB 179 B9
Ivanjska BIH 173 C7
Ivankovo HR 165 F11
Ivano-Frankove UA 160 D8
Ivanovice na Hané CZ 93 D12
Ivanovo BG 177 F7
Ivanovo BG 182 F5
Ivanovo BG 183 C7
Ivanovo SRB 174 D6
Ivanska HR 165 E7
Ivanski BG 183 C8
Ivarrud N 124 F6
Ivarsbjörke S 113 C9
Ivars d'Urgell E 58 D5
Ivaylovgrad BG 187 A10
Iveland N 106 C2
Iver GB 31 D7
Ivești RO 169 E11
Ivești RO 169 F11
Ivrea I 84 C4
İvrindi TR 189 E7
Ivry-la-Bataille F 40 C5
Ivry-sur-Seine F 41 C7
Ivybridge GB 29 E7
Iwaniska PL 159 E11
Iwanowice Włościańskie PL 159 F8
Iwkowa PL 160 D2
Iwye BY 153 F12
Ixelles B 35 C9
Ixworth GB 31 C10
İyaslar TR 193 A10
Iža SK 165 A10
Iza UA 161 G7
Izarra E 56 C6
Izbica PL 160 B7
Izbica Kujawska PL 154 F6
Izbiceni RO 176 F5
Izbicko PL 158 E5
Izbiște MD 170 C4
Izbište SRB 175 C7
Izbižno BIH 173 E10
Izeaux F 47 E7
Izeda P 55 E6
Izegem B 35 C7
Izernore F 47 C8
Izeron F 47 E7
Izgrev BG 177 F9
Izgrev BG 183 E9
Iž Mali HR 83 D11
Izmayil UA 171 C3
İzmir TR 193 C9
Iznájar E 69 B8
Iznalloz E 69 B9
Izola SLO 83 A8
Izsák H 166 D3
Izsófalva H 161 G2
Izvoare RO 176 E2
Izvoarele RO 171 C3
Izvoarele RO 176 E5
Izvoarele RO 176 F6
Izvoarele RO 177 C8
Izvoarele RO 177 E7
Izvoarele Sucevei RO 168 B6
Izvor BG 175 F10
Izvor BG 181 E6
Izvor MK 184 B4
Izvor MK 185 A6
Izvor SRB 175 F8
Izvorovo BG 171 F1
Izvoru RO 176 E6
Izvoru Bârzii RO 175 D10
Izvoru Berheciului RO 169 D10
Izvoru Crișului RO 167 D11

J

Jääjärvi FIN 130 D6
Jaakonvaara FIN 141 D14
Jaala FIN 143 C15
Jaalanka FIN 136 D9
Jaalanka FIN 136 E9
Jääli FIN 135 D15
Jaama EST 148 C2
Jääskänjoki FIN 138 E9
Jääskö FIN 133 D14
Jaatila FIN 135 B14
Jabaga E 63 D8
Jabalanac HR 83 C10
Jabaloyas E 63 D10
Jabalquinto E 69 A9
Jabbeke B 35 B7
Jabel D 99 C13
Jablan Do BIH 178 D5
Jablanica BIH 173 E8
Jabłoń PL 157 G8
Jablonec nad Jizerou CZ 97 E8
Jablonec nad Nisou CZ 97 E8
Jablonica SK 162 D4
Jabłonka PL 163 C9
Jabłonka Kościelna PL 156 E6
Jabłonna PL 155 F10
Jabłonna Lacka PL 157 F6
Jabłonna Pierwsza PL 157 H7
Jablonné nad Orlicí CZ 93 B11
Jablonné v Podještědí CZ 97 E7
Jablonové SK 93 F12
Jabłonowo Pomorskie PL 155 D7
Jablůnka CZ 162 C5
Jablunkov CZ 163 B7
Jabugo E 67 D6
Jabuka BIH 173 E10
Jabuka SRB 174 D6
Jabuka SRB 179 C7
Jabukovac HR 165 F6
Jabukovac SRB 175 E9
Jabukovik SRB 180 D5
Jaca E 48 E4
Jachenau D 88 A3
Jáchymov CZ 92 B3
Jacovce SK 162 D6
Jäderfors S 119 E12
Jadów PL 155 F12
Jädraås S 119 E11
Jadranska Lešnica SRB 174 D3
Jadraque E 63 C7
Jægerspris DK 103 D9
Jægervatnet N 127 A18
Jaén E 69 A9
Jägala EST 147 C10
Jagare BIH 173 C7
Jagerberg A 164 C5
Jagodina SRB 175 F7
Jagodnjak HR 165 E11
Jagodzin PL 97 D8
Jagsthausen D 43 B11
Jagstzell D 91 D7
Jähdyspohja FIN 139 F11
Jahnsfelde D 96 A6
Jahodná SK 162 E5
Jah-Salih AL 179 E9
Jajce BIH 173 D7
Ják H 165 B7
Jakabszállás H 166 D4
Jäkälävaara FIN 137 C10
Jakkukylä FIN 135 D15
Jakkula FIN 138 E8
Jäkkvik S 125 D12
Jaklovce SK 161 F3
Jakobsbakken N 125 B10
Jakobsnes N 130 D8
Jakobstad FIN 138 C9
Jakokoski FIN 141 E13
Jakovlje HR 164 E5
Jakšić HR 165 F9
Jakštaičiai LT 150 D2
Jaktorów PL 157 F3
Jakubany SK 161 E2
Jakubov SK 93 F11
Jakubów PL 157 F5
Jalance E 63 F10
Jalasjärvi FIN 138 F9
Jalhay B 36 C5
Jaligny-sur-Besbre F 46 C4
Jallais F 39 F10
Jalovik SRB 174 D4
Jałówka PL 156 D9
Jalubí CZ 162 C4
Jämaja EST 146 E4
Jämäs FIN 141 B12
Jämejala EST 147 E11
Jameln D 99 D10
Jamena SRB 173 C11
Jamestown IRL 23 F8
Jametz F 35 F11
Jamielnik PL 155 C7
Jämijärvi FIN 142 B8
Jamilena E 69 A9
Jäminkipohja FIN 143 B11
Jämjö S 105 C9
Jammerdal N 112 B7
Jamník SK 161 F2
Jämsä FIN 139 C12
Jämsä FIN 143 B13
Jämsänkoski FIN 143 B13
Jämshög S 104 C7
Jämtön S 134 C8
Jamu Mare RO 175 C7
Janakkala FIN 143 D12
Janapolė LT 150 E4
Jánd H 161 G5
Jandelsbrunn D 92 E5
Janderup DK 102 D2
Jäneda EST 147 C11
Jänickendorf D 96 B4
Janja BIH 174 D3
Janjevo SRB 180 D3
Janjići BIH 174 F3
Janjina HR 178 D3
Jänkä FIN 139 D13
Jänkälä FIN 131 D3
Jänkisjärvi S 132 E10
Jánkmajtis H 161 H6
Janków PL 159 B7
Jankowo Dolne PL 154 E4
Jānmuiža LV 151 B10
Jännevirta FIN 141 E9
Jánoshalma H 166 E3
Jánosháza H 165 B8
Jánoshida H 166 C5
Jánossomorja H 165 A8
Janovice nad Úhlavou CZ 92 D4
Janów PL 156 D8
Janów PL 159 E7
Janowice Wielkie PL 97 E9
Janowiec PL 157 H5
Janowiec Wielkopolski PL 101 E12
Janów Lubelski PL 160 B5
Janowo PL 155 D10
Janów Podlaski PL 157 F8
Jansjö S 123 D10
Jänsmässholmen S 121 D15
Jānuciems LV 151 E13
Janville F 40 D6
Janzé F 39 E9
Japca MD 170 B3
Jäppilä FIN 140 F8
Jaraba E 63 B9
Jaraczewo PL 97 C12
Jarafuel E 63 F10
Jaraicejo E 61 E9
Jaraíz de la Vera E 61 D9
Järämä S 132 B6
Jarandilla de la Vera E 61 D9
Järbo S 119 E12
Járdánháza H 161 G1
Jard-sur-Mer F 44 C2
Jaren N 111 B13
Jarfjordbotn N 130 D8
Járgastat N 129 E16
Jargeau F 40 E7
Jarhoinen FIN 133 E11
Jarhois S 133 E11
Jariștea RO 169 F10
Jarkovac SRB 175 C6
Järkvissle S 119 A12
Järlåsa S 114 C8
Järlepa EST 147 C9
Jarmen D 100 C4
Jarménil F 42 D6
Jarmina HR 165 F11
Järna S 109 A11
Järna S 113 A11
Jarnac F 44 D5
Jarnages F 45 C10
Järnäs S 123 E17
Järnäsklubb S 123 E17
Järnforsen S 108 E7
Jarny F 42 B4
Jarocin PL 158 C4
Jarocin PL 160 B5
Jarok SK 162 E5
Jaroměř CZ 93 B9
Jaroměřice CZ 93 C11
Jaroměřice nad Rokytnou CZ 93 D9
Jaroslavice CZ 93 E10
Jarosław PL 160 C6
Jarosławiec PL 101 A11
Jarošov nad Nežárkou CZ 93 D8
Jarovnice SK 161 E3
Järpås S 107 C12
Järpbyn S 121 E14
Järpen S 121 E14
Järpliden S 118 E3
Jarplund-Weding D 98 A6
Jarque E 57 E8
Jarrow GB 21 F14
Järva-Jaani EST 147 C11
Järvakandi EST 147 D9
Järvberget S 123 D13
Järvenpää FIN 133 C12
Järvenpää FIN 138 E7
Järvenpää FIN 140 C8
Järvenpää FIN 141 D10
Järvenpää FIN 143 E13
Järvikylä FIN 135 F17
Järvikylä FIN 139 C13
Järvikylä FIN 139 C13
Jarville-la-Malgrange F 42 C5
Järvirova FIN 133 D12
Järvsand S 123 C9
Järvsjö S 123 B12
Järvsö S 119 C11
Järvsta S 119 E13
Järvtjärn S 134 E5
Järvträsk S 123 A16
Jarzé F 39 E11
Jaša Tomić SRB 175 C6
Jasen BIH 178 D5
Jasenak HR 83 B11
Jasenica BIH 172 C5
Jasenovac HR 173 B6
Jasenovo SRB 175 D7
Jasenovo SRB 179 B8
Jasień PL 97 C8
Jasień PL 101 B13
Jasienica PL 155 F11
Jasienica PL 163 B7
Jasienica Rosielna PL 160 D4
Jasieniec PL 157 G3
Jasika SRB 175 F7
Jasionka PL 160 C5
Jasionna PL 159 E9
Jasionówka PL 156 D8
Jaśliska PL 161 E4
Jasło PL 160 D3
Jašlūnai LT 153 E11
Jasmuiža LV 151 D13
Jasov SK 161 F2
Jasová SK 162 F6
Jassans-Riottier F 46 D6
Jasseron F 47 C7
Jastarnia PL 154 A6
Jastrebarsko HR 164 E5
Jastrowie PL 101 D11
Jastrząb PL 157 H3
Jastrzębia PL 157 H4
Jastrzębia Góra PL 154 A5
Jastrzębie-Zdrój PL 163 B7
Jászapáti H 166 B5
Jászárokszállás H 166 B4
Jászberény H 166 C4
Jászboldogháza H 166 C4
Jászfényszaru H 166 B4
Jászjákóhalma H 166 B5
Jászkarajenő H 166 C5
Jászkisér H 166 C5
Jászladány H 166 C5
Jászszentandrás H 166 B5
Jászszentlászló H 166 D4
Jásztelek H 166 C5
Jatar E 69 C9
Jättendal S 119 C13
Jättensjö S 119 B10
Jatuni FIN 132 B9
Jatzke D 100 C5
Jatznick D 100 C5
Jaulín E 57 F10
Jaun CH 47 B11
Jaunalūksne LV 149 B2
Jaunanna LV 149 B2
Jaunauce LV 150 D5
Jaunay-Clan F 45 B6
Jaunbērze LV 150 C6
Jaunciems LV 150 B5
Jaundundaga LV 146 F4
Jaungulbene LV 151 B13
Jaunjelgava LV 151 C10
Jaunkalsnava LV 151 C11
Jaunklidzis LV 147 F11
Jaunlaicene LV 147 F13
Jaunlutriņi LV 150 C4
Jaunmārupe LV 151 C7
Jaunmuiža LV 151 C11
Jaunolaine LV 151 C7
Jaunpiebalga LV 151 B12
Jaunpils LV 150 C6
Jaunsāti LV 150 C5
Jaunsēlpils LV 151 C11
Jaunsilava LV 151 D12
Jauntsarats E 48 E2
Jaurakainen FIN 135 D17

Jaurakkajärvi FIN 137 D10
Jaurrieta E 48 E3
Jausiers F 52 C5
Javalí Viejo E 72 F2
Javarus FIN 131 E1
Jávea-Xàbia E 72 D5
Jävenitz D 95 A10
Javerlhac-et-la-Chapelle-St-Robert F 45 D7
Javgur MD 170 D3
Javier E 48 E3
Javorani BIH 173 C7
Javorník CZ 93 B12
Jävre S 134 D6
Javron-les-Chapelles F 39 D11
Jawor PL 97 D10
Jawornik Polski PL 160 D5
Jawor Solecki PL 157 H4
Jaworzno PL 158 D6
Jaworzno PL 159 F7
Jaworzyna Śląska PL 97 E10
Jayena E 69 C9
Jazeneuil F 44 C6
Jebel RO 175 B7
Jebjerg DK 102 B4
Jedburgh GB 21 E11
Jedlanka PL 157 G6
Jedlicze PL 160 D4
Jedlina-Zdrój PL 97 E10
Jedlińsk PL 157 G4
Jedlnia-Letnisko PL 157 H4
Jedlová CZ 93 C10
Jedľové Kostoľany SK 162 E6
Jednorożec PL 155 D11
Jedovnice CZ 93 D11
Jędrzejewo PL 101 E10
Jędrzejów PL 159 E9
Jédula E 68 C5
Jedwabne PL 156 D6
Jedwabno PL 155 C10
Jeesiö FIN 133 D16
Jeesiöjärvi FIN 133 C14
Jegălia RO 177 E11
Jegun F 49 C6
Jegunovce MK 180 E3
Jejsing DK 102 F3
Jēkabpils LV 151 C11
Jektvik N 124 C5
Jelah BIH 173 C8
Jelašca BIH 173 F9
Jelcz-Laskowice PL 97 D12
Jelenia Góra PL 97 E9
Jeleniewo PL 152 E6
Jelenin PL 97 C8
Jelenje HR 83 B9
Jeleśnia PL 163 B8
Jelgava LV 150 C7
Jelka SK 162 E5
Jelling DK 102 D4
Jeloboc MD 170 C3
Jelovica SRB 181 C6
Jełowa PL 158 E5
Jels DK 102 E4
Jelsa HR 173 F6
Jelšane SLO 83 A9
Jelšava SK 161 F1
Jelsi I 79 D7
Jemeppe B 35 D10
Jemgum D 33 B8
Jemielnica PL 158 E5
Jemielno PL 97 C11
Jemnice CZ 93 D9
Jena D 95 E10
Jenbach A 88 B4
Jeneč CZ 92 B6
Jengen D 87 B11
Jenikowo PL 101 C8
Jennersdorf A 164 C6
Jenny S 109 D9
Jenő H 165 B10
Jensvoll N 117 A15
Jeppo FIN 138 D9
Jērcēni LV 147 F11
Jerchel D 95 B9
Jerez de la Frontera E 68 C4
Jerez del Marquesado E 71 E6
Jerez de los Caballeros E 67 C6
Jerfojaur S 125 E16
Jergol N 129 E14
Jergucat AL 184 E3
Jeri LV 147 F10
Jérica E 64 E3
Jerichow D 95 A11
Jerka PL 97 C11
Jernved DK 102 E3
Jerslev DK 103 D8
Jerslev DK 106 E7
Jerstad N 126 C9
Jerte E 61 D9
Jerup DK 106 D7
Jerzens A 87 C11
Jerzmanowa PL 97 C10
Jerzmanowice PL 159 F8
Jerzu I 80 D4
Jesenice CZ 92 B4
Jesenice CZ 93 C7
Jesenice HR 172 D4
Jesenice HR 172 F6
Jesenice SLO 89 D9
Jeseník CZ 93 B12
Jeseník nad Odrou CZ 162 B5
Jesenské SK 163 E10
Jeserig D 95 B11
Jeserig D 95 B12
Jesi I 83 E7
Jesionowo PL 101 D8
Jesolo I 82 A6
Jessen D 96 C3
Jessheim N 111 B14
Jeßnitz D 95 C11
Jesteburg D 99 D7
Jettingen-Scheppach D 91 F7
Jeumont F 35 D9
Jevenstedt D 98 B7
Jever D 33 A9
Jevíčko CZ 93 C11
Jevišovice CZ 93 E10
Jevnaker N 111 B12
Jezera BIH 173 D8
Jezerane HR 83 B11
Jezerce SRB 180 E3
Jezero BIH 173 D7
Jezero HR 172 B3
Jeżewo PL 154 C5
Jeżewo PL 156 D7
Jeziorany PL 152 F2
Jeziorzany PL 157 G6
Jeżów PL 157 G1
Jeżowe PL 160 C5
Jeżów Sudecki PL 97 E9
Jiana RO 175 E10
Jibert RO 168 E6
Jibou RO 167 C11
Jichișu de Jos RO 168 C3
Jičín CZ 93 B8
Jidvei RO 168 E4
Jieznas LT 153 D9
Jihlava CZ 93 D9
Jijila RO 171 C2
Jijona-Xixona E 72 D4
Jilava RO 177 E8
Jilavele RO 177 D9
Jilemnice CZ 97 E9
Jílové CZ 96 E6
Jílové u Prahy CZ 93 C7
Jiltjaur S 125 E12
Jimbolia RO 166 F6
Jimena E 69 A10
Jimena de la Frontera E 69 D6
Jimramov CZ 93 C10
Jina RO 168 F3
Jince CZ 92 C5
Jindřichov CZ 93 B12
Jindřichov CZ 158 F4
Jindřichův Hradec CZ 93 D8
Jiřikov CZ 97 E7
Jirkov CZ 92 A4
Jirlău RO 177 C10
Jirnsum NL 32 B5
Jirny CZ 93 B7
Jisaku EST 147 C14
Jistebnice CZ 93 D7
Jistebník CZ 162 B6
Jitia RO 177 B9
Jlajkovci SRB 179 C10
Joachimsthal D 100 E5
Joane P 54 F3
Job F 46 D4
Jobbágyi H 163 F9
Jobsbo S 113 B13
Jochberg A 88 B5
Jocketa D 95 E11
Jockfall S 132 E9
Jockgrim D 43 B9
Jódar E 71 D6
Jodłowa PL 160 D3
Jodłownik PL 160 D1
Jodoigne B 35 C10
Joensuu FIN 141 E13
Jõepere EST 147 C12
Joesjö S 124 E8
Joeström S 124 E8
Jõesuu EST 147 E9
Jœuf F 36 F6
Jõgeva EST 147 D12
Jõgua EST 147 C14
Johanngeorgenstadt D 91 B12
Johannisfors S 115 B10
Johannishus S 105 C8
Johanniskirchen D 92 E3
Johansfors S 105 B9
John o'Groats GB 19 H10
Johnston GB 28 B5
Johnstone GB 20 D7
Johnstown IRL 25 C7
Johnstown IRL 25 C10
Johovac BIH 174 D3
Jöhstadt D 92 A4
Jõhvi EST 147 C14
Joigny F 41 E9
Joinville F 42 D3
Joița RO 177 E7
Jokela FIN 135 B16
Jokela FIN 135 E16
Jokela FIN 143 D12
Jokelankylä FIN 139 C14
Jøkelfjordeidet N 128 C9
Jokijärvi FIN 137 C12
Jokijärvi FIN 139 D17
Joki-Kokko FIN 135 D16
Jokikunta FIN 143 E11
Jokikylä FIN 137 E11
Jokikylä FIN 138 E8
Jokikylä FIN 139 C13
Jokikylä FIN 139 C15
Jokilampi FIN 137 C12
Jokimaa FIN 143 D12
Jokioinen FIN 143 D9
Jokiperä FIN 138 E8
Jokipii FIN 138 E9
Jokivarsi FIN 139 E11
Jokivarsi FIN 139 E12
Jokkmokk S 132 E3
Jokūbavas LT 150 E2
Jolanda di Savoia I 82 C4
Jolanki FIN 133 E13
Jolda P 54 E3
Joloskylä FIN 135 D16
Joltai MD 170 E3
Jomala FIN 115 B13
Jømna N 117 E15
Jona CH 43 F10
Jönåker S 109 B9
Jonava LT 153 C9
Joncy F 46 B6
Jondal N 110 B4
Jonesborough GB 23 D10
Joniec PL 155 E10
Joniškėlis LT 151 D8
Joniškis LT 150 D7
Joniškis LT 153 C12
Jonkeri FIN 141 C13
Jönköping S 108 D4
Jonkowo PL 155 C9
Jonku FIN 136 D9
Jonquières F 51 B8
Jonsberg S 109 B9
Jonsered S 107 D11
Jonslund S 107 C12
Jonstorp S 103 C11
Jonzac F 44 E5
Joppolo I 75 B8
Jorăști RO 169 F11
Jorba E 59 D7
Jorcas E 58 F2
Jordanów PL 163 B9
Jordanów Śląski PL 97 E11
Jordbro S 115 D10
Jordbru N 124 B9
Jordbrua N 124 D8
Jördenstorf D 99 C13
Jordet N 118 D3
Jork D 98 C7
Jörlanda S 107 D10
Jormvattnet S 121 B16
Jörn S 134 D4
Joroinen FIN 141 F9
Jørpeland N 110 D4
Jorquera E 63 F9
Jørstadmoen N 117 D12
Jošanica BIH 173 E9
Jošanička Banja SRB 179 C10
Jošavka BIH 173 C7
Joseni RO 169 D6
Josenii Bârgăului RO 168 C5
Josifovo MK 185 B7
Josipdol HR 172 B3
Josipovac HR 165 E11
Josnes F 40 E6
Jössefors S 112 C8
Josselin F 38 E6
Jossund N 121 C9
Josvainiai LT 150 F7
Jota N 117 D15
Jou P 54 F5
Jouarre F 41 C9
Joué-lès-Tours F 40 F4
Joué-sur-Erdre F 39 E9
Jougne F 47 B9
Joukokylä FIN 137 D10
Jouques F 51 C10
Joure NL 32 C5
Journiac F 45 F7
Joutenniva FIN 139 B15
Joutsa FIN 143 B15
Joutseno FIN 145 C10
Joutsijärvi FIN 131 E3
Joux-la-Ville F 41 E10
Jouy F 40 C6
Jouy-aux-Arches F 42 B5
Jouy-le-Potier F 40 E6
Jøvik N 127 A18
Jøvik N 127 B13
Joyeuse F 51 B7
Joze F 46 D3
Józefów PL 157 F4
Józefów PL 160 A4
Józefów PL 160 C7
Juankoski FIN 141 D10
Juan-les-Pins F 52 D6
Juban AL 179 E8
Jubë AL 184 B1
Jübek D 98 A6
Jublains F 39 D11
Jubrique E 69 C6
Jüchen D 36 B6
Juchowo PL 101 C10
Jüchsen D 91 B8
Jucu RO 168 D3
Judaberg N 110 D3
Judenbach D 91 B9
Judenburg A 89 B10
Judinsalo FIN 143 B13
Juelsminde DK 102 D6
Jugon-les-Lacs F 39 D7
Jugorje SLO 164 E4
Jugureni RO 177 C8
Juhonpieti S 132 D10
Juhtimäki FIN 143 B9
Juillac F 45 E8
Juillan F 48 D6
Jujurieux F 47 C7
Jukkasjärvi S 132 C5
Juknaičiai LT 150 F3
Juksjaur S 125 E10
Jukua FIN 137 C9
Julåsen S 119 B10
Julbach A 92 E5
Jule N 121 C15
Jülich D 36 C6
Juliénas F 46 C6
Jullouville F 39 C8
Jumaliskylä FIN 137 E13
Jumeaux F 46 E3
Jumilhac-le-Grand F 45 E8
Jumilla E 71 C10
Juminen FIN 141 D9
Jumisko FIN 137 B11
Jumurda LV 151 C11
Juncal P 60 E3
Juncosa E 58 E5
Juneda E 58 D5
Jung S 107 C13
Jungingen D 43 D11
Junglinster L 36 E6
Jungsund FIN 138 D7
Junik SRB 179 E9
Juniskär S 119 B13
Juniville F 35 F9
Jünkerath D 37 D7
Junkerdal N 125 C10
Junnonoja FIN 135 F15
Junosuando S 132 D9
Junqueira P 66 E5
Junsele S 123 D11
Juntinvaara FIN 137 F15
Juntusranta FIN 137 D13
Juodeikiai LT 150 D6
Juodkrantė LT 150 E2
Juodšiliai LT 153 D11
Juodupė LT 151 D11
Juoksengi S 133 E11
Juokseni FIN 133 E11
Juokslahti FIN 143 B13
Juokuanvaara FIN 135 C13
Juonto FIN 137 F13
Juorkuna FIN 136 E8
Juornaankylä FIN 143 D14
Juostinikai LT 151 E9
Juotasniemi FIN 135 B17
Jupânești RO 176 D3
Jupilles F 40 E3
Juprelle B 35 C12
Jurançon F 48 D5
Jurbarkas LT 152 C6
Jurbise B 35 C8
Jürgenshagen D 99 C11
Jürgenstorf D 100 C3
Jurģi LV 150 C5
Jüri EST 147 C9
Jurignac F 44 D5
Jurilovca RO 171 D3
Jurjevo HR 83 C10
Jūrkalne LV 150 B2
Jurkloŝter SLO 164 D4
Jurkowice PL 159 E11
Jūrmala LV 150 C7
Jūrmalciems LV 150 D2
Jurmo FIN 142 D5
Jurmo FIN 142 F6
Jurmu FIN 137 D10
Jurovski Brod HR 164 E4
Jursla S 109 B8
Jurva FIN 138 E7
Jussac F 45 F10
Jussey F 42 E4
Juta H 165 D9
Jüterbog D 96 C4
Jutis S 125 D13
Jutrosin PL 97 C12
Jutsajaure S 132 D3
Juujärvi FIN 136 B9
Juuka FIN 141 D12
Juuma FIN 137 B13
Juupajoki FIN 143 B11
Juupakylä FIN 139 F10
Juurikka FIN 141 G14
Juurikkalahti FIN 141 B10
Juurikkamäki FIN 141 E10
Juurikorpi FIN 144 D6
Juuru EST 147 C9
Juustovaara FIN 133 D13
Juutinen FIN 139 B17
Juva FIN 144 B8
Juvanådammet S 123 D12
Juvigné F 39 D9
Juvigny-le-Tertre F 39 C9
Juvigny-sous-Andaine F 39 C10
Juvola FIN 141 F11
Juzennecourt F 42 D2
Juzet-d'Izaut F 49 E7
Jūžintai LT 151 E11
Jyderup DK 103 D8
Jylhä FIN 139 D17
Jylhämä FIN 135 E17
Jyllinge DK 103 D10
Jyllinkoski FIN 138 F8
Jyllintaival FIN 138 E8
Jyrinki FIN 139 C12
Jyrkänkoski FIN 137 B14
Jyrkänkylä FIN 141 B13
Jyrkkä FIN 141 C9
Jystrup DK 103 D9
Jyväskylä FIN 139 F15

K

Kaagjärve EST 147 F12
Kaakamo FIN 135 C12
Kaalepi EST 147 C11
Kaamanen FIN 129 E19
Kaamasjoki FIN 129 E19
Kaamasmukka FIN 129 E18
Kaanaa FIN 143 B11
Kääntöjärvi S 132 D7
Kääpa EST 147 F14
Kääpälä FIN 144 C6
Kaarakkala FIN 140 C8
Kaaraneskoski FIN 133 E12
Käärdi EST 147 E12
Kaarepere EST 147 D13
Kaaresuvanto FIN 132 B9
Kaarina FIN 142 E7
Kaarlela FIN 139 C10
Käärmelehto FIN 133 D15
Kaarnevaara S 133 C10
Kaarnijärvi FIN 131 F1
Kaarßen D 99 D10
Kaarst D 37 B7
Kaasmarkku FIN 142 C7
Kaatsheuvel NL 32 E4
Kaava FIN 129 D18
Kaavi FIN 141 E10
Kaba H 167 C7
Kabakça TR 189 B9
Kabaklar TR 189 E11
Kabakum TR 193 A8
Kabala EST 147 D11
Kåbdalis S 134 B4
Kabelvåg N 126 D7
Kaberneeme EST 147 B10
Kabile LV 150 C4
Kableshkovo BG 183 D9
Kabli EST 147 E8
Kać SRB 174 C4
Kačanik SRB 180 E3
Kačarevo SRB 174 D6
Kachkivka UA 170 A2
Kachurivka UA 170 B5
Kačice CZ 92 B5
Kačikol SRB 180 D3
Käckelbäcksmon S 119 A13
Kaczory PL 101 D11
Kadaň CZ 92 B4
Kadarkút H 165 D9
Kadıköy TR 189 B9
Kadıköy TR 189 C6
Kadıköy TR 189 C11
Kadıköy TR 193 A9
Kadila EST 147 C12
Kadrifakovo MK 180 F5
Kadrina EST 147 C12
Kadzidło PL 155 D11
Käenkoski FIN 141 E15
Kaerepere EST 147 D9
Kåfjord N 128 D11
Kåfjord N 129 B16
Kåfjorddalen N 128 E6
Kåge S 134 E5
Kågeröd S 103 D12
Kaggebo S 109 D9
Kağıthane TR 189 B10
Kagkadi GR 190 C3
Kahla D 95 E10
Kahl am Main D 203 A7
Kåhög S 107 D11
Kahraman TR 197 A8
Kähtävä FIN 135 F12
Kaïafa GR 190 D4
Käina EST 146 D5
Kainasto FIN 138 F8
Kainourgio GR 190 B3
Kainulasjärvi S 132 D9
Kainuunkylä FIN 135 B11
Kainuunmäki FIN 140 C8
Kaipiainen FIN 144 D7
Kaipola FIN 143 B13
Kairala FIN 131 D2
Kairiai LT 150 E6
Kairiškiai LT 150 D5
Kaisajoki FIN 135 B12
Kaisepakte S 127 D17
Kaisersesch D 37 D8
Kaiserslautern D 37 F9
Kaisheim D 91 E8
Kaišiadorys LT 153 D9
Kaisma EST 147 D9
Kaitainen FIN 140 F9
Kaitainsalmi FIN 137 F11
Kaitajärvi FIN 135 B13
Kaitum S 132 C4
Kaivanto FIN 136 F9
Kaive LV 150 B6
Kaive LV 151 B11
Kajaani FIN 137 F10
Kajal SK 162 E5
Kajanki FIN 133 B11
Kajdacs H 165 C11
Kajew PL 159 B7
Kajoo FIN 141 D12
Kájov CZ 92 E6
Kakanj BIH 173 D9
Kakasd H 165 D11
Kakavi AL 184 E3
Kakenieki LV 150 C6
Kakenstorf D 98 D7
Kakerbeck D 99 E10
Kakhanavichy BY 149 E4
Kakilahti FIN 136 F8
Käkišķe LV 150 D2
Kaklıç TR 193 C8
Kąkolewnica Wschodnia PL 157 G7
Kąkolewo PL 97 C11
Kakovatos GR 190 E4
Kakrukë AL 184 C3
Kakskerta FIN 142 E7
Kakslauttanen FIN 131 B2
Kakucs H 166 C3
Kál H 166 B5
Käl S 123 D12
Kälä FIN 143 B15
Kalabakbaşı TR 189 E7
Kålaboda S 134 F5
Kalače MNE 179 D9
Kala Dendra GR 185 B9
Kalaja FIN 139 C14
Kalajärvi FIN 143 E12
Kalajoki FIN 135 F11
Kalak N 129 B19
Kalakangas FIN 139 C14
Kalakoski FIN 139 F10
Kalamaki GR 185 E8
Kalamaki GR 190 D2
Kalamaki GR 191 D8
Kalamaria GR 185 C8
Kalamata GR 190 E5
Kalamos GR 191 C8
Kalamoti GR 193 C7
Kalamoto GR 185 C9
Kalampaka GR 185 E6
Kalampaki GR 187 B6
Kalana EST 146 D4
Kalandra GR 185 E9
Kala Nera GR 185 F8
Kalanistra GR 190 C4
Kalanti FIN 142 D6
Kälarne S 123 F10
Kalathos GR 197 D8
Kalavarda GR 197 D7
Kalavryta GR 190 C5
Kaława PL 97 B9
Kalbe (Milde) D 99 E10
Kalce SLO 89 E9
Kalchevo BG 183 E7
Káld H 165 B8
Kaldabruņa LV 151 D12
Kaldbak FO 18 A3
Kaldfarnes N 127 B12
Kaldfarnes N 127 B13
Kaldfjord N 127 A16
Kaldslett N 127 A16
Kaldvåg N 127 D10
Kaldvik N 127 D11
Kale TR 197 B9
Kalefeld D 95 C7
Kaleköy TR 187 D9
Kälen S 119 A8
Kälen S 119 B11
Kälen S 134 D6
Kalentzi GR 184 F4
Kalesija BIH 173 D10
Kalesmeno GR 190 B4
Kalēti LV 150 D2
Kalety PL 159 E6
Kalevala RUS 137 D17
Kali GR 185 C7
Kali HR 172 D3
Kalianoi GR 191 D5
Kalimanci MK 181 F6
Kalimash AL 179 E9
Kaliningrad RUS 152 D2
Kalinino RUS 152 E6
Kalinovik BIH 173 F9
Kalinovka RUS 152 D4
Kalinowa PL 158 C5
Kalinowo PL 152 F6
Kaliska PL 154 C5
Kalisz PL 158 C5
Kalisz Pomorski PL 101 D9
Kalita EST 147 E9
Kali Vrysi GR 186 B5
Kalix S 135 C10
Kalixforsen S 132 C4
Kalkar D 32 E6
Kalkhorst D 99 C10
Kalki LV 146 F4
Kalkiainen FIN 131 E3
Kalkım TR 189 E7
Kalkkimaa FIN 135 C12
Kalkkinen FIN 143 C14
Kałków PL 93 B12
Kalkūne LV 151 E12
Kall D 37 C7
Kall S 121 E14
Källa S 105 A11
Kallaste EST 147 D14
Kallax S 134 C8
Källberget S 118 A6
Källbomark S 134 D6
Källby FIN 138 C9
Källby S 107 B13
Kalle N 126 D7
Källeboda S 112 D7
Källekärr S 107 C10
Källered S 107 D11
Källerud S 107 A12
Kallham A 92 F5
Kallifoni GR 185 F6
Kallifytos GR 187 B6
Kallimasia GR 193 C7
Kallinge S 105 C8
Kalliojoki FIN 137 F15
Kalliopi GR 187 E8
Kalliosalmi FIN 133 E17
Kallirachi GR 187 C7
Kallislahti FIN 145 B10
Kallithea GR 185 D8
Kallithea GR 185 D9
Kallithea GR 185 E7
Kallithea GR 190 D4
Kallithea GR 190 F4
Kallithea GR 191 D8
Kallithea GR 193 D8
Kallithiro GR 185 F6
Kalljord N 126 C9
Kallmet i Madh AL 179 F8
Kallmünz D 91 D10
Kallo FIN 133 D12
Kálló H 166 B3
Kallön S 125 E15
Kalloni GR 187 F10
Kalloni GR 191 D7
Kalloni GR 192 D5
Kállósemjén H 161 H4
Kallsedet S 121 D13
Källsjön S 119 E11
Kallträsk FIN 138 F7
Kallunki FIN 131 E5
Kallunki FIN 137 B13
Kálmánháza H 161 H4
Kalmar S 105 B10
Kalmari FIN 139 E14
Kalmthout B 32 F2
Kalna SRB 180 C5
Kalna SRB 180 D5
Kalná nad Hronom SK 163 E7
Kalnciems LV 150 C7
Kalni LV 150 D4
Kalnieši LV 149 E2
Kalnujai LT 150 F6
Kalocsa H 166 D2
Kalofer BG 181 D10
Kaloi Limenes GR 194 F8
Kaloneri GR 185 D5
Kalo Nero GR 190 E4
Kalos Agros GR 186 B6
Kalotina BG 181 C6
Kalotintsi BG 181 D6
Kaloyanovets BG 182 E5
Kaloyanovo BG 181 E10
Káloz H 165 C10
Kalpaki GR 184 E4
Kalpio FIN 137 E10
Kals am Großglockner A 89 B6
Kaltanėnai LT 151 F11
Kaltbrunn CH 43 F11
Kaltene LV 150 B5
Kaltenkirchen D 99 C7
Kaltennordheim D 95 E7
Kaltensundheim D 95 E7
Kaltinėnai LT 150 E4
Kaluđerica SRB 174 D6
Kalugerovo BG 181 E9
Kalundborg DK 103 D8
Kalupe LV 151 D13
Kałuszyn PL 157 F5
Kaluzhskoye RUS 152 D4
Kalvåg N 116 C1
Kalvarija LT 152 E7
Kalvatn N 116 B4
Kalveliai LT 153 D12
Kalvene LV 150 C3
Kalvi EST 147 C13
Kälviä FIN 139 C10
Kalvik N 125 A10
Kalvitsa FIN 144 B7
Kalvola FIN 143 C11
Kalvträsk S 123 B17
Kalwang A 89 B10
Kalwaria Zebrzydowska PL 163 B9
Kalymnos GR 193 F8
Kalyny UA 161 G8
Kalythies GR 197 D8
Kalyves GR 187 C7
Kalyvia GR 190 B3
Kalyvia GR 190 B3
Kalyvia GR 190 D5
Kalyvia Thorikou GR 191 D8
Kamajai LT 151 E11
Kämäränkylä FIN 137 F14
Kamarde LV 151 D8
Kamares GR 190 C4
Kamares GR 191 F10
Kamariotissa GR 187 D8
Kambja EST 147 E13
Kamburovo BG 182 C6
Kamen BG 182 C5
Kamen D 33 E9
Kamenari BG 182 D6
Kamena Vourla GR 191 B6
Kamen Bryag BG 183 C11
Kamencia SRB 174 F6
Kamenec pod Vtáčnikom SK 163 D7
Kamengrad BIH 172 C6
Kamenica BIH 172 D5
Kamenica BIH 173 D9
Kamenica BIH 174 F3
Kamenica MK 180 E6
Kamenica SK 161 E2
Kamenica SRB 174 E4
Kamenica SRB 180 C5
Kamenica nad Cirochou SK 161 F4
Kamenica nad Hronom SK 163 F7
Kamenicë AL 184 C4
Kamenice CZ 93 C7
Kamenice CZ 93 D9
Kamenice nad Lipou CZ 93 D8
Kameničná SK 162 F6
Kamenín SK 163 F7
Kamenka RUS 145 E11
Kamenná Poruba SK 163 C7
Kamennogorsk RUS 145 D11
Kamenný Most SK 163 F7
Kamenný Přívoz CZ 93 C7
Kamenný Újezd CZ 93 E6
Kameno BG 183 D8
Kameno Pole BG 181 C8
Kamenovo BG 177 F8
Kamensko BIH 173 D9
Kamensko HR 165 F8
Kamensko HR 173 E6
Kamenskoye RUS 152 D4
Kamenz D 96 D6
Kamerik NL 198 A5
Kamern D 99 E12
Kames GB 20 D6
Kamëz AL 184 B2
Kamičak BIH 173 C6
Kamicë-Flakë AL 179 E7
Kamień PL 160 C5
Kamieńczyk PL 155 E12
Kamienica PL 161 D1
Kamienica Polska PL 159 E7
Kamieniec PL 97 B10
Kamieniec Ząbkowicki PL 93 A11
Kamienka SK 161 E2
Kamień Krajeński PL 101 C13
Kamienna Gora PL 97 E10
Kamiennik PL 97 E12
Kamień Pomorski PL 101 C7
Kamieńsk PL 159 D8
Kamień Wielkie PL 97 A7
Kamilski Dol BG 187 A10
Kamion PL 155 F9
Kamion PL 157 G2
Kamionka PL 157 H6
Kamiros GR 197 D7
Kamlunge S 135 C9
Kammela FIN 142 D5
Kammen N 128 C4
Kamnik SLO 89 D10
Kamno SLO 89 D8
Kamøyvær N 129 A16
Kamp D 201 D8
Kampanis GR 185 C8
Kampen D 102 F2
Kampen NL 32 C5
Kampenhout B 198 D5
Kämpfelbach D 203 D6
Kampi GR 190 A2
Kampia GR 193 B6
Kampinkylä FIN 138 E8
Kampinos PL 157 F2
Kamp-Lintfort D 33 F7
Kampos GR 190 C5
Kampos GR 190 F5
Kampvoll N 127 B14
Kamsjö S 134 F3
Kamula FIN 139 B16
Kamut H 167 D6
Kam"yane UA 170 A5
Kam"yanka UA 170 D6
Kam"yans'ke UA 170 F4
Kamyanyets BY 157 F9
Kamyanyuki BY 157 E9
Kanaküla EST 147 E10
Kanal SLO 89 D8
Kanala FIN 139 D12
Kanala GR 191 E9
Kanali GR 184 E2
Kanali GR 190 A2
Kanalia GR 185 F8
Kanallaki GR 184 F4
Kanan S 125 F10
Kanatlarci MK 185 B6
Kańczuga PL 160 D5
Kandava LV 150 B5
Kandel D 43 B9
Kandelin D 100 B4
Kandern D 43 E8
Kandersteg CH 86 E5
Kandila GR 190 B2
Kandila GR 190 D5
Kandle EST 147 B12
Kanepi EST 147 F13
Kanestraum N 120 E4
Kanfanar HR 83 B8
Kangas FIN 135 F13
Kangas FIN 138 D9
Kangasaho FIN 139 E13
Kangasala FIN 143 C11
Kangaskylä FIN 135 F16
Kangaskylä FIN 137 E11
Kangaskylä FIN 139 C13
Kangaslahti FIN 141 D10
Kangaslampi FIN 141 F10
Kangasniemi FIN 139 G17
Kangasvieri FIN 139 C13
Kangos S 132 D9
Kangosjärvi FIN 133 C11
Kanianka SK 163 D7
Kaninë AL 184 D2
Kanjiža SRB 166 E5
Kankaanpää FIN 142 B7
Kankaanpää FIN 142 C7
Kankainen FIN 139 F16
Kankari FIN 136 E8
Kånna S 103 B13
Kannas FIN 137 E12
Känne S 119 B9
Kannonjärvi FIN 139 E14
Kannonkoski FIN 139 E14
Kannus FIN 139 C11
Kannusjärvi FIN 144 D7
Kannuskoski FIN 144 D7
Kanpantxua E 57 B6
Kanstad N 127 D10
Kanstadbotn N 127 C10
Kantala FIN 140 F8
Kantanos GR 194 E6
Kantele FIN 143 D14
Kantens NL 33 B7
Kantia GR 191 D6
Kantojärvi FIN 135 C12
Kantojoki FIN 137 B13
Kantokylä FIN 139 B13
Kantola FIN 139 D10
Kantomaanpää FIN 135 B12
Kantorneset N 127 B17
Kantserava BY 149 F4
Kantti FIN 138 F9
Kanturk IRL 24 D5
Kaolinovo BG 177 F10
Kaona SRB 174 F5
Kaonik BIH 173 D8
Kaonik SRB 180 B3
Kapaklı TR 189 B8
Kapaklı TR 189 D10
Kapanbeleni TR 189 D7
Kapandriti GR 191 C8
Kaparelli GR 191 C7
Kapčiamiestis LT 153 F8
Kapelle NL 32 F2
Kapellen B 32 F2
Kapelle-op-den-Bos B 198 C4
Kapellskär S 115 C12
Kapfenberg A 164 B4
Kapıkargın TR 197 C9
Kapitan-Andreevo BG 182 F6
Kapız TR 197 B9
Kaplava LV 149 E2
Kaplice CZ 93 E7
Kapljuh BIH 172 C5
Kápolna H 166 B5
Kápolnásnyék H 165 B11
Kaposfő H 165 D9
Kaposmérő H 165 D9
Kaposszekcső H 165 D10
Kaposvár H 165 D9
Kapp N 117 E13
Kappel D 37 E8
Kappel-Grafenhausen D 202 E4
Kappeln D 99 A7
Kappelrodeck D 202 D5
Kappl A 87 C10
Kåpponis S 134 B4
Kaprijke B 32 F1
Kaprun A 89 B6
Kapshticë AL 184 C5
Kapsia GR 190 D5
Kaptol HR 165 F9
Kaptsyowka BY 156 C9
Kapušany SK 161 E3
Kapusta FIN 135 B12
Kapuvár H 165 A8
Käpylä FIN 135 F14
Karaağaç TR 189 A7
Karaağaç TR 189 F6
Karaağaçlı TR 193 B9
Karabanove UA 170 C5
Karabiga TR 189 D7
Karaböğürtlen TR 197 B9
Karabunar BG 181 E9
Karaburun TR 189 B10
Karaburun TR 193 B7
Karaca TR 197 C8
Karacabey TR 189 D9
Karacadağ TR 183 F9
Karacakılavuz TR 189 B7
Karacaköy TR 189 B9
Karád H 165 C9
Karadzhalovo BG 182 E4
Karahalil TR 189 A9
Karaincirli TR 187 C10
Karainebeyli TR 187 D10

Karaisen *BG* 182 C4
Karakaja *BIH* 173 D11
Karakasım *TR* 188 A6
Karakaya *TR* 189 F9
Karakoca *TR* 189 D10
Karaköy *TR* 193 B9
Karaköy *TR* 197 B9
Karakurt *TR* 197 A13 A10
Karala *EST* 146 E3
Karaman *TR* 189 E9
Karamanovo *BG* 182 B5
Karamehmet *TR* 189 B8
Karamyshevo *RUS* 148 F4
Karamyshevo *RUS* 152 E5
Karancsberény *H* 163 E9
Karancskeszi *H* 163 E9
Karancslapujtő *H* 163 E9
Karancsság *H* 163 E9
Karankämäki *FIN* 140 C8
Karaoğlanlı *TR* 193 B10
Karaorman *TR* 189 E9
Karaova *TR* 193 E10
Karapchiv *UA* 168 A6
Karapelit *BG* 177 F11
Karasjok *N* 129 E15
Karatoulas *GR* 190 D4
Karats *S* 125 C16
Karavas *GR* 194 C5
Karavelovo *BG* 181 D10
Karavelovo *BG* 183 E7
Kärävete *EST* 147 C11
Karavomylos *GR* 191 B6
Karavukovo *SRB* 173 B11
Karben *D* 37 D11
Kårberg *S* 108 B5
Karbinci *MK* 180 F5
Kårböle *S* 119 C9
Kårböleskog *S* 119 C9
Karbow-Vietlübbe *D* 99 D12
Karbunarë e Vogël *AL* 184 C2
Karby *D* 99 A7
Karby *DK* 102 B3
Karby *S* 115 C10
Karcag *H* 167 C6
Karcsa *H* 161 H4
Karczew *PL* 157 F4
Karczmiska Pierwsze *PL* 157 H6
Kärda *S* 103 A13
Kardakata *GR* 190 C1
Kardam *BG* 171 F2
Kardam *BG* 182 C6
Kardamaina *GR* 193 F9
Kardamyli *GR* 190 F5
Kardašova Řečice *CZ* 93 D7
Karden *D* 37 D8
Kardiani *GR* 192 D5
Kardis *S* 133 E11
Karditsa *GR* 185 F6
Karditsomagoula *GR* 185 F6
Kärdla *EST* 146 D5
Kardon *BY* 149 F6
Kardos *H* 166 D6
Kardoskút *H* 166 E6
Karegasnjarga *FIN* 129 E16
Kareļi *LV* 150 D4
Kargowa *PL* 97 B9
Karhi *FIN* 139 C10
Karhila *FIN* 139 F13
Karhujärvi *FIN* 131 F4
Karhunkangas *FIN* 135 F14
Karhula *FIN* 144 D6
Kariani *GR* 186 C6
Karigasniemi *FIN* 129 E16
Karihaugen *N* 127 D12
Karijoki *FIN* 138 F7
Karinainen *FIN* 142 D8
Käringberg *S* 123 A12
Käringen *N* 127 D10
Käringsjön *S* 118 B3
Käringsjövallen *S* 118 A4
Karinkanta *FIN* 135 E13
Karis *FIN* 143 E10
Karise *DK* 103 E10
Karisjärvi *FIN* 143 D11
Karitaina *GR* 190 E5
Karitsa *GR* 185 D7
Karjalaisenniemi *FIN* 137 B11
Karjalan kirkonkylä *FIN* 142 D7
Karjalankylä *FIN* 135 D15
Karjalankylä *FIN* 142 D7
Karjalanvaara *FIN* 135 B9
Karjalanvaara *FIN* 137 F10
Karjalohja *FIN* 143 E10
Kärjenkoski *FIN* 138 F7
Karjulanmäki *FIN* 139 C13
Karkalou *GR* 190 D5
Kärki *LV* 147 F11
Kärkinen *FIN* 135 F12
Kärkkäälä *FIN* 139 E16
Kärkkäälä *FIN* 140 C8
Karkkila *FIN* 143 D9
Karkku *FIN* 143 C9
Kärklinieki *LV* 149 B2
Kärkölä *FIN* 143 D10
Kärkölä *FIN* 143 D11
Karksi *EST* 147 E11
Karksi-Nuia *EST* 147 E11
Kårkul *S* 134 B5
Kärla *EST* 146 E4
Kärlå *FIN* 138 F7
Karlby *FIN* 142 F4
Karlebotn *N* 130 C5
Karleby *FIN* 139 C10
Karlholmsbruk *S* 115 A9
Karlino *PL* 101 B9
Karlobag *HR* 83 C11
Karlovac *HR* 164 F5
Karlovasi *GR* 193 D8
Karlovice *CZ* 158 F3
Karlovo *BG* 181 D10
Karlovy Vary *CZ* 92 B3
Karłowice *PL* 158 E4
Karlsbäck *S* 123 D15
Karlsbad *D* 43 C10
Karlsberg *S* 119 C9
Karlsborg *S* 108 B5
Karlsdal *S* 113 D12
Karlsdorf-Neuthard *D* 43 B10
Karlsfeld *D* 91 F9
Karlsfors *S* 119 C9
Karlshagen *D* 100 B5
Karlshamn *S* 105 C7
Karlshöfen *D* 33 B12
Karlskoga *S* 113 D12
Karlskrona *S* 105 C9
Karlsøy *N* 128 C4
Karlsruhe *D* 43 B9
Karlstad *S* 113 D10
Karlstadt *D* 90 C6

Karlstein an der Thaya *A* 93 E8
Karlstetten *A* 93 F9
Karlukovo *BG* 181 C9
Karmansbo *S* 113 C14
Karmas *S* 125 B17
Karmélava *LT* 153 D9
Kärnä *FIN* 139 D11
Kärnä *FIN* 139 D15
Kärna *S* 107 D10
Karnaliyivka *UA* 170 E6
Karnice *PL* 101 B8
Karniewo *PL* 155 E10
Karnjarga *FIN* 129 D19
Karnobat *BG* 183 D7
Karojba *HR* 83 B8
Karolinka *CZ* 162 C6
Karonsbo *S* 123 B15
Karoti *GR* 187 B10
Karousades *GR* 184 E2
Karow *D* 95 B11
Karow *D* 99 C12
Karpacz *PL* 97 E9
Kärpänkylä *FIN* 137 C14
Karpenisi *GR* 190 B4
Karperi *GR* 185 B9
Karpero *GR* 185 E6
Kärppälä *FIN* 143 C9
Karpuzlu *TR* 187 C10
Karpuzlu *TR* 197 A7
Kärrbackstrand *S* 118 E4
Karrebæksminde *DK* 103 E9
Karrenzin *D* 99 D11
Kärrsjö *S* 123 D15
Karsakiškis *LT* 151 E9
Kärsämä *FIN* 135 E15
Kärsämäki *FIN* 139 C15
Kärsava *LV* 149 C3
Karsikas *FIN* 139 C14
Karsikkoniemi *FIN* 133 C11
Karsikkovaara *FIN* 140 B9
Karsimus *FIN* 131 E2
Karsin *PL* 154 C4
Karşıyaka *TR* 189 C9
Karşıyaka *TR* 193 C9
Karsko *PL* 101 E8
Kårsta *S* 115 C10
Karstädt *D* 99 D10
Karstädt *D* 99 D11
Kärstna *EST* 147 E11
Karstula *FIN* 139 E13
Karszew *PL* 158 B6
Kartal *H* 166 B4
Kartavoll *N* 110 E3
Kartena *LT* 150 E2
Kartitsch *A* 88 C6
Kartuzy *PL* 154 B5
Käru *EST* 147 D11
Käru *EST* 147 D12
Karuna *FIN* 142 E8
Karungi *S* 135 B11
Karunki *FIN* 135 B12
Karup *DK* 102 C4
Kårvåg *N* 120 B5
Karvala *FIN* 139 D11
Kärväskylä *FIN* 139 D11
Karvia *FIN* 138 F9
Kårviskhamn *N* 127 B15
Karviná *CZ* 163 B7
Karvoskylä *FIN* 139 C14
Karvounari *GR* 184 F3
Karwica *PL* 155 D11
Karya *GR* 185 E7
Karya *GR* 190 B2
Karya *GR* 191 D6
Karyes *GR* 187 C6
Karyes *GR* 191 E5
Karyotissa *GR* 185 C7
Karyoupoli *GR* 194 B3
Karystos *GR* 191 C9
Kås *DK* 102 A5
Kašalj *SRB* 179 C10
Kasejovice *CZ* 92 D5
Kasendorf *D* 91 B9
Kasepää *EST* 147 D14
Kasfjord *N* 127 C11
Kashirskoye *RUS* 152 D2
Kaşıkçı *TR* 189 B7
Kašina *HR* 164 E6
Kaskantyú *H* 166 D3
Kåskats *S* 132 F4
Kaskii *FIN* 145 B9
Kaskinen *FIN* 138 F6
Kaskö *FIN* 138 F6
Käsmä *FIN* 137 C12
Käsmo *N* 124 B9
Kåsmolia *N* 124 B9
Kaspakas *GR* 187 E8
Kašperské Hory *CZ* 92 D5
Kaspichan *BG* 183 C8
Kassa *S* 133 D11
Kassandreia *GR* 185 D9
Kasseedorf *D* 99 B9
Kassel *D* 94 D6
Kassiopi *GR* 184 E2
Kastania *GR* 184 D4
Kastania *GR* 184 E5
Kastania *GR* 185 D7
Kastania *GR* 185 E6
Kastanies *GR* 187 A10
Kastanochori *GR* 185 C10
Kastari *FIN* 143 C13
Kastellaun *D* 37 D8
Kastelli *GR* 194 E9
Kastellia *GR* 190 B5
Kaštel Stari *HR* 172 E5
Kaštel Sućurac *HR* 172 E5
Kaštel Žegarski *HR* 172 D4
Kasterlee *B* 32 F2
Kastire *LV* 151 D13
Kastl *D* 91 D10
Kastlösa *S* 105 C10
Kastnaharnn *N* 127 C13
Kastorf *D* 99 C9
Kastoria *GR* 185 C6
Kastorio *GR* 190 E5
Kastraki *GR* 190 B3
Kastraki *GR* 192 E5
Kašträne *LV* 151 C9
Kazichane *BG* 181 D7
Kazıklı *TR* 193 E9
Kazimierz Wielka *PL* 159 F9
Kazimierz Biskupi *PL* 158 B5
Kazimierz Dolne *PL* 157 H5
Kazincbarcika *H* 161 G2
Kazlowshchyna *BY* 149 E4
Kazlų Rūda *LT* 153 D7
Kaznějov *CZ* 92 C4
Kaz'yany *BY* 149 E2
Kaz'yany *BY* 151 F13
Kçirë *AL* 179 E8
Kcynia *PL* 101 E12
Kdyně *CZ* 92 D4

Katarraktis *GR* 193 C7
Keadue *IRL* 22 D6
Keady *GB* 23 D9
Kealkill *IRL* 24 E4
Kebal *S* 107 B9
Kecel *H* 166 D3
Kecerovce *SK* 161 F3
Kechrokampos *GR* 187 B7
Kechros *GR* 187 B9
Kecskéd *H* 165 A10
Kecskemét *H* 166 D4
Kédainiai *LT* 151 F7
Kédros *GR* 190 A5
Keenagh *IRL* 23 E6
Keeni *EST* 147 F12
Kefalos *GR* 193 F8
Kefalovryso *GR* 185 E7
Kefenrod *D* 37 D12
Kefermarkt *A* 93 F7
Kegums *LV* 151 C9
Kegworth *GB* 27 F9
Kehdingbrook *D* 203 A5 Kato Nevrokopi *GR* 185 B10
Kehidakustány *H* 165 C8
Kehl *D* 43 C8
Kehlen *L* 36 E6
Kehra *EST* 147 C10
Kehrig *D* 37 D8
Kehtna *EST* 147 D9
Kehvo *FIN* 140 D8
Keighley *GB* 27 D8
Keihärinkoski *FIN* 139 D15
Keikyä *FIN* 142 C8
Keila *EST* 147 C8
Keila-Joa *EST* 147 C8
Keillmore *GB* 20 D5
Keinäsperä *FIN* 135 D17
Keipene *LV* 151 C10
Keiprod *N* 127 C14
Keiss *GB* 19 H10
Keitele *FIN* 139 D15
Keitelepohja *FIN* 139 D15
Keith *GB* 19 K11
Kék *H* 161 G4
Kékcse *H* 161 G5
Kelankylä *FIN* 137 B11
Kelberg *D* 37 D7
Kelbra (Kyffhäuser) *D* 95 D9
Kelč *CZ* 162 C5
Kělcyrë *AL* 184 D3
Kelebia *H* 166 E4
Kelechyn *UA* 161 H7
Kelheim *D* 91 E10
Kell *D* 37 E7
Kellas *GB* 19 K10
Kellas *GB* 21 B11
Kellenhusen *D* 99 B10
Kelli *GR* 185 C6
Kellinghusen *D* 98 C7
Kellmünz an der Iller *D* 87 A10
Kello *FIN* 135 D14
Kellokoski *FIN* 143 D13
Kelloniemi *FIN* 131 E3
Kelloniemi *FIN* 133 D13
Kelloselkä *FIN* 131 E5
Kells *GB* 20 D4
Kells *IRL* 23 E9
Kells *IRL* 24 E2
Kells *IRL* 25 C8
Kelmė *LT* 150 E5
Kelmis *B* 36 C6
Kelontekemä *FIN* 133 C15
Kelottijärvi *FIN* 132 A8
Kelso *GB* 21 D10
Kelujärvi *FIN* 131 D2
Kelvå *FIN* 141 D13
Kelvedon *GB* 31 D10
Kelvä *FIN* 141 D13
Kemalpaşa *TR* 193 C9
Kemberg *D* 95 C12
Kemecse *H* 161 G4
Kemence *H* 163 E7
Kemer *TR* 189 A9 Kecerovce Kemer *TR* 189 B10
Kémes *H* 165 E10
Kemeten *A* 164 B6
Kemi *FIN* 135 C13
Kemihaara *FIN* 131 C5
Kemijärvi *FIN* 131 D4
Kemilä *FIN* 137 C14
Keminmaa *FIN* 135 C13
Keminperä *FIN* 137 D12
Kemnath *D* 91 D11
Kemnay *GB* 19 L12
Kemnitz *D* 97 D7
Kemnitz *D* 100 B5
Kempele *FIN* 135 D14
Kempen *D* 32 F6
Kempenich *D* 37 D8
Kempsey *GB* 29 A10
Kempston *GB* 31 C8
Kempten (Allgäu) *D* 87 B10
Kendal *GB* 26 C6
Kenderes *H* 166 C6
Kendice *SK* 161 F3
Kenézlő *H* 161 G4
Kenfig *GB* 29 B7
Kengis *S* 133 D10
Kengyel *H* 166 C5
Kenilworth *GB* 29 A11
Kenmare *IRL* 24 E3
Kenmore *GB* 21 B9
Kenn *D* 37 E7
Kennacraig *GB* 20 D6
Kensaleyre *GB* 18 L4
Kensworth *GB* 31 D7
Kentavros *GR* 187 B8
Kentriko *GR* 185 B8
Kentro *GR* 190 D2
Kenyeri *H* 165 B8
Kenzingen *D* 43 D8
Kepez *TR* 187 D10
Kępice *PL* 101 B11
Kępno *PL* 158 D4
Kepsut *TR* 189 E9
Keramitsa *GR* 184 E3
Keramoti *GR* 187 C7
Keräntöjärvi *S* 132 C9
Kerasia *GR* 185 D6
Kerasona *GR* 184 E4
Keräs-Sieppi *FIN* 133 B11
Keratea *GR* 191 D6
Kerava *FIN* 143 E13
Kerecsend *H* 161 F10
Kerekegyháza *H* 166 D3
Kerepestarcsa *H* 166 B3
Kerets'ky *UA* 161 G7
Kergu *EST* 147 D9
Keri *GR* 190 D2

Kerimäki *FIN* 145 B11
Kerisalo *FIN* 141 F9
Kerkdriel *NL* 32 E4
Kerkebakken... Kerkejaure *S* 134 B3
Kerken *D* 32 F6
Kerkini *GR* 185 B9
Kerkkoo *FIN* 143 E14
Kerkonkoski *FIN* 139 E17
Kerkrade *NL* 36 C6
Kerkwijk *NL* 199 B6
Kerkyra *GR* 184 F2
Kerlouan *F* 38 C3
Kerma *FIN* 141 F11
Kermen *BG* 182 D6
Kernascléden *F* 38 D5
Kernhof *A* 164 A5
Kerns *CH* 86 D6
Kerpen *D* 37 C7
Kerrykeel *IRL* 23 B7
Kershopefoot *GB* 21 E11
Kersilö *FIN* 133 C17
Kersleben *D* 95 D9
Kerstinbo *S* 114 B7
Kerteminde *DK* 102 E7
Kertészsziget *H* 167 C7
Kertezi *GR* 190 D4
Kerttuankylä *FIN* 139 D10
Kerzers *CH* 47 B11
Kesälahti *FIN* 145 B12
Kesarevo *BG* 182 C5
Kesasjärv *S* 134 B8
Kesh *GB* 23 C7
Kesh *IRL* 22 C6
Kesik *TR* 193 B8
Keşan *TR* 188 C6
Kesänniemenkylä *FIN* 137 B12
Keşan... Keşiklik... Kesäniemenkylä
Keskikylä *FIN* 141 E14
Keskikylä *FIN* 135 E13
Keskikylä *FIN* 135 F13
Keskikylä *FIN* 135 F13
Keskikylä *FIN* 139 F11
Keskinen *FIN* 137 E13
Keskipiiri *FIN* 135 E14
Keski-Posio *FIN* 137 B11
Keskusvankila *FIN* 140 C8
Kesowo *PL* 154 C4
Kessel *B* 198 C5
Kessel *NL* 199 C8
Kesselinkylä *FIN* 141 C14
Kessingland *GB* 31 C12
Kesteren *NL* 199 B7
Kestilä *FIN* 135 D14
Kestilä *FIN* 135 F15
Kestrini *GR* 184 E3
Keswick *GB* 26 B5
Keszthely *H* 165 C8
Kesztöc *H* 165 A11
Kétegyháza *H* 167 D7
Kéthely *H* 165 C8
Ketola *FIN* 131 E2
Ketomella *FIN* 133 B14
Keträvaara *FIN* 137 D13
Ketrzyn *PL* 152 E3
Ketsch *D* 37 F11
Kétsoprony *H* 167 D6
Kettering *GB* 31 C7
Kettershausen *D* 87 A10
Kettinge *DK* 99 A11
Kettletoft *GB* 19 E11
Kettlewell *GB* 27 C7
Kettwig *D* 199 C9
Kéty *PL* 163 B8
Ketzin *D* 95 B12
Keula *D* 95 D8
Keuruu *FIN* 139 E13
Keväjärvi *FIN* 130 F3
Kevelaer *D* 32 E6
Kevermes *H* 167 D7
Kevo *FIN* 129 D19
Keynsham *GB* 29 C9
Keyritty *FIN* 141 D10
Kežmarok *SK* 161 E1
Khadzhidimovo *BG* 185 A10
Khalamyer"ye *BY* 149 E7
Kharlu *RUS* 145 B14
Kharmanli *BG* 182 F5
Khaskovo *BG* 182 F5
Khayredin *BG* 176 F3
Khelyulya *RUS* 145 B14
Khisarya *BG* 181 D10
Khiytola *RUS* 145 C12
Khlivchany *UA* 160 C3
Kholms'ke *UA* 171 B4
Khorio *GR* 195 B8
Khrabrovo *RUS* 152 D2
Khrishteni *BG* 182 E5
Khust *UA* 161 H6
Khvoyna *BG* 181 F10
Khyriv *UA* 161 E6
Kiannanniemi *FIN* 137 D13
Kiato *GR* 191 C6
Kiaunoriai *LT* 150 E6
Kibæk *DK* 102 C3
Kibworth Harcourt *GB* 27 F10
Kiby *N* 130 C7
Kičevo *MK* 184 A4
Kichenitsa *BG* 177 F8
Kichevo *BG* 183 C9
Kidderminster *GB* 29 A10
Kidlington *GB* 29 B12
Kidričevo *SLO* 164 C5
Kidsgrove *GB* 27 E7
Kidwelly *GB* 28 B5
Kiefersfelden *D* 88 A5
Kiegęlceplis *LV* 151 C10
Kiekinkoski *FIN* 141 B14
Kiekrz *PL* 97 B11
Kiel *D* 99 B8
Kielajoki *FIN* 129 E18
Kielce *PL* 159 E10
Kiełczygłów *PL* 159 D6
Kielder *GB* 21 E11
Kieldrecht *B* 198 C4
Kiełpino *PL* 154 B5
Kienberg *D* 91 F11
Kierspe *D* 37 B8
Kieselbach *D* 95 E7
Kiesilä *FIN* 144 C7
Kiesimä *FIN* 139 E17
Kietrz *PL* 158 F5
Kietz *D* 97 A7
Kifjord *N* 129 B19
Kifisia *GR* 191 C8

Kihlanki *FIN* 133 C11
Kihlanki *S* 133 C10
Kihlepa *EST* 147 E8
Kihlevere *EST* 147 C12
Kihniö *FIN* 139 F10
Kiihtelysvaara *FIN* 141 F14
Kiikala *FIN* 143 E10
Kiikka *FIN* 142 C8
Kiikla *EST* 147 C14
Kiikoinen *FIN* 142 C8
Kiili *EST* 147 C9
Kiiminki *FIN* 135 D15
Kiisa *EST* 147 C9
Kiiskilä *FIN* 139 C13
Kiistala *FIN* 133 C14
Kiiu *EST* 147 C10
Kije *PL* 159 F10
Kijevo *HR* 172 E5
Kijevo *SRB* 179 D10
Kijewo Królewskie *PL* 154 D5
Kikerino *RUS* 148 C6
Kikinda *SRB* 166 F5
Kikół *PL* 154 E7
Kikorze *PL* 101 C8
Kikuri *LV* 150 C3
Kil *S* 113 C9
Kilafors *S* 119 D12
Kilargue *IRL* 22 D6
Kilb *A* 93 F8
Kilbaha *IRL* 24 C3
Kilbeggan *IRL* 23 F8
Kilbeheny *IRL* 24 D6
Kilberry *GB* 20 D5
Kilberry *IRL* 23 F8
Kilbirnie *GB* 20 D6
Kilboghamn *N* 124 D5
Kilbotn *N* 127 C12
Kilbrittain *IRL* 24 E5
Kilby *S* 115 B10
Kilcar *IRL* 22 C5
Kilchoan *GB* 20 B4
Kilchrenan *GB* 20 C6
Kilcock *IRL* 23 F9
Kilcolgan *IRL* 22 F5
Kilcommon *IRL* 25 C8
Kilconney *IRL* 23 E8
Kilcoole *IRL* 23 F10
Kilcormac *IRL* 23 F7
Kilcreggan *GB* 20 D7
Kilcullen *IRL* 23 F9
Kildare *IRL* 23 F9
Kildavin *IRL* 25 C9
Kilden *DK* 106 E7
Kildimo New *IRL* 24 C5
Kildonan Lodge *GB* 19 J9
Kile *N* 106 A2
Kilen *N* 111 D9
Kilfenora *IRL* 22 G4
Kilfinan *GB* 20 D6
Kilfinnane *IRL* 24 D6
Kilforsen *S* 123 D11
Kilgarvan *IRL* 24 E4
Kilgetty *GB* 28 B5
Kilglass *IRL* 22 E6
Kilglass *IRL* 22 F6
Kilham *GB* 21 D12
Kilidülbahir *TR* 187 D10
Kilifarevo *BG* 182 C5
Kilingi-Nõmme *EST* 147 E9
Kiliya *UA* 171 C4
Kilkea *IRL* 23 G9
Kilkee *IRL* 24 C3
Kilkeel *GB* 23 D11
Kilkelly *IRL* 22 E5
Kilkenny *IRL* 25 C8
Kilkhampton *GB* 28 D6
Kilkieran *IRL* 22 F3
Kilkinlea *IRL* 24 D4
Kilkishen *IRL* 24 C5
Kill *IRL* 23 F9
Kill *IRL* 25 D8
Killabunane *IRL* 24 E3
Killadysert *IRL* 24 C4
Killagan Bridge *GB* 20 E4
Killala *IRL* 22 D4
Killaloe *IRL* 24 C6
Killamerry *IRL* 25 D8
Killann *IRL* 25 C9
Killarga *IRL* 22 D6
Killarney *IRL* 24 D4
Killavullen *IRL* 24 D6
Killeagh *IRL* 24 E7
Killean *GB* 20 C5
Killearn *GB* 20 C8
Killeberg *S* 104 C6
Killeenleagh *IRL* 24 E4
Killeigh *IRL* 23 F8
Killen *GB* 23 C7
Killenaule *IRL* 25 C9
Killerig *IRL* 25 C9
Killeshandra *IRL* 23 E7
Killichonan *GB* 21 B8
Killiecrankie *GB* 21 B9
Killimor *IRL* 22 F6
Killin *GB* 21 C8
Killinaboy *IRL* 22 G4
Killinchy *GB* 23 D11
Killinge *S* 132 C4
Killingworth *GB* 21 E13
Killinick *IRL* 25 D10
Killinkoski *FIN* 139 F11
Killorglin *IRL* 24 D3
Killough *GB* 23 D11
Killough *IRL* 23 F10
Killucan *IRL* 23 E8
Killukin *IRL* 22 E6
Killundine *GB* 20 B5
Killurin *IRL* 25 D9
Killybegs *IRL* 22 C6
Killyclogher *GB* 20 F2
Killylea *GB* 23 D9
Kilmacanoge *IRL* 23 F10
Kilmacrenan *IRL* 23 B7
Kilmacthomas *IRL* 25 D9
Kilmaine *IRL* 22 E4
Kilmaley *IRL* 24 C4
Kilmallock *IRL* 24 D5
Kilmaluag *GB* 18 K4
Kilmarnock *GB* 20 D8
Kilmartin *GB* 20 C6
Kilmeage *IRL* 23 F9
Kilmeedy *IRL* 24 D5
Kilmelford *GB* 20 C6
Kilmichael *IRL* 24 E4
Kilmihill *IRL* 24 C4
Kilmona *IRL* 24 E5
Kilmoon *IRL* 23 E10
Kilmore *IRL* 24 C5

Kilmore *IRL* 25 D9
Kilmore Quay *IRL* 25 D9
Kilmuckridge *IRL* 25 C10
Kilmurry *IRL* 24 C5
Kilmurry McMahon *IRL* 24 C4
Kilnaboy *IRL* 22 G4
Kilnaleck *IRL* 23 E8
Kilnamanagh *IRL* 25 C10
Kilninian *GB* 20 B4
Kilninver *GB* 20 C5
Kilnock *IRL* 22 E5
Kiloran *GB* 20 C4
Kilpelä *FIN* 131 C4
Kilpilahti *FIN* 143 E14
Kilpisjärvi *FIN* 128 E6
Kilpua *FIN* 135 F13
Kilquiggin *IRL* 25 C9
Kilrane *IRL* 25 D10
Kilrea *GB* 20 E3
Kilrean *IRL* 22 C6
Kilreekill *IRL* 22 F6
Kilronan *IRL* 22 F3
Kilrush *IRL* 24 C4
Kilsallagh *IRL* 22 E5
Kilsaran *IRL* 23 E10
Kilshanchoe *IRL* 23 F9
Kilshanny *IRL* 22 G4
Kilskeer *IRL* 23 E9
Kilsmo *S* 108 A7
Kilsund *N* 106 B4
Kilsyth *GB* 21 C8
Kiltartan *IRL* 22 F5
Kiltealy *IRL* 25 C9
Kiltegan *IRL* 25 C9
Kiltimagh *IRL* 22 E5
Kiltogan *IRL* 25 C9
Kiltoom *IRL* 22 F6
Kiltsi *EST* 147 C12
Kiltullagh *IRL* 22 F5
Kilvakkala *FIN* 143 C9
Kilvenaapa *FIN* 135 B16
Kilvo *S* 132 E6
Kilwaughter *GB* 20 F5
Kilwinning *GB* 20 D7
Kilworth *IRL* 24 D6
Kimasozero *RUS* 137 F17
Kimberley *GB* 31 B11
Kimbolton *GB* 31 C8
Kiminki *FIN* 139 E13
Kimito *FIN* 142 E8
Kimle *H* 162 F4
Kimmeria *GR* 187 B7
Kimo *FIN* 138 D8
Kimola *FIN* 143 C15
Kimonkylä *FIN* 143 D15
Kimovaara *RUS* 141 C16
Kimpton *GB* 31 D8
Kimstad *S* 108 B7
Kinahmo *FIN* 141 E13
Kinbrace *GB* 19 J9
Kincardine *GB* 21 C9
Kincraig *GB* 19 L9
Kincses *H* 165 B10
Kindberg *A* 164 A4
Kindelbrück *D* 95 D9
Kinderbeuern *D* 37 D8
Kinding *D* 91 E9
Kindsbach *D* 202 C4
Kindsjön *S* 118 E4
Kineta *GR* 191 D7
Kingarrow *IRL* 22 C6
Kingarth *GB* 20 D6
Kingisepp *RUS* 148 C5
Kingsbridge *GB* 29 E7
Kingsclere *GB* 29 C12
Kingscourt *IRL* 23 E9
Kingskerswell *GB* 29 E7
Kingsland *IRL* 22 E6
King's Lynn *GB* 27 F12
Kingsnorth *GB* 31 E10
Kingsteignton *GB* 29 D7
Kingsthorne *GB* 29 B9
Kingston *GB* 19 K10
Kingston Bagpuize *GB* 29 B12
Kingston Seymour *GB* 29 C9
Kingston upon Hull *GB* 27 D11
Kingswear *GB* 29 E7
Kingswood *GB* 29 C9
Kings Worthy *GB* 29 C12
Kington *GB* 29 A8
Kingussie *GB* 21 A8
Kingwilliamstown *IRL* 24 D4
Kınık *TR* 189 A9
Kınık *TR* 193 A9
Kinisjärvi *FIN* 133 D14
Kinloch *GB* 20 A4
Kinlochard *GB* 20 C8
Kinlochewe *GB* 18 K6
Kinlochleven *GB* 20 B7
Kinloch Rannoch *GB* 21 B8
Kinloss *GB* 19 K9
Kinlough *IRL* 22 D6
Kinn *N* 127 C10
Kinna *S* 107 C12
Kinnared *S* 103 A12
Kinnarp *S* 107 C14
Kinnarumma *S* 107 D12
Kinnegad *IRL* 23 F8
Kinnitty *IRL* 23 F7
Kinnula *FIN* 139 D13
Kinnulanlahti *FIN* 140 D8
Kinrooi *B* 35 B12
Kinross *GB* 21 C10
Kinsale *IRL* 24 E5
Kinsalebeg *IRL* 25 E7
Kinsarvik *N* 110 B5
Kintai *LT* 150 F2
Kintaus *FIN* 139 F14
Kintbury *GB* 29 C12
Kintore *GB* 19 L12
Kinvara *IRL* 22 F5
Kinvarra *IRL* 22 E3
Kioni *GR* 190 C2
Kipen' *RUS* 148 B6
Kipfenberg *D* 91 E9
Kipilovo *BG* 182 D6
Kipinä *FIN* 135 D17
Kipoi *GR* 184 E4
Kippel *CH* 86 E5
Kippen *GB* 21 C8
Kippenheim *D* 43 D8
Kir *AL* 179 E8
Kirakkajärvi *FIN* 130 D5
Kirakkaköngäs *FIN* 129 F19
Királd *H* 161 G1
Királyegyháza *H* 165 D9
Királyhegyes *H* 166 E6
Kiran *N* 120 C8
Kıran *TR* 197 B8
Kirazlı *TR* 188 D5
Kırbla *EST* 147 D7

Kirby Muxloe GB 27 F9
Kırcasalih TR 189 B6
Kirchanschöring D 89 A6
Kirchardt D 37 F11
Kirchbach A 89 C7
Kirchbach in Steiermark A 164 C5
Kirchberg CH 43 F11
Kirchberg CH 47 A12
Kirchberg D 92 E4
Kirchberg D 95 E12
Kirchberg (Hunsrück) D 201 E7
Kirchberg am Wagram A 93 F9
Kirchberg am Walde A 93 E8
Kirchberg am Wechsel A 164 A5
Kirchberg an der Jagst D 90 D6
Kirchberg an der Pielach A 93 F8
Kirchberg an der Raab A 164 C5
Kirchbichl A 88 A5
Kirchdorf D 33 C11
Kirchdorf D 99 C10
Kirchdorf an der Iller D 87 A10
Kirchdorf an der Krems A 89 A9
Kirchdorf im Wald D 92 E4
Kirchdorf in Tirol A 88 A5
Kirchehrenbach D 91 C9
Kirchen (Sieg) D 37 C9
Kirchenlamitz D 91 B10
Kirchenthumbach D 91 C10
Kirchgellersen D 99 D8
Kirchhain D 37 C11
Kirchheim D 90 C6
Kirchheim D 94 E6
Kirchheim am Neckar D 203 C7
Kirchheim bei München D 91 F10
Kirchheim-Bolanden D 37 E10
Kirchheim unter Teck D 43 C11
Kirchhundem D 37 B10
Kirchlauter D 91 B8
Kirchlinteln D 33 C12
Kirch Mulsow D 99 C11
Kirchohsen (Emmerthal) D 94 B5
Kirchroth D 91 E12
Kirchschlag in der Buckligen Welt A 164 A6
Kirchseelte D 33 C11
Kirchtimke D 33 B12
Kirchwalsede D 33 B12
Kirchweidach D 91 C12
Kirchwistedt D 33 B11
Kirchzarten D 43 E8
Kirchzell D 37 E12
Kircubbin GB 23 D11
Kireç TR 189 E9
Kiremitçişalih TR 188 B6
Kirillovskoye RUS 145 E11
Kirjais FIN 142 E6
Kirjavala FIN 145 B12
Kırkağaç TR 193 A10
Kirkbean GB 21 F9
Kirkby GB 26 E6
Kirkby in Ashfield GB 27 E9
Kirkby Lonsdale GB 26 C6
Kirkbymoorside GB 27 C10
Kirkby Stephen GB 27 C7
Kirkby Thore GB 21 F11
Kirkcaldy GB 21 C10
Kirkcolm GB 20 F6
Kirkconnel GB 21 E8
Kirkcudbright GB 21 F8
Kirkeby DK 102 E7
Kirkehamn N 110 F5
Kirke Helsinge DK 103 D8
Kirke Hyllinge DK 103 D9
Kirkel-Neuhäusel D 202 C3
Kirkenær N 112 B7
Kirkenes N 130 D8
Kirke Såby DK 103 D9
Kirke Stillinge DK 103 E8
Kirkham GB 26 D6
Kirkinner GB 21 F8
Kirkintilloch GB 21 D8
Kirkjubøur FO 18 B3
Kırkkavak TR 189 B6
Kırkkepenekli TR 189 B8
Kırklareli TR 183 F8
Kirkmichael GB 20 E7
Kirkmichael GB 21 B9
Kirk Michael GBM 26 C2
Kirknewton GB 21 D10
Kirkoswald GB 21 F11
Kirkpatrick-Fleming GB 21 E10
Kirkton GB 20 C5
Kirkton of Durris GB 21 A12
Kirkton of Glenisla GB 21 B10
Kirkton of Skene GB 19 D8
Kirktown of Auchterless GB 19 L12
Kirktown of Deskford GB 19 K11
Kirkwall GB 19 H11
Kirn D 37 E8
Kırnujärvi S 132 D10
Kirovsk RUS 145 F14
Kirriemuir GB 21 B10
Kirschweiler D 37 E8
Kirtik S 134 B5
Kirtlington GB 29 B12
Kirton GB 31 C11
Kirton in Lindsey GB 27 E10
Kirtorf D 37 C12
Kiruna S 132 C4
Kisa S 108 D7
Kisač SRB 174 C4
Kisar S 161 G6
Kisbér H 165 A10
Kiseljak BIH 173 C10
Kiseljak BIH 173 C11
Kiseljak BIH 173 E9
Kisgyőr H 161 G2
Kishkeam IRL 24 D4
Kisielice PL 155 D13
Kisielnica PL 155 D13
Kisko FIN 143 E9
Kisköre H 166 C5
Kiskőrös H 166 D3
Kiskunfélegyháza H 166 D4
Kiskunhalas H 166 E3
Kiskunlacháza H 166 C3
Kiskunmajsa H 166 E4
Kışlacık TR 183 F9
Kıslänge H 165 C10
Kisléta H 167 B8
Kislőd H 165 B9
Kismarja H 167 C8
Kisnána H 163 F10
Kisovec SLO 89 D10
Kissakoski FIN 144 B6
Kissamos GR 194 E6

Kissenbrück D 95 B8
Kißlegg D 87 B9
Kisszállás H 166 E3
Kist D 203 B8
Kistanje HR 172 E4
Kistelek H 166 E4
Kistokaj H 161 G2
Kistrand N 129 C15
Kisújszállás H 166 C6
Kisvárda H 161 G4
Kisvarsány H 161 G5
Kiszkowo PL 97 A12
Kiszombor H 166 E5
Kitee FIN 141 F14
Kitinoja FIN 138 E9
Kitka FIN 137 B12
Kitros GR 185 D8
Kitsi FIN 141 D15
Kittajaur S 134 B3
Kittelfjäll S 122 A8
Kittilä FIN 133 C13
Kittsee A 93 F12
Kitula FIN 143 E10
Kitzbühel A 88 B5
Kitzen D 95 D11
Kitzingen D 91 C7
Kitzscher D 95 D12
Kiuce PL 159 F8
Kiukainen FIN 142 C7
Kiurujärvi FIN 131 D2
Kiuruvesi FIN 139 C17
Kivarinjärvi FIN 137 E10
Kivelä FIN 131 F4
Kiveri GR 191 D6
Kivesjärvi FIN 137 F9
Kiveskylä FIN 137 F9
Kiveslahti FIN 136 F9
Kiviapaja FIN 145 B10
Kivijärvi FIN 139 D14
Kivijärvi S 132 C10
Kivik S 104 D6
Kivikangas FIN 139 D12
Kivilahti FIN 141 E14
Kivilompolo FIN 133 A10
Kivilompolo FIN 135 B12
Kivilompolo N 133 A10
Kivioja FIN 135 B14
Kiviõli EST 147 C13
Kiviperä FIN 137 B14
Kivivaara FIN 137 E13
Kivivaara FIN 141 C14
Kivi-Vigala EST 147 D8
Kivotos GR 184 D5
Kiwity PL 152 B3
Kizilcaova TR 193 C10
Kızılcıkdere TR 183 F8
Kızılpınar TR 189 B8
Kızılyaka TR 197 B8
Kjækan N 128 D9
Kjåmes N 127 D12
Kjeldebotn N 127 D12
Kjelkenes N 116 C2
Kjelkvik N 127 D11
Kjellerup DK 102 C4
Kjelling N 124 B7
Kjemmoen N 118 D9
Kjengsnes N 127 C11
Kjerknesvågen N 121 D10
Kjerret N 112 B7
Kjerringdal N 128 C9
Kjerringholmen N 129 B12
Kjerringøy N 124 A5
Kjerringvåg N 120 D5
Kjerringvik N 126 C9
Kjerringvik N 127 D12
Kjerstad N 120 D4
Kjølebrønn N 106 B5
Kjølen N 107 A9
Kjøllefjord N 129 B19
Kjølstad N 117 D10
Kjøpsvik N 127 D11
Kjøra N 120 D7
Kjøsvika N 121 A12
Kjulaås S 108 C8
Klaaswaal NL 32 E2
Kľačno SK 163 D7
Kladanj BIH 173 D10
Kläden D 95 A10
Kladnica SRB 179 C9
Kladnice HR 172 E5
Kladno CZ 92 B6
Kladovo SRB 175 D9
Kladruby CZ 92 C3
Klagenfurt A 89 C9
Klågerup S 103 D12
Klaipėda LT 150 E2
Kłaj PL 159 G9
Klaksvík FO 18 A3
Klamila FIN 144 D7
Klana HR 83 B9
Klanac HR 172 C4
Klanjec HR 164 D5
Klanxbüll D 102 F3
Klapkalnciems LV 150 B6
Kläppsjö S 123 D12
Klärke S 119 A12
Klarup DK 102 A6
Klašnice BIH 173 C7
Klasov SK 162 E6
Klässbol S 113 C8
Kláštterec nad Ohří CZ 92 B4
Kláštor pod Znievom SK 163 D7
Klátova Nová Ves SK 162 D6
Klatovy CZ 92 D4
Klaukkala FIN 143 E12
Klaus an der Pyhrnbahn A 89 A9
Klausdorf D 96 B4
Klausdorf D 100 B4
Klausen D 37 C7
Klausen Leopoldsdorf A 93 F10
Klausučiai LT 152 D7
Klauvnes N 124 E6
Klazienaveen NL 33 C7
Kłecko PL 97 A12
Kłecko bowiec PL 101 D10
Kleczew PL 154 F5
Kłeczkowo PL 159 F8
Kleemola FIN 139 D12
Kleidi GR 185 C8
Kleinarl A 89 B7
Klein Berßen D 33 C8
Kleinblittersdorf D 37 F7
Klein Bünzow D 100 C5
Kleinfurra D 95 D8
Kleinheubach D 37 E12
Kleinjena D 95 D10
Klein Kreutz D 95 B12

Kleinlobming A 89 B10
Kleinmachnow D 96 B4
Kleinpaschleben D 95 C10
Kleinreifling A 89 A10
Kleinrinderfeld D 203 B8
Klein Rönnau D 99 C8
Kleinwallstadt D 37 E12
Kleinwelka D 96 D6
Kleinzell A 93 G9
Kleio GR 187 F10
Kleisoura GR 184 C5
Kleitoria GR 190 D5
Kleiva N 126 C9
Klejnik PL 159 E8
Klejtrup DK 102 B5
Klek SRB 174 F6
Klembivka UA 170 A2
Klemensker DK 105 E7
Klenčí pod Čerchovem CZ 91 D12
Klenica PL 97 C9
Klenike SRB 180 E4
Klenje SRB 174 D3
Klenovec SK 163 D9
Klenovice na Hané CZ 93 D12
Kleosin PL 156 D8
Klepacze PL 156 D8
Kleppe N 110 E3
Kleppestø N 110 B2
Kleppstad N 126 D7
Klepsk PL 97 B9
Kleszczele PL 157 E8
Kleszczewo PL 97 B12
Kleszczewo PL 152 F6
Kleszczów PL 159 D7
Klettwitz D 96 C5
Kleve D 32 E6
Klevshult S 108 E4
Kličevac SRB 175 D7
Kličevo MNE 179 D6
Klieken D 95 C11
Klietz D 99 E12
Klikuszowa PL 163 B9
Klim D 102 A4
Kliment BG 177 C10
Kliment BG 181 C9
Klimentovo BG 183 C9
Klimkovice CZ 162 B6
Klimontów PL 159 E11
Klimontów PL 159 F9
Klimpfjäll S 122 A7
Klin SK 163 C8
Klina SRB 179 D10
Klinča Sela HR 164 E5
Klingenberg D 96 E5
Klingenberg am Main D 37 E12
Klingenthal D 91 B11
Klingersel S 134 B7
Klingre S 123 E15
Klink D 99 D13
Klinkby DK 102 B3
Klinte S 109 E12
Klintehamn S 109 E12
Klipev DK 102 D7
Klippan S 103 C12
Klippen S 123 C13
Klippen S 124 E9
Klippinge DK 103 E10
Klis HR 172 E6
Klisura BG 181 D9
Klisura BG 181 E7
Klisura SRB 180 D5
Klitmøller DK 102 A3
Klitten D 97 D7
Klitten S 118 D7
Klixbüll D 98 A5
Kljajićevo SRB 166 F3
Ključ BIH 173 C6
Klobouky CZ 93 E11
Kłobuck PL 159 E6
Kłobukowo PL 159 F7
Klöch A 89 B7
Klobenz D 37 D9
Klobouwo PL 97 A8
Klobow D 99 D13
Kłodawa PL 155 F11
Klokkarvik N 110 B2
Klokočava SK 163 D7
Klokočevci HR 165 E10
Klokočov SK 163 C7
Klokot SRB 180 E3
Klokotnica BG 183 D9
Kłomnice PL 159 E8
Klonowa PL 158 D5
Klooga EST 147 C8
Kloosterburen NL 33 B7
Kloosterzande NL 32 F1
Klos AL 179 F9
Klos AL 184 B3
Klöse S 123 D12
Klöster Ivanić HR 165 E6
Klöster Podravski HR 165 E8
Kloster CZ 100 E4
Klosterfelde D 100 E4
Klosterhäseler D 95 D10
Klösterle A 87 C8
Klosterlechfeld D 87 A11
Klostermansfeld D 95 C9
Klosterneuburg A 93 F10
Klosters CH 87 D9
Klöster Zinna D 96 B4
Klöten CH 43 C10
Kloten S 113 C13
Klotten D 37 D8
Klötze (Altmark) D 95 A9
Klovborg DK 102 D4
Klöverträsk S 134 C6
Klövmoen N 124 C6
Klövsjö S 118 A7
Klubbfors S 134 C6
Klubbvik N 130 C6
Kluczbork PL 158 D5
Kluczewsko PL 159 E8
Kluki PL 159 D7
Klukowo PL 157 D7
Klumpen S 122 D7
Klundert NL 32 E3
Klungsten S 115 A14
Klupe BIH 173 C8
Kluse D 33 C8
Kľušov SK 161 G3
Klusy PL 155 C13
Klutsjön S 118 B4
Klütz D 99 C10

Kłwów PL 157 G3
Klyastsitsy BY 149 E5
Klykoliai LT 150 D5
Klynivka UA 169 A7
Knaben N 110 E6
Knåda S 119 D10
Knaften S 123 C15
Knäred S 103 B12
Knaresborough GB 27 C9
Knarrevik N 110 B2
Knarrlagsund N 120 D6
Knätten S 118 B7
Knebel DK 102 C6
Knesebeck D 99 E8
Kneesworth GB 31 C9
Kneiva N 126 C9
Knejnik PL 159 B12
Knetzgau D 91 C8
Kneževi Vinogradi HR 165 E11
Kneža BG 181 C7
Knežha CZ 93 D9
Kněžice CZ 93 B9
Knežina BIH 173 D11
Kněžmost CZ 93 B8
Knić SRB 174 F6
Knidi GR 185 D6
Knighton GB 29 A8
Knin HR 172 D5
Knislinge S 104 C6
Knittelfeld A 89 B10
Knittlingen D 43 B10
Kniveri LV 150 D3
Knivsta S 115 C9
Knizhovnik BG 182 F5
Knjaževac SRB 180 B5
Knock GB 20 C5
Knock IRL 22 E5
Knock IRL 24 C4
Knockalough IRL 24 C4
Knockanevin IRL 24 D6
Knockban GB 18 K7
Knockbrack IRL 23 C7
Knockbridge IRL 23 E10
Knockcroghery IRL 22 E6
Knocklong IRL 24 D6
Knockmoyle IRL 22 F6
Knocknaboul IRL 24 D4
Knocknacarry GB 20 E4
Knocknacree IRL 25 D8
Knocknagree IRL 24 D4
Knocks IRL 24 E5
Knocktopher IRL 25 D8
Knokke-Heist B 35 B7
Knoppe S 119 B12
Knorrendorf D 100 C4
Knottingley GB 27 D9
Knowle GB 29 A11
Knucklas GB 29 A8
Knud DK 102 B4
Knurów PL 158 F6
Knutbränna S 122 D7
Knutsbol S 113 D12
Knutsford GB 27 B7
Knyazevo RUS 149 D5
Knyazhe UA 168 A6
Knyazhevo BG 183 E4
Knyazhitsy RUS 148 E4
Knyszyn PL 156 D7
Kobaky UA 168 A6
Kobarid SLO 89 D8
Kobatovci BIH 173 C7
Kobbelveid N 125 A10
Kobbevågnes N 128 B7
Kölcse H 161 G6
København DK 103 D11
Kobenz A 89 B10
Kobeřice CZ 158 G5
Kobern D 201 D7
Kobersdorf A 165 A6
Kobiele Wielkie PL 159 D8
Kobierzyce PL 97 E11
Kobilyane BG 187 A8
Kobiór PL 159 F6
Koblenz D 37 D9
Kobrow D 99 C11
Kobyla Góra PL 158 D4
Kobylanka PL 101 D7
Kobylany PL 157 G6
Kobyłka PL 155 F11
Kobylnica PL 101 B12
Kobylniki PL 155 F9
Kocaavşar TR 189 E8
Kocahıdır TR 187 B6
Kočani MK 180 F5
Kocapınar TR 189 E8
Koçarlı TR 193 D10
Kocayazı TR 183 F8
Koceljevo SRB 174 E4
Kočerin BIH 173 F7
Kočevje SLO 89 E10
Kočevska Reka SLO 89 E10
Kochanowice PL 158 E6
Kochel am See D 88 A3
Kocherinovo BG 181 E7
Kochmar BG 177 F10
Kochovo BG 183 C7
Kock PL 157 G6
Kočovce SK 162 D5
Kocs H 165 A10
Kocsér H 166 C5
Kocsola H 165 C10
Koczała PL 101 C11
Kodavere EST 147 D14
Kodeń PL 157 G9
Kodersdorf D 97 D7
Kodesjärvi FIN 138 F7
Kodiksami FIN 142 C6
Kodisjoki FIN 142 C6
Kodyma UA 170 A4

Koigi EST 147 D11
Koijärvi FIN 143 D10
Koikkala FIN 144 B8
Koiliomeno GR 190 D2
Koirakoski FIN 140 C9
Koirisi GR 185 B9
Koira GR 194 B3
Koitila FIN 137 C10
Koivu FIN 135 B14
Koivujärvi FIN 139 C16
Koivujärvi FIN 139 D16
Koivumäki FIN 140 D9
Koivumäki FIN 141 F11
Koivuniemi FIN 135 C15
Kõja S 123 F13
Kojanlanti EST 141 E11
Kojetín CZ 162 C5
Kóka H 166 C4
Kökar FIN 142 F4
Kokari LV 151 C13
Kokava nad Rimavicou SK 163 D9
Kokelv N 129 C14
Kokemäki FIN 142 C7
Kokkala FIN 194 B3
Kokkari GR 193 D8
Kokkinochoma GR 187 C6
Kokkino Nero GR 185 E8
Kokkokylä FIN 135 C17
Kokkola FIN 139 C10
Kokkosniva FIN 131 D2
Kokkovaara FIN 133 D13
Köklot FIN 138 C7
Koknese LV 151 C10
Kokonvaara FIN 141 E12
Kokora EST 147 D14
Kokory CZ 162 C4
Kokrica SLO 89 D9
Koksijde B 34 B6
Kola FIN 139 D12
Kolari FIN 133 D11
Kolari S 133 D11
Kolárovice SK 163 E8
Kolarovo BG 185 B9
Kolárovo SK 162 F5
Kolašen S 121 D13
Kolašin MNE 179 D8
Kolbäck S 114 C6
Kolbacz PL 101 D7
Kolbaskowo PL 100 D6
Kolberg N 127 D12
Kolbermoor D 88 A5
Kolbiel PL 157 F4
Kolboltn N 111 C11
Kolbu N 117 E13
Kolbudy Górne PL 154 B5
Kolbuszowa PL 160 C4
Kølby DK 102 B4
Kolczygłowy PL 101 B12
Kolczyn PL 97 A8
Koldby DK 102 B3
Koldere TR 193 B10
Kolding DK 102 E4
Koler S 134 C5
Kölesd H 165 C11
Kolesjan AL 179 F7
Koleška BIH 173 F9
Kolforsen S 119 D12
Kõlga EST 147 C11
Kolga-Jaani EST 147 D11
Kolho FIN 139 E15
Koli FIN 141 D13
Kolín CZ 93 B8
Kolíňany SK 162 E6
Kolinec CZ 92 D4
Kolindros GR 185 D7
Koliri GR 190 D3
Kolisne UA 170 E5
Kolitzheim D 91 C7
Kõljala EST 146 E5
Koljane HR 172 E5
Kolka LV 146 F5
Kølkær DK 102 C4
Kolkku FIN 139 D16
Kolkonjärvi FIN 137 B10
Kolkwitz D 97 C10
Kollaja FIN 135 D17
Kölleda D 95 D9
Kollines GR 190 C5
Kölln-Reisiek D 98 C7
Kolltveit N 110 B2
Kolmisoppi FIN 140 D9
Kolmsbo AL 184 C2
Köln D 37 C7
Kolnica PL 156 C8
Kolno PL 155 D12
Kolo BIH 173 E7
Koło PL 158 B6
Kolobrzeg PL 101 B9
Kolochava UA 161 G8
Kolonje AL 184 C2
Kolonowskie PL 158 E5
Kolosen S 118 B4
Kolpino RUS 145 F14
Kolsätter S 118 B6
Kolsh AL 179 F9
Kölsillre S 119 B9
Kólsjön S 119 B12
Kolsko PL 97 C9
Kolsta S 113 C15
Kolsva S 113 C14
Kölsvallen S 118 C6
Kölsvallen S 118 B5

Kolvik N 129 C15
Kølvrå DK 102 C4
Kolympari GR 194 D6
Kolympia GR 197 D8
Komádi H 167 C7
Komagfjord N 129 C11
Komagvær N 130 C9
Komańcza PL 161 E5
Komanos GR 185 D6
Komar BIH 173 D7
Komara GR 187 A10
Komarani SRB 179 C3
Komarevo SRB 181 B10
Komarica BIH 173 C8
Komárno SK 165 A10
Komarno UA 161 D8
Komárom H 165 A9
Komárov CZ 92 C5
Komarów Osada PL 160 B7
Kombuli LV 149 E2
Komen SLO 89 E8
Komesi AL 184 C4
Komi GR 193 C7
Komi GR 193 D7
Komin HR 164 D6
Komin HR 173 F8
Komiža HR 79 A10
Komjatice SK 162 E5
Komletinci HR 173 B10
Komló H 165 D10
Kömlő H 166 B5
Kömlöd H 165 A10
Kommeno GR 190 A3
Komnina GR 185 C6
Komorane SRB 179 D10
Komornik PL 97 B11
Komorowo PL 155 E12
Komorzno PL 158 D5
Komoshtitsa BG 176 F2
Komossa FIN 138 D9
Komotini GR 187 B8
Kompakka FIN 141 F13
Kompeluvaara S 132 D8
Kömpöc H 166 E4
Kompoti GR 190 A3
Komprachcice PL 158 E4
Kömsi EST 146 D7
Komsomol'sk RUS 152 D2
Komsomol'sk RUS 155 F4
Komsomol's'k UA 161 G8
Komu FIN 139 C16
Komula FIN 141 C10
Komunari BG 183 D8
Komuniga BG 182 F4
Komylio GR 190 B2
Konak SRB 193 C9
Konakpınar TR 189 F8
Konare BG 171 F2
Konare BG 185 A10
Konarzyce PL 155 D13
Konarzyny PL 101 C12
Koncanica HR 165 E8
Konče MK 185 A7
Kondolovo BG 183 E9
Kondoros H 166 D6
Kondratowice PL 97 E11
Kondrat'yevo RUS 145 D9
Kondrić HR 173 B9
Koneck PL 154 E6
Køng DK 103 E10
Konga S 105 B8
Kongas N 129 C14
Kongas FIN 131 E1
Köngäs FIN 133 C13
Kongasmäki FIN 137 E9
Kongens Lyngby DK 103 D11
Konginkangas FIN 139 E15
Kongsberg N 111 C11
Kongselva N 126 D9
Kongsfjord N 130 B6
Kongslia N 117 D9
Kongsmoen N 121 B12
Kongsvik N 127 C11
Kongsvinger N 112 B7
Kongsvoll N 120 E6
Konice CZ 93 C11
Koniecpol PL 159 E8
Königheim D 203 B8
Königsberg in Bayern D 91 B8
Königsborn D 95 B10
Königsbronn D 91 F7
Königsbrück D 96 D5
Königsbrunn D 88 A3
Königsdorf D 88 A3
Königsee D 95 E9
Königsfeld im Schwarzwald D 43 D7
Königshofen D 95 D10
Königshütte D 95 E8
Königsmoos D 91 E9
Königssee D 89 A7
Königstein D 91 C10
Königstein D 96 E6
Königstein im Taunus D 203 A5
Königswartha D 96 D6
Königswiesen A 93 F7
Königswinter D 37 C8
Königs Wusterhausen D 96 B5
Konin PL 158 B5
Konispol AL 184 E3
Konitsa GR 184 D4
Köniz CH 86 D5
Konjevrate HR 172 E5
Konjic BIH 173 E8
Konjsko BIH 173 E7
Konjsko BIH 178 D5
Konkka MK 185 B8
Konnekoski FIN 139 E17
Könnern D 95 C10
Konnevesi FIN 139 E16
Könni FIN 138 D8
Konnunsuo FIN 145 C10
Konnuslahti FIN 141 E9
Könölä FIN 135 C12
Konolfingen CH 86 D5
Konopiska PL 159 E7
Konopki PL 155 E12
Konopnica PL 157 H6
Konopnica PL 158 D6
Konotop PL 97 C9
Kon'ovo BG 182 D6
Końskie PL 157 H2
Końsko MK 185 B7
Końskowola PL 157 H6
Konsmo N 110 E6
Konstancin-Jeziorna PL 157 F4
Konstantinova LV 149 D2
Konstantinovy Lázně CZ 92 C3

Konstantynów PL 157 F8
Konstantynów Łódzki PL 159 C7
Konstanz D 43 E11
Kontariotissa GR 185 D7
Kontiainen FIN 139 E10
Kontias GR 187 E8
Kontinjoki FIN 137 F10
Kontiokoski FIN 135 D15
Kontiolahti FIN 141 E13
Kontiomäki FIN 137 F11
Kontkala FIN 141 E12
Kontopouli GR 187 E8
Kontovazaina GR 190 D4
Konttajärvi FIN 133 E12
Konttila FIN 135 C17
Konttimäki FIN 141 D9
Konush BG 182 F5
Konz D 37 E7
Konzell D 91 D12
Koog aan de Zaan NL 32 D3
Koonga EST 147 D8
Köörtilä FIN 142 B6
Koosa EST 147 D14
Kootstertille NL 32 B6
Kootwijkerbroek NL 199 A7
Kopani GR 184 F4
Kopanica PL 97 B9
Kopanos GR 185 C7
Kopardal N 124 D4
Koparnes N 116 B3
Kopčany SK 93 E12
Koper SLO 83 A8
Kopervik N 110 D2
Kópháza H 165 A7
Kopice PL 158 E3
Kopidlno CZ 93 B8
Kopilovtsi BG 181 C6
Köping S 113 C15
Köpingebro S 104 D6
Köpingsvik S 105 B11
Kopisto FIN 135 F12
Kopki PL 160 C5
Koplik AL 179 E7
Koplik i Sipërm AL 179 E7
Köpmanholm S 115 C11
Köpmanholmen S 123 E15
Koporiće SRB 179 C10
Koposperä FIN 139 C14
Koppang N 117 C11
Kopparberg S 113 C13
Kopparmora S 115 C9
Kopparnäs S 134 C6
Koppelo FIN 130 F3
Koppera N 121 E11
Koppl A 89 A7
Koppom S 112 C7
Koprivets BG 182 C5
Koprivlen BG 185 A10
Koprivnica HR 165 D7
Kopřivnice CZ 162 B6
Koprivshtitsa BG 181 D9
Koprzywnica PL 159 E12
Kopsa FIN 135 E13
Köpstal L 202 B1
Kõpu EST 146 D5
Kõpu EST 147 E10
Koraj BIH 173 C11
Koramoniemi FIN 137 B12
Korbach D 33 G11
Korbevac SRB 180 D5
Korbovo SRB 175 D10
Korčanica BIH 172 C5
Korchiv UA 160 C8
Körchow D 99 D10
Korčula HR 178 E5
Korczew PL 157 F7
Korczyna PL 160 D4
Korenita SRB 174 E3
Koŕeňov CZ 97 E8
Korentokylä FIN 136 D9
Korentovaara FIN 141 E16
Koretin SRB 180 E4
Korfantów PL 158 F4
Korfos GR 191 D7
Korgen N 124 D6
Körgene LV 147 F9
Körgessaare EST 146 D4
Korholanmäki FIN 137 F10
Korhosenniemi FIN 137 C12
Koria FIN 144 D6
Korinos GR 185 D7
Korinth DK 102 E6
Korinthos GR 191 D6
Korisia GR 191 E9
Korisos GR 184 D5
Korita BIH 172 C5
Korita BIH 173 F9
Korita HR 178 E6
Korita MNE 179 D8
Korithi GR 190 D2
Korkana FIN 137 F11
Korkatti FIN 135 F15
Korkeakangas FIN 141 F14
Korkeakoski FIN 143 E13
Korkee FIN 143 D13
Körkvere EST 146 E4
Körle D 94 D6
Körmend H 165 B7
Kormista GR 186 C6
Kormu FIN 143 D12
Korňa SK 163 C7
Kornalovychi UA 161 D7
Körner D 95 D8
Korneuburg A 93 F10
Kornevo RUS 152 C3
Kornhaga FIN 135 C14
Kornofolia GR 187 B10
Kornos GR 187 B8
Kornsjø N 107 A12
Kornwestheim D 43 C11
Környe H 165 A10
Koroleve UA 161 G4
Koromačno HR 83 C10
Korondó H 165 A9
Koroneia GR 191 C6
Koroni GR 194 B2
Koronos GR 193 D10
Koronouda GR 185 C9
Koronowo PL 154 D4
Koropi GR 191 C10
Körösladány H 167 D7
Körösszakál H 167 C8
Körösszegapáti H 167 C8
Köröstarcsa H 167 D7
Koroviya UA 169 A7

Korpela FIN 133 B14
Körperich D 36 E6
Korpi FIN 139 C12
Korpijärvi FIN 135 B13
Korpijoki FIN 139 C16
Korpiksi S 135 C10
Korpijylä FIN 137 E12
Korpikylä S 135 B11
Korpilahti FIN 139 F15
Korpilombolo S 132 E10
Korpilompolo FIN 133 E13
Korpinen FIN 137 D10
Korpinen FIN 141 D10
Korpisel'kya RUS 141 F16
Korpivaara FIN 141 E12
Korpo FIN 142 E6
Korpoström FIN 142 E6
Korsåmon S 119 A12
Korsbäck FIN 138 E6
Korsberga S 105 A8
Korsberga S 107 C15
Korsholm FIN 138 E6
Korskrogen S 119 C10
Korsmyrbränna S 122 E8
Korsnäs FIN 138 E6
Korsnes N 127 D11
Korso FIN 143 E13
Korsør DK 103 E8
Korssjön S 134 F5
Korssund N 116 D1
Korsträsk S 134 C5
Korsveggen N 120 E4
Korsvoll N 120 E4
Korsze PL 152 E3
Kortemark B 35 B7
Korten BG 182 D5
Kortenhoef NL 32 D4
Kortesalmi FIN 137 C14
Kortesjärvi FIN 139 D10
Kortessem B 35 C11
Kortevaara FIN 141 B13
Kortgene NL 32 E1
Korthi GR 192 D4
Kortrijk B 35 C7
Kortteenperä FIN 135 B17
Kortteinen FIN 141 D11
Korubaşı TR 187 E10
Korucu TR 189 F7
Koruköy TR 189 C6
Koruköy TR 193 E10
Korva S 135 B11
Korvakumpu FIN 131 D2
Korvala FIN 133 C16
Korvaluoma FIN 142 B8
Körveküla EST 147 E13
Korvenkylä FIN 135 D15
Korvenkylä FIN 137 C14
Korvenkylä FIN 139 B12
Korvua FIN 137 D12
Koryčany CZ 93 D12
Korycin PL 156 D8
Koryfasi GR 190 E4
Koryfi GR 185 C8
Korytnica PL 155 F12
Korzenna PL 160 D2
Korzeńsko PL 97 C11
Korzunovo RUS 130 E9
Korzybie PL 101 B11
Kos GR 193 F9
Kosakowo PL 154 A6
Kosanica MNE 179 C7
Košarovce SK 161 E4
Kösching D 91 E10
Kościan PL 97 B11
Kościelec PL 158 B6
Kościelna Wieś PL 158 C5
Kościernica PL 101 B10
Kościerzyna PL 154 B4
Kosd H 166 B3
Kose EST 147 C10
Kose EST 147 F14
Košeca SK 162 C6
Košecké Podhradie SK 162 D6
Kösedere TR 187 E10
Kösedere TR 193 B8
Köseilyas TR 189 B8
Kosel D 98 A7
Koselji BIH 173 E9
Koserow D 100 B6
Košetice CZ 93 C8
Kosharevo BG 181 D6
Kóšice SK 161 F3
Kosiv UA 168 A6
Kosivs'ka Polyana UA 161 G9
Kosjerić SRB 174 F4
Koška HR 165 E10
Koskama FIN 133 C14
Koskeby FIN 138 E6
Koskela FIN 135 E15
Koskela FIN 139 D11
Koskenkorva FIN 138 E8
Koskenkylä FIN 133 C16
Koskenkylä FIN 137 C14
Koskenkylä FIN 137 F11
Koskenkylä FIN 140 E8
Koskenkylä FIN 142 D7
Koskenmäki FIN 137 F13
Koskenniska FIN 129 F17
Koskenpää FIN 139 F14
Koskenperä FIN 139 C14
Koski FIN 143 D9
Koski FIN 143 E9
Koskimäki FIN 138 E7
Koskinou GR 197 D8
Koskioinen FIN 143 C9
Koškovce SK 161 E4
Koskue FIN 138 F9
Koskullskulle S 132 D5
Koslovets BG 182 C4
Kosman BIH 173 F10
Kosmas GR 191 E6
Kosmio GR 187 B8
Kosola FIN 138 D9
Kosova Hora CZ 93 C6
Kosovo HR 172 E5
Kosovo Polje SRB 180 D3
Kosovska Kamenica SRB 180 D4
Kosovska Mitrovica SRB 179 D10
Kosów Lacki PL 157 E6
Koßdorf D 96 D4
Kössen A 88 A5
Kosta GR 191 E7
Kosta S 105 B8
Kostakioi GR 190 A2
Košťálov CZ 97 E8
Kostamo FIN 131 E2
Kostandenets BG 182 B6
Kostandovo BG 181 E9

Kostanjevac HR 164 E4
Kostanjevica SLO 164 E4
Kostel SLO 83 A10
Kostelec nad Černými Lesy CZ 93 C7
Kostelec nad Orlicí CZ 93 B10
Kostelec na Hané CZ 93 C12
Kostenets BG 181 E8
Kostenets BG 181 E8
Kostice CZ 93 E12
Kostinbrod BG 181 D7
Kostolac SRB 175 D6
Kostolné Kračany SK 162 F5
Kostomłoty PL 97 D11
Kostrzyn PL 97 A7
Kostrzyn PL 97 B12
Kostyzhitsy RUS 148 F6
Kosula FIN 141 E11
Košute HR 173 E6
Kosy UA 170 B5
Kosyny UA 161 G5
Koszalin PL 101 B10
Koszęcin PL 158 E6
Kőszeg H 165 B7
Koszyce PL 159 F10
Kotajärvi FIN 135 D15
Kotala FIN 131 D5
Kotala FIN 139 F12
Kotalanperä FIN 135 D15
Kotas GR 184 C5
Kotě AL 184 D2
Kötegyán H 167 D7
Kotel BG 183 D6
Kőtelek H 166 C5
Kotelow D 100 D5
Kotešová SK 163 C7
Kothen (Anhalt) D 95 C10
Kotikylä FIN 140 D8
Kotila FIN 137 D10
Kotiranta FIN 137 E13
Kotka FIN 144 E6
Kotlin PL 158 C4
Kotly RUS 148 A7
Kotoriba HR 165 D7
Kotorsko BIH 173 C9
Kotor Varoš BIH 173 C7
Kotovs'k UA 170 B5
Kotraža SRB 174 F5
Kotronas GR 194 B3
Kötschach A 89 C7
Kotsøy N 121 F9
Kottenheim D 201 D7
Kottes A 93 F8
Köttmannsdorf A 89 C9
Köttsjön S 123 E10
Kotuń PL 157 F6
Kötzting D 92 D3
Koudekerke NL 32 F1
Koudum NL 32 C4
Koufalia GR 185 C8
Koufovouno GR 187 B10
Kougsta S 121 E9
Kouklioi GR 184 E4
Koumanis GR 190 D4
Koura FIN 139 E10
Kournas GR 194 E7
Koutaniemi FIN 137 F10
Koutojärvi S 135 B10
Koutsochero GR 185 E7
Koutsopodi GR 191 D6
Koutsouras GR 195 F11
Koutus FIN 133 E12
Kouva FIN 137 C10
Kouvola FIN 144 D6
Kovachevets BG 182 C5
Kovachevitsa BG 181 F8
Kovachevo BG 182 E6
Kovachevtsi BG 181 D6
Kovachitsa BG 176 F2
Kovači BIH 173 E7
Kovačica SRB 174 C6
Kővágószőlős H 165 D10
Kovallberget S 123 B13
Kovanj BIH 173 E10
Kovarce SK 162 E6
Kovářov CZ 92 C6
Kovdor RUS 131 C8
Kovelahti FIN 142 B8
Kovero FIN 141 E15
Kovilj SRB 174 C5
Kovin SRB 175 D6
Kovjoki FIN 138 C9
Kovland S 119 B13
Kövra S 118 A7
Kovren MNE 179 C8
Kowal PL 155 E7
Kowala-Stępocina PL 157 H4
Kowale PL 158 C5
Kowale Oleckie PL 152 E5
Kowale-Pańskie PL 158 C6
Kowalewo Pomorskie PL 154 D6
Kowalów PL 97 B7
Kowary PL 97 E9
Kowiesy PL 157 G2
Köyceğiz TR 197 C9
Köyhäjoki FIN 139 C11
Köyliö FIN 142 C7
Koynare BG 181 D9
Koyundere TR 193 B9
Koyunyeri TR 187 C10
Kozani GR 185 D6
Kozarac BIH 173 C6
Kozarac HR 165 E11
Kozar Belene BG 182 C4
Kozármisleny H 165 D10
Kozárovce SK 163 E7
Kozçeşme TR 189 D6
Kozica HR 173 F7
Koziegłowy PL 159 E7
Kozielice PL 101 D7
Kozienice PL 157 G5
Kozina SLO 89 E8
Kožlany CZ 92 C5
Kozłów Biskupi PL 157 F2
Kozłowo PL 155 D9
Kozluk BIH 173 C11
Koźly PL 155 F11
Koźminek PL 158 C5
Koźmin Wielkopolski PL 158 C3
Koz'ove UA 161 F7
Kozubszczyzna PL 157 H6
Kożuchów PL 97 C9
Kożuhe BIH 173 C9
Kozy PL 163 B8
Kozyörük TR 189 B6
Krabbendijke NL 32 F2
Krabi EST 147 F13
Kräckelbäcken S 118 C7

Krackow D 100 D6
Kraddsele S 125 E12
Kraftsdorf D 95 E10
Krag CZ 93 C7
Kragelund DK 102 C4
Kragerø N 90 A6
Kragi PL 101 C11
Kragujevac SRB 175 E6
Kraj HR 172 E6
Kraj HR 173 F7
Krajenka PL 101 D12
Krajišnik SRB 175 C6
Krajnik Dolny PL 100 D6
Krakača BIH 172 B4
Kråken S 138 C3
Kråkerøy N 107 A8
Krakés LT 150 F7
Krakhella N 116 D2
Kräklingbo S 109 E13
Kråklivollen S 121 E9
Kråkmoen N 127 E10
Krakovets' UA 160 D7
Kraków PL 159 F8
Krakow am See D 99 C12
Kråksmåla S 105 A9
Kråkstad N 111 C13
Kralevo BG 183 C7
Kraljeva BIH 173 D9
Kraljeviča HR 83 B10
Kraljevo SRB 174 F6
Kralovice CZ 92 C4
Kráľovský Chlmec SK 161 G4
Kralupy nad Vltavou CZ 92 B6
Králův Dvůr CZ 92 C6
Kramarzyny PL 101 B12
Kramfors S 119 A14
Kramolin BG 182 C4
Krampenes N 130 C8
Kramsach A 88 B4
Kramsk PL 158 B5
Kramvik N 130 C9
Kranenburg D 32 E6
Kranevo BG 183 C11
Krångfors S 134 E4
Krania GR 184 E5
Krania Elassonas GR 185 E6
Kranichfeld D 95 E9
Kranidi GR 191 E7
Kranj SLO 89 D9
Kranjska Gora SLO 89 D8
Krapanj HR 172 E4
Krapets BG 171 F3
Krapiel PL 101 D8
Krapina HR 164 D5
Krapinske Toplice HR 164 D5
Krapkowice PL 158 F4
Krašić HR 164 E5
Krasiczyn PL 160 D6
Krasiv UA 170 A3
Kråslava LV 149 E2
Kraslice CZ 91 B12
Krasnagorka BY 149 E2
Krásná Hora nad Vltavou CZ 92 C6
Krasnapollye BY 149 E6
Krasne PL 155 D10
Krasne PL 160 C5
Krasne UA 170 B4
Kraśniczyn PL 160 B7
Kraśnik PL 160 B5
Krasni Okny UA 170 B4
Krasnobród PL 160 B7
Krasnogorodskoye RUS 149 C4
Krásnohorské Podhradie SK 161 F2
Krasnoles'ye RUS 152 E5
Krásno nad Kysucou SK 163 C7
Krasnopol PL 152 C7
Krasno Polje HR 83 C11
Krasnosel'skoye RUS 145 D11
Krasnosielc PL 155 D11
Krasnovo BG 181 E9
Krasnoyil's'k UA 169 A7
Krasnoznamensk RUS 152 D5
Krasnystaw PL 160 B7
Krasocin PL 159 E9
Kraszewice PL 158 C5
Kraszewo PL 152 E2
Kratigos GR 189 B8
Kratiškiai LT 151 D9
Kratovo MK 180 E5
Kratte masugn S 114 B6
Krauchenwies D 43 D11
Krauja LV 151 E3
Kraujas UA 151 B9
Kraukļi LV 151 B12
Krauschwitz D 97 C7
Krautheim D 90 D6
Kravaře CZ 162 B6
Kravarsko HR 164 E6
Kravoder BG 181 C7
Kraymorie BG 183 E8
Kražiai LT 150 E5
Krčina BIH 173 C11
Krefeld D 33 F7
Kreiensen D 94 C6
Krekanava LT 151 E8
Krekhovychi UA 161 E9
Krekilä FIN 139 C11
Kremasti GR 197 E8
Kremen BG 181 F8
Kremena BG 171 F2
Kremenica LV 151 E8
Krempe D 98 C7
Kremperheide D 33 A12
Krempna PL 161 D4
Krems an der Donau A 93 F9
Kremsbrücke A 89 C8
Kremsmünster A 92 F6
Křepice PL 159 B8
Krepoljin SRB 175 E8
Kreševo BIH 173 E9
Kreshpan AL 184 C2
Křešice CZ 92 A6
Kresna BG 181 F7
Kresnice SLO 89 D10
Kressbronn am Bodensee D 87 B9
Krestena GR 190 D4
Kretinga LT 150 E2
Kretingalė LT 150 E2
Kreuth D 88 A4
Kreuzau D 36 C6
Kreuzlingen CH 43 E11
Kreuztal D 37 C9
Kreuzwertheim D 90 C6

Kreva BY 153 E13
Krezluk BIH 173 D7
Krichim BG 181 E9
Krieglach A 164 A5
Kriegstetten CH 43 F8
Krien D 100 C4
Kriens CH 86 C6
Krievciems LV 150 B3
Krieza GR 191 C9
Krikello GR 190 B4
Krikellos GR 190 B3
Krimpen aan de IJssel NL 32 E3
Krimūnas LV 150 C6
Křinec CZ 93 B8
Krinida GR 186 C5
Krinides GR 187 B6
Kriškalni LV 151 C11
Kriškovci BIH 173 C7
Kristberg S 108 B6
Kristdala S 109 E8
Kristiansand N 106 C2
Kristianstad S 104 C6
Kristiansund N 120 E3
Kristiinankaupunki FIN 138 F6
Kristinefors S 113 B8
Kristineberg S 123 A15
Kristinehamn S 113 D11
Kristinestad FIN 138 F6
Kristoni GR 185 C8
Kristvallabrunn S 105 B10
Kritinia GR 197 D7
Kritsa GR 195 E10
Kritzmow D 99 B12
Kriukai LT 150 D7
Kriūkai LT 153 C7
Kriva Bara BG 175 F11
Krivača BIH 173 D9
Kriva Feja SRB 180 D5
Krivaja BIH 173 D7
Krivāň SK 163 D8
Krivany SK 161 E2
Kriva Palanka MK 180 E5
Krivelj SRB 175 E9
Krivi Put HR 83 B10
Krivi Vir SRB 175 F8
Krivodol BG 181 C7
Krivogaštani MK 184 B5
Krivolak MK 185 A7
Križ HR 165 E7
Křižanov CZ 93 D9
Križevci HR 165 D7
Křižová CZ 93 C9
Križpolje HR 83 B11
Krk HR 83 B10
Krka SLO 89 E10
Krmčina HR 172 D3
Krnča SK 162 D6
Krnica HR 83 C6
Krnjača SRB 174 D5
Krnjak HR 164 F5
Krnjeuša BIH 172 C5
Krnjevo SRB 175 D7
Krnov CZ 158 F4
Krobia PL 97 C12
Kroczyce PL 159 E8
Krøderen N 111 B11
Krofdorf Gleiberg D 37 C11
Krog S 119 B9
Krogis D 96 D4
Krok S 121 E14
Krokees GR 191 F6
Krokeide N 110 B2
Krokek S 109 B8
Kroken N 116 D6
Kroken N 124 F7
Krokfors S 134 B5
Krokfors S 134 B5
Kroknäs S 118 A8
Kroknes N 130 C8
Krokom S 122 E6
Krokos GR 185 D6
Krokowa PL 154 A5
Kroksjö S 123 B13
Kroksjö S 123 D15
Kroksjö S 134 E4
Krokstadelva N 111 C12
Krokstadøra N 120 D7
Krokstranda N 124 D9
Krokstrømmen S 118 B8
Kroktjärn S 134 D3
Krokträsk S 134 C6
Królowa Most PL 156 D8
Krõlpa D 95 E10
Kroměříž CZ 162 C4
Krommenie NL 32 C3
Krompachy SK 161 F2
Kromsdorf D 95 E9
Kronach D 91 B9
Kronberg im Taunus D 203 A5
Kronburg D 87 B10
Kronoby FIN 139 C10
Kronprinzenkoog D 98 C5
Kronshagen D 99 B8
Kronstadt RUS 145 F12
Kropa SLO 89 D9
Kröpelin D 99 B11
Kropp D 98 B7
Kroppenstedt D 95 C9
Kropstädt D 95 C10
Krościenko nad Dunajcem PL 161 C1
Kröslin D 100 B5
Krosna LT 153 E8
Krośnice PL 97 D12
Krośniewice PL 159 B7
Krosno PL 160 D4
Krosno Odrzańskie PL 97 B8
Krossen N 95 E10
Krossen N 111 C8
Krossmoen N 110 F3
Krote LV 150 C3
Krotoszyce PL 97 D10
Krotoszyn PL 158 C3
Krottendorf A 164 B5
Krouna CZ 93 C10
Krousonas GR 194 E8
Krõv D 37 E8
Krovik N 127 E19
Krovyli GR 187 C8
Krrabë AL 184 B2
Krš HR 172 E7
Kršan HR 83 B9
Krško SLO 164 E4
Krstac MNE 173 F10
Krstinja HR 172 B4
Krtova BIH 173 C9

Kruchowo PL 154 E4
Krüden D 99 E11
Kruft D 201 D7
Kruibeke B 35 B9
Kruiningen NL 32 F2
Kruishoutem B 35 C8
Krujë AL 184 A2
Krukenychi UA 160 D7
Kruklanki PL 152 E4
Krukowo PL 155 D11
Krumbach A 87 C9
Krumbach A 164 A6
Krumbach (Schwaben) D 87 A10
Krumë AL 179 D9
Krummesse D 99 C9
Krumovgrad BG 187 B9
Krumovo BG 181 E10
Krumovo BG 182 C6
Krumpa (Geiseltal) D 95 D10
Krumvíř CZ 93 E11
Krün D 88 A3
Kruonis LT 153 D9
Kruopiai LT 150 D6
Krupac BIH 173 E9
Krupac SRB 181 C5
Krupanj SRB 174 E3
Krupa na Vrbasu BIH 173 C7
Krupava BY 153 F11
Krupe PL 160 A7
Krupina SK 163 E8
Krupište MK 180 F5
Krupka CZ 96 E5
Krupnik BG 181 F7
Kruså DK 98 A6
Kruševac SRB 180 B3
Kruševica SRB 174 E5
Kruševo MK 184 B5
Kruševo Grdo BIH 173 C7
Krushari BG 171 F1
Krushel'nytsya UA 161 E8
Krushevets BG 183 E8
Krushevo BG 182 C4
Krushovene BG 176 F3
Krushovitsa BG 176 F3
Krušovce SK 162 E6
Kruszewo PL 101 E11
Kruszyna PL 101 B12
Kruszyna PL 159 E7
Krutådal N 124 E7
Krute MNE 179 E7
Kruununpyy FIN 139 C10
Krużlov SK 161 E3
Krya Vrysi GR 185 C6
Kryekuq AL 184 C2
Kryezi AL 179 E9
Kryłów PL 160 B9
Krynica PL 161 A6
Krynica Morska PL 155 B7
Krynice PL 160 B7
Krynki PL 156 D9
Krynychne UA 171 B3
Kryoneri GR 191 D6
Kryoneritis GR 191 B7
Kryopigi GR 185 D9
Krypno Kościelne PL 156 D7
Kryry S2 92 B4
Krystad N 126 D5
Krystallopigi GR 184 C5
Kryva Balka UA 170 C5
Kryve Ozero UA 170 B6
Kryvorivnya UA 168 A5
Kryzhopil' UA 170 A3
Kržanja MNE 179 D7
Krzanowice PL 158 F5
Krząstka PL 160 C5
Krzęcin PL 101 D9
Krzelów PL 97 D11
Krzemienewo PL 97 C11
Krzepice PL 158 E6
Krzepielów PL 97 C10
Krzeszów PL 97 E10
Krzeszów PL 160 C5
Krzeszowice PL 159 F8
Krzeszyce PL 97 A8
Krzętów PL 159 E8
Krzykosy PL 97 B12
Krzynowłoga Mała PL 155 D10
Krzystkowice PL 97 C8
Krzywcza PL 160 D6
Krzywda PL 157 G6
Krzywiń PL 97 C12
Krzywin PL 100 D5
Krzywowierzba PL 157 G8
Krzyżanów PL 159 B7
Krzyżanowice PL 162 B6
Krzyż Wielkopolski PL 101 E10
Ksar Sghir MA 69 E5
Ksawerów PL 159 C7
Książ Wielki PL 159 F9
Książ Wielkopolski PL 97 B12
Księżpol PL 160 C7
Kubanovka RUS 152 D5
Kubbe S 123 D14
Kübekháza H 166 E5
Kublichy BY 149 F4
Kublis CH 87 D9
Kubrat BG 177 F8
Kubuļi LV 149 E4
Kuç AL 184 D2
Kučevo SRB 175 D8
Kuchen D 90 C6
Kuchl A 89 A7
Kuchuran UA 170 D5
Kuchyña SK 93 E12
Kucice PL 155 E9
Kuciny PL 159 C7
Kučište HR 178 D3
Küçükanafarta TR 187 D10
Küçükbahçe TR 193 C7
Küçükçekmece TR 189 B10
Küçükkarıştıran TR 189 B7
Küçükkemerdere TR 193 C10
Küçükköy TR 188 F6
Küçükkumla TR 189 D11
Küçükkuyu TR 188 E6
Küçükyoncalı TR 189 B8
Kucura SRB 174 C4
Kudever' RUS 149 C6
Kudirkos Naumiestis LT 152 D6
Kudowa-Zdrój PL 93 B10
Kūdums LV 151 B10
Kufstein A 88 A5
Kuggerud N 112 B4
Kuggören S 119 C14
Kuha FIN 133 C17
Kuhakoski FIN 145 B9
Kühbach D 91 F9

Kuhbier D 99 D12
Kühfelde D 99 E10
Kuhmalahti FIN 143 B12
Kuhmo FIN 137 F14
Kuhmoinen FIN 143 B13
Kühndorf D 95 E7
Kühren D 95 D12
Kuhs D 99 C12
Kuhstedt D 33 B11
Kuijõe EST 147 C7
Kuimetsa EST 147 C10
Kuinre NL 32 C5
Kuivajärvi FIN 137 E15
Kuivajõe EST 147 C10
Kuivakangas S 135 B11
Kuivalahti FIN 142 C6
Kuivaniemi FIN 135 C14
Kuivanto FIN 143 D15
Kuivasjärvi FIN 139 F9
Kuivastu EST 146 E6
Kujakowice Dolne PL 158 D5
Kūkas LV 151 C12
Kukasjärvi FIN 133 D15
Kukasjärvi S 135 B10
Kukës AL 179 D9
Kukko FIN 139 E12
Kukkola FIN 135 C12
Kukkola S 135 C12
Kuklen BG 181 E10
Kuklin PL 155 D10
Kuklinów PL 97 C12
Kukljica HR 172 D3
Kukljin SRB 180 B3
Kukmirn A 164 B6
Kuktiškes LT 151 F11
Kulje BIH 173 C7
Kukur AL 184 C3
Kukurečani MK 184 B5
Kula BG 175 F9
Kula HR 165 F9
Kula SRB 174 C4
Kulaši BIH 173 C8
Kulata BG 185 B9
Kulautuva LT 153 D8
Külciems LV 150 B6
Kuldīga LV 150 C3
Külefli TR 189 C8
Kuleli TR 189 B6
Kulen Vakuf BIH 172 C5
Kulesze PL 156 D7
Kulho FIN 141 E13
Kulia N 121 D9
Kuliai LT 150 E3
Kulju FIN 143 C10
Kullaa FIN 142 C7
Kullamaa EST 147 D8
Kulleseid N 110 C2
Kulltorp S 104 A5
Kulmain D 91 C10
Kulmbach D 91 B9
Kuloharju FIN 137 D11
Külsheim D 43 A12
Kultima FIN 132 B4
Kulu TR 187 D14
Kuluntalahti FIN 137 F10
Kulupenai LT 150 E3
Kulva LT 153 C9
Kulvemäki FIN 140 C9
Kulykiv UA 160 D9
Kumafşarı TR 193 C10
Kumane SRB 174 B5
Kumanovo MK 180 E4
Kumbağ TR 189 C7
Kumberg A 164 B5
Kumbri LT 150 C3
Kumbuļi LV 151 E13
Kumburun TR 187 E10
Kumhausen D 91 E11
Kumkadı TR 189 D7
Kumkale TR 187 D10
Kumköy TR 189 B11
Kumla S 108 A6
Kumla kyrkby S 114 C7
Kumlinge FIN 115 B15
Kummer D 99 D10
Kummerow D 99 C13
Kummersdorf-Alexanderdorf D 96 B4
Kummersdorf Gut D 96 B4
Kummunkylä FIN 139 D16
Kumpuranta FIN 141 G12
Kumpuselkä FIN 139 D16
Kumpuvaara FIN 135 C18
Kumrovec HR 164 D5
Kunadacs H 166 D3
Kunágota H 167 E7
Kunbaja H 166 E3
Kunbaracs H 166 D3
Kunčina CZ 93 C11
Kunda EST 147 B13
Kunes N 129 C18
Kunfehértó H 166 E3
Kungälv S 107 D10
Kungas FIN 139 C11
Kungsängen S 115 D9
Kungsäter S 104 A3
Kungsbacka S 107 E11
Kungsberg S 119 E12
Kungsfors S 119 E12
Kungsgården S 119 D12
Kungsgården S 119 D12
Kungshamn S 105 F6
Kungshult S 103 D12
Kungsör S 114 C4
Kunhegyes H 166 C6
Kunín CZ 162 B5
Kuniów PL 158 E5
Kunmadaras H 166 C6
Kunovice CZ 162 C4
Kunowo PL 97 B7
Kunpeszér H 166 D3
Kunrade NL 199 D7
Kunrau D 95 B9
Kunštát CZ 93 C11
Kunszentmárton H 166 D5
Kunszentmiklós H 166 D3
Kunsziget H 165 A9
Kunvald CZ 93 B11
Kunžak CZ 93 D8
Künzell D 90 C6
Künzelsau D 90 D6
Kunžing D 92 E4

Kuohu FIN 139 F14
Kuoksajärvi FIN 133 E15
Kuoksu S 132 C7
Kuolayarvi RUS 131 E6
Kuolio FIN 137 C12
Kuomiokoski FIN 144 C7
Kuona FIN 139 C15
Kuopio FIN 140 E9
Kuoppala FIN 138 D9
Kuorevesi FIN 143 B12
Kuortane FIN 139 E11
Kuortti FIN 143 C15
Kuosku FIN 131 D4
Kuossakåbba S 132 D4
Kuouka S 132 E5
Kup PL 158 E4
Kupari HR 178 D5
Küpeler TR 189 E8
Kupferberg D 91 B10
Kupferzell D 90 D6
Kupientyn PL 157 F6
Kupinec HR 164 E5
Kupinovo SRB 174 D5
Kupiškis LT 151 E9
Kupjak HR 83 B10
Küplü TR 187 B10
Kuppenheim D 43 C9
Kuprava LV 149 E3
Kupres BIH 173 D7
Kuprešani BIH 173 D7
Küps D 91 B9
Kurapollye BY 151 F13
Kuratën AL 184 B2
Kurbnesh AL 179 F9
Kurd H 165 D10
Kürdzhali BG 187 A8
Kurejoki FIN 139 D11
Kuremaa EST 147 D13
Kuremäe EST 148 C2
Kuressaare EST 146 E3
Kurevere EST 146 E3
Kurienkylä FIN 139 F10
Kurikka FIN 138 E8
Kuřim CZ 93 D11
Kurima SK 161 E3
Kurjala FIN 141 E10
Kurjan AL 184 C2
Kurki FIN 137 D10
Kurkiharju FIN 141 E14
Kurkikylä FIN 137 D11
Kurkimäki FIN 140 E9
Kurmene LV 151 D9
Kürnach D 203 B9
Kürnare BG 181 D10
Kürnbach D 43 B10
Kurolanlahti FIN 140 D8
Kuropta RUS 131 C6
Kurort Bad Gottleuba D 96 E5
Kurort Kipsdorf D 96 E5
Kurort Oberwiesenthal D 92 B3
Kurort Schmalkalden D 79 C9
Kurort Steinbach-Hallenberg D 95 E8
Kurów PL 157 H6
Kurowice PL 159 C7
Kurravaara S 132 C4
Kurrokvejk S 125 E14
Kuršėnai LT 150 D6
Kurši LT 150 D4
Kursu FIN 131 E4
Kuršumlija SRB 180 C3
Kuršumlijska Banja SRB 180 C3
Kurtakko FIN 133 D12
Kurtbey TR 188 B6
Kurtna EST 148 C2
Kurtzea E 56 B6
Kuru FIN 143 B10
Kurvinen FIN 137 C14
Kuryłówka PL 160 C5
Kurzelów PL 159 E8
Kurzeszyn PL 157 G2
Kurzętnik PL 155 D8
Kusa LV 151 C12
Kusadak SRB 175 E6
Kuşadası TR 193 D8
Kuşçayır TR 188 E6
Kusel D 37 E8
Kusey D 95 A9
Kusfors S 134 E4
Kushnytsya UA 161 G7
Kušići SRB 179 C10
Kuside MNE 179 D6
Kuślin PL 97 B10
Kusmark S 134 E5
Küsnacht CH 43 F10
Küssnacht CH 43 F9
Kustavi FIN 142 D6
Küsten D 99 E10
Kusterdingen D 43 C11
Kuštilj SRB 175 C7
Kuta BIH 173 E11
Kutalli AL 184 C2
Kutas H 165 D8
Kutemajärvi FIN 140 F7
Kutenholz D 33 B12
Kuti MNE 179 D8
Kutina H 166 C1
Kutjevo HR 165 F9
Kutlovo SRB 175 E6
Kutná Hora CZ 93 C8
Kutno PL 159 B7
Kutrikko FIN 131 E5
Kuttainen S 132 B9
Kuttanen FIN 132 B9
Kuttura FIN 133 B16
Kúty SK 93 E12
Kúty UA 168 A6
Kuukasjärvi FIN 135 C17
Kuumu FIN 137 E14
Kuurne B 35 C7
Kuurtola FIN 137 D13
Kuusa FIN 139 E15
Kuusaa FIN 139 C15
Kuusajärvi FIN 133 C14
Kuusajoki FIN 133 C13
Kuusalu EST 147 C10
Kuusamo FIN 137 C13
Kuusamonkylä FIN 137 F13
Kuusankoski FIN 144 D6
Kuusijärvi FIN 137 D11
Kuusijoki FIN 142 B8
Kuusiku EST 147 D8
Kuusirati FIN 136 F9
Kuusirata FIN 135 F14
Kuusivaara FIN 131 E2
Kuusjärvi FIN 141 E11
Kuusjoki FIN 143 D9
Kuuslahti FIN 140 D9
Kuvansi FIN 141 F9
Kuvaskangas FIN 142 B6

Kuyka UA 169 A7
Kuyvozi RUS 145 E13
Kužiai LT 150 E6
Kuzmice SK 161 F4
Kuzmin SRB 174 C3
Kuźmina PL 161 D5
Kuz'molovskiy RUS 145 E13
Kuznechnoye RUS 145 C12
Kuźnia Raciborska PL 158 F5
Kuźnica PL 156 C9
Kuźnica Czarnkowska PL 101 E11
Kväcklingen S 119 A12
Kværkeby DK 103 E9
Kværndrup DK 102 E7
Kvalfors N 124 E5
Kvalnes N 126 D6
Kvalnes N 126 E8
Kvalnes N 127 B11
Kvalnes N 130 C8
Kvaløyhamn N 124 E3
Kvaloysletta N 127 A16
Kvaløyvågen N 127 A16
Kvalsaukan N 127 C10
Kvalsund N 129 B12
Kvalsvik N 116 B3
Kvalvåg N 120 E3
Kvalvik N 127 A19
Kvam N 117 C11
Kvannås N 127 B14
Kvanndal N 110 B5
Kvanne N 117 A9
Kvannli N 121 A14
Kvänum S 107 C13
Kvarnberg S 118 D8
Kvarnbyn S 134 F4
Kvarnriset S 134 F5
Kvarnsand S 115 B11
Kvarnsjö S 118 A7
Kvarntäkt S 119 E10
Kvarntorp S 108 A6
Kvarv N 124 B8
Kvarv N 125 B10
Kvasice CZ 162 C4
Kvasy UA 168 A4
Kveaune N 121 C15
Kvėdarna LT 150 E3
Kveinsjøen N 121 A12
Kvelde N 106 A6
Kveli N 121 B15
Kvenvær N 120 D4
Kvevlax FIN 138 D7
Kvibille S 103 B11
Kvicksund S 114 D6
Kvidinge S 103 C12
Kvikkjokk S 125 C14
Kvillsfors S 108 E7
Kvinesdal N 110 F5
Kvinlog N 110 E5
Kvissleby S 119 B13
Kvisvik N 120 E3
Kvitblik N 125 B10
Kviteberg N 128 D8
Kviteseid N 111 D8
Kvitnes N 126 C9
Kvitnes N 128 C5
Kvitsøy N 110 D2
Kvívík FO 18 A2
Kvorning DK 102 C5
Kwaadmechelen B 35 B11
Kwidzyn PL 154 C6
Kwieciszewo PL 154 E5
Kwilcz PL 97 A10
Kyan S 119 D10
Kybartai LT 152 D6
Kycklingvattnet S 121 B16
Kydrasivka UA 170 A5
Kyjov CZ 93 D12
Kyläinpää FIN 138 E8
Kylänlahti FIN 141 D13
Kyläsaari FIN 142 B6
Kyleakin GB 18 L5
Kyle of Lochalsh GB 18 L5
Kylerhea GB 18 L5
Kylestrome GB 18 J6
Kylland N 106 B1
Kyllburg D 37 D7
Kyllini GR 190 D3
Kylmäkoski FIN 143 C10
Kylmälä FIN 135 E16
Kymi GR 191 B9
Kymina GR 185 C8
Kyminlinna FIN 144 D6
Kymönkoski FIN 139 D15
Kyndby Huse DK 103 D9
Kyngäs FIN 135 D17
Kynsiperä FIN 137 C11
Kynsivaara FIN 137 C11
Kynšperk nad Ohří CZ 91 B12
Kypärävaara FIN 137 E12
Kyparissia GR 190 E4
Kypasjärv S 135 B10
Kyprinos GR 187 A10
Kypseli GR 191 D7
Kyrgia GR 187 B6
Kyriaki GR 191 C6
Kyritz D 99 E12
Kyrkås S 122 E7
Kyrkhult S 104 C7
Kyrksæterøra N 120 E6
Kyrkslätt FIN 143 E11
Kyrksten S 113 D11
Kyrnychky UA 171 B4
Kyröskoski FIN 143 B9
Kyrsyä FIN 145 B9
Kyslytsya UA 171 C4
Kysucké Nové Mesto SK 163 C7
Kysucký Lieskovec SK 163 C7
Kytäjä FIN 143 D12
Kythira GR 194 C4
Kythnos GR 191 E9
Kytökylä FIN 135 F15
Kytömäki FIN 137 E11
Kyustendil BG 181 E6
Kyyjärvi FIN 139 D13
Kyynämöinen FIN 139 F14
Kyynärö FIN 143 C12

L

Laa an der Thaya A 93 E10
Laaber D 91 D10
La Adrada E 62 D3
Laage D 99 C12
Laagri EST 147 C9
Laaja FIN 137 E12
Laajoki FIN 142 D7
Laakajärvi FIN 141 C10
La Alberca E 61 C8
La Alberca E 72 F2
La Alberca de Záncara E 63 E8
La Alberguería de Argañán E 61 D7
La Albuera E 67 B6
La Aldehuela E 61 D10
La Algaba E 67 E7
La Aliseda de Tormes E 61 D10
La Aljorra E 72 F2
La Almarcha E 63 E8
La Almolda E 58 D3
La Almunia de Doña Godina E 57 F9
Laanila FIN 131 B2
Lääniste EST 147 E14
La Antilla E 67 E5
Laapas FIN 144 D8
Laarkirchen A 92 G5
Laarne B 35 B8
Laasala FIN 139 E12
Laaslich D 99 D11
Laatre EST 147 E10
Laatre EST 147 F12
Laatzen D 94 B6
Laax CH 87 D8
La Azohía E 72 F2
La Baconnière F 39 D10
Labajos E 62 C3
La Balme-de-Sillingy F 47 D9
La Bañeza E 55 D8
Labanoras LT 151 F11
La Barre-de-Monts F 44 B1
La Barre-en-Ouche F 40 C4
La Barthe-de-Neste F 49 D6
Labarthe-Rivière F 49 D7
La Bassée F 34 C6
La Bastide-Clairence F 48 D3
Labastide-d'Anjou F 49 D9
Labastide-d'Armagnac F 48 C5
La Bastide-de Bousignac F 49 D9
La Bastide-de-Sérou F 49 D8
La Bastide-l'Évêque F 49 B10
Labastide-Murat F 49 A9
Labastide-Puylaurent F 51 A6
Labastide-Rouairoux F 50 D4
Labastide-St-Pierre F 49 C8
La Bastide-sur-l'Hers F 49 E9
La Bâthie F 47 D9
La Bâtie-Neuve F 52 B4
Lábatlan H 165 A10
Labatut-Rivière F 48 C6
La Baule-Escoublac F 39 F7
La Bazoche-Gouet F 40 D4
La Bazoge F 39 D12
L'Abbaye CH 47 B9
Labégude F 51 A7
La Bégude-de-Mazenc F 51 A8
Labenne F 48 C3
La Bérarde F 47 F9
Labergement-lès-Seurre F 47 A7
Laberget N 127 C13
La Bernerie-en-Retz F 44 A1
Laberweinting D 91 E11
Labin HR 83 B9
Labinot-Mal AL 184 B3
La Bisbal de Falset E 58 E5
La Bisbal del Penedès E 59 E6
La Bisbal d'Empordà E 59 D10
Łabiszyn PL 154 E4
Lablachère F 51 B7
Labljane SRB 180 D3
Laboe D 99 B8
La Bonneville-sur-Iton F 40 C5
La Bouëxière F 39 D9
Labouheyre F 48 B4
La Bouilladisse F 51 D10
La Bourboule F 46 D2
Laboutarie F 49 C10
La Bóveda de Toro E 55 F9
Łabowa PL 161 D2
La Brède F 48 A4
La Bréole F 52 C4
La Bresse F 43 D6
La Brillanne F 51 C10
Labrit F 48 B4
La Broque F 43 D7
La Bruffière F 44 A3
Labruguière F 49 C10
L'Absie F 44 B4
La Buisse F 47 E8
Łabunie PL 160 B7
La Bussière F 41 E8
Läby S 115 B9
Laç AL 179 E8
Laç AL 184 A2
La Cabrera E 62 C5
La Caillère-St-Hilaire F 44 B4
Lacalahorra E 71 E6
La Caletta I 80 B4
Lacalm F 46 F2
La Calmette F 51 C7
La Calzada de Oropesa E 61 E10
La Campana E 67 D9
La Cañada de San Urbano E 71 F8
La Cañada de Verich E 58 F3
Lacanau F 44 F3
Lacanau-Océan F 44 E3
Lacanche F 41 F12
La Canourgue F 50 B5
La Capelle F 35 E8
Lacapelle-Barrès F 46 F2
Lacapelle-Marival F 45 F9
Laćarak SRB 174 C4
La Caridad E 55 A6
La Carlota E 69 A7
La Carolina E 70 C5
Lacaune F 50 C4
La Cavada E 56 B4
La Cavalerie F 50 B5
Lacave F 45 F9
Lacco Ameno I 78 F5
Laceby GB 27 D11
Lacedonia I 76 A4
La Cellera de Ter E 59 D9
La Celle-St-Avant F 45 A7
La Cerca E 56 C5
La Cerollera E 58 F3
Laces I 87 D11
La Chaise-Dieu F 46 E4
La Chaize-le-Vicomte F 44 B3
La Chambre F 47 E9
Lachania GR 197 E7
La Chapelaude F 45 C11
La Chapelle F 35 E11
La Chapelle-aux-Bois F 42 D5
La Chapelle-aux-Saints F 45 F9
La Chapelle-d'Abondance F 47 C10
La Chapelle-d'Aligné F 39 E11
La Chapelle-d'Angillon F 41 F7
La Chapelle-de-Guinchay F 46 C6
La Chapelle-des-Fougeretz F 39 D8
La Chapelle-en-Valgaudémar F 47 F9
La Chapelle-en-Vercors F 47 F7
La Chapelle-la-Reine F 41 D8
La Chapelle-Laurent F 46 E3
Lachapelle-sous-Aubenas F 51 A7
La Chapelle-St-André F 41 F9
La Chapelle-St-Laurent F 44 B5
La Chapelle-St-Luc F 41 D11
La Chapelle-St-Quillain F 42 F4
La Chapelle-St-Ursin F 45 A10
La Chapelle-sur-Erdre F 39 F8
Lachar E 69 B9
La Charité-sur-Loire F 41 F9
La Chartre-sur-le-Loir F 40 E4
La Châtaigneraie F 44 B4
La Châtre F 45 B9
La Châtre-Langlin F 45 C8
La Chaume F 41 E12
La Chaussée-St-Victor F 40 E5
La Chaussée-sur-Marne F 41 C12
La Chaux-de-Fonds CH 43 F6
La Chaux-du-Dombief F 47 B8
Lachendorf D 95 A7
Lachen-Speyerdorf D 37 F10
La Cheppe F 41 B12
La Chèze F 38 D6
Lachowo PL 155 D13
Lāči LV 151 E13
Lacići HR 165 E10
La Cierva E 63 D9
La Ciotat F 51 D10
La Cisterniga E 55 E10
Lack GB 23 C7
Łąck PL 155 F8
Lackamore IRL 24 C6
Läckeby S 105 B10
Łącko PL 161 D1
La Clayette F 46 C5
La Clusaz F 47 D9
La Cluse F 51 A10
La Cluse-et-Mijoux F 47 B9
La Codosera E 61 F6
La Concha E 56 B4
La Condamine-Châtelard F 52 C5
Laconi I 80 D3
La Coquille F 45 D7
La Coronada E 67 B8
La Coronada E 67 C9
La Côte-St-André F 47 E7
La-Couarde-sur-Mer F 44 C3
La Couronne F 44 D6
Lacourt F 49 E8
La Courtine F 45 D10
La Couture-Boussey F 40 C5
Lāčplēsis LV 151 C9
Lacq F 48 D4
La Crau F 52 E4
La Crèche F 44 C5
Lacroix-Barrez F 45 F11
La Croixille F 39 D9
La Croix-Valmer F 52 E5
Lacrouzette F 49 C10
La Cumbre E 61 F9
Łączna PL 159 E10
Łącznik PL 158 F4
Ladánybene H 166 C3
Ladbergen D 33 D9
Ladce SK 162 C6
Lądek PL 158 B4
Lądek-Zdrój PL 93 B11
Ladelund D 98 A6
Ladenburg D 37 F11
Lădești RO 176 D4
Ladi GR 187 B10
Ladignac-le-Long F 45 D8
Ladinhac F 45 F11
Ladispoli I 78 D2
Ladoeiro P 61 E6
Ladomirová SK 161 E4
Ladon F 41 D8
Ladozhskoye Ozero RUS 145 E15
Ladushkin RUS 155 A9
Ladybank GB 21 C10
Ladykirk GB 21 D12
Ladysford GB 19 K12
Lādzere LV 150 B5
Ładzice PL 159 D7
Ładzin PL 100 C7
Laekvere EST 147 C13
La Encina E 72 D3
Laer D 33 D8
La Ercina E 55 C9
Lærdalsøyri N 116 D6
Laerma GR 197 D7
Laerru I 80 B2
La Espina E 55 B7
La Estación E 59 D8
La Estrella E 61 E10
Laeva EST 147 E12
La Fare-les-Oliviers F 51 C9
La Farlède F 52 E4
La Fatarrella E 58 E4
La Faurie F 51 A10
La Faute-sur-Mer F 44 C3
La Felipa E 63 F9
La Fère F 35 E7
La Ferrière F 44 B3
La Ferrière-aux-Etangs F 39 C10
La Ferté-Alais F 41 D7
La Ferté-Bernard F 40 D4
La Ferté-Frênel F 40 C4
La Ferté-Gaucher F 41 C9
La Ferté-Imbault F 40 F6
La Ferté-Loupière F 41 E9
La Ferté-Macé F 39 C11
La-Ferté-Milon F 41 B9
La Ferté-sous-Jouarre F 41 C9
La Ferté-St-Aubin F 40 E6
La Ferté-St-Cyr F 40 E6
Laferté-sur-Amance F 42 E4
Laferté-sur-Aube F 41 D12
La Férte-Vidame F 40 C4
La Ferté-Villeneuil F 40 E5
Lafitole F 49 D6
Lafkos GR 191 A7
La Flèche F 39 E11
Lafnitz A 164 B6
La Fontaine-St-Martin F 39 E12
La Font de la Figuera E 72 D3
La Force F 45 F6
La Forêt-sur-Sèvre F 44 B4
La Forge F 42 D6
Laforsen S 119 C10
Lafortunada E 49 E6
La Fouillade F 49 B10
La Foux-d'Allos F 52 C5
Lafrançaise F 49 B8
La Fregeneda E 61 C7
La Fresneda E 58 F4
Lafrimbolle F 43 C7
La Frontera E 63 D8
La Fuente de San Esteban E 61 C8
La Fuliola E 58 D6
La Gacilly F 39 E7
La Galera E 58 F4
Lagan S 103 B13
La Garde F 52 E4
La Garde-Adhémar F 51 B8
La Garde-Freinet F 52 E4
Lagardelle-sur-Lèze F 49 D8
Lagarelhos P 54 E5
Lagares da Beira P 60 D5
La Garnache F 44 B2
La Garriga E 59 D8
Lagarrigue F 49 C10
La Garrovilla E 67 B7
La Gaubretière F 44 B3
Lagavara GB 20 E4
Lage D 33 D7
Lage D 33 E11
Lagedi EST 147 C9
Lage Mierde NL 32 F4
Lagerfors S 107 B15
Lagfors S 119 A13
Lagg GB 20 E6
Laggan GB 20 A7
Laggan GB 21 A8
Lagganulva GB 20 C4
Laggarberg S 119 B13
Laghey IRL 22 C6
Laghtgeorge IRL 22 F5
Łagiewniki PL 97 E11
La Gineta E 63 F9
Lagkada GR 193 C7
Lagkadas GR 185 C9
Lagkadia GR 190 D5
La Glacerie F 39 A8
Lagnieu F 47 D7
Lagny-sur-Marne F 41 C8
Lago I 76 E6
Lagoa P 55 F6
Lagoa P 66 E3
Lagoaça P 61 B7
Lago Menor E 73 B11
Lagonegro I 76 C5
Lagor F 48 D4
Lagorce F 44 E5
Lagord F 44 C3
La Gornal E 59 E7
Lagos GR 187 B8
Lagos P 66 E2
Lagosanto I 82 C5
Łagów PL 97 B8
Łagów PL 159 E11
Lagrán E 57 C6
La Granada de Riotinto E 67 D7
La Granadella E 58 E5
La Grand-Croix F 46 D6
La Grande-Combe F 51 B7
La Grande-Motte F 51 C7
La Granja d'Escarp E 58 E4
La Granjuela E 67 C9
Lagrasse F 50 D4
La Grave F 47 E9
Lägsta S 123 D14
La Guarda E 67 B8
Laguardia E 57 C6
La Guardia E 62 E6
La Guardia de Jaén E 69 A9
Laguarta E 48 F5
Laguenne F 45 E9
Laguépie F 49 B9
La Guerche-de-Bretagne F 39 E9
La Guerche-sur-l'Aubois F 46 B2
Laguiole F 46 F2
Laguna Dalga E 55 D8
Laguna de Duero E 55 E10
Laguna de Negrillos E 55 D8
Lagundo I 88 C3
Lagunilla E 61 D9
Lagyna GR 185 C9
Lagyna GR 187 B10
La Haba E 67 B8
Lahana TR 189 B7
La Haye-du-Puits F 39 B8
La Haye-Pesnel F 39 C9
Lähdejänkkä FIN 135 B12
Lähden D 33 C9
Lahenpää S 132 E10
Laheycourt F 42 C3
La Higuera E 71 B10
Lahinch IRL 24 C4
La Hiniesta E 55 E8
La Hinojosa E 63 E8
Lahnajärvi S 132 E8
Lahnalahti FIN 140 F9
Lahnanen FIN 139 C16
Lahnasjärvi FIN 141 C9
Lahnasuando S 132 E9
Lahnstein D 37 D9
Lahntal-Goßfelden D 37 C11
Laholm S 103 C12
Lahonci SLO 164 D6
La Horcajada E 61 D10
La Horra E 56 E4
Lahr (Schwarzwald) D 43 D8
Lähte EST 147 E13
Lahti FIN 142 D6
Lahti FIN 143 D14
Lahtiranta FIN 135 E13
Laichingen D 90 F6
Laide GB 18 K5
Laidi LV 150 C3
Laidze LV 150 B5
Laifour F 200 E2
L'Aigle F 40 C4
La Iglesuela E 62 D3
La Iglesuela del Cid E 58 G3
Laignes F 41 E11
Laigueglia I 53 D8
L'Aiguillon-sur-Mer F 44 C3
Laihia FIN 138 E8
Laikko FIN 145 C11
Laiksjö S 123 C11
Lailly-en-Val F 40 E6
Laimont F 42 C3
Lainate I 85 B7
Lainio S 132 C8
Laino Borgo I 76 D5
Lairg GB 19 J8
La Iruela E 71 D7
Laisbäck S 123 A12
Laisheden S 125 E14
Laissac F 50 B4
Laisvall S 125 D13
Laisvalls by S 125 D13
Laitala FIN 137 E12
Laitikkala FIN 143 C11
Laitila FIN 142 D6
Laiuse EST 147 D12
Laives I 88 D3
Laižuva LT 150 D5
La Jana E 58 F4
La Jarrie F 44 C3
Lajatico I 82 F2
La Javie F 52 C4
Lajeosa P 61 D7
Lajeosa do Mondego P 61 C6
Lajkovac SRB 174 E5
La Jonchère-St-Maurice F 45 C8
La Jonquera E 50 F4
Lajoskomárom H 165 C10
Lajosmizse H 166 C4
La Jumellière F 39 F10
Lakaluoma FIN 139 E10
Lakatnik BG 181 C7
Lakaträsk S 134 B6
Lakavica MK 179 F10
Lakavica MK 185 A7
Lakenheath GB 31 C10
Lakhdenpokh'ya RUS 145 B13
Laki MK 181 F6
Łąkie PL 101 D12
Lakitelek H 166 D4
Lakka GR 184 F3
Lakki GR 193 E8
Lakkoi GR 194 E6
Lakkoma GR 185 D9
Lakkoma GR 187 D9
Lakkopetra GR 190 C3
Łąkociny PL 158 C4
Lakomäki FIN 139 E15
Łąkorz PL 155 D7
Lakšárska Nová Ves SK 162 D4
Lakselv N 129 C14
Lakselvsletta N 127 B18
Laksfors N 124 E5
Laktaši BIH 173 C7
Lakuntza E 48 E1
La Lantejuela E 67 E9
La Lapa E 67 C6
Lalapaşa TR 183 F7
Lalas GR 190 D4
L'Albagés E 58 E5
Lalbenque F 49 B9
L'Alcora E 64 D4
L'Alcudia E 64 F3
L'Alcudia de Crespins E 72 D3
Lalevade-d'Ardèche F 51 A7
Lalëz AL 184 A2
L'Alfàs del Pi E 72 D4
Lalín E 54 C3
Lalinac SRB 180 C5
Lalinde F 45 F7
La Línea de la Concepción E 69 D6
Lalioti GR 191 C6
Lalling F 35 D7
Lalley F 47 F8
Lalm N 117 C10
La Londe-les-Maures F 52 E4
Laloșu RO 176 D4
Laloubère F 49 D6
La Loupe F 40 D5
Lalouvesc F 46 E6
La Louvière B 35 D9
Lalove UA 161 G6
La Loye F 47 A8
L'Alpe-d'Huez F 47 E9
Lalueza E 58 D3
La Luisiana E 67 D9
Laluque F 48 C4
Lam D 92 D4
Lama I 79 C6
La Machine F 46 B3
La Maddalena I 80 A3
La Magdalena E 55 C8
Lamagistère F 49 B7
La Malène F 50 B5
Lamalou-les-Bains F 50 C5
Lama Mocogno I 82 D2
La Manga del Mar Menor E 72 F3
Lamanon F 51 C9
La Marche F 41 F9
Lamarche F 42 D4
Lamarche-sur-Saône F 42 F3
Lamargelle F 41 E12
Lamarque F 44 E4
Lamas P 60 C3
La Massana AND 49 E9
Lamastre F 46 F6
La Mata E 62 E4
La Mata de los Olmos E 58 F3
La Matilla E 62 B5
Lambach A 92 F5
Lamballe F 38 D6
Lambersart F 34 C7
Lambesc F 51 C9
Lambia GR 190 D4
Łambinowice PL 158 E4
Lamborn S 119 E10
Lambourn GB 29 B11
Lambrecht (Pfalz) D 202 C5
Lambsheim D 37 E10
Lamego P 60 B5
La Meilleraye-de-Bretagne F 39 E9
Lameiras P 61 C6
Lamerdingen D 87 A11
L'Ametlla de Mar E 58 F5
Lamezia I 75 B9
Lamia GR 190 B5
Lamiako E 56 B6
La Milesse F 39 D12
Lamlash GB 20 D6
Lammhult S 104 A7
Lammi FIN 139 D11
Lammi FIN 143 C13
Lamminkoski FIN 139 F10
Lamminmaa FIN 138 F8
Lamminperä FIN 135 C16
Lamminvaara FIN 137 B10
La Mojonera E 71 F7
La Môle F 52 E4
Lamon I 88 D4
La Mongie F 49 E6
La Monnerie-le-Montel F 46 D4
La Morera E 67 B6
Lamothe F 46 E3
La Mothe-Achard F 44 B2
Lamothe-Cassel F 49 A8
La Mothe-St-Héray F 44 C5
Lamotte-Beuvron F 40 E7
La Motte-Chalancon F 51 B9
La Motte-du-Caire F 51 B11
Lamovita BIH 173 C6
Lampaanjärvi FIN 140 D7
Lampaul F 38 D1
Lampaul-Guimiliau F 38 D3
Lampaul-Plouarzel F 38 D2
Lampeland N 111 C11
Lamperila FIN 140 E8
Lampertheim D 37 E10
Lampertswalde D 96 D5
Lampeter GB 28 A6
Lampinou GR 185 F9
Lampinsaari FIN 135 F14
Lampiselkä FIN 131 D1
Lamprechtshausen A 92 G3
Lampsijärvi FIN 133 E13
Lamsfeld-Groß Liebitz D 96 C6
Lamspringe D 95 C7
Lamstedt D 33 A12
Lamu FIN 135 F16
La Mudarra E 55 E10
La Muela E 57 E9
Lamujoki FIN 135 F16
La Mure F 47 F8
Lamure-sur-Azergues F 46 C5
Lana I 88 C3
Lanabukt N 130 D8
Lanaja E 57 E11
Lanaken B 35 C12
Lanarce F 46 F5
Lanark GB 21 D9
La Nava E 67 D6
La Nava de Ricomalillo E 62 E3
La Nava de Santiago E 61 F8
Lancaster GB 26 C6
Lanchester GB 21 F13
Lanciano I 79 C6
Lanckorona PL 163 B9
Łańcut PL 160 C5
Lancy CH 47 C9
Landau an der Isar D 91 E12
Landau in der Pfalz D 37 F10
Landbobyn S 118 E7
Lande N 121 A13
Landeck A 87 C11
Landeleau F 38 D4
Landen B 199 D6
Landerneau F 38 D3
Landersheim F 43 C7
Landeryd S 103 A12
Landesbergen D 33 C12
Landete E 63 E10
Landévant F 38 E5
Landgraaf NL 36 C6
Landiras F 48 A5
Landivisiau F 38 C3
Landivy F 39 D9
Landkirchen auf Fehmarn D 99 B10
Landön S 121 D16
Landos F 46 F4
Landquart CH 87 D9
Landrecies F 35 D8
Landres F 35 F12
Landsberg am Lech D 87 A11
Landsbro S 108 E5
Landscheid D 201 E6
Landshut D 91 E11
Landskrona S 103 D11
Landsmeer NL 198 A5
Landstuhl D 37 F9
Landudec F 38 D3
Landvetter S 107 D11
Landze LV 150 B3
Lanesborough IRL 23 E7
Lanesøyra N 128 C4
Lanester F 38 E5
La Neuve-Lyre F 40 C4
La Neuveville CH 47 A11
La Neuville-au-Pont F 41 B12
Laneuville-sur-Meuse F 35 F11
Lång S 113 D9
Langå DK 102 C5
Langa E 62 B3
Långå S 118 B5
Langa de Duero E 56 E5
Långalma S 115 B10
Långåminne FIN 138 E7
Långan S 121 D16
Langangen N 106 A6
Långås S 103 B10
Långasjö S 105 B8
Langau A 93 E9
Långbäck S 123 A11
Långbäcken S 123 C14
Langballig D 98 A7
Långban S 113 C11
Långbo S 119 C10
Långbo S 119 D12
Langbunes N 130 C9
Langburkersdorf D 96 D6
Langdorf D 92 D4
Langeac F 46 E3
Langeais F 40 F3
Langebæk DK 103 F10
Långed S 123 D17
Langedijk NL 32 C3
Langeid N 106 B2
Längelmäki FIN 143 B12
Langeln D 95 C8
Langelsheim D 95 C7
Langemark B 34 C6
Langemyr N 106 B3
Langen D 33 A11
Langen D 37 E11
Langenaltheim D 91 E8
Langenau D 91 F7
Langenaubach D 201 C9
Langenberg D 33 E10
Langenberg D 199 C10
Langenburg D 90 D6
Langenenslingen D 43 D11
Langenes N 126 B9
Längenfeld A 87 C11
Langenfeld (Rheinland) D 37 B7
Langenhagen D 94 B6
Langenhahn D 201 C8
Langenhorn D 98 A5
Langenleuba-Oberhain D 95 E12
Langenlois A 93 F9
Langenlonsheim D 201 E8
Langennaundorf D 96 C4
Langenneufnach D 87 A11
Langenorla D 95 E10
Langenpreising D 91 F10
Langenselbold D 37 D12
Langenthal CH 43 F8
Langenwang A 164 A5
Langenweddingen D 95 B10
Langenzenn D 91 D8
Langenzersdorf A 93 F10
Langeoog D 33 A8
Langeskov DK 102 E7
Langesund N 106 A6
Langevåg N 110 C2
Langevåg N 116 B4
Langewiesen D 95 E8
Langfjordbotn N 128 C9
Langgöns D 37 D11
Langhagen D 99 C12
Langham GB 27 F10
Langhamn N 127 B14
Långhed S 119 D11
Länghem S 107 D13
Langhirano I 82 C1
Langholm GB 21 E11
Langhus N 111 C13
Långlöt S 105 B11
Långnäs S 114 A6
Langnau CH 86 D5
Langnes N 127 B15
Langnes N 130 C4
Langnes N 130 D7
Langø DK 99 A10
Langogne F 46 F4
Langoiran F 44 F5
Langon F 48 A5
Langport GB 29 C9
Langreo E 55 B8
Langres F 42 E3
Langschlag A 93 E7
Långsel S 134 B8
Långsele S 123 C15
Långsele S 123 E12
Langset N 111 B14
Langset N 124 D5
Langset N 125 B9
Långshyttan S 113 B15
Långsjöby S 123 A11
Långskog S 119 B12
Langslett N 128 D6
Langstrand N 128 B11
Långsund S 134 D7
Langsur D 202 B2
Langtoft GB 27 C11
Långträsk S 123 A16
Långträsk S 134 C7
Långträsk S 134 D4
Langueux F 38 D6
Languidic F 38 E5
Languilla E 56 F5
Langula D 95 D7
Långvattnet S 123 D11
Långvattnet S 123 D13
Långvattnet S 134 E4
Långviken S 125 E15
Långviksmon S 123 D15
Långvinds bruk S 119 D13
Langwarden (Butjadingen) D 33 A10
Langwathby GB 21 F11
Langwedel D 33 C12
Langwedel D 99 B7
Langweid am Lech D 91 F8
Łanięta PL 155 F7
Lanivet GB 28 E5
Lanjarón E 69 C10
Lankojärvi FIN 133 E12
Lanloup F 38 C6
Lanmeur F 38 C4
Lanna S 103 A13
Lanna S 108 A5
Länna S 115 C9
Lannach A 164 C4
Lannavaara S 132 B7
Lannemezan F 49 D6
Lannepax F 49 C6
Lannevesi FIN 139 E14
Lannilis F 38 C2
Lannion F 38 C5
Lannoy F 35 C7
Lanobre F 45 E11
La Nocle-Maulaix F 46 B4
Lanouaille F 45 E8
Lánov CZ 97 E9
Lansån S 132 F8
Lansargues F 51 C7
Lansen D 99 C13
Länsikoski FIN 135 C13
Länsikylä FIN 139 E11
Länsipää FIN 135 B12
Länsiranta FIN 133 D16
Länsi-Teisko FIN 143 B10
Lansjärv S 132 E8
Lanškroun CZ 93 C11
Lanslebourg-Mont-Cenis F 47 E10
Lanta F 49 C9
Lantadilla E 56 D3
Lanton F 48 A3
Lantosque F 53 D6
Lantriac F 46 E5
Lanty F 46 B4
La Nucía E 72 D4
Lanuéjouls F 49 B10
Lanurile RO 171 C1
Lanusei I 80 D4
Lanuvio I 78 D3
Lanvollon F 38 C6
Łany PL 158 F5
Lánycsók H 165 D11
Lanz D 99 D11
Lanzahita E 62 D3
Lanžhot CZ 93 E11
Lanzo Torinese I 47 E11
Laon F 35 E8
Laons F 40 C5
La Paca E 71 D9
La Pacaudière F 46 C4
Lapajärvi FIN 131 E4
Lapalisse F 46 C4
La Pallice F 44 C3
La Palma E 72 F3
La Palma del Condado E 67 E6
La Palme F 50 E4
Lapalud F 51 B8
La Palud-sur-Verdon F 52 D4
Lapanj AL 184 D3
Łapanów PL 160 D1
Lapardha AL 184 C2
La Parra E 67 B6
La Parra de Las Vegas E 63 E8
Lapas GR 190 C3
La Pellerine F 39 D9
La Penne F 52 D5
La Peraleja E 63 D8
La Pesga E 61 D8
La Petite-Pierre F 43 C7
La Peza E 71 E6
Lapford GB 29 D7
Lapijoki FIN 142 C6
La Pinilla E 72 F2
Lapinjärvi FIN 143 D15
Lapinkylä FIN 143 E11
Lapinlahti FIN 140 D8
Lapinneva FIN 139 G9
Lapinsalo FIN 139 C17
La Plagne F 47 D10
La Plaza E 55 B7
Laplume F 49 B7
Lapmežciems LV 150 B7
La Pobla de Claramunt E 59 D7

La Pobla del Duc E 72 D4
La Pobla de Lillet E 59 C7
La Pobla de Montornès E 59 E6
La Pobla de Segur E 58 C5
La Pobla de Vallbona E 64 E3
La Pola de Gordón E 55 C8
La Pommeraye F 39 F10
La Porta F 53 G10
La Portellada E 58 F4
La Portera E 63 F10
Lapos RO 177 C8
La Pouëze F 39 E10
Lapoutroie F 43 D7
Lapovo SRB 175 E7
Lappajärvi FIN 139 D11
Lappe S 108 A7
Lappea FIN 133 D11
Lappersdorf D 91 D11
Lappetelä FIN 140 D8
Lappfjärd FIN 138 F7
Lappfors FIN 139 C10
Lappi FIN 135 E14
Lappi FIN 137 D13
Lappi FIN 142 C6
Lappila FIN 143 D13
Lappo FIN 142 E5
Lappohja FIN 143 F9
Lapptråsk S 135 B11
Lappuluobbal N 129 E13
La Preste F 49 F10
La Proveda de Soria E 57 D7
Lápseki TR 188 D6
Laptevo RUS 149 C5
Lapua FIN 139 E10
La Puebla de Almoradiel E 63 E6
La Puebla de Arganzón E 56 C6
La Puebla de Cazalla E 69 B7
La Puebla de los Infantes E 67 D9
La Puebla del Río E 67 E7
La Puebla de Montalbán E 62 E4
La Puebla de Valdavia E 55 C10
La Puebla de Valverde E 64 D3
La Puerta de Segura E 71 C7
Lăpugiu de Jos RO 167 F10
La Punt CH 87 D9
Lăpuş RO 168 C4
Lăpuşata RO 176 D4
Lăpuşna MD 169 D2
Lăpuşnicel RO 175 D9
Lăpuşnicu Mare RO 175 D8
Lapušnik SRB 179 D10
Łapy PL 156 E7
L'Aquila I 78 C4
Laracha E 54 B2
Laracor IRL 23 E9
Laragh IRL 23 F10
Laragne-Montéglin F 51 B10
La Rambla E 69 A7
Laranueva E 63 C7
La Rasa E 56 E5
La Ravoire F 47 D8
Larbert GB 21 C9
Larçay F 39 E10
L'Arbresle F 46 D6
Lärbro S 109 D13
Larceveau-Arros-Cibits F 48 D3
Larchamp F 39 D9
Larchant F 41 D8
Larche F 45 E8
Larche F 52 C5
Lardaro I 85 B10
Larderello I 82 F2
Lardero E 57 D7
Lardos GR 197 D8
Laredo E 56 B5
La Redorte F 50 D4
Laren NL 32 D4
Laren NL 199 A8
La Réole F 48 A5
Larga MD 169 A9
Largan IRL 22 D5
L'Argentière-la-Bessée F 47 F10
Largoward GB 21 C11
Largs GB 20 D7
Largu RO 177 D10
Lari I 82 E2
Lariano I 78 D3
La Riba E 58 E6
La Riba de Escalote E 56 F6
La Ricamarie F 46 E5
La Riche F 40 F4
La Rinconada E 67 E8
Larino I 79 D7
Larionovo RUS 145 D13
Larisa GR 185 E7
Larkhall GB 21 D9
Larkollen N 111 D13
Larling GB 31 C10
L'Armentera E 59 C10
Larmor-Plage F 38 E5
Larne GB 20 F5
La Robla E 55 C8
La Roca de la Sierra E 61 F7
La Roche CH 47 B11
La Roche-Bernard F 38 E4
La Roche-Canillac F 45 E9
La Roche-Chalais F 44 E6
La Roche-de-Rame F 47 F10
La Roche-Derrien F 38 D5
La Roche-des-Arnauds F 51 A10
La Roche-en-Ardenne B 35 D12
La Rochefoucauld F 45 D6
La Rochelle F 44 C3
Larochemillay F 46 B5
La Roche-Posay F 45 B7
La Roche-sur-Foron F 47 C9
La Roche-sur-Yon F 44 B3
La Rochette F 47 D7
Larochette L 36 E6
La Roda E 63 F8
La Roda de Andalucía E 69 B7
La Roë F 39 E9
Laroles E 71 E7
La Romana E 72 E3
La Romieu F 49 C6
Laroquebrou F 45 F10
La Roque-d'Olmes F 49 E9
La Roque-Ste-Marguerite F 50 B5
Laroque-Timbaut F 49 B7
La Rouquette F 49 B9

Larsnes N 116 B3
Laruns F 48 E5
Laruscade F 44 E5
Larv S 107 C13
Larva E 71 D6
Larvik N 106 A7
Larymna GR 191 B7
Lasà I 87 D11
Lasalle F 47 D11
La Salle I 47 D11
La Salle les Alpes F 47 F10
La Salvetat-Peyralès F 49 B10
La Salvetat-sur-Agout F 50 C4
La Salzadella E 64 D5
Läsänkoski FIN 144 B6
Las Arenas E 55 B10
La Sauvetat-du-Dropt F 49 A6
La Savina E 73 D7
Lasberg A 93 F7
Las Berlanas E 62 C3
Lásby DK 102 C5
Las Cabezas de San Juan E 67 F8
Lascari I 74 D4
Las Casas E 64 E4
Lascuarre E 58 C5
La Seca E 55 F10
La Secuita E 59 E6
La Séguinière F 44 A4
La Selva del Camp E 58 E6
La Selve F 49 B11
La Sénia E 58 F4
La Seyne-sur-Mer F 51 D10
Las Herencias E 62 E3
Łasin PL 154 C7
Lasinja HR 164 E5
Łask PL 159 C7
Łaskarzew PL 157 G5
Laško SLO 164 D4
Laskowa PL 160 D1
Laskowice PL 154 D5
Laskowiec PL 155 D12
Las Labores E 62 F5
Laslea RO 168 E5
Las Majadas E 63 D8
Las Menas E 71 E8
Las Mesas E 63 F7
Las Navas de la Concepción E 67 D9
Las Navas del Marqués E 62 C4
Lasne B 198 D4
Las Negras E 71 F9
La Solana E 71 B6
La Souterraine F 45 C8
Lasovo SRB 175 F9
Lasowice Małe PL 158 E5
Las Palas E 72 F2
Las Pedroñeras E 63 F7
Las Pedrosas E 57 D10
La Spezia I 85 E8
Las Plassas I 80 D2
Las Rotas E 72 D5
Las Rozas de Madrid E 62 C5
Lassahn D 100 C5
Lassan D 100 C5
Lassay-les-Châteaux F 39 D11
Lassemoen N 121 B13
Łasserud S 112 C7
Lasseube F 48 D5
Lassigny F 34 E6
Lassila FIN 142 B7
Lassing A 89 A9
Lassing A 89 A10
Laßnitzhöhe A 164 B5
Lastebasse I 85 B11
Las Terreras E 71 D9
Las Torres de Cotillas E 72 E2
Lastours F 49 D10
Lastovo HR 178 D2
Lastra a Signa I 82 E3
Lastras de Cuéllar E 56 F3
Lastrup D 33 C9
Łastukoski FIN 141 D10
Lastva BIH 178 D5
La Suze-sur-Sarthe F 39 E12
Lašva BIH 173 D8
Lasva EST 147 E14
Las Veguillas E 61 C9
Las Ventas con Peña Aguilera E 62 E4
Las Ventas de San Julián E 61 D10
Łaszczów PL 160 B8
Laszki PL 160 C6
Laterza I 77 F3
Lavala FIN 137 D14
Lavalette F 49 D10
La Valette-du-Var F 51 D10
La Vall d'Uixó E 64 E4
La Valle I 88 C4
Lavamünd A 89 C10
Lavangen N 127 C14
Lavangsnes N 127 C13
Lavara F 187 B10
Lavardac F 49 B6
Lavassaare EST 147 D8
Lavaur F 49 C9
Lavaveix-les-Mines F 45 C10
Lavda GR 184 D5
Lavdar i Korçës AL 184 C4
La Vecilla E 55 C9
La Vega E 55 B8
La Vega E 55 B8
La Vega E 55 B8
Lavelanet F 49 E9
Le Vellés E 61 B9
Lavello I 76 A4
Laven DK 102 C5
La Ventosa E 63 D8
La Verdière F 51 C10
La Vernarède F 51 B6
La Verpillière F 47 D7
La Verrie F 44 B4
La Veuve F 41 B11
Lavia FIN 142 B8
Laviano I 76 B4
La Victoria E 69 A7
La Vid E 56 E5
Lavik N 127 B14
La Villa I 81 C2
La Villa de Don Fadrique E 63 E6
La Ville-aux-Clercs F 40 E5
La Villedieu F 46 F4
La Villedieu-du-Clain F 45 C6
La Villedieu-en-Fontenette F 42 E5
Lavinio-Lido di Enea I 78 E3
Lavis I 85 A11
Lavit F 49 C7
Lavoriškes LT 153 D12

Lauder GB 21 D11
Lauderi LV 149 D4
Laudona LV 151 C12
Laudun F 51 B8
Lauenau D 33 D12
Lauenbrück D 98 D7
Lauenburg (Elbe) D 99 D9
Lauenförde D 37 A12
Lauf D 202 D5
Laufach D 203 A7
Lauf an der Pegnitz D 91 C9
Laufen CH 43 E8
Laufenberg CH 43 E9
Laufenburg CH 43 E9
Lauffen am Neckar D 203 C7
Laugnac F 49 B7
Lauingen (Donau) D 91 E7
Laujar de Andarax E 71 F7
Laukaa FIN 139 F15
Laukeng N 128 D9
Lauker S 134 C3
Laukka FIN 135 E15
Laukkala FIN 139 D17
Laukkoski FIN 143 E13
Laukluspa S 127 E18
Laukna EST 147 D8
Lauksargiai LT 150 A17
Laulett N 127 A17
Laukkien N 128 C6
Laukuva LT 150 E4
Laukvik N 121 C9
Laukvik N 126 D7
Laukvik N 126 E8
Laukvik N 127 A14
Laukvik N 129 C11
Laukvik N 130 B6
Laukžemė LT 150 D2
Launac F 49 C8
Launceston GB 28 D6
La Unión E 72 F3
Launkalne LV 151 B11
Laupen CH 47 B11
Laupheim D 87 A9
Laupstad N 126 D7
Lauragh IRL 24 E3
Lauraguel F 49 D10
Laurbjerg DK 102 C5
Laureana di Borrello I 75 C9
Laurencekirk GB 21 B12
Laurencetown IRL 22 F6
Laurens F 50 C5
Laurenzana I 76 C5
Lauria I 76 C5
Laurière F 45 C8
Laurieston GB 21 F8
Laurino I 76 C4
Lauris F 51 C9
Laurito I 76 C4
Lausanne CH 47 B10
Lauscha D 91 B9
Laußig D 95 C12
Laußnitz D 96 D5
Laussonne F 46 F5
Laussou F 49 A7
Lauta D 96 D6
Lautamaa FIN 135 C12
Lautenbach D 43 C9
Lauter D 95 E12
Lauterbourg F 43 F9
Lauterbrunnen CH 86 D5
Lautere LV 151 C11
Lauterhofen D 91 D10
Lautersbach (Hessen) D 94 C11
Lauterstein D 203 D8
Lautertal D 91 B8
Lautiosaari FIN 135 C13
Lautrec F 49 C10
Lauttavaara FIN 137 E9
Lauttijärvi FIN 142 B6
Lauve N 106 A7
Lauvsnes N 121 C9
Lauvstad N 116 B3
Lauvuskylä FIN 141 C13
Lauvvik N 110 E4
Lauzerte F 49 B8
Lauzès F 49 A9
Lauzun F 49 A6
Lavagna I 53 C10
Laval F 39 D11
La Teste-de-Buch F 48 A3
Lathen D 33 C8
Latheron GB 19 J10
Latheronwheel GB 19 J10
La Thuile I 47 B9
Lathus F 45 C7
Latiano I 77 B9
Latikberg S 123 B12
Latillé F 44 B6
Latina I 78 E3
Latisana I 89 E7
Latorpsbruk S 113 D12
La Torre de Cabdella E 49 F7
La Torre de Esteban Hambrán E 62 D4
La Torre de l'Espanyol E 58 E5
La Tour-d'Auvergne F 45 D10
Latour-de-France F 50 E4
La Tour-du-Crieu F 49 D9
La Tour-du-Pin F 47 D7
La Tour-sur-Orb F 50 C5
Latowicz PL 157 F5
La Tranche-sur-Mer F 44 C3
La Tremblade F 44 D3
La Trimouille F 45 C8
La Trinité F 53 D6
La Trinité-Porhoët F 38 D6
La Trinité-sur-Mer F 38 E5
Latronico I 76 C6
Latronquière F 45 F10
Lattari I 76 B4
Lattes I 51 C6
Lattrop NL 199 A9
La Turballe F 38 F7
Latva FIN 135 F15
Latva FIN 136 C9
Latvajärvenperä FIN 137 D11
Laubach D 37 C11
Laubach D 37 D8
Lauben D 87 A10
Laubere LV 151 C10
Laubrück D 87 B11
Lauchhammer D 96 D5
Lauchringen D 43 E9
Laucienne LV 150 B5
Lauda-Königshofen D 90 C6

La Voulte-sur-Rhône F 46 F6
Lavoûte-Chilhac F 46 E3
Lavoûte-sur-Loire F 46 E4
Lavradio P 66 B1
Lavre P 66 B3
Lavrio GR 191 D9
La Wantzenau F 202 D6
Lawers GB 21 B8
Lawford GB 31 D11
Lawrencetown GB 23 D10
Łask PL 156 D6
Ławszowa PL 97 D8
Ławy PL 101 E7
Laxå S 108 B5
Laxbäcken S 123 B10
Laxe E 54 B2
Laxey GBM 26 C3
Laxford Bridge GB 18 J6
Laxne S 93 A7
Laxo GB 19 E14
Laxou F 42 C5
Laxsjö S 122 D7
Laxvik S 103 B11
Laxviken S 122 D7
Layana E 48 F3
La Yesa E 64 E3
Läyliäinen FIN 143 D11
Layos E 62 E4
Layrac F 49 B7
Laz HR 164 E6
Laza E 54 D5
Laza RO 169 D11
Lazagurría E 48 F1
Lazarata E 190 B2
Lăzarea RO 169 D7
Lăzăreni RO 167 D9
Lazarev Krst MNE 179 D7
Lazarevac SRB 174 E5
Lazarevo SRB 174 C6
Lazdijai LT 153 E8
Lazdona LV 151 C12
Lazdukalns LV 149 C2
Lazeshchyna UA 168 A4
Lazise I 82 B2
Łaziska PL 157 H5
Łaziska Górne PL 158 F6
Lazkao E 48 D1
Lázně Bělohrad CZ 93 B9
Lázně Bohdaneč CZ 93 B8
Lázně Kynžvart CZ 91 B12
Laznica SRB 175 E8
Lazonby GB 21 F11
Lazuri RO 167 B10
Lazuri de Beiuş RO 167 D9
Leabgarrow IRL 22 C5
Leacht Seoirse IRL 22 F5
Leadburn GB 21 D10
Leadenham GB 27 E10
Leadhills GB 21 E9
Leamhcán IRL 23 F10
Leamington Spa, Royal GB 29 A11
Leányfalu H 164 N5
Leap IRL 24 E4
Leasingham GB 27 E11
Leatherhead GB 31 E8
Leavvajohka N 129 D17
Łeba PL 101 A13
Lebach D 37 F7
Lebane SRB 180 D4
Le Ban-St-Martin F 202 C1
Le Barp F 48 A4
Le Bar-sur-Loup F 52 D5
Lebbeke B 35 B9
Le Béage F 46 F5
Le Beausset F 51 D10
Lebedivka UA 170 F6
Lébénymiklós H 165 A8
Lebesby N 129 B18
Le Bez F 49 D10
Le Biot F 47 C10
Le Blanc F 45 B8
Le Bleymard F 51 B6
Łebno PL 154 B5
Le Bois-d'Oingt F 46 D6
Le Bois-Plage-en-Ré F 44 C3
Le Boréon F 53 C6
Le Boulou F 50 E4
Le Boupère F 44 B4
Le Bourg F 45 F9
Le Bourg-d'Oisans F 47 E9
Le Bourget-du-Lac F 47 D8
Le Bousquet-d'Orb F 50 C5
Le Breuil F 46 B5
Le Breuil F 46 C5
Lebrija E 67 F7
Le Brouilh-Monbert F 49 C6
Le Brusquet F 52 C4
Lebução P 54 E5
Le Bugue F 45 F7
Le Buisson-de-Cadouin F 45 F7
Łebunia PL 154 B4
Lebus D 97 B7
Lebusa D 96 C4
Lebyazh'ye RUS 145 F11
Leça da Palmeira P 60 B3
Leça do Bailio P 60 B3

Lechlade GB 29 B11
Lechovo GR 185 C5
Lechtingen (Wallenhorst) D 33 D10
Leciñena E 57 E10
Leck D 98 A5
Leckaun IRL 22 D6
Leckmelm GB 18 K6
Le Clapier F 50 C5
Leclerbtingen D 43 D11
Le Collet-de-Dèze F 51 B6
Le Conquet F 38 D2
Le Coteau F 46 C5
Le Coudray-St-Germer F 34 F4
Lécousse F 39 D9
Le Crès F 51 C6
Le Creusot F 46 B5
Lecrín E 69 C9
Le Croisic F 38 F6
Le Crotoy F 34 D4
Lectoure F 49 C7
Ledaig GB 20 C6
Ledaña E 63 F7
Ledanca E 63 C7
Lēdas LV 150 B5
Ledbury GB 29 A10
Lede B 198 D2
Ledeč nad Sázavou CZ 93 C8
Ledegem B 198 D2
Ledenice BIH 173 C9
Ledenice CZ 93 E7
Léderguès F 49 B10
Ledesma E 61 B9
Lédignan F 51 C7
Ledigos E 55 D10
Ledmore GB 18 J7
Lednica SK 162 C6
Lednice CZ 93 E11
Lednické Rovne SK 162 C6
Le Donjon F 46 C4
Le Dorat F 45 C8
Ledrada E 61 D9
Lēdurga LV 151 B9
Ledusjö S 123 D16
Ledvattsfors S 125 F16
Łędyczek PL 101 C11
Łędziny PL 101 B8
Łędziny PL 159 F7
Leeds GB 27 D8
Leedstown GB 28 E4
Leek GB 27 E7
Leek NL 32 B6
Leeming GB 27 C8
Lee Moor GB 28 E6
Leende NL 32 F5
Leer (Ostfriesland) D 33 B8
Leerdam NL 199 B6
Leersum NL 199 A6
Leese D 33 C12
Leeuwarden NL 32 B5
Leevaku EST 147 E14
Leevi EST 147 F14
Leezen D 99 C8
Leezen D 99 C10
Le Faou F 38 D3
Le Fauet F 38 D5
Le Fenouiller F 44 B2
Leffinge B 198 C1
Le Fleix F 45 F6
Le Folgoët F 38 C3
Leforest F 198 D2
Le Fossat F 49 D8
Le Fousseret F 49 D8
Le Fugeret F 52 C5
Le Fuilet F 39 F9
Leganés E 62 D5
Leganiel E 63 D7
Legau D 87 B10
Le Gault-Soigny F 41 C10
Le Gault-St-Denis F 40 D5
Legazpi E 48 D1
Legde D 99 E11
Legden D 33 D8
Legé F 44 B2
Lège-Cap-Ferret F 44 F3
Le Genest-St-Isle F 39 D10
Leggs GB 23 C7
Legionowo PL 155 F10
Léglise B 35 E11
Legnago I 82 B3
Legnano I 85 B6
Legnica PL 97 D10
Legnickie Pole PL 97 D10
Le Gond-Pontouvre F 45 D6
Łęgowo PL 154 B6
Legrad HR 165 D7
Le Grand-Bornand F 47 D9
Le Grand-Bourg F 45 C9
Le Grand-Lemps F 47 E7
Le Grand-Lucé F 40 E4
Le Grand-Pressigny F 45 B7
Le Grand-Quevilly F 34 F3
Le Grand-Serre F 46 E6
Le Grau-du-Roi F 51 C7
Le Gros Theil F 34 F2
Le Gua F 47 E8
Legutiano E 57 C6
Legyesbénye H 161 G3
Le Havre F 39 A12
Lehe D 98 B6
Lehliu RO 177 E9
Lehliu-Gară RO 177 E9
Lehmäjoki FIN 138 D8
Lehmen D 37 D8
Lehmikumpu FIN 135 B14
Lehmivaara FIN 133 E11
Lehmo FIN 141 E13
Lehmsdorf E 95 E11
Lehnice SK 162 E4
Lehnin D 95 B12
Léhon F 39 D7
Le Horps F 39 D11
Lehota SK 162 E5
Lehrberg D 91 D8
Lehre D 95 B8
Lehrte D 95 B6
Lehsen D 99 D10
Lehtimäki FIN 139 E11
Lehtiniemi FIN 137 B10
Lehto FIN 137 B14
Lehtola FIN 135 F13
Lehtopää N 129 E13

Lehtovaara FIN 133 D17
Lehtovaara FIN 137 C10
Lehtovaara FIN 137 C10
Lehtovaara FIN 137 F14
Lehtovaara FIN 140 B9
Lehtovaara FIN 141 D11
Lehtse EST 147 C11
Leianokladi GR 190 B5
Leibertingen D 43 D11
Leiblfing D 91 E11
Leibnitz A 164 C5
Leicester GB 27 F9
Leichlingen (Rheinland) D 199 C10
Leiden NL 32 D3
Leiderdorp NL 32 D3
Leidschendam NL 32 D2
Leie EST 147 E12
Leifear F 20 F2
Leiferde D 95 B7
Léim an Bhradáin IRL 23 F10
Leimani LV 151 D11
Leimen D 37 F11
Leimuiden NL 198 A5
Leinburg D 91 B9
Leine N 117 E9
Leinefelde D 95 D7
Leinelfelde D 95 D7
Leinì I 84 C4
Leino FIN 137 D12
Leinzell D 90 E6
Leioa E 56 B6
Leipalingis LT 153 E8
Leipheim D 91 F11
Leipivaara FIN 137 E10
Leipojärvi S 132 D6
Leipzig D 95 D11
Leira N 120 E4
Leira N 124 B9
Leirado E 54 D3
Leirâmoen N 124 C8
Leiranger N 126 E8
Leirbotn N 129 C11
Leiria P 60 E3
Leirlia N 121 B15
Leiro E 54 D3
Leirvåg N 116 E2
Leirvik FO 18 A3
Leirvik N 110 C2
Leirvik N 116 E2
Leirvik N 121 B11
Leirvika N 124 C6
Leisach A 89 C6
Leisi EST 146 D5
Leisnig D 96 D3
Leiston GB 31 C12
Leitir Ceanainn IRL 23 C7
Leitir Mhic an Bhaird IRL 22 C6
Leitrim GB 22 F5
Leitza E 48 D2
Leitzkau D 95 B10
Leive FIN 135 B10
Leivonmäki FIN 143 B15
Leivset N 124 B9
Leixlip IRL 23 F10
Lejasciems LV 151 B13
Lejasstrazdi LV 150 C6
Leka GR 193 D8
Lekaj AL 184 B2
Lekangen N 127 B13
Lekani GR 187 B7
Łęka Opatowska PL 158 D5
Lekárovce SK 161 F5
Łękawica PL 163 B8
Lekbibaj AL 179 E8
Lekéčiai LT 153 D7
Lekenik HR 164 E6
Lekeryd S 108 D4
Lekhchevo BG 181 C8
Lekhovo GR 185 C5
Leknes GB 21 E9
Lęknica PL 97 C7
Lekoes N 126 D6
Lekowo PL 101 C9
Leksand S 119 E9
Leksvik N 121 C8
Lekunberri E 48 D2
Leland N 124 C6
Le Langon F 44 C4
Le Lardin-St-Lazare F 45 E8
Le Lauzet-Ubaye F 52 C4
Le Lavandou F 52 E4
Leleasca RO 176 D4
Leles SK 161 G5
Leleşti RO 175 C11
Le Leuy F 48 C4
Lelice PL 155 E8
Le Lion-d'Angers F 39 F11
Leliūnai LT 151 F10
Lelkowo PL 155 B9
Lelle EST 147 D9
Le Locle CH 47 A10
Le Louroux-Béconnais F 39 F10
Lelów PL 159 E8
Le Luc F 52 E5
Le Lude F 39 E12
Lelystad NL 32 C4
Lem DK 102 C2
Le Malzieu-Ville F 46 F3
Le Mans F 39 D12
Le Markstein F 43 E7
Le Martinet F 51 B7
Le Mas-d'Agenais F 49 B6
Le Mas-d'Azil F 49 D8
Le Masnau-Massuguiès F 50 C4
Le Massegros F 50 B5
Le Mayet-de-Montagne F 46 C4
Le May-sur-Èvre F 39 F11
Lembach im Mühlkreis A 92 E5
Lembeke B 198 C3
Lemberg D 43 B8
Lemberg F 43 B8
Lembeye F 48 D5
Lembras F 45 F7
Lembruch D 33 C10
Lemele NL 32 C6
Lemelerveld NL 32 C6
Le Mêle-sur-Sarthe F 40 C3
Le Merlerault F 39 D12
Le Mesnil-sur-Oger F 41 C11
Lemetinvaara FIN 137 F12
Lemgo D 33 D11
Lemi FIN 144 C8
Lemierzyce PL 97 A7

Lemland FIN 115 B14
Lemmenjoki FIN 133 A16
Lemmer NL 32 C5
Le Molay-Littry F 39 B10
Le Monastier F 50 A5
Le Monastier-sur-Gazeille F 46 F4
Le Monêtier-les-Bains F 47 F10
Le Montet F 46 C3
Lempäälä FIN 143 C10
Lempdes F 46 D3
Lempdes F 46 E3
Lemppy FIN 140 E8
Lemu FIN 142 D6
Le Muy F 52 E5
Lemvig DK 102 B2
Lemwerder D 33 B11
Lembyrien IRL 25 D7
Lena N 117 E13
Lenart SLO 164 C5
Lēnas LV 150 C5
Lenauheim RO 166 F6
Lencloître F 45 B6
Lencouacq F 48 B5
Lend A 89 B7
Lendak SK 161 E1
Lendava SLO 165 C6
Lendery RUS 141 D16
Lendinara I 82 B4
Lendum DK 106 A7
Lenē AL 184 B3
Leněsice CZ 92 B5
Le Neubourg F 40 B4
Lengau A 92 F4
Lengau A 92 F4
Lengdorf D 91 F11
Lengenes N 127 D15
Lengenfeld D 95 E11
Lengenwang D 87 B11
Lengerich D 33 C9
Lengerich D 33 D9
Lenggries D 88 A4
Lengnau CH 43 F7
Lengyeltóti H 165 C9
Lenham GB 31 E10
Lenhovda S 105 B8
Lenine UA 170 F5
Léning F 43 C6
Le Nizan F 48 B5
Lenk CH 47 C11
Lenkimai LT 150 D2
Lenna I 85 B8
Lennartsfors S 112 C6
Lennastnäs S 115 C9
Lenne D 94 C6
Lennestadt D 37 B10
Lenningen D 43 C11
Lennsjö S 119 E12
Leno I 82 B1
Le Noirmont CH 43 F6
Lenola I 78 E5
Le Nouvion-en-Thiérache F 35 D8
Lens B 35 C8
Lens F 34 D6
Lensahn D 99 B9
Lensvik N 120 D7
Lent F 47 C7
Lent NL 199 B7
Lentas GR 194 F6
Lenti H 165 C7
Lentiai I 88 D5
Lentiira FIN 137 F14
Lenting D 91 E9
Lentini I 75 E7
Lentvaris LT 153 D11
Lenvik N 127 C13
Lenzburg CH 43 F9
Lenzen D 99 D10
Lenzing A 92 G5
Lenzkirch D 43 E9
Leoben A 89 G11
Leoben A 89 C4
Leobendorf A 93 F10
Leobersdorf A 93 G10
Leogang A 89 B6
Léognan F 44 F4
Leominster GB 29 A9
León E 55 C8
Léon F 48 C3
Leonberg D 43 C11
Léoncel F 47 F7
Leonding A 92 F6
Leonessa I 78 B3
Leonforte I 74 D5
Leonidio GR 191 E5
Leontari GR 190 A5
Leontari GR 190 C5
Leopoldov SK 162 E5
Leopoldsburg B 35 B11
Leopoldsdorf im Marchfelde A 93 F11
Leopoldshagen D 100 C5
Leopoldshöhe D 33 D11
Leorda RO 169 B8
Leordeni RO 176 D6
Leordina RO 168 B4
Leova MD 170 E2
Le Palais F 38 F5
Le Palais-sur-Vienne F 45 D8
Le Pallet F 39 F9
Le Parcq F 34 D5
Lepassaare EST 148 F1
Le Passage F 49 B7
Le Pavillon-Ste-Julie F 41 D10
Lepe E 67 E5
Le Péage-de-Roussillon F 46 E6
Le Pellerin F 39 F8
Le Périer F 47 F8
Le Perthus F 50 F4
Le Pertre F 39 D9
Le Petit-Quevilly F 34 F3
Le Pian-Médoc F 44 E4
Le Pin-au-Haras F 39 C12
L'Épine F 51 B10
Le Pin-la-Garenne F 40 D4
Lepistönmäki FIN 139 D10
Lepitsa BG 181 C9
Le Pizou F 44 E6
Le Plan F 49 E7
Le Plessis-Belleville F 41 B8
Le Poët F 51 B9
Lepoglava HR 164 D6
Le Poinçonnet F 45 B9
Le Poiré-sur-Vie F 44 B3
Le Pont-de-Beauvoisin F 47 D8
Le Pont-de-Claix F 47 E8
Le Pont-de-Montvert F 51 B6

Le Pontet F 51 C8
Leporano I 77 C8
Le Porge F 44 F3
Le Porge-Océan F 44 F3
Le Portel F 31 F12
Leposavić SRB 179 C10
Le Pouldu F 38 E4
Le Pouliguen F 38 F7
Lepoura GR 191 C9
Le Pouzin F 46 F6
Leppäjärvi FIN 133 B10
Leppäkoski FIN 143 D12
Leppälä FIN 129 D19
Leppälä FIN 137 D11
Leppälähkylä FIN 139 E11
Leppälahti FIN 140 D8
Leppälahti FIN 141 F12
Leppäselkä FIN 139 D16
Leppävesi FIN 139 F15
Leppiaho FIN 135 C15
Leppiniemi FIN 135 E16
Lepsala FIN 143 C15
Lepsäma FIN 143 E12
Lepsény H 165 B10
Leptokarya GR 185 D8
Le Puy-en-Velay F 46 E4
Le Puy-Notre-Dame F 39 F11
Le Quesnoy F 35 D8
Lequile I 77 C10
Ler N 120 E8
Le Raincy F 41 C8
Léran F 49 E9
Lerberget S 103 C11
Lercara Friddi I 74 D4
Lerdala S 107 C14
Léré F 41 F8
Le Relecq-Kerhuon F 38 D3
Lereşti RO 176 C6
Lerici I 85 E8
Lérida E 58 D3
Lerín E 48 E2
Lerkaka S 105 B11
Lerma E 56 D4
Lerm-et Musset F 48 B5
Lermoos A 87 C11
Lerot S 112 C7
Le Rouget F 45 F10
Lérouville F 42 C4
Le Rozier F 50 B5
Lerum S 107 D11
Le Russey F 42 F6
Lervik N 111 D13
Lerwick GB 19 E14
Lesa I 84 B6
Les Abrets F 47 D8
Les Aix-d'Angillon F 41 F8
Lešak SRB 179 C10
Lesaka E 48 D2
Les Andelys F 34 F3
Les Angles F 49 E10
Les Angles F 51 C8
Lešani MK 184 B4
Les Arcs F 47 D10
Les Arcs F 52 E4
Les Aubiers F 44 B4
Les Avellanes E 58 D3
Les Avenières F 47 D8
Les Bondons F 51 B6
Les Bordes F 41 E7
Les Borges Blanques E 58 D5
Les Borges del Camp E 58 E6
Les Bouchoux F 47 C8
Les Brenets CH 47 A10
Lesbury GB 21 E13
Les Cabannes F 49 E9
L'Escala E 59 C10
L'Escale F 51 B11
Lescar F 48 D5
L'Escarène F 53 D6
Les Cases d'Alcanar E 58 F5
Lesce SLO 89 D9
Lesconil F 38 E3
Les Contamines-Montjoie F 47 D10
Les Coves de Vinromà E 64 D5
Lescun F 48 D4
Lescure-d'Albigeois F 49 C10
Les Deux-Alpes F 47 E9
Les Diablerets CH 47 C11
Les Échelles F 47 E8
Les Églisottes-et-Chalaures F 44 E5
Le Sel-de-Bretagne F 39 E8
Le Sen F 48 B4
Le Sentier CH 47 B9
Les Éparges F 42 C4
Les Epesses F 44 B4
Les Escaldes AND 49 E9
Les Essards-Taignevaux F 47 B7
Les Essarts F 44 B3
Le Seu d'Urgell E 49 F8
Les Eyzies-de-Tayac-Sireuil F 45 F8
Les Fins F 47 A10
Les Forges F 42 D5
Les Fourgs F 47 B9
Les Gets F 47 C10
Les Hautes-Rivières F 200 E2
Les Herbiers F 44 B3
Les Houches F 47 D10
Lesichovo BG 181 E9
Lesično SLO 148 D4
Lesidren BG 181 D9
Lesina I 79 B8
Les Issambres F 52 E5
Lesja N 117 B9
Lesjöfors S 113 C11
Leskava LT 153 D8
Leskelä FIN 135 F15
Lesko PL 161 E5
Leskoec MK 184 B4
Leskova S 179 C9
Leskovac SRB 180 D4
Leskovik AL 184 D4
Leskovo BG 177 F11
Les Landes-Genusson F 44 B3
Leslie GB 21 C10
Les Lucs-sur-Boulogne F 44 B3
Lesmahagow GB 21 D9
Les Maillys F 42 F3
Les Marches F 47 D8
Les Martres-de-Veyre F 46 D3
Les Matelles F 51 C6
Les Mazures F 200 E2
Les Mées F 51 B10
Les Menuires F 47 E10
Lesmont F 41 D11
Les Mureaux F 40 C6
Lešná CZ 162 B5
Lešnia PL 97 D8

Lesneven F 38 C3
Lešnica PL 158 F5
Lešnica SRB 174 D3
Lešniów Wielki PL 97 C8
Lesogorskiy RUS 145 C10
Lès Òllières-sur-Eyrieux F 46 F4
Lesovaara FIN 137 D13
Lesovo BG 183 B9
Levoča SK 161 E2
Lesparre-Médoc F 44 E4
Les Peintures F 44 E5
Les Pennes-Mirabeau F 51 D9
Lesperon F 48 C3
Les Pieux F 39 A8
Lespignan F 50 D5
Lespinassière F 50 D4
Les Planches-en-Montagne F 47 B9
Les Planes d'Hostoles E 59 C9
L'Espluga Calba E 58 E6
L'Espluga de Francolí E 58 E6
Les Ponts-de-Cé F 39 F10
Les Ponts-de-Martel CH 47 A10
Les Preses E 59 C9
Lespuigue F 49 D7
Les Rosiers-sur-Loire F 39 F11
Les Rousses F 47 C9
Les Sables-d'Olonne F 44 C2
Les Salles-du-Gardon F 51 B7
Lessay F 39 B8
Lessebo S 105 A8
Les Sièges F 41 D10
Lessines B 35 C8
Les Sorinières F 39 F8
Lestene LV 150 C6
Les Ternes F 46 E3
Les Thuiles F 52 C5
Lestijärvi FIN 139 C13
Leština CZ 93 C11
Lestrade F 50 B4
Les Trois-Moutiers F 40 F3
L'Hospitalet-près-l'Andorre F 49 E9
Lešu RO 168 C5
Lesura BG 181 D8
Les Vans F 51 B7
Les Vignes F 50 B5
Leszczyn PL 101 C9
Leszno PL 97 C11
Leszno PL 157 F3
Leszno Górne PL 97 D9
Létavértes H 167 C8
Letca RO 167 C11
Letcani RO 169 C10
Letca Nouă RO 177 E7
Letchworth Garden City GB 31 B8
Letea Veche RO 169 D9
Le Teich F 48 B3
Le Teil F 51 A8
Le Teilleul F 39 D10
Le Temple F 44 F4
Letenye H 165 D7
Le Theil F 40 D4
Le-Theil-de-Bretagne F 39 E9
Le Thillot F 43 E6
Le Tholy F 43 E6
Le Thor F 51 C8
Letino I 79 E6
Letkés H 163 F7
Letnitsa BG 181 C11
Letonice CZ 93 D11
Le Touquet-Paris-Plage F 31 F12
Le Touvet F 47 E8
Letovice CZ 93 C11
L'Étrat F 46 E5
Le Trayas F 52 E5
Le Tréport F 34 D3
Letsbo S 119 C10
Letschin D 81 A7
Letterfinish IRL 24 E3
Letterkenny IRL 23 C7
Lettermacaward IRL 22 C6
Letterston GB 28 B5
Letur F 71 C8
Le Tuzan F 48 B4
Letzlingen D 95 B9
Leu RO 176 E4
Leuc F 49 D10
Leucate F 50 E5
Leuchars GB 21 C11
Leuchtenberg D 91 C11
Leud RO 168 B4
Leuk CH 84 A4
Leukerbad F 84 A4
Leumrabhagh GB 18 J4
Leun D 37 C8
Leuna D 95 D11
Leunen NL 32 B6
Leușeni MD 170 D2
Leutasch A 88 B3
Leutenberg D 95 E9
Leutershausen D 91 D7
Leutkirch im Allgäu D 87 B10
Leuvanjoki FIN 135 D15
Leuven B 35 C10
Leuze-en-Hainaut B 35 C8
Le Val F 52 E4
Le Vallinot-Longeau-Percey F 42 E3
Levan AL 184 C1
Levänen FIN 144 C8
Levang N 124 C3
Levanger N 121 D10
Levanjska Varoš HR 165 F10
Levanto FIN 143 D13
Levanto I 53 C11
Leva Reka MD 181 B7
Levăsjoki FIN 142 B6
Level H 162 F4
Levelek H 161 H4
Leven GB 21 C11
Leven GB 27 D11
Levens F 53 D6
Levenwick GB 19 F14
Leverano I 77 C10
Leverburgh GB 18 J2
Le-Verdon-sur-Mer F 44 D3
Le Vernet F 49 E9
Lèves F 40 D5
Levet F 45 B10
Levice SK 163 E7
Levico Terme I 85 A11
Levidi GR 190 D5
Levie F 53 H10
Levier F 47 B9
Le Vigan F 51 C6
Lévignac F 49 C8

Lévignacq F 48 B3
Levijoki FIN 139 E11
Le Ville I 82 F5
Levinovac HR 165 E8
Le-Vivier-sur-Mer F 39 C8
Levka BG 182 F6
Levkogeia GR 186 B5
Levoča SK 161 E2
Levonperä FIN 139 C14
Levo-oja FIN 135 D16
Levroux F 45 B9
Levski BG 182 C4
Levunovo BG 185 B9
Lewes GB 31 F9
Lewin Brzeski PL 158 E4
Lewin Kłodzki PL 93 B10
Leyburn GB 27 C8
Leyland GB 26 D6
Leyme F 45 E9
Leysin CH 47 C11
Leytron CH 47 C11
Leżajsk F 160 C5
Lézan F 51 C6
Lézat-sur-Lèze F 49 D8
Lezay F 45 C6
Lezhë AL 179 F8
Lézignan-Corbières F 50 D4
Lezoux F 46 D3
Lezuza E 71 B8
Lgota Górna PL 159 E7
Lgota Wielka PL 159 D7
Lhenice CZ 92 B6
Lherm F 49 D8
L'Hermenault F 44 B4
L'Honor-de-Cos F 49 B8
L'Hôpital F 202 C2
L'Horme F 46 E6
L'Hospitalet F 48 B4
L'Hospitalet de l'Infant E 58 F5
L'Hospitalet de Llobregat E 59 E8
Lia N 127 C14
Liabøen N 120 E4
Liancourt F 34 F5
Liapades GR 184 E2
Liart F 35 D8
Liarvåg N 110 D3
Liatorp S 104 B6
Libáň CZ 93 B8
Libatse EST 147 D8
Libberton GB 21 D9
Libčany CZ 93 B9
Libčeves CZ 92 B5
Liberadz PL 155 D9
Liberec CZ 97 E8
Libĕšice CZ 96 E6
Libiąż PL 159 F7
Libice nad Cidlinou CZ 93 B8
Libin B 35 E11
Libina CZ 93 C12
Libochovice CZ 92 B6
Libofshë AL 184 C2
Libohovë AL 184 D4
Libouchec CZ 96 E6
Libourne F 44 F5
Libramont B 35 E11
Librazhd AL 184 B3
Librilla E 71 D10
Libros E 63 D10
Licata I 74 E4
Licciana Nardi I 85 E9
Licenza I 78 C3
Liceras E 56 F5
Lich D 37 C11
Lijar E 71 E8
Lichfield GB 27 F8
Lichnov CZ 158 F4
Lichnowy PL 154 B6
Lichtaart B 198 C5
Lichte D 91 A9
Lichtenau D 33 C9
Lichtenau D 43 C9
Lichtenau im Waldviertel A 93 E8
Lichtenfels D 91 B9
Lichtenstein D 95 E12
Lichtentanne D 95 E12
Lichtenvoorde NL 33 E7
Lichtenwörth A 93 G10
Lichterfelde D 100 E5
Lichtervelde B 35 B7
Liči LV 151 B10
Liči LV 151 B10
Lička Jesenica HR 172 C3
Lički Osik HR 172 C3
Licko Lešće HR 172 C3
Licodia Eubea I 75 E6
Licques F 31 F12
Ličupe LV 151 C10
Licurici RO 176 D3
Lida BY 153 F11
LideČko CZ 162 C6
Liden S 119 A12
Lidhult S 103 B12
Lidingö S 115 D10
Lidköping S 107 B13
Lido I 82 B5
Lido Adriano I 82 D5
Lido di Classe I 82 D5
Lido di Foce Verde I 78 E3
Lido di Jesolo I 82 B6
Lido di Metaponto I 77 C7
Lido di Ostia I 78 D2
Lido di Siponto I 79 D9
Lido di Spina I 82 C5
Lidoríki GR 190 B5
Lidsälen S 118 A6
Lidsjöberg S 122 C4
Lidumnieki LV 149 C3
Lidzbark PL 155 D8
Lidzbark Warmiński PL 152 E2
Liebenau D 95 B7
Liebenau D 94 A6
Liebenburg D 95 B7
Liebenfels A 89 C9
Liebenwalde D 100 E4
Lieberose D 96 C6
Liebertwolkwitz D 95 D11
Liebling RO 175 B9
Lieboch A 164 B4
Liebstadt D 96 E5
Liedakkala FIN 135 C13
Liédena E 48 E3
Liedenpohja FIN 139 F11
Liège B 35 C12
Liegi CZ 150 C2
Liehittäjä S 135 B10

Liekokylä FIN 135 C16
Lieksa FIN 141 D14
Lielauce LV 150 C5
Lielbērze LV 150 C6
Lielirbe LV 146 F4
Lieljumprava LV 151 C9
Lielklapari LV 151 C9
Lielmēmele LV 151 C10
Lielvārde LV 151 C9
Lielvircava LV 150 C7
Liempde NL 199 B6
Lien S 121 D15
Lien S 123 E10
Lienden NL 199 B7
Lienen D 33 D9
Lienz A 89 C6
Liepa LV 151 B10
Liepāja LV 150 C2
Liepāre LV 150 C6
Liepas LV 151 D12
Liepe D 100 E5
Liepen D 100 C4
Liepene LV 150 B4
Liepgarten D 100 C6
Liepiņas FIN 133 B11
Lieplaukalē LT 150 E3
Lieplaukē LT 150 E4
Liepna LV 149 B2
Lieponys LT 153 E10
Liepupe LV 151 B8
Lier B 35 B10
Lier N 111 B7
Lierbyen N 111 C12
Liernais F 41 F11
Lierneux B 35 D12
Liesek SK 163 C9
Lieser D 37 E8
Lieshout NL 199 B7
Lieso FIN 143 C12
Liessel NL 32 F5
Liestal CH 43 F8
Liešťany SK 162 D4
Liešti RO 177 B11
Lietavská Lúčka SK 163 C7
Lietekylä FIN 137 D13
Lieto FIN 142 D7
Liétor F 71 B9
Lievestuore FIN 139 F16
Lievoperä FIN 135 F16
Liezen A 89 A9
Liezēre LV 151 B12
Liffol-le-Grand F 42 D4
Lifford IRL 20 F2
Liffré F 39 D8
Lifton GB 28 D6
Ligardes F 49 B6
Līgatne LV 151 B10
Ligist A 89 C11
Lignano Pineta I 89 E7
Lignano Sabbiadoro I 89 E7
Lignan-sur-Orb F 50 D5
Ligné F 39 F9
Ligneuville B 36 D6
Lignières F 45 B9
Ligny-en-Barrois F 42 C3
Ligny-le-Châtel F 41 E10
Ligonchio I 82 D1
Ligota PL 158 C4
Ligowo PL 155 E7
Ligueil F 45 A7
Ligugé F 45 B6
Lihme DK 102 B3
Lihula EST 146 D7
Liiga EST 146 D6
Lijar E 71 E8
Lijeśće BIH 173 B9
Lijeska BIH 174 F3
Lijeva Rijeka MNE 179 D7
Likavka SK 163 D8
Likenäs S 118 E5
Liksna LV 151 E12
Lilaia GR 191 B5
Liland N 126 D6
Liland N 127 D12
Lilaste LV 151 B8
L'Île-Bouchard F 40 F3
L'Île-Rousse F 53 F8
Lilienfeld A 93 F9
Liljendal FIN 143 D15
Liljak BG 181 F10
Lilla DK 102 D4
Lilla Edet S 107 C11
Lillåfors S 134 B6
Lilla Tjärby S 103 B12
Lillby FIN 139 C11
Lille B 32 F3
Lille F 35 C7
Lillebo N 118 C3
Lillebonne F 34 E2
Lillefjord N 129 A11
Lillehammer N 117 D12
Lillesand N 106 C3
Lilleshall GB 27 F7
Lillestrøm N 111 C14
Lille Værløse DK 103 D10
Lillfjäten S 118 C4
Lillhärdal S 118 C4
Lillholmsjö S 121 D16
Lilli EST 147 D13
Lilliesleaf GB 21 D11
Lillkyrka S 114 C8
Lillkågeträsk S 134 E5
Lillögda S 123 C13
Lillpite S 134 D6
Lillroten S 119 A14
Lillsaivis S 134 B4
Lillselet S 132 E5
Lillskog S 119 C9
Lillsved S 118 A7
Lillviken S 125 C11
Lilyache BG 181 C8
Lilyak BG 183 C6
Lima S 118 E5
Limana I 88 D5
Limanköy TR 183 F10

Limanowa PL 160 D1
Limanu RO 171 F3
Limatola I 79 D7
Limavady GB 20 E3
Limay F 40 B6
Limbach D 37 F12
Limbach D 202 C2
Limbach-Oberfrohna D 95 E12
Limbadi I 75 B8
Limbaži LV 151 A9
Limbourg B 36 C5
Limburg an der Lahn D 37 D10
Limburgerhof D 203 C5
Lime DK 102 B5
Limedsforsen S 118 E5
Limenaria GR 187 C7
Limenas GR 187 C7
Limenas Chersonisou GR 194 E9
Limerick IRL 24 C5
Limingen N 121 B15
Liminka S 135 E14
Liminpuro FIN 136 E9
Limmared S 107 D13
Limmen NL 32 C5
Limni GR 191 B7
Limni I 75 D7
Limnochori GR 185 C6
Limoges F 45 D8
Limogne-en-Quercy F 49 B9
Limone Piemonte I 53 C7
Limonest F 46 D6
Limone sul Garda I 85 B10
Limosano I 79 D7
Limoux F 49 D10
Limpias E 56 B6
Lin AL 184 B4
Lind DK 102 C3
Lindas N 116 E2
Lindau D 95 B11
Lindau D 98 A7
Lindau (Bodensee) D 87 B9
Lindberg D 92 D4
Linde DK 102 C2
Lindelse DK 103 F7
Linden D 95 A10
Linden D 98 B5
Lindenberg D 96 B6
Lindenberg D 99 D12
Lindenberg im Allgäu D 87 B9
Lindenfels D 37 E11
Lindern (Oldenburg) D 33 C9
Lindesberg S 113 C13
Lindesnäs S 113 B12
Lindewitt D 98 A6
Lindfield GB 31 E8
Lindholmen S 115 C10
Lindi EST 147 E8
Lindknud DK 102 D4
Lindkoski FIN 143 D15
Lindlar D 37 B8
Lindome S 107 D11
Lindores GB 21 C10
Lindoso P 54 E3
Lindow D 100 E3
Lindsdal S 105 B8
Lindsjö S 105 D11
Lindstedt D 95 A10
Lindved DK 102 D5
Lindwedel D 94 A6
Linge N 116 B5
Lingen (Ems) D 33 C8
Lingenfeld D 37 F10
Lingfield GB 31 E8
Linghed S 119 E10
Linghem S 108 C7
Lingolsheim F 43 C8
Lingrasmo N 127 B9
Linguaglossa I 75 D7
Linguizzetta F 53 G10
Linhares P 60 C5
Liniewo PL 154 B5
Linkmenys LT 151 F11
Linköping S 108 C7
Linksness GB 19 H10
Linkuva LT 151 D9
Linlithgow GB 21 D10
Linna EST 147 E11
Linnamäe EST 146 D7
Linnamäe EST 147 F13
Linnankylä FIN 139 F10
Linneryd S 105 B8
Linnich D 36 C6
Linow D 99 D13
Linsell S 118 B6
Lintula NL 32 D3
Linthal CH 87 D8
Linthe D 95 B12
Lintig D 33 A11
Lintrup DK 102 D4
Lintula FIN 133 C14
Lintzoain E 48 E3
Linum D 99 D13
Linxe F 48 C3
Linyola E 58 D5
Linz A 92 F7
Linz am Rhein D 37 C8
Lioboml UA 157 H10
Liocan MD 169 A9
Liorac-sur-Louyre F 45 F7
Lios Mór IRL 25 D7
Lios Póil IRL 24 D2
Lios Tuathail IRL 24 D4
Lipa BIH 173 E7
Lipa PL 160 B6
Lipăneşti RO 177 C8
Lipany SK 161 E3
Lipar SRB 174 B4
Lipari I 75 C6
Lipcani MD 169 A9
Lipce Reymontowskie PL 157 C3
Liperi FIN 141 E11
Liphook GB 31 E7
Lipiany PL 101 D7
Lipik HR 165 F6
Lipinki PL 160 D3
Lipinki Łużyckie PL 97 C8
Lipiny PL 97 C9

Lipka PL 101 D12
Lipki Wielkie PL 101 E9
Lipkovo MK 180 E3
Lipljan SRB 180 D3
Lipnica BIH 173 D9
Lipnica PL 101 C12
Lipnica PL 159 E9
Lipnik PL 159 E11
Lipník nad Bečvou CZ 162 B5
Lipniţa RO 177 E11
Lipnita BG 181 C8
Lipno PL 97 C11
Lipno PL 155 E7
Lipolist SRB 174 D4
Liposthey F 48 B4
Lipova RO 169 D10
Lipová SK 162 D5
Lipovac HR 173 B11
Lipovac SRB 180 D4
Lipová-Lázně CZ 93 B12
Lipovǎţ RO 169 D11
Lipovec CZ 93 D11
Lipoveni MD 170 D3
Lipovljani HR 165 F6
Lipovu RO 176 E3
Lipowiec PL 155 D11
Lipowiec Kościelny PL 155 D9
Lipowina PL 155 B8
Lippoldsberg (Wahlsburg) D 94 C6
Lippstadt D 33 C10
Lipsk PL 156 C5
Lipsko PL 157 H5
Liptál CZ 162 C5
Liptovská Kokava SK 163 C9
Liptovská Lúžna SK 163 D8
Liptovská Osada SK 163 C8
Liptovská Teplička SK 163 D9
Liptovské Revúce SK 163 D8
Liptovský Hrádok SK 163 C9
Liptovský Mikuláš SK 163 C9
Lipusz PL 154 B4
Lipůvka CZ 93 D11
Liqenas AL 184 C4
Lirē F 39 F9
Lis AL 184 A3
Lisa RO 168 F5
Lisa RO 176 F6
Lisac BIH 173 D9
Lisac HR 178 D4
Lisacul IRL 22 D5
Lisbane GB 23 C11
Lisbellaw GB 23 D7
Lisboa P 66 B1
Lisburn GB 23 D10
Liscannor IRL 24 C4
Liscarney IRL 22 D3
Liscarroll IRL 24 D5
Lisciano Niccone I 82 F5
Lišĉa Palanka BIH 172 C5
Lişcoteanca RO 177 C11
Lisdoonvarna IRL 22 F4
Liseleje DK 103 C9
Lisets BG 181 C10
Lisewo PL 154 D6
Lisgarode IRL 24 C6
Lisgoold IRL 24 E6
Lisia Góra PL 159 F11
Lisięcice PL 158 F4
Lisieux F 39 B12
Lisiy Nos RUS 145 E13
Liskeard GB 28 E6
Lisková SK 163 C8
Lisków PL 158 C5
Lisky UA 171 C4
Lisle F 45 E7
Lislea GB 20 F3
L'Isle-Adam F 41 B7
L'Isle-de-Noé F 49 C6
L'Isle-d'Espagnac F 45 D6
L'Isle-en-Dodon F 49 D7
L'Isle-Jourdain F 45 C7
L'Isle-Jourdain F 49 C7
L'Isle-sur-la-Sorgue F 51 C9
L'Isle-sur-le-Doubs F 42 F6
L'Isle-sur-Serein F 41 E11
Lisle-sur-Tarn F 49 C9
Lismacaffry IRL 23 E8
Lisma FIN 133 B14
Lismanaapa FIN 133 D17
Lismarka N 117 D13
Lismore GB 20 B6
Lisnagry IRL 24 C5
Lisnakill IRL 25 D8
Lisnarrick GB 23 D7
Lisnaskea GB 23 D8
Lisne UA 170 E4
Lišov CZ 93 C7
Lisów PL 158 F6
Lispole IRL 24 D2
Lisronagh IRL 25 D7
Lisryan IRL 23 E8
Liss GB 31 E7
Lissan GB 20 F3
Lisse NL 32 D3
Lissendorf D 201 D6
Lisskogsbränden S 113 A10
Lissone I 84 B6
Lissycasey IRL 24 C4
List D 102 E2
Listed DK 105 E8
Listerby S 105 C8
Listerlin IRL 25 D8
Listowel IRL 24 D4
Listrac-Médoc F 44 E4
Listry IRL 24 D3
Liszki PL 159 F8
Liszkowo PL 101 D12
Lit S 121 E15
Lita RO 176 F5
Litakovo BG 181 D8
Litava SK 163 E8
Litene LV 149 B3
Liteni RO 169 B9
Litér H 165 B9
Lit-et-Mixe F 48 B3
Lith NL 199 B6
Lithakia GR 190 D2
Lithi GR 193 C7
Lithines GR 195 E11
Litija SLO 89 D10
Litke H 163 E9
Litlefjord N 129 B14
Litmalahti FIN 141 E9
Litmaniemi FIN 141 E10
Litochoro GR 185 D8
Litoměřice CZ 92 A6
Litomyšl CZ 93 C10
Litovel CZ 93 C12

Litschau A 93 E8
Littau CH 86 C6
Littleborough GB 27 D7
Littlehampton GB 31 F7
Littlemill GB 19 K9
Littlemore GB 29 B12
Little Oakley GB 31 D11
Littleport GB 31 C9
Littlestone-on-Sea GB 31 F10
Littleton IRL 25 C7
Littoinen FIN 142 E7
Litva BIH 173 D10
Litvínov CZ 96 E5
Liu-brani F 202 C3
Liudvinavas LT 153 E7
Liukkunen FIN 141 D14
Livada RO 161 H7
Livada RO 167 C3
Livadáki GR 190 D4
Livadeia GR 191 C6
Livădeni MD 169 A11
Livadero GR 185 D6
Livadero GR 187 B6
Livadi GR 191 E10
Livadi GR 191 E10
Livadia GR 185 D7
Livanates GR 191 B7
Līvāni LV 151 D12
Livari MNE 179 E7
Livarot F 39 D12
Livbērze LV 150 C6
Livernon F 49 A9
Liverpool GB 26 E6
Livezeni RO 168 D5
Livezi RO 169 E9
Livezi RO 168 C5
Livezile RO 168 C5
Livezile RO 175 D10
Līvi LV 151 B10
Livigno I 87 D10
Livingston GB 21 D10
Livino BIH 173 F7
Livo FIN 135 C17
Livold SLO 89 E10
Livonniska FIN 137 C10
Livorno I 82 E1
Livorno Ferraris I 84 C5
Livron-sur-Drôme F 46 F4
Livža LV 149 C4
Liw PL 155 F12
Lixing-lès-St-Avold F 202 C2
Lixnaw IRL 24 D4
Lixouri GR 190 C1
Lizard GB 28 F4
Lizarraga E 48 E1
Lizdēni LV 147 F10
Lizums LV 151 B12
Lizy-sur-Ourcq F 41 B9
Lizzanello I 77 C10
Lizzano I 77 C8
Ljaljenča BIH 173 C11
Lješane SRB 179 D9
Ljeskove Vode BIH 173 C8
Ljig SRB 174 E5
Ljønes N 124 B8
Ljørdal N 118 D4
Ljosland N 106 B1
Ljøsne N 116 D7
Ljuberađa SRB 180 C5
Ljubinje BIH 178 D5
Ljubija BIH 172 C5
Ljubina HR 173 D10
Ljubogošta BIH 173 E10
Ljubovija SRB 174 E3
Ljubuški BIH 173 F8
Ljugarn S 109 E13
Ljung S 107 C13
Ljungå S 119 A11
Ljungaverk S 119 A12
Ljungby S 103 B13
Ljungby S 125 F15
Ljungbyhed S 103 C10
Ljungbyholm S 105 B10
Ljungdalen S 118 A4
Ljungsarp S 107 D14
Ljungsbro S 108 B7
Ljungskile S 107 C10
Ljupina HR 173 B9
Ljuša BIH 173 D7
Ljuså S 134 C7
Ljusdal S 119 C11
Ljusfallshammar S 108 B7
Ljusne S 119 D13
Ljusnedal S 118 A4
Ljustorp S 119 A13
Ljusträsk S 134 C3
Ljusvattnet S 134 E6
Ljuti Dolac BIH 173 F8
Ljutomer SLO 164 C6
Llagostera S 59 D9
Llamas de la Ribera E 55 C8
Llanaelhaearn GB 26 F3
Llanarth GB 28 A6
Llananhney GB 28 B6
Llanbadarn Fawr GB 28 A6
Llanbadrig GB 26 E3
Llanbedr GB 26 F3
Llanbedrog GB 26 F3
Llanberis GB 26 E3
Llanbister GB 29 A8
Llanblethian GB 29 B7
Llançà E 50 F5
Llandanwg GB 26 F3
Llandderfel GB 26 F6
Llandeilo GB 28 B7
Llandissilio GB 28 B5
Llandovery GB 29 B7
Llandrillo GB 26 F6
Llandrindod Wells GB 29 A8
Llandudno GB 26 E5
Llandysul GB 28 A6
Llanegwad GB 28 B6
Llanelian GB 26 E5
Llanelli GB 28 B6
Llanelltyd GB 26 F5
Llanes E 55 B10
Llanfaelog GB 26 E3
Llanfair Caereinion GB 26 F5
Llanfairfechan GB 26 E4
Llanfair-pwllgwyngyll GB 26 E4
Llanfair Talhaiarn GB 26 E5
Llanfihangel-ar-arth GB 28 A6
Llanfyllin GB 26 F5
Llangadfan GB 26 F5
Llangadog GB 28 B7
Llangefni GB 26 E3
Llangeler GB 28 A6
Llangelynin GB 26 F3

Llangoed GB 26 E3
Llangollen GB 26 F5
Llangurig GB 29 A7
Llangynidr GB 29 B8
Llanidloes GB 29 A7
Llanilar GB 28 A6
Llanishen GB 29 B8
Llanllwchaiarn GB 26 F5
Llanllyfni GB 26 E4
Llannerch-y-medd GB 26 E3
Llan-non GB 28 A6
Llannon GB 28 B6
Llanrhaeadr-ym-Mochnant GB 26 F5
Llanrhidian GB 28 B6
Llanrhystud GB 28 A6
Llanrug GB 26 E4
Llanrumney GB 29 B8
Llanrwst GB 26 E4
Llansanffraid Glan Conwy GB 26 E4
Llansannan GB 26 E4
Llansawel GB 28 A6
Llantilio Pertholey GB 29 B8
Llantrisant GB 29 B8
Llantwit Major GB 29 C8
Llanuwchllyn GB 26 F4
Llanwddyn GB 26 F5
Llanwenog GB 28 A6
Llanwnda GB 26 E3
Llanwnog GB 26 F5
Llanwrtyd Wells GB 29 A7
Llanybydder GB 28 A6
Llardecans E 58 E5
Llaurí E 64 F4
Llavorsí E 49 E8
Llay GB 26 E5
Lledrod GB 28 A7
Llera E 67 C7
Llerena E 67 C7
Lliria E 64 F3
Llívia E 49 F9
Llodio E 56 B6
Llombai E 64 F3
Lloret de Mar E 59 D9
Lloseta E 65 E10
Llubí E 73 B11
Llucmajor E 73 C10
Lniano PL 154 C5
Lo B 34 C6
Loamnes RO 168 F4
Loano I 53 C8
Loarre E 48 F4
Löbau D 97 D7
Lobbæk DK 105 E7
Lobe LV 151 C10
Löbejün D 95 C10
Lobera de Onsella E 48 F3
Loběrği LV 147 F12
Łobez PL 101 C9
Lobith NL 199 B8
Löbnitz D 99 B13
Łobodno RO 159 E6
Lobón E 67 B6
Lobonäs S 119 C9
Loburg D 95 B11
Łobżenica PL 101 D12
Locana I 47 E11
Locarno CH 84 A6
Locate di Triulzi I 85 C7
Loccum (Rehburg-Loccum) D 33 D12
Loceri I 80 D4
Lochaline GB 20 B5
Lochau A 87 B9
Lochawe GB 20 C6
Lochboisdale GB 18 L2
Lochcarron GB 18 L5
Lochdon GB 20 C5
Lochearnhead GB 21 C8
Lochem NL 32 D6
Lochen A 92 F4
Lochend GB 19 L8
Loches F 40 F4
Loch Garman IRL 25 D10
Lochgelly GB 21 C10
Lochgilphead GB 20 C6
Lochgoilhead GB 20 C7
Lochinver GB 18 J6
Lochmaben GB 21 E10
Lochmaddy GB 18 K2
Lochovice CZ 92 C5
Łochów PL 155 E12
Lochranza GB 20 D6
Lochristi B 35 B8
Loch Sgioport GB 18 L2
Lockenhaus A 165 B6
Lockerbie GB 21 E10
Lockne S 122 E7
Löcknitz D 100 D6
Locks Heath GB 29 D12
Lockton GB 27 C10
Locmaria-Plouzané F 38 D2
Locmariaquer F 38 E6
Locminé F 38 E6
Locorotondo I 77 B8
Locquirec F 38 C4
Locri I 75 C9
Loctudy F 38 E3
Loculi I 80 C4
Löddeköpinge S 103 D12
LöddeN D 95 C10
Loddin D 100 B6
Lødding N 121 B10
Loddiswell GB 29 E7
Loddon GB 31 B11
Lodè I 80 B4
Lode LV 151 B10
Loděnice CZ 92 B6
Löderup S 104 E6
Lodève F 50 C5
Lodi I 85 C8
Løding N 124 B8
Lødingen N 127 D10
Lodi Vecchio I 85 C7
Lodosa E 48 F1
Lödöse S 107 C11
Łodygowice PL 163 B8
Łódź PL 159 C7
Loeches E 62 D6
Loenen NL 199 A8
Löf D 37 D8
Løfallstrand N 110 B4
Lofer A 89 A6
Löffingen D 43 E9
Lofos GR 185 D7
Lofsdalen S 118 B5
Loftahammar S 109 D9
Lofthus N 110 B4
Lofthus N 127 C10
Loftus GB 27 B10

Log SLO 89 D8
Loga N 110 F5
Logan GB 21 E8
Logatec SLO 89 E9
Lögda S 123 C14
Lögdeå S 123 D16
Loggerheads GB 27 F7
Loghill IRL 24 C4
Logkanikos GR 190 E5
Logofteni MD 169 B11
Logreşti RO 176 D3
Logroño E 57 D7
Logrosán E 61 F10
Løgstør DK 102 B4
Løgstrup DK 102 B4
Løgten DK 102 B6
Løgumkloster DK 102 E3
Lohals DK 103 E7
Lohberg D 92 D4
Lohéac F 39 E8
Lohe-Rickelshof D 98 B6
Lohfelden D 94 D6
Lohijärvi FIN 135 B12
Lohilahti FIN 141 F11
Lohiluoma FIN 138 E8
Lohiniva FIN 133 C13
Lohiranta FIN 137 B12
Lohja FIN 143 E11
Lohja kunta FIN 143 E11
Lohmar D 37 C8
Lohme D 100 A5
Lohmen D 96 E6
Lohmen D 99 C12
Löhnberg D 37 C10
Löhne D 33 D11
Lohne (Oldenburg) D 33 C10
Lohra D 37 C11
Lohr am Main D 90 C6
Lohsa D 96 D6
Lohtaja FIN 139 B11
Lohusuu EST 147 D14
Loiano I 82 D3
Loigny-la-Bataille F 40 D6
Loimaa FIN 143 D9
Loimaan kunta FIN 143 D8
Loiré F 39 E10
Loiri-Porto San Paolo I 80 B3
Loiron F 39 D10
Loisy-sur-Marne F 41 C12
Loitz D 100 C4
Loivos I 54 E5
Loivos do Monte P 60 B5
Loja E 69 B8
Loja LV 151 B9
Løjt Kirkeby DK 102 E4
Loka brunn S 113 C11
Lokakylä FIN 139 D14
Lokalahti FIN 142 D5
Lokavec SLO 89 E8
Lokca SK 163 C8
Loke S 122 F7
Løken N 111 C14
Lokeren B 35 B9
Loket CZ 91 B12
Lokev SLO 89 E9
Lokka FIN 131 C3
Løkken DK 106 A6
Løkken N 120 E7
Lokkiperä FIN 139 C13
Łőkösháza H 167 E7
Lokrume S 109 D13
Loksa EST 147 B11
Løksa N 127 C14
Løksebotn N 127 C14
Lokuta EST 147 D9
Lokuti EST 147 C9
Lokve HR 83 B10
Lokve SLO 89 D8
Lokve SRB 159 C7
Løkvoll N 128 D6
Lolishniy Shepit UA 168 A6
Lollar D 37 C11
L'Olleria E 72 D3
Lom BG 175 F11
Lom N 117 C9
Łomazy PL 157 G8
Lombez F 49 C7
Lombheden S 135 B9
Lomborg DK 102 B2
Lomello I 84 C6
Lomen N 117 D9
Łomianki PL 155 E11
Lomma S 103 D12
Lommatzsch D 96 D4
Lomme F 34 C6
Lommel B 35 B11
Łomnica PL 97 B9
Lomnice CZ 93 D10
Lomnice nad Lužnicí CZ 93 D7
Lomnice nad Popelkou CZ 93 A8

Longhoughton GB 21 E13
Long Itchington GB 29 A12
Longlier B 35 E11
Long Melford GB 31 C10
Longmorn GB 19 K10
Longny-au-Perche F 40 C4
Longobardi I 76 E6
Longobucco I 77 E7
Longomel P 60 F5
Longos GR 184 F3
Longos Vales P 54 D3
Long Preston GB 27 C7
Longré F 44 C5
Longridge GB 26 D6
Longroiva P 61 C6
Long Stratton GB 31 C11
Long Sutton GB 27 F12
Longton GB 26 D6
Longtown GB 21 E11
Longueau F 34 E5
Longué-Jumelles F 39 F11
Longuenesse F 34 C5
Longueville F 41 C9
Longueville-sur-Scie F 34 E3
Longuyon F 35 E12
Longwood IRL 23 F9
Longwy F 35 E12
Lonigo I 82 B3
Lonin N 111 C10
Löningen D 33 C9
Lonjica HR 165 E6
Lonkan N 126 C9
Lonkka FIN 137 D13
Lonlay-l'Abbaye F 39 D10
Lönneberga S 108 D7
Lonneker NL 199 A9
Lonny F 200 E2
Lons F 48 D5
Lönsboda S 104 C6
Lonsee D 90 E6
Lons-le-Saunier F 47 B8
Lønstrup DK 106 E6
Lontzen B 199 D8
Lónya H 161 G5
Loo EST 147 C9
Loon op Zand NL 32 E4
Loosdorf A 93 F8
Loose GB 31 E10
Lopadea Nouă RO 168 E3
Lopar HR 83 C10
Lopare BIH 173 D10
Lopate MK 180 E4
Lopatica MK 184 B5
Łopatki PL 159 C7
Lopatnic MD 169 A10
Lopatovo RUS 148 F4
Lopcombe Corner GB 29 C11
Löpe EST 147 D7
Lopera E 69 A8
Łopiennik Górny PL 160 A7
Lopigna F 53 G9
Łopik NL 198 B5
Loppa N 128 C7
Loppersum NL 33 B7
Loppi FIN 143 D11
Lopra FO 18 C3
Lopushna UA 168 A6
Łopuszno PL 159 D9
Lopyan BG 181 D9
Lora N 117 B9
Lora del Río E 67 D8
Loranca de Tajuña E 63 D6
Loràs S 122 E8
Lörby S 104 C7
Lorca E 71 D9
Lorch D 37 D9
Lorch D 90 E6
Lorcha E 72 D4
Lordelo P 54 F4
Lordosa P 60 C5
Lørenskog N 111 C13
Loreo I 82 B5
Loreto I 83 F8
Loreto Aprutino I 78 C5
Lorgues F 52 D4
Lorient F 38 E5
Lorignac F 44 E4
Loriguilla E 64 E3
Lőrinci H 166 B4
Loriol-sur-Drôme F 46 F6
Lormes F 41 F10
Louveigné B 199 D7
Lormont F 44 E5
Lorquin F 202 C2
Lorris F 41 E8
Lorsch D 37 E11
Lørslev DK 106 E7
Lørstrand S 119 C11
Lörrstrand S 123 A10
Lorup D 33 C9
Lorupe LV 151 B9
Los S 119 E12
Losacino E 55 E7
Losa del Obispo E 64 E3
Los Alcázares E 72 F3
Los Algezares E 72 F2
Los Arcos E 48 E1
Losar de la Vera E 61 D9
Los Arenales del Sol E 72 E4
Los Barrios E 69 D6
Los Barrios de Luna E 55 C8
Los Belones E 72 F3
Los Cantareros E 71 D10
Los Corrales E 69 B7
Los Corrales de Buelna E 56 B3
Loscos E 58 E1
Los Dolores E 72 F2
Løset N 117 D14
Los Gallardos E 71 E9
Loshchynivka UA 171 C3
Losheim D 37 E7
Los Hinojosos E 63 E7
Łosice PL 157 F7
Łosiów PL 158 E4
Los Maldonados E 72 F2
Los Molinos E 62 D4
Losna N 117 D12
Los Navalmorales E 62 E3
Los Navalucillos E 62 E3
Løsning DK 102 D5
Losomäki FIN 141 D11
Losone CH 84 A6
Łososina Dolna PL 160 D2
Losova MD 170 C2
Losovaara FIN 137 E11

Los Palacios y Villafranca E 67 E8
Los Pandos E 56 B4
Los Pedrones E 63 F10
Los Pozuelos de Calatrava E 70 B5
Los Rábanos E 57 E7
Los Royos E 71 D9
Los Santos E 61 C9
Los Santos de Maimona E 67 C7
Loßburg D 43 D9
Losse F 48 B5
Losser NL 33 D7
Lossiemouth GB 19 K10
Lößnitz D 95 E12
Lostallo CH 85 A7
Lostice CZ 93 C11
Los Tojos E 56 B3
Lostwithiel GB 28 E5
Los Villares E 69 A9
Los Yébenes E 62 E5
Löt S 105 B11
Lote N 116 C4
Loten N 110 D2
Løten N 117 E14
Lotenhulle B 198 C2
Loth GB 19 G11
Lothmore GB 19 J9
Lotorp S 108 B7
Lotte D 33 D9
Lottefors S 119 D11
Löttorp S 105 A11
Lottstetten D 43 E10
Lottum NL 199 C8
Lotyń PL 101 C11
Lotzorai I 80 D4
Louannec F 38 C5
Louargat F 38 C5
Loučeň CZ 93 B8
Loučná nad Desnou CZ 93 B12
Loučovice CZ 93 E7
Loudéac F 38 D6
Loudes F 46 E4
Loudun F 44 A6
Loué F 39 E11
Loue FIN 135 B13
Louejärvi FIN 135 B13
Louejoki FIN 135 B14
Loughborough GB 27 F9
Loughbrickland GB 23 D10
Lougher IRL 24 D3
Loughgall GB 23 D9
Loughglinn IRL 22 E5
Loughton GB 31 D9
Lougratte F 49 A7
Louhans F 47 B7
Louka CZ 162 D4
Loukas GR 190 D5
Loukisia GR 191 C7
Loukkojärvi FIN 135 D15
Loukusa FIN 137 C10
Loulans F 42 F5
Loulay F 44 C4
Loulé P 66 E3
Louny CZ 92 B5
Loupiac F 48 A5
Lourdes F 48 D5
Lourdoueix-St-Pierre F 45 C9
Louriçal P 60 D3
Lourinhã P 60 F2
Louros GR 190 A2
Loury F 40 E7
Lousã P 60 D4
Lousa P 66 B1
Lousada P 54 F3
Louth GB 27 E11
Louth IRL 23 E9
Loutra GR 191 E9
Loutra GR 193 A8
Loutra Aidipsou GR 191 B7
Loutra Eleftheron GR 186 C6
Loutraki GR 185 C6
Loutraki GR 190 B3
Loutraki GR 191 D6
Loutra Kyllinis GR 190 D3
Loutra Smokovou GR 190 A5
Loutra Ypatis GR 190 B5
Loutro GR 185 E6
Loutro GR 190 B3
Loutros GR 187 C10
Louvain B 35 C10
Louvain B 198 D5
Louveigné B 199 D7
Louverné F 39 D10
Louvie-Juzon F 48 D5
Louviers F 34 F3
Louvigné-du-Désert F 39 D9
Louvroil F 35 D8
Louze F 41 D12
Lov DK 103 E9
Lövånger S 134 F6
Lövåsen S 123 C10
Lovas HR 173 B10
Lovasberény H 165 B11
Lovászi H 165 C7
Lovászpatona H 165 B9
Lovberg S 122 A7
Lövberga S 123 D9
Lovčenac SRB 174 F4
Lovčica-Trubín SK 163 D7
Løve DK 103 E8
Lovech BG 181 C10
Løvel DK 102 B4
Lovendegem B 35 B8
Lovere I 85 B9
Lovero I 85 A9
Lövestad S 104 D5
Loviisa FIN 143 C15
Lovik N 127 C10
Lovikka S 132 D9
Lovinac HR 172 D4
Lovinobaňa SK 163 E9
Lovisa FIN 143 E15
Loviště HR 173 F7
Lovliden S 123 B11
Løvlund N 117 C10
Lövnäs S 118 D5
Lövnäs S 123 B9
Lövnäs S 125 D14
Lövnäsvallen S 118 C6
Lovnidol BG 182 D4
Lövő H 165 A7
Lovosice CZ 96 E6
Lovraeid N 110 D4
Lovran HR 83 B8
Lovreč HR 173 F7
Lovreć HR 173 F7
Lovrenc SLO 164 C4
Lovrin RO 166 B6
Lövsele N 134 F6
Lövsjö S 122 B8
Lövsjön S 113 B13

Lövstabruk S 115 B9
Lövstalöt S 115 C9
Lövstrand S 123 C10
Lovund N 124 D3
Lövvik S 119 A15
Lövvik S 123 C9
Löwenberg D 100 E4
Löwenberg D 100 E4
Löwenstein D 43 B11
Lower Ballinderry GB 23 C10
Lower Cam GB 29 B10
Lower Kilchattan GB 20 C4
Lowestoft GB 31 C12
Lowick GB 21 D13
Lößnitz D 95 E12
Lostallo CH 85 A7
Łowicz PL 157 F1
Low Street GB 31 B11
Łowyń PL 97 B9
Loxstedt D 33 B11
Löyä FIN 139 E11
Loyettes F 47 D7
Loymola RUS 145 B16
Löytö FIN 144 F2
Löytökylä FIN 135 D16
Löytövaara FIN 137 C11
Lozarevo BG 183 D7
Lozen BG 181 D7
Lozen BG 183 E9
Lozenets BG 183 E9
Loznica RO 167 C11
Löttorp S 105 A11
Löttstetten D 43 E10
Loznitsa BG 171 F1
Loznitsa BG 183 C12
Lozorno SK 93 F12
Lozovac HR 172 E4
Lozovik SRB 175 E7
Lozoya E 62 C5
Lozoyuela E 62 C5
Lozuvata UA 170 A6
Lozzo di Cadore I 88 D5
Lü IRL 23 E11
Luanco E 55 A8
Luarca E 55 A6
Lubań PL 97 D8
Lubanowo PL 100 D7
Lübars D 95 B11
Lubartów PL 157 H7
Lubasz PL 101 E11
Łubawa PL 155 C8
Lubawka PL 97 E10
Lübbecke D 33 D9
Lubbeek B 35 C10
Lübben D 96 C5
Lübbenau D 96 C5
Lübbow D 99 E10
Lubczyna PL 101 C7
Lube LV 150 B5
Lubčeła SK 163 C8
Lübeck D 99 C9
Lubenec CZ 92 B4
Lübenik SK 161 F1
Lubersac F 45 E8
Lübesse D 99 D10
Lubezere LV 150 B5
Lubiaj LT 150 E3
Lubián E 55 D6
Łubianka PL 154 D6
Lubichowo PL 154 C5
Lubicz Dolny PL 154 D6
Lubięcin PL 97 C9
Lubień PL 163 B9
Lubień Kujawski PL 155 F7
Lubieszów PL 101 D9
Lubiń PL 97 C11
Lubin PL 97 D10
Lubiszyn PL 101 E7
Lublin PL 157 H7
Lubliniec PL 158 E6
Lubmin D 100 B5
Lubnia PL 154 C4
Lubniany PL 158 E5
Lubnice PL 159 F11
Lubniewice PL 97 A8
Łubno PL 101 D10
Łubno PL 159 B7
Lubochnia PL 157 G2
Lubomierz PL 97 D9
Lubomino PL 155 B9
Luboń PL 97 B11
Luborzyca PL 159 F9
Łubotice SK 161 E3
Łubowidz PL 155 D8
Łubowo PL 101 C11
Łubowo PL 101 E12
Lubraniec PL 154 E6
Lubrín E 71 E8
Lubrza PL 97 B8
Lubrza PL 158 F4
Lubsko PL 97 C7
Lübstorf D 99 C10
Lubstów PL 154 F5
Lubsza PL 158 E4
Lübtheen D 99 D10
Luby CZ 91 B11
Lubycza Królewska PL 160 C8
Lübz D 99 D12
Luc F 49 B11
Luc F 51 A6
Lucainena de las Torres E 71 E8
Lucan IRL 23 F10
Lucani SRB 174 F5
Lúcar E 71 E8
Luçay-le-Mâle F 40 F5
Lucca I 82 E2
Lucca Sicula I 74 D3
Lucé F 40 D5
LucEa F 53 G10
Lucena E 69 B8
Lucena de Jalón E 57 E9
Lucena del Cid E 64 D4
Lucena del Puerto E 67 E6
Lucenay-lès-Aix F 46 B3
Lucenay-l'Évêque F 41 F11
Luc-en-Diois F 51 A9
Lučenec SK 163 E9
Luceni E 57 E9
Lucera I 79 D8
Lucéram F 53 D6
Lucfalva H 163 E9
Luché-Pringé F 39 E12
Luchente E 64 D3
Lüchow D 99 E10
Luchy F 34 E5

Luciana E 70 B4
Lucień PL 155 F7
Lucieni RO 177 D6
Lucignano I 82 F4
Lučine SLO 89 D9
Lucito I 79 D7
Luckau D 96 C5
Luckenwalde D 96 B4
Lucksta S 119 B13
Lučky SK 163 C8
Luco dei Marsi I 78 D4
Luçon F 44 B3
Lucq-de-Béarn F 48 D4
Luc-sur-Mer F 39 B11
Lucy-le-Bois F 41 E10
Ludag GB 18 L2
Ludanice SK 162 E6
Ludányhalászi H 163 E9
Ludbreg HR 165 D7
Lüdenscheid D 37 B9
Lüderitz D 95 A10
Lüdersdorf D 99 C9
Ludeşti RO 176 D6
Ludgershall GB 29 C11
Lüdinghausen D 33 E8
Ludlow GB 29 A9
Ludogortsi BG 177 F9
Ludoni RUS 148 E5
Ludoş RO 168 F3
Ludres F 202 D1
Luduş RO 168 E4
Ludvigsborg S 103 D13
Ludvika S 113 B14
Ludwigsau-Friedlos D 94 E6
Ludwigsburg D 43 C11
Ludwigsfelde D 96 B4
Ludwigshafen D 43 E11
Ludwigshafen am Rhein D 37 F10
Ludwigslust D 99 D10
Ludwigsstadt D 91 B9
Ludwin PL 157 H7
Ludza LV 149 C3
Lüe F 48 B4
Luelmo E 55 F7
Lüerdissen D 94 C6
Luesia E 48 F3
Lueta RO 169 E6
Lug BIH 178 D5
Luga RUS 148 D6
Lugagnano Val d'Arda I 85 D8
Lugano CH 85 A6
Lüganuse EST 147 C14
Lugau D 95 E12
Lugaži LV 147 F11
Lügde D 33 E12
Luglon F 48 B4
Lugnano in Teverina I 78 B2
Lugnås S 107 B14
Lugnvik S 119 A14
Lugnvik S 122 E7
Lugny-lès-Charolles F 46 C5
Lugo E 54 B4
Lugo I 82 D4
Lugo-di-Nazza F 53 G10
Lugoj RO 175 B8
Lugones E 55 B8
Lugros E 71 E6
Luhačovice CZ 162 C5
Luhalahti FIN 143 B9
Luhamaa EST 148 F1
Luhanka FIN 143 B14
Luhden D 33 D11
Luhe-Wildenau D 91 C11
Lühmannsdorf D 100 B5
Luhtapohja FIN 141 E15
Luhtikylä FIN 143 D13
Luhy UA 168 A4
Luhy UA 170 A4
Luica RO 177 E9
Luica RO 177 E9
Luik B 35 C12
Luik B 199 D7
Luikonlahti FIN 141 E11
Luimneach IRL 24 C5
Luino I 84 B6
Luintra E 54 D4
Luiro FIN 131 C4
Luiro FIN 131 C3
Luisant F 40 D5
Luizi Călugăra RO 169 D9
Łukowe PL 161 D6
Łukowica PL 161 D1
Łukowisko PL 157 F7
Lukšiai LT 152 D7
Luky UA 161 F7
Lula I 80 C3
Luleå S 134 C8
Luleburgaz TR 189 B7
Lüllemäe EST 147 F12
Lullymore IRL 23 F9
Lümanda EST 146 E4
Lumbier E 48 E3
Lumbrales E 61 C7
Lumbreras E 57 D6
Lumbres F 34 C5
Lumby DK 102 E6
Lumezzane I 85 B9
Lumijoki FIN 135 E14
Lumimetsä FIN 135 F14
Lumina RO 171 E3
Lumio F 53 F9

Lummelunda S 109 D12
Lummen B 35 C11
Lumparland FIN 115 B14
Lumphanan GB 19 L11
Lumpiaque E 57 E9
Lumpzig D 95 E11
Lumsheden S 119 E11
Luna E 57 D10
Luna RO 168 D3
Lunamatrona I 80 D2
Lunano I 82 E5
Lunas E 50 C5
Lunca MD 170 C4
Lunca RO 167 C3
Lunca RO 168 D6
Lunca RO 169 B9
Lunca RO 176 F5
Lunca Banului RO 170 D2
Lunca Bradului RO 168 D6
Lunca Cernii de Jos RO 175 B10
Lunca Corbului RO 176 D5
Lunca de Jos RO 169 D7
Lunca de Sus RO 169 D7
Luncaviţa RO 171 C2
Luncaviţa RO 175 C9
Luncoiu de Jos RO 167 E10
Lund DK 102 D5
Lund N 121 B11
Lund N 126 E8
Lund N 127 C15
Lund S 103 D12
Lundamo N 120 E8
Lundbjörken S 118 E8
Lundby DK 102 F5
Lundby DK 103 E9
Lunde DK 102 D2
Lunde DK 102 E6
Lunde N 111 D10
Lunde N 127 C16
Lunde S 119 A14
Lundeborg DK 103 E7
Lundebyvollen N 118 E8
Lundegård N 110 F6
Lunden D 98 B6
Lundin Links GB 21 C11
Lundsbrunn S 107 C13
Lundsjön S 122 E7
Lünebach D 37 D6
Lüneburg D 99 D8
Lunel F 51 C7
Lünen D 33 E9
Lunery F 45 B10
Lunéville F 42 C5
Lungani RO 169 C11
Lunger S 113 D14
Lungern CH 86 D6
Lungro I 76 D6
Lungsjön S 123 C10
Lunguleţu RO 177 D7
Lunino RUS 150 E6
L'Union F 49 C8
Lunkkaus FIN 131 D3
Lunna BY 156 D10
Lunnäset S 118 A5
Lünne D 33 D8
Lunneborg N 127 B16
Lunow D 100 E6
Lunteren NL 199 A7
Luogosanto I 80 A3
Luohua FIN 135 E14
Luoke LT 150 E5
Luokkala FIN 135 C15
Luola-aapa FIN 135 C15
Luoma-aho FIN 139 D11
Luopa FIN 138 E9
Luopajärvi FIN 138 E9
Luopioinen FIN 143 C12
Luostari RUS 130 E10
Luosto FIN 131 D1
Luosu FIN 133 C12
Luotolahti FIN 144 C8
Luovankylä FIN 138 F7
Luovttejohka N 129 C21
Lupac RO 175 C8
Lupandi LV 149 E3
Łupawa PL 101 B12
Lupeni RO 168 E8
Lupeni RO 175 C11
Lupiac F 49 C6
Lupiñén E 57 D10
Lupión E 69 A6
Łupków PL 161 E5
Lupoglav HR 83 B9
Łupowo PL 101 E8
Luppa D 96 D3
Luppoperä FIN 137 D9
Luppy F 42 C5
Lupşa RO 167 E11
Lupşanu RO 177 E10
Luque E 69 A8
Luras I 80 B3
Lurbe-St-Christau F 48 D4
Lurcy-Lévis F 46 B2
Lure F 42 E5
Lurgan GB 23 D10
Lurgan IRL 22 E6
Lurí F 53 F10
Lurøy N 124 D4
Lurs F 51 C10
Lurudal N 121 C13
Lury-sur-Arnon F 40 F7
Lusca IRL 23 F11
Lusciano I 76 B2
Luserna San Giovanni I 47 F11
Lushnjë AL 184 C2
Lusi FIN 143 C15
Lusignan F 45 C6
Lusigny-sur-Barse F 41 D11
Lusk IRL 23 E11
Lus-la-Croix-Haute F 51 A10
Lusminki FIN 137 C14
Lusnić BIH 173 E6
Luso P 60 D4
Luspa FIN 132 B8
Luspebryggan S 125 B18
Lussac F 45 F5
Lussac-les-Châteaux F 45 C7
Lussac-les-Églises F 45 C8
Lussan F 51 B7
Lüssow D 99 C12
Lusta GB 18 K3
Lustad N 121 C12
Lustadt D 203 C5
Lustenau A 87 C9
Luster N 116 D6
Lustivere EST 147 D12
Łuszkowo PL 97 B11
Luszyn PL 159 B8
Lutago I 88 C4
Lütau D 99 D9
Lütetsburg D 33 A8

Lutherstadt Wittenberg D 95 C12
Lütjenburg D 99 B9
Lutnes N 118 D4
Lutocin PL 155 E8
Lutomiersk PL 159 C7
Luton GB 31 D8
Lutowiska PL 161 E6
Lutriņi LV 150 C4
Lutry PL 152 E2
Luttenberg NL 199 A8
Lutter am Barenberge D 95 C7
Lutterbach F 43 E7
Lutterworth GB 29 A12
Lututów PL 158 D5
Lützelbach D 37 E12
Lützen D 95 D11
Lutzerath D 37 D8
Lutzingen D 91 E8
Lutzmannsburg A 165 B7
Lützow D 99 C10
Luua EST 147 D13
Luujoki FIN 135 C14
Luukkola FIN 145 C9
Luukkonen FIN 145 B9
Luumäen kk FIN 144 D8
Luumäki FIN 144 D8
Luunja EST 147 E13
Luupujoki FIN 139 C17
Luupuvesi FIN 139 C17
Luusniemi FIN 140 G7
Luusua FIN 131 F2
Luvia FIN 142 C6
Luvos S 125 C16
Lux F 42 F3
Luxembourg L 36 E6
Luxe-Sumberraute F 48 D3
Luxeuil-les-Bains F 42 E5
Luxey F 48 B4
Luyego de Somoza E 55 D7
Luyksgestel NL 199 C6
Luz P 66 E2
Luz P 66 E4
Luz P 67 C5
Luzaga E 63 C8
Lužani HR 173 B8
Luzarches F 41 B7
Luz-Ardiden F 48 E5
Luže CZ 93 C10
Luzech F 49 B8
Lužec nad Vltavou CZ 92 B6
Luzenac F 49 E9
Luzern CH 86 C6
Luzhany UA 169 A7
Luzhki BY 149 F3
Luzianes P 66 D3
Luz i Madh AL 184 B2
Luzino PL 154 A5
Luzmela E 56 B3
Łużna PL 160 D3
Lūžņas LV 146 F3
Lūznava LV 149 D2
Luzón E 63 B8
Luz-St-Sauveur F 48 E6
Luzy F 46 B4
Luzzara I 82 C2
Luzzi I 76 E6
L'viv UA 160 D9
Lwówek PL 97 B10
Lwówek Śląski PL 97 D9
Lyady RUS 148 D4
Lyaskelya RUS 145 B15
Lyaskovets BG 182 C5
Lyavoshki BY 149 E2
Lybokhora UA 161 F6
Lybster GB 19 J10
Lychen D 100 D4
Lycksaberg S 123 A14
Lycksele S 123 B15
Lydd GB 31 F10
Lyderslev DK 103 E10
Lydford GB 28 D6
Lydney GB 29 B9
Lyeninski BY 157 F10
Lyfjord N 127 A16
Lygna N 111 B13
Lygumai LT 150 D7
Lykofi GR 187 B10
Lykoporia GR 191 C6
Lyly FIN 143 B11
Lylykylä FIN 137 E11
Lyman UA 171 B5
Lymans'ke UA 170 D5
Lymans'ke UA 171 C2
Lyme Regis GB 29 D9
Lymington GB 29 D11
Lymm GB 26 E7
Lynäs S 119 D12
Lyndhurst GB 29 D11
Lyne DK 102 D3
Lyneham GB 29 B11
Lynemore GB 19 L9
Lyness GB 19 H10
Lyngby DK 103 C7
Lyngdal N 110 F6
Lyngmoen N 128 D5
Lyngså DK 102 A7
Lyngseidet N 127 A19
Lyngsnes N 121 B10
Lynmouth GB 29 C7
Lynton GB 29 C7
Lyntupy BY 153 C13
Lyökki FIN 142 D5
Lyon F 46 D6
Lyons-la-Forêt F 34 F3
Lyrestad S 107 B15
Lyrkeia GR 191 D6
Lysabild DK 102 F6
Lysá pod Makytou SK 162 C6
Lyse PL 155 D12
Lysebotn N 110 D5
Lysekil S 107 C9
Lyshchytsy BY 157 F9
Lysice CZ 93 D11
Lysnes N 127 B14
Łysomice PL 154 D6
Lysøysund N 120 D7
Lysroll N 127 D11
Lyss CH 47 A11
Lysvik S 113 B9
Łyszkowice PL 157 G1
Lytchett Minster GB 29 D10
Lytham St Anne's GB 26 D5
Lytovezh UA 160 B9
Lyubashivka UA 170 B6
Lyuben BG 181 E10
Lyubimets BG 182 F6
Lyublino RUS 152 D1
Lyubomyrka UA 170 B4
Lyubyntsi UA 161 E8
Lyulyakovo BG 183 D8

M

Maakeski FIN 143 C13
Maalahti FIN 138 E7
Maalismaa FIN 135 D15
Maam IRL 22 E3
Maaninka FIN 140 D8
Maaninkavaara FIN 131 F4
Maanselkä FIN 141 C10
Maaralanpera FIN 139 C16
Maardu EST 147 B10
Maarheeze NL 199 C7
Maaria FIN 142 D7
Maarianvaara FIN 141 E11
Maarn NL 199 A6
Maarssen NL 32 D4
Maarssenbroek NL 199 A6
Maas IRL 22 C6
Maasbracht NL 35 B12
Maasbree NL 32 F6
Maasdam NL 198 B5
Maaseik B 35 B12
Maaselkä FIN 137 F14
Maasen D 33 C11
Maasland NL 32 E2
Maasmechelen B 35 C12
Maassluis NL 32 E2
Maastricht NL 35 C12
Määttälä FIN 139 C12
Määttälänvaara FIN 137 B14
Maavesi FIN 140 F9
Mablethorpe GB 27 E12
Macael E 71 E8
Maçanet de Cabrenys E 50 F4
Maçanet de la Selva E 59 D9
Mação P 60 E5
Măcăreşti MD 169 C11
Macastre E 64 F3
Maccagno I 84 A6
Macchiagodena I 79 D6
Macclesfield GB 27 E7
Macduff GB 19 K12
Macea RO 167 E7
Maceda E 54 D4
Maceda P 60 C3
Macedo de Cavaleiros P 55 E6
Maceira P 60 C6
Maceira P 60 E3
Macelj HR 164 D5
Macerata I 83 F7
Macerata Feltria I 82 E5
Măceşu de Jos RO 176 F3
Măceşu de Sus RO 176 F3
Machados P 66 C5
Machairas GR 190 B3
Machault F 35 F10
Machecoul F 44 B2
Machelen B 198 D4
Machen GB 29 B8
Machern D 95 D12
Machliny PL 101 D10
Machov CZ 93 A10
Machowa PL 159 F11
Machrihanish GB 20 E5
Machynlleth GB 26 F4
Maciejowice PL 157 G5
Măcin RO 171 C2
Macinaggio F 53 F10
Măciuca RO 176 D4
Mačkatica SRB 180 D5
Mackenbach D 37 F9
Mackenrode D 95 C8
Mačkovci SLO 164 C6
Macomer I 80 C2
Mâcon F 46 C6
Macosquin GB 20 E3
Macotera E 61 C10
Macroom IRL 24 E5
Macugnaga I 84 B4
Mačvanska Mitrovica SRB 174 D4
Mačvanski Pričinović SRB 174 D4
Mád H 161 G3
Madan BG 181 B7
Madan BG 187 A7
Mädan S 119 A15
Madängsholm S 107 C14
Madara BG 183 C8
Madaras H 166 E3
Mădăraş RO 167 D8
Mădărjac RO 169 C10
Maddalena Spiaggia I 80 E3
Maddaloni I 76 A2
Made NL 32 E3
Madekoski FIN 135 E15
Madeley GB 26 F7
Mäder A 87 C9
Madetkoski FIN 131 C1
Madiran F 48 C5
Madley GB 29 A9
Madliena LV 151 C10
Madocsa H 166 D2
Madona LV 151 C12
Madonna di Campiglio I 85 A10
Madrid E 62 D5
Madridejos E 62 F5
Madrigal de las Altas Torres E 61 B11
Madrigal de la Vera E 61 D10
Madrigal del Monte E 56 D4
Madrigalejo E 61 F9
Madrigueras E 63 F9
Madroñera E 61 F9
Mădulari RO 176 D4
Madzharovo BG 187 A9
Mæl N 111 C9
Maël-Carhaix F 38 D5
Maella E 58 E4
Maello E 62 C3
Maenclochog GB 28 B5
Maenza I 78 D4
Mære N 121 D10
Măerişte RO 167 C10
Mäetaguse EST 147 C14
Maeztu E 57 C7
Mafra P 66 B1
Magacela E 67 B8
Magallón E 57 E9
Magalluf E 65 E10
Magaña E 57 E7
Magašići BIH 174 E3
Magaz E 56 E3
Magdala D 95 E9
Magdeburg D 95 B10
Magdeburgerforth D 95 B11
Magenta I 85 C6
Magescq F 48 C3
Măgeşti RO 167 C9
Maggia CH 84 A6
Maghera GB 20 F3
Magherafelt GB 20 F3
Magheralin GB 23 D10
Măgherani RO 168 D5
Maghery GB 23 C9
Maghull GB 26 D6
Magione I 82 F5
Mägiotsa EST 148 E1
Măgireşti RO 169 D9
Magisano I 75 A10
Maglaj BIH 173 C9
Magland F 47 C10
Maglavit RO 175 E11
Magliano de'Marsi I 78 C4
Magliano in Toscana I 81 B4
Magliano Sabina I 78 C2
Maglič̌ SRB 174 F6
Maglie I 77 C10
Maglód H 166 C3
Magnac-Laval F 45 C8
Magné F 44 C4
Magnières F 42 D6
Magnor N 112 C7
Magnuszew PL 157 G4
Magny-Cours F 46 B3
Magny-en-Vexin F 40 B6
Mágocs H 165 D10
Magoula GR 190 E5
Magstrup DK 102 E4
Magueija P 60 B5
Maguilla E 67 C8
Maguiresbridge GB 23 D8
Măgura RO 169 D9
Măgura RO 176 E6
Magura SRB 180 D3
Măgura Ilvei RO 168 C5
Măgurele RO 177 C8
Măgurele RO 177 E8
Măgureni RO 177 C7
Măguri-Răcătău RO 167 D11
Magy H 161 H4
Magyaralmás H 165 B10
Magyaratád H 165 D9
Magyarbánhegyes H 167 E6
Magyarbóly H 165 E10
Magyaregregy H 165 D10
Magyarhomorog H 167 C8
Magyarkeszi H 165 C10
Magyarnándor H 163 F8
Magyarpolány H 165 B9
Magyarszék H 165 D10
Mahala UA 169 A8
Maheriv UA 160 C8
Mahíde E 55 E7
Mahlberg D 202 E4
Mahlsdorf D 99 E10
Mahlu FIN 139 E14
Mahlwinkel D 95 B10
Mahmudia RO 171 C4
Mahmudiye TR 187 E10
Mahmutköy TR 189 C6
Mahón E 73 B13
Mahora E 63 F9
Mahovo HR 165 E6
Mähring D 91 C12
Mahtra EST 147 C10
Maia P 60 B3
Maials E 58 E5
Măicăneşti RO 177 C10
Maîche F 43 F6
Maida I 75 B9
Maiden Bradley GB 29 C10
Maidenhead GB 31 D7
Maiden Newton GB 29 D9
Maidens GB 20 E7
Maidstone GB 31 E10
Maienfeld CH 87 C9
Maierato I 75 B9
Maierhöfen D 87 B10
Maieru RO 168 C5
Măierus RO 169 F7
Maigh Chromtha IRL 24 E5
Maigh Cuilinn IRL 22 F4
Maiglean Rátha IRL 23 F8
Maignelay-Montigny F 34 E6
Maijanen FIN 133 D14
Maikammer D 202 C5
Maillas F 48 B5
Maillebois F 40 C5
Maillezais F 44 C4
Mailly-le-Camp F 41 C11
Mailly-le-Château F 41 E10
Mailly-Maillet F 34 D6
Mailovac SRB 175 D7
Mainaschaff D 203 B7
Mainbernheim D 91 C7
Mainburg D 91 E10
Mainham IRL 23 F9
Mainhardt D 90 D6
Mainiemi FIN 143 B16
Mainistir Eimhín IRL 23 F8
Mainistir Fhear Maí IRL 24 D6
Mainistir Laoise IRL 25 C8
Mainistir na Búille IRL 22 E6
Mainistir na Corann IRL 24 E6
Mainistir na Feile IRL 24 D4
Männikkö S 132 D8
Mainsat F 45 C10
Maintenon F 40 C6
Mainua FIN 137 F9
Mainvilliers F 40 D5
Mainz D 37 D10
Maiolati Spontini I 83 F7
Maiorca P 60 D3
Maiorga P 60 E3
Mairena del Alcor E 67 E8
Maisach D 91 F9
Maishofen A 89 B6
Maišiagala LT 153 D11
Maissau A 93 E9
Maisse F 41 D7
Maissin B 200 E3
Maivala FIN 137 B14
Maizières-lès-Metz F 202 C1
Majadahonda E 62 D5
Majadas de Tiétar E 61 E9
Majava FIN 137 C12
Majavatn N 121 A14
Majdan BIH 173 D7
Majdan Królewski PL 160 C4
Majdan Niepryski PL 160 C7
Majdanpek SRB 175 E8
Majovakylä FIN 135 C17
Majs H 165 E11
Majšperk SLO 164 D5
Majtum S 125 D18
Makád H 165 B11
Makarove UA 161 G6
Makarove UA 170 C6
Makarska HR 173 F7
Mäkelänranta FIN 137 E13
Makhnovka RUS 149 B6
Mäkikylä FIN 139 E12
Makkola FIN 141 G11
Makkoshotyka H 161 G4
Makkum NL 32 B4
Maklár H 163 F10
Makljenovac BIH 173 C9
Makó H 166 E5
Mākoņkalns LV 149 D2
Mąkoszyce PL 158 E4
Makov SK 163 C7
Makovac SRB 180 D3
Maków PL 157 G2
Maków PL 157 H4
Mąkowarsko PL 154 D4
Maków Mazowiecki PL 155 E11
Maków Podhalański PL 163 B9
Makrakomi GR 190 B5
Makresh BG 175 F10
Makri GR 187 C9
Makrisia GR 190 D4
Makrochori GR 185 C7
Makrychori GR 185 E7
Makrygialos GR 185 D8
Makrygialos GR 195 E10
Makrynitsa GR 185 F8
Makryrrachi GR 190 A5
Maksamaa FIN 138 D8
Maksniemi FIN 135 C13
Maksymilianowo PL 154 D5
Malá E 69 B9
Mala IRL 24 D5
Mala S 103 C13
Malå S 123 A15
Mala Bosna SRB 166 E4
Mala Čista HR 172 E4
Malacky SK 93 F12
Málaga E 69 C8
Malagón E 62 F5
Malahide IRL 23 F10
Malahvianvaara FIN 137 E14
Malaia RO 176 C4
Mălăieşti MD 170 D5
Málainn Bhig IRL 22 C5
Málainn Mhóir IRL 22 C5
Mala Kladuša BIH 172 B4
Malalbergo I 82 C4
Malá Lehota SK 163 D7
Malamocco I 82 B5
Malancourt F 35 F11
Malandrino GR 190 C5
Malangen N 127 B16
Malangseidet N 127 B16
Malanów PL 158 C5
Malansac F 39 E7
Malaryta BY 157 G10
Mäläskä FIN 135 F16
Mala Subotica HR 165 D7
Malaucène F 51 B9
Malaunay F 34 E3
Malaussanne F 48 C5
Mälävaara FIN 131 E4
Malåvännäs S 123 A14
Mała Wieś PL 155 F9
Malax FIN 138 E7
Malaya Byerastavitsa BY 156 D9
Malbekkvatn N 130 E7
Malbork PL 154 B7
Malborn D 37 E7
Malbouzon F 46 F3
Malbuisson F 47 B9
Malcesine I 85 B10
Malchin D 99 C13
Malchow D 99 D12
Malcocinado E 67 C8
Malcov SK 161 E3
Malczyce PL 97 D10
Măldăeni RO 176 E5
Măldăreşti RO 176 C4
Maldegem B 35 B7
Malden NL 32 E5
Maldon GB 31 D10
Małdyty PL 155 C8
Malè I 87 E11
Malechowo PL 101 B11
Malejan E 57 E8
Maleme GR 194 D6
Malemort-du-Comtat F 51 B9
Malemort-sur-Corrèze F 45 E9
Malente D 99 B9
Målerås S 105 B9
Males GR 195 E10
Malesco I 84 A6
Malesherbes F 41 D7
Malesina GR 191 B7
Malestroit F 39 E7
Maletto I 75 D6
Malevo BG 182 F5
Malexander S 108 C6
Malfa I 75 B6
Malgersdorf D 91 E12
Malgovik S 123 B10
Malgrat de Mar E 59 D9
Malhadas P 55 E7
Malia GR 194 E9
Malicorne-sur-Sarthe F 39 E11
Malijai F 52 C4
Mali Iđoš SRB 174 B4
Målilla S 108 E7
Mali Lošinj HR 83 C9
Mali Mokryany UA 160 D7
Malin IRL 20 E2
Malin Beg IRL 22 C5
Málinec SK 163 D9
Malines B 35 B9
Malines B 198 C4
Mălini RO 169 C8
Malin More IRL 22 C5
Malinovka LV 151 E13
Malinska HR 83 B10
Maliq AL 184 C4
Mališevo SRB 179 E10
Maliskylä FIN 139 C14
Malissard F 46 F6
Maliuc RO 171 C4
Mali Zvornik SRB 173 D11
Maljasalmi FIN 141 E11
Malkara TR 189 C6
Małkinia Górna PL 155 E13
Malko Gradishte BG 182 F5
Malko Tŭrnovo BG 183 F9
Mallaig GB 20 A5
Mållångsbo S 119 D10
Mallén E 57 E9
Mallentin D 99 C10
Mallersdorf D 91 E11
Malles Venosta I 87 D11
Mallica TR 189 F7
Malling DK 102 C6
Malliß D 99 D10
Mallnitz A 89 C7
Mallow IRL 24 D5
Mallusjoki FIN 143 D14
Mallwyd GB 26 F4
Malm N 121 C10
Malmån S 123 E12
Malmbäck S 108 D4
Malmberget S 132 D5
Malmby S 114 D8
Malmédy B 36 D6
Malmein N 110 E4
Malmesbury GB 29 B10
Malmköping S 109 A9
Malmö S 103 D12
Malmslätt S 108 C7
Malnaş RO 169 E7
Malnate I 85 B6
Malnava LV 149 C3
Malnes N 126 C8
Malo I 85 B11
Malo Crniće SRB 175 D7
Małogoszcz PL 159 E9
Malo Konare BG 181 E9
Małomice PL 97 C8
Malomir BG 183 E7
Malomozhayskoye RUS 152 D5
Malón E 57 E8
Malona GR 197 D8
Malonno I 85 A9
Malonty CZ 93 E7
Malorad BG 181 C8
Mološište SRB 180 C4
Malo Titavo BIH 172 D5
Malovăţ RO 175 D10
Måløy N 116 C2
Maloye-Lugovoye RUS 152 D2
Maloye Sitna BY 149 E6
Malpartida P 61 C7
Malpartida de Cáceres E 61 F8
Malpartida de la Serena E 67 B8
Malpartida de Plasencia E 61 E8
Malpas GB 26 E6
Malpica E 54 B2
Malpica de Tajo E 62 E3
Malpica do Tejo P 60 E6
Mālpils LV 151 B9
Malsch D 43 C9
Mălselv N 127 B16
Malsfeld D 94 D6
Malšice CZ 93 D7
Målsnes N 127 B16
Målsryd S 107 D13
Målsta S 122 E7
Malta A 89 C8
Malta LV 149 D2
Malta P 61 C6
Maltastrupi LV 151 D13
Maltby GB 27 E9
Maltby le Marsh GB 27 E12
Maltepe TR 189 D7
Malterdingen D 43 D8
Malters CH 86 C6
Malton GB 27 C10
Malu cu Flori RO 176 C6
Maluenda E 57 F8
Malŭk Izvor BG 182 F5
Malu Mare RO 176 E3
Malung S 118 E6
Malungsfors S 118 E6
Mālupe LV 149 B2
Mălureni RO 176 C5
Mălusteni RO 169 E11
Małuszów PL 97 B8
Maluszyn PL 159 E8
Malva E 55 E9
Malvaglia CH 87 E7
Malveira P 66 B1
Malvik N 121 E9
Malý Horeš SK 161 G4
Mályi H 161 G2
Mały Płock PL 155 D13
Malý Šariš SK 161 E3
Malyy Bereznyy UA 161 F5
Mamaia RO 171 E3
Mamarchevo BG 183 E7
Mamarrosa P 60 D3
Mambrilla de Castejón E 56 E4
Mamer L 36 E6
Mamers F 40 D3
Mamiči BIH 173 F8
Mamirolle F 42 F5
Mammaste EST 147 E14
Mammendorf D 91 F9
Mammola I 75 C9
Mamoiada I 80 C3
Mamone I 80 B3
Mamonovo RUS 155 B8
Mamuras AL 184 A2
Mamuša SRB 179 E10
Mana MD 170 C3
Maňa SK 162 E6
Manacor E 73 B11
Manage B 35 D9
Manamansalo FIN 136 F9
Mañaria E 57 B6
Månås S 113 A9
Manasia RO 177 D9
Manasterz PL 160 D5
Manastir BG 181 F10
Mânăstirea RO 177 E9
Mănăstirea Caşin RO 169 E9
Mănăstirea Humorului RO 169 B7
Manastirica SRB 175 D7
Manastirsko BG 183 C7
Mânăştiur RO 167 F9
Mancera de Abajo E 61 C10
Mancha Real E 69 A9
Manchester GB 27 E7
Manching D 91 E9
Manchita E 67 B7
Manciano I 81 B5
Manciet F 49 C6
Mandal N 106 C1
Måndalen N 116 A6
Mandalo GR 185 C7
Mandas I 80 D3
Mandatoriccio I 77 E7
Mandayona E 63 C7
Mandelbachtal-Ormesheim D 202 C3
Mandelieu-la-Napoule F 52 D5
Mandello del Lario I 85 B7
Manderscheid D 37 D7
Mandeure F 43 F6
Mandino Selo BIH 173 E7
Mándok H 161 G5
Mandra GR 191 C7
Măndra RO 168 F6
Mandraki GR 197 C6
Mandres-en-Barrois F 42 D3
Mandriko GR 197 D7
Mandritsa BG 187 B10
Manduria I 77 C9
Mane F 49 D7
Mane F 51 C10
Manea GB 27 G12
Măneciu RO 177 C7
Manerbio I 82 B1
Mañeru E 48 E2
Măneşti RO 176 D6
Mâneşti RO 177 D7
Manětín CZ 92 C4
Manfredonia I 79 D9
Mangalia RO 171 F3
Manganeses de la Lampreana E 55 E8
Manganeses de la Polvorosa E 55 D8
Mångberg S 118 E8
Mångbyn S 134 F6
Manger N 116 E2
Mangiennes F 35 F12
Mangotsfield GB 29 C9
Mångsbodarna S 118 D6
Mangualde P 60 C5
Manhay B 35 D12
Manhuelles F 42 B4
Mani GR 187 B10
Maniace I 75 D6
Maniago I 89 D6
Maniakoi GR 184 D5
Manieczki PL 97 B11
Manilva E 69 D6
Manisa TR 193 B9
Manises E 64 E4
Manjärvträsk S 134 C4
Manjaur S 123 B16
Mank A 93 F8
Månkarbo S 115 B8
Mankila FIN 135 E15
Manlay F 41 F11
Manlleu E 59 D8
Manna GR 191 D6
Männamaa EST 146 D5
Mannersdorf an der Rabnitz A 165 B7
Mannheim D 37 F10
Männikuste EST 147 E8
Manningtree GB 31 D11
Manolada GR 190 C3
Manole BG 181 E10
Manoleasa RO 169 B10
Manoppello I 78 C6
Manorbier GB 28 B5
Manorhamilton IRL 22 D6
Manosque F 51 C10
Manowo PL 101 B10
Manresa E 59 D7
Månsåsen S 121 E16
Manschnow D 97 A7
Mansfield D 95 C9
Mansfield GB 27 E9
Mansfield Woodhouse GB 27 E9
Mansilla E 56 D6
Mansilla de las Mulas E 55 D9
Mansle F 45 D6
Manso F 53 G9
Mansonville F 49 B7
Mansores P 60 C4
Manston GB 29 D10
Månssträsk S 125 E16
Mantamados GR 187 F10
Mantasia GR 190 A5
Manteigas P 60 D5
Mantel D 91 C11
Manternach L 202 B1
Mantes-la-Jolie F 40 C6
Mantes-la-Ville F 40 C6
Manthelan F 40 F4
Mantila FIN 138 F9
Mantoche F 42 F4
Mantorp S 108 C6
Mantoudi GR 191 B7
Mantova I 82 B2
Mäntsälä FIN 143 D13
Mänttä FIN 139 F13
Mäntyharju FIN 144 C6
Mäntyjärvi FIN 133 E14
Mäntyjärvi FIN 137 B10
Mäntylahti FIN 140 D8
Mäntyluoto FIN 142 B5
Mäntyvaara S 132 E7
Manuel E 72 C4
Manulla IRL 22 E4
Mány H 165 A11
Manyas TR 189 D8
Manzac-sur-Vern F 45 E7
Mânzăleşti RO 177 C9
Manzanal de Arriba E 55 E7
Manzanal del Puerto E 55 C7
Manzanares E 71 A6
Manzanares el Real E 62 C5
Manzaneda E 54 D5
Manzanedo E 56 C4
Manzaneque E 62 E5
Manzanera E 64 D3
Manzanilla E 67 E7
Manzano I 89 E7
Manzat F 46 D2
Manziana I 78 C2
Manziat F 46 C6
Maoča BIH 173 C10
Maqellarë AL 184 A3
Maqueda E 62 D4
Mar P 54 E2
Mara I 80 C2
Marac F 42 E3
Maracalagonis I 80 E3
Marachkova BY 149 E4
Mărăcineni RO 176 D5
Mărăcineni RO 177 C9
Maradik SRB 174 C5
Maråker S 119 D13
Maranchón E 63 B8
Maranello I 82 C2
Marange-Silvange F 202 C1
Maranhão P 66 A4
Marano I 82 D3
Marano di Napoli I 76 B2
Marano sul Panaro I 82 D2
Marans F 44 C4
Maranville F 41 D12
Mărăşeşti RO 169 F10
Mărăşu RO 171 D1
Maratea I 76 D5
Marateca P 66 B2
Marathea GR 185 E6
Marathias GR 190 C5
Marathokampos GR 193 D8
Marathonas GR 191 C8
Marathopoli GR 190 E4
Maraussan F 50 D5
Maraye-en-Othe F 41 D10
Marazion GB 28 E4
Marazliyivka UA 170 E6
Marbach CH 86 D5
Marbach am Neckar D 43 C11
Marbäck S 107 D13
Marbella E 69 C7
Marboz F 47 C7
Marburg an der Lahn D 37 C11
Marby S 121 E16
Marça E 58 E5
Marcali H 165 C8
Marcaltő H 165 B8
Marčana HR 83 C8
Marcaria I 82 B2
Marcăuţi MD 169 A10
Marcellina I 78 C3
Marcelová SK 165 A10
Marcenais F 44 E5
Marcenat F 46 E2
March GB 27 F12
Marchamalo E 63 C6
Marchaux F 42 F5
Marche-en-Famenne B 35 D11
Marchegg A 93 F11
Marchena E 67 E9
Marchenoir F 40 E5
Marcheprime F 44 F4
Marchiennes F 35 D7
Marchin B 35 D11
Marchtrenk A 92 F6
Marciac F 49 C6
Marciana I 81 B2
Marciana Marina I 81 B2
Marcianise I 76 A2
Marciano della Chiana I 82 F4
Mārciena LV 151 C12
Marcigny F 46 C5
Marcilhac-sur-Célé F 49 A9
Marcilla E 48 F2
Marcillac F 44 E4
Marcillac-la-Croisille F 45 E10
Marcillac-Vallon F 49 B10
Marcillat-en-Combraille F 45 C11
Marcilly-en-Gault F 40 F6
Marcilly-en-Villette F 40 E7
Marcilly-le-Hayer F 41 D10
Marcilly-sur-Eure F 40 C5
Marcinkonys LT 153 E9
Marcinkowice PL 101 D10
Marcinkowice PL 160 D2
Marcinowice PL 97 E11
Marciszów PL 97 E10
Marck F 34 C4
Marckolsheim F 43 D8
Marco de Canaveses P 60 B4
Marcoing F 35 D7
Marcòn I 82 A5
Marcoux F 52 C4
Marcq-en-Barœul F 35 C7
Mărculeşti MD 169 B12
Mårdaklev S 103 A11
Mardarivka UA 170 B5
Mardeuil F 41 B10
Mårdsele S 123 B16
Mårdsjö S 122 E9
Mårdsjö S 123 C11
Mårdudden S 134 B6
Marebbe I 88 C4
Marennes F 44 D3
Maresfield GB 31 F9
Mareuil F 45 E6
Mareuil-sur-Arnon F 45 B10
Mareuil-sur-Lay F 41 B11
Mareuil-sur-Lay-Dissais F 44 B3
Marey-sur-Tille F 42 E3
Marga RO 175 B9
Margarites GR 194 E8
Mărgăriteşti RO 177 C9
Margariti GR 184 F3
Margate GB 31 E11
Mărgău RO 167 D10
Margecany SK 161 F3
Margerie-Hancourt F 41 C12
Margherita di Savoia I 76 A6
Marghita RO 167 C9
Margina RO 167 F9
Marginea RO 169 B7
Mărgineni RO 169 D9
Mărgineni RO 169 D9
Margionys LT 153 F9
Margone I 47 E11
Margonin PL 101 E12
Margraten NL 35 C12
Marguerittes F 51 C7
Margut F 35 E11
Marhaň SK 161 E3
María E 71 D8
Mariac F 46 F5
Mariager DK 102 B5
Maria Lankowitz A 89 B11
Maria Luggau A 89 C6
Marialva P 61 C6
Mariampole LV 149 D2
Mariana E 63 D8
Mariannelund S 108 D7
Mariano Comense I 85 B7
Marianopoli I 74 D4
Marianowo PL 101 D8
Mariánské Lázně CZ 91 C12
Mariapfarr A 89 B8
Maria Saal A 89 C9
Mariazell A 164 A4
Maribo DK 99 A10
Maribor SLO 164 C5
Marieberg S 108 A6
Marieby S 122 E7
Mariefred S 114 D8
Mariehamn FIN 115 B13
Marieholm S 103 D12
Marieholm S 107 E14
Mariembourg B 35 D10
Marienberg D 96 E4
Marienhafe D 33 A8
Marienhagen D 94 B6
Marienheide D 37 B9
Mariental D 95 B8
Mariestad S 107 B14
Marifjøra N 116 D6
Marigliano I 76 B2
Marignana F 53 G9
Marignane F 51 D9
Marigné-Laillé F 40 E3
Marigny F 39 B9
Marigny-le-Châtel F 41 D10
Marijampolė LT 152 D7
Marikaj AL 184 B2
Marikostinovo BG 185 B9
Marín E 54 D2
Marina di Alberese I 81 B4
Marina di Amendolara I 77 D7
Marina di Arbus I 80 D1
Marina di Camerota I 76 C4
Marina di Campo I 81 B2
Marina di Carrara I 85 E9
Marina di Castagneto Donoratico I 82 F2
Marina di Cecina I 82 F1
Marina di Chieuti I 79 D8
Marina di Gioiosa Ionica I 75 C9
Marina di Grosseto I 81 B3
Marina di Leuca I 77 D10

Marina di Massa I 85 E9
Marina di Novaglie I 77 D10
Marina di Palma I 74 E4
Marina di Pulsano I 77 C8
Marina di Ragusa I 75 D4
Marina di Ravenna I 82 C5
Marinaleda E 60 B7
Marina Palmense I 83 F8
Marina Romea I 82 C5
Marina Schiavonea I 77 D7
Marinella I 74 D2
Marineo I 74 D3
Marines E 64 E3
Marines F 40 B6
Maringues F 46 D3
Marinha das Ondas P 60 D3
Marinha Grande P 60 E3
Marinhas P 54 E2
Marinići HR 83 B9
Marinka BG 183 E8
Marinkainen FIN 139 C10
Mārinkalns LV 149 B1
Marino I 78 D3
Mar'insko RUS 148 D4
Mariotto I 77 A7
Mărişelu RO 168 C5
Maritsa GR 197 D8
Marizy F 46 B5
Marjaliza E 62 E5
Mārjamaa EST 147 D8
Marjaniemi FIN 135 D13
Marjokylä FIN 137 E14
Marjonieemi FIN 143 C14
Marjovaara FIN 141 E15
Marjusaari FIN 139 D12
Mark GB 29 C9
Mark S 123 B10
Markaryd S 103 C13
Markaz H 163 F10
Markby FIN 138 D9
Markdorf D 43 E11
Markebäck S 108 B5
Markelo NL 33 D7
Market Deeping GB 27 F11
Market Drayton GB 26 F7
Market Harborough GB 31 C7
Markethill GB 23 D9
Market Rasen GB 27 E11
Market Warsop GB 27 E9
Market Weighton GB 27 D10
Markgröningen D 43 C11
Markhus N 110 C4
Marki PL 155 F11
Markina-Xemein E 57 B7
Markinch GB 21 C10
Märkisch Buchholz D 96 B5
Markitta S 132 D7
Marklohe D 33 C12
Marknesse NL 32 C5
Markneukirchen D 91 B11
Markopoulo GR 191 D8
Markovac SRB 175 E7
Markovac SRB 175 E7
Markovac Našički HR 165 E10
Markovac Trojstveni HR 165 E7
Markowa PL 160 C5
Markranstädt D 95 D11
Marksuhl D 95 E7
Markt Allhau A 164 B6
Marktbergel D 91 D7
Markt Berolzheim D 91 D8
Markt Bibart D 91 C7
Marktbreit D 203 B9
Markt Erlbach D 91 D8
Markt Hartmannsdorf A 164 B5
Marktheidenfeld D 90 C6
Markt Indersdorf D 91 F9
Marktjärn S 119 A11
Marktl D 92 F3
Marktleugast D 91 B10
Marktoberdorf D 87 B11
Marktoffingen D 91 E7
Marktredwitz D 91 B11
Markt Rettenbach D 87 B10
Markt Sankt Martin A 165 A6
Markt Schwaben D 91 F10
Marktseft D 91 C7
Markt Wald D 87 A11
Markusevec HR 164 E6
Markušica HR 165 F11
Markuškov SK 161 F2
Markuszów PL 157 H6
Marl D 33 D10
Marl D 33 E8
Marlborough GB 29 C11
Marldon GB 29 E7
Marle F 35 E8
Marlengo I 88 C3
Marlenheim F 43 C8
Marlhes F 46 E5
Marlishausen D 95 E9
Marlow D 99 B13
Marlow GB 31 D7
Marly F 35 D8
Marly F 42 B5
Marma S 115 B8
Marmagne F 41 F7
Marmagne F 46 B5
Marmande F 49 A6
Marmara GR 190 B5
Marmara TR 189 C8
Marmaracik TR 189 B8
Marmaraereğlisi TR 189 C8
Marmari GR 191 C9
Marmaro GR 193 B7
Marmelar P 66 C4
Marmeleira P 60 F3
Marmelete P 66 E2
Marmirolo I 82 B2
Marmolejo E 69 A8
Marmoutier F 43 C7
Marnardal N 106 C2
Marnäs S 119 E10
Marnay F 42 F4
Marne D 98 C6
Marne-la-Vallée F 41 C8
Marnes N 124 B7
Marnheim D 37 E10
Marnitz D 99 D11

Marpingen D 37 F8
Marpissa GR 192 E5
Marple GB 27 E7
Marpod RO 168 F5
Marquartstein D 88 A5
Marquion F 35 D7
Marquise F 31 F12
Marquixanes F 49 E10
Marradi I 82 D4
Marrasjärvi FIN 133 E14
Marraskoski FIN 133 E14
Marrubiu I 80 D2
Marrum NL 32 B5
Mârşa RO 177 E7
Marsac-en-Livradois F 46 E4
Marsac-sur-Don F 39 E8
Marsaglia I 53 B10
Marsal F 42 C6
Marsala I 74 D1
Mârşani RO 176 E4
Marsannay-la-Côte F 42 F2
Marsanne F 51 A8
Marsberg D 33 F11
Marsciano I 78 B2
Marseillan F 51 D6
Marseille F 51 D9
Marseille-en-Beauvaisis F 34 E4
Marsico Nuovo I 76 C5
Marsico Vetere I 76 C5
Marsillargues F 51 C7
Marsjärv S 134 B3
Mârslet DK 102 C6
Mārsnēni LV 151 B11
Marsrac-sur-Tarn F 49 C10
Märsta S 115 C9
Marstal DK 99 F7
Mårstenet S 119 E9
Marston GB 29 B12
Marstrand S 107 D10
Marstrup DK 102 E4
Mârşylä FIN 139 C11
Marta I 78 B1
Mårtanberg S 119 E9
Martano I 77 C10
Martel F 45 F9
Martelange B 35 E12
Martellago I 82 A5
Martello I 87 D11
Mártély H 166 E5
Marten BG 177 F8
Martfeld D 33 C12
Martfö H 166 C5
Marthon F 45 D6
Martiago E 61 D8
Martignacco I 89 D7
Martigné-Briand F 39 F11
Martigné-Ferchaud F 39 E9
Martigné-sur-Mayenne F 39 D10
Martigny CH 47 C11
Martigny-le-Comte F 46 B5
Martigny-les-Bains F 42 D4
Martigny-les-Gerbonvaux F 42 D4
Martigues F 51 D9
Martiherrero E 62 C3
Martil MA 69 E6
Martim Longo P 66 E4
Martin SK 163 C7
Martina Franca I 77 B8
Martin Brod BIH 172 C5
Martinchel P 60 E4
Martinci SRB 174 C3
Martinci Čepinski HR 165 E10
Martín de la Jara E 69 B7
Martín del Río E 58 F2
Martín de Yeltes E 61 C8
Martinengo I 85 B7
Martineşti RO 167 F11
Martinet E 49 F9
Martinfeld D 95 D7
Martingança P 60 E3
Mârtiniş RO 168 D5
Martín Muñoz de las Posadas E 62 B3
Martinniemi FIN 135 D14
Martino GR 191 B7
Martinporra E 55 B8
Martinsberg A 93 F8
Martinščica HR 83 C9
Martinsicuro I 78 B5
Martis I 80 B2
Martizay F 45 B8
Martley GB 29 A10
Martna EST 146 D7
Martock GB 29 D9
Martonvaara FIN 141 D12
Martorell E 59 E7
Martos E 69 A9
Martres-Tolosane F 49 D8
Mårtsbo S 119 E13
Martti FIN 131 D1
Marttila FIN 143 D8
Marttila FIN 143 D13
Marttisenjärvi FIN 140 C7
Marugán E 62 C4
Maruggio I 77 C9
Marum NL 32 B6
Marum S 115 C12
Mărunţei RO 176 E4
Mărupe LV 151 C8
Maruszów PL 159 D12
Maruszów PL 160 B4
Marvão P 60 F6
Marvejols F 50 A5
Marville F 35 F11
Marxheim D 91 E8
Marxzell D 43 C9
Mâry FIN 143 E9
Mar'yanivka UA 170 C6
Marykirk GB 21 B11
Marynychi UA 168 A6
Maryport GB 19 L10
Marywell GB 21 A11
Marzabotto I 82 D3
Marzahna D 95 B12
Marzahne D 95 A12
Marzamemi I 75 F7
Marzan F 39 E7
Mârzăneşti RO 177 F6
Marzling D 91 F10
Masa E 56 C4
Masainas I 80 E2
Masari GR 197 D8
Mas-Cabardès F 49 D10
Mascali I 75 D7
Mascalucia I 75 D7
Mascaraque E 62 E5
Maschito I 76 B5
Masclat F 45 F8

Mas de Barberans E 58 F4
Mas de las Matas E 58 F3
Masegosa E 63 C8
Masegoso E 71 B8
Masegoso de Tajuña E 63 C7
Maselheim D 87 A9
Masera I 84 A5
Maserada sul Piave I 88 E5
Masevaux F 43 E6
Masfjorden N 116 E2
Masham GB 27 C8
Masi N 129 C11
Masi Lombarda I 82 D4
Maside E 54 D3
Masi Torello I 82 C4
Maskalyanyaty BY 149 E7
Maskaur S 125 E14
Masku FIN 143 D8
Maslenica HR 172 D4
Maslinica HR 172 F5
Masloc RO 167 E7
Maslovare BIH 173 C8
Masone I 53 B9
Masquefa E 59 E7
Massa I 85 E9
Massa Fiscaglia I 82 C5
Massafra I 77 B8
Massa Lombarda I 82 D4
Massa Lubrense I 76 B2
Massamagrell E 64 E4
Massa Marittimo I 81 A3
Massa Martana I 78 B3
Massarosa I 82 E1
Massat F 49 E8
Massay F 40 F6
Maßbach D 91 B7
Masseret F 45 D9
Masseube F 49 D7
Massford GB 23 D10
Massiac F 46 E3
Massiari EST 147 F9
Massimino I 53 B8
Massing D 91 F12
Mas-St-Chély F 50 B5
Mâştăcani RO 171 B2
Mastershausen D 201 D7
Masterud N 112 B7
Mastichari GR 193 F9
Mastrevik N 116 E1
Masua I 80 E1
Masugnsbyn S 132 D8
Masullas I 80 D2
Mâsvik N 128 D2
Masyevichy BY 157 G9
Maszewo PL 97 B7
Maszewo PL 101 B13
Maszewo PL 101 D8
Maszewo Duże PL 155 E8
Matabuena E 62 B5
Matadepera S 59 E8
Mataguži MNE 179 E7
Matala FIN 135 C14
Matala GR 194 F4
Matalalahti FIN 140 C8
Matalascañas E 67 E6
Matalebreras E 57 F7
Matallana de Valmadrigal E 55 D9
Matamala de Almazán E 57 E6
Matamorosa E 56 C3
Mataporquera E 56 C3
Matapozuelos E 55 F10
Matara FIN 141 D12
Mataragka GR 185 F7
Mataragka GR 190 B3
Mataraselkä FIN 133 C17
Mataró E 59 E8
Mataruge MNE 173 E7
Mataruška Banja SRB 174 F6
Mătăsari RO 175 D11
Mătăsaru RO 177 D6
Mătăsvaara FIN 141 D13
Matca RO 169 F11
Mateeşti RO 176 C3
Matei RO 168 D4
Matelica I 83 F7
Matera I 77 B7
Materija SLO 89 E9
Mateševo MNE 179 D7
Mátészalka H 161 H5
Mateuţi MD 169 B11
Matfors S 119 B13
Matha F 44 D5
Mathay F 43 F6
Mathi I 84 C4
Matignon F 39 C7
Matigny F 34 E7
Matilda FIN 143 E8
Matinlompolo FIN 133 E12
Matino I 77 C10
Matisi I 78 B1
Matišši SI 119 E13
Matkaniva FIN 135 F14
Matkavaara FIN 137 E12
Matku FIN 143 D10
Matlock GB 27 E8
Matosinhos P 60 B3
Matour F 46 C5
Mátraballa H 163 F10
Mátraderecske H 163 F10
Mátramindszent H 163 F9
Matrand N 112 B7
Mátraszele H 163 F9
Mátraszőlős H 163 F9
Mátraterenye H 163 F9
Mátraverebély H 163 F9
Matre N 110 C3
Matre N 116 E3
Matrei am Brenner A 88 B3
Matrei in Osttirol A 88 B6
Matsdal S 125 F10
Matsouki GR 190 B3
Matt D 87 D8
Mattaincourt F 42 D5
Mattersburg A 165 A6
Mattighofen A 92 F4
Mattila S 88 A9
Mattilanmäki FIN 131 E4
Mattinata I 79 D10
Mattinen FIN 135 B13
Mattisudden S 132 E3
Mattmar S 121 E15
Mattmyra S 119 D9
Mâttsund S 134 C7
Matulji HR 83 B9
Matuškovo SK 162 E5
Matyrzyna BY 149 F5
Maubert-Fontaine F 35 E9
Maubeuge F 35 D8
Maubourguet F 48 D6
Maubuisson F 44 E3
Mauchline GB 21 D8

Maud GB 19 K12
Mauerbach A 93 F10
Mauerkirchen A 92 F4
Mauerstetten D 87 B11
Maughold GBM 26 C3
Mauguio F 51 C7
Maukkula FIN 141 E15
Maula FIN 135 C13
Maulbronn D 43 C10
Mauléon F 44 B4
Mauléon-Barousse F 49 E7
Mauléon-d'Armagnac F 48 C5
Mauléon-Licharre F 48 D4
Maulévrier F 44 A4
Maum IRL 22 E3
Mauna FIN 132 E3
Maunu S 132 B8
Maunujärvi FIN 133 D14
Maunula FIN 135 D15
Maura N 111 B13
Maure-de-Bretagne F 39 E8
Maureillas-las-Illas F 50 A4
Mâureni RO 175 C8
Maurens F 45 F6
Mauriac F 44 E5
Mauriac F 45 E10
Mauricemills IRL 24 C4
Maurik NL 199 B6
Maurnes N 126 C9
Mauron F 39 D7
Mauroux F 49 B8
Maurs F 45 E10
Maurset N 110 B6
Maurstad N 116 C2
Mauru FIN 135 B15
Maury F 50 E4
Mautern an der Donau A 93 F9
Mauterndorf A 89 B8
Mautern in Steiermark A 89 B10
Mauth D 92 E5
Mauthausen A 93 F7
Mauthen A 89 C6
Mauves F 46 E6
Mauvezin F 39 D7
Mauvoisin CH 47 C11
Mauzé-sur-le-Mignon F 44 C4
Mavranaioi GR 184 D5
Mavrochori GR 184 C5
Mavrodendri GR 185 D6
Mavrodin RO 176 E6
Mavromati GR 190 E4
Mavrommati GR 185 F6
Mavrommati GR 191 C7
Mavrothalassa GR 185 C10
Mavrovë AL 184 D2
Mavrovo MK 179 F5
Mavrovouni GR 185 E7
Mavrovouni GR 185 E7
Mavsdode SLO 89 D9
Mawdka PL 160 C5
Maxent F 39 E7
Maxéville F 202 D1
Maxial P 60 F2
Maxieira P 60 E5
Mâxineni RO 177 C11
Maxmo FIN 138 D8
Maxsain D 201 C8
Mayakovskoye RUS 152 D5
Maybole GB 20 E7
Mayen D 37 D8
Mayenne F 39 D10
Mayet F 39 E12
Mayfield GB 31 E7
Mayobridge GB 23 D10
Mayorga E 55 D9
Mâyrânperä FIN 135 F14
Mayres F 51 A7
Mayrhofen A 88 B4
Mâyry FIN 139 E11
Mayschoss D 37 C8
May's Corner GB 23 D10
Máza H 165 D10
Mazagón E 67 E6
Mazagran F 35 F10
Mažaičiai LT 150 D3
Mazaleón E 58 E4
Mazamet F 49 D10
Mazan F 51 B9
Mazara del Vallo I 74 D2
Mazarakia GR 184 F3
Mazarambroz E 62 E4
Mazarete E 63 C8
Mazarrón E 72 F2
Mazé F 39 F11
Mažeikiai LT 150 C3
Maženiai LT 151 E8
Mazères F 49 D9
Mazerolles F 48 D5
Mazeyrolles F 49 A8
Mazi TR 197 D8
Mazières-en-Gâtine F 44 B5
Mazirbe LV 146 F4
Mažonai LT 150 E4
Mazsalaca LV 147 F10
Mažučište MK 185 B5
Mazzano I 82 A1
Mazzano Romano I 78 C2
Mazzarino I 74 E5
Mazzarone I 75 E6
Mazzo di Valtellina I 85 A9

Međas BIH 173 D10
Meddersheim D 37 E9
Meddo NL 199 A9
Mede I 84 C6
Medebach D 37 B11
Medeikiai LT 151 D9
Medelås S 123 B14
Medelim P 61 D6
Medellín E 67 B8
Membrook D 33 F7
Medemblik NL 32 C4
Medena-Selišta BIH 173 D6
Medeno Polje BIH 173 D6
Medenychi UA 161 E8
Medeş BIH 174 D3
Medesano I 82 C1
Medgidia RO 171 E2
Medgyesbodzás H 167 D6
Medgyesegyháza H 167 D7
Medhamn S 107 A14
Mediana E 57 F10
Mediaş RO 168 E4
Medicina I 82 D4
Medieşu Aurit RO 167 B11
Medinaceli E 63 B8
Medina de las Torres E 67 C7
Medina del Campo E 55 F10
Medina de Pomar E 56 C5
Medina de Rioseco E 55 E9
Medina-Sidonia E 68 D5
Medinilla E 61 D9
Medininkai LT 153 D12
Mediona E 59 E7
Médis F 44 D4
Medkovets BG 175 F11
Medle S 134 E5
Medlov CZ 93 C12
Medneva LV 149 B3
Medolla I 82 C3
Medousa GR 187 B8
Medovoye RUS 136 D4
Medulin HR 83 E8
Medumi LV 151 E12
Meduno I 89 D6
Međurečje SRB 179 B9
Medvede SRB 180 C3
Medveda SRB 175 F7
Medvedev SRB 175 E7
Medveda SRB 180 E5
Medviđa HR 172 D4
Medvode SLO 89 D9
Medyka PL 160 D5
Medze LV 150 C2
Medzev SK 161 F2
Medzibrod SK 163 D8
Medzilaborce SK 161 E4
Meenaclady IRL 22 B6
Meenavean IRL 22 C5
Meer B 198 C5
Meerane D 95 E11
Meerapalu EST 148 E1
Meerbeck D 33 D12
Meerbusch D 33 F7
Meerhout B 199 C6
Meerkerk NL 198 B5
Meerle B 198 C5
Meerlo NL 199 B8
Meersburg D 43 E11
Meerssen NL 35 C12
Meetkerke B 198 C2
Meeuwen B 35 B12
Mefjordvær N 127 A13
Mega Dereio GR 187 B10
Megala Kalyvia GR 185 F6
Megali Panagia GR 185 D9
Megali Volvi GR 185 C8
Megalochori GR 185 E6
Megalo Chorio GR 190 B4
Megalo Chorio GR 197 C8
Megalo Livadi GR 191 E8
Megalopoli GR 190 E5
Megara GR 191 C7
Megardssætra N 121 C13
Megen NL 199 B7
Mège I 165 D10
Megève F 47 D10
Megyaszó H 161 G3
Mehadia RO 175 D9
Mehadica RO 175 C9
Mehamn N 129 A20
Mehedeby S 115 B8
Mehikoorma EST 148 E1
Méhkerék H 167 D7
Mehren D 37 D7
Mehring D 37 F7
Mehrstetten D 90 F6
Mehtäkylä FIN 135 F12
Mehun-sur-Yèvre F 41 F7
Meidrim GB 28 B3
Meigh GB 23 D10
Meigle GB 21 B10
Meijel NL 32 F5
Meikleour GB 21 B10
Meilen CH 43 F10
Meilhan F 48 C4
Meillac F 39 D8
Meillant F 45 C10
Meillerie F 47 C10
Meimoa P 61 D6
Meina I 84 B6
Meine D 79 B8
Meinersen D 95 B7
Meinerzhagen D 201 B8
Meiningen D 95 F7
Meira E 54 B5
Meiringen CH 86 D6
Meisburg D 37 D7
Meisdorf D 95 C9
Meise B 198 D4
Meisenheim D 37 E9
Meißen D 96 D4
Meißenheim D 202 E4
Meitingen D 91 E8
Meix-devant-Virton B 35 E11
Méjanes F 51 D8
Mejannes-le-Clap F 51 B8
Mejdan-Obrovac BIH 173 C7
Mejorada E 62 D3
Mejorada del Campo E 62 D6
Meka Gruda BIH 173 F9
Mekinje SLO 89 D9
Mel I 88 D5
Mela S 109 A10
Melalahti FIN 137 D10
Melampes GR 194 E5
Melanthi GR 184 D5
Melay F 46 C5
Melay F 42 E4

Melazzo I 53 B8
Melbå N 127 C11
Melbârži LV 151 B11
Melbourn GB 31 C9
Melbu N 126 C8
Melby DK 97 D10
Melchow D 100 E5
Melcice-Lieskové SK 162 D5
Meldal N 120 E7
Meldola I 82 D5
Meldorf D 98 B6
Mele I 53 B9
Melegnano I 85 C7
Melenci SRB 174 C5
Melendugno I 77 C10
Melfi I 76 B5
Melfjordbotn N 124 C6
Melgaço P 54 E3
Melgar de Arriba E 55 D9
Melgar de Fernamental E 56 D3
Melgar de Tera E 55 E7
Melgven F 38 E4
Melhus N 120 E8
Melia GR 185 E8
Meliana E 64 E4
Melick NL 36 B6
Melicucco I 75 C9
Mélida E 48 F2
Melide E 54 C3
Melides P 66 C2
Meligalas GR 190 E4
Meliki GR 185 C7
Melilli I 75 E7
Melineşti RO 176 D3
Mélisey F 42 E6
Meliskerke NL 198 B3
Melissa GR 187 B7
Melissa I 77 E8
Melissano I 77 D10
Melissochori GR 191 C7
Melissopetra GR 184 C4
Melitaia GR 190 A5
Meliti GR 185 C6
Melito di Porto Salvo I 75 D8
Melivoia GR 185 E8
Melivoia GR 187 B7
Melk A 93 F8
Melkadalen N 127 D12
Melkefoss N 130 E7
Melksham GB 29 C10
Mellac F 38 E4
Mellajärvi FIN 135 B13
Mellakoski FIN 135 B12
Mellanfjärden S 119 C13
Mellansel S 123 E14
Mellansjö S 119 B10
Mellanström S 125 E15
Mellau A 87 C9
Melle B 35 B8
Melle D 33 B8
Melle F 44 C5
Mellen D 99 D7
Mellenbach-Glasbach D 95 E9
Mellendorf (Wedemark) D 94 A6
Mellensee D 96 B3
Mellerud S 107 B11
Mellgård S 119 A9
Mellilä FIN 143 D8
Mellin D 95 A8
Mellingen D 95 E9
Mellôsa S 109 A9
Mellrichstadt D 91 B7
Melmerby GB 21 F11
Melnica SRB 175 E7
Mělník CZ 93 B6
Mel'nikovo RUS 145 D12
Melnitsa BG 183 E7
Melnsils LV 146 F5
Melón E 54 D3
Meløy N 126 C9
Meløysund N 124 C6
Melrand F 38 E5
Melres P 60 B4
Melrose GB 21 D11
Mels CH 87 C8
Melsdorf D 99 B8
Melsungen D 94 D6
Melsvik N 128 C11
Meltaus FIN 133 D14
Meltham GB 27 D8
Melton GB 31 C11
Melton Mowbray GB 27 F10
Meltosjärvi FIN 133 E13
Melun F 41 D8
Melvaig GB 18 K5
Melvich GB 19 H9
Mélykút H 166 E3
Melzo I 85 C7
Memaliaj AL 184 D2
Membrey F 42 E4
Membrilla E 71 B6
Membrío E 61 E6
Mêmele LV 151 D8
Memleben D 95 D9
Memmelsdorf D 91 C8
Memmingen D 87 B10
Memmingerberg D 87 B10
Memsie GB 19 K12
Menaggio I 85 A7
Menai Bridge GB 26 E3
Menaldum NL 32 B5
Menars F 40 E5
Menasalbas E 62 E4
Menat F 46 C2
Menata I 82 C5
Mendavia E 48 F1
Mende F 50 A6
Menden (Sauerland) D 33 F8
Mendenitsa GR 191 B6
Menderes TR 193 C9
Mendig D 37 D8
Mendiga P 60 E3
Mendigorría E 48 E2
Menditte F 48 D4
Mendrisio CH 85 B6
Ménéac F 38 D7
Menemen TR 193 B9
Menesjärvi FIN 133 A16
Ménessaire F 41 F11
Menet F 45 E11
Menetes GR 197 F6
Menfi I 74 D2
Mengabril E 67 B8
Mengele LV 151 C10
Mengen D 87 A9
Mengerskirchen D 37 C10
Mengeš SLO 89 D10
Mengíbar E 69 A9

Menidi GR 190 A3
Ménigoute F 44 C5
Ménil-la-Tour F 42 C4
Ménil-sur-Belvitte F 42 D6
Menin B 35 C7
Menin B 198 D2
Menkijärvi FIN 139 E11
Meškulas AL 184 C4
Mennecy F 41 C7
Mennetou-sur-Cher F 40 F6
Menou F 41 F8
Mens F 47 F9
Mensignac F 45 E7
Menslage D 33 C9
Mentana I 78 C3
Menteroda D 95 D8
Menteşe TR 197 B8
Menton F 53 D7
Méntrida E 62 D4
Menznau CH 86 D6
Méobecq F 45 B8
Meolo I 88 E5
Méounes-les-Montrieux F 51 D10
Meppel NL 32 C6
Meppen D 33 C8
Mequinenza E 58 E4
Mer F 40 E5
Mera RO 169 F9
Merag HR 83 C9
Meråker N 121 E11
Meråkervollen N 121 E11
Merano I 88 C3
Méraq F 48 C5
Merasjärvi S 132 C7
Merasjärvi S 133 C10
Merate I 85 B7
Merbes-le-Château B 35 D9
Mercadillo E 56 B5
Mercatale I 82 E5
Mercatello sul Metauro I 82 E5
Mercatino Conca I 82 E6
Mercato San Severino I 76 B3
Mercato Saraceno I 82 E5
Merćez SRB 179 C11
Merching D 87 A11
Merchtem B 35 C9
Mercœur F 45 E9
Mercogliano I 76 B3
Mercuès F 49 B8
Merdrignac F 38 D7
Mërdzene LV 149 C3
Mere S 35 C8
Mere GB 29 D10
Méreau F 40 F7
Merei RO 177 C9
Merelbeke B 35 C8
Meremäe EST 148 F2
Merenberg D 201 C9
Mereni MD 170 D4
Mereni RO 171 E2
Mereni RO 169 E6
Méréville F 40 D7
Merghindeal RO 168 F5
Mergozzo I 84 B5
Meria F 53 F2
Méribel-les-Allues F 47 E10
Meriç TR 187 B10
Merichas GR 191 E8
Merijärvi FIN 135 F12
Merikarvia FIN 142 B6
Meriläinen FIN 139 D12
Merimasku FIN 142 E6
Měřín CZ 93 D9
Mering D 87 A11
Merişani RO 176 D5
Mereşti RO 169 F6
Mérk H 167 B9
Merkendorf E 164 C4
Merkendorf D 91 D8
Merkenes S 125 C11
Merkinė LT 153 E9
Merklín CZ 92 C4
Merklingen D 90 E6
Merksplas B 198 C5
Merlara I 82 B3
Merlevenez F 38 E5
Merlines F 45 D10
Mern DK 103 E10
Mērnieki LV 147 F5
Mernye H 165 D9
Merošina SRB 180 C4
Merrey F 42 D4
Mersch L 36 E6
Merseburg (Saale) D 95 D10
Mersinbeleni TR 193 D10
Mers-les-Bains F 34 D3
Mērsrags LV 150 B6
Mertajärvi S 132 B8
Mertert L 36 E6
Mertesdorf D 201 D7
Merthyr Tydfil GB 29 B8
Mertingen D 91 E8
Mertloch D 201 D7
Mértola P 66 D4
Mertzwiller F 202 D4
Méru F 34 F5
Mervans F 47 B9
Mervent F 44 B4
Merville F 34 C6
Merville F 49 C8
Méry-sur-Seine F 41 C10
Merzen D 33 D9
Merzig D 37 F7
Mesagne I 77 B9
Mesagros GR 191 C8
Mésanger F 39 F9
Mesão Frio P 60 B5
Mesaria GR 193 B7
Mesariá GR 193 D10
Mesariá GR 191 E8
Meschede D 33 F10
Meschers-sur-Gironde F 44 D4
Mešeišta MK 184 B4
Meselefors S 123 C14
Mesenikolas GR 185 E6
Meseşenii de Jos RO 167 C10
Mesgrigny F 41 D10
Mesi GR 187 C8
Mesići BIH 173 E11
Mesihovina BIH 173 E7
Mesimeri GR 185 D8
Mesinge DK 102 E7
Meškla GR 194 E6
Meškučiai LT 150 D6
Meslay-du-Maine F 39 E10
Mesocco CH 87 E8
Mesochora GR 184 F5
Mesochori GR 185 E7
Mesochori GR 197 E6
Mesola I 82 C5

Mesolongi GR 190 C3
Mesongi GR 184 F2
Mesopotamia GR 184 C5
Mesopotamos GR 184 F4
Mesoraca I 75 A10
Mesotopos GR 193 A7
Mespelbrunn D 203 B7
Mesquer F 38 F7
Messac F 39 E8
Messanges F 48 C3
Meßdorf D 99 E11
Messei F 39 C10
Messeix F 45 D11
Messejana P 66 D3
Messina I 75 C8
Messincourt F 35 E11
Messingen D 33 D8
Messini GR 190 E5
Meßkirch D 43 E11
Messlingen S 118 A4
Meßstetten D 43 D10
Mesta I 76 B2
Mesta GR 193 C6
Mestanza E 70 B4
Městec Králové CZ 93 B8
Mestervik N 127 B16
Mesti GR 187 C9
Mestlin D 99 C11
Město Albrechtice CZ 158 F4
Město Touškov CZ 92 C4
Mestre I 82 B5
Mesves-sur-Loire F 41 F8
Mesztegnyő H 165 C8
Meta I 76 B2
Métabief F 47 B9
Metagkitsi GR 185 D10
Metajna HR 83 C11
Metallika GR 185 B8
Metallostroy RUS 145 F14
Metaxades GR 187 B10
Metelen D 33 D8
Meteş RO 167 E11
Metfield GB 31 C11
Methana GR 191 E7
Metheringham GB 27 E11
Methlick GB 19 L12
Methoni GR 194 B2
Methven GB 21 C9
Methwold GB 27 F13
Metković HR 173 F8
Metlika SLO 164 E4
Metnitz A 89 C9
Metochi GR 190 C3
Metochi GR 191 A6
Metovnica SRB 175 F9
Mētriena LV 151 C12
Metsäkansa FIN 143 C10
Metsäkylä FIN 137 D11
Metsäkylä FIN 144 D7
Metsälä FIN 136 C9
Metsämaa FIN 143 D9
Metschow D 100 C3
Metsküla EST 146 D5
Metslawier NL 32 B6
Metsovo GR 184 E5
Mettäjärvi S 133 E11
Mettendorf D 36 E6
Mettenheim D 91 F11
Mettet B 35 D10
Mettevoll N 128 D7
Mettingen D 33 D9
Mettlach D 37 F7
Mettmann D 33 F7
Mettray F 40 F4
Metz F 42 B5
Metzervisse F 36 F6
Metzingen D 43 C11
Meudt D 201 D8
Meulan F 40 B6
Meulebeke B 35 C7
Meung-sur-Loire F 40 E6
Meursault F 46 B6
Meuselwitz D 95 D11
Meuzac F 45 D8
Mevagissey GB 28 E5
Mexborough GB 27 E9
Meximieux F 47 D7
Mey GB 19 H10
Meyenburg D 99 D12
Meylan F 47 E8
Meymac F 45 D10
Meyrargues F 51 C10
Meyreuil F 51 D10
Meyronnes F 52 C5
Meyrueis F 50 B5
Meyssac F 45 E9
Meysse F 51 A8
Meythet F 47 D9
Mezapos GR 194 B3
Mežāre LV 151 C12
Mežciems LV 150 C7
Mezdra BG 181 C8
Mèze F 51 D6
Mézel F 52 D4
Mežgale LV 151 D11
Mezhdurech'ye RUS 152 D4
Mezhdurech'ye RUS 152 D4
Mezbořī CZ 96 E5
Mežica SLO 164 E4
Mézidon-Canon F 39 B11
Mézières-en-Brenne F 45 B8
Mézières-sur-Issoire F 45 C7
Mézilhac F 46 F5
Mézilles F 41 E9
Mezmiešti CZ 97 E10
Mézin F 49 B6
Mezio P 60 C5
Mezőberény H 167 D7
Mezőcsát H 163 F11
Mezőcsokonya H 165 D9
Mezőfalva H 165 C11
Mezőgyán H 167 D8
Mezőhegyes H 166 E6
Mezőkeresztes H 161 H2
Mezőkovácsháza H 167 E6
Mezőkövesd H 163 F11
Mezőlak H 165 B8
Mezőnyárád H 161 H2
Mezőörs H 165 A9
Mézos F 48 B3
Mezőszemere H 166 B6
Mezőszentgyörgy H 165 B10
Mezőszilas H 165 C10
Mezőtárkány H 166 B5
Mezőtúr H 166 D6
Mezőzombor H 161 G3
Mezquita de Jarque E 58 F2
Mežvāle LV 150 C4
Mežvidi LV 149 C3
Mežvidi LV 150 C4
Mezzana I 85 A10
Mezzanego I 53 C10
Mezzano I 88 D4

Mezzocorona I 85 A11
Mezzojuso I 74 D3
Mezzoldo I 85 A8
Mezzolombardo I 85 A11
Mga RUS 145 F15
Miączyn PL 160 B8
Miajadas E 61 F9
Mialet F 45 D7
Miały PL 101 E7
Miasteczko Krajeńskie PL 101 D12
Miastko PL 101 B11
Miastków Kościelny PL 157 G5
Miastkowo PL 155 D12
Miavaig GB 18 J3
Mica RO 168 C3
Mica RO 168 E4
Micăsasa RO 168 E4
Micești RO 176 D5
Micești de Câmpie RO 168 D4
Michałany SK 161 F4
Michalová SK 163 D9
Michalovce SK 161 F4
Michałów PL 159 F9
Michałów Górny PL 157 G4
Michałowice PL 159 F8
Michałowice PL 159 F8
Michałowo PL 156 D9
Michelau in Oberfranken D 91 B9
Michelbach an der Bilz D 90 D6
Micheldorf A 89 C9
Micheldorf in Oberösterreich A 89 A9
Michelfeld D 90 D6
Michelstadt D 37 E12
Michendorf D 96 B4
Michorzewo PL 97 B10
Michów PL 157 G6
Mickelspiltom FIN 143 D15
Mickleton GB 21 F12
Mickleton GB 29 A11
Miclești RO 169 C10
Midbea GB 19 G11
Middagsbukt N 127 B17
Middelbeers NL 199 C6
Middelburg NL 32 E1
Middelfart DK 102 D5
Middelharnis NL 32 E2
Middelkerke B 34 B6
Middelstum NL 33 B7
Middenbeemster NL 32 C3
Middenmeer NL 32 C4
Middleham GB 27 C8
Middlemarsh GB 29 D10
Middlesbrough GB 27 B9
Middleton GB 27 C7
Middleton GB 27 E7
Middleton Cheney GB 29 A12
Middleton in Teesdale GB 21 F12
Middletown GB 23 D9
Middlewich GB 26 E7
Midhurst GB 31 F7
Midleton IRL 24 E6
Midlum D 33 A11
Midtgård N 130 D8
Midtskogberget N 118 D3
Miðvágur FO 18 A2
Midwolda NL 33 B8
Mid Yell GB 19 D14
Miechów PL 159 F9
Miechów Charsznica PL 159 F8
Miedes E 57 F9
Miedziana Góra PL 159 E10
Miedzichowo PL 97 B9
Miedzna PL 155 F13
Miedzna PL 159 G7
Miedźno PL 159 E6
Międzybórz PL 158 D4
Międzychód PL 97 A9
Międzylesie PL 93 E11
Międzyrzec Podlaski PL 157 G7
Międzyrzecz PL 97 B9
Międzyzdroje PL 100 C6
Miehikkälä FIN 144 D8
Miehlen D 201 D8
Miejsce Piastowe PL 161 D4
Miejska Górka PL 97 C11
Miękinia PL 97 D11
Miękojārvi S 135 B10
Miélan F 49 D6
Mielec PL 159 F11
Mielęcin PL 101 D10
Mielęszyn PL 101 E12
Mielno PL 101 B10
Mieluskylä FIN 135 F14
Miełżyn PL 154 F3
Mieming A 87 C12
Mierasjärvi FIN 129 D19
Mieraslompolo FIN 129 D19
Miercurea-Ciuc RO 169 C7
Miercurea Nirajului RO 168 D5
Miercurea Sibiului RO 168 F3
Mieres E 55 B8
Mieres E 59 C9
Mierlo NL 32 F5
Mierojávri N 129 E11
Mieroszów PL 97 E10
Miers F 45 E9
Mierzęcice PL 159 F7
Mierzyn PL 100 D6
Miesau D 202 C3
Miesbach D 88 A4
Mieścisko PL 101 E12
Miesenbach D 202 C4
Mieslahti FIN 137 F10
Miessaure S 132 E4
Mieste D 95 B9
Mieszków PL 158 B3
Mieszkowice PL 100 E6
Mietingen D 87 A9
Mietków PL 97 E11
Mietoinen FIN 142 D6
Miettilä FIN 145 C11
Mieussy F 47 C10
Mieza E 61 B7
Migennes F 41 E10
Miglianico I 78 C6
Migliarino I 82 C4
Migliaro I 82 C4
Miglionica I 77 B6
Mignaloux-Beauvoir F 45 B6
Migné-Auxances F 45 B6
Mignovillard F 47 B9
Miguel Esteban E 62 F6
Miguelturra E 70 B5
Migushino RUS 149 E7
Mihăești RO 168 F5
Mihăești RO 176 C6
Mihăești RO 176 E5

Mihai Bravu RO 171 D3
Mihai Bravu RO 177 E8
Mihăileni RO 169 B8
Mihăileni RO 169 E7
Mihăilești RO 169 E7
Mihăilești RO 177 E7
Mihail Kogălniceanu RO 171 C3
Mihail Kogălniceanu RO 171 D1
Mihail Kogălniceanu RO 171 C2
Mihailovca MD 170 D3
Mihai Viteazu RO 168 D3
Mihai Viteazu RO 171 C3
Mihajlovac SRB 175 D6
Mihajlovac SRB 175 E9
Mihajlovo SRB 174 C5
Mihălăşeni RO 169 B10
Mihăld H 165 D8
Mihalţ RO 168 E3
Mihályi H 165 A8
Mihla D 95 D7
Miilluranta FIN 139 C16
Mijares E 62 D3
Mijas E 69 C7
Mijdrecht NL 32 D3
Mijoska MNE 179 D7
Mikașéws F 149 F6
Mikepércs H 167 C8
Mikhalishki BY 153 D13
Mikhalkovo BG 181 F9
Mikhaltsi BG 182 C4
Mikhaylovo BG 181 B8
Mikhaylovo BG 182 C4
Mikitamäe EST 148 E2
Mikitsikha BY 149 F6
Mikkeli FIN 144 B7
Mikkola mlk FIN 144 B7
Mikkelvik N 128 C3
Mikkola FIN 133 D16
Mikladalur FO 18 A3
Miklavž SLO 164 C5
Mikleuš HR 165 E9
Mikljaki PL 152 F4
Mikołajki Pomorskie PL 155 C7
Mikołów PL 159 F6
Mikoszewo PL 154 B6
Mikre BG 181 C10
Mikri Volvi GR 185 C10
Mikro Dereio GR 187 B10
Mikrokambos GR 185 C8
Mikromilia GR 186 B6
Mikropoli GR 185 B10
Mikrothives GR 185 F8
Mikrovalto GR 185 D6
Mikstat PL 158 C4
Mikulāš CZ 96 E6
Mikulasovice CZ 96 E6
Mikulčice CZ 93 E12
Mikulov CZ 93 E11
Mikulovice CZ 158 F3
Mikušovce SK 162 C6
Miladinovci MK 180 F4
Milagro E 57 F9
Milagros E 56 F4
Miłakowo PL 155 B9
Milano I 85 C7
Milano Marittima I 82 D5
Milanówek PL 157 F3
Milaş RO 168 D4
Milas TR 197 E7
Milatkoviće SRB 179 C10
Milazzo I 75 C7
Milborne Port GB 29 D10
Milcoiu RO 176 C6
Milcov RO 176 E4
Milcovul RO 177 B10
Mildenhall GB 31 C10
Mildstedt D 98 B6
Mileanca RO 169 A9
Milejczyce PL 157 E8
Milejewo PL 155 B8
Milejów PL 157 H7
Milena I 74 E4
Milești MD 169 C12
Milestone IRL 24 C6
Mileto I 75 B9
Mílevsko CZ 92 D6
Milford GB 31 E8
Milford IRL 23 B7
Milford IRL 24 D5
Milford Haven GB 28 B4
Milhão P 55 E6
Milhaud F 51 C7
Milići BIH 173 D11
Milicz PL 97 D12
Milies GR 185 F9
Milíkov CZ 163 B7
Milina GR 191 A7
Milis I 80 C2
Milievre UA 168 A6
Milizac F 38 C2
Miljana HR 164 D5
Miljevina BIH 173 E10
Milkel D 97 D6
Miłki PL 152 F4
Milkovitsa BG 176 F5
Milk'ovtsi BG 181 D6
Mill NL 32 E5
Millares E 64 F3
Millas F 50 E4
Millau F 50 B5
Millay F 46 B5
Millbrook GB 28 E6
Millbrook IRL 23 E8
Millesimo I 53 C8
Millevaches F 45 D10
Millford GB 23 D7
Millhouse GB 20 D6
Millières F 42 D3
Millingen aan de Rijn NL 199 B8
Millisle GB 23 C11
Millom GB 26 C5
Millport GB 20 D7
Millstreet IRL 24 D4
Millstreet IRL 24 E6
Milltown IRL 22 E5
Milltown IRL 24 D2
Milltown IRL 24 D5
Milltown Malbay IRL 24 C4
Milly-la-Forêt F 41 D7
Milmarcos E 63 D11
Milmersdorf D 100 D5
Milmort D 199 D7

Milna HR 172 F5
Milnathort GB 21 C10
Milngavie GB 21 D8
Milnthorpe GB 26 C6
Milo I 75 D7
Miłocice PL 101 C11
Miłomłyn PL 155 C8
Miłoradz PL 154 B6
Miłosław PL 158 B3
Miloševo SRB 180 D3
Miłowka PL 163 B8
Miltach D 91 D12
Miltiņi LV 150 C6
Milton GB 18 L8
Milton GB 21 B9
Milton Keynes GB 31 C7
Miltzow D 100 B4
Milutinovac SRB 175 F7
Milverton GB 29 C8
Milz D 91 B8
Mimetiz E 56 B5
Mimizan F 48 B3
Mimizan-Plage F 48 B3
Mimoń CZ 97 E7
Mina de São Domingos P 66 D5
Mín an Chladaigh IRL 22 B6
Minas de Riotinto E 67 D6
Minateda E 71 C9
Minaya E 63 F8
Minde P 60 E3
Mindelheim D 87 A10
Mindelstetten D 91 E10
Minden D 33 D11
Minderhout B 198 C5
Mindnes N 124 E3
Mîndreşti MD 170 B2
Mindszent H 166 D5
Mindszentgodisa H 165 D10
Mindtangen N 124 E3
Mindūnai LT 151 F11
Mindya BG 182 C5
Minehead GB 29 C8
Mineo I 75 E6
Mineralni Bani BG 182 F4
Minerbio I 82 C3
Minervino Murge I 76 A6
Minfeld D 43 B9
Minger MD 170 D2
Minglanilla E 63 E9
Mingorría E 62 C3
Miniac-Morvan F 39 C8
Miničevo SRB 175 D6
Mín na bhFiann IRL 22 C5
Minne S 119 B9
Minnertsga NL 32 B4
Minnesund N 111 B14
Minnigaff GB 20 F8
Minot F 41 E12
Mińsk Mazowiecki PL 157 F5
Minsterley GB 26 F6
Mintilogllio GR 190 C4
Mintiu Gherlii RO 168 C3
Mintlaw GB 19 K13
Mintraching D 91 E11
Minturno I 78 E5
Minucciano I 82 D1
Minusio CH 84 A6
Mioarele RO 176 C6
Mionica SRB 174 E5
Mionnay F 46 D6
Mios F 48 A4
Mira E 63 E10
Mira I 82 B5
Mira P 60 D3
Mirabeau F 51 C10
Mirabel E 61 E8
Mirabel F 49 B8
Mirabella Eclano I 76 A4
Mirabella Imbaccari I 74 E5
Miradoux F 49 C7
Miraflores de la Sierra E 62 C5
Miralcamp E 58 D5
Miramare I 82 D6
Mirambeau F 44 E4
Mirambel E 58 F3
Miramont-de-Guyenne F 49 A6
Miranda de Arga E 48 F2
Miranda de Ebro E 56 D6
Miranda do Corvo P 60 D4
Miranda do Douro P 55 E7
Mirande F 49 C6
Mirandela P 54 F4
Mirandilla E 67 A7
Mirandola I 82 C2
Mirandol-Bourgnounac F 49 A10
Miranje HR 172 E4
Mirano I 82 B5
Miras AL 184 C4
Miraş SRB 180 E3
Mirăslău RO 168 E3
Miratovac SRB 180 E4
Miravci MK 185 B7
Miravete de la Sierra E 58 F2
Mircea Vodă RO 171 E3
Mircea Vodă RO 177 C10
Mirceşti RO 169 C9
Mircze PL 160 B8
Mirebeau F 42 F3
Mirebeau F 45 B6
Mirecourt F 42 D5
Miren SLO 89 E8
Mirepoix F 49 D9
Mireşu Mare RO 167 C11
Mireval F 51 C6
Miribel F 46 D6
Mirič na BIH 173 B10
Mirkovci HR 165 F6
Mirkovo BG 181 D9
Mirlović Zagora HR 172 E5
Mirna SLO 89 E11
Mirna Peč SLO 89 E11
Mirocin PL 160 C6
Mirocin Górny PL 97 C9
Miroševce SRB 180 D4
Miroşi RO 176 E5
Miroslava LT 153 E8
Miroslavas LT 153 E8
Miroslaveşti RO 169 C9

Mirošov CZ 92 C5
Mirotice CZ 92 D6
Mirovice CZ 92 D6
Mirovtsi BG 183 C8
Mirow D 99 D13
Mirsk PL 97 E8
Mirsk HR 83 B9
Mirto Crosia I 77 D7
Miruena de los Infanzones E 61 C10
Mirzec PL 157 H4
Misano Adriatico I 83 E6
Mişca RO 167 D8
Mischii RO 176 E3
Miserey-Salines F 42 F4
Mishnyevichy BY 149 F7
Misi FIN 133 C17
Misilmeri I 74 C3
Mišinci BIH 173 C8
Miske H 166 E3
Miskolc H 161 G2
Mislina HR 178 D4
Mislinja SLO 89 D10
Mišnjak HR 83 C11
Mison F 51 B10
Missanello I 76 C6
Missenträsk S 123 A17
Missillac F 39 F7
Misso EST 147 F14
Mistelbach A 93 E11
Mistelgau D 91 C9
Misten N 124 B8
Misterbianco I 75 D7
Misterhult S 109 E9
Misterton GB 27 E10
Mistretta I 74 D5
Mistros GR 191 B8
Misurina I 88 C5
Misvær N 124 B9
Mitandersfors S 112 B7
Mitchelstown IRL 24 D6
Mithymna GR 187 A8
Mitoc RO 169 A10
Mitrašinci MK 184 B5
Mitreni RO 177 E9
Mitropoli GR 185 E6
Mitrousi GR 185 B9
Mitrova Reka SRB 179 C9
Mitry-Mory F 41 C9
Mittādalen S 118 A4
Mittelberg A 87 D11
Mittelberg A 87 C12
Mittelbiberach D 87 A9
Mittelkalbach D 90 B6
Mittelsinn D 203 A8
Mittenwald D 88 B3
Mittenwalde D 96 B5
Mittenwalde D 100 D5
Mitterbach am Erlaufsee A 164 A4
Mitterding A 92 F4
Mitterdorf im Mürztal A 164 A5
Mittersheim F 43 C6
Mittersill A 88 B5
Mitterkirchen D 91 F12
Mitterteich D 91 C11
Mittet N 116 A7
Mittilden S 121 B16
Mittweida D 96 E3
Mittwitz D 91 B9
Mizhhir"ya UA 161 F8
Mizil RO 177 C8
Miziya BG 181 C8
Mjällby S 104 C7
Mjällom S 119 A14
Mjaudnes N 126 E9
Mjöbäck S 104 A3
Mjölby S 108 C6
Mjølfjell N 116 A7
Mjøndalen N 111 C12
Mjønes N 124 B8
Mjøsjøby S 123 D15
Mjøsund FIN 142 E7
Mjøträsk S 135 B9
Mjøvattnet S 119 A14
Mjøvattnet S 134 E5
Mladá Boleslav CZ 93 B7
Mladá Vožice CZ 93 C7
Mladé Buky CZ 97 E8
Mladenovac SRB 174 E6
Mladenovo SRB 174 C3
Mladikovine BIH 173 D8
Mladinovo BG 182 F6
Mlado Nagoričane MK 180 E4
Mława PL 155 D9
Mlekarevo BG 182 E6
Mlinice BIH 173 D8
Mlinište BIH 173 D6
Młodzieszyn PL 157 F2
Młynary PL 155 B8
Młynarze PL 155 E11
Mlyns'ka UA 161 E9
Mnichovice CZ 92 C6
Mnichovo Hradiště CZ 93 A7
Mnichów PL 159 F9
Mniów PL 159 D9
Mníšek nad Hnilcom SK 161 F2
Mníšek pod Brdy CZ 92 C6
Mniszew PL 157 G4
Mniszków PL 157 H2
Mo N 116 E3
Mo S 119 D11
Mo S 119 E12
Mo S 123 D11
Mo S 123 D11
Moacşa RO 169 F7
Moaña E 54 D2
Moara RO 169 B8
Moara Domnească MD 169 B10
Moara Vlăsiei RO 177 D8
Moate IRL 23 E7
Mobberley GB 27 E7
Moča SK 165 A10
Močanin I 80 D2
Moçarria P 60 F3
Moceş E 62 E5
Močenok SK 162 E5
Mochales E 63 B9
Mochos GR 194 B4
Mochowo PL 155 E8
Mochy PL 97 C10
Mociu RO 168 D4
Möckern D 95 B10
Möckmühl D 43 B11
Mockrehna D 95 C12
Mocksträsk S 134 C7
Moclin E 69 B9
Moclinejo E 69 C8
Mocra MD 170 B4

Mocsa H 165 A10
Modane F 47 E10
Modave B 35 D11
Modbury GB 29 E7
Modelu RO 177 E10
Modi GR 191 B6
Modica I 75 F6
Modigliana I 82 D4
Modliborzyce PL 160 B5
Mödling A 93 F10
Modliszewice PL 157 H2
Modra SK 162 E4
Modran BIH 173 C8
Modrany SK 165 A9
Modřice CZ 93 D9
Modrište MK 184 A5
Modruš HR 172 B3
Modrý Kameň SK 163 E8
Modugno I 77 A7
Moëlan-sur-Mer F 38 E4
Moelfre GB 26 E3
Moelv N 117 E13
Moen N 121 D12
Moen N 127 B16
Moena I 88 D4
Moerbeke B 198 C3
Moergestel NL 32 E4
Moerkerke B 198 C2
Moers D 33 F7
Moffat GB 21 E10
Mofreita P 55 F6
Moftin RO 167 B10
Mogadouro P 55 F6
Mogata S 109 C9
Møgelin D 95 A11
Møgeltønder DK 102 F3
Mogenstrup DK 103 E9
Moggio Udinese I 89 D7
Mögglingen D 203 D8
Mogielnica PL 157 G3
Mogila MK 184 B5
Mogilany PL 163 B9
Mogilishte BG 183 C10
Mogilno S 154 E2
Moglia I 82 C2
Mogliano I 83 F7
Mogliano Veneto I 82 A5
Mogón E 71 C6
Mogoro I 80 D2
Mogoşani RO 176 D6
Mogoşeşti RO 169 C9
Mogoşeşti-Siret RO 169 C9
Mogoşoaia RO 177 D7
Moguer E 67 E6
Mogyoród H 166 B3
Mohács H 165 E11
Moharque F 71 C9
Mohed S 119 D12
Mohedas de Granadilla E 61 D8
Mohedas de la Jara E 61 E10
Mohelnice CZ 93 C11
Mohelno CZ 93 D10
Mohernando E 63 C6
Mohill IRL 23 E7
Möhkö FIN 141 E16
Möhlau D 95 C11
Möhlin CH 43 E8
Moholm S 107 B15
Mohora H 163 E8
Mohorn D 96 E5
Mohyliv Podil's'kyy UA 170 A1
Moi N 110 F5
Moi N 110 F5
Moià E 59 D8
Moiano I 76 A3
Moieciu RO 176 C6
Moimenta da Beira P 60 C5
Moineşti RO 169 E8
Moingt F 46 D5
Móinteach Mílie IRL 23 F8
Moira GB 23 D10
Moi i Rana N 124 D7
Moirans F 47 E7
Moirans-en-Montagne F 47 C8
Moirax F 49 B7
Moires GR 194 E8
Mõisaküla EST 147 E10
Moisburg D 98 D7
Moisdon-la-Rivière F 39 E9
Moisei RO 168 B5
Moisiovaara FIN 137 E13
Moislains F 34 E6
Moissac F 49 B8
Moissac-Bellevue F 52 D4
Moissey F 42 F4
Moïta S 53 G10
Moïta F 60 D4
Moïta P 60 E3
Moïta P 66 B2
Moixent-Mogente E 72 D3
Mojácar F 71 C9
Mojados E 55 F10
Mojkovac MNE 179 D8
Mojmírovce SK 162 E5
Mojstrana SLO 89 C9
Mojzeso SK 162 B6
Møkkevik N 126 D6
Möklinta S 114 B7
Mokobody PL 157 F6
Mokrá Hora CZ 93 D11
Mokrance SK 161 F3
Mokre PL 159 F10
Mokren BG 183 D7
Mokrievo MK 185 B8
Mokrin SRB 166 F5
Mokronog SLO 89 E11
Mokronoge BIH 172 D5
Mokronoge BIH 173 E7
Mokrous SLO 89 C11
Moksy FIN 139 D12
Mol B 35 B11
Mol SRB 166 F5
Mola di Bari I 77 A8
Molai GR 194 B4
Molare I 53 B9
Molares P 54 F1
Molas F 49 D7
Molbergen D 33 C9
Mölbling A 89 C9
Mølby DK 102 E4
Mold GB 26 E5
Moldava nad Bodvou SK 161 F2
Molde N 116 A6
Moldjord N 124 B8
Moldova Nouă RO 175 D8
Moldova-Suliţa RO 168 B6

Moldoveni RO 169 D9
Moldoviţa RO 169 B7
Møldrup DK 102 B5
Moldvik N 127 C11
Moledo P 54 E2
Moledo E 60 C5
Molelos P 60 C4
Molenbeek-St-Jean B 198 D4
Molenstede B 199 C6
Molescroft GB 27 D11
Molesmes F 41 E11
Moleşti MD 170 D3
Molétai LT 151 F10
Molfetta I 77 A7
Molfsee D 99 B8
Moliden S 123 E14
Molières F 45 B8
Molières F 49 B8
Molières-sur-Cèze F 51 B7
Moliets-et-Maa F 48 C3
Molina Aterno I 78 C5
Molina de Aragón E 63 C9
Molina de Segura E 72 E2
Molina di Ledro I 85 B10
Molinara I 76 A3
Molinaseca E 55 C7
Molinella I 82 C4
Molines-en-Queyras F 47 F10
Molinet F 46 C4
Molinges F 47 C8
Molinicos E 71 C8
Molini di Tures I 88 C4
Molino de Villobas E 48 F5
Molinos E 58 F3
Molino de Rei E 59 E8
Moliterno I 76 C5
Molitg-les-Bains F 49 E10
Molkojärvi FIN 133 D14
Molkom S 113 C10
Mollas AL 184 C3
Mölle S 103 C11
Molledo E 56 B3
Möllenbeck D 100 D4
Möllenhagen D 100 C3
Mollerussa E 58 D5
Molles F 46 C4
Mollet del Vallès E 59 D8
Molliens-Dreuil F 34 E5
Mollis CH 43 F11
Molln A 89 A9
Mölln D 99 C9
Mölln D 100 C4
Molló E 49 F10
Mollösund S 107 C9
Mölltorp S 108 C4
Mölnbo S 109 A10
Mölnlycke S 107 D11
Molnytsya UA 169 A8
Moloha UA 170 E3
Molompize F 46 E3
Molos GR 191 B6
Moloy F 42 E2
Molpe FIN 138 E3
Molsheim F 202 D3
Molunat HR 178 E5
Molve HR 165 D6
Molveno I 85 A10
Molvízar E 71 F8
Mombaldone I 53 B8
Mombeltrán E 61 D10
Mombercelli I 53 B8
Mömbris D 37 D12
Mombuey E 55 D7
Momchilgrad BG 187 A8
Momignies B 35 D9
Momo I 84 B5
Moná FIN 138 D5
Monachil E 69 B9
Monaco-d'Auléne F 53 H10
Monaghan IRL 23 D9
Monamolin IRL 25 C10
Monäs FIN 138 D4
Monashi UA 170 E6
Monasterace I 75 C10
Monasterevin IRL 23 F8
Monastir I 80 E3
Monastiraki GR 190 B2
Monbahus F 49 A7
Monbazillac F 45 F6
Moncada E 64 F4
Moncalieri I 53 A7
Moncalvo I 84 C5
Monção P 54 D3
Moncarapacho P 66 E4
Moncaut F 49 B6
Moncel-sur-Seille F 42 C5
Mönchengladbach D 36 B6
Mönchhof A 93 G11
Monchio delle Corti I 82 D1
Monchique P 66 E2
Mönchsdeggingen D 91 E8
Monclar F 49 B7
Monclar-de-Quercy F 49 C9
Moncofa E 64 E4
Moncontour F 38 D6
Moncontour F 44 B5
Moncoutant F 44 B4
Moncrabeau F 49 B6
Monda E 69 C7
Mondariz E 54 D3
Mondariz-Balneario E 54 D3
Mondavezan F 49 D7
Mondavio I 83 E6
Mondéjar E 63 D6
Mondello I 74 C3
Mondeville F 39 B11
Mondolfo I 83 E7
Mondoñedo E 54 B5
Mondorf-les-Bains L 36 E6
Mondoubleau F 40 E4
Mondovì I 53 C7
Mondragon F 51 B8
Mondragone I 78 F5
Mondsee A 89 A7
Monea GB 23 D7
Moneasa RO 167 E9
Moneglia I 53 C10
Monegrillo E 57 E11
Monein F 48 D5
Monemvasia GR 194 B5
Monesiglio I 53 C8
Monesterio E 67 C7
Monestier-de-Clermont F 47 F8
Monestiés F 49 B10
Monéteau F 41 E10
Moneygall IRL 25 C7
Moneymore GB 20 F3
Moneyneany GB 20 F3
Moneyreagh GB 23 C11
Monfalcone I 89 E8
Monfero Corvino Rovella I 76 B3
Monflanquin F 49 A7

Monfort F 49 C7
Monforte P 60 F6
Monforte da Beira P 61 E6
Monforte d'Alba I 53 B7
Monforte del Cid E 72 E3
Monforte de Lemos E 54 C4
Monforte de Moyuela E 58 E2
Monfortinho P 61 D7
Monghidoro I 82 D3
Mongrando I 84 B5
Mongstad N 116 E2
Monguelfo I 88 C5
Monheim D 91 E8
Moniaive GB 21 E9
Monieux F 51 B9
Monifieth GB 21 C11
Monilea IRL 23 E8
Mõniste EST 147 F13
Monistrol-d'Allier F 46 F4
Monistrol de Calders E 59 D8
Monistrol de Montserrat E 59 D7
Monistrol-sur-Loire F 46 E5
Monivea IRL 22 F5
Mönkeberg D 99 B8
Mońki PL 156 D7
Monkokehampton GB 28 D6
Monléon-Magnoac F 49 D7
Monmouth GB 29 B9
Monnaie F 40 E4
Mönni FIN 141 E14
Monninkylä FIN 143 E14
Monok H 161 G3
Monolithos GR 197 D7
Monopoli I 77 B8
Monor H 166 C3
Monor RO 168 D5
Monostorapáti H 165 C9
Monostorpályi H 167 C8
Monóvar E 72 E3
Monpazier F 49 A7
Monreal E 48 E3
Monreal del Campo E 63 C10
Monreale I 74 C3
Monreith GB 20 F7
Monroy E 61 E8
Monroyo E 58 F3
Mons B 35 D8
Mons F 50 C4
Mons F 52 D5
Monsampolo del Tronto I 78 B5
Monsaraz P 67 C5
Monschau D 36 C6
Monsec F 45 E7
Monségur F 49 A6
Monselice I 82 B4
Monsempron-Libos F 49 B7
Monserrat E 64 F3
Monsheim D 203 B5
Mönsheim D 203 D6
Mønsted DK 102 C4
Monster NL 32 D2
Mönsterås S 105 A10
Monsummano Terme I 82 E2
Monta I 53 B7
Montabaur D 37 D9
Montaberner E 72 D4
Montady F 50 D5
Montagnac F 50 D5
Montagnana I 82 B3
Montagne F 44 F5
Montagney F 42 F4
Montagnol F 50 C5
Montagrier F 45 E6
Montaigu F 44 B3
Montaigu-de-Quercy F 49 B8
Montaigut F 46 C2
Montaigut-sur-Save F 49 C8
Montaione I 82 E2
Montalbán E 58 F2
Montalbán de Córdoba E 69 A7
Montalbano Elicona I 75 C7
Montalbano Jonico I 77 C7
Montalbo E 63 E7
Montalcino I 81 A4
Montale I 82 E3
Montalegre P 54 E4
Montalieu-Vercieu F 47 D7
Montalivet-les-Bains F 44 E3
Montallegro I 74 E3
Montalto delle Marche I 78 B5
Montalto di Castro I 81 C5
Montalto Marina I 81 C5
Montalto Uffugo I 76 E6
Montalvão P 60 E5
Montamarta E 55 E8
Montana BG 181 C7
Montana CH 47 C11
Montanejos E 64 D3
Montaner F 48 D5
Montano Antilia I 76 C4
Montans F 49 C9
Montaquila I 78 D6
Montargil P 60 F4
Montargis F 41 E8
Montastruc-la-Conseillère F 49 C9
Montataire F 34 F5
Montauban F 49 B8
Montauban-de-Bretagne F 39 D7
Montaudin F 39 D10
Montauriol F 49 A7
Montauroux F 52 D5
Montaut F 48 C4
Montaut F 48 D5
Montaut F 49 D9
Montayral F 49 B7
Montazzoli I 79 D6
Montbard F 41 E11
Montbarrey F 47 A8
Montbazens F 49 B10
Montbazin F 51 C6
Montbazon F 40 F4
Montbéliard F 43 E6
Montbenoît F 47 B9
Montbeton F 49 B8
Montblanc E 58 E6
Montboucher-sur-Jabron F 51 A8
Montbozon F 42 F5
Montbrió del Camp E 58 E6
Montbrison F 46 D5
Montbron F 45 D7
Montbrun F 49 A9
Montbrun-les-Bains F 51 B9
Montcada i Reixac E 59 E8
Montcavrel F 31 F12
Montceau-les-Mines F 46 B5
Montcenis F 46 B5
Montchanin F 46 B5
Montcornet F 35 E9
Montcresson F 41 E8
Montcuq F 49 B8
Montcy-Notre-Dame F 35 E10
Montdardier F 51 C6
Mont-Dauphin F 52 B5
Mont-de-Marsan F 48 C5
Montdidier F 34 E6
Mont-Dore F 46 D2
Monteagudo E 57 E8
Monteagudo de las Salinas E 63 E9
Monteagudo de las Vicarías E 57 F7
Montealegre del Castillo E 71 B10
Montebello Ionico I 75 D8
Montebello Vicentino I 82 B3
Montebelluna I 88 E5
Montebourg F 39 B9
Montebruno I 53 B10
Montecalvo in Foglia I 82 E6
Montecalvo Irpino I 76 A4
Monte-Carlo MC 53 D6
Montecarotto I 83 E7
Montecassiano I 83 F7
Monte Castello di Vibio I 78 B2
Montecastrilli I 78 B2
Montecatini Terme I 82 E2
Montecatini Val di Cecina I 82 F2
Montecchio I 83 E6
Montecchio Emilia I 82 C1
Montecchio Maggiore I 82 A3
Montech F 49 C8
Montechiaro d'Asti I 53 A8
Montechiarugolo I 82 C1
Montecilfone I 79 D7
Montecorice I 76 C3
Montecosaro I 83 F8
Montecreale Valcellina I 89 D6
Montecreto I 82 D2
Monte da Pedra P 60 F5
Monte das Flores P 66 B4
Montederramo E 54 D5
Monte di Procida I 76 B2
Monte do Trigo P 66 C4
Montefalco I 78 B3
Montefalcone I 79 D7
Montefalcone di Val Fortore I 76 A4
Montefano I 83 F7
Montefelcino I 83 E6
Montefiascone I 78 B2
Montefiore dell'Aso I 78 A5
Montefiorino I 82 D2
Montefortino I 78 B4
Montefranco I 78 B3
Montefrío E 69 B8
Montegiordano I 77 C7
Montegiorgio I 83 F8
Monte Gordo P 66 E5
Montegranaro I 83 F8
Montegrotto Terme I 82 B4
Montehermoso E 61 D8
Monteiasi I 77 C8
Monteils F 49 B9
Monteiros P 60 A5
Montejaque E 69 C6
Montejícar E 69 A10
Montejo de la Sierra E 62 B5
Montelabbate I 83 E6
Montelanico I 78 D4
Montelavar P 66 B1
Montel-de-Gelat F 45 D11
Monteleone di Puglia I 76 A4
Monteleone di Spoleto I 78 B3
Monteleone d'Orvieto I 78 B2
Monteleone Rocca Doria I 80 C2
Montelepre I 74 C3
Montelibretti I 78 C3
Montélier F 47 F7
Montélimar F 51 A8
Montella I 76 B4
Montellano E 67 E8
Montels F 49 D8
Montelupo Fiorentino I 82 E3
Montelupone I 83 F8
Montemaggiore Belsito I 74 D4
Montemagno I 53 B8
Montemarciano I 83 E7
Montemayor E 69 A7
Montemayor de Pililla E 56 E3
Montembœuf F 45 D7
Montemesola I 77 B8
Montemiletto I 76 A3
Montemilone I 76 A5
Montemolín E 67 C7
Montemonaco I 78 B4
Montemor-o-Novo P 66 B3
Montemurlo I 82 E3
Montemurro I 76 C5
Montenay F 39 D10
Montendre F 44 E5
Montenegro de Cameros E 56 D6
Montenero di Bisaccia I 79 D7
Montenerodomo I 79 C6
Monte Porzio I 83 E7
Monteprandone I 78 B5
Montepulciano I 78 A1
Monterblanc F 38 E6
Monterchi I 82 F5
Monte Real P 60 E3
Montereale I 78 B4
Montereau-fault-Yonne F 41 D8
Monte Redondo P 60 E3
Monterenzio I 82 D3
Monteriggioni I 82 F3
Monteroduni I 79 D6
Monte Romano I 78 C1
Monteroni d'Arbia I 82 F3
Monteroni di Lecce I 77 C10
Monterosso Almo I 75 E6
Monterosso Calabro I 75 B9
Monterotondo I 78 C3
Monterotondo Marittimo I 82 F2
Monterrei E 54 E5
Monterroso E 54 C4
Monterrubio de la Serena E 67 B9
Monterubbiano I 78 A5
Montesa E 72 D3
Monte San Biagio I 78 E4
Monte San Giovanni Campano I 78 D5
Montesano Salentino I 77 D10
Montesano sulla Marcellana I 76 C5
Monte San Savino I 82 F4
Monte Santa Maria Tiberina I 82 F5
Monte Sant'Angelo I 79 D9
Monte San Vito I 83 E7
Montesarchio I 76 A3
Montescaglioso I 77 B7
Montesclaros E 62 D3
Montescudaio I 82 F2
Montese I 82 D2
Montesilvano I 79 B6
Montespertoli I 82 E3
Montesquieu F 49 B8
Montesquieu-Volvestre F 49 D8
Montesquiou F 49 C6
Montes Velhos P 66 D3
Monteux F 51 B8
Montevago I 74 D2
Montevarchi I 82 E4
Montevecchia I 80 D2
Monteverde I 76 A5
Montevil P 66 C2
Montfaucon F 39 F9
Montfaucon F 45 F9
Montfaucon-d'Argonne F 35 F11
Montfaucon-en-Velay F 46 E5
Montferran-Savès F 49 C7
Montferrat F 52 D4
Montferrier F 49 E9
Montfoort NL 198 A5
Montfort F 39 D8
Montfort F 48 D4
Montfort NL 199 C7
Montfort-en-Chalosse F 48 C4
Montfort-l'Amaury F 40 C6
Montfort-le-Gesnois F 40 D3
Montfort-sur-Risle F 34 F2
Montgai E 58 D5
Montgaillard F 49 D6
Montgaillard F 49 E9
Montgenèvre F 47 F10
Montgeron F 41 C7
Montgiscard F 49 D9
Montgivray F 45 B9
Montgomery GB 26 F5
Montguyon F 44 E5
Monthermé F 35 E10
Monthey CH 47 C10
Monthois F 35 F10
Monthureux-sur-Saône F 42 D4
Monti I 80 B3
Monticelli d'Ongina I 85 C8
Monticello F 53 F9
Montichiari I 82 B1
Monticiano I 81 A4
Montiel E 71 B7
Montier-en-Der F 41 D12
Montieri I 81 A4
Montiers-sur-Saulx F 42 C3
Montiglio I 84 C5
Montignac F 45 E8
Montignies-le-Tilleul B 35 D9
Montignoso I 82 D1
Montigny F 43 C6
Montigny-la-Resie F 41 E10
Montigny-le-Roi F 42 D3
Montigny-lès-Metz F 42 B5
Montigny-Mornay-Villeneuve-sur-Vingeanne F 42 E3
Montigny-sur-Aube F 41 E12
Montijo E 67 B6
Montijo P 66 B2
Montilla E 69 A7
Montillana E 69 A9
Montivilliers F 39 A12
Montizón E 71 C6
Montjaux F 50 B4
Montjean F 39 D10
Montjovet I 84 B4
Montlaur F 50 D4
Montlieu-la-Garde F 44 E5
Mont-Louis F 49 E10
Montluçon F 45 C11
Montluel F 47 D7
Montmarault F 46 C2
Montmartin-sur-Mer F 39 C8
Montmédy F 35 E11
Montmélian F 47 D9
Montmelo E 59 D8
Montmeyran F 47 F6
Montmeyan F 52 D4
Montmirail F 40 D4
Montmirail F 41 C10
Montmirey-le-Château F 42 F4
Montmoreau-St-Cybard F 45 E6
Montmorillon F 45 C7
Montmorin F 51 B10
Montmorot F 47 B8
Montmort-Lucy F 41 C10
Montoir-de-Bretagne F 39 F7
Montoire-sur-le-Loir F 40 E4
Montoison F 46 F6
Montoito P 66 B4
Montola FIN 140 F8
Montón E 63 B10
Montone I 82 F5
Montopoli di Sabina I 78 C3
Montorio al Vomano I 78 B5
Montoro E 69 A8
Montory F 48 D4
Montournais F 44 B4
Montpelier IRL 24 C6
Montpellier F 51 C6
Montpeyroux F 50 A4
Montpezat F 49 B7
Montpézat F 49 D7
Montpezat-de-Quercy F 49 B8
Montpezat-sous-Bauzon F 46 F5
Montpon-Ménestérol F 45 E6
Montpont-en-Bresse F 47 B7
Mont-ras E 59 D10
Montréal F 41 E11
Montréal F 49 C6
Montréal F 49 D10
Montredon-Labessonnié F 49 C10
Montregard F 46 E5
Montréjeau F 49 D7
Montrésor F 40 F5
Montresta I 80 C2
Montret F 47 B7
Montreuil F 31 G12
Montreuil-Bellay F 39 F11
Montreuil-Juigné F 39 E10
Montreux CH 47 C10
Montrevault F 39 F9
Montrevel-en-Bresse F 47 C7
Montrichard F 40 F5
Montricoux F 49 B9
Montriond F 47 C10
Mont-roig del Camp E 58 E5
Montrond F 47 B8
Montrond-les-Bains F 46 D5
Montrose GB 21 B12
Montroy E 64 F3
Monts F 40 F4
Montsalvy F 45 F10
Montsauche-les-Settons F 41 F11
Montségur F 49 E9
Montseny E 59 D8
Montsoué F 48 C4
Mont-sous-Vaudrey F 47 B8
Monts-sur-Guesnes F 45 B6
Mont-St-Aignan F 34 F3
Mont-St-Jean F 41 F11
Mont-St-Martin F 35 E12
Mont-St-Vincent F 46 B5
Montsûrs F 39 D10
Montsuzain F 41 D11
Montuïri E 73 B10
Montvalent F 45 F9
Montville F 34 E3
Montzen B 199 D7
Montzéville F 36 F4
Monza I 85 B7
Monzelfeld D 37 E8
Monzingen D 37 E9
Monzón E 58 D4
Monzón de Campos E 56 D3
Mook NL 199 B7
Moone IRL 23 G9
Moorbad Lobenstein D 91 B10
Moordorf (Südbrookmerland) D 33 B8
Moorends GB 27 D10
Moorenweis D 91 F9
Moorfields GB 20 F4
Moorrege D 98 C7
Moorslede B 35 C7
Moorweg D 33 A9
Moos D 92 E3
Moosbach D 91 C11
Moosburg A 89 C9
Moosburg an der Isar D 91 F10
Moosinning D 91 F10
Mooste EST 147 E14
Mór H 165 B10
Mora E 62 E5
Mora P 66 B3
Mora S 113 B14
Mora S 118 D8
Mora de Rubielos E 64 D3
Moradillo de Roa E 56 E4
Morąg PL 155 C8
Mórahalom H 166 E4
Moraice MNE 179 C7
Moraira E 72 D5
Morais P 55 E6
Moraïtika GR 184 E2
Morakovo MNE 179 D7
Móra la Nova E 58 E5
Moral de Calatrava E 70 B5
Moraleda de Zafayona E 69 B9
Moraleja E 61 D7
Moraleja del Vino E 55 F8
Moraleja de Sayago E 61 B9
Morales de Campos E 55 E9
Morales del Vino E 55 F8
Morales de Toro E 55 E9
Morales de Valverde E 55 E8
Moralina E 55 F7
Moräng S 134 D3
Morano Calabro I 76 D6
Morano sul Po I 84 C5
Morar GB 20 B5
Morărești RO 176 C5
Morasverdes E 61 C8
Morata de Jalón E 57 F9
Morata de Tajuña E 62 D6
Moratalla E 71 C9
Morava BG 182 C4
Morava MD 170 C4
Morava SLO 89 E10
Moravany CZ 93 B9
Moravany CZ 93 D11
Moravany SK 161 F4
Moravče SLO 89 E10
Moravice HR 83 B11
Moravița RO 175 C7
Moravka BG 182 C6
Morávka CZ 163 B7
Moravská Třebová CZ 93 C11
Moravské Budějovice CZ 93 D9
Moravské Lieskové SK 162 D5
Moravský Beroun CZ 162 B4
Moravský Svätý Ján SK 93 E12
Morawica PL 159 E10
Morbach D 37 E8
Morbegno I 85 A8
Morbier F 47 B9
Mörbisch am See A 165 A7
Mörby S 115 C10
Mörbylånga S 105 B10
Morcenx F 48 B4
Morciano di Leuca I 77 D10
Morciano di Romagna I 82 E6
Morcone I 76 A3
Mordelles F 39 D8
Mordoğan TR 193 B8
Mordy PL 157 F7
More LV 151 B10
Moréac F 38 E6
Moreanes P 66 D4
Morebattle GB 21 D12
Morecambe GB 26 C6
Moreda E 55 B8
Moreda E 71 E6
Morée F 40 E5
Mörel CH 86 E6
Morella E 58 F3
Moreni RO 177 D7
Morenish GB 21 C8
Morentín E 48 E1
Moreruela de Tábara E 55 E8
Mores I 80 B2
Morestel F 47 D7
Moretonhampstead GB 29 D7
Moreton-in-Marsh GB 29 B11
Moret-sur-Loing F 41 D8
Moretta I 53 B7
Moreuil F 34 E5
Morez F 47 B9
Morfa Nefyn GB 26 F2
Morfasso I 85 D8
Mörfelden D 203 B6
Morfi GR 184 D5
Morfi GR 184 F3
Morfovouni GR 185 F6
Morgat F 38 D2
Morgedal N 111 D8
Morges CH 47 B10
Morgex I 47 D11
Morgongåva S 114 C7
Morhange F 42 C6
Mori I 85 B10
Moria GR 193 A8
Moricone I 78 C3
Morienval F 34 F6
Moriles E 69 B7
Morina SRB 179 E9
Morinë AL 179 E10
Moringen D 94 C6
Morino I 78 D4
Moritzburg D 96 D5
Morjärv S 134 B9
Mork N 120 F3
Mørke DK 102 C6
Morkkaperä FIN 131 E1
Mørkøv DK 103 D9
Morkovice CZ 93 D12
Mörkret S 118 C4
Morlaàs F 48 D5
Morlaix F 38 C4
Morlanne F 48 C4
Morlanwelz B 35 D9
Mörlenbach D 37 E11
Morley F 42 C3
Morley GB 27 D8
Morley's Bridge IRL 24 E4
Mörlunda S 105 A9
Mormanno I 76 D6
Mormant F 41 C8
Mormoiron F 51 B9
Mornant F 46 D6
Mornas F 51 B8
Mornese I 53 B9
Moroeni RO 177 C6
Morolo I 78 D4
Morón de Almazán E 57 F7
Morón de la Frontera E 67 E9
Moros E 57 F8
Morosaglia F 53 G10
Morottaja FIN 131 E4
Morović SRB 174 C3
Morozova RUS 145 F14
Morozovo BG 182 D4
Morozzo I 53 C7
Morpeth GB 21 E13
Mørrevatnet N 120 D8
Morrfjord N 126 D8
Morriston GB 29 B7
Morrovalle I 83 F8
Mörrum S 105 C7
Morsbach D 37 C9
Morschen D 94 D6
Morshyn UA 161 E8
Mörsil S 121 E15
Morskoga S 113 C13
Morskogen N 111 B14
Morsum D 33 C12
Mørsvikbotn N 127 E10
Mortagne-au-Perche F 40 C4
Mortagne-sur-Gironde F 44 E4
Mortagne-sur-Sèvre F 44 A4
Mortágua P 60 D4
Mortain F 39 C10
Mortara I 84 C6
Morteau F 47 A10
Morteaux-Coulibœuf F 39 C11
Mörtebo S 119 E12
Mortegliano I 89 E7
Mortelle I 75 C8
Morteni RO 176 D6
Mortensnes N 128 C11
Mortensnes N 130 C6
Mortimer's Cross GB 29 A9
Morton GB 27 F11
Mortrée F 39 C12
Mörtschach A 89 C6
Mortsel B 35 B9
Mörtsjön S 122 D7
Mortsund N 126 D6
Morud DK 102 E6
Morunglav RO 176 E4
Morville GB 26 F7
Mor'ye RUS 145 E15
Moryń PL 100 E6
Morzeszczyn PL 154 C6
Morzine F 47 C10
Moșana MD 169 A11
Mosar BY 149 F2
Mosås S 108 A6
Mosätt S 118 B7
Mosbach D 37 F12
Mosborough GB 27 E9
Mosbjerg DK 106 D7
Mosby N 106 C2
Moscavide P 66 B1
Moščenica HR 165 F6
Moščenička Draga HR 83 B9
Moschopotamos GR 185 D7
Mosciano Sant'Angelo I 78 B5
Mościcha PL 156 C8
Moscovei MD 170 F2
Moscow GB 21 D8
Moseby DK 102 A5
Mosėdis LT 150 D3
Mosel D 95 E11
Möser D 95 B10
Mosina PL 97 B11
Mosjö S 123 E13
Mosjøen N 124 E5
Moskaret N 117 B12
Mosko BIH 178 D5
Moskorzew PL 159 E8
Moskosel S 125 E17
Moskuvaara FIN 131 C1
Moslavna Podravska HR 165 E9
Moșna RO 168 E4
Moșna RO 169 D11
Moșnița Nouă RO 175 B7
Moșoaia RO 176 D5
Moso in Passiria I 88 C3
Mosonmagyaróvár H 162 F4
Mosonszolnok H 162 F4
Mošovce SK 163 D7
Mosqueruela E 64 D4
Moss N 111 D13
Mossala FIN 142 E5
Mossat GB 19 L11
Mossbo S 119 D11
Mössingen D 43 D11
Mossley GB 20 F5
Mossley GB 27 D7
Moss-side GB 20 E4
Mosstakan S 112 C7
Most BG 182 F5
Most CZ 92 A5
Mostar BIH 173 F8
Mosteiro E 54 B5
Mosteiro P 60 E5
Mosteiro P 66 D4
Mostek CZ 93 B9
Moșteni RO 177 E7
Mosterhamn N 110 C2
Mostkowo PL 101 E8
Mostkowo PL 155 C9
Most na Soči SLO 89 D8
Móstoles E 62 D5
Mosty PL 157 G8
Mostys'ka UA 160 D7
Mosty u Jablunkova CZ 163 B7
Mosvik N 121 D10
Mosyr UA 160 A9
Moszczenica PL 159 C8
Mota del Cuervo E 63 F7
Mota del Marqués E 55 E9
Moțăieni RO 176 C6
Motala S 108 B6
Motarzyno PL 101 B12
Moțăței RO 175 E11
Moțca RO 169 C9
Motherwell GB 21 D9
Môtiers CH 47 B10
Motike BIH 172 D6
Motike BIH 173 C7
Motilla del Palancar E 63 E9
Motilleja E 63 F9
Motjärnshyttan S 113 C10
Motoșeni RO 169 E10
Motovun HR 83 B8
Motril E 69 C9
Motru RO 175 D10
Mõtsu EST 146 D7
Motta Montecorvino I 79 D8
Motta San Giovanni I 75 C8
Motta Visconti I 85 C6
Motten D 90 B6
Möttingen D 91 E8
Mottola I 77 B8
Möttönen FIN 139 D13
Mötz A 87 C11
Mou DK 102 B6
Moucha GR 190 A4
Mouchamps F 44 B3
Mouchan F 49 C6
Moudon CH 47 B10
Moudros GR 187 E8
Mougins F 52 D6
Mouhijärvi FIN 143 B9
Moularès F 49 B10
Moulay F 39 D10
Mouleydier F 45 F7
Mouliherne F 39 F12
Moulin-Neuf F 49 D9
Moulins F 46 B3
Moulins-Engilbert F 46 B4
Moulins-la-Marche F 40 C3
Moulis-en-Médoc F 44 E4
Moulismes F 45 C7
Moult F 39 B11
Moulton GB 31 C7
Moulton GB 31 C9
Mountbellew IRL 22 F6
Mount Bellew IRL 22 F6
Mountbenger GB 21 D10
Mountcharles IRL 22 C6
Mountcollins IRL 24 D4
Mount Hamilton GB 20 F2
Mountjoy GB 20 F2
Mountjoy GB 23 C9
Mountmellick IRL 23 F8
Mount Norris GB 23 D10
Mount Nugent IRL 23 E8
Mountrath IRL 23 F8
Mountshannon IRL 24 C6
Mountsorrel GB 27 F9
Moura P 66 C5
Mourão P 67 C5
Mourenx F 48 D4
Mouriès F 51 C8
Mouries GR 185 B8
Mouriki GR 191 C7
Mourisca do Vouga P 60 C4
Mouriscas P 60 E4
Mournies GR 194 E7
Mourujärvi FIN 137 B11
Mouscron B 35 C7
Moussac F 51 C7
Moussey F 43 D7
Moussoulens F 49 D10
Moussy F 41 F9
Moustéru F 38 C5
Moustey F 48 B4
Moustheni GR 186 C6
Moustiers-Ste-Marie F 52 D4
Mouthe F 47 B9
Mouthier-Haute-Pierre F 47 A9
Mouthiers-sur-Boëme F 45 D6
Mouthoumet F 50 E4
Moutier CH 43 F7
Moutier-d'Ahun F 45 C10
Moûtiers F 47 E10
Moutiers-les-Mauxfaits F 44 C3
Moutnice CZ 93 D11
Moutsouna GR 193 E6
Moux F 50 D4
Moux-en-Morvan F 41 F11
Mouy F 34 F5
Mouzaki GR 185 F6
Mouzaki GR 190 D4
Mouzay F 35 F11
Mouzon F 35 E11
Moviken S 119 C12
Movila RO 171 D1
Movila Miresii RO 171 C1
Movileni RO 169 C10
Movileni RO 169 F10
Movileni RO 176 E5
Movilița RO 169 F10
Movilița RO 177 D8
Moville IRL 20 E2
Movollen N 121 F11
Mowtie GB 21 B12
Moy GB 19 L8
Moy GB 23 D9
Moya E 63 E10
Moyard IRL 22 E2
Moyasta IRL 24 C3
Moycullen IRL 22 F4
Moy-de-l'Aisne F 35 E7
Moyenmoutier F 43 D6
Moyenneville F 34 D4
Moygashel GB 23 D9
Moyivka UA 170 A2
Möykkylänperä FIN 135 E13
Möykkylänperä FIN 135 F17
Moylaw IRL 22 D4
Moylett IRL 23 E8
Moylough IRL 22 F5
Moymore IRL 24 C5
Moyne IRL 23 E7
Moyvalley IRL 23 F9
Moyvore IRL 23 E7
Mozac F 46 D3
Mozăceni RO 176 D6
Mozárbez E 61 C9
Mozelj SLO 89 E10
Mozelos P 60 C5
Mozgovo SRB 175 F8
Mozirje SLO 89 D10
Mozoncillo E 62 B4
Mozsgó H 165 D9
Mozyr' RUS 152 E3
Mračaj BIH 173 E7
Mrągowo PL 152 F3
Mrákov CZ 92 D3
Mrakovica BIH 173 B6
Mramor BIH 173 F8
Mramorak SRB 175 D6
Mratinje MNE 173 F10
Mrčajevci SRB 174 F6
Mrežičko MK 185 B6
Mrkalji BIH 173 D10
Mrkonjić-Grad BIH 173 D7
Mrkopalj HR 83 B10
Mrmoš SRB 180 B3
Mrocza PL 101 D13
Mroczeń PL 158 D4
Mroczków PL 157 H3
Mroczno PL 155 D8
Mrozy PL 157 F5
Mścice PL 101 B10
Mściwojów PL 97 D10
Mšené Lázně CZ 92 B6
Mšeno CZ 93 B7
Mshinskaya RUS 148 C6
Mstów PL 159 E7
Mszana PL 163 B7
Mszana Dolna PL 160 D1
Mszczonów PL 157 G3
Muccia I 78 A4
Much D 37 C8
Muchalls GB 21 A12
Mucharz PL 163 B9
Mücheln (Geiseltal) D 95 D10
Muchow D 99 D11
Muchówka PL 160 D1
Much Wenlock GB 26 F6
Mucientes E 55 E10
Mücka D 97 D7
Mücke Große-Eichen D 37 C12
Mücke-Nieder-Ohmen D 37 C12
Muckross IRL 24 D4
Múcsony H 161 G2
Mudanya TR 189 D10
Mudau D 203 B7
Müdelheim D 199 C9
Müden (Aller) D 95 A7
Müden (Örtze) D 99 E8
Mudersbach D 201 C8
Mŭdrets BG 182 E6
Muel E 57 F9
Muelas del Pan E 55 E8
Muff IRL 20 E2
Muga de Sayago E 55 F7
Mugardos E 54 B3
Muge P 60 F3
Mügeln D 96 C4
Mügeln D 96 D4
Mugeni RO 168 E6
Muggensturm D 203 D5
Muggia I 89 E8
Muğla TR 197 B8
Müglen BG 183 D8
Müglizh BG 182 D5
Mugron F 48 C4
Mühlacker D 43 C10
Mühlanger D 95 C12
Mühlbachl A 88 B3
Mühlberg D 95 E8
Mühlberg D 96 D4
Mühldorf A 89 C7
Mühldorf am Inn D 91 F12
Mühldorf bei Feldbach A 164 C5
Mühlen A 89 B10
Mühlenbeck D 100 E4
Mühlhausen D 37 F11
Mühlhausen D 91 D9
Mühlhausen (Thüringen) D 95 D7
Mühltroff D 91 A10
Muhola FIN 139 D14
Muhos FIN 135 E15
Muhr am See D 91 D8
Muhur AL 179 F9
Muineachán IRL 23 D9
Muine Bheag IRL 25 C9
Muiños E 54 E4
Muirdrum GB 21 B11
Muirhead GB 21 C10
Muirkirk GB 21 D8
Muir of Ord GB 18 K8
Muizon F 35 F8
Mujdić BIH 173 D7
Mujejärvi FIN 141 C12
Mukacheve UA 161 G6
Mukařov CZ 93 C7
Mukhavyets BY 157 F9
Mukhovo BG 181 E8
Mukkala FIN 131 D5
Mukkavaara FIN 131 D4
Mula E 71 C10
Mulbarton GB 31 B11
Muleby DK 104 E7
Mulešići BIH 173 C9
Mulfingen D 90 D6
Mülheim an der Ruhr D 33 F7
Mülheim-Kärlich D 201 D7
Mulhouse F 43 E7
Muljava SLO 89 E10
Mullach Íde IRL 23 F10
Mullagh IRL 23 E9
Mullagh IRL 23 F9
Mullaghroe IRL 22 E6
Mullany's Cross IRL 22 D5
Mullartown GB 23 D11
Müllheim D 43 E8
Mullhyttan S 108 A5
Mullingar IRL 23 E8
Mullion GB 28 E4
Müllrose D 96 B6
Mullsjö S 107 D14
Mulrany IRL 22 E3
Mulsanne F 39 E12
Mulseryd S 107 D14
Multia FIN 139 F13
Multiperä FIN 137 C15
Mümliswil CH 43 F8
Munakka FIN 138 E9
Muñana E 61 C10
Munapirtti FIN 144 E6
Münchberg D 91 B10
Müncheberg D 96 A6
München D 91 F10
Münchenbernsdorf D 95 E10
Münchenbuchsee CH 47 A11
Münchhausen D 37 C11
Münchsteinach D 91 C8
Münchweiler an der Rodalb D 202 C4
Münchwilen CH 43 F11
Mundaka E 57 B6
Munderkingen D 203 E8
Mundesley GB 31 B11
Mundford GB 31 B10
Mundheim N 110 B3
Mundolsheim F 43 C8
Munebrega E 57 F8

Munera E 71 A8
Mungia E 56 B6
Mungret IRL 24 C5
Muñico E 61 C10
Muniesa E 58 E2
Munilla E 57 D7
Munka-Ljungby S 103 C11
Munkbyn S 119 B11
Munkebakken N 130 D6
Munkebo DK 102 E7
Munkedal S 107 C10
Munken N 120 D6
Munkflohögen S 122 D7
Munkfors S 113 C10
Munklia N 127 D14
Munksund S 134 D7
Munktorp S 114 C6
Munkzwalm B 35 C8
Munne FIN 144 C7
Münnerstadt D 91 B7
Munningen D 91 E8
Muñogalindo E 62 C3
Munsala FIN 138 D8
Münsingen CH 47 B12
Münsingen D 90 F5
Münster A 88 B4
Münster CH 86 E6
Münster D 33 E9
Münster D 37 E11
Münster D 99 E8
Munster F 43 D7
Münsterdorf D 98 C7
Munstergeleen NL 199 D7
Münsterhausen D 91 F7
Münstermaifeld D 201 D7
Muntendam NL 33 B7
Munteni RO 169 F10
Munteni-Buzău RO 177 D9
Muntenii de Jos RO 169 D11
Münzenberg D 37 D11
Münzkirchen A 92 F5
Muodoslompolo S 133 C10
Muonio FIN 133 C11
Muonionalusta S 133 C11
Muotathal CH 87 D7
Muotkajärvi FIN 133 B10
Muotkavaara FIN 133 C12
Mur SRB 179 C9
Muradiye TR 189 D9
Muradiye TR 193 B9
Murakeresztúr H 165 D7
Muráň SK 163 D10
Muras E 54 B4
Murasson F 50 C4
Muraste EST 147 C8
Muraszemenye H 165 D7
Murat F 46 E2
Muratlar TR 197 B9
Muratlı TR 189 B7
Murato F 53 F10
Murat-sur-Vèbre F 50 C4
Murau A 89 B9
Muravera I 80 E4
Murazzano I 53 C8
Murça P 54 F5
Murchante E 57 D8
Mŭrchevo BG 181 B7
Murchin D 100 C5
Murcia E 72 F2
Murczyn PL 154 E4
Mur-de-Barrez F 45 F11
Mûr-de-Bretagne F 38 D6
Mur-de-Sologne F 40 F6
Mureck A 164 C5
Mürefte TR 189 C7
Muret F 49 D8
Murgeni RO 169 E12
Murgenthal CH 43 F8
Murgești RO 177 C9
Murgia E 56 C6
Muri CH 43 F9
Muri CH 47 B11
Murias de Paredes E 55 C7
Muriedas E 56 B4
Murighiol RO 171 C4
Murillo de Río Leza E 48 F1
Murillo el Fruto E 48 F3
Murino MNE 179 D8
Murisengo I 84 C5
Murjāni LV 151 B9
Murjek S 132 F5
Murley GB 23 D8
Murlo I 82 F3
Murmastiene LV 151 C13
Murnau am Staffelsee D 88 A3
Muro E 73 B11
Muro F 53 F9
Muro P 54 F2
Muro de Alcoy E 72 D4
Murol F 46 D2
Murole FIN 143 B10
Muro Lucano I 76 B4
Muron F 44 C4
Murony H 167 D7
Muros E 54 C1
Muros E 55 A7
Muros I 80 B2
Murovane UA 160 C9
Murów PL 158 E4
Murowana Goślina PL 97 A12
Murrë AL 184 A3
Murrhardt D 90 E6
Murronkylä FIN 135 E16
Murroogh IRL 22 F4
Mursallı TR 193 D10
Mûrs-Erigné F 39 F10
Murska Sobota SLO 164 C6
Mursko Središće HR 165 C6
Murtas E 71 F6
Murtede P 60 D4
Murten CH 47 B11
Murter HR 172 E4
Murtino MK 185 B8
Murto FIN 135 E15
Murtolahti FIN 141 D9
Murtomäki FIN 140 B9
Murtovaara FIN 137 C13
Murumoen N 121 C16
Murvica HR 172 D3
Murviel-lès-Béziers F 50 D5
Mürzsteg A 164 A5
Murzynowo PL 97 A8
Mürzzuschlag A 164 A5
Mūsa LV 151 D8
Musbury GB 29 D8
Müschenbach D 201 C8
Musei I 80 E2
Muselievo BG 176 F5
Musile di Piave I 88 E6
Muskö S 109 B12
Mussalo FIN 144 E6
Musselburgh GB 21 D10
Musselkanaal NL 33 C8
Mussidan F 45 E6
Mussomeli I 74 D4
Musson B 35 E12
Mussy-sur-Seine F 41 E12
Mustafakemalpaşa TR 189 D9
Müstair CH 87 D10
Mustamaa FIN 135 F17
Mustamaa FIN 139 D10
Mustasaari FIN 138 D7
Mustavaara FIN 137 D12
Mustavaara FIN 137 F12
Mustinlahti FIN 141 E10
Mustjala EST 146 E4
Mustla EST 147 E11
Mustola FIN 130 F4
Mustolanmäki FIN 141 C10
Mustolanmutka FIN 141 B10
Mustvee EST 147 D13
Mušutište SRB 179 E10
Muszaki PL 155 D10
Muszyna PL 161 E2
Muta SLO 89 C11
Mutala FIN 143 B10
Mutalahti FIN 141 F16
Mütevelli TR 193 B10
Muthill GB 21 C9
Mutilva Baja E 48 E2
Mutné SK 163 C8
Mutriku E 48 D1
Mutterstadt D 37 F10
Mutxamel E 72 E4
Mutzig F 43 C7
Mutzschen D 96 D3
Muuga EST 147 C13
Muukajärvi S 132 E10
Muuksi EST 147 B11
Muurame FIN 139 F15
Muurasjärvi FIN 139 C14
Muurikkala FIN 144 D8
Muurla FIN 143 E9
Muurola FIN 135 B14
Muurola FIN 144 D8
Muuruvesi FIN 141 D10
Muxía E 54 B1
Muzillac F 38 E7
Mužla SK 165 A11
Myahuny BY 153 C14
Myakishevo RUS 149 C5
Myaretskiya BY 149 F3
Myazhany BY 151 E13
Mybster GB 19 J10
Myckelgensjö S 123 D13
Myckle S 134 E5
Myedna BY 157 G9
Myggenäs S 107 C10
Myggsjö S 118 C8
Myhinpää FIN 140 F7
Myjava SK 162 D5
Mykanów PL 159 E7
Mykhal'cha UA 169 A7
Mykhaylivka UA 170 F5
Myki GR 187 B7
Myklebostad N 126 E9
Mykolayiv UA 161 D8
Mykolayivka UA 170 E4
Mykolayivka-Novorosiys'ka UA 170 E5
Mykonos GR 192 E5
Mykulychyn UA 168 A5
Mykytychi UA 160 B9
Myllykoski FIN 144 D6
Myllykylä FIN 138 E8
Myllykylä FIN 143 E10
Myllykylä FIN 144 D7
Myllylahti FIN 137 D13
Myllymäki FIN 139 E12
Myloi GR 191 D6
Mylopotamos GR 194 C4
Mynämäki FIN 142 D7
Mynttilä FIN 144 C6
Myon F 47 A8
Myory BY 149 E3
Myra GR 185 F8
Myrås S 125 E14
Myre N 126 C9
Myre N 127 B10
Myresjö S 108 E5
Myrhaug N 117 A14
Myrheden S 134 D4
Myrhult S 108 B4
Myrina GR 187 E8
Myriokefala GR 194 E7
Myrkky FIN 138 F7
Myrland N 126 D5
Myrland N 126 D9
Myrland N 127 C10
Myrlandshaugen N 127 C13
Myrmoen N 117 A15
Myrne UA 171 B4
Myrnes N 128 C9
Myrnopillya UA 170 E4
Myrsini GR 190 D3
Myrsini GR 194 B3
Myrskylä FIN 143 D14
Myrties GR 193 F8
Myrtos GR 195 E10
Myrviken S 121 E16
Mysen N 111 C14
Myshall IRL 25 C9
Myślachowice PL 159 F7
Mysłakowice PL 97 E9
Myślenice PL 163 B9
Myślibórz PL 101 E7
Myślice PL 155 C8
Mysłowice PL 159 F7
Mysovka RUS 150 F2
Myssjö S 118 A7
Mystegna GR 193 A7
Mystras GR 190 E5
Myszków PL 159 E7
Myszyniec PL 155 D11
Mytikas GR 190 B2
Mytilini GR 193 A8
Mytilinioi GR 193 D8
Mýtna SK 163 E9
Mýto CZ 92 C5

N

Nå N 110 B5
Naaldwijk NL 32 E2
Naamankylä FIN 135 E17
Naamijoki FIN 133 E11
Naantali FIN 142 E7
Naapurinvaara FIN 137 F11
Naarden NL 199 A6
Näärinki FIN 144 B8
Naarn im Machlande A 93 F7
Naartijärvi S 135 C11
Naarva FIN 141 D16
Naas IRL 23 F9
Näätämö FIN 130 D6
Näätänmaa FIN 141 F10
Näätävaara FIN 137 E13
Nabburg D 91 D11
Nábrád H 161 G5
Na Cealla Beaga IRL 22 C6
Načeradec CZ 93 C7
Nacha BY 153 E10
Náchod CZ 93 B10
Nacina Ves SK 161 F4
Näckådalen S 118 D7
Nackel D 99 E13
Nackenheim D 201 E9
Näcksjö S 119 C12
Na Clocha Liathe IRL 23 F10
Nacpolsk PL 155 E9
Nad IRL 24 D5
Nadalj SRB 174 C4
Nadarzyce PL 101 D11
Nadarzyn PL 157 F3
Naddvik N 116 D7
Nadeș RO 168 E5
Nădlac RO 166 E6
Nădrag RO 175 B9
Nadrichne UA 170 E4
Nádudvar H 167 C7
Năeni RO 177 C8
Nærbø N 110 E3
Næroset N 117 E13
Nærsnes N 111 C13
Næsbjerg DK 102 D3
Næstved DK 103 E9
Näfels CH 43 F11
Nafferton GB 27 C11
Nafpaktos GR 190 C4
Nafplio GR 191 D6
Nagele NL 32 C5
Naggen S 119 B11
Naglarby S 113 B14
Na Gleannta IRL 22 C6
Nagļi LV 149 C1
Nagłowice PL 159 E9
Nagold D 43 C10
Nagore E 48 E3
Nago-Torbole I 85 B10
Nagu FIN 142 E6
Nagyatád H 165 D8
Nagybajom H 165 D9
Nagybánhegyes H 167 E6
Nagybaracska H 165 D11
Nagybarca H 161 G2
Nagyberény H 165 C10
Nagyberki H 165 D10
Nagycenk H 165 A7
Nagycsécs H 161 H2
Nagycserkesz H 161 H4
Nagydobos H 161 G5
Nagydorog H 165 C11
Nagyecsed H 161 H5
Nagyfüged H 166 B5
Nagyhalász H 161 G4
Nagyharsány H 165 E10
Nagyhegyes H 167 B7
Nagyigmánd H 165 A10
Nagyiván H 167 C6
Nagykálló H 161 H4
Nagykanizsa H 165 D7
Nagykapornak H 165 C7
Nagykáta H 166 C4
Nagykereki H 167 C8
Nagykónyi H 165 C10
Nagykőrös H 166 C4
Nagykörű H 166 C5
Nagykovácsi H 165 A11
Nagylak H 166 E6
Nagylóc H 163 E9
Nagylók H 165 C11
Nagylózs H 165 A7
Nagymágocs H 166 D5
Nagymaros H 165 A11
Nagynyárád H 165 E11
Nagyoroszi H 163 F8
Nagyrécse H 165 C8
Nagyréde H 166 B4
Nagyszénás H 166 D6
Nagyszokoly H 165 C10
Nagytarcsa H 166 B3
Nagytőke H 166 D5
Nagyvarsány H 161 G5
Nagyvázsony H 165 C9
Nagyvisnyó H 161 G1
Naha EST 148 E1
Naharros E 63 D8
Nahe D 99 C8
Nahirne UA 171 C2
Nahrendorf D 99 D9
Naidăș RO 175 D8
Naila D 91 B10
Nailloux F 49 D9
Nailsworth GB 29 B10
Naimakka S 132 A7
Naintré F 45 B6
Naipköy TR 189 C7
Nairn GB 19 K9
Naives-Rosières F 42 C3
Naizin F 38 E6
Najac F 49 B9
Nájera E 56 D6
Näkkälä FIN 133 A11
Nakkerud N 111 B12
Nakkila FIN 142 C7
Náklo CZ 93 C12
Nakło PL 159 E8
Naklo SLO 89 D9
Nakło nad Notecią PL 101 D13
Nakomiady PL 152 E3
Näkotne LV 150 C6
Nakovo SRB 166 F6
Nakskov DK 99 A10
Nalbach D 202 C2
Nalbant RO 171 C3
Nalda E 57 D7
Nälden S 121 E16
Nałęczów PL 157 H6
Nálepkovo SK 161 F2
Näljänkä FIN 137 D11
Nalkki FIN 137 E10
Nalliers F 44 C3
Nalžovské Hory CZ 92 D5
Namborn D 37 E8
Nambroca E 62 E5
Namdalseid N 121 C10
Náměšť nad Oslavou CZ 93 D10
Náměšť na Hané CZ 93 C12
Námestovo SK 163 C8
Nämpnäs FIN 138 E6
Namsos N 121 C11
Namsskogan N 121 B14
Namsvatn N 121 B15
Namur B 35 D10
Namysłów PL 158 D4
Nana RO 177 E9
Nána SK 163 F7
Nançay F 40 F7
Nanclares de la Oca E 56 C6
Nancy F 42 C5
Nandrin B 199 D6
Nănești RO 177 B10
Nangis F 41 C9
Nannestad N 111 B13
Nanov RO 176 F6
Nans-les-Pins F 51 D10
Nant F 50 B5
Nanterre F 41 C7
Nantes F 39 F8
Nanteuil-le-Haudouin F 41 B8
Nantiat F 45 C8
Nantua F 47 C8
Nantwich GB 26 E6
Naousa GR 185 C7
Naousa GR 192 E5
Napajedla CZ 162 C5
Napiwoda PL 155 D9
Napkor H 161 H4
Napola I 74 D2
Napoli I 76 B2
Napp N 126 D5
Năpradea RO 167 C11
Náquera E 64 E4
När S 109 E13
Nåra N 116 D1
Nárai H 165 B7
Narberth GB 28 B5
Narbolia I 80 C2
Narbonne F 50 D5
Narbonne-Plage F 50 D5
Narborough GB 31 B10
Narbuvoll N 117 B14
Narcao I 80 E2
Narcy F 41 F9
Nardò I 77 C10
Narechenski Bani BG 181 F10
Narew PL 156 E9
Narewka PL 157 E9
Närhilä FIN 139 E16
Narin IRL 22 C6
Nārupclems LV 150 B5
Narkaus FIN 135 B16
Narken S 132 E9
Narlıdere TR 193 C9
Narni I 78 B3
Naro I 74 E4
Narol PL 160 C7
Närpes FIN 138 F6
Narrosse F 48 C3
Narta HR 165 E7
Nartë AL 184 D1
Năruja RO 169 F9
Naruska FIN 131 D6
Naruszewo PL 155 E9
Narva EST 148 C3
Narva FIN 143 C10
Narva-Jõesuu EST 148 C3
Närvijoki FIN 138 E7
Narvik N 127 D13
Narzole I 53 B7
Narzym PL 155 D9
Näs FIN 115 B14
Nås N 106 A5
Näs S 109 E12
Näs S 113 B12
Näs S 118 A8
Näsåker S 123 E11
Năsăud RO 168 C4
Nasavrky CZ 93 C9
Näsberg S 119 C10
Nasbinals F 50 A5
Näs bruk S 114 B6
Näsby S 105 C10
Na Sceirí IRL 23 E10
Našec SRB 179 E10
Näset S 119 D9
Našice HR 165 F10
Nasielsk PL 155 E10
Näske S 123 E15
Näsliden S 123 A16
Naso I 75 C6
Nassau D 37 D9
Nassereith A 87 C11
Nässja S 108 C5
Nässjö S 108 D5
Nässjö S 123 D10
Nassogne B 35 D11
Nästansjö S 123 B11
Nastätten D 201 D8
Nästeln S 118 A7
Nastola FIN 143 D14
Năsturelu RO 177 F6
Näsum S 104 C7
Nasutów PL 157 H6
Näsviken S 119 C12
Näsviken S 122 D9
Naszály H 165 A10
Natalinci SRB 175 E6
Nateby GB 27 C7
Naters CH 84 A4
Nattavaara S 132 E5
Nattavaara by S 132 E6
Nattheim D 91 E7
Nättraby S 105 C9
Naturno I 87 D11
Naucelle F 49 B10
Naucelles F 45 F10
Naudaskalns LV 149 B2
Nauders A 87 D11
Naudīte LV 150 C6
Nauen D 95 A12
Nauendorf D 95 C10
Nauheim D 37 E10
Naujac-sur-Mer F 44 E3
Naujamiestis LT 151 E8
Naujasis Daugėliškis LT 151 F12
Naujoji Akmenė LT 150 D5
Naujoji Vilnia LT 153 D11
Naukšēni LV 147 F10
Naul IRL 23 E10
Naulaperä FIN 137 E10
Naulavaara FIN 141 C10
Naumburg (Hessen) D 33 F12
Naumburg (Saale) D 95 D10
Naundorf D 96 D4
Naundorf D 96 E4
Naunhof D 95 D12
Nauroth D 37 C9
Naurstad N 124 B8
Naustbukta N 121 B11
Naustdal N 116 C3
Nauste N 117 A8
Nautijaur S 125 C17
Nautsi RUS 130 E6
Nautsund N 116 D2
Nava E 55 B9
Navacepeda de Tormes E 61 D10
Navaconcejo E 61 D9
Nava de Arévalo E 62 C3
Nava de la Asunción E 62 B4
Nava del Rey E 55 F9
Nava de Sotrobal E 61 C10
Navadrutsk BY 149 F2
Navafría E 62 B5
Navahermosa E 62 E4
Navajas E 64 E4
Naval E 58 C4
Navalagamella E 62 D4
Navalcaballo E 57 E6
Navalcán E 61 D10
Navalcarnero E 62 D4
Navalero E 56 E6
Navalmanzano E 62 B4
Navalmoral E 62 D3
Navalmoral de la Mata E 61 E9
Navalonguilla E 61 D10
Navalosa E 62 D3
Navalperal de Pinares E 62 C4
Navalpino E 62 F3
Navaluenga E 62 D3
Navalvillar de Ibor E 61 E10
Navalvillar de Pela E 61 F10
Navamorcuende E 62 D3
Navan IRL 23 E9
Navapolatsk BY 149 E5
Navarcles E 59 D7
Navardún E 48 E3
Navarredonda de la Rinconada E 61 C8
Navarrenx F 48 D4
Navarrés E 64 F3
Navarrete E 57 D6
Navarrevisca E 62 D3
Navàs E 59 D7
Navascués E 48 E3
Navas de Estrena E 62 E3
Navas de Jorquera E 63 F9
Navas del Madroño E 61 E7
Navas del Rey E 62 D4
Navas de Oro E 62 B4
Navas de San Juan E 71 C6
Navasfrías E 61 D7
Navata E 59 C9
Navatalgordo E 62 D3
Nave I 85 B9
Nave P 66 E2
Nave de Haver P 61 C7
Nävekvarn S 109 B9
Navelli I 78 C5
Nåverdal N 117 A12
Näverede S 122 E8
Nave Redonda P 66 E3
Näverkärret S 113 C14
Näverrys FIN 135 C15
Naverstad S 107 B10
Navès E 59 D7
Naves F 45 E9
Navezuelas E 61 E10
Navia E 55 A6
Navilly F 47 B7
Navit N 128 D8
Năvodari RO 171 E3
Nävragöl S 105 C9
Nawojowa PL 161 D2
Naxos GR 192 E5
Nay-Bourdettes F 48 D5
Nazaré P 60 E2
Nazelles-Négron F 40 F4
Nazza D 95 D7
Ndroq AL 184 B2
Nea Agathoupoli GR 185 D8
Nea Alikarnassos GR 194 E9
Nea Anchialos GR 185 F8
Nea Apollonia GR 185 C9
Nea Artaki GR 191 B8
Nea Efesos GR 185 D7
Nea Epidavros GR 191 D7
Nea Figaleia GR 190 E4
Nea Filadelfeia GR 191 C8
Nea Fokaia GR 185 D9
Nea Ionia GR 185 F8
Nea Iraklitsa GR 187 C6
Nea Kallikrateia GR 185 D9
Nea Karvali GR 187 C6
Nea Karya GR 187 C7
Nea Kerdylia GR 185 C10
Nea Kios GR 191 D6
Nea Koroni GR 190 F4
Nea Lampsakos GR 191 C8
Neale IRL 22 E4
Nea Liosia GR 191 C8
Nea Madytos GR 185 C10
Nea Makri GR 191 C8
Nea Malgara GR 185 C8
Nea Mesimvria GR 185 C8
Nea Michaniona GR 185 D8
Nea Moudania GR 185 D9
Nea Olynthos GR 185 D9
Nea Pella GR 185 C8
Nea Peramos GR 187 C6
Nea Peramos GR 191 C7
Nea Plagia GR 185 D9
Neapoli GR 184 D5
Neapoli GR 194 B5
Neapoli GR 195 E10
Nea Poteidaia GR 185 D9
Nea Roda GR 186 D5
Nea Santa GR 185 C8
Nea Santa GR 187 B9
Nea Silata GR 185 D9
Nea Styra GR 191 C9
Neath GB 29 B7
Nea Tiryntha GR 191 D6
Nea Triglia GR 185 D9
Neaua RO 168 E5
Nea Vravrona GR 191 D9
Nea Vyssa GR 187 A11
Nea Zichni GR 185 B10
Nebel D 98 A4
Nébias F 49 E10
Nebljusi HR 172 C4
Nebra (Unstrut) D 95 D10
Nebreda E 56 E4
Nechanice CZ 93 B9
Neckarbischofsheim D 203 C6
Neckargemünd D 37 F11
Neckarsteinach D 37 F11
Neckarsulm D 37 F12
Neckartenzlingen D 43 C11
Necșești RO 176 E6
Necton GB 31 B10
Nečujam HR 172 F5
Neda E 54 B3
Nedansjö S 119 B12
Nedašov CZ 162 C6
Neddemin D 100 C4
Neded SK 162 E5
Nedelino BG 187 B8
Nedelišće HR 165 D6
Nederby DK 102 B4
Nederhögen S 118 B7
Nederhorst den Berg NL 199 A6
Neder Hvam DK 102 C4
Nederlangbroek NL 199 A6
Nedervetil FIN 139 C10
Neder Vindinge DK 103 E9
Nederweert NL 32 F5
Nedlitz D 95 B11
Nedožery-Brezany SK 163 D7
Nedrebø N 110 E4
Nedre Saxnäs S 125 F14
Nedre Soppero S 132 B7
Nedstrand N 110 D3
Nedvědice CZ 93 D10
Nedyalsko BG 183 E7
Nędza PL 158 F5
Neede NL 33 D7
Needham Market GB 31 C11
Neer NL 199 C8
Neerijnen NL 199 B6
Neermoor D 33 B8
Neeroeteren B 199 C7
Neerpelt B 35 B11
Neetze D 99 D9
Nefyn GB 26 F2
Negenborn D 94 C6
Negoi RO 176 F2
Negomir RO 175 D11
Negorci MK 185 B7
Negoslavci HR 173 B11
Negotin SRB 175 E10
Negotino MK 179 F10
Negotino MK 185 B7
Negrar I 82 A2
Negrași RO 176 D6
Negredo E 63 B7
Negreira E 54 C2
Nègrepelisse F 49 B9
Negrești RO 169 D10
Negrești-Oaș RO 161 H7
Negri RO 169 D9
Negru Vodă RO 171 F2
Nehoiu RO 177 C8
Neiden N 130 D6
Neidín IRL 24 E3
Neitaskaite S 132 E8
Neitsuanto S 132 D5
Neittävä FIN 135 E17
Neive I 53 B8
Nejdek CZ 91 B12
Nekézseny H 161 G1
Nekla PL 97 B12
Neksø DK 105 E8
Nelas P 60 C5
Nellim FIN 130 F4
Nellingen D 90 E6
Nelson GB 27 D7
Nemaitonys LT 153 D9
Neman RUS 152 C5
Nemanjica MK 180 F4
Nemanskoye RUS 152 C5
Nembro I 85 B8
Nemea GR 191 D6
Nemenčine LT 153 D11
Nemesgulács H 165 C8
Nemesnádudvar H 166 E3
Nemesvámos H 165 B9
Nemesvid H 165 C8
Nemétkér H 165 C11
Nemėžis LT 153 D11
Nemours F 41 D8
Nemsdorf-Göhrendorf D 95 D10
Nemšová SK 162 D6
Nemunaitis LT 153 E9
Nemunėlio Radviliškis LT 151 D9
Nemyriv UA 160 C7
Nenagh IRL 24 C6
Nendaz CH 47 C11
Neninice SK 163 E8
Nenita GR 193 C7
Nennhausen D 95 A12
Nennslingen D 91 D9
Nenonpelto FIN 140 F8
Nentershausen D 37 D9
Nentershausen D 94 D6
Nenthead GB 21 F12
Nenzing A 87 C9
Neo Agioneri GR 185 C8
Neochoraki GR 191 C7
Neochori GR 185 B9
Neochori GR 185 F6
Neochori GR 187 B10
Neochori GR 190 A3
Neochori GR 190 C3
Neo Erasmio GR 187 C7
Neoi Epivates GR 185 C8
Neo Monastiri GR 185 F7
Neoneli I 80 C2
Neo Petritsi GR 185 B9
Neorić HR 172 E6
Neos Kafkasos GR 184 C5
Neos Marmaras GR 185 D10
Neos Mylotopos GR 185 C7
Neo Souli GR 185 B10
Neos Pagontas GR 191 B8
Neos Pyrgos GR 191 B7
Neos Skopos GR 185 B10
Néoules F 52 E4
Nepi I 78 C2
Nepomuk CZ 92 D5
Nérac F 49 B6
Neratovice CZ 93 B7
Nerău RO 166 F6
Neravai LT 153 E9
Nerchau D 95 D12
Nercillac F 44 D5
Nerdal N 117 A9
Nerde Gärdsjö S 119 E9
Néré F 44 D5
Nereju RO 169 F9
Neresheim D 91 E7
Neresnica SRB 175 E8
Neresnytsya UA 161 G8
Nereta LV 151 D10
Nereto I 78 B5
Nerezine HR 83 C9
Nerežišće HR 172 F6
Néris-les-Bains F 45 C11
Nerja E 69 C9
Nerkoo FIN 140 D8
Nerlia N 124 E7
Nerokouros GR 194 E7
Néronde F 46 D5
Nérondes F 46 B2
Neroth D 37 D7
Nerpio E 71 C8
Nersac F 44 D6
Nersingen D 91 F7
Nerskogen N 117 A11
Nerushay UA 171 B5
Nerva E 67 D6
Nervesa della Battaglia I 88 E5
Nervieux F 46 D5
Nes FO 18 A3
Nes N 111 D9
Nes N 112 A2
Nes N 126 D9
Nes N 127 D10
Nes NL 32 B5
Nesbyen N 117 E10
Neschwitz D 96 D6
Nesebŭr BG 183 D9
Neset N 128 C7
Nes Flaten N 110 C5
Nesgrenda N 106 B4
Nesheim N 110 D3
Nesje N 126 D6
Nesjegjerde N 116 A6
Nesland N 126 D5
Neslandsvatn N 106 B5
Nesle F 34 E6
Nesna N 124 D5
Nesovice CZ 93 D12
Nessa F 53 F9
Nesse D 33 A8
Nesseby N 130 C6
Nesselwang D 87 B11
Nesslau CH 43 F11
Nessodtangen N 111 C13
Nestani GR 191 D5
Nestby N 124 B9
Nesterov RUS 152 D6
Neston GB 26 E5
Nestorio GR 184 D5
Nestoyita UA 170 B4
Nesttun N 110 B2
Nesvady SK 162 F6
Nesvatnstemmen N 106 B3
Nesvik N 110 D4
Nethy Bridge GB 19 L9
Netolice CZ 92 D6
Netphen D 37 C10
Netra (Ringgau) D 95 D7
Netretić HR 164 E4
Netstal CH 87 C8
Nettancourt F 41 C12
Nettersheim D 37 D7
Nettetal D 32 F6
Nettuno I 78 E3
Netvořice CZ 93 C7
Neu-Anspach D 37 D11
Neuberend D 98 A7
Neuberg an der Mürz A 164 A5
Neubeuern D 88 A5
Neubiberg D 91 F10
Neubrandenburg D 100 C4
Neubruchhausen D 33 C11
Neubrunn D 203 B8
Neubukow D 99 B11
Neubulach D 43 C10
Neuburg am Rhein D 203 D5
Neuburg an der Donau D 91 E9
Neuburg-Steinhausen D 99 C11
Neuburxdorf D 96 D4
Neuchâtel CH 47 B10
Neu Darchau D 99 D9
Neudietendorf D 95 E8
Neudorf A 162 F2
Neudrossenfeld D 91 B10
Neuenbürg D 43 C10
Neuendettelsau D 91 D8
Neuenhagen Berlin D 96 A5
Neuenhaus D 33 D7
Neuenhof CH 43 F9
Neuenkirch CH 43 F9
Neuenkirchen D 33 A11
Neuenkirchen D 33 C11
Neuenkirchen D 33 D8
Neuenkirchen D 33 D9
Neuenkirchen D 98 B6
Neuenkirchen D 98 D7
Neuenkirchen D 100 A4
Neuenkirchen D 100 B4
Neuenkirchen (Oldenburg) D 33 C10
Neuenkirchen-Seelscheid D 37 C8
Neuenrade D 201 B8
Neuenstadt am Kocher D 43 B11
Neuenstein D 203 C8
Neuenwalde D 33 A11
Neuerburg D 36 D6
Neufahrn bei Freising D 91 F10
Neufahrn in Niederbayern D 91 E11
Neufchâteau B 35 E11
Neufchâteau F 42 D4
Neufchâtel-en-Bray F 34 E3
Neufchâtel-Hardelot F 31 F12
Neufchâtel-sur-Aisne F 35 F9
Neufeld D 33 A12
Neufeld an der Leitha A 93 G10
Neuffen D 43 C11
Neufmanil F 200 E2
Neufra D 43 D11
Neugersdorf D 97 E7
Neuharlingersiel D 33 A9
Neuhaus A 89 A11
Neuhaus A 89 C10
Neuhaus (Oste) D 33 A12
Neuhaus am Inn D 92 F4
Neuhaus am Klausenbach A 164 C6
Neuhaus am Rennweg D 91 A9
Neuhaus an der Pegnitz D 91 C10
Neuhausen CH 43 E10
Neuhausen D 96 E4
Neuhausen D 203 D6
Neuhausen ob Eck D 43 E10
Neuhof D 90 B6
Neuhof an der Zenn D 91 D8
Neuhofen D 203 C5
Neuhofen an der Krems A 92 F6
Neuillé-Pont-Pierre F 40 E4
Neuilly F 41 F10
Neuilly-en-Thelle F 34 F5
Neuilly-le-Réal F 46 C3
Neuilly-l'Évêque F 42 E3
Neuilly-St-Front F 41 B9
Neu-Isenburg D 203 A6
Neukalen D 99 C13
Neu Kaliß D 99 D10
Neukirch D 96 D6
Neukirchen D 37 C12
Neukirchen D 96 E3
Neukirchen D 99 B10
Neukirchen D 102 F3
Neukirchen am Großvenediger A 88 B5
Neukirchen an der Enknach A 92 F4
Neukirchen an der Vöckla A 92 F5
Neukirchen-Balbini D 91 D11
Neukirchen beim Heiligen Blut D 92 D3
Neukirchen vorm Wald D 92 E4

Neukloster D 99 C11
Neulengbach A 93 F9
Neuler D 91 E7
Neulewin D 100 E6
Neulikko FIN 137 E10
Neulise F 46 D5
Neu Lübbenau D 96 B5
Neum BIH 178 D4
Neumagen D 201 E6
Neumark D 95 E11
Neumarkt am Wallersee A 89 A7
Neumarkt im Mühlkreis A 93 F6
Neumarkt in der Oberpfalz D 91 D9
Neumarkt in Steiermark A 89 B9
Neumarkt-Sankt Veit D 91 F12
Neu Mukran D 100 B5
Neumünster D 99 B7
Neunburg vorm Wald D 91 D11
Neundorf D 91 A11
Neung-sur-Beuvron F 40 E6
Neunkirch CH 43 E10
Neunkirchen A 164 A6
Neunkirchen D 37 E10
Neunkirchen D 37 F8
Neunkirchen am Brand D 91 C9
Neunkirchen am Sand D 91 C9
Neuötting D 91 F12
Neupetershain D 96 C6
Neupölla A 93 E8
Neureichenau D 92 E5
Neuruppin D 99 E13
Neuschönau D 92 E4
Neusiedl am See A 93 G11
Neusorg D 91 C10
Neuss D 37 B7
Neussargues-Moissac F 46 E2
Neustadt D 43 E9
Neustadt D 95 E10
Neustadt D 99 E12
Neustadt (Harz) D 95 C8
Neustadt (Hessen) D 37 C12
Neustadt (Wied) D 37 C8
Neustadt am Kulm D 91 C10
Neustadt am Rübenberge D 94 A5
Neustadt an der Aisch D 91 C8
Neustadt an der Donau D 91 E10
Neustadt an der Waldnaab D 91 C11
Neustadt an der Weinstraße D 37 F10
Neustadt bei Coburg D 91 B9
Neustadt-Glewe D 99 D11
Neustadt in Holstein D 99 B9
Neustadt in Sachsen D 96 D6
Neustift im Stubaital A 88 B3
Neustrelitz D 100 D4
Neutraubling D 91 E11
Neutrebbin D 96 A6
Neu-Ulm D 90 F7
Neuvéglise F 46 F2
Neuves-Maisons F 202 D1
Neuvic F 45 E6
Neuvic F 45 E10
Neuville-aux-Bois F 40 D7
Neuville-de-Poitou F 45 B6
Neuville-les-Dames F 47 C7
Neuville-lès-Dieppe F 34 E3
Neuville-sur-Saône F 46 D6
Neuvilly-en-Argonne F 42 B3
Neuvy-Grandchamp F 46 B4
Neuvy-le-Roi F 40 E4
Neuvy-Pailloux F 45 B9
Neuvy-St-Sépulchre F 45 B9
Neuvy-sur-Barangeon F 41 F7
Neuweiler D 43 C10
Neuwied D 37 D8
Neuwittenbek D 99 B8
Neu Wulmstorf D 99 D7
Neu Zauche D 96 C6
Neuzelle D 97 B7
Neu Zittau D 96 B5
Névache F 47 E10
Nevarénai LT 150 D4
Neveja LV 146 F4
Neveklov CZ 93 C7
Nevel' RUS 149 D7
Nevele B 35 B8
Neverfjord N 129 C12
Nevernes N 124 F4
Neverness N 126 C9
Neveronys LT 153 D9
Nevers F 46 A3
Nevesinje BIH 173 F9
Nevestino BG 181 E6
Névez F 38 E4
Neviano I 77 C10
Néville F 34 E2
Nevlunghavn N 106 B6
Nevsha BG 183 C8
New Abbey GB 21 E9
New Aberdour GB 19 K12
New Alresford GB 29 D12
Newark-on-Trent GB 27 E10
Newbawn IRL 25 D9
Newbiggin-by-the-Sea GB 21 E13
Newbliss IRL 23 D8
Newborough GB 27 F11
Newbridge GB 29 B8
Newbridge IRL 23 F9
New Buildings GB 20 F2
Newburgh GB 19 J11
Newburgh GB 21 C10
Newbury GB 29 C12
Newby Bridge GB 26 C6
Newcastle GB 23 D11
Newcastle GB 29 A8
Newcastle IRL 23 F10
Newcastle IRL 25 D8
Newcastle Emlyn GB 28 A6
Newcastleton GB 21 E11
Newcastle-under-Lyme GB 27 E7
Newcastle upon Tyne GB 21 F13
Newcastle West IRL 24 D4
New Cumnock GB 21 E8
New Deer GB 19 K12
Newel D 37 E7
Newent GB 29 B10
New Galloway GB 21 E8
New Inn IRL 22 F6
New Inn IRL 23 E8
Newinn IRL 25 D7
New Kildimo IRL 24 C5
Newmarket GB 18 J4
Newmarket GB 31 C9
Newmarket IRL 24 D4
Newmarket IRL 25 D8
Newmarket-on-Fergus IRL 24 C5

Newmill GB 19 K11
New Milton GB 29 D11
Newnham GB 29 B10
New Pitsligo GB 19 K12
Newport GB 18 J7
Newport GB 27 F7
Newport GB 28 A5
Newport GB 29 D9
Newport GB 29 D12
Newport GB 31 D9
Newport IRL 22 E3
Newport IRL 24 C6
Newport-on-Tay GB 21 C11
Newport Pagnell GB 31 C7
Newport Trench GB 20 F3
New Quay GB 28 A6
Newquay GB 28 E4
New Radnor GB 29 A8
New Romney GB 31 F10
New Ross IRL 25 D9
Newry GB 23 D10
Newton GB 20 C6
Newton GB 26 D7
Newton Abbot GB 29 D7
Newton Aycliffe GB 21 F13
Newton Ferrers GB 28 E6
Newtonhill GB 21 A12
Newton-le-Willows GB 26 E6
Newton Mearns GB 21 D8
Newtonmore GB 21 A8
Newton Stewart GB 20 F6
Newtown GB 26 F5
Newtown GB 29 A9
Newtown IRL 24 D5
Newtown IRL 24 D5
Newtown IRL 25 C8
Newtownabbey GB 20 F5
Newtownards GB 23 C11
Newtownbarry IRL 25 C9
Newtownbutler GB 23 D8
Newtown Crommelin GB 20 F4
Newtown Forbes IRL 23 E7
Newtownmountkennedy IRL 23 F10
Newtown Mount Kennedy IRL 23 F10
Newtown St Boswells GB 21 D11
Newtownstewart GB 20 F2
Nexon F 45 D8
Neyland GB 28 B5
Nezamyslice CZ 93 D12
Nezavertailovca MD 170 D5
Nézsa H 163 F8
Nezvěstice CZ 92 C5
Niance GR 191 F6
Nianfors S 119 C12
Niata GR 191 F6
Nibbiano I 53 B10
Nibe DK 102 B5
Níča LV 150 D2
Nicastro I 75 B9
Nice F 53 D6
Nīcgale LV 151 D12
Nichelino I 53 A7
Nickelsdorf A 93 G12
Nicolae Bălcescu RO 169 B9
Nicolae Bălcescu RO 169 F9
Nicolae Bălcescu RO 171 D3
Nicolae Bălcescu RO 171 D6
Nicolae Bălcescu RO 176 D4
Nicolae Bălcescu RO 176 D4
Nicolae Titulescu RO 176 C5
Nicolaevca MD 170 B2
Nicolosi I 75 D7
Nicoreni MD 169 B11
Nicorești RO 169 F10
Nicosia I 74 D5
Nicotera I 75 B8
Nicşeni RO 169 B9
Niculești RO 177 D7
Niculițel RO 171 C2
Nida LT 150 E1
Nidau CH 43 F7
Nidda D 37 D12
Nidzica PL 155 D9
Niebla E 67 E6
Nieborów PL 157 F2
Niebüll D 98 A5
Niebylec PL 160 D4
Niechanowo PL 154 F4
Niechcice PL 159 D8
Niechłonin PL 155 D9
Niechłów PL 97 C10
Niechorze PL 101 B8
Niederaichbach D 91 E11
Niederanven L 36 E6
Niederau D 96 D5
Niederaula D 94 E6
Niederbipp CH 43 F8
Niederbrechen D 37 D10
Niederbreitbach D 201 C7
Niederbronn-les-Bains F 43 C8
Niederfinow D 100 E5
Niederfischbach D 201 C8
Niedergörsdorf D 96 C3
Niederkassel D 37 C8
Niederkirchen D 37 E9
Niederkrüchten D 36 B6
Niederndorf A 88 A5
Niederneisen D 37 D10
Niedernhall D 90 D6
Niedernhausen D 37 D7
Niederoderwitz D 97 E7
Nieder-Olm D 201 E9
Nieder-Rodenbach D 37 D12
Niederroßla D 95 D9
Niedersachswerfen D 95 C8
Niederselters D 37 D10
Niederstetten D 90 D6
Niederunnen CH 43 F11
Niederviehbach D 91 E11
Niederwerrn D 91 B7
Niederwörresbach D 202 B3
Niederzissen D 37 D8
Niedrzwica Duża PL 157 H6
Niedźwiada PL 155 C13
Niedźwiedź PL 161 C9
Niefern-Öschelbronn D 43 C10
Niegosław PL 101 E9
Niegosławice PL 97 C9
Niegowa PL 159 E7
Niegripp D 95 B10
Nieheim D 33 E12
Niekerk NL 32 B6
Niekłań Wielki PL 157 H3
Niekursko PL 101 D10
Niel B 198 C4
Nielisz PL 160 B7
Niemberg D 95 C11
Niemce PL 157 H7
Niemcza PL 97 E11
Niemegk D 95 B12
Niemelä FIN 129 C20

Niemelä FIN 131 E5
Niemelänkylä FIN 135 F12
Niemenkylä FIN 138 E7
Niemenkylä FIN 142 C6
Niemenpää FIN 135 B11
Niemis S 135 B11
Niemisel S 134 B7
Niemisjärvi FIN 139 E15
Niemisjärvi FIN 140 E8
Niemiskylä FIN 139 C17
Niemodlin PL 158 E4
Nienadówka PL 160 C5
Nienburg (Saale) D 95 C10
Nienburg (Weser) D 33 C12
Niepars D 100 B3
Niepołomice PL 159 F9
Nieporęt PL 155 F11
Nierstein D 37 E10
Niesa FIN 133 D11
Niesi FIN 133 D15
Niesky D 97 D7
Nieświń PL 157 H2
Nieszawa PL 154 E6
Nietsak S 132 E4
Nietulisko Duże PL 159 E11
Nieul F 45 D8
Nieuw-Amsterdam NL 33 C7
Nieuw-Bergen NL 32 E6
Nieuwegein NL 32 D4
Nieuwe-Niedorp NL 32 C3
Nieuwe Pekela NL 33 B7
Nieuwerkerk NL 32 E2
Nieuwerkerk aan de IJssel NL 32 E3
Nieuwerkerken B 35 C11
Nieuwe-Tonge NL 32 E2
Nieuwkoop NL 32 D3
Nieuw-Loosdrecht NL 199 A6
Nieuw-Milligen NL 199 A7
Nieuw-Namen NL 198 C5
Nieuwolda NL 33 B7
Nieuwpoort B 34 B6
Nieuwveen NL 198 A5
Nieuw-Vennep NL 32 D3
Nieuw-Vossemeer NL 198 B4
Nieuw-Weerdinge NL 33 C7
Nievern D 201 D8
Niewęgłosz PL 157 G7
Niezabyszewo PL 101 B12
Nigrán E 54 D2
Nigrita GR 185 C10
Nigüelas E 69 C9
Niherne F 45 B9
Niinilahti FIN 139 E15
Niinimaa FIN 139 E16
Niinimäki FIN 141 F10
Niinisalo FIN 142 B6
Niinivaara FIN 141 D11
Niinivesi FIN 139 E16
Niirokumpu FIN 137 B11
Níjar E 71 F8
Nijemci HR 173 B11
Nijkerk NL 32 D4
Nijlen B 35 B10
Nijmegen NL 32 E5
Nijverdal NL 33 D6
Nikaia GR 185 E7
Nikaranperä FIN 139 E14
Nikel' RUS 130 E8
Niki GR 184 C5
Nikisiani GR 186 C6
Nikiti GR 185 D10
Nikkala S 135 C11
Nikkaluokta S 127 E17
Nikkaroinen FIN 143 C14
Nikkeby N 128 C6
Nikodin MK 185 B6
Nikokleia GR 185 C10
Nikola-Kozlevo BG 177 F10
Nikolovo BG 177 F9
Nikolsdorf A 89 C6
Nikopol BG 176 F5
Nikopoli GR 190 A2
Nīkrāce LV 150 C3
Nikšić MNE 179 D6
Nikyup BG 182 C5
Niliivaara FIN 133 C14
Niliivaara S 132 D7
Nilsiä FIN 141 D10
Nilvange F 36 F6
Nim DK 102 D5
Nîmes F 51 C7
Nimigea RO 168 C4
Nimis I 89 C7
Nimolimo FIN 137 B11
Nimsenkangas FIN 141 C11
Nimisjärvi FIN 135 E17
Nimtofte DK 102 C7
Nin HR 83 D11
Nina EST 147 D14
Nindorf D 98 B6
Ninemile Bar GB 21 E9
Ninemilehouse IRL 25 D8
Ninove B 35 C9
Niort F 44 C5
Nirza LV 149 D3
Niš SR 180 C4
Nisa P 60 E5
Niscemi I 74 E5
Niška Banja SRB 180 C5
Niskankorpi FIN 139 C13
Niskanpera FIN 135 B15
Nisko PL 160 B5
Niskos FIN 139 F10
Nismes B 35 D10
Nispen NL 32 F2
Nisporeni MD 169 C11
Nissafors S 107 E14
Nissan-lez-Enserune F 50 D5
Nissilä FIN 139 C17
Nissinvaara FIN 137 B13
Nissoria I 74 D5
Nissumby DK 102 B2
Nissum Seminariebuy DK 102 B2
Nistelrode NL 32 E5
Nistorești RO 169 F9
Nītaure LV 151 B10
Nitra SK 162 E6
Nitrianske Hrnčiarovce SK 162 E6
Nitrianske Pravno SK 163 D7
Nitrianske Rudno SK 162 D6
Nitrianske Sučany SK 162 D6
Nitry F 41 E10
Nitta S 107 D13
Nittedal N 111 B13
Nittel D 36 E6
Nittenau D 91 D11

Nittendorf D 91 D10
Nittorp S 107 D14
Niukkala FIN 145 B12
Nivå DK 103 D11
Niva FIN 137 F14
Nivala FIN 139 C13
Nivankylä FIN 133 E11
Nivanpää FIN 133 E11
Nivelles B 35 C9
Nivenskoye RUS 152 D2
Nivillac F 39 E7
Nivillers F 34 F5
Nivnice CZ 162 D5
Nivolas-Vermelle F 47 D7
Nivyanin BG 181 C8
Nižbor CZ 92 C6
Nížná SK 163 C9
Nižná Slaná SK 161 F1
Nižný Hrabovec SK 161 F4
Nižný Hrušov SK 161 F4
Nižný Žipov SK 161 F4
Nizza di Sicilia I 75 D7
Nizza Monferrato I 53 B8
Njavve S 125 C15
Njegovuđa MNE 179 C7
Njé Maj AL 184 C3
Njetjavare S 132 E4
Njivice HR 83 B10
Njurundabommen S 119 B13
Njutånger S 119 C13
No DK 102 C2
Noailhan F 48 B5
Noailles F 34 F5
Noain E 48 E2
Noale I 82 A5
Noalejo E 69 A9
Noasca I 47 E11
Nöbbele S 105 B8
Nobber IRL 23 E9
Nobitz D 95 E11
Noblejas E 62 E6
Noćaj SRB 174 D4
Nocé F 40 D4
Nocera Inferiore I 76 B3
Nocera Terinese I 75 A9
Nocera Umbra I 78 A3
Noceto I 82 C1
Noci I 77 B8
Nociglia I 77 B10
Nociūnai LT 151 F8
Nocrich RO 168 F4
Nødebo DK 103 D10
Nodeland N 106 C2
Nødinge S 107 D11
Nodland N 110 F4
Nods F 42 F5
Noé F 49 D6
Noepoli I 77 C6
Noer D 99 B8
Nœux-les-Mines F 34 D6
Noez E 62 E4
Nofuentes E 56 C5
Nogales E 67 B6
Nogara I 82 B3
Nogaro F 48 C5
Nogent F 42 D3
Nogent-le-Bernard F 40 D3
Nogent-le-Roi F 40 C6
Nogent-le-Rotrou F 40 D4
Nogent-sur-Aube F 41 D11
Nogent-sur-Oise F 34 F5
Nogent-sur-Seine F 41 D10
Nogent-sur-Vernisson F 41 E8
Nogersund S 105 C7
Nógrád H 163 F8
Nógrádmegyer H 163 E9
Nógrádsáp H 163 F8
Nograles E 56 F6
Noguera de Albarracín E 63 D9
Noguères F 48 D4
Nogueruelas E 64 D3
Nohant-Vic F 45 B9
Nohfelden D 37 E8
Nohic F 49 C6
Noia E 54 C2
Noicattaro I 77 A7
Noidans-lès-Vesoul F 42 E5
Noilhan F 49 C6
Noiretable F 46 D4
Noirmoutier-en-l'Île F 44 A1
Noisseville F 42 B5
Noja E 56 B6
Nojorid RO 167 C8
Nokia FIN 143 C10
Nol S 107 D11
Nolay F 46 B6
Noli I 53 C8
Nolimo FIN 137 B11
Nolmyra S 115 B8
Nólsoy FO 18 A3
Nombela E 62 D4
Nomeland N 106 A2
Nomenij SLO 89 D9
Nomeny F 42 C5
Nomexy F 42 D5
Nomia GR 194 B5
Nonancourt F 40 C5
Nonantola I 82 C3
Nonaspe E 58 E4
None I 53 B7
Nonnenweier D 202 E4
Nonnweiler D 37 E7
Nontron F 45 D7
Nonza F 53 F10
Nõo EST 147 E13
Noordwijk aan Zee NL 198 A4
Noordwijk-Binnen NL 32 D2
Noordwijkerhout NL 32 A5
Noordwolde NL 32 C6
Noormarkku FIN 142 B6
Nopankylä FIN 138 E5
Noppikoski S 118 D4
Nor S 119 C11
Nora S 113 C13
Nora S 119 A12
Norberg S 113 B14
Norcia I 78 B4
Nordagutu N 111 D10
Nordală S 119 A13
Nordanås S 119 A11
Nordanås S 125 E16
Nordankäl S 123 D10
Nordannälden S 121 E16
Nordano S 114 B6
Nordborg DK 102 E5
Nordbotn N 128 D9
Nordby DK 102 D7

Nordby DK 102 E2
Norddeich D 33 A8
Nørddepil FO 18 A3
Norddorf D 98 A4
Norddyrøy N 120 D5
Nordeide N 116 D3
Nordeidet N 128 D4
Norden D 33 A8
Nordendorf D 91 E8
Nordenham D 33 B10
Nordenskov DK 102 D3
Norderåsen S 122 E7
Norderney D 33 A8
Norderö S 121 E16
Nordersteдt D 99 C8
Nordfjord N 130 B8
Nordfjordbotn N 127 B17
Nordfjordeid N 116 C3
Nordfold N 126 E6
Nordhalben D 91 B10
Nordhallen S 121 E13
Nordhastedt D 98 B6
Nordhausen D 95 D8
Nordheim D 43 B11
Nordholz D 33 A11
Nordhorn D 33 D8
Nordhuglo N 110 C3
Nordingrå S 119 A15
Nordkil N 127 D10
Nordkirchen D 33 E9
Nordkisa N 111 B14
Nordkjosbotn N 127 B18
Nordland N 126 C4
Nord-Leirvåg N 132 E4
Nordlenangen N 127 A19
Nordli N 121 C15
Nördlingen D 91 E7
Nordmaling S 123 D17
Nordmannvik N 128 D5
Nordmela N 127 B10
Nordmela N 127 B10
Nordnesøy N 124 C4
Nordøyvågen N 124 D6
Norðragøta FO 18 A3
Nordrak N 111 B13
Nordsand N 127 C12
Nordsinni N 117 E11
Nordsjö S 119 C12
Nordsjö S 123 D10
Nordsjona N 124 D5
Nordskáli FO 18 A2
Nordskjør N 120 C8
Nordskot N 126 E8
Nordstemmen D 94 B6
Nord-Værnes N 124 C5
Nordvik N 124 C4
Nordvik S 119 A14
Nordvika N 120 D6
Nordwalde D 33 D8
Nore S 119 C11
Norem N 121 D10
Noreña E 55 B8
Noresund N 111 B11
Norg NL 33 B6
Norheimsund N 110 B4
Norinkylä FIN 138 E6
Norje S 104 C7
Norma I 78 D3
Norn S 113 B14
Nornäs S 118 D5
Noroy-le-Bourg F 42 E5
Norppa FIN 139 C11
Norra Åsum S 104 D6
Norra Blommaberg S 119 C9
Norra Bredåker S 134 C6
Norra bro S 108 A6
Norra Fjällnäs S 125 E10
Norra Holmnäs S 134 C3
Norråker S 122 C9
Norra Klagshamn S 103 D11
Norra Malånäs S 123 A15
Norra Prästholm S 134 C8
Norra Rödupp S 134 B9
Norra Skärvången S 121 D16
Norra Vi S 108 D7
Norra Vallgrund FIN 138 C5
Norra Vi S 108 D6
Norrbäck S 119 B12
Norrbäck S 123 B13
Norrbo S 119 C12
Norrboda HR 123 D7
Norrbo S 119 B10
Norrby DK 198 C9
Norrby S 115 B11
Norrbyberg S 123 B14
Norrbyn S 138 F4
Norrbyskär S 138 C5
Nørre Aaby DK 102 E5
Nørre Alslev DK 100 A1
Nørreballe DK 99 A10
Nørre Bork DK 102 D2
Nørre Broby DK 102 E6
Nørre Felding DK 102 C3
Nørre Halne DK 102 A5
Nørre Kongerslev DK 102 B6
Nørre Nebel DK 102 D2
Norrent-Fontes F 34 C5
Nørre Snede DK 102 D4
Nørresundby DK 102 A5
Nørre Vejrup DK 102 D3
Nørre Vorupør DK 102 B2
Norrfällsviken S 123 F15
Norrfjärden S 119 B13
Norrfjärden S 138 C5
Norrflärke S 123 D14
Norrforsen S 123 C14
Norrfors S 123 D15
Norrgårdssälen S 118 E6
Norr-Greningen S 122 E8
Norrhult-Klaverström S 105 A8
Norrköping S 109 B8
Norrländ N 121 B4
Norrlångträsk S 134 C3
Norrnäs FIN 138 E6
Norrsjön S 122 E3
Norrskedika S 115 B10
Norrstig S 119 A14
Norrstrand S 125 E16
Norrsunnet S 119 E11
Norrtälje S 115 C11
Norrtärn S 123 C14
Norrvåge S 123 E15
Norrvik S 123 B13
Nors DK 102 A3
Norsholm S 108 B7
Norsjö S 123 B17
Norsminde DK 102 C6
Norstrup DK 102 B5

Nordby DK 102 E2
North Cave GB 27 D10
North Dell GB 18 J4
North Duffield GB 27 D10
Northeim D 95 C6
North Ferriby GB 27 D10
North Grimston GB 27 C10
North Hykeham GB 27 E10
North Leigh GB 29 B12
North Shields GB 21 E14
North Somercotes GB 27 E12
North Sunderland GB 21 D13
North Tidworth GB 29 C11
Northton GB 18 K2
North Walsham GB 31 B11
Northwich GB 26 E6
Nortmoor D 33 B9
Norton GB 27 C10
Norton GB 31 C10
Norton Fitzwarren GB 29 C8
Nortorf D 99 B8
Nortrup D 33 C9
Nort-sur-Erdre F 39 F8
Norup DK 102 B6
Norvasalmi FIN 133 E15
Norwich GB 31 B11
Norwick GB 19 C15
Noşlac RO 168 E3
Nossa Senhora da Boa Fé P 66 B3
Nossa Senhora da Graça de Póvoa e Meadas P 60 E5
Nossa Senhora da Graça do Divor P 66 B4
Nossa Senhora da Graça dos Degolados P 61 F6
Nossa Senhora das Neves P 66 C4
Nossa Senhora de Machede P 66 B4
Nossebro S 107 C12
Nossen D 96 D4
Nossentiner Hütte D 99 C12
Noszlop H 165 B9
Noszvaj H 161 H1
Notaresco I 78 B5
Notia GR 185 B7
Nótincs H 163 F8
Nötö FIN 142 F6
Noto I 75 F7
Notodden N 111 C10
Notre-Dame-de-Bellecombe F 47 D10
Notre-Dame-de-Gravenchon F 34 F2
Notre-Dame-de-Monts F 44 B1
Notre-Dame-d'Oé F 40 F3
Nötsch im Gailtal A 89 C8
Nottensdorf D 98 D7
Nottingham GB 27 F9
Nottuln D 33 E8
Notviken S 134 C8
Nouan-le-Fuzelier F 40 E7
Nouans-les-Fontaines F 40 F5
Nouart F 35 F11
Nõuni EST 147 F11
Nousiainen FIN 142 D7
Nousionmäki FIN 141 D10
Nousu FIN 131 D5
Nouvion F 34 D4
Nouzilly F 40 E4
Nouzonville F 35 E10
Nõva EST 146 C7
Nova H 165 C7
Nová Baňa SK 163 E7
Nova Breznica MK 180 F3
Nova Bukovica HR 165 E9
Nová Bystřice CZ 93 D8
Nová Cerekev CZ 93 D8
Novachene BG 181 D8
Novachene BG 181 D8
Novaci MK 185 B5
Novaci RO 176 C3
Nova Crnja SRB 174 B6
Novadnieki LV 150 C4
Nová Dubnica SK 162 D6
Novafeltria I 82 E5
Nova Gorica SLO 89 D8
Nova Gradiška HR 173 B7
Nova Ivanivka UA 170 F4
Novaj H 161 H1
Novajidrány H 161 G3
Nová Kamena BG 177 F10
Nova Kasaba BIH 173 D11
Novaki HR 165 E6
Novakovo BG 182 F4
Nováky SK 163 D7
Novales E 56 B3
Novales E 57 D11
Nova Levante I 88 D4
Novalja HR 83 C11
Novallas E 57 E8
Nova Makhala BG 181 F9
Nova Nadezhda BG 182 E5
Nova Nekrasivka UA 171 C3
Nova Paka CZ 93 B9
Nova Pazova SRB 174 D5
Nova Pokrovka UA 171 B4
Nova Role CZ 92 B3
Nova Sela HR 173 F8
Nova Siri I 77 C7
Novate Mezzola I 85 A7
Nova Topola BIH 173 B7
Nova Varoš SRB 179 C8
Nova Vas SLO 89 E9
Nová Včelnice CZ 93 D8
Nová Ves CZ 93 B8
Nová Ves nad Žitavou SK 162 E6
Nova Zagora BG 182 E6
Novelda E 72 E3
Novellara I 82 C2
Nové Hrady CZ 93 E7
Nové Mesto nad Metují CZ 93 B10
Nové Mesto nad Váhom SK 162 D5
Nové Město na Moravě CZ 93 C10
Nové Město pod Smrkem CZ 97 E8
Nove Misto UA 161 D6
Noventa di Piave I 88 E6
Noventa Vicentina I 82 B4
Novés E 62 D4
Noves F 51 C8
Nové Veselí CZ 93 C9
Nové Zámky SK 162 F6
Novgorod RUS 149 B5
Novgorodka RUS 149 D5

Novgrad BG 177 F7
Novi Banovci SRB 174 D5
Novi Bečej SRB 174 B5
Novi di Modena I 82 C2
Novi Dojran MK 185 B8
Noviergas E 57 E7
Novi Grad BIH 173 B9
Novigrad HR 83 B8
Novigrad HR 172 D4
Novigrad Podravski HR 165 D7
Novi Iskür BG 181 D7
Novi Karlovci SRB 174 D5
Novi Khan BG 181 D8
Novi Kneževac SRB 166 F5
Novi Kozarci SRB 174 B5
Novi Ligure I 53 B9
Novillars F 42 F5
Novi Marof HR 165 D6
Novion-Porcien F 35 E9
Novi Pazar BG 183 C8
Novi Pazar SRB 179 C10
Novi Sad SRB 174 C4
Novi Šeher BIH 173 D8
Novi Slankamen SRB 174 C5
Novi Travnik BIH 173 D8
Novi Vinodolski HR 83 B10
Novo Beograd SRB 174 D5
Novo Miloševo SRB 174 B5
Novomoskovskiy RUS 155 A9
Novomykolaivka UA 171 B5
Novo Orahovo SRB 166 F4
Novo Oryakhovo BG 183 D9
Novopetrivka UA 170 D5
Novo Poljance SRB 179 D10
Novorzhev RUS 149 B6
Novosamarka UA 170 C5
Novosedly CZ 93 E11
Novoselë AL 179 F10
Novoselë AL 184 C1
Novoselets BG 182 E6
Novoselija BIH 173 C7
Novoselivka UA 170 D5
Novoselivka UA 170 D5
Novo Selo BG 175 E10
Novo Selo BG 177 F8
Novo Selo BG 182 D5
Novo Selo BIH 173 B8
Novo Selo BIH 173 B9
Novo Selo MK 185 B8
Novo Selo SRB 175 F6
Novoselovo RUS 155 B9
Novoseltsi BG 182 E6
Novoselye RUS 148 A3
Novoselytsya UA 170 A6
Novosil's'ke UA 171 C3
Novostroyevo RUS 152 D4
Novot SK 163 C8
Novo Virje HR 165 D8
Novovolyns'ka UA 160 B6
Novoyavorivs'ke UA 160 D8
Novska HR 165 F7
Nový Bor CZ 97 E7
Nový Bydžov CZ 93 B8
Novy-Chevrières F 35 E9
Nový Dvor BY 153 F10
Nový Hrozenkov CZ 162 C6
Nový Jičín CZ 162 B5
Nový Knín CZ 92 C6
Nový Malín CZ 93 F12
Nový Pahost BY 149 F2
Nový Rychnov CZ 93 D8
Novyya Kruki BY 149 E3
Novyy Izborsk RUS 148 F2
Novyy Rozdil UA 161 D6
Nový Život SK 162 E4
Nowa Brzeźnica PL 159 D7
Nowa Cerekwia PL 156 C8
Nowa Chodorówka PL 156 C8
Nowa Dęba PL 159 F12
Nowa Karczma PL 154 B5
Nowa Ruda PL 97 E11
Nowa Sarzyna PL 160 C5
Nowa Słupia PL 159 E11
Nowa Sól PL 97 C9
Nowa Sucha PL 157 F2
Nowa Wieś Ełcka PL 156 C5
Nowa Wieś Lęborska PL 101 A13
Nowa Wieś Wielka PL 154 E5
Nowa Wola PL 156 E5
Nowa Wola Gołębiowska PL 157 H4
Nowe PL 154 C6
Nowe Brusno PL 160 C7
Nowe Brzesko PL 159 F9
Nowe Czarnowo PL 100 E6
Nowe Miasteczko PL 97 C9
Nowe Miasto PL 155 F10
Nowe Miasto Lubawskie PL 155 D8
Nowe Miasto nad Pilicą PL 157 G3
Nowe Miasto nad Wartą PL 97 B12
Nowe Ostrowy PL 159 B7
Nowe Piekuty PL 157 E7
Nowe Skalmierzyce PL 158 C4
Nowe Warpno PL 100 C6
Nowinka PL 152 F6
Nowogard PL 101 C9
Nowogród PL 155 D12
Nowogród Bobrzański PL 97 C8
Nowogródek Pomorski PL 101 E8
Nowogrodziec PL 97 D8
Nowosady PL 157 E9
Nowosielce PL 161 D5
Nowosolna PL 159 C8
Nowotaniec PL 161 D5
Nowowola PL 156 D6
Nowy Bartków PL 157 F7
Nowy Duninów PL 155 F7
Nowy Dwór PL 154 D4
Nowy Dwór Gdański PL 154 B7
Nowy Dwór Mazowiecki PL 155 F10
Nowy Kawęczyn PL 157 F3
Nowy Korczyn PL 159 F10
Nowy Lubliniec PL 160 C7
Nowy Sącz PL 161 D2
Nowy Staw PL 154 B7
Nowy Targ PL 163 C10

Nowy Tomyśl PL 97 B10
Nowy Wiśnicz PL 160 D1
Nowy Żmigród PL 161 D4
Noyal-Muzillac F 38 E7
Noyalo F 38 E6
Noyal-Pontivy F 38 D6
Noyant F 39 E12
Noyarey F 47 E8
Noyen-sur-Sarthe F 39 E11
Noyers F 41 E10
Noyers-sur-Cher F 40 F5
Noyers-sur-Jabron F 51 B10
Noyon F 34 E6
Nozay F 39 E8
Nozdrzec PL 160 D5
Nozeroy F 47 B9
Nuaillé-d'Aunis F 44 C4
Nuasjärvi FIN 133 E13
Nubledo E 55 A8
Nucet RO 167 E10
Nuci RO 177 D8
Nucșoara RO 176 C5
Nudersdorf D 95 C12
Nüdlingen D 91 B7
Nudyzhe UA 157 H10
Nueil-sur-Argent F 44 B4
Nuenen NL 32 F5
Nueno E 57 D11
Nueva E 55 B10
Nueva-Carteya E 69 A8
Nueva Jarilla E 68 C4
Nuez de Ebro E 57 E10
Nufăru RO 171 C3
Nughedu di San Nicolò I 80 B3
Nuijamaa FIN 145 D10
Nuillé-sur-Vicoin F 39 E10
Nuits F 41 E11
Nuits-St-Georges F 42 F2
Nukari FIN 143 D12
Nukši LV 149 D3
Nuland NL 32 E4
Nule I 80 C3
Nules E 64 E4
Nulvi I 80 B2
Numana I 83 E8
Numansdorp NL 32 E2
Nummela FIN 143 E11
Nummi FIN 142 D7
Nummi FIN 143 E10
Nummijärvi FIN 138 F8
Nummikoski FIN 138 F9
Nünchritz D 96 D4
Nuneaton GB 27 F9
Nunkirchen D 202 C2
Nunnanen FIN 133 B12
Nunnanlahti FIN 141 D12
Nuñomoral E 61 D8
Nunsdorf D 96 B4
Nunspeet NL 32 D5
Nuojua FIN 135 E17
Nuoksujärvi S 132 E9
Nuolijärvi FIN 141 C11
Nuoramoinen FIN 143 C14
Nuorgam FIN 129 C20
Nuoritta FIN 135 D16
Nuoro I 80 C3
Nuorunka FIN 136 C9
Nuottavaara FIN 133 D12
Nuottikylä FIN 137 E12
Nur PL 157 E6
Nuragus I 80 D3
Nurallao I 80 D3
Nuraminis I 80 E3
Nureci I 80 D2
Nuriye TR 193 B10
Nurmaa FIN 144 C6
Nurmes FIN 141 C12
Nurmesperä FIN 139 C15
Nurmijärvi FIN 141 C13
Nurmijärvi FIN 143 E12
Nurmo FIN 139 E9
Nürnberg D 91 D9
Nurney IRL 23 F9
Nurri I 80 D3
Nurste EST 146 D4
Nürtingen D 43 C11
Nurzec-Stacja PL 157 F8
Nus I 47 D11
Nusco I 76 B4
Nușeni RO 168 C4
Nușfalău RO 167 C10
Nusfjord N 126 D5
Nusnäs S 118 E8
Nusplingen D 43 D10
Nußbach A 92 G6
Nußdorf D 89 A6
Nußdorf am Inn D 88 A5
Nuštar HR 165 F11
Nustrup DK 102 E4
Nuth NL 35 C12
Nutheim N 111 C9
Nuttuperä FIN 139 C15
Nuuksujärvi S 132 C8
Nuupas FIN 135 B16
Nuutajärvi FIN 143 C9
Nuutila FIN 135 F16
Nuutilanmaki FIN 144 B8
Nuvsvåg N 128 C9
Nuvvus FIN 129 D17
Nuxis I 80 E2
Nüziders A 87 C9
Nya Bastuselet S 125 F16
Nyåker S 123 D13
Nyåker S 123 D16
Nyárád H 165 B8
Nyáregyháza H 166 C4
Nyárlőrinc H 166 D4
Nyársapát H 166 C4
Nybble S 107 A15
Nybergsund N 118 D3
Nyborg DK 103 E7
Nyborg N 130 C5
Nyborg S 135 C10
Nybro S 105 B9
Nybrostrand S 104 E5
Nyby FIN 138 E6
Nyby N 129 C15
Nyby S 122 E8
Nybyn S 119 C9
Nybyn S 123 E14
Nybyn S 134 D6
Nýdek CZ 163 B7
Nydri GR 190 B2
Nye S 105 A8
Nyékládháza H 161 H2
Nyelv N 130 C5
Nyergesújfalu H 165 A11
Nyhammar S 113 B12
Nyhem S 119 A10
Nyhem S 125 E14
Ny Højen DK 102 D5
Nyhus N 127 B15
Nyhyttan S 113 C12
Nyírábrány H 167 B9
Nyíracsád H 167 B8
Nyírád H 165 B8
Nyíradony H 167 B8
Nyírbátor H 167 B9
Nyírbéltek H 167 B9
Nyírbogát H 167 B9
Nyírbogdány H 161 G4
Nyíregyháza H 161 H4
Nyírgelse H 167 B8
Nyírgyulaj H 161 H5
Nyíribrony H 161 G4
Nyírkáta H 161 H5
Nyírmada H 161 G5
Nyírmeggyes H 161 H5
Nyírmihályi H 167 B8
Nyírpazony H 161 H4
Nyírtass H 161 G5
Nyírtelek H 161 G4
Nyírtét H 161 G4
Nyírtura H 161 G4
Nyírvasvári H 167 B9
Nykarleby FIN 138 C9
Nyker DK 105 E7
Nykil S 108 C6
Nykøbing DK 99 A11
Nykøbing Mors DK 102 B3
Nykøbing Sjælland DK 103 D9
Nyköping S 109 B10
Nykrogen S 114 B6
Nykroppa S 113 C11
Nyksund N 126 C9
Nykvåg N 126 C7
Nykvarn S 109 A10
Nykyrke S 108 B5
Nyland S 123 D16
Nyland S 123 E13
Nyland S 138 C3
Nylars DK 105 E7
Nyliden S 123 D15
Nymburk CZ 93 B8
Nymfes GR 184 E2
Nymindegab DK 102 D2
Nymoen N 128 C6
Nynäshamn S 109 B11
Nyneset N 121 C13
Ny Nørup DK 102 D4
Nyoiseau F 39 E10
Nyon CH 47 C9
Nyons F 51 B9
Nyråd DK 103 E9
Nýřany CZ 92 C4
Nýrsko CZ 92 D4
Nyrud N 130 E6
Nysa PL 158 F3
Nysäter S 113 D8
Nysätern S 118 A5
Nysättra S 115 C11
Nysted DK 99 A11
Nysted N 127 C15
Nystrand S 134 C5
Nyträsk S 134 E4
Nytrøa N 127 B16
Nyúl H 165 A9
Nyvoll N 129 C11
Nyzhankovychi UA 160 D6
Nyzhni Petrivtsi UA 169 A7
Nyzhni Vorota UA 161 F7
Nyzhniy Bystryy UA 161 G8
Nyzhnya Vysots'ke UA 161 E7
Nyzhnya Yablun'ka UA 161 E6

O

Oadby GB 27 F9
Oakengates GB 26 F7
Oakham GB 27 F10
Oakley GB 29 B12
Oakley GB 29 C12
Oakley GB 31 C7
Oancea RO 170 F2
Oandu EST 147 C13
Oarja RO 176 D5
O Arrabal E 54 D2
Oarța de Jos RO 167 C11
Obal' BY 149 E7
Obal' BY 149 F6
Obalj BIH 173 F9
Oban GB 20 C6
O Barco E 55 D6
Obârșia RO 176 F4
Obârșia-Cloșani RO 175 C10
Obârșia de Câmp RO 175 E11
Obbola S 138 C4
Obdach A 89 B10
Obecnice CZ 92 C5
Obedinenie BG 182 C5
Obejo E 70 C3
Obeliai LT 151 E11
Oberaich A 89 B11
Oberalm A 89 A7
Oberammergau D 87 B12
Oberasbach D 91 D8
Oberau D 88 A3
Oberaudorf D 88 A5
Obercunnersdorf D 97 D7
Oberderdingen D 43 B10
Oberding D 91 F10
Oberdorla D 95 D7
Oberdrauburg A 89 C6
Oberegg CH 87 C9
Oberelsbach D 91 B7
Oberfell D 201 D7
Obergebra D 95 D8
Obergösgen CH 43 F8
Ober-Grafendorf A 93 F9
Obergriesbach D 91 F9
Obergünzburg D 87 B10
Obergurgl A 88 C3
Obergurig D 96 D6
Oberhaag A 164 C4
Oberhaid D 91 C8
Oberharmersbach D 43 D9
Oberhausen D 33 F7
Oberhausen D 91 E9
Oberhausen-Rheinhausen D 203 C5
Oberheldrungen D 95 D9
Oberhof D 95 E8
Oberhofen CH 86 D5
Oberhoffen-sur-Moder F 202 D4
Oberkirch D 43 C9
Oberkochen D 91 E7
Oberkotzau D 91 B10
Oberlangen D 33 C8
Oberlungwitz D 95 E12
Obermarchtal D 87 A9
Obermaßfeld-Grimmenthal D 91 A7
Obermoschel D 37 E9
Obernai F 43 D7
Obernberg am Inn A 92 F4
Obernburg am Main D 203 B7
Oberndorf D 33 A12
Oberndorf am Lech D 91 E8
Oberndorf am Neckar D 43 D10
Oberndorf bei Salzburg A 89 A6
Oberneukirchen A 92 F6
Obernfeld D 95 C7
Obernheim D 43 D10
Obernheim-Kirchenarnbach D 202 C4
Obernkirchen D 33 D12
Obernzell D 92 E5
Ober-Olm D 201 E9
Oberpullendorf A 165 A7
Oberried D 43 E8
Oberrieden D 87 A10
Oberriet CH 87 C9
Ober-Roden D 37 E11
Oberrot D 203 C8
Oberrotweil D 43 D8
Oberschneiding D 91 E12
Oberschützen A 164 B6
Obersiebenbrunn A 93 F11
Obersinn D 90 B6
Obersontheim D 203 C8
Oberspier D 95 D8
Oberstadion D 87 A9
Oberstaufen D 87 B10
Oberstdorf D 87 C10
Oberstenfeld D 43 B11
Oberthal D 37 E8
Oberthulba D 203 A8
Obertilliach A 89 C6
Obertraubling D 91 E11
Obertrubach D 91 C9
Obertshausen D 37 D11
Oberursel (Taunus) D 37 D11
Obervellach A 89 C7
Oberviechtach D 91 D11
Oberwald CH 86 D6
Oberwart A 164 B6
Oberwesel D 37 D9
Oberwolfach D 203 E5
Oberwölz A 89 B9
Óbidos P 60 F2
Obilić SRB 180 D3
Obing D 91 F11
Obinitsa EST 148 F1
Obitel BG 183 C7
Objat F 45 E8
Objazda PL 101 A12
Öblarn A 89 B8
Obleševo MK 180 F5
Oblikë e Madhe AL 179 E7
Obnova BG 181 C10
Obodivka UA 170 A4
Oboga RO 176 E4
O Bolo E 54 D5
Obón E 58 F2
Oborci BIH 173 D7
Oborín SK 161 F4
Oborishte BG 181 D9
Oborniki PL 97 A11
Oborniki Śląskie PL 97 D11
Obrazów PL 159 E12
Obreja RO 175 C9
Obrenovac SRB 174 D5
Obretenik BG 182 B5
Obrež SRB 174 D4
Obrež SRB 175 F7
Obrigheim D 37 F12
Obrigheim (Pfalz) D 203 B5
Obrnice CZ 92 A5
Obrochishte BG 183 C10
Obrov SLO 83 A9
Obrovac HR 172 D4
Obrovac SRB 174 C3
Obrowo PL 154 E6
Obrtići BIH 173 E10
Obruchishte BG 182 E5
Obryte PL 155 E11
Obrzycko PL 101 E11
Obsza PL 160 C6
Obudovac BIH 173 C10
Obyce SK 162 E6
Obzor BG 183 D9
O Cádavo E 54 B5
Ocaklar TR 189 D8
O Campo da Feira E 54 B3
Ocaña E 62 E6
Ocana F 53 H9
O Carballiño E 54 D3
O Castelo E 54 D3
O Castro E 54 C3
O Castro de Ferreira E 54 C4
Occhiobello I 82 C4
Occimiano I 84 C6
Očevlja BIH 173 D9
Ochagavía E 48 E3
O Chao E 54 B4
Ochiltree GB 21 E8
Ochla PL 97 C8
Ochodnica SK 163 C7
Ocholt D 33 B9
Ochsenfurt D 91 C7
Ochsenhausen D 87 A9
Ochtrup D 33 D8
Ocke S 121 E15
Ockelbo S 119 E12
Öckerö S 107 D10
Ockholm D 98 A5
Ocksjön S 118 A8
Ocland RO 168 E6
Ocna de Fier RO 175 C8
Ocna Mureș RO 168 E3
Ocna Sibiului RO 168 F4
Ocna Șugatag RO 168 B3
Ocnele Mari RO 176 C4
Ocnița RO 177 D7
Ocolina MD 170 A2
Ocoliș RO 167 E11
O Convento E 54 D2
O Corgo E 54 C5
Ocrkavlje BIH 173 E10
Öcsa H 166 C3
Öcsény H 165 D11
Öcsöd H 166 D5
Octeville F 39 A8
Octeville-sur-Mer F 39 A12
Ocypel PL 154 C5
Odăile RO 177 C9
Ödåkra S 103 C11
Odda N 110 B5
Odden N 128 D5
Oddense DK 102 B3
Odder DK 102 D6
Oddsta GB 19 D15
Ödeborg S 107 B10
Odeceixe P 66 E2
Odeleite P 66 E5
Odelouca P 66 E3
Odelzhausen D 91 F9
Odemira P 66 D2
Òdena E 59 D7
Odensbacken S 108 A7
Odensberg S 107 C13
Odense DK 102 E6
Odensjö S 108 D4
Odensvi S 109 D8
Oderberg D 100 E6
Oderin D 96 B5
Odernheim am Glan D 37 E9
Oderzo I 88 E5
Ödeshog S 108 C5
Odiáxere P 66 E2
Odiham GB 31 E7
Ødis DK 102 E4
Odivelas P 66 B1
Odivelas P 66 C3
Ödkarby FIN 115 B13
Odobești RO 169 F10
Odobești RO 177 D7
Odolanów PL 158 C4
Odolena Voda CZ 92 B6
Odón E 63 C9
Odoorn NL 33 C7
Odorheiu Secuiesc RO 168 E6
Odry CZ 162 B5
Odrzywół PL 157 G3
Ödsmål S 107 C10
Ødsted DK 102 D4
Odŭrne BG 181 C10
Odžaci BIH 173 E9
Odžaci SRB 174 B3
Odžak BIH 173 B9
Odžak BIH 173 E6
Odžak BIH 173 F9
Odžak MNE 179 C7
Odziena LV 151 C11
Oebisfelde D 95 B8
Oedelem B 198 C2
Oedelsheim (Oberweser) D 94 C6
Oederan D 96 E4
Oeffelt NL 32 E5
Oegstgeest NL 32 D3
Oeiras P 66 B1
Oelde D 33 E10
Oelixdorf D 98 C7
Oelsnitz D 91 B11
Oelsnitz D 95 E12
Oene NL 199 A8
Oenkerk NL 32 B5
Oensingen CH 43 F8
Oerel D 33 B12
Oering D 99 C8
Oerlenbach D 91 B7
Oerlinghausen D 33 E11
Oestrich-Winkel D 37 D9
Oettersdorf D 95 E10
Oettingen in Bayern D 91 E8
Oetz A 87 C11
Oetzen D 99 D9
Oeversee D 98 A6
Œyreluy F 48 C3
Ofatinți MD 170 B4
Öfehértó H 161 H5
Ofena I 78 C5
Offanengo I 85 C8
Offemont F 43 E6
Offenbach am Main D 37 D11
Offenbach an der Queich D 203 C5
Offenberg D 92 E3
Offenburg D 43 D8
Offerdal S 121 E16
Offersøy N 127 D10
Offida I 78 B5
Offingen D 91 F7
Offranville F 34 E3
O Forte E 54 C3
Ofte N 111 D8
Ofterdingen D 43 D11
Oftersheim D 37 F11
Ogenbargen D 33 A9
Oger F 41 C11
Ogeu-les-Bains F 48 D4
Ogéviller F 42 C6
Oggevatn N 106 C3
Ogliastro F 53 F10
Ogliastro Cilento I 76 C4
Ogmore GB 29 C7
Ognyanovo BG 185 A10
Ogonelloe IRL 24 C6
Ogošte SRB 180 D4
Ogoya BG 181 D8
Ogra RO 168 E4
Ogre LV 151 C9
Ogren AL 184 D3
Ogresgals LV 151 C9
Ogrezeni RO 177 E7
Ogrodniki PL 155 E12
Ogrodzieniec PL 159 F8
Ogrosen D 96 C6
O Grove E 54 D2
Ogulin HR 83 B11
Oğulpaşa TR 188 A6
Ohaba RO 168 E3
Ohaba Lungă RO 167 F8
Ohanes E 71 E7
Ohey B 35 D11
Ohkola FIN 143 D13
Ohlsbach D 43 D8
Ohlstadt D 88 A3
Ohne D 33 D8
Ohorn D 96 D6
Ohrady SK 162 E5
Ohrdruf D 95 E8
Ohrid MK 184 B4
Öhringen D 43 B11
Ohtaanniemi FIN 141 E11
Ohtanajärvi S 132 E10
Ohukotsu EST 147 C9
Oia GR 195 C9
Oiã P 60 C3
Oiartzun E 48 D2
Oichalia GR 185 E6
Øie N 121 B12
Oignies F 34 D6
O Igrexario E 54 D3
Oijärvi FIN 135 C15
Oijen NL 199 B6
Oijusluoma FIN 137 C13
Oikarainen FIN 135 B16
Oileán Ciarraí IRL 24 D4
Oilgate IRL 25 D9
Oímbra E 54 E5
Oinacu RO 177 F8
Oinas FIN 131 E2
Oinasjärvi FIN 140 C9
Oinofyta GR 191 C8
Oinoi GR 191 C7
Oion E 57 C7
O Irixo E 54 C3
Oiron F 44 B5
Oirschot NL 199 B6
Oiselay-et-Grachaux F 42 F4
Oisemont F 34 E4
Oisseau F 39 D10
Oissel F 34 F3
Oisterwijk NL 199 B6
Oisu EST 147 D11
Õisu EST 147 E11
Oitti FIN 143 D13
Oituz RO 169 E9
Oitylo GR 194 B3
Oivanki FIN 137 B13
Oizon F 41 F8
Öja FIN 139 C9
Öja S 109 E12
Ojakkala FIN 143 E11
Ojakylä FIN 135 D13
Ojakylä FIN 135 D14
Ojakylä FIN 135 F15
Ojanperä FIN 136 F8
Öjarn S 122 D8
Ojdula RO 169 F8
Öje S 118 E6
Öjebyn S 134 D6
Öjeforsen S 119 B9
Ojén E 69 C7
Öjingsvallen S 119 C8
Ojos Negros E 63 C10
Ojrzeń PL 155 E10
Öjung S 119 C10
Okalewo PL 155 D8
Okány H 167 D7
Okçular TR 197 C9
Økdal N 117 A12
Okehampton GB 28 D6
Okhotnoye RUS 152 D4
Oklaj HR 172 E5
Oknö S 105 A11
Okoč SK 162 F5
Okonek PL 101 C11
Okopy PL 157 H9
Ököritófülpös H 161 H6
Okorsh BG 177 F10
Okříšky CZ 93 D9
Okrouhlice CZ 93 C8
Okrúhle SK 161 E4
Oksa PL 159 E9
Öksajärvi S 132 C8
Oksakoski FIN 139 D12
Oksava FIN 139 C14
Oksbøl DK 102 D2
Oksbøl DK 102 E5
Øksfjord N 128 C9
Øksnes N 126 C8
Øksneshamn N 126 D9
Oksvoll N 120 D7
Oktonia GR 191 B9
Okučani HR 173 B7
Olague E 48 E2
Olaine LV 151 C7
Olalhas P 60 E4
Oland N 106 B3
Olănești MD 170 E5
Olanu RO 176 D4
Olargues F 50 C4
Olari RO 167 E8
Olaszliszka H 161 G3
Olave E 48 E2
Oława PL 97 E12
Olazti E 48 E1
Olba E 64 D3
Olbendorf A 164 B6
Olbernhau D 96 E4
Olbersdorf D 97 E7
Olbersleben D 95 D9
Olbia I 80 B3
Olbięcin PL 160 B5
Olbramovice CZ 93 C7
Olcea RO 167 D8
Oldcastle IRL 23 E8
Old Dailly GB 20 E7
Oldebroek NL 32 D5
Oldedalen N 116 C5
Oldehove NL 32 B6
Oldeide N 116 C2
Oldemarkt NL 32 C5
Olden N 116 C5
Olden S 121 D15
Oldenbrok D 33 B10
Oldenburg D 33 B10
Oldenburg in Holstein D 99 B9
Oldendorf D 33 A12
Oldenswort D 98 B5
Oldenzaal NL 33 D7
Olderdalen N 128 D6
Oldereid N 124 B8
Olderfjord N 129 C15
Oldernes N 129 C13
Oldervik N 124 C5
Oldervik N 127 A18
Oldervik N 129 B13
Oldham GB 27 D7
Old Head IRL 24 E5
Oldisleben D 95 D9
Old Leake GB 27 E12
Oldmeldrum GB 19 L12
Oldsum D 98 A4
Oldtown IRL 23 E10
Oleby S 113 B9
Olecko PL 152 E6
Oleggio I 84 B6
Oleiros P 60 E5
Oleksandrivka UA 170 C6
Olekseyivka UA 170 B3
Olemps F 49 B11
Olen B 35 B10
Ølen N 110 C3
Olesa de Montserrat E 59 D7
Oleśnica PL 158 D3
Oleśnica PL 159 F11
Olešnice CZ 93 C10
Olesno PL 158 E5
Olesno PL 159 F10
Oleszyce PL 160 C7
Olette F 49 E10
Olevano Romano I 78 D4
Olfen D 33 E8
Olgina EST 148 C3
Olginate I 85 B7
Ølgod DK 102 D3
Olgrinmore GB 19 J9
Olhalvo P 60 F2
Olhão P 66 E4
Olhava FIN 135 D14
Ølholm DK 102 D5
Olho Marinho P 60 F2
Ol'hopil' UA 170 A5
Oliana E 59 C6
Olías del Rey E 62 E5
Oliena I 80 C3
Oliete E 58 E2
Oligastro Marina I 76 C3
Olingdal S 118 C7
Olingsjövallen S 118 C7
Oliola E 58 D6
Olite E 48 F2
Oliva E 72 D4
Oliva de la Frontera E 67 C6
Oliva de Mérida E 67 B7
Olival P 60 E3
Olivares E 67 E7
Olivares de Júcar E 63 E8
Oliveira de Azeméis P 60 C4
Oliveira de Frades P 60 C4
Oliveira do Arda P 60 B4
Oliveira do Bairro P 60 C4
Oliveira do Conde P 60 D5
Oliveira do Douro P 60 B3
Oliveira do Hospital P 60 D5
Olivenza E 67 B5
Oliveri I 75 C7
Olivet F 40 E6
Oliveto Citra I 76 B4
Oliveto Lucano I 76 B6
Olivone CH 87 D7
Ol'ka SK 161 E4
Olkijoki FIN 135 E13
Olkiluoto FIN 142 C5
Olkkajärvi FIN 133 E16
Olkusz PL 159 F8
Ollaberry GB 19 D14
Ollerton GB 27 E9
Ollerup DK 102 E7
Olliergues F 46 D4
Ollila FIN 137 B13
Ollila FIN 143 D8
Ollilanniemi FIN 137 E12
Ollioules F 51 D10
Ollo E 48 E2
Öllölä FIN 141 F15
Ollolai I 80 C3
Ollon CH 47 C10
Ollsta S 122 E8
Ölmbrotorp S 113 D13
Ölme S 113 D11
Olmedilla de Roa E 56 E4
Olmedo E 55 F10
Olmedo I 80 B1
Olmeta-di-Tuda F 53 F10
Olmeto F 53 H9
Olmos de Ojeda E 56 C3
Olney GB 31 C7
Olocau E 64 E3
Olocau del Rey E 58 F3
Olofsfors S 123 D16
Olofstorp S 107 D11
Olofström S 104 C7
Olombrada E 56 F3
Olomouc CZ 162 B4
Olonne-sur-Mer F 44 B2
Olonzac F 50 D4
Oloron-Ste-Marie F 48 D4
Olost E 59 D8
Olot E 59 C8
Oloví CZ 91 B12
Olovo BIH 173 D10
Olpe D 37 B9
Olřišov CZ 158 G4
Olšany CZ 93 C11
Olšany u Prostějova CZ 93 C12
Olsätter S 113 C10
Olsbenning S 113 B15
Olsberg D 33 F10
Olsberg N 127 B16
Ölsboda S 108 A4
Olsfors S 107 D12
Olshammar S 108 B5
Olsøy N 120 D8
Olst NL 32 D6
Ølsted DK 102 D5
Ølsted DK 103 D10
Ølstykke DK 103 D10
Olszanica PL 161 E5
Olszanka PL 158 E3
Olszany PL 160 D6
Olszewo-Borki PL 155 D12
Olsztyn PL 152 F1
Olsztyn PL 159 E7
Olsztynek PL 155 C9
Olszyn PL 157 F8
Olszyna PL 97 D8
Olszyny PL 160 D2
Oltedal N 110 E4
Olten CH 43 F8
Oltenești RO 169 D11
Olteni RO 176 E6
Oltenița RO 177 E9
Oltina RO 171 E1
Olula del Río E 71 E8
Olustvere EST 147 D11
Olvan E 59 C7
Olvasjärvi FIN 136 D9
Ólvega E 57 E8
Olvena E 58 C4
Olvera E 67 F9
Olympiada GR 185 C10
Olympiada GR 185 E7
Olympos GR 197 E6
Olzai I 80 C3
Oma N 110 B3
Omagh GB 20 F2
Omalos GR 194 E6
Omarchevo BG 182 E6
Omarska BIH 173 C6
Ombersley GB 29 A10
Omedu EST 147 D14
Omegna I 84 B5
Ömerköy TR 189 E9
Ömerli TR 189 D9
O Mesón do Vento E 54 B3
Omessa F 53 G10
Omiš HR 173 F6
Omišalj HR 83 B10
Ommen NL 32 C6
Omne S 123 F14
Omolio GR 185 E8
Omoljica SRB 175 D6
Omont F 35 E10
Omossa FIN 138 F7
O Mosteiro E 54 C2
Omurtag BG 183 C6
Omvriaki GR 190 A5
Oña E 56 C5
Ona N 116 A5
Onani I 80 C3
Onano I 78 B1
Oñati E 48 D1
Oncala E 57 E7
Oncești RO 169 E10
Onchan GBM 26 C3
Onda E 64 E4
Ondara E 72 D5
Ondarroa E 48 D1
Ondřejov CZ 93 C7
Ondres F 48 C3
Oneglia I 53 D8
Onesse-et-Laharie F 48 B3
Onești RO 169 E9
Onet-le-Château F 49 B11
Ongles F 51 B10
Oniceni RO 169 D10
Onich GB 20 B6
Onifai I 80 C4
Oniferi I 80 C3
Onițcani MD 170 C4
Onkamaa FIN 144 D7
Onkamo FIN 131 E6
Onkamo FIN 135 D15
Onkamo FIN 141 F14
Onkiniemi FIN 143 C15
Önnestad S 104 C6
Önningby FIN 115 B14
Ónod H 161 G2
Onøya N 124 D4
Onsala S 107 E11
Onsbjerg DK 102 D7
Ønslev DK 99 A11
Onslunda S 104 D6
Onstmettingen D 43 D10
Onstwedde NL 33 B8
Ontiñena E 58 D4
Ontinyent E 72 D3
Ontojoki FIN 141 B11
Ontronvara RUS 141 E16
Onttola FIN 141 E13
Ontur E 71 B10
Onuškis LT 151 D11
Onuškis LT 153 E10
Onzain F 40 E5
Onzonilla E 55 C8
Oola IRL 24 C6
Ooltgensplaat NL 32 E2
Oonurme EST 147 C13
Oostakker B 35 B8
Oostburg NL 35 B7
Oostende B 34 B6
Oostendorp NL 32 D5
Oosterbeek NL 199 B7
Oosterend NL 32 B3
Oosterhesselen NL 33 C7
Oosterhout NL 32 E3
Oosterland NL 32 E2
Oosterwolde NL 32 C6
Oosterzele B 35 C8
Oostham B 199 C6
Oosthuizen NL 32 C3
Oostkamp B 35 B7
Oostkapelle NL 32 E1
Oostmalle B 198 C5
Oost-Souburg NL 32 F1
Oostvleteren B 34 C6
Oost-Vlieland NL 32 B4
Oostvoorne NL 198 B4
Ootmarsum NL 33 D7
Opaka BG 182 C6
Opalenica PL 97 B10
Opalenie PL 154 C6
Opályi H 161 H5
Opan BG 182 E5
Opařany CZ 93 D6
Opatija HR 83 B9
Opatov CZ 93 C10
Opatovice nad Labem CZ 93 B9
Opatów PL 158 D5
Opatów PL 158 E6
Opatów PL 159 E11
Opatówek PL 158 C5
Opatowiec PL 159 F10
Opava CZ 162 B5
O Pazo E 54 D3
O Pazo de Irixoa E 54 B3
Ope S 122 E7
O Pedrouzo E 54 C3
Opeinde NL 32 B6
Opfenbach D 87 B9
Opglabbeek B 199 C7
Opheusden NL 199 B7
Opi I 78 D5
Opitter B 199 C7
Oploo NL 199 B7
Oplotnica SLO 164 D4
Opmeer NL 32 C3
Opochka RUS 149 C5
Opočno CZ 93 B10
Opoczno PL 157 H2
Opoeteren B 199 C7
Opole PL 158 E4
Opole Lubelskie PL 157 H5
Oporelu RO 176 D4
Oporets' UA 161 F7
O Porriño E 54 D2
Opoul-Périllos F 50 E4
Opovo SRB 174 C5
Oppach D 97 D7
Oppala S 119 E13
Oppdal N 117 A11
Oppeano I 82 B3
Oppeby S 108 C7
Oppedal N 116 D3
Oppegard N 111 C13
Oppenau D 43 D9
Oppenheim D 37 E10
Oppenweiler D 203 D7
Opphaug N 120 D7
Opphus N 117 D14
Oppido Lucano I 76 B5
Oppido Mamertina I 75 C8
Oppin D 95 C11
Opponitz A 89 A10
Oppurg D 95 E10
Oprisavci HR 173 B9
Oprișor RO 175 E11
Oprtalj HR 83 B8
Opsa BY 151 E13
Opsaheden S 113 B10
Optași-Măgura RO 176 D5
Ópusztaszer H 166 E5
Opuzen HR 173 F8
Opwijk B 35 C9
Ór H 161 H5
Ora I 88 D3
Øra N 128 C8
Orada P 66 B5
Oradea RO 167 C8
Oradour-sur-Glane F 45 D8
Oradour-sur-Vayres F 45 D7
Orah BIH 173 F7
Orah BIH 178 D5
Orahovičko Polje BIH 173 D8
Orahova BIH 173 B7
Orahovac SRB 179 E10
Orahov Do BIH 178 D4
Orahovica HR 165 E9
Oraio GR 187 B7
Oraiokastro GR 185 C8
Oraison F 51 C10
Orajärvi FIN 133 E12
Orakylä FIN 131 D1
Orange F 51 B8
Orani I 80 C3

Oranienburg D 100 E4
Órán Mór IRL 22 F5
Oranmore IRL 22 F5
Orašac BIH 172 C5
Orašac HR 178 D5
Orašac SRB 180 C5
Orašje BIH 173 B10
Orăştie RO 167 F11
Orăştioara de Sus RO 167 F11
Oraşu Nou RO 161 H7
Oraţjärn S 119 C10
Orava EST 148 F1
Orava FIN 139 D10
Oravainen FIN 138 D8
Oravala FIN 144 D6
Öravan S 123 B14
Oravankylä FIN 139 C15
Öravattnet S 122 E9
Oravi FIN 141 F11
Oravikoski FIN 140 E9
Oravisalo FIN 141 F13
Oraviţa RO 175 C8
Oravivaara FIN 137 E11
Oravská Polhora SK 163 B8
Oravské Veselé SK 163 C8
Oravský Podzámok SK 163 C8
Orba E 72 D4
Orbacém P 54 E2
Örbäck S 113 C15
Orbaden S 119 C11
Ørbæk DK 102 E7
Orbais-l'Abbaye F 41 C10
Orbara E 48 C1
Orbe CH 47 B10
Orbeasca RO 176 E6
Orbec F 40 B3
Orbeni RO 169 E10
Orbetello I 81 C4
Örbyhus S 115 B9
Orca P 60 D6
Orce E 71 D8
Orcera E 71 C7
Orchamps-Vennes F 42 F6
Orchies F 35 D7
Orchomenos GR 191 C6
Orchów PL 159 C7
Orchowo PL 154 E5
Orciano di Pesaro I 83 E6
Orcières F 52 B4
Orcival F 46 D2
Ordan-Larroque F 49 C6
Ordes E 54 B3
Ordizia E 48 D1
Ordona I 76 A5
Ordzhonikidze UA 170 C6
Orea E 63 C9
O Real E 54 B3
Örebäcken S 118 C4
Orebić HR 173 G7
Örebro S 113 D13
Ořechov CZ 93 D11
Öregcsertő H 166 D3
Öreglak H 165 C9
Öregrund S 115 B10
Orehoved DK 103 F9
Oreini GR 185 B10
Orekhovitsa BG 181 B9
Orellana de la Sierra E 67 A8
Orellana la Vieja E 67 A8
Ören TR 193 C10
Ören TR 197 B7
Orenhofen D 201 E6
Oreoi GR 191 B7
Orés E 48 F3
Oresh BG 182 B4
Oreshak BG 181 D10
Orestiada GR 187 B11
Öreström S 123 C16
Öretjändalen S 119 A10
Oreye B 35 C11
Orezu RO 177 D9
Orford GB 31 C12
Organi GR 187 B9
Organyà E 59 C6
Orgaz E 62 E5
Orgelet F 47 B8
Ørgenvika N 111 B11
Orgères-en-Beauce F 40 D6
Orgita EST 147 D8
Orgiva E 69 C10
Orgon F 51 C9
Orgosolo I 80 C3
Orhaneli TR 189 E10
Orhaniye TR 187 C10
Orhaniye TR 197 C8
Orhanlar TR 189 E8
Orhei MD 170 C3
Oria E 71 E8
Oria I 77 C9
O Rial E 54 C2
Origny-Ste-Benoîte F 35 E7
Orihuela E 72 E3
Orihuela del Tremedal E 63 C9
Orikhiva UA 170 F4
Orikum AL 184 D1
Orimattila FIN 143 D14
Oriniemi FIN 143 C9
Orio E 48 D1
Oriola E 54 D5
Oriolo I 77 C6
Oriolo Romano I 78 C2
Oripää FIN 142 D8
Orismala FIN 138 E8
Orissaare EST 146 D6
Oristà E 59 D8
Oristano I 80 D2
Oristown IRL 23 E9
Őriszentpéter H 165 C6
Oriv UA 161 E3
Oriveden asema FIN 143 B11
Orivesi FIN 143 B11
Orizare BG 183 D9
Orizari MK 180 F5
Ørjarvik N 120 F2
Ørje N 112 D6
Orkanger N 120 E7
Örkelljunga S 103 C12
Örkény H 166 C3
Orla PL 157 E6
Orlamünde D 95 E10
Orlat RO 168 F3
Orléans F 40 E6
Orlivka UA 171 C2
Orlová CZ 162 B6
Orlov Dol BG 182 E6
Orły PL 160 D6
Orlyak BG 177 F10

Orlyane BG 181 C10
Orma GR 185 C6
Ormanlı TR 189 B9
Ormaryd S 108 C7
Ormea I 53 C8
Örményes H 166 C6
Örménykút H 166 D6
Ormos GR 192 D4
Ormos Panormou GR 192 D5
Ormos Prinou GR 187 C7
Ormož SLO 164 D6
Ormskirk GB 26 D6
Ormylia GR 185 D10
Ornaisons F 50 D4
Ornans F 42 F5
Ornäs S 113 A14
Örnäsudden S 125 E13
Ornavasso I 84 B5
Ornbau D 91 D8
Ornes N 121 B15
Ørnes N 124 C6
Orneta PL 155 D7
Ørnhøj DK 102 C3
Ornö S 109 A12
Ornontowice PL 158 F6
Örnsköldsvik S 123 E15
Orodel RO 175 D10
Orolik HR 173 B11
Orom SRB 166 F4
Oron-la-Ville CH 47 B10
Oronoz E 48 D2
Orońsko PL 157 H3
Oropa I 84 B4
Oropesa E 61 F10
Oropesa del Mar E 64 C5
Ororbia E 48 E2
Orosei I 80 C4
Orosháza H 166 D6
Oroslavje HR 164 E5
Oroszlány H 165 B10
Orpierre F 51 B10
Orreaga E 48 D3
Orrefors S 105 B9
Orrios E 58 F2
Orroli I 80 D3
Orrmo S 118 C7
Orrviken S 122 E6
Orsa S 118 C8
Orsara di Puglia I 76 A4
Orsay F 40 C7
Örsbäck S 123 C17
Orsennes F 45 C9
Örserum S 108 C5
Orsières CH 47 C11
Örsjö S 105 B9
Ørslev DK 103 E9
Ørsnes N 116 A5
Orsogna I 79 C6
Orsomarso I 76 D5
Ørsta N 116 B4
Örsundsbro S 115 C8
Ortaca TR 197 C9
Ortacesus I 80 D3
Ortakent TR 193 E9
Ortaklar TR 189 D9
Ortaköy TR 189 B9
Ortala S 115 C11
Orta Nova I 76 A4
Orte I 78 C2
Ortenberg D 37 D12
Ortenberg D 43 D8
Ortenburg D 92 E4
Orth an der Donau A 93 F11
Orthez F 48 D4
Ortholmen S 118 B6
Orthovouni GR 184 E5
Ortigosa E 57 D6
Ortigueira F 54 A4
Ørting DK 102 D6
Ortisei I 88 C4
Orţişoara RO 167 F7
Ortnevik N 116 C3
Orton GB 26 C6
Ortona I 79 C6
Ortovera I 53 C8
Ortrand D 96 D5
Örträsk S 123 C15
Ortueri I 80 C2
Örtülüce TR 189 D7
Ørum DK 102 C5
Ørum DK 102 C7
Orune I 80 C3
Orusco E 63 D6
Orval F 45 B8
Orvalho P 60 D5
Orvault F 39 F8
Orvieto I 78 B2
Örviken S 134 A6
Orvinio I 78 C3
Oryakhovo BG 176 F3
Orzesze PL 158 F6
Orzinuovi I 85 C8
Orzyny PL 155 C11
Orzysz PL 152 F4
Os N 117 B14
Osa N 116 E6
Osa de Vega E 63 E7
Oşani LV 151 D11
Osaonica SRB 179 C9
Osbaldwick GB 27 D9
Os Blancos E 54 D4
Osburg D 202 B2
Øsby DK 102 E5
Osby S 104 C5
Osbyholm S 103 D13
Oščadnica SK 163 C7
Oschatz D 96 D4
Oschiri I 80 B3
Ościsłowo PL 155 E9
Os Dices E 54 C2
Osdorf D 99 B8
Osečina SRB 174 E4
O Seixo E 54 E2
Oseja de Sajambre E 55 B9
Osek CZ 92 C5
Osek CZ 96 E5
Osen N 121 C9
Osenets BG 182 B6
Ošenieki LV 150 C4
Osera E 57 E10
Oşeşti RO 169 D10
Oset N 117 D10
Osetno PL 97 C10
Ōsi H 165 B10
Osica de Sus RO 176 E4
Osidda I 80 B3
Osie PL 154 C5
Osięciny PL 154 E6

Osieck PL 157 G4
Osieczna PL 97 C11
Osieczna PL 154 C5
Osiecznica PL 97 D8
Osiek PL 154 C5
Osiek PL 155 D7
Osiek PL 159 E11
Osiek PL 163 B8
Osiek Jasielski PL 161 D3
Osiek Mały PL 158 B6
Osiek nad Notecią PL 101 D12
Osielsko PL 154 D5
Osiglia I 53 C8
Osijek HR 165 E11
Osikovitsa BG 181 D9
Osilo I 80 B2
Osimo I 83 F7
Osina PL 101 C8
Osini I 80 D3
Osio Sotto I 85 B8
Osipaonica SRB 175 D7
Osjaków PL 158 D6
Oskar S 105 B9
Oskar-Fredriksborg S 115 D10
Oskarshamn S 109 E8
Oskarström S 103 B11
Oskava CZ 93 C12
Oskořínek CZ 93 B8
Osľany SK 163 D8
Oslättfors S 119 E12
Osli H 165 A8
Oslo N 111 C13
Osloß D 79 B8
Osma E 56 C5
Osma FIN 133 D15
Osmancalı TR 193 C9
Osmancık TR 189 D11
Osmangazi TR 189 D11
Osmaniye TR 189 F10
Osmaniye TR 189 F10
Osmanki FIN 139 C16
Osmanlı TR 189 A6
Os'mino RUS 148 C5
Ösmo S 109 B11
Osmolin PL 157 F1
Osmoloda UA 161 F9
Osnabrück D 33 D10
Osno Lubuskie PL 97 B7
Osny F 40 B7
Osoblaha CZ 158 F4
Osogna I 85 A10
Osojnik HR 178 D5
Osoppo I 89 D7
Osor E 59 D9
Osor HR 83 B11
Oşorhei RO 167 C9
Osorno E 56 D3
Osowa PL 152 E6
Osowa Sień PL 97 C10
Osøyri N 110 B2
Ospitaletto I 85 B9
Oss NL 32 E5
Ossa GR 185 C9
Ossa de Montiel E 71 B7
Ossana I 85 A10
Osséja F 49 F9
Ossendrecht NL 198 C4
Ossès F 48 D3
Ossiach A 89 C7
Oßmannstedt D 95 D9
Ossun F 48 D5
Østa S 114 B7
Ostana I 53 C8
Östanå S 103 C8
Östanfjärden S 135 C10
Ostanjö S 108 A5
Ostanjö S 125 D16
Östanskär S 119 A13
Ostanvik S 119 D9
Oštarije HR 172 B3
Ostaszewo PL 154 B6
Östavall S 119 B9
Ostbevern D 33 D9
Østbirk DK 102 D5
Östbjörka S 119 C8
Østby N 107 A9
Østby N 118 D4
Østby S 123 D13
Osted DK 103 D9
Østerby DK 98 A5
Osterby D 98 B7
Østerby DK 102 A5
Osterbybruk S 115 B9
Österbymo S 108 D6
Osterede S 123 E11
Österfärnebo S 114 B7
Osterfeld D 95 D10
Österforse S 123 E14
Ostergarn S 109 E13
Östergraninge S 123 F12
Österhankmo FIN 138 D7
Osterhever D 98 B5
Osterhofen D 92 E4
Osterholz-Scharmbeck D 33 B11
Øster Hornum DK 102 B5
Øster Hurup DK 102 B6
Øster Jølby DK 102 B3
Østerild DK 102 A3
Österjörn S 134 D4
Øster Lindet DK 102 E4
Österlars DK 105 E7
Østerlisa S 115 C11
Østermarie DK 105 E8
Østermark FIN 142 E6
Ostermiething A 92 F3
Ostermundigen CH 47 B11
Östernorn S 123 C12
Östero FIN 138 D8
Osterode am Harz D 95 D7
Osterrönfeld D 98 B7
Österskär S 115 D10
Osterstad FIN 143 C13
Østervrå DK 102 A6
Øster Vrøgum DK 102 D2

Ostfildern D 203 D7
Östhammar S 115 B10
Ostheim vor der Rhön D 91 B7
Ostellerv NL 32 D5
Osthofen D 37 E10
Ostia I 78 D2
Ostiano I 82 B1
Ostiglia I 82 B3
Ostiz E 48 E2
Östloning S 119 A13
Östmark S 113 B8
Östmark S 123 E14
Østnor S 118 D7
Ostojićevo SRB 166 F5
Ostoros I 165 H1
Ostra I 83 E7
Ostra RO 169 C7
Östra Äliden S 134 D4
Östra Ed S 109 C9
Östra Frölunda S 107 E13
Östra Granberg S 134 C4
Östra Grevie S 103 E12
Östra Husby S 109 B9
Östra Ljungby S 103 C12
Östra Lovsjön S 122 C7
Östra Löa S 113 C13
Östra Ormsjö S 123 C10
Östra Ryd S 109 C8
Östra Skrämträsk S 134 E5
Östra Sönnarslöv S 104 D6
Östra Stugusjö S 119 A9
Östrau D 95 C11
Ostrau D 96 D4
Östra Vemmerlöv S 104 D6
Ostravice S 162 B6
Östra Yttermark FIN 138 E6
Oštřelj BIH 173 D5
Ostren AL 184 B3
Oštřetín CZ 93 B10
Ostrhauderfehn D 33 B9
Ostricourt F 198 C2
Östringen D 37 F11
Ostritsa BG 182 B6
Ostritz D 97 D7
Ostróda PL 155 C8
Ostromecko PL 154 D5
Ostroměř CZ 93 B9
Ostroróg PL 97 A10
Ostrov CZ 176 F4
Ostrov CZ 92 B3
Ostrov RO 177 E10
Ostrov RO 177 E10
Ostrov RUS 149 B4
Ostroveni RO 176 F3
Ostrovo BG 177 F9
Ostrovo BG 177 F9
Ostrov u Macochy CZ 93 D11
Ostrów PL 159 F12
Ostrówek PL 157 G7
Ostrówek PL 158 D4
Ostrowice PL 101 C9
Ostrowiec PL 101 B8
Ostrowiec Świętokrzyski PL 159 E11
Ostrowite PL 154 F5
Ostrowite PL 155 D7
Ostrów Lubelski PL 157 H7
Ostrów Mazowiecka PL 155 E12
Ostrowo PL 154 E5
Ostrów Wielkopolski PL 158 C4
Ostrowy nad Okszą PL 159 E7
Ostrožac BIH 172 C4
Ostrožac BIH 173 E8
Ostrożeń PL 157 G5
Ostrozub SRB 179 E10
Østrup DK 102 B4
Ostrzeszów PL 158 D4
Ostuni I 77 C10
Ostvik S 134 E6
Ostwald F 202 D4
Osula EST 147 F13
Osuna E 69 B8
Oŝupe LV 151 C13
Osvallen S 118 A4
Osvica BIH 173 C8
Oswaldkirk GB 27 C9
Oswestry GB 26 F5
Oświęcim PL 159 F7
Ota S 53 G9
Otaci MD 170 A1
Otalampi FIN 143 E12
Otanki LV 150 D2
Otanmäki FIN 136 F9
Otaslavice CZ 93 D11
Otava FIN 144 B7
Otavice HR 172 E5
Oteiza E 48 E2
Oţeleni RO 169 C9
Oţelu Roşu RO 175 B9
Otepää EST 147 E12
Oteren N 127 B18
Oterma FIN 136 E6
Otero de Bodas E 55 E7
Otervik N 121 A11
Oteşani RO 176 C4
Oteševo MK 184 C4
Otfinów PL 159 F10
Othem S 109 D13
Ötigheim D 43 C10
Otisheim D 43 C10
Otišić HR 172 E5
Otívar E 69 C9
Otley GB 27 D8
Otley GB 31 C11
Otmuchów PL 93 B12
Otnes N 117 C14
Otočac HR 172 C3
Otok HR 173 B10
Otok HR 173 E6
Otoka BIH 172 C5
Otopeni RO 177 D8
Otorowo PL 97 A10
Otovica MK 180 F4
Otradnoye RUS 145 E12
Otranto I 77 C10
Otricoli I 78 B3
Otrokovice CZ 162 C5
Otta I 80 C3
Ottana I 80 C3
Ottaviano I 76 B3
Ottenby S 105 C10
Ottendorf-Okrilla D 96 D5
Ottenheim D 202 E4
Ottenschlag A 93 F8
Ottensheim A 92 F6
Ottenstein D 94 C5
Ottervrå D 106 F7
Ottenhöfen im Schwarzwald D 43 C9
Ottenschlag A 93 F8
Otterbach D 202 C4
Otterbäcken S 107 B15
Otterberg D 37 E9

Otterburn GB 21 E12
Otter Ferry GB 20 C6
Otterfing D 88 A4
Otterlo NL 32 D5
Otterndorf D 33 A11
Ottersberg D 33 B12
Ottersøy N 121 B10
Otterstad S 107 B13
Otterswick GB 19 D14
Otterswijk GB 19 D14
Otterup DK 102 D6
Otterwisch D 95 D12
Ottevény H 165 A9
Ottignies B 35 C10
Ottmarsheim F 43 E8
Ottobeuren D 87 B10
Ottobrunn D 91 F10
Ottömös H 166 E4
Ottone I 53 B9
Ottrau D 37 C12
Ottsjö S 121 E14
Ottsjön S 122 D7
Ottweiler D 37 F8
Otwock PL 157 F4
Otxandio E 57 B6
Otyń PL 97 C9
Otzing D 92 E3
Ouanne F 41 E9
Ouarville F 40 D6
Ouca P 60 C3
Oucques F 40 E5
Oud-Beijerland NL 32 E2
Ouddorp NL 198 B3
Oudehaske NL 32 C5
Oudemirdum NL 32 C5
Oudenaarde B 35 C8
Oudenbosch NL 32 E3
Oudenburg B 35 B7
Oudeschild NL 32 B3
Oude-Tonge NL 32 E2
Oudewater NL 198 A5
Oud-Gastel NL 32 E3
Oudon F 39 F9
Oud-Turnhout B 32 F3
Oud-Vossemeer NL 32 E2
Oudzele B 198 C2
Oued Laou MA 69 F6
Ouffet B 35 D11
Oughterard IRL 22 F4
Ougney F 42 E4
Ouguela E 61 F6
Ouistreham F 39 B11
Oulainen FIN 135 F13
Oulanka FIN 131 F5
Oulchy-le-Château F 41 B9
Oulder B 36 D6
Oullins F 46 D6
Oulton GB 31 C12
Oulu FIN 135 D14
Oulunsalo FIN 135 E14
Oulx I 47 E10
Oundle GB 31 C8
Oupeye B 35 C11
Ouranoupoli GR 186 D5
Oure DK 103 E7
Ourense E 54 D4
Ourique P 66 D3
Ourol E 54 A4
Ouroux-en-Morvan F 41 F10
Ouroux-sur-Saône F 47 B6
Ourville-en-Caux F 34 E2
Oust F 49 E8
Outakoski FIN 129 D16
Outarville F 40 D7
Outeiro P 54 B4
Outeiro P 55 E6
Outeiro de Rei E 54 B4
Outeiro Seco P 54 E5
Outokumpu FIN 141 E12
Outomuro E 54 D3
Outreau F 31 F12
Outwell GB 27 F12
Ouveillan F 50 D4
Ouzouer-le-Marché F 40 E6
Ouzouer-sur-Loire F 41 E7
Ovada I 53 B9
Ovanåker S 119 D10
Ovanmo S 123 D10
Ovar P 60 C3
Ovaro I 89 D6
Ovča SRB 174 D6
Ovcha Mogila BG 182 B5
Ovcharovo BG 182 B6
Ovchepoltsi BG 181 E9
Ove DK 102 B5
Ovelgönne D 33 B10
Överammer S 123 E9
Överäng S 121 D14
Överås N 116 B6
Overath D 37 C8
Overberg S 118 B7
Øverbygd N 127 C17
Øverbyn S 119 C12
Overdinkel NL 199 A10
Over Feldborg DK 102 C3
Øvergard N 122 B4
Overhalla N 121 B11
Överhogdal S 118 B8
Overheda GR 123 E15
Over Hornbæk DK 102 C5
Overijse B 35 C10
Överissjö S 123 C13
Over Jerstal DK 102 E4
Øverkalix S 135 B9
Øverlade DK 102 B4
Överlännäs S 123 E14
Överlida S 107 D12
Overloon NL 199 B7
Övermalax FIN 138 E6
Övermark FIN 138 E6
Övermorjärv S 134 B9
Övernäs S 125 D14
Överö FIN 115 B15
Overøye N 116 B6
Overpelt B 35 C11
Over Simmelkær DK 102 C3
Överstbyn S 134 B7
Övertänger S 119 E10
Overton GB 26 F6
Overton GB 29 C12
Övertorneå S 135 B11
Överturingen S 118 B8
Överum S 109 D8
Ovezande NL 32 F1
O Viceido E 54 A4
Oviedo E 55 B8
Oviglio I 53 B8
Oviken S 122 E6
Ovindoli I 78 C5
Oviši LV 146 F3
Öv Långträsk S 125 E16

Ovodda I 80 C3
Övrа S 123 D11
Padsvillye BY 149 F3
Øvre Alta N 129 D11
Øvre Ärdal N 116 D7
Øvre Åstbru N 117 D13
Övre Bredåker S 134 B7
Øvre Flåsjön S 134 B7
Øvre Kildal N 128 C7
Övrella N 111 C10
Övre Soppero S 132 B7
Øvre Tværåsel S 134 C5
Ovria GR 190 C4
Ovrå S 123 E9
Ovtrup DK 102 D2
Owen D 43 C11
Owingen D 43 E11
Owińska PL 97 A11
Owschlag D 98 B7
Öxabäck S 107 E12
Oxberg S 118 D7
Oxelösund S 109 B10
Oxenhope GB 27 D8
Oxentea MD 170 C4
Oxford GB 29 B12
Oxhalsö S 115 C11
Oxie S 103 D12
Oxkangar FIN 138 D8
Oxshott GB 31 E8
Oxted GB 31 E9
Oxton GB 21 D9
Oxylithos GR 191 B9
Øyangen N 120 E7
Oydegarden N 120 D4
Øyenkilen N 107 A8
Øyer N 117 D12
Øyeren N 112 B7
Øyfjord N 124 B9
Øynes N 124 B9
Øynes N 127 C11
Oyonnax F 47 C8
Øyslebø N 106 C2
Oyten D 33 B12
Øyvatnet N 127 C12
Oza E 54 B3
Ozaeta E 57 C7
Ozalj HR 164 E4
Ożarów PL 159 E12
Ożarów Mazowiecki PL 157 F3
Ožbalt SLO 164 C4
Özbaşı TR 193 D9
Özbek TR 193 C8
Ózd H 161 G1
Oždany SK 163 E9
Özdere TR 193 D8
Ożenna PL 161 E3
Ozersk RUS 152 E5
Ozieri I 80 B3
Ozimek PL 158 E6
Ozimica BIH 173 D9
Özlüce TR 197 B9
Ozoir-la-Ferrière F 41 C8
Ozolaine LV 147 F9
Ozoli LV 147 F9
Ozoli LV 151 C12
Ozolmuiža LV 149 D2
Ozolnieki LV 150 C7
Ozora H 165 C10
Ozorków PL 159 C7
Ozun RO 169 F7
Ozzano dell'Emilia I 82 D3
Ozzano Monferrato I 84 C5

P

Pääaho FIN 137 D10
Pääjärvi FIN 123 E13
Paakinmäki FIN 137 F11
Paakkila FIN 141 E11
Paakkola FIN 135 C13
Paal B 199 C6
Paalasmaa FIN 141 D12
Paaso FIN 143 C15
Paasvere EST 147 C13
Paatela FIN 145 B9
Paattinen FIN 142 D7
Paatus FIN 129 C17
Paavola FIN 135 E14
Pabaiskas LT 151 F9
Paberžė LT 153 D11
Pabianice PL 159 C7
Pabillonis I 80 D2
Pabirže LT 151 D9
Pabradė LT 153 D12
Pabu F 38 C5
Pacanow PL 159 F11
Paceco I 74 C3
Pacheia Ammos GR 195 E10
Pachino I 75 F7
Pachni GR 187 B7
Paciano I 78 A2
Pačlavice CZ 93 D12
Pacos de Ferreira P 54 F3
Pacov CZ 93 D8
Pacsa H 165 C8
Păcureţi RO 177 C8
Pacy-sur-Eure F 40 B5
Paczków PL 93 B12
Padasjoki FIN 143 C13
Padborg DK 98 A6
Padbury GB 30 D7
Padej SRB 166 F5
Pădene HR 172 E5
Paderborn D 33 E11
Paderne P 66 E3
Paderne de Allariz E 54 E8
Padeş RO 175 C10
Padesh BG 181 F7
Padew Narodowa PL 159 F12
Padežine BIH 173 F8
Padiham GB 27 D7
Pădina RO 175 E11
Padina RO 177 D10
Padina SRB 174 D6
Padinska Skela SRB 174 D5
Padirac F 45 F9
Padise EST 147 C8
Padoby BY 149 F2
Padornelo P 54 E5
Padova I 82 B4
Padoux F 42 D6
Padria I 80 C2
Padrón E 54 C2
Padru I 80 B4

Padstow GB 28 D5
Padul E 69 B9
Padula I 76 C5
Paduli I 76 A3
Padure LV 150 C3
Paesana I 53 B6
Paese I 88 E5
Pag HR 83 D11
Pagani I 76 B3
Paganica I 78 C4
Paganico I 81 B4
Pagėgiai LT 150 E4
Pagham GB 31 E8
Pagiriai LT 151 F8
Pagiriai LT 153 D11
Paglieta I 79 C6
Pagny-sur-Moselle F 42 C5
Pagondas GR 193 D8
Pagouria GR 187 B8
Pagramantis LT 150 E4
Paharova S 132 E4
Páhi H 166 D3
Pahkakoski FIN 135 D16
Pahkakumpu FIN 131 E3
Pahkakumpu FIN 137 C12
Pahkala FIN 135 F11
Pahkamäki FIN 139 D16
Pähl D 88 A3
Pahlen D 98 B6
Pahranichny BY 156 D9
Pahtaoja FIN 135 C14
Paião P 60 D3
Paide EST 147 D11
Paignton GB 29 E7
Paihola FIN 141 E13
Päijälä FIN 143 B12
Paikuse EST 147 E9
Pailhès F 49 D8
Paillet F 48 A5
Paimbœuf F 39 F7
Paimela FIN 143 C14
Paimio FIN 142 E7
Paimpol F 38 C5
Paimpont F 39 D7
Painswick GB 29 B10
Painten D 91 E10
Paipis FIN 143 E13
Paisley GB 21 D8
Paistu EST 147 E11
Paisua FIN 140 C9
Päiväjoki FIN 131 F2
Pajala S 133 D10
Pajares de la Lampreana E 55 E8
Pajarón E 63 E9
Pajęczno PL 159 D6
Pajukoski FIN 141 C11
Pajukoste FIN 129 C20
Pajūris LT 150 F4
Pajukylä FIN 140 D7
Pajuvaara FIN 137 D14
Páka H 165 C7
Pakaa FIN 143 D14
Pakalné S 152 E5
Pakalne LV 147 F9
Pakalniai LT 151 F10
Pakapė LT 150 E6
Pakarila FIN 139 C17
Pakistjärvi FIN 133 E12
Pakkala FIN 143 C11
Pakod H 165 C8
Pakość PL 154 E5
Pakosław PL 97 C12
Pakoštane HR 172 E4
Päkozd H 165 B11
Pakrac HR 165 E8
Pakruojis LT 150 E7
Paks H 165 C11
Paksuniemi S 132 C5
Pala EST 147 D13
Palacios del Sil E 55 C7
Palacios de Sanabria E 55 D6
Palaciosrubios E 61 B10
Palade EST 146 D5
Palafrugell E 59 D10
Palagianello I 77 B7
Palagiano I 77 B8
Palagonia I 75 D6
Palaia I 82 E2
Palaia Fokaia GR 191 D6
Palaikastro GR 195 E11
Palaiochora GR 194 E6
Palaiochori GR 185 B10
Palaiochori GR 185 D10
Palaiochori GR 191 C7
Palaiokastritsa GR 184 E1
Palaiokastro GR 193 D9
Palaiokipos GR 193 A7
Palaiokomi GR 186 C5
Palaiomonastiro GR 185 E6
Palaiopoli GR 192 D4
Palaiopyrgos GR 185 E6
Palaiopyrgos GR 185 E8
Palaiopyrgos GR 190 C4
Palaiovracha GR 190 B5
Palairos GR 190 C4
Palaiseau F 41 C7
Palamas GR 185 F7
Palamós E 59 D10
Palamuse EST 147 D13
Palanca RO 169 D9
Palanga LT 150 E2
Pălânge S 135 C9
Palanzano I 82 D1
Palárikovo SK 162 E6
Palas de Rei E 54 C4
Palata BY 149 E6
Palata I 79 D7
Pălatca RO 168 D4
Palau I 80 A3
Palavas-les-Flots F 51 C6
Palazzo Adriano I 74 D3
Palazzolo Acreide I 75 E6
Palazzolo sull'Oglio I 85 B8
Palazzo San Gervasio I 76 B6
Paldiski EST 147 C8
Pale BIH 173 E10
Pãle LV 147 E9
Paleičiai LT 150 F2
Palena I 79 D6
Palencia E 56 D2
Palenciana E 69 B7
Palenzuela E 56 D3
Palermo AL 184 D2
Palermo I 74 C3
Palešnica PL 160 D2
Palestrina I 78 D3
Palèvenelė LT 151 E10
Palež BIH 174 E3
Palhaça P 60 C3
Pálháza H 161 G4
Palia Kavala GR 187 C6
Paliano I 78 D4

Palić SRB 166 E4
Palinges F 46 B5
Palinuro I 76 C4
Paliouri GR 185 E10
Paliouria GR 185 E6
Palis F 41 D10
Palivere EST 147 D7
Palizzi I 75 D9
Paljakka FIN 137 B14
Paljakka FIN 137 E11
Pålkäne FIN 143 C11
Pålkem S 134 B7
Palkino RUS 148 F3
Palkisoja FIN 131 A2
Palkovice CZ 162 B6
Palladio GR 187 B8
Pallagorio I 77 E7
Pallarés E 67 C7
Pallas Grean New IRL 24 C6
Pallas Green IRL 24 C6
Pälli FIN 135 E16
Palling D 91 F12
Palluau F 44 B2
Palluau-sur-Indre F 45 B8
Palma P 66 C2
Palma Campania I 76 B3
Palma del Río E 67 D9
Palma de Mallorca E 65 E10
Palma di Montechiaro I 74 E4
Palmadula I 80 B1
Palmanova E 65 E10
Palmanova I 89 E7
Palmaz P 60 C4
Palmeira P 54 E3
Palmela P 66 B2
Palmi I 75 C8
Pálmonostora H 166 D4
Palmse EST 147 B11
Palnackie GB 21 F9
Palnieca Г 53 H10
Palo del Colle I 77 A7
Palohuornas S 132 E6
Palojärvi FIN 131 E2
Palojärvi FIN 133 A10
Palojärvi FIN 133 E14
Palojoensuu FIN 132 B10
Palokki FIN 141 E11
Palomaa FIN 129 E19
Palomäki FIN 141 D11
Palomar de Arroyos E 58 F2
Palomares del Río E 67 E7
Palomas E 67 B7
Palombara Sabina I 78 C3
Palombaro I 79 C6
Palomene LT 153 D9
Palomera E 63 D8
Palomeras del Campo E 63 E7
Palomonte I 76 B4
Palonoja FIN 131 B2
Palonselkä FIN 133 D13
Palonurmi FIN 141 D10
Paloperä FIN 131 F4
Palos de la Frontera E 67 E6
Palosenjärvi FIN 135 E16
Palotabozsok H 165 D11
Palotáshalom H 166 B4
Palovaara FIN 135 B12
Palovaara FIN 135 B16
Palovaara FIN 137 E13
Palovaara FIN 141 E14
Pals E 59 D10
Pålsboda S 108 A6
Palsmane LV 151 B12
Palsselkä FIN 133 D16
Pålsträsk S 134 C6
Paltamo FIN 137 F10
Paltanen FIN 140 F7
Paltaniemi FIN 137 F10
Paltin RO 169 F9
Pǎltiniş RO 169 A9
Pǎltiniş RO 175 C9
Pǎltinoasa RO 169 B7
Pal'tsevo RUS 145 D10
Paludi I 77 D7
Paluel F 34 E2
Paluknys LT 153 E10
Paluzza I 89 C7
Palyatskishki BY 153 E11
Palyessye BY 157 F12
Palzem D 186 B2
Pambukovica SRB 174 E4
Pameče SLO 89 C11
Pamfylla GR 193 A8
Pamhagen A 165 A7
Pamiers F 49 D9
Pampäji LV 150 C4
Pamparato I 53 C7
Pampelonne F 49 B10
Pampilhosa P 60 D4
Pampilhosa da Serra P 60 D5
Pampliega E 56 D4
Pamplona E 48 E2
Pampow D 99 C10
Pamproux F 44 C5
Pamukçu TR 189 E8
Panaci RO 168 C6
Panagia GR 187 C7
Panagia GR 187 E8
Panagia GR 194 E9
Panaguyurishte BG 181 D9
Panagyurski Kolonii BG 181 D9
Panahor AL 184 C2
Panaitolio GR 190 B3
Panaja AL 184 C1
Pǎnǎşeşti MD 170 C3
Panassac F 49 D7
Pǎnǎtǎu RO 177 C8
Panazol F 45 D8
Pancalieri I 53 B7
Pancar TR 193 C9
Pance TR 189 B7
Pǎnceşti RO 169 E10
Pančevo SRB 174 D6
Pancharevo BG 181 D7
Panciu RO 169 F10
Pancorbo E 56 C5
Pâncota RO 167 E8
Pancrudo E 58 F1
Pánd H 166 C4
Pandělys LT 151 D10
Pandino I 85 C8
Pandrup DK 102 A5
Pandy GB 29 B9
Panelia FIN 142 C6
Panemunė LT 152 C4
Panemunėlis LT 151 E10
Panes E 55 B10
Pǎnet RO 168 D4
Panevėžys LT 151 E8
Panga FIN 131 F4
Pǎngǎrati RO 169 D8
Pange F 202 C1

Panicale I 78 A2
Panichkovo BG 182 F4
Panissières F 46 D5
Paniza E 57 F9
Panjas F 48 C5
Panjevac SRB 175 E8
Panjik BIH 173 C9
Panka FIN 140 D7
Pankajärvi FIN 141 D14
Pankakoski FIN 141 D14
Panker D 99 B9
Panki PL 158 E6
Pannarano I 76 A3
Pannes F 41 D8
Panni I 76 A4
Panningen NL 32 F5
Pannonhalma H 165 A9
Panóias P 66 D3
Panorama GR 185 C9
Panormos GR 194 E8
Panschwitz-Kuckau D 96 D6
Pantanassa GR 194 B4
Päntäne FIN 138 F8
Pantelimon RO 171 D2
Pantelimon RO 177 E8
Panticeu RO 168 C3
Pantoja E 62 D5
Pantoja E 62 D5
Panttikylä FIN 138 F8
Panttila FIN 138 E8
Pant-y-dwr GB 29 A8
Paola I 76 E6
Pap H 161 G5
Pápa H 165 B8
Papadianika GR 194 B4
Papasidero I 76 D5
Pápateszér H 165 B9
Papenburg D 33 B8
Papendorf D 99 B12
Papendrecht NL 32 E3
Papilė LT 150 D4
Papilys LT 151 D10
Papín SK 161 E5
Papkeszi H 165 B10
Paplaka LV 150 D2
Papowo Biskupie PL 154 D6
Pappades GR 191 B7
Pappados GR 193 A7
Pappenheim D 91 E8
Paprotnia PL 157 F6
Par GB 28 E5
Parabita I 77 C10
Paraćin SRB 175 F7
Paracuellos E 63 E9
Paracuellos de Jarama E 62 C5
Parád H 163 F10
Parada P 61 C6
Parada de Ester P 60 C4
Parada de Pinhão P 54 F4
Parada de Rubiales E 61 B10
Parada de Sil E 54 D4
Paradeisi GR 197 D8
Paradeisia GR 190 E5
Paradeisos GR 187 B7
Paradela E 54 C5
Paradela P 54 E4
Paradela P 60 B5
Paradyż PL 157 H2
Parainen FIN 142 E7
Parakalamos GR 184 E4
Parakka S 132 D7
Parakoila GR 193 A7
Paralepa EST 146 D7
Paralia GR 190 C4
Paralia GR 191 F6
Paralia Avdiron GR 187 C7
Paralia Saranti GR 191 C6
Paralia Tyrou GR 191 E6
Paralio Astros GR 191 E6
Paramé F 39 C8
Parâmio P 55 E6
Páramo del Sil E 55 C7
Paramythia GR 184 E4
Paranhos P 60 D5
Parantala FIN 139 E15
Parapotamos GR 184 E3
Paras N 127 B19
Pârâu RO 168 F6
Parava RO 169 E9
Paravola GR 190 B4
Paray-le-Monial F 46 C5
Parcani MD 170 B3
Parcent F 72 C7
Parcé-sur-Sarthe F 39 E11
Parchen D 95 B11
Parchim D 99 D11
Parchovany SK 161 F4
Parchów PL 97 D9
Parchowo PL 101 B13
Parciaki PL 155 D11
Parcoul F 44 E6
Parczew PL 157 G7
Pardais P 66 B5
Pardies F 48 D4
Pardilhó P 60 C3
Pardoşi RO 177 C9
Parechcha BY 153 F9
Paredes de Coura P 54 E2
Paredes de Nava E 55 D10
Pareja E 63 C7
Parempuyre F 44 F4
Parenti I 77 E6
Parentis-en-Born F 48 B3
Parets del Vallès E 59 D8
Parey D 95 B10
Parga GR 184 F3
Pârgǎreşti RO 169 E9
Pargas FIN 142 E7
Parghelia I 75 B8
Pargny-sur-Saulx F 41 C12
Pargolovo RUS 145 E13
Parhalahti FIN 135 E13
Päri EST 147 E11
Parigné-l'Évêque F 40 E3
Parikkala FIN 145 B12
Parincea RO 169 E10
Paris F 41 C7
Parisot F 49 B9
Parisot F 49 C9
Parissavaara FIN 141 E16
Pärjänsuo FIN 136 C9
Pärjol RO 169 D9
Park GB 20 F2
Parkajoki S 133 C10
Parkano FIN 139 C14
Parkkila FIN 137 D11
Parkkila FIN 139 C14
Parkkila FIN 144 B7

Parkkima FIN 139 C15
Parkkuu FIN 143 B10
Parksepa EST 147 F13
Parkstein D 91 C11
Parkua FIN 141 B9
Parkumäki FIN 145 B10
Parla E 62 D5
Parlan F 45 F10
Parma I 82 C1
Parndorf A 93 G11
Pärnu EST 147 E8
Pärnu-Jaagupi EST 147 D9
Paroikia GR 192 E5
Parola FIN 143 C11
Paron F 41 D9
Parowa PL 97 D8
Parrillas E 61 D10
Parsau D 95 A8
Parsberg D 91 D10
Pârscov RO 177 C9
Pârşcoveni RO 176 E4
Parşecko PL 101 C11
Parstein D 100 E6
Partakko FIN 129 E20
Partaloa E 71 E8
Partanna I 74 D2
Parteboda S 119 A10
Partenen A 87 D10
Partenstein D 90 B6
Pârteştii de Jos RO 169 B7
Parthenay F 44 B5
Partheni GR 193 E8
Partinello F 53 G9
Partinico I 74 C3
Partizani I 78 C3
Partizani SRB 174 E5
Partizánska Ľupča SK 163 C8
Partizánske SK 162 D6
Partney GB 27 E8
Parton GB 26 B4
Partry IRL 22 E4
Partsi EST 147 E14
Parudaminys LT 153 D11
Parup DK 102 C4
Parva RO 168 C5
Parvaiainen S 135 C11
Pâryd S 105 B9
Parysów PL 157 G5
Parzęczew PL 159 C7
Pasai Donibane E 48 D2
Paşaköy TR 187 C10
Paşaköy TR 187 E10
Paşaköy TR 189 E8
Paşaköy TR 193 B10
Pasalanakylä FIN 141 D10
Paşayiğit TR 187 C10
Paşcani RO 169 C9
Pasching A 92 F6
Paskevalkan FIN
Pasiǎn di Prato I 89 D7
Pasiano di Pordenone I 89 E6
Pasieki PL 155 F5
Pasiene LV 149 D4
Pasikovci HR 165 F9
Paskalevets BG 182 C4
Paskalevo BG 171 F1
Påskallavik S 105 A10
Pastęk PL 155 B8
Pasmajärvi FIN 133 D12
Pašman HR 172 E3
Passage East IRL 25 D9
Passail A 164 B5
Passais F 39 C10
Passau D 92 E4
Passignano sul Trasimeno I 82 F5
Passow D 100 D6
Passy F 47 D10
Pastavy BY 151 F13
Pastende LV 150 B4
Pasto FIN 139 E10
Pastoriza E 54 B5
Pastrana E 63 D7
Păstrăveni RO 169 C8
Pašuliene LV 151 E12
Pasvalys LT 151 D7
Pašvitinys LT 150 D7
Pasym PL 155 C9
Pasytsely UA 170 A5
Paszab H 161 G4
Paszowice PL 97 D10
Pásztó H 163 F9
Pasztowa Wola PL 157 H4
Pata SK 162 E5
Pataias P 60 E3
Patak H 163 E8
Patana FIN 139 D11
Pătârlagele RO 177 C8
Patay F 40 D6
Patchway GB 29 B9
Pateley Bridge GB 27 C8
Paternek DK 105 E7
Pateniemi FIN 135 D14
Patergassen A 89 C8
Paterna E 64 E4
Paterna del Campo E 67 E7
Paterna del Madera E 71 B8
Paterna del Río E 71 E7
Paterna de Rivera E 68 C5
Paternion A 89 C8
Paternò I 75 D6
Paterno I 76 C5
Paternopoli I 76 B4
Patersdorf D 92 D3
Pǎterud S 112 C7
Patişka Reka MK 180 F3
Pátka H 165 B11
Patmos GR 193 E8
Patna GB 20 E7
Patnów PL 158 D6
Patokoski FIN 133 E14
Patoniemi FIN 137 B12
Patoniva FIN 129 D19
Patos AL 184 C2
Patra GR 190 C4
Pǎtrǎuti RO 169 B8
Patrica I 78 D4
Patrick GB 26 C2
Patrimonio F 53 F10
Patrington GB 27 D11
Pátroha H 161 G4
Pattada I 80 B3
Pattensen D 94 B6
Patterdale GB 26 B6
Patti I 75 C6
Pattijoki FIN 135 E13
Pättikkä FIN 132 A7
Pǎtulele RO 175 E10
Patumǎšiai LT 150 E5
Păturages B 198 E3

Páty H 165 A11
Pau F 48 D5
Pǎuca RO 168 E3
Paudorf A 93 F9
Pauilhac F 49 C7
Pauillac F 44 E4
Paukarlahti FIN 140 E9
Paukkaja FIN 141 E10
Paukkeri FIN 136 D9
Paul P 60 D5
Paularo I 89 C7
Pǎuleni-Ciuc RO 169 E7
Pǎuleşti MD 170 C2
Pǎuleşti RO 167 B10
Paulhac-en-Margeride F 46 F3
Paulhan F 50 C5
Paulilatino I 80 C2
Paulinenaue D 99 E13
Pǎuliş RO 167 E8
Paulistrôm S 108 E7
Paŭls E 58 F4
Paulx F 44 B2
Pǎuneşti RO 169 E10
Pausa D 95 E11
Pǎuşeşti RO 176 C4
Pǎuşeşti-Mǎglaşi RO 176 C4
Pautrask S 123 B13
Pauvres F 35 E10
Pavel BG 182 C5
Pavel Banya BG 182 D4
Pavia I 85 C7
Pavia P 66 B3
Pavia di Udine I 89 E7
Pavías E 64 E4
Pavie F 49 C7
Pavilly F 34 E2
Pāvilosta LV 150 C2
Pavlikeni BG 182 C4
Pavliani GR 190 B5
Pavlikeni BG 182 C4
Pavliš SRB 175 C7
Pavlivka UA 170 C5
Pavlivka UA 170 F4
Pavlos GR 191 B7
Pavlovac HR 165 E8
Pavlovce nad Uhom SK 161 F5
Pavllo GR 190 B5
Pavullo nel Frignano I 82 D2
Pavy RUS 148 E6
Päwesin D 95 A12
Pawfosiów PL 159 C7
Pawłówek PL 154 D4
Pawłowice PL 97 C11
Pawłowiczki PL 158 F5
Pawonków PL 158 E6
Paxton GB 21 D12
Payerne CH 47 B11
Paymogo E 67 D5
Payrin-Augmontel F 49 C10
Payzac F 45 E8
Pazardzhik BG 181 D9
Pazarič BIH 173 E9
Pazarköy TR 189 E7
Pazin HR 83 B8
Paziols F 50 E4
Pázmánd H 165 B11
Pazos E 54 C2
Pchelarovo BG 182 F4
Pchelin BG 181 E8
Pcim PL 163 B9
Pčinja MK 180 F3
Peacehaven GB 31 F7
Peal de Becerro E 71 D6
Péaule F 39 E7
Pébrac F 46 E3
Peč SRB 179 D9
Peccia CH 87 E7
Peccioli I 82 E2
Pécel H 166 C3
Peceneaga RO 171 C2
Pečenjevce SRB 180 C4
Pechea RO 171 B1
Pechenga RUS 130 D10
Pechina E 71 F8
Pechory RUS 148 F2
Peci BIH 172 D5
Pecica RO 167 E7
Pečigrad BIH 172 B4
Pečinci SRB 174 D4
Pecineaga RO 171 F2
Peciu Nou RO 175 B7
Pecka CZ 93 B9
Pecka SRB 174 E4
Pečky CZ 93 B8
Pęcław PL 97 D10
Pečovská Nová Ves SK 161 E3
Pecq B 35 C7
Pécs H 165 D10
Pécsvárad H 165 D10
Pečurice MNE 179 E8
Pęczniew PL 158 C6
Pedaso I 78 A5
Pedrogão P 60 E3
Pedrógão P 61 D6
Pedrógão SK 162 C6
Pedrógão Grande P 60 E4
Pedrógão Pequeno P 60 E4
Pedro-Martínez E 71 D6
Pedro Muñoz E 63 F7
Pedrosa E 56 B4
Pedrosa del Príncipe E 56 D3
Pedrosillo de los Aires E 61 C9
Pedroso E 57 D6
Pedroso E 60 B3
Pedrouzos E 54 C2
Pedasó I 78 A5
Peebles GB 21 D10
Peel GBM 26 C2
Peenemünde D 100 B5
Peer B 35 B11
Peera FIN 128 F2
Pefki GR 191 A7
Pefkofyto GR 184 D4
Pefkoi GR 195 E10
Pefkos GR 184 E9
Pega P 61 D6
Pegalajar E 69 A9
Pegau D 95 D11
Peggau A 164 B4
Pegli I 53 C9

Pegnitz D 91 C10
Pego E 72 D4
Pego P 60 F4
Pegões P 66 B2
Pegôw D 97 D11
Peguera E 65 E9
Pehčevo MK 181 F6
Pehkolanlahti FIN 136 F9
Pehlivanköy TR 189 B6
Peillac F 39 E7
Peille F 53 D6
Peine D 95 B7
Peio I 87 E11
Peipin F 51 B10
Peipohja FIN 142 C6
Peïra-Cava F 53 D6
Peiraias GR 191 D8
Peißen D 95 C11
Peißen D 95 C11
Peißenberg D 88 A3
Peiting D 87 B11
Peitz D 96 C6
Peize NL 33 B7
Pekankylä FIN 137 E13
Pekanpää FIN 135 B11
Pekkala FIN 135 B17
Pelagićevo BIH 173 C10
Pelago I 82 E4
Pelahustán E 62 D3
Pelarrodríguez E 61 C8
Pelasgia GR 191 B6
Pelčii LV 150 C3
Pełczyce PL 101 D9
Peleagonzalo E 55 F9
Pelēči LV 151 D13
Pelekas GR 184 E2
Peleta GR 191 E6
Pelhřimov CZ 93 D8
Pelinei MD 170 F2
Pelinia MD 169 A10
Pelishat BG 181 C10
Pélissanne F 51 C9
Pelitköy TR 189 F6
Pelkoperä FIN 135 F15
Pelkosenniemi FIN 131 D2
Pella GR 185 C8
Pellaro I 75 C8
Pellegrino Parmense I 85 D8
Pellegrue F 44 F6
Pellérd H 165 D10
Pellesmäki FIN 140 E9
Pellestrina I 82 B6
Pellevoisin F 45 B8
Pellinki FIN 143 E14
Pellizzano I 85 A10
Pello FIN 133 E11
Pello S 133 E11
Pellosniemi FIN 144 C7
Pelm D 37 D7
Peloche E 61 F10
Pelovo BG 181 C9
Pelplin PL 154 C6
Pelsin D 100 C5
Pelso FIN 135 E16
Peltokangas FIN 139 D12
Peltosalmi FIN 140 C8
Peltovuoma FIN 133 B12
Pélussin F 46 E6
Pelvoux F 47 F9
Pély H 166 C5
Pelynt GB 28 E5
Pembrey GB 28 B5
Pembridge GB 29 A9
Pembroke GB 28 B5
Pembroke Dock GB 28 B5
Pembury GB 31 E9
Pemfling D 91 D12
Pempelijärvi S 132 E8
Peñacerrada E 57 C6
Penacova P 60 D4
Peñafiel E 56 E4
Peñafiel P 60 B4
Peñaflor E 67 D9
Peñaflor de Hornija E 55 E10
Penagos E 56 B4
Peñalba E 58 E3
Peñalén E 63 D8
Peñalsordo E 67 B9
Penalva do Castelo P 60 C5
Penamacor P 61 D6
Peñaranda de Bracamonte E 61 C10
Peñaranda de Duero E 56 E5
Peñarroya de Tastavins E 58 F4
Peñarroya-Pueblonuevo E 67 C9
Peñarrubia E 71 C8
Penarth GB 29 C8
Peñascosa E 71 B8
Peñas de San Pedro E 71 B9
Peñausende E 55 F8
Penc H 166 B3
Pencader GB 28 A6
Pencoed GB 28 B2
Pendeen GB 28 E3
Pendilhe P 60 C5
Pendine GB 28 B5
Pendlebury GB 27 D7
Penedo Gordo P 66 D4
Penedono P 60 C6
Penela P 60 D4
Pénestin F 38 E7
Néni GB 20 E5
Penikkajärvi FIN 137 C14
Peninki FIN 139 D15
Peninver GB 20 E5
Peñíscola E 64 E5
Penistone GB 27 D7
Penkridge GB 27 F7
Penkule LV 150 D6
Penly F 34 E3
Penmarch F 38 E3
Pennabilli I 82 E5
Penna in Teverina I 78 C2
Pennapiedimonte I 79 C6
Pennautier F 49 D10
Penne F 49 B9
Penne I 78 C5
Penne-d'Agenais F 49 B7
Pennyghael GB 20 C4
Penrhiw-pâl GB 28 A6
Penrhyn Bay GB 28 E4
Penrith GB 22 F11
Penryn GB 28 E4
Pensala FIN 138 D8
Pentalofo GR 190 C3
Pentalofos GR 184 D5

Pentalofos GR 187 A10
Pentapoli GR 185 B10
Pentaoria GR 190 D5
Pentinniemi FIN 135 C16
Pentir GB 28 E3
Pentone I 75 B10
Pentraeth GB 28 E4
Pentre GB 29 B8
Pentrefoelas GB 26 E4
Penttäjä S 133 E11
Penttilänvaara FIN 137 C12
Penvénan F 38 C5
Penybont GB 29 A8
Penybontfawr GB 26 F5
Pen-y-fai GB 29 B7
Penzance GB 28 E3
Penzberg D 88 A3
Penzlin D 100 D4
Péone F 52 C5
Pepelow D 99 B11
Pepeni MD 170 B2
Pepingen B 35 C9
Pepinster B 35 C12
Peplos GR 187 C10
Pępowo PL 97 C12
Pēqin AL 184 C2
Peque E 55 D7
Pêra P 66 E3
Peraboddze BY 149 E2
Perachora GR 191 C6
Perafita E 59 C8
Perä-Hyyppä FIN 138 F8
Peraia GR 185 C6
Peraia GR 185 C8
Perais P 60 E5
Perälä FIN 138 F7
Peralada E 59 C10
Peraleda de la Mata E 61 E10
Peraleda del Zaucejo E 67 C8
Peralejos E 58 G1
Peralejos de las Truchas E 63 C9
Perales del Alfambra E 58 F2
Perales del Puerto E 61 D7
Peralta E 48 F2
Peralta de Alcofea E 58 D3
Peralta de la Sal E 58 D4
Peraltilla E 58 D3
Peralva P 66 E4
Peralveche E 63 C8
Perama GR 184 E4
Perama GR 191 D8
Perama GR 194 D8
Perämäki FIN 138 D9
Peramola E 58 C6
Peranka FIN 137 D13
Peränne FIN 139 F11
Perä-Posio FIN 137 B10
Peraroli di Cadore I 88 D5
Peräseinäjoki FIN 139 E10
Perast MNE 179 E6
Perävaara FIN 133 E11
Perbál H 165 A11
Perchtoldsdorf A 93 F10
Percy F 39 C9
Perdasdefogu I 80 D3
Perdaxius I 80 E2
Perdifumo I 76 B4
Perdiguera E 57 E10
Perdika GR 184 F3
Perdika GR 191 D7
Perdiki GR 193 D7
Perdikkas GR 185 C6
Perduhovo Selo BIH 173 D6
Perechyn UA 161 F5
Peredo P 55 F6
Peregu Mare RO 167 E6
Perehin's'ke UA 161 F9
Pereiras P 66 E3
Pereiro E 54 A4
Pereiro P 66 E4
Pereiro de Aguiar E 54 D4
Perekhrestove UA 170 C5
Pererita MD 169 A9
Pereruela E 55 F8
Peresecina MD 170 C3
Peressaare EST 147 C13
Peretu RO 176 E6
Pereyma UA 170 A5
Perfugas I 80 B2
Perg A 93 F7
Pergine Valdarno I 82 F4
Pergine Valsugana I 85 A11
Pergola I 83 E6
Perho FIN 139 D12
Periam RO 167 E6
Periana E 69 C8
Pericei RO 167 C10
Périers F 39 B8
Perieţi RO 176 E5
Perieţi RO 177 D10
Périgueux F 45 E7
Periklia GR 185 B7
Perila EST 147 C10
Perín-Chym SK 161 F3
Periprava RO 171 C5
Periş RO 177 D7
Perişani RO 176 C4
Perişor RO 176 E2
Perişoru RO 177 E11
Perissa GR 195 C9
Peristasi GR 185 D8
Peristera GR 185 C9
Peristeri GR 191 C8
Perithori GR 185 B10
Perivoli GR 184 E5
Perivoli GR 190 A5
Perivoli GR 190 A5
Perivolia GR 194 E7
Perjasica HR 172 B3
Perkáta H 165 B10
Perkiömäki FIN 139 D9
Perl D 36 F6
Perleberg D 99 D11
Perlejewo PL 157 E7
Perlez SRB 174 C5
Perloja LT 153 E9
Perły PL 152 E4
Permani RO 83 B9
Permantokoski FIN 133 F16
Përmet AL 184 D3
Pernå FIN 143 E15
Pernarava LT 150 F7
Pernarec CZ 92 C4
Pernegg an der Mur A 164 B4
Pernersdorf A 93 E9
Pernes P 60 F3
Pernes-les-Fontaines F 51 C9
Perni GR 187 C8
Pernik BG 181 D7
Pernió FIN 143 E9
Perniön asema FIN 143 E9
Pernitz A 93 G9
Pernu FIN 137 B10
Pero I 85 B7
Peroguarda P 66 C3
Pérols F 51 C6
Péron F 47 C8
Perondi AL 184 C2
Péronnas A 47 C7
Péronne F 34 E5
Perosa Argentina I 47 F11
Pero Viseu P 60 D6
Perpignan F 50 E4
Perranporth GB 28 E4
Perreux F 46 C5
Perrigny F 47 B8
Perrogney-les-Fontaines F 42 E3
Perros-Guirec F 38 C5
Perrum-Åbmir FIN 129 C13
Persan F 41 B7
Persåsen S 118 A7
Persberg S 113 C11
Persbo S 113 B13
Persenbeug A 93 F8
Pershagen S 109 A11
Pershamawskaya BY 149 E4
Pershore GB 29 A10
Pershotravneve UA 171 C4
Pershyttan S 113 D13
Persnäs S 105 A11
Persön S 134 C8
Perstorp S 103 C12
Perth GB 21 C10
Perthes F 41 D8
Pertouli GR 184 E5
Perttaus FIN 133 D15
Pertteli FIN 143 E12
Perttula FIN 143 E12
Pertuis F 51 C10
Pertunmaa FIN 143 C15
Peruca S 58 C3
Peruc CZ 92 B5
Perucǎcke SRB 174 F3
Perucica BIH 173 F10
Perugia I 82 F5
Perukka FIN 135 F17
Perunkajärvi FIN 133 E15
Perushtitsa BG 181 E10
Perušić HR 172 C3
Péruwelz B 35 C8
Pervalka LT 150 F2
Pervenchères F 40 D3
Pervomaisc MD 170 D5
Pervomayskoye RUS 145 E12
Perwez B 35 C10
Pesadas de Burgos E 56 C4
Pesaro I 83 E6
Pescaglia I 82 E1
Pescantina I 82 B2
Pescara I 79 C6
Pescasseroli I 78 D5
Pesceana RO 176 C4
Peschadoires F 46 D3
Peschici I 79 D9
Peschiera del Garda I 82 B2
Pescia I 82 E2
Pescina I 78 C5
Pescocostanzo I 78 D4
Pescolanciano I 79 D6
Pescopennataro I 79 D6
Pescorocchiano I 78 C4
Pesco Sannita I 76 A3
Peseux CH 47 B10
Peshkopi AL 179 F9
Peshtera BG 181 E9
Pesiökylä FIN 137 E12
Pesiönranta FIN 137 E12
Pesmes F 42 F4
Pesnica SLO 164 C5
Pesochnyy RUS 145 E13
Peso da Régua P 60 B5
Pesquera de Duero E 56 E3
Pessac F 44 F4
Pessalompolo FIN 133 F12
Pessan F 49 C7
Pesse NL 33 C6
Pessin D 96 A3
Peštani MK 184 B4
Peştera RO 171 E2
Peştişani RO 175 C11
Peştişu Mic RO 167 F10
Pesués E 56 B3
Pešurići BIH 173 E11
Petacciato I 79 C7
Petäikkö FIN 135 E16
Petäiskylä FIN 141 C12
Petäjäjärvi FIN 135 C17
Petäjäkangas FIN 135 D14
Petäjäkoski FIN 135 B14
Petäjäkoski FIN 135 F13
Petäjävesi FIN 139 F14
Petalax FIN 138 E6
Petalidi GR 190 F4
Pétange L 36 E5
Petas GR 190 A3
Petelea RO 168 D5
Peterborough GB 27 F11
Peterculter GB 19 L12
Peterhead GB 19 K13
Péteri H 166 C3
Peterlee GB 21 F14
Petersberg D 90 A6
Petersdorf D 91 E9
Petersdorf auf Fehmarn D 99 B9
Petersfield GB 31 E7
Petershagen D 33 D11
Petershagen D 96 B6
Peterswell IRL 22 F5
Pétervására H 163 E10
Pethelinos GR 185 B10
Petilia Policastro I 75 A10
Petín E 54 C5
Petisträsk S 123 B17
Petite-Rosselle F 202 C2
Petit-Mars F 39 F9
Petitmont F 202 D2
Petit-Noir F 47 B7
Petko Karavelovo BG 182 C5
Petko Slaveykov BG 182 C10
Petkula FIN 131 C1
Petkus D 96 C4
Petlovača SRB 174 D3
Pet Mogili BG 182 E6
Petnehása H 161 G5
Petőfibánya H 166 B4
Petra E 73 D11
Petrǎchioaia RO 177 D8

Petrades GR 188 B6
Petralia-Soprana I 74 D5
Petran AL 184 D3
Petrana GR 185 D6
Petrella Salto I 79 D7
Petrella Tifernina I 79 D7
Petrer E 72 E3
Petreşti RO 167 B9
Petreşti RO 176 D6
Petreştii de Jos RO 168 D3
Petreto-Bicchisano F 53 H9
Petriano I 83 E6
Petricani RO 169 C8
Petrijevci HR 165 E11
Petrila RO 176 C2
Petrinja HR 164 F6
Petriş RO 167 E9
Petritoli I 78 A5
Petrivka UA 170 D4
Petrivs'k UA 170 D3
Petrochori GR 190 B4
Petrodvorets RUS 145 F12
Pétrola E 71 B9
Petromäki FIN 141 E9
Petronà I 75 A10
Petroşani RO 176 C2
Petroşe RO 182 F6
Petroussa GR 186 B6
Petrova RO 168 B4
Petrovac MNE 179 E6
Petrovac SRB 175 E7
Petrovany SK 161 F3
Petrovaradin SRB 174 C4
Petrovec MK 180 F4
Petrovice CZ 92 C6
Petrovice u Karviné CZ 163 B7
Petrovići BIH 173 D10
Petrovići MNE 178 D6
Petrovo BG 185 B9
Petrovo RUS 152 D1
Petrovo Selo SRB 175 D9
Petruma FIN 141 F11
Petru Rareş RO 168 C4
Petruşeni MD 169 B10
Petřvald CZ 162 B6
Petřvald CZ 162 B6
Petsakoi GR 190 C5
Petsmo FIN 138 D7
Petten NL 32 C3
Pettigo GB 23 C7
Pettineo I 74 D5
Petting D 89 A6
Pettnau am Arlberg A 87 C10
Pettorano sul Gizio I 78 D5
Petŭrch BG 181 D7
Petworth GB 31 F7
Peuerbach A 92 F5
Peujard F 44 E5
Peura FIN 135 B14
Peurajärvi FIN 135 B16
Pevensey GB 31 F9
Peveragno I 53 C7
Pewsey GB 29 C11
Pewsum (Krummhörn) D
33 B8
Pexonne F 43 D6
Peymeinade F 52 D5
Peynier F 51 D10
Peypin F 51 D10
Peyrat-le-Château F 45 D9
Peyrehorade F 48 C3
Peyriac-Minervois F 50 D4
Peyrieu F 47 D8
Peyrins F 47 E7
Peyrolles-en-Provence F 51 C10
Peyruis F 51 B10
Pézenas F 50 D5
Pezinok SK 162 E4
Pezuls F 45 F7
Pfaffenberg D 91 E11
Pfaffendorf D 96 B6
Pfaffenhausen D 87 A10
Pfaffenhofen an der Ilm D
91 E10
Pfaffenhofen an der Roth D
203 E9
Pfaffenhoffen F 43 C8
Pfäffikon CH 43 F10
Pfaffing D 91 F11
Pfalzfeld D 201 D8
Pfalzgrafenweiler D 43 C10
Pfarrkirchen D 92 F3
Pfarrweisach D 91 B8
Pfarrwerfen A 89 B7
Pfedelbach D 43 B11
Pflach A 87 B11
Pfons A 88 B3
Pförring D 91 E10
Pforzen D 87 B10
Pforzheim D 43 C10
Pfreimd D 91 D10
Pfronstetten D 43 D11
Pfronten D 87 B11
Pfullendorf D 43 E11
Pfullingen D 43 D11
Pfunds A 87 D11
Pfungstadt D 37 E11
Pfyn CH 43 E10
Phalsbourg F 43 C7
Philippeville B 35 D10
Philippine NL 198 C3
Philippsburg D 203 C5
Philippsreut D 92 E5
Piacenza I 85 C8
Piadena I 82 B1
Piana F 53 G9
Piana GR 190 D5
Piana Crixia I 53 C8
Piana degli Albanesi I 74 D3
Piancastagnaio I 78 B1
Piandimeleto I 82 E3
Piàn di Scò I 82 E4
Pianella I 78 C5
Pianello Val Tidone I 53 B10
Piano del Voglio I 82 D3
Pianoro I 82 D3
Pianosa I 81 B2
Pianotolli-Caldarello F 53 J10
Pians A 87 C11
Piansano I 78 B1
Pianu RO 168 F2
Pias P 66 C5
Piaseczno PL 101 D7
Piaseczno PL 157 F4
Piasek PL 100 E6
Piaski PL 97 C12
Piaski PL 157 H7
Piastów PL 157 F3
Piątek PL 159 B7

Piątnica Poduchowna PL
155 D13
Piatra RO 176 F6
Piatra Neamţ RO 169 D8
Piatra Olt RO 176 E4
Piatra Şoimului RO 169 D8
Piau-Engaly F 49 E6
Piazza al Serchio I 82 D1
Piazza Armerina I 74 E5
Piazza Brembana I 85 B8
Piazzatorre I 85 B8
Piazzola sul Brenta I 82 A4
Pibrac F 49 C8
Piçan HR 83 B9
Picar AL 184 D3
Picassent E 64 F4
Picauville F 39 B9
Picerno I 76 B5
Picher D 99 D10
Pichl bei Wels A 92 F5
Pichler D 99 D11
Pickering GB 27 C10
Pico I 78 E5
Picón E 70 A4
Picoto P 60 B3
Picquigny F 34 E5
Pidbuzh UA 161 E7
Pidhorodtsi UA 161 E7
Pidlisne UA 169 A7
Piebalgas LV 151 C8
Piechcin PL 154 E5
Piechowice PL 97 E9
Piecki PL 155 C11
Piecnik PL 101 D10
Piediclorte-di-Gaggio F 53 G10
Piedicroce F 53 G10
Piedimonte Etneo I 75 D7
Piedimonte Matese I 76 A2
Piedimulera I 84 A5
Piedrabuena E 70 A4
Piedrafita de Babia E 55 C7
Piedrahíta E 61 D10
Piedralaves E 62 D3
Piedras Albas E 61 E7
Piedras Blancas E 55 A8
Piedruja LV 149 E2
Piegaro I 78 B2
Piégut-Pluviers F 45 D7
Piehinki FIN 135 E12
Piekary Śląskie PL 159 F6
Piekielnik PL 163 C9
Pielavesi FIN 139 D17
Pieleşti RO 176 E3
Pielgrzymka PL 97 D9
Pienava LV 150 C6
Pieniężna PL 101 C11
Pieniężno PL 155 B9
Pieńkowo PL 101 B11
Pienza I 78 A1
Pieranica I 85 C8
Pieranie PL 154 E4
Pieralba I 53 F10
Pietra Ligure I 53 C8
Pietralunga I 82 E5
Pietramelara I 76 A2
Pietramontecorvino I 79 D8
Pietraperzia I 74 E5
Pietraporzio I 52 C6
Pietrari RO 176 C4
Pietrasanta I 82 E1
Pietravairano I 76 A2
Pietroasa RO 167 D10
Pietroasele RO 177 C9
Pietroşani RO 177 F7
Pietrosella F 53 H9
Pietroşiţa RO 177 C6
Pietrowice Wielkie PL 158 F5
Pieve d'Alpago I 88 D5
Pieve del Cairo I 84 C6
Pieve di Bono I 85 B10
Pieve di Cadore I 88 D5
Pieve di Cento I 82 C3
Pieve di Soligo I 88 E5
Pieve di Teco I 53 C7
Pieve Fosciana I 82 D1
Pievepelago I 82 D2
Pieve Santo Stefano I 82 E5
Pieve Torina I 78 A4
Pieve Vergonte I 84 A5
Piffonds F 41 D9
Piges GR 190 E5
Pigi GR 185 E6
Pigi GR 193 A7
Piglio I 78 D4
Pigna I 53 D7
Pignans F 52 E4
Pignataro Interamna I 78 E5
Pignataro Maggiore I 76 A2
Pignola I 76 B5
Pihlajakoski FIN 143 B13
Pihlajalahti FIN 143 B13
Pihlajalahti FIN 145 B9
Pihlajavesi FIN 139 F12
Pihlava FIN 142 B6
Pihtipudas FIN 139 D15
Piikkiö FIN 142 E8
Piilijärvi S 132 C6
Piiloperä FIN 137 B12

Piippola FIN 135 F15
Piipsjärvi FIN 135 F13
Piirsalu EST 147 C8
Piispa FIN 141 D11
Piispajärvi FIN 137 D13
Piittisjärvi FIN 135 B17
Pijnacker NL 32 D2
Pikkala FIN 135 E15
Pikkula FIN 135 C8
Piktupėnai LT 150 F3
Piła PL 101 D11
Pilar de la Mola E 73 D8
Pilas E 67 E7
Pilawa PL 157 G5
Piława Górna PL 97 E11
Pilchowice PL 158 F6
Pilda LV 149 D3
Piles E 72 D1
Pilgramsberg D 91 D12
Pili GR 191 B8
Pilica PL 159 F8
Pilis I 166 C4
Piliscsaba H 165 A11
Pilisszántó H 165 A11
Pilisszentiván H 165 A11
Pilisvörösvár H 165 A11
Pill A 88 B4
Pilling GB 26 D6
Pilníkov CZ 93 A9
Pilpala FIN 143 D11
Pilsach D 91 D10
Pilskalns LV 151 B13
Pilsting D 91 E12
Piltene LV 150 B3
Pilträsk S 134 C4
Pilu RO 167 D7
Pilviškiai LT 152 D7
Piłzno PL 159 G11
Pimentel I 80 E3
Pimperne GB 29 D10
Pimpiö S 133 L10
Piña de Campos E 56 D3
Piña de Esgueva E 56 E3
Piñar E 69 B10
Pınarbaşı TR 187 D10
Pınarca TR 189 B9
Pinarejo E 63 E8
Pınarhisar TR 189 A8
Pınarköy TR 189 A7
Pınarlıbelen TR 193 D10
Pinasca I 47 F11
Pincehely H 165 C10
Pinchbeck GB 27 F11
Pińczów PL 159 E10
Pindstrup DK 102 C6
Pineda de Cigüela E 63 D7
Pineda de la Sierra E 56 D5
Pineda de Mar E 59 D9
Pinela P 55 E6
Piñel de Abajo E 56 E3
Pinerolo I 47 F11
Pineto I 78 B6
Piney F 41 D11
Pinggau A 164 B6
Pinhal Novo P 66 B2
Pinhanços P 60 D5
Pinhão P 60 B5
Pinheiro P 66 C2
Pinheiro Grande P 60 F4
Pinhel P 61 C6
Pinhoe GB 29 D8
Pinilla de Molina E 63 C9
Pinilla de Toro E 55 E9
Pinkafeld A 164 B6
Pinneberg D 98 C7
Pinnow D 97 C7
Pino E 55 E7
Pino F 53 F10
Pino del Río E 55 C10
Pinofranqueado E 61 D8
Pinols F 46 E3
Piñor E 54 C3
Pinoso E 72 E2
Pinos-Puente E 69 B9
Pinsac F 45 F9
Pinsiö FIN 143 B9
Pintamo FIN 137 D10
Pintano E 48 E3
Pinto E 62 D5
Pinwherry GB 20 E7
Pinzano al Tagliamento I 89 D6
Pinzio P 61 C6
Pinzolo I 85 A10
Piobbico I 82 E6
Piolenc F 51 B8
Pioltello I 85 C7
Piombino I 81 B3
Piombino Dese I 88 E4
Pionerskiy RUS 155 A9
Pionki PL 157 H4
Pionsat F 45 C11
Pioraco I 83 F6
Piornal E 61 D9
Piossasco I 47 F11
Piossasco I 76 A2
Piotrasele RO 167 D10
Piotrkowice PL 97 D11
Piotrków Kujawski PL 154 E5
Piotrków Trybunalski PL 159 D8
Piove di Sacco I 82 B5
Piovene Rocchette I 85 A3
Piperskärr S 109 D9
Pipirig RO 169 C8
Pipriac F 39 E8
Piqeras AL 184 D2
Pir RO 167 C9
Piraino I 75 C6
Piran SLO 83 A8
Pirčiupiai LT 153 E10
Pirg AL 184 C4
Pirgovo BG 177 F7
Piriac-sur-Mer F 38 F6
Piricse H 161 H4
Pirin BG 185 A10
Pirinççi TR 189 B10
Pirkkala FIN 143 C11
Pîrlița MD 169 C11
Pîrlița MD 170 C2
Pirmasens D 37 F9
Pirna D 96 E5
Pirnmill GB 20 D6
Pirot SRB 180 C6
Pirovac HR 172 E4
Pirtó H 166 E3
Pirttijoki FIN 137 E9
Pirttikoski FIN 135 B18
Pirttikoski FIN 135 C13
Pirttikoski FIN 143 C10
Pirttimäki FIN 139 C17
Pirttimäki FIN 141 C10
Pirttimäki FIN 140 E7
Pirttimäki FIN 141 C10
Pirttinen FIN 139 D10

Pirttivaara FIN 137 D14
Pirttivuopio S 127 E17
Pisa FIN 135 B14
Pisa I 82 E1
Pisanets BG 177 F8
Pisarovina HR 164 E5
Pisarovo BG 181 C9
Pischelsdorf in der Steiermark A
164 B5
Pischia RO 167 F7
Pisciotta I 76 C4
Pişcolt RO 167 B9
Piscu RO 171 B1
Piscu Vechi RO 175 F11
Pišece SLO 164 D5
Písečná CZ 93 B12
Písek CZ 92 D6
Písek CZ 163 B7
Pishcha UA 170 A5
Pishchana UA 170 A5
Pishchanka UA 170 A3
Pisisaare EST 147 D11
Piskokefalo GR 195 E11
Piškorevci HR 173 B9
Pisoderi GR 184 C5
Pisogne I 85 B9
Pissonas GR 191 B8
Pissos F 48 B4
Pistiana GR 184 F5
Pisticci I 77 C7
Pisto FIN 137 D13
Pistoia I 82 E2
Pisz PL 155 C12
Piszczac PL 157 G8
Pitagowan GB 21 B9
Pitäjänmäki FIN 139 C15
Pitarque E 58 F2
Piteå S 134 D6
Piteşti RO 176 D5
Pithiviers F 41 D7
Pitigliano I 81 B5
Pitkäjärvi FIN 143 C10
Pitkälä FIN 145 B11
Pitkälahti FIN 140 E9
Pitkäsenkylä FIN 135 F12
Pitkyaranta RUS 145 B15
Pitlochry GB 21 B9
Pitomača HR 165 E8
Pitrags LV 146 F4
Pitres E 71 F6
Pîtres F 34 F3
Pitscottie GB 21 C11
Pitsinaiika GR 190 C5
Pitstone GB 31 C7
Pitsund S 134 D7
Pitt GB 29 C12
Pittem B 35 C7
Pitten A 164 A6
Pittentrail GB 19 K8
Pittenweem GB 21 C11
Pitvaros H 166 E6
Pivashiivka UA 170 A5
Pivašiūnai LT 153 E9
Pivka SLO 89 E9
Pivnice SRB 174 C3
Piwniczna-Zdrój PL 161 E2
Pizarra E 69 C7
Pizzighettone I 85 C8
Pizzo I 75 B9
Pizzoferrato I 79 D6
Pizzoli I 78 C4
Pjedsted DK 102 D5
Pjelax FIN 138 F6
Pjenovac BIH 173 D11
Pjesker S 134 C3
Plaaz D 99 C12
Plabennec F 38 C3
Placencia de las Armas E 48 D1
Plachkovtsi BG 182 D4
Plăcis LV 151 B9
Plaffeien CH 47 B11
Plagia GR 185 B10
Plaidt D 37 D8
Plăieşii de Jos RO 169 E8
Plaintel F 38 D6
Plaisance F 49 C6
Plaisance-du-Touch F 49 C8
Plaisir F 40 C6
Plaka GR 184 F5
Plaka GR 187 D8
Plaka GR 191 E6
Plaka GR 195 B7
Plakhtiyivka UA 170 A5
Plakovo BG 182 D5
Plana BIH 173 G9
Planá CZ 91 C7
Plana GR 185 D10
Planá nad Lužnicí CZ 93 D7
Plaňany CZ 93 B8
Plancher-Bas F 43 E6
Plancoët F 39 C7
Plancy-l'Abbaye F 41 D10
Plan-de-Baux F 47 F7
Plan-de-la-Tour F 52 E5
Plandište SRB 175 C7
Plan-d'Orgon F 51 C8
Planeja SRB 179 B10
Planès F 49 F10
Planegg D 91 F9
Plañi LV 147 F11
Planos GR 190 D7
Plasencia E 61 D8
Plasencia del Monte E 57 D10
Plaški HR 172 B4
Plassen N 118 D4
Plášťovce SK 163 E7
Plasy CZ 92 C4
Plataies GR 191 C7
Platamona Lido I 80 B1
Platamonas GR 185 E8
Platamonas GR 187 B7
Platania I 75 A9
Platanias GR 194 B4
Platanistos GR 191 D9
Platanorrevma GR 185 D7
Platanos GR 190 D4
Platanos GR 191 A6
Platanos GR 194 E8
Platanos GR 190 C4
Platanovrysi GR 187 B7
Plataria GR 184 F3
Plate D 99 C11
Plateliai LT 150 D3
Platerów PL 157 F7
Plati GR 187 A10
Platì I 75 C9

Platiana GR 190 D4
Platičevo SRB 174 D4
Platja d'Aro E 59 D10
Platja de Nules E 64 E4
Platone LV 150 C6
Plattling D 92 E3
Platy GR 185 C8
Platykampos GR 185 E8
Platys Gialos GR 192 D4
Platys Gialos GR 192 E5
Plau D 99 D12
Plaue D 95 E8
Plauen D 91 E10
Plav MNE 179 D8
Plava SRB 175 E9
Plavecký Štvrtok SK 93 F12
Plavinas LV 151 C11
Plavna SRB 175 E9
Plavno RO 172 D5
Plavy CZ 97 E8
Pławno PL 101 C10
Plaza E 56 B6
Plazac F 45 E8
Plazów PL 160 C7
Pleaux F 45 E10
Plech D 91 C9
Plecka Dąbrowa PL 159 B8
Pleine-Fougères F 39 D9
Plekšņi LV 149 D2
Plélan-le-Grand F 39 D7
Plélo F 38 D6
Plémet F 38 D6
Plénée-Jugon F 39 D7
Pléneuf-Val-André F 38 C6
Pleniţa RO 175 E11
Plentzia E 56 B6
Plérin F 38 C6
Plescop F 38 E6
Pleşcuţa RO 171 E8
Pleşeni MD 170 E2
Pleševec SK 161 F1
Plesná CZ 91 B11
Plesná D 96 D3
Pleşoiu RO 176 E4
Plessa D 96 D5
Plessé F 39 E8
Plestin-les-Grèves F 38 C4
Pleszew PL 158 C4
Pleternica HR 173 B8
Plettenberg D 37 B9
Pleubian F 38 C5
Pleudihen-sur-Rance F 39 C8
Pleumartin F 45 B7
Pleumeur-Bodou F 38 C4
Pleurs F 41 C10
Pleuven F 38 E3
Pleven BG 181 C10
Plevnik-Drienové SK 163 C7
Pleyben F 38 D4
Pleyber-Christ F 38 C4
Pliego F 72 E2
Plieniems LV 150 B4
Pliešovce SK 163 D8
Pliezhausen D 203 D7
Plikati GR 184 E4
Plisa S 149 F3
Pliska BG 183 C8
Plitvica HR 172 C4
Pljevlja MNE 179 C7
Ploaghe I 80 B2
Plobannalec F 38 E3
Plobsheim F 202 E4
Ploče HR 177 F7
Ploce LV 150 C2
Plochingen D 203 D7
Pločica SRB 175 D6
Płociczno PL 152 E6
Plodovoye RUS 145 D13
Ploegsteert B 198 D1
Ploemeur F 38 E5
Ploeren F 38 E6
Ploërmel F 39 E7
Plœuc-sur-Lié F 38 D6
Plogonnec F 38 D3
Plogshagen D 100 A4
Ploieşti RO 177 D7
Plomari GR 193 B7
Plombières-les-Bains F 42 E5
Plomeur F 38 E3
Plomin HR 83 B9
Plomodiern F 38 D3
Plön D 99 B8
Plonéour-Lanvern F 38 E3
Plonévez-du-Faou F 38 D4
Plonévez-Porzay F 38 D3
Płońsk PL 155 E9
Plop MD 169 A11
Plopana RO 169 D9
Plopeni RO 177 C7
Plopi MD 170 B4
Plopii-Slăviteşti RO 176 F5
Plopşoru RO 176 D2
Plopu RO 177 C8
Plosca RO 176 E6
Ploscoş RO 168 D3
Ploska UA 168 B4
Płoskinia PL 155 B8
Płośnica PL 155 D8
Plößberg D 91 C11
Płoty PL 101 C11
Plötzin D 95 B12
Plötzky D 95 B10
Plou E 58 F2
Plouagat F 38 C6
Plouaret F 38 C5
Plouarzel F 38 D2
Plouay F 38 D5
Ploubalay F 39 C7
Ploubazlanec F 38 C5
Ploubezre F 38 C5
Ploudalmézeau F 38 C2
Ploudiry F 38 D3
Plouescat F 38 C3
Plouézec F 38 C6
Ploufragan F 38 D6
Plougasnou F 38 C4
Plougastel-Daoulas F 38 D3
Plougonvelin F 38 D2
Plougonven F 38 C4
Plougrescant F 38 C5
Plouguenast F 38 D6
Plouguerneau F 38 C2
Plouguernével F 38 D5
Plouha F 38 C6
Plouhinec F 38 D3
Plouhinec F 38 E5

Platiana GR 190 D4
Podvysoká SK 163 C7
Podwilk PL 163 B9
Poederlee B 198 C5
Poeni RO 176 E5
Poenţa MD 169 A11
Pofi I 78 D4
Pogăceaua RO 168 D4
Pogana RO 169 E10
Pogar BIH 173 D9
Poggendorf D 100 B4
Poggiardo I 77 C10
Poggibonsi I 82 F3
Poggio Berni I 82 D5
Poggio Bustone I 78 C3
Poggio Catino I 78 C3
Poggiodomo I 78 B3
Poggio Imperiale I 79 D8
Poggio-Mezzana F 53 G10
Poggio Mirteto I 78 C3
Poggio Moiano I 78 C3
Poggio Picenze I 78 C5
Poggio Renatico I 82 C4
Poggio Rusco I 82 C3
Pöggstall A 93 F8
Pogny F 41 C11
Pogoanele RO 177 D9
Pogoniani GR 184 E3
Pogorzela PL 97 C12
Pogorzelice PL 101 B13
Pogradec AL 184 C4
Pogrodzie PL 155 B8
Pohja FIN 143 E9
Pohja FIN 143 C10
Pohja-Lankila FIN 145 C11
Pohjasenvaara FIN 133 D11
Pohjaslahti FIN 135 B17
Pohjaslahti FIN 139 F12
Pohjavaara FIN 137 F11
Pohjois-Ii FIN 135 D14
Pohjoisjärvi FIN 139 F13
Pohorelá SK 163 D10
Pohořelice CZ 93 E11
Pohronská Polhora SK 163 D9
Pohronský Ruskov SK 163 F7
Poian RO 169 E8
Poiana RO 177 D7
Poiana Blenchii RO 168 C3
Poiana Câmpina RO 177 C7
Poiana Cristei RO 177 B9
Poiana Lacului RO 176 D5
Poiana Mare RO 175 F11
Poiana Mărului RO 176 B6
Poiana Sibiului RO 168 F3
Poiana Stampei RO 168 C6
Poiana Teiuliu RO 169 C7
Poiana Vadului RO 167 E10
Poibrene BG 181 E8
Põide EST 146 D6
Poienarii RO 177 D8
Poienarii Burchii RO 177 D8
Poienarii de Argeş RO 176 C5
Poieneşti RO 169 D10
Poieni RO 167 D10
Poienile de Sub Munte RO
168 B4
Poijula FIN 137 D10
Poikajärvi FIN 133 E15
Põikva EST 147 D10
Poinçon-lès-Larrey F 41 E11
Poing D 91 F10
Pointis-Inard F 49 D7
Poirino I 53 B7
Poiseux F 41 F9
Poissons F 42 D3
Poissy F 40 C7
Poitiers F 45 B6
Poix-de-Picardie F 34 E4
Poix-Terron F 35 E10
Pojan AL 184 C4
Pojanluoma FIN 138 E9
Pojatno RO 164 E5
Pojejena RO 175 D8
Pojo FIN 143 E10
Pojorâta RO 168 B6
Pókaszepetk H 165 C7
Poki LV 150 C7
Pokka FIN 133 B15
Poklečani BIH 173 E7
Pokoj BIH 172 C4
Pokój PL 158 E4
Pokrówka PL 157 H8
Pokupsko HR 164 F5
Polača HR 172 C5
Polače HR 178 E3
Pola de Allande E 55 B6
Pola de Laviana E 55 B8
Pola de Lena E 55 B8
Pola de Siero E 55 B8
Pola de Somiedo E 55 B7
Polaincourt-et-Clairefontaine F
42 E5
Połajewo PL 101 E11
Polán E 62 E4
Polanica-Zdrój PL 93 B10
Połaniec PL 159 F11
Polanów PL 101 B11
Polatsk BY 149 F5
Polch D 37 D8
Polcirkeln S 132 E6
Polczyno PL 154 A5
Połczyn-Zdrój PL 101 C10
Polegate GB 31 F9
Polena BG 181 F7
Poleñino E 57 E11
Polepy CZ 92 B6
Polesella I 82 C4
Polessk RUS 152 D3
Polgár H 161 H3
Polgárdi H 165 B10
Polia I 75 B9
Poliçan AL 184 C4
Police PL 100 C7
Police nad Metují CZ 97 E10
Polichni GR 185 C8
Polička CZ 93 C10
Policoro I 77 C7
Polientes E 56 C4
Polignano a Mare I 77 B8
Poligny F 47 B8
Polikrayshte BG 182 C5
Polisot F 41 C11
Polistena I 75 C9
Politika GR 191 B8
Pölitz D 99 C8
Polizzi Generosa I 74 D5
Põlja SRB 175 D7
Poljana HR 172 C4
Poljana Pakračka HR 165 F7

Poljane SLO 89 D9
Poljčane SLO 164 D5
Polje BIH 173 C8
Poljica HR 172 D3
Poljice BIH 173 D10
Poljice-Popovo BIH 178 D5
Polkowice PL 97 D10
Polla I 76 B4
Pölläkkä FIN 141 F11
Pöllau A 164 B5
Pöllauberg A 164 B5
Polle D 94 C5
Pollença E 73 B11
Pollenfeld D 91 E9
Pollenza I 83 F7
Pollfoss N 116 C7
Polliat F 47 C7
Pollica I 76 C4
Pollina I 74 D5
Pollitz D 99 E11
Pollos E 55 F9
Polmak N 129 C20
Polminhac F 45 F11
Polmont GB 21 D9
Polo FIN 137 C12
Polomka SK 163 D9
Polop E 72 D4
Pölöske H 165 C7
Połoski PL 157 G8
Polovragi RO 176 C3
Polperro GB 28 E5
Pöls A 89 B10
Polsbroek NL 198 B5
Polsingen D 91 E8
Polska Cerekiew PL 158 F5
Polski Gradets BG 182 E6
Polski Trŭmbesh BG 182 C5
Polsko Kosovo BG 182 C5
Polso FIN 139 D12
Poltár SK 163 E9
Põltsamaa EST 147 D11
Põlula EST 147 C13
Polumir SRB 179 B10
Połupin PL 97 B8
Põlva EST 147 E14
Polvela FIN 141 D12
Polvenkylä FIN 138 E8
Polverigi I 83 E7
Polvijärvi FIN 141 E12
Polyana UA 161 F6
Polyanets'ke UA 170 A6
Polyantho GR 187 B8
Polyany RUS 145 E11
Polyatsite BG 183 D8
Polydendro GR 185 D7
Polydrosos GR 191 B6
Polygyros GR 185 D9
Polykarpi GR 185 C7
Polykastano GR 184 D5
Polykastro GR 185 C8
Polymylos GR 185 D7
Polyneri GR 184 D5
Polypotamo GR 184 C5
Polzela SLO 89 D11
Pölzig D 95 E11
Pomaluengo E 56 B4
Pomarance I 82 F2
Pomarão P 66 D4
Pomarez F 48 C4
Pomarico I 77 B7
Pomarkku FIN 142 B7
Pomârla RO 169 A8
Pomáz H 166 B3
Pombal P 54 F5
Pombal P 60 E3
Pomer E 57 E8
Pomeroy GB 23 C9
Pomezeu RO 167 D9
Pomezí CZ 93 C10
Pomezia I 78 D3
Pomi RO 167 B11
Pomiechówek PL 155 F10
Pömiö FIN 135 C14
Pommard F 46 A6
Pommelsbrunn D 91 C10
Pommersfelden D 91 C8
Pomol BIH 173 D11
Pomorie BG 183 D9
Pomorsko PL 97 B8
Pompaire F 44 B5
Pompei I 76 B3
Pompey F 42 C5
Pompia GR 194 E8
Pompignan F 51 C6
Pomysk Mały PL 101 B13
Poncin F 47 C7
Ponferrada E 55 C6
Poniatowa PL 157 H6
Poniatowo PL 155 D8
Poniec PL 97 C11
Poniklá CZ 97 E8
Poniky SK 163 D8
Ponoarele RO 175 D10
Ponor RO 167 E11
Ponoševac SRB 179 E9
Pons F 44 D4
Ponsa FIN 143 B11
Ponsacco I 82 E2
Pont-à-Celles B 35 C9
Pontacq F 48 D5
Pontailler-sur-Saône F 42 F3
Pontaix F 47 F7
Pont-à-Marcq F 35 C7
Pont-à-Mousson F 42 C5
Pontardawe GB 29 B7
Pontarion F 45 D9
Pontarlier F 47 B9
Pontassieve I 82 E3
Pontaubault F 39 C9
Pont-Audemer F 34 F2
Pontault-Combault F 41 C8
Pontaumur F 45 D11
Pont-Aven F 38 E4
Pont-Canavese I 84 C4
Pontcharra F 47 E9
Pontchâteau F 39 F7
Pont-Croix F 38 D3
Pont-d'Ain F 47 C7
Pont-de-Buis-lès-Quimerch F 38 D3
Pont-de-Chéruy F 47 D7
Pont-de-Larn F 49 C10
Pont-de-l'Isère F 46 E6
Pont-de-Loup B 198 E5
Pont-de-Poitte F 47 B8
Pont-de-Roide F 43 F6
Pont-de-Salars F 50 B4
Pont de Suert E 49 F7
Pont-de-Vaux F 47 C6
Pont-de-Veyle F 46 C6
Pont-d'Hérault F 51 B6
Pont-d'Ouilly F 39 C11
Pont-du-Casse F 49 B7
Pont-du-Château F 46 D3
Pont-du-Navoy F 47 B8
Ponte I 76 A3
Ponte Aranga E 54 B4
Ponteareas E 54 D3
Pontebba I 89 C7
Pontecagnano Faiano I 76 B3
Ponte Caldelas E 54 D3
Ponteceso E 54 B2
Pontechianale I 52 B6
Pontecorvo I 78 E5
Pontecurone I 53 B9
Ponte da Barca P 54 E3
Pontedassio I 53 D8
Pontedecimo I 53 B9
Ponte de Lima P 54 E2
Ponte dell'Olio I 53 B11
Pontedera I 82 E2
Ponte de Sor P 60 F4
Pontedeume E 54 B3
Ponte di Legno I 85 A10
Ponte di Piave I 88 E5
Ponte do Rol P 60 F2
Pontefract GB 27 D9
Ponte Gardena I 88 C4
Pontelagoscuro I 82 C4
Ponteland GB 21 E13
Pontelandolfo I 76 A3
Ponte-Leccia F 53 G10
Pontelongo I 82 B5
Ponte nelle Alpi I 88 D5
Ponte Nizza I 53 B10
Ponte Nossa I 85 B8
Ponte Nova I 88 D3
Pont-en-Royans F 47 E7
Pontenure I 85 C8
Pontenx-les-Forges F 48 B3
Ponte San Nicolò I 82 B4
Ponte San Pietro I 85 B8
Ponte Valga E 54 C2
Pontevedra E 54 D2
Pontével P 60 F3
Pont-Évêque F 46 D6
Pontevico I 82 B1
Pont-Farcy F 39 C9
Pontfaverger-Moronvilliers F 35 F9
Pontgibaud F 46 D2
Pont-Hébert F 39 B9
Pontinha P 66 B1
Pontinia I 78 E4
Pöntiö FIN 136 F2
Pontivy F 38 D6
Pont-l'Abbé F 38 E3
Pont-la-Ville F 41 D12
Pont-les-Moulins F 42 F5
Pont-l'Évêque F 39 B12
Pontlevoy F 40 F5
Pontoise F 40 B7
Pontokomi GR 185 D6
Pontones E 71 C7
Pontonnyy RUS 145 F14
Pontonx-sur-l'Adour F 48 C4
Pontoon IRL 22 E4
Pontorson F 39 C8
Pontpoint F 34 F6
Pontremoli I 85 E8
Pontresina CH 87 E9
Pontrhydfendigaid GB 29 A7
Pontrieux F 38 C5
Pontrilas GB 29 B9
Ponts E 58 D6
Pöntsö FIN 133 C12
Pont-Ste-Marie F 41 D11
Pont-Ste-Maxence F 34 F6
Pont-St-Esprit F 51 B8
Pont-St-Martin I 84 B4
Pont-sur-Yonne F 41 D9
Pontvallain F 39 E12
Pontyberem GB 28 B6
Pontycymer GB 29 B7
Pontypool GB 29 B8
Pontypridd GB 29 B8
Ponyatívka UA 170 D6
Ponza I 78 F3
Ponzone I 53 B8
Poola FIN 138 E7
Poole GB 29 D11
Poolewe GB 18 K5
Pooley Bridge GB 21 F11
Pool of Muckhart GB 21 C9
Pootsi EST 147 E8
Pope LV 150 B3
Popeasca MD 170 D5
Poperinge B 34 C6
Popești RO 167 C9
Popești RO 169 C10
Popești RO 176 C4
Popești RO 176 E6
Popești-Leordeni RO 177 E8
Popielów PL 158 E4
Popina BG 177 E9
Popintsi BG 181 E9
Popitsa BG 181 C8
Poplaca RO 168 F4
Popoli I 78 C5
Popovača HR 165 E7
Popovica SRB 175 E9
Popovitsa BG 182 E4
Popovo BG 182 C6
Popów PL 157 F1
Popów PL 159 D6
Poppenhausen D 91 B7
Poppenricht D 91 D10
Poppi I 82 E4
Poprad SK 161 E1
Popricani RO 169 C11
Poproč SK 161 F2
Popsko BG 187 A9
Pópulo P 54 F5
Populonia I 81 B2
Porąbka PL 163 B8
Poraj PL 159 E7
Porcari I 82 E2
Porcia I 89 E6
Porcsalma H 161 H6
Porcuna E 69 A8
Pordenone I 89 E6
Pordim BG 181 C10
Poręba PL 159 F7
Poręba-Kocęby PL 155 E12
Poreč HR 83 B8
Pori FIN 142 C6
Porice BIH 173 D7
Porjus S 132 E3
Porkhov RUS 148 F6
Porkkala FIN 143 F11
Porkuni EST 147 C12
Porlammi FIN 143 D15
Porlezza I 85 A7
Porlock GB 29 C7
Pornainen FIN 143 E13
Pornassio I 53 C7
Pornic F 39 F7
Pornichet F 39 F7
Poroina Mare RO 175 E10
Poros GR 190 C2
Poros GR 191 D7
Poroschia RO 176 F6
Poroshkove UA 161 F6
Poroszló H 166 B6
Porozina HR 83 B9
Porpi GR 187 B8
Porqueres E 59 C9
Porras FIN 143 D10
Porraskoski FIN 143 C12
Porrentruy CH 43 F7
Porreres E 73 B11
Porretta Terme I 82 D2
Porsangmoen N 129 D14
Pörsänmäki FIN 140 D8
Porsåsen N 118 E3
Porsgrunn N 106 A6
Porsi S 134 B5
Porspoder F 38 C2
Port N 129 D17
Porta F 49 E9
Portadown GB 23 D10
Portaferry GB 23 D11
Portaje E 61 E7
Portakallık TR 197 B8
Portalegre P 60 F6
Portals Vells E 65 F10
Portaria GR 185 D9
Portaria GR 185 F8
Portarlington IRL 23 F8
Port Askaig GB 20 D4
Portavogie GB 23 D12
Portbail F 39 B8
Port-Barcarès F 50 E5
Portbou E 50 F5
Port Brillet F 39 D10
Portchester GB 29 D12
Port d'Andratx E 65 E9
Port-de-Bouc F 51 D8
Port-de-Piles F 45 A7
Port de Pollença E 73 B11
Port-des-Barques F 44 D3
Port de Sóller E 65 E10
Portel P 66 C4
Portel-des-Corbières F 50 D4
Portell de Morella E 58 F3
Port Ellen GB 20 D4
Port-en-Bessin-Huppain F 39 B10
Portencross GB 20 D7
Port Erin GBM 26 C2
Portes-lès-Valence F 46 F6
Portets F 44 F5
Portet-sur-Garonne F 49 C8
Port Eynon GB 28 B6
Port Glasgow GB 20 D7
Porth GB 29 B8
Porthcawl GB 29 C7
Port Henderson GB 18 K5
Porthleven GB 28 E4
Porthmadog GB 26 F3
Porticcio F 53 H9
Portici I 76 B2
Portieux F 42 D5
Portilla E 63 D8
Portilla de la Reina E 55 B10
Portillo E 56 F2
Portillo de Toledo E 62 D4
Portimão P 66 E2
Portimo FIN 135 B16
Portimojärvi FIN 135 B11
Portishead GB 29 C9
Port-Joinville F 44 B1
Portknockie GB 19 K11
Port Láirge IRL 25 D8
Portland IRL 22 F6
Port-la-Nouvelle F 50 D5
Port Laoise IRL 23 F8
Portlaoise IRL 23 F8
Portlethen GB 21 A12
Port-Leucate F 50 E5
Port Logan GB 20 F7
Port-Louis F 38 E5
Portmagee IRL 24 E2
Portmahomack GB 19 K9
Portman E 72 F3
Portmarnock IRL 23 F10
Port Mearnóg IRL 23 F10
Portmuck GB 20 F5
Port-na-Con GB 18 H7
Portnaguran GB 18 J4
Portnahaven GB 20 D3
Portnalong GB 18 L4
Port-Navalo F 38 E6
Porto E 55 D6
Porto F 53 G9
Porto P 60 B3
Porto Alto P 66 B2
Porto Azzurro I 81 B2
Porto Botte I 80 E2
Portobravo E 54 C2
Porto Cervo I 80 A4
Porto Cesareo I 77 C9
Portocheli GR 191 E7
Portocolom E 73 C11
Porto Covo da Bandeira P 66 D2
Porto Cristo E 73 B11
Porto d'Ascoli I 78 B5
Porto de Lagos P 66 E2
Porto de Mós P 60 E3
Porto do Barqueiro E 54 A4
Porto do Son E 54 C1
Porto Empedocle I 74 E4
Porto Ercole I 81 C4
Portoferraio I 81 B2
Portofino I 53 C10
Port of Ness GB 18 J4
Porto Garibaldi I 82 C5
Porto Germeno GR 191 C7
Portogruaro I 89 E6
Porto Koufo GR 186 E5
Porto Levante I 75 C6
Porto Levante I 82 B5
Pörtom FIN 138 E7
Portomaggiore I 82 C4
Portomarín E 54 C4
Port Omna IRL 22 F6
Portopalo di Capo Passero I 75 F7
Porto Petro E 73 C11
Portør N 106 B5
Porto Rafti GR 191 D9
Porto Recanati I 83 F8
Porto Rotondo I 80 A4
Portorož SLO 83 A8
Porto San Giorgio I 83 F8
Porto San Paolo I 80 B4
Porto Sant'Elpidio I 83 F8
Porto Santo Stefano I 81 C4
Portoscuso I 80 E1
Porto Tolle I 82 C5
Porto Torres I 80 B1
Porto-Vecchio F 53 H10
Portovenere I 85 E8
Portpatrick GB 20 F6
Portrane IRL 23 F10
Port Reachrann IRL 23 F10
Portreath GB 28 E4
Portree GB 18 L4
Portroe IRL 24 C6
Portrush GB 20 E3
Portsalon IRL 20 E1
Portsmouth GB 29 D12
Portsoy GB 19 K11
Port-Ste-Marie F 49 B6
Portstewart GB 20 E3
Port-St-Louis-du-Rhône F 51 D8
Port St Mary GBM 26 C2
Port-St-Père F 39 F8
Port-sur-Saône F 42 E5
Port Talbot GB 29 B7
Portugalete E 56 B5
Portumna IRL 22 F6
Port-Vendres F 50 E5
Port William GB 20 F7
Poruba SK 163 D7
Porubne UA 169 A8
Porumbacu de Jos RO 168 F4
Porvoo FIN 143 E14
Porządzie PL 155 E11
Porzuna E 62 F4
Posada E 55 B8
Posada I 80 B4
Posada de Valdeón E 55 B10
Posadas E 69 A6
Poșaga RO 167 E11
Poschiavo CH 85 A9
Posedarje HR 172 D3
Poseidonia GR 192 E4
Poseritz D 100 B4
Posești RO 177 C8
Pösing D 91 D12
Posio FIN 137 B11
Positano I 76 B2
Possagno I 88 E4
Posseberg S 113 D11
Possendorf D 96 E5
Possesse F 41 C12
Pößneck D 95 E10
Posta I 78 B4
Poșta Câlnău RO 177 C9
Postal I 88 C3
Posta Piana I 76 A5
Postau D 91 E11
Posterholt NL 36 B6
Postiglione I 76 B4
Postojna SLO 89 E9
Postoliska PL 155 F11
Postoloprty CZ 92 B5
Postomino PL 101 B11
Postřelmov CZ 93 C11
Postupice CZ 93 C7
Posušje BIH 173 F7
Poświętne PL 156 E7
Poświętne PL 157 G2
Potamia GR 187 C7
Potamia GR 190 F5
Potamochori GR 187 B8
Potamoi GR 186 B6
Potamos GR 184 E2
Potamos GR 194 C4
Potashnya UA 170 A5
Potcoava RO 176 E5
Potęgowo PL 101 B12
Potenza I 76 B5
Potenza Picena I 83 F8
Potes E 55 B10
Potidania GR 190 C5
Potigny F 39 C11
Potkraj BIH 173 E7
Potku FIN 135 E17
Potlogi RO 177 D7
Potočac SRB 175 F7
Potočani BIH 173 E7
Potoci BIH 172 D6
Potoci BIH 173 F8
Potok Złoty PL 159 E7
Potsdam D 96 B4
Pötsönvaara FIN 141 D16
Potštát CZ 162 B5
Pottendorf A 93 G10
Pottenstein A 93 G10
Pottenstein D 91 C9
Potterne GB 29 C10
Potters Bar GB 31 D8
Pöttmes D 91 E9
Potton GB 31 C8
Pöttsching A 162 F2
Potworów PL 157 G3
Pouancé F 39 E9
Pougny F 41 F9
Pougues-les-Eaux F 46 A3
Pougy F 41 D11
Pouillon F 48 C4
Pouilly-en-Auxois F 41 F12
Pouilly-sous-Charlieu F 46 C5
Pouilly-sur-Loire F 41 F8
Pouilly-sur-Saône F 47 A7
Poulaines F 40 F6
Pouldreuzic F 38 E3
Poulgorm Bridge IRL 24 E4
Pouligny-St-Pierre F 45 B8
Poulithra GR 191 E6
Poullaouen F 38 D4
Poulnamucky IRL 25 D7
Poulstrup DK 106 E7
Poulton-le-Fylde GB 26 D6
Pounta GR 192 E5
Poupas F 49 C7
Pourcieux F 51 D10
Pouri GR 185 F9
Pourrain F 41 E9
Pourrières F 51 C10
Pousada P 61 C6
Pousos P 60 E3
Poussan F 51 D6
Poussay F 42 D5
Poussu FIN 137 C13
Pouxeux F 42 D6
Pouyastruc F 49 D6
Pouydesseaux F 48 C5
Pouzauges F 44 B4
Pouzay F 40 F4
Považská Bystrica SK 162 C6
Povedilla E 71 B7
Poviglio I 82 C2
Povlja HR 173 F6
Póvoa de Lanhoso P 54 E3
Póvoa de São Miguel P 67 C5
Póvoa de Varzim P 54 F2
Póvoa do Concelho P 61 C6
Povoletto I 89 D7
Povrly CZ 96 E6
Powburn GB 21 E13
Power's Cross IRL 22 F6
Powick GB 29 A10
Powidz PL 154 F4
Powmill GB 21 C9
Poyales del Hoyo E 61 D10
Poyatos E 63 D8
Poyntz Pass GB 23 D10
Poyrazcık TR 193 A9
Poysdorf A 93 E11
Pöytyä FIN 142 D8
Poza de la Sal E 56 C5
Pozaldez E 55 F10
Požaranje SRB 180 E3
Požarevac SRB 175 D7
Požarnica BIH 173 C10
Požega HR 165 F9
Požega SRB 174 F5
Požerė LT 150 E4
Pozezdrze PL 152 E4
Pozherevitsy RUS 149 B7
Poznań PL 97 B11
Pozo Alcón E 71 D7
Pozoamargo E 63 F8
Pozoantiguo E 55 E9
Pozoblanco E 70 C3
Pozo Cañada E 71 B9
Pozo de Guadalajara E 63 D6
Pozohondo E 71 B9
Pozo-Lorente E 63 F10
Pozondón E 63 C10
Pozořice CZ 93 D11
Pozorrubio E 63 E7
Poźrzadło Wielkie PL 101 D9
Pozuel del Campo E 63 C10
Pozuelo E 71 B8
Pozuelo de Alarcón E 62 D5
Pozuelo de Aragón E 57 E9
Pozuelo del Páramo E 55 D8
Pozuelo del Rey E 62 D6
Pozuelo de Zarzón E 61 D8
Pozuelos de Calatrava E 70 B4
Pozza di Fassa I 88 D4
Pozzallo I 75 F6
Pozzolo Formigaro I 53 B9
Pozzomaggiore I 80 C2
Pozzuoli I 76 B2
Pozzuolo del Friuli I 89 E7
Prabuty PL 155 C7
Prača BIH 173 E10
Prachatice CZ 92 D6
Pracht D 37 C9
Prackenbach D 92 D3
Prádanos de Ojeda E 56 C3
Pradejón E 48 F1
Pradelles F 46 F4
Prádena E 62 B5
Prades F 49 E9
Prades F 49 E10
Prades-d'Aubrac F 50 A4
Pradillo E 57 D6
Pradines F 49 B8
Prado P 54 E3
Prado de la Guzpeña E 55 C9
Prado del Rey E 69 C5
Pradoluengo E 56 D5
Præstbro DK 102 A6
Præstø DK 103 E10
Pragelato I 47 E10
Pragersko SLO 164 D5
Prägraten A 88 B5
Praha CZ 93 B6
Prahecq F 44 C5
Prahovo SRB 175 E10
Praia a Mare I 76 D5
Praia da Barra P 60 C3
Praia da Rocha P 66 E2
Praia da Tocha P 60 D3
Praia de Esmoriz P 60 C3
Praia de Mira P 60 D3
Praiano I 76 B3
Praid RO 168 D6
Prăjeni RO 169 B10
Prakovce SK 161 F2
Pralognan-la-Vanoise F 47 E10
Pralyetarsk BY 149 E7
Pramanta GR 184 E5
Prambachkirchen A 92 F5
Pranjani SRB 174 E5
Prapatnica HR 172 E5
Prašice SK 162 D6
Praszka PL 158 D5
Prata di Pordenone I 89 E6
Pratau D 95 C12
Prat de Comte E 58 F4
Pratdip E 58 E5
Pratella I 76 A2
Prato I 82 E3
Prato allo Stelvio I 87 D11
Pratola Peligna I 78 C5
Pratovecchio I 82 E4
Prats de Lluçanès E 59 C8
Prats-de-Mollo-la-Preste F 49 F10
Pratteln CH 43 E8
Prauliena LV 151 C12
Prauthoy F 42 E3
Pravda BG 177 F10
Pravdinsk RUS 152 E3
Pravets BG 181 D8
Pravia E 55 B7
Prayssas F 49 B7
Prazaroki BY 149 F4
Praz-sur-Arly F 47 D10
Prebold SLO 89 D11
Préchac F 48 B5
Preci I 78 B4
Précigné F 39 E11
Prečín SK 163 C7
Précy-sous-Thil F 41 F11
Predappio I 82 D4
Predazzo I 88 D4
Predeal RO 177 B7
Predeal-Sărari RO 177 C8
Predejane SRB 180 D5
Predești RO 176 E3
Preding A 164 C4
Predlitz A 89 B8
Predmeja SLO 89 E8
Předměřice nad Labem CZ 93 B9
Predosa I 53 B9
Pré-en-Pail F 39 D11
Prees GB 26 F6
Preetz D 99 B8
Préfailles F 39 F7
Preganziòl I 88 E5
Pregarten A 93 F7
Pregrada HR 164 D5
Preignan F 49 C7
Preiļi LV 151 D13
Preitenegg A 89 C10
Preiviiki FIN 142 C6
Preixan F 49 D10
Prejmer RO 169 F7
Prekaja BIH 172 D6
Preko HR 172 D3
Prekopa HR 164 F6
Preljina SRB 174 F5
Prelog HR 165 D7
Prelošćica HR 165 F6
Přelouč CZ 93 B9
Prem SLO 89 E9
Premantura HR 83 C8
Prémery F 41 F9
Premia I 84 A5
Premià de Mar E 59 E8
Premilcuore I 82 E4
Prémilhat F 45 C11
Premnitz D 95 A11
Premosello Chiovenda I 84 A5
Prenzlau D 100 D5
Préporché F 46 B4
Přerov CZ 162 C4
Prerow am Darß, Ostseebad D 99 B13
Preselentsi BG 171 F2
Preševo SRB 180 E4
Presicce I 77 D10
Prešov SK 161 F3
Pressac F 45 C7
Pressath D 91 C10
Pressbaum A 93 F10
Presseck D 91 B10
Pressel D 95 C12
Pressig D 91 B9
Prestatyn GB 26 E5
Prestbakken N 127 C15
Prestbury GB 29 B10
Pre-St-Didier I 47 D10
Prestebakke N 107 B10
Presteigne GB 29 A8
Prestfoss N 111 B11
Přeštice CZ 92 C4
Preston GB 21 D12
Preston GB 26 D6
Prestwick GB 20 E7
Prettin D 96 C3
Pretushë AL 184 C4
Pretzfeld D 91 C9
Pretzier D 99 E10
Pretzsch D 95 C12
Pretzschendorf D 96 E5
Preuilly-sur-Claise F 45 B7
Preutești RO 169 C8
Prevalje SLO 89 C10
Prévenchères F 51 A6
Préveranges F 45 C10
Prevešt SRB 175 F7
Preveza GR 190 B2
Prevršac HR 172 B5
Prežganje SLO 89 D10
Prezid HR 89 E10
Prez-sous-Lafauche F 42 D3
Priaranza del Bierzo E 55 C6
Pribelja BIH 173 D6
Pribeta SK 162 F6
Pribinić BIH 173 C8
Pribislavec HR 165 D6
Priboieni RO 176 D6
Priboj BIH 173 C10
Priboj SRB 179 B8
Příbor CZ 162 B6
Priborn D 99 D13
Priboy BG 181 D6
Příbram CZ 92 C6
Pribrezhnoye RUS 152 D1
Pribude HR 172 E5
Pribylina SK 163 C9
Přibyslav CZ 93 C9
Prichaly RUS 150 F2
Prichsenstadt D 91 C7
Pridvorci BIH 173 F9
Priedaine LV 150 C3
Priedes LV 147 F9
Priego E 63 D8
Priego de Córdoba E 69 B8
Priekulė LT 150 E2
Priekule LV 150 D3
Priekuļi LV 151 B10
Prienai LT 153 D8
Prienai LT 153 D12
Prien am Chiemsee D 88 A5
Prieros D 96 B5
Prießnitz D 95 D10
Prießnitz D 95 D12
Priestewitz D 96 D5
Prievidza SK 163 D7
Priežmale LV 149 D2
Prignac-et-Marcamps F 44 E5
Prigor RO 175 D9
Prigoria RO 176 C3
Prigradica HR 178 D2
Prigrevica SRB 174 B3
Prijeboj HR 172 C4
Prijedor BIH 173 C6
Prijepolje SRB 179 C8
Prikuli LV 151 D13
Priladozhskiy RUS 145 F15
Prilep MK 185 B6
Prilike SRB 174 F5
Prillimäe EST 147 C9
Priluka BIH 173 E6
Přimda CZ 91 C12
Primišlje HR 172 B3
Primolano I 88 E4
Primorsk RUS 145 E10
Primorsk RUS 155 A9
Primorsko BG 183 E9
Primor'ye RUS 155 A9
Primošten HR 172 E4
Princes Risborough GB 31 D7
Princetown GB 28 D7
Prinos GR 187 C7
Prinsenbeek NL 32 E3
Prinzhöfte D 33 C11
Priolithos GR 190 D5
Priolo Gargallo I 75 E7
Prioro E 55 C10
Priozersk RUS 145 C13
Priponești RO 169 E10
Prirechnyy RUS 130 E8
Prisăcani RO 169 C11
Priseaca RO 176 D4
Priseltsi BG 183 C9
Prisjan SRB 180 C6
Prisoja MNE 179 D8
Prisoje BIH 173 E7
Příšovice CZ 97 E8
Prissac F 45 B8
Prissé F 46 C6
Priština SRB 180 D3
Pristol RO 175 E10
Prittriching D 87 A11
Pritzerbe D 95 B11
Pritzier D 99 D10
Pritzwalk D 99 D12
Privas F 46 F6
Priverno I 78 E4
Privlaka HR 83 D11
Privlaka HR 173 B10
Prizna HR 83 C10
Prizren SRB 179 E10
Prizzi I 74 D3
Prkosi BIH 172 C5
Prnjavor BIH 173 C8
Prnjavor SRB 174 D3
Proaza E 55 B7
Probištip MK 180 E5
Probota RO 169 C10
Probsteierhagen D 99 B8
Probus GB 28 E5
Proceno I 78 B1
Prochoma GR 185 C8
Prochowice PL 97 D10
Procida I 76 B2
Prodromos GR 191 C6
Produlești RO 177 D7
Proença-a-Nova P 60 E5
Proença-a-Velha P 61 D6
Profen D 95 D11
Profesor-Ishirkovo BG 177 F10
Profilia GR 197 D7
Profitis GR 185 C9
Profitis Ilias GR 194 E9
Profondeville B 35 D10
Progonat AL 184 D2
Prohn D 100 B4
Prokhladnoye RUS 150 F2
Prokopi GR 191 B7
Prokuplje SRB 180 C4
Prolaz BG 183 C6
Prolog BIH 173 E6
Promachoi GR 185 B7
Promachonas GR 185 B9
Promna PL 157 G3
Promyri GR 191 A7
Pronsfeld D 36 D6
Propriano F 53 H9
Proseč CZ 93 C10
Prosek AL 179 F8
Prosenik BG 183 D8
Prosenjakovci SLO 165 C6
Prosetín CZ 93 C9
Proshkava BY 149 F4
Proskynites GR 187 C8
Prosotsani GR 186 B5
Prosperous IRL 23 F9
Prossedi I 78 D4
Prostějov CZ 93 D12
Prostki PL 156 C6
Prostřední Bečva CZ 162 C6
Prószków PL 158 E4
Proszowice PL 159 F9
Proszówki PL 159 F9
Proti GR 186 C5
Protići BIH 173 D6
Protivanov CZ 93 D11
Protivín CZ 92 D6
Protokklisi GR 187 B10
Protoria GR 194 E9
Prötzel D 96 A5
Provadiya BG 183 C8
Provatas GR 185 B9
Provenchères-sur-Fave F 43 D7
Provins F 41 C9
Provo SRB 174 D4
Prozor BIH 173 E8
Prozor HR 172 C3
Prrenjas AL 184 B4
Pruchnik PL 160 D6
Prudhoe GB 21 F13
Prudnik PL 158 F4
Prudzinki BY 149 E4
Prugovac SRB 180 D3
Prügy H 161 G3
Prüm D 36 D6
Pruna E 67 F9
Prundeni RO 176 D4
Prundu RO 177 E8
Prundu Bârgăului RO 168 C5
Prunières F 52 B4
Pruniers-en-Sologne F 40 F6
Prunișor RO 175 D10
Prusac BIH 173 D7
Prušánky CZ 93 E11
Prusice PL 97 D11
Prusinovice CZ 162 C5
Prūsīši LV 151 B13
Pruszcz PL 154 D4
Pruszcz PL 154 D5
Pruszcz Gdański PL 154 B6
Pruszków PL 157 F3
Prutz A 87 C11
Pružina SK 162 C6
Prvačina SLO 89 E8
Pryamobalka UA 170 F4
Prymors'ke UA 171 B5
Prymors'ke UA 171 B5
Pryozerne UA 171 B4
Prypruttya UA 169 A8
Przasnysz PL 155 D10
Przechlewo PL 101 C12
Przeciszów PL 159 F7
Przecław PL 159 F11
Przedbórz PL 159 D8
Przedecz PL 154 F6
Przejazdowo PL 154 B6
Przelewice PL 101 D8
Przemęt PL 97 B10
Przemków PL 97 C9
Przemyśl PL 160 D6
Przerośl PL 152 E6
Przewale PL 160 B8
Przewłoka PL 157 G8
Przeworno PL 97 E12
Przeworsk PL 160 C5
Przewóz PL 97 D7
Przeździatka PL 157 F6
Przezdzięk Wielki PL 155 D10
Przezmark PL 155 C7
Przine-Zdralovac BIH 172 D6
Przodkowo PL 154 B5
Przybiernów PL 101 C7
Przyborów PL 97 C9
Przyborowice PL 155 E9
Przybranowo PL 154 E6
Przygodzice PL 158 C4
Przykona PL 158 C6
Przyłęk PL 157 G1
Przylep PL 97 C8
Przylesie PL 158 E3
Przyrów PL 159 E8
Przysieki PL 160 D3
Przystajń PL 158 E6
Przystałowice Duże PL 157 H3
Przysucha PL 157 H3
Przyszów PL 160 C4
Przytoczna PL 97 A9

Przytoczno PL 157 G6
Przytuły PL 156 D6
Przytyk PL 157 H3
Przywidz PL 154 B5
Psača MK 180 E5
Psachna GR 191 B8
Psara GR 193 B6
Psarades GR 184 C5
Psari GR 190 E4
Psari GR 191 D6
Psathopyrgos GR 190 C4
Psinthos GR 197 D8
Pskov RUS 148 F3
Psychiko GR 185 B10
Psychro GR 194 E9
Pszczew PL 97 B9
Pszczółki PL 154 B6
Pszczonów PL 157 G1
Pszczyna PL 163 B7
Pteleos GR 191 A6
Pteri GR 190 C5
Ptolemaïda GR 185 C6
Ptuj SLO 164 D5
Publier F 47 C10
Puchberg am Schneeberg A 162 F1
Pucheni RO 176 C6
Puchenii Mari RO 177 D8
Puchheim D 91 F9
Púchov SK 162 C6
Pucioasa RO 177 C6
Pučišće HR 173 F6
Puck PL 154 A5
Puckaun IRL 24 C6
Puçol E 64 E4
Pudasjärven kirkko FIN 135 D17
Pudasjärvi FIN 135 D17
Puddletown GB 29 D10
Puderbach D 201 C8
Pudinava LV 149 C3
Pudsey GB 27 D8
Puebla de Albortón E 57 F10
Puebla de Alcocer E 67 B9
Puebla de Alfindén E 57 E10
Puebla de Almenara E 63 E7
Puebla de Beleña E 63 C6
Puebla de Don Fadrique E 71 D8
Puebla de Don Rodrigo E 62 F3
Puebla de Guzmán E 67 D5
Puebla de la Calzada E 67 B6
Puebla de la Reina E 67 B7
Puebla de Lillo E 55 B9
Puebla del Maestre E 67 C7
Puebla del Príncipe E 71 B7
Puebla del Prior E 67 B7
Puebla del Salvador E 63 E9
Puebla de Obando E 61 F7
Puebla de Sanabria E 55 D6
Puebla de Sancho Pérez E 67 C7
Puebla de San Miguel E 63 D10
Puebla de Yeltes E 61 C8
Puente de Domingo Flórez E 55 D6
Puente de Génave E 71 C7
Puente del Congosto E 61 D9
Puente de Montañana E 58 C5
Puente de San Miguel E 56 B3
Puente-Genil E 69 B7
Puente la Reina E 48 E2
Puentenansa E 56 B3
Puente Viesgo E 56 B4
Puerto de Béjar E 61 D9
Puerto de Mazarrón E 72 F2
Puerto de San Vicente E 61 E10
Puerto Lápice E 62 F6
Puertollano E 70 B4
Puerto Lumbreras E 71 D9
Puertomingalvo E 64 D4
Puerto Real E 68 C4
Puerto Seguro E 61 C7
Puerto Serrano E 67 F8
Pueyo E 48 E2
Pueyo de Santa Cruz E 58 D4
Pufești RO 169 E10
Puget-Théniers F 52 D5
Puget-Ville F 52 E4
Pugnochiuso I 79 D10
Puhja EST 147 E12
Puhoi MD 170 D4
Puhos FIN 137 D10
Puhos FIN 141 F13
Puhovac BIH 173 D9
Pui RO 175 B11
Puiatu EST 147 E10
Puiești RO 169 E11
Puiești RO 177 C10
Puig E 64 E4
Puigcerdà E 49 F9
Puigpunyent E 65 E10
Puig-reig E 59 D7
Puikkola FIN 131 E3
Puikule LV 147 F9
Puimoisson F 52 D4
Puiseaux F 41 D7
Puisieux F 34 D6
Puisseguin F 44 F5
Puisserguier F 50 D5
Puivert F 49 E10
Pujaut F 51 B8
Pujols F 44 F5
Pujols F 49 B7
Puka EST 147 E12
Pukanec SK 163 E7
Pukaro FIN 143 D15
Pukavik S 104 C7
Pukë AL 179 E8
Pukiš BIH 173 C10
Pukkila FIN 143 D14
Pula HR 83 C8
Pula I 80 E3
Puławy PL 157 H5
Pulborough GB 31 F7
Pulfero I 89 D7
Pulgar E 62 E4
Pulheim D 37 B7
Pulju FIN 133 B13
Pulkau A 93 E9
Pulkkaviita FIN 131 D5
Pulkkila FIN 135 F15
Pulkkinen FIN 139 D11
Pulkonkoski FIN 140 D8
Pulpí E 71 E9
Pulsa FIN 144 D8
Pulsano I 77 C8
Pulsen D 96 D4
Pulskala FIN 131 D4
Pulsnitz D 96 D6
Pulsujärvi S 132 B6
Pułtusk PL 155 E11
Pulversheim F 43 E7
Pumpėnai LT 151 E8
Pumpuri LV 150 C4
Pumsaint GB 29 A7
Pūņas LV 150 B4
Punat HR 83 B10
Pundsvik N 127 D12
Punduri LV 149 D3
Pungești RO 169 D10
Punghina RO 175 E10
Punia LT 153 D9
Punkaharju FIN 145 B11
Punkalaidun FIN 143 C9
Punkka FIN 144 C7
Punta Ala I 81 B3
Punta Križa HR 83 C9
Punta Sabbioni I 82 B5
Punta Umbría E 67 E6
Puokio FIN 136 E9
Puolakkovaara FIN 131 D1
Puolanka FIN 137 E10
Puoliväli FIN 140 D9
Puoltikasvaara S 132 D6
Puottaure S 134 B4
Pūpoli LV 149 D2
Puraći BIH 173 C8
Puračić BIH 173 C10
Purani RO 177 F6
Puras FIN 137 E14
Purbach am Neusiedler See A 93 G11
Purcari MD 170 D5
Purchena E 71 E8
Pūre LV 150 B5
Purgstall an der Erlauf A 93 F8
Purila EST 147 C9
Purkersdorf A 93 F10
Purkijaur S 125 C18
Pürksi EST 146 C7
Purley GB 31 E8
Purmerend NL 32 C3
Purmo FIN 139 C9
Purmojärvi FIN 139 D10
Purmsāti LV 150 D3
Purnu S 132 E6
Purnumukka FIN 131 B2
Purnuvaara FIN 137 C12
Purnuvaara S 132 D6
Purola FIN 144 E6
Purontaka FIN 139 C12
Purujärvi FIN 145 B12
Purujosa E 57 E8
Purullena E 71 E6
Pŭrvenets BG 181 E10
Purviniške LT 153 D7
Pŭrvomay BG 182 E4
Pŭrvomay BG 185 B9
Puša LV 149 D2
Pušalotas LT 151 E8
Puschendorf D 91 C8
Pushkinskiye Gory RUS 149 B5
Pušmucova LV 149 C3
Püspökladány H 167 C7
Püssi EST 147 C14
Pusterwald A 89 B9
Pusté Úľany SK 162 E5
Pustków PL 159 F11
Pustomyty UA 160 D8
Pustoshka RUS 149 D6
Pŭstrovo BG 182 E4
Pusula FIN 143 E10
Puszcza Mariańska PL 157 G2
Puszczykowo PL 97 B11
Pusztaföldvár H 166 D6
Pusztakovácsi H 165 C9
Pusztamérges H 166 E4
Pusztamonostor H 166 B4
Pusztaszabolcs H 165 B11
Pusztaszer H 166 D4
Pusztavacs H 166 C4
Pusztavám H 165 B10
Putaja FIN 142 C8
Putanges-Pont-Écrepin F 39 C11
Putbus D 100 B4
Putifigari I 80 B1
Putignano I 77 B8
Putikko FIN 145 B11
Putinci SRB 174 C4
Putineiu RO 176 F5
Putineiu RO 177 F7
Putkivaara FIN 135 B17
Putlitz D 99 D12
Putna RO 169 B7
Putnok H 161 G1
Putte B 35 B10
Putte NL 32 F2
Puttelange-aux-Lacs F 43 B6
Putten NL 32 D5
Puttgarden D 99 A10
Püttlingen D 37 F7
Putula FIN 143 C13
Putyla UA 168 B6
Putzar D 100 C5
Putzkau D 96 D6
Puukari FIN 141 C11
Puukkokumpu FIN 135 C14
Puumala FIN 145 B9
Puurmani EST 147 D12
Puurs B 35 B9
Puurtila FIN 141 F9
Puutossalmi FIN 140 E9
Puutturinjärvi FIN 135 E17
Puybrun F 45 F9
Puycasquier F 49 C7
Puygouzon F 49 C10
Puylaroque F 49 B9
Puylaurens F 49 C10
Puy-l'Évêque F 49 A8
Puymirol F 49 B7
Puymoyen F 45 D6
Puyôo F 48 C4
Pwllheli GB 26 F3
Pyaozerskiy RUS 137 C17
Pyatidorozhnoye RUS 155 B9
Pyatirech'ye RUS 145 D14
Pyelishcha BY 157 F9
Pyershamayski BY 153 F11
Pyhäjärvi FIN 129 F16
Pyhäjärvi FIN 131 D2
Pyhäjoki FIN 135 F12
Pyhäjoki FIN 142 C7
Pyhäkylä FIN 137 D12
Pyhältö FIN 144 D7
Pyhämaa FIN 142 D5
Pyhänkoski FIN 135 F12
Pyhäntä FIN 135 F16
Pyhäntä FIN 137 F11
Pyhäntaka FIN 143 C14
Pyhäranta FIN 142 D5
Pyhäsalmi FIN 139 C15
Pyhäselkä FIN 141 F13
Pyhe FIN 142 D6
Pyhra A 93 F9
Pyhtää FIN 144 E6
Pyle GB 29 B7
Pyles GR 197 E6
Pyli GR 185 F6
Pyli GR 191 C8
Pyli GR 193 F9
Pylkönmäki FIN 139 E13
Pylos GR 190 F4
Pylypets' UA 161 F7
Pyntäinen FIN 142 B6
Pyrbaum D 91 D9
Pyrgetos GR 185 E8
Pyrgi GR 193 C6
Pyrgiotika GR 191 D6
Pyrgoi GR 185 C6
Pyrgoi GR 186 B6
Pyrgos GR 190 D3
Pyrgos GR 192 D5
Pyrgos GR 193 D8
Pyrgos GR 194 E9
Pyrgos Dirou GR 194 B3
Pyrrönperä FIN 139 B15
Pyrsogianni GR 184 D4
Pyrzyce PL 101 D7
Pyšely CZ 93 C7
Pyskowice PL 158 F6
Pyssyperä FIN 137 D10
Pystan' UA 168 A6
Pysznica PL 160 B5
Pytalovo RUS 149 B3
Pythagoreio GR 193 D8
Pythio GR 185 D7
Pythio GR 188 B6
Pyykkölänvaara FIN 137 E12
Pyykköskylä FIN 137 D13
Pyyli FIN 141 F11

Q

Qafzez AL 184 D4
Qelëz AL 179 E8
Qeparo AL 184 D2
Qerret AL 184 B2
Quadrazais P 61 D7
Quadri I 79 D6
Quakenbrück D 33 C9
Qualiano I 76 B2
Quaregnon B 198 E3
Quargnento I 53 B9
Quarona I 84 B5
Quarrata I 82 E2
Quarré-les-Tombes F 41 F10
Quarteira P 66 E3
Quartell E 64 E4
Quarten CH 43 F11
Quartu Sant'Elena I 80 E3
Quatre-Champs F 35 F10
Quatretonda E 72 D4
Quattro Castella I 82 C1
Quedlinburg D 95 C9
Queenborough GB 31 E10
Queensbury GB 27 D8
Queenstown IRL 24 E6
Queidersbach D 37 F9
Queige F 47 D9
Queiriga P 60 C5
Quel E 57 D7
Quelaines-St-Gault F 39 E10
Quellendorf D 95 C11
Queluz P 66 B1
Quemada E 56 E4
Quend F 34 D4
Quendorf D 33 D8
Queralbs E 49 F10
Quercianella I 82 F1
Querenhorst D 95 B8
Querfurt D 95 D10
Quérigut F 49 E10
Quern D 98 A7
Quernheim D 33 D10
Quero E 63 E6
Quero I 88 E4
Querrieu F 34 E5
Quesa E 64 F3
Quesada E 71 D6
Quesnoy-sur-Deûle F 34 C7
Quessoy F 38 D6
Questembert F 38 E7
Quettehou F 39 A9
Quettreville-sur-Sienne F 39 C9
Quevauvillers F 34 E5
Queyrac F 44 E4
Quézac F 45 F10
Quiaios P 60 D3
Quiberon F 38 F5
Quickborn D 99 C7
Quierschied D 37 F8
Quiévrain B 35 D8
Quiévrechain F 198 E3
Quiliano I 53 C8
Quillan F 49 E10
Quillebeuf-sur-Seine F 34 F2
Quimper F 38 E3
Quimperlé F 38 E4
Quin IRL 24 C5
Quincinetto I 84 B4
Quincy-Voisins F 41 C8
Quingey F 42 F4
Quinson F 52 D4
Quinssaines F 45 C11
Quintana de la Serena E 67 B8
Quintana del Castillo E 55 C7
Quintana del Pino E 56 C4
Quintana del Puente E 56 D3
Quintana de Rueda E 55 C9
Quintana-Martín Galíndez E 56 C5
Quintanapalla E 56 D4
Quintanar de la Orden E 63 E6
Quintanar de la Sierra E 56 E5
Quintanar del Rey E 63 F9
Quintana Redonda E 57 E6
Quintanilla de Onésimo E 56 E3
Quintenas F 46 E6
Quintin F 38 D6
Quinto CH 87 D7
Quinto E 57 F11
Quintos P 66 D4
Quinzano d'Oglio I 85 C9
Quiroga E 54 D5
Quiruelas de Vidriales E 55 D8
Quismondo E 62 D4
Quissac F 51 C7
Quittebeuf F 40 B4
Qukës AL 184 B3

R

Raab A 92 F5
Raabs an der Thaya A 93 E8
Raahe FIN 135 E12
Raajärvi FIN 131 E1
Rääkkylä FIN 141 F13
Raalte NL 32 D6
Raamsdonksveer NL 32 E3
Raanujärvi FIN 133 E13
Raappananmäki FIN 137 E10
Raasiku EST 147 C10
Raate FIN 137 E14
Raattama FIN 133 B12
Rab HR 83 C10
Rabac HR 83 B9
Rabaçal P 60 D4
Rabaçal P 61 C6
Rábade E 54 B4
Răbăgani RO 167 D9
Rábahidvég H 165 B7
Rábakecöl H 165 B8
Rabanales E 55 E7
Rábapaty H 165 B7
Rabastens F 49 C9
Rabastens-de-Bigorre F 49 D6
Rábatamási H 165 A8
Raba Wyżna PL 163 B9
Rabbalshede S 107 B9
Rabča SK 163 C8
Rabčice SK 163 B9
Rabe SRB 166 E5
Rabenstein an der Pielach A 93 F8
Raben Steinfeld D 99 C11
Råberg S 123 B13
Rąbino PL 101 C9
Rabisha BG 175 F10
Rabivere EST 147 C9
Rabka PL 163 B9
Räbke D 95 B8
Rabrovo BG 175 E10
Rabrovo SRB 175 D8
Rača SRB 175 E6
Rača SRB 180 D3
Răcăciuni RO 169 E9
Racale I 77 D10
Rácalmás H 165 B11
Racalmuto I 74 E4
Răcari RO 177 D7
Răcășdia RO 175 D8
Racconigi I 53 B7
Rače SLO 164 D5
Rachanie PL 160 B8
Rachecourt-sur-Marne F 42 C3
Raches GR 191 B6
Raches GR 193 D7
Răchiți RO 169 B9
Răchitoasa RO 169 E10
Răchitova RO 175 B10
Rachoni GR 187 C7
Raciąż PL 154 C4
Raciąż PL 155 E9
Racibórz PL 158 F5
Raciechowice PL 160 D1
Racimierz PL 101 C7
Račinovci HR 173 C10
Račišće HR 178 D3
Răciu RO 168 D4
Răciula MD 170 C2
Ráckeve H 165 B11
Racksätter S 113 D14
Racksund S 125 D14
Racławice PL 159 F9
Răcoasa RO 169 F9
Racoș RO 168 E6
Racova RO 169 D9
Racovița RO 175 B8
Racovița RO 176 B4
Racovița RO 177 C10
Racovițeni RO 177 C9
Raczki PL 152 F6
Rączki PL 155 D9
Rád H 166 B3
Råda S 107 C13
Råda S 113 B9
Råda S 113 B10
Rada de Haro E 63 E7
Radalj SRB 174 E3
Radanovo BG 182 C5
Radapole LV 149 C1
Rădășeni RO 169 C8
Rădăuți RO 169 B7
Rădăuți-Prut RO 169 A9
Raddestorf D 33 D11
Raddi in Chianti I 82 F3
Raddusa I 75 E6
Radë AL 184 B2
Rade N 111 D13
Radeberg D 96 D5
Radebeul D 96 D5
Radeburg D 96 D5
Radeče SLO 89 D11
Radęcin PL 101 D9
Radefeld D 95 D11
Radegast D 95 C11
Rådelsbråten S 118 E3
Radenci SLO 164 C6
Rădeni MD 169 C12
Radensleben D 100 E3
Radenthein A 89 C8
Rădești RO 168 E3
Radevormwald D 37 B8
Radibor D 96 D6
Radići BIH 173 C7
Radicofani I 78 B1
Radicondoli I 82 F3
Radilovo BG 181 E9
Radiměř CZ 93 C10
Radiovce MK 179 F10
Radis D 95 C12
Radizelj SLO 164 D5
Radko Dimitrievo BG 183 C8
Radków PL 93 A10
Radlje ob Dravi SLO 89 C11
Radłów PL 158 E6
Radłów PL 159 F10
Radnejaur S 125 E15
Radnevo BG 182 E5
Radnice CZ 92 C5
Rădoaia MD 169 B12
Radoč BIH 173 F8
Radohova BIH 173 D8
Rădoiești RO 176 E6
Radojevo SRB 166 F6
Radolfzell am Bodensee D 43 E10
Radom PL 157 H4
Rådom S 123 E11
Radomin PL 155 D7
Radomir BG 181 D6
Radomirești RO 176 E5
Radomirtsi BG 181 C9
Radomsko PL 159 D7
Radomyšl CZ 92 D5
Radomyśl nad Sanem PL 160 B4
Radomyśl Wielki PL 159 F11
Radonice CZ 92 B4
Radošina SK 162 D5
Radošovce SK 162 D4
Radoszyce PL 159 D9
Radoszyn PL 97 B8
Radovan RO 176 E3
Radovanu RO 177 E9
Radovets BG 183 F6
Radovići MNE 179 E6
Radoviš MK 185 A7
Radovljica SLO 89 D9
Radovnica SRB 180 E5
Radowo Małe PL 101 C8
Radožda MK 184 B4
Radslavice CZ 162 C5
Radstadt A 89 B7
Radstock GB 29 C10
Răducăneni RO 169 D11
Radučić HR 172 D5
Raduil BG 181 E8
Radujevac SRB 175 E10
Radun' BY 153 E10
Radvanice CZ 97 E10
Radvaň nad Laborcom SK 161 E4
Radviliškis LT 150 E7
Radwanice PL 97 C9
Radymno PL 160 D6
Radzanów PL 155 E9
Radzanów PL 157 G3
Radzanowo PL 155 E8
Radzice Duże PL 157 H2
Radzicz PL 101 D12
Radzieje PL 152 E4
Radziejów PL 154 E6
Radziejowice PL 157 F3
Radziemice PL 159 F9
Radzików PL 97 B7
Radziłów PL 156 D6
Radzymin PL 155 F11
Radzyń Chełmiński PL 154 D6
Radzyń Podlaski PL 157 G7
Ræhr DK 102 A3
Rækker Mølle DK 102 C3
Raeren B 36 C6
Raesfeld D 33 E7
Rafelbunyol E 64 E4
Raffadali I 74 E4
Rafford GB 19 K9
Rafina GR 191 C9
Råforsen S 113 B10
Răfov RO 177 D8
Rafsbotn N 129 C12
Raften N 126 D9
Raftsjöhöjden S 122 D8
Ragaciems LV 150 B6
Rágama E 61 C10
Ragana LV 151 B9
Rageliai LT 151 E11
Rägelin D 99 D13
Raglan GB 29 B9
Råglanda S 107 A13
Ragösen D 95 B12
Raguhn D 95 C11
Ragunda S 123 E10
Ragunda S 123 E10
Ragusa I 75 F6
Raguva LT 151 E9
Rahden D 33 D11
Rahkio FIN 143 D8
Rahkonen FIN 139 C12
Rahman RO 171 D2
Råholt N 111 B14
Rahumäe EST 148 E1
Raiano I 78 C5
Raikuu FIN 141 F12
Räimä FIN 140 D9
Rain D 91 E8
Rain D 91 E11
Rainbach im Mühlkreis A 93 E6
Raippo FIN 145 D9
Räisälä FIN 131 E3
Raisdorf D 99 B8
Raisio FIN 142 E7
Raiskio FIN 135 C16
Raiskio FIN 141 B12
Raismes F 35 D7
Raistakka FIN 137 B11
Rait GB 21 C10
Raitajärvi S 135 B10
Raja EST 147 D13
Raja-Jooseppi FIN 131 B4
Rajala FIN 133 C16
Rajamäki FIN 143 D12
Rajastrand S 122 B8
Rajcza PL 163 B8
Rájec CZ 93 D11
Rajec SK 163 C7
Rajecká Lesná SK 163 C7
Rajgród PL 156 C7
Rajhrad CZ 93 D11
Rajince SRB 180 E4
Rajka H 162 E4
Raka EST 147 C9
Raka SLO 164 E4
Rakamaz H 161 G3
Rakek SLO 89 E9
Rakevo BG 181 C7
Rakhiv UA 168 A4
Rakh'ya RUS 145 E14
Rakita BG 181 C9
Rakita BG 181 D6
Rakitna SLO 89 E9
Rakitovec SLO 83 B8
Rakitovo BG 181 F9
Rakke EST 147 D12
Rakkeby DK 106 E6
Rakkestad N 111 D14
Raklitsa BG 183 D7
Rákóczifalva H 166 C5
Rákócziújfalu H 166 C5
Rakoniewice PL 97 B10
Rakoshyn UA 161 G6
Rakova Bara SRB 175 D8
Rakovica HR 172 C4
Rakovina SRB 179 E10
Rakovitsa BG 175 F9
Rakovník CZ 92 B5
Rakovo BG 181 E6
Rakovski BG 181 E10
Rakow D 100 B4
Raków PL 159 E11
Rakvere EST 147 C12
Ralingen D 37 E7
Ralja SRB 174 D6
Rälla S 105 B11
Ram SRB 175 D7
Ramacca I 75 E6
Rämälä FIN 139 E12
Ramales de la Victoria E 56 B5
Ramalhal P 60 F2
Ramatuelle F 52 E5
Ramberg N 126 D5
Rambervillers F 42 D6
Rambin D 100 B4
Rambouillet F 40 C6
Rambrouch L 35 E12
Rambucourt F 42 C4
Ramelton IRL 23 B7
Râmeț RO 168 E3
Ramillies B 198 D5
Ramingstein A 89 B8
Ramirás E 54 D4
Ramløse DK 103 C10
Rämma S 118 D6
Ramme DK 102 C2
Rammelsbach D 202 B3
Rammingen D 91 E7
Râmna RO 175 C8
Ramnäs S 114 C6
Ramnes N 111 D12
Râmnicelu RO 177 C10
Râmnicelu RO 177 C11
Râmnicu Sărat RO 177 C10
Râmnicu Vâlcea RO 176 C4
Ramonville-St-Agne F 49 C8
Ramosch CH 87 D10
Rämpsänkylä FIN 137 F13
Rampside GB 26 C5
Ramså N 127 B11
Ramsau im Zillertal A 88 B4
Ramsberg S 113 C13
Ramsbottom GB 27 D7
Ramsele S 123 C17
Ramsele S 123 D10
Ramsen CH 43 E10
Ramsey GB 31 C8
Ramsey GBM 26 C3
Ramsey St Mary's GB 31 C8
Ramsgate GB 31 E11
Ramsi EST 147 E11
Ramsing DK 102 B3
Ramsjö S 119 B10
Ramsloh (Saterland) D 33 B9
Ramstadlandet N 121 B10
Ramstein D 37 F9
Ramsund N 127 D12
Ramučiai LT 150 F3
Ramundberget S 118 A3
Ramvik S 119 A14
Ramygala LT 151 E8
Råna N 127 D13
Rånäs S 115 C10
Rånäs S 118 C5
Rånåsfoss N 111 B14
Rance B 35 D9
Randaberg N 110 E3
Randalstown GB 20 F4
Randan F 46 C3
Randaträsk S 134 B6
Randazzo I 75 D6
Rånddalen S 118 B5
Randegg A 93 F7
Randen N 117 C9
Randen N 117 C11
Randers DK 102 C6
Randersacker D 203 B8
Randijaur S 125 C17
Randonnai F 40 C4
Randsjö S 118 B6
Randsverk N 117 C10
Råne N 127 E11
Råneå S 134 C8
Rânes F 39 C11
Rångedala S 107 D13
Rangendingen D 203 E6
Rangersdorf A 89 C6
Rangsby FIN 138 E6
Rangsdorf D 96 B4
Ranhados P 60 C5
Ranilović SRB 174 E6
Ranis D 95 E10
Ranizów PL 160 C4
Ranka LV 151 B12
Ranķi LV 150 C3
Rankinen FIN 135 F14
Rankweil A 87 C9
Ranna EST 147 D14
Rannankylä FIN 139 C15
Rannankylä FIN 139 C16
Rannapungerja EST 147 D14
Rånnaväg S 107 D13
Ränneslöv S 103 C12
Rännö S 119 B12
Rannsundet S 118 B5
Rannu EST 147 E12
Ranovac SRB 175 E7
Ransbach-Baumbach D 37 D9
Ransberg S 108 C4
Ransby S 118 E4
Ranskill GB 27 E9
Ranst B 198 C5
Ransta S 114 C7
Ranta FIN 129 F19
Rantajärvi S 133 E11
Rantakangas FIN 139 E11
Rantasalmen asema FIN 141 F10
Rantasalmi FIN 141 F10
Ranta-Töysä FIN 139 E11
Ranten A 89 B9
Rantsila FIN 135 E15
Ranttila FIN 129 E16
Rantum D 98 A4
Rantzausminde DK 102 E7
Ranua FIN 135 C17
Ranum DK 102 B4
Rånvassbotn N 127 D13
Ranxë AL 179 F8
Raon-l'Étape F 43 D6
Raossi I 85 B11
Rapakkojoki FIN 139 C17
Rapallo I 53 C10
Raphoe IRL 20 F1
Rapice PL 97 B7
Räpina EST 148 E1
Rapla EST 147 D9
Rapolano Terme I 82 F4
Rapolla I 76 B5
Rapoltu Mare RO 167 F11
Raposa P 60 F3
Raposeira P 66 E2
Rapotín CZ 93 B12
Rapoula do Côa P 61 D6
Rapperswil CH 43 F10
Räpplinge S 105 B11
Rapsani GR 185 E8
Raron CH 84 A4
Raša HR 83 B9
Räsälä FIN 141 E9
Rasanovci BIH 172 D5
Rașca RO 169 C8
Rascafría E 62 C5
Rascăieți MD 170 D5
Raschau D 91 A12
Rașcov MD 170 B3
Rasdorf D 94 E6
Raseiniai LT 150 F6
Råsele S 123 C11
Rasen N 112 A6
Rasharkin GB 20 F4
Rašica SLO 89 E10
Rasina EST 147 E14
Rășinari RO 176 B4
Rasines E 56 B5
Rasinja HR 165 D7
Rasinkylä FIN 137 E10
Rasinvaara FIN 137 D14
Rasivaara FIN 141 F13
Råsjö S 119 B10
Raška SRB 179 C10
Rask Mølle DK 102 D5
Raškovice CZ 162 B6
Raslavice SK 161 E3
Rășmirești RO 177 F7
Rasno SRB 179 C9
Râșnov RO 177 B6
Rasony BY 149 E5
Rasova RO 171 E1
Rasovo BG 175 F11
Raspenava CZ 97 E8
Rasquera E 58 E5
Rast RO 176 F2
Raštani BIH 173 F8
Rastatt D 43 C9
Rastdorf D 33 C9
Rasteby N 127 B19
Råsted DK 102 B5
Rastede D 33 B10
Rastenfeld A 93 E8
Rastević HR 172 D4
Rasti FIN 133 C14
Rasti FIN 141 G13
Rastinkylä FIN 141 C13
Răstolița RO 168 D5
Rastošnica BIH 173 C10
Rastovac MNE 179 D6
Rastow D 99 D10
Råstrand S 123 A14
Răsuceni RO 177 E7
Rasueros E 61 B10
Rasvåg N 110 F5
Raszków PL 158 C4
Raszyn PL 157 F3
Rataje SRB 180 C3
Rätan S 118 B8
Ratan S 138 C5
Rätansbyn S 118 B8
Ratasjärvi FIN 133 E11
Ratasvuoma FIN 135 B12
Rateče SLO 89 C8
Ratekau D 99 C9
Rătești RO 176 D6
Rathangan IRL 23 F9
Ráth Bhoth IRL 20 F1
Ráth Caola IRL 24 C5
Rathconrath IRL 23 E7
Rathcoole IRL 23 F10
Ráth Cúil IRL 23 F10
Ráth Domhnaigh IRL 25 C7
Rathdowney IRL 25 C7
Ráth Droma IRL 25 C10
Rathdrum IRL 25 C10
Rathenow D 95 A11
Rathfriland GB 23 D10
Rathgormuck IRL 25 D7
Ráth Iomgháin IRL 23 F9
Rathkeale IRL 24 C5
Rathkeevin IRL 25 D7
Rathlee IRL 22 D4
Rathluirc IRL 24 D5
Ráth Mealtain IRL 23 B7
Rathmolyon IRL 23 F9
Rathmore IRL 24 D4
Rathmullan IRL 20 E1
Ráth Naoi IRL 23 G10
Rathnew IRL 23 G10
Rathnure IRL 25 D9
Ratho GB 21 D10
Rathowen IRL 23 E7
Rathstock D 97 A7
Rathumney IRL 25 D9
Rathvilly IRL 25 C9
Ratiboř CZ 162 C5
Ratić BIH 174 D3
Ratingen D 33 F7
Ratíškovice CZ 93 E12
Rátka H 161 G3
Ratkovac SRB 179 E10
Ratkovo SRB 174 C3
Ratnieki LV 149 D2
Ratoath IRL 23 E10
Rattelsdorf D 91 B8
Ratten A 164 B5
Rattenberg A 88 B4
Rattosjärvi FIN 133 E13
Rattray GB 21 B10
Rättsel S 134 C3
Rättvik S 119 E9
Ratvika N 120 D8
Ratzeburg D 99 C9
Rätzlingen D 95 B9
Raubach D 201 C8
Rauda LV 151 E12
Raudåna N 106 B4
Raudanjoki FIN 133 D16
Raudaskylä FIN 139 B13
Raudasmäki FIN 139 B13
Raudeberg N 116 C2
Râu de Mori RO 175 C10
Raudėnai LT 150 D5
Raudondvaris LT 153 D8
Raudonė LT 152 C7
Rauen D 96 B6
Raufoss N 117 E13
Rauha FIN 145 C10
Rauhala FIN 133 C12
Raulhac F 45 F11
Rauma FIN 142 C6
Rauna LV 151 B11
Raunds GB 31 C7
Rauris A 89 B7
Râu Sadului RO 176 B4
Rauschenberg D 37 C11
Raussila FIN 144 D6
Rautajärvi FIN 143 C12
Rautalampi FIN 140 E7
Rautaperä FIN 130 E4
Rautas S 127 D18
Rautavaara FIN 141 C10
Rautenkranz D 91 B11
Rautila FIN 135 F11
Rautila FIN 142 D6
Rautio FIN 136 F3
Rautionmäki FIN 139 E16
Rautjärven kk FIN 145 C11
Rautjärvi FIN 145 C11
Rautuskylä FIN 133 C13
Rauvanniemi FIN 145 B11
Rauzan F 44 F5
Ravadinovo BG 183 E9
Ravanusa I 74 E4
Rava-Rus'ka UA 160 C8
Ravasd H 165 A9

Ravča HR 173 F7
Ravda BG 183 D9
Ravels B 32 F3
Ravelsbach A 93 E9
Rävemåla S 105 B8
Ravenglass GB 26 C5
Ravenna I 82 D5
Ravensburg D 87 B9
Ravenstein NL 32 E5
Ravières F 41 E11
Ravijoki FIN 144 D8
Ravik N 124 B7
Rävlanda S 107 D12
Ravna Dubrava SRB 180 C5
Ravna Gora HR 83 B10
Ravna Reka SRB 175 E8
Ravne SLO 89 D11
Ravne na Koroškem SLO 89 C10
Ravnets BG 183 D8
Ravni BIH 173 F8
Ravnište SRB 180 C3
Ravnje SRB 174 D3
Ravnkilde DK 102 B5
Ravno BIH 173 E7
Ravno BIH 178 D4
Ravnogor BG 181 F9
Ravno Selo SRB 174 C4
Ravnshøj DK 106 E7
Ravnstrup DK 102 C4
Rävsön S 119 A15
Ravsted DK 102 E4
Rawa Mazowiecka PL 157 G2
Rawicz PL 97 C11
Rawmarsh GB 27 E9
Rawtenstall GB 27 D7
Raykovo BG 187 A7
Rayleigh GB 31 D10
Rayol-Canadel-sur-Mer F 52 E4
Räyrinki FIN 139 D11
Ražana SRB 174 E4
Ražanac HR 172 D3
Ražanj SRB 175 F8
Războieni RO 169 C9
Razboj BIH 173 B7
Razbojna SRB 180 C3
Razdelna BG 183 C9
Razdol BG 185 A9
Razdrto SLO 89 E9
Razès F 45 C8
Razgrad BG 176 F2
Razgrad BG 183 B7
Ražljevo BIH 173 C10
Razlog BG 181 F7
Razlovci MK 181 F6
Ražňany SK 161 E3
Ráztočno SK 163 D7
Răzvad RO 177 D6
Reading GB 30 E7
Reaghstown IRL 23 E9
Real P 54 F3
Réalmont F 49 C10
Realmonte I 74 E3
Réalville F 49 B8
Rear Cross IRL 24 C6
Réaup F 49 B6
Reay GB 19 H9
Rebais F 41 C9
Rebbenesbotn N 128 C2
Rebecq B 35 C9
Rébénacq F 48 D5
Rebild DK 102 B5
Rebollosa de Jadraque E 63 B7
Reboly RUS 141 C15
Rebordelo E 54 B3
Rebordelo P 54 E5
Rebra RO 168 C4
Rebricea RO 169 D11
Rebrișoara RO 168 C4
Rebrovo BG 181 D7
Rebŭrkovo BG 181 C8
Reca SK 162 E4
Recanati I 83 F8
Rečane SRB 179 E10
Recaș RO 167 F8
Recco I 53 C10
Recea MD 169 B11
Recea MD 170 C3
Recea RO 167 B12
Recea RO 168 F5
Recea RO 176 D6
Recea-Cristur RO 168 C3
Recess IRL 22 F3
Recey-sur-Ource F 41 E12
Réchicourt-le-Château F 43 C6
Rechlin D 99 D13
Rechnitz A 165 B6
Recht B 36 D6
Rechtenbach D 90 C6
Reci RO 169 F7
Rečica SLO 89 D11
Rečice BIH 173 F8
Recke D 33 D9
Reckingen CH 86 E6
Recklinghausen D 33 E8
Recoaro Terme I 85 B11
Recoubeau-Jansac F 51 A9
Recsk H 163 F10
Recuerda E 56 F6
Recz PL 101 D9
Ręczno PL 157 H1
Reda PL 154 A5
Redalen N 117 E13
Redange L 36 E5
Redcar GB 27 B9
Redcastle IRL 20 E2
Redcross IRL 25 C10
Reddelich D 99 B11
Redditch GB 29 A11
Réde H 165 B9
Redea RO 176 E4
Redefin D 99 D10
Redhill GB 31 E8
Rédics H 165 C6
Réding F 43 C7
Redinha P 60 D3
Rediu RO 169 C11
Rediu RO 169 D9
Rediu RO 169 F11
Rediul Mare MD 169 A11
Rednitzhembach D 91 D9
Redon F 39 E7
Redondela E 54 D2
Redondelo P 54 E4
Redondo P 66 B4
Redován E 72 E3
Red Point GB 18 K5
Redruth GB 28 E4
Redsted DK 102 B3
Reduzum NL 32 B5
Rędzikowo PL 101 B12
Rędziny PL 159 E7
Reen IRL 24 E3
Reens IRL 24 C5
Reepham GB 31 B11
Rees D 32 E6
Reeßum D 33 B12
Reetz D 33 E9
Reetz D 95 B11
Reetz D 99 D11
Reftele S 103 A13
Regalbuto I 75 D6
Regen D 92 E4
Regensburg D 91 D11
Regensdorf CH 43 F9
Regenstauf D 91 D11
Reggello I 82 E4
Reggio di Calabria I 75 C8
Reggiolo I 82 C2
Reggio nell'Emilia I 82 C2
Reghin RO 168 D5
Reghiu RO 169 F9
Regna S 108 B7
Regnitzlosau D 91 B11
Régny F 46 D5
Regöly H 165 C10
Regozero RUS 137 D17
Regstrup DK 103 D9
Reguengo E 54 D2
Reguengos de Monsaraz P 66 C4
Rehau D 91 B11
Rehburg (Rehburg-Loccum) D 33 D12
Rehden D 33 C10
Rehling D 91 F8
Rehlingen-Siersburg D 37 F7
Řehlovice CZ 96 E5
Rehmsdorf D 95 D11
Rehna D 99 C10
Rehula FIN 145 C9
Reibitz D 95 C11
Reichelsheim (Odenwald) D 203 B6
Reichenau an der Rax A 164 A5
Reichenbach CH 86 D5
Reichenbach D 95 E11
Reichenbach D 203 B6
Reichenberg D 90 C6
Reichenfels A 89 B10
Reichenthal A 92 E6
Reichertsheim D 91 F11
Reichia GR 194 B5
Reichling D 87 B11
Reichmannsdorf D 91 A9
Reicholzheim D 90 C6
Reichraming A 89 A9
Reichshoffen F 43 C8
Reichstett F 202 D4
Reiden CH 43 F8
Reigada P 61 C7
Reigate GB 31 E8
Reignac F 44 E4
Reignier F 47 C9
Reil D 37 D8
Reilingen D 203 C6
Reillanne F 51 C10
Reillo E 63 E9
Reims F 35 F9
Reina E 67 C8
Reinach CH 43 F8
Reinach CH 43 F9
Reinbek D 99 C8
Reinberg D 100 B4
Reine N 126 E5
Reinfeld (Holstein) D 99 C8
Reinheim D 37 E11
Reinosa E 56 C3
Reinøysund N 130 D8
Reinsfeld D 37 E7
Reinskard N 128 D4
Reinskloster N 120 D7
Reinstad N 127 C10
Reinsvik N 120 E3
Reinsvoll N 117 E13
Reipa N 124 C6
Reisbach D 91 E12
Reischach D 91 F12
Reisjärvi FIN 139 C13
Reiskirchen D 37 C11
Reiss GB 19 J10
Reitan N 116 B8
Reitan N 117 A14
Reitano I 74 D5
Reith bei Seefeld A 88 B3
Reit im Winkl D 88 A5
Reittiö FIN 141 D9
Reivyčiai LT 150 D4
Rejmyre S 108 B7
Rejowiec PL 157 H8
Rejsby DK 102 E3
Reka HR 165 D7
Rekava LV 149 B3
Rekavice BIH 173 C7
Reken D 33 E8
Rekijoki FIN 143 E9
Rekken NL 33 D7
Reklynets' UA 160 C9
Rekovac SRB 175 F7
Rekowo PL 101 B12
Rekvik N 127 A15
Rėkyva LT 150 E6
Reliquias P 66 D3
Relletti FIN 135 E13
Relleu E 72 D4
Rellingen D 99 C7
Rém H 166 E3
Remagen D 37 C8
Rémalard F 40 D4
Rembercourt-Sommaisne F 42 C3
Remda D 95 E9
Remels (Uplengen) D 33 B9
Remennikovo RUS 149 C5
Remeskylä FIN 139 C16
Remetea RO 167 D9
Remetea RO 168 D6
Remetea Chioarului RO 168 B3
Remetea Mare RO 167 F7
Remeți RO 161 H8
Remetinec HR 165 D6
Remetské Hámre SK 161 F5
Remich L 36 E6
Remicourt B 199 D6
Remiremont F 42 D6
Remmam S 123 D14
Remmen S 118 B8
Remmet S 118 B7
Remnes N 124 E4
Remolinos E 57 E9
Remouchamps B 199 E7
Remoulins F 51 C8
Remplin D 99 C13
Remptendorf D 91 A10
Remscheid D 37 B8
Remte LV 150 C5
Remungol F 38 E6
Rémuzat F 51 B9
Rena E 61 F9
Rena N 117 D14
Renaison F 46 C4
Renålandet S 122 D8
Renazé F 39 E9
Renčēni LV 147 F10
Renchen D 43 C9
Renda LV 150 B4
Rende I 76 E6
Rendsburg D 98 B7
Renedo E 55 E10
Renedo E 56 B4
Renedo de la Vega E 55 D10
Renens CH 47 B10
Renesse NL 32 E1
Renfrew GB 21 D8
Renginio GR 191 B6
Rengsdorf D 37 C8
Rengsjö S 119 D12
Renholmen S 134 D6
Reni UA 171 C2
Renko FIN 143 D11
Renkomäki FIN 143 D14
Renkum NL 199 B7
Renndal N 120 E5
Rennerod D 37 C10
Rennertshofen D 91 E9
Rennes F 39 D8
Rennes-les-Bains F 49 E10
Renningen D 43 C10
Rennweg A 89 B8
Renòn I 88 C3
Rens DK 102 F4
Rensjön S 127 D18
Reńska Wieś PL 158 F5
Renström S 134 E4
Renswoude NL 199 A7
Rentina GR 190 A4
Rentjärn S 123 A15
Rentweinsdorf D 91 B8
Renwez F 35 E10
Renzow D 99 C10
Repbäcken S 113 A13
Répcelak H 165 B8
Repedea RO 168 B4
Repino RUS 145 E12
Repki PL 157 F6
Replot FIN 138 D6
Repojoki FIN 133 B15
Repolka RUS 148 C6
Reposaari FIN 142 B5
Repparfjord N 129 C13
Reppelin D 99 B12
Reppen N 124 C6
Reppenstedt D 99 D8
Reps AL 179 F9
Repton GB 27 F8
Repvåg N 129 B16
Requejo E 55 D6
Requena E 63 F10
Réquista F 49 B11
Rerik, Ostseebad D 99 B11
Resana I 88 E4
Resarö S 115 D10
Resavica SRB 175 E8
Resele S 123 E12
Resen BG 182 C5
Resen MK 184 B5
Resenbro DK 102 C5
Resende P 60 B5
Rešetari HR 173 B7
Reșița RO 175 C8
Resko PL 101 C8
Resna MNE 179 E6
Resolven GB 29 B7
Respenda de la Peña E 55 C10
Resse (Wedemark) D 94 A6
Ressons-sur-Matz F 34 E6
Restelica SRB 179 F10
Restinga MA 69 E6
Reston GB 21 D12
Resuttano I 74 D5
Retamal E 67 B8
Retford GB 27 E10
Rethel F 35 E9
Rethem (Aller) D 33 C12
Rethymno GR 194 E7
Retie B 32 F4
Retiers F 39 E9
Retje SLO 89 E10
Retortillo E 61 C8
Retortillo de Soria E 56 F6
Retournac F 46 E5
Rétság H 163 F8
Retuerta del Bullaque E 62 F4
Retunen FIN 141 E11
Retz A 93 E9
Reuden D 95 B11
Reuilly F 40 F7
Reurieth D 91 B8
Reus E 58 E6
Reusel NL 32 F4
Reut D 92 F3
Reute D 43 D8
Reuțel MD 169 B11
Reuterstadt Stavenhagen D 100 C3
Reutlingen D 43 D11
Reutte A 87 C11
Reutuaapa FIN 135 B15
Reuver NL 32 F6
Revel F 49 D10
Revello I 53 B6
Revest-du-Bion F 51 B10
Révfülöp H 165 C9
Revholmen N 107 A8
Reviga RO 177 D10
Revigny-sur-Ornain F 42 C2
Revilla de Collazos E 56 C3
Revilla del Campo E 56 D4
Revin F 35 E10
Revine-Lago I 88 E5
Řevnice CZ 92 C6
Řevničov CZ 92 B5
Revò I 88 D3
Revonlahti FIN 135 E13
Revsnes N 116 D6
Revsnes N 127 C11
Revsund S 119 A9
Revúca SK 163 D10
Rewal PL 101 B8
Rexbo S 119 E9
Reyrieux F 46 D6
Rezé F 39 F8
Rēzekne LV 149 C2
Rezi H 165 C8
Rezina MD 170 B3
Rēzna LV 149 D2
Rezovo BG 183 F10
Rezzato I 82 A1
Rezzo I 53 C7
Rezzoaglio I 53 B10
Rgotina SRB 175 E9
Rhade D 33 B12
Rhaunen D 37 E8
Rhayader GB 29 A7
Rheda-Wiedenbrück D 33 E10
Rhede D 33 E7
Rhede (Ems) D 33 B8
Rheden NL 199 A8
Rheinau D 43 C8
Rheinbach D 37 C7
Rheinberg D 33 E7
Rheinböllen D 201 E8
Rheinbreitbach D 37 C8
Rheinbrohl D 201 D7
Rheine D 33 D8
Rheinfelden (Baden) D 43 E8
Rheinsberg D 100 D3
Rheinstetten D 43 C9
Rheinzabern D 203 C5
Rhêmes-Notre-Dame I 47 D11
Rhêmes-St-Georges I 47 D11
Rhenen NL 32 E5
Rhens D 201 D8
Rhiconich GB 18 J7
Rhinau F 43 D8
Rhinow D 99 E12
Rhisnes B 198 D5
Rho I 85 B7
Rhode IRL 23 F8
Rhoden (Diemelstadt) D 33 F12
Rhoon NL 198 B4
Rhoose GB 29 C8
Rhosllanerchrugog GB 26 E5
Rhôs-on-Sea GB 26 E4
Rhossili GB 28 B6
Rhuddlan GB 26 E5
Rhydaman GB 28 B7
Rhyl GB 26 E5
Rhymney GB 29 B8
Riace I 75 C9
Riachos P 60 F3
Riaillé F 39 E9
Rialp E 49 F8
Riaño E 55 C10
Riano I 78 C3
Rians F 51 C10
Riantec F 38 E5
Rianxo E 54 C2
Riaz CH 47 B11
Riba E 56 B4
Ribadavia E 54 D3
Ribadelago E 55 D6
Riba de Mouro P 54 D3
Ribadeo E 54 A5
Riba de Saelices E 63 C8
Ribadesella E 55 B9
Ribaforada E 57 D8
Ribafrecha E 48 F1
Ribarci SRB 180 E6
Ribare SRB 180 C4
Ribari SRB 174 D3
Ribaritsa BG 181 D9
Riba-roja d'Ebre E 58 E4
Riba-roja de Turia E 64 E3
Ribbåsen S 118 D7
Ribchester GB 26 D6
Ribe DK 102 E3
Ribeauvillé F 43 D7
Ribécourt-Dreslincourt F 34 E6
Ribeira P 54 E3
Ribeira de Pena P 54 E4
Ribemont F 35 E7
Ribera I 74 E3
Ribérac F 45 E6
Ribera del Fresno E 67 B7
Ribesalbes E 64 D4
Ribes de Freser E 49 F10
Ribița RO 167 E10
Ribnica BIH 173 D9
Ribnica SLO 89 E10
Ribnica SLO 164 C4
Ribnica SRB 174 F4
Ribnik HR 164 E4
Rîbnița MD 170 B4
Ribnitz-Damgarten D 99 B12
Ribnovo BG 181 F8
Ribota E 56 F5
Ricadi I 75 B8
Říčany CZ 93 C7
Říčany CZ 93 D10
Riccia I 79 E7
Riccio I 82 F5
Riccione I 82 D6
Riccò del Golfo di Spezia I 85 E8
Richardménil F 42 C5
Richelieu F 45 A6
Richhill GB 23 D9
Richka UA 168 A5
Richmond GB 27 C8
Richvald SK 161 E3
Rickebo S 119 D11
Rickenbach D 43 E8
Rickinghall GB 31 C10
Rickling D 99 B8
Rickmansworth GB 31 D8
Ricla E 57 E9
Ricse H 161 G4
Ridala EST 146 D7
Ridasjärvi FIN 143 D13
Riddarhyttan S 113 C14
Ridderkerk NL 32 E3
Riddes CH 47 C11
Riđica SRB 166 F3
Rīdzene LV 151 B10
Riebiņi LV 151 D13
Riebnesluspen S 125 D13
Riec-sur-Belon F 38 E4
Ried CH 84 A5
Riede D 33 C11
Riedenburg D 91 E10
Rieder D 95 C9
Ried im Innkreis A 92 F4
Ried im Oberinntal A 87 C11
Ried im Zillertal A 88 B4
Ried in der Riedmark A 93 F7
Riedlingen D 87 A8
Riegelsberg D 37 F7
Riegersburg A 164 B5
Riego de la Vega E 55 D8
Riehe (Suthfeld) D 94 B5
Riehen CH 43 E8
Rielasingen-Worblingen D 43 E10
Riello E 55 C8
Rielves E 62 E4
Riemst B 35 C12
Rieneck D 203 A8
Rieni RO 167 D9
Rieponlahti FIN 140 E7
Riepsdorf D 99 B9
Riesa D 96 D4
Rieseby D 99 A7
Riesi I 74 E5
Riestedt D 95 D9
Rietavas LT 150 E3
Rietberg D 33 E10
Rieth D 100 C6
Riethoven NL 199 C6
Rieti I 78 C3
Rietschen D 97 D7
Rieumes F 49 D8
Rieupeyroux F 49 B10
Rieutort-de-Randon F 50 A5
Rieux F 39 E7
Rieux F 49 D8
Riez F 52 D4
Rifiano I 88 C3
Rīga LV 151 C8
Rigaio GR 185 F8
Rigaud F 52 D5
Riggisberg CH 47 B11
Rignac F 49 B10
Rignano Flaminio I 78 C2
Rignano Garganico I 79 D9
Rignano sull'Arno I 82 E3
Rigny-le-Ferron F 41 D10
Rigny-sur-Arroux F 46 B5
Rigny-Ussé F 40 F3
Rigside GB 21 D9
Rihtniemi FIN 142 C5
Riihimäki FIN 143 D12
Riihivaara FIN 141 C14
Riikonkumpu FIN 133 C14
Riipi FIN 133 D16
Riippi FIN 138 F7
Riisipere EST 147 C8
Riistavesi FIN 141 E10
Riitiala FIN 143 B8
Riječa BIH 173 E10
Rijeka BIH 173 D9
Rijeka BIH 173 F11
Rijeka HR 83 B9
Rijeka Crnojevića MNE 179 E7
Rijen NL 32 E3
Rijkevorsel B 32 F3
Rijnsburg NL 32 D2
Rijsbergen NL 32 E3
Rijssen NL 33 D7
Rijswijk NL 32 D2
Rikava LV 149 C2
Riksgränsen S 127 D15
Rila BG 181 E7
Rilhac-Rancon F 45 D8
Rilland NL 198 C4
Rillé F 39 F12
Rillieux-la-Pape F 46 D6
Rillo E 58 F2
Rillo de Gallo E 63 C9
Rimavská Baňa SK 163 D9
Rimavská Seč SK 161 G1
Rimavská Sobota SK 163 E10
Rimavské Janovce SK 163 E10
Rimbach D 92 D3
Rimbach D 203 B6
Rimbo S 115 C10
Rimetea RO 168 E3
Rimforsa S 108 C7
Rimicāni LV 151 D12
Rimini I 82 D6
Rimjokk S 134 B5
Rimmilä FIN 143 D11
Rimóc H 163 E9
Rimogne F 200 E2
Rimont F 49 E8
Rimpar D 90 C6
Rimsbo S 119 D11
Rimšė LT 151 E12
Rimšėnai LT 151 F12
Rimske Toplice SLO 89 D11
Rimsting D 88 A5
Rinchnach D 92 E4
Rincón de la Victoria E 69 C8
Rincón de Soto E 57 D8
Rinda LV 150 A3
Rindal N 120 E6
Rindsholm DK 102 C4
Rineia GR 192 E5
Rinella I 75 B6
Ringarum S 109 C8
Ringaudai LT 153 D8
Ringe D 33 C7
Ringe DK 102 E6
Ringebu N 117 C12
Ringelia N 117 E12
Ringen N 111 B12
Ringford GB 21 F8
Ringhals S 103 A10
Ringkøbing DK 102 C2
Ringleben D 95 D9
Ringsend GB 20 E3
Ringsta S 122 E7
Ringsted DK 103 E9
Ringvattnet S 122 C8
Ringville IRL 25 D7
Ringwood GB 29 D11
Rinkaby S 104 D6
Rinkabyholm S 105 B10
Rinkenæs DK 102 F5
Rinkilä FIN 145 B10
Rinloan GB 21 A10
Rinn S 113 B9
Rinneen IRL 24 C4
Rinøyvåg N 127 D10
Rintala FIN 139 D10
Rinteln D 33 D12
Rio GR 190 C4
Rio Caldo P 54 E3
Rio de Mel P 60 C6
Rio de Moinhos P 66 B4
Rio de Moinhos P 66 C3
Rio de Moinhos P 66 D3
Rio de Onor P 55 E6
Rio di Pusteria I 88 C4
Riofrío E 62 C3
Riofrío de Aliste E 55 E7
Riogordo E 69 C8
Rioja E 71 F8
Riola Sardo I 80 D2
Riolobos E 61 E8
Riolo Terme I 82 D4
Riols F 50 C4
Riom F 46 D3
Riomaggiore I 85 E8
Rio Maior P 60 F3
Rio Marina I 81 B2
Riom-ès-Montagnes F 45 E11
Rion-des-Landes F 48 C4
Rionegro del Puente E 55 D7
Rio nell'Elba I 81 B2
Rionero in Vulture I 76 B5
Rionero Sannitico I 79 D6
Rions F 48 A5
Riorges F 46 C5
Ríos E 54 E5
Rioseco de Tapia E 55 C8
Rio Tinto P 60 B3
Rio Torto P 54 E5
Rioz F 42 F5
Ripač BIH 172 C4
Ripacandida I 76 B5
Ripalimosano I 79 D7
Ripanj SRB 174 D6
Riparbella I 82 F2
Ripatransone I 78 B5
Ripe I 83 E7
Ripi I 78 D4
Ripiceni RO 169 B10
Ripley GB 27 C8
Ripley GB 27 E9
Ripoll E 59 C8
Ripon GB 27 C8
Riposto I 75 D7
Rips NL 199 B7
Riquewihr F 43 D7
Risan MNE 179 D6
Risarven S 119 C10
Risbäck S 122 B9
Risberg S 118 D6
Risca GB 29 B8
Rișca RO 167 D11
Rîșcani MD 169 B11
Riscle F 48 C5
Risdal N 106 B3
Risede S 122 C8
Rish BG 183 D7
Risinge S 108 B7
Risliden S 123 B16
Risnabben S 134 D3
Risnes N 110 E5
Risør N 106 B5
Risøyhamn N 127 C10
Rissa N 120 D7
Rissna S 122 E8
Rissnaben S 134 D4
Riste FIN 142 C7
Risteli FIN 141 B12
Risti EST 147 D8
Ristiina FIN 144 B7
Ristijärvi FIN 137 F11
Ristilä FIN 137 B11
Ristilampi FIN 133 E17
Ristinen FIN 140 D7
Ristinkylä FIN 141 E12
Ristioja FIN 133 E13
Ristonmännikkö FIN 133 D16
Risträsk S 123 B12
Risudden S 135 B11
Risum-Lindholm D 98 A5
Rītausma LV 151 D8
Rite LV 151 D10
Rīteri LV 151 C11
Ritini GR 185 D7
Ritola FIN 139 E11
Ritterhude D 33 B11
Rittersdorf D 201 D5
Rittersgrün D 91 B12
Riudarenes E 59 D9
Riudecols E 58 E5
Riudoms E 58 E6
Riutta FIN 139 C12
Riutula FIN 129 F18
Rīva LV 150 C2
Riva del Garda I 85 B10
Riva di Solto I 85 B9
Riva di Tures I 88 C5
Rivanazzano I 53 B10
Rivardo Ligure I 53 C9
Rivarolo Canavese I 84 C4
Rivarolo Mantovano I 82 B1
Rivas-Vaciamadrid E 62 D6
Rive-de-Gier F 46 D6
Rivedoux-Plage F 44 C3
Rivello I 76 C5
Riverchapel IRL 25 C10
Rivergaro I 53 B11
Rivero E 56 B3
Riverstown IRL 23 F7
Riverstown IRL 24 E6
Rivery F 34 E5
Rives F 47 E8
Rivesaltes F 50 E4
Rivière-sur-Tarn F 50 B5
Rivignano I 89 E7
Rivinperä FIN 135 F16
Rivodutri I 78 B3
Rivoli I 84 C4
Rivolta d'Adda I 85 C8
Rixensart B 35 C10
Rixheim F 43 E7
Rixö S 107 C9
Riza GR 191 C6
Rizes GR 190 E5
Rizia GR 187 A10
Rizomata GR 185 D7
Rizomylos GR 185 F8
Rizziconi I 75 C8
Rjånes N 116 B3
Rjukan N 111 C9
Rø DK 105 E7
Ro I 82 C4
Rö S 119 A14
Roa E 56 E4
Roa N 111 B13
Roade GB 31 C7
Roadside GB 19 H10
Roadside of Kinneff GB 21 B12
Roager DK 102 E3
Roaillan F 48 B5
Roald N 116 A4
Roan N 120 C8
Roanne F 46 C5
Roata de Jos RO 177 E7
Roath GB 29 C8
Röbäck S 138 C4
Robănești RO 176 E4
Robbio I 84 C6
Robeasca RO 177 C10
Robecco d'Oglio I 85 C9
Röbel D 99 D13
Robella I 84 C5
Robert-Espagne F 42 C3
Roberton GB 21 D9
Roberton GB 21 E11
Robertsfors S 134 F5
Robežnieki LV 149 E3
Robiac-Rochessadoule F 51 B7
Robilante I 53 C6
Robin Hood's Bay GB 27 C10
Robion F 51 C9
Robledo E 71 B8
Robledo de Chavela E 62 C4
Robledo del Mazo E 62 E3
Robledollano E 61 E9
Robles de la Valcueva E 55 C9
Robliza de Cojos E 61 C9
Robøle N 117 E11
Robregordo E 62 B5
Robres E 57 E11
Robres del Castillo E 48 F1
Roč HR 83 B9
Rocafort de Queralt E 59 E6
Rocamadour F 45 F9
Roca Vecchia I 77 C10
Roccabianca I 82 B1
Roccadaspide I 76 C4
Rocca d'Evandro I 76 A1
Rocca di Cambio I 78 C4
Rocca di Mezzo I 78 C5
Rocca di Neto I 77 E7
Rocca di Papa I 78 D3
Roccafranca I 85 C8
Roccagloriosa I 76 C4
Roccagorga I 78 D4
Rocca Grimalda I 53 B9
Rocca Imperiale I 77 C7
Roccalbegna I 81 B5
Roccalumera I 75 D7
Roccamandolfi I 79 D6
Rocca Massima I 78 D3
Roccamena I 74 D3
Roccamonfina I 76 A1
Roccamontepiano I 78 C6
Roccanova I 76 C6
Roccapalumba I 74 D4
Rocca Pia I 78 D5
Roccaraso I 78 D6
Rocca San Casciano I 82 D4
Rocca San Giovanni I 79 C6
Roccasecca I 78 D5
Roccasecca dei Volsci I 78 E4
Rocca Sinibalda I 78 C3
Roccastrada I 81 A4
Roccavione I 53 C6
Roccella Ionica I 75 C9
Rocchetta Sant'Antonio I 76 A4
Rochdale GB 27 D7
Roche GB 28 E5
Rochechouart F 45 D7
Rochefort B 35 D11
Rochefort F 44 D4
Rochefort-en-Terre F 39 E7
Rochefort-Montagne F 46 D2
Rochefort-sur-Nenon F 42 F4
Rochehaut B 200 E3
Roche-la-Molière F 46 E5
Rochemaure F 51 A8
Roches-Bettaincourt F 42 D3
Rocheservière F 44 B2
Rochester GB 21 E12
Rochester GB 31 E10
Rochetaillée F 42 E3
Rochford GB 31 D10
Rochfortbridge IRL 23 F8
Rochin F 35 C7
Rochlitz D 95 D12
Rociana del Condado E 67 E6
Ročinj SLO 89 D8
Rociu RO 176 D6
Rockanje NL 198 B4
Rockchapel IRL 24 D4
Rockcliffe GB 21 F9
Rockcorry IRL 23 D8
Rockenhausen D 37 E9
Rockesholm S 113 C12
Rockhammar S 113 C13
Rockhill IRL 24 D5
Rockingham GB 27 F10
Rockmills IRL 24 D6
Rockneby S 105 B10
Röcknitz D 95 D12
Rocourt-St-Martin F 41 B9
Rocroi F 35 E10
Rodach bei Coburg D 91 B8
Roda de Bara E 59 E6
Roda de Ter E 59 D8
Rodalben D 37 F9
Rodaljice HR 172 D4
Rödåsel S 134 F3
Rodberg N 111 B9
Rødbergshamn N 127 B15
Rødby DK 99 A10
Rødbyhavn DK 99 A10
Rødding DK 102 B3
Rødding DK 102 C5
Rødding DK 102 E4
Rödeby S 105 C9
Rodeiro E 54 C4
Rødekro DK 102 E4
Rodel GB 18 K3
Rodellar E 48 F5
Rodelle F 50 A4
Roden NL 33 B6
Ródenas E 63 C10
Rodenkirchen (Stadland) D 33 B10
Rödental D 91 B9
Rodewald D 98 E6
Rodewisch D 91 A11
Rodez F 49 B11
Rodi Garganico I 79 D9
Roding D 91 D12
Rodingträsk S 123 C14
Rödjebro S 114 B8
Rødkærsbro DK 102 C4
Rodleben D 95 C11
Rødlia N 124 E7
Rödmyra S 119 C11
Rodna RO 168 C5
Rododafni GR 190 C5
Rodolivos GR 186 C5
Rödön S 121 E16
Rodopoli GR 185 B9
Rodopos GR 194 D6
Rodos GR 197 D8
Rødovre DK 103 D10
Rødsand N 127 B13
Rødsand N 130 D8
Rødseidet N 121 B11
Rödvattnet S 123 D13
Rødvig DK 103 E10
Roela EST 147 C13
Roermond NL 36 B5
Roeselare B 35 C7
Roești RO 176 D4
Roetgen D 36 C6
Röfors S 108 B5
Rofrano I 76 C4
Rogač HR 172 F5
Rogačica SRB 174 E4
Rogaška Slatina SLO 164 D5
Rogaszyce PL 158 D4
Rogate GB 31 E7
Rogatec SLO 164 D5
Rogatica BIH 173 E11
Rogätz D 95 B10
Roggel NL 32 F5
Roggenburg D 91 F7
Roggendorf D 99 C10
Roggentin D 100 D3
Roggiano Gravina I 76 D6
Roghudi I 75 C8
Rogienice Wielkie PL 155 D13
Rogil P 66 E2

Rogliano F 53 F10
Rogliano I 77 E6
Rognac F 51 D9
Rognan N 124 B9
Rognes F 51 C9
Rognes N 120 E8
Rognonas F 51 C8
Rogova RO 175 E10
Rogovka LV 149 C2
Rogovo SRB 179 E10
Rogów PL 157 G1
Rogowo PL 154 E4
Rogowo PL 155 E7
Rogozen BG 181 B8
Rogoznica HR 172 E4
Rogoźnica PL 97 D10
Rogoźniczka PL 157 F7
Rogoźno PL 101 E12
Rogslösa S 108 C5
Rogsta S 118 A8
Rogsta S 119 C13
Roguszyn PL 155 F12
Rohan F 38 D6
Röhlingen D 91 E7
Rohlsdorf D 99 D11
Rohlsdorf D 99 D12
Rohod H 161 G5
Rohovce SK 162 E4
Rohožník SK 93 F12
Rohr D 95 E8
Rohrau A 93 F11
Rohrbach D 91 E10
Rohrbach in Oberösterreich A 92 E5
Rohrbach-lès-Bitche F 43 B7
Rohrberg D 99 E10
Rohr in Niederbayern D 91 E10
Röhrmoos D 91 F9
Röhrnbach D 92 E5
Rohrsen D 33 C12
Roiffieux F 46 E6
Roisel F 35 E7
Roismala FIN 143 C8
Roivainen FIN 131 B2
Roiz E 56 B3
Roja LV 150 A5
Rojales E 72 E3
Röjan S 118 B7
Röjdåfors S 113 B8
Rojewo PL 154 E5
Rökå S 123 A15
Rokai LT 153 D8
Rokiciny PL 159 C8
Rokietnica PL 97 A11
Rokietnica PL 160 D6
Rokiškis LT 151 E11
Rokitno PL 157 F8
Rokksøy N 127 C10
Røkkum N 117 A8
Røkland N 124 C9
Roklum D 95 B8
Roknäs S 134 D6
Rokycany CZ 92 C5
Rokytnice CZ 162 C4
Rokytnice v Orlických Horách CZ 93 B10
Rolampont F 42 E3
Rold DK 102 B5
Røldal N 110 C5
Rolde NL 33 C7
Rolfs S 135 C10
Rolfstorp S 103 A10
Rollag N 111 B10
Rollán E 61 C9
Rolle CH 47 C9
Rolsted DK 102 E7
Rolvåg N 124 D3
Rolvsnes N 110 C2
Rolvsøy N 111 D14
Rom D 99 D11
Rom F 45 C6
Roma I 78 D3
Roma RO 169 B9
Roma S 109 D12
Romagnano Sesia I 84 B5
Romagné F 39 D9
Romainmôtier CH 47 B9
Romakkajärvi FIN 133 E13
Roman BG 181 C8
Roman RO 169 D9
Romana I 80 C2
Românași RO 167 C11
Românești RO 169 B10
Români RO 169 D9
Romanija BIH 173 E10
Romano d'Ezzelino I 88 E4
Romano di Lombardia I 85 B8
Romanones E 63 C7
Romanovce MK 180 E4
Romanovo RUS 152 D1
Romanowo PL 101 E11
Romanshorn CH 43 E11
Romans-sur-Isère F 47 E7
Romanu RO 171 C1
Romazy F 39 D9
Rombas F 36 F6
Rombiolo I 75 B9
Romeira P 60 F3
Rometta I 75 C7
Romeu P 54 E5
Romford GB 31 D9
Romhány H 163 F8
Römhild D 91 B8
Romillé F 39 D8
Romilly-sur-Seine F 41 C10
Rommerskirchen D 37 B7
Romont CH 47 B10
Rømonysæter N 118 C3
Romorantin-Lanthenay F 40 F6
Romos RO 167 F11
Romppala FIN 141 E13
Romrod D 37 C12
Romsey GB 29 D12
Rømskog N 112 C6
Romsley GB 29 A10
Romstad N 121 C11
Romuli RO 168 B4
Rona de Jos RO 161 H9
Rona de Sus RO 161 H9
Rönäs S 124 E8
Rønbjerg DK 102 B3
Roncade I 88 E5
Roncadelle I 82 A1
Roncal E 48 E4
Roncegno I 85 A11
Ronce-les-Bains F 44 D3
Ronchamp F 42 E6
Ronchi dei Legionari I 89 E7
Ronciglione I 78 C2
Ronco Canavese I 84 C4
Roncone I 85 B10
Ronco Scrivia I 53 B9
Ronda E 69 C6
Rønde DK 102 C6
Rondissone I 84 C4
Rone S 109 E12
Ronehamn S 109 E12
Rong N 110 A1
Rõngu EST 147 E12
Rönnäng S 107 D10
Rönnäs S 123 B10
Rönnbacken S 119 E11
Rönnberg S 125 E17
Rönnberget S 134 D6
Rønne DK 104 E7
Rønnebæk DK 103 E9
Ronneburg D 95 E11
Ronneby S 105 C8
Ronnebyhamn S 105 C8
Rønnede DK 103 E10
Ronnenberg D 94 B6
Rönneshytta S 108 B6
Rönnholm S 123 D16
Rønningen N 127 C15
Rönnliden S 125 F17
Rönnöfors S 121 D15
Rönö S 109 C9
Ronov nad Doubravou CZ 93 C9
Ronsberg D 87 B10
Ronse B 35 C8
Ronshausen D 94 E6
Ronvik N 124 B7
Rooaun IRL 22 F6
Roodeschool NL 33 B7
Rookchapel IRL 24 D4
Roosendaal NL 32 E2
Roosinpohja FIN 139 F13
Roosky IRL 23 E7
Roosna-Alliku EST 147 C11
Ropa PL 161 D3
Ropaži LV 151 C9
Ropcha UA 169 A7
Ropczyce PL 159 F12
Ropeid N 110 D4
Roperuelos del Páramo E 55 D8
Ropienka PL 161 D5
Ropinsalmi FIN 132 A7
Ropotovo MK 184 B5
Roquebillière F 53 C6
Roquebrun F 50 C5
Roquebrune-Cap-Martin F 53 D6
Roquebrune-sur-Argens F 52 E5
Roquecor F 49 B7
Roquecourbe F 49 C10
Roquefort F 48 B5
Roquemaure F 51 B8
Roquesteron F 52 D6
Roquetas E 58 F5
Roquetas de Mar E 71 F7
Roquevaire F 51 D10
Rørbakken N 127 C14
Rörberg S 119 E12
Rørby DK 103 D8
Rore BIH 173 D6
Røros N 117 A14
Rorschach CH 87 C9
Rörvattnet S 121 D16
Rørvig DK 103 D9
Rørvik N 110 F5
Rørvik N 121 B10
Rørvik N 126 D7
Rörvik S 104 A7
Rosà I 88 E4
Rosala FIN 142 F7
Rosal de la Frontera E 67 D5
Rosans F 51 B9
Rosapenna IRL 23 B7
Rosário P 66 D3
Rosarno I 75 C8
Rosavci BIH 173 C6
Rosbach vor der Höhe D 37 D11
Roscanvel F 38 D2
Ros Cathail IRL 22 F4
Rosche D 99 E9
Roscigno I 76 C4
Rościszewo PL 155 E8
Roscoff F 38 C4
Ros Comáin IRL 22 E6
Roscommon IRL 22 E6
Ros Cré IRL 25 C7
Roscrea IRL 25 C7
Rosdorf D 94 D6
Rose I 76 E6
Rose MNE 178 E6
Rosée B 200 D2
Rosehearty GB 19 K12
Rosemarkie GB 19 K8
Rosen BG 183 E9
Rosenallis IRL 23 F8
Rosendal N 110 C4
Rosenfeld D 43 D10
Rosenfors S 108 E7
Rosengarten D 99 D7
Rosenheim D 88 A5
Rosenlund S 107 D13
Rosenow D 100 C4
Rosenthal D 37 C11
Roserberg S 115 C9
Roses E 59 C10
Roseți RO 177 E10
Roseto Capo Spulico I 77 D7
Roseto degli Abruzzi I 78 B6
Roseto Valfortore I 76 A4
Roshchino RUS 145 E12
Rosheim F 43 C7
Roshven GB 20 B5
Roșia RO 167 D9
Roșia RO 168 F4
Roșia de Amaradia RO 176 C3
Roșia de Secaș RO 168 E3
Roșia Montană RO 167 E11
Rosica LV 149 D3
Rosice CZ 93 C9
Rosice CZ 93 D10
Rosières F 46 E4
Rosières-en-Santerre F 34 E6
Roșiești RO 169 E11
Rosignano Marittimo I 82 F1
Roșiile RO 176 D3
Roșiori RO 169 D10
Roșiori RO 177 D10
Roșiori de Vede RO 176 E6
Rositsa BG 171 F1
Rositsa BY 149 E3
Rositz D 95 D11
Rosiyanivka UA 170 C5
Roskhill GB 18 L3
Roskilde DK 103 D10
Rosko PL 101 E10
Roskovec AL 184 C2
Roskow D 95 B12
Röslau D 91 B10
Roslev DK 102 B3
Rosmalen NL 32 E4
Rosmaninhal P 61 E6
Ros Mhic Thriúin IRL 25 D9
Rosnowo PL 101 B10
Rosolina I 82 B5
Rosolina Mare I 82 B5
Rosolini I 75 F6
Rosoman MK 185 A6
Rosoy F 41 D9
Rosporden F 38 E4
Rösrath D 37 C8
Rossano I 77 D7
Rossano Veneto I 88 E4
Roßbach D 92 E3
Rossbol S 122 E7
Rosscahill IRL 22 F4
Ross Carbery IRL 24 E4
Rosscarbery IRL 24 E4
Rosscor GB 22 D6
Roßdorf D 37 E11
Rossell E 58 F4
Rosselló E 58 D5
Rosses Point IRL 22 D5
Rossett GB 26 E6
Rossfjord N 127 B15
Roßhaupten D 87 B11
Rossiglione I 53 B9
Rossignol B 35 E11
Rössing (Nordstemmen) D 94 B6
Rossington GB 27 E9
Rossio ao Sul do Tejo P 60 F4
Roßla D 95 D9
Rosslare IRL 25 D10
Rosslare Harbour IRL 25 D10
Roßlau D 95 C11
Rosslea GB 23 D8
Roßleithen A 89 A9
Rossnowlagh IRL 22 C6
Rossön S 123 D10
Ross-on-Wye GB 29 B9
Rossosz PL 157 G8
Rossoszyca PL 158 C6
Rossow D 99 D13
Roßtal D 91 D8
Rossum NL 199 B6
Røssvassbukta N 124 E7
Rossvik N 121 A11
Rossvoll N 120 E4
Rossvoll N 127 B15
Roßwein D 96 D4
Røst N 124 A3
Röstabo S 119 D11
Röstånga S 103 C12
Rostarzewo PL 97 B10
Röste S 119 D11
Rostellan IRL 24 E6
Rostock D 99 B12
Rostrenen F 38 D5
Rostrevor GB 23 D10
Röström S 123 C10
Rostrup DK 102 B5
Rostundelva N 128 D6
Rosturk IRL 22 E3
Rostuša MK 184 A4
Røstvollen N 118 B3
Røsvik N 125 B9
Rosvik S 134 D7
Röszke H 166 E5
Rot S 118 D7
Rota E 68 C4
Rota N 127 E10
Rota Greca I 76 E6
Rot am See D 90 D7
Rot an der Rot D 87 A10
Rotava CZ 91 B12
Rotberget N 113 A8
Roteberg S 119 D10
Rotello I 79 D7
Rotenburg (Wümme) D 33 B12
Rotenburg an der Fulda D 94 D6
Rötgesbüttel D 95 B8
Rotgülden A 89 B7
Roth D 91 D9
Rothbury GB 21 E13
Röthenbach an der Pegnitz D 91 D9
Rothenberg D 37 E11
Rothenbuch D 90 C5
Rothenburg (Oberlausitz) D 97 D7
Rothenburg ob der Tauber D 91 D7
Rothéneuf F 39 C8
Rothenfels D 90 C6
Rothenschirmbach D 95 D10
Rothenstein D 95 E10
Rotherham GB 27 E9
Rothes GB 19 K10
Rothesay GB 20 D6
Rotheux-Rimière B 35 C11
Rothiesholm GB 19 G11
Rothley GB 27 F9
Rothrist CH 43 F8
Rothwell GB 27 D9
Rothwell GB 31 C7
Rothwesten (Fuldatal) D 94 D6
Rotimlja BIH 173 F8
Rotimojoki FIN 139 C17
Rotnäset S 122 C9
Rotonda I 76 D6
Rotondella I 77 C7
Rotselaar B 35 C10
Rotsjö S 119 A10
Rotsjön S 134 F4
Rotsund N 128 D6
Rott D 87 B11
Rottach-Egern D 88 A4
Rott am Inn D 91 G11
Røttangen N 127 E10
Rottenacker D 87 A9
Röttenbach D 91 D9
Rottenbach D 95 E9
Rottenbuch D 87 B11
Rottenburg am Neckar D 43 D10
Rottenburg an der Laaber D 91 E11
Rottendorf D 90 C7
Rottenmann A 89 A9
Rotterdam NL 32 E3
Rotthalmünster D 92 F4
Röttingen D 90 C6
Rottleberode D 95 C8
Rottne S 105 A7
Rottnemon S 112 B8
Rottneros S 113 C9
Rottofreno I 85 C8
Rottweil D 43 D10
Rotunda RO 176 F4
Rotviken S 121 D16
Rötz D 91 D12
Rouans F 39 F8
Roubaix F 35 C7
Rouchovany CZ 93 D10
Rõude EST 147 D7
Roudnice nad Labem CZ 92 B6
Rouen F 34 F3
Rouffach F 43 E7
Rouffignac F 45 E7
Rõuge EST 147 F13
Rougé F 39 E9
Rougemont F 42 F5
Rougemont-le-Château F 43 E6
Roughton GB 31 B11
Rougnac F 45 D6
Rouillac F 44 D5
Rouillé F 44 C6
Roujan F 50 C5
Roukala FIN 135 F11
Roukalahti FIN 141 F13
Roulans F 42 F5
Roulers B 35 C7
Roulers B 198 D2
Roumazières-Loubert F 45 D7
Roumoules F 52 D4
Roundstone IRL 22 F3
Roundway GB 29 C11
Roundwood IRL 23 F10
Rouravaara FIN 133 C14
Roure I 47 E11
Rousínov CZ 93 D11
Rousky GB 20 F2
Rousset F 51 D10
Roussillon F 46 E6
Roussillon F 51 C9
Rousson F 51 B7
Routot F 34 F2
Rouvroy F 198 E1
Rouvroy-sur-Audry F 35 E10
Rouy F 46 A4
Rovala FIN 131 C5
Rovala FIN 131 E1
Rovaniemi FIN 133 F15
Rovanpää FIN 133 C15
Rovanpää FIN 133 E12
Rovapää FIN 131 D2
Rovastinaho FIN 135 C16
Rovato I 85 B9
Rovegno I 53 B10
Roverbella I 82 B2
Roveredo CH 85 A7
Rovereto I 85 B11
Rövershagen D 99 B12
Roverud N 112 B7
Roviano I 78 C3
Rovies GR 191 B7
Rovigo I 82 B4
Rovinari RO 175 D11
Rovine BIH 173 B7
Rovinj HR 83 B8
Rovinka SK 162 E4
Rovišće HR 165 E7
Rovisuvanto FIN 129 E16
Rovsättra S 115 B10
Rów PL 101 E7
Rowde GB 29 C10
Równa PL 158 C6
Rownaye BY 149 F6
Roxmo S 109 A8
Roxton GB 31 C8
Royan F 44 D3
Royat F 46 D3
Roybon F 47 E7
Roybridge GB 20 B7
Roydon GB 31 C11
Roye F 34 E6
Royère-de-Vassivière F 45 D9
Røyken N 111 C12
Røykenes N 127 C10
Röykkä FIN 143 E12
Roylyanka UA 170 E5
Røyrvik N 121 B15
Røyse N 111 B12
Royston GB 31 C8
Royton GB 27 D7
Röyttä FIN 135 C12
Roytvollen N 121 A12
Royuela E 63 D10
Roza BG 182 E6
Rožaje MNE 179 D9
Rozalén del Monte E 63 E7
Rozalimas LT 150 E7
Różan PL 155 E11
Różanki PL 101 E8
Rozavlea RO 168 B4
Rozay-en-Brie F 41 C8
Rožďalovice CZ 93 B8
Rozdil UA 161 E9
Rozdil'na UA 170 D6
Rozdrażew PL 158 C4
Rozenburg NL 198 B4
Rozendaal NL 199 A7
Roženica HR 164 E5
Rozes LV 151 B11
Rozhniv UA 168 A6
Rozhnyativ UA 161 F9
Rozino BG 181 D10
Rožmitál pod Třemšínem CZ 92 C5
Rožňava SK 161 F2
Rożniatów PL 158 B6
Roznov RO 169 D9
Rožnov pod Radhoštěm CZ 162 C6
Roznowo PL 101 E11
Rozogi PL 155 D11
Rozovets BG 182 E4
Rozoy-sur-Serre F 35 E9
Rozprza PL 159 D8
Roztoka Wielka PL 161 E2
Roztoky CZ 92 B5
Roztoky UA 168 A6
Rozula LV 151 B9
Rožupe LV 151 D12
Roźwienica PL 160 D6
Rozzano I 85 C7
Rrëshen AL 179 F8
Rrogozhinë AL 184 B2
Rromanat AL 184 B2
Rtkovo SRB 175 D10
Rtyně v Podkrkonoší CZ 93 B10
Ru E 54 B3
Rua P 60 C5
Ruabon GB 26 F5
Ruaudin F 39 E12
Ruba LV 150 D5
Rúbaň SK 162 F6
Rubano I 82 B4
Rubashki BY 149 F3
Rubayo E 56 B4
Rubbestadneset N 110 C2
Rubena E 56 D4
Rübenau D 96 E4
Rubene LV 151 B10
Rubeņi LV 151 D11
Rubí E 59 E8
Rubiá E 55 D6
Rubí de Bracamonte E 56 F2
Rubielos de la Cérida E 63 C10
Rubielos de Mora E 64 D3
Rubiera I 82 C2
Rubik AL 179 F8
Rublacedo de Abajo E 56 C5
Rucăr RO 176 C6
Rucava LV 150 D2
Ruciane-Nida PL 155 C12
Rückersdorf D 96 C5
Ruda PL 158 D6
Ruda S 105 A10
Rudabánya H 161 G2
Ruda Maleniecka PL 157 H2
Rudamina LT 153 D11
Rudamina LT 153 E7
Ruda Różaniecka PL 160 C7
Rudartsi BG 181 D7
Ruda Śląska PL 158 F6
Rudbārži LV 150 C3
Ruddervoorde B 198 C2
Rude LV 150 B5
Rude LV 150 D2
Rudelzhausen D 91 E10
Rudersberg D 90 E6
Rudersdorf A 164 B6
Rüdersdorf Berlin D 96 B5
Rüdesheim D 201 E8
Rudice BIH 172 C5
Rudina SK 163 C7
Rūdiškės LT 153 D10
Rudka PL 157 E7
Rudkøbing DK 103 F7
Rudky UA 161 D7
Rudná CZ 92 B6
Rudna PL 97 C10
Rudna Glava SRB 175 E9
Rudňany SK 161 F2
Rudna Wielka PL 97 C11
Rudne UA 160 D8
Rudnica PL 97 A8
Rudnica SRB 179 C10
Rudnik BG 183 D9
Rudnik PL 158 F5
Rudnik SRB 174 E5
Rudnik SRB 179 D10
Rudniki PL 158 D6
Rudnik nad Sadem PL 160 C5
Rüdnitz D 100 E5
Rudno PL 157 G6
Rudno SRB 179 C9
Rudnyky UA 161 E8
Rudnytsya UA 170 A3
Rudo BIH 174 F3
Rudolfov CZ 93 E7
Rudolstadt D 95 E9
Rudozem BG 187 B7
Rudsgrendi N 111 C9
Rudsjön S 123 D10
Rudston GB 27 C11
Ruds Vedby DK 103 D8
Rudzāti LV 151 D13
Rudziczka PL 158 F4
Rudziniec PL 158 F5
Rue F 34 D4
Rueda E 55 F10
Rueda de Jalón E 57 E9
Rueil-Malmaison F 40 C7
Ruelle-sur-Touvre F 45 D6
Ruen BG 183 D8
Ruente E 56 B3
Ruffano I 77 D10
Ruffec F 45 B8
Ruffec F 45 C6
Ruffey-lès-Echirey F 42 F3
Ruffiac F 39 E7
Ruffieu F 47 C8
Ruffieux F 47 D8
Rufford GB 26 D6
Rufina I 82 E3
Rugāji LV 149 B2
Rugby GB 29 A12
Rugeley GB 27 F8
Rugge N 126 C8
Rugince MK 180 E4
Ruginești RO 169 E10
Ruginoasa RO 169 C9
Rügland D 91 D8
Rugles F 40 C4
Rugvica HR 164 E6
Ruha FIN 139 E9
Ruhala FIN 140 G2
Ruhla D 95 E7
Ruhland D 96 D5
Ruhmannsfelden D 92 E3
Rühn D 99 C11
Ruhpolding D 89 A6
Ruhstorf an der Rott D 92 F4
Ruidera E 71 B7
Ruikka FIN 135 B14
Ruinas I 80 D2
Ruinen NL 32 C6
Ruinerwold NL 32 C6
Ruiselede B 35 B7
Ruismäki FIN 139 E10
Ruivães P 54 E3
Ruja PL 97 D10
Rūjiena LV 147 F10
Rujišta BIH 173 F8
Ruka FIN 137 B13
Rukajärvi FIN 137 B13
Rukkisperä FIN 135 E14
Rulbo S 118 C8
Rullbo S 118 E7
Rullnäs S 123 D15
Rully F 46 B6
Rülzheim D 43 B9
Rum A 88 B3
Rum BY 149 E6
Rum H 165 B7
Ruma SRB 174 C4
Rumboci BIH 173 E7
Rumburk CZ 97 E7
Rumelange L 36 F6
Rumelifeneri TR 189 B11
Rumenka SRB 174 C4
Rumes B 35 C7
Rumia PL 154 A5
Rumigny F 35 E9
Rumilly F 47 D8
Rummu EST 147 C8
Rummukkala FIN 141 F12
Rumo FIN 141 D11
Rumont F 42 C3
Rumšiškės LT 153 D9
Rumskulla S 108 D7
Rumst B 35 B9
Rumyantsevo BG 181 C9
Runaberg S 123 E11
Runcorn GB 26 E6
Runcu RO 171 D2
Runcu RO 176 C4
Runcu RO 176 C6
Rundēni LV 149 D3
Rundfloen N 118 D4
Rundhaug N 127 B16
Rundmoen N 124 D8
Rundvik S 123 D16
Rungsted DK 103 D11
Runhällen S 114 B7
Runkel D 201 D9
Runni FIN 140 C7
Runović HR 173 F7
Runsten S 105 B11
Runtuna S 109 B10
Ruohokangas FIN 131 A3
Ruohola FIN 135 C15
Ruokojärvi FIN 133 D12
Ruokojärvi FIN 145 B11
Ruokojärvi S 133 E10
Ruokolahti FIN 145 C10
Ruokoniemi FIN 145 B10
Ruokotaipale FIN 144 C8
Ruolahti FIN 143 B13
Ruoms F 51 B7
Ruona FIN 135 B17
Ruona FIN 139 E11
Ruonajärvi FIN 133 D13
Ruopsa FIN 131 E2
Ruorasmäki FIN 143 B15
Ruotaanmäki FIN 140 D7
Ruoti I 76 B5
Ruotsalo FIN 139 C10
Ruotsinkylä FIN 143 D15
Ruotsinpyhtää FIN 143 D15
Ruottisenharju FIN 136 D9
Ruovesi FIN 139 G12
Rupa HR 83 B9
Rupea RO 168 E6
Ruppovaara FIN 141 F14
Rupt-sur-Moselle F 42 E6
Rus E 71 C6
Rus RO 168 C3
Rusånes N 124 C9
Rusănești RO 176 F5
Rusca Montană RO 175 B9
Ruscova RO 168 B4
Rusdal N 110 E4
Ruse BG 177 F7
Ruše SLO 164 C5
Rusele S 123 B14
Ruseni MD 169 A10
Rusețu RO 177 D10
Ruševo HR 165 F9
Rush IRL 23 E10
Rushden GB 31 C7
Rusiec PL 159 D6
Rușii-Munți RO 168 D5
Rusinovo MK 181 F6
Rusinów PL 157 H3
Rusinowo PL 101 D10
Ruskeala RUS 145 B14
Ruskele S 123 B15
Ruski Krstur SRB 174 B3
Rusko FIN 142 D7
Rusko Selo SRB 166 F6
Ruskov SK 161 F3
Ruskträsk S 123 B15
Rusnė LT 150 F2
Rusokastro BG 183 E8
Rušona LV 149 D1
Rüsselsheim D 37 D10
Russeluft N 129 C11
Russelv N 128 D5
Russhaugen N 127 D11
Russi I 82 D5
Rust A 93 G11
Rustad N 111 B13
Rustad N 117 D14
Rustrel F 51 C9
Ruswil CH 43 F9
Ruszów PL 97 D8
Rutalahti FIN 139 G15
Rute E 69 B8
Rute S 109 D13
Rutesheim D 203 D6
Rüthen D 33 F10
Ruthin GB 26 E5
Rüti CH 43 F10
Rutigliano I 77 A8
Rutino I 76 C4
Rutka-Tartak PL 152 E6
Rutki-Kossaki PL 156 D6
Rutledal N 116 D2
Rutoši SRB 179 B8
Rutten NL 32 C5
Rütten-Scheid D 199 C9
Rutvik S 134 C8
Ruuhensuo FIN 137 C9
Ruuhijärvi FIN 143 E13
Ruuhijärvi FIN 143 C15
Ruukki FIN 135 E14
Ruunaa FIN 141 D14
Ruurlo NL 33 D6
Ruusa EST 147 E14
Ruusmäe EST 147 F14
Ruutana FIN 139 C17
Ruutana FIN 143 B11
Ruuvaoja FIN 131 C5
Ruvanaho FIN 131 F6
Ruvaslahti FIN 141 E12
Ruvo del Monte I 76 B5
Ruvo di Puglia I 77 A6
Ruy F 47 D7
Ruynes-en-Margeride F 46 E3
Rŭzhevo Konare BG 181 E10
Ruzhintsi BG 175 F10
Ružina LV 149 D2
Ružindol SK 162 E5
Ružomberok SK 163 C8
Ruzsa H 166 E4
Ry DK 102 C5
Ryabovo RUS 145 E10
Ryakhovo BG 177 F8
Ryakhovtsite BG 181 C11
Rybachiy RUS 150 F1
Rybany SK 162 D6
Rybczewice Drugie PL 160 A6
Rybitví CZ 93 B9
Rybnik PL 158 F6
Rybno PL 155 C11
Rybno PL 155 D8
Rybno PL 157 F2
Ryboły PL 156 E8
Rychliki PL 155 C8
Rychnov nad Kněžnou CZ 93 B10
Rychnowo PL 155 C9
Rychtal PL 158 D4
Rychvald CZ 162 B6
Rychwał PL 158 B5
Ryczywół PL 101 E11
Ryczywół PL 157 G4
Ryd S 104 C7
Rydaholm S 104 B6
Rydal S 107 D12
Rydboholm S 107 D12
Ryde DK 102 C3
Ryde GB 29 D12
Rydet S 107 E11
Rydöbruk S 103 B12
Rydsgård S 103 E13
Rydsnäs S 108 D6
Rydułtowy PL 158 F5
Rydzyna PL 97 C11
Rye GB 31 F10
Ryen N 106 C3
Ryeng N 130 D8
Ryes F 39 B10
Rygge N 111 D13
Ryggesbro S 119 D10
Ryglice PL 160 D3
Rygnestad N 110 D6
Ryhälä FIN 145 B9
Ryhall GB 27 F11
Ryjewo PL 154 C6
Rykene N 106 C4
Ryki PL 157 G5
Rymań PL 101 C9
Rymanów PL 161 D4
Rýmařov CZ 97 G12
Rymättylä FIN 142 E6
Rymnio GR 185 D6
Ryn PL 152 F4
Rynarzewo PL 154 D4
Rynkeby DK 102 E7
Ryńsk PL 154 D6
Ryomgård DK 102 C7
Rypefjord N 129 B12
Rypin PL 155 D7
Rysjedal N 116 D2
Ryslinge DK 102 E7
Ryssby S 104 B6
Rysum (Krummhörn) D 33 B8
Rytel PL 154 C4
Rytilahti FIN 131 E3
Rytinki FIN 136 C9
Rytky FIN 139 C17
Rytkynkylä FIN 135 F14
Ryttylä FIN 143 D12
Rytwiany PL 159 E11
Ržanovo MK 184 B4
Rząśnik PL 155 E11
Rzeczenica PL 101 C12
Rzeczyca PL 157 G2
Rzeczyca PL 158 C6
Rzegnowo PL 155 D10
Rzejowice PL 159 D8
Rzekuń PL 155 D11
Rzepiennik Strzyżewski PL 160 D3
Rzepin PL 97 B7
Rzerzęczyce PL 159 E7
Rzesznikowo PL 101 C8
Rzeszów PL 160 C5
Rzgów PL 159 C8
Rzgów Pierwszy PL 158 B5
Rzuców PL 157 H3

S

Sääksjärvi FIN 139 D11
Sääksjärvi FIN 143 C10
Sääksjärvi FIN 143 D13
Sääksmäki FIN 143 C11
Saal D 99 B12
Saal an der Donau D 91 E10
Saalbach-Hinterglemm A 89 B6
Saalburg D 91 B10
Saales F 43 D7
Saalfeld D 95 E9
Saalfelden am Steinernen Meer A 89 B6
Saanen CH 47 C11
Saarbrücken D 37 F7
Saarburg D 37 E7
Sääre EST 146 F4
Saarela FIN 141 C13
Saaren kk FIN 145 B12
Saarenkylä FIN 133 E15
Saaresmäki FIN 140 B7
Saari FIN 145 B12
Saariharju FIN 136 C9
Saarijärvi FIN 139 E14
Saari-Kämä FIN 135 B16
Saarikoski FIN 128 F7
Saarikoski FIN 135 C15
Saarikoski FIN 135 E14
Saarikylä FIN 137 D13
Saario FIN 141 F14
Saaripudas FIN 133 D11
Saariselkä FIN 131 B2
Saarivaara FIN 137 E14
Saarivaara FIN 141 F15
Saarlouis D 37 F7
Saarwellingen D 37 F7
Saas CH 87 D9
Sääse EST 147 C12
Saas Fee CH 84 A4
Saas Grund CH 84 A4
Sääskjärvi FIN 143 D15
Säävälä FIN 135 D16
Šabac SRB 174 D4
Sabadell E 59 D8
Săbăoani RO 169 C9
Sabarat F 49 D8
Sabatynivka UA 170 A6
Sabaudia I 78 E4
Sabbionetta I 82 C1
Sabero E 55 C9
Sabile LV 150 B5
Sabiñánigo E 48 E5
Sabinov SK 161 E3
Sabiote E 71 C6
Sables-d'Or-les-Pins F 39 C7
Sablé-sur-Sarthe F 39 E11
Sablet F 51 B9
Sabnie PL 157 E6
Sabres F 48 B4
Sabro DK 102 C6
Sabrosa P 54 F4
Sabugal P 61 D6
Sabugueiro P 60 D5
Sabugueiro P 66 B3
Săcădat RO 167 C9
Săcălășeni RO 168 B3
Săcălaz RO 167 F7
Sacañet E 64 E3
Săcășeni RO 167 C10
Sacavém P 66 B1
Sacecorbo E 63 C8
Sacedón E 63 D7
Săcel RO 168 B4
Săcel RO 168 E5
Săcele RO 171 E3
Săcele RO 177 B7
Săcelu RO 176 C3

Săceni RO 176 E6
Saceruela E 70 B3
Sachseln CH 86 D6
Sachsenberg (Lichtenfels) D 37 B11
Sachsenbrunn D 91 B8
Sachsenburg A 89 C7
Sachsenhagen D 33 D12
Sachsenhausen (Waldeck) D 33 F12
Sachsenheim D 43 C11
Sacile I 88 E5
Sacoșu Turcesc RO 175 B7
Sacović BIH 172 E6
Sacquenay F 42 E3
Sacramenia E 56 E4
Sacu RO 175 B9
Săcueni RO 167 C9
Săcuieu RO 167 D10
Sačurov SK 161 F4
Sada E 54 B3
Sádaba E 48 F3
Sadala EST 147 D13
Sadali I 80 D3
Saddell GB 20 D5
Sadina BG 182 C6
Sadki PL 101 D12
Sadkowice PL 157 G3
Sadkowo PL 101 C10
Sadlinki PL 154 C6
Sadova MD 170 C2
Sadova RO 168 B6
Sadova RO 176 F3
Sadove UA 170 E4
Sadovets BG 181 C9
Sadovo BG 181 E10
Sadowie PL 159 E11
Sadowne PL 155 E12
Sadská CZ 93 B7
Sadu RO 176 B4
Sădvaluspen S 125 D12
Sæbo N 110 B6
Sæbø N 116 B4
Sæbøvik N 110 C3
Sæby DK 103 D8
Sæby DK 106 E8
Sæd DK 102 F3
Saelices E 63 E7
Saelices de la Sal E 63 C8
Saelices del Rio E 55 C9
Saelices de Mayorga E 55 D9
Saerbeck D 33 D9
Særslev DK 102 D6
Sæter N 120 C8
Sætra N 120 E6
Sætre N 111 C13
Saeul L 36 E5
Sævareid N 110 B3
Safaalan TR 189 B9
Safara P 67 C5
Säffle S 107 A12
Saffré F 39 E8
Saffron Walden GB 31 C9
Sâg RO 167 C10
Şag RO 175 B7
Sagama I 80 C2
Sagard D 100 A5
Sage D 33 C10
Săgeata RO 177 C9
Sågen S 113 B11
Sagiada GR 184 E3
Sağırlar TR 189 F9
Sağlamtaş TR 189 C7
Sågmyra S 119 E9
Sagna RO 169 D10
Sagone F 53 G9
Sagres P 66 E2
Sagstua N 111 B15
Şagu RO 167 E7
Sagunto E 64 E4
Sagvåg N 110 C2
Ságvár H 165 C10
Sagy F 47 B7
Sahagún E 55 D9
Sahaidac MD 170 D3
Sahalahti FIN 143 C11
Sahankylä FIN 138 F8
Saharna Nouă MD 170 B3
Săhăteni RO 177 C8
Şahin TR 189 B6
Şahinli TR 188 D6
Sahl DK 102 C5
Sahrajärvi FIN 139 F14
Sahun E 49 E6
Sahune F 51 B9
Šahy SK 163 E7
Saiakopli EST 147 C12
Saighdinis GB 18 K2
Saija FIN 131 D5
Säijä FIN 143 C10
Saikari FIN 140 E7
Saillagouse-Llo F 49 F10
Saillans F 51 A9
Sail-sous-Couzan F 46 D4
Saimaanharju FIN 145 C9
Säimen FIN 141 F12
Sains-Richaumont F 35 E8
St Abbs GB 21 D12
St-Affrique F 50 C4
St-Agnan F 46 B4
St-Agnan-en-Vercors F 47 F7
St-Agnant F 44 D4
St-Agnant-de-Versillat F 45 C9
St Agnes GB 28 E4
St-Agrève F 46 E5
St-Aignan F 40 F5
St-Aignan-sur-Roë F 39 E9
St-Aigulin F 44 E5
St-Albain F 46 C6
St-Alban F 38 C6
St-Alban-Leysse F 47 D8
St Albans GB 31 D8
St-Alban-sur-Limagnole F 46 F3
St-Amand-en-Puisaye F 41 E9
St-Amand-les-Eaux F 35 D7
St-Amand-Longpré F 40 E5
St-Amand-Montrond F 45 B11
St-Amand-sur-Fion F 41 C12
St-Amans F 50 A5
St-Amans-des-Cots F 46 F2
St-Amans-Soult F 49 D10
St-Amant-de-Boixe F 45 D6
St-Amant-Roche-Savine F 46 D4
St-Amant-Tallende F 46 D3
St-Amarin F 43 E7
St-Ambroix F 51 B7
St-Amour F 47 C7
St-Andiol F 51 C8
St-André F 50 E4
St-André-de-Corcy F 47 D6
St-André-de-Cruzières F 51 B7
St-André-de-Cubzac F 44 F5
St-André-de-l'Eure F 40 C5
St-André-de-Sangonis F 50 C6
St-André-de-Valborgne F 51 B6
St-André-le-Gaz F 47 D8
St-André-les-Alpes F 52 D5
St-André-les-Vergers F 41 D11
St Andrews GB 21 C11
St-Angel F 45 D10
St Anne GBG 39 A7
St-Anthème F 46 D4
St-Antonin-Noble-Val F 49 B9
St-Août F 45 B9
St-Apollinaire F 42 F3
St-Arcons-d'Allier F 46 E4
St-Arnoult-en-Yvelines F 40 C6
St Asaph GB 26 E5
St-Astier F 45 E7
St-Astier F 45 F6
St Athan GB 29 C8
St-Auban F 52 D5
St-Auban-sur-l'Ouvèze F 51 B9
St-Aubin F 47 A7
St-Aubin-Château-Neuf F 41 E9
St-Aubin-d'Aubigné F 39 D8
St-Aubin-de-Blaye F 44 E4
St-Aubin-du-Cormier F 39 D9
St-Aubin-lès-Elbeuf F 34 F3
St-Aubin-sur-Mer F 39 B11
St-Aulaye F 45 E6
St Austell GB 28 E5
St-Avé F 38 E6
St-Avertin F 40 F4
St-Avold F 42 B6
St-Ay F 40 E6
St-Aygulf F 52 E5
St-Barthélemy-d'Agenais F 49 A6
St-Barthélemy-de-Vals F 46 E6
St-Bauzille-de-Putois F 51 C6
St-Béat F 49 E7
St-Beauzély F 50 B4
St Bees GB 26 C4
St-Benin-d'Azy F 46 A3
St-Benoît F 45 B6
St-Benoît F 49 D10
St-Benoît-du-Sault F 45 C8
St-Benoît-sur-Loire F 41 E7
St-Béron F 47 D8
St-Berthevin F 39 D10
St-Bertrand-de-Comminges F 49 D7
St-Blaise CH 47 A10
St-Blaise-la-Roche F 43 D7
St-Blin-Semilly F 42 D3
St-Boil F 46 B6
St-Bonnet-de-Bellac F 45 C7
St-Bonnet-de-Joux F 46 C5
St-Bonnet-en-Bresse F 47 B7
St-Bonnet-en-Champsaur F 52 B4
St-Bonnet-le-Château F 46 E5
St-Bonnet-le-Froid F 46 E5
St-Bonnet-sur-Gironde F 44 E4
St-Branchs F 40 F4
St Brelade GBJ 39 B7
St-Brevin-les-Pins F 39 F7
St-Briac-sur-Mer F 39 C7
St-Brice-en-Coglès F 39 D9
St Brides Major GB 29 C7
St-Brieuc F 38 C6
St-Bris-le-Vineux F 41 E10
St-Brisson F 41 F11
St-Broing-les-Moines F 41 E12
St Buryan GB 28 E3
St-Calais F 40 E4
St-Cannat F 51 C9
St-Céré F 45 F9
St-Cergue CH 47 C9
St-Cergues F 47 C9
St-Cernin F 45 E10
St-Chaffrey F 47 F10
St-Chamarand F 49 A8
St-Chamas F 51 C9
St-Chamond F 46 E6
St-Chaptes F 51 C7
St-Chef F 47 D7
St-Chély-d'Apcher F 46 F3
St-Chély-d'Aubrac F 50 A4
St-Chinian F 50 D4
St-Christol F 51 B9
St-Christol-lès-Alès F 51 B7
St-Christoly-Médoc F 44 E4
St-Christophe I 47 D11
St-Christophe-en-Bazelle F 40 F6
St-Christophe-en-Brionnais F 46 C5
St-Ciers-sur-Gironde F 44 E4
St-Cirq-Lapopie F 49 B9
St-Clair-du-Rhône F 46 E6
St-Clar F 49 C7
St-Claud F 45 D6
St-Claude F 47 C8
St Clears GB 28 B6
St-Clément F 41 D9
St-Clément F 42 C6
St-Clément F 45 E9
St Clement GBJ 39 B7
St-Clément-de-Rivière F 51 C6
St Columb Major GB 28 E5
St Combs GB 19 K13
St-Constant F 45 F10
St-Cosme-en-Vairais F 40 D3
St-Cricq-Chalosse F 48 C4
St-Cyprien F 45 F8
St-Cyprien F 49 B8
St-Cyprien F 50 E5
St-Cyr-sur-Loire F 40 F4
St-Cyr-sur-Mer F 51 D10
St Cyrus GB 21 B12
St David's GB 25 E12
St Day GB 28 E4
St-Denis F 41 C7
St-Denis-d'Anjou F 39 E11
St-Denis-de-Gastines F 39 D10
St-Denis-de-Jouhet F 45 B9
St-Denis-de-Pile F 44 F5
St-Denis-d'Oléron F 44 C3
St-Denis-en-Bugey F 47 D7
St-Denis-lès-Bourg F 47 C7
St Dennis GB 28 E5
St-Désert F 46 B6
St-Didier-en-Velay F 46 E5
St-Didier-sur-Chalaronne F 46 C6
St-Dié F 43 D6
St-Dier-d'Auvergne F 46 D3
St-Dizier F 41 C12
St-Dizier-Leyrenne F 45 C9
St-Dolay F 39 E7
St-Donat-sur-l'Herbasse F 47 E6
St-Doulchard F 41 F7
Ste-Adresse F 39 A12
Ste-Alvère F 45 F7
Ste-Bazeille F 49 A6
Ste-Cécile-les-Vignes F 51 B8
Ste-Croix CH 47 B10
Ste-Croix F 47 B7
Ste-Croix F 47 F7
Ste-Croix-Volvestre F 49 D8
Ste-Engrâce F 48 D4
Ste-Énimie F 50 B5
Ste-Eulalie d'Olt F 50 B4
Ste-Eulalie-en-Born F 48 B3
Ste-Feyre F 45 C9
Ste-Foy-de-Peyrolières F 49 D8
Ste-Foy-la-Grande F 45 F6
Ste-Foy-l'Argentière F 46 D5
Ste-Foy-lès-Lyon F 46 D6
Ste-Foy-Tarentaise F 47 D10
Ste-Geneviève F 34 F5
Ste-Geneviève-sur-Argence F 46 F2
St-Égrève F 47 E8
Ste-Hélène F 44 F4
Ste-Hermine F 44 B3
Ste-Livrade-sur-Lot F 49 B7
St-Élix-le-Château F 49 D8
St-Élix-Theux F 49 D6
Ste-Lizaigne F 45 A10
St-Éloy-les-Mines F 46 C2
Ste-Lucie-de-Tallano F 53 H10
Ste-Marguerite F 202 E2
Ste-Marie F 50 E5
Ste-Marie-aux-Mines F 43 D7
Ste-Maure-de-Peyriac F 49 B6
Ste-Maure-de-Touraine F 40 F4
Ste-Maxime F 52 E5
Ste-Menehould F 41 B12
Ste-Mère-Église F 39 B9
St-Émiland F 46 B5
St Endellion GB 28 D5
St Enoder GB 28 E5
Ste-Orse F 45 E8
Ste-Pazanne F 39 F8
Ste-Radegonde F 44 B5
St-Erme-Outre-et-Ramecourt F 35 E8
St Erth GB 28 E4
Saintes F 44 D4
Ste-Sabine F 41 F12
Ste-Savine F 41 D11
Ste-Sévère-sur-Indre F 45 C10
St-Esteben F 48 D3
St-Estèphe F 44 E4
St-Estève F 50 E4
Ste-Suzanne F 39 D11
St-Étienne F 46 E5
St-Étienne-de-Baïgorry F 48 D3
St-Étienne-de-Fontbellon F 51 A7
St-Étienne-de-Fursac F 45 C9
St-Étienne-de-Montluc F 39 F8
St-Étienne-de-St-Geoirs F 47 E7
St-Étienne-de-Tinée F 52 C5
St-Étienne-du-Bois F 47 C7
St-Étienne-du-Rouvray F 34 F3
St-Étienne-en-Dévoluy F 51 A10
St-Étienne-les-Orgues F 51 B10
St-Étienne-lès-Remiremont F 42 D6
St-Étienne-Vallée-Française F 51 B6
Ste-Tulle F 51 C10
Ste-Vertu F 41 E10
St-Fargeau F 41 E9
St-Félicien F 46 E6
St-Félix-Lauragais F 49 D9
St Fergus GB 19 K13
St-Ferme F 44 F6
Saintfield GB 23 D11
St Fillans GB 21 C8
St-Firmin F 42 D5
St Firmin F 47 F9
St-Flavy F 41 D10
St-Florent F 53 F10
St-Florent-des-Bois F 44 B3
St-Florentin F 41 D10
St-Florent-le-Vieil F 39 F9
St-Florent-sur-Cher F 45 B10
St-Flour F 46 E3
St-Flovier F 45 B8
St-Fons F 46 D6
St-Fort-sur-Gironde F 44 E4
St-Frajou F 49 D7
St-François-Longchamp F 47 E9
St-Front-de-Pradoux F 45 E6
St-Fulgent F 44 B3
St-Galmier F 46 D5
St-Gaudens F 49 D7
St-Gaultier F 45 B8
St-Gein F 48 C5
St-Gély-du-Fesc F 51 C6
St-Genest-Malifaux F 46 E5
St-Geniez F 52 C4
St-Geniez-d'Olt F 50 B4
St-Genis-de-Saintonge F 44 E4
St-Genis-Laval F 46 D6
St-Genis-Pouilly F 47 C9
St-Genix-sur-Guiers F 47 D8
St-Genou F 45 B8
St-Geoire-en-Valdaine F 47 E8
St-Georges-Buttavent F 39 D10
St-Georges-d'Aurac F 46 E4
St-Georges-de-Commiers F 47 E8
St-Georges-de-Didonne F 44 D4
St-Georges-de-Luzençon F 50 B4
St-Georges-de-Mons F 46 D2
St-Georges-de-Reneins F 46 C6
St-Georges-des-Groseillers F 39 C10
St-Georges-d'Oléron F 44 D3
St-Georges-du-Vièvre F 34 F2
St-Georges-en-Couzan F 46 D4
St-Georges-lès-Baillargeaux F 45 B6
St-Georges-sur-Baulche F 41 E10
St-Georges-sur-Cher F 40 F5
St-Georges-sur-Loire F 39 F10
St-Geours-de-Maremne F 48 C3
St-Gérand-le-Puy F 46 C4
St-Germain-Chassenay F 46 B3
St-Germain-de-Calberte F 51 B6
St-Germain-de-la-Coudre F 40 D4
St-Germain-des-Fossés F 46 C3
St-Germain-d'Esteuil F 44 E4
St-Germain-du-Bel-Air F 49 A8
St-Germain-du-Bois F 47 B7
St-Germain-du-Corbéis F 39 D12
St-Germain-du-Plain F 47 B6
St-Germain-du-Puy F 41 F7
St-Germain-du-Teil F 50 B5
St-Germain-en-Laye F 40 C7
St-Germain-Laval F 46 D5
St-Germain-Lembron F 46 E3
St-Germain-les-Belles F 45 D8
St-Germain-les-Vergnes F 45 E9
St-Germain-l'Herm F 46 E4
St Germans GB 28 E6
St-Germé F 48 C5
St-Gervais F 44 B1
St-Gervais F 47 E7
St-Gervais-d'Auvergne F 46 C2
St-Gervais-la-Forêt F 40 E5
St-Gervais-les-Bains F 47 D10
St-Gervais-les-Trois-Clochers F 45 B6
St-Gervais-sur-Mare F 50 C5
St-Géry F 49 B9
St-Ghislain B 35 D8
St-Gildas-de-Rhuys F 38 E6
St-Gildas-des-Bois F 39 E7
St-Gilles F 51 C7
St-Gilles-Croix-de-Vie F 44 B2
St-Gingolph F 47 C10
St-Girons F 49 E8
St-Girons-Plage F 48 C3
St-Gobain F 35 E7
St-Guénolé F 38 E3
St-Guilhem-le-Désert F 51 C6
St-Haon-le-Châtel F 46 C4
St-Héand F 46 D5
St Helens GB 26 E6
St Helier GBJ 39 B7
St-Herblain F 39 F8
St-Hilaire F 49 D10
St-Hilaire-de-Brethmas F 51 B7
St-Hilaire-de-Riez F 44 B2
St-Hilaire-des-Loges F 44 C4
St-Hilaire-de-Villefranche F 44 D4
St-Hilaire-du-Harcouët F 39 C9
St-Hilaire-du-Rosier F 47 E7
St-Hilaire-Fontaine F 46 B4
St-Hilaire-le-Grand F 41 B11
St-Hilaire-St-Florent F 39 F11
St-Hippolyte F 43 D7
St-Hippolyte F 43 F6
St-Hippolyte-du-Fort F 51 C6
St-Honoré-les-Bains F 46 B4
St-Hostien F 46 E5
St-Hubert B 35 D11
St-Imier CH 43 F6
St-Ismier F 47 E8
St Ive GB 28 E6
St Ives GB 28 E4
St Ives GB 31 C8
St-Izaire F 50 C4
St-Jacques-de-la-Lande F 39 D8
St-James F 39 C9
St-Jean F 49 C8
St-Jean-Bonnefonds F 46 E5
St-Jean-Brévelay F 38 E6
St-Jean-d'Angély F 44 D4
St-Jean-d'Assé F 39 D12
St-Jean-de-Bournay F 47 D7
St-Jean-de-Braye F 40 E6
St-Jean-de-Daye F 39 B9
St-Jean-de-la-Ruelle F 40 E6
St-Jean-de-Losne F 42 F3
St-Jean-de-Luz F 48 D2
St-Jean-de-Marsacq F 48 C3
St-Jean-de-Mauréjols-et-Avéjan F 51 B7
St-Jean-de-Maurienne F 47 E9
St-Jean-de-Monts F 44 B1
St-Jean-de-Sixt F 47 D9
St-Jean-de-Védas F 51 C6
St-Jean-d'Illac F 44 F4
St-Jean-du-Bruel F 50 B5
St-Jean-du-Falga F 49 D9
St-Jean-du-Gard F 51 B6
St-Jean-le-Centenier F 51 A8
St-Jean-Pied-de-Port F 48 D3
St-Jean-Poutge F 49 C6
St-Jean-sur-Erve F 39 D11
St-Jeoire F 47 C9
St-Jeure-d'Ay F 46 E6
St-Jeures F 46 E5
St-Joachim F 39 F7
St John GBJ 39 B7
St John's Chapel GB 21 F12
St John's Town of Dalry GB 21 E8
St-Jores F 39 B9
St-Jorioz F 47 D9
St-Jory F 49 C8
St-Jouan-des-Guérets F 39 C8
St-Jouin-Bruneval F 39 A12
St-Jouin-de-Marnes F 44 B5
St-Julien F 47 C7
St-Julien F 49 D8
St-Julien-Beychevelle F 44 E4
St-Julien-Boutières F 46 F5
St-Julien-Chapteuil F 46 E5
St-Julien-de-Concelles F 39 F9
St-Julien-de-Vouvantes F 39 E9
St-Julien-du-Sault F 41 D9
St-Julien-du-Verdon F 52 D5
St-Julien-en-Beauchêne F 51 A10
St-Julien-en-Born F 48 B3
St-Julien-en-Genevois F 47 C9
St-Julien-l'Ars F 45 B7
St-Junien F 45 D7
St-Just F 51 B8
St Just GB 28 E3
St-Just-en-Chaussée F 34 E5
St-Just-en-Chevalet F 46 D4
St-Just-Ibarre F 48 D3
St-Justin F 48 C5
St Just in Roseland GB 28 E4
St-Just-la-Pendue F 46 D5
St-Just-Luzac F 44 D3
St-Just-Sauvage F 41 C10
St-Just-St-Rambert F 46 E5
St Keverne GB 28 E4
St-Lambert-des-Levées F 39 F11
St-Lary-Soulan F 49 E6
St-Laurent F 52 C5
St-Laurent-Bretagne F 48 D5
St-Laurent-d'Aigouze F 51 C7
St-Laurent-de-Carnols F 51 B8
St-Laurent-de-Cerdans F 50 F4
St-Laurent-de-Chamousset F 46 D5
St-Laurent-de-la-Cabrerisse F 50 D4
St-Laurent-de-la-Salanque F 50 E4
St-Laurent-de-Neste F 49 D6
St-Laurent-des-Autels F 39 F9
St-Laurent-du-Pont F 47 E8
St-Laurent-du-Var F 53 D6
St-Laurent-en-Caux F 34 E2
St-Laurent-en-Grandvaux F 47 B8
St-Laurent-les-Bains F 51 A6
St-Laurent-Médoc F 44 E4
St-Laurent-Nouan F 40 E6
St-Laurent-sur-Gorre F 45 D7
St-Laurent-sur-Sèvre F 44 B4
St-Léger B 35 E12
St-Léger-des-Vignes F 46 B3
St-Léger-en-Yvelines F 40 C6
St-Léger-sous-Beuvray F 46 B5
St-Léonard F 43 D6
St-Léonard-de-Noblat F 45 D8
St Leonards GB 29 D11
St-Lizier F 49 D8
St-Lô F 39 B9
St-Lon-les-Mines F 48 C3
St-Loubès F 44 F5
St-Louis-lès-Bitche F 202 D3
St-Loup-de-la-Salle F 46 B6
St-Loup-Lamairé F 44 B5
St-Loup-sur-Semouse F 42 E5
St-Lubin-des-Joncherets F 40 C5
St-Lunaire F 39 C7
St-Lupicin F 47 C8
St-Lyé F 41 D11
St-Lys F 49 C8
St-Macaire F 48 A5
St-Macaire-en-Mauges F 39 F10
St-Magne F 48 A4
St-Magne-de-Castillon F 44 F5
St-Maime F 51 C10
St-Maixent-l'École F 44 C5
St-Malo F 39 C7
St-Malo-de-la-Lande F 39 B8
St-Mamert-du-Gard F 51 C7
St-Marcel F 40 B5
St-Marcel F 45 B9
St-Marcel F 46 B6
St-Marcel-d'Ardèche F 51 B8
St-Marcel-lès-Annonay F 46 E6
St-Marcel-lès-Sauzet F 51 A8
St-Marcel-lès-Valence F 47 F6
St-Marcellin F 47 E7
St-Marc-sur-Seine F 41 E12
St-Mards-en-Othe F 41 D10
St Margaret's Hope GB 19 H11
St-Marsal F 50 E4
St-Mars-d'Outillé F 40 E3
St-Mars-du-Désert F 39 F9
St-Mars-la-Brière F 40 D3
St-Mars-la-Jaille F 39 E9
St-Martial F 51 B6
St-Martial-de-Nabirat F 45 F8
St-Martial-de-Valette F 45 D7
St-Martin F 51 C10
St Martin GBG 38 B6
St Martin GBJ 39 B7
St-Martin-Boulogne F 31 F12
St-Martin-d'Ablois F 41 B10
St-Martin-d'Arrossa F 48 D3
St-Martin-d'Auxigny F 41 F7
St-Martin-de-Belleville F 47 E10
St-Martin-de-Castillon F 51 C10
St-Martin-de-Crau F 51 C8
St-Martin-de-Landelles F 39 C9
St-Martin-de-Londres F 51 C6
St-Martin-d'Entraunes F 52 C5
St-Martin-de-Ré F 44 C3
St-Martin-des-Besaces F 39 B10
St-Martin-des-Champs F 38 C4
St-Martin-de-Seignanx F 48 C3
St-Martin-de-Valamas F 46 F5
St-Martin-de-Valgalgues F 51 B7
St-Martin-d'Hères F 47 E8
St-Martin-d'Oney F 48 C4
St-Martin-du-Mont F 47 C7
St-Martin-du-Var F 53 D6
St-Martin-en-Bresse F 47 B7
St-Martin-le-Beau F 40 F4
St-Martin-sur-Ouanne F 41 E9
St-Martin-Valmeroux F 45 E10
St-Martin-Vésubie F 53 C6
St-Martory F 49 D7
St Mary's GB 19 H11
St-Mathieu F 45 D7
St-Mathurin F 44 B2
St-Maur F 45 B9
St-Maurice CH 47 C10
St-Maurice-de-Lignon F 46 E5
St-Maurice-des-Lions F 45 D7
St-Maurice-la-Souterraine F 45 C8
St-Maurice-l'Exil F 46 E6
St-Maurice-Navacelles F 51 C6
St-Maurin F 49 B7
St Mawes GB 28 E4
St-Max F 42 C5
St-Maximin-la-Ste-Baume F 51 D10
St-Médard-en-Jalles F 44 F4
St-Méen-le-Grand F 39 D7
St-Méloir-des-Ondes F 39 C8
St-Memmie F 41 C11
St-Menoux F 46 B3
St Merryn GB 28 D5
St-Mesmin F 41 D10
St-Mesmin F 45 E8
St-Michel F 35 E9
St-Michel F 44 D6
St-Michel F 49 D6
St-Michel-Chef-Chef F 39 F7
St-Michel-de-Castelnau F 48 B5
St-Michel-de-Maurienne F 47 E9
St-Michel-en-l'Herm F 44 C3
St-Michel-sur-Meurthe F 43 D6
St-Mihiel F 42 C4
St Monans GB 21 C11
St-Montant F 51 B8
St-Nabord F 42 D6
St-Nauphary F 49 C8
St-Nazaire F 39 F7
St-Nazaire-le-Désert F 51 A9
St-Nectaire F 46 D2
St Neots GB 31 C8
St-Nicolas B 199 D7
St-Nicolas F 34 D6
St-Nicolas-d'Aliermont F 34 E3
St-Nicolas-de-la-Grave F 49 B8
St-Nicolas-de-Port F 42 C5
St-Nicolas-de-Redon F 39 E7
St-Nicolas-du-Pélem F 38 D5
St-Oedenrode NL 32 E4
St-Omer F 34 C5
St-Orens-de-Gameville F 49 C9
St-Ost F 49 D6
St Osyth GB 31 D11
St-Ouen F 34 D5
St-Ouen F 40 E5
St Ouen GBJ 39 B7
St-Ouen-des-Toits F 39 D10
St-Pair-sur-Mer F 39 C8
St-Palais F 48 D3
St-Palais-sur-Mer F 44 D3
St-Pal-de-Chalancon F 46 E4
St-Pal-de-Mons F 46 E5
St-Pantaléon F 46 B5
St-Pantaléon F 49 B8
St-Papoul F 49 D10
St-Pardoux-Isaac F 49 A6
St-Pardoux-la-Rivière F 45 E7
St-Parize-le-Châtel F 46 B3
St-Parres-lès-Vaudes F 41 D11
St-Paterne F 39 D12
St-Paterne-Racan F 40 E3
St-Paul F 52 B5
St-Paul-Cap-de-Joux F 49 C9
St-Paul-de-Fenouillet F 49 E11
St-Paul-de-Jarrat F 49 E9
St-Paul-en-Born F 48 B3
St-Paul-en-Forêt F 52 D5
St-Paul-et-Valmalle F 51 C6
St-Paulien F 46 E4
St-Paul-le-Jeune F 51 B7
St-Paul-lès-Dax F 48 C3
St-Paul-lès-Durance F 51 C10
St-Paul-Trois-Châteaux F 51 B8
St-Pé-de-Bigorre F 48 D5
St-Pée-sur-Nivelle F 48 D2
St-Péray F 46 F6
St-Père F 41 F10
St-Père-en-Retz F 39 F7
St Peter in the Wood GBG 38 B6
St Peter Port GBG 38 B6
St-Phal F 41 D10
St-Philbert-de-Bouaine F 44 B2
St-Philbert-de-Grand-Lieu F 44 A2
St-Pierre I 47 D11
St-Pierre-d'Albigny F 47 D9
St-Pierre-de-Chignac F 45 E7
St-Pierre-de-Côle F 45 E7
St-Pierre-de-la-Fage F 50 C5
St-Pierre-de-Maillé F 45 B7
St-Pierre-de-Plesguen F 39 D8
St-Pierre-des-Champs F 50 D4
St-Pierre-des-Corps F 40 F4
St-Pierre-des-Échaubrognes F 44 A4
St-Pierre-des-Landes F 39 D9
St-Pierre-des-Nids F 39 D11
St-Pierre-de-Trivisy F 49 C10
St-Pierre-d'Irube F 48 D3
St-Pierre-d'Oléron F 44 D3
St-Pierre-du-Chemin F 44 B4
St-Pierre-du-Mont F 48 C4
St-Pierre-Église F 39 A9
St-Pierre-en-Faucigny F 47 C9
St-Pierre-en-Port F 34 E1
St-Pierre-le-Moûtier F 46 B3
St-Pierre-lès-Elbeuf F 34 F3
St-Pierre-lès-Nemours F 41 D8
St-Pierre-Montlimart F 39 F9
St-Pierre-Quiberon F 38 E5
St-Pierre-sur-Dives F 39 B11
St-Plancard F 49 D7
St-Pois F 39 C9
St-Poix F 39 E9
St-Pol-de-Léon F 38 C4
St-Pol-sur-Mer F 34 B5
St-Pol-sur-Ternoise F 34 D5
St-Pompont F 45 F8
St-Pons F 52 C5
St-Pons-de-Thomières F 50 D4
St-Porchaire F 44 D4
St-Pourçain-sur-Sioule F 46 C3
St-Prex CH 47 C9
St-Priest F 46 D6
St-Priest-de-Champs F 46 D2
St-Priest-Laprugne F 46 D4
St-Priest-Taurion F 45 D8
St-Privat F 45 E10
St-Privat-d'Allier F 46 F4
St-Prix F 46 C4
St-Projet F 49 B9
St-Puy F 49 C6
St-Quentin F 35 E7
St-Quentin-la-Poterie F 51 B7
St-Quirin F 43 C7
St-Rambert-d'Albon F 46 E6
St-Rambert-en-Bugey F 47 D7
St-Raphaël F 52 E5
St-Remèze F 51 B7
St-Rémy F 46 B6
St-Rémy-de-Provence F 51 C8
St-Remy-en-Bouzemont-St-Genest-et-Isson F 41 C12
St-Rémy-sur-Avre F 40 C5
St-Rémy-sur-Durolle F 46 D4
St-Renan F 38 D2
St-Révérien F 41 F10
St-Rhemy I 47 D11
St-Riquier F 34 D4
St-Romain-en-Gal F 46 D6
St-Romain-sur-Cher F 40 F5
St-Romans F 47 E7
St-Rome-de-Cernon F 50 B4
St-Rome-de-Tarn F 50 B4
St-Saëns F 34 E3
St Sampson GBG 38 B6
St-Saturnin-lès-Apt F 51 C9
St-Saud-Lacoussière F 45 D7
St-Saulge F 41 F10
St-Sauves-d'Auvergne F 45 D11
St-Sauveur F 38 D3
St-Sauveur F 42 E5
St-Sauveur-de-Montagut F 46 F6
St-Sauveur-en-Puisaye F 41 E9
St-Sauveur-Gouvernet F 51 B9
St-Sauveur-Lendelin F 39 B9
St-Sauveur-le-Vicomte F 39 B8
St-Sauveur-sur-Tinée F 52 C6
St-Sauvy F 49 C7
St-Savin F 44 E5
St-Savin F 45 B7
St-Savinien F 44 D4
St Saviour GBJ 39 B7
St-Sébastien-de-Morsent F 40 B5
St-Sébastien-sur-Loire F 39 F8
St-Seine-l'Abbaye F 41 F12
St-Sernin F 51 A7
St-Sernin-sur-Rance F 50 C4
St-Seurin-sur-l'Isle F 44 E5
St-Sever F 48 C4
St-Sever-Calvados F 39 C9
St-Siméon-de-Bressieux F 47 E7
St-Simon F 35 E7
St-Simon F 45 F11
St-Sorlin-d'Arves F 47 E9
St-Souplets F 41 B8
St-Sulpice F 49 C9
St-Sulpice-Laurière F 45 C8
St-Sulpice-les-Champs F 45 D10
St-Sulpice-les-Feuilles F 45 C8
St-Sulpice-sur-Lèze F 49 D8
St-Sulpice-sur-Risle F 40 C4
St-Sylvain F 39 B11
St-Symphorien F 46 F4
St-Symphorien F 48 B5
St-Symphorien-de-Lay F 46 D5
St-Symphorien-sur-Coise F 46 D5
St Teath GB 28 D5
St-Thégonnec F 38 C4
St-Thibéry F 50 D5
St-Thiébault F 42 D4
St-Thurien F 38 E4
St-Trivier-de-Courtes F 47 C7
St-Trivier-sur-Moignans F 46 C6
St-Trojan-les-Bains F 44 D3
St-Tropez F 52 E5
St-Uze F 46 E6
St-Valérien F 41 D9
St-Valery-en-Caux F 34 E2
St-Valery-sur-Somme F 34 D4
St-Vallier F 46 B5
St-Vallier F 46 E6
St-Vallier-de-Thiey F 52 D5
St-Varent F 44 B5
St-Vaury F 45 C9
St-Victor F 46 E6
St-Victor-de-Cessieu F 47 D7
St-Victoret F 51 D9
St-Victor-la-Coste F 51 B8
St Vigeans GB 21 B11
St-Vigor-le-Grand F 39 B10
St-Vincent I 84 B4
St-Vincent-de-Connezac F 45 E6
St-Vincent-de-Paul F 48 C4
St-Vincent-les-Forts F 52 C4
St-Vit F 42 F4
St-Vite F 49 B7
St-Vith B 36 D6
St-Vivien-de-Médoc F 44 E3
St-Xandre F 44 C3
St-Yan F 46 C5
St-Ybars F 49 D8
St-Yorre F 46 C3
St-Yrieix-la-Perche F 45 D8
St-Yrieix-sur-Charente F 45 D6
St-Yvy F 38 E4
St-Zacharie F 51 D10
Sainville F 40 D6
Saissac F 49 D10
Saittarova S 132 D8
Saivomuotka S 132 B10
Saïx F 49 C10
Sajaniemi FIN 143 D11
Šajince SRB 180 E5
Šajkaš SRB 174 C5
Sajóbábony H 161 G2
Sajókaza H 161 G2
Sajókeresztúr H 161 G2
Sajólád H 161 G2
Sajószentpéter H 161 G2
Sajószöged H 161 H3
Sajóvámos H 161 G2
Säjvis S 135 C11
Saka LV 150 C2
Sakajärvi S 132 D5
Sakalishcha BY 149 E5
Sakaravaara FIN 137 E12
Šakiai LT 152 D7
Säkinmäki FIN 139 F16
Sakızköy TR 189 B7
Säkkilä FIN 137 B13
Sakshaug N 121 D10
Saksild DK 102 D6
Sakskøbing DK 99 A11
Saksun FO 18 A2
Saku EST 147 C9
Šakule SRB 174 C6
Säkylä FIN 142 C7
Šakyna LT 150 D6
Sala LV 150 C7
Sala LV 151 C11
Sala S 114 C7
Šaľa SK 162 E5
Salaca LV 147 F10
Sălacea RO 167 C9
Salacgrīva LV 147 F8
Sala Consilina I 76 C5
Salagnac F 45 E8
Salahmi FIN 140 C7
Salaise-sur-Sanne F 46 E6
Salakas LT 151 E12
Salakos GR 197 D7
Salakovac BIH 173 F8
Salamajärvi FIN 139 D13
Salamanca E 61 C9
Salamina GR 191 D7
Salandra I 77 B6
Salanki FIN 133 B13
Salantai LT 150 D3
Salar E 69 B8
Sălard RO 167 C9
Salardu E 49 E7
Salarlı TR 188 B6
Salas E 55 B7
Salaš SRB 175 E9
Salas de los Infantes E 56 D5
Salash BG 180 B6
Salaspils LV 151 C8
Sălașu de Sus RO 175 C10
Sălățig RO 167 C11
Sălătrucel RO 176 C4
Sălătrucu RO 176 C5
Salaunes F 44 F4
Salberg S 123 D16
Salbertrand I 47 E10
Sälboda S 113 C8
Salbohed S 114 C6
Salbris F 40 F7
Salbu N 116 D2
Salcea RO 169 B8
Salching D 91 E12
Salcia RO 175 E10
Salcia RO 176 F5
Salcia RO 177 C8
Salcia Tudor RO 177 C10
Sălciile RO 177 D8
Šalčininkai LT 153 E11
Šalčininkėliai LT 153 E11
Sălciua RO 167 E11
Salcombe GB 29 E7
Sălcuța MD 170 D4
Sălcuța RO 176 E2
Saldaña E 55 C10
Saldenburg D 92 E4
Saldón E 63 D10
Salduero E 56 E6
Saldus LV 150 C4
Sale GB 27 E7
Sale I 53 B9
Saleby S 107 C13
Salem D 43 E11

Salem D 99 C9
Salemi I 74 D2
Salen GB 20 B5
Salen GB 20 B5
Sälen S 118 D5
Salernes F 52 D4
Salerno I 76 B3
Salers F 45 E10
Salettes F 46 F4
Saleux F 34 E5
Salford GB 27 E7
Şalgamlı TR 189 B6
Salgótarján H 163 E9
Salgueiro P 60 E5
Salhus N 110 A2
Sali HR 172 E3
Salice Salentino I 77 C9
Saliceto I 53 C8
Saliena LV 151 C7
Saliena LV 151 E13
Salies-de-Béarn F 48 D4
Salies-du-Salat F 49 D7
Salignac-Eyvignes F 45 F8
Salillas de Jalón E 57 E9
Salinas E 55 A8
Salinas E 72 D3
Salinas del Manzano E 63 D9
Salinas de Pamplona E 48 E2
Salinas de Pisuerga E 56 C3
Salin-de-Giraud F 51 D8
Saline di Volterra I 82 F2
Sälinkää FIN 143 D13
Salins F 45 E10
Salins-les-Bains F 47 B8
Salir P 66 E3
Salisbury GB 29 C11
Săliște RO 168 F3
Săliștea RO 167 F11
Săliștea de Sus RO 168 B4
Salka SK 163 F7
Sal'kove UA 170 A5
Sall DK 102 C5
Salla EST 147 D12
Salla FIN 131 E5
Sallanches F 47 D10
Sallent E 59 D7
Sallent de Gállego E 48 E5
Salles F 48 A4
Salles-Curan F 50 B4
Salles-d'Angles F 44 D5
Salles-la-Source F 49 B11
Salles-sur-l'Hers F 49 D9
Sallgast D 96 C5
Sälliku EST 147 C14
Sallingberg A 93 F8
Sallins IRL 23 F9
Sällsjö S 121 E15
Sallypark IRL 24 C6
Salme EST 146 E4
Salmerón E 63 C8
Salmeroncillos de Abajo E 63 C7
Salmi FIN 139 E10
Salmi S 135 B10
Salmijärvi FIN 137 D10
Salminen FIN 137 B12
Salminen FIN 140 E8
Salmivaara FIN 131 E4
Salmiyarvi RUS 130 E8
Salmoral E 61 C10
Salmtal D 37 E7
Salnava LV 149 C3
Salnö S 115 C11
Salo FIN 143 E9
Salò I 85 B10
Salobre E 71 B7
Salobreña E 69 C9
Saločiai LT 151 D8
Saloinen FIN 135 E12
Salon F 41 C11
Salon-de-Provence F 51 C9
Salonkylä FIN 139 C11
Salonpää FIN 135 E14
Salonta RO 167 D8
Salorino E 61 F6
Salornay-sur-Guye F 46 B6
Salorno I 85 A11
Salou E 58 E6
Salouël F 34 E5
Šalovci SLO 164 C6
Salsåker S 123 F14
Salsbruket N 121 B11
Salsburgh GB 21 D9
Salses-le-Château F 50 E4
Sălsig RO 167 B11
Salsomaggiore Terme I 85 D8
Salt E 59 D9
Saltara I 83 E6
Saltash GB 28 E6
Saltburn-by-the-Sea GB 27 B10
Saltcoats GB 20 D7
Salteras E 67 E7
Salthill IRL 22 F4
Salto P 54 E4
Saltoniškės LT 153 D11
Saltrød N 106 C4
Saltsjöbaden S 115 D10
Saltum DK 106 E6
Saltvik FIN 115 B14
Saltvik S 119 C13
Saludecio I 83 E6
Saluggia I 84 C5
Salur TR 189 D8
Salussola I 84 C5
Saluzzo I 53 B6
Salva RO 168 C4
Salvacañete E 63 D10
Salvagnac F 49 C9
Salvaleón E 67 B6
Salvaterra de Magos P 66 A2
Salvaterra do Extremo P 61 E7
Salvatierra E 48 E1
Salvatierra de los Barros E 67 C6
Salvatierra de Santiago E 61 F8
Salve I 77 D10
Salviac F 49 A8
Sály H 161 H2
Salzburg A 89 A7
Salzgitter D 95 B7
Salzhausen D 99 D8
Salzhemmendorf D 94 B6
Salzkotten D 33 E11
Salzmünde D 95 C10
Salzwedel D 99 E10
Salzweg D 92 E4
Samadet F 48 C5
Samaila SRB 174 F6
Samarate I 84 B6
Samarica HR 165 E7
Samarina GR 184 D5
Samarinești RO 175 D11
Samassi I 80 E2
Samatan F 49 D7
Sambade P 55 F6
Sâmbăta RO 167 D9
Sambiase I 75 B9
Sambir UA 161 D7
Samboal E 56 F3
Samborzec PL 159 E12
Sambuca di Sicilia I 74 D3
Sambuca Pistoiese I 82 D3
Sambuco I 52 C6
Sâmbureşti RO 176 D4
Samedan CH 87 D9
Sameiro P 60 D6
Samer F 31 F12
Sames E 55 B9
Sami GR 190 C2
Samil P 55 E6
Samir de los Caños E 55 E7
Şamlı TR 189 E8
Sammakko S 132 E7
Sammakkola FIN 141 C10
Sammaljoki FIN 143 C9
Sammatti FIN 143 E10
Sammichele di Bari I 77 B7
Samnaun CH 87 D10
Samobor HR 164 E5
Samoëns F 47 C10
Samões P 54 F5
Samokov BG 181 E8
Samokov MK 180 F3
Samolaco I 85 A7
Samora Correia P 66 B2
Šamorín SK 162 E4
Samos E 54 C5
Samos GR 193 D8
Samoš SRB 175 C6
Samothraki GR 187 D9
Samovodene BG 182 C5
Samper de Calanda E 58 E3
Sampeyre I 53 B6
Sampierdarena I 53 C9
Sampieri I 75 F6
Sampigny F 42 C4
Şamşud RO 167 C10
Samswegen D 95 B10
Samtens D 100 B4
Samuelsberg N 128 D6
Samugheo I 80 D2
Samuil BG 183 B7
Samuilovo BG 182 E5
San Adrián E 48 F2
San Agustín de Guadalix E 62 C5
Sanaigmore GB 20 D4
San Amaro E 54 D3
Sânandrei RO 167 F7
San Andrés del Rabanedo E 55 C8
San Antolín E 55 B6
San Antonio E 63 E10
Sanary-sur-Mer F 51 D10
San Asensio E 56 C6
San Bartolomé de las Abiertas E 62 E3
San Bartolomé de la Torre E 67 E5
San Bartolomé de Pinares E 62 C3
San Bartolomeo al Mare I 53 D8
San Bartolomeo in Galdo I 76 A4
San Basilio I 80 D3
San Benedetto dei Marsi I 78 C5
San Benedetto del Tronto I 78 B5
San Benedetto Po I 82 B2
San Benito E 70 B3
San Benito de la Contienda E 67 B5
San Biagio di Callalta I 88 E5
San Biagio Platani I 74 D4
San Bonifacio I 82 B3
San Buono I 79 D7
San Candido I 88 C5
San Carlos del Valle E 71 B6
San Casciano dei Bagni I 78 B1
San Casciano in Val di Pesa I 82 E3
San Cataldo I 74 E4
San Cataldo I 77 C10
San Cebrián de Castro E 55 E8
Sâncel RO 168 E3
Sancergues F 41 F8
Sancerre F 41 F8
San Cesario sul Panaro I 82 C3
Sancey-le-Grand F 42 F6
Sancheville F 40 D6
Sanchidrián E 62 C3
San Chirico Nuovo I 76 B6
San Chirico Raparo I 76 C6
San Cibrão das Viñas E 54 D4
San Cipirello I 74 D3
San Cipriano d'Aversa I 76 B2
San Clemente E 63 F8
San Clodio E 54 D5
Sancoins F 46 B2
San Colombano al Lambro I 85 C7
San Cosme E 54 A5
San Costantino Albanese I 77 C6
San Costanzo I 83 E7
Sâncrăieni RO 169 E7
Sâncraiu RO 167 D10
Sâncraiu de Mureș RO 168 D5
San Cristóbal de Entreviñas E 55 D8
San Cristóbal de la Vega E 62 B3
Sancti-Spíritus E 61 C8
Sancti-Spíritus E 67 B9
Sand N 110 D4
Sand N 111 B15
Sand N 126 D5
Sand (Bad Emstal) D 33 F12
Sanda S 109 E12
Sandager DK 102 E5
Sandamendi E 56 B5
San Damiano d'Asti I 53 B8
San Damiano Macra I 53 C6
Sandane N 116 C4
San Daniele del Friuli I 89 D7
San Daniele Po I 82 B1
Sandanski BG 185 A9
Sandared S 107 D12
Sandarne S 119 D13
Sandau D 99 E12
Sandbach GB 27 E7
Sandberg D 90 B7
Sandby DK 103 F8
Sande D 33 B10
Sande N 111 C12
Sande N 116 D3
Sande P 60 B4
Sandefjord N 106 A7
Sandeggen N 127 A17
Sandeid N 110 C3
Sandelva N 128 D7
San Demetrio Corone I 77 D6
San Demetrio ne Vestini I 78 C5
Sander N 112 B6
Sandersdorf D 95 C11
Sandershausen (Niestetal) D 94 D6
Sandersleben D 95 C10
Sandes N 126 C8
Sandes N 126 C9
Sandfjord N 130 B9
Sandfors S 134 E5
Sandgarth GB 19 G11
Sandhausen D 37 F11
Sandhead GB 20 F7
Sandhem S 107 D14
Sandhult S 107 D12
Sandhurst GB 31 E7
Sandiás E 54 D4
Sandillon F 40 E7
Sandkrug D 100 E5
Sandl A 93 E7
Sandland N 128 C8
Sandnäset S 118 A8
Sandnes N 106 A5
Sandnes N 110 E3
Sandnes N 121 C12
Sandneshamn N 127 A15
Sandness GB 19 E13
Sandness N 127 C11
Sandnessjøen N 124 D4
Sando E 61 C8
Sandomierz PL 159 E12
Sândominic RO 169 D7
Sandon GB 27 F7
San Donaci I 77 C9
San Donà di Piave I 88 E6
San Donato di Lecce I 77 C10
San Donato di Ninea I 76 D6
San Donato Milanese I 85 C7
San Donato Val di Comino I 78 D5
Sándorfalva H 166 E5
Sandown GB 29 D12
Sandøy N 116 A5
Sandplace GB 28 E6
Šandrovac HR 165 E8
Sandsele S 123 A13
Sandsend GB 27 B10
Sandsjö S 118 C8
Sandsjöfors S 108 E5
Sandsjönäs S 123 A13
Sandslån S 123 E13
Sandstad N 120 D6
Sandstedt D 33 B11
Sandstrak N 124 D3
Sandstrand N 127 C12
Sandtangen N 130 D7
Sandtorg N 127 C12
Sandträsk S 134 B6
Sânduleni RO 169 E9
Sândulești RO 168 D3
Sandur FO 18 B3
Sandvatn N 110 F5
Sandved DK 103 E9
Sandvik FO 18 B3
Sandvik N 117 D15
Sandvik N 124 B7
Sandvik N 127 A16
Sandvik N 127 B14
Sandvik N 129 B16
Sandvik S 119 C11
Sandvika N 111 C13
Sandvika N 121 D12
Sandviken S 119 E12
Sandviken S 123 E15
Sandviken S 123 F13
Sandviksjön S 122 D7
Sandvikvåg N 110 C2
Sandwich GB 31 E11
Sandwick GB 19 F14
Sandy GB 31 C8
Sanem L 36 E5
San Emiliano E 55 C8
San Esteban de Gormaz E 56 E5
San Esteban de la Sierra E 61 C9
San Esteban de Litera E 58 D4
San Esteban del Molar E 55 E8
San Esteban del Valle E 62 D3
San Fele I 76 B5
San Felice a Cancello I 76 A2
San Felice Circeo I 78 E4
San Felices de los Gallegos E 61 C7
San Felice sul Panaro I 82 C3
San Ferdinando I 75 C8
San Ferdinando di Puglia I 76 A6
San Fernando E 68 D4
San Fernando de Henares E 62 D5
San Fili I 76 E6
San Filippo del Mela I 75 C7
Sanfins do Douro P 54 F5
San Francisco Javier E 73 D7
San Fratello I 75 C6
Sanfront I 53 B6
Sânga S 123 E13
Sangarcía E 62 C4
Sangaste EST 147 F12
Sangatte F 31 F12
San Gavino Monreale I 80 D2
Sångbäcken S 118 B7
San Gemini I 78 B3
Sângeorgiu de Mureș RO 168 D5
Sângeorgiu de Pădure RO 168 E5
Sângeorz-Băi RO 168 C5
Sânger RO 168 D4
Sangerhausen D 95 D9
San Germano Chisone I 47 F11
Sângeru RO 177 C8
Sangijän S 135 C11
San Gimignano I 82 F3
San Ginesio I 78 A4
Sanginjoki FIN 135 E16
Sanginkylä FIN 135 E17
San Giorgio a Liri I 78 E5
San Giorgio della Richinvelda I 89 D6
San Giorgio del Sannio I 76 A3
San Giorgio di Lomellina I 84 C6
San Giorgio di Nogaro I 89 E7
San Giorgio di Piano I 82 C3
San Giorgio Ionico I 77 C8
San Giorgio la Molara I 76 A3
San Giorgio Lucano I 77 C6
San Giovanni a Piro I 76 C4
San Giovanni Bianco I 85 B8
San Giovanni d'Asso I 82 F4
San Giovanni Gemini I 74 D4
San Giovanni Incarico I 78 D4
San Giovanni in Croce I 82 B1
San Giovanni in Fiore I 77 E7
San Giovanni in Persiceto I 82 C3
San Giovanni Lupatoto I 82 B3
San Giovanni Rotondo I 79 D9
San Giovanni Suegiu I 80 E2
San Giovanni Teatino I 79 C6
San Giovanni Valdarno I 82 E4
Sangis S 135 C10
San Giuliano Terme I 82 E1
San Giuseppe Jato I 74 D3
San Giuseppe Vesuviano I 76 B3
San Giustino I 82 E5
San Godenzo I 82 E4
San Gregorio I 75 C8
San Gregorio Magno I 76 B4
San Gregorio Matese I 76 A2
Sangüesa E 48 E3
San Guiliano Milanese I 85 C7
San Guim de Freixenet E 59 D6
Sanguinet F 48 B3
Sanguinetto I 82 B3
Sani GR 185 D9
San Ildefonso E 62 C5
Sanislău RO 167 B9
Sanitz D 99 B12
San Javier E 72 F3
San Jordi E 58 F3
San Jorge de Alor E 67 B5
San José E 71 F8
San José del Valle E 68 C5
San José de Malcocinado E 68 D5
San Juan E 57 B6
San Juan de Alicante E 72 E4
San Juan de Aznalfarache E 67 E7
San Juan de la Nava E 62 D3
San Juan del Puerto E 67 E6
San Justo de la Vega E 55 D7
Sankt Aegyd am Neuwalde A 93 G9
Sankt Andrä A 89 C10
Sankt Andrä am Zicksee A 165 A7
Sankt Andreasberg D 95 C8
Sankt Anna S 109 C9
Sankt Anna am Aigen A 164 C5
Sankt Anton an der Jeßnitz A 93 G8
Sankt Augustin D 37 C8
Sankt Gallen A 89 A10
Sankt Gallen CH 43 F11
Sankt Gallenkirch A 87 C9
Sankt Gangloff D 95 E10
Sankt Georgen am Walde A 93 F7
Sankt Georgen im Schwarzwald D 43 D9
Sankt Gilgen A 89 A7
Sankt Goar D 37 D9
Sankt Goarshausen D 37 D9
Sankt Ingbert D 37 F8
Sankt Jakob im Rosental A 89 C9
Sankt Jakob im Walde A 164 B5
Sankt Jakob in Defereggen A 88 C5
Sankt Johann am Tauern A 89 B9
Sankt Johann im Pongau A 89 B7
Sankt Johann im Walde A 89 C6
Sankt Johann in Tirol A 88 A5
Sankt Julian D 37 E9
Sankt Katharinen D 201 C7
Sankt Lambrecht A 89 B9
Sankt Leonhard am Forst A 93 F8
Sankt Leonhard am Hornerwald A 93 E9
Sankt Leonhard im Pitztal A 87 C11
Sankt Lorenz A 89 A7
Sankt Lorenzen im Gitschtal A 89 C7
Sankt Lorenzen im Lesachtal A 89 C6
Sankt Lorenzen im Mürztal A 164 B4
Sankt Lorenzen ob Murau A 89 B9
Sankt Marein im Mürztal A 164 B4
Sankt Margarethen D 33 A12
Sankt Margarethen an der Raab A 164 B5
Sankt Margarethen bei Knittelfeld A 89 B10
Sankt Margarethen im Burgenland A 93 G11
Sankt Märgen D 43 D9
Sankt Martin A 89 B7
Sankt Martin A 93 E7
Sankt Martin im Mühlkreis A 92 F6
Sankt Michael im Burgenland A 164 B6
Sankt Michael im Lungau A 89 B8
Sankt Michael in Obersteiermark A 89 B11
Sankt Michaelisdonn D 98 C6
Sankt Moritz CH 87 D9
Sankt Nikolai im Saustal A 164 C4
Sankt Nikolai im Sölktal A 89 B9
Sankt Olof S 104 D6
Sankt Oswald bei Freistadt A 93 E7
Sankt Oswald ob Eibiswald A 89 C11
Sankt Pankraz A 89 A9
Sankt Paul im Lavanttal A 89 C10
Sankt Peter am Kammersberg A 89 B9
Sankt Peter am Ottersbach A 164 C5
Sankt-Peterburg RUS 145 F13
Sankt Peter-Freienstein A 89 B11
Sankt Peter in der Au A 93 F7
Sankt Peter-Ording D 98 B5
Sankt Pölten A 93 F9
Sankt Radegund A 92 F3
Sankt Ruprecht an der Raab A 164 B5
Sankt Stefan im Gailtal A 89 C8
Sankt Stefan ob Leoben A 89 B10
Sankt Stefan ob Stainz A 164 C4
Sankt Ulrich bei Steyr A 92 F6
Sankt Valentin A 93 F7
Sankt Veit am Vogau A 164 C5
Sankt Veit an der Glan A 89 C9
Sankt Veit an der Gölsen A 93 F9
Sankt Veit im Pongau A 89 B7
Sankt Veit in Defereggen A 88 C5
Sankt Wendel D 37 F8
Sankt Wolfgang D 91 F11
Sankt Wolfgang im Salzkammergut A 89 A7
San Lazzaro di Savena I 82 D3
San Leo I 82 E5
San Leonardo de Yagüe E 56 E5
San Leonardo in Passiria I 88 C3
San Lorenzo I 75 D8
San Lorenzo al Mare I 53 D7
San Lorenzo Bellizzi I 77 D6
San Lorenzo de Calatrava E 70 C5
San Lorenzo de El Escorial E 62 C4
San Lorenzo de la Parrilla E 63 E8
San Lorenzo di Sebato I 88 C4
San Lorenzo in Campo I 83 E6
San Lorenzo Nuovo I 78 B1
San Luca I 75 C9
Sanlúcar de Barrameda E 68 C4
Sanlúcar de Guadiana E 66 E5
Sanlúcar la Mayor E 67 E7
San Lucido I 76 E6
Sanluri I 80 D2
San Maddalena Vallalta I 88 C5
San Mamés de Campos E 56 D2
San Marcello I 83 E7
San Marcello Pistoiese I 82 D2
San Marco Argentano I 76 D6
San Marco dei Cavoti I 76 A3
San Marco in Lamis I 79 D9
San Marcos E 54 B3
San Marino RSM 82 E5
San Martin E 48 D1
San Martín E 56 B4
Sânmartin RO 167 C8
Sânmartin RO 168 C4
Sânmartin RO 169 E7
San Martín de la Vega E 62 D5
San Martín de la Vega del Alberche E 61 D10
San Martin del Pimpollar E 61 D10
San Martín de Montalbán E 62 E4
San Martín de Pusa E 62 E3
San Martin de Unx E 48 E2
San Martín de Valdeiglesias E 62 D4
San Martino Buon Albergo I 82 B3
San Martino di Castrozza I 88 D4
San Martino di Lupari I 88 E4
San Martino di Venezze I 82 B4
San Martino in Badia I 88 C4
San Martino in Passiria I 88 C3
San Martino in Pensilis I 79 D8
San Mateo de Gállego E 57 E10
San Mauro Castelverde I 74 D5
San Mauro Forte I 76 C6
San Mauro Marchesato I 77 E7
San Mauro Pascoli I 82 D5
San Mauro Torinese I 84 C4
San Menaio I 79 D9
San Michele al Tagliamento I 89 E6
San Michele Mondovì I 53 C7
San Michele Salentino I 77 B9
San Miguel de Arroyo E 56 F3
San Miguel de Bernuy E 56 F4
San Miguel de Salinas E 72 F3
Sânmihaiu Almașului RO 167 C11
Sânmihaiu de Câmpie RO 168 D4
Sânmihaiu Român RO 175 B7
San Millán de la Cogolla E 56 D6
San Miniato I 82 E2
Sänna S 108 B5
Sannahed S 108 A6
Sannazzaro de'Burgondi I 85 C6
Sannicandro di Bari I 77 B7
Sannicandro Garganico I 79 D9
Sannicola I 77 C10
San Nicola dell'Alto I 77 E7
San-Nicolao F 53 G10
San Nicolás del Puerto E 67 C8
Sânnicolau Mare RO 166 E6
San Nicolò I 82 C4
San Nicolò d'Arcidano I 80 D2
San Nicolò Gerrei I 80 E3
Sanniki PL 155 F8
Sanok PL 161 D5
San Pablo de los Montes E 62 E4
San Pancrazio I 88 C3
San Pancrazio Salentino I 77 C9
San Paolo di Civitate I 79 D8
Sânpaul RO 167 D11
Sânpaul RO 168 E4
San Pedro E 71 B8
San Pedro de Alcántara E 69 D7
San Pedro de Ceque E 55 D7
San Pedro del Arroyo E 62 C3
San Pedro de Latarce E 55 E9
San Pedro del Pinatar E 72 F3
San Pedro del Romeral E 56 B4
San Pedro de Rozados E 61 C9
San Pedro Manrique E 57 D7
San Pedro Palmiches E 63 D8
San Pellegrino Terme I 85 B8
Sânpetru RO 169 F7
Sânpetru de Câmpie RO 168 D4
Sânpetru Mare RO 166 E6
San Piero a Sieve I 82 E3
San Piero Patti I 75 C6
San Pietro I 75 B7
San Pietro di Cadore I 89 C6
San Pietro in Cariano I 82 A2
San Pietro in Casale I 82 C3
San Pietro in Guarano I 77 E6
San Pietro Vernotico I 77 C10
San Polo d'Enza I 82 C1
San Prospero I 82 C3
Sanquhar GB 21 E9
San Quirico d'Orcia I 81 A5
San Rafael del Río E 58 F4
San Remo I 53 D7
San Román E 54 C5
San Román de Cameros E 57 D7
San Román de la Cuba E 55 D10
San Román de los Montes E 62 D3
San Roque E 54 B2
San Roque E 54 D3
San Roque E 69 D6
San Rufo I 76 C4
Sansac-de-Marmiesse F 45 F10
San Salvador de Cantamunda E 56 C3
San Salvatore I 80 D1
San Salvatore Monferrato I 53 B9
San Salvatore Telesino I 76 A2
San Salvo I 79 C7
San Sebastián de los Ballesteros E 69 A7
San Sebastián de los Reyes E 62 C5
San Secondo Parmense I 82 C1
Sansepolcro I 82 E5
San Severa I 78 C1
San Severino Lucano I 76 C6
San Severino Marche I 83 F7
San Severo I 79 D8
San Silvestre de Guzmán E 67 E5
Sânsimion RO 169 E7
Sanski Most BIH 173 C6
Sansol E 48 E1
San Sosti I 76 D6
San Sperate I 80 E3
San Spirito I 77 A7
Sanț RO 168 C5
Santa Amalia E 67 A7
Santa Ana E 71 B9
Santa Ana de Pusa E 62 E3
Santa Ana la Real E 67 D6
Santa Bàrbara E 58 F5
Santa Bárbara de Casa E 67 D5
Santacara E 48 F2
Santa Cataliña de Armada E 54 B2
Santa Catarina P 66 C3
Santa Catarina da Fonte do Bispo P 66 E4
Santa Caterina dello Ionio I 75 B10
Santa Caterina di Pittinuri I 80 C2
Santa Caterina Villarmosa I 74 D5
Santa Cesarea Terme I 77 C10
Santa Cilia de Jaca E 48 E4
Santa Clara-a-Nova P 66 E3
Santa Clara-a-Velha P 66 D3
Santa Clara de Louredo P 66 D4
Santa Coloma de Farners E 59 D9
Santa Coloma de Queralt E 59 D6
Santa Colomba de Somoza E 55 D7
Santa Columba de Curueño E 55 C9
Santa Comba Dão P 60 D4
Santa Comba de Rossas P 55 E6
Santa Cristina d'Aro E 59 D9
Santa Cristina de la Polvorosa E 55 D8
Santa Croce Camerina I 75 F6
Santa Croce del Sannio I 76 A3
Santa Croce di Magliano I 79 D8
Santa Croce sull'Arno I 82 E2
Santa Cruz P 66 C2
Santa Cruz da Tapa P 60 C4
Santa Cruz de Bezana E 56 B4
Santa Cruz de Campézo E 48 E1
Santa Cruz de la Serós E 48 E4
Santa Cruz de la Sierra E 61 F9
Santa Cruz de la Zarza E 63 E6
Santa Cruz de los Cáñamos E 71 B7
Santa Cruz del Retamar E 62 D4
Santa Cruz de Moya E 63 E10
Santa Cruz de Mudela E 71 B6
Santadi I 80 E2
Santa Domenica Talao I 76 D5
Santa Domenica Vittoria I 75 D6
Santa Elena E 71 C5
Santa Elena de Jamuz E 55 D8
Santa Elisabetta I 74 E4
Santaella E 69 A7
Santa Engracia E 48 F1
Santa Eufemia E 70 B3
Santa Eugèni E 65 E10
Santa Eulalia E 55 B8
Santa Eulalia E 55 B9
Santa Eulalia E 63 C10
Santa Eulália P 67 A5
Santa Eulalia del Río E 73 D8
Santa Eulalia de Oscos E 54 B5
Santa Eulàlia de Riuprimer E 59 D8
Santa Fé E 69 B9
Santa Fiora I 81 B5
Sant'Agata de'Goti I 76 A3
Sant'Agata del Bianco I 75 C9
Sant'Agata di Esaro I 76 D5
Sant'Agata di Militello I 75 C6
Sant'Agata di Puglia I 76 A4
Sant'Agata Feltria I 82 E5
Santa Giusta I 80 D2
Santa Giustina I 88 D5
Sant'Agostino I 82 C3
Sant Agustí de Lluçanès E 59 C8
Santahamina FIN 143 E13
Santa Iria P 66 D4
Santa Justa P 66 A3
Sant'Alberto I 82 C5
Santalha P 54 E5
Santa Liestra y San Quílez E 49 F6
Santa Luce I 82 F2
Santa Lucia I 80 B4
Santa Lucia del Mela I 75 C7
Santa Lucía de Moraña E 54 C2
Santa Luzia P 66 D3
Santa Magdalena de Pulpís E 64 D5
Santa Mare RO 169 B10
Santa Margalida E 73 B11
Santa Margarida da Serra P 66 C2
Santa Margarida de Montbui E 59 D7
Santa Margarida do Sádão P 66 C3
Santa Margherita di Belice I 74 D3
Santa Margherita Ligure I 53 C10
Santa Maria CH 87 D10
Santa Maria E 48 F4
Santa Maria Capua Vetere I 76 A2
Santa Maria da Feira P 60 C3
Santa Maria de Cayón E 56 B4
Santa Maria de Corcó E 59 C8
Santa María de Huertas E 57 F7
Santa Maria del Berrocal E 61 C10
Santa María del Camí E 65 E10
Santa María del Campo E 56 D4
Santa María del Campo Rus E 63 E8
Santa María del Cedro I 76 D5
Santa Maria della Versa I 53 B10
Santa María de los Llanos E 63 F7
Santa María del Páramo E 55 D8
Santa María del Val E 63 C8
Santa María de Nieva E 71 E9
Santa Maria de Palautordera E 59 D8
Santa Maria di Castellabate I 76 C3
Santa Maria di Sala I 82 A5
Santa María la Real de Nieva E 62 B4
Santa Maria Maggiore I 84 A5
Santa Maria Navarrese I 80 D4
Santa Maria Nuova I 83 F7
Sântămăria-Orlea RO 175 B10
Santa Maria Rezzonico I 85 A7
Santa-Maria-Siché F 53 H9
Santa Marina I 76 C5
Santa Marina del Rey E 55 C8
Santa Marina Salina I 75 B6
Santa Marinella I 78 C1
Santa Marta E 63 F8
Santa Marta E 67 B6
Santa Marta de Penaguião P 60 B5
Santa Marta de Tormes E 61 C9
Sant'Ambroggio F 53 F9
Santana P 60 D3
Santana P 66 C1
Sântana RO 167 E8
Santana da Serra P 66 D3
Santana de Cambas P 66 D4
Santana do Mato P 66 B3
Sant'Anastasia I 76 B2
Sant'Anatolia di Narco I 78 B3
Santander E 56 B4
Sant'Andrea Apostolo dello Ionio I 75 B10
Sant'Andrea Frius I 80 E3
Sântandrei RO 167 C8
Sant'Angelo I 75 B9
Sant'Angelo a Fasanella I 76 C4
Sant'Angelo dei Lombardi I 76 B4
Sant'Angelo di Brolo I 75 C6
Sant'Angelo in Lizzola I 83 E6
Sant'Angelo in Vado I 82 E5
Sant'Angelo Lodigiano I 85 C7
Sant'Angelo Muxaro I 74 E4
Santa Ninfa I 74 D2
Sant'Anna Arresi I 80 E2
Sant'Antimo I 76 B2
Sant'Antioco I 80 E1
Sant Antoni de Portmany E 73 D7
Sant'Antonio Abate I 76 B3
Sant'Antonio di Gallura I 80 B3
Sant'Antonio di Santadi I 80 D1
Santanyí E 73 C11
Santa Olalla E 62 D4
Santa Oliva E 59 E7
Santa Ollala del Cala E 67 D7
Santa Pau E 59 C9
Santa Pola E 72 E3
Santar P 60 C5
Sant'Arcangelo I 76 C6
Santarcangelo di Romagna I 82 D5
Santarém P 60 F3
Sant'Arsenio I 76 C4
Santa Severina I 77 E7
Santas Martas E 55 D9
Santa Sofia I 82 E4
Santa Sofia P 66 B3
Santa Sofia d'Epiro I 77 D6
Santa Susana P 66 B4
Santa Susana P 66 C3
Santa Teresa di Gallura I 80 A3
Santa Teresa di Riva I 75 D7
Santău RO 167 C10
Santa Uxía de Ribeira E 54 C2
Santa Venerina I 75 D7
Santa Vitória P 66 D3
Santa Vitória do Ameixial P 66 B4
Sant Boi de Llobregat E 59 E8
Sant Carles de la Ràpita E 58 F5
Sant Celoni E 59 D8
Sant Cugat del Vallès E 59 E8
Sant'Egidio alla Vibrata I 78 B5
Sant'Elia a Pianisi I 79 D7
Sant'Elia Fiumerapido I 78 D5
Sant Elm E 65 E9
San Telmo E 67 D6
Sant'Elpidio a Mare I 83 F8
San Teodoro I 80 B4
Santeramo in Colle I 77 B7
Santervás de la Vega E 55 C10
Santes Creus E 59 E6
Sant Feliu de Guíxols E 59 D10
Sant Feliu de Pallerols E 59 C9
Sant Feliu Sasserra E 59 D8
Santhià I 84 C5
Sant Hilari Sacalm E 59 D9
Sant Hipòlit de Voltregà E 59 C8
Santiago de Alcántara E 61 E6
Santiago de Calatrava E 69 A8
Santiago de Compostela E 54 C2
Santiago de Covelo E 54 D3
Santiago de la Espada E 71 C7
Santiago de la Ribera E 72 F3
Santiago del Campo E 61 E8
Santiago do Cacém P 66 C2
Santiago do Escoural P 66 B3
Santiagomillas E 55 D7
Santibáñez de Béjar E 61 D9
Santibáñez de la Peña E 55 C10
Santibáñez de la Sierra E 61 C9
Santibáñez de Tera E 55 E8
Santibáñez de Vidriales E 55 D7
Santibáñez el Bajo E 61 D8
Santibáñez Zarzaguda E 56 D4
Sant'Ilario d'Enza I 82 C1
Santillana E 56 B3
Sântimbru RO 168 E3
Santiponce E 67 E7
Santisteban del Puerto E 71 C6

Santiuste de San Juan Bautista E 62 B3
Santiz E 61 B9
Sant Jaime Mediterráneo E 73 B13
Sant Jaume d'Enveja E 58 F5
Sant Joan de Labritja E 65 F8
Sant Joan de les Abadesses E 59 C8
Sant Joan de Vilatorrada E 59 D7
Sant Joan les Fonts E 59 C9
Sant Josep de sa Talaia E 73 D7
Sant Julià de Lòria AND 49 F9
Sant Llorenç de Morunys E 59 C7
Sant Llorenç des Cardassar E 73 B11
Sant Lluís E 73 B13
Sant Martí de Tous E 59 D7
Sant Martí Sarroca E 59 E7
Sant Mateu E 58 G4
Sant Miquel de Balansat E 73 C7
Santo Aleixo P 66 B5
Santo Aleixo da Restauração P 67 C5
Santo Amador P 67 C5
Santo André P 66 C2
Santo Antoniño E 54 C2
Santo António dos Cavaleiros P 66 B1
Santo Domingo de la Calzada E 56 D6
Santo Domingo de Silos E 56 E5
Santo Estêvão P 66 B2
Santo Estêvão P 66 E4
Santo Isidro de Pegões P 66 B2
Santok PL 101 E8
Santomera E 72 E2
Sant Omero I 78 B5
Santoña E 56 B5
Santo Pietro I 74 E6
Santo-Pietro-di-Tenda F 53 F10
Santo-Pietro-di-Venaco F 53 G10
Santo Stefano al Mare I 53 D7
Santo Stefano Belbo I 53 B8
Santo Stefano d'Aveto I 53 B10
Santo Stefano di Cadore I 88 C6
Santo Stefano di Camastra I 74 C5
Santo Stefano di Magra I 85 E8
Santo Stefano Quisquina I 74 D3
Santo Stino di Livenza I 89 E6
Santo Tirso P 54 F3
Santo Tomé E 71 C6
Santovenia E 55 E8
Santpedor E 59 D7
Sant Pere de Ribes E 59 E7
Sant Pere de Torelló E 59 C8
Sant Pere Pescador E 59 C10
Sant Pol de Mar E 59 D9
Santpoort NL 198 A5
Sant Privat d'en Bas E 59 C8
Sant Quintí de Mediona E 59 E7
Sant Quirze de Besora E 59 C8
Sant Sadurní d'Anoia E 59 E7
Santullano E 55 B8
Santu Lussurgiu I 80 C2
Santurtzi E 56 B5
Sant Vicenç dels Horts E 59 E8
Sant Vicenç de Castellet E 59 D7
San Venanzo I 78 B2
San Vendemiano I 88 E5
San Vero Milis I 80 C2
San Vicente de Alcántara E 61 F6
San Vicente de Arana E 48 E1
San Vicente de la Barquera E 56 B3
San Vicente de la Sonsierra E 56 C6
San Vicente del Raspeig E 72 E3
San Vicente de Palacio E 62 B3
San Vicente de Toranzo E 56 B4
San Vicenzo E 54 C2
San Vincenzo I 75 B7
San Vincenzo I 81 A3
San Vincenzo Valle Roveto I 78 D5
San Vitero E 55 E7
San Vito I 80 E4
San Vito al Tagliamento I 89 E6
San Vito Chietino I 79 C6
San Vito dei Normanni I 77 B9
San Vito di Cadore I 88 D5
San Vito lo Capo I 74 C2
San Vito Romano I 78 D3
San Vito sullo Ionio I 75 B9
San Vittoria in Matenano I 78 A4
Sanxenxo E 54 D2
Sanxhax AL 184 A2
Sanza I 76 C5
Sânzieni RO 169 E8
Sanzoles E 55 F8
São Barnabé P 66 E3
São Bartolomeu P 60 F5
São Bartolomeu da Serra P 66 C2
São Bartolomeu de Messines P 66 E3
São Bento do Cortiço P 66 B4
São Brás P 66 D4
São Brás de Alportel P 66 E4
São Brás do Regedouro P 66 C3
São Brissos P 66 C4
São Cosmado P 60 B5
São Domingos P 66 D2
São Facundo P 60 F4
São Francisco da Serra P 66 C2
São Geraldo P 66 B3
São Gregório P 66 B4
São Jacinto P 60 C3
São João da Madeira P 60 C4
São João da Pesqueira P 60 B6
São João da Venda P 66 E4
São João do Campo P 60 D4
São João dos Caldeireiros P 66 D4
São José da Lamarosa P 60 F4
São Lourenço de Mamporcão P 66 B4
São Luís P 66 D2
São Manços P 66 C4
São Marcos da Ataboeira P 66 D4
São Marcos da Serra P 66 E3
São Marcos do Campo P 66 C4
São Martinho da Cortiça P 60 D4
São Martinho das Amoreiras P 66 D3
São Martinho de Angueira P 55 E7
São Martinho do Porto P 60 E2
São Matias P 66 C4
São Miguel de Acha P 61 D6
São Miguel de Machede P 66 B4
São Miguel de Rio Torto P 60 F4
São Miguel do Outeiro P 60 C4
São Miguel do Pinheiro P 66 D4
Saône F 42 F5
São Pedro da Cadeira P 60 F2
São Pedro de Muel P 60 E2
São Pedro de Solis P 66 E4
São Pedro do Sul P 60 C4
Saorge F 53 D7
São Romão P 67 B5
São Romão do Sado P 66 C3
São Sebastião dos Carros P 66 D4
São Teotónio P 66 D2
Saou F 51 A9
São Vicente P 54 E5
São Vicente da Beira P 60 D5
Sáp H 167 C7
Sapanca TR 187 E10
Săpânța RO 161 H8
Sapareva Banya BG 181 E7
Saparevo BG 181 E7
Săpata RO 176 D5
Sapes GR 187 B9
Sapna BIH 173 C11
Sa Pobla E 73 B11
Săpoca RO 177 C9
Sapotskin BY 153 F8
Sappada I 89 C6
Sap'parjåkka N 129 D17
Sappee FIN 143 C11
Sappen N 128 D7
Sappetavan S 123 A13
Sappetsele S 123 A13
Sappisaasi S 132 C7
Sapri I 76 C5
Sapsalampi FIN 139 F11
Sapsoperä FIN 141 B11
Sara FIN 138 F9
Saraby N 129 C12
Saracena I 76 D6
Saračinec HR 164 D6
Sarafovo BG 183 D9
Saraiķi LV 150 C2
Säräisniemi FIN 135 F17
Saraiu RO 171 D2
Sarajärvi FIN 136 C9
Sarajärvi FIN 145 B11
Sarajevo BIH 173 E9
Saramo FIN 141 C12
Saramon F 49 C7
Saran F 40 E6
Sáránd H 167 C8
Sarandë AL 184 E3
Sarantaporo GR 185 D7
Sarantsi BG 181 D8
Sa Ràpita E 73 C10
Sarasău RO 161 H8
Sarata UA 170 E5
Sărata Galbenă MD 170 D2
Sărata-Monteoru RO 177 C9
Sărata Nouă MD 170 E2
Sărăteni MD 170 D2
Sărătenii Vechi MD 170 B3
Saray TR 189 B8
Sarayakpınar TR 183 F7
Saraylar TR 189 C8
Šarbanovac SRB 175 F9
Sărbeni RO 177 E6
Sárbogárd H 165 C11
Sarcelles F 41 C7
Sarconi I 76 C5
Sardara I 80 D2
Šardice CZ 93 E12
Sardinia GR 190 B3
Sardoal P 60 E4
Sare F 48 D2
S'Arenal E 65 E10
Šarengrad HR 174 C3
Sarentino I 88 C3
Särevere EST 147 D10
Sarezzo I 85 B9
Sargans CH 87 C8
Sariai LT 153 C13
Sarıbeyler TR 189 F8
Sarıcaali TR 187 C10
Sarıçam TR 193 B9
Sarichioi RO 171 D3
Sarıdanişment TR 183 F7
Sariegos E 55 C8
Sarıkemer TR 193 D9
Sarıköy TR 189 D8
Sariñena E 58 D3
Šarišské Michaľany SK 161 E3
Sarıyer TR 189 B11
Sarjankylä FIN 139 B14
Sarkad H 167 D7
Sarkadkeresztúr H 167 D7
Särkelä FIN 137 C12
Sárkeresztúr H 165 B11
Särkijärvi FIN 133 C11
Särkijärvi FIN 135 C15
Särkijärvi FIN 136 E9
Särkikorpi FIN 141 D12
Särkikylä FIN 139 D11
Särkilahti FIN 143 B14
Särkilahti FIN 145 B11
Särkiluoma FIN 137 B14
Särkimo FIN 138 D8
Särkisalmi FIN 145 B11
Särkisalo FIN 139 E16
Särkisalo FIN 143 E8
Şarköy TR 189 C7
Sarlat-la-Canéda F 45 F8
Sarliac-sur-l'Isle F 45 E7
Sărmaş RO 168 D6
Sărmăşag RO 167 C10
Sărmaşu RO 168 D4
Sármellék H 165 C8
Sarmijärvi FIN 130 F4
Sarmizegetusa RO 175 B10
Särna S 118 C5
Sarnadas do Ródão P 60 E5
Sarnaki PL 157 F7
Sarnano I 78 A4
Sārnate LV 150 B2
Sarnen CH 86 D6
Sarnıç TR 193 C9
Sarnico I 85 B8
Sarno I 76 B3
Sarnowa PL 97 C11
Särnstugan S 118 C5
Särö S 107 D10
Sarochyna BY 149 F5
Saronno I 85 B7
Sárosd H 165 B11
Sárospatak H 161 G4
Šarovce SK 163 E7
Sarow D 100 C4
Sarpsborg N 111 D14
Sarracín E 56 D4
Sarral E 58 E6
Sarralbe F 43 C7
Sarrance F 48 D4
Sarrancolin F 49 E6
Sarraquinhos P 54 E4
Sarras F 46 E6
Sarre GB 31 E11
Sarre I 47 D11
Sarreaus E 54 D4
Sarrebourg F 43 C7
Sarreguemines F 43 B7
Sárrétudvari H 167 C7
Sarre-Union F 43 C7
Sarria E 54 C5
Sarrià de Ter E 59 C9
Sarrians F 51 B8
Sarrión E 64 D3
Sarroca de Lleida E 58 E5
Sarròch I 80 E3
Sarród H 165 A7
Sarrola-Carcopino F 53 G9
Sarron F 48 C5
Sarry F 41 C11
Sarsina I 82 E5
Sarstedt D 94 B6
Sárszentágota H 165 C11
Sárszentlőrinc H 165 C11
Sart B 199 D7
Sartaguda E 48 F1
Sarteano I 78 B1
Sartène F 53 H9
Sarti GR 186 D5
Sartilly F 39 C9
Sartininkai LT 150 F3
Sarud H 166 B6
Şaru Dornei RO 168 C6
Saruhanlı TR 193 B10
Sarule I 80 C3
Sărulești RO 177 C9
Sărulești RO 177 E9
Sárvár H 165 B7
Sarvela FIN 138 F9
Sarvijoki FIN 138 E7
Sarvikumpu FIN 141 F12
Sarviluoma FIN 138 F8
Sarvinki FIN 141 E14
Sarvisé E 48 E5
Sarvisvaara S 132 E6
Särvsjön S 118 A5
Sar"ya BY 149 E3
Sarzana I 85 E8
Sarzeau F 38 E6
Sarzedas P 60 E5
Sarzedo P 60 B5
Sasa MK 180 E6
Sasalli TR 193 C8
Sasamón E 56 D3
Sasbach D 43 C9
Sasbachwalden D 202 D5
Sasca Montană RO 175 D8
Saschiz RO 168 E5
Săsciori RO 168 F3
Sascut RO 169 E10
Sásd H 165 D10
Sasina BIH 173 C6
Sasnava LT 153 D7
Sassali FIN 133 D15
Sassano I 76 C5
Sassari I 80 B2
Sassello I 53 C8
Sassen D 100 B4
Sassenage F 47 E8
Sassenberg D 33 E10
Sassenheim NL 32 D3
Sassetta I 81 A3
Sassnitz D 100 A5
Sassocorvaro I 82 E5
Sassoferrato I 83 F6
Sasso Marconi I 82 D3
Sassuolo I 82 C2
Sástago E 57 F11
Šaštín-Stráže SK 93 E12
Sas Van Gent NL 32 F1
Sáta H 161 G1
Satão P 60 C5
Sătchinez RO 167 F7
Šateikiai LT 150 E3
Såtenäs villastad S 107 C12
Säter S 113 B14
Sätervallen S 118 A5
Sāti LV 150 C5
Satiķi LV 150 C5
Sātiņa S 107 D11
Satillieu F 46 E6
Satkūnai LT 150 D7
Satnica Đakovačka HR 165 F10
Sätofta S 103 D13
Sátoraljaújhely H 161 G4
Satovcha BG 186 A5
Satow D 99 C11
Sätra brunn S 114 C6
Satriano di Lucania I 76 B5
Satrup D 98 A7
Sattajärvi FIN 135 B12
Sattajärvi S 133 D10
Sattanen FIN 133 D17
Satteins A 87 C9
Satteldorf D 91 D7
Satter S 132 E7
Sattledt A 92 F6
Satulung RO 167 B11
Satu Mare RO 167 B10
Saubusse F 48 C3
Saúca E 63 B7
Sauca MD 170 A1
Săuca RO 167 C9
Saucats F 48 A4
Săucești RO 169 D9
Sauclières F 50 C5
Sauda N 110 C4
Saue EST 147 C9
Sauerlach D 91 G10
Sauga EST 147 E8
Saugnacq-et-Muret F 48 B4
Saugos LT 150 F2
Saugues F 46 F4
Saujon F 44 D4
Sauk AL 184 B2
Sauka LV 151 D10
Šaukėnai LT 150 E5
Saukko FIN 141 C11
Saukkoaapa FIN 131 D2
Saukkojärvi FIN 135 B16
Saukkola FIN 143 E10
Saukkoriipi FIN 133 E12
Saukonkylä FIN 139 E11
Sauland N 111 C9
Saulce-sur-Rhône F 51 A8
Sauldorf D 43 E11
Saulepi EST 146 E7
Săulești RO 176 D2
Saulgau D 87 A9
Saulgrub D 87 B12
Saulheim D 37 E10
Šaulia RO 168 D4
Saulieu F 41 F11
Saulkalne LV 151 C8
Saulkrasti LV 151 B8
Sault F 51 B9
Sault-de-Navailles F 48 C4
Sault-lès-Rethel F 35 F9
Saulx F 42 E5
Saulxures-sur-Moselotte F 43 E6
Saulzais-le-Potier F 45 B11
Saumos F 44 F3
Saumur F 39 F11
Saunajärvi FIN 141 C13
Saunakylä FIN 139 D13
Saunavaara FIN 131 D3
Saundersfoot GB 28 B5
Saurat F 49 E9
Saurieši LV 151 C8
Sauris I 89 D6
Saursfjord N 126 E9
Sausnēja LV 151 C11
Sausset-les-Pins F 51 D9
Saussy F 42 F2
Sautens A 87 C11
Sautiņi LV 151 B8
Sautron F 39 F8
Sautso Kraftverk N 129 D12
Sauvagnon F 48 D5
Sauve F 51 C6
Sauveterre-de-Béarn F 48 D4
Sauveterre-de-Guyenne F 44 F5
Sauveterre-la-Lémance F 49 A8
Sauviat-sur-Vige F 45 D9
Sauvo FIN 142 E8
Sauxillanges F 46 D3
Sauzet F 49 B8
Sauzé-Vaussais F 45 C6
Sauzon F 38 F5
Sava I 77 C9
Sava SLO 89 D10
Săvădisla RO 167 D11
Savalia GR 190 D3
Savaloja FIN 135 E15
Sävar S 138 C5
Săvârșin RO 167 E9
Sävast S 134 C7
Savaştepe TR 189 F8
Säve S 107 D10
Savelli I 77 E7
Savenay F 39 F8
Săveni RO 169 B9
Săveni RO 177 D11
Saverdun F 49 D9
Saverna EST 147 E13
Saverne F 43 C7
Sävi FIN 142 B8
Säviä FIN 139 D17
Saviaho FIN 141 C10
Savières F 41 D10
Savigliano I 53 B7
Savignac-les-Églises F 45 E7
Savignano Irpino I 76 A4
Savignano sul Rubicone I 82 D5
Savigné-l'Évêque F 39 D12
Savigneux F 46 D5
Savigny-en-Sancerre F 41 F8
Savigny-lès-Beaune F 41 F12
Savigny-sur-Braye F 40 E4
Savijärvi FIN 141 C13
Savikylä FIN 141 C11
Savilahti FIN 145 C10
Savimäki FIN 140 C7
Savines-le-Lac F 52 B4
Săvinești RO 169 D8
Savino Selo SRB 174 B4
Saviranta FIN 137 F10
Saviselkä FIN 139 B16
Savitaipale FIN 144 C8
Săvja S 115 C9
Šavnik MNE 173 G11
Savognin CH 87 D9
Savoisy F 41 E11
Savona I 53 C8
Savonlinna FIN 145 B10
Savonranta FIN 141 F12
Savran' UA 170 A6
Sävsjö S 108 E5
Sävsjön S 113 C12
Savudrija HR 83 B7
Savukoski FIN 131 D4
Sawin PL 157 H8
Sawston GB 31 C9
Sax E 72 D3
Saxdalen S 113 B12
Saxen A 93 F7
Saxhyttan S 113 C11
Saxilby GB 27 E10
Saxmundham GB 31 C11
Saxnäs S 122 B8
Saxon CH 47 C11
Saxthorpe GB 31 B11
Saxvallen S 121 D12
Sayalonga E 69 C8
Sayatón E 63 D7
Sayda D 96 E4
Säynäjä FIN 137 B13
Säynätsalo FIN 139 F15
Säyneinen FIN 141 D10
Sázava CZ 93 C7
Sazlı TR 187 E10
Sazlı TR 193 D9
Sazoba TR 189 D7
Sazoba TR 193 B10
Scaër F 38 D4
Scăești RO 176 E3
Scafa I 78 C6
Scalasaig GB 20 C4
Scalby GB 27 C11
Scalea I 76 D5
Scaletta Zanclea I 75 C7
Scalloway GB 19 E14
Scandale I 77 E7
Scandiano I 82 C2
Scandicci I 82 E3
Scandriglia I 78 C3
Scanno I 78 D5
Scano di Montiferro I 80 C2
Scansano I 81 B4
Scânteia RO 169 D11
Scânteia RO 177 D10
Scânteiești RO 169 F12
Scanzano Jonico I 77 C7
Scapa GB 19 H11
Scarborough GB 27 C11
Scardovari I 82 C5
Scarinish GB 20 B3
Scario I 76 C4
Scărișoara RO 176 F5
Scarlino I 81 B3
Scarperia I 82 E3
Scartaglen IRL 24 D4
Scartaglin IRL 24 D4
Ščenica-Bobani BIH 178 D5
Scerni I 79 C7
Scey-sur-Saône-et-St-Albin F 42 E4
Schaafheim D 203 B7
Schaan FL 87 C9
Schaarsbergen NL 199 A7
Schaerbeek B 35 C9
Schaesberg NL 36 C6
Schaffhausen CH 43 E10
Schafflund D 98 A6
Schafstädt D 95 D10
Schafstedt D 98 B6
Schäftlarn D 91 G9
Schagen NL 32 C3
Schaijk NL 199 B7
Schalchen A 92 F4
Schalkau D 91 B9
Schalkhaar NL 199 A8
Schalksmühle D 33 F9
Schänis CH 43 F11
Schapen D 33 D9
Schaprode D 100 A4
Scharbeutz D 99 B9
Schardenberg A 92 E4
Schärding A 92 F4
Scharendijke NL 32 E1
Scharnebeck D 99 D9
Scharnitz A 88 B3
Scharnstein A 89 A8
Scharrel (Oldenburg) D 33 B9
Scharwoude NL 32 C4
Schashagen D 99 B9
Schattendorf A 165 A7
Schebheim D 91 C7
Scheemda NL 33 B7
Scheer D 43 D11
Scheeßel D 98 D6
Schefflenz D 37 F12
Scheggia e Pascelupo I 83 F6
Scheggino I 78 B3
Şcheia RO 169 B8
Şcheia RO 169 D11
Scheibbs A 93 F8
Scheiblingkirchen A 164 A6
Scheidegg D 87 B9
Scheifling A 89 B9
Scheinfeld D 91 C7
Schela RO 171 B1
Schela RO 176 C2
Schelklingen D 90 F6
Schellerten D 95 B7
Schemmerhofen D 87 A9
Schenefeld D 98 B6
Schenefeld D 99 C7
Schenkenfelden A 92 E6
Schenkenzell D 203 E5
Schenklengsfeld D 94 E6
Schermbeck D 33 E7
Schermen D 95 B10
Schermerhorn NL 32 C3
Scherpenheuvel B 35 C10
Scherpenzeel NL 32 D4
Scherwiller F 43 D7
Scherzingen CH 43 E11
Scheßlitz D 91 C9
Schiavi di Abruzzo I 79 D6
Schiedam NL 32 E2
Schieder-Schwalenberg D 33 E12
Schieren L 36 E6
Schierling D 91 E11
Schiermonnikoog NL 32 B6
Schiers CH 87 D9
Schiffdorf D 33 A11
Schifferstadt D 37 F10
Schifflange L 36 E6
Schiffweiler D 202 C3
Schijndel NL 32 E4
Schilde B 32 F3
Schillingen D 202 B2
Schillingsfürst D 91 D7
Schilpario I 85 A9
Schiltach D 43 D9
Schiltigheim F 43 C8
Schimatari GR 191 C8
Schinnen NL 199 D7
Schinos GR 190 B3
Schinveld NL 36 C5
Schio I 85 B11
Schipkau D 96 C5
Schipluiden NL 198 B4
Schirmeck F 43 D7
Schirmitz D 91 C11
Schitu RO 176 E5
Schitu RO 177 E7
Schitu Duca RO 169 C11
Schitu Golești RO 176 C6
Schkeuditz D 95 D11
Schkölen D 95 D10
Schköna D 95 C12
Schkopau D 95 D10
Schlabendorf D 96 C5
Schladen D 95 B8
Schlangen D 33 E11
Schlangenbad D 37 D10
Schleching D 88 A5
Schleiden D 36 C6
Schleife D 97 C7
Schleinbach A 93 F10
Schleitheim CH 43 E9
Schleiz D 95 E10
Schlema D 95 E12
Schlepzig D 96 B5
Schleswig D 98 A7
Schleusingen D 91 A8
Schlieben D 96 C4
Schliengen D 43 E8
Schlier D 87 B9
Schlierbach A 89 A9
Schlieren CH 43 F9
Schliersee D 88 A4
Schlitters A 88 B4
Schlitz D 94 E6
Schlossberg A 164 C4
Schloss Holte-Stukenbrock D 33 E11
Schlossvippach D 95 D9
Schlosswil CH 86 D5
Schlotheim D 95 D8
Schluchsee D 43 E9
Schlüchtern D 90 B6
Schlüsselfeld D 91 C8
Schmallenberg D 37 B10
Schmelz D 37 F7
Schmidgaden D 91 D11
Schmidmühlen D 91 D10
Schmiedeberg D 96 E5
Schmölln D 95 E11
Schmölln D 100 D6
Schnabelwaid D 91 C10
Schnackenburg D 99 D11
Schnaittach D 91 C9
Schneeberg D 95 E12
Schneidlingen D 95 C9
Schneizlreuth D 89 A6
Schnelldorf D 203 C9
Schnellmannshausen D 95 D7
Schneverdingen D 98 D7
Schnürpflingen D 203 E8
Schobüll D 98 A6
Schodnia PL 158 E5
Schoenberg B 36 D6
Scholen D 33 C11
Schollene D 99 E12
Schöllkrippen D 203 A7
Schöllnach D 92 E4
Schömberg D 43 D10
Schömberg D 203 D6
Schönaich D 203 D7
Schönau D 92 F3
Schönau im Schwarzwald D 43 E8
Schönbach A 93 F8
Schönberg A 99 C9
Schönberg D 99 C9
Schönberg D 100 E3
Schönberg (Holstein) D 99 B8
Schönberg am Kamp A 93 E9
Schönberg im Stubaital A 88 B3
Schönborn D 96 C5
Schondra D 90 B6
Schönebeck D 99 D12
Schönebeck (Elbe) D 95 B10
Schöneck D 91 B11
Schönecken D 36 D6
Schönenberg-Kübelberg D 202 C3
Schönermark D 100 D5
Schönewalde D 96 C4
Schönewörde D 95 A8
Schongau D 87 B11
Schönhausen D 95 A11
Schöningen D 95 B8
Schönkirchen D 99 B8
Schönow D 100 E5
Schönsee D 91 C12
Schöntal D 90 D6
Schönthal D 91 D12
Schönwalde D 96 C5
Schönwalde am Bungsberg D 99 B9
Schönwies A 87 C11
Schoondijke NL 32 F1
Schoonebeek NL 33 C7
Schoonhoven NL 32 E3
Schoorl NL 32 C3
Schopfheim D 43 E8
Schopfloch D 91 D7
Schöppenstedt D 95 B8
Schoppernau A 87 C10
Schöppingen D 33 D8
Schörfling am Attersee A 89 A8
Schorndorf D 90 E6
Schorndorf D 91 D12
Schortens D 33 A9
Schoten B 32 F2
Schotten D 37 D12
Schramberg D 43 D9
Schrecksbach D 37 C12
Schrems A 93 E8
Schrepkow D 99 E12
Schriesheim D 37 F11
Schrobenhausen D 91 E9
Schröder A 89 B9
Schrozberg D 90 D6
Schruns A 87 C9
Schübelbach CH 43 F10
Schuby D 98 A6
Schulenberg im Oberharz D 95 C7
Schull IRL 24 E3
Schulzendorf D 100 E6
Schüpfheim CH 86 D6
Schuttertal D 202 E4
Schutterwald D 202 E4
Schüttorf D 33 D8
Schwaan D 99 C12
Schwabach D 91 D9
Schwäbisch Gmünd D 90 E6
Schwäbisch Hall D 90 D6
Schwabmünchen D 87 A11
Schwabstedt D 98 B6
Schwaförden D 33 C11
Schwaigern D 43 B11
Schwalbach D 37 F7
Schwalmstadt-Treysa D 37 C12
Schwalmstadt-Ziegenhain D 37 C12
Schwanberg A 89 C11
Schwanden CH 87 C8
Schwandorf D 91 D11
Schwanebeck D 95 C9
Schwanenstadt A 92 F5
Schwanewede D 33 B11
Schwangau D 87 B11
Schwanstetten D 91 D9
Schwarme D 33 C12
Schwarmstedt D 98 E7
Schwarz D 99 D13
Schwarza D 95 E8
Schwarzach D 92 E3
Schwarzau im Gebirge A 164 A5
Schwarzenau A 93 E8
Schwarzenbach A 165 A6
Schwarzenbach am Wald D 91 B10
Schwarzenbek D 99 C8
Schwarzenberg D 95 E12
Schwarzenborn D 94 E5
Schwarzenburg CH 47 B11
Schwarzenfeld D 91 D11
Schwarzheide D 96 D5
Schwaz A 88 B4
Schwechat A 93 F10
Schwedeneck D 99 B8
Schwedt an der Oder D 100 D6
Schwegenheim D 203 C5
Schwei (Stadland) D 33 B10
Schweiburg D 33 B10
Schweich D 37 E7
Schweigen-Rechtenbach D 43 B8
Schweighouse-sur-Moder F 202 D4
Schweinfurt D 91 B7
Schweinitz D 96 C4
Schweinrich D 99 D13
Schwelm D 33 F8
Schwendau A 88 B4
Schwendi D 87 A9
Schwenningen D 43 D10
Schwepnitz D 96 D5
Schwerin D 99 C10
Schweringen D 33 C12
Schwerte D 33 F9
Schwichtenberg D 100 C5
Schwieberdingen D 43 C11
Schwiesau D 95 A9
Schwindegg D 91 F11
Schwinkendorf D 99 C13
Schwoich A 88 A5
Schwyz CH 87 C7
Sciacca I 74 D3
Sciara I 74 D4
Scicli I 75 F6
Sciez F 47 C9
Scigliano I 77 E6
Scilla I 75 C8
Ścinawa PL 97 D10
Scionzier F 47 C10
Scoarța RO 176 C2
Scobinți RO 169 C9
Scoglitti I 74 F5
Scolaticci I 75 C6
Scole GB 31 C11
Scone GB 21 C10
Sconser GB 18 L4
Scopello I 84 B5
Scoppito I 78 C4
Scorbé-Clairvaux F 45 B6
Scordia I 75 E6
Scornicești RO 176 D5
Scorrano I 77 C10
Scorțaru Nou RO 177 C11
Scorțeni MD 170 C3
Scorțeni RO 169 D9
Scorțeni RO 177 C7
Scorțoasa RO 177 C9
Scorton GB 27 C8
Scorzè I 82 A5
Scotch Corner GB 27 C8
Scotch Corner IRL 23 D9
Scotshouse IRL 23 D8
Scourie GB 18 J6
Scousburgh GB 19 F14
Scrabster GB 19 H9
Screeb IRL 22 F3
Screggan IRL 23 F7
Scremerston GB 21 D13
Scribbagh GB 22 D6
Scrioaștea RO 176 E5
Scriob IRL 22 F3
Sculeni MD 169 C11
Scundu RO 176 D4
Scunthorpe GB 27 D10
Scuol CH 87 D10
Scurcola Marsicana I 78 C4
Scurtu Mare RO 176 E6
Scutelnici RO 177 D9
Seaca RO 176 E5
Seaca RO 176 F6
Seaca de Pădure RO 176 E2
Seaford GB 31 F9
Seaham GB 21 F14
Seahouses GB 21 D13
Seamer GB 27 C11
Seapatrick GB 23 D10
Seara P 54 E2
Seascale GB 26 C5
Seaton GB 21 F9
Seaton GB 29 D8
Seaton Delaval GB 21 E13
Seaton Sluice GB 21 E14
Seaview GB 29 D12
Sebal P 60 D3
Sébazac-Concourès F 50 B4
Sebbersund DK 102 B5
Sebechleby SK 163 E7
Sebedražie SK 163 D7
Sebeș RO 168 F3
Šebetov CZ 93 C11
Sebezh RUS 149 D4
Sebiș RO 167 E9
Sebnitz D 96 E6
Seč CZ 93 C9
Sečanj SRB 175 C6
Seča Reka SRB 174 E4
Secăria RO 177 C7
Secaș RO 167 F8
Sece LV 151 C10
Secemin PL 159 E8
Seckach D 43 B11
Seckau A 89 B10
Seclin F 35 C7
Secondigny F 44 B5
Sečovce SK 161 F4
Sečovská Polianka SK 161 F4
Secu RO 176 E2
Secuieni RO 168 E5
Secuieni RO 169 D9
Secuieni RO 169 D10
Secusigiu RO 167 E6
Seda LT 150 D4
Seda LV 147 F11
Sedan F 35 E10
Sedano E 56 C4
Sedbergh GB 26 C6
Seddülbahir TR 187 D10
Seden DK 102 E6
Sēdere LV 151 E12
Séderon F 51 B10
Sedgefield GB 21 F14
Sedico I 88 D5
Sedilo I 80 C2
Sedini I 80 B2
Sedlarica HR 165 E8
Sedlčany CZ 93 C6
Sedlec Prčice CZ 93 C7
Sedlice CZ 92 D5
Sedlice SK 161 F3
Sedliská SK 161 F4
Sedlnice CZ 162 B6
Sedrina I 85 B8
Šeduva LT 150 E7
Sędziejowice PL 159 C7
Sędzin PL 154 E6
Sędziszów PL 159 E9
Sędziszów Małopolski PL 159 F12
See A 87 C10
See A 89 B7
Seebach D 95 E7
Seebach D 203 D5
Seebergen D 95 E8
Seeboden A 89 C8
Seebruck D 88 A5
Seeburg D 95 C7
Seedorf D 99 C9
Seefeld D 91 F9
Seefeld D 96 A5
Seefeld (Stadland) D 33 B10
Seefeld in Tirol A 88 B3
Seeg D 87 B11
Seehausen D 95 B9
Seehausen D 100 D5

Seehausen (Altmark) D 99 E11
Seeheim-Jugenheim D 37 E11
Seekirchen am Wallersee A 89 A7
Seelow D 96 A6
Seelze D 94 B6
Seend GB 29 C10
Seeon D 88 A5
Sées F 39 C12
Seesen D 95 C7
Seeshaupt D 88 A3
Seethal A 89 B8
Seevetal D 99 D8
Seewiesen A 164 A4
Séez F 47 D10
Seferihisar TR 193 C8
Sefkerin SRB 174 C6
Sefrivatn N 121 A14
Seftigen CH 47 B12
Segalstad N 117 D12
Segarcea RO 176 E3
Segarcea-Vale RO 176 F5
Segeletz D 99 E13
Segersäng S 109 A11
Segersta S 119 D12
Segerstad S 105 C11
Segesd H 165 D8
Seggiano I 81 B5
Séglien F 38 D5
Seglinge FIN 115 B15
Seglingsberg S 114 C6
Seglodden N 130 C9
Seglvik N 128 C7
Segmon S 113 D9
Segni I 78 D4
Segonzac F 44 D5
Segorbe E 64 E4
Segovia E 62 C4
Segré F 39 D12
Ségrie F 39 D12
Ségur F 50 B4
Segura P 61 E7
Segura de la Sierra E 71 C7
Segura de León E 67 C6
Segura de los Baños E 58 F2
Segurilla E 62 D3
Sehlde D 95 B7
Sehma D 92 A3
Sehnde D 95 B6
Seia P 60 D5
Șeica Mare RO 168 E4
Șeica Mică RO 168 E4
Seiches-sur-le-Loir F 39 E11
Seiersberg A 164 B4
Seierstad N 121 B10
Seifhennersdorf D 97 E7
Seignelay F 41 E10
Seignelégier CH 43 F6
Seilhac F 45 E9
Seillans F 52 D5
Seilles B 199 E6
Seimeni RO 171 E2
Seinäjoki FIN 138 E9
Seini RO 161 B11
Seinsheim D 91 C7
Seipäjärvi FIN 133 D16
Seirijai LT 153 E8
Seissan F 49 D7
Seitajärvi FIN 131 C3
Şeitin RO 166 E6
Șeix F 49 E8
Seixal P 66 B1
Sejerby DK 103 D8
Sejerslev DK 102 B3
Sejet DK 102 D5
Sejny PL 152 E2
Sekkemo N 128 C8
Şękowa PL 161 D3
Sękowo PL 97 A10
Sel S 123 E10
Sel S 123 E13
Sela HR 165 E6
Selänger S 119 B13
Selanovtsi BG 176 F3
Selänpää FIN 144 C6
Selargius I 80 E3
Șelaru RO 176 E6
Șelattyn GB 26 F5
Selaya E 56 B4
Selb D 91 B11
Selbekken N 120 E7
Selbitz D 91 B10
Selbu N 121 E10
Selbustrand N 121 E9
Selby GB 27 D9
Selcë AL 179 D8
Selce HR 83 B10
Selce SK 163 D8
Selci Đakovački HR 165 F10
Selçuk TR 193 C8
Selde DK 102 B4
Selegas I 80 D3
Selenicë AL 184 C2
Selent D 99 B8
Selero GR 187 B7
Sélestat F 43 D7
Selet S 134 C7
Selet S 138 B3
Seleuş RO 167 E8
Seleuş SRB 175 C6
Selevac SRB 175 E6
Seleznevo RUS 145 D10
Selfjord N 126 D5
Selji LV 147 F10
Selice SK 162 E5
Seligenstadt D 203 A6
Șelimbăr RO 168 F4
Şelimiye TR 193 E10
Selimpaşa TR 189 B9
Selimşahlar TR 193 B9
Selishtë AL 184 A3
Selishte BG 181 E7
Selişte SRB 175 F9
Selitë AL 184 C2
Selja S 118 D7
Selje N 116 B2
Seljeli N 124 D6
Seljelynes N 127 B17
Seljenes N 129 B15
Seljord N 111 D9
Selkäjärvi S 132 E8
Selkälä FIN 131 E6
Selkirk GB 21 D11
Selkopp N 129 B14
Selkoskylä FIN 137 D13
Sella E 72 D4
Sellano I 78 D3
Sellasia GR 190 E5
Sellia GR 194 E7
Sellia Marina I 75 B10

Sellières F 47 B8
Sellin, Ostseebad D 100 B5
Sellindge GB 31 E10
Selling DK 102 C6
Sellingen NL 33 C8
Sellrain A 88 B3
Sellye H 165 E9
Selm D 33 E8
Selmes P 66 C4
Selmsdorf D 99 C9
Selnes N 120 D7
Selnes N 127 B17
Selnes N 127 C11
Selo BIH 173 D10
Selommes F 40 E5
Selongey F 42 E3
Selonnet F 52 C4
Selow D 99 C11
Seløy N 124 D3
Selsey GB 31 E7
Selsingen D 33 B12
Seljsön S 123 E12
Selsøyvika N 124 C4
Seltjärn S 123 D9
Seltz F 43 C9
Selva I 77 B8
Selva N 120 D7
Selva dei Molini I 88 C4
Selva di Progno I 85 B11
Selva di Val Gardena I 88 C4
Selvær N 124 C3
Selvåg N 120 D6
Selvazzano Dentro I 82 B4
Selvino I 85 B8
Selyatyn UA 168 B6
Selzthal A 89 A9
Sem N 111 D12
Semanić MK 185 B7
Semeac F 49 D6
Sémelay F 46 B4
Semeliškės LT 153 D10
Semeljci HR 165 F11
Semeni MD 169 C11
Semenivka UA 170 E6
Semerovo SK 162 E6
Semič SLO 89 E11
Semide P 60 D3
Semily CZ 97 E8
Seminara I 75 C8
Semizovac BIH 173 E9
Semlac RO 167 E6
Semlow D 99 B13
Semmenstedt D 95 B8
Semoutiers-Montsaon F 42 D3
Sempach CH 43 F9
Sempeter SLO 89 E8
Semproniano I 81 B5
Semriach A 164 B4
Šemša SK 161 F3
Šemšovo MK 180 E3
Semur-en-Auxois F 41 F11
Semur-en-Brionnais F 46 C5
Semussac F 44 D4
Sena E 58 D3
Seña SK 161 F3
Senales I 87 D11
Sénas F 51 C9
Sencelles E 73 B10
Šenčur SLO 89 D9
Send GB 31 E7
Senden D 91 F7
Sendenhorst D 33 E9
Sendim P 54 F3
Sendim P 55 F7
Șendreni RO 171 C1
Șendriceni RO 169 B8
Šenec SK 162 E4
Seneffe B 35 C9
Seneghe I 80 C2
Senes E 71 E8
Senez F 52 D4
Senftenberg A 93 F9
Senftenberg D 96 D6
Sengouagnet F 49 E7
Senhora do Rosário P 61 F6
Senica SK 162 D4
Senice na Hané CZ 93 C12
Senigallia I 67 E7
Senis I 80 D2
Senise I 76 C6
Senj HR 83 C10
Senje SRB 175 F7
Senjehesten N 127 B12
Senjehopen N 127 B13
Senjski Rudnik SRB 175 F8
Sen'kava SU 151 B8
Šenkvice SK 162 E4
Sery F 35 E9
Serzedo P 60 B3
Sennan S 103 B11
Sennariolo I 80 C2
Sennecey-le-Grand F 46 B6
Sennels DK 102 B3
Sennen GB 28 E3
Sennik BG 181 D11
Sennori I 80 B2
Sennwald CH 87 C8
Sennybridge GB 29 B7
Senohrad SK 163 E8
Senokos BG 183 B10
Sênonches F 40 C5
Senonbi I 80 D5
Senones F 43 D6
Senouillac F 49 C9
Senovo BG 177 D8
Senožeče SLO 89 E9
Sens F 41 D9
Sens-de-Bretagne F 39 D8
Senta SRB 166 F5
Sentein F 49 E8
Senterada E 49 F7
Šentilj SLO 164 C5
Šentjernej SLO 164 E4
Šentjur pri Celju SLO 164 D4
Senuc F 35 F10
Seon CH 43 F9
Šepak DK 173 E8
Sepino I 76 A3
Seppois-le-Bas F 43 E7
Şepreuş RO 167 D8
Septemvri RO 177 D8
Septemvri BG 181 E8
Septernes N 116 A6
Setiles E 63 D7
Setivoho BIH 174 F3
Šetonje SRB 175 E7
Septfonds F 49 B9

Setter GB 19 E14
Settimo San Pietro I 80 E3
Settimo Torinese I 84 C4
Settimo Vittone I 84 B4
Settle GB 27 C7
Setúbal P 66 B2
Seubersdorf in der Oberpfalz D 91 D10
Seui I 80 D3
Seuil-d'Argonne F 42 C3
Seulo I 80 D3
Seurre F 47 A7
Seva E 59 D8
Sevar BG 177 F9
Sevaster AL 184 D2
Sevel DK 102 C3
Sevenoaks GB 31 E9
Sevenum NL 32 F6
Sévérac-le-Château F 50 B5
Sever do Vouga P 60 C4
Severin HR 165 E7
Severinovca MD 170 A3
Severnyak BG 171 F1
Seveso I 85 B7
Ševětín CZ 93 D7
Sevettijärvi FIN 130 E5
Sevid HR 172 E4
Sévignacq F 48 D5
Sevilla E 67 E8
Sevilla la Nueva E 62 D4
Sevilleja de la Jara E 62 E3
Şevketiye TR 189 C8
Sevlievo BG 182 C4
Sevnica SLO 164 D4
Sevojno SRB 174 F4
Sévrier F 47 D9
Sexdrega S 107 D13
Seyches F 49 A6
Seyda D 95 C12
Seymen TR 189 B8
Seymen TR 189 B9
Seyne F 52 C4
Seynes F 51 B7
Seynod F 47 D8
Seyrek TR 193 B8
Seyssel F 47 D8
Seysses F 49 C8
Sežana SLO 89 E8
Sézanne F 41 C10
Sezemice CZ 93 B9
Sezimovo Ústí CZ 93 D7
Sezze I 78 E4
Sfaka GR 195 E10
Sfântu Gheorghe RO 169 F7
Sfântu Gheorghe RO 177 D9
Sfendami GR 185 D8
Sfintesti RO 176 E5
Sgiogarstaigh GB 18 J4
's-Gravendeel NL 32 E3
's-Gravenhage NL 32 D2
's-Gravenmoer NL 198 B5
's-Gravenpolder NL 32 F2
's-Gravenvoeren B 199 D7
's-Gravenzande NL 32 E2
Sgurgola I 78 D4
Shabla BG 171 F3
Shaftesbury GB 29 C10
Shalfleet GB 29 D11
Shalwy IRL 22 C5
Shanacrane IRL 24 E4
Shanagolden IRL 24 C4
Shanavogh IRL 24 C4
Shankill IRL 23 F10
Shanklin GB 29 D12
Shanlaragh IRL 24 E4
Shantonagh IRL 23 D9
Shanvus IRL 22 D6
Sharashova BY 157 E10
Sharavogue IRL 23 F7
Sharkawshchyna BY 149 F2
Sharkovo BG 183 E7
Shatilava BY 149 F6
Shats'k UA 157 H9
Shaverki RUS 141 D17
Shawbost GB 18 J3
Shawford GB 29 C12
Sheelin, Lough GB 18 J8
Sheerness GB 31 E10
Sheffield GB 27 F9
Shefford GB 31 C8
Shelekhove UA 170 B6
Shëmri AL 179 E9
Shëngjergj AL 184 B3
Shëngjin AL 179 F8
Shepit UA 168 B6
Shepshed GB 27 F9
Shepton Mallet GB 29 C9
Sherborne GB 29 D9
Sherborne St John GB 29 C12
Sherburn in Elmet GB 27 D9
Shercock IRL 23 E9
Sheringham GB 31 B11
Sherston GB 29 B10
's-Hertogenbosch NL 32 E4
Shetaj AL 184 A2
Shevchenkove UA 171 B4
Shieldaig GB 18 K5
Shifnal GB 27 F7
Shijak AL 184 B2
Shildon GB 21 F13
Shillelagh IRL 24 E5
Shillington GB 31 C8
Shinfield GB 31 E7
Shinness Lodge GB 18 J8
Shinrone IRL 23 G7
Shipka BG 182 D4
Shipkovo BG 181 D10
Shipley GB 27 D8
Shipston on Stour GB 29 A11
Shipton GB 26 F6
Shiroka Lûka BG 181 F10
Shirokë AL 179 E8
Shivachevo BG 182 D6
Shkodër AL 179 E8
Shkorpilovtsi BG 183 D6
Shlissel'burg RUS 145 F15
Shmoylovo RUS 148 F4
Sho BY 149 F4
Shoreham-by-Sea GB 31 F8
Shotts GB 21 D9
Shrewsbury GB 26 F6
Shrewton GB 29 C11
Shrigley GB 20 D3
Shrivenham GB 29 B11
Shrule IRL 22 E4
Shtërmen AL 184 C3
Shtiqën AL 179 E9
Shtit BG 182 F6
Shtrûklevo BG 177 D8
Shumen BG 183 C7
Shumilina BY 149 F7

Shushicë AL 184 B3
Shymkove UA 170 B6
Shyroke UA 161 G7
Shyroke UA 170 F6
Shyryayeve UA 170 C6
Siamanov D 80 D2
Sianów BG 101 B9
Siatista GR 185 D6
Šiauliai LT 150 E6
Šiauliai LT 150 C4
Šibari I 77 D6
Sibbhult S 104 C6
Sibbo FIN 143 E13
Šibenik HR 172 E4
Sibinj HR 173 B8
Sibiu RO 168 F4
Sible Hedingham GB 31 D10
Sibnica SRB 174 E5
Sic RO 168 D3
Siciany I 85 B7
Šibotović D 91 D10
Sicienko PL 154 D4
Siciny PL 97 C10
Sickte D 95 B8
Sicula RO 167 E8
Šiculeni RO 169 E7
Siculiana I 74 E3
Šid SK 163 F11
Šid SRB 174 C3
Sidari GR 184 E2
Sidbury GB 29 D8
Sidcup GB 31 E9
Siddeburen NL 33 B7
Siddi I 80 D2
Sideby FIN 138 F6
Sidensjö S 123 E14
Siderno I 75 C9
Sidgunda LV 151 C9
Sidirokastro GR 185 B9
Sidirokastro GR 190 E4
Sidironero GR 187 B6
Sidmouth GB 29 D8
Sidrabini LV 151 C11
Sidsjö S 119 A9
Sidskogen S 119 C10
Sidzina PL 158 E3
Siebe N 128 C11
Siebengewald NL 199 B9
Siebenlehn D 96 D4
Sieciborzyce PL 97 C9
Sieciechów PL 157 G5
Siedlanka PL 159 F12
Siedlce PL 157 F6
Siedlec PL 97 C6
Siedlisko PL 97 B8
Siedlisko PL 101 E10
Siedlisko PL 157 H8
Siedliszcze PL 157 H8
Siedliszcze PL 160 B5
Siegburg D 37 C8
Siegen D 37 C10
Siegenburg D 91 E10
Sieggraben A 165 A6
Sieghartskirchen A 93 F10
Siegsdorf D 88 A6
Sieima N 128 E8
Siek D 99 D8
Siekasjärvi S 133 E10
Siekkinen FIN 137 C11
Sielec PL 160 A8
Sielnica SK 163 D8
Siemianowice Śląskie PL 159 F7
Siemianówka PL 157 E10
Siemiatycze PL 157 F7
Siemień PL 157 G7
Siemkowice PL 159 D6
Siemyśl PL 101 B9
Siena I 82 F3
Sieniawa PL 160 A7
Sieniec PL 158 D6
Siennica PL 157 F6
Siennica Różana PL 160 A7
Sienno PL 159 D11
Sieppijärvi FIN 133 D11
Siepraw PL 163 B9
Sieradz PL 158 C6
Sieraków PL 97 A10
Sieraków PL 158 E6
Sierakówek PL 155 F7
Sierakowice PL 154 B4
Sierck-les-Bains F 36 F6
Sierentz F 43 E7
Sierksdorf D 99 B9
Sierńczyno PL 101 C10
Sierndorf A 93 F10
Sierning A 92 F6
Sieroszewice PL 158 C4
Sierpc PL 155 E8
Sierra de Fuentes E 61 F8
Sierra de Luna E 57 D10
Sierra de Yeguas E 69 B7
Sierra Engarcerán E 64 D5
Sierre CH 47 C12
Sierro E 71 E7
Siershahn D 201 D8
Siersleben D 95 C10
Siete Iglesias de Trabancos E 55 F9
Sietow D 99 D13
Şieu RO 168 C5
Şieu RO 168 C5
Şieu-Măgheruş RO 168 C4
Şieu-Odorhei RO 168 C4
Şieuț RO 168 C5
Sieversdorf D 99 D11
Sieverstedt D 98 A6
Sievi FIN 123 C13
Sievin asema eli Korhoskylä FIN 139 C12
Siewierz PL 159 F7
Sifferbo S 113 A13
Sifjord N 127 B13
Sig RO 161 C10
Sigean F 50 D4
Sigerfjord N 127 C10
Siggelkow D 99 D11
Sigglesthorne GB 27 D11
Sighetu Marmaţiei RO 161 H8
Sighişoara RO 168 E5
Sigillo I 83 F6
Sigmaringen D 43 D11
Sigmaringendorf D 43 D11
Sigmen BG 183 D7
Sigmundsherberg A 93 E9
Signa I 82 E3
Signau CH 86 D5
Signes F 51 D10
Signy-l'Abbaye F 35 E9
Signy-le-Petit F 35 E9

Simos GR 190 C4
Simpelveld NL 36 C5
Simplon CH 84 A5
Simrishamn S 104 D6
Simskardet N 122 A5
Sinabelkirchen A 164 B5
Sinaia RO 177 C7
Sinalepa EST 146 D7
Sinalunga I 82 F4
Sinanlı TR 189 B7
Sinarades GR 184 E2
Sinarcas E 63 E10
Şinca RO 168 F6
Sindal DK 106 E7
Sindel BG 183 C9
Sindelfingen D 43 C10
Sindi EST 147 E9
Sindia I 80 C2
Sindos GR 185 C8
Sinekçi TR 189 C7
Sinekli TR 189 B9
Sinemorets BG 183 E9
Sines P 66 D2
Sineşti RO 169 C10
Sineşti RO 176 D3
Sineşti RO 177 D8
Sinetänsalmi FIN 133 E14
Sinetta FIN 133 E14
Sineu E 73 B11
Singen (Hohentwiel) D 43 E10
Singera MD 170 D3
Singereí MD 169 C9
Singhofen D 37 D9
Singsjön S 122 E8
Singureni RO 177 E2
Singusdal N 106 A4
Sinimäe EST 148 C2
Siniscola I 80 B4
Sinj HR 173 E6
Sinlabajos E 62 B3
Sin-le-Noble F 35 D7
Sinn D 37 C10
Sinnai I 80 E3
Sinnes N 110 E5
Sinoie RO 171 D3
Sinole LV 151 B12
Sinopoli I 75 C8
Sins CH 43 F9
Sinsheim D 37 F11
Sint Annaland NL 32 E2
Sint Annaparochie NL 32 B5
Sint Anthonis NL 32 E5
Sintautai LT 152 D7
Sintava SK 162 E5
Sintea Mare RO 167 D8
Sintereag RO 168 C4
Sinteu RO 167 C10
Sint-Genesius-Rode B 198 D4
Sint-Gillis-Waas B 32 F2
Sint-Huibrechts-Lille B 199 C6
Sint Jansteen NL 198 C4
Sint-Katelijne-Waver B 35 B10
Sint-Laureins B 198 C3
Sint-Lenaarts B 198 C5
Sint Maartensdijk NL 32 E2
Sint-Margriete B 198 C3
Sint-Maria-Lierde B 35 C8
Sint-Martens-Latem B 35 B8
Sint Michielsgestel NL 199 B6
Sint Nicolaasga NL 32 C5
Sint-Niklaas B 35 B9
Sint Odilienberg NL 199 C8
Sint-Pauwels B 198 C4
Sint Philipsland NL 32 E2
Sint-Pieters-Leeuw B 35 C9
Sintra P 66 B1
Sint-Truiden B 35 C11
Sint Willebrord NL 32 E3
Sinzheim D 43 C9
Sinzig D 37 C8
Sióagárd H 165 D11
Siófok H 165 C10
Sion CH 47 C11
Sion RO 177 C8
Sion Mills GB 20 D1
Şipca MD 170 C5
Sipinen FIN 137 F12
Šipkovica MK 179 B7
Sipola FIN 135 F15
Sipote RO 169 C10
Şipotina MD 170 C2
Šipovo BIH 173 D7
Sipplingen D 43 E11
Sippola FIN 144 D7
Sira N 110 F5
Siracë HR 165 E8
Siracusa I 75 E7
Siran F 45 F10
Sirbmá N 129 C19
Siret RO 169 B8
Sireţel RO 169 C9
Sirevåg N 110 F3
Sirgala EST 148 C3
Şiria RO 167 E8
Širig SRB 174 C4
Sirineasa RO 176 D4
Širitovci HR 172 E5
Siriu RO 177 C8
Sirkka FIN 133 C13
Sirkkakoski FIN 133 E12
Sirkkamäki FIN 139 E16
Sirmione I 82 B2
Şirna RO 177 D7
Širnach CH 43 F11
Sirniö FIN 137 C11
Sirnitz A 89 C9
Sirod F 47 B8
Sirogojno SRB 174 F4
Sirok H 161 H1
Široki Brijeg BIH 173 F8
Širolo I 83 E8
Sirotsina BY 149 F7
Siruela E 70 B2
Sirutiškis LT 151 F7
Širvintos LT 153 C10
Sisak HR 165 F6
Sisante E 63 F8
Şişcani MD 170 D2
Şisco F 53 F10
Sişeşti RO 168 B4
Şişeşti RO 175 D10
Şişli TR 189 B10
Sissa I 82 C1
Sissach CH 43 F8
Sisses GR 194 E8
Sissonne F 35 E8
Şiştarovăţ RO 167 E8
Şişteron F 51 C10
Sistranda N 120 D5
Sistrans A 88 B3
Sita Buzăului RO 177 B8

Sitaniec PL 160 B7
Siteia GR 195 E11
Sitges E 59 E7
Sitkówka-Nowiny PL 159 E10
Sitnica BIH 173 C7
Sitochori GR 185 C10
Sitovo BG 177 E10
Sitsyenyets BY 149 E6
Sittard NL 35 C12
Sittensen D 98 D7
Sittersdorf A 89 C10
Sittingbourne GB 31 E10
Sitzendorf an der Schmida A 93 E9
Sitzenroda D 96 D3
Siulaisiadar GB 18 J4
Siuntio FIN 143 E11
Siuro FIN 143 C9
Siurua FIN 135 D16
Siurunmaa FIN 131 D1
Sivac SRB 174 B3
Sivakka FIN 141 C13
Sivakkajoki FIN 135 B13
Sivakkavaara FIN 141 E11
Siverić HR 172 E5
Siverskiy RUS 148 C7
Sivertgården N 124 E7
Sivry B 35 D9
Sivry-sur-Meuse F 35 F11
Sixarby S 115 B9
Six-Fours-les-Plages F 51 D10
Sixmilebridge IRL 24 C5
Sixmilecross GB 23 C8
Six Road Ends GB 20 F5
Sixt-Fer-à-Cheval F 47 C10
Sizun F 38 D3
Sjemeć BIH 174 F3
Sjenica SRB 179 C9
Sjetlina BIH 173 E10
Sjoa N 117 C11
Sjøåsen N 121 C10
Sjöbo S 103 D13
Sjöbotten S 134 E6
Sjöbrånet S 123 C17
Sjøholt N 116 B5
Sjølund DK 102 E5
Sjömarken S 107 D12
Sjonbotn N 124 D6
Sjørring DK 102 B3
Sjørslev DK 102 C4
Sjørup DK 102 C4
Sjösa S 109 B10
Sjösäter S 115 B11
Sjötofta S 107 E13
Sjötorp S 107 B14
Sjoutnäset S 122 B7
Sjøvassbotn N 127 B17
Sjøvegan N 127 C14
Sjövik S 107 D11
Sjulsåsen S 122 C7
Sjulsmark S 134 C7
Sjunnen S 108 E6
Sjuntorp S 107 C11
Sjursvik N 127 B12
Skademark S 123 E16
Skælsør DK 103 E8
Skærbæk DK 102 E3
Skævinge DK 103 D10
Skaftung FIN 138 F6
Skagen DK 106 D8
Skagersvik S 107 B15
Skäggebyn S 107 A12
Skagshamn S 123 E16
Skaidi N 129 C13
Skaidiškės LT 153 D11
Skaill GB 19 H11
Skaista LV 149 E2
Skaistgiriai LT 151 E8
Skaistgirys LT 150 D6
Skaistkalne LV 151 D9
Skala GR 190 C2
Skala GR 191 B7
Skala GR 191 F6
Skala GR 193 E8
Skała PL 159 F8
Skala Eresou GR 193 A6
Skala Kallonis GR 193 A7
Skala Marion GR 187 C7
Skålan S 118 A7
Skaland N 127 B13
Skala Oropou GR 191 C8
Skålavik FO 18 B3
Skalbmierz PL 159 F9
Skåle N 121 C15
Skålevik N 106 C3
Skälgården S 119 A12
Skáli FO 18 A3
Skalica SK 162 D4
Skalice CZ 97 E7
Skalité SK 163 C7
Skalitsa BG 182 E6
Skallelv N 130 C8
Skällinge S 103 A10
Skallvik S 109 C9
Skalmodal S 124 F8
Skalmsjö S 123 D13
Skalná CZ 91 B11
Skålö S 113 A11
Skaloti GR 187 B6
Skals DK 102 B4
Skålsjön S 119 D10
Skalstugan S 121 D12
Skålsvik N 124 B7
Skålvallen S 119 C10
Skån S 119 B11
Skanderåsen S 118 A7
Skanderborg DK 102 C5
Skånes-Fagerhult S 103 C12
Skåne-Tranås S 104 D5
Skånevik N 110 C3
Skåningen N 128 C4
Skankalne LV 147 F10
Skänninge S 108 C6
Skanör med Falsterbo S 103 E11
Skansbacken S 113 B11
Skansen N 121 D9
Skansholm S 123 B10
Skansnäs S 123 A10
Skansnäs S 125 E13
Skansnäset S 122 C9
Skåpafors S 107 A11
Skąpe PL 97 B8
Skapiškis LT 151 E10
Skår N 110 D4
Skara S 107 C13
Skäran S 134 F6
Skarberget N 127 D11
Skärblacka S 108 B7
Skarda S 123 C15
Skardmodalen N 124 F7
Skardmunken N 127 A18
Skardstein N 127 B11
Skardsvåg N 129 A16
Skare N 110 C5
Skåre S 113 D9
Skärhamn S 107 D10
Skarkdalen S 118 A4
Skärkind S 108 C7
Skarnes N 112 B6
Skärplinge S 115 B9
Skarp Salling DK 102 B4
Skarrild DK 102 D3
Skärså S 119 D13
Skarsfjord N 128 D2
Skärsjövålen S 118 B5
Skarstad N 127 D11
Skärstad S 108 D4
Skarsvåg N 127 B15
Skarszewy PL 154 B5
Skårup DK 102 E7
Skarv N 128 C11
Skärvången S 121 D16
Skarvfjordhamn N 128 B11
Skarvsjöby S 123 B12
Skaryszew PL 157 H4
Skarżysko-Kamienna PL 157 H3
Skasenden N 112 B7
Skästra S 119 C11
Skatamark S 134 C7
Skatan S 119 B13
Skattkärr S 113 D10
Skattungbyn S 118 D8
Skatvik N 127 B14
Skaudvilė LT 150 F5
Skaugvoll N 124 C7
Skaulo S 132 D6
Škaune LV 149 D3
Skavdal N 127 B10
Skave DK 102 C3
Skavnakk N 128 C7
Skawina PL 159 G8
Skebobruk S 115 C11
Skebokvarn S 109 A9
Skeda udde S 108 C7
Šķēde LV 150 C4
Skede S 108 E6
Skedevi S 108 B7
Skedsmokorset N 111 B14
Skee S 107 B9
Skegness GB 27 E12
Skegrie S 103 E12
Skei N 116 C4
Skei N 121 A11
Skela SRB 174 D5
Skelby DK 103 E9
Skelde DK 98 A7
Skelhøje DK 102 C4
Skellefteå S 134 E5
Skelleftehamn S 134 E6
Skelmersdale GB 26 D6
Skelton GB 27 B10
Šķeltova LV 149 D2
Skelund DK 102 B6
Skelwick GB 19 G11
Skėmiai LT 150 E7
Skender Vakuf BIH 173 D7
Skenfrith GB 29 B9
Skepasto GR 190 C5
Skępe PL 155 E7
Skepplanda S 107 D11
Skeppshamn S 119 B14
Skeppshult S 103 A12
Skeppsmalen S 123 E16
Skerries IRL 23 E10
Skhidnytsya UA 161 E7
Ski N 111 C13
Skiathos GR 191 A7
Skibbereen IRL 24 E4
Skibbild DK 102 C3
Skibby DK 103 D9
Šķibe LV 150 C6
Skibinge DK 103 E10
Skibotn N 127 B19
Skidal' BY 156 C10
Skiemonys LT 151 F10
Skien N 106 A6
Šķieneri LV 151 B13
Skierbieszów PL 160 B7
Skierniewice PL 157 G2
Skiippagurra N 130 C4
Šķilbēni LV 149 B3
Skillebotn N 124 F3
Skillefjordnes N 129 C11
Skillingaryd S 108 E4
Skillinge S 104 E6
Skillvassbakk N 127 D10
Skinias GR 194 E9
Skinnarud N 117 E12
Skinnskatteberg S 113 C14
Skipmannvik N 125 B9
Skipness GB 20 D6
Skipsea GB 27 D11
Skipton GB 27 D7
Skiptvet N 111 D14
Skirlaugh GB 27 D11
Skitenelv N 127 A17
Skiti GR 185 E8
Skivarp S 103 E13
Skive DK 102 B4
Skivjane SRB 179 E9
Skivsjön S 123 C16
Skiwy Duże PL 157 F7
Skjærhalden N 107 A9
Skjåholmen N 129 B12
Skjånes N 129 B18
Skjånes N 129 B21
Skjåvika N 124 E6
Skjeberg N 107 A9
Skjeggedal N 106 B3
Skjelelv N 127 C13
Skjellbreid N 121 C14
Skjelnan N 127 A17
Skjelnes N 127 A18
Skjelstad N 121 D10
Skjelvik N 124 B7
Skjern DK 102 D3
Skjern N 121 C9
Skjerstad N 124 B9
Skjervøy N 128 C6
Skjød DK 102 C5
Skjold N 127 B17
Skjoldastraumen N 110 D3
Skjolden N 116 D7
Skjombotn N 127 D13
Skjøtningberg N 129 A19
Sklithro GR 185 E8
Skobelevo BG 182 D4
Skoby S 115 B10
Skočivir MK 185 C6
Škocjan SLO 164 E4
Skoczów PL 163 B7
Skodborg DK 102 E4
Skodje N 116 A5
Skøelv N 127 B15
Škofja Loka SLO 89 D9
Škofljica SLO 89 E10
Skog S 119 D12
Skogaholm S 108 A6
Skoganvarri N 129 D15
Skoger N 111 C12
Skogfoss N 130 E7
Skoghall S 113 D9
Skogly N 130 E6
Skogmo N 121 B12
Skogn N 121 D10
Skogså S 134 C7
Skogsby S 105 B11
Skogsfjord N 128 C3
Skogshöjden S 107 C11
Skogstorp S 103 B10
Skogstorp S 114 D6
Skogstue N 128 D11
Skogum N 130 E6
Skoki PL 101 E12
Sköldinge S 109 A8
Skole UA 161 E8
Skollenborg N 111 C11
Sköllersta S 108 A6
Skoltenes N 126 C8
Skoltevatn N 130 E7
Skołyszyn PL 160 D3
Skomlin PL 158 D5
Skonseng N 124 D7
Skönvik S 119 E12
Skopelos GR 191 A8
Skopelos GR 193 A7
Skopi GR 195 E11
Skopje MK 180 F3
Skopos GR 185 C6
Skopos GR 187 B7
Skopun FO 18 B3
Skórcz PL 154 C6
Skorica SRB 175 F8
Skorild N 120 E6
Skorogoszcz PL 158 E4
Skoroszyce PL 158 E3
Skorovatn N 121 B14
Skorped S 123 E13
Skorpetorp S 105 A10
Skørping DK 102 B5
Skorstad N 121 B10
Skórzec PL 157 F6
Skoteini GR 190 D5
Skotfoss N 106 A6
Skotina GR 185 D8
Skotoussa GR 185 B9
Skotselv N 111 C11
Skotterud N 112 C7
Skottsund S 119 B13
Skoura GR 191 E5
Skourta GR 191 C8
Skoutari GR 185 B10
Skoutari GR 194 B4
Skoutaros GR 187 F10
Skovby DK 102 C5
Skövde S 107 C14
Skoved S 123 E14
Skovlund DK 102 D3
Skovsgård DK 102 A4
Skra GR 185 B7
Skräddrabo S 119 D10
Skradin HR 172 E4
Skråmestø N 116 E1
Skranstad N 126 E9
Skravena BG 181 D8
Skrea S 103 B11
Skreia N 117 E13
Skriaudžiai LT 153 D8
Skrinyano BG 181 E6
Skřipov CZ 162 B5
Skrīveri LV 151 C10
Skröven S 132 E7
Skrøytnes N 130 E7
Skrudaliena LV 151 E13
Skrunda LV 150 C4
Skruv S 105 B8
Skrwilno PL 155 D8
Skrzatusz PL 101 D11
Skrzyńsko PL 157 H3
Skrzyszów PL 159 G11
Skucani BIH 173 E6
Skudeneshavn N 110 D2
Skuhrov nad Bělou CZ 93 B10
Skujene LV 151 B10
Skujetnieki LV 149 C2
Skuki LV 149 E3
Skuldelev DK 103 D10
Skule S 123 E14
Skulerud N 111 C15
Skulgammen N 127 A17
Skulsfjord N 127 A16
Skulsk PL 154 F5
Skulte LV 151 B8
Skulte LV 151 C7
Skultorp S 107 C14
Skultuna S 114 C6
Skuodas LT 150 D3
Skurträsk S 123 C16
Skurup S 103 E13
Skuteč CZ 93 C10
Skutskär S 119 E13
Skutvik N 126 D9
Skutvik N 127 B16
Skwierzyna PL 97 A9
Skýcov SK 162 D6
Skydra GR 185 C7
Skyllberg S 108 B6
Skylnäs S 119 A9
Skyros GR 191 B10
Skyttmon S 122 E9
Skyttorp S 115 B9
Slabodka BY 149 E2
Sławoszów PL 159 F9
Sládkovičovo SK 162 E5
Slagavallen S 118 B5
Slagelse DK 103 E8
Slagnäs S 125 E15
Slaidburn GB 26 D7
Slaka S 108 C7
Slampe LV 150 C6
Slane IRL 23 E9
Slanec SK 161 F3
Slangerup DK 103 D10
Slănic RO 177 C7
Slănic Moldova RO 169 E8
Slano HR 178 D4
Slantsy RUS 148 C3
Slaný CZ 92 B6
Slap BIH 174 F3
Slap MNE 179 D7
Slap SLO 89 D8
Šlapaberžė LT 151 F7
Šlapanice CZ 93 D11
Släppträsk S 123 A15
Slate LV 151 D12
Slatina BIH 173 C7
Slatina BIH 173 C8
Slatina BIH 173 E8
Slatina BIH 173 E10
Slatina HR 165 E9
Slatina RO 169 C8
Slatina RO 176 E4
Slatina SRB 174 E4
Slatiňany CZ 93 C9
Slatina-Timiş RO 175 C9
Slatino MK 184 B4
Slatinski Drenovac HR 165 E9
Slătioara RO 176 C3
Slătioara RO 176 E4
Slato BIH 173 F9
Slättberg S 118 D8
Slåttholmen N 126 D8
Slättmon S 119 A13
Slattum N 111 C13
Slava Cercheză RO 171 D3
Slava Rusă RO 171 D3
Slaveino BG 181 F10
Slavičín CZ 162 C5
Slavinja SRB 181 C6
Slavkov CZ 162 B5
Slavkovichi RUS 148 F5
Slavkov u Brna CZ 93 D11
Slavonice CZ 93 E8
Slavonski Brod HR 173 B9
Slavošovce SK 161 F1
Slavotin BG 181 B7
Slavovitsa BG 176 F4
Slavovitsa BG 181 E9
Slavsk RUS 152 C4
Slavs'ke UA 161 F7
Slavsko Polje HR 164 F5
Slavyani BG 181 C10
Slavyanovo BG 181 C10
Slavyanovo BG 182 C6
Slavyanovo BG 182 F5
Sława PL 97 C10
Sławatycze PL 157 G9
Sławęcin PL 101 C13
Sławków PL 159 F7
Sławno PL 101 B11
Sławoborze PL 101 C9
Sławsko PL 101 B11
Sleaford GB 27 F11
Sledmere GB 27 C10
Sleen NL 33 C7
Sleidinge B 198 C3
Sleights GB 27 C10
Slemmestad N 111 C12
Ślesin PL 154 D4
Ślesin PL 154 F5
Sletta N 128 C9
Slevik N 107 A8
Sliač SK 163 D8
Slidre N 117 D9
Sliedrecht NL 32 E3
Slienava LT 153 D9
Sligachan GB 18 L4
Sligeach IRL 22 D6
Sligo IRL 22 D6
Slimminge DK 103 E9
Slimnic RO 168 F4
Slinfold GB 31 E8
Slipra N 121 D9
Slišane SRB 180 D4
Slite S 109 D13
Sliven BG 182 D6
Slivileşti RO 175 D11
Slivnitsa BG 181 D7
Slivo Pole BG 177 F8
Śliwice PL 154 C5
Slobidka UA 170 B4
Slobozia MD 170 D5
Slobozia RO 176 D6
Slobozia RO 177 D10
Slobozia RO 177 F7
Slobozia Bradului RO 177 C10
Slobozia Ciorăşti RO 177 B10
Slobozia Conachi RO 171 B1
Slobozia Mândra RO 176 F5
Slobozia Mare MD 171 B2
Slobozia Moară RO 177 D7
Slochteren NL 33 B7
Slöinge S 103 B11
Słomniki PL 159 F9
Słonowice PL 101 C9
Słońsk PL 97 A7
Slootdorp NL 32 C3
Slottsskogen S 115 C9
Slough GB 31 D7
Sloupnice CZ 93 C10
Sløvåg N 116 E2
Slovenj Gradec SLO 89 C11
Slovenska Bistrica SLO 164 D5
Slovenská Ľupča SK 163 D8
Slovenská Ves SK 161 E1
Slovenske Konjice SLO 164 D4
Slovenské Nové Mesto SK 161 G4
Slovenský Grob SK 162 E4
Slovinci HR 173 B6
Slovinky SK 161 F2
Slørva N 126 D8
Slov"yanoserbka UA 170 D5
Słowik PL 159 C7
Słubice PL 97 B7
Słubice PL 155 F8
Sluderno I 87 D11
Sluis NL 35 B7
Sluiskil NL 32 F1
Šluknov CZ 97 D6
Slunj HR 172 B4
Słupca PL 158 B4
Słupcza PL 160 B4
Słupia PL 157 G1
Słupia PL 159 D9
Słupia PL 159 E8
Słupno PL 155 E8
Słupsk PL 101 B12
Slušovice CZ 162 C5
Slussfors S 125 F11
Słuszków PL 158 C5
Slyuda RUS 131 D8
Smailholm GB 21 D11
Smålandsstenar S 103 A12
Smalåsen N 121 A14
Smalfjord N 129 C21
Smalininkai LT 152 C6
Smalvos LT 151 E12
Smârdan RO 171 C1
Smârdan RO 171 C2
Smârde LV 150 C6
Smârdioasa RO 177 F6
Smardzewice PL 157 H2
Smardzewo PL 97 B9
Smardzko PL 101 C9
Smarhon' BY 153 E13
Šmarje pri Jelšah SLO 164 D5
Šmarjeta SLO 164 E4
Šmartno SLO 89 D10
Šmartno SLO 89 D11
Smarves F 45 B6
Smedby S 105 B10
Smederevo SRB 175 D6
Smederevska Palanka SRB 175 E6
Smedjebacken S 113 B13
Smedsbyn S 134 C8
Smedvik N 126 D6
Smeeni RO 177 C9
Smęgorzów PL 159 F11
Smelror N 130 C10
Smelteri LV 151 D13
Smętowo Graniczne PL 154 C6
Smidary CZ 93 B8
Smidstrup DK 102 D5
Smidstrup DK 103 C10
Śmigiel PL 97 B11
Smilčić HR 172 D4
Smilde NL 33 C6
Smilets BG 181 E9
Smilevo MK 184 B5
Smilgiai LT 151 D9
Smilgiai LT 151 E8
Smilgiai LT 153 D8
Smilgynai LT 150 E2
Smilovci SRB 181 C6
Śmiłowice PL 154 E7
Śmiłowo PL 101 D11
Smiltene LV 151 B11
Smiltynė LT 150 E2
Smilyan BG 187 A7
Smines N 126 C8
Smiřice CZ 93 B9
Smirnenski BG 175 F11
Smirnenski BG 177 F8
Smiugard N 117 D11
Smižany SK 161 F2
Smögen S 107 C9
Smokvica HR 178 D2
Smokvica MK 185 B7
Smołdzino PL 101 A12
Smolenice SK 162 D4
Smolice PL 97 C12
Smolmark S 112 C7
Smolnica PL 100 E7
Smolník SK 161 F2
Smolyan BG 187 A7
Smolyanovtsi BG 181 C6
Smørfjord N 129 B15
Smulţi RO 169 F11
Smyadovo BG 183 C8
Smygehamn S 103 E12
Smyków PL 159 D9
Snagov RO 177 D8
Snainton GB 27 C10
Snaith GB 27 D9
Snålroa N 118 E2
Snappertuna FIN 143 E10
Snaptun DK 102 D6
Snarby N 127 A18
Snåre FIN 139 C10
Snartemo N 110 F6
Snåsa N 121 C12
Snave Bridge IRL 24 E4
Snedsted DK 102 B3
Sneek NL 32 B5
Sneem IRL 24 E3
Snejbjerg DK 102 C3
Snēpele LV 150 C3
Snerta N 117 C15
Snertinge DK 103 D8
Snesslinge S 115 B10
Snesudden S 134 B4
Snettisham GB 27 F13
Śniadowo PL 155 D12
Snikere LV 150 D6
Snina SK 161 F5
Šnjegotina Velika BIH 173 C8
Snøde DK 103 E7
Snøfjord N 129 B14
Snogebæk DK 105 E8
Snoghøj DK 102 D5
Snoldelev DK 103 D10
Soajo P 54 E3
Şoarş RO 168 F5
Soave I 82 B3
Søberg N 126 C7
Soběslav CZ 93 D7
Sobienie-Jeziory PL 157 G4
Sobolew PL 157 G5
Sobota PL 159 B8
Soboth A 89 C11
Sobotín CZ 93 B12
Sobotište SK 162 D4
Sobotka CZ 93 B8
Sobótka PL 97 E11
Sobótka PL 158 C4
Sobótka PL 159 E12
Sobowidz PL 154 B6
Sobra HR 178 D4
Sobradelo E 55 D6
Sobradiel E 57 E9
Sobrado E 54 B3
Sobrado E 54 D3
Sobral da Adiça P 67 C5
Sobral de Monte Agraço P 66 A1
Sobrance SK 161 F5
Sobreira Formosa P 60 E5
Søby DK 102 F6
Soča SLO 89 D8
Sočanica SRB 179 C10
Socchieve I 89 D6
Sočerga SLO 83 B8
Sochaczew PL 157 F2
Sochaux F 43 E6
Sochocin PL 155 E9
Sochos GR 185 C9
Socodor RO 167 D7
Socol RO 175 D7
Socond RO 167 B10
Socovos E 71 C9
Socuéllamos E 63 F7
Sodankylä FIN 133 D17
Söderåkra S 105 C10
Söderala S 119 D12
Söderås S 119 E9
Söderbärke S 113 B14
Söderboda S 115 B10
Söderby-Karl S 115 C11
Söderfors S 114 B8
Söderhamn S 119 D13
Söderköping S 109 C8
Söderkulla FIN 143 E13
Södersvik S 115 C11
Södertälje S 109 A11
Södra Åbyn S 134 E5
Södra Brännträsk S 134 C4
Södra Drängsmark S 134 E5
Södra Harads S 134 B5
Södra Johannisberg S 125 F15
Södra Löten S 118 E4
Södra Sandby S 103 D12
Södra Sandträsk S 123 A16
Södra Sunderbyn S 134 C7
Södra Tresund S 123 B11
Södra Vallgrund FIN 138 D6
Södra Vi S 108 D7
Sodražica SLO 89 E10
Soerendonk NL 32 F5
Soest D 33 E10
Soest NL 32 D4
Soesterberg NL 199 A6
Sofades GR 185 F7
Sofia MD 169 B11
Sofiko GR 187 B11
Sofiko GR 191 D7
Sofiya BG 181 D7
Sofporog RUS 137 C17
Şofrîncani MD 169 A10
Şofronea RO 167 E7
Sofronievo BG 176 F3
Søften DK 102 C6
Søftestad N 106 A4
Sofular TR 197 A9
Sögel D 33 C9
Sogndalsfjøra N 116 D6
Søgne N 106 C2
Soğucak TR 189 A8
Soğucak TR 189 F8
Soğucak TR 193 D9
Soğukoluk TR 197 A7
Söğüt TR 197 C8
Söğütalan TR 189 D10
Soham GB 31 C9
Sohatu RO 177 E9
Soheit-Tinlot B 35 D11
Sohland D 96 D6
Sohodol RO 167 E11
Sohren D 37 E8
Soidinkumpu FIN 137 B12
Soidinvaara FIN 137 F12
Soignies B 35 C9
Soikko FIN 135 C14
Şoimari RO 177 C8
Şoimi RO 167 D9
Şoimuş RO 167 F10
Soing F 42 E4
Soings-en-Sologne F 40 F6
Soini FIN 139 E12
Soinilansalmi FIN 141 F10
Soinlahti FIN 140 C8
Soissons F 35 F7
Soivio FIN 137 C13
Soizy-aux-Bois F 41 C10
Sójkowa PL 160 C5
Söjtör H 165 C7
Sokal' UA 160 C9
Söke TR 193 D9
Soklot FIN 138 C9
Sokna N 111 B11
Soknedal N 120 F8
Sokobanja SRB 175 F8
Sokojärvi FIN 141 D14
Sokolac BIH 173 E10
Sokolany PL 156 D8
Sokolce SK 162 F5
Sokolivka UA 170 A3
Sokółka PL 156 D9
Sokółki PL 152 E5
Sokolnice CZ 93 D11
Sokolniki PL 158 D5
Sokolov CZ 91 B12
Sokolovac HR 165 D7
Sokolovce SK 162 D5
Sokolovici BIH 173 E10
Sokolovo BG 182 C5
Sokolovo BG 183 C10
Sokolovo BIH 173 C6
Sokołów Małopolski PL 160 C5
Sokołów Podlaski PL 157 F6
Sokoły PL 156 E7
Sokorópátka H 165 B9
Sokyrnytsya UA 161 G7
Sól PL 160 B6
Soľ SK 161 F4
Sola N 110 E3
Solacolu RO 177 E9
Solana de los Barros E 67 B6
Solana del Pino E 70 C4
Solana de Rioalmar E 61 C11
Søland N 111 B10
Solarino I 75 E7
Solaro F 53 H10
Solberg N 117 E15
Solberg N 127 B14
Solberg S 123 D11
Solberg S 123 D13
Solberga S 108 D5
Solbjerg DK 102 C6
Solca RO 169 B7
Solčava SLO 89 D10
Solda I 87 D11
Şoldăneşti MD 170 B3
Şoldanu RO 177 E9
Soldatnes N 129 D14
Sölden A 87 D12
Soldeu AND 49 E9
Solec Kujawski PL 154 D5
Solec-Zdrój PL 159 F10
Solenzara F 53 H10
Solesino I 82 B4
Solesmes F 35 D7
Solesmes F 39 E11
Soleşti RO 169 D11
Soleto I 77 C10
Solf FIN 138 D7
Solférino F 48 B4
Solferino I 82 B2
Solfjellsjøen N 124 D4
Soliera I 82 C2
Solignano I 85 D8
Solihull GB 29 A11
Solin HR 172 E5
Solina PL 161 E5
Solingen D 37 B8
Solivella E 58 E6
Soljani HR 173 C10
Sölje S 113 D8
Solkei FIN 144 C8
Söll A 88 A5
Sollacaro F 53 H9
Sollas GB 18 K2
Sollebrunn S 107 C12
Sollefteå S 123 E12
Sollenau A 93 G10
Sollenkroka S 115 D11
Sollentuna S 115 D9
Sollér E 65 E10
Sollerön S 118 E8
Søllested DK 99 A10
Söllichau D 95 C12
Solliès-Pont F 52 E4
Solliès-Toucas F 52 E4
Sollihøgda N 111 C12
Söllingen D 95 B8
Sollstedt D 95 D8
Solmaz TR 197 B9
Solms D 37 C10
Solnice CZ 93 B10
Solnik BG 183 D9
Solofra I 76 B3
Solojärvi FIN 129 F18
Solomiac F 49 C7
Solomos GR 191 D6
Solopaca I 76 A3
Solórzano E 56 B4
Solosancho E 62 C3
Sološnica SK 162 E4
Solothurn CH 43 F8
Solotvyna UA 161 H8
Soløy N 127 C14
Solre-le-Château F 35 D9
Solsem N 121 A11
Solskjela N 120 E4
Sølsnes N 116 A6
Solsona E 58 D7
Solsvik N 110 B1
Solt H 166 D3
Soltau D 99 E7
Soltendieck D 99 E9
Sol'tsy RUS 148 E7
Soltszentimre H 166 D3
Soltvadkert H 166 D3
Solumshamn S 119 A14
Solva GB 25 E12
Solvalla S 115 C10
Solvarbo S 113 B14
Sölvesborg S 104 C7
Solvorn N 116 D6
Solymár H 165 A11
Soma TR 193 A10
Somain F 35 D7
Somberek H 165 D11
Sombernon F 41 F12
Sombor SRB 166 F3
Sombreffe B 35 C10
Şomcuţa Mare RO 167 B11
Somercotes GB 27 E9
Someren NL 32 F5
Somerniemi FIN 143 D10
Somero FIN 143 D10
Someronkylä FIN 135 F12
Somerovaara FIN 135 D16
Sõmerpalu EST 147 F13
Somerton GB 29 C9
Sõmeru EST 147 C12
Someş-Odorhei RO 167 C11
Somianka PL 155 E11
Sominy PL 101 B13
Somlóvásárhely H 165 B8
Sommacampagna I 82 B2
Somma Lombardo I 84 B6
Sommariva del Bosco I 53 B7
Sommarøy N 126 C9
Sommarøy N 127 A15
Sommarset N 125 A10
Sommatino I 74 E4
Somme-Leuze B 35 D11
Sommen S 108 C5
Sommepy-Tahure F 35 F10
Sömmerda D 95 D9
Sommerfeld D 100 E4
Sommersted DK 102 E4
Sommesous F 41 C11
Somme-Suippe F 41 B12
Sommevoire F 41 D12
Sommières F 51 C7
Sommières-du-Clain F 45 C6
Somogyapáti H 165 D9
Somogyjád H 165 D9
Somogyszob H 165 D8
Somogyudvarhely H 165 D8
Somogyvár H 165 C9
Somonino PL 154 B5
Somontín E 71 E8
Somotor SK 161 G4
Somova RO 171 C3
Somovit BG 176 F5
Sompa EST 147 C14
Sompolno PL 154 F6
Sompujärvi FIN 135 C14
Somzée B 35 D9
Son N 111 C13
Son NL 32 E4
Sona I 82 B2
Sona N 121 E10
Şona RO 168 E4
Sonceboz CH 43 F7
Soncillo E 56 C4
Soncino I 85 C8
Sonda EST 147 C13
Sondalo I 85 A9
Søndeled N 106 B5
Sønder Balling DK 102 B3
Sønder Bjerre DK 102 D5
Sønder Bjert DK 102 E5
Sønderborg DK 102 F5
Sønderby DK 103 D10
Sønder Dråby DK 102 B3
Sønder Felding DK 102 D3
Sønderho DK 102 E2
Sønderholm DK 102 A5
Sønder Hygum DK 102 E3
Sønder Nissum DK 102 C2
Sønder Omme DK 102 D3
Sønder Onsild DK 102 B5
Sønder Rubjerg DK 106 E6
Sondershausen D 95 D8
Søndersø DK 102 E6
Sønder Stenderup DK 102 E5
Sønder Vilstrup DK 102 E5
Sønder Vissing DK 102 C5
Sønder Vium DK 102 D2
Sondori LV 149 C2
Sondrio I 85 A8
Soneja E 64 E4
Songe N 106 B5
Songeons F 34 E4
Sonim P 54 E5
Sonka FIN 133 E14
Sonkajärvi FIN 140 C9
Sonkakoski FIN 140 B9
Sonkamuotka FIN 133 B10
Sonneberg D 91 B9
Sonneborn D 95 E8
Sonnefeld D 91 B9
Sonnewalde D 96 C5
Sonnino I 78 E4
Sonntag A 87 C9
Sonntagberg A 93 G7
Sonseca E 62 E5
Son Servera E 73 B11
Sońsk PL 155 E10
Sonstorp S 108 B7
Sonta SRB 173 A11
Sontheim an der Brenz D 91 E7
Sonthofen D 87 B10
Sontra D 94 D6
Soodla EST 147 C10
Söörmarkku FIN 142 B6
Soorts-Hossegor F 48 C3

Sopeira E 49 F7
Sopelana E 56 B6
Sopilja BIH 173 F9
Sopište MK 180 F3
Soponya H 165 B10
Šoporňa SK 162 E5
Sopot BG 181 C9
Sopot BG 181 D10
Sopot PL 154 B6
Sopot RO 176 E3
Sopot SRB 174 D6
Sopotnica MK 184 B5
Sopotu Nou RO 175 D8
Šoppela FIN 131 E3
Sopron H 165 A7
Sopronkövesd H 165 A7
Sora I 78 D5
Soraga I 88 D4
Soragna I 82 C1
Söräker S 119 A14
Söräng S 119 D11
Sorano I 78 B3
Sørarnøy N 124 B6
Sør-Audnedal N 106 C1
Sorbas E 71 E8
Sorbie GB 21 F8
Sorbiers F 46 E5
Sörbo S 119 D11
Sörböle S 119 B13
Sorbolo I 82 C1
Sörby S 113 C9
Sörbygden S 119 A11
Sørbymagle DK 103 E8
Sörbyn S 134 B7
Sörbyn S 134 E4
Sorcy-St-Martin F 42 C4
Sord IRL 23 F10
Sørdal N 125 C11
Sorde-l'Abbaye F 48 C3
Sore F 48 B4
Sørebo N 116 D3
Sören S 134 C9
Søreng N 127 B19
Soresina I 85 C8
Sorèze F 49 D10
Sörfjärden S 119 B13
Sørfjord N 124 D5
Sørfjord N 127 C14
Sørfjorden N 127 C10
Sørfjordmoen N 125 A10
Sörflärke S 123 E13
Sörfors S 119 B13
Sörfors S 138 C4
Sörforsa S 119 C12
Sorge D 95 C8
Sorges F 45 E7
Sorgono I 80 C3
Sorgues F 51 B8
Sørheim N 116 D6
Soria E 57 E7
Soriano Calabro I 75 B9
Soriano nel Cimino I 78 C2
Sorihuela E 61 D9
Sorihuela del Gaudalimar E 71 C6
Sorisdale GB 20 B4
Sørkjosen N 128 D6
Sørkjosen N 128 D6
Sorkwity PL 152 F3
Sørland N 126 E4
Sørlenangen N 127 A19
Sørli N 121 C15
Sørli N 127 D14
Sörmark S 113 B8
Sörmjöle S 138 C4
Sørmo N 127 C16
Sorn GB 21 D8
Sornac F 45 D10
Sörnoret S 123 C12
Sorø DK 103 E8
Soroca MD 170 A2
Sorokino RUS 149 B7
Soroni GR 197 D7
Sorradile I 80 C2
Sørreisa N 127 B15
Sorrento I 76 B2
Sorring DK 102 C5
Sørrollnes N 127 C12
Sorsakoski FIN 140 F9
Sorsele S 125 E14
Sörsjön S 118 D5
Sorso I 80 B2
Sörstafors S 114 C6
Sørstraumen N 128 D8
Sort E 49 F8
Sortavala RUS 145 B14
Sortelha P 61 D6
Sortino I 75 E7
Sörtjärn S 118 B8
Sortland N 126 C9
Sør-Tverrfjord N 128 C8
Sõru EST 146 D5
Sørum N 117 E11
Sorumsand N 117 C14
Sorunda S 109 A11
Sörup D 98 A7
Sørvad DK 102 C3
Sørvær N 128 B8
Sørvåge S 123 E15
Sørvågen N 126 E5
Sørvágur FO 18 A2
Sörvattnet S 118 B4
Sørvik N 127 C13
Sörvik S 113 B13
Sørvika N 117 B15
Sörviken S 123 D9
Sorvilán E 71 F6
Sos F 49 B6
Sosandra GR 185 C7
Sösdala S 103 C13
Sos del Rey Católico E 48 E3
Sosedno RUS 148 E4
Soses E 58 D4
Soshe-Ostrivs'ke UA 170 C5
Sösjö S 119 A9
Sóskút H 165 B11
Sośnica PL 101 D10
Sośnie PL 158 D4
Sośno PL 154 D4
Sosnovka RUS 152 D3
Sosnovo RUS 145 D13
Sosnovyy Bor RUS 145 F11
Sosnowica PL 157 G8
Sosnowiec PL 159 F7
Sosnówka PL 157 G5
Soso FIN 135 E15
Sospel F 53 D6
Sossonniemi FIN 137 C14
Sost F 49 E7
Šoštanj SLO 89 D11
Sostis GR 187 B8
Sot N 112 C6
Şotânga RO 176 D6

Sotés E 57 D6
Sotiel Coronada E 67 D6
Sotillo de la Adrada E 62 D3
Sotillo del Rincón E 57 E6
Sotin HR 173 B11
Sotkajärvi FIN 135 E16
Sotkamo FIN 137 F11
Soto E 55 B7
Soto de la Vega E 55 D8
Soto del Real E 62 C5
Soto de Ribera E 55 B8
Soto en Cameros E 57 D7
Sotopalacios E 56 D5
Sotos E 63 D8
Sotoserrano E 61 D8
Soto y Amío E 55 C8
Sotres E 55 B10
Sotresgudo E 56 C3
Sotrile RO 177 C7
Sotrondio E 55 B8
Sotta F 53 H10
Sotteville-lès-Rouen F 34 F3
Sottomarina I 82 B5
Sottrum D 33 B12
Sottunga FIN 115 B15
Sotuélamos E 71 A7
Soual F 49 C10
Soubès F 50 C5
Soucy F 41 D9
Souda GR 194 E7
Soudan F 39 E9
Soueix F 49 E8
Souesmes F 40 F7
Soufflenheim F 43 C8
Soufli GR 187 B10
Sougia GR 194 E6
Souillac F 45 F8
Souilly F 42 B3
Souk el Had el Rharbia MA 68 E5
Souk-Khémis-des-Anjra MA 69 E5
Soukolojärvi S 135 B11
Souk Tleta Taghramet MA 69 E6
Soulac-sur-Mer F 44 D3
Soulaines-Dhuys F 41 D12
Soulatgé F 49 E11
Souli GR 191 D6
Soullans F 44 B2
Souloum F 48 E5
Soultz-Haut-Rhin F 43 E7
Soultz-sous-Forêts F 43 C8
Soumagne B 35 C12
Soumoulou F 48 D5
Souppes-sur-Loing F 41 D8
Souprosse F 48 C4
Sourdeval F 39 C10
Soure P 60 D3
Sournia F 49 E10
Souro Pires P 61 C6
Sourpi GR 191 A6
Sours F 40 D6
Sourzac F 45 E6
Sousceyrac F 45 F10
Sousel P 66 B4
Soustons F 48 C3
Southam GB 29 A12
Southampton GB 29 D12
South Anston GB 27 E9
South Bank GB 27 B9
Southborough GB 31 E9
South Cave GB 27 D10
South Chard GB 29 D9
Southend GB 20 E5
Southend-on-Sea GB 31 D10
Southery GB 27 A11
Southgate GB 31 D8
South Harting GB 31 F7
South Kelsey GB 27 E11
South Kirkby GB 27 D9
Southminster GB 31 D10
South Molton GB 29 C7
South Ockendon GB 31 D9
Southport GB 26 D5
South Queensferry GB 21 C10
South Shields GB 21 F14
Southwell GB 27 E10
Southwold GB 31 C12
South Woodham Ferrers GB 31 D10
Souto E 54 C4
Souto E 54 E2
Souto P 60 E4
Souto P 61 D7
Souto da Casa P 60 D5
Soutupera FIN 139 B13
Souvala GR 191 D8
Sovarna RO 175 D10
Šǎvassli N 120 E6
Sovata RO 168 D6
Soveja RO 169 E9
Soverato I 75 B10
Soveria F 53 G10
Soveria Mannelli I 75 A9
Sovetsk RUS 152 C4
Sovetskiy RUS 145 C11
Soviči BIH 173 F7
Sovicille I 82 F3
Søvik N 116 A4
Søvind DK 102 D5
Sowno PL 101 B11
Sowno PL 101 D10
Soyaux F 45 D6
Soye F 42 F5
Soylu TR 189 B7
Soymy UA 161 F7
Soyons F 46 E6
Sozopol BG 183 E9
Spa B 35 D12
Spa IRL 24 D3
Spabrücken D 37 E8
Špačince SK 162 E5
Spačva HR 173 B10
Spadafora I 75 C7
Spaichingen D 43 F9
Spalding GB 27 F11
Spálené Poříčí CZ 76 C4
Spalt D 91 D8
Spangenberg D 94 D6
Spanish Point IRL 24 C4
Spantekow D 100 C5
Spanţov RO 177 E9
Sparanise I 76 A2
Sparbu N 121 D10
Spåre LV 150 B3
Sparreholm S 109 A9
Spartà I 75 C8
Sparti GR 190 E5
Sparto GR 190 B3
Spartylas GR 184 E2
Spasovo BG 171 F2
Spata GR 191 D8

Spay D 201 D8
Spean Bridge GB 20 B7
Specchia I 77 D10
Speen GB 29 C12
Speia MD 170 D4
Speicher D 37 E7
Speichersdorf D 91 C10
Spello I 78 B3
Spenge D 33 D10
Spennymoor GB 21 F13
Spentrup DK 102 B6
Spercheiada GR 190 B5
Sperlinga I 74 D5
Sperlonga I 78 E4
Spermezeu RO 168 C4
Spersboda S 115 C11
Spetalen N 111 D13
Spetses GR 191 E7
Spey Bay GB 19 K10
Speyer D 37 F9
Spezzano Albanese I 77 D6
Spiczyn PL 157 H7
Spiddal IRL 22 F4
Spielberg bei Knittelfeld A 89 B10
Spiere B 198 D2
Spiesen-Elversberg D 37 F8
Spiez CH 86 D5
Spigno Monferrato I 53 B8
Spigno Saturnia I 78 E5
Spiinigied'di N 129 E15
Spijk NL 33 B7
Spijkenisse NL 32 E2
Spikberg S 134 C5
Spilamberto I 82 C3
Spili GR 194 E8
Spilimbergo I 89 D6
Spilinga I 75 B8
Spillersboda S 115 C11
Spillum N 121 C11
Spilsby GB 27 E12
Spinazzola I 76 B6
Spincourt F 35 F12
Spinea I 82 B5
Spineni RO 176 D4
Spinetoli I 78 B5
Spink IRL 25 C8
Spinus RO 167 C9
Špionica BIH 173 C9
Spišić-Bukovica HR 165 E8
Spiss A 87 D10
Spišská Belá SK 161 E1
Spišská Nová Ves SK 161 F2
Spišské Bystré SK 161 F2
Spišská Stará Ves SK 161 E1
Spišská Teplica SK 161 E1
Spišské Podhradie SK 161 F2
Spišské Vlachy SK 161 F2
Spišský Hrušov SK 161 F2
Spital am Pyhrn A 89 A9
Spital am Semmering A 164 A5
Spitsyno RUS 148 D2
Spittal GB 19 J10
Spittal an der Drau A 89 C7
Spittal of Glenshee GB 21 B10
Spitz A 93 F8
Spjald DK 102 C3
Spjelkavik N 116 B4
Spjutsbygd S 105 C9
Spjutsund FIN 143 E14
Split HR 172 E5
Splügen CH 87 D8
Spodnja Idrija SLO 89 D9
Spodnje Hoče SLO 164 C5
Spodsbjerg DK 103 F7
Spofforth GB 27 D9
Spoleto I 78 B3
Spoltore I 79 B6
Spondigna I 87 D11
Spontin B 35 D10
Spornitz D 99 D11
Spotorno I 53 C8
Spraitbach D 90 E6
Sprakensehl D 99 E8
Sprâncenata RO 176 D4
Sprängsviken S 119 A14
Spreenhagen D 96 B5
Spremberg D 96 C6
Sprendlingen D 201 E8
Spresiano I 88 E5
Spriana I 85 A8
Sprimont B 35 C12
Spring RO 168 F3
Springe D 94 B6
Springholm GB 21 E9
Springliden S 123 A16
Sproatley GB 27 D11
Sprockhövel D 33 F8
Sproge S 109 E12
Sproxton GB 27 C9
Spunġëni LV 151 C11
Spuž MNE 179 D7
Spychowo PL 155 C11
Spydeberg N 111 C14
Spytihněv CZ 162 C5
Spytkowice PL 159 G7
Spytkowice PL 163 B9
Squillace I 75 B10
Squinzano I 77 C10
Sráid an Mhuilinn IRL 24 D4
Sraith Salach IRL 22 F3
Sranea IRL 22 D6
Srath an Urláir IRL 23 C7
Srbac BIH 173 B8
Srbica SRB 179 D10
Srbobran SRB 174 B4
Srbovac SRB 179 D10
Srdevići BIH 173 E7
Srebrenica BIH 174 E3
Srebrenik BIH 173 C9
Srebûrna BG 177 E10
Sredets BG 177 E9
Sredets BG 183 E8
Središče SLO 164 D6
Srednje BIH 173 E10
Srednjevo SRB 175 D8
Srednogorie BG 181 D10
Sredno Gradishte BG 182 E4
Šrem PL 97 B12
Sremčica SRB 174 D5
Sremska Kamenica SRB 174 C4
Sremska Mitrovica SRB 174 D4
Sremski Karlovci SRB 174 C4
Srnica BIH 173 C10
Srnice BIH 173 B8
Środa Śląska PL 97 D11
Środa Wielkopolska PL 97 B12

Srpska Crnja SRB 174 B6
Srpski Itebej SRB 175 B6
Srpski Miletić SRB 173 A11
Sta S 121 E13
Staatz A 93 E10
Stabbfors S 124 E8
Stabbursnes N 129 C14
Stabroek B 32 F2
Stabulnieki LV 151 D13
Staburags LV 151 C11
Staburnäs S 123 B11
Staby DK 102 C2
Stachy CZ 92 D5
Stade D 33 A12
Staden B 34 C7
Stadl-Paura A 92 F5
Stadra S 113 C12
Stadsbygd N 120 E7
Stadskanaal NL 33 C7
Stadtallendorf D 37 C12
Stadtbergen D 91 F8
Stadthagen D 33 D12
Stadtilm D 95 E9
Stadtkyll D 37 D7
Stadtlauringen D 91 B7
Stadtlohn D 33 E7
Stadtoldendorf A 164 B6
Hradiště CZ 162 C4
Stäfa CH 43 F10
Staffanstorp S 103 D12
Staffelstein D 91 B8
Staffin GB 18 K4
Staffolo I 83 F7
Stafford GB 27 F7
Stahovica SLO 89 D10
Stai N 117 D14
Staicele LV 147 F9
Staig D 90 F6
Stainach GB 27 B8
Staindrop GB 27 B8
Staines GB 31 E7
Stainforth GB 27 C7
Stainforth GB 27 D7
Staintondale GB 27 C11
Stainville F 42 C3
Stainz A 164 C4
Staiti I 75 D9
Stakčín SK 161 F5
Stakevtsi BG 180 B6
Stäki LV 151 B13
Stakiai LT 150 E6
Stakkvik N 128 C4
Stakliškės LT 153 D9
Stalać SRB 175 F7
Stalbe LV 151 B10
Stålbo S 114 B7
Stalbridge GB 29 D10
Stalden CH 84 A4
Staldzene LV 150 B2
Stalgenai LT 150 E3
Stalgene LV 151 C7
Stalham GB 31 B12
Staliga CZ 163 A12
Staliogargo N 129 B12
Stall A 89 C7
Stallarholmen S 114 D8
Ställberg S 113 C12
Ställdalen S 113 C12
Stalkroge DK 102 D3
Stalon S 123 B9
Stalowa Wola PL 160 B5
Stâlpeni RO 176 C5
Stâlpu RO 177 C9
Stamboliyski BG 181 E10
Stambulčić BIH 173 E10
Stamford GB 27 F11
Stamford Bridge GB 27 D10
Stamfordham GB 21 E13
Stammham D 91 E9
Stamna GR 190 B3
Stamovo BG 182 E5
Stams A 87 C11
Stamstik N 126 E9
Stamsund N 126 D6
Stânceni RO 168 D6
Stăncuţa RO 171 D1
Standdaarbuiten NL 198 B5
Standish GB 26 D6
Stănești RO 175 C11
Stănești RO 177 D7
Stânga S 109 E12
Stângǎceaua RO 176 D2
Stangnes N 127 B13
Stångviken S 123 D9
Stanhoe GB 31 B10
Stanhope GB 21 F12
Stănilești RO 170 D4
Staniśc SRB 166 F3
Stanišinci SRB 179 B10
Stanisławów PL 157 F5
Stănița RO 169 C10
Stânjel SLO 89 E8
Stanków CZ 92 C4
Stankovany SK 163 C8
Stanley GB 21 F13
Stanley GB 27 E9
Stanley GB 21 F13
Stannington GB 21 E13
Stanomino PL 101 C8
Stanos GR 185 C10
Stanos GR 190 B3
Stan'ovsti BG 181 D6
Stans CH 87 D6
Stansted Mountfitchet GB 31 D9
Stanton GB 31 C9
Stanzach A 87 C11
Stanz im Mürztal A 164 B5
Stapar SRB 174 B3
Stapel D 99 D9
Stapelburg D 95 C8
Staplehurst GB 31 E10
Staporków PL 157 H3
Stara Błotnica PL 157 G3
Stará Bystrica SK 163 C7
Starachowice PL 157 H3
Stara Gradina HR 165 E8
Stará Huť CZ 92 D6
Stara Kamienica PL 97 E9
Stara Kamionka PL 156 D9
Stara Kiszewa PL 154 C5
Stara Kornica PL 157 F7
Stara Kul'na UA 170 B4
Stará Ľubovňa SK 161 E2
Stara Łubianka PL 101 D11
Stara Moravica SRB 166 F3
Stara Novalja HR 83 C10

Stara Pazova SRB 174 D5
Stara Ploščica HR 165 E7
Stara Reka BG 182 E6
Stara Rudnica PL 100 E6
Stara Sil' UA 161 E6
Stara Tsarychanka UA 170 E5
Stará Turá SK 162 D5
Stara vas-Bizeljsko SLO 164 E5
Stará Ves nad Ondřejnicí CZ 162 B6
Staravina MK 185 B6
Stara Wieś PL 160 B6
Stara Zagora BG 182 E5
Stara Zhadova UA 169 A7
Starčevo SRB 174 D6
Starchiojd RO 177 C8
Starcross GB 29 D8
Stare Babice PL 157 F3
Stare Budkowice PL 158 E5
Střeč CZ 93 D9
Stare Czarnowo PL 101 D7
Stare Dąbrowa PL 101 D8
Stare Dolistowo PL 156 C7
Stare Hołowczyce PL 157 F7
Stare Kurowo PL 101 E9
Staré Město CZ 93 B11
Staré Město u Uherského Hradiště CZ 162 C4
Stare Miasto PL 158 B5
Stare Pole PL 155 B7
Stare Puchaly PL 157 E8
Stare Selo UA 160 D9
Stare Stracze PL 97 C10
Stargard Szczeciński PL 101 D8
Star Huta SK 163 E8
Stari LV 151 B13
Stari Banovci SRB 174 D5
Stařič CZ 162 B6
Stari Dulići BIH 173 F10
Starigrad HR 83 C10
Starigrad HR 172 F6
Stari Gradac HR 165 E8
Stari Log SLO 89 E11
Stari Majdan BIH 172 C6
Stari Mikanovci HR 173 B10
Stari Trg SLO 83 B11
Stari Trg SLO 89 E9
Stari Trg SRB 179 D10
Stari Troyany UA 171 B4
Starkenberg D 95 E11
Stärkesmark S 138 B3
Starnberg D 91 G9
Starogard PL 101 C9
Starogard Gdański PL 154 C6
Staroglavice BIH 174 E3
Starokozache UA 170 E5
Staro Oryakhovo BG 183 D9
Staropatitsa BG 175 F9
Staro Petrovo Selo HR 173 B8
Starosel BG 181 E10
Staro Selo BG 177 F9
Staro Selo BIH 173 D7
Staro Selo SRB 175 E7
Staroseltsi BG 181 D10
Starosiedle PL 97 C7
Starowa Góra PL 159 C7
Staroye Syalo BY 149 F7
Staro Zhelezare BG 181 E10
Starozreby PL 155 E8
Startforth GB 27 B8
Starup DK 102 E5
Stary Brus PL 157 H8
Stary Dzierzgoń PL 155 C7
Stary Dzikowiec PL 160 C4
Stary Kisielin PL 97 C9
Stary Kobrzyniec PL 155 E7
Stary Kolín CZ 93 B8
Stary Majdan PL 160 C3
Starynovichy BY 149 F3
Stary Pahost PL 155 C11
Stary Plzenec CZ 92 C5
Stary Sącz PL 161 D2
Stary Smokovec SK 161 E1
Stary Szelków PL 155 E11
Stary Targ PL 155 C7
Stary Uścimów PL 157 H7
Staryy Sambir UA 161 E6
Stary Zamość PL 160 B7
Starzyno PL 154 A5
Staškov SK 163 C7
Staßfurt D 95 C10
Staszów PL 159 E11
Stăţheile N 106 A6
Statland N 121 C10
Statsås S 123 B11
Statzendorf A 93 F9
Stăuceni MD 170 C3
Stăuceni RO 169 B9
Stauchitz D 96 D4
Staufenberg D 37 C11
Staupitz D 96 C5
Štavalj SRB 179 C9
Stavang N 116 C2
Stavanger N 110 E3
Stavaträsk S 134 D4
Stavchany UA 169 A8
Stave N 127 B10
Staveley GB 27 E9
Staveley GB 27 C9
Stavelot B 35 A10
Staven S 114 F6
Stavenhagen D 99 C13
Staven RO 181 D6
Stavern NL 32 E2
Stavern N 106 B7
Stavertsi BG 181 B9
Stavky UA 160 A9
Stavning DK 102 D2
Stavoren D 202 C4
Stavre S 119 A9
Stavre S 121 C16
Staveninge S 103 B11
Stavrodromi GR 190 D4
Stavros GR 185 C7
Stavros GR 185 F7
Stavros GR 190 C2
Stavroupoli GR 187 B7
Stavrove UA 160 B5
Stavsätra S 119 C10
Stavsnäs S 115 D11
Stavtrup DK 102 C6
Staw PL 101 B7
Stawiguda PL 155 C9
Stawiski PL 155 D6
Stawiszyn PL 158 C5
Stąbark PL 155 C9
Steane N 111 D9
Stebbins DK 103 A17
Steblev PL 155 C9
Šteblje SLO 164 D5
Štebnyk UA 161 E6
Steccato I 77 B7
Štěchovice CZ 92 C6

Stechow D 95 A11
Steckborn CH 43 E10
Stedesdorf D 33 A9
Stedten D 95 D10
Steeg A 87 C10
Steenbergen NL 32 E2
Steenderen NL 199 A8
Steenvoorde F 34 C6
Steenwijk NL 32 C6
Steeton GB 27 D8
Stefanaconi I 75 B9
Ştefan cel Mare RO 169 D9
Ştefan cel Mare RO 169 D11
Ştefan cel Mare RO 171 E1
Ştefan cel Mare RO 176 F4
Ştefănești MD 170 E5
Ştefănești RO 169 B9
Ştefănești RO 177 D9
Ştefăneşti de Jos RO 177 D8
Ştefani GR 191 C5
Stefan Karadzha BG 183 C8
Stefan-Karadzhovo BG 183 F7
Ştefanov SK 162 D4
Stefanovikeio GR 185 F8
Stefanovouno GR 185 E7
Ştefan Vodă MD 170 D5
Ştefan Vodă RO 177 E10
Ştefești RO 177 C7
Steffisburg CH 86 D5
Stegaurach D 91 C8
Stege DK 103 F10
Stegelitz D 95 B10
Stegersbach A 164 B6
Stegna PL 154 B7
Stegny PL 155 B8
Stehag S 103 D12
Steigra D 95 D10
Steimbke D 33 C12
Stein D 91 D9
Steinach D 91 E12
Steinach D 202 D5
Steinach am Brenner A 88 B3
Stein am Rhein CH 43 E10
Steinau D 33 A11
Steinau an der Straße D 90 B5
Steinbach D 37 C11
Steinbach am Attersee A 89 A8
Steinbach am Wald D 91 B9
Steinbakk N 130 E7
Steinberg D 91 D11
Steinberg D 98 A7
Steine N 121 D11
Steine N 126 C7
Steinen D 43 E8
Steinfeld A 89 C7
Steinfeld D 202 C5
Steinfeld D 203 B8
Steinfeld (Oldenburg) D 33 C10
Steinfjord N 127 B13
Steinfort L 36 E5
Steinfurt D 33 D8
Steingaden D 87 B11
Steinhagen D 33 D10
Steinhagen D 100 B3
Steinheim D 33 E12
Steinheim D 127 B15
Steinheim am Albuch D 203 D9
Steinheim an der Murr D 203 D7
Steinhöring D 91 F11
Steinhorst D 99 E8
Steinigtwolmsdorf D 96 D6
Steinkirchen D 98 D7
Steinkjer N 121 C11
Steinland N 126 D7
Steinløysa N 116 A7
Steinsdorf D 97 B7
Steinsfeld D 91 D7
Steinshamn N 116 A5
Steinsholt N 111 D11
Steinskjærnes N 130 D7
Steinsland N 110 B2
Steinsvik N 116 C2
Steinwenden D 202 C4
Steinwiesen D 91 B9
Stejaru RO 171 D3
Stejaru RO 176 F5
Stekene B 35 B9
Stelle D 99 D8
Stellendam NL 32 E2
Stelnica RO 171 E1
Stelpe LV 151 C9
Stemland N 124 B8
Stemmen D 98 D7
Stemnes N 127 D17
Stemnitsa GR 190 D5
Stemshorn D 33 D10
Stenåsa S 105 B11
Stenay F 35 F11
Stenbacken S 127 D17
Stenbjerg DK 102 B2
Stenbo S 109 C8
Stendal D 95 A10
Stende LV 150 B5
Stenderup DK 102 D3
Steneset N 124 C4
Stengelse N 129 D11
Stenhammar S 107 B13
Stenhamra S 115 D9
Stenhousemuir GB 21 C9
Stenico I 85 A10
Steninge S 103 B11
Stenis S 118 F7
Stenkumla S 109 D12
Stenkyrka S 109 D13
Stenlille DK 103 D9
Stenløse DK 103 D10
Stennäs S 123 D14
Stenness GB 19 E13
Steno GR 190 D5
Steno GR 191 E5
Stensån D 119 B9
Stensele S 123 A12
Stensjö S 123 A17
Stensjön S 108 D5
Stenskär S 115 A10
Stenstorp S 107 C14
Stenstrup DK 102 E6
Stensund S 125 D15
Stensund S 125 F13
Stensved DK 103 F10
Stenton GB 21 D11

Stenträsk S 134 B3
Stenudden S 125 C14
Stenum DK 106 E6
Stenungsund S 107 C10
Stenvad DK 102 C7
Stenzharychi UA 160 B9
Stepanci MK 185 B6
Stepanivka UA 170 D5
Štěpánov CZ 93 C12
Stepen BIH 173 F10
Stepnica PL 100 C7
Stepojevac SRB 174 D5
Stepping DK 102 E4
Sterdyń-Osada PL 157 E6
Sterfawki-Wielkie PL 152 E4
Sterna GR 187 A10
Sterna GR 191 D6
Sterna HR 83 B8
Sternberg D 99 C11
Šternberk CZ 162 B4
Sternes GR 194 D7
Stes-Maries-de-la-Mer F 51 D7
Stęszew PL 97 B11
Štětí CZ 92 B6
Stetten am kalten Markt D 43 D11
Steuerberg A 89 C9
Steutz D 95 C11
Stevenage GB 31 D8
Stevenston GB 20 D7
Stevensweert NL 199 D7
Stevnstrup DK 102 C5
Stewarton GB 20 D7
Stewartstown GB 23 C9
Steyerberg D 33 C12
Steyning GB 31 F8
Steyr A 92 F6
Steyregg A 92 F6
Stężary CZ 93 B9
Stezherovo BG 182 C4
Stężyca PL 154 B4
Stężyca PL 157 G5
Stia I 82 E4
Stibb Cross GB 28 D6
Stickney GB 27 E12
Stidsvig S 103 C12
Stiege D 95 C8
Stiens NL 32 B5
Stienta I 82 C4
Stigen S 107 D11
Stigliano I 76 C6
Stignano I 75 C9
Stigsjö S 119 A14
Stigtomta S 109 B9
Stijena BIH 172 C5
Stikli LV 150 B4
Stilligarry GB 18 L2
Stilling DK 102 C5
Stillington GB 27 C9
Stillorgan IRL 23 F10
Stilo I 75 C9
Stilton GB 27 G11
Štimlje SRB 180 E3
Stimpfach D 91 D7
Stintino I 80 B1
Stio I 76 C4
Stirfaka GR 190 B5
Stiring-Wendel F 37 F7
Stirling GB 21 C9
Štitar HR 173 B11
Štitar SRB 174 D4
Štítina CZ 162 B6
Štítnik SK 161 F1
Štíty CZ 93 C11
Ştiubieni RO 169 B9
Štiuca RO 175 B8
Štivan HR 83 C9
Stjær DK 102 C5
Stjärnfors S 113 C13
Stjärnhov S 109 A9
Stjärnorp S 108 B7
Stjørdalshalsen N 121 E9
Støa N 117 E14
Støa N 118 D4
Stobiecko Miejskie PL 159 D7
Stobreč HR 172 E6
Stoby S 103 C13
Stochov CZ 92 B5
Stocka S 119 C13
Stockach D 43 E11
Stockamöllan S 103 D12
Stockaryd S 104 C7
Stöcke S 138 C4
Stockelsdorf D 99 C9
Stockenboi A 89 C8
Stockerau A 93 F10
Stockheim D 91 B9
Stockholm S 115 D10
Stocking A 164 C5
Stockport GB 27 E7
Stocksfield GB 21 F13
Stockstadt am Rhein D 37 E10
Stockton-on-Tees GB 27 B9
Stockvik S 119 B13
Stoczek PL 155 E12
Stoczek Łukowski PL 157 G5
Stod CZ 92 C4
Stöde S 119 B12
Stoenești RO 176 C4
Stoenești RO 176 E5
Stoenești RO 176 E5
Stoenești RO 177 E7
Stoer GB 18 J6
Stoholm DK 102 C4
Stoianovca MD 170 E2
Stoicănești RO 176 E5
Stoilești RO 176 D4
Stoina RO 176 D3
Stojakovo MK 185 B8
Stojdraga HR 164 E5
Stojnci SLO 164 D5
Stoke Ash GB 31 C11
Stoke-on-Trent GB 27 E7
Stokesay GB 29 A9
Stokesley GB 27 C9
Stokite BG 182 D4
Stokka N 124 A4
Stokkasjøen N 124 A4
Stokkdal N 127 D12
Stokke N 106 A7
Stokkemarke DK 99 A10
Stokkvågen N 124 D5
Stokmarknes N 126 C8
Štoky CZ 93 D9
Stolac BIH 173 F8
Stolberg (Harz) Kurort D 95 C8
Stolberg (Rheinland) D 36 C6
Stołczno PL 101 C12
Stolerova LV 149 D3
Stollberg D 95 E12
Stöllet S 113 B9
Stolmen N 110 B2

Stolniceni MD 170 D3
Stolniceni-Prăjescu RO 169 C9
Stolnici RO 176 D5
Stolnik BG 181 D8
Stolno PL 154 D6
Stolpe D 99 B8
Stolpe D 100 E6
Stolpen D 96 D6
Stolzenau D 33 C12
Stomio GR 185 E8
Stömne S 113 D8
Ston HR 178 D4
Stone GB 27 F7
Stone GB 29 B10
Stonehaven GB 21 B12
Stonehouse GB 21 D9
Stong N 110 D3
Stongfjorden N 116 C2
Stonglandseidet N 127 B13
Stonybreck GB 19 F13
Stoob A 165 A7
Stöpen S 107 C14
Stopiče SLO 164 E4
Stopki PL 152 E3
Stopnica PL 159 F10
Storå N 127 D11
Storå S 113 C13
Stora Åby S 108 C5
Storåbränna S 122 D7
Stora Höga S 107 C10
Stora Levene S 107 C12
Stora Melby S 107 C12
Stora Mellösa S 108 A6
Storarmsjö S 123 C16
Storås N 120 E7
Storåsen S 119 A10
Störåsen S 122 D7
Stora Skedvi S 113 B14
Stora Tallberg S 125 E17
Stora Vika S 109 B11
Storbäck S 122 B9
Storbacka FIN 139 D10
Storbäcken S 118 C4
Storberg S 125 C16
Stor-Blåsjön S 121 B16
Storbo S 118 C3
Storbogaren S 123 D14
Storbränna S 122 D7
Storbrännan S 134 E4
Storbukt N 129 B12
Storby FIN 115 B13
Stordal N 116 B6
Štore SLO 164 D4
Storebø N 110 B2
Storebro S 108 D7
Storebru N 116 C3
Store Damme DK 100 A2
Store Heddinge DK 103 E10
Storeidet N 127 E10
Storekorsnes N 128 C11
Storelv N 128 B10
Store Merløse DK 103 D9
Store Molvik N 130 B5
Støren N 120 E8
Storenga N 128 D7
Store Rise DK 99 A8
Store Rørbæk DK 102 B5
Storfjäten S 118 C5
Storfjord N 127 B18
Storfjordbotn N 129 C18
Storfors S 113 C11
Storforshei N 124 D8
Storhågna S 118 A7
Storhallaren N 120 D5
Stor-Hallen S 118 A7
Storhogen S 122 D6
Stor-Hulljsön S 119 A12
Štorje SLO 89 E8
Storjola S 122 B7
Storjord N 125 C9
Storjorda N 124 C6
Storjorda N 127 C11
Storkow D 96 B3
Storli N 117 A10
Storlien S 121 E12
Stormi FIN 143 C9
Stornara I 76 A5
Stornarella I 76 A5
Stornäs S 122 A8
Stornäs S 123 A11
Stornäset S 123 C10
Stornes N 127 C11
Stornoway GB 18 J4
Storo I 85 B10
Štorobănească RO 177 F6
Storodden N 120 E6
Storöhamn S 135 C12
Storrington GB 31 F8
Storøsta N 117 B13
Storsand S 119 C13
Storsand S 134 B5
Storsandsjö S 123 C17
Störsätern S 118 B3
Storsävarträsk S 134 F3
Storsele S 123 D14
Storseleby S 123 B11
Storselsøy N 124 C4
Storsjö S 118 A5
Storskog S 125 E10
Storslett N 128 D6
Storsletta N 128 D6
Storsteinnes N 127 A18
Storsteinnes N 127 B17
Storsund S 134 C5
Storuman S 123 A12
Storvik N 124 C6
Storvik N 126 C9
Storvik N 128 C9
Storvik N 128 D7
Storvik S 119 E12
Storvorde DK 102 A6
Storvreta S 115 C9
Stós SK 161 F2
Stößen D 95 D10
Stössing A 93 F9
Stoszowice PL 97 E11
Støtt N 124 C5
Stötten am Auerberg D 87 B11
Stotternheim D 95 D9
Stouby DK 102 D5
Stoumont B 35 D12
Stourbridge GB 29 A10
Stourport-on-Severn GB 29 A10
Støvran N 124 B8
Støvring DK 102 B5
Støvset N 124 B8
Stow GB 21 D11
Stowięcino PL 101 A12
Stowmarket GB 31 C10
Stow-on-the-Wold GB 29 B11

Stoyan Mikhalovski BG 183 C8
Stoyanovo BG 181 D8
Stoykite BG 181 F10
Stozher BG 183 C8
Stożne PL 152 E5
Stra I 82 B5
Straach D 95 C12
Strabane GB 20 F2
Strabla PL 157 E8
Strachan GB 21 A11
Strachówka PL 155 F12
Strachur GB 20 C6
Stracin MK 180 E5
Stračiūnai LT 153 E9
Strackholt (Großefehn) D 33 B9
Strączno PL 101 D10
Stradalovo BG 181 E6
Stradbally IRL 23 E8
Stradbroke GB 31 C11
Stradella I 85 C7
Stradi LV 151 B13
Stradishall GB 31 C10
Stradone IRL 23 E8
Stradsett GB 27 F12
Straelen D 32 F6
Stragari SRB 174 E6
Strai N 106 C2
Straimont B 35 E11
Straja RO 169 B7
Strakhilovo BG 182 C5
Strakonice CZ 92 D5
Straldzha BG 183 D7
Stralki BY 149 E4
Straloch GB 21 B9
Strålsnäs S 108 C6
Stralsund D 100 B4
Strambino I 84 C4
Stramproy NL 35 B12
Strâmtura RO 168 B4
Stråñavy SK 163 C7
Strančice CZ 93 C7
Strand N 117 D15
Strand N 126 C9
Strand S 122 D7
Stranda N 116 B5
Strandå N 124 A8
Strandby DK 102 B4
Strandby DK 106 E3
Strande D 99 B8
Strandnorum S 107 C10
Strandval S 123 B10
Strangford GB 20 E7
Stranghele N 116 E3
Strangolagalli I 78 D4
Strångsjö S 109 B8
Stráni CZ 162 D5
Stranocum GB 20 E4
Stranorlar IRL 23 C7
Stranraer GB 20 F6
Stråoane RO 169 E9
Strasatti I 74 D2
Strasbourg F 43 C8
Strasburg D 100 D3
Strășeni MD 170 C3
Strašice CZ 92 C5
Stråssa S 113 D11
Straßberg D 43 D11
Straßberg D 95 C9
Straßburg A 89 C9
Strassen L 36 E6
Straßengel A 164 B4
Straßenhaus D 37 C9
Strasshof an der Norbahn A 93 F11
Straßkirchen D 91 E12
Straßwalchen A 92 G4
Stratford IRL 23 E8
Stratford-upon-Avon GB 29 A11
Strathaven GB 21 D8
Strathblane GB 21 D8
Strathpeffer GB 18 K7
Strathy GB 19 H9
Strathyre GB 21 C8
Stratinska BIH 173 C6
Stratoni GR 185 C10
Stratos GR 190 B3
Stratton GB 28 D5
Stratton St Margaret GB 29 B11
Straubing D 91 E12
Straum N 120 E5
Straum N 124 E5
Straume N 106 A2
Straumen N 120 E4
Straumen N 121 D10
Straumen N 124 B8
Straumen N 125 D10
Straumen N 127 A19
Straumen N 127 C11
Straumen N 130 B7
Straumfjord N 126 C9
Straumgjerde N 116 B5
Straumsnes N 124 B8
Straumsnes N 126 C8
Straumsnes N 127 B13
Straumstad N 127 B17
Straunen N 127 B15
Straupe LV 151 B9
Straupitz D 96 C6
Strausberg D 96 A5
Straußfurt D 95 D8
Stravaj AL 184 C4
Strawczyn PL 159 E9
Straža SRB 175 D7
Strazhitsa BG 182 C5
Stráž nad Nežárkou CZ 93 D7
Stráž nad Nisou CZ 97 E8
Strážnice CZ 162 D4
Stráž pod Ralskem CZ 97 E7
Štrba SK 163 C10
Streatley GB 29 C9
Strečno SK 163 C7
Streda nad Bodrogom SK 161 G4
Streek D 33 B10
Street GB 29 C9
Strehaia RO 175 D11
Strehla D 96 D4
Strejești RO 176 D4
Strekov SK 162 F6
Strelac SRB 180 D5
Strelcha BG 181 D9
Strélnieki LV 151 C8
Strem I 85 A10
Stremț RO 168 E3
Strenči LV 147 F11

Strendur FO 18 A3
Strengberg A 93 F7
Strengelvåg N 126 C9
Strengen A 87 C10
Strengen N 111 D9
Stresa I 84 B6
Stretford GB 27 E7
Stretham GB 31 C9
Streufdorf D 91 B8
Strezimirovtsi BG 180 D5
Strib DK 102 D5
Striberg S 113 C12
Stříbro CZ 92 C3
Stříhen D 33 C11
Striki RO 168 D3
Stroieşti RO 176 C3
Stroiești RO 169 B8
Strokestown IRL 22 E6
Ström S 124 E8
Strömbäck S 138 C4
Strömbacka S 119 C12
Stromberg D 201 E8
Stromeferry GB 18 L5
Strömfors S 134 E4
Strömholm S 125 E15
Stromiec PL 157 G4
Strommen N 111 C13
Strömmen N 111 C13
Strömnäs S 123 B10
Strömnäs S 134 F6
Stromness GB 19 H10
Strömsberg S 115 B9
Strömsbro S 119 C13
Strömsbruk S 119 C13
Strömsholden S 114 C6
Strömsnäs S 123 A14
Strömsnäsbruk S 103 B13
Strömstad S 107 B9
Strömsund S 122 D9
Strömsund S 123 C10
Stronachlachar GB 20 C7
Stroncone I 78 C3
Strongoli I 77 E8
Stronie Śląskie PL 93 B11
Stronsdorf A 93 E10
Strontian GB 20 B5
Stropi LV 151 E13
Stropkov SK 161 E4
Stroppiana I 84 C5
Stroppo I 52 B6
Stroud GB 29 B10
Strövelstorp S 103 C11
Strovija MK 184 A5
Štrpce SRB 180 E5
Strücklingen (Saterland) D 33 B9
Struer DK 102 C3
Struga MK 184 B4
Strugi-Krasnyye RUS 148 C3
Strullendorf D 91 C8
Strumë AL 184 C2
Strumica MK 185 B8
Strumień PL 163 B7
Strumkivka UA 161 G5
Strumyani BG 185 B6
Strumok UA 171 B4
Strunjan HR 173 F7
Strunkovice nad Blanicí CZ 92 D6
Strupli LV 149 C1
Struth D 95 D7
Stružani LV 149 C2
Stružec HR 165 E7
Stryama BG 181 E10
Stryków PL 159 C8
Stryksele S 123 C16
Stryn N 116 C5
Strøby DK 103 E10
Strzała PL 157 F6
Strzałkowo PL 158 B4
Strzebień PL 159 E6
Strzegocin PL 155 F10
Strzegom PL 97 E10
Strzegowo PL 155 E9
Strzelce PL 159 B7
Strzelce Krajeńskie PL 101 E9
Strzelce Opolskie PL 158 E5
Strzelce Wielkie PL 159 D7
Strzeleczki PL 158 F4
Strzelin PL 97 E12
Strzelno PL 154 E5
Strzepcz PL 154 B5
Strzyżewice PL 160 A5
Strzyżów PL 161 D9
Sts-Geosmes F 42 E3
Stubbæk DK 102 F4
Stubbekøbing DK 100 A2
Stubben D 33 B11
Stubel BG 181 C7
Stubenberg A 164 B5
Stubica SRB 175 E7
Štubik SRB 175 D9
Stubline SRB 174 D5
Stubno PL 160 D6
Stuchowo PL 101 C8
Studena HR 173 E7
Studena BG 181 D7
Studena BG 182 F6
Studená CZ 93 D8
Studena UA 170 A3
Studenci HR 173 E7
Studenec CZ 97 E8
Studeníz D 99 E12
Studénka CZ 162 B6
Studénka SK 93 C11
Studina RO 176 F4
Studley GB 29 A11
Studsvik S 109 B10
Studziana PL 101 B13
Studzieniec PL 157 G6
Stugudal N 121 E12
Stugun S 122 E9
Stühlingen D 43 E9

Stuhr D 33 B11
Stukmaņi LV 151 C11
Stülpe D 96 B4
Stulpicani RO 169 C7
Stumm A 88 B4
Stumsnäs S 118 E8
Stuorajavrre N 128 E10
Stuorragár'zi N 129 E16
Stupava SK 93 F12
Stupari BIH 173 D9
Stupnik PL 155 F12
Stupsk PL 155 D9
Stupurai LT 150 D7
Sturefors S 108 C7
Stūri LT 150 C5
Sturkö S 105 C9
Šturlić BIH 172 C5
Sturminster Newton GB 29 D10
Šturovo MK 180 F5
Šťúrovo SK 165 A11
Sturry GB 31 E11
Sturzelbronn F 43 B8
Stuttgart D 43 C11
Stützerbach D 95 E8
Styggedalen N 127 B19
Stylida GR 191 B6
Stypsi GR 187 F10
Styra GR 191 C9
Styrkesnes N 125 A9
Styrnäs S 123 E13
Styrrmanstø N 127 A18
Suances E 56 B3
Suaningi S 133 E10
Suatu RO 168 D3
Subačius LT 151 E9
Subaşı TR 187 B10
Subaşı TR 189 B9
Subaşı TR 189 C11
Subate LV 151 D11
Subbiano I 82 E4
Suben A 92 F4
Subiaco I 78 D4
Subkowy PL 154 B6
Subotica SRB 166 E4
Subotište SRB 174 D4
Subotniki BY 153 E12
Sučany SK 163 C7
Suceava RO 169 B8
Suceveni RO 169 E12
Sucevița RO 169 B7
Sucha Beskidzka PL 163 B9
Suchacz PL 155 B7
Suchá Hora SK 163 C9
Suchá Loz CZ 162 D5
Suchań PL 101 D8
Suchá nad Parnou SK 162 E4
Suchdol CZ 93 C8
Suchdol nad Lužnicí CZ 93 E7
Suchdol nad Odrou CZ 162 B5
Suchedniów PL 159 D10
Suchowola PL 156 C8
Suchożebry PL 157 F6
Suchy Dąb PL 154 B6
Suchy Las PL 97 B11
Sucina E 72 F3
Suciu de Sus RO 168 C4
Suckow D 99 D11
Sucleia MD 170 D4
Sučuraj HR 173 F7
Sudanell E 58 D5
Sudargas LT 152 C6
Sudbury GB 31 C10
Suddendorf D 199 A10
Suddesjaur S 125 E17
Süden D 98 B5
Süderbrarup D 98 B7
Süderhastedt D 98 B6
Süderlügum D 102 F3
Süderstapel D 98 B6
Suderve LT 153 D11
Sudiți RO 177 D11
Sudkov CZ 93 C11
Südlohn D 33 E7
Sudok S 134 B4
Sudoměřice CZ 162 D4
Sudova Vyshnya UA 160 D7
Sudovec HR 165 D6
Sudrabkalns LV 151 D12
SuđuradØ HR 178 D4
Sudwalde D 33 C11
Sueca E 64 F4
Süedinenie BG 181 E10
Suelli I 80 D3
Suèvres F 40 E5
Şugag RO 168 F3
Suha BIH 173 D10
Suha BIH 173 F10
Suhaia RO 176 F6
Suharău RO 169 A8
Suhl D 95 E8
Suhlendorf D 99 E9
Suhmura FIN 141 F13
Suho Polje BIH 173 C11
Suhopolje HR 165 E8
Šuica BIH 173 E7
Şuici RO 176 C5
Šuijavaara S 132 B9
Suilly-la-Tour F 41 F9
Suinula FIN 143 B11
Suinula FIN 143 B12
Suippes F 41 B12
Sukeva FIN 140 C8
Sukhindol BG 182 C4
Sukhodil UA 161 D9
Sukhodil UA 161 D9
Sukošan HR 172 D3
Sükösd H 165 A4
Sukovo SRB 181 C6
Sukow D 99 C11
Sul N 121 D12
Suldrup DK 102 B5
Sulechów PL 97 C9
Sulęcin PL 97 B8
Sulęcin Szlachecki PL 155 E12
Sulęczyno PL 154 B4
Sulejów PL 157 H1
Sulejówek PL 157 F4
Suleskar N 110 D5
Sulesund N 116 B4
Suletea RO 169 E11
Süleymani TR 189 B6
Süleymaniye TR 189 D9
Süleymanlı TR 193 B10
Sulików PL 97 D7
Sulingen D 33 C11
Suliszewo PL 101 D9
Suliţa RO 169 B9
Sulkava FIN 139 D17
Sulkava FIN 145 B9
Sulkavankylä FIN 139 D16
Sulkavanjärvi FIN 139 D17

Sulkavankylä FIN 139 F11
Sułkowice PL 163 B9
Sullington GB 31 F8
Sully F 46 A5
Sully GB 29 C8
Sully-sur-Loire F 41 E7
Sulmierzyce PL 158 C4
Sulmierzyce PL 159 D7
Sulmona I 78 C5
Sulniac F 38 E6
Sułoszowa PL 159 F8
Sułów PL 97 D12
Sułów PL 160 B6
Sulsted DK 102 A5
Sultaniça TR 187 C10
Sultaniye TR 189 D9
Sultanköy TR 187 B8
Sultanköy TR 189 B8
Suluca TR 187 C11
Suluca TR 188 D6
Sulvik S 113 C7
Sulviken S 121 D14
Sulz A 87 C9
Sulz am Neckar D 43 D10
Sulzbach am Main D 37 E12
Sulzbach an der Murr D 43 B11
Sulzbach-Laufen D 90 E6
Sulzbach-Rosenberg D 91 C10
Sulzbach/Saar D 202 C2
Sulzdorf an der Lederhecke D 91 B8
Sulzemoos D 91 F9
Sulzfeld D 91 B6
Sulzfeld D 203 C6
Sulzheim D 91 C7
Sulzthal D 91 B7
Sumartin HR 173 F6
Sumba FO 18 C3
Sumburgh GB 19 F12
Šumećani HR 165 E6
Šümeg H 165 C8
Sumène F 51 C6
Šumiac SK 161 F1
Sumiainen FIN 139 E16
Sumice CZ 162 C5
Sumiswald CH 86 C5
Summer Bridge GB 27 C8
Summerhill IRL 23 E9
Šumperk CZ 93 C11
Sumsa FIN 137 F14
Šumvald CZ 93 C11
Sumvitg CH 87 D7
Sunäkste LV 151 D11
Šuñava SK 163 C10
Sunbilla E 48 D2
Šuncuius RO 167 D10
Šund FIN 115 B14
Sund N 124 B7
Sund N 126 D5
Sund S 108 D6
Sund S 119 B10
Sund S 123 E14
Sundborn S 119 E10
Sundby DK 102 B3
Sundby DK 102 B3
Sundby FIN 138 C9
Sundby N 124 B9
Sunde N 110 C3
Sunde N 120 E6
Sunderland GB 21 F14
Sundern (Sauerland) D 33 F10
Sundet S 121 D13
Sundklakk N 126 D7
Sundnäs S 125 D14
Sundom FIN 138 D7
Sundom S 134 C8
Sundre S 109 F12
Sunds DK 102 C4
Sundsbruk S 119 B13
Sundsjö S 119 A9
Sundsli N 106 A4
Sundsvall S 119 C10
Sundvollen N 111 B12
Sungurlare BG 183 D7
Sunhultsbrunn S 108 D5
Suni I 80 C2
Sunja HR 165 F7
Sunnan S 135 B9
Sünna D 95 E7
Sunnan N 121 C11
Sunnanfors S 113 B14
Sunnansjö S 113 B12
Sunnansjö S 123 E14
Sunnäs S 119 A12
Sunndal N 110 B4
Sunndalsøra N 117 A9
Sunne S 113 C9
Sunne S 119 A14
Sunne S 122 E6
Sunnemo S 113 C10
Sunnersta S 123 D12
Sunningen S 107 C10
Suntaži LV 151 C9
Suodenniemi FIN 142 B8
Suojanperä FIN 130 E4
Suojoki FIN 138 F7
Suolahti FIN 139 E15
Suolijärvi FIN 137 D11
Suolijärvi FIN 135 B14
Suoluvuobmi N 129 D12
Suomela FIN 135 D3
Suomenniemi FIN 144 C7
Suomijärvi FIN 138 F9
Suommu FIN 131 E4
Suomussalmi FIN 137 E10
Suoniemi FIN 143 C9
Suonnankylä FIN 137 B11
Suontee FIN 140 F9
Suopajärvi FIN 133 B13
Suorajärvi FIN 137 B13
Suorsa FIN 135 B9
Šuosja'v'ri N 129 E13
Suostola FIN 131 D2
Suovaara FIN 137 E11
Suovanlahti FIN 139 E15
Supersano I 77 D10
Supertarska Draga HR 83 C10
Supetar HR 172 F6
Supino I 78 D4
Suplac RO 168 E5
Suplacu de Barcău RO 167 C10
Suplai RO 168 C4
Supru FIN 130 E4
Supru RO 167 C10
Súr H 165 B10
Şura Mare RO 168 F4

Şura Mică RO 168 F4
Şurani RO 169 D7
Surany SK 162 E6
Suraż PL 157 E7
Surčin SRB 174 D4
Surdegis LT 151 E9
Surdila-Găiseanca RO 177 C10
Surdila-Greci RO 177 C10
Surduc RO 167 C11
Surdulica SRB 180 D5
Surfleet GB 27 F11
Surgères F 44 C4
Surhuisterveen NL 32 B6
Surier I 47 D11
Surmatura RO 168 B4
Surnadalsøra N 120 F5
Surnevets BG 182 E5
Sürnevo BG 182 E5
Sürnitsa BG 181 F9
Šúrovce SK 162 E5
Sursee CH 86 C5
Surte S 107 D11
Surviliškis LT 151 E8
Surwold D 33 C9
Sury-le-Comtal F 46 D5
Surzur F 38 E6
Susa I 47 E11
Suşani RO 176 D4
Šušara SRB 175 D7
Susch CH 87 D10
Susegana I 88 E5
Susek SRB 174 C4
Süsel D 99 B9
Suseni RO 168 D5
Suseni RO 169 D7
Suseni RO 176 D5
Sushitsa BG 182 C5
Sušice CZ 92 D5
Susiec PL 160 C7
Šuškova LV 149 D4
Suslen MD 170 C3
Susteren NL 35 B12
Sustinente I 82 B3
Sustrum D 33 C8
Susurluk TR 189 C10
Susz PL 155 C7
Susuzmüsellim TR 189 B7
Susz PL 155 C7
Sutera I 74 D4
Suteşti RO 176 D4
Suteşti RO 177 C10
Sutina FIN 137 F14
Sutjeska SRB 174 C6
Sütlüce TR 189 A8
Sutri I 78 C2
Sutri LV 151 D12
Sutterton GB 27 F11
Süttő H 165 A10
Sutton GB 31 D9
Sutton Bridge GB 27 F12
Sutton Coldfield GB 27 F8
Sutton in Ashfield GB 27 E9
Sutton-on-the-Forest GB 27 C9
Suure-Jaani EST 147 D10
Suurejõe EST 147 D9
Suuremõisa EST 146 D5
Suurmäki FIN 141 E11
Suur-Miehikkälä FIN 144 D8
Suurpea EST 147 B11
Suutarinkylä FIN 135 D17
Suutarinkylä FIN 135 F17
Suvainiškis LT 151 D7
Suvanto FIN 131 D2
Suvantokumpu FIN 133 C15
Suva Reka SRB 179 E10
Suvereto I 81 A3
Suviekas LT 151 E12
Suvodol MK 185 B6
Suvorov RO 171 B2
Suvorove UA 171 B3
Suvorovo BG 183 C9
Suwałki PL 152 B5
Suystamo RUS 145 B15
Suze-la-Rousse F 51 B8
Suzzara I 82 C2
Svabensverk S 119 D10
Svalboviken S 109 A8
Svalenik BG 182 B6
Svallerup DK 103 D8
Svalöv S 103 D12
Svalsta S 109 B8
Svalvik S 104 C7
Svalyava UA 161 F6
Svaneke DK 105 E8
Svanesund S 107 C10
Svängsta S 105 C7
Svaningen S 122 C8
Svännäs S 125 B11
Svannäs S 125 D15
Svanselet S 123 B17
Svansele S 123 B17
Svanskog S 107 D12
Svanstein S 133 E11
Svanström S 134 E5
Svantjärnåsen S 118 B7
Svappavaara S 132 C6
Svardal N 117 A12
Svärdsjö S 119 E10
Svarinci LV 149 D3
Svärtå S 108 A5
Svartå FIN 143 E10
Svartå S 108 A5
Svartberget S 119 D11
Svartbyn S 135 B9
Svartemyr N 116 D3
Svartisdalhytta N 124 D7
Svartlå S 134 B7
Svartnäs N 124 B8
Svartnäs S 119 D11
Svartnes N 130 C10
Svartöstaden S 134 C8
Svärttrask S 123 A12
Svartvik S 119 B13
Svatava CZ 91 B12
Svätuše SK 161 G4
Svätý Jur SK 162 E4
Svätý Peter SK 162 F6
Sveballe DK 103 D8
Svedala S 103 D12
Svedja S 119 D12

Svedja S 119 C12
Svedje S 122 C9
Svedje S 123 D15
Svedjebo S 119 C12
Švedlár SK 161 F2
Sveg S 118 B7
Sveggesundet N 120 E3
Sveicarija LT 153 F9
Sveindal N 106 C1
Sveio N 110 C2
Svejbæk DK 102 C5
Sveki LV 151 B13
Švekšna LT 150 E3
Svelgen N 116 C2
Svellingen N 120 D5
Svelvik N 111 C12
Švenčionėliai LT 151 F11
Švenčionys LT 151 F12
Svendborg DK 102 E7
Svene N 111 C11
Svenljunga S 107 E12
Svenningdal N 124 F5
Svensbu N 127 A18
Svensby S 134 D6
Svenshögen S 107 C10
Svenstavik S 118 A7
Svenstrup DK 102 B5
Svenstrup DK 102 E5
Svenstrup DK 103 D8
Svente LV 151 E12
Šventežeris LT 153 E8
Šventoji LT 150 D2
Sverepec SK 162 C6
Sveta Marija HR 165 D7
Svētciems LV 147 F8
Svēte LV 150 C7
Sveti Nikola BG 183 C10
Sveti Nikola BG 183 C9
Sveti Nikole MK 180 F4
Sveti Rok HR 172 D5
Sveti Štefan MNE 179 E6
Světlá Hora CZ 158 F3
Světlá nad Sázavou CZ 93 C8
Svetlen BG 182 C6
Svetlogorsk RUS 155 A9
Svetlyy RUS 155 A9
Svetogorsk RUS 145 C10
Svetozar Miletić SRB 166 F3
Svetvinčenat HR 83 B8
Svezhen BG 181 D11
Švica HR 83 C11
Svidník SK 161 E4
Svihov CZ 92 D4
Sviibi EST 146 D6
Sviljanac SRB 175 E7
Svilengrad BG 182 F6
Svindvik DK 102 E7
Svinesund S 107 A9
Svingen N 127 C14
Svingstad N 117 E12
Svinhult S 108 D6
Svinia SK 161 E3
Svinița RO 175 D9
Svinnå S 134 D6
Svinnersta S 108 B5
Svinninge DK 103 D9
Svinninge N 120 E8
Svinninge S 115 D10
Svínoy FO 18 A4
Svinvika N 120 E4
Svir BY 151 G13
Svirkos LT 151 F12
Svishtov BG 176 F6
Svislach BY 156 D10
Svit SK 161 E1
Svitávka CZ 93 C11
Svitavy CZ 93 C10
Svitene LV 151 D7
Svitlodolyns'ke UA 170 E5
Svityaz' UA 157 H9
Svoboda BG 171 F1
Svoboda BG 182 E4
Svoboda BG 182 F4
Svoboda nad Úpou CZ 97 E9
Svobodinovo BG 182 F4
Svođe SRB 180 D5
Svodín SK 162 F6
Svodna BIH 172 B6
Svoge BG 181 D8
Svogerslev DK 103 D9
Svolvær N 126 D6
Svorkmo N 120 E7
Svratka CZ 93 C10
Svrčinovec SK 163 C7
Svrljig SRB 180 C5
Svullrya N 112 B7
Swadlincote GB 27 F8
Swaffham GB 31 B10
Swalmen NL 36 B6
Swan IRL 25 C8
Swanage GB 29 D11
Swanley GB 31 E9
Swanlinbar IRL 23 C7
Swansea GB 29 B7
Swanton Morley GB 31 B10
Swarożyn PL 154 B6
Swarzędz PL 97 B12
Swatragh GB 20 F3
Sway GB 29 D11
Świątki PL 155 C9
Świbno PL 154 B6
Świderki PL 157 G6
Świdnica PL 97 C8
Świdnica PL 97 E10
Świdnik PL 157 H7
Świdwin PL 101 C9
Świebodzice PL 97 C11
Świebodzin PL 97 B9
Świecie PL 154 D5
Święciechów PL 97 C11
Świeciechów-Duży PL 160 B4
Świedziebnia PL 155 D8
Świekatowo PL 154 D5
Świeradów-Zdrój PL 97 E8
Świercze PL 155 E10
Świerczów PL 158 D4
Świerklaniec PL 159 F6
Świerklany Górne PL 158 F6
Świerzawa PL 97 D9
Świerże PL 157 H9
Świerzenko PL 101 D11
Świerzno PL 101 C7
Świeszyno PL 101 B10
Świętajno PL 155 C11
Świętajno PL 155 C11
Świętochłowice PL 159 F6
Świętoszów PL 97 D8
Świfterbant NL 32 C5
Świlcza PL 160 C4
Swindon GB 29 B11
Swineshead GB 27 F11

Swinford IRL 22 E5
Świnna PL 163 B8
Świnoujście PL 100 C6
Swinton GB 21 D12
Swinton GB 27 D7
Swobnica PL 100 D7
Swords IRL 23 F10
Swornegacie PL 101 C13
Syalyawshchyna BY 149 E5
Sycewice PL 101 B11
Syców PL 158 D4
Sydalen N 126 D7
Sydänmaa FIN 139 E10
Sydänmaankylä FIN 139 C16
Sydnes N 110 C3
Syelishcha BY 149 F4
Syfteland N 110 B2
Sykaminia GR 187 F10
Sykäräinen FIN 139 C12
Syke D 33 C11
Sykea GR 194 B4
Syki GR 185 F9
Sykia GR 185 E7
Sykia GR 186 D5
Sykies GR 185 F7
Sykkylven N 116 B5
Sykorrachi GR 187 C9
Sykourio GR 185 E8
Sylling N 111 C12
Sylte N 116 B6
Symbister GB 19 E14
Symi GR 197 C7
Synej AL 184 B2
Synevyr UA 161 G8
Synevyrs'ka Polyana UA 161 F8
Synod Inn GB 28 A6
Synsiö FIN 139 F17
Synyak UA 161 F6
Syötekylä FIN 137 C10
Sypniewo PL 101 D11
Sypniewo PL 155 D11
Syrau D 91 A11
Syre GB 19 J8
Syrgenstein D 91 E7
Syri FIN 139 C13
Syrjä FIN 141 F10
Sysmä FIN 143 B14
Sysslebäck S 118 E4
Syston GB 27 F9
Syväjärvi FIN 133 D15
Syvänniemi FIN 140 E8
Syvärinpää FIN 141 D9
Syvde N 116 B3
Syvdsnes N 116 B3
Syvota GR 184 F3
Syvros GR 190 B2
Syvsten DK 106 E7
Syyspohja FIN 145 C10
Szabadegyháza H 165 B11
Szabadhidvég H 165 C10
Szabadkígyós H 167 D7
Szabadszállás H 166 D3
Szabolcsbáka H 161 G5
Szada H 166 B3
Szadek PL 159 C6
Szaflary PL 163 C10
Szajol H 166 C5
Szakály H 165 C10
Szakcs H 165 C10
Szakmár H 166 D3
Szakoly H 167 B8
Szákszend H 165 A10
Szalánta H 165 E10
Szalaszend H 161 G3
Szalkszentmárton H 166 D3
Szalonna H 161 G2
Szamocin PL 101 D12
Szamosszeg H 161 G5
Szamotuły PL 97 A11
Szank H 166 D4
Szany H 165 B8
Szár H 165 B11
Szarvas H 166 D6
Szászberek H 166 C5
Szatmárcseke H 161 G6
Szatymaz H 166 E5
Százhalombatta H 165 B11
Szczaniec PL 97 B9
Szczawin Kościelny PL 155 F8
Szczawne PL 161 E5
Szczawnica PL 161 E2
Szczawno-Zdrój PL 97 E10
Szczebrzeszyn PL 160 B6
Szczecin PL 100 D7
Szczecinek PL 101 C11
Szczekociny PL 159 E8
Szczepankowo PL 155 D12
Szczepanowo PL 154 E4
Szczerców PL 159 D7
Szczucin PL 159 F11
Szczuczyn PL 156 C6
Szczurkowo PL 152 E2
Szczurowa PL 159 F10
Szczutowo PL 155 E8
Szczyrk PL 163 B8
Szczytna PL 93 B10
Szczytniki PL 158 C5
Szczytno PL 155 C10
Szécsény H 163 E9
Szederkény H 165 D10
Szedres H 165 D11
Szeged H 166 E5
Szeghalom H 167 C7
Szegi H 161 G3
Szegvár H 166 D5
Székely H 161 G4
Székesfehérvár H 165 B10
Székkutas H 166 D6
Szekszárd H 165 D11
Szemud PL 154 B5
Szendehely H 163 F8
Szendrő H 161 G2
Szendrőlád H 161 G2
Szentendre H 166 B3
Szentes H 166 D5
Szentgál H 165 B9
Szentgotthárd H 164 C6
Szentistván H 166 B6
Szentkirály H 166 D4
Szentlászló H 165 D9
Szentőrinc H 165 D9
Szentpéterfa H 165 B6
Szepetnek H 165 D7
Szepietowo PL 157 E7
Szerecseny H 165 B9
Szeremle H 165 D11
Szerencs H 161 G3
Szerep H 167 C7
Szerzyny PL 160 D3
Szestno PL 152 F3
Szigetbecse H 165 B11
Szigetcsép H 165 B11
Szigethalom H 166 C2
Szigetszentmiklós H 166 C3
Szigetvár H 165 D9
Szigliget H 165 C8
Szihalom H 166 B5
Szikszó H 161 G2
Szil H 165 A8
Szilvásvárad H 161 G1
Szirák H 163 F9
Szirmabesenyő H 161 G2
Szkaradowo PL 97 C12
Szklarska Poręba PL 97 E9
Szklary Górne PL 97 D10
Szlichtyngowa PL 97 C10
Szob H 163 F7
Sződ H 166 B3
Szögliget H 161 F2
Szokolya H 163 F8
Szolnok H 166 C5
Szőlősgyörök H 165 C9
Szombathely H 165 B7
Szomód H 165 A10
Szomolya H 161 H1
Szówsko PL 160 C6
Szpetal Górny PL 154 E7
Szprotawa PL 97 C9
Szreńsk PL 155 D9
Szropy PL 155 C7
Sztabin PL 156 C8
Sztum PL 154 C7
Sztutowo PL 155 B7
Szubin PL 154 D4
Szőcsi H 166 B4
Szudziałowo PL 156 D9
Szügy H 163 E8
Szuhogy H 161 G2
Szulborze Wielkie PL 157 E6
Szumowo PL 155 E13
Szurdokpüspöki H 163 F9
Szydłów PL 159 E11
Szydłowiec PL 157 H3
Szydłowo PL 101 D11
Szydłowo PL 155 D9
Szymanów PL 157 F2
Szymonka PL 152 F4
Szynkielów PL 158 D6
Szypliszki PL 152 E7

T

Taagepera EST 147 F11
Taalintehdas FIN 142 E8
Taapajärvi FIN 133 D13
Taastrup DK 103 D10
Tab H 165 C10
Tabajd H 165 B11
Tabaky UA 171 B3
Tabanera de Cerrato E 56 D3
Tábara E 55 E8
Tabarz D 95 E8
Tabasalu EST 147 C9
Tabdi H 166 D3
Taberg S 107 D15
Tabernas E 71 E8
Taberno E 71 E8
Tabivere EST 147 D13
Taboada E 54 C4
Taboadela E 54 D4
Tábor CZ 93 D7
Táborfalva H 166 C3
Tábua P 60 D4
Tabuaço P 60 B5
Tabuenca E 57 E8
Täby S 115 D10
Tác H 165 B10
Tacen SLO 89 D9
Tacherting D 91 F12
Tachov CZ 91 C12
Tackåsen S 119 C9
Tăcuta RO 169 D11
Tadasuni I 80 C2
Tadcaster GB 27 D9
Tadley GB 29 C12
Taebla EST 146 D7
Tælavåg N 110 B1
Taevaskoja EST 147 E14
Tafalla E 48 E2
Tafers CH 47 B11
Taff's Well GB 29 B8
Tafjord N 116 B6
Täftea S 123 E15
Täfteå S 138 C4
Taga RO 168 D4
Tagaranna EST 146 D4
Taggia I 53 D7
Taghmon IRL 25 D9
Tagliacozzo I 78 C4
Taglio di Po I 82 B5
Taglio-Isolaccio F 53 G10
Tagnon F 35 F9
Tägsjöberg S 123 D11
Tahal E 71 E8
Tähemaa EST 147 E14
Tahilla IRL 24 E3
Tahitótfalu H 166 B3
Tähtelä FIN 133 D17
Taibòn Agordino I 88 D5
Taíde P 54 E3
Tain GB 19 K8
Tainiemi FIN 135 C15
Tainijoki FIN 135 C15
Tain-l'Hermitage F 46 E6
Taintrux F 43 D6
Taio I 88 D3
Taipale FIN 135 B15
Taipale FIN 135 C14
Taipale FIN 139 D17
Taipale FIN 140 D8
Taipale FIN 142 B8
Taipaleenharju FIN 135 D17
Taipalsaari FIN 145 C9
Taipalus FIN 139 E10
Taivalkoski FIN 137 C11
Taivassalo FIN 142 D6
Taizé F 46 B6
Tajmište MK 184 A4
Tajno Łanowe PL 156 C7
Takácsi H 165 B8
Takamaa FIN 143 B10
Takeley GB 31 D9
Takene S 113 C9
Takene S 113 D10
Taklax FIN 138 E6
Taksony H 166 C3
Taktakenéz H 161 G3
Taktaszada H 161 G3
Talais F 44 E3
Talamantes E 57 E8
Talamona I 81 B4
Talamone I 81 B4
Talange F 202 C1
Talant F 42 F3
Talarrubias E 67 A9
Talaván E 61 E8
Talavera de la Reina E 62 E3
Talavera la Real E 67 B6
Talayuela E 61 E9
Talayuelas E 63 E10
Talea RO 177 C7
Talence F 44 F4
Talensac F 39 D8
Tales E 64 E4
Taleža BIH 178 D5
Talgarreg GB 28 A6
Talgarth GB 29 B8
Talhadas P 60 C4
Tali EST 147 E9
Taliard F 52 C4
Taliesin GB 26 F4
Táliga E 67 B5
Tälje S 119 A10
Talla I 82 E4
Tallås S 119 E11
Tallås S 125 E14
Tallåsen S 119 C11
Tällberg S 119 E8
Tallberg S 134 B8
Taller F 48 C3
Tallinn EST 147 C9
Talljärv S 134 B8
Talloires F 47 D9
Tallone F 53 G11
Tallós E 54 C2
Tallow IRL 24 D6
Tallsjö S 123 C14
Talluskylä FIN 140 D7
Tallvik S 135 B9
Tállya H 161 G3
Tălmaciu RO 176 B4
Talmay F 42 F3
Talmaz MD 170 D5
Talmont F 44 D4
Talmont-St-Hilaire F 44 C2
Talpa RO 176 E6
Talsano I 77 C8
Talsi LV 150 B5
Taluskylä FIN 135 F12
Talviainen FIN 143 B12
Talvik N 128 C10
Tama E 55 B10
Tămădău Mare RO 177 E9
Tamajón E 63 B6
Tamames E 61 C8
Tamarë AL 179 E8
Tamarino BG 183 E7
Tamarite de Litera E 58 D4
Tamashowka BY 157 G9
Tamási H 165 C10
Tamași RO 169 D10
Tambach-Dietharz D 95 E8
Tâmboești RO 177 B10
Tâme S 134 E4
Tamins CH 87 D8
Tamış TR 187 E10
Tamm D 43 C11
Tammela FIN 137 C15
Tammela FIN 143 D10
Tammensiel D 98 A5
Tammijärvi FIN 143 B14
Tammiku EST 147 C12
Tammisaari FIN 143 F9
Tammispää EST 147 D14
Tammneeme EST 147 B9
Tâmna RO 175 D11
Tamnay-en-Bazois F 46 A4
Tamnes N 117 A15
Tamnič SRB 175 E9
Tampere FIN 143 C10
Tamsalu EST 147 C12
Tamsweg A 89 B8
Tamurejo E 70 B3
Tamworth GB 27 F8
Tana Bru N 129 C21
Tanacu RO 169 D11
Tanaji LV 151 E13
Tananes N 130 B4
Tananger N 110 E3
Tânăsoaia RO 169 E10
Tanaunella I 80 B4
Tancarville F 34 F1
Tandådalen S 118 D4
Tăndărei RO 177 D11
Tandö S 118 E5
Tandragee GB 23 D10
Tandsbyn S 122 E7
Tandsjöborg S 118 C8
Tang IRL 23 E7
Tångaberg S 103 A10
Tangaveane IRL 22 C6
Tångböle S 121 E13
Tange DK 102 C5
Tangen N 111 A12
Tangen N 117 E14
Tangen N 127 B14
Tanger MA 68 E5
Tångeråsen S 121 D15
Tangerhütte D 95 B10
Tangermünde D 95 A10
Tångstamon S 123 E11
Tangstedt D 99 C8
Tängvattnet S 124 E8
Tanhua FIN 131 C3
Taninges F 47 C10
Tankapirtti FIN 131 B2
Tankavaara FIN 131 B2
Tanlay F 41 E11
Tann D 92 F3
Tann (Rhön) D 95 E7
Tanna D 91 B10
Tannadice GB 21 B11
Tännäs S 118 B4
Tannay F 35 E10
Tannay F 41 F10
Tänndalen S 118 A3
Tanne D 95 C8
Tannenbergsthal D 91 B11
Tännesberg D 91 C11
Tannhausen D 91 E7
Tannheim A 87 C11
Tannila FIN 135 D15
Tännö S 104 A6
Tannroda D 95 E9
Tannsjön S 122 D9
Tanowo PL 100 C6
Tansa RO 169 D10
Țânțăreni RO 176 D2
Tantonville F 42 D5
Tanumshede S 107 B9
Tanvald CZ 97 E8
Taormina I 75 D7
Tapa EST 147 C11
Tapanikylä FIN 137 F13
Tapfheim D 91 E8
Tapia de Casariego E 55 A6
Tápióbicske H 166 C4
Tápiógyörgye H 166 C4
Tapionkylä FIN 133 E14
Tapionniemi FIN 131 E2
Tápióság H 166 C4
Tápiószecső H 166 C4
Tápiószele H 166 C4
Tápiószentmárton H 166 C4
Tápiószőlős H 166 C4
Táplánszentkereszt H 165 B7
Tapojärvi FIN 133 C11
Tapolca H 165 C8
Tappeluft N 128 C9
Tappenbeck D 95 B8
Tappernøje DK 103 E9
Taps DK 102 E4
Tapsony H 165 D8
Tar H 163 F9
Taracena E 63 C6
Taraclia MD 170 D4
Taraclia MD 170 F3
Taradeau F 52 E4
Taradell E 59 D8
Taramundi E 54 B5
Tarancón E 63 D6
Tarano I 78 C3
Taranto I 77 C8
Tarany H 165 D8
Tarare F 46 D5
Tarascon F 51 C8
Tarascon-sur-Ariège F 49 E9
Tarashany UA 169 A8
Tarazona E 57 E8
Tarazona de la Mancha E 63 F9
Tárbena E 72 D4
Tarbert GB 18 K3
Tarbert GB 20 D5
Tarbert GB 20 D6
Tarbert IRL 24 C4
Tarbes F 49 D6
Tarbja EST 147 D11
Tarbolton GB 20 D8
Tărcaia RO 167 D9
Tarcal H 161 G3
Tarcău RO 169 D8
Tarcea RO 167 C9
Tarcento I 89 D7
Tarčin BIH 173 E9
Tarczyn PL 157 G3
Tard H 161 H2
Tardajos E 56 D4
Tardelcuende E 57 E6
Tardets-Sorholus F 48 D4
Tardienta E 57 E10
Tardona H 161 G2
Tărendö S 132 D9
Tareuca MD 170 B3
Târgale LV 150 B3
Targon F 44 F5
Târgoviște RO 177 D6
Targowa Górka PL 101 F12
Târgu Bujor RO 169 F11
Târgu Cărbunești RO 176 D3
Târgu Frumos RO 169 C9
Târgu Jiu RO 175 C11
Târgu Lăpuș RO 168 C3
Târgu Mureș RO 168 E5
Târgu Neamț RO 169 C8
Târgu Ocna RO 169 E9
Târgu Secuiesc RO 169 E8
Târgușor RO 171 E2
Târgu Trotuș RO 169 E9
Tarhos H 167 D7
Tarifa E 69 D5
Tarigrad MD 169 A11
Tarján H 165 A11
Tárkány H 165 A9
Tarleton GB 26 D6
Târlișua RO 168 C4
Tarłów PL 159 D12
Tărlungeni RO 177 B7
Tarm DK 102 D3
Tarmstedt D 33 B12
Tärnaby S 124 E9
Tärnafors S 124 E9
Tarnala FIN 145 B12
Tarnalelesz H 161 G1
Tarna Mare RO 161 G7
Tarnaméra H 166 B5
Tärnamo S 124 E9
Tarnaörs H 166 B5
Tarnaszentmiklós H 166 B5
Târnăveni RO 168 E4
Tarnawa Duża PL 160 B6
Tarnawatka PL 160 B7
Tarnazsadány H 166 B5
Tårnelv N 127 B15
Tårnes N 120 D7
Tårnet N 130 D8
Tarnobrzeg PL 159 E12
Tarnogród PL 160 C6
Tárnok H 165 B11
Tarnos F 48 C3
Tarnoszyn PL 160 C8
Târnova RO 167 E8
Târnova RO 175 E9
Tarnow D 99 C12
Tarnów PL 101 E7
Tarnów PL 159 F10
Tarnowiec PL 160 D4
Tarnówka PL 101 D11
Tarnówko PL 101 E11
Tarnowo Podgórne PL 97 B11
Tarnów Opolski PL 158 E5
Tarnowskie Góry PL 158 F6
Tärnsjö S 114 B7
Tärnvik N 124 A9
Tärnvik N 129 C18
Taron-Sadirac-Viellenave F 48 C5
Tarouca P 60 B5
Tarp D 98 A6
Tarp DK 102 D2
Tarpa H 161 G6
Tarprubežiai LT 152 E7
Tarquinia I 78 C1
Tarquinia Lido I 78 C1
Tarragona E 58 E6
Tårrajaur S 125 D18
Tàrrega E 58 D6
Tarrel GB 19 K9
Tarrenz A 87 C11
Tarrio E 54 B3
Tarroja de Segarra E 58 D6
Tårs DK 103 F8
Tårs DK 106 E7
Tarsele S 123 D11
Tarsia I 76 D6
Târșolț RO 161 H7
Tårstad N 127 D12
Tartas F 48 C4
Tărtășești RO 177 D7
Tartu EST 147 E13
Tårup DK 103 E7
Tarutyne UA 170 E4
Tarvaala FIN 139 E14
Tarvasjoki FIN 142 D8
Tarves GB 19 L12
Tarvisio I 89 C8
Tarvola FIN 139 D11
Taşağıl TR 189 A7
Tașca RO 169 D8
Täsjö S 123 C9
Taşlîc MD 170 C4
Tășnad RO 167 C10
Tass H 166 C3
Tassagh GB 23 D9
Tassin-la-Demi-Lune F 46 D6
Taszár H 165 D9
Tát H 165 A11
Tata H 165 A10
Tatabánya H 165 A10
Tataháza H 166 E3
Tătărani RO 169 D11
Tătărani RO 176 D6
Tătăranu RO 177 B10
Tătărăști RO 169 E10
Tătărăștii de Jos RO 176 E6
Tătărăștii de Sus RO 176 E6
Tătăruca MD 169 A12
Tatarbunary UA 170 F5
Tătărești MD 170 E2
Tatarevo BG 182 E4
Tatarköy TR 189 B7
Tatarlar TR 183 F7
Tatárszentgyörgy H 166 C3
Tating D 98 B5
Tatlısu TR 189 D8
Tatranská Javorina SK 161 E1
Tattershall GB 27 E11
Tătuleşti RO 176 D5
Tau N 110 D3
Tauberbischofsheim D 90 C6
Taucha D 95 D11
Tauche D 96 B6
Tauer D 97 C6
Taufkirchen D 91 F10
Taufkirchen D 91 F11
Taufkirchen (Vils) D 91 F11
Taujėnai LT 151 F9
Țaul MD 169 A11
Taulé F 38 C4
Taulignan F 51 B8
Taunton GB 29 C8
Tauplitz A 89 A9
Tauragė LT 150 F4
Tauragnai LT 151 F11
Tauralaukis LT 150 E2
Taurasi I 76 A3
Taurene LV 151 B11
Tăureni RO 168 D4
Taurianova I 75 C9
Taurisano I 77 D10
Taurupe LV 151 C10
Tauste E 57 E9
Tăuț RO 167 E8
Tăuteu RO 167 C9
Tăuții-Măgherăuș RO 167 B12
Tauves F 45 D11
Tauvo FIN 135 E13
Tauzhne UA 170 A6
Tavaco F 53 G9
Tavagnacco I 89 D7
Tavaklı TR 187 E10
Tavankut SRB 166 E4
Tavannes CH 43 F7
Tavant F 40 F3
Tavarnelle Val di Pesa I 82 E3
Tavastila FIN 144 D6
Tavastkenkä FIN 135 F16
Tavaux F 47 A7
Taveiro P 60 D4
Tavel F 51 B8
Tavelsjö S 138 B4
Tavera F 53 G9
Taverham GB 31 B11
Taverna I 75 A10
Tavernay F 46 A5
Tavernelle I 78 A2
Tavernes F 52 D4
Tavernes de la Valldigna E 72 C4
Tavernspite GB 28 B5
Taverny F 41 B7
Tavertet E 59 D8
Taviano I 77 D10
Tavira P 66 E4
Tavistock GB 28 D6
Tavullia I 83 E6
Tawern D 202 B2
Taxenbach A 89 B6
Taxiarchis GR 185 D10
Taxobeni MD 169 C11
Tayfur TR 187 D10
Tayinloan GB 20 D5
Taylor's Cross IRL 23 F7
Taynuilt GB 20 C6
Tayport GB 21 C11
Tayvallich GB 20 C5
Tázlár H 166 D4
Tazlău RO 169 D8
Tazones E 55 A9
Tczew PL 154 B6
Tczów PL 157 H4
Teaca RO 168 D5
Teano I 76 A2
Tearce MK 180 E3
Teasc RO 176 E3
Teba E 69 C7
Tebar E 63 E8
Tebay GB 26 C6
Tebstrup DK 102 D5
Techendorf A 89 C7
Techirghiol RO 171 E3
Tecuci RO 169 F10
Tedavnet IRL 23 D8
Teeriranta FIN 137 C14
Teerivaara FIN 136 B9
Tefeli GR 194 E9
Tegelen NL 32 F6
Tegelträsk S 123 D13
Teggiano I 76 C5
Téglás H 167 B8
Teglio I 85 A9
Tegnäset S 123 C16
Teichwolframsdorf D 95 E11
Teignmouth GB 29 D8
Teijo FIN 143 E8
Teikosuvanto FIN 133 E11
Teillay F 39 E8
Teillet F 49 C10
Teișani RO 177 C8
Teisendorf D 89 A6
Teisko FIN 143 B10
Teisnach D 92 D4
Teistungen D 95 D7
Teiu RO 176 D6
Teiuș RO 168 E3
Teixeiro E 54 B3
Teixoso P 60 D6
Tejadillos E 63 D9
Tejado E 57 E7
Tejeda de Tiétar E 61 D9
Tejn DK 105 E7
Tekeler TR 197 A7
Tekeli TR 193 C9
Tekeriš SRB 174 D4
Tekija BIH 173 D11
Tekija SRB 175 D9
Tekirdağ TR 189 C7
Tekovské Lužany SK 163 E7
Teksdal N 120 D7
Telaki PL 157 E6
Telatyn PL 160 B8
Telč CZ 93 D8
Telciu RO 168 C4
Teldau D 99 D9
Telečka SRB 166 F3
Telega RO 177 C7
Telekgerendás H 167 D6
Teleneşti MD 170 B2
Telerig BG 177 F11
Telese I 76 A3
Telești RO 175 C11
Telford GB 26 F7
Telfs A 88 B3
Telgárt SK 161 F1
Telgte D 33 E9
Telhado P 60 D5
Telish BG 181 C9
Teliu RO 169 F7
Teliucu Inferior RO 175 B10
Teljo FIN 141 C13
Telkkälä FIN 135 C17
Tellancourt F 35 E12
Tellejåkk S 134 B3
Tellin B 35 D11
Tellingstedt D 98 B6
Telneset N 117 B13
Telnice CZ 93 D11
Telões P 54 F4
Telšiai LT 150 E4
Telti I 80 B3
Teltow D 96 B4
Tembleque E 62 E6
Temeleuți MD 169 C12
Temeni GR 190 C5
Temerin SRB 174 C4
Temmes FIN 135 E15
Tempi GR 185 E8
Tempio Pausania I 80 B3
Temple Bar GB 28 A6
Templeboy IRL 22 D5
Temple Ewell GB 31 E11
Templemore IRL 25 C7
Templepatrick GB 20 F4
Temple Sowerby GB 21 F11
Templeton GB 28 B5
Templetuohy IRL 25 C7
Templeuve F 198 D2
Templin D 100 D5
Tempo GB 23 D8
Temse B 35 B9
Temska SRB 180 C6
Temů I 85 A9
Tenala FIN 143 E9
Tenay F 47 D8
Ten Boer NL 33 B7
Tenbury Wells GB 29 A9
Tenby GB 28 B5
Tence F 46 E5
Tende F 53 C7
Tendilla E 63 C7
Tendu F 45 B9
Teneniai LT 150 F3
Tenevo BG 183 E7
Tengelic H 165 C11
Tengen D 43 E10
Tengesdal N 110 C4
Tenhult S 108 D4
Teningen D 43 D8
Tenja HR 165 F11
Tenk H 166 B5
Tennänget S 118 D6
Tennenbronn D 43 D9
Tennevik N 127 C12
Tenneville B 35 D12
Tennevoll N 127 C14
Tennilä FIN 135 B16
Tennilä FIN 143 D13
Tennskjer N 127 B15
Tennstrand N 126 D9
Tenterden GB 31 E10
Tentúgal P 60 D3
Teora I 76 B4
Teovo MK 185 A6
Tepasto FIN 133 C13
Tépe H 167 C8
Tepeboz TR 193 B7
Tepecik TR 189 B10
Tepecik TR 189 E10
Tepelenë AL 184 D3
Teplá CZ 92 C3
Teplice CZ 96 E5
Teplice nad Metuj CZ 97 E10
Teplička SK 161 F2
Teplička nad Váhom SK 163 C7
Tepsa FIN 133 C15
Țepu RO 169 F10
Ter Aar NL 198 A5
Teramo I 78 B5
Térande LV 150 B3
Ter Apel NL 33 C8
Teratyn PL 160 B8
Tërbaç AL 184 D2
Terborg-Silvolde NL 32 E6
Terchová SK 163 C8
Terebești RO 167 B10
Tereblya UA 161 G8
Teregova RO 175 C9
Teremia Mare RO 166 F6
Terena P 66 B5
Teresa E 64 E3
Teresa de Cofrentes E 63 F10
Teresin PL 157 F2
Terespol PL 157 F9
Teresva UA 161 G8
Terezín CZ 92 A6
Terezino Polje HR 165 E8
Tergnier F 35 E7
Tergu I 80 B2
Terheijden NL 198 B5
Terikeste EST 147 E14
Terjärv FIN 139 C11
Terka PL 161 E5
Terlano I 88 C3
Těrlicko CZ 162 B6
Terlizzi I 77 A7
Terme Luigiane I 76 E5
Térmens E 58 D5
Termignon F 47 E10
Terminiers F 40 D6
Termini Imerese I 74 D4
Termoli I 79 D7
Termon IRL 23 B7
Termonfeckin IRL 23 E10
Ternaard NL 32 B5
Ternavka UA 169 A8
Ternberg A 92 G6
Terndrup DK 102 B6
Terneuzen NL 32 F1
Terni I 78 B3
Ternitz A 164 A6
Ternove UA 161 G8
Terovo GR 184 F4
Terpezița RO 176 E3
Terpni GR 185 C9
Terpsithea GR 185 E7
Terpyllos GR 185 B8
Terracina I 78 E4
Terrades E 59 C9
Terråk N 121 A12
Terralba I 80 D2
Terranova da Sibari I 77 D6
Terranova di Pollino I 76 D6
Terranuova Bracciolini I 82 E4
Terrasini I 74 C3
Terrassa E 59 D8
Terrasson-Lavilledieu F 45 E8
Terraube F 49 C7
Terravecchia I 77 E7
Terricciola I 82 E2
Terriente E 63 D10
Terrin IRL 23 E8
Terrinches E 71 B7
Terrou F 45 F9
Terrugem P 66 B1
Terrugem P 67 B5
Terryglass IRL 22 F6
Terslev DK 103 E9
Tertenia I 80 D4
Teruel E 63 D10
Tervajoki FIN 138 D8
Tervakoski FIN 143 D12
Tervavaara FIN 137 D11
Tervel BG 177 F10
Terves F 44 B4
Tērvete LV 150 D6
Tervo FIN 139 E17
Tervola FIN 135 B13
Tervolan asema FIN 135 B13
Tervuren B 35 C10
Tés H 165 B10
Tešanj BIH 173 C8
Těšany CZ 93 D11
Tešedíkovo SK 162 E5
Tesero I 88 D4
Tešica SRB 180 C4
Tesimo I 88 C3
Tesjoki FIN 143 E15
Teslić BIH 173 C8
Teslui RO 176 D4
Teslui RO 176 E4
Tespe D 99 D8
Tessenderlo B 35 B11
Tessin D 99 B12
Tesson F 44 D4
Tessy-sur-Vire F 39 C9
Testa del Gargano I 79 D10
Testa dell'Acqua I 75 F6
Testelt B 198 C5
Teşvikiye TR 189 C11
Tét H 165 A9
Tetbury GB 29 B10
Teţcani MD 169 A9
Teţchea RO 167 C9
Teteringen NL 198 B5
Teterow D 99 C13
Tetétlen H 167 C7
Teteven BG 181 D9
Teti I 80 C3
Tetney GB 27 E11
Tetoiu RO 176 D3
Tétouan MA 69 E6
Tetovo BG 177 F8
Tetovo MK 179 E10
Tettens D 33 A9
Tettnang D 87 B9
Tetyń PL 101 D7
Teublitz D 91 D11
Teuchern D 95 D11
Teufen CH 43 F11
Teufenbach A 89 B9
Teulada E 72 D5
Teulada I 80 F2
Teunz D 91 D11
Teupitz D 96 B5
Teurajärvi FIN 133 D11
Teurajärvi S 132 E9
Teuro FIN 143 D10
Teuschnitz D 91 B9
Teutschenthal D 95 D10
Teuva FIN 138 F7
Tevaniemi FIN 143 B9
Tevansjö S 119 B9
Tevel H 165 D10
Tēvenāni LV 149 C1
Tevfikiye TR 187 E10
Teviothead GB 21 E11
Tewkesbury GB 29 B10
Teyssieu F 45 F9
Thal D 95 E7
Thale (Harz) D 95 C9
Thaleischweiler-Fröschen D 202 C4
Thalfang D 37 E7
Thalheim D 95 C11
Thalheim bei Wels A 92 F6
Thaljina BIH 173 F7
Thalmässing D 91 D9
Thalwil CH 43 F10
Thame GB 30 D7
Thann F 43 E7
Thannhausen D 91 F7
Thaon-les-Vosges F 42 D5
Tharandt D 96 E5
't Harde NL 32 D5
Tharsis E 67 D5
Thasos GR 187 C7
Thatcham GB 29 C12
Thaumiers F 45 B11
Thaxted GB 31 D9
Thaya A 93 E8
Thayngen CH 43 E10
Theale GB 29 C12
Thedinghausen D 33 C12
Theillay F 40 F7
Theißen D 95 D11
Theix F 38 E6
Them DK 102 C5
Themar D 91 A8
The Mumbles GB 28 B6
Thenay F 45 B8
Thénezay F 44 B5
Thenon F 45 E8
Theologos GR 187 C7

Théoule-sur-Mer F 52 D5
The Pike IRL 25 D7
Therma GR 187 D9
Thermi GR 185 C9
Thermisia GR 191 E7
Thermo GR 190 B4
Thermopyles GR 191 B6
Thérouanne F 34 C5
The Sheddings GB 20 F4
Thespies GR 191 C7
Thesprotiko GR 188 D4
Thessaloniki GR 185 C8
The Stocks GB 31 E10
Thetford GB 31 C10
Theth AL 179 E8
Theux B 35 C12
Thèze F 48 D5
Thèze F 51 B10
Thiaucourt-Regniéville F 42 C4
Thiberville F 40 B3
Thibie F 41 C11
Thiéblemont-Farémont F 41 C12
Thiendorf D 96 D5
Thiene I 88 E3
Thierhaupten D 91 E8
Thierrens CH 47 B10
Thiers F 46 D4
Thiersee A 88 A5
Thiersheim D 91 B11
Thiesi I 80 B2
Thießow D 100 B5
Thiézac F 45 E11
Thimert-Gâtelles F 40 C5
Thin-le-Moutier F 35 E10
Thionville F 36 F6
Thiron Gardais F 40 D4
Thirsk GB 27 C9
Thisted DK 102 B3
Thisvi GR 191 C6
Thiva GR 191 C7
Thivars F 40 D5
Thiviers F 45 E7
Thizy F 46 C5
Thoirette F 47 C8
Thoiry F 40 C6
Thoissey F 46 C6
Tholen NL 32 F2
Tholey D 37 F8
Thomastown IRL 25 C8
Thommen B 36 D6
Thônes F 47 D9
Thonnance-lès-Joinville F 42 D3
Thonon-les-Bains F 47 C9
Thorame-Haute F 52 C5
Thoras F 46 F4
Thoré-la-Rochette F 40 E4
Thorenc F 52 D5
Thorigny-sur-Oreuse F 41 D9
Thörl A 89 A11
Thorn NL 35 B12
Thornaby-on-Tees GB 27 B9
Thornbury GB 29 B9
Thorne GB 27 D10
Thorney GB 27 F11
Thornhill GB 21 E9
Thorning DK 102 C4
Thornton GB 26 D5
Thorpe-le-Soken GB 31 D11
Thorpe Market GB 31 B11
Thorpeness GB 31 C12
Thorsager DK 102 C6
Thorshøj DK 106 E7
Thorsø DK 102 C5
Thouarcé F 39 F11
Thouaré-sur-Loire F 39 F9
Thouars F 44 B5
Thouria GR 190 E5
Thourotte F 34 F6
Thrapston GB 31 C7
Threshfield GB 27 C7
Thropton GB 21 E13
Thrumster GB 19 J10
Thuès-entre-Valls F 49 E10
Thueyts F 51 A7
Thuin B 35 D9
Thuine D 33 D9
Thuir F 50 E4
Thum D 96 E3
Thundersley GB 31 D10
Thüngen D 90 C6
Thüngersheim D 90 C6
Thuré F 45 B6
Thuret F 46 D3
Thurey F 47 B7
Thüringen A 87 C9
Thurins F 46 D6
Thürkow D 99 C13
Thurlby GB 27 F11
Thurles IRL 25 C7
Thurnau D 91 B9
Thursby GB 21 F10
Thurso GB 19 H9
Thury-Harcourt F 39 C11
Thusis CH 87 D8
Thwaite GB 27 C7
Thyborøn DK 102 B2
Thyez F 47 C10
Thymiana GR 193 C7
Thyregod DK 102 D4
Thyrnau D 92 E5
Tia Mare RO 176 F5
Tiana I 80 C2
Ţibana RO 169 D10
Ţibăneşti RO 169 D10
Tibble S 115 D9
Tiberget S 118 D6
Tibi E 72 D3
Tibolddaróc H 161 H2
Tibro S 108 C4
Ţibucani RO 169 C9
Tice BIH 172 D6
Ticehurst GB 31 E10
Ticha BG 183 D6
Tichá CZ 162 B6
Tichileşti RO 171 C1
Ţičići BIH 173 D9
Ticknall GB 27 F9
Ticleni RO 176 D2
Ţicuşu RO 168 F6
Ticvaniu Mare RO 175 C8
Tidaholm S 107 C14
Tidan S 107 B15
Tiddische D 95 A8
Tidenham GB 29 B9
Tidersrum S 108 D7
Tiebas E 32 F2
Tiedra E 55 E9
Tiefenbach D 91 D12
Tiefenbach D 92 E4
Tiefenbronn D 43 C10
Tiefencastel CH 87 D9
Tiefensee D 100 E5

Tiel NL 32 E4
Tielen B 198 C5
Tielt B 35 C7
Tiemassaari FIN 141 F10
Tienen B 35 C10
Tiengen D 43 E9
Tiercé F 39 E10
Tierga E 57 E8
Tierp S 115 B9
Tierzo E 63 C9
Tifeşti RO 169 F10
Tigănaşi RO 169 C10
Tigăneşti RO 176 F6
Tigare BIH 174 C5
Tighina MD 170 D4
Tighira MD 169 C11
Tignale I 85 B10
Tignes F 47 E10
Tigveni RO 176 C5
Tigy F 41 E7
Tiha Bârgăului RO 168 C5
Tihany H 165 C9
Tihemetsa EST 147 E10
Tihilä FIN 139 D18
Tihusniemi FIN 140 F9
Tiistenjoki FIN 139 E10
Tiitilänkylä FIN 139 E17
Tijesno HR 172 E4
Tijnje NL 32 B5
Tijola E 71 E8
Tikkakoski FIN 139 F15
Tikkala FIN 139 F14
Tikkala FIN 141 F14
Tikkurila FIN 143 E13
Tikob DK 103 C10
Tilburg NL 32 E4
Tilbury GB 31 E9
Til-Châtel F 42 E3
Tildarg GB 20 F4
Tileagd RO 167 C9
Tilehurst GB 29 C12
Tilh F 48 C4
Tilişca RO 168 F3
Tillac F 49 D6
Tillberga S 114 C7
Tillicoultry GB 21 C9
Tillières-sur-Avre F 40 C5
Tilloy-et-Bellay F 41 B12
Tillyfourie GB 19 L11
Tilly-sur-Seulles F 39 B10
Tilvikai FIN 139 E10
Tilža LV 149 C2
Tim DK 102 C2
Timahoe IRL 23 G8
Timár H 161 G3
Timau I 89 C7
Timelkam A 92 F5
Timiryazevo RUS 152 C4
Timişeşti RO 169 C9
Timişoara RO 167 F7
Timmele S 107 D13
Timmendorfer Strand D 99 C8
Timmernabben S 105 B10
Timmersdala S 107 B14
Timola FIN 141 F9
Timoleague IRL 24 E5
Timolin IRL 23 G9
Timoniemi FIN 137 F13
Timovaara FIN 141 D12
Timrå S 119 A13
Timring DK 102 C3
Timsgearraidh GB 18 J2
Tinahely IRL 25 C10
Tinajas E 63 D7
Tinalhas P 60 E5
Tinca RO 167 D8
Tinchebray F 39 C10
Tineo E 55 B7
Tingere LV 150 B5
Tinglev DK 102 F4
Tingsryd S 105 B7
Tingstad S 109 B8
Tingstäde S 109 D13
Tingvatn N 110 F6
Tingvoll N 104 E5
Tingwall GB 19 G10
Tinja BIH 173 C9
Tinjan HR 83 B8
Tinn N 111 C9
Tinnoset N 111 C10
Tinos GR 192 D5
Tinosu RO 177 D8
Tinqueux F 35 F8
Tintagel GB 28 D5
Ţinténiac F 39 D8
Tintern Parva GB 29 B9
Ţinţeşti RO 177 C9
Tintigny B 35 E12
Tinūži LV 151 C9
Tioabraid Árann IRL 24 D4
Tione di Trento I 85 B10
Tipasoja FIN 141 B11
Tipperary IRL 24 D6
Tiptree GB 31 D10
Tipu EST 147 E10
Tira MD 170 B2
Tiranë AL 184 B2
Tiranges F 46 E4
Tirano I 85 B9
Tiraspol MD 170 D5
Tiraspolul Nou MD 170 D5
Tire TR 193 D10
Tiream RO 167 B9
Tireli LV 150 C7
Tirgo E 40 D5
Tiriez E 71 B8
Tirig E 64 D5
Tiriolo I 75 B10
Tirkšliai LT 150 C3
Tirnova MD 169 A11
Tishono RUS 152 E2
Tišnjevica BG 181 D8
Tišnov CZ 93 D11
Tisovec SK 163 D9
Tistrup DK 102 D3
Tisvilde DK 103 C10
Tiszaalpár H 166 D4
Tiszabecs H 161 G6
Tiszabezdéd H 161 G5
Tiszabő H 166 C5
Tiszabura H 166 C5

Tiszacsege H 167 B7
Tiszadada H 161 G3
Tiszaderzs H 166 B6
Tiszadob H 161 G3
Tiszaeszlár H 161 G3
Tiszaföldvár H 166 D5
Tiszafüred H 166 B6
Tiszagyenda H 166 C6
Tiszaigar H 166 B6
Tiszajenő H 166 C5
Tiszakanyár H 161 G4
Tiszakarád H 161 G4
Tiszakécske H 166 C5
Tiszakerecseny H 161 G5
Tiszakeszi H 167 B6
Tiszakürt H 166 C5
Tiszalök H 161 G3
Tiszalúc H 161 G3
Tiszanagyfalu H 161 G3
Tiszanána H 166 B6
Tiszapalkonya H 161 H3
Tiszapüspöki H 166 C5
Tiszaroff H 166 C5
Tiszasas H 166 D5
Tiszasüly H 166 C5
Tiszaszalka H 161 G5
Tiszaszentimre H 166 C6
Tiszasziget H 166 E5
Tiszatarján H 163 F12
Tiszatelek H 161 G4
Tiszatenyő H 166 C5
Tiszaug H 166 D5
Tiszaújváros H 161 H3
Tiszavárkony H 166 C5
Tiszavasvári H 161 H3
Titaguas E 63 E10
Titel SRB 174 C5
Tiţeşti RO 176 C6
Tithorea GR 191 B6
Tito I 76 B5
Titova Korenica HR 172 C4
Titov Drvar BIH 172 D5
Titran N 120 D4
Tittelsnes N 110 C3
Titting D 91 E9
Tittmoning D 92 F3
Titu RO 177 D7
Titulcia E 62 D5
Tiukuvaara FIN 133 C13
Tiurajärvi FIN 133 C12
Tivat MNE 179 E6
Tiverton GB 29 D8
Tivissa E 58 E5
Tivoli I 78 D3
Tizzano F 53 H9
Tjæreborg DK 102 E3
Tjåkkjokk S 125 E15
Tjällmo S 108 B6
Tjåmotis S 125 C16
Tjappsälve S 125 E17
Tjärmyrberget S 122 C9
Tjärn S 123 C13
Tjärnäs S 114 A6
Tjärnberg S 123 C15
Tjärstad S 108 C7
Tjäruträsk S 134 B8
Tjautas S 132 D5
Tjeldnes N 127 D11
Tjeldstø N 116 E1
Tjentište BIH 173 F10
Tjöck FIN 138 E6
Tjøme N 106 A7
Tjønnefoss N 106 B6
Tjorhom N 110 E5
Tjörnarp S 103 D13
Tjøtta N 124 E3
Tjuda FIN 142 E6
Tjuvskjær N 127 C13
Tkon HR 172 E3
Tleń PL 154 C5
Tłmače SK 163 E7
Tłuchowo PL 155 E7
Tlumačov CZ 162 C5
Tłuszcz PL 155 F11
Toab GB 19 F14
Toaca RO 168 D5
Tóalmás H 166 C4
Toano I 82 D2
Tobar an Choire IRL 22 D5
Tobarra E 71 B9
Tobercurry IRL 22 D5
Tobermore GB 20 F3
Tobermory GB 20 B4
Tobo S 115 B9
Tobyn S 113 C9
Tocane-St-Apre F 45 E6
Tocco da Casauria I 78 C5
Tocha P 60 D2
Töcksfors S 112 C6
Tocón E 69 B10
Todal N 120 E5
Toddington GB 29 B11
Todi I 78 B2
Todireni RO 169 B8
Todireşti RO 169 B8
Todireşti RO 169 C9
Todireşti RO 169 D10
Todmorden GB 27 D7
Todolella E 58 F3
Todorići BIH 173 D7
Todor-Ikonomovo BG 177 F10
Todorovo BG 177 F9
Todtmoos D 43 E8
Todtnau D 43 E8
Toén E 54 D4
Toft GB 19 E14
Toft N 124 F3
Tofta S 103 A10
Tofta S 109 D12
Tofte N 111 C11
Tøftedal S 107 B10
Toftir FO 18 A3
Toftlund DK 102 E4
Tofyeli BY 149 E5
Togher IRL 23 E10
Togher IRL 23 F7
Togher IRL 24 E14
Togston GB 21 E13
Tohmajärvi FIN 141 F14
Tohmo FIN 131 D2
Toholampi FIN 139 C12
Toija FIN 143 C10
Toijala FIN 143 C10
Toila EST 148 C2
Toirano I 53 C8
Toivakka FIN 139 F16
Toivala FIN 140 E9
Toivola FIN 144 C6

Tojaci MK 185 B6
Tōjby FIN 138 E6
Tōk H 165 A11
Tokachka BG 187 B9
Tokaj H 161 G3
Tokarnia PL 159 E9
Tokarnia PL 163 B9
Tokod H 165 A11
Tököl H 165 B11
Tokrajärvi FIN 141 E15
Toksovo RUS 145 E14
Tolastadh Úr GB 18 J4
Tolbaños E 62 C3
Tolbert NL 32 B6
Tolcsva H 161 G3
Toledo E 62 E4
Tolentino I 83 F7
Tolfa I 78 C1
Tolga N 117 B14
Toliejai LT 151 F10
Tolja FIN 135 B17
Tolk D 98 A7
Tolkmicko PL 155 B8
Tollarp S 104 C2
Tollered S 107 D11
Tollesbury GB 31 D10
Tollo I 79 C6
Tølløse DK 103 D9
Töllsjö S 107 D12
Tolmachevo RUS 148 D6
Tolmezzo I 89 D7
Tolmin SLO 89 D8
Tolna H 165 D11
Tolnanémedi H 165 C10
Tolne DK 106 E7
Tolo GR 191 D6
Tolocăneşti MD 169 A11
Tolonen FIN 133 E14
Tolosa E 48 D1
Tolosa P 60 F5
Tolosenmäki FIN 141 F14
Tolox E 69 C7
Tolšiči BIH 173 D10
Tolva E 58 C5
Tolva FIN 137 B2
Tolvayarvi RUS 141 F16
Tolve I 76 B6
Tomai MD 170 D2
Tomai MD 170 E3
Tomar P 60 E4
Tomares E 67 E7
Tomaševac SRB 174 C6
Tomaševo MNE 179 C8
Tomašica BIH 173 C6
Tomášikovo SK 162 E5
Tomášovce SK 163 E9
Tomaszów Lubelski PL 160 C7
Tomaszów Mazowiecki PL 157 G2
Tomatin GB 19 L9
Tombebœuf F 49 A6
Tomelilla S 104 D5
Tomelloso E 63 F6
Tomeşti RO 167 E10
Tomeşti RO 167 F9
Tomeşti RO 169 C11
Tomice PL 163 B8
Tomintoul GB 19 L10
Tomislavgrad BIH 173 E7
Tømmerneset N 127 E10
Tommerup DK 102 E6
Tomnavoulin GB 19 L10
Tömörkény H 166 D5
Tompa H 166 E4
Tomra N 116 A5
Tomşani RO 177 D8
Tona E 59 D8
Tonara I 80 C3
Tonbridge GB 31 E9
Tondela P 60 C4
Tønder DK 102 F3
Tonezza del Cimone I 85 B11
Tongeren B 35 C11
Tongland GB 21 F8
Tongue GB 18 J8
Tonisvorst D 199 C8
Tonkopuro FIN 131 E4
Tonna GB 29 B7
Tonnay-Boutonne F 44 D4
Tonnay-Charente F 44 D4
Tonnerre F 41 E10
Tønnes N 124 C5
Tönning D 98 B5
Tonstad N 110 F5
Tonsvik N 127 A17
Toombeola IRL 22 F3
Toomebridge GB 20 F4
Tootsi EST 147 D9
Topalu RO 171 D2
Topana RO 176 D5
Topares E 71 D8
Toparlar TR 197 C8
Topchii BG 177 F9
Topçin D 96 B5
Topçic-Polje BIH 173 D8
Topcliffe GB 27 C9
Topen D 91 B10
Topeno FIN 143 D11
Tophisar TR 189 D9
Topleţ RO 175 D9
Topliceni RO 177 C10
Topli Do SRB 181 C6
Topliţa RO 168 D6
Topliţa RO 175 D10
Töplitz D 95 B12
Topojë AL 184 C1
Topola SRB 174 E6
Topolčani MK 184 B5
Topolčany SK 162 E6
Topolčianky SK 162 E6
Topole GR 194 E6
Topólka PL 154 E6
Topolnica SRB 175 E9
Topol'niky SK 162 F5
Topolog RO 171 D2
Topolovăţu Mare RO 167 F8
Topoloveni RO 176 D5
Topolovgrad BG 182 E6
Topolovnik SRB 175 D7
Topolovo BG 182 B5
Toponica SRB 174 F6
Toporivtsi UA 169 A8
Toporów PL 97 B8
Toporu RO 177 E7
Toporzyk PL 101 C10
Topraisar RO 171 E2

Topsham GB 29 D8
Topusko HR 172 B4
Torá E 59 D6
Toral de los Guzmanes E 55 D8
Toral de los Vados E 55 C6
Torano Castello I 76 E6
Torasalo FIN 141 F10
Toras-Sieppi FIN 133 C11
Torbalı TR 193 C9
Torbjörntorp S 107 C14
Torbygget S 118 A4
Torchiara I 76 C4
Torchiarolo I 77 C10
Torcy F 46 B5
Torda SRB 174 B5
Tordas H 165 B11
Tordehumos E 55 E9
Tordera E 59 D9
Tordesillas E 55 E10
Tordesilos E 63 C9
Töre S 134 C6
Töreboda S 107 B15
Toreby DK 99 A11
Torekov S 103 C11
Torella del Sannio I 79 D6
Torellano E 72 E3
Torelló E 59 C8
Toreno E 55 C6
Torestorp S 107 E12
Torgau D 96 C3
Torgelow D 100 C6
Torgiano I 78 A2
Torhamn S 105 C9
Torhout B 35 B7
Tori EST 147 E9
Torigni-sur-Vire F 39 B10
Torija E 63 C6
Torino I 84 C4
Toritto I 77 B7
Torkanivka UA 170 A4
Torkovichi RUS 148 D7
Torla E 48 E5
Torma EST 147 D13
Törmänen FIN 129 B9
Tormac RO 175 B7
Törmänen FIN 131 A2
Törmänki FIN 133 E13
Törmänmäki FIN 137 E10
Törmäsenvaara FIN 137 C13
Törmäsjärvi FIN 135 B12
Tormestorp S 103 C13
Tormón E 63 D10
Tormore GB 20 D6
Tornadizos de Ávila E 62 C3
Tornal'a SK 161 G1
Tornavacas E 61 D9
Tornby DK 106 D6
Tornemark DK 103 E9
Tornes N 116 A6
Tørnes N 127 D11
Tornesch D 98 C7
Torneträsk S 127 D18
Tornio FIN 135 C11
Tornjoš SRB 166 F4
Torno I 85 B7
Tornos E 63 C10
Tornow D 100 D4
Toro E 55 E9
Torö S 109 B11
Törökbálint H 165 B11
Törökszentmiklós H 166 C5
Torony H 165 B7
Toros BG 181 C9
Toroshino RUS 148 F4
Torp FIN 115 B3
Torpa S 108 D6
Torphins GB 19 L11
Torpo N 117 C9
Torpoint GB 28 E6
Torpsbruk S 104 A7
Torpshammar S 119 B11
Torquay GB 29 E8
Torquemada E 56 D3
Torraiba de Calatrava E 70 A5
Torralba E 63 D8
Torralba I 80 B2
Torralba de Aragón E 57 E10
Torralba de El Burgo E 56 E6
Torralba de los Sisones E 63 C10
Torralba de Oropesa E 61 E10
Torrão P 66 C3
Torrböle S 123 D17
Torre-Alháquime E 67 F9
Torre Annunziata I 76 B2
Torrebaja E 63 D10
Torreblanca E 64 D5
Torreblascopedro E 69 A9
Torrebruna I 79 D7
Torrecaballeros E 62 C4
Torrecampo E 70 C3
Torre Canne I 77 B8
Torre-Cardela E 71 D6
Torrecilla de Alcañiz E 58 F3
Torrecilla de la Jara E 62 E3
Torrecilla de la Orden E 61 B10
Torrecilla del Rebollar E 58 F1
Torrecillas de la Tiesa E 61 E9
Torrecuso I 76 A3
Torre da Gadanha P 66 B3
Torre das Vargens P 60 F5
Torre de Coelheiros P 66 C4
Torre de Dona Chama P 54 E5
Torre de Embesora E 64 D4
Torredeita P 60 C4
Torre de Juan Abad E 71 B6
Torre del Bierzo E 55 C7
Torre del Burgo E 63 C6
Torre del Campo E 69 A9
Torre del Greco I 76 B2
Torre del Mar E 69 C8
Torredembarra E 59 E6
Torre de Miguel Sesmero E 67 B6
Torre de Moncorvo P 61 B6
Torre do Terrenho P 60 C5
Torrefarrera E 58 D5
Torregamones E 55 F7
Torregrossa E 58 D5
Torreiglesias E 62 B4
Torreira P 60 C3
Torrejoncillo E 61 E8
Torrejoncillo del Rey E 63 D7
Torrejón de Ardoz E 62 D5
Torrejón del Rey E 62 C5
Torrejón el Rubio E 61 E9
Torrelacarcel E 63 C10
Torrelaguna E 62 C5
Torrelapaja E 57 E8
Torrelavega E 56 B3

Torrellas E 57 E8
Torrelles de Foix E 59 E7
Torrelobatón E 62 C5
Torrelodones E 62 C5
Torremaggiore I 79 D8
Torremanzanas-La Torre de les Macanes E 72 D4
Torremayor E 67 B6
Torremegía E 67 B7
Torre Mileto I 79 D9
Torremocha E 61 F8
Torremocha de Jiloca E 63 C10
Torremolinos E 69 C7
Torremormojón E 56 D2
Torrenostra E 64 D5
Torrent E 64 F4
Torrente del Cinca E 58 E4
Torrenueva E 71 B6
Torreorgaz E 61 F8
Torre Orsaia I 76 C5
Torre Pellice I 47 F11
Torreperogil E 71 C6
Torres E 69 A9
Torresandino E 56 E4
Torre San Giovanni I 77 D10
Torre Santa Susanna I 77 C8
Torres de Albánchez E 71 C7
Torres de Berrellén E 57 E9
Torres de la Alameda E 62 D6
Torres del Carrizal E 55 E8
Torresmenudas E 61 B9
Torres Novas P 60 F3
Torres Vedras P 60 F2
Torrevelilla E 58 F3
Torrevieja E 72 F3
Torrice I 78 D4
Torricella I 77 C9
Torricella in Sabina I 78 C3
Torricella Peligna I 79 C6
Torricella Sicura I 78 B5
Torricella Taverne CH 85 A6
Torrico E 61 E10
Torri del Benaco I 85 B10
Torridon GB 18 K5
Torriglia I 53 B10
Torrijas E 64 D3
Torrijo E 62 E4
Torrijo del Campo E 63 C10
Torrijos E 62 E4
Torrín GB 18 L4
Torrita di Siena I 82 F4
Torroal P 66 C2
Torroella de Montgrí E 59 C10
Torrox E 69 C9
Torrubia del Campo E 63 E7
Torrubia de Soria E 57 E7
Tørrvika N 124 B7
Torsåker S 114 A6
Torsång S 113 B14
Torsås S 105 C10
Tørsbøl DK 102 F4
Törsbole S 123 A15
Torsby S 113 B10
Torsby S 113 C9
Torsebro S 104 C6
Torshälla S 114 D6
Tórshavn FO 18 A3
Torsholma FIN 142 E5
Torsken N 127 B12
Torslanda S 107 D10
Torsminde DK 102 C2
Torsö S 107 B14
Torsvåg N 128 C4
Törtel H 166 C4
Tortella E 59 C9
Torteval GBG 38 B6
Torthorwald GB 21 E9
Tortinmäki FIN 142 D7
Tórtola de Henares E 63 C6
Tórtoles de Esgueva E 56 E3
Tortolì I 80 D4
Tortomanu RO 171 E2
Tortona I 53 B9
Tortora I 76 C4
Tortoreto I 78 B5
Tortorici I 75 C6
Tortosa E 58 F5
Tortozendo P 60 D5
Tortuera E 63 C9
Tortuna S 114 C7
Toruń PL 154 D6
Torun' UA 161 F8
Torup S 103 B12
Tõrva EST 147 E11
Tor Vaianica I 78 D2
Torvandi EST 147 E13
Torvenkylä FIN 135 F11
Torvik N 116 B3
Torvik N 120 F3
Torvikbukt N 110 B4
Torvinen FIN 133 D17
Torvizcón E 71 F6
Torvsjö S 123 C12
Torysa SK 161 E2
Torzym PL 97 B8
Tosbotn N 124 E4
Toscolano-Maderno I 85 B10
Tossa S 59 D9
Tossåsen S 118 A5
Tóssåsen S 118 A7
Tossavanlahti FIN 139 D16
Tosse F 48 C3
Tösse S 107 B12
Tossicia I 78 B5
Tosside GB 27 C7
Tõstamaa EST 147 E7
Tostedt D 98 D7
Tószeg H 166 C5
Toszek PL 158 F6
Totana E 71 D10
Totebo S 109 D8
Tótkomlós H 166 E6
Totland GB 29 D11
Totnes GB 29 E8
Totra S 119 E13
Tótszerdahely H 165 D7
Tøttdal N 121 C10
Tottijärvi FIN 143 C9
Totton GB 29 D12
Tótvázsony H 165 B9
Touça P 61 B6
Toucy F 41 E9
Touffailles F 49 B8
Touget F 49 C7
Toul F 42 C4
Toulon F 51 D10
Toulon-sur-Allier F 46 B3

Toulon-sur-Arroux F 46 B5
Toulouges F 50 E4
Toulouse F 49 C8
Tounj HR 172 B3
Tourch F 38 D4
Tourcoing F 35 C7
Tourlaville F 39 A8
Tournai B 35 C7
Tournan-en-Brie F 41 C8
Tournay F 49 D6
Tournecoupe F 49 C7
Tournefeuille F 49 C8
Tournon-d'Agenais F 49 B7
Tournon-St-Martin F 45 B7
Tournon-sur-Rhône F 46 E6
Tournus F 46 B6
Tourny F 40 D4
Tourouvre F 40 C4
Tours F 40 F4
Tourteron F 35 E10
Tourtoirac F 45 E8
Toury F 40 D6
Tous E 64 F3
Touvois F 44 B2
Toužim CZ 92 B3
Tovačov CZ 162 C4
Tovariševo SRB 174 C3
Tovarné SK 161 F4
Tovarnik HR 173 B11
Toven N 124 D5
Tovrljane SRB 180 C3
Towcester GB 30 C7
Tower IRL 24 E5
Toymskardlia N 122 A5
Töysä FIN 139 E11
Traar D 199 C9
Trabada E 54 B5
Trabanca E 61 B8
Trabazos E 55 E7
Traben D 37 E8
Trąbki PL 160 D1
Trąbki Wielkie PL 154 B6
Traboch A 89 B10
Trabotivište MK 181 F6
Traby BY 153 E12
Trachili GR 191 B9
Tradate I 85 B6
Trädet S 107 D13
Trædal N 127 D14
Trafrask IRL 24 E3
Traguera E 64 D5
Tragwein A 93 F7
Traian RO 169 D10
Traian RO 171 C1
Traian RO 176 E4
Traian RO 176 F6
Traian Vuia RO 167 F9
Traid E 63 C9
Traiguera E 58 F4
Train D 91 E10
Traînel F 41 D9
Traisen A 93 F9
Traiskirchen A 93 F10
Traismauer A 93 F9
Traitsching D 91 D12
Trakai LT 153 D10
Trakovice SK 162 E5
Trakšėdžiai LT 150 F2
Tralee IRL 24 D3
Trá Li IRL 24 D3
Tramacastilla E 63 D9
Tramagal P 60 F4
Tramatza I 80 C2
Tramayes F 46 C6
Tramelan CH 43 F7
Trá Mhór IRL 25 D8
Tramonti di Sopra I 89 D6
Tramonti di Sotto I 89 D6
Tramore IRL 25 D8
Tramutola I 76 C5
Tranås S 108 C5
Tranbjerg DK 102 C6
Trancoso P 60 C6
Tranebjerg DK 102 D7
Tranemo S 107 E13
Trången S 121 C9
Trånghalla S 108 D4
Trångslet S 118 D6
Trångsviken S 121 E16
Trani I 77 A6
Trannes F 41 D12
Tranovalto GR 185 D6
Tranøy N 127 D10
Trans F 39 D7
Trans-en-Provence F 52 D4
Transtrand S 118 D4
Transtrand S 118 E1
Tranum DK 102 A4
Tranvik S 115 D11
Trapani I 74 C2
Trapene LV 151 B13
Traplice CZ 162 C4
Trappes F 40 C7
Trarbach D 201 A7
Traryd S 103 B13
Trasacco I 78 D5
Träskvik FIN 138 F7
Trasmiras E 54 D4
Trasobares E 57 E8
Tratalias I 80 F2
Traun A 92 F6
Traunreut D 89 A6
Traunstein D 89 A6
Traunstein D 89 A6
Traupis LT 151 E9
Trava SLO 89 E10
Tråvad S 107 C13
Travagliato I 82 A2
Travanca do Mondego P 60 D4
Travassô P 60 C4
Travemünde D 99 C8
Travenbrück D 99 C8
Travers CH 47 B10
Traversetolo I 82 C1
Trávnica SK 162 E6
Travnik BIH 173 D8
Travo I 53 B10
Trawniki PL 157 H8
Trawsfynydd GB 26 F4
Trbuk BIH 173 C9
Trebaseleghe I 88 E5
Trebatice SK 162 D5
Trebatsch D 96 B6
Trebbin D 96 B4

Třebechovice pod Orebem CZ 93 B9
Trebel D 99 E10
Treben D 95 D11
Třebenice CZ 92 B5
Trebenow D 100 D5
Trèbes F 49 D10
Trébeurden F 38 C4
Třebíč CZ 93 D9
Trebisacce I 77 D7
Trebišov SK 161 F4
Trebnje SLO 89 E11
Trebolle E 54 C4
Třeboň CZ 93 D7
Trebsen D 95 D12
Trebujena E 67 F7
Trebur D 37 E10
Trecastagni I 75 D7
Trecate I 84 C6
Trecchina I 76 C5
Trecenta I 82 B3
Tredegar GB 29 B8
Tredington GB 29 A11
Tredozio I 82 D4
Treehoo IRL 23 D8
Trefaldwyn GB 26 F5
Trefeglwys GB 26 F4
Treffen A 89 C8
Treffort-Cuisiat F 47 C7
Treffurt D 95 D7
Trefriw GB 26 E4
Trefynwy GB 29 B9
Tregaron GB 29 A7
Trégastel F 38 C4
Tregde N 106 C2
Tregony GB 28 E5
Trégueux F 38 D6
Tréguier F 38 C5
Trégunc F 38 E4
Tregynon GB 26 F5
Trehörna S 108 C5
Trehörningsjö S 123 D15
Treia D 98 A6
Treia I 83 F7
Treignac F 45 D9
Treigny F 41 E9
Treimani EST 147 F8
Treis D 201 D7
Trekanten S 105 B10
Treklyano BG 181 D6
Trélazé F 39 F11
Trelech GB 28 B6
Trélissac F 45 E7
Trelleborg S 103 E12
Trelleck GB 29 B9
Trélon F 35 D9
Tremadog GB 26 F3
Tremblay-les-Villages F 40 C5
Tremedal de Tormes E 61 B8
Tremelo B 35 C10
Trémentines F 39 F10
Tremês P 60 F3
Trémeven F 38 E4
Tremezzo I 85 B11
Trémolat F 45 F7
Třemošná CZ 92 C4
Trémouilles F 50 B4
Tremp S 58 C5
Trenance GB 28 E4
Trenčianska Turná SK 162 D6
Trenčianske Jastrabie SK 162 D6
Trenčianske Stankovce SK 162 D5
Trenčianske Teplice SK 162 D6
Trenčín SK 162 D6
Trendelburg D 37 A12
Trengereid N 110 B3
Trensacq F 48 B4
Trent D 100 A4
Trenta SLO 89 D9
Trentels F 49 B7
Trento I 85 A11
Tréon F 40 C5
Treorchy GB 29 B7
Trepča HR 164 F5
Treppeln D 97 B7
Trept F 47 D7
Trepuzzi I 77 C10
Trequanda I 82 F4
Trescléoux F 51 B10
Trescore Balneario I 85 B8
Tresenda I 85 A9
Tresfjord N 116 A6
Tresigallo I 82 C4
Tresjuncos E 63 E7
Treskog S 113 C8
Trešnjevica SRB 174 F5
Tresnuraghes I 80 C2
Trespaderne E 56 C5
Tressait GB 21 B9
Třešť CZ 93 D8
Tretower GB 29 B8
Trets F 51 D10
Tretten N 117 D12
Treuchtlingen D 91 B8
Treuenbrietzen D 95 B12
Treungen N 106 A4
Trévé F 38 D6
Trevélez E 71 F6
Tréveray F 42 C3
Trèves F 50 B5
Trevi I 78 B3
Treviana E 56 C5
Trévières F 39 B8
Treviglio I 85 B8
Trevignano Romano I 78 C2
Trévillers F 43 F6
Treviño E 56 C6
Treviso I 88 E5
Trevllazër AL 184 C2
Trevões P 60 B6
Trévoux F 46 D6
Trézelles F 46 C4
Trezzo sull'Adda I 85 B8
Trgovište SRB 180 E5
Trhová Hradská SK 162 F5
Trhové Sviny CZ 93 E7
Trhovište SK 161 F4
Trhový Štěpánov CZ 93 C8
Triacastela E 54 C5
Triaize F 44 C3
Trianta GR 197 D8
Triantaros GR 192 D5
Tribalj HR 83 B10
Tribanj-Krušćica HR 172 D3
Tribehou F 39 B9
Tribsees D 99 B13
Tribunj HR 172 E4
Tricarico I 76 B6
Tricase I 77 D10
Tricesimo I 89 D7
Trichiana I 88 D5
Tricot F 34 E6
Trieben A 89 A9
Triebes D 95 E11
Trie-Château F 34 F4
Trier D 37 E7
Trierweiler D 202 B2
Trieste I 89 E8
Trie-sur-Baïse F 49 D6
Trieux F 36 F5
Trifești RO 169 C11
Trifești RO 169 E9
Triften D 92 F14
Trigaches P 66 C4
Trigance F 52 D4
Triggiano I 77 A7
Triglitz D 99 D12
Trignac F 39 F7
Trigrad BG 181 F8
Triguères F 41 E8
Trigueros E 67 E6
Trigueros del Valle E 55 E10
Trikala GR 185 E6
Trikāta LV 147 F10
Trikeri GR 191 A7
Trilj HR 173 E6
Trillevallen S 121 E14
Trillick GB 23 D8
Trillo E 63 C7
Trilofo GR 190 E5
Trilofos GR 185 D8
Trilport F 41 C8
Trim IRL 23 E9
Trimdon GB 21 F14
Trimley St Mary GB 31 D11
Trimmis CH 87 D9
Trimsaran GB 28 B6
Trindade P 54 F5
Trindade P 66 D5
Třinec CZ 163 B7
Tring GB 31 D7
Trinità d'Agultu I 80 B2
Trinitapoli I 76 A6
Trino I 84 C5
Trins A 88 B3
Trinta P 61 C6
Trinwillershagen D 99 B13
Triollo E 55 C10
Triora I 53 D7
Tripkau D 99 D10
Tripoli GR 190 D5
Tripotama GR 190 D4
Tripotamos GR 185 C7
Trippstadt D 37 F9
Triptis D 95 E10
Tritenii de Jos RO 168 D4
Trittau D 99 D8
Trittenheim D 37 E7
Trivalea-Moșteni RO 176 E6
Trivento I 76 B5
Trivero I 84 B5
Trivigno I 76 B5
Trizac F 45 E11
Trnakovac HR 173 B7
Trnava CZ 162 D5
Trnava SK 162 E5
Trnava SRB 174 E5
Trnava Hora SK 163 D7
Trnjani BIH 173 C6
Trnovci MK 184 B5
Trnovec Bartolovečki HR 165 D6
Trnovec nad Váhom SK 162 E5
Trnovica BIH 173 F9
Trnovo BIH 173 E9
Tro N 124 E4
Troarn F 39 B11
Tröbitz D 96 D4
Trochtelfingen D 43 D11
Trödje S 119 E13
Troense DK 102 E7
Trofa P 54 F2
Trofaiach A 89 B11
Trofors N 124 C5
Trogir HR 172 E5
Trøgstad N 111 C14
Troia I 76 A4
Tróia P 66 C2
Troianul RO 176 F6
Troina I 75 D6
Troisdorf D 37 C8
Troisfontaines F 202 D3
Trois-Ponts B 35 D12
Troissereux F 34 F5
Trois-Vièvres F 36 D6
Troistorrents L 36 D6
Troitșoe MD 170 D4
Trojane SLO 89 D10
Trojanów PL 157 G5
Troldhede DK 102 D3
Trollbukta N 129 C19
Trollhättan S 107 C11
Trollvik N 128 D6
Tromello I 85 C6
Tromsdalen N 127 A16
Tromsø N 127 A16
Tromvik N 127 A15
Tronco P 54 E5
Trondenes N 127 C12
Trondheim N 120 E8
Trones N 121 B13
Trongisvágur FO 18 B3
Tronnes N 124 C8
Trönninge S 103 B11
Trönningeby S 103 A10
Tronö S 119 D12
Trontano I 84 A5
Tronvik N 121 D9
Tronville-en-Barrois F 42 C3
Tronzano Vercellese I 84 C5
Troo F 40 E4
Troon GB 20 D7
Trooz B 35 D12
Tropaia GR 190 D4
Tropea I 75 B8
Trory GB 23 D7
Trosa S 109 B11
Troshan AL 179 F8
Tröskien S 118 F9
Troškūnai LT 151 E9
Trošmarija HR 164 F4
Trossin D 95 C12
Tröstau D 91 B10
Trostberg D 88 A6
Trostyanets' UA 161 E9
Trostyanets' UA 169 A12
Troszyn PL 155 D12
Troubky CZ 162 C4
Troubsko CZ 93 D10
Troutbeck GB 26 C6
Trouville-sur-Mer F 39 B12
Trouy F 45 A10
Troviscal P 60 E4
Trowbridge GB 29 C10
Troyan BG 181 D10
Troyanovo BG 183 D8
Troyes F 41 D11
Troyits'ke UA 170 B6
Troyits'ke UA 170 D6
Troyon F 42 B3
Trpanj MNE 173 F8
Trpejca MK 184 C4
Trpezi MNE 179 D7
Trpinja HR 173 B10
Trsa MNE 173 F10
Trstená SK 163 C9
Trstené pri Hornáde SK 161 F3
Trstenik HR 178 D3
Trstenik SRB 179 B11
Trstenik SRB 179 D10
Trstice SK 162 E5
Trstín SK 162 D4
Trubar BIH 172 D5
Trubia E 55 B8
Truchas E 55 D7
Truchtersheim F 43 C8
Trud BG 181 E10
Trudovets BG 181 D8
Trudy BY 149 E6
Trujillanos E 67 B7
Trujillo E 61 F9
Trulben D 43 B8
Trün BIH 181 D6
Trun CH 87 D7
Trun F 39 C12
Trůnchovitsa BG 181 C11
Truro GB 28 E4
Trușești RO 169 B10
Trusetal D 95 E7
Trush AL 179 F7
Truskava LT 151 F8
Truskavets' UA 161 E8
Trūstenik BG 177 F7
Trūstenik BG 181 C9
Trustrup DK 103 C7
Trutnov CZ 97 E9
Try N 106 C2
Tryavna BG 182 D4
Trybusivka UA 170 A3
Tryfos GR 190 B3
Trygona GR 184 F5
Tryńcza PL 160 C6
Tryserum S 109 A11
Trysil N 118 D3
Tryškiai LT 150 C5
Trysunda S 123 E15
Tržac HR 172 C4
Trzcianka PL 101 D10
Trzcianka PL 155 E12
Trzcianne PL 156 D7
Trzciel PL 97 B9
Trzciana PL 101 D10
Trzciano PL 155 E12
Trzcinica PL 158 D3
Trzebiatów PL 101 B8
Trzebiechów PL 97 B9
Trzebiel PL 97 C7
Trzebielino PL 101 B12
Trzebień PL 97 D9
Trzebieszów PL 157 G7
Trzebieszowice PL 93 B11
Trzebież PL 100 D6
Trzebinia PL 159 F7
Trzebiszewo PL 97 A8
Trzebnica PL 97 D12
Trzebownisko PL 160 C5
Trzeciewiec PL 154 D5
Trzemeszno PL 154 E4
Trzemeszno Lubuskie PL 97 B8
Trześcianka PL 156 E8
Trześniów PL 161 D4
Trzeszczany Pierwsze PL 160 B8
Tržič SLO 89 D9
Trzcińsko-Zdrój PL 100 E7
Trzyciąż PL 159 F8
Trzydnik Duży PL 160 B5
Tsagkarada GR 185 F9
Tsakarisianos GR 190 C2
Tsalapitsa BG 181 E10
Tsamantas GR 184 E3
Tsaparevo BG 185 A9
Tsareva Livada BG 182 D4
Tsarevo BG 183 E9
Tsarimir BG 181 E10
Tsaritsani GR 185 E6
Tsar Kaloyan BG 177 F8
Tsar-Petrovo BG 175 F10
Tschagguns A 87 C9
Tschernitz D 97 C7
Tsebrykove UA 170 C6
Tselina BG 182 B4
Tsenovo BG 182 B5
Tserovo BG 181 D8
Tserovo BG 181 E9
Tsiistre EST 147 F13
Tsirguliina EST 147 F12
Tsivaras GR 194 F7
Tsotili GR 184 F5
Tsoukalades GR 190 B2
Tsūrvaritsa BG 181 F8
Tsvetino BG 181 F8
Tsyatsyerki BY 149 G2
Tua N 121 D9
Tuaim IRL 22 E5
Tuaim Beola IRL 22 F3
Tuam IRL 22 E5
Tuamgraney IRL 24 C5
Tubbercurry IRL 22 D5
Tubbergen NL 33 D7
Tubilla del Agua E 56 C4
Tübingen D 43 C11
Tubize B 35 C9
Tubre I 87 D10
Tučepi HR 173 F7
Tuchan F 50 E4
Tüchen D 99 D12
Tuchheim D 95 B11
Tuchola PL 154 C4
Tuchomie PL 101 B12
Tuchów PL 160 D6
Tuchowicz PL 157 G6
Tuckur FIN 138 D8
Tuczno PL 101 D10
Tudela E 57 D7
Tudela de Duero E 56 E2
Tudora RO 169 B9
Tudor Vladimirescu RO 171 B1
Tudu EST 147 C13
Tudulinna EST 147 C14
Tudweiliog GB 26 F2
Tuejar E 63 E10
Tuenno I 88 D3
Tufeni RO 176 E5
Tufești RO 171 D1
Tuffé F 40 D4
Tufjord N 129 A12
Tuhkakylä FIN 141 B10
Tui E 54 D2
Tuili I 80 D2
Tuin MK 184 A5
Tuiskula FIN 138 E8
Tūja LV 151 B8
Tukhkala RUS 137 C16
Tukhol'ka UA 161 F7
Tukums LV 150 C6
Tula I 80 B2
Tulach Mhór IRL 23 F8
Tulare SRB 180 D3
Tulbing A 93 F10
Tulca RO 167 D8
Tulce PL 97 B12
Tulcea RO 171 C3
Tulčík SK 161 E3
Tulette F 51 B8
Tulghes RO 169 D7
Tuli BIH 178 D5
Tuliszków PL 158 B5
Tulje BIH 178 D5
Tulka S 115 B11
Tulla IRL 24 C5
Tullaghan IRL 22 D6
Tullamore IRL 23 F8
Tulle F 45 E9
Tullebølle DK 103 F7
Tulleng N 127 A15
Tulleråsen S 121 E16
Tullingså S 122 D9
Tullins F 47 E8
Tulln A 93 F10
Tullow IRL 25 C9
Tully GB 23 D7
Tully GB 23 D8
Tullyallen IRL 23 E10
Tullyvin IRL 23 D8
Tulnici RO 169 F9
Tulos RUS 141 C14
Tulovo BG 182 D5
Tułowice PL 158 D5
Tułowice PL 158 E4
Tulppio FIN 131 D13
Tulsk IRL 22 E6
Tulstrup DK 103 D10
Tuluceşti RO 171 B2
Tumba S 109 A11
Tumbo S 114 D6
Tume LV 150 C6
Tummel Bridge GB 21 B8
Tumšupe LV 151 B9
Tun S 107 C12
Tunadal S 119 B13
Tuna-Hästberg S 113 B13
Tunari RO 177 E8
Tunbridge Wells, Royal GB 31 E9
Tunga GB 18 J4
Tungozero RUS 137 C17
Tunnerstad S 108 C4
Tunnhovd N 111 B9
Tunnsjø-Røyrvika N 121 B14
Tunsjön S 123 E12
Tunstall GB 31 C11
Tuntenhausen D 88 A5
Tunvägen S 118 A8
Tuohikotti FIN 144 C7
Tuohikylä FIN 131 E5
Tuolluvaara S 132 C4
Tuomikylä FIN 138 E9
Tuomioja FIN 135 E14
Tuorila FIN 142 B6
Tuoro sul Trasimeno I 82 F5
Tuovilanlahti FIN 140 D8
Tupilați RO 169 C9
Tupinești GB 29 A7
Tura H 166 B4
Turanlar TR 193 D10
Turany SK 163 C8
Turawa PL 158 E5
Turba EST 147 C8
Turbe BIH 173 D8
Turbenthal CH 43 F10
Turburea RO 176 D3
Turceni RO 176 D2
Turcia I 55 C8
Turčianske Teplice SK 163 D7
Turcifal P 60 F2
Turcineşti RO 176 C2
Turcoaia RO 171 C2
Turda RO 168 D3
Turdaş RO 167 F11
Turégano E 62 B4
Turek PL 158 B5
Tureni RO 168 D3
Turenki FIN 143 D10
Turew PL 97 B11
Turgeliai LT 153 E12
Tŭrgovishte BG 183 C7
Turgut TR 197 B8
Turgutalp TR 193 A10
Turgutbey TR 189 B7
Turgutlu TR 193 C10
Turgutreis TR 193 F9
Türi EST 147 C9
Turia RO 169 E8
Turić BIH 173 C10
Turie SK 163 C7
Turija SRB 174 B4
Turija SRB 175 D8
Turis E 64 F3
Turiya BG 182 D4
Türje H 165 C8
Turka UA 161 E7
Türkeve H 166 C6
Türkgücü TR 189 B7
Türkheim D 87 A11
Turki LV 151 D12
Turkmenli TR 187 E10
Turkova BY 149 E6
Turkovići BIH 178 D4
Turku FIN 142 E7
Turlava LV 150 C3
Turleque E 62 E5
Turmantas LT 151 E13
Turmenti BIH 178 D5
Turna LV 147 F11
Tūrnak BG 181 C9
Turňa nad Bodvou SK 161 F2
Turnau A 164 A4
Türnava BG 181 B8
Turnberry GB 20 E7
Turners Hill GB 31 E8
Turnhout B 32 F3
Türnitz A 93 G9
Turnov CZ 97 E8
Turnu Măgurele RO 176 F5
Turnu Roşu RO 176 D4
Turnu Ruieni RO 175 C9
Turobin PL 160 B6
Turośl PL 155 C12
Turośl PL 155 D12
Turów PL 157 G7
Turowo PL 101 C11
Turquel P 60 F3
Turrach A 89 C8
Turre E 71 E9
Turri I 80 D2
Turriff GB 19 K12
Tursi I 77 C6
Turț RO 161 H7
Turtel MK 180 F5
Turtola FIN 133 C11
Turulung RO 161 H8
Turup DK 102 E5
Tur'ya-Bystra UA 161 F6
Tur'ya-Polyana UA 161 F6
Turyatka UA 169 A8
Tur'ye UA 161 E7
Tur'yi Remety UA 161 F6
Turynka UA 160 C9
Turza Wielka PL 155 D9
Turzovka SK 163 C7
Tusa I 74 D5
Tuscania I 78 C1
Tuse DK 103 D9
Tuset N 121 E10
Tušilović HR 164 F5
Tușnad RO 169 E7
Tussenhausen D 87 A11
Tüßling D 91 F12
Tuszów Narodowy PL 159 F11
Tuszyma PL 159 F12
Tuszyn PL 159 C8
Tutbury GB 27 F8
Tutjunniemi FIN 141 F13
Tuțora RO 169 C11
Tutova RO 169 E11
Tutow D 99 C13
Tutrakan BG 177 E9
Tuttlingen D 43 E10
Tütüncü TR 189 D8
Tutzing D 88 A3
Tützpatz D 100 C4
Tuukkala FIN 143 B16
Tuuliharju FIN 133 D13
Tuulimäki FIN 137 F11
Tuulos FIN 143 C12
Tuupovaara FIN 141 F15
Tuuri FIN 139 E11
Tuusniemi FIN 141 E10
Tuusula FIN 143 E12
Tuv N 117 B8
Tuv N 124 B8
Tuvattnett S 122 D7
Tuve S 107 D10
Tuvnes N 120 D5
Tuvtråsk S 123 B15
Tuxford GB 27 E10
Tuzburgazi TR 193 B8
Tuzculu TR 193 B8
Tūzha BG 182 D4
Tuzi MNE 179 E7
Tužina SK 163 D7
Tuzla BIH 173 C10
Tuzla RO 171 E3
Tuzla TR 187 E10
Tužno HR 164 D6
Tuzora MD 170 C2
Tuzsér H 161 G5
Tvååker S 103 A10
Tvärålund S 123 C17
Tvärån S 134 C6
Tväråträsk S 123 A13
Tvardița MD 170 E3
Tvärsele S 122 B4
Tvärskog S 105 B10
Tvede DK 102 B6
Tvedestrand N 106 B4
Tveit N 110 C3
Tveit N 110 D4
Tverai LT 150 E4
Tverečius LT 151 F13
Tverråga N 124 D7
Tverråmo N 125 D3
Tverrelmo N 127 C18
Tversted DK 106 D7
Tving S 105 D9
Tvis DK 102 C3
Tvøroyri FO 18 B3
Tvorozhkovo RUS 148 E4
Tvrdošín SK 163 C9
Tvrdošovce SK 162 E6
Tvůrditsa BG 182 D5
Twardogóra PL 158 D3
Twatt GB 19 G10
Tweedmouth GB 21 D12
Tweedsmuir GB 21 D10
Twello NL 32 D6
Twist D 33 C8
Twiste (Twistetal) D 33 F11
Twistringen D 33 C10
Two Mile Borris IRL 25 C7
Twomileborris IRL 25 C7
Two Mile Bridge IRL 23 F8
Tworóg PL 158 D6
Twyford GB 29 C12
Twyford GB 31 C7
Twyning GB 29 A10
Tyachiv UA 161 G8
Tychero GR 187 B10
Tychowo PL 101 C10
Tychowo PL 101 C10
Tychy PL 159 F6
Tyczyn PL 160 C5
Tydal N 121 D11
Tydavnet IRL 23 D8
Tyfors S 113 B11
Tygelsjö S 103 D11
Tyinkrysset N 117 D8
Tykocin PL 156 D7
Tylawa PL 161 D4
Tylissos GR 194 E9
Tyllinge S 109 C8
Tylmanowa PL 161 D1
Tylösand S 103 B11
Tylstrup DK 102 A5
Tymbark PL 161 D1
Tymień PL 101 B9
Tymowa PL 97 D10
Tympaki GR 194 F8
Tynaarlo NL 33 B7
Tynderö S 119 B14
Tyndrum GB 20 B8
Týnec nad Labem CZ 93 B8
Týnec nad Sázavou CZ 93 C7
Tynemouth GB 21 E14
Tyngsjö S 113 B10
Tyniewicze Małe PL 157 E8
Týniště nad Orlicí CZ 93 B10
Tynkä FIN 135 F12
Tynset N 117 B13
Typpö FIN 135 F12
Typpyrä FIN 133 E14
Tyrämäki FIN 137 D12
Tyrävaara FIN 137 D12
Tyrawa Wołoska PL 161 D5
Tyresö S 115 D9
Tyringe S 103 C13
Tyristrand N 111 B12
Tyrjänsaari FIN 141 E15
Tyrnävä FIN 135 E15
Tyrnavos GR 185 E7
Tyrrellspass IRL 23 F8
Tyrväntö FIN 143 C11
Tysnes N 127 D10
Tysse N 110 B5
Tysse N 116 D2
Tyssebotnen N 116 E3
Tyssedal N 110 B5
Tystberga S 109 B10
Tytuvėnai LT 150 E5
Tyukod H 161 H6
Tyulenovo BG 183 B11
Tywyn GB 26 F3

U

Uachdar GB 18 L2
Uachtar Ard IRL 22 F4
Ub SRB 174 E5
Übach-Palenberg D 199 D8
Ubby DK 103 D8
Úbeda E 69 A10
Überherrn D 37 F7
Überlingen D 43 E11
Übersee D 88 A6
Ubli HR 178 D2
Ubli MNE 179 D6
Ubli MNE 179 D7
Ubrique E 69 B7
Ubstadt-Weiher D 37 F11
Ucciani F 53 G9
Uccle B 35 C9
Ucea RO 168 F5
Uceda E 62 C6
Ucel F 51 A7
Ucero E 56 E5
Uchanie PL 160 B8
Uchaux F 51 B8
Uchizy F 46 B6
Uchte D 33 D11
Üchtelhausen D 91 B7
Uchtspringe D 95 A10
Uckange D 202 C2
Uckfield GB 31 F9
Uckro D 96 C5
Uclés E 63 E7
Üçpınar TR 193 B9
Uda RO 176 D5
Udanin PL 97 D10
Udavské SK 161 F4
Udbina HR 172 C4
Udby DK 103 D9
Uddebo S 107 E13
Uddeholm S 113 B9
Uddel NL 199 A7
Uddevalla S 107 C10
Uddheden S 113 C8
Uddington GB 21 D9
Uden NL 32 E5
Udenhout NL 32 E4
Udenisht AL 184 C4
Uderns A 88 B4
Üdersdorf D 37 D7
Udeşti RO 169 B8
Udine I 89 D7
Udorpie PL 101 B13
Udruma N 116 B3
Udrycze PL 160 B7
Uebigau D 96 C4
Ueckermünde D 100 C6
Uehlfeld D 91 C8
Uelsen D 33 D7
Uelzen D 99 E9
Uetendorf CH 47 B12
Uetersen D 98 C7
Uettingen D 90 C6
Uetze D 95 B7
Uffculme GB 29 D8
Uffenheim D 91 C7
Uffing am Staffelsee D 88 A3
Uftrungen D 95 C8
Ugale LV 150 B4
Ugao SRB 179 C9
Ugarana E 56 B6
Uge DK 102 F4
Ugelbølle DK 102 C6
Ugento I 77 D10
Ugerløse DK 103 D9
Uggdal N 110 B2
Uggelheden S 118 E3
Uggelhuse DK 102 C6
Uggerby DK 106 D7
Uggerslev DK 102 D6
Uggiano la Chiesa I 77 C10
Ugijar E 71 F6
Ugine F 47 D9
Uglev DK 102 B3
Ugljan HR 83 D11
Ugljevik BIH 173 C11
Ugod H 165 B9
Uğurchin BG 181 C9
Uğurlu TR 187 C9
Uharte-Arakil E 48 E2
Úherce Mineralne CZ 162 C4
Uherské Hradiště CZ 162 C4
Uherský Brod CZ 162 C5
Uhingen D 90 C6
Uhldingen D 43 E11
Uhlířské Janovice CZ 93 C8
Uhlstädt D 95 E9
Uhniv UA 160 C8
Uhtna EST 147 C13
Uig GB 18 K4
Uimaharju FIN 141 E14
Uimila FIN 143 C15
Uitgeest NL 32 C3
Uithoorn NL 32 D3
Uithuizen NL 33 B7
Uitvar RO 175 B6
Ujazd PL 157 G1
Ujazd PL 158 F5
Újec CZ 93 C12
Újezd CZ 162 C5
Újfehértó H 167 B8
Újhartyán H 166 C3
Újkér H 165 B7
Újkígyós H 167 D7
Újléta H 167 C8
Ujma-Major H 166 E5
Ujnász H 166 E5
Újsolý PL 163 C8
Újszalonta H 167 D7
Újszász H 166 C5
Újszentiván H 166 E5
Ujszentmargita H 167 B7
Újszilvás H 166 C4
Újtikos H 161 H3
Újudvar H 165 C7
Ukhozhany UA 169 A5
Ukkola FIN 141 E14
Ukmergė LT 151 F9
Ukri LV 150 D5
Ula BY 149 F6
Ula TR 197 B8
Ulamış TR 193 C8
Uland S 119 A14
Ulan-Majorat PL 157 G6
Ulanów PL 160 C5
Ulaş TR 189 B8
Ulassai I 80 D4
Ula Tirso I 80 C2
Ulbjerg DK 102 B4
Ulbroka LV 151 C8
Ulbster GB 19 J10
Ulcinj MNE 179 E6
Uldum DK 102 D5
Ulefoss N 111 D10
Uleila del Campo E 71 E8
Ulenurme EST 147 E13
Ulëz AL 179 F8
Ulfborg DK 102 C3
Ulhówek PL 160 C8
Uličе SK 161 F5
Ulieş RO 168 D6
Ulieşti RO 177 D6
Ulila EST 147 E12
Uljanik HR 165 E8
Uljma SRB 175 C7
Ullånger S 123 E14
Ullapool GB 18 K6
Ullared S 103 A11
Ullatti S 132 D7
Ullava FIN 139 C11
Ullbergsträsk S 123 A17
Ulldecona E 58 F4
Ulldemolins E 58 E5
Ullersløv DK 102 E7
Ullervad S 107 B14
Úlles H 166 E4
Ulleskelf GB 27 D9
Ullisjaur S 123 A10
Ullits DK 102 B4
Üllő H 166 C3
Ullsfjord N 127 A18
Ulm D 90 F6
Ulma RO 168 A6
Ulmbach D 90 B5
Ulme P 60 F4
Ulmen D 37 D7
Ulmeni RO 167 C11
Ulmeni RO 177 C9
Ulmeni RO 177 E7
Ulmi RO 177 D6
Ulmu RO 177 D7
Ulmu RO 177 E9
Ulog BIH 173 F9
Uløybukta N 128 D6
Ulricehamn S 107 D13
Ulrichsberg A 92 E5
Ulrichstein D 37 C12
Ulrika S 108 C6
Ulriksberg S 113 B12
Ulriksfors S 122 D9
Ulrum NL 32 B6
Ulsberg N 117 A11
Ulsta GB 19 D14
Ulsted DK 102 A6
Ulsteinvik N 116 B3
Ulstrup DK 102 C5
Ulstrup DK 103 D7
Ulsvåg N 127 D10
Ultrå S 123 E16
Uluabat TR 189 D9
Ulucak TR 193 B9
Ulucak TR 193 C9
Ulukonak TR 197 A7
Ulväker S 107 C14
Ulvenhout NL 32 E3
Ulverston GB 26 C5
Ulvik N 116 B3
Ulvila FIN 142 C6
Ulvöhamn S 123 E15
Ulvsjön S 118 C12
Ulvsjön S 119 B11
Ulvvik S 119 A14
Ul'yanovka UA 170 A6
Ul'yanovo RUS 152 D5
Umag HR 83 B8
Umberleigh GB 28 D7
Umbertide I 82 F5
Umbrărești RO 169 F10
Umbriatico I 77 E7
Umbukta N 124 D6
Umčari SRB 174 D6
Umeå S 123 C18
Umeh S 123 C18
Umgransele S 123 B11
Umin Dol MK 180 D4
Umka SRB 174 D5
Umkirch D 43 E8
Umljanović HR 172 E5
Ummeljoki FIN 144 D6
Ummern D 95 A7
Umnäs S 125 F11
Ümraniye TR 189 B11
Umurbey TR 188 D6
Umurga LV 151 A9
Uña E 63 D9
Uña de Quintana E 55 D7
Unaja FIN 142 C6
Ūnanov CZ 93 E10
Unapool GB 18 J6
Unari FIN 133 D15
Unbyn S 134 C7
Uncastillo E 48 F3
Undenäs S 108 A4
Undersåker S 121 E14
Underidet N 128 D9
Underfossen N 129 C18

Undersåker S 121 E14
Undingen D 43 D11
Undløse DK 103 D9
Undva EST 146 D3
Undy GB 29 B9
Unelanperä FIN 136 F9
Ungerhausen D 87 A10
Ungheni MD 169 C11
Ungheni RO 168 E4
Ungheni RO 176 E5
Ungra RO 168 F6
Unguraşi RO 168 C4
Ungureni RO 169 B9
Ungureni RO 169 D10
Ungurpils LV 147 F9
Unhais da Serra P 60 D5
Unhais-o-Velho P 60 D5
Unhošť CZ 92 B6
Uničov CZ 93 C12
Uniejów PL 158 C6
Unieux F 46 E5
Unín SK 162 D4
Unirea RO 168 E3
Unirea RO 171 C1
Unirea RO 171 F3
Unirea RO 175 B10
Unirea RO 175 E11
Unirea RO 177 E11
Unisław PL 154 D5
Unkel D 37 C8
Unken A 89 A6
Unlingen D 87 A9
Unna D 33 E9
Unnaryd S 103 B13
Unnau D 201 C8
Unntorp S 118 D7
Unset N 117 C14
Unsholtet N 117 A14
Unstad N 126 D6
Untamala FIN 138 D9
Untamala FIN 142 D6
Unţeni RO 169 B9
Unterägeri CH 43 F10
Unterammergau D 87 B12
Unterdießen D 87 B11
Untergriesbach D 92 E5
Unterhaching D 91 F10
Unterkulm CH 43 F9
Unterlüß D 99 E8
Untermaßfeld D 91 A7
Untermerzbach D 91 B8
Untermünkheim D 90 D6
Unterneukirchen D 91 F12
Unterpleichfeld D 91 C7
Unterreit D 91 F11
Unterschächen CH 87 D7
Unterschleißheim D 91 F10
Untersiemau D 91 B8
Untersteinach D 91 B10
Unterweißenbach A 93 F7
Unterwössen D 88 A5
Unverre F 40 D5
Upavon GB 29 C11
Upenieki LV 150 C5
Upesgrīva LV 150 B6
Upgant-Schott D 33 A8
Úpice CZ 93 A10
Upinniemi FIN 143 E11
Uplyme GB 29 D9
Upninkai LT 153 C10
Upper Knockando GB 19 L10
Upperlands GB 20 F3
Upphärad S 107 C11
Uppingham GB 27 F10
Upplanda S 115 B9
Upplands-Väsby S 115 C9
Uppsala S 115 C9
Uppsälje S 113 A11
Uppsete N 116 E5
Uppsjö S 119 C12
Upton upon Severn GB 29 A10
Upyna LT 150 E5
Upyna LT 150 F4
Upytė LT 151 E8
Urafirth GB 19 E14
Urago d'Oglio I 85 B8
Uraiújfalu H 165 B7
Uras I 80 D2
Ura Vajgurore AL 184 C2
Uraz PL 97 D11
Urbach D 37 C9
Urbania I 82 E6
Urbar D 201 D8
Urbe I 53 C9
Urberach D 203 B6
Urbino I 82 E6
Urbisaglia I 83 F7
Urbise F 46 C4
Určice CZ 93 D12
Urda E 62 F5
Urdari RO 176 D2
Urdax-Urdazuli E 48 D2
Urdorf CH 43 F9
Urdos F 48 E4
Urduña E 56 C6
Ure N 126 D6
Urecheni RO 169 C9
Urecheşti RO 169 E10
Urecheşti RO 177 B10
Urë e Shtrenjtë AL 179 E8
Urepel F 48 D3
Ureterp NL 32 B6
Urga LV 147 F9
Úrhida H 165 B10
Úri H 166 C4
Uri I 80 B2
Uricani RO 175 C11
Uriménil F 42 D5
Uringe S 109 A11
Uriu RO 168 C4
Urjala FIN 143 C10
Urk NL 32 C5
Ürkmez TR 193 C8
Úrkút H 165 B9
Urla TR 193 C8
Urlaţi RO 177 D8
Urlingford IRL 25 C7
Urmeniş RO 168 D4
Urmince SK 162 D6
Urnäsch CH 43 F11
Urnieta E 48 D2
Üröm H 166 B3
Uroševac SRB 180 E3
Urovica SRB 175 E9
Urrea de Gaén E 58 E3
Urrea de Jalón E 57 E9
Urretxu E 48 D1
Urriés E 48 E3
Urros P 61 B6
Urroz E 48 E3
Urrugne F 48 D2
Ursberg D 87 A10
Ursensollen D 91 D10
Urshult S 105 B7
Ursviken S 134 E6
Urszulin PL 157 H8
Urt F 48 D3
Urtenen CH 47 A11
Urtimjaur S 132 E5
Urueña E 55 E9
Ururi I 79 D8
Urville Nacqueville F 39 A8
Urzędów PL 160 B5
Urzica RO 176 F4
Urziceni RO 167 B9
Urziceni RO 177 D9
Urzicuţa RO 176 E3
Urzulei I 80 C4
Urzy F 46 A3
Usagre E 67 C7
Ušari BIH 173 C7
Ušće SRB 179 C10
Uschlag (Staufenberg) D 94 D6
Uście Gorlickie PL 161 D3
Uście Solne PL 159 F10
Uscio I 53 C10
Usedom D 100 C5
Usellus I 80 D2
Useras E 64 D4
Ushachy BY 149 F5
Uši LV 146 F5
Usingen D 37 D11
Usini I 80 B2
Usk GB 29 B9
Uskali FIN 141 F14
Uskedal N 110 C3
Üsküdar TR 189 B11
Üsküp TR 183 F8
Uslar D 94 C6
Usma LV 150 B4
Úsov CZ 93 C12
Uspenivka UA 170 E5
Usquert NL 33 B7
Ussana I 80 E3
Ussassai I 80 D3
Usseglio I 47 E11
Ussel F 45 D10
Ussel F 46 E2
Usson-du-Poitou F 45 C7
Usson-en-Forez F 46 E4
Ustaoset N 111 B8
Ustaritz F 48 D3
Ust'-Chorna UA 161 G8
Ust'-Dolyssy RUS 149 D7
Úštěk CZ 96 E6
Uster CH 43 F10
Ustibar BIH 179 B7
Ustica I 74 B3
Ustikolina BIH 173 E10
Ústí nad Labem CZ 96 E6
Ústí nad Orlicí CZ 93 C10
Ustiprača BIH 173 E11
Ustirama BIH 173 E8
Ustka PL 101 A11
Ust'-Luga RUS 148 B3
Ustou F 49 E8
Ustovo BG 187 A7
Ustrem BG 183 E6
Ustroń PL 163 B7
Ustronie Morskie PL 101 B9
Ustrzyki Dolne PL 161 E6
Ustya UA 170 A5
Ustyluh UA 160 B9
Usurbil E 48 D1
Uszew PL 160 D2
Uszód H 165 C11
Utajärvi FIN 135 E16
Utåker N 110 C3
Utakleiv N 126 D6
Utanede S 119 A12
Utanen FIN 135 E16
Utansjö S 119 A14
Utanskog S 123 E14
Utarp D 33 A8
Utbjoa N 110 C3
Utebo E 57 E10
Utelle F 53 D6
Utena LT 151 F11
Utersum D 98 A4
Uthaug N 120 D7
Uthleben D 95 D8
Uthlede D 33 B11
Utiel E 63 E10
Utne N 110 B5
Utö S 109 B12
Utoropy UA 168 A6
Utrecht NL 32 D4
Utrera E 67 E8
Utrillas E 58 F2
Utrine SRB 166 F4
Utro N 120 C8
Utsjoki FIN 129 D18
Utskor N 126 C8
Uttendorf A 88 B6
Uttendorf A 92 F4
Uttenweiler D 87 A9
Utterbyn S 113 B9
Utterliden S 125 F17
Uttersberg S 113 C14
Uttersjö S 123 D14
Utterslev DK 103 F8
Utti FIN 144 D6
Utting am Ammersee D 87 A12
Uttoxeter GB 27 F8
Utula FIN 145 C9
Utvalnäs S 119 E13
Utvik N 116 C5
Utvorda N 121 B9
Utzedel D 100 C4
Uuemõisa EST 146 D7
Uukuniemi FIN 145 B13
Uulu EST 147 E9
Uura FIN 137 F10
Uurainen FIN 139 E14
Uuro FIN 138 F8
Uusikaarlepyy FIN 138 C9
Uusikartano FIN 142 D7
Uusikaupunki FIN 142 D5
Uusikylä FIN 139 D12
Uusikylä FIN 143 D15
Uusi-Värtsilä FIN 141 F14
Uva FIN 137 E11
Uvac BIH 174 F4
Uvåg N 126 C8
Úvaly CZ 93 B7
Uvanå S 113 B10
Uvdal N 111 B9
Üvecik TR 187 E10
Uvernet-Fours F 52 C5
Uv'jarätto N 129 D12
Uxbridge GB 31 D8
Uxeau F 46 B5
Üxheim D 37 D7
Uyeasound GB 19 D15
Uza F 48 B3
Užava LV 150 B2
Uzdin SRB 174 C6
Uzel F 38 D6
Uzer F 51 A7
Uzerche F 45 E9
Uzès F 51 B7
Uzhhorod UA 161 F5
Uzhok UA 161 F6
Užice SRB 174 F4
Uzlovoye RUS 152 D5
Uznovë AL 184 C2
Užpaliai LT 151 E11
Uzrechcha BY 149 F3
Uzundzhovo BG 182 F5
Uzunköprü TR 188 B6
Uzunkuyu TR 193 C8
Užventis LT 150 E5

V

Vaadinselkä FIN 131 E5
Vaajakoski FIN 139 F15
Vaajasalmi FIN 140 E7
Vääkiö FIN 137 D12
Vaala FIN 135 E17
Vaalajärvi FIN 133 D16
Vaale D 98 C6
Vaalimaa FIN 144 D8
Vaals NL 36 C6
Vaarakylä FIN 137 C11
Vaarankylä FIN 137 F10
Vaaranniva FIN 137 D11
Vaaraperä FIN 137 C13
Vaaraslahti FIN 139 D17
Väärinmaja FIN 140 G2
Vaartsi EST 148 F2
Vaas F 40 E3
Vaasa FIN 138 D7
Vaassen NL 32 D5
Väätäiskylä FIN 139 E13
Väätsa EST 147 D10
Vaattojärvi FIN 133 D12
Vabalninkas LT 151 E9
Vabole LV 151 D12
Vabre F 49 C10
Vabres-l'Abbaye F 50 C4
Vác H 166 B3
Văcăreşti RO 177 D6
Vaccarizzo Albanese I 77 D6
Váchartyán H 166 B3
Vacheresse F 47 C10
Vachlia GR 190 D4
Väckelsång S 105 B7
Vacov CZ 92 D5
Vacqueyras F 51 B8
Vácrátót H 166 B3
Văculeşti RO 169 B8
Vad RO 168 C3
Vad S 113 B14
Vadakste LV 150 D5
Vadaktai LT 151 E7
Vădastra RO 176 F4
Vădăstriţa RO 176 F4
Vaddas gruver N 128 D8
Vădeni RO 171 C1
Väderstad S 108 C5
Vad Foss N 106 B5
Vadheim N 116 D3
Vadla N 110 D4
Vadocondes E 56 E4
Vadokliai LT 151 F8
Vado Ligure I 53 C8
Vadskinn N 127 C11
Vadsø N 130 C7
Vadstena S 108 C5
Vadu Crişului RO 167 D10
Vadu lui Isac MD 171 B2
Vadu Izei RO 161 H8
Vadul lui Vodă MD 170 C4
Vadul Turcului MD 170 B3
Vadum DK 102 A5
Vadu Moldovei RO 169 C8
Vadu Moţilor RO 167 E10
Vadu Paşii RO 177 C9
Vaduz FL 87 C9
Vadžgirys LT 150 F5
Væggerløse DK 99 A11
Vafaïka GR 187 B8
Vafiochori GR 185 B8
Våg N 110 D2
Vågaholmen N 124 C5
Vågåmo N 117 C10
Vagan BIH 173 D6
Vågan N 127 B14
Vågdalen S 122 D9
Våge N 110 B3
Våge N 110 G6
Vaggatem N 130 E6
Vaggeryd S 108 E4
Vågholmane N 116 A4
Vagia GR 191 C7
Văgiuleşti RO 175 D11
Vaglia I 82 E3
Vaglio Basilicata I 76 B5
Vagli Sotto I 82 D1
Vagney F 42 D6
Vagnhärad S 109 B11
Vagnsunda S 115 C11
Vagos P 60 C3
Vågseidet N 116 E2
Vågsele S 123 B14
Vågsodden N 124 E3
Vágur FO 18 C3
Vähäjoki FIN 135 B14
Vähäkangas FIN 139 B13
Vähäkyrö FIN 138 D8
Vähäniva FIN 132 B9
Vahanka FIN 139 E13
Vahastu EST 147 D10
Vahenurme EST 147 D8
Vähikkälä FIN 143 D12
Vahojärvi FIN 143 B9
Váhovce SK 162 E5
Vahterpää FIN 143 E15
Vahto FIN 142 D7
Vaiamonte P 60 F6
Vaiano I 82 E3
Vaickūniškės LT 153 D10
Vaida EST 147 C9
Vaidava LV 151 B10
Vaideeni RO 176 C3
Vaidotai LT 153 D11
Vaiges F 39 D11
Vaiguva LT 150 E5
Väike-Maarja EST 147 C12
Väike-Punperja EST 147 C14
Vaikijaur S 132 E3
Vaikko FIN 141 D11
Vailly-sur-Aisne F 35 F8
Vailly-sur-Sauldre F 41 F8
Vaimastvere EST 147 D12
Väimela EST 147 F14
Vaimõisa EST 147 D8
Vainikkala FIN 145 D9
Vaiņode LV 150 D3
Vainotiškiai LT 150 F7
Vairano Patenora I 76 A2
Vairano Scalo I 76 A2
Väisälä FIN 137 E11
Vaison-la-Romaine F 51 B9
Vaïssac F 49 B9
Vaišvydava LT 153 D9
Vaivio FIN 141 E12
Vaivre-et-Montoille F 42 E5
Vaja H 161 H5
Vajangu EST 147 C12
Vajdácska H 161 G4
Våje N 106 B4
Våje N 126 D5
Vajkal AL 184 A3
Vajmat S 125 C18
Vajska SRB 173 B11
Vajszló H 165 E9
Vajta H 165 C11
Vakarel BG 181 D8
Vakern S 113 B11
Vakıflar TR 189 B8
Vaklino BG 171 F2
Vaksdal N 110 B3
Vaksevo BG 181 E6
Vaksince MK 180 E4
Vál H 165 B11
Valada P 60 F3
Vålådalen S 121 E13
Valadares P 54 D3
Valajanaapa FIN 135 C15
Valajaskoski FIN 135 B14
Valaliky SK 161 F3
Valand N 106 C2
Valandovo MK 185 B8
Vålånger S 119 A14
Valanida GR 185 E7
Valanjou F 39 F10
Valareña E 57 D9
Vålåsjø N 117 B10
Valaská SK 163 D9
Valaská Belá SK 162 D6
Valašská Bystřice CZ 162 C6
Valašská Polanka CZ 162 C5
Valašské Klobouky CZ 162 C6
Valašské Meziříčí CZ 162 C5
Vålax FIN 143 E14
Valberg F 52 C5
Valberg N 126 D6
Vålberg S 113 D9
Valbiska HR 83 B9
Valbo S 119 E13
Valbom P 60 B3
Valbona E 64 D3
Valbondione I 85 A9
Valbonë AL 179 E8
Valbonnais F 47 F8
Valbonne F 52 D6
Valbuena de Duero E 56 E3
Valča SK 163 C7
Valcabrère F 49 D7
Valcău de Jos RO 167 C10
Vâlcele RO 169 F7
Vâlcele RO 176 E5
Vâlcelele RO 177 C10
Vâlcelele RO 177 E10
Valdagno I 85 B11
Valdahon F 42 F5
Valdaora I 88 C5
Valddak N 129 C14
Valdealgorfa E 58 E3
Valdeblore F 53 C6
Valdecaballeros E 61 F10
Valdecañas de Tajo E 61 E9
Valdecarros E 61 C10
Valdecilla E 56 B4
Valdecuenca E 63 D10
Valdefuentes E 61 F8
Valdeganga E 63 F9
Valdeķi LV 150 C5
Valdelacasa E 61 C9
Valdelacasa de Tajo E 61 E10
Valdelamusa E 67 D6
Valdelinares E 64 D3
Valdemanco del Esteras E 70 B3
Valdemārpils LV 150 B5
Valdemarsvik S 109 C9
Valdemeca E 63 D9
Valdemorillo E 62 C4
Valdemoro E 62 D5
Valdemoro-Sierra E 63 D9
Valdenoches E 63 C6
Valdeobispo E 61 D8
Valdeolivas E 63 C8
Valdepeñas E 71 B6
Valdepeñas de Jaén E 69 A9
Valderas E 55 D9
Val-de-Reuil F 34 F3
Valderice I 74 C2
Valderiès F 49 B10
Valderøy N 116 A4
Valderrobres E 58 F4
Val de Santo Domingo E 62 D4
Valdestillas E 55 F10
Valdetormo E 58 F4
Valdetorres E 67 B7
Valdeverdeja E 61 E10
Valdevimbre E 55 D8
Valdgale LV 150 B5
Valdice CZ 93 B8
Valdidentro I 87 E10
Valdilecha E 63 D6
Val-d'Isère F 47 E10
Valdisotto I 87 E10
Valdivienne F 45 B7
Val-d'Izé F 39 D9
Valdobbiadene I 88 E4
Valdoie F 43 E6
Valdunquillo E 55 D9
Vale GBG 38 B6
Våle N 111 D12
Våle S 119 A8
Valea Adîncă MD 170 A3
Valea Argovei RO 177 E9
Valea Călugărească RO 177 D8
Valea Chioarului RO 167 C11
Valea Ciorii RO 177 D11
Valea Crişului RO 169 F7
Valea Danului RO 176 C5
Valea Doftanei RO 177 C7
Valea Dragului RO 177 E8
Valea Ierii RO 167 D11
Valea Largă RO 168 D4
Valea lui Mihai RO 167 B9
Valea Lungă RO 168 E4
Valea Lungă RO 177 C7
Valea Măcrişului RO 177 D9
Valea Mare MD 169 C11
Valea Mare RO 176 D3
Valea Mare RO 176 D6
Valea Mare RO 176 E4
Valea Mare-Pravăţ RO 176 C6
Valea Mărului RO 169 F11
Valea Moldovei RO 169 C8
Valea Nucarilor RO 171 C3
Valea Râmnicului RO 177 C10
Valea Salciei RO 177 C9
Valea Sării RO 169 F9
Valea Seacă RO 169 C9
Valea Seacă RO 169 E10
Valea Stanciului RO 176 F3
Valea Teilor RO 171 C3
Valea Ursului RO 169 D10
Valea Viilor RO 168 E4
Valea Vinului RO 167 B11
Vale da Rosa P 66 E4
Vale das Mós P 60 F4
Vale de Açor P 60 F5
Vale de Açor P 66 D4
Vale de Cambra P 60 C4
Vale de Cavalos P 60 F3
Vale de Espinho P 61 D7
Vale de Estrela P 61 C6
Vale de Figueira P 60 F3
Vale de Lobo P 66 E3
Vale de Prazeres P 60 D6
Vale de Reis P 66 C3
Vale de Salgueiro P 54 E5
Vale de Santarém P 60 F3
Vale do Peso P 60 F5
Válega P 60 C3
Valeggio sul Mincio I 82 B2
Valen N 110 C3
Valença P 54 D2
Valença do Douro P 60 B5
Valençay F 40 F6
Valence F 46 F6
Valence F 49 B7
Valence-d'Albigeois F 49 B10
Valence-sur-Baïse F 49 C6
Valencia E 64 F4
Valencia de Alcántara E 61 F6
Valencia de Don Juan E 55 D8
Valencia de las Torres E 67 C7
Valencia del Mombuey E 67 C5
Valencia del Ventoso E 67 C7
Valenciennes F 35 D8
Văleni RO 169 D11
Văleni RO 176 E5
Vălenii de Munte RO 177 C8
Valensole F 51 C10
Valentano I 78 B1
Valentigney F 43 F6
Valenza I 53 A9
Valenzano I 77 A7
Valenzuela E 69 A8
Valenzuela de Calatrava E 70 B5
Våler N 111 D13
Våler N 117 E15
Valera de Arriba E 63 E8
Valernes F 51 B10
Vales Mortos P 66 D5
Valestrand N 110 A2
Valevåg N 110 C2
Valfabbrica I 82 F6
Valfarta E 58 D3
Valfroicourt F 42 D5
Valfurva I 87 E10
Valga EST 147 F12
Valgalciems LV 150 B5
Valgale LV 150 B4
Valgrisenche I 47 D11
Valgu EST 147 D9
Valguarnera Caropepe I 74 E5
Valgunde LV 150 C7
Valhelhas P 60 D6
Valhermoso E 63 C9
Vålhovd N 117 E12
Välijoki FIN 135 B15
Välikangas FIN 135 B16
Väli-Kannus FIN 139 C11
Valikardhë AL 184 A3
Välikylä FIN 139 C11
Valimi GR 190 C5
Välitalo FIN 133 C16
Văliug RO 175 C9
Väli-Viirre FIN 139 C11
Valjala EST 146 E5
Valjevo SRB 174 E4
Valjok N 129 D16
Valjunquera E 58 F4
Valka LV 147 F12
Valkeajärvi FIN 139 F12
Valkeakoski FIN 143 C11
Valkeakoski S 133 E11
Valkeala FIN 144 D6
Valkeiskylä FIN 140 C8
Valkeiskylä FIN 141 D10
Valkenburg NL 35 C12
Valkenswaard NL 32 F4
Valkininkai LT 153 E10
Valkla EST 147 C10
Valko FIN 143 E15
Valkó H 166 B4
Valla S 109 A8
Valla S 123 E10
Valladolid E 55 E10
Valladolises E 72 F2
Vállaj H 167 B9
Vallåkra S 103 D11
Vallargärdet S 113 D10
Vallata I 76 A4
Vallauris F 52 D6
Vallberga S 103 C12
Vallbo S 121 E14
Vallbona d'Anoia E 59 D7
Vallda S 107 E10
Valldal N 116 B6
Vall d'Alba E 64 D4
Valldemossa E 65 E10
Valle E 56 B3
Valle LV 151 C9
Valle N 106 A2
Valle N 110 B6
Valle N 124 B6
Valle Castellana I 78 B5
Vallecorsa I 78 E4
Valle de Abdalajís E 69 C7
Valle de la Serena E 67 B8
Valle de Matamoros E 67 C6
Valle de Santa Ana E 67 C6
Valle di Cadore I 88 D5
Valledolmo I 74 D4
Valledoria I 80 B2
Valleiry F 47 C8
Vallelunga Pratameno I 74 D4
Valle Mosso I 84 B5
Vallen S 123 D11
Vallen S 134 F6
Vallenca E 63 D10
Vallendar D 201 D8
Vallentuna S 115 C10
Vallerås S 118 E6
Valleraugue F 51 B6
Vallermosa I 80 E2
Vallerotonda I 78 D5
Vallersund N 120 D7
Vallervatnet N 121 B15
Vallet F 39 F9
Valley D 88 A4
Valley GB 26 E2
Vallfogona de Riucorb E 58 D6
Vallières F 45 D10
Vallioniemi FIN 137 B12
Vallmoll E 58 E6
Valløby DK 103 E10
Vallo della Lucania I 76 C4
Vallo di Nera I 78 B3
Valloire F 47 E9
Vallombrosa I 82 E4
Vallon-en-Sully F 45 B11
Vallon-Pont-d'Arc F 51 B7
Vallorbe CH 47 B9
Vallorcine F 47 C10
Vallouise F 47 F9
Vallrun S 121 D16
Valls E 58 E6
Vallsbo S 119 E12
Vallsjön S 119 A11
Vallsta S 119 C11
Vallstena S 109 D13
Vallvik S 119 D13
Valmadrera I 85 B7
Valmadrid E 57 F10
Valmen N 117 D15
Valmiera LV 147 F10
Valmiermuiža LV 147 F10
Valmojado E 62 D4
Valmont F 34 E2
Valmontone I 78 D3
Valmorel F 47 E9
Valmy F 41 B12
Valnes N 124 B7
Valognes F 39 A9
Valongo P 60 B4
Valongo P 60 F5
Válor E 71 F6
Valoria la Buena E 56 E2
Valøy N 121 B9
Valøy N 121 C11
Valpaços P 54 E5
Valpalmas E 57 D10
Valpelline I 47 D11
Valperga I 84 C4
Valpovo HR 165 E10
Valpperi FIN 142 D7
Valras-Plage F 50 D5
Valréas F 51 B8
Valros F 50 D5
Vals CH 87 D8
Valsavarenche I 47 D11
Valse DK 103 F9
Valseca E 62 B4
Valsequillo E 67 C9
Valsgård DK 102 B5
Valsgarth GB 19 D15
Valshed S 119 E9
Valsinni I 77 C6
Valsjöbyn S 121 C16
Valsjön S 119 B11
Valška SRB 174 E6
Valskog S 113 D14
Vals-les-Bains F 51 A7
Valsøybotn N 120 E5
Välsta S 119 C13
Valstagna I 88 E4
Val-Suzon F 42 F2
Valtablado del Río E 63 C8
Valtero GR 185 B9
Valtesiniko GR 190 D5
Valtice CZ 93 E11
Valtiendas E 56 F4
Valtierra E 57 D8
Valtimo FIN 141 C11
Valtola FIN 144 C7
Valtopina I 78 A3
Valtos GR 187 A10
Valtotopi GR 185 C10
Valtournenche I 84 B4
Valtura HR 83 C8
Valu lui Traian RO 171 E2
Valun HR 83 C9
Väluste EST 147 E11
Valverde de Burguillos E 67 C6
Valverde de Júcar E 63 E8
Valverde de la Virgen E 55 C8
Valverde del Camino E 67 D6
Valverde de Leganés E 67 B6
Valverde del Fresno E 61 D7
Valverde de Llerena E 67 C8
Valverde del Majano E 62 C4
Valverde de Mérida E 67 B7
Valvika N 124 B8
Valvträsk S 134 B7
Valyra GR 190 E4
Vama RO 161 H7
Vama RO 169 B7
Vama Buzăului RO 177 B7
Vamberk CZ 93 B10
Vamdrup DK 102 E4
Våmhus S 118 D7
Vamlingbo S 109 F12
Vammala FIN 143 C8
Vammen DK 102 B5
Vamos GR 194 E7
Vámosmikola H 163 F7
Vámospércs H 167 B8
Vámosújfalu H 161 G3
Vampula FIN 142 C8
Vamvakofyto GR 185 B9
Vamvakou GR 185 F7
Vanaja FIN 143 D12
Vana-Koiola EST 147 F14
Vânători RO 168 E5
Vânători RO 169 C9
Vânători RO 169 F10
Vânători RO 171 B2
Vânători RO 175 E10
Vânătorii Mici RO 177 E7
Vânători-Neamţ RO 169 C8
Vanault-les-Dames F 41 C12
Vana-Vigala EST 147 D8
Vana-Võidu EST 147 E11
Váncsod H 167 C8
Vanda FIN 143 E12
Vandel DK 102 D4
Vandellós E 58 E5
Vandenesse F 46 B4
Vandenesse-en-Auxois F 41 F12
Vandœuvre-lès-Nancy F 202 D1
Vandoies I 88 C4
Vändra EST 147 D10
Vändträsk S 134 C6
Vandzene LV 150 B5
Vandžiogala LT 151 F7
Väne LV 150 C5
Väne-Åsaka S 107 C11
Vänersborg S 107 C11
Vañes E 56 C3
Vang N 117 D9
Vånga S 108 B7
Vangaži LV 151 B9
Vänge S 109 E13
Vängel S 123 D10
Vangshamn N 127 B15
Vangshylla N 121 D10
Vangsnes N 116 D5
Vangsvik N 127 B14
Vanha-Kihlanki FIN 133 C10
Vanhakylä FIN 138 F7
Vänjaurbäck S 123 C15
Vänjaurträsk S 123 C15
Vânjuleţ RO 175 E10
Vânju Mare RO 175 E10
Vannareid N 128 C4
Vännäs S 138 C3
Vännäsberget S 134 B9
Vännäsby S 138 C3
Vannavalen N 128 C4
Vänne N 106 B2
Vannes F 38 E6
Vannvåg N 128 C4
Vannvikan N 120 D8
Vänö FIN 142 F7
Vansbro S 113 A11
Vanse N 110 F5
Vänsjö S 119 C9
Vantaa FIN 143 E12
Vanttausjärvi FIN 135 B17
Vanttauskoski FIN 135 B17
Vanvey F 41 E12
Vanyarc H 163 F8
Vanzone I 84 B5
Vaour F 49 B9
Vápenná CZ 93 B12
Vaplan S 121 E16
Vaqueiros P 66 E4
Vara EST 147 D13
Vara S 107 C12
Vara del Rey E 63 F8
Varades F 39 F9
Vărădia RO 175 C8
Vărădia de Mureş RO 167 E9
Varages F 51 C10
Varaire F 49 B9
Varajärvi FIN 135 B13
Varajoki FIN 137 F14
Varakļāni LV 151 C13
Varallo I 84 B5
Varangerbotn N 130 C5
Varano de'Melegari I 85 D8
Varapayeva BY 149 F2
Varapodio I 75 C8
Vărăşti RO 177 E8
Vărătec RO 169 C8
Varaždin HR 165 D6
Varaždinske Toplice HR 165 D6
Varazze I 53 C9
Varberg S 103 A10
Vărbilău RO 177 C7
Varbla EST 146 E7
Varbó H 161 G2
Varbola EST 147 C8
Varces-Allières-et-Risset F 47 E8
Vârciorog RO 167 D9
Varda GR 190 C3
Vardali GR 190 A5
Varde DK 102 D2
Vardim BG 177 F6
Vardište BIH 174 F3
Vårdö FIN 115 B14
Vardø N 130 C10
Várdomb H 165 D11
Varejoki FIN 135 B13
Varekil S 107 C10
Varel D 33 B10
Varėna LT 153 E10
Varengeville-sur-Mer F 34 E2
Varenna I 85 A7
Varennes-en-Argonne F 35 F11
Varennes-St-Sauveur F 47 C7
Varennes-sur-Allier F 46 C3
Varennes-Vauzelles F 46 A3
Vareš BIH 173 D9
Varese I 85 B6
Varese Ligure I 53 C11
Varetz F 45 E8
Vârfu Câmpului RO 169 B8
Vârfuri RO 177 C7
Vârfurile RO 167 E10
Vårgårda S 107 C12
Vargata RO 168 D5
Vârghiş RO 169 E7
Vargön S 107 C11
Vargträsk S 123 C15
Varhaug N 110 E3
Vari GR 191 D8
Vari GR 192 E4
Variaş RO 167 E6
Varik NL 199 B6
Variku EST 146 C7
Varilhes F 49 D9
Varín SK 163 C7
Väring S 107 B14
Variņi LV 151 B12
Variskylä FIN 137 F9
Varislahti FIN 141 E11
Varistaipale FIN 141 E11
Varjakka FIN 135 E14
Varjisträsk S 125 D18
Varkalai LT 150 E3
Varkaus FIN 141 F9
Värkava LV 151 D13
Varkhi BY 149 E7
Vârlezi RO 169 F11
Varlosen (Niemetal) D 94 D6
Värme LV 150 C4
Värmlandsbro S 107 A13
Varna BG 183 C9
Varna I 88 C4
Varna SRB 174 D4
Värnamo S 104 A6
Värnäs S 113 B9
Varnavas GR 191 C8
Varnhem S 107 C14
Varniai LT 150 E4
Varnja EST 147 E14
Varnsdorf CZ 97 E7
Varntresken N 124 E7
Varnyany BY 153 D13
Varöbacka S 103 A10
Varonichy BY 149 F5
Varonka BY 149 F2
Városföld H 166 D4
Varoška Rijeka BIH 172 B5
Városlőd H 165 B9
Várpaisjärvi FIN 140 D9
Várpalota H 165 B10
Varpanen FIN 144 C6
Varparanta FIN 141 G11

Varpasalo FIN 141 F12
Varpsjö S 123 C11
Varpuselkä FIN 131 E5
Varpuvaara FIN 131 E4
Värriö FIN 131 D3
Varrio FIN 131 E2
Vars F 45 D6
Vars F 52 B5
Vărşand RO 167 D7
Varsány H 163 E8
Värsås S 107 C15
Varsi I 85 D8
Värska EST 148 F2
Vărşolţ RO 167 C10
Varsseveld NL 33 E6
Vårst DK 102 B6
Vårsta S 109 A11
Varstu EST 147 F13
Varteig N 111 D14
Vartemyagi RUS 145 E13
Vårteşcoiu RO 169 F10
Vartholomio GR 190 D3
Vartius FIN 137 E14
Vårtoape RO 176 E6
Vartofta S 107 C14
Vårtop RO 176 E2
Värtsilä FIN 141 F15
Varuträsk S 134 C4
Varvara BG 181 E9
Varvara BG 183 E9
Varvara GR 185 C10
Varvarin SRB 175 F7
Varvasaina GR 190 D4
Värve LV 150 B3
Varvikko FIN 131 E4
Várvölgy H 165 C8
Vårvoru de Jos RO 176 E3
Varyazh UA 160 B6
Vărzărești MD 170 C2
Varzi I 53 B10
Varzo I 84 A5
Varzy F 41 F9
Vasa FIN 138 D7
Vasalemma EST 147 C8
Vasanello I 78 C2
Vasaniemi FIN 131 D2
Vasankari FIN 135 F11
Vasaraperä FIN 137 B12
Vásárosdombó H 165 D10
Vásárosnamény H 161 G5
Vaşcău RO 167 E10
Våse S 113 D10
Vashkivtsi UA 169 A7
Vashtëmi AL 184 C4
Vasilati RO 177 E8
Vasilika GR 185 D9
Vasilika GR 193 A7
Vasiliki GR 190 B2
Vasiliko GR 191 C8
Vasilikos GR 190 D2
Vasilis GR 185 F7
Vasilitsi GR 194 B2
Vasil Kolarov BG 181 F10
Vasil Levski BG 182 E5
Vasilopoulo GR 190 B3
Vasilovtsi BG 175 F11
Vasil'yevo RUS 148 F2
Vaškai LT 151 D8
Vaski LV 150 C6
Vaškiai LT 150 E2
Väskinde S 109 D12
Vaskio FIN 143 E9
Vaskivesi FIN 139 F11
Vasknarva EST 148 C1
Vaskút H 166 E2
Vaskuu FIN 139 F11
Vasles F 44 B5
Vaslui RO 169 D11
Vasmegyer H 161 G4
Vassaras GR 191 E6
Vassbo S 118 C4
Vassbotn N 127 C13
Vassbygdi N 116 E6
Vassdalen N 127 C14
Vassdalsvik N 124 C6
Vassenden N 116 D4
Vassieux-en-Vercors F 47 F7
Vassmolösa S 105 B10
Vassnäs S 121 D14
Vassor FIN 138 D8
Vasstrand N 127 A15
Vassy F 39 C10
Vasszécseny H 165 B7
Västana S 119 A12
Västanå S 119 B13
Västanå S 123 E16
Västanbäck S 123 D2
Västanfjärd FIN 142 E8
Västannäs S 134 B9
Västansjö S 119 A12
Västansjö S 119 C12
Västansjö S 123 A9
Västansjö S 123 C13
Västansjö S 123 E12
Västansjö S 124 E9
Västansjön S 119 B12
Västanvik S 119 E8
Vastemõisa EST 147 E10
Västerås S 114 C7
Västeråsen S 123 F11
Västerberg S 119 E12
Västerby S 113 B14
Västerbyn S 115 B10
Västerfärnebo S 114 C6
Västerhällan S 118 A5
Västerhaninge S 109 A12
Västerhejde S 109 D12
Västerhus S 123 E15
Västerlandsjö S 123 E15
Västerljung S 109 B10
Västermyckeläng S 118 D7
Västerottna S 113 C8
Västerträsjö S 119 C11
Västervik S 109 D9
Västilä FIN 143 B12
Vastinki FIN 139 E14
Västinniemi FIN 141 E10
Vasto I 79 C7
Vastorf D 99 D9
Västra Åmtervik S 113 C9
Västra Bodarna S 107 D11
Västra Eneby S 108 D7
Västra Fagelberget S 121 C17
Västra Harg S 108 C6
Västra Hjäggböle S 134 C4
Västra Husby S 109 C8
Västra Karup S 103 C11
Västra Kiilisjärvi S 133 C8
Västra Lainejaure S 123 A15
Västra Ormsjö S 123 C10
Västra Sjulsmark S 134 F5
Västra Stugusjö S 119 A19
Västra Täsjö S 122 C9

Västra Torup S 103 C13
Västra Yttermark FIN 138 E6
Vastse-Kuuste EST 147 E13
Vastseliina EST 148 F1
Vasvár H 165 B7
Vasylivka UA 171 B3
Vasylivka UA 171 B4
Vaszar H 165 B9
Vatan F 45 A9
Vátava RO 168 D5
Våte S 109 E12
Vatera GR 193 A7
Vatero GR 185 C6
Vaterholmsbru N 121 D11
Vaterstetten D 91 F10
Vatheia GR 194 C3
Vathy GR 191 C8
Vathy GR 193 D8
Vathylakkos GR 185 C8
Vathylakkos GR 185 D6
Vathys GR 193 F9
Vati GR 197 D2
Vatican City E 78 D2
Vatici MD 170 C3
Vatjusjärvi FIN 139 B14
Vatla EST 146 D7
Vatland N 110 F6
Vatnahalsen N 116 E6
Vatne N 116 B8
Vatne N 110 E3
Vatolakkos GR 185 D5
Vatoussa GR 193 A7
Vatra Dornei RO 168 C6
Vatra Moldoviței RO 169 B7
Vats N 117 B8
Vatta H 161 H2
Vattholma S 115 B9
Vattjom S 119 B13
Vattlång S 119 C14
Vattrång S 119 C13
Vattukylä FIN 135 F11
Vatula FIN 143 B8
Våtvoll N 127 C10
Vaubadon F 39 B10
Vaubecourt F 42 C3
Vauchassis F 41 D10
Vauclaix F 41 F9
Vauconcourt-Nervezain F 42 E4
Vaucouleurs F 42 C4
Vaudémont F 42 D5
Vaugneray F 46 D6
Vauldalen N 117 A16
Vaulx-en-Velin F 46 D6
Vaulx-Milieu F 47 D7
Vauvenargues F 51 C10
Vauvert F 51 C7
Vauvillers F 42 E4
Vaux-le-Pénil F 41 C8
Vaux-sur-Mer F 44 D3
Vaux-sur-Sûre B 35 E12
Vavdos GR 185 D9
Vayrac F 45 F9
Vayres F 45 D7
Väyrylä FIN 137 E10
Vaysal TR 183 F7
Väystäjä FIN 135 B12
Včelná CZ 93 E6
Veåskoonjarga FIN 129 F20
Veauche F 46 D5
Veavågen N 110 E2
Vebbestrup DK 102 B5
Veberöd S 103 D13
Vebomark S 134 F6
Vecate LV 147 F10
Vecauce LV 150 D4
Vecchiano I 82 E1
Vechelde D 95 B7
Vechta D 33 C10
Veckerhagen (Reinhardshagen) D 94 D4
Veckrape LV 151 C10
Veclaicene LV 147 F14
Vecmikeļi LV 150 D6
Vecpiebalga LV 151 B11
Vecpils LV 150 C2
Vecsaikava LV 151 C12
Vecsalaca LV 147 F8
Vecsaule LV 151 D8
Vecsés H 166 C3
Vecskulte LV 151 B8
Vecslabada LV 149 D3
Vecumnieki LV 151 C9
Veda S 119 A14
Vedde DK 103 D9
Veddelev DK 103 D10
Veddige S 104 A2
Veddum DK 102 B6
Vēde LV 150 B3
Vedea RO 176 D5
Vedea RO 177 F7
Vedelago I 88 E5
Vedevåg S 113 C13
Vedjeön S 122 C8
Vedra S 54 C3
Védrines-St-Loup F 46 E3
Vedro Polje BIH 172 D5
Vedsted DK 102 E4
Vedum S 107 C11
Veendam NL 33 B7
Veenendaal NL 32 D5
Veenhusen D 33 B8
Veensgarth GB 19 E14
Veere NL 198 B3
Veerle B 198 C5
Veflinge DK 102 E6
Vegacervera E 55 C8
Vega de Espinareda E 55 C6
Vegadeo E 54 B5
Vega de Pas E 56 B4
Vega de Tirados E 61 B9
Vegadel Valcarce E 55 C6
Vega de Valdetronco E 55 E9
Veganzones E 62 B5
Vegaquemada E 55 C7
Vegarienza E 55 C7
Vegarshei N 106 B4
Vegas del Condado E 55 C9
Vegas de Matute E 62 C4
Vegby S 107 D13
Végegyháza H 166 E6
Veggen N 127 D13
Vegger DK 102 B5
Veghel NL 32 E5

Veği LV 150 B4
Veglie I 77 C9
Vegset N 121 C12
Vehkajärvi FIN 143 B12
Vehkalahti FIN 143 B15
Vehkalahti FIN 144 D7
Vehkataipale FIN 145 C9
Vehlow D 99 D12
Vehmaa FIN 142 D6
Vehmaa FIN 144 B8
Vehmasjärvi FIN 141 C9
Vehmersalmi FIN 141 E10
Vehniä FIN 139 F15
Vehu FIN 139 E13
Vehvilä FIN 140 E8
Veidholmen N 120 D3
Veidneset N 129 B13
Veigy-Foncenex F 47 C9
Veihtivaara FIN 137 E14
Veikkola FIN 143 E11
Veimo N 121 D11
Veinge S 103 B12
Veiros P 66 B4
Veisiejis LT 153 E8
Veitastrond N 116 D6
Veitsbronn D 91 C8
Veitsch A 164 A5
Veitservasa FIN 133 C13
Veiveriai LT 153 D8
Veiviržėnai LT 150 E3
Vejano I 78 C2
Vejby DK 103 C10
Vejbystrand S 103 C11
Vejen DK 102 D4
Vejer de la Frontera E 68 D5
Vejle DK 102 D5
Vejle DK 102 E6
Vejprnice CZ 92 C4
Vejrum DK 102 C5
Vejstrup DK 103 E7
Vekilski BG 177 F10
Vela RO 176 E2
Velagići BIH 173 C6
Vela Luka HR 178 D2
Velamazán E 57 F6
Velanda S 107 C11
Velanidia GR 194 C5
Veľaty SK 161 F4
Velaux F 51 C9
Velbastaður FO 18 B3
Velbert D 33 F8
Velburg D 91 D10
Velçë AL 184 D2
Veldegem B 198 C2
Velden N 91 F11
Velden NL 199 B7
Velden am Wörther See A 89 C9
Veldhoven NL 32 F4
Velefique E 71 E8
Velehrad CZ 162 C4
Velen D 33 E7
Velence H 165 B10
Velenje SLO 89 D11
Veles MK 180 F4
Velešević HR 164 E6
Velešín CZ 93 E6
Velešta MK 184 B4
Velestino GR 185 F8
Vélez-Blanco E 71 D8
Vélez de Benaudalla E 69 C10
Vélez-Málaga E 69 C8
Vélez-Rubio E 71 D8
Velgast D 99 B13
Velika HR 165 F9
Velika Brijesnica BIH 173 C9
Velika Drenova SRB 175 F7
Velika Gorica HR 164 E6
Velika Greda SRB 175 C7
Velika Ilova BIH 173 C8
Velika Ivanča SRB 174 E6
Velika Kladuša BIH 172 B4
Velika Kopanica HR 173 B9
Velika Krsna SRB 175 D7
Velika Mlaka HR 164 E6
Velika Obarska BIH 173 C11
Velika Pisanica HR 165 E8
Velika Plana SRB 174 E6
Velika Plana SRB 180 C2
Velika Račna SLO 89 E10
Velika Slatina SRB 180 E3
Velika Trnovitica HR 165 E7
Velike Lašče SLO 89 E10
Veliki Drvenik HR 172 F5
Veliki Gaj SRB 175 C7
Veliki Grđevac HR 165 E8
Veliki Preslav BG 183 C7
Veliki Prolog HR 173 F7
Veliki Radinci SRB 174 C4
Veliki Šiljegovac SRB 180 B4
Veliki Troyany UA 170 A6
Velikiy Lyubin' UA 160 D8
Veliki Zdenci HR 165 E7
Veliko Gradište SRB 175 D8
Veliko Laole SRB 175 E7
Veliko Srediste SRB 175 C7
Veliko Trojstvo HR 165 E7
Velikönig TR 189 B8
Velilla de Cinca E 58 D4
Velilla del Río Carrión E 55 C10
Veli Lošinj HR 83 D11
Velimče TR 189 B8
Velimeşe TR 189 B8
Velimlje MNE 179 D6
Vélines F 44 F6
Velingrad BG 181 E9
Velipojë AL 179 F7
Velise EST 147 D9
Veliuona LT 152 C7
Velje Duboko MNE 179 D7
Veljun HR 172 B4
Velká Bíteš CZ 93 D10
Velká Bystřice CZ 162 B4
Velká Dobrá CZ 92 B6
Velká Hleďsebe CZ 91 C12
Veľká Ida SK 161 F3
Veľká Lomnica SK 161 E1
Veľká Mača SK 162 E4
Veľka nad Ipľom SK 163 E9
Veľká nad Veličkou CZ 162 D5
Velké Pavlovice CZ 93 E11
Veľké Ripňany SK 162 E5
Veľké Svatoňovice CZ 97 E10
Veľké Úľany SK 162 E4
Veľký Beranov CZ 93 D9
Veľký Blh SK 163 E10
Veľký Cetín SK 162 E6
Veľký Ďur SK 162 E6
Veľký Kríš SK 163 E8
Veľký Lapáš SK 162 E5
Veľký Kýr SK 162 E6
Veľký Meder SK 162 F5
Velký Osek CZ 93 B8
Veľký Šenov CZ 96 D6
Veľký Slavkov SK 161 E1
Veľký Týnec CZ 162 B4
Veľký Újezd CZ 162 B4
Vellahn D 99 D9
Vellberg D 90 D6
Velletri I 78 D3
Vellevans F 42 F6
Velling DK 102 C3
Vellinge S 103 E12
Vellisca E 63 D7
Vellmar D 94 D6
Velo GR 191 D6
Velosnes F 35 E11
Velp NL 199 B7
Velpke D 95 B8
Velten D 100 E4
Velturno I 88 C4
Velušina MK 184 C5
Velvary CZ 92 B6
Velventos GR 185 D7
Velyatyn UA 161 G7
Velyka Horozhanna UA 161 D7
Velyka Kisnytsya UA 170 A2
Velyka Kopanya UA 161 G6
Velyka Mykhaylivka UA 170 D4
Velyka Tur"ya UA 161 E8
Velyki Kom"yaty UA 161 G6
Velyki Mosty UA 160 C6
Velykokomarivka UA 170 C5
Velykoploske UA 170 C6
Velykozymenove UA 170 C6
Velykyy Bereznyy UA 161 F6
Velykyy Bychkiv UA 161 H9
Velykyy Rakovets' UA 161 G7
Velžys LT 151 E8
Vemb DK 102 C2
Vemdalen S 118 B6
Vemdalsskalet S 118 B5
Vémhänd H 165 D11
Vemhån S 118 B7
Vemmenæs DK 103 E7
Vemundvik N 121 B11
Vena S 108 D7
Venaco F 53 G10
Venafro I 78 E6
Venansault F 44 B2
Venarey-les-Laumes F 41 E11
Venaria I 84 C4
Venarotta I 78 B4
Venäs S 119 C11
Venasca I 53 B6
Venčane SRB 174 E5
Vence F 52 D6
Venciūnai LT 153 B3
Vendargues F 51 C6
Vendas Novas P 66 B3
Vendays-Montalivet F 44 E3
Vendenheim F 202 D4
Vendeuvre-du-Poitou F 45 B6
Vendeuvre-sur-Barse F 41 D11
Vendinha P 66 B4
Vendœuvres F 45 B8
Vendôme F 40 F4
Veneheitto FIN 135 F17
Venejärvi FIN 133 D12
Venelles F 51 C9
Vénès F 49 C10
Venesjärvi FIN 142 B7
Veneskoski FIN 139 D8
Venetmäki FIN 140 D7
Venetmäki FIN 141 E9
Venetpalo FIN 139 C15
Venets BG 183 C7
Venets BG 183 D7
Venevere EST 147 C13
Venezia I 82 B5
Vengasaho FIN 135 D16
Vengsoy N 127 A16
Venhuizen NL 32 C4
Venialbo E 55 F8
Vénissieux F 46 D6
Venizel F 35 F7
Venjan S 118 E6
Venlo NL 32 F6
Venna GR 187 B9
Vennesla N 106 C2
Vennesund N 121 A12
Venosa I 76 B5
Venoy F 41 E10
Venray NL 32 E5
Vensac F 44 E3
Verucchio I 82 E5
Verviers B 35 C12
Vervins F 35 E8
Verwood GB 29 C11
Verzino I 77 D10
Verzuolo I 53 B6
Verzy F 41 B11
Vesajärvi FIN 142 B8
Vesala FIN 135 D16
Vesanto FIN 139 D17
Vesanka FIN 139 F15
Vesanto FIN 139 E16
Vescovato I 82 B1
Vése H 165 D8
Vesela Dolyna UA 170 E4
Veselava LV 151 B10
Veselé SK 162 D5
Veselets BG 183 E9
Veselie BG 183 E9
Veselí nad Lužnicí CZ 93 D7
Veselí nad Moravou CZ 162 D4
Vesijako FIN 143 C13
Vesijärvi FIN 138 F7
Vesilahti FIN 143 C10
Vesime I 53 B8
Vesivehmaa FIN 143 C14
Vesløs DK 102 A3
Vesnovo RUS 152 D3
Vesoul F 42 E5
Vespolate I 84 C6
Vessa GR 193 C7
Vessem NL 32 F4

Verba UA 170 A4
Verceia I 85 A7
Vercelli I 84 C5
Vercel-Villedieu-le-Camp F 42 F5
Verchen D 100 C3
Verd SLO 89 E9
Verdaches F 52 C4
Verdalen N 110 E3
Verdalsøra N 121 D10
Verden (Aller) D 33 C12
Verdikoussa GR 185 E6
Vërdovë AL 184 C4
Verdun F 42 B3
Verdun-sur-Garonne F 49 C8
Verdun-sur-le-Doubs F 47 B7
Verebiejai LT 153 E9
Veresegyház H 166 B3
Verești RO 169 B8
Verfeil F 49 B9
Verfeil F 49 C9
Vergale LV 150 C2
Vergaville F 43 C6
Vergato I 82 D3
Vergèze F 51 C7
Verghereto I 82 E5
Vergi GR 185 C10
Vergina GR 185 D7
Vergongheon F 46 E3
Vergt F 45 E7
Verguleasa RO 176 D4
Verići BIH 173 C6
Verín E 54 E5
Veringenstadt D 43 D11
Veriora EST 148 E1
Verkebro S 114 A8
Verkhivka UA 170 A4
Verkhni Petrivtsi UA 169 A7
Verkhniy Bereziv UA 168 A5
Verkhniy Yaseniv UA 168 A5
Verkhnya Vysots'ke UA 161 F7
Verkhnya Vyznytsya UA 161 H6
Verkhnya Yablun'ka UA 161 E6
Verkhnye Syn'ovydne UA 161 E8
Verkhovyna UA 168 A5
Verl D 33 E11
Verla FIN 144 C6
Verlaine B 35 C11
Verma N 116 B8
Vermand F 35 E7
Vermenton F 41 E10
Vermeş RO 175 B8
Vermiglio I 85 A10
Vermiosa P 60 E3
Vermoil P 60 E3
Vermosh AL 179 E8
Vermuntila FIN 142 C6
Vernante I 53 C7
Vernantes F 39 F12
Vernayaz CH 47 C11
Vern-d'Anjou F 39 E10
Verneřice CZ 96 E6
Vernești RO 177 C9
Vernet F 49 D8
Vernet-les-Bains F 49 E10
Verneuil-sur-Avre F 40 C4
Verneuil-sur-Vienne F 45 D8
Vernier CH 47 C9
Verningen N 106 A7
Vernio I 82 D3
Verniolle F 49 D9
Vernole I 77 C10
Vernon F 40 B5
Vernouillet F 40 C5
Vernoux-en-Vivarais F 46 F6
Vern-sur-Seiche F 39 D8
Verny F 42 B5
Vero F 53 G9
Veröcemaros H 163 F8
Veroia GR 185 D7
Verolanuova I 85 C9
Veroli I 78 D4
Verona I 82 B2
Verosvres F 46 C5
Verpelėt H 161 H1
Verrabotn N 121 D9
Verran N 121 D9
Verres I 84 B4
Verrières F 45 C6
Versailles F 40 C7
Versam CH 71 D8
Verseg H 166 B4
Vers-en-Montagne F 47 B8
Versmold D 33 D10
Versoix CH 47 C9
Versols-et-Lapeyre F 50 C4
Verson F 39 B11
Vers-Pont-du-Gard F 51 C8
Vert F 48 C7
Verteillac F 45 E6
Vértesacsa H 165 B11
Vértesboglár H 165 B11
Vértessomló H 165 A10
Vértesszőlős H 165 A10
Verteuil-d'Agenais F 49 B6
Vertheuil F 44 E4
Verton F 34 D4
Vertou F 39 F8
Vertus F 41 C11

Verka UA 170 A4
Vertrian F 82 E5
Veulettes-sur-Mer F 34 E2
Veurne B 34 B6
Vevang N 120 E2
Vevey CH 47 C10
Vevi GR 185 C6
Vex CH 47 C11
Vexala FIN 138 D8
Veynes F 51 B9
Veyre-Monton F 46 D3
Veyrier CH 47 C9
Vezdemarbán E 55 E9
Vézelay F 41 F10
Vézelise F 42 D5
Vézénobres F 51 B7
Vezins F 39 F11
Vézins-de-Lévézou F 50 B4
Vezirhan TR 189 C10
Vezirköprü TR 23 F8
Vezzani F 53 G10
Vezzano I 85 A11
Viadana I 82 C2
Viala du Tarn F 50 B4
Vialas F 51 B6
Viana E 48 E1
Viana de Cega S 55 E10
Viana do Alentejo P 66 C4
Viana do Bolo E 54 D5
Viana do Castelo P 54 E2
Vianden L 36 E6
Viane F 50 C4
Vianen NL 32 E4
Viannos GR 194 F2
Viaño Pequeno E 54 B3
Vianos E 71 B8
Viantie FIN 135 C13
Viareggio I 82 E1
Viarmes F 41 B7
Vias F 50 D5
Viasvesi FIN 142 C6
Viatodos P 54 F2
Viator E 71 F8
Vibble S 109 D12
Vibbyn S 134 C7
Vibonati I 76 C5
Viborg DK 102 C4
Vibo Valentia I 75 B9
Vibraye F 40 D4
Viby DK 103 D10
Viby S 104 C4
Vic E 59 D8
Vícar E 71 F7
Vicari I 74 D4
Vic-en-Bigorre F 49 D6
Vicarstown IRL 23 F8
Vicchio I 82 E3
Vicdessos F 49 F8
Vic-Fezensac F 49 C6
Vichy F 46 C3
Vickan S 107 E11
Vic-le-Comte F 46 D3
Vico F 53 G9
Vico del Gargano I 79 D9
Vico Equense I 76 B2
Vicoforte I 53 C7
Vicolungo I 84 C6
Vicovaro I 78 C3
Vicovu de Jos RO 169 B7
Vicovu de Sus RO 169 B7
Vicq-Exemplet F 45 B10
Vic-sur-Aisne F 35 F7
Vic-sur-Cère F 45 F11
Vic-sur-Seille F 42 C6
Victoria RO 169 B10
Victoria RO 176 B5
Victoria RO 177 D11
Victor Vlad Delamarina RO 175 B8
Vidaga LV 151 B12
Vidago P 54 E4
Vidais P 60 F2
Vīdale LV 146 F4
Vidamlya BY 157 F9
Vidángoz E 48 E3

Viðareiði FO 18 A3
Vidauban F 52 E4
Vidče CZ 162 B5
Viddal N 116 B5
Viddalba I 80 B2
Videbæk DK 102 C3
Videle RO 177 E7
Videm SLO 164 D5
Videm SLO 164 E5
Videmonte P 60 C6
Videniškiai LT 151 F10
Vidhas AL 184 B3
Vidigueira P 66 C4
Vidin BG 175 F10
Vidiškiai LT 151 F9
Vidlin GB 19 E14
Vidnava CZ 93 B12
Vidovec HR 164 D6
Vidovice BIH 173 C10
Vidra RO 167 E10
Vidra RO 169 F9
Vidra RO 177 E8
Vidrare BG 181 C9
Vidrek N 127 D13
Vidrenjak HR 165 E7
Vidriēres S 59 D9
Vidriži LV 151 B9
Vidsala LV 151 D11
Vidsel S 134 C5
Vidstrup DK 106 D6
Viduklė LT 150 E5
Vidzy BY 151 F13
Viechtach D 92 D3
Vieille-Brioude F 46 E3
Vieira de Leiria P 60 E3
Vieira do Minho P 54 E3
Vieki FIN 141 D13
Viekšniai LT 150 D5
Vielank D 99 D10
Vielha E 49 F7
Vielle-Aure F 49 E6
Vielle-St-Girons F 48 C3
Vielmur-sur-Agout F 49 C10
Vielsalm B 36 D5
Vielverge F 42 F3
Vienenburg D 95 C8
Vienība LV 150 C6
Vienne F 46 D6
Viereck D 100 C6
Vieremä FIN 140 C8
Vieritz D 43 D7
Vierraden D 100 D6
Viereth-Trunstadt D 91 C8
Vierlingsbeek NL 32 E5
Viernau D 95 E8
Viernheim D 37 E11
Vierraden D 100 D6
Viersen D 32 F6
Vierumäki FIN 143 C14
Vierville-sur-Mer F 39 B10
Vierzon F 40 F7
Viesecke D 99 D12
Viešintos LT 151 E11
Vieste I 79 D10
Viešvėnai LT 150 E4
Viešvilė LT 152 C7
Vietas S 125 A15
Vietri di Potenza I 76 B5
Vietri sul Mare I 76 B3
Vieux-Boucau-les-Bains F 48 C3
Vieux-Condé F 198 E3
Vievis LT 153 D10
Vif F 47 E8
Vig DK 103 D10
Vīganti LV 151 D13
Vigarano Mainarda I 82 C3
Vigasio I 82 B2
Vigaun A 89 A7
Vigdenes N 121 D9
Vigeland N 110 F6
Vigeois F 45 E9
Vigevano I 85 C6
Vigge S 118 A7
Vigge S 119 B12
Viggianello I 76 D6
Viggiano I 76 C5
Vígľaš SK 163 D8
Vigliano Biellese I 84 B5
Vignacourt F 34 D5
Vignale Monferrato I 53 A8
Vignanello I 78 C2
Vigneulles-les-Hattonchâtel F 42 C4
Vignola I 82 D3
Vignola Mare l'Agnata I 80 A3
Vignory F 42 D3
Vigny F 40 B6
Vigo E 54 D2
Vigo di Cadore I 88 D5
Vigo di Fassa I 88 D4
Vigone I 47 F11
Vigonza I 82 B4
Vigo Rendena I 85 A10
Vigrestad N 110 E3
Viguzzolo I 53 B9
Vigy F 36 F6
Vihalsen N 120 E5
Vihanti FIN 135 F13
Vihiers F 39 F11
Vihtari FIN 141 F11
Vihtasuo FIN 141 D12
Vihtavuori FIN 139 F15
Vihteljärvi FIN 142 B8
Vihti FIN 143 E11
Vihtijärvi FIN 143 E12
Vihula EST 147 B12
Viiala FIN 143 C10
Viiksimo FIN 137 F15
Viile Satu Mare RO 167 B10
Viimsi EST 147 C9
Viinamäki FIN 141 B10
Viinijärvi FIN 141 E12
Viinikka FIN 139 D16
Viinikkala FIN 139 D16
Viinikoski FIN 135 D17
Viiratsi EST 147 E11
Viirre FIN 135 F12
Viisarimäki FIN 139 F16
Viişoara MD 169 B10
Viişoara RO 168 E3
Viişoara RO 168 E5
Viişoara RO 169 A9
Viişoara RO 169 D9
Viişoara RO 176 E1
Viitaila FIN 143 C13
Viitala FIN 139 E10
Viitamäki FIN 139 C16
Viitaniemi FIN 141 D10
Viitapohja FIN 143 B11
Viitaranta FIN 131 D3

Viitaranta *FIN* 137 B12
Viitasaari *FIN* 139 D15
Viitavaara *FIN* 137 E13
Viitavaara *FIN* 137 F12
Viitka *EST* 148 F1
Viitna *EST* 147 C10
Viivikonna *EST* 148 C2
Vijciems *LV* 147 F11
Vik *N* 106 C4
Vik *N* 110 B2
Vik *N* 124 B9
Vik *N* 124 F3
Vik *N* 126 D7
Vik *S* 104 D6
Vika *FIN* 133 E16
Vika *N* 117 A15
Vika *S* 113 A14
Vikajärvi *FIN* 133 E16
Vikan *N* 120 E5
Vikan *N* 121 B10
Vikarbyn *S* 113 B15
Vikarbyn *S* 119 E9
Vikartovce *SK* 161 F1
Vikbyn *S* 113 B15
Vike *N* 116 E3
Vike *S* 119 A12
Vikebukt *N* 116 A6
Vikedal *N* 110 D3
Viken *S* 103 C11
Viken *S* 119 B9
Viken *S* 119 B11
Vikersund *N* 111 C11
Vikeså *N* 110 E4
Vikevåg *N* 110 D3
Vikholmen *N* 124 D4
Vikï *LV* 147 F9
Vikingstad *S* 108 C6
Vikmanshyttan *S* 113 B14
Vikna *N* 121 B9
Vikoč *BIH* 173 F10
Vikøyri *N* 116 D5
Vikran *N* 127 A16
Vikran *N* 127 C12
Vikran *N* 129 A12
Viksberg *S* 113 B14
Viksjö *S* 119 A13
Viksjöfors *S* 119 D10
Viksmon *S* 123 E12
Viksna *LV* 149 B2
Viktarinas *LT* 153 E8
Vikten *N* 126 D5
Viktorivka *UA* 170 A9
Vikýřovice *CZ* 93 C11
Vila *E* 54 E3
Vila Boa *P* 61 D7
Vila Boa do Bispo *P* 60 B4
Vila Caiz *P* 54 F3
Vila Chã de Sá *P* 60 C5
Vila Cova da Lixa *P* 54 F3
Vilada *S* 97 C7
Viladamat *E* 59 C10
Vila da Ponte *P* 54 E4
Viladecans *E* 59 E8
Vila de Cruces *E* 54 C2
Vila de Rei *P* 60 E4
Vila do Bispo *P* 66 E2
Vila do Conde *P* 54 F2
Viladrau *E* 59 D8
Vilafamés *E* 64 D4
Vilafant *E* 59 C9
Vila Fernando *P* 61 E5
Vila Flor *P* 54 F5
Vila Franca das Naves *P* 61 C6
Vilafranca de Bonany *E* 73 B11
Vilafranca del Penedès *E* 59 E7
Vila Franca de Xira *P* 66 B2
Vilagarcía de Arousa *E* 54 C2
Vilajuïga *E* 50 F5
Vilaka *LV* 149 B3
Vilalba *E* 54 B4
Vilallonga *E* 49 F10
Vilamartín *E* 50 F5
Vilamarxant *E* 64 E3
Vilamoura *P* 66 E3
Viļāni *LV* 149 C1
Vila Nogueira de Azeitão *P* 66 B1
Vilanova *E* 54 B5
Vila Nova da Baronia *P* 66 C3
Vilanova d'Alcolea *E* 64 D5
Vilanova de Arousa *E* 54 C2
Vila Nova de Cacela *P* 66 E4
Vila Nova de Famalicão *P* 54 F2
Vila Nova de Foz Coa *P* 61 B6
Vila Nova de Gaia *P* 60 B3
Vilanova de la Barca *E* 58 D5
Vilanova de L'Aguda *E* 58 D6
Vila Nova de Meià *E* 58 D6
Vila Nova de Paiva *P* 60 C5
Vila Nova de Poiares *P* 60 D4
Vilanova de Prades *E* 58 E5
Vila Nova de São Bento *P* 66 D5
Vilanova de Sau *E* 59 D8
Vilanova i la Geltrú *E* 59 E7
Vila Pouca da Beira *P* 60 D5
Vila Pouca de Aguiar *P* 54 E4
Vila Praia de Âncora *P* 54 E2
Vilar *P* 54 E3
Vilar *P* 60 C2
Vilarandelo *P* 54 E5
Vilarchao *E* 54 C4
Vilar da Veiga *P* 54 E3
Vilar de Andorinho *P* 60 B3
Vilar de Barrio *E* 54 D4
Vilar de Santos *E* 54 D4
Vilardevós *E* 54 E5
Vila Real *P* 54 F4
Vila Real de Santo António *P* 66 E5
Vilarelho da Raia *P* 54 E5
Vilar Formoso *P* 61 C7
Vilarinho da Castanheira *P* 61 B6
Vilarinho do Bairro *P* 60 D3
Vilariño de Conso *E* 54 D5
Vila-rodona *E* 59 E6
Vila Ruiva *P* 66 C4
Vila Seca *P* 54 E2
Vilaseca de Solcina *E* 58 E6
Vilassar de Mar *E* 59 D8
Vilasund *S* 124 C8
Vitka Velha de Ródão *P* 60 E5
Vila Verde *P* 54 E3
Vila Verde *P* 54 F4
Vila Verde *P* 60 D3
Vila Verde da Raia *P* 54 E5
Vila Verde de Ficalho *P* 67 D5
Vila Viçosa *P* 66 C5
Vilce *E* 71 C6
Vildbjerg *DK* 102 C3

Vilémov *CZ* 93 C9
Vilgale *LV* 150 C3
Vilhelmina *S* 123 B11
Vilia *GR* 191 C7
Viljakkala *FIN* 143 B9
Viljevo *HR* 165 E10
Viljolahti *FIN* 141 F10
Viļķene *LV* 147 F9
Viļķija *LT* 153 C8
Vilkijärvi *FIN* 144 D8
Vilkyškiai *LT* 150 F4
Villa Bartolomea *I* 82 B3
Villabate *I* 74 C3
Villablanca *E* 67 E5
Villablino *E* 55 C7
Villabona *E* 48 D1
Villabrágima *E* 55 E10
Villac *E* 45 E8
Villacañas *E* 62 E6
Villa Carcina *I* 85 B7
Villacarriedo *E* 56 B4
Villacarrillo *E* 71 C6
Villa Castelli *I* 77 B7
Villacastín *E* 62 C4
Villach *A* 89 C8
Villacidro *I* 80 E2
Villaciervos *E* 57 E6
Villaconejos *E* 62 D6
Villaconejos de Trabaque *E* 63 D8
Villada *E* 55 D10
Villa d'Almè *I* 85 B8
Villa del Prado *E* 62 D4
Villa del Río *E* 69 A8
Villadepera *E* 55 E7
Villa de Ves *E* 63 F10
Villadiego *E* 56 C3
Villadose *I* 82 B4
Villadossola *I* 84 A5
Villaeles de Valdavia *E* 55 C10
Villaescusa de Haro *E* 63 E7
Villaescusa la Sombría *E* 56 D5
Vilafáfila *E* 55 E8
Villafeliche *E* 63 B10
Villaflores *E* 55 F9
Villafranca d'Asti *I* 53 B8
Villafranca de Córdoba *E* 69 A7
Villafranca de Ebro *E* 57 E10
Villafranca del Bierzo *E* 55 C7
Villafranca del Campo *E* 63 C10
Villafranca del Cid *E* 64 D4
Villafranca de los Barros *E* 67 B7
Villafranca de los Caballeros *E* 62 F6
Villafranca di Verona *I* 82 B2
Villafranca in Lunigiana *I* 85 E8
Villafranca-Montes de Oca *E* 56 D5
Villafranca Tirrena *I* 75 C7
Villafranco del Guadalquivir *E* 67 E7
Villafrati *I* 74 D3
Villafrechos *E* 55 E9
Villafruela *E* 56 E4
Villafuerte *E* 56 E4
Villagarcía de Campos *E* 55 E9
Villagarcía de la Torre *E* 67 C7
Villagarcía del Llano *E* 63 F9
Villagio Mancuso *I* 75 A10
Villagonzalo *E* 67 B7
Villagrande Strisaili *I* 80 D4
Villaharta *E* 70 C3
Villähde *I* 83 D14
Villahermosa *I* 71 B7
Villahermosa del Campo *E* 63 B10
Villahermosa del Río *E* 64 D4
Villaherreros *E* 56 D3
Villahizán *E* 56 D4
Villahoz *E* 56 D4
Villaines-en-Duesmois *F* 41 E12
Villaines-la-Juhel *F* 39 D11
Villajoyosa-La Vila Joiosa *E* 72 D4
Villala *FIN* 141 F13
Villalán *FIN* 145 D9
Villa Lagarina *I* 85 B11
Villalago *I* 78 D5
Villalar de los Comuneros *E* 55 E9
Villa Latina *I* 78 D5
Villalba de Duero *E* 56 E4
Villalba de Guardo *E* 55 C10
Villalba del Alcor *E* 67 E7
Villalba de la Sierra *E* 63 D8
Villalba de los Alcores *E* 55 E10
Villalba de los Barros *E* 67 B6
Villalba del Rey *E* 63 D7
Villalba dels Arcs *E* 58 E4
Villalba de Rioja *E* 56 C6
Villalcampo *E* 55 E7
Villalcázar de Sirga *E* 56 D2
Villalengua *E* 57 F8
Villalgordo del Júcar *E* 63 F8
Villa Literno *I* 76 A2
Villalobos *E* 55 E9
Villalón de Campos *E* 55 D9
Villalonga *E* 72 D4
Villalpando *E* 55 E9
Villalpardo *E* 63 F9
Villaluenga de la Sagra *E* 62 D5
Villalumbroso *E* 55 D10
Villalmanla *E* 58 D8
Villamañán *E* 55 D8
Villamanrique *E* 71 B7
Villamanrique de la Condesa *E* 67 E7
Villamanta *E* 62 D4
Villamar *I* 80 D2
Villamartín *E* 67 E8
Villamartín de Campos *E* 55 D10
Villamassargia *I* 80 E2
Villamayor *E* 61 C9
Villamayor de Calatrava *E* 70 B4
Villamayor de Campos *E* 55 E9
Villamayor de Santiago *E* 63 E7
Villamayor de Treviño *E* 56 D3
Villamblard *F* 45 E7
Villamediana *E* 56 D2
Villamediana de Iregua *E* 48 F1
Villamejil *E* 55 C7
Villamesías *E* 61 F9
Villamejil *E* 61 D7
Villa Minozzo *I* 82 D1
Villamo *FIN* 138 F7
Villamor de los Escuderos *E* 55 F8
Villamuelas *E* 62 E5

Villamuriel de Cerrato *E* 56 E3
Villandraut *F* 48 B5
Villanova *I* 77 B9
Villanova d'Albenga *I* 53 C8
Villanova d'Asti *I* 53 B7
Villanova del Battista *I* 76 A4
Villanovafranca *I* 80 D3
Villanova Monferrato *I* 84 C5
Villanova Monteleone *I* 80 B1
Villanova Truschedu *I* 80 D2
Villanova Tulo *I* 80 D3
Villanterio *I* 85 C7
Villanúa *E* 48 E4
Villanubla *E* 55 E10
Villanueva de Alcardete *E* 63 E6
Villanueva de Alcorón *E* 63 C8
Villanueva de Algaidas *E* 69 B8
Villanueva de Argaño *E* 56 D4
Villanueva de Bogas *E* 62 E5
Villanueva de Cameros *E* 57 D6
Villanueva de Castellón *E* 72 C4
Villanueva de Córdoba *E* 70 C3
Villanueva de Gállego *E* 57 E10
Villanueva de Gómez *E* 62 C3
Villanueva de la Cañada *E* 62 D5
Villanueva de la Concepción *E* 69 C7
Villanueva de la Fuente *E* 71 B7
Villanueva de la Jara *E* 63 F9
Villanueva de la Reina *E* 69 A9
Villanueva del Arzobispo *E* 71 C6
Villanueva de las Cruces *E* 67 D5
Villanueva de la Serena *E* 67 B8
Villanueva de la Sierra *E* 61 D8
Villanueva de las Torres *E* 71 D6
Villanueva de la Vera *E* 61 F10
Villanueva del Campo *E* 55 E9
Villanueva del Duque *E* 70 C2
Villanueva del Fresno *E* 67 C5
Villanueva de los Castillejos *E* 67 D5
Villanueva de los Infantes *E* 71 B7
Villanueva del Rey *E* 67 C9
Villanueva del Río Segura *E* 71 C10
Villanueva del Río y Minas *E* 67 D8
Villanueva del Rosario *E* 69 C8
Villanueva del Trabuco *E* 69 C8
Villanueva de Mesía *E* 69 B8
Villanueva de San Carlos *E* 70 B5
Villanueva de San Juan *E* 67 F9
Villanueva de Tapia *E* 69 B8
Villanueva de Valdegovia *E* 56 C5
Villanuño de Valdavia *E* 56 C2
Villány *H* 165 E10
Villa Opicina *I* 89 E8
Villapalacios *E* 71 B7
Villaperuccio *I* 80 E2
Villapiana *I* 77 D6
Villapiana Lido *I* 77 D6
Villa Poma *I* 82 C3
Villapourçon *F* 46 B4
Villaputzu *I* 80 E4
Villaquejida *E* 55 D8
Villaquilambre *E* 55 C8
Villaralbo *E* 55 F8
Villaralto *E* 70 C3
Villarcayo *E* 56 C4
Villard-Bonnot *F* 47 E8
Villard-de-Lans *F* 47 E8
Villar de Cañas *E* 63 E7
Villar de Chinchilla *E* 71 B9
Villar de Ciervo *E* 61 C7
Villardeciervos *E* 55 E7
Villardefrades *E* 55 E9
Villar del Arzobispo *E* 64 E3
Villar de la Yegua *E* 61 C7
Villar del Buey *E* 55 F7
Villar del Cobo *E* 63 D9
Villar del Humo *E* 63 E9
Villar de los Barrios *E* 55 C6
Villar de los Navarros *E* 58 E1
Villar del Pedroso *E* 61 E10
Villar del Rey *E* 61 F7
Villar del Salz *E* 63 C10
Villar de Olalla *E* 63 D8
Villar de Peralonso *E* 61 B8
Villar de Rena *E* 61 F9
Villar de Torre *E* 56 D6
Villardompardo *E* 69 A8
Villareal *E* 64 E4
Villarejo de Fuentes *E* 63 E7
Villarejo de Montalbán *E* 62 E3
Villarejo de Órbigo *E* 55 D8
Villarejo de Salvanés *E* 63 D6
Villarente *E* 55 C8
Villares de la Reina *E* 61 B9
Villargordo *E* 69 A9
Villargordo del Cabriel *E* 63 E10
Villarino de los Aires *E* 55 F7
Villarluengo *E* 64 D3
Villarosa *I* 74 D5
Villarquemado *E* 63 C10
Villarramiel *E* 55 D10
Villarrasa *E* 67 E6
Villarreal de Huerva *E* 63 B10
Villarrín de Campos *E* 55 E8
Villarrobledo *E* 63 F7
Villarrodrigo *E* 71 C7
Villarroya de la Sierra *E* 57 F8
Villarroya de los Pinares *E* 58 F2
Villarrubia de los Ojos *E* 62 F5
Villarrubia de Santiago *E* 62 E6
Villars *E* 63 E7
Villars *F* 45 E7
Villars-Colmars *F* 52 C5
Villars-les-Dombes *F* 47 D7
Villars-sur-Var *F* 52 D5
Villarta de los Montes *E* 62 F3
Villarta de San Juan *E* 62 F6
Villasalto *I* 80 E4
Villasana de Mena *E* 56 B5
Villasandino *E* 56 D3
Villa San Giovanni *I* 75 C8
Villa San Pietro *I* 80 E3
Villasante de Montija *E* 56 B5
Villa Santina *I* 89 D6
Villasarracino *E* 56 D2
Villasavary *F* 49 D10
Villasayas *E* 57 F6
Villasbuenas *E* 61 B7

Villasdardo *E* 61 B8
Villaseca de Laciana *E* 55 C7
Villaseca de la Sagra *E* 62 E5
Villaseco de los Gamitos *E* 61 B8
Villaseco de los Reyes *E* 61 B8
Villaseco del Pan *E* 55 F8
Villasequilla de Yepes *E* 62 E5
Villasimius *I* 80 E4
Villasmundo *I* 75 E7
Villasor *I* 80 E2
Villaspeciosa *I* 80 E2
Villasrubias *E* 61 D7
Villastar *E* 63 D10
Villasur de Herreros *E* 56 D5
Villatobas *E* 62 E6
Villatoro *E* 61 C10
Villatoya *E* 63 F10
Villatuerta *E* 48 E2
Villaturiel *E* 55 C9
Villava *E* 48 E2
Villavallelonga *I* 78 D5
Villavelayo *E* 56 D6
Villaverde de Guadalimar *E* 71 C7
Villaverde del Río *E* 67 D8
Villaverde y Pasaconsol *E* 63 E8
Villavernia *I* 53 B9
Villaviciosa *E* 55 B9
Villaviciosa de Córdoba *E* 70 C2
Villaviciosa de Odón *E* 62 D5
Villavieja *E* 64 E4
Villavieja de Yeltes *E* 61 C8
Villaviudas *E* 56 E3
Villayón *E* 55 B6
Villazanzo de Valderaduey *E* 55 C10
Villé *F* 43 D7
Villebois-Lavalette *F* 45 E6
Villebrumier *F* 49 C8
Villecomtal-sur-Arros *F* 49 D6
Villecomte *F* 42 E3
Villecroze *F* 52 D4
Villedaigne *F* 50 D4
Villedieu-la-Blouère *F* 39 F9
Villedieu-les-Poêles *F* 39 C9
Villedieu-sur-Indre *F* 45 B9
Ville-en-Tardenois *F* 36 F1
Villefagnan *F* 44 C6
Villefontaine *F* 47 D7
Villefort *F* 51 B6
Villefranche-d'Albigeois *F* 49 C10
Villefranche-d'Allier *F* 46 C2
Villefranche-de-Lauragais *F* 49 D9
Villefranche-de-Lonchat *F* 44 F6
Villefranche-de-Panat *F* 50 B4
Villefranche-de-Rouergue *F* 49 B10
Villefranche-du-Périgord *F* 49 A8
Villefranche-sur-Cher *F* 40 F6
Villefranche-sur-Mer *F* 53 D6
Villefranche-sur-Saône *F* 46 D6
Villefranque *F* 48 D3
Villegas *E* 56 D3
Villel *E* 63 D10
Villelaure *F* 51 C9
Villemandeur *F* 41 E8
Villemorien *F* 41 D11
Villemoustaussou *F* 49 D10
Villemur-sur-Tarn *F* 49 C9
Villena *E* 72 D3
Villenauxe-la-Grande *F* 41 C10
Villeneuve *CH* 47 C10
Villeneuve *F* 49 B10
Villeneuve *F* 51 C10
Villeneuve-au-Chemin *F* 41 D10
Villeneuve-d'Allier *F* 46 E3
Villeneuve-d'Ascq *F* 35 C7
Villeneuve-de-Berg *F* 51 A8
Villeneuve-de-Marsan *F* 48 C5
Villeneuve-de-Rivière *F* 49 D7
Villeneuve-la-Guyard *F* 41 D10
Villeneuve-l'Archevêque *F* 41 D10
Villeneuve-lès-Avignon *F* 51 C8
Villeneuve-lès-Béziers *F* 50 D5
Villeneuve-Loubet *F* 52 D6
Villeneuve-sur-Allier *F* 46 B3
Villeneuve-sur-Lot *F* 49 B7
Villeneuve-sur-Yonne *F* 41 D9
Villeneuve-Tolosane *F* 49 C8
Villepinte *F* 49 D10
Villercomtal *F* 49 A11
Villeréal *F* 49 A7
Villerest *F* 46 D5
Villerías *E* 55 E10
Villerouge-Termenès *F* 50 D4
Villers-Bocage *F* 34 C5
Villers-Bocage *F* 39 B10
Villers-Bretonneux *F* 34 E6
Villers-Carbonnel *F* 34 E6
Villers-Cotterêts *F* 35 F7
Villers-Écalles *F* 34 E3
Villers-en-Argonne *F* 41 B12
Villersexel *F* 42 E5
Villers-Farlay *F* 47 A8
Villers-le-Bouillet *B* 199 D6
Villers-le-lac *F* 47 A9
Villers-lès-Nancy *F* 42 C5
Villers-Outréaux *F* 35 D7
Villers-Semeuse *F* 35 E10
Villers-sur-Mer *F* 39 B11
Villerville *F* 39 B11
Villery *F* 41 D11
Villeseneux *F* 41 C11
Ville-sur-Tourbe *F* 36 F3
Villetta Barrea *I* 78 D5
Villeurbanne *F* 46 D6
Villeveyrac *F* 51 C6
Villevocance *F* 46 E6
Villié-Morgon *F* 46 D6
Villiers-Charlemagne *F* 39 E10
Villiers-en-Lieu *F* 41 C12
Villiers-le-Sec *F* 41 D9
Villiers-St-Benoît *F* 41 E9
Villiers-St-Georges *F* 41 C9
Villikkala *FIN* 144 D6
Villingen *D* 43 D9
Villingsberg *S* 113 D12
Villmar *D* 201 D9
Villoldo *E* 55 D10
Villora *E* 63 E9
Villoruela *E* 61 B10

Villasdardo *E* 61 B8
Villshärad *S* 103 B11
Villvattnet *S* 118 F4
Vilmány *H* 161 G3
Vilnius *LT* 153 D11
Vilovi d'Onyar *E* 59 D9
Vilppula *FIN* 139 F12
Vilpulka *LV* 147 F10
Vils *A* 87 B11
Vils *DK* 102 B3
Vilsbiburg *D* 91 F11
Vilseck *D* 91 C10
Vilshofen *D* 92 E4
Vil'shanka *UA* 170 A3
Vilsted *DK* 102 B4
Vilusi *BIH* 173 C7
Vilusi *MNE* 178 D6
Viluste *EST* 148 F1
Vilvestre *E* 61 B7
Vilvoorde *B* 35 C9
Vilzēni *LV* 147 F10
Vima Mică *RO* 168 C3
Vimbodí *E* 58 E6
Vimeiro *P* 60 F2
Vimercate *I* 85 B7
Vimianzo *E* 54 B1
Vimieiro *P* 66 B4
Vimioso *P* 55 E6
Vimmarvattnet *S* 123 D9
Vimmerby *S* 108 D7
Vimory *F* 41 E8
Vimoutiers *F* 39 C12
Vimpeli *FIN* 139 D11
Vimperk *CZ* 92 E5
Vimy *F* 34 D6
Vinac *BIH* 173 D8
Vinadio *I* 52 C4
Vinaixa *E* 58 E5
Vinařice *CZ* 92 B6
Vinaròs *E* 58 G4
Vinarsko *BG* 183 D8
Vinäs *S* 118 E8
Vinassan *F* 50 D5
Vinay *F* 47 E7
Vinberg *S* 103 B11
Vinça *F* 50 E4
Vinča *SRB* 174 D6
Vincey *F* 42 D5
Vinchiaturo *I* 79 E7
Vinci *I* 82 E2
Vind *DK* 102 C3
Vindblæs *DK* 102 B4
Vindeballe *DK* 102 F6
Vindeby *DK* 102 E7
Vindel-Ånäset *S* 134 F3
Vindeln *S* 123 C17
Vinderei *RO* 169 E11
Vinderslev *DK* 102 C3
Vinderup *DK* 102 C3
Vindsvik *N* 110 D3
Vindtved *S* 108 A7
Vinebre *E* 58 E5
Vineuil *F* 40 E5
Vineuil *F* 45 B9
Vinga *RO* 167 E7
Vingåker *S* 108 A7
Vingäng *S* 118 E4
Vingrau *F* 50 E4
Vingrom *N* 117 D12
Vingsand *N* 120 C8
Vinhais *P* 55 E6
Vinhas *P* 55 E6
Vinica *HR* 164 D6
Vinica *MK* 180 F5
Vinica *SLO* 83 B11
Vinica *SK* 163 E8
Viničné *SK* 162 E4
Viniegra de Arriba *E* 56 D6
Vinine *BIH* 173 D8
Viniśce *HR* 172 F5
Vinje *N* 110 C7
Vinje *N* 116 E4
Vinjeøra *N* 120 E5
Vinkovci *HR* 165 F11
Vinkt *B* 199 C7
Vinliden *S* 123 B13
Vinné *SK* 161 F4
Vinnes *N* 110 B1
Vinnesvåg *N* 110 B2
Vinni *EST* 147 C11
Vinning *S* 107 C13
Vinningen *D* 43 B8
Vinodol *SK* 162 E6
Vinograd *BG* 182 C5
Vinogradets *BG* 181 E9
Vinon-sur-Verdon *F* 51 C10
Vinsa *S* 132 E9
Vinslöv *S* 103 C13
Vinsobres *F* 51 B9
Vinsternes *N* 120 E4
Vinstra *N* 117 C11
Vintervollen *N* 130 D8
Vintilă Vodă *RO* 177 C9
Vintjärn *S* 119 E11
Vintrosa *S* 113 D12
Vintturi *FIN* 139 C11
Vinţu de Jos *RO* 168 E2
Viñuelas *E* 62 C6
Vinuesa *E* 56 E6
Vinzelberg *D* 95 A10
Viöl *D* 98 A6
Violay *F* 46 D5
Violès *F* 51 B8
Vipava *SLO* 89 E8
Vīpe *LT* 151 D12
Vipereşti *RO* 177 C8
Vipiteno *I* 88 E3
Vipperow *D* 99 D13
Vir *BIH* 173 E11
Vir *HR* 83 D11
Vir *SLO* 89 D10
Vira *S* 109 B8
Virawlya *BY* 149 E3
Virazeil *F* 49 A6
Virbalis *LT* 152 D6
Virbi *LV* 150 D4
Virče *MK* 181 F6
Vire *F* 39 C10
Vireši *LV* 151 B12
Vireux-Molhain *F* 200 D2
Vireux-Wallerand *F* 35 D10
Virey-sous-Bar *F* 41 D11
Virgen *A* 88 B5
Vīrįąt *F* 47 C7
Virieu-le-Grand *F* 47 D8

Villotte-sur-Aire *F* 42 C3
Villshärad *S* 103 B11
Villvattnet *S* 118 F4
Vilmány *H* 161 G3
Vilnius *LT* 153 D11
Vilovi d'Onyar *E* 59 D9
Vilppula *FIN* 139 F12
Vilpulka *LV* 147 F10
Vils *A* 87 B11
Vils *DK* 102 B3
Vilsbiburg *D* 91 F11
Vilseck *D* 91 C10
Vilshofen *D* 92 E4
Vil'shanka *UA* 170 A3
Vilsted *DK* 102 B4
Vilusi *BIH* 173 C7
Vilusi *MNE* 178 D6
Viluste *EST* 148 F1
Vilvestre *E* 61 B7
Vilvoorde *B* 35 C9
Vilzēni *LV* 147 F10
Vima Mică *RO* 168 C3
Vimbodí *E* 58 E6
Vimeiro *P* 60 F2
Vimercate *I* 85 B7
Vimianzo *E* 54 B1
Vimieiro *P* 66 B4
Vimioso *P* 55 E6
Vimmarvattnet *S* 123 D9
Vimmerby *S* 108 D7
Vimory *F* 41 E8
Vimoutiers *F* 39 C12
Vimpeli *FIN* 139 D11
Vimperk *CZ* 92 E5
Vimy *F* 34 D6
Vinac *BIH* 173 D8
Vinadio *I* 52 C4
Vinaixa *E* 58 E5
Vinařice *CZ* 92 B6
Vinaròs *E* 58 G4
Vinarsko *BG* 183 D8
Vinäs *S* 118 E8
Vinassan *F* 50 D5
Vinay *F* 47 E7
Vinberg *S* 103 B11
Vinça *F* 50 E4
Vinča *SRB* 174 D6
Vincey *F* 42 D5
Vinchiaturo *I* 79 E7
Vinci *I* 82 E2
Vind *DK* 102 C3
Vindblæs *DK* 102 B4
Vindeby *DK* 102 E7
Vindel-Ånäset *S* 134 F3
Vindelgransele *S* 123 A14
Vindeln *S* 123 C17
Vinderei *RO* 169 E11
Vinderslev *DK* 102 C3
Vinderup *DK* 102 C3
Vindsvik *N* 110 D3
Vindtved *S* 108 A7
Vinebre *E* 58 E5
Vineuil *F* 40 E5
Vineuil *F* 45 B9
Vinga *RO* 167 E7
Vingåker *S* 108 A7
Vingäng *S* 118 E4
Vingrau *F* 50 E4
Vingrom *N* 117 D12
Vingsand *N* 120 C8
Vinhais *P* 55 E6
Vinhas *P* 55 E6
Vinica *HR* 164 D6
Vinica *MK* 180 F5
Vinica *SLO* 83 B11
Vinica *SK* 163 E8
Viničné *SK* 162 E4
Viniegra de Arriba *E* 56 D6
Vinine *BIH* 173 D8
Viniśce *HR* 172 F5
Vinje *N* 110 C7
Vinje *N* 116 E4
Vinjeøra *N* 120 E5
Vinkovci *HR* 165 F11
Vinkt *B* 199 C7
Vinliden *S* 123 B13
Vinné *SK* 161 F4
Vinnes *N* 110 B1
Vinnesvåg *N* 110 B2
Vinni *EST* 147 C11
Vinning *S* 107 C13
Vinningen *D* 43 B8
Vinodol *SK* 162 E6
Vinograd *BG* 182 C5
Vinogradets *BG* 181 E9
Vinon-sur-Verdon *F* 51 C10
Vinsa *S* 132 E9
Vinslöv *S* 103 C13
Vinsobres *F* 51 B9
Vinsternes *N* 120 E4
Vinstra *N* 117 C11
Vintervollen *N* 130 D8
Vintilă Vodă *RO* 177 C9
Vintjärn *S* 119 E11
Vintrosa *S* 113 D12
Vintturi *FIN* 139 C11
Vinţu de Jos *RO* 168 E2
Viñuelas *E* 62 C6
Vinuesa *E* 56 E6
Vinzelberg *D* 95 A10
Viöl *D* 98 A6
Violay *F* 46 D5
Violès *F* 51 B8
Vipava *SLO* 89 E8
Vīpe *LT* 151 D12
Vipereşti *RO* 177 C8
Vipiteno *I* 88 E3
Vipperow *D* 99 D13
Vir *BIH* 173 E11
Vir *HR* 83 D11
Vir *SLO* 89 D10
Vira *S* 109 B8
Virawlya *BY* 149 E3
Virazeil *F* 49 A6
Virbalis *LT* 152 D6
Virbi *LV* 150 D4
Virče *MK* 181 F6
Vire *F* 39 C10
Vireši *LV* 151 B12
Vireux-Molhain *F* 200 D2
Vireux-Wallerand *F* 35 D10
Virey-sous-Bar *F* 41 D11
Virgen *A* 88 B5
Vīrįąt *F* 47 C7
Virieu-le-Grand *F* 47 D8

Virigneux *F* 46 D5
Viriginin *F* 47 D8
Viriville *F* 47 E7
Virķēni *LV* 147 F10
Virkkala *FIN* 143 E11
Virkkula *FIN* 137 C10
Virklund *DK* 102 C3
Virmaanpää *FIN* 140 E8
Virmaila *FIN* 143 C13
Virmutjoki *FIN* 145 C10
Virolahden kk *FIN* 144 D8
Virolahti *FIN* 144 D8
Virovitica *HR* 165 E8
Virpazar *MNE* 179 E7
Virpe *LV* 150 B4
Virrat *FIN* 139 F11
Virsbo *S* 113 C15
Virserum *S* 105 A9
Virtaniemi *FIN* 130 F4
Virtasalmi *FIN* 140 F8
Virton *B* 35 E12
Virtsu *EST* 146 D7
Virttaa *FIN* 142 D8
Viru-Jaagupi *EST* 147 C12
Viru-Nigula *EST* 147 C13
Viry *F* 47 C9
Vis *HR* 79 A10
Visaginas *LT* 151 E12
Višakio Rūda *LT* 153 D7
Visan *F* 51 B8
Vişani *RO* 177 C10
Visåsen *S* 119 A13
Visbek *D* 33 C10
Visborg *DK* 102 B6
Visby *DK* 102 E3
Visby *S* 109 D12
Visé *B* 35 C12
Višegrad *BIH* 174 F3
Visegrád *H* 165 A11
Viserba *I* 82 D6
Viseu *P* 60 C5
Vişeu de Jos *RO* 168 B4
Vişeu de Sus *RO* 168 B4
Vishnyeva *BY* 153 E13
Vishovgrad *BG* 182 C4
Visiedo *E* 58 F1
Visikums *LV* 149 B3
Vişina *RO* 176 D6
Vişina *RO* 176 F4
Visingsö *S* 108 C5
Visjövalen *S* 121 E12
Viskafors *S* 107 D12
Viskan *S* 119 B11
Viški *LV* 151 D13
Vislanda *S* 104 B6
Visnes *N* 110 D2
Višnja Gora *SLO* 89 E10
Višnjićevo *SRB* 174 D3
Višňová *CZ* 97 E8
Višňové *CZ* 93 E10
Visočka Ržana *SRB* 180 D6
Visočani *BIH* 173 D7
Visočani *BIH* 173 D8
Visočka *CZ* 93 E10
Viso del Marqués *E* 71 B5
Visoké *AL* 184 C2
Visoko *BIH* 173 E9
Visone *I* 53 B9
Visonta *H* 166 B5
Visp *CH* 84 A4
Vissac-Auteyrac *F* 46 E4
Vissani *GR* 184 E4
Visselfjärda *S* 105 B9
Visselhövede *D* 98 D7
Vissenbjerg *DK* 102 E6
Visso *I* 78 B4
Vissoie *CH* 84 A4
Vist *N* 121 D10
Vistabella del Maestrazgo *E* 64 D4
Vistbäcken *S* 134 C3
Vişţea *RO* 168 F5
Vistheden *S* 134 C5
Visthus *N* 124 E4
Vištytis *LT* 152 E6
Visuvesi *FIN* 139 F11
Viszneķ *H* 166 B5
Vita *I* 74 D2
Vită *S* 134 C8
Vitaby *S* 104 D6
Vităfors *S* 134 C8
Vitanovä *SK* 163 C9
Vitanovac *SRB* 175 F6
Vitanovac *SRB* 180 C5
Vítaz *SK* 161 F2
Vitberget *S* 134 C4
Viterbo *I* 78 C2
Viterne *F* 42 C5
Vitez *BIH* 173 D8
Vítězná *CZ* 93 B9
Vitigudino *E* 61 B8
Vitina *BIH* 173 F8
Vitina *SRB* 180 E3
Vītini *LV* 150 D5
Vitis *A* 93 E8
Vítkov *CZ* 162 B5
Vitkovići *BIH* 173 E10
Vitolini *LV* 150 C7
Vitolište *MK* 185 B6
Vitomirica *SRB* 179 D9
Vitorchiano *I* 78 C2
Vitoria-Gasteiz *E* 57 C6
Vitoševac *SRB* 175 F3
Vitovlje *BIH* 173 D8
Vitré *F* 39 D9
Vitrey-sur-Mance *F* 42 E4
Vitrolles *F* 51 D9
Vitry-en-Artois *F* 34 D6
Vitry-en-Perthois *F* 41 C12
Vitry-le-François *F* 41 C12
Vitry-sur-Loire *F* 46 B4
Vittangi *S* 132 C7
Vittaryd *S* 103 B13
Vitteaux *F* 41 F12
Vittel *F* 42 D4
Vittikko *FIN* 131 E4
Vittikko *FIN* 135 B13
Vittikkovuoma *FIN* 133 D12
Vittinge *S* 114 C7
Vittjärv *S* 134 C7
Vittoria *I* 75 F6
Vittorio Veneto *I* 88 E5
Vittsjö *S* 103 C13
Vitulano *I* 76 A3
Vitulazio *I* 76 A2
Vitvattnet *S* 118 B8
Vitvattnet *S* 123 D16
Vitvattnet *S* 135 B10
Viù *I* 84 C3
Vive *HR* 164 F5

Vivastbo *S* 114 B7
Viveiro *E* 54 A4
Vivel del Río Martín *E* 58 F2
Viver *E* 64 E3
Viverols *E* 46 E4
Viveros *E* 71 B7
Vivier-au-Court *F* 35 E10
Viviers *F* 51 B8
Viviez *F* 49 A11
Vivild *DK* 102 C6
Viv-le-Fesq *F* 51 C7
Vivonne *F* 45 C6
Vix *F* 41 E12
Vix *F* 44 C4
Vizantea-Livezi *RO* 169 F10
Vize *TR* 189 A8
Vizille *F* 47 E8
Vižinada *HR* 83 B8
Viziru *RO* 171 C1
Vizitsa *BG* 183 E9
Vizovice *CZ* 162 C5
Vizslás *H* 163 E9
Vizsoly *H* 161 G2
Vizzini *I* 75 E6
Vlaardingen *NL* 32 E2
Vlachata *GR* 190 C2
Vlacherna *GR* 190 D5
Vlachia *GR* 191 B8
Vlachiotis *GR* 191 E6
Vlachokerasia *GR* 190 E5
Vlachovice *CZ* 162 C5
Vlădaia *RO* 175 E11
Vladaya *BG* 181 D7
Vlădeni *RO* 169 B9
Vlădeni *RO* 169 C10
Vlădeni *RO* 171 D1
Vlădeşti *RO* 170 F2
Vlădeşti *RO* 176 C4
Vlădeşti *RO* 176 C5
Vladičin Han *SRB* 180 D5
Vlădila *RO* 176 E3
Vladimir *MNE* 179 E7
Vladimir *RO* 176 D3
Vladimirci *SRB* 174 D4
Vladimirescu *RO* 167 E7
Vladimirovac *SRB* 175 C6
Vladimirovo *BG* 181 C10
Vladinya *BG* 181 C10
Vladislav *CZ* 93 D9
Vlad Ţepeş *RO* 177 E10
Vladychen' *UA* 171 B3
Vlăhiţa *RO* 168 E5
Vlahovići *BIH* 173 F8
Vlanduk *BIH* 173 D8
Vlaole *SRB* 175 E8
Vlase *SRB* 180 D4
Vlasenica *BIH* 173 D10
Vlašici *HR* 172 D3
Vlašim *CZ* 93 C7
Vlasina Okruglica *SRB* 180 D5
Vlăsineşti *RO* 169 B9
Vlasotince *SRB* 180 D5
Vlatkovići *BIH* 173 D7
Vlčany *SK* 162 E5
Vlčnov *CZ* 162 D5
Vledder *NL* 32 C6
Vleuten *NL* 32 D4
Vlijmen *NL* 32 E4
Vlissingen *NL* 32 F1
Vlochos *GR* 185 E7
Vlorë *AL* 184 D2
Vlotho *D* 33 D11
Vlycho *GR* 190 B2
Vnanje Gorice *SLO* 89 D9
Vnorovy *CZ* 162 D4
Vöčin *HR* 165 E9
Vöcklabruck *A* 92 F4
Vöcklamarkt *A* 92 F4
Voden *BG* 177 F9
Voden *BG* 183 D7
Voderady *SK* 162 E5
Vodica *BIH* 173 C7
Vodice *HR* 83 B9
Vodice *HR* 172 E4
Vodňaci *HR* 83 C10
Vodinci *HR* 173 E11
Vodnjany *BG* 182 C6
Vodjenica *BIH* 172 C5
Vodnany *CZ* 92 D6
Vodnjan *HR* 83 C8
Vodskov *DK* 102 A6
Vodstrup *DK* 102 B3
Voe *GB* 191 C4
Voel *DK* 102 C5
Voerde (Niederrhein) *D* 33 E7
Voerendaal *NL* 199 D9
Voerladegård *DK* 102 C5
Voerså *DK* 102 A6
Vogatsiko *GR* 184 D6
Vogelbeck *NL* 198 A5
Vogelgrun *F* 43 D8
Vogelsang *D* 100 D4
Vogelsdorf *D* 96 B5
Vogelweh *D* 37 F9
Voghera *I* 82 C4
Voghiera *I* 82 C4
Vognill *N* 117 A11
Vognsild *DK* 102 B4
Vogošća *BIH* 173 E9
Vogt *D* 87 B9
Vogtareuth *D* 88 A5
Voguë *F* 51 A7
Vohburg an der Donau *D* 91 E10
Vohenstrauß *D* 91 C11
Vöhl *D* 37 B11
Võhma *EST* 146 D11
Võhma *EST* 147 D11
Vohonjoki *FIN* 136 B9
Vöhringen *D* 43 D10
Vöhringen *D* 91 F7
Voiceşti *RO* 176 D4
Void-Vacon *F* 42 C4
Voikkaa *FIN* 144 D6
Voikoski *FIN* 144 C6
Voila *RO* 168 F5
Voillecomte *F* 41 C12
Voineasa *RO* 176 C1
Voineasa *RO* 176 E3
Voineşti *RO* 176 C6
Voiron *F* 47 E8
Võisiku *EST* 147 E8
Voiteg *RO* 175 C7
Voiteur *F* 47 B8
Voitsberg *A* 89 B7
Voivodeni *RO* 168 D5
Vojakkala *FIN* 135 B10
Vojakkala *FIN* 143 D11
Vojenice *DK* 102 B4
Vojens *DK* 102 E4
Vojka *SRB* 174 D5
Vojkovic *BIH* 173 E9
Vojnić *HR* 164 F5

Vojnik MK 180 E4
Vojnik SLO 164 D4
Vojtjajaure S 124 E9
Voka EST 148 C2
Vokány H 165 E10
Vokil BG 177 F10
Voknavolok RUS 137 E16
Voksa N 116 B2
Volakas GR 186 B5
Volary CZ 92 E5
Volda N 116 B4
Voldby DK 102 C5
Voldby DK 103 C7
Voldum DK 102 C6
Volendam NL 32 D4
Volgsele S 123 B11
Volimes GR 190 D2
Volintiri MD 170 E5
Volissos GR 193 C6
Voljevac BIH 173 E8
Voljice BIH 173 E8
Volkach D 91 C7
Volkel NL 199 B7
Völkermarkt A 89 C10
Volketswil CH 43 F10
Völklingen D 37 F7
Volkmarsen D 33 F12
Volkovija MK 179 F10
Voll N 117 E13
Völlen D 33 B8
Vollenhove NL 32 C5
Vollersode D 33 B11
Vollsjö S 103 D13
Volmunster F 43 B7
Voloiac RO 175 D11
Voloka UA 169 A7
Volonne F 51 B11
Volos GR 185 F8
Voloshcha UA 161 D8
Volosovo RUS 148 C5
Volosyanka UA 161 F6
Volováţ RO 169 B7
Volovets' UA 161 F7
Volovo BG 182 B5
Volpago del Montello I 88 C5
Volpedo I 53 B9
Volpiano I 84 C4
Völs A 88 B3
Völschow D 100 C4
Voltaggio I 53 B9
Volta Mantovana I 82 B2
Volterra I 82 F2
Voltlage D 33 D9
Voltri I 53 C9
Voltti FIN 138 D9
Volturara Appula I 79 E13
Volturara Irpina I 76 B3
Volturino I 79 E8
Voluntari RO 177 E8
Volvic F 46 D3
Volx F 51 C10
Volya Arlamivs'ka UA 160 D7
Volyně CZ 92 D5
Vomp A 88 B4
Voneshta Voda BG 182 D5
Vonge DK 102 D4
Vonges F 42 F3
Voni GR 194 E9
Vonitsa GR 190 B2
Vōnnu EST 147 E14
Vööpste EST 147 E14
Vööpsu EST 148 E2
Voorburg NL 32 D2
Voore EST 147 D13
Voorhout NL 198 A4
Voorschoten NL 32 D2
Voorst NL 32 D6
Voorthuizen NL 199 A7
Võrra FIN 138 D8
Voranava BY 153 E11
Vorbasse DK 102 D4
Vorchdorf A 92 F5
Vorden NL 32 D6
Vordernberg A 89 A10
Vordingborg DK 103 E9
Vordorf D 95 B8
Vorë AL 184 B2
Voreppe F 47 E8
Vorey F 46 E4
Vorgod DK 102 C3
Vormsele S 123 B15
Vormstad N 120 E7
Vormsund N 111 B14
Vormträsk S 123 B15
Vorna FIN 135 F15
Vorniceni RO 169 B9
Voroi GR 194 E8
Vorokhta UA 168 A5
Vorona RO 169 B9
Vorra D 91 C9
Vorsau A 164 B5
Vorst B 35 B11
Vorţa RO 167 E10
Vorwerk D 33 B12
Voskopojë AL 184 C4
Voşlăbeni RO 169 D7
Voss N 116 E4
Vosselaar B 32 F3
Voştane HR 173 E6
Võsu EST 147 B11
Votice CZ 93 C7
Votonosi GR 184 E5
Voudia GR 195 B8
Vougeot F 42 F2
Vouillé F 44 C5
Vouillé F 45 B6
Voukolies GR 194 E6
Voula GR 191 D8
Voulaines-les-Templiers F 41 E12
Vouliagmeni GR 191 D8
Voulpi GR 190 A4
Voulx F 41 D8
Vouneuil-sous-Biard F 45 B6
Vouneuil-sur-Vienne F 45 B7
Vourgareli GR 184 F5
Vourvourou GR 185 D10
Voutenay-sur-Cure F 41 E10
Voutezac F 45 E8
Voutianoi GR 190 E5
Vouvant F 44 B4
Vouvray F 40 F4
Vouvry CH 47 C10
Vouzela P 60 C4
Vouzi GR 190 A5
Vouziers F 35 F10
Vouzon F 40 D6
Vowchyn BY 157 F9
Vowkawshchyna BY 149 E2
Voxna S 119 D10
Voynika BG 183 E7

Voynitsa RUS 137 D15
Voynovo BG 177 F10
Voynyagovo BG 181 D10
Vozmediano E 57 E8
Vozneshka-Persha UA 170 E4
Vrå DK 106 E6
Vrabevo BG 181 D10
Vráble SK 162 E6
Vračev Gaj SRB 175 D7
Vrachasi GR 195 E10
Vrachesh BG 181 D8
Vrachnaiika GR 190 C4
Vrachos GR 184 D5
Vracov CZ 162 D4
Vrådal N 111 D8
Vrakúň SK 162 F5
Vrané nad Vltavou CZ 92 C6
Vranino BG 183 B10
Vranino BG 183 D7
Vranje AL 179 E9
Vranisht AL 184 D2
Vranjak BIH 173 C9
Vranje SLO 89 C11
Vranjska Banja SRB 180 D5
Vranovice CZ 93 E11
Vranov nad Topľou SK 161 F4
Vransko SLO 89 D10
Vrapčište MK 179 F10
Vrapčići BIH 173 F8
Vrasene B 198 C4
Vrasna GR 185 C10
Vratarnica SRB 175 F9
Vratimov CZ 162 D4
Vratnica MK 180 E3
Vratsa BG 181 C8
Vrattsa BG 181 E6
Vražogrnac SRB 175 F9
Vrbanja BIH 173 C7
Vrbanja HR 173 C10
Vrbanjci BIH 173 C7
Vrbas SRB 174 B4
Vrbaška BIH 173 B9
Vrbica SRB 166 E5
Vrbice CZ 93 E11
Vrbnik HR 83 B10
Vrbnik HR 172 D5
Vrbno pod Pradědem CZ 158 F3
Vrbovac SRB 175 F9
Vrbovce SK 162 D4
Vrbové SK 162 D5
Vrbovec HR 165 E6
Vrbovsko HR 83 B11
Vrchlabí CZ 97 E9
Vrčín SRB 174 D6
Vrdy CZ 93 C8
Vrebac HR 172 C4
Vrécourt F 42 D4
Vreden D 33 D7
Vreeland NL 199 A6
Vrees D 33 C9
Vrela SRB 179 D9
Vrelo SRB 180 C4
Vrena S 109 B9
Vrensted DK 106 E6
Vřesina CZ 162 B6
Vresse B 35 E10
Vresthena GR 191 E6
Vretstorp S 108 A5
Vrgorac HR 173 F7
Vrhnika SLO 89 E9
Vrhopolje BIH 173 C6
Vrhovine HR 172 C3
Vridsted DK 102 C4
Vries NL 33 B7
Vriezenveen NL 33 D7
Vrigstad S 108 E4
Vrinners DK 102 C6
Vrísa GR 193 A7
Vrizy F 35 F10
Vrlika HR 172 E5
Vrnjačka Banja SRB 179 B10
Vrnograč BIH 172 B4
Vron F 34 D4
Vrontados GR 193 C7
Vrontero GR 184 C5
Vrontou GR 185 D7
Vroomshoop NL 33 D7
Vrosina GR 184 E4
Vrouchas GR 195 E10
Vroutek CZ 92 B4
Vrouwenpolder NL 32 E1
Vrpolje HR 172 E5
Vrpolje HR 173 B9
Vrrin AL 184 B1
Vršac SRB 175 C7
Vršani BIH 173 C11
Vrsar HR 83 B8
Vrsi HR 172 D3
Vrtoče BIH 172 C5
Vrulja MNE 179 E7
Vrútky SK 163 C7
Vrutok MK 179 F10
Vrův BG 175 E10
Vrysia GR 185 F7
Vrysoula GR 184 F4
Všemina CZ 162 C4
Všeruby CZ 92 C4
Všetaty CZ 93 C7
Vsetín CZ 162 C5
Vsevolozhsk RUS 145 E14
Vūbel BG 176 F5
Vučijak BIH 173 C8
Vučitrn SRB 179 D10
Vučja Lokva SRB 179 C10
Vučje SLO 180 D4
Vught NL 32 E4
Vuğlevtsi BG 182 D5
Vuka HR 165 F10
Vukova Gorica HR 164 F4
Vukovar HR 173 B11
Vuku N 121 D11
Vulcan RO 175 C11
Vulcan RO 176 B6
Vulcana-Băi RO 176 C6
Vülchedrüm BG 181 C9
Vülchidol BG 183 C9
Vulpeni RO 176 E3
Vultureni RO 168 D3
Vultureni RO 169 C8
Vultureşti RO 169 B8
Vultureşti RO 169 D11
Vultureşti RO 176 D4
Vulturu RO 177 E11
Vulturu RO 177 B10
Vuobmaved FIN 129 C16
Vuohijärvi FIN 144 C6
Vuohtomäki FIN 139 C16
Vuojärvi FIN 133 D12
Vuokatti FIN 137 F11

Vuokko FIN 141 D12
Vuolenkoski FIN 143 C15
Vuolijoki FIN 139 C16
Vuolle FIN 139 C11
Vuollerim S 134 B5
Vuonisjärvi FIN 141 D14
Vuonislahti FIN 141 D13
Vuonos FIN 141 E12
Vuontisjärvi FIN 133 B11
Vuorenmaa FIN 140 G9
Vuorenmaa FIN 142 C8
Vuoreslahti FIN 137 F9
Vuorimäki FIN 139 E11
Vuorimäki FIN 140 C9
Vuoriniemi FIN 145 B11
Vuosaari FIN 143 E13
Vuosanka FIN 137 F13
Vuostimo FIN 131 E2
Vuostimojärvi FIN 131 E2
Vuotner S 134 C3
Vuotso FIN 131 B2
Vuottas S 134 B7
Vuottolahti FIN 136 F9
Vuotunki FIN 137 B14
Vurpar RO 168 F4
Vürshets BG 181 C7
Vustsye BY 149 E5
Vutcani RO 169 E11
Vuzenica SLO 89 C11
Vuzlove UA 161 G5
Vvedenka UA 170 E5
Vyalets BY 149 F7
Vyalikaya Byerastavitsa BY 156 D10
Vyalikaya Stayki BY 149 F7
Vyalikaye Syalo BY 149 F3
Vyarkhovichy BY 157 F9
Vyartsilya RUS 141 F15
Vyaz RUS 149 C12
Vyborg RUS 145 D10
Vyčapy-Opatovce SK 162 E6
Východná SK 163 D9
Vydeniai LT 153 E10
Vydrany SK 162 F5
Vyerkhnyadzvinsk BY 149 E3
Vyetryna BY 149 F7
Vyhne SK 163 D7
Vyhoda UA 161 F8
Vylkove UA 171 C5
Vylok UA 161 G6
Vynnyky UA 160 D6
Vynohradiv UA 161 G7
Vynohradivka UA 170 F4
Vyritsa RUS 148 C7
Vyronas GR 191 D8
Vyroneia GR 185 B9
Vyshgorodok RUS 149 B3
Vyshka UA 161 F6
Vyshkiv UA 161 F8
Vyshkove UA 161 G7
Vyshneve UA 161 F6
Vyshniv UA 157 H10
Vyskod' SK 161 F4
Výškov CZ 93 D12
Vyšné Ružbachy SK 161 E2
Vyšný Mirošov SK 161 E3
Vyšný Orlík SK 161 E3
Vyšný Žipov SK 161 F4
Vysoká nad Kysucou SK 163 C7
Vysoké Mýto CZ 93 C10
Vysokoye RUS 152 D4
Vysotsk RUS 145 D11
Vyssínia GR 184 C5
Vytina GR 190 D5
Vyzhnytsya UA 168 A6
Vyžuonos LT 151 E11
Vzmor'ye RUS 155 A9

W

Waabs D 99 A7
Waal D 87 B11
Waalre NL 32 F4
Waalwijk NL 32 E4
Waarschoot B 35 B8
Wabern D 37 F12
Wąbrzeźno PL 154 D6
Wachenheim an der Weinstraße D 203 C5
Wachow D 95 A11
Wachtebeke B 35 B8
Wächtersbach D 37 D12
Wacken D 98 B6
Wackersdorf D 91 D12
Waddeweitz D 99 D9
Waddington D 37 D11
Waddinxveen NL 32 D3
Wadebridge GB 28 D5
Wädenswil CH 43 F10
Wadern D 37 E7
Wadersloh D 33 E10
Wadgassen D 37 F7
Wadhurst GB 31 E9
Wadlew PL 159 C7
Wadowice PL 163 B9
Wadowice Górne PL 159 F11
Wądroże Wielkie PL 97 D10
Waganiec PL 154 E6
Wagenfeld D 33 C11
Wagenhoff D 95 A8
Wageningen NL 32 E5
Waghäusel D 37 F11
Waging am See D 89 A6
Wagna A 164 C5
Wągrowiec PL 101 E12
Wahlhausen D 95 D6
Wahlsdorf D 96 C4
Wahlstedt D 99 C8
Wahrenholz D 95 A8
Waiblingen D 43 C11
Waibstadt D 203 C6
Waidhofen an der Thaya A 93 E8
Waidhofen an der Ybbs A 93 G7
Waigolshausen D 91 C7
Waimes B 36 D6
Wain D 87 A10
Wainfleet All Saints GB 27 E12
Wainhouse Corner GB 28 D5
Waischenfeld D 91 C9
Wakefield GB 27 D8
Wakendorf II D 99 C8
Walberswick GB 31 C12
Wałbrzych PL 97 E10
Walburg D 94 D6

Walchum D 33 C8
Walcourt B 35 D9
Wałcz PL 101 D10
Wald CH 43 F10
Wald D 43 E11
Wald D 91 D11
Waldachtal D 43 D10
Waldböckelheim D 201 E8
Waldbreitbach D 201 C7
Waldbröl D 37 C9
Waldbrunn-Lahr D 37 C10
Waldburg D 87 B9
Waldbüttelbrunn D 90 C6
Walddrehna D 96 C5
Waldeck D 201 D8
Waldegg A 93 G10
Waldenbuch D 43 C11
Waldenburg CH 43 F8
Waldenburg D 90 D6
Walderbach D 91 D11
Waldershof D 91 C11
Waldesch D 201 D8
Waldfischbach-Burgalben D 37 F9
Waldhausen A 93 E8
Waldhausen im Strudengau A 93 F7
Waldheim D 96 D4
Walding A 92 F6
Waldkappel D 94 D6
Waldkirch D 43 D8
Waldkirchen D 92 E5
Waldkraiburg D 91 F11
Wald-Michelbach D 203 B6
Waldmohr D 37 F8
Waldmünchen D 91 D12
Wałdowo-Szlacheckie PL 154 D6
Waldrach D 37 E7
Waldsassen D 91 C11
Waldsee D 203 C5
Waldshut D 43 F9
Waldstatt CH 43 F11
Waldstetten D 91 F7
Waldstetten D 203 D8
Walenstadt CH 43 F11
Walferdange L 36 E6
Walim PL 97 E10
Walkendorf D 99 C13
Wallasey GB 26 E5
Walldorf D 37 D11
Walldorf D 37 F11
Walldorf D 95 E7
Walldürn D 43 A11
Wallenfels D 91 B9
Wallerfing D 92 E3
Wallern im Burgenland A 165 A7
Wallersdorf D 91 E12
Wallerstein D 91 E7
Wallgau D 88 A3
Wallhausen D 91 D7
Wallhausen D 201 E8
Wallisellen CH 43 F10
Wallmer GB 31 E11
Walls GB 19 E13
Wallsbüll D 98 A6
Wallstawe D 99 D8
Walmer GB 31 E11
Walsall GB 27 F7
Walschleben D 95 D8
Walsleben D 99 E13
Walsoken GB 27 F12
Walsrode D 98 E7
Waltenhofen D 87 B10
Waltershausen D 95 E7
Waltham on the Wolds GB 27 F10
Walton-on-Thames GB 31 E8
Walton on the Naze GB 31 D11
Wamba E 55 E10
Wamel NL 199 B6
Wanderup D 98 A6
Wandlitz D 100 E5
Wandre B 199 D7
Wang A 93 B7
Wang CH 43 F8
Wangen im Allgäu D 87 B9
Wängi CH 43 F10
Wankendorf D 99 B8
Wanna D 33 A11
Wanne-Eikel D 199 B10
Wanroij NL 199 B7
Wanssum NL 199 B8
Wantage GB 29 B12
Wanze B 35 C11
Wanzleben D 95 B9
Wapenveld NL 32 D6
Wapiersk PL 101 C9
Wapenik PL 155 C9
Wapnica PL 101 E12
Wapno PL 101 E12
Warberg D 95 B9
Warboys GB 31 C8
Warburg D 33 F12
Warcop GB 27 B7
Warcq F 36 F5
Wardenburg D 33 B10
Wardington GB 29 A12
Ware GB 31 D8
Waregem B 35 C7
Wareham GB 29 D10
Waremme B 35 C11
Waren D 99 C13
Warendorf D 33 E9
Warffum NL 33 B7
Warin D 99 C11
Waringstown GB 23 D10
Wark GB 21 E11
Warka PL 157 G4
Warkworth GB 21 E13
Warlingham GB 31 E8
Warloy-Baillon F 34 D6
Warlubie PL 154 C6
Warmenhuize B 198 D4
Warmington GB 29 A12
Warminster GB 29 C10
Warmond NL 198 A5
Warmsen D 33 D11
Warnemünde D 99 B12
Warngau D 88 A4
Warnice PL 101 D7
Warnice PL 101 D10
Warnino PL 101 C10
Warnow D 99 C11
Warnsveld NL 32 D6
Warrenpoint GB 23 D10
Warrington GB 26 E6
Warsingsfehn D 33 B8
Warslow GB 27 E8
Warstein D 33 F10
Warszawa PL 157 F4
Warszkowo PL 101 B11
Warta PL 158 C5
Warta Bolesławiecka PL 97 D9

Wartberg an der Krems A 92 G6
Wartberg D 91 F10
Wartenberg-Angersbach D 94 E5
Warth A 87 C10
Wartin D 100 D6
Wartkowice D 158 C6
Wartmannsroth D 90 B6
Warwick GB 29 A11
Warwick Bridge GB 21 F11
Warzyce PL 160 D4
Wasbek D 99 B7
Wasbister GB 19 G10
Washington GB 21 F13
Wasigny F 35 E9
Wasilków PL 156 D8
Waśniów PL 159 E11
Wąsosz PL 97 C11
Wąsosz PL 156 C6
Wąsowo PL 97 B10
Waspik NL 32 E3
Wasseiges B 199 D6
Wasselonne F 43 C7
Wassen CH 87 D7
Wassenaar NL 32 D2
Wassenberg D 36 B6
Wasseralfingen D 91 E7
Wasserbillig D 202 B2
Wasserburg am Inn D 91 F11
Wasserliesch D 202 B2
Wasserlosen D 90 B7
Wassertrüdingen D 91 D8
Wassigny F 35 D8
Wassy F 42 C2
Wasungen D 95 E7
Watchet GB 29 C7
Watchgate GB 26 C6
Waterbeck GB 21 E10
Waterford IRL 25 C8
Watergrasshill IRL 24 D6
Wateringen NL 198 A4
Waterland-Oudeman B 198 C3
Waterloo B 35 C9
Waterlooville GB 30 F6
Waterville IRL 24 E2
Watford GB 31 D8
Wathlingen D 95 A7
Watlington GB 30 D6
Watten F 34 C5
Watten GB 19 J10
Wattenbek D 99 B8
Wattens A 88 B4
Watten-Scheid D 199 C10
Wattenwil CH 47 B12
Wattlebridge GB 23 D8
Watton D 33 E9
Wattwil CH 43 F11
Wavre B 35 C10
Wavrin F 34 C6
Wawelno PL 101 D13
Wąwelno PL 158 E4
Wąwolnica PL 157 H6
Wawrów PL 101 E8
Wawrzeńczyce PL 159 F9
Waxweiler D 36 D6
Waziers F 198 C2
Weaverham GB 26 E6
Wechmar D 95 E8
Wechselburg D 95 D12
Wedde NL 33 B8
Weddingstedt D 98 B6
Wedel (Holstein) D 99 C7
Wedemore GB 29 C9
Wednesbury GB 27 F7
Weede D 99 C8
Weedon Bec GB 29 A12
Weelde B 198 C5
Weem GB 21 B9
Weener D 33 B8
Weerberg A 88 B4
Weerselo NL 33 D7
Weert NL 32 F5
Weesen CH 43 F11
Weesp NL 32 D4
Weeze D 32 E6
Weferlingen D 95 B9
Wegberg D 36 B6
Wegenstedt D 95 B9
Weggis CH 87 C7
Węgierska Górka PL 163 B8
Wegliniec PL 97 D8
Węgorzewo PL 152 E4
Węgorzyno PL 101 C9
Węgrów PL 155 F13
Węgrzynowo PL 155 F9
Wegscheid A 164 A4
Wegscheid D 92 E5
Wehdel D 33 A11
Wehl NL 32 E6
Wehr D 43 E8
Wehrbleck D 33 C11
Wehringen D 87 A11
Weibern D 199 C10
Weibersbrunn D 90 C5
Weichering D 91 E9
Weichs D 91 F9
Weida D 95 E10
Weidenberg D 91 C10
Weiden in der Oberpfalz D 91 C11
Weidenstetten D 203 D8
Weidenthal D 37 F9
Weiding D 91 D12
Weierbach D 37 F8
Weiersbach D 37 F8
Weigersdorf D 97 D7
Weihmichl D 91 E11
Weikersheim D 90 D6
Weil D 87 A11
Weilbach D 37 E12
Weilburg D 37 D10
Weil der Stadt D 43 C10
Weilerbach D 202 C4
Weilerswist D 37 C7
Weilheim an der Teck D 90 C6
Weilheim in Oberbayern D 88 A3
Weilmünster D 37 D10
Weimar D 95 E9
Weinbach D 201 D9
Weinböhla D 96 D5
Weinfelden CH 43 E11
Weingarten (Baden) D 203 C6
Weinheim D 37 E11
Weinsberg D 37 F12
Weinstadt D 43 C11
Weira D 95 E9

Weisen D 99 D11
Weiskirchen D 37 E7
Weismain D 91 B9
Weissach D 43 C10
Weißbriach A 89 C7
Weißenbach am Lech A 87 C11
Weißenberg D 97 D7
Weißenbrunn D 91 B9
Weißenburg in Bayern D 91 D8
Weißenfels D 95 D10
Weißenhorn D 91 F7
Weißensee D 95 D9
Weißenstadt D 91 B10
Weißenstein A 89 C8
Weißenthurm D 201 D7
Weißig D 96 D5
Weißkeißel D 97 D7
Weißkirchen in Steiermark A 89 B10
Weißkollm D 96 D6
Weißwasser D 97 C7
Weistrach A 93 F7
Weiswampach L 36 D6
Weisweil D 43 D8
Weitbruch F 202 D3
Weitefeld D 201 C8
Weiten A 93 F8
Weitensfeld A 89 C9
Weiterstadt D 203 B6
Weitra A 93 E7
Weixdorf D 96 D5
Weiz A 164 B5
Wejherowo PL 154 A5
Wekerom NL 32 D5
Welkenraedt B 36 C5
Well NL 32 E6
Wellaune D 95 C12
Welle D 98 D7
Wellen B 199 D6
Wellesbourne GB 29 A11
Wellheim D 91 E9
Wellin B 35 D11
Welling D 37 D8
Wellingborough GB 31 C7
Wellington GB 26 F6
Wellington GB 29 D8
Wellingtonbridge IRL 25 D9
Wellington Bridge IRL 25 D9
Wells GB 29 C9
Wells-next-the-Sea GB 31 B10
Welney GB 27 F12
Welshampton GB 26 F6
Welschbillig D 37 E7
Welshpool GB 26 F5
Welsickendorf D 96 C4
Welsleben D 95 C10
Welver D 33 E9
Welwyn GB 31 D8
Welwyn Garden City GB 31 D8
Welzheim D 90 E6
Welzow D 96 C6
Wem GB 26 F6
Wembdon GB 29 C8
Wemding D 91 E8
Wemeldinge NL 198 B4
Wemyss Bay GB 20 D7
Wendeburg D 95 B7
Wendelsheim D 37 E10
Wendelstein D 91 D9
Wenden D 37 C9
Wendens Ambo GB 31 C9
Wendisch Priborn D 99 D12
Wendisch Rietz D 96 B6
Wendlingen am Neckar D 43 C11
Wendover GB 31 D7
Wenduine B 198 C2
Wengen CH 86 D5
Wengsel (Isterberg) D 33 D8
Wennigsen (Deister) D 94 B6
Wenningstedt D 102 F2
Wenns A 87 C12
Wentorf D 99 C8
Wentorf bei Hamburg D 99 D8
Wenzenbach D 91 D11
Wenzlow D 95 B11
Wépion B 198 E5
Werbach D 90 C6
Werben D 96 C6
Werben (Elbe) D 99 E11
Werbig D 96 C4
Werbkowice PL 160 B8
Werbomont B 35 D12
Werdau D 95 E11
Werder D 95 B12
Werder D 100 C4
Werdohl D 33 F9
Werfen A 89 B7
Werkendam NL 198 B5
Werl D 33 E9
Werlte D 33 C9
Wermelskirchen D 201 B7
Wermsdorf D 96 D3
Wernau D 43 C11
Wernberg-Köblitz D 91 C11
Werndorf A 164 C5
Werne D 33 E9
Werneck D 91 C7
Werneuchen D 96 A5
Wernigerode D 95 C8
Wernshausen D 95 E7
Werpeloh D 33 C9
Wertach D 87 B10
Wertheim D 90 C6
Werther CH 86 C6
Werther D 95 D8
Werther (Westfalen) D 33 D10
Wertingen D 91 E8
Wervershof NL 32 C4
Wervik B 35 C7
Wesel D 32 E6
Wesenberg D 100 D3
Wesendorf D 95 A8
Wesepe NL 199 A8
Wesoła PL 157 F4
Wesselburen D 98 B5
Wesseling D 37 C7
Wesseln D 98 B6
Wessem NL 199 C7
Weßling D 91 F9
Wessobrunn D 87 B12
West Auckland GB 21 F13
West Bridgford GB 27 F9
West Bromwich GB 27 F8
Westbury GB 29 C10
Westendorf A 88 B5
Westensee D 99 B7
Westerbeck (Sassenberg) D 95 A4
Westerbork NL 33 C7
Westerburg D 37 C9

Westerdale GB 19 J10
Westeregeln D 95 C9
Westerende-Kirchloog (Ihlow) D 33 B8
Westergate GB 31 F7
Westergellersen D 99 D8
Westerhaar NL 33 D7
Westerheim D 203 D8
Westerholt D 33 A8
Westerhorn D 98 C7
Westerhoven NL 199 C6
Westerland D 102 F2
Westerlo B 35 B10
Westerrönfeld D 98 B7
Westerstede D 33 B9
Westerstetten D 90 E6
Westervoort NL 32 E5
Westgate GB 21 F12
West Grinstead GB 31 F8
West Haddon GB 29 A12
Westhausen D 91 E7
Westhill GB 19 L12
Westhofen D 203 B5
Westhoffen F 202 D3
Westkapelle NL 35 A7
West Kilbride GB 20 D7
West Kirby GB 26 E5
West Knapton GB 27 C10
West Lavington GB 29 C11
Westleton GB 31 C12
West Linton GB 21 D10
West Looe GB 28 E5
West Lulworth GB 29 D10
Westmalle B 32 F3
West Malling GB 31 E9
West Meon Hut GB 29 C12
West Mersea GB 31 D10
West Moors GB 29 D11
Westness GB 19 G10
Westnewton GB 21 F10
Weston GB 27 F7
Weston GB 29 D10
Weston-super-Mare GB 29 C9
Westonzoyland GB 29 C9
Westport IRL 22 E3
Westport Quay IRL 22 E3
West Somerton GB 31 B12
West Tarbert GB 20 D6
West-Terschelling NL 32 B4
Westward Ho! GB 28 C6
West Wellow GB 29 D11
West Winch GB 27 F12
Wethau D 95 D10
Wetheral GB 21 F11
Wetherby GB 27 D9
Wetlina PL 161 F5
Wetter (Hessen) D 37 C11
Wetter (Ruhr) D 201 B7
Wetteren B 35 C8
Wetterzeube D 95 D11
Wettin D 95 C10
Wettingen CH 43 F9
Wetzikon CH 43 F10
Wetzlar D 37 C11
Wevelgem B 35 C7
Wewelsfleth D 33 A12
Wexford IRL 25 D10
Weyarn D 88 A4
Weybridge GB 31 E8
Weyerbusch D 37 C9
Weyer Markt A 89 A10
Weyersheim F 43 C8
Weyhausen D 95 B8
Weyhe D 33 C11
Weymouth GB 29 D10
Whalton GB 21 E12
Whauphill GB 20 F8
Wheddon Cross GB 29 C7
Wherwell GB 29 C12
Whiddon Down GB 29 D7
Whitburn GB 21 D9
Whitby GB 27 C10
Whitchurch GB 26 F6
Whitchurch GB 29 B8
Whitchurch GB 31 D7
Whitecross GB 23 D10
Whitegate IRL 24 E6
Whitegate IRL 24 E6
Whitehall GB 19 G11
Whitehall IRL 25 C8
Whitehaven GB 26 B4
Whitehead GB 20 F5
Whitehill GB 31 E7
Whitehills GB 19 K11
Whitfield GB 31 E11
Whithorn GB 21 F1
Whiting Bay GB 20 E6
Whitland GB 28 B5
Whitley Bay GB 21 E14
Whitstable GB 31 E11
Whittington GB 26 F5
Whittlesey GB 27 F11
Wiartel PL 155 C12
Wiatrowo PL 101 E12
Wiązów PL 97 E12
Wiązowna PL 157 F4
Wiązownica PL 160 C6
Wichelen B 35 B8
Wick GB 19 J10
Wick GB 29 C7
Wick GB 31 F7
Wickede (Ruhr) D 201 B8
Wickenrode (Helsa) D 94 D6
Wickford GB 31 D10
Wickham GB 29 D12
Wickham Market GB 31 C11
Wicklow IRL 23 G10
Wicko PL 101 A13
Widawa PL 159 D6
Widecombe in the Moor GB 29 D7
Widnau CH 87 C9
Widnes GB 26 E6
Widuchowa PL 100 D6
Więcbork PL 101 D12
Wieck am Darß PL 99 B13
Wieczna Kościelna PL 155 D9
Wieda D 95 C8
Wiedensahl D 33 C12
Wiederau D 96 E3
Wiednitz D 96 D6
Wiefelstede D 33 B10
Wiehe D 95 D9
Wiehl D 37 C9
Wiek D 100 A4
Więsszyce PL 158 F5
Wielbark PL 155 D10
Wieleń PL 101 E10
Wielenbach D 88 A3
Wielgie PL 155 E2
Wielgomłyny PL 159 D8
Wielichowo PL 97 B10

Wieliczka PL 159 G9
Wieliczki PL 152 F6
Wielka Wieś PL 159 F8
Wielkie Oczy PL 160 C7
Wielki Klincz PL 154 B5
Wielopole Skrzyńskie PL 159 G12
Wielowieś PL 158 E6
Wielsbeke B 198 D2
Wieluń PL 158 D6
Wiemersdorf D 99 C7
Wien A 93 F10
Wienerbruck A 93 G8
Wiener Neustadt A 93 G10
Wieniawa PL 157 H3
Wieniec PL 154 E6
Wienrode D 95 C8
Wiepke D 95 A9
Wieprz PL 163 B8
Wieprz PL 163 B8
Wierciań Duży PL 157 F7
Wierden NL 33 D7
Wieren D 99 E9
Wieringerwerf NL 32 C4
Wiernsheim D 203 D6
Wieruszów PL 158 D5
Wierzawice PL 160 C5
Wierzbica PL 157 H4
Wierzbica PL 157 H8
Wierzbica Górna PL 158 D4
Wierzbięcin PL 101 C8
Wierzbinek PL 154 F6
Wierzbnik PL 158 E3
Wierzbno PL 155 F12
Wierzbowa PL 97 D9
Wierzchlas PL 158 D6
Wierzchosławice PL 154 E5
Wierzchosławice PL 159 F10
Wierzchowo PL 101 C11
Wierzchowo PL 101 D10
Wierzchucino PL 154 A5
Wies A 164 C4
Wiesa D 96 E3
Wiesau D 91 C11
Wiesbaden D 37 D10
Wieselburg A 93 F8
Wiesen A 165 A6
Wiesen CH 87 D9
Wiesen D 90 B5
Wiesenau D 97 C6
Wiesenburg D 95 B11
Wiesenfelden D 91 D11
Wiesensteig D 203 D8
Wiesent D 91 D11
Wiesenthau D 91 C9
Wiesentheid D 91 C7
Wiesloch D 37 F11
Wiesmath A 164 A6
Wiesmoor D 33 B9
Wieszowa PL 158 F6
Wietmarschen D 33 C8
Wietze D 94 A6
Wietzen D 33 C12
Wietzendorf D 99 E7
Wiewiórczyn PL 159 C7
Wigan GB 26 D6
Wiggensbach D 87 B10
Wigmore GB 29 A9
Wigston GB 27 F9
Wigton GB 21 F10
Wigtown GB 21 F8
Wijchen NL 32 E5
Wijewo PL 97 C10
Wijhe NL 199 A8
Wijk aan Zee NL 32 C3
Wijk bij Duurstede NL 32 E4
Wijk en Aalburg NL 199 B6
Wil CH 43 F11
Wilamowice PL 163 B8
Wilczęta PL 155 B8
Wilczogóra PL 154 F5
Wilczyn PL 154 F5
Wildalpen A 89 A10
Wildau D 96 B5
Wildberg D 43 C10
Wildberg D 99 E13
Wildberg D 100 C4
Wildeck-Richelsdorf D 95 E7
Wildendürnbach A 93 E10
Wildenfels D 95 E11
Wildeshausen D 33 C10
Wildflecken D 90 B6
Wildon A 164 C5
Wildpoldsried D 87 B10
Wildshut A 92 F3
Wilga PL 157 G4
Wilhelminadorp NL 199 C6
Wilhelmsburg A 93 F9
Wilhelmsburg D 100 C5
Wilhelmsdorf D 43 E11
Wilhelmshaven D 33 A10
Wilkau-Haßlau D 95 E12
Wilkinstown IRL 23 E9
Wilkołaz Pierwszy PL 160 A5
Wilków PL 157 H5
Wilków PL 158 D4
Wilkowice PL 163 B8
Wilkowo PL 97 B8
Willand GB 29 D8
Willebadessen D 33 E12
Willebroek B 35 B9
Willemstad NL 32 E2
Willich D 33 F7
Willingdon GB 31 F9
Willingen (Upland) D 33 F11
Willingshausen D 37 C12
Willisau CH 43 F9
Williton GB 29 C8
Willstätt D 43 D8
Wilmslow GB 27 C7
Wilnis NL 198 A5
Wilsdruff D 37 C10
Wilp NL 199 A8
Wilsdruff D 37 C10
Wilster D 98 C6
Wilsum D 33 C7
Wiltersdorf A 93 E11
Wiltingen D 37 E7
Wilton GB 29 C11
Wiltz L 36 E5
Wimblington GB 27 F12
Wimborne Minster GB 29 D11
Wimereux F 31 F12
Wimmelburg D 95 C10
Wimmis CH 86 D5
Wimpassing A 164 A6
Wincanton GB 29 C10
Winchburgh GB 21 D10
Winchelsea GB 31 F10
Wincheringen D 202 B1
Winchester GB 29 C12

Wincrange L 36 D5
Winda PL 152 E3
Windach D 87 A12
Windeby D 99 B7
Windermere GB 26 C6
Windesheim D 37 E9
Windhagen D 37 C8
Windhausen D 99 H3
Windischeschenbach D 91 C11
Windischgarsten A 89 A9
Windorf D 92 E4
Windsbach D 91 D8
Windsor GB 31 E7
Wingate GB 21 F14
Wingene B 35 B7
Wingen-sur-Moder F 43 C7
Winklarn D 91 D11
Winkleigh GB 29 D7
Winklern A 89 C6
Winklern bei Oberwölz A 89 B9
Winnenden D 43 C11
Winnert D 98 B6
Winnica PL 155 E10
Winningen D 95 C9
Winningen D 201 D8
Winnweiler D 202 B4
Winschoten NL 33 B8
Winsen (Aller) D 99 E7
Winsen (Luhe) D 99 D8
Winsford GB 26 E6
Wińsko PL 97 D11
Winslow GB 31 D7
Winssen NL 199 B7
Winston GB 27 B8
Winsum NL 32 B5
Winterberg D 37 B11
Winterbourne Abbas GB 29 D9
Winterfeld D 99 E10
Winterswijk NL 33 E7
Winterthur CH 43 E10
Winterton GB 27 D10
Winton GB 27 C7
Wintrich D 201 E6
Wintzenheim F 43 D7
Winwick GB 31 C8
Winzenburg D 94 C6
Winzer D 92 E4
Wipperdorf D 95 D8
Wipperfürth D 37 B8
Wippra Kurort D 95 C9
Wirdumer (Wirdum) D 33 B8
Wirges D 201 D8
Wirksworth GB 27 E8
Wirsberg D 91 B10
Wischhafen D 33 A12
Wishaw GB 21 D9
Wiskitki PL 157 F2
Wisła PL 163 B10
Wiślica PL 159 F10
Wiśniew PL 157 F6
Wiśniewo PL 155 D9
Wiśniowa PL 160 D1
Wiśniowa PL 160 D4
Wissant F 31 F12
Wissembourg F 43 B8
Wissen D 37 C8
Wissenkerke NL 32 E1
Wistedt D 98 D7
Wisznia Mała PL 97 D12
Wisznice PL 157 G4
Witaszyce PL 158 C4
Witham GB 31 D10
Witheridge GB 29 D7
Withernsea GB 27 D12
Witkowo PL 101 D9
Witkowo PL 154 F4
Witley GB 31 E7
Witmarsum NL 32 B4
Witney GB 29 B12
Witnica PL 101 B6
Witnica PL 101 E7
Witonia PL 159 B7
Witosław PL 101 D12
Witry-lès-Reims F 35 F9
Wittdün D 98 A4
Witten D 33 F8
Wittenbach CH 43 F11
Wittenberge D 99 E11
Wittenburg D 99 C10
Wittenförden D 99 C10
Wittenhagen D 100 B4
Wittenheim F 43 E7
Wittibreut D 92 F3
Wittichenau D 96 D6
Wittighausen D 90 C6
Wittingen D 99 E9
Wittlich D 37 E7
Wittmar D 95 B8
Wittmund D 33 A9
Wittorf D 99 C11
Witzwort D 98 B5
Wiveliscombe GB 29 C8
Wivenhoe GB 31 D10
Wiżajny PL 152 E5
Wizna PL 156 D6
Władysławowo PL 158 B5
Władysławowo PL 154 A5
Wleń PL 97 D9
Włocławek PL 154 E7
Włodawa PL 157 G7
Włodzienin PL 158 F4
Włodzimierzów PL 159 D8
Włostów PL 159 E11
Włoszakowice PL 97 C10
Włoszczowa PL 159 E8
Wöbbelin D 99 D11
Woburn GB 31 D7
Wodynie PL 157 F5
Wodzierady PL 159 C7
Wodzisław PL 159 E9
Wodzisław Śląski PL 158 F5
Woensdrecht NL 198 C4
Woerden NL 32 D3
Wœrth F 43 C8
Wohlen CH 43 F9
Wohlen CH 47 B11
Wohlmirstedt D 95 D9
Wohltorf D 99 D8
Wöhrden D 98 B6
Wohyń PL 157 G7
Woippy F 42 B5
Wojaszówka PL 160 D4
Wojcieszków PL 157 G6
Wojcieszów PL 97 E9
Wójcin PL 154 E4
Wojkowice PL 159 F7
Wojnicz PL 159 G10
Wojnowo PL 154 D4

Wojsławice PL 160 B8
Woking GB 31 E7
Wokingham GB 31 E7
Wola PL 154 E7
Wola Mołodycka PL 160 C6
Wola Mysłowska PL 157 G5
Wolanów PL 157 H3
Wola Rębkowska PL 157 G5
Wola Uhruska PL 157 H9
Wola Wierzbowska PL 155 E10
Wolbórz PL 157 H1
Wolbrom PL 159 F8
Wołczyn PL 158 D5
Woldegk D 100 D5
Woldendorp NL 33 B8
Wolfach D 43 D9
Wolfegg D 87 B9
Wolfen D 95 C11
Wolfenbüttel D 95 B8
Wolfersheim D 37 D11
Wolfhagen D 33 F12
Wolfi's D 95 F9
Wolfpassing A 88 A3
Wolfsberg A 89 C10
Wolfsburg D 95 B8
Wolfstein D 37 E9
Wolfurt A 87 C9
Wolgast D 100 B5
Wolhusen CH 86 C6
Wolin D 100 C7
Wólka PL 155 E7
Wólka PL 157 H7
Wólka Dobryńska PL 157 F8
Wolkenstein D 97 D11
Wollaston GB 27 F11
Wollau CH 43 F11
Wolmirstedt D 95 B10
Wolnzach D 91 E11
Wołomin PL 155 F11
Woloskowola PL 157 H8
Wołów PL 97 D11
Wolpertshausen D 90 D6
Wolpertswende D 87 B9
Wolphaartsdijk NL 198 B3
Wölpinghausen D 33 D12
Wolsingham GB 21 F13
Wolsztyn PL 97 B10
Woltersdorf D 96 B4
Woltersdorf D 99 E10
Wolvega NL 32 C6
Wolverhampton GB 27 F7
Wombwell GB 27 D9
Wommelgem B 35 B10
Wommels NL 32 B5
Wonfurt D 91 B7
Wonsees D 91 C9
Woodbridge GB 31 C11
Woodcote GB 29 B12
Woodford IRL 22 F6
Woodhall Spa GB 27 E11
Woodland GB 21 F13
Woodley GB 31 E7
Woodstock GB 29 B12
Woodton GB 31 C11
Woodtown IRL 23 E9
Wool GB 29 D10
Wooler GB 21 D12
Wootton Bassett GB 29 B11
Worb CH 47 B12
Worbis D 95 D7
Worcester GB 29 A10
Wördern A 93 F10
Worfield GB 27 F7
Wörgl A 88 B5
Workington GB 21 F9
Worksop GB 27 D9
Workum NL 32 C4
Wörlitz D 95 C11
Wormeldange L 36 E6
Wormerveer NL 32 D3
Wormhout F 34 C5
Worms D 37 E10
Worpswede D 33 B11
Wörrstadt D 37 E10
Wörschach A 89 A9
Wörth A 89 B6
Wörth D 91 E8
Wörth am Main D 203 B7
Wörth am Rhein D 43 B9
Worthing GB 31 F8
Woudenberg NL 199 A6
Woudrichem NL 32 E3
Woudsend NL 32 C5
Woustviller F 43 B7
Wouw NL 32 E2
Woźniki PL 159 E7
Wragby GB 27 E11
Wrangle GB 27 E12
Wrecsam GB 26 E6
Wręczyca Wielka PL 159 E6
Wredenhagen D 99 D13
Wrelton GB 27 C10
Wremen D 33 A11
Wrestedt D 99 E9
Wrexham GB 26 E6
Wriedel D 99 D8
Wriezen D 100 E6
Wrist D 99 F7
Wróblew PL 158 C6
Wrocław PL 97 D12
Wrohm D 98 B6
Wronki PL 101 E10
Wronki PL 152 E5
Wrotnów PL 155 E13
Wrząelka PL 158 B6
Wrzelowiec PL 160 A4
Wrzeście PL 101 A12
Września PL 101 F13
Wrzosowo PL 101 B9
Wschowa PL 97 C10
Wulfen D 95 C10
Wulfersdorf D 92 E4
Wülfershausen an der Saale D 91 B7
Wulfsen D 99 D8
Wulften D 95 C7
Wulkau D 99 E12
Wullersdorf A 93 E9
Wundschuh A 164 C4
Wünnenberg D 33 E11
Wünsdorf D 96 B4
Wunsiedel D 91 B11
Wunstorf D 94 B5
Wuppertal D 33 F8
Wurmlingen D 43 E9
Würselen D 36 C6
Wurzbach D 91 B10
Wurzen D 95 D12
Wüstenrot D 43 B11

Wusterhausen D 99 E12
Wusterhusen D 100 B5
Wustermark D 95 A12
Wusterwitz D 95 B11
Wustrau-Altfriesack D 100 E3
Wustrow D 99 E9
Wustrow D 100 D3
Wustrow, Ostseebad D 99 B12
Wutha D 95 E7
Wutöschingen D 43 E9
Wuustwezel B 32 F2
Wyczechy PL 101 C12
Wydminy PL 152 F5
Wye GB 31 E10
Wygoda PL 159 D7
Wygon PL 101 D9
Wyhl D 43 D8
Wyk auf Föhr D 98 A5
Wylatowo PL 154 E4
Wylye GB 29 C11
Wymondham GB 31 B11
Wyre Piddle GB 29 A10
Wyrozęby-Konaty PL 157 F6
Wyry PL 159 F6
Wyryki-Połód PL 157 G8
Wyrzysk PL 101 D12
Wyśmierzyce PL 157 G3
Wysoka PL 101 D12
Wysoka PL 101 E8
Wysoka Kamieńska PL 101 C9
Wysokie PL 160 B6
Wysokie PL 160 B6
Wysokie Mazowieckie PL 157 E7
Wysowa PL 161 E3
Wyszanów PL 158 D5
Wyszki PL 157 E7
Wyszków PL 155 E11
Wyszogród PL 155 F9
Wyszyny PL 101 E11
Wytyczno PL 157 H8

X

Xanceda E 54 B3
Xanten D 33 E6
Xanthi GR 187 B7
Xarrë AL 184 E3
Xàtiva E 72 C3
Xeraco E 72 C4
Xeresa E 72 C4
Xermade E 54 B4
Xerta E 58 F5
Xertigny F 42 D5
Xifiani GR 185 C7
Xino Nero GR 185 C6
Xinzo de Limia E 54 D4
Xirivella E 64 F4
Xirochori GR 190 D4
Xirokampi GR 190 F5
Xirokampo GR 193 E8
Xiropotamos GR 186 B6
Xonrupt-Longemer F 43 D6
Xove E 54 A4
Xunqueira de Ambía E 54 D4
Xylagani GR 187 C8
Xylokastro GR 191 C6
Xyloupoli GR 185 C9

Y

Yablanitsa BG 181 C9
Yablanovo BG 183 D7
Yabluniv UA 168 A5
Yabŭlchevo BG 183 D8
Yabŭlkovo BG 182 E4
Yağcı TR 189 C7
Yağcılar TR 189 F8
Yağcılı TR 189 F8
Yagoda BG 182 D5
Yakimovo BG 176 F2
Yakoruda BG 181 E8
Yakovo BG 185 A9
Yalıçiftlik TR 189 D10
Yalıkavak TR 193 E9
Yalıköy TR 189 B9
Yalova TR 187 D10
Yambol BG 183 E7
Yamkino RUS 148 F5
Yamm RUS 148 E3
Yampil' UA 170 A2
Yangı TR 197 C9
Yanguas E 57 D7
Yanıkağıl TR 189 B8
Yaniskoski RUS 130 F5
Yankavichy BY 149 E5
Yankovo BG 183 D7
Yantarnyy RUS 155 A8
Yapıldak TR 188 D6
Yaraş TR 197 B8
Yareva BY 151 F13
Yarlovo BG 181 E7
Yarm GB 21 F13
Yarnton GB 29 B12
Yarrow GB 21 D10
Yarove UA 170 E4
Yasen BG 181 C10
Yasen' UA 161 A3
Yasenovo BG 183 B7
Yasenovets BG 177 F9
Yasinya UA 168 A4
Yas'ky UA 170 D4
Yasna Polyana BG 183 E9
Yasnoye RUS 152 E5
Yassıören TR 189 B10
Yasski RUS 148 F7
Yatağan TR 197 B8
Yate GB 29 B10
Yatova E 64 F3
Yatton GB 29 B9
Yavora UA 161 E7
Yavoriv UA 168 A5
Yaxley GB 27 F11
Yaylagöne TR 188 C6
Yazıbaşı TR 193 C10
Yazıköy TR 197 C6
Yazna BY 149 F7
Yazvina BY 149 F7
Ybbs an der Donau A 93 F8
Ybbsitz A 93 G7
Ychoux F 48 B4
Ydby DK 102 B2
Ydes F 45 E10
Ydra GR 191 E7
Ydrefors S 108 D7
Yealand DK 26 F5
Yealmpton GB 28 E7
Yebra E 63 D7

Wusterhausen D 99 E12
Yebra de Basa E 48 F5
Yecla E 72 D2
Yecla de Yeltes E 61 C8
Yedy BY 149 F2
Yémeda E 63 E9
Yemişendere TR 197 B9
Yenice TR 187 C10
Yenice TR 189 D7
Yenice TR 189 D7
Yenice TR 197 B8
Yeniçiftlik TR 189 B8
Yeniçiftlik TR 189 D7
Yeniçiftlik TR 193 C10
Yenifoça TR 193 B8
Yenihisar TR 193 E9
Yeniköy TR 188 D6
Yeniköy TR 189 A9
Yeniköy TR 189 B6
Yeniköy TR 189 B9
Yeniköy TR 193 B9
Yeniköy TR 193 B10
Yeniköy TR 193 C10
Yeniköy TR 193 D10
Yeniköy TR 197 B8
Yenimuhacirköy TR 188 C6
Yenişakran TR 193 B9
Yenne F 47 D8
Yeovil GB 29 D9
Yepes E 62 E5
Yerkesik TR 197 B8
Yersekе NL 32 F2
Yershovo RUS 148 F7
Yerville F 34 E2
Yesa E 48 E3
Yeşilsırt TR 189 B7
Yeşilyurt TR 197 B8
Yeste E 71 C7
Yevtodiya UA 170 B4
Yezyaryshcha BY 149 E7
Y Fenni GB 29 B8
Ygos-St-Saturnin F 48 C4
Ygrande F 46 B2
Ykspihlaja FIN 139 C10
Ylakiai LT 150 D3
Ylä-Luosta FIN 141 D11
Ylämaa FIN 145 D9
Ylämylly FIN 141 E11
Yläne FIN 142 D7
Ylä-Valtimo FIN 141 C11
Ylihärmä FIN 138 D9
Yli-Ii FIN 135 D15
Ylijärvi FIN 144 D8
Yli-Kärppä FIN 135 C15
Ylikiiminki FIN 135 D16
Yli-Körkkö FIN 135 B11
Ylikulma FIN 143 E9
Yli-Kurki FIN 137 D10
Yli-Lesti FIN 139 D13
Yli-Liakka FIN 135 C12
Yli-Livo FIN 136 C9
Yli-Muonio FIN 133 E16
Yli-Nampa FIN 133 E16
Ylinenjärvi S 133 E10
Yli-Olhava FIN 135 C15
Ylipää FIN 135 E13
Ylipää FIN 135 E13
Ylipää FIN 135 E13
Ylipää FIN 135 E14
Ylipää FIN 135 F13
Ylipää FIN 139 C13
Ylipää FIN 139 D11
Yli-Paakkola FIN 135 B13
Ylistaro FIN 138 D9
Yli-Siurua FIN 135 C17
Yli-Tannila FIN 135 D16
Ylitornio FIN 135 B11
Yli-Utos FIN 136 D8
Yli-Valli FIN 139 F9
Ylivieska FIN 139 B13
Yli-Vuotto FIN 135 E17
Ylläsjärvi FIN 133 C12
Ylöjärvi FIN 143 B10
Ylönkylä FIN 143 E9
Ylvingen N 124 E3
Ymonville F 40 D6
Yngsjö S 104 D6
Yoğuntaş TR 183 A8
Yolageldi TR 189 A6
Yonkovo BG 177 F9
York GB 27 D9
Youghal IRL 26 E7
Yovkovo BG 171 F2
Yoxford GB 31 C12
Ypäjä FIN 143 D9
Ypäjänkylä FIN 143 D9
Ypati GR 190 B5
Yport F 34 E1
Yppäri FIN 135 F12
Ypsos GR 184 E2
Ypyä FIN 139 C13
Yrittäperä FIN 137 D10
Yrttivaara S 132 E2
Ysane S 104 C7
Ysbyty Ystwyth GB 29 A7
Yset N 117 A12
Yssel E 58 D4
Yssel'steyn NL 199 C7
Yssingeaux F 46 E5
Ystad S 103 E13
Ystalyfera GB 29 B7
Ytre Arna N 110 B2
Ytre Billefjord N 129 C15
Ytre Kjæs N 129 B16
Ytre Sandvik N 129 C15
Ytterän S 121 D14
Ytterberg S 118 A7
Ytter-Busjö S 123 B15
Ytterhogdal S 118 B8
Ytterjeppo FIN 138 D8
Yttermalung S 118 E6
Ytterstat S 134 D6
Ytterträsk S 134 F4
Ytterturingen S 119 B9
Yttervik S 125 C13
Yttre Lansjärv S 132 F4
Yukanbey TR 193 A9
Yukanthos GR 190 D2
Yukarıkızılca TR 193 C9
Yukhavichy BY 149 E7
Yuncler E 62 D5
Yuncos E 62 D5
Yundola BG 181 E8
Yunquera E 69 C7
Yunquera de Henares E 63 C6

Yuper BG 177 F8
Yuratsishki BY 153 E12
Yuravichy BY 149 F5
Yürücekler TR 189 E10
Yürük TR 189 C7
Yuzhnyy RUS 152 D2
Yverdon CH 47 B10
Yvetot F 34 E2
Yvignac F 39 D7
Yvoir B 35 D10
Yvoire F 47 C9
Yvonand CH 47 B10
Yxnerum S 109 C8
Yxsjö S 123 C13
Yxsjöberg S 113 B12
Yxskaftkälen S 122 D8
Yzeure F 46 B3
Yzeures-sur-Creuse F 45 B7

Z

Zaamslag NL 198 C3
Zaandam NL 32 D3
Zaazyer"ye BY 149 F5
Zăbala RO 169 F8
Żabalj SRB 174 C5
Zabalova E 48 F1
Žabari SRB 175 E7
Zabeltitz-Treugeböhla D 96 D5
Żabia Wola PL 157 F3
Żabica BIH 178 D5
Žabice SLO 83 A9
Žabiele PL 155 D12
Zabierzów PL 159 F8
Ząbki PL 157 F4
Żabno PL 159 F10
Żabno PL 160 B6
Zabok HR 164 C7
Žabokreky SK 163 C7
Žabokreky nad Nitrou SK 162 D6
Zabór PL 97 C9
Zabor"ye BY 149 E6
Ząbów PL 101 D7
Żabowo PL 101 D8
Zăbrani RO 167 E8
Zăbreni MD 169 A10
Zábřeh CZ 93 C11
Ząbrowo PL 101 E10
Zabrze PL 158 F6
Zabŭrdo BG 181 F10
Zabuzhzhya UA 157 H9
Zacharo GR 190 E4
Zaclău RO 171 C2
Žacléř CZ 97 E9
Zaczopki PL 157 F8
Zadar HR 83 C11
Zadunayivka UA 170 F4
Zádveřice CZ 162 C5
Zadzim PL 158 C6
Zadzyezhzha BY 149 E4
Zafarraya E 69 C8
Zafferana Etnea I 75 D7
Zafirovo BG 177 E9
Zafra E 67 B7
Zafra de Záncara E 63 E7
Zafrilla E 63 D9
Żagań PL 97 C8
Żagare RO 168 E5
Żagareli SK 185 C9
Zagarise I 75 A10
Zagklivери GR 185 C9
Žaglav HR 83 E11
Zagnańsk PL 159 E10
Zagon RO 169 F8
Zagora GR 185 F9
Zagora SLO 89 A7
Zagorje ob Savi SLO 89 D10
Zagórów PL 158 B4
Zagortsi BG 183 E8
Zagórz PL 161 D5
Zagra RO 168 C4
Zagra RO 168 C4
Zagrazhden BG 176 F5
Zagrazhden BG 182 F3
Zagreb HR 164 E5
Žagrović HR 172 D5
Zagvozd HR 173 F7
Žagubica SRB 175 E8
Zagvozd HR 173 F7
Zagvárékas H 166 C5
Zahara E 67 F9
Zahara de los Atunes E 68 D5
Zahinos E 67 C6
Zahna D 95 C12
Zahnitkiv UA 170 A3
Záhony H 161 G5
Záhorská Ves SK 93 F11
Zahor"ye BY 149 E5
Zăicani MD 169 B10
Zaiceva LV 149 B2
Zaidín E 58 D4
Żaiginys LT 150 F6
Zaim MD 170 D6
Zajas MK 184 A4
Zaječar SRB 175 F9
Zaječov CZ 92 C5
Zákamené SK 163 C8
Zákány H 165 D7
Zakaryan SRB 175 F7
Zakhar'ino BY 149 F5
Zákinthos GR 190 D2
Zaklíczyn PL 160 D1
Zaklików PL 160 B5
Zakłopača BIH 173 D11
Zakoma BIH 173 D6
Zakopane PL 163 B9
Zakros GR 195 E11
Zakrzew PL 157 H4
Zakrzew PL 160 B5
Zakrzewo PL 101 D13
Zakrzewo PL 154 E5
Zakrzów-Wieś PL 160 B5
Zákupy CZ 97 E7
Zala HR 173 F6
Zalaapáti H 165 C6
Zalaegerszeg H 165 C7
Zalakaros H 165 C6
Zalakomár H 165 C7
Zalalövő H 165 C7

Zalaszántó H 165 C8
Zalaszentbalázs H 165 C7
Zalaszentgrót H 165 C7
Zalaszentiván H 165 C7
Zalău RO 167 C11
Zalavár H 165 C8
Zalavas LT 153 D13
Załazy PL 157 H5
Zaldíbar E 57 B6
Žalec SLO 89 D11
Załenięki LV 150 C5
Zalesie PL 101 E13
Zalesie PL 157 F8
Zalesie Śląskie PL 158 F5
Zalęsje LV 149 C4
Zales'ye RUS 152 D4
Zaleszany PL 160 B4
Zalewo PL 155 C8
Zalha RO 168 C3
Zālīte LV 151 C8
Zalivnoye RUS 152 D2
Zaltbommel NL 32 E4
Žalužije BIH 174 E3
Zalužnica HR 172 C3
Zalve LV 151 D10
Zalyessye BY 149 F3
Zalyessye BY 153 E13
Zam RO 167 E9
Zamárdi H 165 C9
Zamarte PL 101 C12
Žamberk CZ 93 B10
Zambrana E 56 C6
Zâmbreasca RO 176 E6
Zambrów PL 156 E6
Zambujal de Cima P 66 C1
Zambujeira do Mar P 66 D2
Zamęcin PL 101 D9
Zamfirovo BG 181 C7
Zamogil'ye RUS 148 D2
Zámoly H 165 B10
Zamora E 55 E8
Zamość PL 155 D12
Zamość PL 160 B7
Zamoshsha BY 149 F2
Zamostea RO 169 B8
Zams A 87 C11
Zámutov SK 161 F4
Zandhoven B 35 B10
Zandov CZ 96 E6
Zandvliet B 32 F1
Zandvoort NL 32 D3
Zanести RO 169 D9
Zaniemyśl B 97 B12
Zante LV 150 C5
Zaorejas E 63 C9
Zaovine SRB 174 F3
Zapałów PL 160 C6
Zaplanik BIH 178 E6
Zaplyus'e RUS 148 E6
Zăpodeni RO 169 D11
Zapole PL 158 C6
Zapolyarnyy RUS 130 E3
Zapol'ye RUS 148 E4
Zaporozhskoye RUS 145 D14
Zappeio GR 185 F7
Zapponeta I 76 A5
Zaprešić HR 164 E5
Zapruddze BY 149 F3
Zapytiv UA 160 B5
Zaragoza E 57 E10
Zărand RO 167 E9
Zarańsko PL 101 C9
Zaratamo E 56 B6
Zaratán E 55 E10
Zarautz E 48 D1
Zarcilla de Ramos E 71 D9
Zaręby PL 155 D11
Zaręby-Kościelne PL 155 E13
Zarechcha BY 149 E7
Zărеnai LT 150 F4
Zaricheve UA 161 F6
Żarki PL 159 E7
Żarki Wielkie PL 97 C7
Zărnești RO 176 B6
Zărnești RO 177 C9
Zarnovica SK 163 D7
Żarnów PL 157 H2
Zarnowiec PL 159 F8
Zaronava BY 149 F7
Zaros GR 194 E4
Żarošice CZ 93 E11
Żarów PL 97 E10
Zarpen D 99 C9
Zarra E 63 F10
Zarren B 198 C1
Zarrentin D 99 C9
Zarszyn PL 161 D5
Žáry PL 97 C8
Zarza Capilla E 67 B9
Zarza de Alange E 67 B7
Zarza de Granadilla E 61 D8
Zarza de Tajo E 63 D6
Zarzadilla de Totana E 71 D9
Zarza la Mayor E 61 D6
Zarzecze PL 160 D6
Zarzuela del Monte E 62 C4
Zarzuela del Pinar E 56 F3
Zas E 54 B2
Zasa LV 151 D11
Zaskarki BY 149 F5
Žaškov SK 163 D7
Žasliai LT 153 D10
Zásmuky CZ 93 C8
Zasów PL 159 F11
Zastražišče HR 173 F6
Žatec CZ 92 B5
Zaton HR 172 D4
Zaton HR 178 E6
Zátor CZ 158 F4
Zatory PL 155 F10
Zátreni RO 176 D3
Zatyshshya UA 170 C3
Zaube LV 151 C10
Zau de Câmpie RO 168 D4
Zavadka UA 161 E7
Závadka nad Hronom SK 163 D9
Zavala BIH 178 D4
Zavala HR 173 F6
Zavalje BIH 172 C4
Zavalla UA 169 A7
Zavallya UA 170 A6
Zavattarello I 53 B10
Zaventem B 35 C9
Zavet BG 177 F9
Zavidoviči BIH 173 D9

Zavlaka SRB 174 E3
Zăvoaia RO 177 D10
Závod SK 93 E12
Zăvoi RO 175 B9
Zavoj SRB 181 C7
Zavutstsye BY 149 F4
Zavyachellye BY 149 F5
Zavydovychi UA 160 D8
Zawada PL 97 C9
Zawada PL 157 G1
Zawada PL 158 E4
Zawada PL 159 E7
Zawada PL 160 B7
Zawady PL 156 D7
Zawadzkie PL 158 E5
Zawichost PL 160 B4
Zawidów PL 97 D8
Zawidz Kościelny PL 155 E8
Zawiercie PL 159 F7
Zawoja PL 163 B9
Zawonia PL 97 D12
Zaytsevo RUS 148 F4
Žažina HR 164 E6
Zázrivá SK 163 C8
Žažvic HR 172 E4
Zbąszyn PL 97 B9
Zbąszynek PL 97 B9
Zbehy SK 162 E6
Zberoaia MD 169 D12
Zbiczno PL 155 D7
Zbiersk PL 158 C5
Zbiroh CZ 92 C5
Zblewo PL 154 C5
Zbludowice PL 159 F10
Zbójna PL 155 D12
Zbójno PL 155 D7
Zborov RUS 161 B3
Zborovice CZ 162 C4
Zbraslav CZ 93 D10
Zbraslavice CZ 93 C8
Zbrzeźnica PL 156 D6
Zbuczyn Poduchowny PL 157 F6
Ždala HR 165 D8
Žďánice CZ 93 D12
Žďár CZ 93 A8
Žďár nad Sázavou CZ 93 C9
Zdenci HR 165 E9
Ždiar SK 161 E1
Zdice CZ 92 C5
Zdihovo HR 83 B11
Zdíkov CZ 92 D5
Žďírec nad Doubravou CZ 93 C9
Zdounky CZ 162 C4
Ždralovac BIH 173 E6
Zdravets BG 183 C9
Zdravinje SRB 180 C3
Ždrelac HR 172 D3
Ždrelo SRB 175 E8
Zdunje MK 180 F3
Zduńska Wola PL 159 C6
Zduny PL 97 C12
Zduny PL 157 F1
Zdynia PL 161 E3
Zdziarzec PL 159 F11
Zdziechowa PL 101 E13
Zdzieszowice PL 158 F5
Zdzisłowice PL 160 B6
Zębowice PL 158 E5
Żebrák CZ 92 C5
Zebreira P 61 E6
Zebrene LV 150 C5
Zebrzydowa PL 97 D8
Zechlin Dorf D 99 D13
Zechlinerhütte D 100 D3
Zeddam NL 199 B8
Zeddiani I 80 D2

Zedelgem B 35 B7
Zederhaus A 89 B8
Žednik SRB 166 F4
Żędowice PL 158 E6
Zeebrugge B 35 B7
Zeeland NL 32 E5
Zeewolde NL 199 A7
Zegama E 48 E1
Żegiestów PL 161 G5
Žegocina PL 160 D1
Žegra SRB 180 E3
Zehdenick D 100 E4
Zehna D 99 C12
Žehra SK 161 F2
Zehren D 96 D4
Zeilarn D 92 F3
Žeimelis LT 151 D8
Žeimiai LT 151 F8
Zeiselmauer A 93 F10
Zeiskam D 203 C5
Zeist NL 32 D4
Zeithain D 96 D4
Zeitlofs D 90 B6
Zeitz D 95 D11
Zejmen AL 179 F8
Želazków PL 158 C5
Zele B 35 B9
Żelechlinek PL 157 G2
Żelechów PL 157 G5
Zelena UA 168 A5
Zelena UA 168 A5
Zelena UA 169 A9
Zelenče SK 162 E5
Zeleni Jadar BIH 174 E3
Zelenikovo BG 182 E4
Zelenikovo MK 180 F4
Zelenogorsk RUS 145 E12
Zelenogradsk RUS 152 D1
Zelenohirs'ke UA 170 B6
Żeletava CZ 93 D9
Železná Ruda CZ 92 D4
Železné SK 163 D8
Železnice CZ 93 B8
Železniki SLO 89 D9
Železný Brod CZ 97 E8
Zelhem NL 32 D6
Želiezovce SK 163 E7
Zelina HR 164 E6
Zelinja BIH 173 C9
Želino MK 180 F3
Željuša BIH 173 F8
Żelków-Kolonia PL 157 F6
Zell D 91 B10
Zell (Mosel) D 37 D8
Zella-Mehlis D 95 E8
Zell am Harmersbach D 43 D9
Zell am Main D 203 B8
Zell am See A 89 B6
Zell am Ziller A 88 B4
Zell im Wiesental D 43 E10
Zellingen D 90 C6
Zell-Pfarre A 89 D9
Zelmeni LV 150 D6
Želovce SK 163 E8
Zelów PL 159 D7
Zeltingen-Rachtig D 37 E8
Zeltini LV 151 B13
Zeltweg A 89 B10
Želva LT 151 F10
Zelzate B 35 B8
Žemaičiu Naumiestis LT 150 F3
Žemberovce SK 163 E7
Zemblak AL 184 C4
Zembrów PL 157 E6
Zembrzyce PL 163 B9

Zemen BG 181 E6
Zemeno GR 191 C6
Zemeş RO 161 D9
Zemianska Olča SK 162 F5
Zemîte LV 150 C5
Zemitz D 100 C5
Zemmer D 37 E7
Zemné SK 162 F6
Zemplénagárd H 161 G5
Zemplínske Hámre SK 161 F5
Zemst B 35 C9
Zemun SRB 174 D5
Zenica BIH 173 D8
Zennor GB 28 E3
Zentene LV 150 B5
Žepa BIH 173 E11
Žepče BIH 173 D9
Žeravice CZ 162 C4
Zerbst D 95 C11
Zerf D 37 E7
Zerind RO 167 D9
Żerków PL 158 B4
Zernez CH 87 D10
Zernien D 99 D9
Zernitz D 99 E12
Zero Branco I 88 E5
Zerpenschleuse D 100 E5
Zerrenthin D 100 D5
Zestoa E 48 D1
Žetale SLO 164 D5
Zetea RO 161 E6
Zetel D 33 B9
Zeťovo BG 182 E4
Zeulenroda D 95 E10
Zeven D 33 B12
Zevenaar NL 32 E6
Zevenbergen NL 32 E3
Zevgolatio GR 191 D6
Zevio I 82 B3
Zeytinalanı TR 197 C9
Zeytinbağı TR 189 D10
Zeytindağ TR 193 B9
Zeytineli TR 193 C8
Zeytinli TR 189 E6
Zeytinliova TR 193 B10
Zgierz PL 159 C9
Zgłobice PL 159 G10
Zgornje Bitnje SLO 89 D9
Zgornje Jezersko SLO 89 D9
Zgornji Duplek SLO 164 C5
Zgorzelec PL 97 D8
Zgropolci MK 185 A6
Žgurița MD 169 A11
Zhabinka BY 157 F10
Zhabokrychka UA 170 A3
Zheleznodorozhnyy RUS 152 E3
Zhelyazkovo BG 183 D6
Zhelyu Voyvoda BG 183 D6
Zheravna BG 183 D6
Zhilino RUS 152 E1
Zhitkovo RUS 145 D11
Zhitnitsa BG 183 C9
Zhitom AL 184 C2
Zhodzishki BY 153 D13
Zhorany UA 157 H9
Zhovkva UA 160 C9
Zhovtantsi UA 160 D9
Zhovtneve UA 161 B3
Zhovtneve UA 171 B3
Zhovtyy Yar UA 170 F3
Zhuprany BY 153 E13
Zhvyrka UA 160 C9
Zhydachiv UA 161 E9
Zhyrmuny BY 153 E11
Žiar nad Hronom SK 163 D7
Zibalai LT 153 C10

Zibello I 82 B1
Zibreira P 60 F3
Zicavo F 53 H10
Žichovice CZ 92 D5
Zidani Most SLO 89 D11
Zidarovo BG 183 D6
Žídikai LT 150 D4
Židlochovice CZ 93 D11
Ziduri RO 177 C10
Žiębice PL 97 E12
Ziedkalne LV 150 D6
Ziegelroda D 95 D9
Ziegendorf D 99 D11
Ziegenrück D 95 E10
Ziegra D 96 D4
Zieleniewo PL 101 B9
Zieleniewo PL 101 D9
Zielitz D 95 C11
Zielkowice PL 157 F2
Zielona PL 155 D8
Zielona Chocina PL 101 C12
Zielona Góra PL 97 C9
Zielona Góra PL 101 E11
Zielonka PL 155 F11
Zielonki PL 159 F8
Zieluń PL 155 D8
Ziemeris LV 147 F14
Ziemnice Wielkie PL 158 E4
Ziemupe LV 150 C2
Zierenberg D 33 F12
Zierikzee NL 32 E1
Ziersdorf A 93 E9
Zierzow D 99 D11
Ziesar D 95 B11
Ziežmariai LT 153 D9
Žigljen HR 83 C10
Žiguri LV 149 B3
Žihárec SK 162 E5
Žihle CZ 92 B4
Zilaiskalns LV 147 F10
Žilina SK 163 C7
Žilinai LT 153 E10
Zillis CH 87 D8
Ziltendorf D 97 B7
Zilupe LV 149 D4
Zimandu Nou RO 167 E7
Zimbor RO 167 C11
Zimmersrode (Neuental) D 37 B12
Zimnicea RO 176 F6
Zimnitsa BG 183 D7
Žindaičiai LT 150 F5
Zingst am Darß, Ostseebad D 99 B13
Zinkgruvan S 108 B6
Zinnowitz D 100 B5
Ziras LV 150 B3
Zirc H 165 B9
Zirchow D 100 C6
Žiri SLO 89 D9
Zirndorf D 91 D8
Zirnești MD 170 E2
Zirņi LV 149 D4
Ziros GR 195 E11
Žirovnice CZ 93 D8
Zistersdorf A 93 E11
Žitište SRB 174 C5
Žitkovac SRB 180 C4
Žitni Potok SRB 180 C4
Žitomislići BIH 173 F8
Žitorsđa SRB 180 C4
Žitoše MK 184 B5
Zitsa GR 184 E4
Zittau D 97 E7
Zitz D 95 B11
Živaja HR 173 B6

Živinice BIH 173 D10
Živogošće HR 173 F7
Žiželice CZ 93 B8
Zizers CH 87 D9
Zizurkil E 48 D1
Zlarin HR 172 E4
Zlata SRB 180 C5
Zlatar BG 183 C7
Zlatar HR 164 D6
Zlatar-Bistrica HR 164 D6
Zlataritsa BG 182 C5
Zlaté Hory CZ 158 F3
Zlaté Klasy SK 162 E4
Zlaté Moravce SK 162 E6
Zlaten Rog BG 175 E10
Zlatna RO 167 E11
Zlatna Panega BG 181 C9
Zlatograd BG 187 B8
Zlatokop SRB 180 D4
Zławieś Wielka PL 154 D5
Žlebič SLO 89 E10
Žleby CZ 93 C8
Zlēkas LV 150 D4
Zliobinai LT 150 E4
Zlín CZ 162 C5
Zliv CZ 92 D6
Žljebovi BIH 173 D10
Złocieniec PL 101 C10
Złoczew PL 158 D6
Zlokućane SRB 179 D10
Zlokuchene BG 181 E8
Zlonice CZ 92 B6
Złota PL 157 G2
Złota PL 159 F10
Złotniki Kujawskie PL 154 E5
Złotoryja PL 97 D9
Złotów PL 101 D12
Złoty Stok PL 93 B11
Zlozela BIH 173 D7
Žlutice CZ 92 B4
Zmajevac BIH 172 C5
Zmajevac HR 165 E11
Zmajevo SRB 174 C4
Zmeyovo BG 182 E5
Žmigród PL 97 D11
Žmijavci HR 173 F7
Žminj HR 83 B8
Żmudź PL 160 A8
Zmamensk RUS 152 D3
Żnin PL 154 E4
Znojmo CZ 93 E10
Zoagli I 53 C10
Zöblitz D 96 E4
Zoelen NL 199 B6
Zoersel B 32 F3
Zoetermeer NL 32 D2
Zofingen CH 43 F8
Zogno I 85 B9
Zografou GR 191 D8
Zola Predosa I 82 C3
Zolder B 35 B11
Zoldo Alto I 88 D5
Żółkiewka-Osada PL 160 B6
Zölkow D 99 C11
Zollikofen CH 47 A11
Zollikon CH 43 F10
Zolotkovychi UA 160 D6
Żółynia PL 160 C5
Zomba H 165 D11
Zomergem B 35 B8
Zonhoven B 35 C11
Zoni GR 187 A10
Zoniana GR 194 E3
Zonnebeke B 34 C6
Zonza F 53 H10

Żórawina PL 97 E12
Zörbig D 95 C11
Županja HR 173 B10
Žur SRB 179 E10
Žūras LV 150 B3
Zürich CH 43 F10
Zürnevo BG 177 F10
Zörnigall D 95 C12
Zorleni RO 169 E11
Zorlenţu Mare RO 175 C8
Zorneding D 91 F10
Zornheim D 37 E10
Zornitsa BG 183 C9
Żory PL 158 F6
Zossen D 96 B4
Zottegem B 35 C8
Zoutkamp NL 32 B6
Zoutleeuw B 199 D6
Zovi Do BIH 173 F9
Zovka RUS 148 E4
Zreče SLO 164 D4
Zrenjanin SRB 174 C5
Zrin HR 172 C5
Zrinski Topolovac HR 165 D7
Zrmanja Vrelo HR 172 D5
Zrnovci MK 180 F5
Zruč CZ 92 B4
Zruč nad Sázavou CZ 93 C8
Zsadány H 167 D7
Zsáka H 167 C7
Zsámbék H 165 A11
Zsámbok H 166 B4
Zsana H 166 E4
Zscherben D 95 D10
Zschopau D 96 E4
Zschortau D 95 D11
Zsombó H 166 E4
Zuberec SK 163 C9
Zubia E 69 B9
Zubiaur E 56 B6
Zubiči BIH 173 D8
Zubiena I 84 C5
Zubieta E 48 D1
Zubin Potok SRB 179 D10
Zubiri E 48 E2
Zubří CZ 162 C6
Zubrohlava SK 163 C9
Żuchlów PL 97 B8
Žuć SRB 180 C3
Zucaina E 64 D4
Zuchwil CH 43 F8
Zudaire E 48 E1
Zudar D 100 B4
Zufre E 67 D7
Zug CH 43 F10
Zuhatzu-Kuartango E 56 C6
Zuheros E 69 B8
Zuid-Beijerland NL 198 B4
Zuidhorn NL 32 B6
Zuidland NL 198 B4
Zuidlaren NL 33 B7
Zuidwolde NL 33 C6
Zuienkerke B 198 C2
Zújar E 71 D7
Żuków PL 157 F2
Żuków PL 157 F9
Żukowice PL 160 D6
Żukowo PL 154 B5
Żuljana HR 178 D3
Žulová CZ 93 B12
Zülpich D 37 C7
Zulte B 35 C7
Zumaia E 48 D1
Zumarraga E 48 D1
Zundert NL 32 F3
Zungri I 75 B8

Zunzarren E 48 E3
Zuoz CH 87 D9
Zúrgena E 71 E8
Zurndorf A 93 G12
Zurow D 99 C11
Zurzach CH 43 E9
Zusmarshausen D 91 F8
Züssow D 100 C5
Žuta Lokva HR 83 C11
Žutautai LT 150 E2
Zutendaal B 35 C12
Zutphen NL 32 D6
Žužemberk SLO 89 E10
Zvečan SRB 179 D10
Zvejniekciems LV 151 B8
Zverino BG 181 D8
Zvezdal AL 184 C4
Zvezdel BG 187 A8
Zvezdets BG 183 E8
Zvolen SK 163 D8
Zvolenská Slatina SK 163 D8
Zvonce SRB 180 D6
Zvorişte RO 169 B8
Zvornik BIH 173 D11
Zwartemeer NL 33 C8
Zwartsluis NL 32 C6
Zweeloo NL 33 C7
Zweibrücken D 37 E8
Zweisimmen CH 47 B11
Zwenkau D 95 D11
Zwethau D 96 C4
Zwettl A 93 E8
Zwevegem B 35 C7
Zwevezele B 198 C2
Zwickau D 95 E12
Zwiefalten D 43 D11
Zwierzyn PL 101 E9
Zwierzyniec PL 160 B6
Zwiesel D 92 D4
Zwijndrecht B 35 B9
Zwijndrecht NL 32 E3
Zwinge D 95 D7
Zwingen CH 43 F8
Zwingenberg D 37 E11
Zwochau D 95 D11
Zwoleń PL 157 H5
Zwolle NL 32 C6
Zwönitz D 95 E12
Zwota D 91 B11
Zyabki BY 149 F4
Zyal'ki BY 149 F4
Zyalyonka BY 149 E5
Zychlin PL 159 B8
Żydowo PL 101 B11
Żydowo PL 101 F13
Žygaičiai LT 150 F4
Zygos GR 187 B6
Zygry PL 159 C6
Žyniai LT 150 F4
Żyraków PL 159 F11
Żyrardów PL 157 F2
Żyrzyn PL 157 H6
Żytkiejmy PL 152 E6
Żytniów PL 158 D6
Žytno PL 159 E8
Żywiec PL 163 B8
Żywocice PL 158 F4

Æ

Ærøskøbing DK 102 F6

Ø

Ødis DK 102 E4
Ødsted DK 102 D4
Øie N 121 B12
Økdal N 117 A12
Øksfjord N 128 C9
Øksnes N 126 C8
Øksneshamn N 126 D9
Ølen N 110 C3
Ølgod DK 102 D3
Ølholm DK 102 D5
Ølsted DK 102 D5
Ølstykke DK 103 D10
Ønslev DK 99 A11
Øra N 128 C8
Ørbæk DK 102 E7
Ørgenvika N 111 B11
Ørjavik N 120 F2
Ørje N 112 D6
Ørnes N 124 C6
Ørnhøj DK 102 C3
Ørslev DK 103 E9
Ørsnes N 116 A5
Ørsta N 116 B4
Ørsted DK 102 C6
Ørting DK 102 D6
Ørum DK 102 C5
Ørum DK 102 C7
Øsby DK 102 E5
Østbirk DK 102 D5
Østby N 107 A9
Østby N 118 D4
Østengård DK 102 D4
Øster Assels DK 102 B3
Øster Bjerregrav DK 102 C5
Øster Brønderslev DK 102 B5
Østerby DK 102 A5
Øster Hornum DK 102 B5
Øster Hurup DK 102 B6
Øster Højst DK 102 E4
Østerild DK 102 A3
Øster Jølby DK 102 B3
Østerlars DK 105 E7
Øster Lindet DK 102 E4
Øster Tørslev DK 102 C6
Øster Ulslev DK 99 A11
Øster Vedsted DK 102 E3
Østervrå DK 106 E7
Øster Vrøgum DK 102 D2
Østese N 110 B4
Østrup DK 102 B4
Øvergård N 127 C17
Øvrebygd N 127 B18

Øvre Alta N 129 D11
Øvre Kildal N 128 D7
Øvrella N 111 C10
Øvre Rendal N 117 C14
Øvre Årdal N 116 D12
Øvre Åstbru N 117 D13
Øyangen N 120 E7
Øydegarden N 120 E4
Øyenkilen N 107 A8
Øyer N 117 D12
Øyeren N 112 B7
Øyjord N 124 B9
Øynes N 124 B9
Øynes N 127 C11
Øyslebø N 106 C2
Øyvatnet N 127 C12

Å

Å N 120 F7
Å N 126 E4
Å N 127 B12
Å N 127 C13
Åberget S 125 E18
Åbo S 119 C10
Åbodarna S 123 E14
Åbogen N 112 B7
Åbosjö S 123 D13
Åby S 105 A7
Åby S 109 B8
Åbyen DK 106 D7
Åbyggeby S 119 E13
Åbyn S 134 D6
Åbytorp S 108 A6
Ådalsliden S 123 E11
Ådum DK 102 D3
Åfarnes N 116 A7
Åfjord N 120 D8
Åfoss N 106 A6
Ågerup DK 103 D10
Ågotnes N 110 B2
Ågskaret N 124 C5
Åheim N 116 B3
Åhus S 104 D6
Åkarp S 103 D12
Åkerbränna S 123 D11
Åkerby S 115 B9
Åkerholmen S 134 C6
Åkersberga S 115 D10
Åkers styckebruk S 114 D8
Åkerström N 117 C14
Åknes N 126 C9
Åkran N 121 D12
Åkrehamn N 110 D2
Åkullsjön S 134 C5
Åkvisslan S 123 E13
Ål N 117 E9
Ålberga S 109 B9
Ålbo S 114 D7
Ålbæk DK 106 D7
Åle DK 102 D5

Åled S 103 B11
Ålem S 105 B10
Ålen N 117 A14
Ålesund N 116 B4
Ålgnäs S 119 D12
Ålgård N 110 E3
Ålhult S 108 D7
Ålloluokta S 125 B17
Ålmo N 120 E4
Ålsrode DK 103 C7
Ålstad N 126 D9
Ålund S 134 D6
Ålvik N 110 B4
Ålvund N 117 A9
Ålvundeid N 117 A9
Ålåsen S 122 D7
Åmdals Verk N 111 D4
Åminne FIN 138 E7
Åminne S 103 A14
Åmland N 110 F5
Åmli N 106 A3
Åmli N 106 B3
Åmmeberg S 108 B6
Åmot N 110 C7
Åmot N 111 B11
Åmot N 111 C11
Åmot S 103 A10
Åmotfors S 112 C7
Åmsele S 123 B16
Åmsosen N 110 D3
Åmynnet S 123 E15
Åmål S 107 A12
Åmål S 107 B12
Åmøyhamn N 124 C5
Åna-Sira N 110 F4
Åndalsnes N 116 A7
Åneby N 111 B13
Ånes N 120 E4
Ånge S 119 A10
Ånge S 125 E14
Ångersjö S 113 C15
Ångersjö S 118 C8
Ånn S 121 E13
Ånsvik N 125 B9
Ånäset S 134 F6
Åpta N 110 C7
Årby DK 103 D8
Årbyn S 134 C6
Årdal N 116 C4
Årdalstangen N 116 D7
Åre S 121 E14
Årför N 121 B11
Årgård N 121 C10
Århult S 105 A10
Århus DK 102 C6
Årjäng S 112 C5
Årnes N 111 B14
Årnes N 120 F5
Årnes N 127 B15
Årnäs S 107 B14

Åros N 111 C12
Årosjåkk S 127 E17
Årre DK 102 D3
Årrenjarka S 125 C15
Årsandøy N 121 A12
Årsdale DK 105 E4
Årset N 121 C11
Årslev DK 102 E6
Årstein N 127 C14
Årsunda S 114 A7
Årvik N 116 B3
Årviksand N 128 C6
Årvågen N 120 E5
Åryd S 105 B7
Åryd S 105 C8
Årøybukta N 127 A19
Årøysund N 106 A7
Ås N 111 C13
Ås N 121 E11
Ås S 112 C7
Ås S 113 C12
Ås S 122 E7
Ås S 123 E11
Åsa N 111 C13
Åsa S 107 E11
Åsan N 121 B12
Åsarna S 118 A7
Åsby S 103 A10
Åse N 127 B10
Åsebyn S 112 D7
Åseda S 105 A8
Åsegg N 121 C9
Åsele S 123 C12
Åselet S 134 D4
Åsen N 121 D10
Åsen S 118 D6
Åsen S 125 E16
Åsenbruk S 107 B11
Åseral N 106 B1
Åshammar S 119 E12
Åskilje S 123 B13
Åskogen S 134 C7
Åsli N 117 E11
Åsljunga S 103 C12
Åsmansbo S 113 B13
Åsmarka N 117 D11
Åsskard S 120 E5
Åsta N 117 D14
Åstan N 120 E7
Åsteby S 113 B9
Åstorp S 103 C11
Åstrand S 113 B9
Återvänningen S 119 A13
Åtorp S 108 A4
Åträsk S 134 B7
Åträsk S 134 D5
Åttonträsk S 123 C14
Åtvidaberg S 108 C7
Åva FIN 142 E5
Åvestbo S 113 C14

Åvist FIN 138 D9

Ä

Äetsä FIN 142 C8
Ähtäri FIN 139 E12
Ähtärinranta FIN 139 E12
Äijäjoki FIN 132 B10
Äijälä FIN 139 E16
Äkäsjokisuu FIN 133 C11
Äkäslompolo FIN 133 C12
Älandsbro S 119 A14
Älgarås S 108 B7
Älgered S 119 B12
Älghult S 105 A9
Älmestad S 107 D13
Älmhult S 104 B6
Älmsta S 115 C11
Älta S 115 D11
Älvdalen S 118 D7
Älvho S 118 D6
Älvkarleby S 119 E13
Älvkarleö S 115 A8
Älvros S 118 B5
Älvsbyn S 134 C4
Älvsered S 103 A11
Älvängen S 107 D11
Ämmälänkylä FIN 139 E9
Ämmänsaari FIN 137 E12
Åmådalen S 118 D8
Äng S 121 E16
Ängbe S 119 C11
Ängelholm S 103 C11
Ängersjö S 118 D8
Ängeslevä FIN 135 E15
Ängesträsk S 134 B6
Ängeså S 132 E8
Ängom S 119 B13
Äppelbo S 113 B11
Ärla S 114 D7
Ärnäs S 118 D5
Ärtrik S 123 E11
Ärtled S 119 E9
Åsarp S 107 C14
Äsbacka S 119 D11
Äsbjörka S 119 E9
Äsby S 113 D13
Äsköping S 108 A8
Äsjö S 119 B12
Ätran S 103 A11
Äyskoski FIN 139 E15
Äystö FIN 138 F7
Äänekoski FIN 139 E15

Ö

Öckerö S 107 D10
Ödeborg S 107 B10
Ödeshog S 108 C5
Ödkarby FIN 115 B13

Ödsmål S 107 C10
Ödåkra S 103 C11
Öja FIN 139 C9
Öja S 109 E12
Öjarn S 122 D8
Öjebyn S 134 C6
Öjeforsen S 119 B9
Öjingsvallen S 119 C8
Öjung S 119 C10
Öksajärvi S 132 C5
Öllölä FIN 141 F15
Ölmbrotorp S 113 D13
Ölme S 113 D11
Ölsboda S 108 A4
Ömossa FIN 138 F7
Önnestad S 104 C6
Öratjärn S 119 C10
Öravan S 123 B14
Öravattnet S 122 E9
Örbyhus S 115 B9
Örbäck S 118 C4
Örebro S 113 D13
Öregrund S 115 B10
Öreström S 123 C16
Öretjändalen S 119 A10
Örkelljunga S 103 C12
Örnsköldsvik S 123 E15
Örnäsudden S 123 D17
Örsbäck S 123 D17
Örserum S 108 C5
Örsjö S 105 B8
Örsundsbro S 115 C8
Örträsk S 123 C15
Örviken S 134 E6
Ösmo S 109 B11
Östa S 114 B7
Östanfjärden S 135 C10
Östansjö S 108 A5
Östanskär S 119 A13
Östanvik S 119 D9
Östanå S 104 C6
Östavall S 119 B9
Östbjörka S 119 E9
Östby S 123 D13
Österbybruk S 115 B9
Österbymo S 108 D6
Österede S 123 E11
Österfärnebo S 114 B7
Östergran S 109 E13
Österhankmo FIN 138 D7
Österjörn S 134 D4
Österlisa S 115 C11
Östermark FIN 142 E8
Östernoret S 123 C12
Östero FIN 138 D8
Österskucku S 118 A8

Östersund S 122 E7
Östersundom FIN 143 E13
Östervåla S 114 B8
Österås S 123 E12
Östhammar S 115 B10
Östloning S 119 A13
Östmark S 113 B8
Östmarkum S 123 E14
Östnor S 118 D7
Östra Ed S 109 C9
Östra Frölunda S 107 E13
Östra Granberg S 134 C4
Östra Grevie S 103 D12
Östra Husby S 109 B9
Östra Ljungby S 103 C12
Östra Lovsjön S 122 D7
Östra Ljusne S 113 C13
Östra Ormsjö S 123 C10
Östra Ryd S 109 C8
Östra Skråmträsk S 134 E5
Östra Stugusjö S 119 A9
Östra Sönnarslöv S 104 D6
Östra Vemmerlöv S 104 D6
Östra Yttermark FIN 138 E6
Östra Åliden S 134 D4
Överammer S 123 E9
Överberg S 118 B7
Överbyn S 119 C12
Överhogdal S 118 B8
Överhörnäs S 123 E15
Överissjö S 123 C13
Överkalix S 135 B8
Överlida S 107 E12
Överlännäs S 123 E12
Övermalax FIN 138 E7
Övermark FIN 138 E6
Övermorjärv S 134 B9
Övernäs S 125 D14
Överstbyn S 134 B7
Övertorneå S 135 B8
Överturingen S 118 B8
Övertänger S 119 E10
Överum S 109 D8
Överäng S 121 D14
Överö FIN 115 B15
Öv Långträsk S 123 E16
Övra S 123 D11
Övre Bredåker S 134 C6
Övre-Konås S 121 D14
Övre Soppero S 132 B7
Övre Tväråsel S 134 C5
Övsjöbyn S 123 D12
Öxabäck S 107 E12